UNDERSTANDING
FAMILY LAW

UNDERSTANDING FAMILY LAW

Fourth Edition

John DeWitt Gregory
Distinguished Professor of Law Emeritus
Maurice A. Deane School of Law at Hofstra University

Peter Nash Swisher
Professor of Law
University of Richmond School of Law

Robin Fretwell Wilson
Class of 1958 Law Alumni Professor of Law
Washington and Lee University School of Law

CAROLINA ACADEMIC PRESS
Durham, North Carolina

ISBN: 978-0-7698-4744-3
eBook ISBN: 978-1-4224-8661-0

Library of Congress Cataloging-in-Publication Data

Gregory, John DeWitt
Understanding family law / John DeWitt Gregory, Emeritus Distinguished Professor of Family Law, Hofstra University Maurice Deane School of Law, Peter Nash Swisher, Professor of Law, University of Richmond School of Law, Robin Fretwell Wilson, Class of 1958 Law Alumni Professor of Law, Washington and Lee University School of law -- Fourth edition.
    p.cm.
  Includes index.
  ISBN 978-0-7698-4744-3
1. Domestic relations--United States. I. Swisher, Peter N., 1944- II. Wilson, Robin Fretwell. III. Title.
  KF505.G734 2013
  346.7301'5--dc23

2013001038

This publication is designed to provide authoritative information in regard to the subject matter covered. It is sold with the understanding that the publisher is not engaged in rendering legal, accounting, or other professional services. If legal advice or other expert assistance is required, the services of a competent professional should be sought.

Carolina Academic Press, LLC
700 Kent Street
Durham, North Carolina 27701
Telephone (919) 489-7486
Fax (919) 493-5668
www.caplaw.com

Printed in the United States of America
2018 printing

DEDICATION

To William Wilford Gregory, who taught me whatever I know about the unbought grace of life

— John DeWitt Gregory

To Karen and Stephanie

— Peter Nash Swisher

To Walter Wadlington, a teacher and scholar to emulate

— Robin Fretwell Wilson

TABLE OF CONTENTS

TABLE OF CONTENTS

TABLE OF CONTENTS

TABLE OF CONTENTS

TABLE OF CONTENTS

TABLE OF CONTENTS

TABLE OF CONTENTS

TABLE OF CONTENTS

TABLE OF CONTENTS

TABLE OF CONTENTS

TABLE OF CONTENTS

Chapter 1

AN INTRODUCTION TO FAMILY LAW

§ 1.01 GENERAL INTRODUCTION

In its traditional sense, family law, also called domestic relations law, involves the legal relationships between husband and wife and parent and child as a social, political, and economic unit. In recent years, the boundaries of family law have grown to encompass legal relationships among persons who live together but are not married — so-called nontraditional families. The legal aspects of family relationships, whether traditional[1] or nontraditional,[2] necessarily include principles of constitutional law, property law, contract law, tort law, civil procedure, statutory regulations, equitable remedies, and, of course, marital property and support rights.

Increasingly, the theoretical and practical implications of family law have been shifting from moral to economic issues, and accordingly, a general practitioner or business lawyer must now understand and master important family law concepts and principles, separate and apart from any divorce litigation. For example, the validity or invalidity of a marriage has far-reaching social, legal, and economic implications in wrongful death actions, since most state wrongful death statutes limit economic recovery to the legal spouse as statutory beneficiary, rather than the de facto spouse.[3] Other areas of the law, including intestate succession and probate law, workers' compensation awards, social security benefits, pensions and retirement plans, medical benefits, insurance payments, loss of consortium actions, state and federal tax law, and marital property and support rights, are also directly affected by the validity or invalidity of a marriage,[4] although some of these benefits are also being covered through domestic partnership legislation in some states and municipalities.[5] American family law currently is in a state of flux and transition based upon the dynamic interplay of three interrelated factors: (1) state and federal legislatures that regulate by statute many important family relationships; (2) courts that interpret these statutes or determine equitable remedies in the absence of such statutes; and (3) family law practitioners who must ultimately decide what strategic alternatives exist in favor of their clients, and who must persuasively plead and prove these alternate remedies before the courts, and increasingly before the legislatures, based upon the law, facts, and social need in each particular case.

---

[1] *See infra* § 1.02[A].

[2] *See infra* § 1.02[B].

[3] *See generally infra* § 2.05[D].

[4] *See generally infra* §§ 2.05[D], 2.10[C], 3.01-3.14.

[5] *See infra* § 2.02[C].

[A]   Legislative Regulation of Family Law

State legislatures traditionally have regulated important family law relationships such as marriage and divorce based upon the state's important nexus with the family unit, and based upon the general welfare of its citizens. As the United States Supreme Court stated in *Maynard v. Hill*:

> Marriage, as creating the most important relation in life, as having more to do with the morals and civilization of a people than any other institution, has always been subject to the control of the legislature. That body prescribes the age at which the parties may contract to marry, the procedure or form essential to constitute marriage, the duties and obligations it creates, its effects upon the property rights of both . . . and the acts which may constitute grounds for its dissolution.[6]

However, since marriage and divorce are fundamental rights subject to constitutional protection, a state cannot arbitrarily prohibit or interfere with the exercise of these marital rights without a compelling reason for doing so.[7] Additionally, although the state legislatures continue to regulate many important family law relationships, Congress in its federal capacity has also entered the field of family law regulation, especially in the areas of child custody[8] and child support[9] enforcement remedies, and federal domestic violence legislation.[10]

[B]   Judicial Regulation of Family Law

State courts, on the other hand, must interpret and apply state family law statutes to each particular legal controversy, or attempt to find equitable remedies in the absence of such statutory remedies.

Most family law statutes are drafted as general guidelines. Consequently, state court judges normally have broad discretion in resolving many family law disputes, including spousal support and the division of marital property on divorce, and in child custody litigation. However, the *extent* of such judicial discretion in family law matters has come under increased scrutiny in recent years. For example, family court judges, from their equity heritage as triers of both law and fact, traditionally

---

[6] 125 U.S. 190, 205 (1888). Implicit throughout *Maynard* is the traditional view that marriage is a status relationship involving three parties: Husband, Wife, and the State. *See also Simms v. Simms*, 175 U.S. 162, 167 (1899) ("The whole subject of the domestic relations of husband and wife, parent and child, belongs to the laws of the State, and not the laws of the United States."). *See generally infra* § 1.03.

[7] *See, e.g., Skinner v. Oklahoma*, 316 U.S. 535 (1942) (protecting the fundamental freedom to procreate from state infringement); *Loving v. Virginia*, 388 U.S. 1 (1967) (declaring state statutes prohibiting interracial marriages to be unconstitutional); *Zablocki v. Redhail*, 434 U.S. 374 (1978) (requiring less onerous state enforcement means than prohibiting the marriage of a father who had not paid child support). *See generally infra* § 1.05.

[8] *See, e.g.*, The Federal Parental Kidnapping Prevention Act of 1980, 28 U.S.C. § 1738A. *See generally infra* § 11.02[C].

[9] *See, e.g.*, The Child Support Enforcement Amendments of 1984, 42 U.S.C. §§ 651-67. *See generally infra* §§ 3.14[C], 8.06[F].

[10] *See, e.g.*, The Violence Against Women Act, Pub. L. No. 103-322 (1994). *See generally infra* § 7.08[A].

possess very wide discretion in adjudicating many family law disputes.[11] However, the American Law Institute's recently proposed *Principles of the Law of Family Dissolution*[12] argues that since judicial discretion in family law matters can be "inherently limitless," a major theme of the *Principles* is an effort to improve the consistency and predictability of such trial court decisions.[13]

Moreover, a particular judge's interpretation of family law issues will be guided by the law of the state whose family law governs a particular case, and the underlying law is by no means uniform from state to state. A judge, for example, may be bound to apply a particular state's "traditional" family law statutes and judicial precedents, a more "modern" approach, or a "centrist" combination of the two.[14] A family court judge's analysis of the relevant facts and law may also be influenced by whether he or she is a judicial "formalist" or a judicial "functionalist."

Under the theory of legal formalism, also known as legal positivism, correct legal decisions are determined by pre-existing legislative and judicial precedents, and the court must reach its decision based upon a logical application of the facts to these pre-existing rules. The formalist judge, embracing the principle of judicial restraint, must apply the existing law to the particular facts and remain socially neutral. Judging under this formalistic theory is thus a matter of logical necessity rather than a matter of choice.[15]

Under the countervailing theory of legal functionalism, also referred to as legal realism or legal pragmatism, the formalistic view of legal certainty and uniformity is viewed as rarely attainable, and perhaps even undesirable, in a changing society. Thus, the paramount concern of the legal functionalists is not logical and legal consistency, as the formalists believe, but socially desirable consequences.[16]

---

[11] For example, H. Clark, The Law of Domestic Relations in the United States 644-45 (2d ed. 1988):

> It is axiomatic that the trial courts have wide discretion in determining the propriety and the amount of [spousal support]. The relevant factors are so numerous and their influence so incapable of precise evaluation that the trial court's decision in a particular case will be affirmed unless it amounts to an abuse of discretion or is based upon an erroneous application of legal principles . . . . As a result, claims for [spousal support] are won or lost in the trial courts, which have a corresponding heavy responsibility to deal fairly with the spouses in such cases . . . .

This broad judicial discretion also applies to the classification, valuation, and distribution of marital property on divorce, *see id.* at 589-94, and to child custody determinations as well, *see id.* at 796-97:

> In most states the award of [child] custody is held to be a matter for the discretion of the trial court, to be upset on appeal only where an abuse of that discretion is shown . . . Certainly any appellate court should be reluctant to substitute its judgment for that of a trial court in cases so entirely dependent upon particular facts and the subtle differences to be drawn from those facts.

[12] *See generally* ALI, *Principles of the Law of Family Dissolution: Analysis and Recommendations* (2000).

[13] *Id.* at 69-70, 83, 259.

[14] *See, e.g.*, Hobbs & Mulligan, *Centrist Judging and Traditional Family Values*, 49 Wash. & Lee L. Rev. 345 (1992).

[15] *See, e.g.*, G. Paton & D. Dorham, Jurisprudence 3-14 (3d ed. 1972), Weinrib, *Legal Formalism: On the Imminent Rationality of Law*, 97 Yale L.J. 949 (1988). *See generally* M. Jori, Legal Positivism (1992).

[16] *See, e.g.*, W. Rumble, American Legal Realism (1968); G. Aichele, Legal Realism and Twentieth Century American Jurisprudence (1990).

Put another way, where legal formalism is logically-based and precedent-oriented, legal functionalism is sociologically-based and result-oriented to validate society's needs and expectations. According to various commentators, the current transition in family law theory and practice is based upon the need to make American family law more rational and less harsh concerning the reasonable expectations of contemporary society.[17]

It remains open to debate whether state legislatures should remain preeminent in determining current family law needs and goals, as the formalists generally believe, or whether the judiciary should take a more active role in determining current family law goals and remedies, as the functionalists generally believe.[18] For example, in the 2003 case of *Goodridge v. Massachusetts Department of Public Health*[19] the Massachusetts Supreme Judicial Court held in a 4-3 decision that the Commonwealth of Massachusetts had "failed to identify any constitutionally adequate reason for denying civil marriages to same-sex couples" according to the Court's definition of what constituted a "civil marriage," and therefore recognized the validity of same-sex marriage in Massachusetts. Three dissenting judges in *Goodridge*, however, opined that "What is at stake in this case is not the unequal treatment of individuals or whether individual rights have been impermissibly burdened, but the power of the Legislature to effectuate social change without interference from the courts." Moreover, disagreement persists as to which family law principles should be retained, and which should be changed to meet the needs of contemporary American society.

These questions are of more than academic importance, since although legal functionalism has been the dominant legal theory of American jurisprudence for most of the twentieth century,[20] legal formalism is far from a dead issue, and seems to be enjoying a remarkable resurgence:

> Not since the late 1920s and 1930s has there been such widespread interest in American jurisprudence. But it is no longer the [legal functionalists] who are challenging established norms. The victories at the polls of political conservatives like Richard Nixon and Ronald Reagan [and George Herbert

---

There is yet a third school of American legal theory, the Critical Legal Studies Movement, which generally calls for the dismantling of existing political and legal institutions in favor of newly empowered forms of social democracy. *See, e.g.*, White, *From Realism to Critical Legal Studies*, 40 Sw. U. L. Rev. 819 (1986); Comment, *Round and Round the Bramble Bush: From Legal Realism to Critical Legal Scholarship*, 95 Harv. L. Rev. 1669 (1982); Tushnet, *Critical Legal Studies: A Political History*, 100 Yale L. J. 1515 (1991).

[17] *See, e.g.*, M. Glendon, The New Family and the New Property (1981); M. Glendon, The Transformation of Family Law: State, Law, and Family in the United States and Western Europe (1990); Schneider, *The New Step: Definition, Generalization, and Theory of American Family Law*, 18 U. Mich. J.L. Ref. 1039 (1985).

[18] *Compare Hewitt v. Hewitt*, 394 N.E.2d 1204 (Ill. 1979) ("We believe that [family law] questions are appropriately within the province of the legislature, and that, if there is to be a change in the law of this State on this matter, it is for the legislature and not the courts to bring about that change."), *with Frey v. Frey*, 471 A.2d 705 (Md. 1984) ("it is within the power of this court to change the common law").

[19] 798 N.E.2d 941 (Mass. 2003). *See also infra* § 2.08[B].

[20] *See generally* K. Llewellyn, Jurisprudence: Realism in Theory and Practice (1962); Rumble, *supra* note 16; Aichele, *supra* note 16.

Walker Bush and George W. Bush and a Republican-controlled Congress], and the corresponding ideological commitments of many recent appointments to the [state and] federal bench, now threaten the continued prominence of a theory of judicial interpretation first articulated and advanced by the [legal functionalists]. Impossible only a decade ago, "mechanical jurisprudence" has made a remarkable comeback, and a new legal formalism may [or may not] triumph as the principal mode of judicial interpretation.[21]

Thus, a family law student and practitioner must be aware of both the dichotomy between "traditional" and "modern" family law statutes and judicial opinions, and how these statutes and opinions will be interpreted by a formalist or a functionalist family court judge.

The role of the federal judiciary in family law matters is discussed later in this chapter.[22]

[C] The Role of the Family Law Practitioner

The ultimate client-representation role of the family law practitioner is to argue the client's case persuasively before the court. In the court setting, the attorney will employ various alternate remedies and legal strategies to advance the client's interests. Presentation of the client's position, as well as the analysis that went into preparation for court proceedings, will often find the attorney confronting, and deciding upon, an amalgam of theories best suited to the client's case. In each case, the family law practitioner must determine what "traditional" family law principles ought to be retained or abolished, what "modern" family law trends ought to be adopted or rejected, and what ultimate public policy goals are to be achieved through these various laws.

This process of analysis, repeated on behalf of various clients, can ultimately lead the practitioner to pronounced views of how the law should be structured and, once structured, how it should be implemented. In a very real sense, then, the family law practitioner is in the forefront of any movements for reform of the substance and procedure of American family law.[23]

These interrelated family law problems facing the legislator, the jurist, and the family law practitioner resist easy solution. For example, to remove some of the worst vestiges of long-standing fault-based divorce statutes, most jurisdictions have enacted "no-fault" divorce legislation and marital property distribution statutes. These no-fault divorce statutes currently allow divorces to be granted

---

[21] Aichele, *supra* note 16, at x. *See also* Schaier, *Formalism*, 97 Yale L.J. 509 (1988) (discussing how legal formalism still serves a useful function in limiting judicial discretion and judicial activism); Weinrib, *Legal Formalism: On the Imminent Rationality of Law*, 97 Yale L.J. 949 (1988) (questioning whether the law is essentially rational as the formalists believe, or whether law is essentially political as the functionalists believe). *See generally* Symposium, *Formalism Revisited*, 66 U. Chi. L. Rev. 527-942 (1999).

[22] *See generally infra* §§ 1.04, 1.05.

[23] *See, e.g.*, Monroe Inker, *Changes in Family Law: A Practitioner's Perspective*, 33 Fam. L. Q. 515 (1999); *see also* Louise Raggio, *Women Lawyers in Family Law*, 33 Fam. L. Q. 501 (1999).

without regard to fault if the marriage has become insupportable because of discord or irreconcilable differences that destroy the legitimate ends of the marriage relationship and prevent any reasonable expectation of reconciliation. Modern property distribution statutes likewise focus on establishing a roughly equitable "no fault" distribution of marital property based on each party's contribution to the marriage. Although these no-fault procedures arguably are more efficient, and these marital property distribution guidelines have a ring of fairness to them, some commentators have argued that divorced wives and their children may actually be more economically disadvantaged under this "modern" family law legislation than under a more "traditional" approach.[24] Likewise, there is still continuing controversy involving what role (if any) marital fault should play in a "no fault" divorce regime.[25] Indeed, some commentators have concluded that the no-fault divorce revolution in America "has failed."[26]

Thus the quest continues to determine which family law principles are obsolete and which family law principles are relevant to the changing needs of our

---

[24] *See, e.g.*, L. Weitzman, The Divorce Revolution in America: The Unexpected Social and Economic Consequences for Women and Children in America (1985). Although the accuracy of Professor Weitzman's statistical studies have been questioned, other studies have corroborated this "feminization of poverty" resulting from divorce. *See also* McLindon, *Separate But Unequal: The Economic Disaster of Divorce for Women and Children*, 21 Fam. L.Q. 351 (1987); K. Winner, Divorced from Justice: The Abuse of Women and Children by Divorce Lawyers and Judges (1996). Minor children also suffer from divorce:

> Two-thirds of all divorces involve minor children, and according to Columbia law professor Martha Fineman, author of *The Illusion of Equality*, the average annual child support payment is only around $3,000. "Equality is being applied with a vengeance against women", she says. Ultimately, the average household income for children of divorce drops thirty percent, while the poverty rate for children living with single mothers is five times as high as for those in intact families.

Elizabeth Gleick, *Hell Hath No Fury*, Time Magazine, Oct. 7, 1996 at 84. *See also* Scott, *Rational Decision-Making About Marriage and Divorce*, 76 Va. L. Rev. 9, 29 (1990) ("There is substantial evidence that the process of going through their parents' divorce and resulting changes in their lives are psychologically costly for most children"); Judith Wallerstein, The Unexpected Legacy of Divorce: A Twenty Five Year Landmark Study (2000) (discussing the long-term negative effects of divorce on children); Judith Wallerstein & Sandra Blakeslee, Second Chances: Men, Women, and Children a Decade After Divorce (1989) (same).

[25] *Compare* ALI *Principles of the Law of Family Dissolution: Analysis and Recommendations* (2000), *and* Ellman, *The Place of Fault in Modern Divorce Law*, 28 Ariz. St. L.J. 773 (1996) (arguing for the total abolition of all fault-based factors in marital dissolution or divorce), *with* Woodhouse, *Sex, Lies, and Dissipation: The Discourse of Fault in a No-Fault Era*, 82 Geo. L.J. 2525 (1994) (arguing that fault factors on divorce still have a legitimate purpose to counteract egregious marital fault), *and* Swisher, *Reassessing Fault Factors in No-Fault Divorce*, 31 Fam. L. Q. 269 (1997) (same). *See also* Wardle, *No-Fault Divorce and the Divorce Conundrum*, 1991 BYU L. Rev. 79; DiFonzo, Beneath the Fault Line: The Popular and Legal Culture of Divorce in Twentieth Century America (1997).

[26] See for example, Council on Families in America, *Marriage in America: A Report to the Nation* (1995):

> The divorce revolution- the steady displacement of a marriage culture by a culture of divorce and unwed parenthood- has failed. It has created terrible hardships for children, incurred unsupportable social costs, and failed to deliver on its promise of greater adult happiness. The time has come to shift the focus of national attention from divorce to marriage and to rebuild a family culture based on enduring marital relationships.

But see Divorce Reform at the Crossroads (Sugarman & Hill ed. 1990) (arguing that serious problems within a no-fault divorce regime need to be corrected, but without abandoning no-fault divorce *per se*).

contemporary society. But while embarking on this legitimate quest, the legislator, jurist, scholar, and family law practitioner ought not be too hasty, in the absence of sound empirical evidence, to "throw the baby out with the bath water" in assessing and reassessing present and future family law needs and goals.

§ 1.02 WHAT IS A FAMILY?

In order to understand the legal relationships existing in a family law context, we must first define what a "family" is. Narrowly defined, "family" can mean a group related by blood or by marriage, such as a traditional family involving a husband and wife or a parent and child.[27] Broadly defined, a "family" may include a nontraditional family, meaning one of a group living in the same household.[28]

A "family" can also be analyzed under an "organic" model or under an "individualistic" model. An organic family model emphasizes the good of the family unit at the expense of its individual members, and it is frequently associated with a hierarchically-ordered "traditional" family unit. An individualistic family model, on the other hand, views the family as composed of discrete and separate individuals, who are basically complete apart from the family unit.[29]

Regardless of how it has been defined, however, the remarkable resilience of the family unit has been primarily related to its role in the raising and socialization of children, and in the mutual social and economic support of its members.[30]

Arguably, a family is also morally justifiable under a "community" model, where the family finds its justification not only in its function of raising children and contributing to the economic well-being of its members, but also in the benevolence and the psychological satisfactions a family brings. Thus, family law finds its ultimate justification in reducing the uncertainties and inequities that are associated with conjugal relationships without rules, in establishing custody of children, in preventing harm to children, in providing economic rights and obligations for family members, and in establishing rules that will optimize human happiness within a family relationship.[31]

---

[27] *See, e.g., Village of Belle Terre v. Boraas,* 416 U.S. 1 (1974) (holding that a single family dwelling for zoning purposes, under a village ordinance, was limited to persons related by blood, adoption, or marriage).

[28] *See, e.g., Braschi v. Stahl Associates,* 543 N.E.2d 49 (N.Y. 1989) (for rent control purposes, a family included "two adult lifetime partners whose relationship is long-term and characterized by an emotional and financial commitment and interdependence"); *see also* Note, *Legal Rights of Unmarried Heterosexual and Homosexual Couples and the Evolving Definitions of "Family,"* 29 J. Fam. L. 417 (1990-91); Chambers & Polikoff, *Family Law and Gay and Lesbian Family Issues in the Twentieth Century,* 33 Fam. L. Q. 523 (1999); *infra* notes 51, 69 (and accompanying text).

[29] *See generally* L. Houlgate, Family and State: The Philosophy of Family Law (1988).

[30] J. Eekelaar, Family Law and Social Policy 20-23 (2d ed. 1984).

[31] Houlgate, *supra* note 29, at 49.

[A] The Traditional Family

Marriage, or the public bonding of a man and a woman to give legitimacy to their conjugal relationship, has existed since Biblical times. The nature of the marital union, and the rights and obligations arising from this familial relationship, have undergone a long, but surprisingly resilient, evolutionary process.

Unlike most other branches of the law, the evolution of family law has experienced the intertwining of secular and religious principles, and has carried forward elements of both. From the ancient Hebrew ceremonial requirement of a marriage contract or *Ketubah*,[32] to the Medieval Church's ecclesiastical canon law[33] which treated marriage as a holy sacrament rather than as a civil contract,[34] marriage and family law principles have come down through the centuries as an enduring and conservative body of law.

A more recent example of the Roman Catholic Church's attitude toward marriage is illustrated in a 1930 Encyclical by Pope Pius XI:

> . . . [L]et it be repeated as an immutable and inviolable fundamental doctrine that matrimony was not instituted or restored by man but by God; not by man were the laws to strengthen and confirm and elevate it but by God . . . . [T]his is the constant tradition of the Universal Church . . . .
>
> . . . Yet, although matrimony is of its very nature of divine institution, the human will, too, enters into it and performs a most noble part. For each individual marriage, inasmuch as it is a conjugal union of a particular man and woman, arises only from the free consent of each of the spouses; and this free act of the will, by each party hands over and accepts those rights proper to the state of marriage . . . . [A]mongst the blessings of marriage, the child holds the first place.[35]

Marriage requirements thus remained remarkably unchanged through the centuries leading up to the Protestant Reformation. However, when Henry VIII and the English Reformation transformed the Roman Catholic Church into an English Church, the regulation of the ecclesiastical courts in family law matters was transferred to the English civil courts, and to Parliament.[36]

In 1753, Parliament enacted Lord Hardwicke's Act which required that all marriages must be celebrated in accordance with the rules of the Church of England: that there be a publication of the marriage announcement, that a marriage license be obtained, and that there be two witnesses to the ceremony.[37]

---

[32] *See generally* L. Epstein, The Jewish Marriage Contract (1927).

[33] *See* O'Connor, *The Origin and Development of Canon Law*, 4 Jurist 54 (1944).

[34] For example, *Matthew* 19:6 "What therefore God hath joined together, let no man put asunder."

[35] Pope Pius XI, *Encyclical Letter on Christian Marriage* (1930).

[36] *See generally* S. Green & J. Long, Marriage and Family Law Agreements 8-12 (1984); T. Plucknett, A Concise History of the Common Law 628-29 (5th ed. 1956).

[37] J. Davies & R. Lawry, Institutions and Methods of Law 72-74 (1982).

English law concerning marriage and family law generally was largely adopted by the American colonies, and was later readopted by most American states. However, there were no counterparts to the English ecclesiastical courts to resolve disputes regarding the validity of marriage and the application of other family law concepts. Also, after the seventeenth century, there was the increasing recognition of the concept of divorce in America. The ultimate result in America was the assignment of legal issues concerning marriage and divorce to the state legislatures and to the equity jurisdiction of state courts.[38]

By the turn of the twentieth century, European and American legal systems had come to share a common set of traditional assumptions regarding marriage and the traditional family unit as a basic social institution: (1) marriage was a primary support institution and a decisive determinant of the social, economic, and legal status of the spouses and children; (2) marriage in principle was to last until the death of a spouse, and would be terminated during the lives of the spouses only for serious cause; (3) the community aspect of marriage and the family was to be emphasized over the individualistic personalities of each member; (4) within the family, the standard pattern of authority and role allocation was that the husband-father was predominant in decision-making and was to provide for the material needs of the family, while the wife-mother cared for the household and the children; and (5) procreation and child rearing were assumed to be major purposes of marriage.[39]

However, as women began entering the salaried work force in increasing numbers, and their economic vulnerability lessened, it became easier for both men and women to dissolve their marriage. Thus, as a result of recent social and economic developments, "two paycheck" families have now become the norm, rather than the exception, and the modern American family is now being redefined by gender-neutral laws, new lifestyles, new realities, and new expectations — with a resulting decrease in the number of children per family, and a resulting increase in the divorce rate.[40] Concurrently, according to Professor Glendon, the notion is beginning to appear that now "the family exists for the benefit of the individual, rather than the individual existing for the benefit of the family."[41]

The traditional concept of marriage and the family has been further questioned by various feminist writers who claim that the traditional family structure was

---

[38] *See* Clark, *supra* note 11, at 72; S. Green & J. Long, Marriage and Family Law Agreements 12-13 (1984); B. Whitehead, The Divorce Culture (1997).

[39] *See* Glendon, The New Family, *supra* note 17, at 1-35.

[40] *See, e.g.*, *Orr v. Orr*, 440 U.S. 268, 279-80 (1979) (holding that old notions that "generally it is the man's primary responsibility to provide a home and its essentials" can no longer justify family laws that discriminate on the basis of gender, and no longer "is the female destined solely for the home and the rearing of family, and only the male for the marketplace and the world of ideas"); *see also* Minow, *Toward a History of Family Law*, 1985 Wis. L. Rev. 819; Mather, *Evolution and Revolution in Family Law*, 25 St. Mary's L. J. 405 (1993). However, true gender equality in American family law and social policy is not yet a reality. *See, e.g.*, Fineman, *Implementing Equality*, 1983 Wis. L. Rev. 789; Minow, *Toward a History of Family Law, supra.*

[41] Glendon, The New Family, *supra* note 17, at 33.

originally perpetuated to maintain male dominance,[42] and some feminist writers
have argued for the abolition of marriage *per se* in favor of other alternatives.[43]
Marxist scholars also have argued that the laws supporting these marital institutions were exploitive instruments by which the ruling class maintained its economic
and political power.[44]

But even those Marxist and former Marxist societies once committed to radical
social change have been unable to alter the traditional family structure significantly.
For example, the hope of early Soviet Communists was to weaken family ties and
promote equality in sexual roles by allowing either spouse to escape marriage by a
single *ex parte* application at a registrar's office, or alternately, it was not necessary
to enter into a formal marriage, since Soviet *de facto* cohabitation was also
recognized. However, subsequent Soviet legislation found it necessary to restore
state supervision over entering marriage, and to put formidable obstacles in the
way of divorce,[45] and a similar progression of events has been evident in other
Marxist, and former Marxist, countries as well.[46]

Likewise, the United Nations, in its Universal Declaration of Human Rights, also
recognizes that the family "is the natural and fundamental group unit of society and
is entitled to protection by society and the State."[47]

Yet the present-day traditional American family, even with an increased pattern
among husbands and wives of dual decision-making and dual economic support, has
been battered by current social and economic developments. For example, according to the U.S. Census Bureau, where in 1970 about 12 percent of children lived with
only one parent, by 2000 about one in four, more than sixteen million children, lived
with only one parent. Currently one in four children is now born outside of
marriage, compared to one in twenty in 1960. Moreover, children living with only
one parent, usually the mother, are six times more likely to be poor as those living

---

[42] *See, e.g.*, Rifkin, *Toward a Theory of Law and Patriarchy*, 3 Harv. Women's L.J. 83 (1980); Stark,
Divorce Law, Feminism, and Psychoanalysis: In Dreams Begin Responsibilities, 38 UCLA L. Rev.
1483 (1991); Carbone & Brinig, *Rethinking Marriage: Feminist Ideology, Economic Chance, and
Divorce Reform*, 65 Tulane L. Rev. 953 (1991); Bartlett, *Feminism and Family Law*, 33 Fam. L. Q. 475
(1999).

[43] *See, e.g.* Martha Fineman, *Why Marriage?*, 9 Va. J. Soc. Pol'y & L. 239 (2001) (arguing that the
concept of marriage limits the development of family policy by precluding consideration of other viable
solutions to social problems); Nancy Polikoff, *Ending Marriage As We Know It*, 32 Hofstra L. Rev. 201
(2003) (arguing for other relationship options than marriage in order to better allocate legal and
economic rights and responsibilities between various parties).

[44] *See generally* Marxism and Law (P. Beirne & R. Quinny, eds. 1982).

[45] *See generally* Eekelaar, *supra* note 30, at 20-23 ("There are striking similarities between [the
Soviet experience] and the position into which modern Western family law is moving."). *See also*
Dyuzheva, *International Marriage and Divorce Regulation and Recognition in Russia*, 29 Fam. L. Q.
645, 646-48 (1995).

[46] *See, e.g.*, Palmer, *The People's Republic of China: New Marriage Regulations*, 26 J. Fam. L. 39
(1987-88); Soltesz, *Hungary: Toward a Strengthening of Marriage*, 26 J. Fam. L. 113 (1987-88); Zace,
Albania: Family Law Under the Dictatorship of the Proletariat, 33 U. Louisville J. Fam. L. 259 (1995);
Gec-Korosec & Rijavec, *Slovenia: Post-Independence Changes in Family Law*, 33 U. Louisville J. Fam.
L. 485 (1995).

[47] U.N. General Assembly, *Universal Declaration of Human Rights*, Article 16(3).

with both parents.[48]

These statistics suggest that the traditional American family may be at risk, and this trend toward nontraditional family arrangements has generated a high-level reevaluation of the basic premises underlying the traditional family, resulting in strong endorsements of a rededicated commitment to the traditional structure.[49] For example, a report issued by the bipartisan National Commission on Children concluded that "Families formed by marriage, where two caring adults are committed to one another and to their children, provide the best environment for bringing children into the world and supporting their growth and development."[50]

Accordingly, a number of states have explored various ways to strengthen or "reinstitutionalize" traditional marriage. Louisiana and Arizona, for example, have enacted so-called "covenant marriage" statutes as an alternative to "regular" marriage, where the parties agree to attend premarital counseling from a clergy member or marital counselor, and further agree to dissolve their marriage based on traditional fault grounds, rather than through no-fault divorce. And in 1998 Florida passed a bipartisan Marriage Preparation and Preservation Act providing that: (1) all Florida high school students must take a required course in "marriage and relationship skill based education"; (2) engaged couples are strongly encouraged to take a "premarital preparation course" which may include instruction in conflict resolution, communication skills, financial responsibilities, children and parenting, and data on problems married couples face, and those parties taking such a premarital preparation course are entitled to a reduction in the cost of their marriage license fee; (3) each couple applying for a marriage license will also be given a handbook prepared by the Florida Bar Association informing couples of "the rights and responsibilities under Florida law of marital partners to each other and to their children, both during a marriage and upon its dissolution"; and (4) couples with children who file for divorce in Florida must take a "Parent Education and Family Stabilization Course" that covers the legal and emotional impact of divorce on adults and children, financial responsibility, laws regarding child abuse and neglect, and conflict resolution skills.[51]

These studies, among many others, suggest that the traditional family unit still continues to play an important role in our present-day society, and the traditional family unit therefore should continue to function as, and be legally protected as, a valuable social and institutional structure. Accordingly, a number of states have begun to enact bipartisan legislative measures to "reinstitutionalize" marriage and

---

[48] *See generally* U.S. Dept. of Commerce, Current Population Reports, Series P-70 No. 126 *Living Arrangements of Children* at 1-4 (2009).

[49] *See, e.g.*, Council on Families in America, *Marriage in America: A Report to the Nation* (1995): ("The time has come to shift the focus of national attention from divorce to marriage and to rebuild a family culture based on enduring marital relationships.").

[50] National Commission on Children, Beyond Rhetoric (1991). *See also* Linda Waite & Maggie Gallagher, The Case for Marriage: Why Married People are Happier, Healthier, and Better-Off Financially (2000).

[51] *See* Michael McManus, *Florida Passes Nation's Most Sweeping Reform of Marriage Laws*, Ethics and Religion Advance (May 16, 1998) (predicting that this law will inspire many other states to pass similar laws).

the traditional family structure, primarily by: (1) changing state laws that would make it harder for couples to divorce through so-called "covenant marriage" statutes; and (2) encouraging or mandating couples to participate in premarital education and counseling prior to marriage.[52] To date, the success or failure of these legislative initiatives have not yet been ascertained.

[B] The Nontraditional Family

An analysis of contemporary American family law, however, cannot be limited solely to the traditional family structure. As Professor Marjorie Schultz aptly observes:

> Marriage has undergone tremendous change in recent decades . . . . Only a small percentage of American families still have all the characteristics associated with the nuclear family ideal. In place of a single socially approved ideal we have compelling demands for autonomy and privacy, and multiple levels of intimacy: single parents, working wives, house husbands, homosexual couples, living together arrangements without marriage, serial marriage, stepchildren. The changes are legion, and their message is clear: the destruction of traditional marriage as the sole model for adult intimacy is irreversible.[53]

More recently, in 2001, the Law Commission of Canada in its report *Beyond Conjugality: Recognizing and Supporting Personal Adult Relationships*, concluded that:

> [Marriage] is no longer a sufficient model to respond to the variety of relationships that exist . . . today. Whether we look at older people living with their adult children, adults with disabilities living with their caretakers, or siblings cohabiting in the same residence, the marriage model is inadequate. Some of these other relationships are also characterized by emotional and economic interdependence, mutual care and concern and the

---

[52] *See, e.g.*, Stanley & Markman, Can Government Rescue Marriages? (1997). *See generally infra* § 2.03. *See also* David Collidge & William Duncan, *Reaffirming Marriage: A Presidential Priority*, 24 Harv. J. L. & Pub. Pol'y 623 (2001) (criticizing attempts to expand the definition of marriage and calling for a reaffirmation of marriage as a union between a man and a woman); George Dent, *The Defense of Traditional Marriage*, 15 J. L. & Policy 581 (1999) (stating various arguments for upholding traditional marriage); Brian Bix, *State of the Union: The State's Interest in the Marital Status of Their Citizens*, 55 U. Miami L. Rev. 1 (2000); Elizabeth Scott, *Social Norms and the Legal Regulation of Marriage*, 86 Va. L. Rev. 1901 (2000).

[53] Schultz, *Contractual Ordering of Marriage: A New Model for State Policy*, 70 Cal. L. Rev. 204, 207 (1982). *See also* Minow, *Redefining Families: Who's In and Who's Out*, 62 U. Colo. L. Rev. 269 (1991); Treuthart, *Adopting a More Realistic Definition of "Family,"* 26 Gonz. L. Rev. 91 (1990-91); Post, *The Question of Family: Lesbians and Gay Men Reflecting a Redefined Society*, 19 Fordham Urb. L.J. 747 (1992); Fineman, *Intimacy Outside the Natural Family: the Limits of Privacy*, 23 Conn. L. Rev. 955 (1991) (discussing single mother families); Note, *Looking for a Family Resemblance: The Limits of the Functional Approach to the Legal Definition of Family*, 104 Harv. L. Rev. 1640 (1991); *The 21st Century Family*, Newsweek, Winter/Spring 1990, at 15-46; Family Law Symposium, *A More Perfect Union? Marriage and Marriage-Like Relationships in Family Law*, 30 N.M. L. Rev. 1 (2000); Summer L. Nastich, *Questioning the Marriage Assumptions*, 21 J. Law & Inequality 114 (2003); Harry Krause & David Meyer, *What Family for the 21st Century?*, 50 Am. J. Comp. L. 101 (2002).

expectation of some duration. All of these personal adult relationships could also benefit from [alternative] legal frameworks to support peoples' need for certainty and stability.[54]

Accordingly, this treatise will also analyze various nontraditional family law concepts including: nonmarital cohabitation;[55] domestic partnership legislation;[56] same sex marriage;[57] *de facto* "marriage";[58] "marriage" by estoppel;[59] paternity and legitimacy issues;[60] single parent adoption;[61] homosexual parent adoption;[62] and sexual preference issues related to child custody determinations on divorce.[63]

For example, unmarried heterosexual and homosexual cohabitants in many states may now contractually agree to define their property and support rights separate and apart from any marital rights and obligations;[64] and a growing number of American cities and states have recently passed various "domestic partnership" ordinances and statutes[65] that recognize an unmarried domestic partnership status for municipal and state purposes.[66] Although some other countries have recognized a legal status for unmarried domestic partners,[67] only a minority of American jurisdictions to date have fully recognized a nonmarital

---

[54] The Law Commission of Canada, Beyond Conjugality: Recognizing and Supporting Personal Adult Relationships at 129 (2001). *See also* Linda McClain, *Intimate Affiliation and Democracy: Beyond Marriage?*, 32 Hofstra L. Rev. 379, 411 (2003) ("I believe that this call to move 'beyond conjugality' issues a valuable challenge that provides the opportunity for critical reflection upon the facilitative role of government in supporting intimate affiliation").

[55] *See infra* § 2.02.

[56] *See infra* § 2.02[C].

[57] *See infra* § 2.08[B].

[58] *See infra* § 2.05[D].

[59] *See infra* § 2.05[E].

[60] *See infra* § 5.02.

[61] *See infra* § 6.01[H].

[62] *See infra* § 6.01[I].

[63] *See infra* § 11.05[C].

[64] *See generally infra* §§ 2.02[A], 2.02[B], 2.05[D].

[65] For example, Seattle, Washington; Madison, Wisconsin; New York City; Takoma Park, Maryland; and Berkeley, West Hollywood, Santa Cruz, and San Francisco, California among many other municipalities. Hawaii and Vermont have enacted statewide domestic partnership legislation. *See infra* § 2.02[C].

[66] *See, e.g.*, Note, *Domestic Partnership Recognition in the Workplace: Equitable Employee Benefits for Gay Couples (and Others)*, 51 Ohio St. L.J. 1067 (1990); Note, *Legal Rights of Unmarried Heterosexual and Homosexual Couples and the Evolving Definitions of "Family,"* 29 J. Fam. L. 497 (1990-91); Note, *A Legal and Social Analysis of Domestic Partnership Ordinances*, 92 Colum. L. Rev. 1164 (1992); O'Brien, *Domestic Partnership: Recognition and Responsibility*, 32 San Diego L. Rev. 163 (1995). *See generally infra* § 2.02[C].

[67] *See, e.g.*, Fawcett, *Taking the Middle Path: Recent Swedish Legislation Grants Minimal Property Rights to Unmarried Cohabitants*, 24 Fam. L.Q. 179 (1990); Bradley, *Unmarried Cohabitants in Sweden: A Renewed Social Institution*, 11 J. Legal Hist. 300 (1990). Norway, Denmark, and France have also passed similar legislation. The Netherlands, Belgium, and Canada also have recognized same-sex marriage.

domestic partnership status on a state-wide basis.[68]

As a result of this societal change in lifestyles found in the rapid growth of nontraditional families, commentators such as Professor Lenore Weitzman have questioned the continuing viability of traditional families *per se*:

> [O]ur society has undergone profound transformations in the past century, and the long-standing legal structure of marriage may now be anachronistic. The state's interest in preserving the traditional family may not be important enough to offset new societal and individual needs which require more flexibility and choice in family forms.[69]

Nevertheless, it seems unlikely that the majority of state legislatures will abolish these "anachronistic" marriage requirements in the foreseeable future.[70] And even if the parties were able to contract privately free from all state regulation of marriage, what legal protection would be afforded to prevent the possible exploitation of one contracting party by the other contracting party?[71]

Finally, is present family law only a "patchwork attempt" stretching "old law to deal with modern realities" as Professor Weitzman argues, or can American family law adequately address, rectify, and subsume many of Professor Weitzman's legitimate concerns?[72]

In conclusion, it is becoming clear that the preferable approach is for state legislatures and courts to recognize and protect the legal rights and obligations of *both* traditional *and* nontraditional families as they currently coexist in American society, by providing alternative legal rights and remedies for each social structure

---

[68] *See generally infra* § 2.02[C].

[69] Weitzman, *Legal Regulation of Marriage: Tradition and Change, A Proposal for Individual Contracts and Contracts in Lieu of Marriage*, 62 Cal. L. Rev. 1169, 1170 (1974). *See also* L. Weitzman, The Marriage Contract — Spouses, Lovers, and the Law (1981); Martha Fineman, *Why Marriage?*, 9 Va. J. Soc. Pol'y & L. 239 (2001); Nancy Polikoff, *Ending Marriage As We Know It*, 32 Hofstra L. Rev. 201 (2003) (arguing for the abolition of marriage in favor of other viable relationship alternatives).

[70] *See* Clark, *supra* note 11, at 75 ("Notwithstanding these developments, a majority of Americans still marry in the traditional way and continue to regard marriage as the most important relationship in their lives."); *see also infra* §§ 2.03-2.05.

[71] *See* Glendon, *Marriage and the State: The Withering Away of Marriage*, 62 Va. L. Rev. 663, 666 (1976) ("If the state is in the process of divesting itself of its marriage regulation business, then, of course, it is not likely to set up shop as an enforcer to heretofore unenforceable contracts."); *see also* Lynne Wardle, *The Bonds of Matrimony and the Bonds of Constitutional Democracy*, 32 Hofstra L. Rev. 349 (2003) (arguing that marriage is based on a number of fundamental core institutions within our constitutional democracy, rather than being based on mere contractual arrangements). However, it seems unlikely that many states today will choose to legislate themselves out of the marriage regulation business. *See, e.g., infra* § 2.03. Nevertheless, the parties may still privately order many of their marital rights and obligations through marital contracts and agreements, as long as they are not unconscionable to the parties or the state. *See generally infra* Chapter 4.

[72] *See, e.g.*, Dan Browning, *Critical Familism, Civil Society, and the Law*, 32 Hofstra L. Rev. 313 (2003); Linda McClain, *Intimate Affiliation and Democracy: Beyond Marriage?*, 32 Hofstra L. Rev. 379 (2003) (opposing the abolition of marriage as a legal category, but also arguing that state legislatures and courts must move beyond "traditional" marriage to incorporate and embrace greater equality and responsibility within families, as well as extending governmental support and recognition to other forms of committed intimate relationships).

according to the public policy of each state, and based upon the present and future needs of its citizens.[73]

§ 1.03　STATE REGULATION OF FAMILY LAW

Historically in the United States, the marital relationship has always been controlled and regulated by the individual states. Marriage is therefore more than a mere contractual relationship between a man and a woman. It is a status, based on contract, and established by law. It constitutes an institution involving the highest interests of society, and it is therefore subject to state regulation based upon the general welfare of its citizens.[74]

Since the prevailing view is that marriage is a status based on contract, even when a court is faced with a purely economic or contractual issue within the marital relationship, there is the continuing recognition of a state's power to regulate a marital relationship, and all the incidents of that marital relationship.[75]

The state may therefore prescribe the age at which parties may contract to marry, the procedure or form essential to constitute marriage, the duties and obligations created by marriage, the effect of marriage on the parties' property and support rights and obligations, and the acts which may constitute grounds for the dissolution of marriage.[76]

Various commentators, however, have questioned some of these traditional assumptions involving state regulation of marriage. They have questioned whether the legal *status* of marriage has now become obsolete, and whether the incidents of marriage should now move from *status* to *contract* implications, with a corresponding de-emphasis in the state's regulation of marriage.[77]

---

[73] *See generally* Comment, *Prohibiting Marital Status Discrimination: A Proposal for the Protection of Unmarried Couples*, 42 Hastings L.J. 1415 (1991); Minow, *Redefining Families*, 62 U. Colo. L. Rev. 269 (1991); Treuthart, *Adopting a More Realistic Definition of "Family,"* 26 Gonz. L. Rev. 91 (1990-91); Note, *Looking for a Family Resemblance: The Limits of the Functional Approach to the Legal Definition of Family*, 104 Harv. L. Rev. 1640 (1991); Note, *Family Law — Expansion of the Term "Family" to Include Nontraditional Relationships*, 20 Mem. St. U. L. Rev. 135 (1989); Note, *Legal rights of Unmarried Heterosexual and Homosexual Couples and the Evolving Definitions of "Family,"* 29 J. Fam. L. 417 (1990-91); O'Brien, *Domestic Partnership: Recognition and Responsibility*, 32 San Diego L. Rev. 163 (1995); Family Law Symposium, *A More Perfect Union? Marriage and Marriage-Like Relationships in Family Law*, 30 N.M. L. Rev. 1 (2000); *Conference on Marriage, Families, and Democracy*, 32 Hofstra L. Rev. 1-421 (2003).

To date, Hawaii, Vermont, California, and New Jersey have enacted statewide domestic partnership legislation, and a number of other states are considering similar legislative action. *See infra* § 2.02[C].

[74] *See, e.g.*, *Maynard v. Hill*, 125 U.S. 190, 205 (1888); *Griswold v. Connecticut*, 381 U.S. 479, 486 (1965); *Boddie v. Connecticut*, 401 U.S. 371, 376 (1971); *see also Simms v. Simms*, 175 U.S. 162, 167 (1899) (family law is normally subject to the laws of the states, not federal law); Restatement (Second) of Conflicts § 283 (1969).

[75] *See, e.g.*, *Boddie v. Connecticut*, 401 U.S. 371, 376 (1971) ("Without a prior judicial imprimatur, individuals may fully enter into and rescind commercial contracts, for example, but we are unaware of any jurisdiction where private citizens may covenant for or dissolve marriages without state approval."), quoted with approval in *Cramer v. Commonwealth*, 202 S.E.2d 911, 915 (Va. 1974).

[76] *Maynard v. Hill*, 125 U.S. 190, 205 (1888).

[77] *See, e.g.*, Schultz, *Contractual Ordering of Marriage: A New Model for State Policy*, 70 Cal. L. Rev.

To date, however, the majority of states have *not* adopted this contractual approach, and most jurisdictions continue to regulate marriage and divorce as a status relationship consisting of three parties: husband, wife, and the state.[78]

Although American state legislatures and state courts have traditionally regulated family law relationships such as marriage and divorce based upon a state's strong public policy involving the general welfare of its citizens, the state's right to regulate such marital relationships is not absolute, and cannot be arbitrary, unreasonable, or capricious. Because marriage has been recognized by the United States Supreme Court to be a fundamental right, a state cannot prohibit certain marital rights and obligations without demonstrating a compelling state interest for doing so.[79]

§ 1.04   FEDERAL REGULATION OF FAMILY LAW

As discussed above, the individual states traditionally have regulated important family law relationships such as marriage and divorce.[80] Accordingly, on various occasions, the United States Supreme Court has reiterated the "domestic relations exception" rule — that federal courts do *not* have the jurisdiction to grant divorces, award spousal support, or determine child custody issues, even though there may in fact be diversity of citizenship, and even though the required amount in controversy for federal jurisdiction is met.[81]

---

204 (1982); Wright, *Marriage: From Status to Contract?*, 13 Anglo-Am. L. Rev. 17 (1984); Comment, *Marriage as a Contract: Toward a Functional Redefinition of the Marital Status*, 9 Colum. J. L. & Soc. Probs. 607 (1973); Singer, *The Privatization of Family Law*, 1992 Wis. L. Rev. 1443; *see also Ponder v. Graham*, 4 Fla. 23 (1851); *Ryan v. Ryan*, 277 So. 2d 266 (Fla. 1973) (where two Florida courts viewed marriage more in terms of a contract than a status relationship, and questioned whether state legislation regulating marriage might arguably impair the parties' contractual rights if it detrimentally affected their vested property or support rights). *See generally* W. O'Donnell & D. Jones, The Law of Marriage and Marital Alternatives 1-4 (1982).

[78] *See, e.g., Sosna v. Iowa*, 419 U.S. 393, 404 (1975) (the inception and termination of marriage "has long been regarded as a virtually exclusive province of the State" within constitutional limitations); *see also* Sugarman, Divorce Reform at the Crossroads 138 (1990) ("Marriage, at least in this century, is typically said to be best understood as a status, rather than as a contractual relationship"). However, the parties may still privately order many of their marital rights and obligations through marital agreements. *See generally infra* Chapter 4; *infra* § 2.02[A] (or through nonmarital agreements).

[79] *See, e.g., Griswold v. Connecticut*, 381 U.S. 479 (1965) (striking down a state law prohibiting contraceptives to married couples and recognizing a fundamental right of privacy within the marital relationship free from state interference); *Loving v. Virginia*, 388 U.S. 1 (1967) (holding that under a constitutional right to marry, any state prohibition of interracial marriage violated the Equal Protection and Due Process Clauses of the Fourteenth Amendment of the Constitution); *Zablocki v. Redhail*, 434 U.S. 374 (1978) (holding that a state statute prohibiting a person from marrying if he had an unpaid child support obligation was unconstitutional since there were less onerous means of enforcing the child support obligation other than prohibiting the marriage per se); *see also infra* § 1.05.

[80] *See supra* § 1.03; *see also Simms v. Simms*, 175 U.S. 162, 167 (1899) ("The whole subject of the domestic relations of husband and wife, parent and child, belongs to the laws of the State, and not the laws of the United States").

[81] *See, e.g., Barber v. Barber*, 62 U.S. 582 (1858); *Ex parte Burrus*, 136 U.S. 586 (1890); *Simms v. Simms*, 175 U.S. 162 (1899); *Ohio ex rel. Popovici v. Agler*, 280 U.S. 379 (1930). *See generally* C. Wright et al., Federal Practice and Procedure § 3609 (1975).

One rationale for this "domestic relations exception" rule to federal diversity jurisdiction in family law matters has been that divorce was not a suit "of a civil nature at common law or equity" at the time the original Judiciary Act, which conferred jurisdiction on the federal courts, was passed.[82] Although this rationale has been criticized by some federal courts as "not convincing" and "dubious,"[83] the Supreme Court has limited its scope in *Akenbrandt v. Richards*,[84] and Congress has not amended the statute.[85]

Nevertheless, important inroads have been made toward overcoming this "domestic relations exception" obstacle, and significant monetary recoveries in federal court have been recognized for family-related *tortious* conduct, including child enticement actions,[86] and the unlawful taking of a child.[87]

For example, in *Cole v. Cole*,[88] it was held that federal diversity cases having intrafamily aspects could not be dismissed merely upon that basis alone. In *Cole*, the husband brought a claim against his ex-wife for malicious prosecution, abuse of process, arson, conspiracy, and conversion. Noting that such claims could have arisen between strangers with no marital relationship whatever, and noting that this case did not require an adjustment of family status, the court found that the federal domestic relations exception was inapplicable in this particular case.[89]

Likewise, a federal court may take diversity jurisdiction whenever a cause of action sounds in tort or contract, even though there are important interrelated family law issues that must be resolved by the court in order to properly adjudicate the case. For example, in *Hewitt v. Firestone Tire & Rubber Co.*,[90] a federal district court took diversity jurisdiction in a wrongful death action dealing with the underlying issue of which of two women was the legal wife, qualifying her as beneficiary under a state wrongful death statute.[91] And in *Metropolitan Life Ins. Co. v. Holding*,[92] a federal court had to determine the validity of a marriage in order

---

[82] *See, e.g.,* 28 U.S.C. § 1332(a), Revisor's Note. *See generally* Clark, *supra* note 11, at 705-13.

[83] *See, e.g., Spindel v. Spindel*, 283 F. Supp. 797 (E.D.N.Y. 1968); *Lloyd v. Loeffler*, 694 F.2d 489 (7th Cir. 1982).

[84] 504 U.S. 655 (discussed *infra* § 8.02, at notes 34-38 and accompanying text). But see *Spindel v. Spindel*, 283 F. Supp. 797 (E.D.N.Y. 1968), where a federal court held that it *did* have jurisdiction to hear a case to invalidate a husband's Mexican divorce and award the wife damages for an alleged fraudulent inducement to marry action. *See also Vann v. Vann*, 294 F. Supp. 193 (E.D. Tenn. 1968) (federal jurisdiction found to determine the validity of a divorce decree attacked for fraud).

[85] 28 U.S.C. § 1332(a).

[86] *See, e.g.,* W. Keeton, Prosser & Keeton on the Law of Torts 925-26 (5th ed. 1984).

[87] *See, e.g.,* Restatement (Second) of Torts § 700 (1979).

[88] 633 F.2d 1083 (4th Cir. 1980).

[89] *Id. See also Wasserman v. Wasserman*, 671 F.2d 832 (4th Cir. 1982) (federal diversity action for child enticement, intentional infliction of mental distress, and civil conspiracy in a child custody dispute was upheld).

[90] 490 F. Supp. 1358 (E.D. Va. 1980).

[91] *Id.*

[92] 293 F. Supp. 854 (E.D. Va. 1968).

to ascertain the legal beneficiary of a life insurance policy.[93]

Federal courts, of course, also have jurisdiction to adjudicate the constitutionality of state statutes regulating the marital relationship.[94] Federal regulation of family law may also be found in federal statutory enactments, particularly in the field of child support[95] and child custody[96] enforcement remedies.[97]

§ 1.05 CONSTITUTIONAL PARAMETERS TO FAMILY LAW REGULATION

Although family law relationships involving marriage and divorce traditionally have been regulated by the individual states,[98] the state's right to regulate such marital relations is not absolute, and is subject to constitutional limitations if the state regulation is arbitrary, unreasonable, or capricious.[99]

In 1923, for example, the Supreme Court in *Meyer v. Nebraska*[100] recognized that the right to marry was a liberty guaranteed by the Due Process Clause of the Fourteenth Amendment of the United States Constitution.[101] The *Meyer* case, citing earlier Supreme Court precedent, justified this constitutional protection of the marital relationship based upon the importance of marriage to society in general. However, more recent Supreme Court cases have emphasized the importance of the marital relationship to the individual as well,[102] and many important Supreme Court cases beginning in the 1960s have evidenced a growing concern for the constitutional protection of the marital relationship from unreasonable state intrusion.

For example, in *Griswold v. Connecticut*,[103] the Supreme Court held that marriage is a "relationship lying within the zone of privacy created by several fundamental constitutional guarantees,"[104] and therefore a Connecticut state law

---

[93] *Id. See also Renshaw v. Heckler*, 787 F.2d 50 (2d Cir. 1986) (also determining the validity of an underlying common law marriage).

[94] *See generally infra* § 1.05.

[95] *See, e.g.*, The Federal Child Support Enforcement Amendments of 1984, 42 U.S.C. §§ 651-67. *See generally infra* §§ 3.12[C], 9.06[F].

[96] *See, e.g.*, The Federal Parental Kidnapping Prevention Act of 1980, 28 U.S.C. § 1738A. *See generally infra* § 11.02[C].

[97] *See generally* K. Redden, Federal Regulation of Family Law (1982).

[98] *See supra* §§ 1.01, 1.03.

[99] *See generally* Strickman, *Marriage, Divorce and the Constitution*, 15 Fam. L.Q. 259 (1982); Note, *The Constitution and the Family*, 93 Harv. L. Rev. 1156 (1980).

[100] 262 U.S. 390 (1923).

[101] *Id.* at 399-400. *See also Skinner v. Oklahoma*, 316 U.S. 535 (1941) (marriage and procreation "involves one of the basic civil rights of man" which is "fundamental to the very existence and survival of the race").

[102] *See, e.g.*, Glendon, The New Family, *supra* note 17, at 32 (the emphasis of family law is now that the family exists for the benefit of the individual, rather than that the individual exists for the benefit of the family); *see also* Strickman, *Marriage, Divorce and the Constitution*, 15 Fam. L.Q. 259 (1982).

[103] 381 U.S. 479 (1965).

[104] *Id.* at 485.

forbidding the use of contraceptives to married couples was found to violate the constitutional right to marital privacy.[105]

Although this constitutional right to privacy, as enunciated in *Griswold*, is not mentioned in the Constitution, seven justices nevertheless found that there was constitutional protection for the right to privacy, although they could not agree as to where they found it. Justice Douglas, writing for the Court, found the right to privacy in a "penumbra" of other fundamental and enumerated rights. Justice Goldberg found protection for the right to privacy in the inherent fabric of the Constitution, specifically in the Ninth Amendment concept of reserved rights. And Justice Harlan utilized a *Meyer*-type constitutional analysis by finding that the Connecticut statute violated the Due Process Clause of the Fourteenth Amendment by violating "basic values implicit in the concept of ordered liberty."[106] Two justices, however, Black and Stewart, applied a more formalistic judicial analysis[107] and declined to rule that the Connecticut statute was unconstitutional because they could find no express provision of the Constitution that it violated, although both found the statute to be personally repugnant.[108]

This important constitutional debate over the right to privacy in *Griswold* might be moot today if it were only limited to the use of contraceptives.[109] However, the constitutional debate found in *Griswold* remains crucially important today since the landmark abortion case of *Roe v. Wade*[110] also rests upon a constitutional right to privacy argument.[111]

Constitutional protection of the marital relationship against arbitrary and unreasonable state infringement was again reaffirmed by the Supreme Court in *Loving v. Virginia*,[112] where the Court held that Virginia's miscegenation laws violated the Equal Protection and Due Process Clauses of the Fourteenth Amendment. And in *Zablocki v. Redhail*[113] the Court held that a Wisconsin state statute prohibiting a person from marrying if he had an unpaid child support obligation was unconstitutional since there were less onerous means of enforcing the child support obligation other than prohibiting the marriage per se.

Thus, in both *Loving* and *Zablocki* the Supreme Court reiterated that the right to marry is a fundamental constitutional right subject to strict judicial scrutiny, and the state would have the burden of demonstrating a compelling state interest in order to prohibit such marriages.[114]

---

[105] *Id.* at 486.

[106] Griswold, 381 U.S. 479.

[107] *See supra* § 1.01[B].

[108] Griswold, 381 U.S. 479.

[109] *See also Eisenstadt v. Baird*, 405 U.S. 438 (1972) (striking down a Massachusetts statute that prohibited supplying contraceptives to unmarried persons). *See generally infra* § 5.04.

[110] 410 U.S. 113 (1973).

[111] *See generally infra* § 5.05.

[112] 388 U.S. 1 (1967).

[113] 434 U.S. 374 (1978).

[114] For a discussion of same-sex marriage in the United States, see *infra* § 2.08[B].

However, when a state is merely regulating, rather than prohibiting, certain marital rights and obligations, then the state ordinarily must only show a rational reason, rather than a compelling state interest, for its actions. For example, in *Moe v. Dinkins*,[115] a New York federal district court upheld a New York marriage statute which required that applicants under the age of 18 obtain parental consent. The court reasoned that the statute's rational purpose was to protect minors from making immature decisions, and thereby prevent unstable marriages. The court also held that the New York statute only delayed the minors' decision to marry, and did not prohibit that fundamental right per se.[116]

---

[115] 533 F. Supp. 623 (S.D.N.Y. 1981), *aff'd* 669 F.2d 67 (2d Cir. 1981), *cert. denied* 459 U.S. 827 (1982).

[116] *Id.*

Chapter 2

MARRIAGE AND MARRIAGE ALTERNATIVES

§ 2.01 INTRODUCTION

Marriage is more than a personal relationship between a man and a woman. It is a legal status, founded on contract, and established by law.[1] It constitutes a social institution involving the highest interests of society, and therefore is subject to state regulation based upon the general welfare of the people of the state.[2]

The validity or invalidity of a marriage has far-reaching social, legal, and economic implications in such diverse areas as wrongful death actions, intestate succession and probate law, real property law, contract law, criminal law, constitutional law, social security benefits, worker's compensation awards, insurance coverage, pension plans, loss of consortium actions, state and federal tax law and, of course, marital property and support rights.[3]

Despite the growing diversity of family relationships and alternative family forms in contemporary American society, marriage still remains an important legal and social institution. A significant majority of Americans will marry at some point in their lives, and most Americans still regard marriage as an important part of their life plan.[4] Moreover, the law continues to encourage, support, and regulate the institution of marriage in contemporary American society as an important criterion for allocating a wide range of social and economic benefits. Indeed, contemporary debates over "family values" often center on the question of who may marry, and what legal and economic consequences should follow from the decision to marry.[5] Thus, decisions about who may marry, what relationships will be recognized as valid marriages, and what economic, social, political, and legal rights should devolve upon the parties through marriage, continue to be of significant importance to legislators, jurists, scholars, family law practitioners, and the vast majority of Americans today.

---

[1] *See infra* § 2.03.

[2] *See, e.g., Maynard v. Hill*, 125 U.S. 190, 205 (1888); *Griswold v. Connecticut*, 381 U.S. 479, 486 (1965); *Boddie v. Connecticut*, 401 U.S. 371, 376 (1971); *see also supra* §§ 1.01[A], 1.03.

[3] *See generally infra* Chapters 3, 6, 8, 9.

[4] *See* Clark, *supra* note 4, at 26 ("Notwithstanding [consensual alternatives to marriage], a majority of Americans still marry in the traditional way and continue to regard marriage as the most important relationship in their lives").

[5] *See, e.g.,* Weyrauch, *Metamorphoses in Marriage*, 13 Fam. L. Q. 415 (1980) (discussing the changing role of formal and informal marriages in the United States); Whitehead, The Divorce Culture (1997); *Symposium, Law and the New American Family*, 73 Ind. L. J. 393 (1998). Historical evidence also suggests that access to marriage was at the core of the values that motivated those who fought for, and framed, the Fourteenth Amendment of the U.S. Constitution. *See* Davis, Neglected Stories: Family Values and the Constitution (1997).

Yet although marriage remains a central legal and social institution in America, an increasing number of Americans are establishing family relations outside of marriage.[6]

The reasons for the rise in nonmarital cohabitation are as varied as the couples themselves. For same-sex couples, formal marriage is not currently an option in most states. Surveys suggest, however, that a large number of American adults who identify themselves as lesbian or gay live with another person of the same sex and regard that person as their life partner.[7] For younger heterosexual couples, cohabitation is often a prelude to marriage, which tends to occur later today than in the past, both for women and men.[8] And for older heterosexual Americans, many of whom have been previously divorced and are cautious about recommitting to marriage again, long-term nonmarital cohabitation is often viewed as a viable alternative to marriage for a number of practical and philosophical reasons.[9]

State courts and legislatures therefore are increasingly asked to determine the legal rights and obligations of nonmarital cohabitants or domestic partners in the same manner as they would determine the legal rights and obligations of married spouses. Accordingly, this Chapter will analyze and discuss the essential characteristics of marriage and marriage-like relationships including: nonmarital cohabitation and domestic partnerships as alternatives to marriage; formal statutory marriages; informal marriages; the last-in-time marriage presumption; proof of marriage; the capacity and intent to marry; marital conflicts of law; and annulment of marriage.

§ 2.02   CONSENSUAL ALTERNATIVES TO MARRIAGE

Nonmarital cohabitation, as an American social development, has experienced an eight-fold increase from 1970-1990,[10] and there are strong indications that this trend may continue in the future.[11] Unlike marriage, where marital property and

---

[6] *See generally* Dr. Naomi Gerstel, Fact Sheet, Council on Contemporary Families, *Single and Unmarried Americans as Family and Community Members*, Sept. 15, 2011 (discussing diverse family structures that include single or unmarried members, and providing current statistics on family composition).

[7] *See, e.g.*, Chambers, *What If? The Legal Consequences of Marriage and the Legal Needs of Lesbian and Gay Male Couples*, 95 Mich. L. Rev. 447, 449 (1996).

[8] In 1997, the median age of first marriage for men was 26.8 years, up from 23.2 years in 1970. For women, the median age for first marriage was 25.0 years, compared to 20.8 years in 1970. Bureau of the Census, U.S. Dept. of Commerce, *Current Population Reports, Series P20-506, Marital Status and Living Arrangements* (Mar. 1997) (Table 1).

[9] *See, e.g.*, Parks, *Middle Age Couples: Committed, Unmarried*, Dallas Morning News, Sept. 11, 1994 at F-1; Steinhauer, *More Older Couples Move in Together*, Dallas Morning News, July 15, 1995 at C-11.

[10] *See, e.g.*, Bureau of the Census, U.S. Department of Commerce, Current Population Reports Series P-20, No. 445 *Marital Status and Living Arrangements* (1990); *see also* Council on Family Law, *The Future of Family Law: Law and the Marriage Crisis in North America*, available at www.marriagedebate.com/pdf/future_of_family_law.pdf (detailing the current trends surrounding marriage, cohabitation, and divorce in American family law and proposing that what is missing in family law is "any real understanding of the central role of marriage as a social institution in protecting the well-being of children").

[11] *See, e.g.*, Bureau of the Census, U.S. Department of Commerce, Current Population Reports Series

support rights are legally recognized and protected through state legislative and judicial authority,[12] a nonmarital relationship or domestic partnership between unmarried heterosexual or homosexual couples, in the vast majority of states, traditionally lacked any legal recognition based upon the legal status of the unmarried cohabitants, although this traditional rule has begun to moderate somewhat.[13] In the absence of state recognition of nonmarital cohabitation as a legal status, however, the parties might still have certain contractual rights and other equitable remedies based upon their nonmarital cohabitation.[14]

American legal treatment of nonmarital cohabitation has changed significantly over the past 25 years. Traditionally, the law viewed unmarried cohabitation relationships with disfavor, characterizing them as meretricious, and often criminal as well. Couples engaged in such relationships could not look to the courts to define their legal rights and obligations, nor to resolve their disputes in the event their relationship failed. Nor were unmarried cohabitants entitled to any of the statutory or common law benefits traditionally accorded to married couples. More recently, however, this traditional view has been replaced by an increased willingness on the part of the courts to resolve financial and property disputes between unmarried cohabitants. These judicial approaches to such disputes still vary considerably, however, and disagreement exists as to the extent to which nonmarital cohabitation should be analogized to marriage for the purpose of determining the unmarried partners' legal rights and obligations toward one another. Courts, in particular, disagree about whether the relationship between unmarried cohabitants should be governed primarily by principles of contract law, or whether the law should treat nonmarital cohabitation as a status relationship.[15]

In disputes between unmarried cohabitants and third parties, however, courts have been reluctant to extend to cohabitants many of the legal and economic benefits traditionally associated with marriage, although there have been some judicial exceptions to this general rule. Many courts have suggested that decisions regarding the extension of benefits to unmarried cohabitants are more properly made in the legislative area, rather than by the courts; and recently some state and local legislative bodies have responded to this need by passing "domestic partnership" statutes and ordinances designed to grant to unmarried cohabitants some, but not all, of the legal rights and benefits traditionally available to married couples. A number of public and private employers also have extended some employment-related benefits to unmarried couples, both heterosexual and homosexual.[16] These measures, in turn, have engendered debate about the appropriate definition of family, and about the role of the law in regulating and channeling intimate behavior.

P-20 No. 506 *Marital Status and Living Arrangements* (1997).

[12] *See generally infra* Chapters 4, 8, 9.

[13] *See generally infra* § 2.02[C].

[14] *See generally infra* § 2.02[A].

[15] *See generally* Swisher, Miller & Shapo, Family Law: Cases, Materials and Problems 171-73 (3d ed. 2012).

[16] *Id.* at 191. *See generally* Cox, *Alternative Families: Obtaining Traditional Family Benefits Through Litigation, Legislation, and Collective Bargaining*, 15 Wis. Women's L.J. 93 (2000).

[A]   Nonmarital Cohabitation: Contract Implications

Since the widely publicized case of *Marvin v. Marvin*,[17] numerous state courts increasingly have been asked to evaluate and enforce nonmarital contracts, oral or written, express or implied, which purportedly cover the contractual rights and obligations of unmarried cohabiting heterosexual or homosexual couples.

The *Marvin* cases involved actor Lee Marvin and singer Michelle Triola Marvin, who cohabited together for approximately six years. Although Michelle legally changed her last name to Marvin, the parties were never married. After the couple's cohabiting relationship broke up, Michelle sued Lee in a contract action, alleging that Lee contractually had promised to support her in consideration of her companionship services during their cohabiting relationship, and Michelle argued that even if this alleged agreement was not an express contract, then it should be actionable as an implied contract.

The California Supreme Court in *Marvin I*[18] held that an express or implied contractual cause of action based upon a cohabiting nonmarital relationship was actionable in California, and in the absence of a contractual action the courts could also employ other equitable remedies:

> We conclude: (1) The Provisions of the Family Law Act do *not* govern the distribution of property acquired during a nonmarital relationship; such a relationship remains subject solely to [contractual] judicial decision. (2) The courts should enforce express contracts between nonmarital partners except to the extent that the contract is explicitly founded on the consideration of meretricious sexual services. (3) In the absence of an express contract, the courts should inquire into the conduct of the parties to determine whether that conduct demonstrates an implied contract, agreement of partnership or joint venture, or some other tacit understanding between the parties. The courts may also employ the doctrine of quantum meruit, or equitable remedies such as constructive or resulting trusts, when warranted by the facts of the case.[19]

However, a subsequent trial court in *Marvin II*,[20] and an appellate court in *Marvin III*,[21] both held that Michelle had not met her factual burden of proof in demonstrating that any implied or express contract existed in her particular case, nor was the trial court justified in giving Michelle any type of equitable rehabilitative award under California law.[22]

---

[17]   *Marvin v. Marvin*, 557 P.2d 106 (Cal. 1976) (*Marvin I*); *Marvin v. Marvin*, Case C23303, 5 Fam. L. Rep. 3079 (1979) (*Marvin II*); *Marvin v. Marvin*, 176 Cal. Rptr. 555 (Cal. Ct. App. 1981) (*Marvin III*).

[18]   557 P.2d 106.

[19]   *Id.*

[20]   Case C23303, 5 Fam. L. Rep. 3079 (1979).

[21]   176 Cal. Rptr. 555 (Cal. Ct. App. 1981).

[22]   Michelle Marvin's attorney had, for some reason, dismissed her quantum meruit cause of action in *Marvin II*, thereby removing that equitable remedy from the court's consideration.

Although the general public has largely misinterpreted the *Marvin* decision as creating a type of quasi-marriage alternative,[23] in reality the *Marvin* decision was a basic contract case, and was decided utilizing a basic contractual analysis.[24] The *Marvin* decision was also important in illustrating the "severance" doctrine, which separates any meretricious sexual activities that generally would constitute illegal consideration in nonmarital cohabitation agreements, from legally recognized contractual consideration such as companionship and homemaking services.[25]

There were some dire predictions that *Marvin* would "open the door" to a flood of nonmarital contractual claims, that it would change the way society looks at marriage, and that it would put marital rights and obligations in jeopardy. In general, however, post-*Marvin* judicial decisions have taken a more conservative approach to nonmarital cohabitation agreements; and most courts have dealt only with contractual issues, and have basically ignored the larger social policy issues of the nonmarital relationship per se.

For example, in the case of *Morone v. Morone*,[26] the New York Court of Appeals rejected the concept of an implied nonmarital contract as recognized in *Marvin*, and held that it would only recognize express nonmarital contracts not based upon sexual conduct. The *Morone* court justified its decision based upon the fact that there would be difficulties of proof and risk of fraud in recognizing implied nonmarital contracts. The problem for the *Morone* court, therefore, was not one of failure to recognize a nonmarital relationship, but the difficulty in quantifying the remedy. A number of other state courts have followed this New York limitation to *Marvin*.[27]

---

[23] Indicative of this common misunderstanding is the widespread use of the term "palimony" by the press and lay public when discussing *Marvin*-type cases.

[24] *See generally* Marital and Nonmarital Contracts: Preventative Law for the Family (J. Krauskopf ed., 1979). *See also* Prince, *Public Policy Limitations on Cohabitation Agreements: Unruly Horse or Circus Pony?*, 70 Minn. L. Rev. 163 (1986); Comment, *Property Rights Upon Termination of Unmarried Cohabitation:* Marvin v. Marvin, 90 Harv. L. Rev. 1708 (1977); Allen Parkman, *The Contractual Alternative to Marriage*, 32 N. Ky. L. Rev. 125 (2005); Brian Bix, *The Public and Private Ordering of Marriage*, 2004 U. Chi. Legal F. 295 (discussing private and public ordering or marriage and marriage-like relationships).

A number of cases predating *Marvin* dealt with a similar nonmarital contractual analysis. *See, e.g., Tyranski v. Piggins*, 205 N.W.2d 595 (Mich. Ct. App. 1973); *Walker v. Walker*, 47 N.W.2d 633 (Mich. 1951). *But see* Comment, *Applying* Marvin v. Marvin *to Same-Sex Couples: A Proposal for a Sex-Preference Neutral Cohabitation Contract Statute*, 25 U.C. Davis L. Rev. 1029 (1992).

[25] Some other cases recognizing this "severance" doctrine as applied to nonmarital cohabitation contracts include: *Kozlowski v. Kozlowski*, 395 A.2d 913 (N.J. Super. Ct.), *aff'd*, 403 A.2d 902 (N.J. 1979); *Hierholzer v. Sardy*, 340 N.W.2d 91 (Mich. Ct. App. 1983); *Cook v. Cook*, 691 P.2d 664 (Ariz. 1984).

[26] 413 N.E.2d 1154 (N.Y. 1980).

[27] *See, e.g., Carnes v. Sheldon*, 311 N.W.2d 747 (Mich. Ct. App. 1981); *Merrill v. Davis*, 673 P.2d 1285 (N.M. 1983); *In re Estate of Alexander*, 445 So. 2d 836 (Miss. 1984). Minnesota, by state statute, requires an express written nonmarital agreement before it will be enforced. Minn. Stat. Ann. §§ 513.075, 513.076. *But see also Carney v. Hansell*, 831 A.2d 128 (N.J. Super. 2003) (holding that an unmarried woman was *not* entitled to compensation for services rendered to the owner of a towing business with whom she had cohabited for more than sixteen years. She was entitled, however, to *quantum meruit* compensation for services rendered as a "key employee" of his towing business).

Still other states have totally rejected the *Marvin* rationale, either because nonmarital contracts purportedly violate state public policy, or because the "severance" doctrine regarding meretricious sexual relationships is not recognized in those jurisdictions. For example in *Hewitt v. Hewitt*[28] the Illinois Supreme Court stated that nonmarital cohabitation cases cannot be characterized solely in terms of contract law, since major public policy questions are involved in determining whether, under what circumstances, and to what extent it is desirable to accord some type of legal status to claims arising from nonmarital relationships.

The *Hewitt* court conceded that traditional public policy prohibitions on contracts based in whole or in part on illicit sexual intercourse[29] would not necessarily prevent the parties from forming valid contracts regarding independent matters for which sexual relations do *not* form any part of the consideration.[30] Nevertheless, the court held that "we believe that these questions are appropriately within the province of the legislature, and that, if there is to be a change in the law of this State on this matter, it is for the legislature and not the courts to bring about that change."[31] A number of other courts have followed the *Hewitt* rationale, holding that nonmarital contracts are unenforceable.[32]

A better reasoned approach, however, is found in *Watts v. Watts*,[33] where the Wisconsin Supreme Court expressly rejected the *Hewitt* rationale, holding that since courts regularly settle contract and property disputes between unmarried persons, some of whom have cohabited, they should also do the same for people who specifically indicate the existence of such a nonmarital cohabitation relationship.[34]

[B] Nonmarital Cohabitation: Property Issues

Although the *Marvin* decisions[35] rested primarily, though not exclusively, on principles derived from contract law, in other more recent unmarried cohabitation cases, litigants also have invoked property and partnership theories. Another important issue regarding nonmarital cohabitation therefore involves property rights acquired during a nonmarital cohabitation period, after the parties later marry one another, and then sue for divorce. As discussed in a subsequent chapter, on divorce most jurisdictions allow a family court judge to divide and distribute

---

[28] 394 N.E.2d 1204 (Ill. 1979).

[29] *See, e.g., Wallace v. Rappleye*, 103 Ill. 229, 249 (1882) ("An agreement in consideration of future illicit cohabitation between the plaintiffs is void"); Restatement of Contracts § 589 (1932) ("a bargain in whole or in part for or in consideration of illicit sexual intercourse or a promise thereof is illegal").

[30] *See, e.g.*, Restatement of Contracts §§ 589, 597; 6A Corbin on Contracts § 1476 (1962).

[31] *Hewitt v. Hewitt*, 394 N.E.2d 1204 (Ill. 1979) (citing with approval *Mogged v. Mogged*, 302 N.E.2d 293, 295 (Ill. 1973)).

[32] *See, e.g., Rehak v. Mathis*, 238 S.E.2d 81 (Ga. 1977); *Roach v. Buttons*, 6 Fam. L. Rep. 2355 (Tenn. 1980); *Thomas v. LaRosa*, 400 S.E.2d 809 (W. Va. 1990).

[33] 405 N.W.2d 303 (Wis. 1987).

[34] *Id.* (holding, therefore, that a party's allegations were sufficient to state a cause of action for a breach of express or implied contract, unjust enrichment, and statutory or common law partition). *See generally* Burch, *Cohabitation in the Common Law Countries a Decade After* Marvin*; Settled In or Moving Ahead?*, 22 U.C. Davis L. Rev. 717 (1989).

[35] *See supra* § 2.02[A].

certain property acquired during the marriage which is classified as either "marital property" or "community property."[36] However, a family court judge in most states cannot divide or distribute property acquired prior to the marriage, which is still classified as "separate property" in most states.[37] Nevertheless, some courts have held that a "legal merger" may have taken place upon the marriage of nonmarital cohabitants, thus allowing a family court judge to consider both premarital *and* postmarital property in an equitable distribution of property award on divorce.[38]

Conversely, if unmarried cohabitants do not subsequently marry each other, the courts are split on whether or not state marriage-related property statutes ought to apply by analogy in adjudicating property claims between unmarried cohabitants as well. Some courts have held in the affirmative.[39] A majority of courts to date, however, have held in the negative.[40] And in contexts other than property division, the courts generally have refused to allow unmarried cohabitants to invoke statutory remedies generally available to divorcing couples.[41] Consequently, several commentators have suggested the creation of a legal status known as nonmarital cohabitation. When such a status is established, by the state courts or legislatures, the courts could then proceed to apportion the assets of the members of that status according to traditional principles of community property or equitable distribution.[42]

[C] Nonmarital Cohabitation: Status Implications of Domestic Partnerships and Civil Unions

Although nonmarital cohabiting couples traditionally had few, if any, legal rights and obligations other than private contractual remedies,[43] a growing number of cities[44] have enacted domestic partnership ordinances. These ordinances extend

---

[36] *See generally infra* §§ 10.02, 10.03.

[37] *See generally infra* § 10.03. *See also In re Marriage of Lindsey*, 676 P.2d 328 (Wash. 1984).

[38] *See, e.g., Chestnut v. Chestnut*, 499 N.E.2d 783 (Ind. App. 1986); *Easton v. Johnson*, 681 P.2d 606 (Kan. 1984). *But see Wilen v. Wilen*, 486 A.2d 775 (Md. Ct. App. 1985); *Crouch v. Crouch*, 410 N.E.2d 580 (Ill. Ct. App. 1980).

[39] *See, e.g., Connell v. Francisco*, 898 P.2d 831 (Wash. 1995); *Western States Constr. Co. v. Michoff*, 840 P.2d 1220 (Nev. 1992); *Shuraleff v. Donnelly*, 817 P.2d 764 (Or. Ct. App. 1991); *Gormley v. Robertson*, 83 P.3d 1042 (Wash. Ct. App. 2004).

[40] *See, e.g., Davis v. Davis*, 643 So. 2d 931 (Miss. 1994).

[41] *See, e.g., Friedman v. Friedman*, 24 Cal. Rptr. 2d 892, 898 (Cal. Ct. App. 1993) (holding that a trial court lacks authority to award temporary support to a disabled cohabitant pending trial of her express and implied contract claims, since such temporary relief was available only in the context of marriage and divorce); *Crowe v. DeGioia*, 495 A.2d 889 (N.J. Super. Ct. App. Div. 1985), *aff'd* 505 A.2d 591 (N.J. 1986) (ruling that a state statute permitting an award of attorneys' fees on divorce was inapplicable to an action to distribute property following a nonmarital cohabitation relationship).

[42] *See, e.g.,* Blumberg, *Cohabitation Without Marriage: A Different Perspective*, 28 UCLA L. Rev. 1125 (1981); Bruch, *Property Rights of De Facto Spouses Including Thoughts on the Value of Homemakers' Services*, 10 Fam. L. Q. 101 (1976).

[43] *See generally supra* § 2.02[A].

[44] For example, Berkeley, San Francisco, Los Angeles, Santa Cruz, and West Hollywood, California; New York City; Chicago; Boston; Seattle; Madison, Wisconsin; and Takoma Park, Maryland among numerous other municipalities.

various municipal benefits to an individual's spousal equivalent without regard to sex, as though the two persons were legally married, and as an effective means for conferring certain legally recognized *status* benefits on unmarried heterosexual and homosexual domestic partners.[45] As one commentator has explained:

> In its simplicity, domestic partnership is one step more than cohabitation, but one step less than marriage. Its essential ingredient is a business or government recognition of benefits conferred on a nonmarital adult couple of the same or opposite sex because of conformity with a procedure established by the business or government.[46]

Likewise, various corporations recently have made employment benefits applicable not only to married spouses of their employees, but also to unmarried cohabiting domestic partners as well.[47] Although these modest initiatives have not yet enjoyed substantial support from the majority of other American cities or states, they nevertheless constitute a first major step in the recognition of nonmarital cohabitation as a legally protected status.[48]

Some critics, however, have opposed any legal recognition of nonmarital cohabitation on the ground that de jure legal recognition of nonmarital cohabitation would have a destabilizing effect on the traditional family unit, which is already at risk.[49] But whatever these theoretical rationales may be, American society today consists

---

[45] *See, e.g.,* Berger, *Domestic Partnership Initiatives,* 40 DePaul L. Rev. 417 (1991); Bowman & Cornish, *A Legal and Social Analysis of Domestic Partnership Ordinances,* 92 Colum. L. Rev. 1164 (1992); Note, *Legal Rights of Unmarried Heterosexual and Homosexual Couples and the Evolving Definition of "Family,"* 29 J. Fam. L. 497 (1990-91).

[46] O'Brien, *Domestic Partnership: Recognition and Responsibility,* 32 San Diego L. Rev. 163, 165 (1995).

[47] *See, e.g.,* Note, *Domestic Partnership Recognition in the Workplace: Equitable Employee Benefits for Gay Couples (and Others),* 51 Ohio St. L. J. 1067 (1990). Among the employers offering domestic partnership benefits are more than 100 colleges and universities, as well as an increasing number of law firms, particularly in major cities. *See* Barge, *More Firms Offer Benefits for Gay Couples,* ABA J., June 1995, at 81.

[48] *See generally* Blumberg, *Cohabitation Without Marriage: A Different Perspective,* 28 UCLA L. Rev. 1125 (1981); Minow, *Redefining Families,* 62 U. Colo. L. Rev. 269 (1991); Note, *Expansion of the Term "Family" to Include Nontraditional Relationships,* 20 Mem. St. U. L. Rev. 135 (1989); Comment, *Prohibiting Marital Status Discrimination: A Proposal for the Protection of Unmarried Couples,* 42 Hastings L.J. 1415 (1991); Christensen, *Legal Ordering of Family Values: The Case for Gay and Lesbian Families,* 18 Cardozo L. Rev. 1299 (1997); Ertman, *Contractual Purgatory for Sexual Marginorities: Not Heaven, but Not Hell Either,* 73 Denver U. L. Rev. 1107 (1996); Family Law Symposium, *A More Perfect Union? Marriage and Marriage-Like Relationships in Family Law,* 30 N. M. L. Rev. 1 (2000). *See also* Jeffrey Sherman, *Domestic Partnership and ERISA Preemption,* 76 Tulane L. Rev. 373 (2001).

[49] *See, e.g.,* Sullivan, *Here Comes the Groom,* New Republic, Aug. 28, 1989 at 20.

> Society has good reason to extend legal advantages to heterosexuals who marry . . . . They make a deeper commitment to one another and to society; in exchange, society extends certain benefits to them . . . . We rig the law in its favor not because we disparage all forms of relationships other than the nuclear family, but because we recognize that not to promote marriage would be to ask too much of human virtue . . . . Enshrining in the law a vague principle like domestic partnership is an invitation to qualify at little personal cost for entitlement . . . .

See also Lynne Wardle, *The Bonds of Matrimony and the Bonds of Constitutional Democracy,* 32 Hofstra L. Rev. 349 (2003).

of approximately 30% of households that are composed of traditional families, defined as two heterosexual parents living with their children.[50] The remaining 70% of American households now constitute nontraditional families, defined as one parent families (approximately 30% of all households), single persons, and unmarried heterosexual and homosexual couples.[51]

Consequently, a number of American courts are now granting more legal recognition to unmarried domestic cohabitation on a statewide level, as well as on a municipal level, in loss of consortium actions, workers' compensation actions, and zoning or rental disputes involving real property.[52]

A better reasoned approach would be for more state legislatures and courts to recognize and protect the legal rights and obligations of *both* traditional *and* nontraditional families, as they currently coexist in American society today, by providing alternative legal rights and remedies for each social structure, according to the public policy of each state, and based upon the present and future needs of all its citizens.

For example, in July of 1997, Hawaii became the first state in the United States to enact comprehensive, state-wide domestic partnership legislation. The Hawaii statute allows same-sex couples, and others who are legally prohibited from marrying, to register with the state as "reciprocal beneficiaries." Once registered, reciprocal beneficiaries are eligible for a wide range of benefits previously reserved for married couples. These benefits include: health insurance, retirement benefits, inheritance rights, workers' compensation benefits, family and funeral leave, joint automobile insurance, property rights, and legal standing relating to wrongful death benefits and victims' rights.[53] This legislation was passed in response to the Hawaii Supreme Court's decision in *Baehr v. Lewin*,[54] suggesting that restricting marriage to opposite sex couples in Hawaii may be in violation of the Hawaii

---

[50] *See* Berger, *Domestic Partner Initiatives*, 40 DePaul L. Rev. 417 (1991).

[51] Gutis, *What Is a Family?*, N.Y. Times, Aug. 31, 1989, at C6.

[52] For example, although a loss of consortium action traditionally depends upon proof of a valid marriage, *Curry v. Caterpillar Tractor Co.*, 577 F. Supp. 991 (E.D. Pa. 1984), some courts have allowed loss of consortium claims to be filed by unmarried cohabitants as well. *See, e.g., Bulloch v. United States*, 487 F. Supp. 1078 (D.N.J. 1980). *See generally infra* § 3.05[D].

And although the prevailing traditional view is that state workers compensation statutes generally exclude unmarried cohabitants from any statutory benefits, a minority of states have awarded worker's compensation benefits to dependent unmarried de facto spouses as well. *See, e.g., Kempf v. State Accident Ins. Fund*, 580 P.2d 1032 (Or. Ct. App. 1978). *See generally infra* § 3.05[D].

Finally, the renting or purchasing of a home that is zoned or covenanted as a "family residence" has traditionally presented many legal problems for unmarried cohabitants. *See, e.g., Maryland Comm'n on Human Rights v. Greenbelt Homes*, 475 A.2d 1192 (Md. 1984) (holding that enforcement of a cooperative housing regulation that prohibited unmarried couples did not constitute discrimination based upon marital status). However, on the other hand, the case of *Braschi v. Stahl Assocs.*, 543 N.E.2d 49 (N.Y. 1989), held that, for rent control purposes, a family would include "two adult lifetime partners whose relationship is long-term and characterized by an emotional and financial commitment and interdependence."

[53] 1997 Hawaii H.B. 118 (July 1997).

[54] 852 P.2d 44 (Haw. 1993).

constitution.[55]

Likewise in 1999, the Vermont Supreme Court held in *Baker v. State*,[56] that Vermont "is constitutionally required to extend to same-sex couples the common benefits and protections that flow from marriage under Vermont law," but whether "this takes the form of inclusion within the marriage laws themselves or a parallel domestic partnership system or some equivalent statutory alternative, rests with the Legislature."[57] Consequently, a year later the Vermont legislature passed state legislation recognizing a "civil union" alternative to marriage. Under this domestic partnership legislation, partners in a civil union would be eligible for hundreds of state benefits normally given to married couples. They could transfer property, make medical decision for each other, inherit estates, and oversee burials. They would be required to accept the joint debt of their partners, and dissolve their civil union in Family Court in a proceeding equivalent to divorce.[58]

A number of other states also have enacted similar domestic partnership or civil union legislation, based on the statutory models found in Hawaii and Vermont.[59] Indeed, the American Law Institute's *Principles of the Law of Family Dissolution*,[60] recently proposed a number of statutory recommendations relating to domestic partnership law for the possible adoption and enactment by state legislatures.[61] The scope of these proposed family law principles is to govern the

---

[55] In the wake of the *Baehr* decision, a number of Hawaiian legislators in 1997 proposed a state constitutional amendment banning same-sex marriages in Hawaii, which was subsequently approved by the Hawaiian voters. *See also* Julianna Gonen, *Same-Sex Unions and Domestic Partnerships*, 2 Geo. J. Gender & L. 329 (2001) (reviewing court decisions in Hawaii, Alaska, and Vermont).

[56] 744 A.2d 864 (Vt. 1999).

[57] *Id.* at 867.

[58] *See. e.g.*, Ferdinand, *Gay Civil Unions Near Legality*, The Washington Post, April 19, 2000 at A-3. Subsequently, California and New Jersey also enacted similar state-wide domestic partnership legislation. *See also* Symposium, *Vermont Civil Unions*, 25 Vt. L. Rev. 1 (2000). Whether or not sister states will recognize Vermont civil unions is another largely unresolved issue. *See, e.g.*, Elaine Defranco, *Choice of Law: Will a Wisconsin Court Recognize a Vermont Civil Union?*, 85 Marq. L.Rev. 251 (2001). *But see Brown v. Perez*, 30 Fam. L. Rep. 1094 (BNA 2003) (an Iowa trial judge dissolved a civil union between two same-sex persons, entered into in Vermont, holding that he did so because of the Iowa state constitution's full faith and credit clause). *See also Miller-Jenkins v. Miller-Jenkins*, 637 S.E.2d 330 (Va. Ct. App. 2006) (recognizing the dissolution of a same-sex civil union in Vermont in an interstate child custody dispute).

[59] The Hawaii and Vermont experience, as well as public opinion polls in other states, suggest that while many Americans support the concept of domestic partnership legislation and other legal remedies for same-sex couples, many Americans still remain opposed to same-sex marriage. *See, e.g.*, Garcia, *Californians Accepting Gay Rights, But Poll Finds Opposition to Same-Sex Marriages*, San Francisco Chronicle, March 3, 1997 at A-1. Currently, domestic partnership or civil union statutes on a state-wide basis have been enacted in Hawaii, Vermont, California, Connecticut, New Jersey, Washington State, Oregon, New Hampshire, Rhode Island, and the District of Columbia. Proposed domestic partnership legislation is being considered in a number of other states as well. *Query*: Should civil unions or domestic partnership legislation apply only to same-sex couples, or to heterosexual couples as well? *See* Erin Cleary, *New Jersey's Domestic Partnership Act in the Aftermath of* Lewis v. Harris: *Should New Jersey Expand the Act to Include All Unmarried Cohabitants?*, 60 Rutgers L. Rev. 519 (2008).

[60] ALI, *Principles of the Law of Family Dissolution: Analysis and Recommendations* (Tentative Draft No. 4, April 10, 2000).

[61] *Id.* at Chapter 6, Domestic Partners.

financial claims of domestic partners against one another at the termination of their relationship.[62] Domestic partners are defined under the *Principles* as two persons of the same sex or opposite sex, not married to one another, who for a significant period of time share a primary residence and a life together as a couple.[63] "Domestic partnership property" is defined under the *Principles* as that property which would have been marital property had the domestic partners been married to one another during their domestic partnership period,[64] but nothing in the *Principles* would foreclose contract claims between such persons who have formed a contract that is enforceable under applicable state law.[65]

§ 2.03 MARRIAGE: A STATUS OR CONTRACT?

The vast majority of states have held that marriage constitutes a legal *status* based upon contract. Accordingly, there are three parties to any marriage: Husband, Wife, and the State; and the public policy of the State is to regulate marriage based upon the general welfare of its citizens.[66]

The states therefore can prescribe the age at which parties may contract to marry, the procedures essential to constitute a valid marriage under state law, the duties and obligations created by the marriage, the effect of marriage on the parties' property and support rights and obligations, and the acts which may constitute grounds for the dissolution of marriage.[67] Thus, even when a court is faced with a purely economic or contractual issue within the marital relationship, there is a continuing recognition of the state's power to regulate *all* the incidents of the marital relationship.[68]

Some commentators, however, have questioned these traditional assumptions involving the state's regulation of marriage, and they have argued that the legal *status* of marriage has now become obsolete, and the incidents of marriage should therefore move from *status* to *contract* implications, with a corresponding de-emphasis in the state's regulation of marriage.[69] To date, however, only a small

---

[62] *Id.* at § 6.01(A).

[63] *Id.* at § 6.03.

[64] *Id.* at § 6.04, 6.05.

[65] *Id.* at § 6.01(B).

[66] *See, e.g., Maynard v. Hill*, 125 U.S. 190, 205 (1888); *Boddie v. Connecticut*, 401 U.S. 371, 376 (1971); *see also supra* § 1.03; Symposium, *Marriage Law: Obsolete or Cutting Edge?*, 10 Mich. J. Gender & L. 21 (2003); Anita Bernstein, *For and Against Marriage: A Revision*, 102 Mich. L. Rev. 129 (2003) (examining the benefits and drawbacks of state-sponsored marriage).

[67] *Id. See also Fearon v. Treanor*, 5 N.E.2d 815, 816 (N.Y. 1936); *Cramer v. Commonwealth*, 202 S.E.2d 911, 915 (Va. 1974).

[68] *See, e.g., Boddie v. Connecticut*, 401 U.S. 371, 376 (1971) ("Without a prior judicial imprimatur, individuals may fully enter into and rescind commercial contracts, for example, but we are unaware of any jurisdiction where private citizens may covenant for or dissolve marriage without state approval.").

[69] *See, e.g.,* Wright, *Marriage: From Status to Contract?*, 13 Anglo-Am. L. Rev. 17 (1984); Schultz, *Contractual Ordering of Marriage: A New Model for State Policy*, 70 Cal. L. Rev. 204 (1982); Singer, *The Privatization of Family Law*, 1992 Wis. L. Rev. 1443; Comment, *Marriage as a Contact: Toward a Functional Redefinition of the Marital Status*, 9 Colum. J. L. & Soc. Probs. 607 (1973); *see also* W. O'Donnell & D. Jones, The Law of Marriage and Marriage Alternatives 1-4 (1982).

minority of jurisdictions have viewed marriage more in terms of a contract than a legal status.[70]

Nevertheless, the current statutory regulation of marriage has a number of critics. Professor Lenore Weitzman, for example, argues that "prospective spouses are neither informed of the terms of a [marriage] contract, nor are they allowed any options about these terms . . . . [O]ur society has undergone profound transformations in the past century, and the long-standing legal structure of marriage may now be anachronistic. The state's interest in preserving the traditional family may not be important enough to offset new societal and individual needs which require more flexibility and choice in family forms."[71] Marriage and the traditional nuclear family have been battered by current social and economic factors, and one commentator believes that "our society [may be] moving in the direction of a post-marriage or post-nuclear family system, where the married couple, father-mother unit will no longer be held up as the dominant cultural ideal and will no longer refect the empirical reality for all, or even most, children."[72] Some feminist writers have argued for the uncoupling of marriage and child rearing[73] while other commentators believe that many of our current social ills are caused in large part by father absence.[74] Writes Professor David Blankenhorn:

> What is society going to do about this state of affairs? Given the increasing recognition of the trend toward the post-marriage, post-nuclear family and the obviously negative consequences of this trend, especially for children, a new family debate is now emerging . . . . There are two fault lines that I believe will characterize this new debate in the coming months and years. On one side of the fault line will be those who argue that we cannot reverse the trend-that is, that we cannot reinstitutionalize marriage. Therefore, we must instead deal with the consequences of the weakening of marriage,

---

[70] *See, e.g., Ponder v. Graham,* 4 Fla. 23 (1851); *Ryan v. Ryan,* 277 So. 2d 266 (Fla. 1973); *see also Seizer v. Sessions,* 915 P.2d 553, 561 (Wash. Ct. App. 1996) *rev'd on other grounds* 940 P.2d 261 (Wash. 1997) (comparing Washington and Texas law and pointing out that under Washington State law "the spouses by mutual consent can terminate a marriage, or can mutually treat the community property presumptions as terminated by agreeing to live separate and apart" whereas under Texas law "the institution of marriage is a status, more than a mere contract"); Stephen Sugarman, Divorce Reform at the Crossroads 138 (1990) ("Marriage, at least in this century, is typically said to be best understood as a status, rather than as a contractual relationship").

[71] Weitzman, *Legal Regulation of Marriage: Tradition and Change, A Proposal for Individual Contract and Contracts in Lieu of Marriage,* 62 Cal. L. Rev. 1169, 1170 (1974). *See also* Shultz, *Contractual Ordering of Marriage: A New Model for State Policy,* 70 Cal. L. Rev. 204, 207 (1982) ("Marriage has undergone tremendous change in recent decades . . . only a small percentage of American families still have all the characteristics associated with the nuclear family ideal. In place of a single socially approved ideal we have competing demands for autonomy and privacy, and multiple models of intimacy: single parents, working wives, house husbands, homosexual couples, living together arrangements without marriage, serial marriage, and stepchildren. The changes are legion, and their message is clear: the destruction of traditional marriage as the sole model for adult intimacy is irreversible").

[72] Blankenhorn, *The State of the Family and the Family Law Debate,* 36 Santa Clara L. Rev. 431, 431-32 (1996).

[73] *See, e.g.,* Carbone & Brinig, *Rethinking Marriage: Feminist Ideology, Economic Change, and Divorce,* 65 Tul. L. Rev. 953 (1991); Martha Fineman, The Neutered Mother (1995).

[74] *See, e.g.,* David Blankenhorn, Fatherless America (1995).

especially the economic consequences, recognizing the reality that more and more of our children are simply not going to be growing up with their two married parents . . . Those on the other side of this fault line will insist that we must seek to reverse this trend. They will direct their efforts to strengthening the institution of marriage and seeking to create cultural change in favor of the idea that unwed childbearing is wrong, that our divorce rate is far too high, and that every child deserves a father.[75]

Consequently, some states have attempted to "reinstitutionalize" or strengthen marriage through so-called "covenant marriage" legislation as an alternative to "regular" marriage.[76] Under a Louisiana "covenant" marriage, for example, the parties consensually agree not to obtain a no-fault divorce, and can only dissolve their marriage based upon traditional fault grounds or a separation for two years or more. The couple also agrees to obtain premarital counseling from a clergy member or marital counselor prior to marriage.[77] A number of other states have expressed interest in this Louisiana approach.[78] In 1998, the Florida state legislature, by a bipartisan vote of 91 to 16 in the House and a unanimous vote in the Senate, enacted a "Marriage Preparation and Preservation Act" providing that: (1) all Florida high school students must take a required course in "marriage and relationship skill based education"; (2) engaged couples are encouraged (but not required) to take a "premarital preparation course" of at least four hours in length, which may include instruction in conflict resolution, communication skills, financial responsibilities, children and parenting, and data on problems that married couples face — and those who take this premarital preparation course from a religious or secular marriage counselor are entitled to a reduction in the cost of their marriage license; (3) each couple applying for a marriage license will also be given a handbook prepared by the Florida Bar Association, informing couples of "the rights and responsibilities under Florida law of marital partners to each other and to their children, both during marriage and upon dissolution"; and (4) couples with children who file for divorce must take a "Parent Education and Family Stabilization Course" that covers the legal and emotional impact of divorce on adults and children, financial responsibility, laws regarding child abuse and neglect, and conflict resolution skills.[79]

---

[75] Blankenhorn, *The State of the Family*, *supra* note 72, at 436-37.

[76] *See, e.g.*, La. Rev. Code § 9-224 *et seq*; Ariz. Rev. Stat. § 25-901 *et seq.*

[77] *See generally* Louisiana House Bill 756 (1997). *But see* Katherine Shaw Spaht, *Covenant Marriage Seven Years Later: Its as Yet Unfulfilled Promise*, 65 La. L. Rev. 605 (2005).

[78] *See* Jeter, *Covenant Marriages Tie the Knot Tightly*, The Washington Post, Aug. 15, 1997 at A-1 ("I don't think there's any question that you're going to see a lot of activity around the country as other state legislatures will be studying the concept and trying to adopt it," said Jeff Atkinson, a University of Chicago law professor and a member of the American Bar Association's Family Law Council"); Corey, *States Explore Making Breaking Up Hard to Do*, Baltimore Sun, May 19, 1997 at A-1 (reporting that legislators in at least 20 states have introduced bills to modify no-fault divorce); *see also* Peter Hay, *The American "Covenant Marriage" in the Conflict of Laws*, 64 La. L. Rev. 43 (2003).

[79] *See, e.g.*, McManus, *Florida Passes Nation's Most Sweeping Reform of Marriage Laws*, Ethics and Religion Advance (May 16, 1998) (predicting that this law will inspire many other states to pass similar laws).

Other legislators, sociologists, and clergy have also argued that more states should require premarital counseling prior to marriage. *See, e.g.*, Time Magazine, October 7, 1996 at 84 ("Marriage is a

This recent legislative trend to "reinstitutionalize" and strengthen marriage —
and to discourage divorce — has not been without its critics:

> The notion that the public has a vested interest in seeing families succeed
> is hardly a point of contention. Rather, the issue for opponents of [these
> legislative measures] is whether discouraging divorce is enough to improve
> the quality of marriage, either for parents or their children . . . "It's a
> laudable goal," says [Professor] Atkinson of the ABA. "But is divorce
> automatically worse than every alternative? I don't think these kinds of
> measures are going to be adding to the happiness or longevity of
> marriage."[80]

Although the evidence is not yet in whether this legislative trend to strengthen
and "reinstitutionalize" marriage will be successful or not, it is nevertheless true
that the vast majority of Americans today still support the institution of marriage,[81]
and that the state legislatures and courts, while providing a number of legal rights
and remedies for unmarried cohabitants,[82] currently show no sign of abandoning
state regulation of marriage in the foreseeable future.[83]

---

commitment," says Brian Willats, a spokesman for the Michigan Family Forum, which supports
premarital counseling. "It's not just notarized dating."). And in an August 1997 Time Magazine/CNN
national poll, over two-thirds of those Americans polled favored mandatory premarital counseling.

[80] Jeter, *supra*, note 78, at A-19. *See also* Bradford, *The Counterrevolution: A Critique of Recent
Proposals to Reform No-Fault Divorce Laws*, 49 Stan. L. Rev. 607 (1997) (predicting that such legislative
proposals "will not increase moral behavior" and that fault-based divorce regimes may have a negative
impact on women); Ellman, *Divorce Rates, Marriage Rates, and the Problematic Persistence of
Traditional Marital Roles*, 34 Fam. L. Q. 1, 1-2 (2000) ("The evidence certainly offers little reason to
believe that divorce rates are much affected by divorce laws. The same may prove true about the law's
impact on marriage formation").

[81] *See, e.g.*, Clark, *supra* note 4, at 26 ("Notwithstanding these developments, a majority of Americans
still marry in the traditional way and continue to regard marriage as the most important relationship in
their lives"); Ellman, *supra* note 80, at 2 ("I conclude that women's improved economic position, relative
to men, may indeed contribute to declining marital rates, but only because of the surprising persistence
of traditional marital roles. This persistence in Americans' adherence to traditional marital roles is itself
relevant to policy choices governing the law of divorce and cohabitation").

[82] *See infra* § 2.02.

[83] *See, e.g.*, Stanley & Markman, Can Government Rescue Marriages? 1-2 (1997):

> There is a trend sweeping the country to make changes in legal codes to strengthen and
> stabilize marriages. There are two key thrusts emerging in state legislatures: the first involves
> changes in laws that would make it harder for couples to divorce; the second involves efforts
> to encourage or mandate couples to participate in premarital counseling . . . While strange
> bedfellows, there is a growing consensus among both liberal and conservative political and
> religious leaders that something must be done . . . [Recent empirical studies] strongly
> suggest that couples can learn skills and enhance ways of thinking- prior to marriage- that
> significantly improves their odds of having good marriages . . . . With a growing national
> consensus, a large scale public health education campaign could bring together educators,
> clergy, mental health professionals, and politicians to focus on two key goals: 1) To extol strong
> and happy marriages as a high value and a high priority, and 2) to encourage couples to take
> advantage of effective tools to make their marriages not just more stable, but truly better . . .
> We are talking about values here. Values that say marriage is important. Values that say
> working to resolve differences is good. Values that say preparing for marriage is wise. Values
> that lead to increased dedication for the task of building strong and happy marriages. These
> things can be done if we have the collective will. Let's get to it.

But see also Marsha Garrison, *The Decline of Formal Marriage: Inevitable or Reversible?*, 41 Fam. L.Q.
491 (2007) (arguing that "although policy[holders] can expect only limited results from initiatives

§ 2.04   FORMAL STATUTORY MARRIAGE

Marriage traditionally has been defined as the "voluntary union of a man and a woman to the exclusion of all others"[84] and the vast majority of states therefore prohibit same-sex marriages.[85]

Most Americans who marry do so in a formal statutory marriage in accordance with applicable state statutes. Each state generally requires that: (1) the parties obtain a license prior to the marriage; and (2) the parties be married by an authorized priest, rabbi, minister, or other authorized religious, judicial, or civil officer according to state statute. A blood test for sexually transmitted diseases is also required in many states, and in other states a test for rubella (German measles) is required for women of child-bearing years.[86]

Depending upon the particular state, marriage licenses are valid from 30 to 60 days before they must be renewed; and there is a waiting period in the majority of states averaging from three to five days before the parties can be married. The marriage license is normally issued by a clerk of court or a county clerk where the parties, or either of them, reside, or where the marriage ceremony is to be celebrated. But since a residency or domiciliary requirement is not required for marriage in the vast majority of states, the parties may also be married in another state of their choice.[87]

The marrying official must be duly authorized by the state, and he or she must comply with the applicable state statutes. If the parties wish to be married according to the tenets of a religious denomination that does not have an acknowledged minister or celebrant, then so-called "Quaker statutes" in many states will recognize such a marriage if performed according to the tenets of that particular religious denomination. Other state statutes will recognize the marriage of native American Indians if performed according to tribal custom or law.[88]

If the parties do not fully comply with these statutory requirements for marriage — for example, if the marriage license is invalid, or if the celebrant is not authorized by state law to perform the marriage — such a marriage may be valid or invalid. A majority of states, in order to promote marriage and to validate the marital expectations of the parties, provide that state marital statutes are only *directory* statues, requiring only substantial compliance to constitute a valid marriage.[89]

---

designed to promote formal marriage . . . . they may have the capacity to make a difference at the margins.")

[84] *See, e.g., Hyde v. Hyde*, L.R. 1 P & D 130 (1866).

[85] *See generally infra* § 2.08[B].

[86] *See, e.g.,* The Uniform Marriage and Divorce Act, §§ 201-06. *See generally* Clark, *supra* note 4, at 85-100; S. Green & J. Long, Marriage and Family Law Agreements 18-20 (1984).

[87] *Id.*

[88] *Id.*

[89] *See, e.g., Picarella v. Picarella*, 316 A.2d 826 (Md. Ct. Spec. App. 1974); *Carabetta v. Carabetta*, 438 A.2d 109 (Conn. 1980); *Wright v. Vales*, 613 S.W.2d 850 (Ark. Ct. App. 1981); *Maxwell v. Maxwell*, 273 N.Y.S.2d 728 (N.Y. Sup. Ct. 1966); *see also* Annot., 61 A.L.R.2d 847 (1958) (Later Case Service).

A minority of states, however, have held that state marital statutes are *mandatory* statutes, requiring strict compliance to constitute a valid marriage.[90] However, these mandatory statute jurisdictions often include a curative or "savings" statute, providing that if there is a defect in the license, or a defect in the marrying official, but the parties consummate their marriage with a good faith belief that they have been lawfully joined in marriage, then the marriage is valid, despite their statutory noncompliance.[91]

A party who knew that an impediment existed in the marriage license or the marrying official at the time of the marriage may also be estopped from asserting such a marital impediment at a later date.[92]

§ 2.05   INFORMAL MARRIAGES

An alternative to formal statutory marriage,[93] and to nonmarital cohabitation,[94] is informal marriage which may include common law marriage, putative marriage, marriage by proxy, de facto "marriage," and "marriage" by estoppel.

Although some courts have traditionally viewed informal marriages with suspicion and mistrust, other courts have recognized the validity of such marriages under the public policy rationale of promoting marriage in general, and of validating the marital expectations of the parties in particular, especially with respect to the parties' marital property and support rights and obligations.[95]

[A]   Common Law Marriage

A so-called common law marriage is an informal marriage that does not meet the requirements of a formal statutory marriage. All that is required for a common law marriage is a present intent and agreement of the parties to enter into a matrimonial relationship. In the absence of any express evidence of this present intent and agreement, most courts will infer such present intent and agreement through cohabitation and community repute as husband and wife.[96] Thus, common

---

[90] *See, e.g.*, Minn. Stat. Ann. § 517.01; Va. Code Ann. § 20-13; *see also Williams v. Williams*, 460 N.E.2d 1226 (Ind. App. 1984); *Nelson v. Marshall*, 869 S.W.2d 132 (Mo. Ct. App. 1993); Annot., 61 A.L.R.2d 847 (1958) (Later Case Service).

[91] *See, e.g.*, Va. Code Ann. § 20-31. Consummation, or sexual intercourse, is *not* generally required for a valid marriage. But it *is* often required under various "curative" statutes.

[92] *See infra* § 2.05[E]. *See generally* Clark, *supra* note 4, at 94-96.

[93] *See supra* § 2.04.

[94] *See infra* § 3.02.

[95] *See, e.g.*, Weyrauch, *Informal and Formal Marriage — An Appraisal of Trends in Family Organization*, 28 U. Chi. L. Rev. 88 (1960); Weyrauch, *Metamorphoses of Marriage*, 13 Fam. L.Q. 415 (1980).

[96] *See, e.g., Adams v. Adams*, 559 So. 2d 1084 (Ala. 1990); *Crosson v. Crosson*, 668 So. 2d 868 (Ala. Ct. App. 1995); *In re Estate of Fischer*, 176 N.W.2d 801 (Iowa 1970). *But see Canady v. Russell*, 138 S.W.3d 412 (Tex. App. 2004) (holding that the parties' intent to live together in the future was *not* sufficient to establish a common law marriage, which requires *present* intent and agreement). *See generally* Stein, *Common Law Marriage: Its History and Certain Contemporary Problems*, 9 J. Fam. L. 271 (1969); Hall, *Common Law Marriage*, 46 Cambridge L.J. 106 (1987).

law marriages are as valid as formal statutory marriages in the thirteen American jurisdictions where common law marriages are legally recognized.[97]

Moreover, even if most other American jurisdictions do not recognize common law marriages if contracted within their own state, nevertheless they will recognize common law marriages if contracted in one of the jurisdictions that do recognize such marriages.[98] The rationale for this recognition of sister state common law marriages is the doctrine that a marriage valid where celebrated is valid everywhere, unless such a marriage is against a state's strong public policy;[99] and that common law marriages which validate the present marital expectations of the parties do *not* violate a sister state's strong public policy, which is to promote and protect marriages generally.[100]

Some courts have held that the party claiming a common law marriage must have resided in, or must have established a significant relationship with, the common law marriage state.[101] Other courts, however, have held that visits of short duration to a common law marriage state, where the parties held themselves out as husband and wife, would suffice to create a legally valid common law marriage.[102] This latter approach arguably validates the reasonable expectations of the parties in the marriage, as well as reaffirming state public policy of promoting and protecting marriages in general.[103]

The courts generally require that proof of a common law marriage be established by clear and convincing evidence in order to prevent any fraudulent claims.[104]

---

[97] According to Green & Long, *supra* note 86, at 80-86, the following jurisdictions still recognize common law marriages if contracted within that state: Alabama, Colorado, Georgia (until 1997), Idaho, Iowa, Kansas, Montana, Ohio (until 1991]) Oklahoma, Pennsylvania (until 2003), Rhode Island, South Carolina, Texas, Utah, and the District of Columbia. *See, e.g., Smereczynski v. Dep't of Health & Human Services*, 944 F.2d 296 (6th Cir. 1991) (applying Ohio law). Ohio, however, subsequently abolished common law marriage by statute in 1991. Pennsylvania no longer recognizes common law marriages after 2003. *See PNC Bank v. Workers' Compensation Appeal Board*, 831 A.2d 1269 (Pa. Com. 2003); *Stackhouse v. Stackhouse*, 862 A.2d 102 (Pa. Super. Ct. 2004).

[98] *See, e.g., In re Estate of Burroughs*, 486 N.W.2d 113 (Mich. Ct. App. 1992); *Blaw-Knox Constr. Co. v. Morris*, 596 A.2d 679 (Md. 1991); *Farah v. Farah*, 429 S.E.2d 626 (Va. Ct. App. 1993); *Michelli v. Michelli*, 527 So. 2d 359 (Fla. Dist. Ct. App. 1991); *Brack v. Brack*, 329 N.W.2d 432 (Mich. Ct. App. 1982); *Chatman v. Ribicoff*, 169 F. Supp. 931 (N.D. Cal. 1961); *In re Catapano*, 794 N.Y.S.2d 401 (App. Div. 2005).

[99] *See, e.g.,* Restatement Conflict of Laws §§ 121-23 (1934); Restatement (Second) Conflict of Laws § 283(2) (1971); *see also infra* § 2.09.

[100] *Id. See also Metropolitan Life Ins. Co. v. Holding*, 293 F. Supp. 854 (E.D. Va. 1968); *Kersey v. Gardner*, 264 F. Supp. 887 (M.D. Ga. 1967).

[101] *See, e.g., Hesington v. Estate of Hesington*, 640 S.W.2d 824 (Mo. Ct. App. 1982); *Kennedy v. Damron*, 268 S.W.2d 22 (Ky. 1954); *Kelderhaus v. Kelderhaus*, 467 S.E.2d 303 (Va. Ct. App. 1996).

[102] *See, e.g., Renshaw v. Heckler*, 787 F.2d 50 (2d Cir. 1986); *Metropolitan Life Ins. Co. v. Holding*, 293 F. Supp. 854 (E.D. Va. 1968); *Ventura v. Ventura*, 280 N.Y.S.2d 5 (N.Y. Sup. Ct. 1967).

[103] *Id.* These sister state common law marriages are most often found to exist when the parties, in good faith, have been cohabiting as husband and wife for a number of years.

[104] *See, e.g., In re Estate of Fischer*, 176 N.W.2d 801 (Iowa 1970); and *DeMelo v. Zompa*, 844 A.2d 174 (R.I. 2004).

Another problem often arises in the context of a common law marriage when the purported husband and wife attempt to contract a common law marriage at a time when a legal impediment exists in their common law marriage. For example, a man and a woman begin to live together in a purported common law relationship when one or both of the parties have not yet been legally divorced from a prior spouse. In this situation, some courts have held that the initial meretricious relationship — when the marital impediment still existed — *cannot* ripen into a valid common law marriage, absent proof of a *new* agreement to marry after the impediment is removed.[105] The better reasoned view, however, to validate the marital expectations of the parties, is to hold that the common law marriage still exists after the legal impediment to marriage is removed, under a "continuing agreement" rationale.[106]

Although some courts have traditionally viewed common law marriage with suspicion and mistrust, and although — until recently — the recognition of common law marriage in the United States seemed to be on a decline, now with more cohabiting couples and alternate lifestyles, the recognition and enforcement of common law marriages by various courts may reverse this trend.[107]

[B] Putative Marriage

A putative marriage is an informal "curative" marriage when one or both of the parties were ignorant of an impediment that made their formal statutory marriage invalid. This concept was well explained in an 1847 decision of the Texas Supreme Court:

> Putative matrimony is defined to be a marriage, which being null on account of some dissolving impediment, is held, notwithstanding, for a true marriage, because of its having been contracted in good faith, by both or one of the spouses being ignorant of the impediment. Good faith is always presumed, and he who would impede its effects, must prove that it did not exist.[108]

A putative marriage must be contracted with a good faith belief of one or both of the parties that their formal statutory marriage was valid. But unlike common law

---

[105] *See, e.g., Dandy v. Dandy,* 234 So. 2d 728 (Fla. Dist. Ct. App. 1970); *Byers v. Mount Vernon Mills, Inc.,* 231 S.E.2d 699 (S.C. 1977).

[106] *See, e.g., Richard v. Trousdale,* 508 So. 2d 260 (Ala. 1987); *Parker v. Parker,* 265 S.E.2d 237 (N.C. Ct. App. 1980); *see also Travers v. Rinehardt,* 205 U.S. 423 (1907).

[107] *See, e.g.,* Note, *Common Law Marriage and Unmarried Cohabitators: An Old Solution to a New Problem,* 39 U. Pitt. L. Rev. 579 (1978); Caudill, *Legal Recognition of Unmarried Cohabitation: A Proposal to Update and Reconsider Common Law Marriage,* 49 Tenn. L. Rev. 537 (1982); Sonya Garza, *Common Law Marriage: A Proposal for the Revival of a Dying Doctrine,* 40 New Eng. L. Rev. 541 (2006). For example, common law marriage actions have been brought against such celebrities as actor William Hurt and New York Yankee outfielder Dave Winfield. *See* Newsweek, July 24, 1989, at 46-47. The claim against Hurt was later dismissed, *see Jennings v. Hurt,* 554 N.Y.S.2d 220 (N.Y. App. Div. 1990), but the claim against Winfield was held to be actionable.

[108] *Smith v. Smith,* 1 Tex. 621 (1847). *See also In re Foy's Estate,* 240 P.2d 685 (Cal. Dist. Ct. App. 1952); *Wilkinson v. Wilkinson,* 91 Cal. Rptr. 372 (Cal. Dist. Ct. App. 1970).

marriages, cohabitation of the parties is not always required.[109]

The putative marriage doctrine is most frequently found in those states following a French or Spanish civil law tradition, such as California, Louisiana, and Texas, but various other states following an English common law tradition have also adopted the putative marriage concept by statute.[110] The federal government has also adopted a putative spouse test regarding social security benefits.[111] Like a spouse in any other marriage, a putative spouse may claim marital property and support rights, loss of consortium and personal injury awards, wrongful death benefits, and he or she may inherit from the other putative spouse.[112]

A state that does not recognize the putative marriage doctrine within its own jurisdiction would probably recognize a putative marriage contracted within another state under the well-established conflict of laws doctrine that a marriage valid where celebrated ought to be valid everywhere, unless it is against a state's strong public policy.[113] Accordingly, any imperfection in the marriage license or marrying official probably would not invalidate the putative marriage in most other states, either under a directory marriage statute,[114] or under a mandatory state "curative" statute.[115]

However, some states recognizing the putative marriage doctrine have also held that a putative bigamous or polygamous marriage would also constitute a valid marriage.[116] But in states where bigamous or incestuous marriages are held to be *void ab initio* marriages and against a state's strong public policy,[117] such bigamous putative marriages may *not* be recognized irrespective of their recognition in the sister state.[118]

---

[109] *See, e.g., Vryonis v. Vryonis*, 248 Cal. Rptr. 807 (Cal. Ct. App. 1988); *Garduno v. Garduno*, 760 S.W.2d 735 (Tex. Civ. App. 1988); *Rebouche v. Anderson*, 505 So. 2d 808 (La. Ct. App. 1987); *Hicklin v. Hicklin*, 509 N.W.2d 627 (Neb. 1994). *But see Damon v. Ashcroft*, 360 F.3d 1084 (9th Cir. 2004) (finding no objective criteria of wife's good faith belief in an immigration dispute); *Cardwell v. Cardwell*, 195 S.W.3d 856 (Tex. App. 2006) (finding no putative marriage since the wife did not have a reasonable belief that she was no longer married at the time of her subsequent marriage). *See also* Annot., 34 A.L.R.2d 1255 (Later Case Service); Monica Hof Wallace, *The Pitfalls of a Putative Marriage and the Call for Putative Divorce*, 64 La. L. Rev. 71 (2003).

[110] For example, Illinois, Minnesota, and Wisconsin. The Uniform Marriage and Divorce Act, § 209, also recognizes putative marriages.

[111] *See* 42 U.S.C. § 416(h)(1)(B).

[112] *See generally* Blakesley, *The Putative Marriage Doctrine*, 60 Tul. L. Rev. 1 (1985); Luther & Luther, *Support and Property Rights of the Putative Spouse*, 24 Hastings L. J. 311 (1973); Note, *Rights of the Putative Spouse*, 1978 S. Ill. U. L. J. 423. *See also* Annot., 34 A.L.R.2d 1255, 1291 (Later Case Service); Wallace, *supra* note 109.

[113] *See, e.g.*, Restatement, Conflict of Laws §§ 121-23 (1934); Restatement (Second) Conflict of Laws § 283(2) (1971); *see also infra* § 2.09.

[114] *See supra* note 14 (accompanying text).

[115] *See supra* note 15 (accompanying text).

[116] *See, e.g., In re Dalip Singh Bir's Estate*, 188 P.2d 499 (Cal. Dist. Ct. App. 1948).

[117] *See infra* §§ 2.08[C], 2.08[D].

[118] *Cf. Hager v. Hager*, 349 S.E.2d 908 (Va. Ct. App. 1986) (*void ab initio* marriages, such as a bigamous South Carolina marriage, cannot be affirmed in Virginia). *But see In re Estate of Shippy*, 678 P.2d 848 (Wash. Ct. App. 1984) (the Washington court, in recognizing a *nunc pro tunc* California divorce

[C] Marriage by Proxy

A marriage by proxy is an attempt to comply with state statutory marriage requirements by designating a "stand in" who appears for the absent prospective spouse or, alternately, where the absent party "participates" in the ceremony via telephone or another similar form of communication.[119] The validity of a marriage by proxy is normally governed by the law of the jurisdiction where the ceremony takes place.[120]

Although a marriage by proxy is not uncommon in countries following a Spanish or French civil law tradition,[121] there is remarkably little case authority on the validity of proxy marriages contracted in American states.[122] Even within these cases there is a split of authority.

Some courts, for example, have construed state marriage statutes to require that both parties be present in person, either at the time the marriage license is obtained, or at the time of the marriage ceremony.[123] The better reasoned view, however, would be to recognize a marriage by proxy in order to validate the parties' marital expectations, and promote, rather than discourage, marriage in general.[124]

If a marriage by proxy takes place while an absent spouse is in another country, however, federal immigration law will not recognize such a "spouse, wife, or husband by reason of any marriage ceremony where the contracting parties thereto are not physically present in the presence of each other, unless the marriage shall have been consummated."[125]

---

decree, in effect *was* recognizing a bigamous putative marriage, that under Alaska law would *not* be recognized). *See generally* Annot., 19 A.L.R.3d 648 (1968); Fine, *The Rights of Putative Spouses: Choice of Law Issues and Comparative Insights*, 32 Int'l & Comp. L.Q. 708 (1983).

[119] *See, e.g.*, Comment, *Validity of Proxy Marriages*, 25 S. Cal. L. Rev. 181 (1952); Howery, *Marriage by Proxy and Other Informal Marriages*, 13 UMKC L. Rev. 48 (1944); *see also* Annot., 170 A.L.R. 947 (1947).

[120] *Id. See also* Dan Barry, *Trading Vows in Montana, No Couple Required*, N.Y. Times, Mar. 10, 2008.

[121] *See, e.g., Torres v. Torres*, 366 A.2d 713 (N.J. Super. Ct. Ch. Div. 1976) (New Jersey recognition of a Cuban marriage by proxy). Explorers Christopher Columbus and Vasco de Balboa were both married by proxy, but not presumably while en route to America.

[122] *See, e.g.*, Clark, *supra* note 4, at 124-25.

[123] *See, e.g., Blankenship v. Blankenship*, 133 B.R. 398 (N.D. Ohio 1991) (applying Ohio law); *Respole v. Respole*, 70 N.E.2d 465 (Ohio Ct. C.P. 1946) (purportedly applying W. Va. law).

[124] *See, e.g., Barrons v. United States*, 191 F.2d 92 (9th Cir. 1951) (discussing Texas, California, Nevada, West Virginia, and D.C. law, and upholding a marriage by proxy); Moore, *The Case for Marriage by Proxy*, 11 Clev. Mar. L. Rev. 313 (1962).

[125] 8 U.S.C. § 1101(a)(35).

[D] De Facto "Marriage"

A de facto "marriage," or a relationship between unmarried cohabitants, traditionally lacks any legal recognition as a valid marriage, because: (1) it does not comply with state statutory requirements for a formal marriage;[126] (2) it does not possess the present intent and agreement requirement, nor the community repute requirement for a common law marriage;[127] and (3) it lacks the good faith belief requirement needed for a putative marriage.[128] Thus, in the absence of a contractual nonmarital agreement,[129] or another nonmarital remedy,[130] the de facto "spouse" had few, if any, legal remedies.

For example, in the vast majority of states, only a legal spouse, and *not* a de facto "spouse," would qualify as a beneficiary under state wrongful death statutes,[131] and the prevailing view is likewise that a loss of consortium action[132] depends upon proof of a valid marriage.[133] However, a minority of states have held that loss of consortium actions *may* be brought by unmarried de facto "spouses."[134]

Likewise, the prevailing traditional view is that state workers' compensation statutes are only for the benefit of legal spouses; unmarried de facto "spouses" are therefore excluded from any statutory benefits.[135] However, a minority of jurisdictions have awarded workers' compensation benefits to dependent unmarried de facto "spouses."[136] The rationale for the minority view is that state workers' compensation statutes should be liberally construed, including the words "family" and "dependents" under an "elastic" view that would *not* exclude unmarried de facto "spouses."[137]

---

[126] *See supra* § 2.04.

[127] *See supra* § 2.05[A].

[128] *See supra* § 2.05[B].

[129] *See supra* § 2.02[A].

[130] *See supra* § 2.02[B], [C].

[131] *See, e.g., Nieto v. Los Angeles*, 188 Cal. Rptr. 31 (Cal. Ct. App. 1982); *Hewitt v. Firestone Tire & Rubber Co.*, 490 F. Supp. 1358 (E.D. Va. 1980).

[132] *See infra* § 3.13.

[133] *See, e.g., Felch v. Air Florida*, 562 F. Supp. 383 (D.D.C. 1983); *Curry v. Caterpillar Tractor Co.*, 577 F. Supp. 991 (E.D. Pa. 1984).

[134] *See, e.g., Bulloch v. United States*, 487 F. Supp. 1078 (D.N.J. 1980). In *Bullock*, the court did recognize a loss of consortium claim by an unmarried de facto "spouse," but on unique factual grounds. The cohabitants in this case had been married for 23 years and were then divorced. They began cohabiting again, but were not remarried when the former husband was injured and rendered impotent. *See also Butcher v. Superior Court*, 188 Cal. Rptr. 503 (Cal. Ct. App. 1983) (the nonmarital relationship was both "stable and significant" and "possessed the characteristics of marriage"). The *Butcher* rationale was expressly rejected in *Elden v. Sheldon*, 210 Cal. Rptr. 755 (Cal. Ct. App. 1985), where the court stated that the *Butcher* decision adopts a "vague, indefinite standard that would be incapable of a just or predictable application."

[135] *See, e.g., Caudle-Hyatt, Inc. v. Mixon*, 260 S.E.2d 193 (Va. 1979).

[136] *See, e.g., Kempf v. State Accident Ins. Fund*, 580 P.2d 1032 (Or. Ct. App. 1978); *West v. Barton Malow Co.*, 230 N.W.2d 545 (Mich. 1975).

[137] *Id.*

The renting or purchasing of a home that is zoned or covenanted as a single family residence has also presented legal problems to unmarried cohabitants and de facto "spouses."[138] On the other hand, the New York Court of Appeals has recently held that a homosexual couple who had lived together for ten years could be considered a "family," at least for purposes of avoiding eviction under New York City's rent control regulations.[139] The Court held that "In the context of eviction, a realistic, and certainly valid, view of a family includes two adult life-time partners whose relationship is long-term and characterized by an emotional and financial commitment and interdependence."[140]

Whether these initial decisions will be expanded to provide more legal recognition and protection for unmarried cohabitants and de facto "spouses" in the future, or whether these cases will be limited on their facts in a minority of states, remains to be seen. It is clear, however, that the legal rights and obligations of the nontraditional family[141] need to be addressed in a realistic manner by the courts, and needs to be decisively addressed by the state and federal legislatures.[142]

[E] "Marriage" by Estoppel

A so-called "marriage" by estoppel is most frequently found when a husband or wife has obtained an invalid divorce from a prior spouse and then remarries. Since the prior divorce is legally invalid, the second bigamous marriage is also invalid.[143]

If, however, the parties knew about, or had participated in, the invalid prior divorce and invalid second marriage, they may be estopped by their conduct from questioning the legal validity of the second marriage. Thus, they are still "married" by estoppel principles, even though they are *not legally* married.[144]

The equitable estoppel theory in family law is a way to validate the parties' present expectations in the contested "marriage." It is based upon a personal

---

[138] *See, e.g., Maryland Comm'n on Human Relations v. Greenbelt Homes*, 475 A.2d 1192 (Md. 1984) (a cooperative housing regulation that prohibited unmarried couples did not constitute discrimination based upon marital status); *Village of Belle Terre v. Boraas*, 416 U.S. 1 (1974) (a zoning ordinance restricting land use only to single family dwellings was held not to be unconstitutional). *See generally* Smith, *The Wages of Living in Sin: Discrimination in Housing against Unmarried Couples*, 25 U.C. Davis L. Rev. 1055 (1992).

[139] *See, e.g., Braschi v. Stahl Assocs.*, 543 N.E.2d 49 (N.Y. 1989).

[140] *Id.*

[141] *See supra* §§ 1.02[B], 2.02.

[142] *See generally* Green & Long, *supra* note 86, at 158-210; Wade, *Void and De Facto Marriages*, 9 Sydney L. Rev. 356 (1981). *See also* Minow, *Redefining Families*, 62 U. Colo. L. Rev. 269 (1991); Treuthart, *Adopting a More Realistic Definition of "Family,"* 26 Gonz. L. Rev. 91 (1990-91); Note, *Looking for a Family Resemblance: The Limits of the Functional Approach to the Legal Definition of Family*, 104 Harv. L. Rev. 1640 (1991); *supra* §§ 1.02, 2.02.

[143] *See infra* § 2.08[C].

[144] *See, e.g., In re Marriage of Recknor*, 187 Cal. Rptr. 887 (Cal. Ct. App. 1982). *But see Crosby v. Crosby*, 769 F. Supp. 197 (D. Md. 1991) (in Maryland, silence in the absence of a duty to speak will not give rise to estoppel). *See also* Clark, *Estoppel Against Jurisdictional Attack on Decrees of Divorce*, 70 Yale L.J. 45 (1960); Rosenberg, *How Void is a Void Decree, or the Estoppel Effect of Invalid Divorce Decrees*, 8 Fam. L.Q. 207 (1974); Annot., 81 A.L.R.3d 110 (1977).

disability of the party attacking the void divorce decree and the subsequent invalid marriage under the theory that one who has taken a prior position regarding the divorce and subsequent marriage, and who has obtained a benefit from it, cannot later take an inconsistent position which would prejudice the other party.[145]

This "marriage" by estoppel doctrine is broader than a traditional estoppel theory in that one party does not necessarily have to rely to his or her detriment upon factual representations made by the other party. It is sufficient, in many cases, that a court find only that it would be unfair to let a party take advantage of the legal invalidity of a divorce decree and the invalidity of the subsequent marriage.[146]

The doctrine of "marriage" by estoppel is further complicated because there are no less than three different rules regarding the validity or invalidity of a "marriage" by estoppel, especially when it involves a void migratory divorce. The courts are often split as to which of these three rules should govern, even within the same jurisdiction.

Under the "traditional" rule, the domiciliary state and the parties are *not* bound by any estoppel defense in collaterally attacking a void divorce and subsequent remarriage.[147] The rationale behind this traditional rule is that estoppel, even for a limited purpose, ultimately results in the de facto recognition of a void divorce, usually granted by a court lacking any jurisdiction whatever, and therefore violates the domiciliary state's strong public policy.[148]

Under the "sociological" or "Restatement" rule of "marriage" by estoppel, a court will attempt to validate the parties' "real" expectations of divorce and remarriage, rather than relying on a purely theoretical, and perhaps "unreal" legal basis.[149] The Second Restatement of Conflict of Laws § 74, states the general rule that "A person may be precluded from attacking the validity of a foreign divorce decree if, under the circumstances, it would be inequitable for him [or her] to do so."[150]

Although this "sociological" or "Restatement" rule of "marriage" by estoppel appears to be the majority view in a growing number of jurisdictions, it has been criticized by one commentator for resulting in "uncertainty and ambiguity as to a person's marital status and his capacity to marry . . . . Then, too, estoppel can prevent a valid dissolution of a prior dead marriage and, consequently, the

---

[145] *Id.*

[146] *Id.* Clark, *supra* note 144, at 46-49; Rosenberg, *supra*, note 144, at 208-09.

[147] *See, e.g., Everett v. Everett*, 345 So. 2d 586 (La. Ct. App. 1977); *In re Estate of Steffke*, 222 N.W.2d 628 (Wis. 1974).

[148] *Id.*

[149] *See* Clark, *supra* note 144, at 56-57.

[150] Restatement (Second) Conflict of Laws § 74 (1971). The First Restatement of Conflict of Laws, § 112 (1934), also prohibits the questioning of an invalid divorce "either by the spouse who has obtained such decree of divorce from a court which has no jurisdiction, or by a spouse who takes advantage of such decree by remarrying."

regularization of a bigamous marriage that has been attempted."[151]

A third rule of "marriage" by estoppel is called the "status vs. property right" rule. Under this rule, if the action deals with the marital status, including actions to declare the nullity of a void marriage, separation, or divorce; then estoppel is not appropriate since the parties are trying to clarify their legal status — who is married to whom. But if the action deals with a property right, such as taking against a deceased spouse's will, or enforcing an alleged right to support, then estoppel may apply.[152]

Whatever specific rule a court utilizes, however, "the application of the principles of equitable estoppel cannot be subjected to fixed and settled rules of universal application, but rests largely on the facts and circumstances of each particular case."[153]

Finally, even if husband and wife may be estopped from collaterally attacking a void migratory divorce and a subsequent remarriage, under the traditional majority rule, the state itself would not be estopped from prosecuting a bigamy or unlawful cohabitation action.[154] Some commentators believe, however, that the state should not be able to challenge a void out-of-state divorce.[155]

§ 2.06 THE LAST-IN-TIME MARRIAGE PRESUMPTION

The typical scenario for a last-in-time marriage presumption is not as uncommon as one might suppose: A husband or wife has unexpectedly died, and the bereaved surviving spouse is in the process of bringing a legal proceeding that may include a wrongful death action, a suit for social security benefits, workers' compensation benefits, other insurance benefits, or a probate action. During the pendency of such an action, however, a former wife (or husband) comes forward, claiming that she has never been divorced from the deceased spouse, and that she, rather than the subsequent wife, should recover in any legal proceedings as the legal wife. *Query*: Which wife should prevail?

To many lawyers and lay persons, the initial conclusion might be that because American family law in the vast majority of jurisdictions prohibits bigamy and other plural marriages,[156] the first-in-time wife should recover all the proceeds. But this conclusion would be wrong.

---

[151] *See* Phillips, *Equitable Preclusion of Jurisdictional Attacks on Void Divorces*, 37 Fordham L. Rev. 355, 365-66 (1969).

[152] *See, e.g., Caldwell v. Caldwell*, 81 N.E.2d 60 (N.Y. 1948); *Rabourn v. Rabourn*, 385 P.2d 581 (Alaska 1963).

[153] *Weber v. Weber*, 265 N.W.2d 436, 441 (Neb. 1978). *See also* Swisher, *Foreign Migratory Divorces: A Reappraisal*, 21 J. Fam. L. 9, 37-48 (1982-83).

[154] *See, e.g., State v. DeMeo*, 118 A.2d 1 (N.J. 1955); *see also* Von Mehren, *The Validity of Foreign Divorces*, 45 Mass. L.Q. 23, 29 (1960); Currie, *Suitcase Divorce in the Conflict of Laws*, 34 U. Chi. L. Rev. 26, 54-55 (1966).

[155] *See, e.g.,* A. Ehrenzweig, Conflict of Laws 253 (1962); Goodrich, Handbook on the Conflict of Laws 259 (1964); *see also infra* § 8.02[E].

[156] *See infra* § 2.08[C].

The last-in-time marriage presumption is based upon "one of the strongest presumptions of law" that an existing marriage, once shown, is valid. A subsequent marriage therefore raises the strong presumption that any former marriage was terminated by divorce, and the *former* spouse has the burden of proving that there was no divorce. Thus, if the former spouse fails to rebut this last-in-time marriage presumption, then the subsequent spouse will prevail.[157] An earlier spouse will only be able to rebut this last-in-time marriage presumption by searching all the divorce records where the deceased resided, or might have resided, in order to prove that no divorce decree was ever granted to the deceased spouse. Otherwise, the presumption will not be rebutted.[158] However, if the prior wife does present evidence that no divorce proceedings were instituted in any jurisdiction where the husband might reasonably have pursued them, then the presumption would be rebutted.[159]

Nevertheless, this last-in-time marriage presumption in the vast majority of American jurisdictions continues to exist as "one of the strongest presumptions known to the law" since "the law presumes morality and legitimacy, not immorality and bastardy."[160] Accordingly, this last-in-time marriage presumption applies with equal force to valid common law marriages,[161] as well as to valid statutory marriages.[162]

§ 2.07   PROOF OF MARRIAGE

A valid marriage license or a certified copy of the marriage record will normally constitute prima facie evidence of such a marriage. Also, a presumption of marriage is based upon marital cohabitation and repute, and this strong presumption can be overcome only by cogent and satisfactory proof that there was *no* valid marriage.[163] According to *Wigmore on Evidence*, a valid marriage may be proven by: (1) offering a valid marriage certificate or a record of the marriage;[164] (2) offering testimony of

---

[157] *See generally* Swisher & Jones, *The Last-in-Time Marriage Presumption*, 29 Fam. L. Q. 409 (1995); Annot., *Presumption as to the Validity of Second Marriage*, 14 A.L.R.2d 7 (Later Case Service).

[158] *See, e.g., Hewitt v. Firestone Tire & Rubber Co.*, 490 F. Supp. 1358 (E.D. Va. 1980); *Miller v. Harley-Davidson Motor Co.*, 328 N.W.2d 348 (Iowa Ct. App. 1982). This is the majority view. There is a minority view in a small number of states, however, that all the prior spouse has to do to rebut the last-in-time marriage presumption is offer evidence of a valid marriage, and the burden of proof then shifts to the subsequent spouse to demonstrate that there *was* a divorce. *See, e.g., Tatum v. Tatum*, 241 F.2d 401 (9th Cir. 1957) (applying Cal. law); *Glover v. Glover*, 322 S.E.2d 755 (Ga. Ct. App. 1984). The *Glover* rationale, however, is criticized in 21 Mercer L. Rev. 465.

[159] *See, e.g., Davis v. Davis*, 521 S.W.2d 603 (Tex. 1975).

[160] *See, e.g., Parker v. Am. Lumber Co.*, 56 S.E.2d 214 (Va. 1949).

[161] *See supra* § 2.05[A].

[162] *See supra* § 2.04. *See generally* Swisher & Jones, *supra* note 157.

[163] *See, e.g., McClaugherty v. McClaugherty*, 21 S.E.2d 761 (Va. 1942) ("In the interest of morality and decency the law presumes marriage between a man and a woman when they live together as man and wife . . . . While it is true, however, that cohabitation and repute do not constitute marriage, they do constitute strong evidence tending to raise a presumption of marriage, and the burden is on him who denies the marriage to offer countervailing evidence."); *see also* Swisher, *Proving the Validity of a Marriage*, 43 Virginia Lawyer 29 (Dec. 1994).

[164] 5 Wigmore on Evidence § 1645 (1974 ed.)

eyewitnesses who were present at the marriage ceremony;[165] or (3) offering evidence of matrimonial cohabitation and community repute.[166]

§ 2.08   CAPACITY AND INTENT TO MARRY

Assuming that the parties have met the legal requirements for a formal[167] or informal[168] marriage, they still must possess the legal *capacity* and *intent* to marry. If either the husband or the wife lacks this legal capacity or intent to marry, then the marriage may be *void* (also referred to as *void ab initio* or absolutely void), or *voidable*, depending on the seriousness of the marital impediment.[169] These marital impediments may therefore constitute grounds to *annul* the marriage.[170]

[A]   Void and Voidable Marriages

The historical distinction between void and voidable marriages, based upon a lack of capacity or intent to marry, arose as a result of jurisdictional conflicts between English ecclesiastical courts and English civil courts: If the marriage could be attacked after the death of one of the spouses, then it was a void *ab initio* marriage. But if the marriage could *not* be attacked after the death of either spouse, even though it was invalid under canon law, then the marriage was voidable only, and the surviving spouse was entitled to all marital property and support rights. When Henry VIII and the Church of England broke away from the Roman Catholic Church, however, no annulment of marriage — including Henry's — could be appealed to the Pope in Rome, and thus void and voidable marriages both came under English common law jurisdiction. Under present-day American family law, a defective marriage is classified as either *void ab initio* or *voidable* based upon the seriousness of the marital defect.[171]

A void *ab initio* marriage is a legal nullity, incapable of possessing any marital consequences. Thus, the parties to a void *ab initio* marriage can never ratify it, and such marriages may be collaterally attacked by either "spouse," by any interested third party, or by the State — even after the death of either "spouse."[172]

Examples of void *ab initio* marriages in the majority of states are: same sex marriage; bigamous or polygamous marriage; and incestuous marriage. In a minority of states, underage marriage is also void *ab initio*. Since a void *ab initio*

---

[165] 7 Wigmore on Evidence §§ 2082-88 (1978 ed.)

[166] 9 Wigmore on Evidence § 2505 (1981 ed.). This would constitute evidence of a common law marriage, but it would only raise a *presumption* of a formal statutory marriage.

[167] *See supra* § 2.04.

[168] *See supra* § 2.05.

[169] *See infra* § 2.08[A].

[170] *See infra* § 2.10.

[171] *See generally* Goda, *The Historical Evolution of the Concepts of Void and Voidable Marriages*, 7 J. Fam. L. 297 (1967); Note, *The Void and Voidable Marriage: A Study in Judicial Method*, 7 Stan. L. Rev. 529 (1955); Wrenn, *In Search of a Balanced Procedural Law for Marriage and Nullity Cases*, 46 Jurist 602 (1986).

[172] *Id.*

marriage is a legal nullity from its inception, no formal annulment action is necessary, but an annulment action may still be brought to establish a legal record of the void *ab initio* marriage.[173]

A voidable marriage, on the other hand, is valid for all civil purposes unless it is annulled[174] in a direct proceeding by either the husband or the wife. The marital defect in a voidable marriage may therefore be condoned and ratified by the parties, and when one of the spouses dies, an annulment action cannot be brought by the other spouse. Likewise, interested third parties and the State generally cannot attack a voidable marriage.[175] Examples of voidable marriages in most jurisdictions are: underage marriage; fraudulent marriage; marriage under duress; marriage to a mental incompetent; sham marriage; and marriage in jest. In some states a voidable marriage may also be annulled for: natural and incurable impotency of the body; marriage to a felon or prostitute; or marriage to a spouse who is pregnant by another man, or who has at a time close to the marriage impregnated another woman. When a voidable marriage is annulled in a formal proceeding, this voidable marriage then becomes a void marriage.

This traditional common law distinction between void and voidable marriages is therefore of crucial importance in determining any spousal support or marital property rights, because with a void *ab initio* marriage there are no marital rights, but with a voidable marriage, in the absence of a formal annulment action, both spouses still retain all property and support rights that normally devolve upon them by reason of their marriage.[176]

[B] Same Sex Marriage

Historically, marriage has been defined as the voluntary union of one man and one woman to the exclusion of all others, and most states therefore have refused to permit marriages between two persons of the same sex.[177] Thus, same sex marriages are held to be void *ab initio* in the vast majority of states, since state prohibitions against marriages between persons of the same sex were held not to offend state or federal constitutional due process rights or equal protection rights.[178] For example, in a family law context, a constitutional right to privacy has been applied to married couples,[179] and to unmarried heterosexuals.[180] But until 2003 such a constitutional right to privacy had not been recognized to include

---

[173] *Id. But see supra* § 2.05[E].

[174] *See infra* § 2.10.

[175] *Id.*

[176] *See generally infra* § 2.10[C].

[177] *See generally* Clark, *supra* note 4, at 75-80.

[178] *See, e.g., Baker v. Nelson*, 191 N.W.2d 185 (Minn. 1971); *Dean v. District of Columbia*, 653 A.2d 307 (D.C. Ct. App. 1995); *Jones v. Hallahan*, 501 S.W.2d 588 (Ky. Ct. App. 1973); *De Santo v. Barnsley*, 476 A.2d 952 (Pa. Super. Ct. 1982); *Slayton v. State*, 633 S.W.2d 934 (Tex. Ct. App. 1982). *But see* M.T. v. J.T., 355 A.2d 204 (N.J. Super Ct. App. Div. 1976) (transsexual marriage held to be valid).

[179] *See, e.g., Griswold v. Connecticut*, 381 U.S. 479 (1965).

[180] *See, e.g., Eisenstadt v. Baird*, 405 U.S. 438 (1972).

consensual homosexual relationships.[181] However, in the subsequent case of *Lawrence v. Texas*,[182] the United States Supreme Court overruled *Bowers v. Hardwicke* in striking down a Texas sodomy statute. Although the majority opinion in Lawrence arguably found a familial resemblance between the intimate sexual relationships of heterosexual couples and those of same-sex couples, it nevertheless carefully avoided giving any official recognition to same-sex marriage.[183] However, Justice Scalia, in a strong dissenting opinion, warned readers not to believe the majority's disclaimer about same-sex marriage, and suggested that after *Lawrence* the Supreme Court would have much difficulty in offering a principled analysis of why the United States Constitution would not protect the right to marry a same-sex partner.[184]

In the 1993 case of *Baehr v. Lewin*,[185] the Hawaii Supreme Court found that sex was a suspect category for purposes of equal protection analysis under the Hawaii Constitution, and therefore any prohibition of same-sex marriage in Hawaii must be subject to a strict scrutiny constitutional analysis.[186] The Hawaii Supreme Court remanded the case back to the trial court, which subsequently held that the State of Hawaii had *not* established a compelling state interest to prohibit same-sex marriages in Hawaii, and thus the trial court recognized the validity of same-sex marriages in Hawaii.[187]

In the wake of the *Baehr* decision, a number of states enacted legislation providing that they would not recognize same-sex marriages if validly contracted in another state (such as Hawaii) under the rationale that same-sex marriages would be against the state's strong public policy.[188] Congress further enacted a so-called

---

[181] *See, e.g., Bowers v. Hardwick*, 478 U.S. 186 (1986) (upholding a Georgia sodomy statute). Justice Powell, the swing vote in this 5-4 decision, later admitted that he had probably erred in voting to uphold the constitutionality of the state sodomy statute. *See, e.g.*, John Jeffries Jr., Justice Lewis F. Powell Jr. 530 (1994) ("I think I probably made a mistake on that one," Powell said of *Bowers* . . . "When I had the opportunity to reread the opinions a few months later, I thought the dissent had the better of the arguments").

[182] 539 U.S. 558 (2003).

[183] *Id.*

[184] *Id.* (Scalia, J. dissenting). *See also* Mark Strasser, Lawrence, *Same-Sex Marriage and the Constitution: What is Protected and Why?*, 38 New Eng. L. Rev. 667 (2004) (opining that "Justice Scalia is correct" in this assessment, since both "existing right-to-marry jurisprudence and the existing equal protection jurisprudence require the recognition of same-sex marriage").

[185] *Baehr v. Lewin*, 852 P.2d 44 (Haw. 1993).

[186] *Id.; Baehr et al. v. Miike*, 910 P.2d 112 (Haw. 1996). Not surprisingly, the *Baehr* case has received both support and criticism from a number of legal scholars. *See, e.g.*, Coolridge, *Same-Sex Marriage?* Baehr v. Mike *and the Meaning of Marriage*, 38 S. Tex. L. Rev. 1 (1997); Wardle, *The Potential Impact of Homosexual Parenting on Children*, 1997 U. Ill. L. Rev. 8, 884-91 (arguing that the decision "leaves much to be desired in terms of fair summarization of the evidence, and thorough legal analysis"). For a rather spirited dialogue, pro and con, on same-sex marriage, see Kendle, *Principles and Prejudice: Lesbian and Gay Civil Marriage and the Realization of Equality*, 22 J. Comp. L. 81 (1996), and Kohm, *A Reply to "Principles and Prejudice": Marriage and the Realization that Principles Win Over Political Will*, 22 J. Comp. L. 293 (1996).

[187] *Baehr v. Miike*, 910 P.2d 112 (Haw. 1996).

[188] *See, e.g.*, Ariz. Rev. Stat. Ann. § 25-101[C] (1996); Conn. Gen. Stat. Ann. § 46a-81r (1995); Ill. Comp. Stat. Ann. § 5/213.1 (1996); Utah Code Ann. § 30-1-2 (1995); Va. Code Ann. § 20-45.2 (1997).

Defense of Marriage Act,[189] which amended 28 U.S.C. Section 1738C to provide that no state, territory, or possession of the United States shall be required to give full faith and credit to any sister state same-sex marriage.[190] Some commentators, however, have questioned whether these state and federal legislators have the constitutional power to enact such laws.[191] The *Baehr* decision was rendered moot when the Hawaiian voters subsequently passed a constitutional amendment prohibiting same-sex marriages in Hawaii, although the Hawaiian legislature also passed corresponding domestic partnership legislation relating to homosexual and heterosexual cohabiting couples.[192]

In 1999, the Vermont Supreme Court in the case of *Baker v. State*[193] declared that the State of Vermont was constitutionally required to extend to same-sex couples "the common benefits and protections that flow from marriage under Vermont law," but "whether this ultimately takes the form of inclusion within the marriage laws themselves or a parallel domestic partnership system or some equivalent statutory alternative, rests with the Legislature."[194] The Vermont legislature subsequently enacted "civil union" domestic partnership legislation in lieu of recognizing same-sex marriage in Vermont.[195]

In November 2003 the Massachusetts Supreme Judicial Court in the case of *Goodridge v. Massachusetts Department of Public Health*,[196] held in a 4-3 decision that the Commonwealth of Massachusetts had "failed to identify any constitutionally adequate reason for denying civil marriages to same-sex couples" and therefore the Court legally recognized the validity of same-sex marriages in Massachusetts. Three dissenting judges in *Goodridge* opined that "What is at stake in this case is not the unequal treatment of individuals, or whether individual rights have been impermissibly burdened, but the power of the Legislature to effectuate social change without interference from the courts." When the Massachusetts legislature subsequently queried the Massachusetts Supreme Judicial Court on whether civil union or domestic partnership legislation (such as found in Hawaii

---

[189] 110 Stat. 2419 (1996).

[190] *Id.* The Act also amended 1 U.S.C. § 7 by adding a definition of "marriage" and "spouse" that would affect any ruling, regulation, or interpretation made by any federal bureau or administrative agency in the United States. The term *marriage* under the statute means only a legal union between one man and one woman as husband and wife, and the term *spouse* refers only to a member of the opposite sex who is either a husband or wife.

[191] *See, e.g.*, Kramer, *Same Sex Marriage, Conflict of Laws, and the Unconstitutional Public Policy Exception*, 106 Yale L.J. 1965, 2008 (1997) (arguing that "if states cannot selectively discriminate against each other's laws, Congress cannot authorize them to do it"); *see also* Guillerman, *Comment, The Defense of Marriage Act: The Latest Maneuver in the Continuing Battle to Legalize Same-Sex Marriage*, 34 Houston L. Rev. 425 (1997); Note, *The Defense of Marriage Act and the Overextension of Congressional Authority*, 97 Colum. L. Rev. 1435 (1997). In 2012, the First and Second Circuits Courts of Appeals found DOMA to be unconstitutional. *See, e.g.*, *Massachusetts v. United States HHS*, 682 F.3d 1 (1st Cir. 2012); *Windsor v. United States*, 2012 U.S. App. LEXIS 21785 (2d Cir. 2012).

[192] *See generally supra* § 2.02[C].

[193] *Baker v. State*, 744 A.2d 864 (Vt. 1999).

[194] *Id.* at 867.

[195] *See generally supra* § 2.02[C].

[196] 798 N.E.2d 941 (Mass. 2003).

and Vermont) would be a viable alternative in Massachusetts to a same-sex civil marriage, the Court replied that it would not.[197] Accordingly, in May of 2004, Massachusetts became the first American state to legally recognize same-sex marriage.

A number of state appellate court decisions subsequent to *Goodridge*, however, have rejected the *Goodridge* legal rationale for recognizing same-sex marriages,[198] Congress has further enacted the so-called Defense of Marriage Act (DOMA) stating that no state must give full faith and credit to a sister state's same-sex marriage.[199] Over the past decade, however, more states, mostly in the Northeast, have also recognized same-sex marriage, either by judicial decree or through legislative action.[200] On the other hand, forty-four states still refuse to recognize same-sex marriage, and more than thirty states have passed recent amendments to

---

[197] *Opinions of the Justices to the Senate*, 802 N.E.2d 565 (Mass. 2004).

[198] *See, e.g., Anderson v. State of Washington*, 138 P.3d 963 (Wash. 2006) (holding that there was no fundamental constitutional right to marry a person of the same sex, and the appropriate standard of review was a rational basis review; and encouraging procreation between opposite sex individuals within the framework of marriage was a legitimate governmental interest); *Standhardt v. Superior Court*, 77 P.3d 451 (Ariz. Ct. App. 2003) (similar holding); *Morrison v. Sadler*, 821 N.E.2d 15 (Ind. Ct. App. 2005) (similar holding); *Li v. State*, 110 P.3d 91 (Or. 2005) (similar holding); *Conaway v. Deane*, 932 A.2d 571 (Md. 2007) (similar holding).

[199] *See supra* note 189 (and accompanying text); Note, *Litigating the Defense of Marriage Act: The Next Battlefield for Same-Sex Marriage*, 117 Harv. L. Rev. 2684 (2004); Mark Strasser, *"Defending" Marriage in Light of the Moreno-Cleburne-Romer-Lawrence Jurisprudence: Why DOMA Cannot Pass Muster After* Lawrence, 38 Creighton L. Rev. 421 (2005). *But see* Lynn Wardle, *Nonrecognition of Same-Sex Marriage Judgments Under DOMA and the Constitution*, 38 Creighton L. Rev. 365 (2005); Anita Woudenberg, *Giving DOMA Some Credit*, 38 Val. U. L. Rev. 1509 (2004) (both articles arguing that DOMA is constitutional). *See also Massachusetts v. United States HHS*, 682 F.3d 1 (1st Cir. 2012) (holding DOMA unconstitutional); *Windsor v. United States*, 2012 U.S. App. LEXIS 21785 (2d Cir. 2012) (same).

[200] *See, e.g., Goodridge v. Department of Public Health*, 798 N.E.2d 941 (Mass. 2003); *Kerrigan v. Commissioner of Public Health*, 957 A.2d 407 (Conn. 2008); *Varnum v. Brien*, 763 N.W.2d 862 (Iowa 2009); *Massachusetts v. United States HHS*, 682 F.3d 1 (1st Cir. 2012). From 2009 to 2012, Vermont, New Hampshire, the District of Columbia, and New York also recognized same-sex marriage in their respective jurisdictions through legislative enactment, and Maryland and Maine by voter ratification in November 2012. The California Supreme Court also initially recognized same-sex marriage as a fundamental right in California, rather than under a rational basis test, in the case of *In re Marriage Cases*, 76 Cal. Rptr. 3d 683 (2008). Subsequently, however, California voters approved a constitutional amendment banning same-sex marriage in California under Proposition 8 in 2008. Over 47 million dollars were spent by proponents and opponents of Proposition 8, making it the most expensive social and political issue in American history. In 2009 the California Supreme Court, in the case of *Strauss v. Horton*, 207 P.3d 48 (Cal. 2009) upheld the constitutionality of Proposition 8, which added a new section to Article I of the California Constitution, stating that only valid marriages in California would be between a man and a woman. However, in 2010, a federal district court judge held that California's ban on same-sex marriage violated *federal* constitutional rights to equal protection and due process and "fails to advance any rational basis in singling out gay men and lesbians for denial of a marriage license." *See Perry v. Schwarzenegger*, 704 F. Supp. 2d 921, 994-1003 (N.D. Cal. 2010), *rev'd sub nom. Perry v. Brown*, 671 F.3d 1052 (9th Cir. 2012). Same-sex marriage is also recognized in Canada, the Netherlands, Belgium, Norway, Sweden, Spain, Portugal, and Argentina. *See also* Katharina Boele-Woelki, *The Legal Recognition of Same-Sex Relationships Within the European Union*, 82 Tul. L. Rev. 1949 (2008) (analyzing how European Union member states deal with issues arising when same-sex couples cross borders).

their state constitutions prohibiting same-sex marriage.[201]

Thus it appears that although a large number of legal scholars and other commentators support the principle of same-sex marriage on legal, social, and constitutional grounds,[202] a large number of Americans and most state and federal legislators remain opposed to the recognition of same-sex marriage. Why this apparent dichotomy? Professor William Galston, speaking of American family law reform generally, observes:

> [I]n a democratic society, we are compelled to reflect on the public culture of that society. We can, of course, draw moral principles from our scholarly work and from our philosophical speculation, which is entirely appropriate. But there are also moral principles at work in the culture as a whole. The balance that is to be struck between our private philosophical and scholarly conceptions of what is just, or where responsibility lies, for example, and what the public culture of society believes, about those same issues is an important question. I would submit that in a democracy, we are not free to ignore the public culture in which people believe. We cannot end our moral and practical reflection with that, but we must take it into account.[203]

---

[201] *See generally* Anita Bernstein, *Subverting the Marriage-Amendment Crusade with Law and Policy Reform*, 24 Wash. U. J.L. & Pol'y 79 (2007) (examining anti-same-sex marriage state constitutional amendments, and arguing that public policy reform is the best method of opposing this movement). *But see* Lynn Wardle, *The Attack on Marriage as the Union of a Man and a Woman*, 83 N.D. L. Rev. 1365 (2007) (advocating for the preservation of marriage as a union between a man and a woman).

[202] *See, e.g.*, Friedman, *The Necessity for State Recognition of Same Sex Marriage*, 3 Berkeley Women's L.J. 134 (1987-88); Buchanan, *Same Sex Marriage: The Linchpin Issue*, 10 U. Dayton L. Rev. 541 (1985); Note, *From This Day Forward: A Feminine Moral Discourse on Homosexual Marriage*, 97 Yale L.J. 1783 (1988); Note, *Homosexual's Right to Marry: A Constitutional Text and a Legislative Solution*, 128 U. Pa. L. Rev. 193 (1979); Note, *The Legality of Homosexual Marriage*, 82 Yale L.J. 573 (1973). *See generally* Same Sex Marriage: Pro and Con (Andrew Sullivan, ed. 1997); William Eskridge, The Case for Same Sex Marriage: From Sexual Liberty to Civilized Commitment (1997); *and see* Carlos Ball, *The Positive in the Fundamental Right to Marry: Same-Sex Marriage in the Aftermath of Lawrence v. Texas*, 88 Minn. L. Rev. 1184 (2004); Brenda Feigen, *Same-Sex Marriage: An Issue of Constitutional Rights Not Moral Opinions*, 27 Harv. Women's L.J. 345 (2004); Larry Ribstein, *A Standard Form Approach to Same-Sex Marriage*, 38 Creighton L. Rev. 309 (2005); Symposium, *Can Anyone Show Just Cause Why These Two Should Not be Lawfully Joined Together?*, 38 New Eng. L. Rev. 487 (2004).

Not all advocates of gay and lesbian rights, however, support the concept of same-sex marriage. *See, e.g.*, Polikoff, *We Will Get What We Ask For: Why Legalizing Gay and Lesbian Marriage Will Not Dismantle the Legal Structure of Gender in Every Marriage*, 79 Va. L. Rev. 1535, 1549 (1993) ("Advocating lesbian and gay marriage will detract from, even contradict, efforts to unhook economic benefits from marriage and make basic health care and other necessities available to all"); *see also* Homer, *Against Marriage*, 29 Harv. C.R.-C.L. L. Rev. 505, 515-16 (1994); Ettelbrick, *Wedlock Alert: A Comment on Lesbian and Gay Family Recognition*, 5 J. L. & Policy 107 (1996) (favoring the attempt to broaden a definition of family to include gay and lesbian relationships, but rejecting any efforts to bring such relationships within a marriage rubric).

[203] Galston, *Public Morality and Public Policy: The Case of Children and Family Policy*, 36 Santa Clara L. Rev. 313, 314-15 (1996). *See also* Posner, *Should There be Homosexual Marriage? And If So, Who Should Decide?*, 95 Mich. L. Rev. 1578 (1997) (critiquing William Eskridge's *The Case for Same Sex Marriage: From Sexual Liberty to Civilized Commitment* (1997) and finding Eskridge's argument for state legislative reform to be persuasive and compelling, but rejecting Eskridge's contention that the Constitution should be interpreted as granting the right to same-sex marriage); Same-Sex Marriage Symposium, 18 BYU J. Pub. L. 273-693 (2004).

[C]   Bigamous and Polygamous Marriage

Bigamous, polygamous, or plural marriages are void *ab initio* in the vast majority of American jurisdictions, and are further proscribed by state bigamy statutes.[204]

Polygamy has been defined as having several spouses at the same time, while bigamy has been defined as contracting a second marriage while the first marriage is still subsisting. Traditionally, state bigamy statutes do not require specific intent for a criminal conviction, but the Model Penal Code and a few recent judicial cases now require a guilty intent for a bigamy conviction.[205]

To prevent an innocent spouse who in good faith erroneously believes the other spouse to be dead, and remarries, from being found guilty of violating a state's traditional bigamy statute, many states have adopted a so-called "Enoch Arden" statute.[206] "Enoch Arden" statutes establish a time period — normally five to seven years — after which a spouse may remarry with a good faith belief that the absent spouse is dead. However, it is important to note that "Enoch Arden" statutes do *not* validate the subsequent marriage; they only prevent a criminal prosecution for bigamy.[207]

Although bigamous or polygamous marriages are prohibited in the vast majority of American states, such marriages are legally recognized in many African, Asian, and Muslim countries, and although the practice of polygamy is in a decline throughout the Muslim world due to various social and economic factors, arguments in favor of its legality and morality are still being made. Four most commonly advanced arguments supporting polygamy are as follows:

(1) The Koran, like the Old Testament of the Bible, gives religious authority to a man having more than one wife;

(2) Polygamy is justified when the wife is barren or unwell, allowing the husband to have children without divorcing his first wife or leaving her illprovided for;

(3) Polygamy helps to prevent immorality, such as prostitution, rape, fornication, adultery, and the high divorce rate found in many Western monogamous societies; and

(4) Polygamy protects widows and orphans by catering to the possibility of a greater excess of women over men in time of war or other disasters.[208]

---

[204] *See, e.g., Reynold v. United States*, 98 U.S. 145 (1878); *Potter v. Murray City*, 760 F.2d 1065 (10th Cir. 1985) (applying Utah law); *Rance v. Rance*, 587 N.E.2d 150 (Ind. Ct. App. 1992); *see also* Slovenko, *The De Facto Decriminalization of Bigamy*, 17 J. Fam. L. 297 (1978).

[205] *See generally* Green & Long, *supra* note 86, at 37-40.

[206] So named after Alfred Lord Tennyson's 1864 poem entitled *Enoch Arden*.

[207] *See, e.g., Anonymous v. Anonymous*, 62 N.Y.S.2d 130 (N.Y. Sup. Ct. 1946); *see also* Fenton & Kaufman, *Enoch Arden Revisited*, 13 J. Fam. L. 245 (1973-74). *But see infra* § 2.06.

[208] *See generally* K. Hodkinson, Muslim Family Law: A Sourcebook 107-08 (1981).

Similar arguments have been made supporting plural marriages in the United States, including the rising incidence of extra-marital sex, and a soaring American divorce rate.[209] Other commentators have suggested that judicial decisions subsequent to *Reynolds v. United States* that have upheld an individual's fundamental right to the free exercise of religion[210] might now make the *Reynolds* prohibition against plural marriage a candidate for judicial reconsideration.[211]

Finally, even though most American jurisdictions will not recognize a bigamous or polygamous marriage, even though it may be valid in the country where the plural marriage was celebrated, some states nevertheless may recognize such a bigamous or polygamous marriage as a putative marriage.[212]

[D] Incestuous Marriage: Prohibited Degrees of Kinship

Incestuous marriages are proscribed in Biblical teachings,[213] and they are prohibited in a majority of states as void *ab initio* marriages. The problem, however, is ascertaining what particular degrees of kinship are prohibited by state statute.

Incestuous marriages can be prohibited either by consanguinity (relationship through bloodlines, such as marrying one's parent or one's sibling) or by legal affinity (relationship by marriage, such as marrying one's mother-in-law). An

---

[209] *See, e.g.*, Nedrow, *Polygamy and the Right to Marry: New Life for an Old Lifestyle*, 11 Mem. St. U. L. Rev. 303 (1981); *see also* Ryan Tenney, *Tom Green, Common Law Marriage, and the Illegality of Putative Polygamy*, 17 BYU J. Pub. L. 141 (2002); Maura Strassberg, *The Challenge of Post-Modern Polygamy*, 31 Capital U. L. Rev. 439 (2003).

[210] *See, e.g., Sherbert v. Verner*, 374 U.S. 398 (1963) (involving the wrongful discharge of a Seventh Day Adventist from her state job for refusing to work on Saturdays, the Sabbath Day of her faith); *Wisconsin v. Yoder*, 406 U.S. 205 (1972) (involving Amish whose religious beliefs exempted them from attending public schools beyond the eighth grade).

[211] In a concurring and dissenting opinion to *Yoder*, Justice Douglas noted that *Yoder* opened the way to give religious beliefs a broader base than previously recognized, and he opined that in time *Reynolds* would be overruled. 406 U.S. 205, 247. Professor Lawrence Tribe has suggested that after *Sherbert* the *Reynolds* case may be a candidate for constitutional reconsideration. L. Tribe, American Constitutional Law 853-54 (1978). To date, however, few courts have seriously questioned the *Reynolds* rationale for prohibiting bigamous or polygamous marriage. *See, e.g., Bronson v. Swensen*, 394 F. Supp. 2d 1329 (D. Utah 2005) (prohibiting a polygamous or plural marriage, and stating "*Lawrence [v. Texas]* can[not] be read to require the state of Utah to give formal recognition to . . . a polygamous marriage"); *see also* Davis, *Plural Marriage and Religious Freedom: The Impact of* Reynolds v. United States, 15 Ariz. L. Rev. 287 (1973); *see also* Stephanie Forbes, *Why Have Just One? An Evaluation of the Anti-Polygamy Laws Under the Establishment Clause*, 39 Houston L. Rev. 1517 (2003); Bozzuti, *The Constitutionality of Polygamy Prohibitions after* Lawrence v. Texas: *Is Scalia a Punchline or a Prophet?*, 43 Cath. Law. 409 (2004); Ward, Lawrence v. Texas *and the Practice of Polygamy in Modern America* 11 Wm. & Mary J. Women & L. 131 (2004).

[212] *See, e.g., In re Dalip Singh Bir's Estate*, 188 P.2d 499 (Cal. Ct. App. 1948); and *In re Estate of Shippy*, 678 P.2d 848 (Wash. Ct. App. 1984) (both recognizing a bigamous putative marriage for interstate succession purposes). *But see contra Moustafa v. Moustafa*, 888 A.2d 1230 (Md. Ct. Spec. App. 2005) (refusing to recognize a foreign bigamous marriage based upon the forum state's strong public policy). *See generally* Michele Alexandre, *Lessons from Islamic Polygamy: A case for Expanding the American Concept of Surviving Spouse so as to Include De Facto Polygamous Spouses*, 64 Wash. & Lee L. Rev. 1461 (2007).

[213] *See Leviticus* 18:6-24.

example of a traditional statute is found in a provision of the Annotated Laws of Massachusetts (1983) that was first enacted in 1785:

(1) No man may marry his mother, grandmother, daughter, granddaughter, sister, stepmother, grandfather's wife, grandson's wife, wife's mother, wife's grandmother, wife's daughter, wife's granddaughter, brother's daughter, sister's daughter, father's sister, or mother's sister. (In 1983, son's wife was deleted.)

(2) No woman shall marry her father, grandfather, son, grandson, brother, stepfather, grandmother's husband, daughter's husband, granddaughter's husband, husband's grandfather, husband's son, husband's grandson, brother's son, sister's son, father's brother, or mother's brother. (In 1983, husband's father was deleted.)[214]

In approximately half the states, first-cousin marriages are also prohibited.[215]

A growing number of states, however, have adopted a less restrictive and better reasoned approach to incestuous marriage based upon section 207 of the Uniform Marriage and Divorce Act. With minor amendments, these statutes generally provide that a marriage is incestuous and void only if it is between: (1) an ancestor and descendent; (2) a brother and sister of either half or whole blood, or, in some states, by adoption; or (3) an uncle and niece, or aunt and nephew.[216]

In addition to its religious proscription, incest prohibitions have also been justified based upon genetic and eugenics grounds, but this rationale has been seriously questioned by various writers.[217] Perhaps the strongest basis for justifying a prohibition against such marriages is the historical and sociological incest taboo, where survival of family harmony is dependent on prohibiting sexual rivalries.[218]

In some instances, close relatives, such as first cousins, procure an evasionary incestuous marriage in a sister state that legally recognizes such marriages, and then return to their domiciliary state. Some domiciliary states will not recognize such an evasionary incestuous marriage, on the grounds that it is against the

---

[214] Mass. Ann. Laws Ch. 207, §§ 1-2 (1983).

[215] See, e.g., In re Marriage of Adams, 604 P.2d 332 (Mont. 1979). But see Moore, A Defense of First Cousin Marriage, 10 Clev. Mar. L. Rev. 139 (1961). In Cook v. Cook, 104 P.3d 857 (Ariz. Ct. App. 2005), husband and wife, who were first cousins, were married in Virginia, where first cousin marriages are legal. They moved to Arizona, where first cousin marriages are prohibited, and the Arizona court ordered their marriage dissolved as void ab initio under Arizona law. But see Etheridge v. Shaddock, 706 S.W.2d 395 (Ark. 1986) (recognizing a Texas first cousin marriage, although prohibited under Arkansas law).

[216] See, e.g., Cal. Civ. Code § 4400 (1970); N.Y. Dom. Rel. Law § 5 (McKinney 1971); Va. Code Ann. § 20-38.1 (Michie 1975).

[217] See, e.g., C. Stem, Principles of Human Genetics (3d ed. 1973); H. Maisch, Incest (1972).

[218] See, e.g., Murdock, Social Structure 292-313 (1949). See generally Storke, The Incestuous Marriage — Relic of the Past, 36 U. Colo. L. Rev. 473 (1964); Bratt, Incest Statutes and the Fundamental Right to Marry: Is Oedipus Free to Marry?, 18 Fam. L.Q. 257 (1984); Annot., 72 A.L.R.2d 706 (Later Case Service).

domiciliary state's strong public policy.[219] Other states, however, would recognize such an evasionary marriage in order to validate the parties' marital expectations.[220]

Professor Carolyn Bratt has questioned many of the moral and legal difficulties in defining and justifying various statutory prohibitions against incestuous marriages. She writes:

> The mere word "incest" triggers strong feelings of revulsion in most people. Therefore, any *a priori* labeling of a marriage as incestuous tends to preclude objective thought about the permissibility of the particular form of the marriage prohibition at issue. Such revulsion stems largely from the confusion of incest with sexual abuse of children. This confusion is not limited to the general public, but extends to the courts as well . . . . Nevertheless, one must understand the distinction between state incest statutes as a vehicle for prohibiting and punishing sexual abuse of minors and state incest statutes as a marriage prohibition for adults. The rightful condemnation of the intrinsically abusive nature of adult-child sexual relationships must not be used to shield incest statutes prohibiting marriage between certain adults from an objective evaluation . . . . Once one recognizes these analytical difficulties-reflexive fears, shifting definitions of incest itself, ambivalent attitudes, and facile underlying generalizations — one can begin to rationally evaluate the validity of state incest statutes in the light of the constitutional right to marry. After making such an analysis, this author has concluded that neither the civil marriage bar nor the criminal bar against incestuous acts serves any valid purpose which cannot be better served by statutes which do not impinge on the constitutional right to marry.[221]

[E] Underage Marriage

Under the early common law, a marriage before the age of discretion rendered that marriage void *ab initio*. However, a majority of American jurisdictions now treat an underage marriage as merely voidable.[222] Statutory age restrictions for marriage are widely considered necessary to prevent minor, immature persons from entering into unstable marriages that are likely to fail. Accordingly, in most American jurisdictions, a man and a woman are free to marry without parental consent at the age of majority, normally 18 years of age, or older. The consent of a

---

[219] *See, e.g.*, *In re Estate of Stiles*, 391 N.E.2d 1026 (Ohio 1979); *In re Marriage of Adams*, 604 P.2d 332 (Mont. 1979); *see also infra* § 2.09.

[220] *See, e.g.*, *Etheridge v. Shaddock*, 706 S.W.2d 395 (Ark. 1986) (first-cousin marriage); *In re May's Estate*, 114 N.E.2d 4 (N.Y. 1953) (uncle-niece marriage); *see also infra* § 2.09.

[221] Bratt, *supra* note 218, at 257-58. *See also* Christine Metteer, *Some "Incest" is Harmless Incest: Determining the Fundamental Right to Marry of Adults Related by Affinity Without Resorting to State Incest Statutes*, 10 Kan. J. L. & Pub. Policy 262 (2000); Brett McDonnell, *Privacy Rights in a Post* Lawrence *World: Responses to* Lawrence v. Texas: *Is Incest Next?*, 10 Cardozo Women's L.J. 337 (2004); Courtney Megan Cahill, *A Critical Perspective on Contemporary Family Discourse and the Incest Taboo*, 99 Nw. U. L. Rev. 1543 (2005) (examining how the incest taboo has shaped American law, politics, and public perception).

[222] *See, e.g.*, *Holbert v. West*, 730 F. Supp. 50 (E.D. Ky. 1990) (applying Ky. law).

parent or a parent substitute, however, is required for certain underage marriages, most often for 16- and 17-year-olds, and a majority of states also provide for additional "exceptional circumstances," such as when the expectant bride is pregnant.[223]

Age restrictions to marriage have been held to be constitutional. In the case of *Moe v. Dinkins*,[224] a federal court judge, applying New York law, held that although the right to marry is a fundamental constitutional right, nevertheless there was no total deprivation of a minor's right to marry without parental consent, only a delay. Therefore the judge applied a rational relationship test in light of the state interest in protecting minors in particular and marriage in general.[225]

The courts have split on the issue of whether an underage spouse is able to annul his or her own marriage. Some courts have held that the minor's fraudulent misrepresentation of age bars such an annulment action based upon estoppel, or an "unclean hands," argument.[226]

Should a domiciliary state recognize an underage evasionary marriage of its citizens in a sister state? Again, the courts have split on this issue. On one hand, some courts have granted an annulment based upon the fact that such an evasionary underage marriage was against the domiciliary state's strong public policy.[227] But other courts have held that a domiciliary state has no strong public policy that would require the court to invalidate a sister state underage evasionary marriage, even though that marriage was contrary to the domiciliary state's law.[228]

[F] Mental and Physical Incapacity

[1] Mental Incapacity

Under the common law, marriage to a mentally incompetent person was held to be void *ab initio*, and this view is still recognized in a minority of states. An increasing number of jurisdictions, however, by statutory or case law, have treated marriage to a mentally incapacitated person as voidable, rather than void *ab initio*. For example, Section 208 of the Uniform Marriage and Divorce Act provides in part that:

---

[223] *See generally* Wardle, *Rethinking Marital Age Restrictions*, 22 J. Fam. L. 1 (1983-84); Comment, *Capacity, Parental Power, and a Minor's Right to Remain Married*, 22 Santa Clara L. Rev. 447 (1982). Prof. Wardle argues, however, that although legal policy should still discourage underage marriages, once the underage marriage has occurred, it ought to be vindicated, rather than annulled under an "escape valve" annulment proceeding.

[224] 533 F. Supp. 623 (S.D.N.Y. 1981).

[225] *Id.*

[226] *Compare Ruiz v. Ruiz*, 85 Cal. Rptr. 674 (Cal. Ct. App. 1970) (annulment was granted to the parent, acting as the minor's guardian ad litem, who was not a party to the minor's fraudulent misrepresentation of his age), *with Duley v. Duley*, 151 A.2d 255 (D.C. 1959) (the petition for annulment was denied, apparently based on an "unclean hands" defense).

[227] *See, e.g., Wilkins v. Zelichowski*, 140 A.2d 65 (N.J. 1958); *see also infra* § 2.09.

[228] *See, e.g., State v. Graves*, 307 S.W.2d 545 (Ark. 1957); *see also infra* § 2.09.

(a) The . . . court shall enter its decree declaring the invalidity of a marriage entered into under the following circumstances: (1) a party lacked capacity to consent to the marriage at the time the marriage was solemnized, either because of mental incapacity or infirmity or because of the influence of alcohol, drugs, or other incapacitating substances . . . .

The test for mental capacity to consent at the time the marriage is performed has been defined by some courts as a capacity to understand the nature of the marital contract, as well as a capacity to understand the duties and responsibilities of marriage.[229] Other courts, however, have held that the only legal requirement is the ability to consent at the time of the marriage, without any additional duties or responsibilities test, in order to validate the marital expectations of the parties.[230]

Indeed, a number of courts have held that even though a person might have been previously adjudged to be legally incompetent to handle his or her business affairs, nevertheless such a person might still be competent to marry, by applying a lesser test of competency for marriage than for other business purposes, again to validate the public policy of promoting marriage in general, and to validate the marital expectations of the parties in particular.[231]

[2] Physical Incapacity

Physical incapacity, defined as the natural and incurable impotency of the body, also generally results in a voidable marriage whenever a party lacks the physical capacity to consummate the marriage by sexual intercourse, and at the time the marriage was solemnized the other party did not know of the incapacity.[232]

It has been held that "incurable impotency" under a state annulment statute includes the inability to copulate, whether such inability arose from a physical or mental defect.[233] Moreover, under a common law doctrine of triennial cohabitation, if the couple lived together for three years or more, but the wife is still a virgin, the husband will be presumed to be impotent, and he would have the burden of proving that he was not at fault.[234]

A wife may be impotent, even though she had become pregnant and miscarried, according to the case of *T. v. M.*,[235] where a New Jersey judge held that a wife may

---

[229] *See, e.g., Kerckhoff v. Kerckhoff*, 805 S.W.2d 937 (Tex. Civ. App. 1991); *Homan v. Homan*, 147 N.W.2d 630 (Neb. 1967); *Forbis v. Forbis*, 274 S.W.2d 800 (Mo. 1955).

[230] *See, e.g., Young v. Colorado Nat'l Bank*, 365 P.2d 701 (Colo. 1961).

[231] *See, e.g., Geitner v. Townsend*, 312 S.E.2d 236 (N.C. Ct. App. 1984); *Edmunds v. Edwards*, 287 N.W.2d 420 (Neb. 1980); *Riddell v. Edwards*, 76 P.3d 847 (Alaska 2003). *See generally* Shaman, *Persons who are Mentally Retarded: Their Right to Marry and Have Children*, 12 Fam. L.Q. 61 (1978); Linn & Bowers, *Historical Fallacies Behind Legal Prohibitions of Marriage Involving Mentally Retarded Persons*, 13 Gonz. L. Rev. 625 (1978); Note, *The Right of the Mentally Disabled to Marry*, 15 J. Fam. L. 463 (1977).

[232] Uniform Marriage and Divorce Act § 208(a)(2).

[233] *See, e.g., Rickards v. Rickards*, 166 A.2d 425 (Del. 1960).

[234] *See, e.g., Tompkins v. Tompkins*, 111 A. 599 (N.J. Ch. Ct. 1920); *see also* Annot., 28 A.L.R.2d 499 (Later Case Service).

[235] 242 A.2d 670 (N.J. Super Ct. Ch. Div. 1968).

be incurably impotent, due to vaginismus, a vaginal disorder preventing inter-course, despite her ability to conceive. Thus, impotence is not necessarily equated to sterility.[236]

[G] Fraudulent Marriage

A marriage procured by fraud is a voidable marriage according to case and statutory law in most states. The problem, however, is to ascertain the *degree* of fraud necessary to annul such a marriage.

The influential early case of *Reynolds v. Reynolds*[237] established a two-prong test for determining a fraudulent marriage: (1) there must be material fraud; and (2) the fraud must affect the essentials of the present marriage. Material fraud generally means "but for" the fraud, there would have been no marriage. The "essentials of the present marriage" test is harder to define, because the fraud must adversely affect "the *possibility* of normal marital cohabitation."[238] Thus, examples of material fraud that *do* affect the essentials of the marriage have included: lying about an intent not to have sexual intercourse, or not to have children during the marriage; concealment of impotency or venereal disease; concealment of pregnancy by another person; and lying about one's religious beliefs. However, examples of material fraud that do not affect the essentials of the marriage under the traditional rule have included lying about a party's character, chastity, age, health, wealth, citizenship, ancestry, number of prior marriages and divorces, or lack of love and affection.[239]

A more modern approach to fraudulent marriage, primarily adopted by the courts in New York, encompasses this material fraud test, but rejects the essentials of the present marriage test.[240]

If the wife misrepresents to the husband that she is pregnant at the time of the marriage, when in fact she is not pregnant, the majority of courts have held that the marriage is not fraudulent. Under a traditional majority rule, the courts have generally held that the representation of false pregnancy does *not* go to the

---

[236] *Id. See generally* Annot., *Incapacity for Sexual Intercourse as a Ground for Annulment*, 52 A.L.R.3d 589 (1973).

[237] 85 Mass. 605 (1862). The *Reynolds* case was commented upon in 13 Harv. L. Rev. 110 (1899).

[238] *See* Kingsley, *What are the Proper Grounds for Granting Annulments?*, 18 Law & Contemp. Probs. 39 (1953).

[239] *See, e.g., V.J.S. v. M.J.B.*, 592 A.2d 328 (N.J. Super. Ct. Ch. Div. 1991); *E.D.M. v. T.A.M.*, 415 S.E.2d 812 (S.C. 1992); *Haacke v. Glenn*, 814 P.2d 1157 (Utah 1991); *see also* Kingsley, *Fraud as a Ground for Annulment of Marriage*, 18 S. Cal. L. Rev. 213 (1945); Vanmeman, *Annulment of Marriage for Fraud*, 9 Minn. L. Rev. 497 (1925).

[240] *See, e.g., Tacchi v. Tacchi*, 195 N.Y.S.2d 892 (N.Y. Sup. Ct. 1959) (misrepresentation of age); *Schinker v. Schinker*, 68 N.Y.S.2d 470 (N.Y. App. Div. 1947) (misrepresentation of love and affection). *But see Sangimino v. Sangimino*, 575 N.Y.S.2d 515 (N.Y. App. Div. 1991) (annulment action brought on the basis of fraud was denied since husband's alleged fraud did not evince a high degree of moral turpitude). Most cases following this "modern" approach to fraudulent marriage come from New York, and some commentators have pointed out that due to the extreme difficulty of getting a divorce in New York prior to 1970, far more New Yorkers sued for annulment to end their marriage, or obtained a migratory divorce in another state. *See* Note, *Annulments for Fraud — New York's Answer to Reno?*, 48 Colum. L. Rev. 900 (1948).

"essentials" of the marriage, since the wife is not prevented from performing her other marital duties.[241] Nor will the courts extricate the husband who has created his "own dilemma" based upon his illicit premarital intercourse, and he is therefore barred from bringing an annulment action based on such fraud under the *in pari delicto* or "unclean hands" doctrine.[242]

Other courts, however, have adopted an opposing view, holding that a misrepresentation of pregnancy would indeed constitute material fraud, and that the gravity of such fraud should *not* be barred by any *in pari delicto* or "unclean hands" defense.[243]

[H]　Marriage Under Duress

In most states, by case or statutory law, a marriage where the consent of one of the parties was obtained by duress is a voidable marriage. Duress must have existed at the time of the marriage, where the complaining party could not act as a free agent in entering into the marriage due to coercive force or fear from another person. Moreover, many courts have held that the test for duress is a subjective test, rather than being based on the reasonable person of ordinary prudence standard.[244]

There have been various situations where a young man seduces a young woman, and she becomes pregnant. The judge then threatens to prosecute the young man under a state criminal seduction statute, under a state fornication statute, and contributing to the delinquency of a minor. Alternately, the court gives the young man the option of marrying the young woman in lieu of going to jail. Most courts have held that such a scenario would *not* constitute duress, since the young man still has a choice.[245]

[I]　Sham Marriage

A sham marriage is a marriage for limited purposes and with a limited intent, such as a man marrying a pregnant woman only to legitimize their child, but without intending to consent to any of the other normal essentials of marriage. In this situation, many courts have held that such a marriage with limited intent and for a limited purpose is valid for *all* purposes, regardless of the parties' motive for

---

[241] *See, e.g., Hill v. Hill*, 398 N.E.2d 1048 (Ill. App. Ct. 1979); *Husband v. Wife*, 262 A.2d 656 (Del. Super. Ct. 1970); *see also* Annot., 15 A.L.R.2d 706 (Later Case Service).

[242] *See, e.g., Tyminski v. Tyminski*, 221 N.E.2d 486 (Ohio Ct. C.P. 1966); *Brandt v. Brandt*, 167 So. 524 (Fla. 1936).

[243] *See, e.g., Parks v. Parks*, 418 S.W.2d 726 (Ky. Ct. App. 1967); *Masters v. Masters*, 108 N.W.2d 674 (Wis. 1961). For fraudulent inducement to marry actions, see *supra* § 3.02[B].

[244] *See, e.g., Stakelum v. Terral*, 126 So. 2d 689 (La. Ct. App. 1961); *Worthington v. Worthington*, 352 S.W.2d 80 (Ark. 1962); *see also* Kingsley, *Duress as a Ground for Annulment of Marriage*, 33 S. Cal. L. Rev. 1 (1959); Brown, *The Shotgun Marriage*, 42 Tul. L. Rev. 837 (1968); Bradley, *Duress and Arranged Marriages*, 46 Mod. L. Rev. 499 (1983); Annot., 16 A.L.R.2d 1430 (Later Case Service).

[245] *See, e.g., Figueroa v. Figueroa*, 110 N.Y.S.2d 550 (N.Y. Sup. Ct. 1952); *Jones v. Jones*, 314 S.W.2d 448 (Tex. Civ. App. 1958); *see also* Wadlington, *Shotgun Marriage by Operation of Law*, 1 Ga. L. Rev. 183 (1967); Note, *Coercive Power of the Criminal Seduction Statute*, 16 S.D. L. Rev. 166 (1971).

marriage, and therefore no annulment of marriage may be granted.[246]

Sham marriages have also been utilized by various foreign nationals who marry American citizens in order to circumvent American immigration laws, and these so-called "green card" marriages may also constitute voidable sham marriages.[247] Accordingly, some courts have held that "green card" sham marriages for immigration purposes are invalid marriages.[248] Other courts, however, have held that the validity or invalidity of a "green card" sham marriage is irrelevant, since the foreign national can still be deported by the Immigration and Naturalization Service based upon the fraudulent purpose of the marriage.[249]

The confusion resulting from these conflicting court decisions regarding "green card" sham marriages has resulted in federal legislation and investigatory procedures that now cover all such marriages. Under the Immigration Marriage Fraud Amendments Act of 1986,[250] the granting of permanent residency based upon marital status now provides for a "conditional" permanent residency of two years before the alien attains "permanent" residence status. This provision of the Immigration Marriage Fraud Act thus only affects aliens who have been married for less than two years.[251]

[J] Marriage in Jest

A marriage in jest, although it is based upon the apparent consent of the parties, actually involves no consent, since at least one of the parties realizes the marriage is no more than a "joke". However, because a marriage is presumed to be valid and possess the necessary element of mutual consent, the burden is on the party attempting to annul this voidable marriage to demonstrate that it was in fact a marriage in jest.[252]

The fact situation involving marriages in jest typically involves young people who, after a tennis match, dance, or another social engagement, dare each other to get married, and do so. In the relatively small number of reported cases, if such marriages remain unconsummated and the parties do not cohabit after the marriage, then the courts generally will be inclined to grant an annulment based

---

[246] *See, e.g., Schibi v. Schibi*, 69 A.2d 831 (Conn. 1949); *Bishop v. Bishop*, 308 N.Y.S.2d 998 (N.Y. Sup. Ct. 1970). *See generally* Wade, *Limited Purpose Marriages*, 45 Mod. L. Rev. 259 (1982); Comment, *Sham Marriages*, 20 U. Chi. L. Rev. 710 (1953); Annot., 14 A.L.R.2d 624 (Later Case Service).

[247] Indeed, House Report No. 99-906 (1986) stated that approximately 30% of all petitions for immigrant visas involve suspect marital relationships. *Id.* at 6.

[248] *See, e.g., United States v. Rubenstein*, 151 F.2d 915 (2d Cir.), *cert. denied*, 326 U.S. 766 (1945); *United States v. Lutwak*, 195 F.2d 748 (7th Cir. 1952), *aff'd* 344 U.S. 604 (1953). *But see United States v. Diogo*, 320 F.2d 898 (2d Cir. 1968) (two consummated "green card" marriages were held to be valid marriages).

[249] *See, e.g., Johl v. United States*, 370 F.2d 174 (9th Cir. 1967); *Roe v. Immigration & Naturalization Serv.*, 771 F.2d 1328 (9th Cir. 1985).

[250] Pub. L. No. 99-639, 100 Stat. 3537 (1986).

[251] *See generally* Note, *Immigration Marriage Fraud Amendments of 1986: Till Congress Do Us Part*, 41 U. Miami L. Rev. 1087 (1987).

[252] *See generally* Annot., 14 A.L.R.2d 624 (Later Case Service).

upon the lack of voluntary consent, and based upon the parties' relative immaturity.[253]

However, other courts have taken the marriage relationship more seriously, and will not annul any marriage in jest, absent clear proof of fraud, duress, or mental incapacity. For example, in the case of *Hand v. Berry*,[254] a young couple dared each other to marry "in a spirit of hilarity and without serious intent," "in a spirit of fun, braggadocio, and levity," and "in a spirit of misguided fun and jest." The Georgia court was not amused, found no fraud, and held that the marriage was valid.[255]

§ 2.09   CONFLICT OF LAWS: WHICH MARRIAGE LAWS GOVERN?

Americans, as a migratory people, often move from state to state. Due to the large number and variety of differing state statutes that regulate marriage,[256] it becomes necessary to determine which particular law will govern the solemnization of marriage under applicable conflict of laws principles.

The traditional *lex loci contractus* rule states that the law of the place of celebration governs the legal requirements for marriage: that is to say, a marriage valid where celebrated is valid everywhere, unless that marriage violates a forum state's strong public policy.[257]

The more recent Restatement (Second) Conflict of Laws approach, adopted in a majority of the states, holds that the validity of a marriage is to be determined by the local law of the state which has the "most significant relationship" to the spouses and the marriage.[258] Section 283 (2) of the Second Restatement also provides that a marriage "which satisfies the requirements of the state where the marriage was contracted will everywhere be recognized as valid unless it violates the strong public policy of another state which has the most significant relationship to the spouses and the marriage."[259]

The corollary to this general rule that a marriage valid where contracted is valid everywhere would seem to be that a marriage not valid where contracted is not valid everywhere else, and a number of courts have adopted this corollary rule.[260] Other courts, however, in order to uphold marriage in general, and in order to validate the

---

[253] *Id. See also Meredith v. Shakespeare*, 122 S.E. 520 (W. Va. 1924); *Davis v. Davis*, 175 A. 574 (Conn. 1934).

[254] 154 S.E. 239 (Ga. 1930).

[255] *Id. See also Lannamann v. Lannamann*, 89 A.2d 897, 898 (Pa. Super. Ct. 1952) ("since there was no fraud, duress, or lack of mental capacity, the marriage is valid").

[256] *See supra* § 1.03.

[257] *See, e.g.*, Restatement Conflict of Laws §§ 121-23 (1934).

[258] *See* Restatement (Second) Conflict of Laws § 283(1) (1971).

[259] Restatement (Second) Conflict of Laws § 283(2). *See also id.* at § 6.

[260] *See, e.g., Randall v. Randall*, 345 N.W.2d 319 (Neb. 1984); *Singh v. Singh*, 325 N.Y.S.2d 590 (N.Y. Sup. Ct. 1971). *See generally* Maddaugh, *Validity of Marriage and the Conflict of Laws*, 23 U. Toronto L. Rev. 117 (1973); Da Costa, *The Formalities of Marriage in the Conflict of Laws*, 7 Int'l & Comp. L.Q. 217 (1958).

present expectations of the parties in particular, will look to the best of several possible forum rules to validate the marriage, even if such a marriage was invalid where contracted.[261]

§ 2.10 ANNULMENT OF MARRIAGE

[A] Annulment Jurisdiction

Annulment is the legal determination that a void or voidable marriage was a legal nullity from its inception. An annulment action thus differs from a divorce action in that divorce is the dissolution of a legally valid marriage, where annulment is the legal declaration that a marriage never existed in the first place.

In order to annul a voidable marriage,[262] or in order to create a judicial record of a void *ab initio* marriage,[263] a court must have valid jurisdiction over the parties in the annulment proceeding.

The traditional minority rule is that the state where the marriage was contracted should have jurisdiction in an annulment action, unless the parties were domiciled in another state at the time of the marriage, in which case that domiciliary state should have jurisdiction.[264]

The modern majority view, however, is that the state where the parties, or either of them, are domiciled at the time of the annulment proceeding would have jurisdiction. Thus, a number of states now have jurisdictional statutes applying both to divorce and annulment, and effective at the time the action is actually brought.[265]

Another problem with annulment jurisdiction is whether it must be a bilateral proceeding, or whether it can also be an ex parte proceeding. Traditionally, under a "relation back" doctrine, since an annulment meant that no marriage existed, such an annulment action could not be based upon the nonexistent marriage for any subject matter jurisdiction *in rem*, and *in personam* bilateral jurisdiction over both the parties was therefore required for any annulment action.[266]

The landmark annulment case of *Perlstein v. Perlstein*,[267] however, attacked this traditional legal fiction that a judgment in an annulment case should "relate back" to the inception of the marriage. Rather, the *Perlstein* court made a persuasive analogy to the ex parte divorce case of *Williams v. North Carolina [I]*,[268] stating

---

[261] *See generally* Clark, *supra* note 4, at 98-100.

[262] *See supra* § 2.08[A].

[263] *Id.*

[264] *See, e.g.*, Goodrich, *Jurisdiction to Annul a Marriage*, 32 Harv. L. Rev. 806 (1919); *see also* *Worthington v. Worthington*, 352 S.W.2d 80 (Ark. 1962).

[265] *See, e.g.*, Vernon, *Labyrinthine Ways: Jurisdiction to Annul*, 10 J. Pub. L. 47 (1961); Clark, *supra* note 4, at 222-37.

[266] *See generally* 2 Bishop, Marriage, Divorce and Separation 2-14 (1891).

[267] 204 A.2d 909 (Conn. 1964).

[268] 317 U.S. 287 (1942).

that annulment actions may also be ex parte as well as bilateral, based upon the petitioner's domicile and the questionable marriage as the dual basis for annulment jurisdiction.[269]

The *Perlstein* rationale has been adopted in the vast majority of American jurisdictions.

[B]   Annulment Grounds and Defenses

Annulment is the legal determination that a void or voidable marriage was a nullity from its inception. An annulment action thus differs from a divorce action in that divorce is the dissolution of a legally valid marriage, whereas annulment is the legal declaration that a marriage never existed in the first place.[270]

A void *ab initio* marriage,[271] such as a same sex marriage,[272] a bigamous or polygamous marriage,[273] or an incestuous marriage,[274] does *not* require a formal annulment proceeding, but a party may still petition the court for a formal judicial record that such a marriage was void *ab initio*.

A voidable marriage,[275] on the other hand, is legally valid for all civil purposes unless it is annulled by the parties themselves. Thus, voidable marriages *do* require a formal annulment proceeding, and a voidable marriage may include: an underage marriage,[276] a marriage to a spouse who is mentally or physically incompetent,[277] a fraudulent marriage,[278] a marriage under duress,[279] a sham marriage,[280] and a marriage in jest.[281]

There are certain defenses to annulment actions. First, if the parties fail to bring an annulment action for a voidable marriage during the lifetime of either party, or within a reasonable period of time, they are deemed to have condoned and ratified any marital imperfection, and the marriage remains a legally valid marriage.[282] However, the parties can *never* ratify a void *ab initio* marriage, which is a legal nullity from its inception based upon a state's strong public policy rationale.

---

[269] *Perlstein v. Perlstein*, 204 A.2d 909 (Conn. 1964). *See also Whealton v. Whealton*, 432 P.2d 979 (Cal. 1967).

[270] *See generally* Clark, *supra* note 4, at 219-77.

[271] *See supra* § 2.08[A].

[272] *See supra* § 2.08[B].

[273] *See supra* § 2.08[C].

[274] *See supra* § 2.08[D].

[275] *See supra* § 2.08[A].

[276] *See supra* § 2.08[E].

[277] *See supra* § 2.08[F].

[278] *See supra* § 2.08[G].

[279] *See supra* § 2.08[H].

[280] *See supra* § 2.08[I].

[281] *See supra* § 2.08[J].

[282] *See, e.g., Woods v. Woods*, 638 S.W.2d 403 (Tenn. Ct. App. 1982).

A number of states have enacted a specific statute of limitations affecting annulment actions.[283] Other courts have held that in the absence of a specific annulment statute, a general statute of limitations would apply.[284] In the absence of any statute of limitations defense, a defense may also be raised based upon the unreasonable delay in bringing an annulment action under the equitable doctrine of laches.[285]

Estoppel by judgment or res judicata may also constitute another defense to annulment. For example, in *Statter v. Statter*,[286] the court dismissed the wife's annulment action on bigamy grounds based upon a prior divorce action where the court found the Statter's marriage to be a valid marriage. Therefore, res judicata principles will generally override any mistake of law or mistake of fact, as long as the parties had their day in court on the merits of the case.[287] Estoppel by conduct may also bar the parties from contesting the validity of their marriage based upon a prior invalid divorce.[288]

Finally, are children born into a void *ab initio* marriage, or born into a voidable marriage that is annulled, legitimate or illegitimate under the law? Under the common law, such children were deemed to be illegitimate since, under a traditional "relation back" doctrine the marriage was a nullity, and anything depending on the void marriage would also be void.[289] However, this unfortunate common law rule has now been abrogated by statute in almost every state, providing that children of void or voidable marriages are legitimate by statute.[290]

[C] Property and Support Rights on Annulment

If a marriage is void *ab initio*, or if a voidable marriage is annulled, then the marriage is a nullity. Thus, a majority of jurisdictions have held that permanent spousal support and marital property rights *cannot* be granted on annulment, absent specific statutory authority to the contrary.[291] Lacking such marital property and support rights on annulment, a needy "spouse" in these traditional jurisdictions would only have very limited contractual or equitable remedies.[292]

---

[283] *See, e.g.*, Va. Code Ann. § 20-89.1(c) (a two-year statute of limitations for voidable marriages from the date of the marriage); Cal. Fam. Code § 4425(d) (a four-year statute of limitations after discovery of fraud).

[284] *See, e.g.*, *Witt v. Witt*, 72 N.W.2d 748 (Wis. 1955) (the statute begins to run from the time the marital defect is discovered). *But see Munger v. Munger*, 95 A.2d 153 (N.J. Super. Ct. App. Div. 1953). *See also* Annot., 52 A.L.R.2d 1163 (Later Case Service).

[285] *See, e.g.*, Annot. 34 A.L.R.2d 1306 (Later Case Service).

[286] 143 N.E.2d 10 (N.J. 1957).

[287] *C.f. Aldrich v. Aldrich*, 378 U.S. 540 (1964) (divorce case).

[288] *See supra* § 2.05[E].

[289] *See* Bishop, *supra* note 266 at 313; *see also* Note, *Status of the Issue of Void Marriages*, 56 Harv. L. Rev. 624 (1943).

[290] *See, e.g.*, N.Y. Dom. Rel. Law § 24; Pa. Stat. Ann. tit. 48, § 169.1; Wis. Stat. Ann. § 767.60.

[291] *See generally* Annot., 54 A.L.R.2d 1410 (Later Case Service).

[292] *See, e.g.*, *In re Estate of Thorton*, 499 P.2d 864 (Wash. 1972) (property awarded on an "implied partnership" theory); *Marvin v. Marvin*, 557 P.2d 106 (Cal. 1976) (cause of action based on expressed or

Fortunately, a growing number of states have recognized this financial plight of a needy "spouse" at the time of annulment, and have enacted legislation allowing permanent spousal support and marital property division to be granted on annulment, similar to divorce legislation.[293]

Another recurring problem with spousal support and annulment is based upon the following scenario: Husband and wife are divorced and the divorce decree provides that the payor spouse will pay spousal support to the needy spouse until the payor or payee dies, or until the payee remarries. The payee spouse then remarries, but this second marriage is subsequently annulled.

The states are split as to the effect of the annulment on the payor's initial spousal support obligation. Some courts, applying a traditional "relation back" annulment doctrine to both void *ab initio* and voidable marriages, hold that the prior spousal support obligation is *not* terminated, since there has been no second marriage.[294] Other courts would deny spousal support payments to the payee spouse when the second marriage was voidable, but not void *ab initio*.[295] Still other courts would terminate the prior spousal support obligation whether the remarriage was voidable or void *ab initio*.[296]

A number of courts have granted temporary spousal support to a needy spouse during the pendency of an annulment action when that spouse was attempting to protect and validate the marriage. These courts often have denied temporary spousal support *pendente lite* if the spouse requesting support was the one bringing the annulment action in order to invalidate the marriage.[297] However, this traditional approach normally is not applied in those states where spousal support and marital property rights are recoverable in annulment actions by statutory authority.[298]

---

implied contractual basis); *Walker v. Walker*, 47 N.W.2d 633 (Mich. 1951) (monetary award based upon equitable principle of unjust enrichment); *see also supra* §§ 2.02, 2.05[D].

[293] *See, e.g.*, Conn. Gen. Stat. Ann. § 46b-60; N.Y. Dom. Rel. Law § 236; Va. Code Ann. §§ 20-107.1 to 107.3; Wis. Stat. Ann. § 767.26; *see also* Clark, *supra* note 4, at 245-46 ("It is difficult to understand why more states have not enacted these statutes."). *See generally* Comment, *The Aftereffects of Annulment: Alimony, Property Division, Provision for Children*, 1968 Wash. U. L. Rev. 148.

[294] *See, e.g.*, *Sutton v. Leib*, 199 F.2d 163 (7th Cir. 1952); *Redmann v. Redmann*, 376 N.W.2d 803 (N.D. 1985).

[295] *See, e.g.*, *McConkey v. McConkey*, 215 S.E.2d 640 (Va. 1975) (annulment for fraud terminated spousal support from the prior husband); *Johnston v. Johnston*, 592 P.2d 132 (Kan. Ct. App. 1979) (void *ab initio* marriage did not terminate spousal support payments, but a voidable marriage would).

[296] *See, e.g.*, *Glass v. Glass*, 546 S.W.2d 738, 742 (Mo. Ct. App. 1977) ("We conclude . . . that remarriage . . . refers to the ceremony of marriage and not to the status or relationship — invalid, voidable, or void — which actually results."); *Gaines v. Jacobsen*, 124 N.E.2d 290 (N.Y. 1954); *Hutton v. Hutton*, 118 S.W.3d 176 (Ky. 2003) (also rejecting the void/voidable distinction for the restatement of spousal support). *Sefton v. Sefton*, 291 P.2d 439 (Cal. 1955). However, the *Sefton* court held that spousal support may be reinstated in certain situations for the protection of innocent parties. *See also Weintraub v. Weintraub*, 213 Cal. Rptr. 159 (Cal. Ct. App. 1985). *See generally* Annot., 45 A.L.R.3d 1033 (1972); Note, *The Annulment Controversy: Revival of Prior Alimony Payments*, 13 Tulsa L.J. 127 (1977).

[297] *See generally* Comment, *The Aftereffects of Annulment: Alimony, Property Division, Provision for Children*, 1968 Wash. U.L. Rev. 148.

[298] *See supra* note 193 (and accompanying text).

Chapter 3

PROPERTY AND SUPPORT RIGHTS DURING MARRIAGE

§ 3.01 INTRODUCTION

The legal status of marriage gives rise to rights and obligations affecting spouses during the marriage. Property rights arise out of the parties' ownership interests in marital assets, while support obligations recognize the duty of a spouse to provide ongoing provision of goods and services necessary for daily living. These incidents of marriage involve a variety of concepts relating to the economic relationship of the spouses, both between each other and with respect to third parties.

Two systems of marital property co-exist in the United States: (1) the common law system, which is followed by the majority of states, and (2) the community property system, recognized by a minority of jurisdictions. While the two regimes currently overlap upon dissolution of marriage under equitable distribution principles, they remain distinct during the existence of marriage, and have unique applications on the death of a spouse.[1]

Traditionally, the common law regarded a married couple as one legal entity, with the husband as the head of the household. Accordingly, it allocated the duty of protection and support of the wife and children to the husband and granted him the right to their services and most of their property.

During the 1970s, the United States Supreme Court struck down many gender-based laws that unconstitutionally distinguished between males and females under the Equal Protection Clause of the Fourteenth Amendment of the federal Constitution.[2] In *Orr v. Orr*,[3] the Supreme Court held that an Alabama statute authorizing alimony for women, but not for men, was unconstitutional. *Orr* signaled the demise of many gender-based statutes regulating family support and property matters.[4] Since *Orr*, the Supreme Court has made it clear that statutory differences

---

[1] *See infra* §§ 3.02, 3.03[B], 3.05, 3.06.

[2] *See, e.g., Reed v. Reed*, 404 U.S. 71 (1971) (Idaho statutory classifications that preferred men over women in appointment of administrators for decedents' estates violated Equal Protection Clause of the Fourteenth Amendment); *Stanton v. Stanton*, 421 U.S. 7 (1975) (Utah statute fixing age of majority for termination of child support at twenty-one for male children and eighteen for female children violated equal protection).

[3] 440 U.S. 268 (1979).

[4] *See, e.g.*, Cal. Civ. Code § 2581. *See generally* G. Michael Bridge, Note, *Uniform Probate Code Section 2-202: A Proposal to Include Life Insurance Assets Within the Augmented Estate*, 74 Cornell L. Rev. 511, 543, n.26 (1989).

based on gender as must satisfy "an exceedingly persuasive justification."[5] To withstand constitutional scrutiny, gender-based classifications must at least serve "important governmental objectives," and must be "substantially related to the achievement of those objectives."[6] Although statutory classifications based on gender may be justified, in limited circumstances, to compensate women "for particular economic disabilities [they have] suffered,"[7] the same heightened scrutiny applies even where a statute's objective is to compensate for past discrimination or to balance the burdens borne by males and females.[8]

Both spousal and child support rights and obligations are now generally regarded as gender-neutral concepts, imposing support obligations on both spouses and parents regardless of sex.[9] Property ownership during marriage, however, continues to be allocated under title theory principles in common law jurisdictions.[10]

§ 3.02 THE COMMON LAW THEORY OF PROPERTY RIGHTS

During marriage, common law states apply a "title theory" of property, allocating ownership to the spouse who holds title to, or who has otherwise acquired, the asset in question.[11] The owner of property may manage, control, and dispose of the asset without the consent of, or notice to, the other spouse. Unless transformed by gift, contract, or court decree, title to a marital asset is held by the party who earned the funds used to purchase the asset. Usually title can be traced to the primary wage earner who in the past was, and to a significant extent remains, the husband.

Common law generally regarded any services rendered by one spouse to the other as either obligatory or gratuitous.[12] Therefore, spousal services, such as homemaker services, did not entitle the rendering spouse to rights in the "earning" spouse's property. The presumption that such services were a gift could be rebutted by factual evidence demonstrating that the services were *not* intended to be gratuitous.[13] Thus, a spouse was permitted to prove that certain property of the marriage was held in partnership, quasi-partnership, joint venture, or trust, or that a constructive trust should be imposed to prevent unjust enrichment of the

---

[5] *Mississippi University for Women v. Hogan*, 458 U.S. 718, 724 (1982); *United States v. Virginia*, 518 U.S. 515, 515 (1996). For a discussion of how some judges and scholars have interpreted *Virginia* to announce a higher level of constitutional scrutiny for cases involving gender (*i.e.*, Justice Ginsburg's "skeptical scrutiny"), see David K. Bowsher, *Cracking the Code of* United States v. Virginia, 48 Duke L.J. 305 (1998).

[6] *Hogan*, 458 U.S. at 724. *See also J.E.B. v. Alabama*, 511 U.S. 127, 131-46 (1994).

[7] *Califano v. Webster*, 430 U.S. 313, 320 (1977).

[8] *Hogan*, 458 U.S. at 728.

[9] *See infra* § 9.01.

[10] *Cf. infra* § 3.06.

[11] Homer Clark, The Law of Domestic Relations in the United States 589-94 (2d ed. 1987).

[12] *Id.* at 289-304.

[13] *See, e.g., Eggleston v. Eggleston*, 47 S.E.2d 243, 248 (N.C. 1948).

title-holding spouse.[14]

§ 3.03   THE *"FEME SOLE* ESTATE" AND THE MARRIED WOMEN'S PROPERTY ACTS

Prior to the statutory reforms collectively known as the Married Women's Property Acts, women faced a number of economic disabilities upon marrying. This part reviews those disabilities under the early common law and then describes the limited reforms made in the Married Women's Property Acts.

[A]   The *"Feme Sole* Estate"

Married women suffered severe economic disabilities under early common law, while no corresponding disabilities were imposed on husbands. Upon marriage, the husband acquired title to all the wife's personal property, except for her incidental personal "paraphernalia," such as clothing and ornaments. He was also granted possession of her real property, including the rents and profits, and the rights to manage, control, alienate, and encumber that property. Other disabilities imposed on married women included the legal incapacity to contract, to execute wills, to vote, and to sue or be sued. According to Blackstone, the reason for the married woman's legal incapacity was the "unity" theory of marriage where the husband and wife "became one" person under the law.[15] The law granted the husband control over his wife with corresponding duties to support and protect her.

However, as early as the seventeenth century, courts of equity began to ameliorate the harsh common law disabilities by allowing specific property to be held in trust for the wife's "sole and separate use." This equitable trust arrangement created what was known as the *"feme sole* estate," or the "equitable separate estate." The *feme sole* estate accorded married women the same property rights enjoyed by their single female counterparts, enabling them to own and manage their own assets. The early *feme sole* estate was in the form of a trust and was often created by the wife's father, but could also be established by her husband or by others.[16] This equitable doctrine permitted any type of property to be transferred into trust, thereby allowing the wife to retain her property rights after marriage and to contract, convey, devise, and sue or be sued with respect to that property, while safeguarding her from exposure to the claims of her husband or his

---

[14] *See, e.g., McGehee v. McGehee*, 85 So. 2d 799 (Miss. 1956) (upholding formal, written partnership agreement between spouses relating to ownership of business assets). *But see Chaachou v. Chaachou*, 135 So. 2d 206 (Fla. 1961). In *Chaachou*, where the couple had no written partnership agreement with respect to business property, the court held that any partnership that may have been agreed to "became merged in their larger partnership of marriage and its terms are now too indistinct to be specifically enforced as such." *Id.* at 214. The court concluded, however, that the husband would be unjustly enriched if he were allowed to retain all the business assets without compensating the wife, and the wife was awarded a three-twentieths value of four hotel properties, as well as permanent alimony, a residence, and attorney fees. *Id.* at 215.

[15] *See* 1 William Blackstone, Commentaries on the Laws of England 445 (Cooley 3d ed. 1884).

[16] *See* Clark, *supra* note 11 at 288–89.

creditors.[17]

American courts later adopted the English Chancery Courts' method of creating separate estates for married women without the use of trustees. Therefore, married women who held separate property were sometimes free to manage some of their own financial affairs. However, oftentimes separate estates were created by male relatives who structured the estate to curtail the woman's managerial authority over her own assets.[18] Despite these limitations, the *feme sole* estate had gained considerable popularity in this country by the mid-nineteenth century.

[B] The Married Women's Property Acts

By the late 1800s, state legislatures began to enact a series of statutes collectively known as the Married Women's Property Acts.[19] Like the privately created *feme sole* estate, these statutes were intended to reduce or eliminate the economic disabilities imposed on wives under common law. Commentators have disagreed as to whether the Married Women's Property Acts have rendered the separate equitable *feme sole* estate obsolete.[20]

Although the Married Women's Property Acts varied in detail from one state to another, in general, they extended further than the *feme sole* estate. The Acts not only granted wives the rights to acquire, own, and transfer all types of real and personal property to the same extent as unmarried women, but many Acts further allowed married women to enter into contracts in their own names, to engage in business or employment and retain their own earnings, to make wills, to sue and be sued, and to be fully responsible for their own tortious and criminal conduct.[21] Typically, the Married Women's Property Acts shielded the woman's assets from the creditors of her husband.[22] The Acts had no effect, however, on the husband's position as head of the household, his duty to support the wife, or her reciprocal duty to provide him with household services. Nor did they give her any interests in property owned or earned by the husband. Therefore, because the typical wife was not employed outside the home and brought little, if any, property into the marriage, the economic position of married women in general was not greatly improved.

Because most family law doctrines are now gender neutral, features of the *feme sole* equitable estate and the Married Women's Property Acts which give women greater economic rights than men are subject to constitutional attack. Marital

---

[17] *Id.* at 289.

[18] *See* Richard Chused, Cases, Materials and Problems in Property 198 (2010).

[19] Clark, *supra* note 11, at 489-90.

[20] *Compare* 1 American Law of Property §§ 5.55-.56 (1952), *with* Jack Rappeport, *The Equitable Separate Estate and Restraints on Anticipation*, 11 Miami L.Q. 85 (1956). *See also Andes v. Roller*, 37 S.E. 297 (Va. 1900) (the separate equitable *feme sole* estate continues to have an independent existence distinct from the Married Women's Property Acts).

[21] *See generally* Clark, *supra* note 11, at 290, 293-304.

[22] *See* Richard Chused, *supra* note 18, at 198.

property and support rights and obligations now apply equally to both husbands and wives.[23]

§ 3.04   CO-OWNERSHIP: HOW PROPERTY IS HELD VIS-À-VIS SPOUSES

The law recognizes three methods for holding property concurrently: tenancy by the entirety, joint tenancy, and tenancy in common.[24] Each type of property ownership confers varying rights upon spouses vis-à-vis themselves and third parties.

[A]   Tenancy by the Entirety

The estate of tenancy by the entirety is a form of concurrent property ownership available exclusively to married couples: "A tenancy by the entirety has been described as essentially a joint tenancy, modified by the common-law theory that husband and wife are one person."[25] Tenancy by the entirety has never been recognized in states adhering to the community property system.

Tenancy by the entirety is a means of protecting a married couple's property, both from each other and from their creditors. In a tenancy by the entirety, each spouse holds an equal, undivided interest in the property during the lifetimes of both parties. The estate incorporates a survivorship interest which gives the surviving spouse sole ownership of the whole property at the death of the other spouse.[26] Neither spouse can unilaterally transfer, encumber, sever, or partition property held in tenancy by the entirety, nor destroy the other spouse's right of survivorship. Historically, the individual creditors of one spouse could not reach that spouse's interest in the property held by entirety.[27] The husband, as head of the marital unit, however, had the power to manage the property held in tenancy by the entirety.

Traditionally, a tenancy by the entirety was created whenever property was conveyed simultaneously to a husband and wife,[28] although some states now require it to be expressly created.[29] Originally, the tenancy by the entirety estate was limited to real property, but some states expanded it to include personal

---

[23] *See infra* § 9.01.

[24] *See generally* Abraham Bell & Gideon Parchomovsky, *Of Property and Federalism*, 115 Yale L.J. 72, 82 (2005); Megan D. Randolph, *Let No Man Put Asunder: Divorce, Joint Tenancy, and Notices of Severance*, 47 U. Louisville L. Rev. 607 (2009). *See also* Warren G. Lamont & Susan J. Chan, *Determining When Spousal Joint Tenancies Should be Used to Meet Estate Planning Goals*, 14 Est. Plan. 160 (1991). Spouses should carefully consider which mode of ownership best suits their needs, including their estate planning needs.

[25] *See* Francis C. Amendola, et al., 41 C.J.S. Husband and Wife § 20 (2012). It is important to note that the three modes of property ownership apply to both real and personal property (*e.g.*, bank accounts can be held between spouses as joint tenants or tenants in common).

[26] *See* Paul Haskell, Preface to Wills, Trusts and Administration 118 (1987).

[27] *See id.* at 118-19.

[28] *See* Clark, *supra* note 11, at 295.

[29] Those states are Hawaii, Illinois, Maryland, Massachusetts, Michigan, New Hampshire, Oregon,

property, and some presumed a tenancy by the entirety whenever spouses acquired property together.[30] The United States Supreme Court held in *United States v. Craft*[31] that federal law controlled the nature of property rights for purposes of a federal tax lien and refused to shield property held as tenants by the entirety. The *Craft* court refused to recognize state law provisions which would have ordinarily prohibited the husband from unilaterally alienating his interest in the property.

Currently, fewer than half the common law property states recognize the tenancy by the entirety estate.[32] Where it is recognized, both spouses now have equal rights to property held in the entirety. The majority of states which continue to recognize tenancy by the entirety shield the entirety property both from the unilateral acts of either spouse and from their individual creditors.[33] A few jurisdictions allow either spouse to transfer his or her individual interest and allow separate creditors to reach that spouse's interest, while preserving both the present interest and the survivorship right of the other spouse.[34] Because only married couples may hold property as tenants by the entirety, the estate generally is converted into a tenancy in common upon dissolution of the marriage.[35]

[B] Joint Tenancy

Joint tenancies in property are not limited to married couples. However, after the decline of the tenancy by the entirety, many married couples began to hold property as joint tenants. Historically, in order for a joint tenancy in property to be created, there have been four strict requirements: unity of interest, unity of title, unity of time, and unity of possession.[36] Both separate and marital property may be held in a joint tenancy with each spouse owning an undivided one-half interest.[37]

Tennessee, Virginia, and Wyoming. *See Recognition of Tenants by the Entirety for Real and Personal Property*, 50 State Statutory Surveys, 0130 SURVEYS 17, tbl. 1 (2011) (Westlaw).

[30] *See* Jesse Dukeminier, et al., Property 276-77 (6th ed. 2006).

[31] 535 U.S. 274 (2002).

[32] Tenancy by the entirety is still recognized in Alaska, Delaware, the District of Columbia, Florida, Guam, Hawaii, Illinois, Indiana, Maryland, Massachusetts, Michigan, Mississippi, Missouri, Nebraska, New Jersey, New York, North Carolina, Oklahoma, Oregon, Pennsylvania, Rhode Island, Tennessee, Vermont, Virginia, the U.S. Virgin Islands, and Wyoming. *Recognition of Tenants by the Entirety for Real and Personal Property*, 50 State Statutory Surveys, 0130 SURVEYS 17, tbl. 1 (2011) (Westlaw).

[33] *See, e.g., Sawada v. Endo*, 561 P.2d 1291 (Haw. 1977) (reviewing present state of tenancy by the entirety law and adopting majority position).

[34] *See* Paul Haskell, *supra* note 26, at 118-19.

[35] *See, e.g., Union Grove Milling & Mfg. Co. v. Faw*, 404 S.E.2d 508 (N.C. Ct. App. 1991); *V.R.W., Inc. v. Klein*, 503 N.E.2d 496 (N.Y. 1986).

[36] 4 Horner Probate Prac. & Estates § 73:10; John V. Orth, *Joint Tenancy Law: Plus ca Change . . .* , 5 Green Bag 2d 173 (2002). Most states no longer rigidly follow the four unities requirement, especially where a rigid construction of the rule would defeat the parties' intent. *See* 2 Tiffany Real Prop. § 418 (2011); *In re Estate of Baker*, 78 N.W.2d 863 (Iowa 1956); *In re Estate of Ledwidge*, 358 N.W.2d 18 (Mich. Ct. App. 1984).

[37] 2 Tiffany Real Prop. § 418. *Swink v. Fingado*, 850 P.2d 978 (N.M. 1993), provides an illustration. In *Swink*, a wife inherited $50,000 from her father which is her separate property. The husband and wife purchased a $100,000 house as joint tenants and the wife used her $50,000 inheritance. The wife specifies

However, absent a written agreement designating a spouse's individual interest as separate property, many states presume that property held by a joint tenancy is marital property.[38] Either spouse in a joint tenancy has the right to make contracts and manage the property independently of the other spouse.

Some states require that the instrument conveying the property explicitly create a joint tenancy with the right of survivorship.[39] Other states take a more liberal approach, looking also at the parties' intent to create a joint tenancy.[40] The right of survivorship is the product of the conveyance of property to the joint tenants, not a result of the state's probate laws. The decedent spouse cannot defeat the living spouse's survivorship interest by devising his or her interest to another party. Instead, the property automatically passes to the surviving spouse as a product of the joint tenancy. Nevertheless, one spouse can unilaterally break the joint tenancy by alienating his or her one-half interest through an inter vivos transfer.[41] Oftentimes, spouses would sever the joint tenancy through secret, "straw-man" conveyances creating a tenancy in common and defeating the other spouse's survivorship interest. In order to remedy this problem, many states explicitly prohibit a spouse from unilaterally alienating property held by joint tenancy.[42]

[C]   Tenancy in Common

Most states have a presumption against joint tenancy, making tenancy in common the default rule.[43] Therefore, married couples wishing to hold property a certain way must carefully define their intent. The only requirement for possessing

---

in writing that her half interest, representing the $50,000 investment of her separate property, will remain her separate property. Therefore, upon dissolution of the marriage the wife's half interest is her separate property, whereas the husband's half interest is marital property that may be equitably divided between the couple.

[38]   2 Tiffany Real Prop. § 418.

[39]   *See, e.g.,* Md. Code Ann., Real Prop. § 2-117 (West 2012) ("No deed, will, or other written instrument which affects land or personal property, creates an estate in joint tenancy, unless the deed, will, or other written instrument expressly provides that the property granted is to be held in joint tenancy.").

[40]   *Matter of Estate of Ingram,* 874 P.2d 1282 (Okla. 1994) (joint tenancy may be created by express language in instrument and by actions of party creating joint tenancy which show intention to create essential elements of joint ownership and survivorship.).

[41]   W. W. Allen, *What Acts by One or More of Joint Tenants Will Sever or Terminate the Tenancy,* 64 A.L.R.2d 918 (Originally published in 1959); *Riddle v. Harmon,* 102 Cal. App. 3d 524 (1980) ("Wife who held real property in joint tenancy with husband could unilaterally terminate joint tenancy by conveying her interest from herself as joint tenant to herself as tenant in common.").

[42]   W. W. Allen, *supra* note 41; *Clark v. Carter,* 265 Cal. App. 2d 291 (1968) ("A joint tenant cannot terminate tenancy in real property and in note secured by deed of trust, jointly held by herself and husband, by quit-claiming one-half undivided interest in real property to herself as grantee and tenant in common and assigning one-half undivided interest in note and deed of trust to herself as assignee and tenant in common."); *Knoche v. Morgan,* 664 P.2d 258 (Colo. Ct. App. 1983) ("Colorado statute rendered void any attempt by one of two joint tenants of properly homesteaded property to destroy the joint tenancy by unilateral conveyance."); Colo. Rev. Stat. Ann. § 38-41-202 (West 2012) (renders void attempts by one joint tenant to destroy the joint tenancy by unilateral conveyance).

[43]   Glenda K. Harnad, 48A C.J.S. Joint Tenancy § 10 (2012).

property as tenants in common is unity of possession.[44] Spouses holding property as tenants-in-common need not hold equal shares.[45] Unlike a tenancy by the entirety or a joint tenancy, a tenancy in common does not contain a survivorship interest for co-tenants.[46] Therefore a surviving spouse is only entitled to inherit his or her spouse's interest in a common tenancy property if the interest was devised to the surviving spouse or the interest passed to the surviving spouse through intestacy.[47] Furthermore, each tenant holds an undivided, but separate, interest. There are no restrictions on whether one co-tenant may alienate his or her own interest, but one co-tenant may not contractually bind the other co-tenant(s) with regard to the property.[48]

§ 3.05 COMMON LAW PROPERTY RIGHTS ON DEATH OF A SPOUSE

At death, subject to certain restrictions,[49] a spouse may transfer by will any property that he or she owns individually. Historically, under the common law system of marital property ownership, a surviving spouse could be left without any property or means of support if the deceased spouse left his or her estate to someone outside the marriage. Traditionally, widows were most vulnerable to disinheritance because their husbands usually owned most or all of a married couple's assets. Making matters worse, spouses were not designated as each other's heirs at early common law. Today, however, all American states recognize a surviving spouse as an heir, who will inherit a portion of property passing by intestacy. To alleviate the possibility that a surviving spouse would be left destitute, the common law developed methods of protecting surviving spouses in the form of dower and curtesy. More recently, many state legislatures have provided additional protection to surviving spouses by enacting elective share laws.[50]

---

[44] *See* 2 Tiffany Real Prop. § 426.

[45] *Id.*

[46] *Id.*

[47] *Id.*

[48] *Id.*

[49] Most states legislatures have now passed mandatory "spousal share" laws that discourage complete disinheritance of a surviving spouse. *See Intestate Succession*, 50 State Statutory Surveys, 0160 SURVEYS 1 (2011) (Westlaw); Kenneth Rampino, *Spousal Disinheritance in Rhode Island:* Barrett v. Barrett *and the (De)evolution of the Elective Share Law*, 12 Roger Williams U. L. Rev. 420 (2007); Andra J. Hedrick, *Protection Against Spousal Disinheritance: A Critical Analysis of Tennessee's New Forced Share System*, 28 U. Mem. L. Rev. 561 (1998).

[50] *See supra* note 49. Most states have a homestead law that also protects surviving spouses and minor children against claims from third-party creditors that would dislodge them from the home. The extent of protection varies dramatically from state to state and has been described as "ridiculously small in some states." Dukeminier, Sitkoff & Lindgren, Wills, Trusts, and Estates 474 (8th ed. 2009). *See also* Richard A. Leiter, *Homestead*, 50 State Statutory Surveys, 0130 SURVEYS 5, tbl. 1 (2007) (Westlaw).

[A] Common Law Dower and Curtesy

Although the common law afforded wives no rights in their husband's property during marriage, it did protect wives from total disinheritance on their husband's death in the form of dower. Dower entitled a widow to possession of a life estate in one-third of certain real property that the husband owned at any time during the marriage, regardless of when or how the husband had acquired the property. Even if the husband had disposed of the property during his lifetime, unless she released those rights by voluntarily joining in the deed, the widow's dower rights attached to that land and became possessory upon the husband's death.[51]

Common law dower was limited to inheritable real property that the husband held as a possessory freehold estate. Thus, dower did not attach to personal property or real property in which the husband merely held a leasehold estate, life estate, future interest, or joint tenancy.[52] Dower gave the wife no rights during the husband's lifetime, during which time her dower interest was regarded as "inchoate." Nor did it grant her a property interest that she could transfer to her heirs or devisees if she predeceased him. Once dower became choate on the husband's death, the court assigned to the widow a specific one-third portion of each parcel of land to which dower had attached for her lifetime use. If such assignment was impractical, some courts awarded her one-third of the income from that land for her lifetime.[53] At the wife's death, her dower interest expired.

Although the common law already gave the husband the right to manage and control the wife's real property during the marriage,[54] it further granted the husband a continued interest upon her death in the form of curtesy. Like dower, curtesy was limited to the wife's inheritable freehold real property interests. Curtesy, however, gave the husband a life estate in *all* of the wife's qualified property, although the husband's curtesy rights only attached once a child of the marriage was born alive.[55]

During the past century, as people more commonly began to hold their accumulated wealth in the form of financial investments rather than in real

---

[51] *See* 2 Tiffany Real Property 3d ed. § 487 (Tiffany and Jones eds., 2003); 3 Thompson on Real Property § 21.02 (Thomas ed., 2011).

[52] Thompson, *supra* note 51.

[53] Haskell, *supra* note 26, at 134. A wife's interest in her husband's personal property has changed over time. Before the Norman Conquest, Anglo-Saxon law guaranteed a widow one-third of the property (real and personal) of her husband after his death. *See* Courtney S. Kenny, The History of the Law of England as to the Effects of Marriage on Property 36 (1879). This, however, was abandoned in favor of the land-based system of dower during the medieval period. *Id.* at 21-93. The English Statute of Distributions, 22 & 23 Car. II, c. 10. (1670), gave the surviving spouse a one-third share of the deceased spouse's personal property, if he died intestate. Julian R. Kossow, *The New York Law of Intestate Succession Compared with the Uniform Probate Code: Where There's No Will There's a Way*, 4 Fordham Urb. L.J. 233, 239-40 (1976). The practice of giving the surviving spouse an intestate share of one-third of the personal property apparently was a part of the common law long before 1670. *See* Charles Gross, *The Medieval Law of Intestacy*, 18 Harv. L. Rev. 120 (1904). However, such an interest was not a protection against a husband who sought to disinherit his wife. Only dower played that role.

[54] *See supra* § 3.03.

[55] George L. Haskins, *Curtesy in the United States*, 100 U. Pa. L. Rev. 196 (1951).

property, dower and curtesy became a largely ineffective means for providing protection to a surviving spouse. Most states have abolished both dower and curtesy, and where they still exist, usually in a statutory form, equivalent rights are accorded to both husbands and wives. Dower and curtesy have been replaced or supplemented in most common law states with some variation of an "elective" or "forced" share statute.[56]

[B] Elective Share Statutes

Elective share statutes entitle a surviving spouse to a statutorily prescribed minimum fraction of the decedent spouse's property owned at death. Typically, the fraction is one-third to one-half of the decedent's probate estate, but may vary depending on whether the decedent spouse left descendants or parents.[57] Although the statutes are sometimes referred to as "forced share" statutes, because the surviving spouse can renounce the will and demand a minimum portion of the deceased spouse's estate, the survivor must affirmatively assert this right during a specified time period or it will expire; hence, the term "elective share," as used by the Uniform Probate Code, is more appropriate.[58]

Unlike common law dower and curtesy, elective share statutes apply to both real and personal property and the elective share property is awarded outright to the surviving spouse, rather than as a life estate. Elective share statutes do not give the non-owning spouse property interests in the owning spouse's separate property during the marriage. The non-owning spouse does not receive any devisable or inheritable interests if the non-owning spouse dies first. While the elective share originally applied only to property which the decedent spouse disposed of by will, increasingly, states subject certain lifetime transfers to the spousal elective share as well.[59] Furthermore, if the decedent spouse dies without a will that effectively devises all of his or her property, the intestacy statutes of every state designate a

---

[56] Haskell, *supra* note 26, at 135-36. *See also Intestate Succession, supra* note 49.

[57] Haskell, *supra* note 26, at 136.

[58] *See* Lawrence Waggoner, et al., Family Property Law: Cases and Materials on Wills, Trusts, and Future Interests §§ 10-12 to 10-25 (4th ed. 2006). From 1930 until 1992, the New York elective share obligation could be met by the deceased spouse leaving the surviving spouse a life interest in a testamentary trust funded by an amount equal to the survivor's elective share, which could be as low as one-quarter of the estate if there were children from another marriage. New York adopted a more conventional elective share law in 1992. *Compare* New York Decedent Estate Law § 18(1)(b) (1992), *with* 3-1 New York Civil Practice: EPTL §§ 5-1.1, 5-1.1-A (2011). Other current variations in the elective share include Connecticut, where the elective share includes a life estate in one-third of the probate estate, *see* Conn. Gen. Stat. § 45a-436 (2011), and Rhode Island, where the surviving spouse is entitled to a life estate in all real estate owned at death by the deceased spouse, *see* R.I. Gen. Laws § 33-25-2 (2011). Georgia is the only separate property state without an elective share statute; however, even in the absence of an elective share statute, the living spouse is statutorily entitled to one year of support. Dukeminier, Sitkoff & Lindgren, Wills, Trusts, and Estates, *supra* note 23, at 476 n.2 (8th ed. 2009).

[59] *See, e.g.*, Elias Clark, *The Recapture of Testamentary Substitutes to Preserve the Spouse's Elective Share: An Appraisal of Recent Statutory Reforms*, 2 Conn. L. Rev. 513 (1970); Rena C. Seplowitz, *Transfers Prior to Marriage and the Uniform Probate Code's Redesigned Elective Share — Why the Partnership Is Not Yet Complete*, 25 Ind. L. Rev. 1, 13-18 (1991); Ralph C. Brashier, *Disinheritance and the Modern Family*, 45 Case W. Res. L. Rev. 83, 88 (1994).

surviving spouse as an heir, entitling that spouse to a specified portion of the intestate estate.[60]

The Uniform Probate Code (UPC) sets out a more thorough and complex approach, known as the "augmented estate" elective share,[61] adopted by several states.[62] In its original version, the UPC included in the value of the estate certain enumerated lifetime transfers made by the decedent in which the decedent had retained some economic benefits, and allocated a one-third share of that amount to the surviving spouse. It then deducted from that sum any *inter vivos* gifts from the decedent spouse to the surviving spouse and any non-testamentary benefits passing to the surviving spouse due to the decedent's death.[63] It satisfied the one-third share of an electing spouse first from property already transferred by the decedent spouse to the surviving spouse before distributing funds from the decedent's probate estate. Thus, the augmented estate approach reaches not only the decedent's probate estate, but accounts for certain *inter vivos* transfers, while deducting from the spouse's share most economic benefits already transferred by the decedent to the surviving spouse.[64]

The 1990 UPC redesigned the elective share, attempting to better correlate the elective share with the partnership theory of marriage.[65] The 1990 version retains and expands the augmented estate approach by combining the assets of both spouses in calculating the augmented estate. Further, it adjusts the percentage of the surviving spouse's entitlement according to the length of the couple's marriage, reaching a maximum of fifty percent after fifteen years of marriage. Moreover, it takes into account the surviving spouse's own separate assets, which are counted first in calculating the final amount to be awarded.[66]

---

[60] *See Intestate Succession, supra* note 49.

[61] Unif. Probate Code § 2-202 (2010); *see* Chused, *supra* note 15, at 281. For a full discussion of how state and federal courts have interpreted the UPC's augmented estate provision, see 63 A.L.R.4th 1173 (2009).

[62] *See, e.g.*, Colo. Rev. Stat. Ann. § 15-11-202(2) (2011); Neb. Rev. Stat. § 30-2314 (2011).

[63] Unif. Probate Code §§ 2-201, 2-202.

[64] Unif. Probate Code § 2-202. *See generally* J. Thomas Oldham, *Should the Surviving Spouse's Forced Share Be Retained?*, 38 Case W. Res. L. Rev. 223 (1988).

[65] Unif. Probate Code § 2-202 (2011). The partnership theory of marriage is sometimes characterized "as an expression of the presumed intent of husbands and wives to pool their fortunes on an equal basis, share and share alike." Mary Ann Glendon, The Transformation of Family Law: State, Law, and Family in the United States and Western Europe (1st ed. 1989). The comments to the UPC themselves reflect that "[t]he pre-1990 provisions granted the surviving spouse a one-third share of the augmented estate. The one-third fraction was largely a carryover from common-law dower, under which a surviving widow had a one-third interest for life in her deceased husband's land . . . . The revision of this section is the first step in the overall plan of implementing a partnership or marital-sharing theory of marriage, with a support theory back-up. [The revision] implements the partnership theory by providing that the elective-share amount is 50 percent of the value of the marital-property portion of the augmented estate." Unif. Probate Code § 2-202, cmt. Judge Posner has argued that elective share statutes reduce the transactional costs implicit in contractual negotiations between husbands and wives. *See* Richard A. Posner, Economic Analysis of Law § 18.8 (7th ed. 2007).

[66] *See generally* Lawrence Waggoner, et al., Family Property Law 80-113 (2d ed. 1997); Rena C. Seplowitz, *Transfers Prior to Marriage and the Uniform Probate Code's Redesigned Elective Share — Why the Partnership Is Not Yet Complete*, 25 Ind. L. Rev. 1 (1991).

§ 3.06   THE COMMUNITY PROPERTY SYSTEM

Nine American states and Puerto Rico historically have followed the community property principles developed in Spain and France, rather than the common law property title theory imported from England. These nine states are Arizona, California, Idaho, Louisiana, Nevada, New Mexico, Texas, Washington, and Wisconsin.[67] Since its adoption of the Uniform Marital Property Act[68] in 1983, Wisconsin, traditionally a common law property jurisdiction, is now generally regarded as a community property state.[69]

The community property system is based on a sharing or partnership theory of marriage, which presumes that each spouse contributes equally, in a direct or an indirect manner, to the accumulation of assets during the marriage.[70] Ownership interests are allocated equally to each spouse, recognizing the value of nonmonetary contributions to the marriage relationship, like homemaking services, as well as income-producing activity. Although details vary considerably from one community property state to another, the system, in general, regards most property acquired through the efforts of either spouse during marriage as owned equally by both spouses as community property.

The community property system also designates some assets as a spouse's separate property. Separate property generally includes assets that a spouse acquired prior to or after the dissolution of the marriage, by individual gift or inheritance during the marriage, by designation as separate property by valid contract between the spouses, or by a court decree.[71] Community property states differ as to how they classify passive income and profits from separate property, but every community property state defines earnings attributable to the labor of either spouse and the assets procured with those earnings as community property.[72]

Despite equality of ownership, historically, the husband alone had the right to manage and control community property.[73] For example, in *Brown v. Boeing Co.*,[74]

---

[67] *See* Richard A. Leitner, *Marital Property*, 50 State Statutory Surveys, 0080 SURVEYS 10 (2007) (Westlaw). In Alaska, a couple can elect to hold property either as community property or in any other form permitted by law, including a "concurrent form or a form that provides for survivorship ownership." Alaska Stat. Ann. § 34.77.110 (2011).

[68] Uniform Marital Property Act (2011).

[69] Wis. Stat. Ann. § 766 (2011); Clark, *supra* note 11, at 296 n.58.

[70] *See also infra* § 3.08.

[71] *See, e.g.*, N.M. Stat. Ann. § 40-3-8 (2011); Nev. Rev. Stat. Ann. § 123.130 (2010). *See generally* W. S. McClanahan, Community Property Law in the United States § 410 (1982). In *State ex rel. Industrial Comm. v. Wright*, 43 P.3d 203 (Ariz. Ct. App. 2002), the spouses agreed, in a premarital agreement, to designate the earnings of each spouse as separate property rather than community property. When a judgment was obtained against husband, they modified their agreement to designate their earnings as community property. The husband then objected to a garnishment on his wages to satisfy the judgment, claiming that his community property earnings were not attachable by a separate creditor. The court held that the modification of the premarital agreement constituted a fraudulent conveyance under the circumstances and did not bar the creditor's rights. *Id.* at 208.

[72] *See* Idaho Code Ann. § 32-906 (2011); La. Civ. Code Ann. art. 2338 (2011). *See generally* William DeFuniak & Michael Vaughn, Principles of Community Property § 67 (2d ed. 1971).

[73] *See, e.g.*, *Wilcox v. Wilcox*, 98 Cal. Rptr. 319 (Cal. Ct. App. 1971); *see also* Susan Prager, *The*

a wife argued that her deceased husband had breached his fiduciary duty to act in her best interest and had committed a constructive fraud upon her by electing an employee pension benefit "straight-life" option that did not include a survivor benefit, despite her objections. The Washington Court of Appeals held that under the state's community property statute, either spouse was entitled to manage and control community assets, such as the interest in the pension plan, subject to certain exceptions not applicable in this situation. Despite the fact that the wife ultimately received less money from the option selected than she would have under a joint-survivor option, the court held that the husband had not acted improperly, as his election did not attempt to make a bequest or gift of community property, nor did it transform the asset into the husband's separate property.[75]

Under contemporary, gender-neutral community property principles developed during the 1970s, rights of management and control are allocated to either or both spouses, regardless of sex.[76] The particulars of these management rights and powers differ considerably among community property states, which frequently have different rules for real and personal property.[77]

The right to manage and control community property is not unlimited and gifts of community property by one spouse alone may fall outside the managerial authority. In California, a spouse may rescind a unilateral gift of community property made by the other spouse. Other community property states allow a spouse to make "reasonable" gifts of community property. The American Law Institute's (ALI) *Principles of the Law of Family Dissolution* propose that a spouse should be able to rescind a unilateral gift of marital property when the gift is "substantial relative to the total value of the marital property at the time of the gift."[78] Furthermore, a fiduciary relationship between spouses is recognized by statute in California and is developing by judicial law in other community property states. However, in *Andrews v. Andrews*,[79] the Texas Court of Appeals refused to hold that, absent a fraud on the community, poor investments of community funds made in good faith justified an unequal division of community property on divorce.[80]

Difficult tracing and characterization problems arise when assets are acquired with both separate property and community property funds and when separate

---

Persistence of Separate Property Concepts in California's Community Property System, 1849-1975, 24 UCLA L. Rev. 1 (1976).

[74] 622 P.2d 1313 (Wash. Ct. App. 1980).

[75] *Id.* at 1316-17.

[76] *See Kirchberg v. Feenstra*, 450 U.S. 455 (1981) (holding that Louisiana's statutory designation of the husband as manager of community assets unconstitutionally discriminated on the basis of sex).

[77] *See, e.g.*, Ariz. Rev. Stat. Ann. § 25-214 (2011); Tex. Fam. Code § 3.101 (2011); *see also* Carol S. Bruch, *Protecting the Rights of Spouses in Intact Marriages: The 1987 California Community Property Reform and Why It Was So Hard to Get*, 1990 Wis. L. Rev. 731; Carol S. Bruch, *Management Powers and Duties Under California's Community Property Laws: Recommendations for Reform*, 34 Hastings L.J. 227 (1982).

[78] ALI *Principles of the Law of Family Dissolution* § 4.10(1) (2000).

[79] 677 S.W.2d 171 (Tex. App. 1984).

[80] *See also* J. Thomas Oldham, *Management of the Community Estate During an Intact Marriage*, 56 L. & Contemp. Prob. 99 (1993).

property has been commingled with community property.[81] Therefore, community property law presumes that an asset acquired during marriage is community property unless the spouse claiming a separate property interest can rebut the presumption by proving that all or a portion of the asset falls within the definition of separate property and has not been transformed into community property by gift or transmutation.[82]

During marriage, an individual spouse's ownership interest in community property is undivided, but when the community dissolves, either by divorce or by death, the ownership interests in community property are severed and each spouse is entitled to an individual one-half share. Thus, after termination of the marriage, each spouse owns his or her own separate property and one-half of the former community assets, although many community property states have modified property division on divorce with equitable distribution principles.[83]

Upon death, the decedent spouse in a community property state may dispose of his or her one-half of the community property by will, along with his or her separate property, with no survivorship interest in that property accruing to the surviving spouse.[84] Because community property law, in theory, furnishes built-in protection for a non-wage-earning spouse, community property states do not recognize the tenancy by the entirety estate, nor provide for dower, curtesy, or an elective share.

§ 3.07 THE UNIFORM MARITAL PROPERTY ACT

The Uniform Marital Property Act (UMPA), promulgated in 1983, incorporates the partnership concept of marriage.[85] The UMPA was adopted, with some modifications, by Wisconsin in 1983[86] and has been considered, but not enacted, by some other states.[87] Because the UMPA is based on principles of shared property

---

[81] *See* J. Thomas Oldham, Divorce, Separation and the Distribution of Property § 11.03 (1992); *see also infra* § 10.02.

[82] *See* J. Thomas Oldham, *Tracing, Commingling, and Transmutation*, 23 Fam. L.Q. 219 (1989).

[83] Strict equality of community property division on divorce has been modified by equitable distribution statutes in all but three community property states, California, Louisiana, and New Mexico. *See* Brett R. Turner, 1 Equitable Distribution of Property 3d § 2:5, note 4 (2011). *See generally infra* Chapter 9.

[84] To the extent that a spouse dies intestate in a community property state, the surviving spouse will be entitled to a share of the decedent's separate and community property as an intestate heir. *See, e.g.,* Unif. Probate Code § 2-102A (2010). Additionally, both community and common law property states generally allow a surviving spouse a family allowance and personal property allotment from the decedent spouse's probate estate. *See, e.g.,* Unif. Probate Code § 2-403 (2010).

[85] *See, e.g.,* Uniform Marital Property Act §§ 4, 17 (2010). *See generally* John DeWitt Gregory, The Law of Equitable Distribution § 1.04 (1989).

[86] Wis. Stat. Ann. §§ 766.01-.97 (2011). *See generally* Howard Erlanger & June Weisberger, *From Common Law Property to Community Property: Wisconsin's Marital Property Act Four Years Later*, 1990 Wis. L. Rev. 769.

[87] Wisconsin is the only state to have adopted the UMPA. Colorado, Illinois, Indiana, Michigan, and Missouri have considered but not enacted variations of the UMPA. *See* Wendy A. Wake, Note, *Uniform Marital Property Act: Suggested Revisions for Equality Between Spouses*, 1987 U. Ill. L. Rev. 471, 474 n.11. *See generally* Uniform Law Commission, Uniform Marital Property Act, *available at* http://uniformlaws.org/Act.aspx?title=Marital%20Property%20Act.

ownership during marriage, it is generally regarded as a community property law.[88] The UMPA sought to improve on community property acts elsewhere, incorporating "the best solutions to various problems found among the eight [now nine and Puerto Rico] community property states."[89]

The UMPA provides for a dual classification system of a married couple's property, which categorizes property as either marital property or individual property.[90] Each spouse has a present undivided one-half interest in marital property.[91] All property of spouses is presumed to be marital property,[92] and income from any source is designated marital property.[93] Individual property consists of property acquired prior to marriage[94] and property obtained during the marriage by gift or inheritance by either spouse from a third party.[95] Individual property retains its character if it is exchanged for other assets.[96] Appreciation of individual property remains individual property unless substantial appreciation is attributed to the substantial uncompensated efforts of the other spouse.[97] If marital and individual property are commingled, the asset is classified as marital property unless the individual property interest can be traced.[98]

Management and control rights to property under the UMPA are based on title. A spouse may manage and control his or her individual property and, with some exceptions, marital property that is held in that spouse's name.[99] Property held in both spouses' names must be managed and controlled by the spouses together, unless it is held in their names alternatively, in which case either may act alone.[100]

---

[88] *See* William Reppy, *The Uniform Marital Property Act: Some Suggested Revisions for a Basically Sound Act*, 21 Hous. L. Rev. 679 (1984).

[89] *Id.* at 683. *See generally* Howard Erlanger & June Weisberger, *supra* note 60, at 776-82; Puerto Rico and nine states — Arizona, California, Idaho, Louisiana, New Mexico, Nevada, Texas, Washington, and Wisconsin — follow a community property system. *See, e.g.,* Cal. Fam. Code § 751 (2011); Idaho Code Ann. § 32-906 (2011); P.R. Laws Ann. tit. 31, § 3647 (2008). *See generally* Richard A. Leitner, *Marital Property*, 50 State Statutory Surveys, 0080 SURVEYS 10 (2007) (Westlaw). As noted earlier, in Alaska a couple can elect to hold property either as community property or in any other form permitted by law, including a "concurrent form or a form that provides for survivorship ownership." Alaska Stat. Ann. § 34.77.110 (2011). Fourteen states — Alaska, Arkansas, Colorado, Connecticut, Florida, Hawaii, Kentucky, Michigan, Montana, New York, North Carolina, Oregon, Virginia, and Wyoming — have adopted the Uniform Disposition of Community Property at Death Act, which protects couples who move from a community property state to a non-community property state from dramatic changes in the disposition of property upon a spouse's death. *See* Leitner, *supra* at tbl. 30.

[90] Unif. Marital Prop. Act § 4 (2010).

[91] *Id.* at § 4(c).

[92] *Id.* at § 4(b).

[93] *Id.* at § 4(d).

[94] *Id.* at § 4(f).

[95] *Id.* at § 4(g)(1).

[96] *Id.* at § 4(g)(2).

[97] *Id.* at §§ 4(g)(3), 14(b).

[98] *Id.* at § 14(a).

[99] *Id.* at § 5.

[100] *Id.*

The UMPA imposes a duty on each spouse to act in good faith.[101]

The UMPA permits spouses to alter most of their property rights through marital property agreements.[102] Different fairness standards are set out for agreements made before and during marriage.[103] A spouse may not contractually impair certain creditors' or bona fide purchasers' rights,[104] nor adversely affect a child's right to support.[105]

The UMPA limits an individual spouse's ability to gift marital property to third parties.[106] It further contains detailed provisions relating to life insurance policies and deferred employment benefits.[107]

While the UMPA regulates spousal property rights during marriage and at death,[108] it does not alter the law that governs property distribution on divorce.[109] The Wisconsin courts have held that the state's equitable distribution laws continue to apply to property division upon dissolution of marriage.[110]

§ 3.08   MARRIAGE AS AN "ECONOMIC PARTNERSHIP"

Dissatisfaction with the inequities inherent in the traditional common law concepts of property ownership during marriage[111] resulted in a trend toward viewing marriage as an economic partnership. In 1963, the Report of the Committee on Civil and Political Rights to the President's Commission on the Status of Women observed that:

> Marriage is a partnership to which each spouse makes a different but equally important contribution. This fact has become increasingly recognized in the realities of American family living. While the laws of other countries have reflected this trend, family laws in the United States have lagged behind. Accordingly, the Committee concludes that during marriage each spouse should have a legally defined and substantial right in the earnings of the other spouse and in the real and personal property acquired as a result of such earnings, as well as in the management of such earnings and property. Such right should survive the marriage and be legally recognized in the event of its termination by annulment, divorce, or death.

---

[101]   *Id.* at § 2.

[102]   *Id.* at § 10.

[103]   *Id.*

[104]   *Id.* at §§ 8, 9.

[105]   *Id.* at § 10(b).

[106]   *Id.* at § 6.

[107]   *Id.* at §§ 12, 13.

[108]   *Id.* at § 18.

[109]   *See id.* at § 17, *Prefatory Note.*

[110]   *See Steinmann v. Steinmann*, 749 N.W.2d 145 (Wis. 2008); *Kuhlman v. Kuhlman*, 432 N.W.2d 295 (Wis. Ct. App. 1988).

[111]   *See supra* § 3.02.

This policy should be appropriately implemented by legislation which would safeguard either spouse against improper alienation of property by the other.[112]

This concept, based on principles of shared ownership of property during marriage embedded in community property law and incorporated into the Uniform Marital Property Act, has influenced the development of equitable distribution of property in common law states, but has not yet infiltrated the law governing property rights during marriage in those states.

Observing that the traditional common law view of marriage devalues home-maker services and the law of spousal support inadequately protects wives, some scholars have advocated a theory of family partnership based on a modified version of the business partnership model. This model borrows fundamental tenets of community property law to assure the equality of both spouses' rights during marriage.[113] Although the parties would be free to tailor their property rights by contract prior to marriage, this proposal acknowledges equal rights and obligations of both husbands and wives with respect to services, management, property ownership, and creditors' rights during marriage.[114] Under the economic partner-ship model, the parties can assign family roles based upon their individual skills and interests, placing minimum restrictions on individual freedom.[115] The partnership model would allow married women to pursue careers or other activities outside the home, while protecting those who opt for a traditional role in the home or spend a portion of their lives rearing children.[116]

Over the past several decades, the structure of marriage and parenthood has changed considerably. The traditional role-divided family, in which the husband was breadwinner and the wife was homemaker, has become the exception rather than the rule. By 2011, in 47.8 percent of two-parent families, both parents were employed.[117] Only about 20 percent of American married couples conformed to the traditional pattern of a sole, male wage-earner married to a non-wage-earning female spouse. Interestingly, in 8.6 percent of American marriages, the wife was the only employed spouse.[118] In addition, in 2010, more than 70 percent of married mothers participated in the paid labor market, as compared to less than 40 percent

---

[112] Report of the Committee on Civil and Political Rights to the President's Commission on the Status of Women (1963), *quoted in Prefatory Note*, Unif. Marital Property Act (2010).

[113] Joan Krauskopf & Rhonda Thomas, *Partnership Marriage: The Solution to an Ineffective and Inequitable Law of Support*, 35 Ohio St. L.J. 558 (1974).

[114] *Id.* at 587-88.

[115] *Id.* at 590-94.

[116] *Id.* at 594. The theory provides that spouses are partners who each make a set of meaningful, although perhaps different, contributions to the marital enterprise. As a result, each spouse is entitled to share in the marital estate because each participated in its acquisition. Alicia Brokars Kelly, *The Martial Partnership Pretense and Career Assets: The Ascendancy of Self over the Martial Community*, 81 B.U. L. Rev. 59, 60 (2001). *See also* Marjorie E. Kornhauser, *Theory Versus Reality: The Partnership Model of Marriage in Family and Income Tax Law*, 69 Temp. L. Rev. 1413, 1413 (1996).

[117] *See* U.S. Department of Labor, Bureau of Labor Statistics, Employment Characteristics of Families — 2011, *available at* http://www.bls.gov/news.release/pdf/famee.pdf.

[118] *Id.*

in 1970.[119] This includes more than 63 percent of married mothers with children under six years old, and more than 56 percent of married mothers with children younger than one year.[120] In addition, the percentage of families maintained by one unmarried parent has almost doubled since 1973, accounting for more than 27 percent of all families with children in 2011.[121]

Scholars have offered varied commentaries on the economic partnership theory of marriage.[122] Its principles have been reflected in divorce reform legislation and judicial opinions relating to spousal support, property division, and other legal issues on divorce.[123]

One scholar has criticized the partnership theory of marriage and equality model as a "symbolic expression" that does not necessarily produce fair and just results when applied to women who have assumed traditional roles during marriage. She has urged courts to treat spouses unequally upon dissolution of the marriage in recognition of the economic and social discrimination women still face.[124] Other commentators have objected to equating the family relationship to a business because it may stimulate competition rather than sharing and encourage people to view marriage in financial terms.[125] Yet others have expressed concern that the equality theory, in reality, preserves traditional marital roles, fails to encourage self-sufficiency, and merely lessens the suffering faced by the disadvantaged spouse after divorce instead of encouraging role equality during the marriage.[126] Some have noted the continuing societal and legal assumptions regarding gender roles in marriage and child-rearing, and the decline of the importance of marriage as a forum for raising children.[127] Finally, many scholars have criticized the ALI's

---

[119] *Id.* at Table 5.

[120] *Id.* at Table 6.

[121] *See* Bureau of the Census, *America's Families and Living Arrangements: 2011*, tbl. FG5 (2011), *available at* http://www.census.gov/population/www/socdemo/hh-fam/cps2011.html.

[122] *See, e.g.*, Marsha Garrison, *Toward a Contractarian Account of Family Governance*, 1998 Utah L. Rev. 241; Alicia Brokars Kelly, *The Marital Parnership Pretense and Career Assets: The Ascendancy of Self over the Marital Community*, 81 B.U. L. Rev. 59 (2001); Alicia Brokars Kelly, *Rehabilitating Partnership Marriage as a Theory of Wealth Distribution at Divorce: In Recognition of a Shared Life*, 19 Wis. Women's L.J. 141 (2004); Gaytri Kachroo, *Mapping Alimony: From Status to Contract and Beyond*, 5 Pierce L. Rev. 163 (2007).

[123] *See, e.g.*, Unif. Marriage and Divorce Act, 9A U.L.A. 238-39 (2011); *Price v. Price*, 503 N.E.2d 684 (N.Y. 1986).

[124] Martha Fineman, *Implementing Equality: Ideology, Contradiction and Social Change. A Study of Rhetoric and Results in the Regulation of the Consequences of Divorce*, 1983 Wis. L. Rev. 789, 885. *See also* Joan Williams, *Is Coverture Dead? Beyond A New Theory of Alimony*, 82 Georgetown L. J. 2227, 2236-41, 2245-46 (1994).

[125] *See* Jane Rutherford, *Duty in Divorce: Shared Income as a Path to Equality*, 58 Fordham L. Rev. 539 (1990).

[126] Bea Ann Smith, *The Partnership Theory of Marriage: A Borrowed Solution Fails*, 68 Tex. L. Rev. 689 (1990).

[127] *See, e.g.*, Gary S. Becker, *Nobel Lecture: The Economic Way of Looking at Behavior*, 101 J. Pol. Econ. 385, 397-98 (1993); Arlie Hochschild & Anne Machung, The Second Shift 11-13 (1989); June Carbone, *Morality, Public Policy and the Family: The Role of Marriage and the Public/Private Divide*, 36 Santa Clara L. Rev. 265, 267-69, 275-78 (1996); David Blankenhorn, *The State of the Family and the Family Policy Debate*, 36 Santa Clara L. Rev. 431, 436-37 (1996).

approach to property division, which has adopted many aspects of the equality and partnership theories of marriage, because of its "unprecedented proposal to re-characterize separate property as marital when a long-term marriage dissolves."[128]

§ 3.09   SUPPORT RIGHTS AND OBLIGATIONS

Under the traditional common law, wives had few, if any, property rights. However, the common law attempted to protect wives by imposing a duty of support on their husbands. That duty arose solely from the status of marriage and required a man to support his wife. The wife, in exchange, had a corresponding duty to provide household and other services to the husband, although that duty was rarely, if ever, specifically defined or enforced.[129]

The common law similarly imposed the duty on fathers to support their children. In return, the father had a right to control his children and was entitled to their services and income.[130]

While the family unit remained intact, the courts seldom interfered with the standard of support provided by the husband or father. For example, in *McGuire v. McGuire*,[131] Lydia McGuire brought an action for maintenance and support against her husband of more than thirty years, Charles. The trial court ordered Charles to purchase a number of specific items for improving and repairing the home and a new automobile with an effective heater. It further granted Lydia a personal allowance and ordered Charles to pay for Lydia's travel expenses to visit her daughters. The Nebraska Supreme Court reversed, adopting a nonintervention policy that discouraged courts from interfering with the husband's administration of the family's finances. It held that a couple must be separated or living apart before a court may set a precise standard of family support. The court reasoned:

> The living standards of a family are a matter of concern to the household and not for the courts to determine, even though the husband's attitude toward his wife, according to his wealth and circumstances, leaves little to be said in his behalf. As long as the home is maintained and the parties are living as husband and wife it may be said that the husband is legally supporting his wife and the purpose of the marriage relation is being carried out. Public policy requires such a holding.[132]

In cases similar to *McGuire*, courts have refused to intervene in family governance except in extreme circumstances, because of notions of family autonomy

---

[128] John DeWitt Gregory, *The A.L.I. Property Division Principles: A Model of Radical Paternalism?*, *in* Reconceiving the Family: Critique on the American Law Institute's Principles of the Law of Family Dissolution 163 (Robin Fretwell Wilson ed. 2006). *See also* David Westfall, *Unprincipled Family Dissolution: The A.L.I.'s Recommendations for Division of Property*, *in* Reconceiving the Family, *supra*.

[129] *See* Reva B. Siegel, *Home as Work: The First Woman's Rights Claims Concerning Wives' Household Labor, 1850-1880*, 103 Yale L.J. 1073, 1155-56 (1994).

[130] Clark, *supra* note 11, at 259.

[131] 59 N.W.2d 336 (Neb. 1953).

[132] *Id.* at 342.

and privacy and apprehension that the courts would be over-burdened with "trivial" family matters if family members were provided a legal forum for airing their grievances against each other.[133]

Courts have made exceptions to their policy of non-interference in family support matters by applying the doctrine of necessaries[134] and separate maintenance.[135] Legislatures have also intervened by enacting family support statutes.[136] Furthermore, the common law provided limited property rights to wives in the form of the tenancy by the entirety estate[137] and through the doctrine of dower.[138]

§ 3.10 THE DOCTRINE OF NECESSARIES

Although the common law rarely directly enforced the husband's duty to support his wife, or the father's duty to support his children, by dictating the level of support he must provide, it indirectly intervened in family autonomy through the doctrine of necessaries. Under the doctrine of necessaries, the wife and children could purchase any essential goods or services, including food, clothing, shelter, and medical and legal services, on the husband's credit and the husband became directly liable to the provider of these necessary items. Unlike agency law principles, the doctrine of necessaries held the husband responsible regardless of his consent to, or knowledge of, the purchases.[139]

The family's economic status and standard of living and the husband's ability to provide defined the scope of the necessaries doctrine. Thus, the application of the doctrine varied from one household to another and created uncertainty in an individual case.[140] In *Sharpe Furniture, Inc. v. Buckstaff*,[141] the wife purchased a sofa on credit without her husband's knowledge. The family was economically and socially prominent and the husband had always provided his wife with necessaries. However, he had previously written to the credit bureau stating that he would not

---

[133] *See, e.g., Commonwealth v. George*, 56 A.2d 228 (Pa. 1948); *Balfour v. Balfour*, [1919] 2 K.B. 571 (reversing a support award upon divorce to the wife, in part because "the small courts of this country would have to be multiplied one hundred fold if these arrangements were held to result in legal obligations"). However, a Florida Court allowed a lump-sum alimony award despite the fact that the parties did not seek a permanent dissolution because of the equities of the case and societal changes. *See Coltea v. Coltea*, 856 So. 2d 1047 (Fla. Dist. Ct. App. 2003).

[134] *See infra* § 3.10.

[135] *See infra* § 3.11.

[136] *See infra* § 3.12.

[137] *See supra* § 3.04.

[138] *See supra* § 3.05[A].

[139] *See generally* Margaret Mahoney, *Economic Sharing During Marriage: Equal Protection, Spousal Support and the Doctrine of Necessaries*, 22 J. Fam. L. 221 (1983-84); Note, *The Unnecessary Doctrine of Necessaries*, 82 Mich. L. Rev. 1767 (1984); Clark, *supra* note 11, at 265.

[140] *Compare Gimbel Bros. v. Pinto*, 145 A.2d 865 (Pa. Super. Ct. 1958) (mink coat necessary), *and Sharpe Furniture Co. v. Buckstaff*, 299 N.W.2d 219 (Wis. 1980) (sofa necessary), *with Chipp v. Murray*, 379 P.2d 297 (Kan. 1963) (private detective services not necessary), *and Sharon Clinic v. Nelson*, 394 N.Y.S.2d 118 (N.Y. Sup. Ct. 1977) (no showing that abortion was necessary because of wife's medical condition).

[141] 299 N.W.2d 219 (Wis. 1980).

be responsible for any credit extended to his wife. Despite this warning Sharpe Furniture demanded payment for the sofa and Mr. Buckstaff refused. Affirming the trial court's award to Sharpe Furniture, the Wisconsin Supreme Court held that ample evidence showed that the sofa was necessary to this household and that the husband is primarily liable for any item or service obtained for the benefit of his family. Justice Abrahamson, concurring, disagreed with the rule placing primary liability on the husband for necessaries, arguing that the rule denigrates the contribution of women and denies equal protection to husbands.

In *State v. Clark*,[142] the Wisconsin Supreme Court held that a husband's assets could be considered in determining whether the wife could be declared indigent for the purpose of having her criminal appeal paid for at public expense. The court, applying the doctrine of necessaries, concluded that although the act giving rise to the conviction on a drug charge occurred prior to marriage, the husband was aware of the pending proceedings at the time of marriage and the conviction occurred after marriage. Therefore, the husband was liable for necessary legal expenses of the wife.

The necessaries doctrine denied recovery by the third party when that party furnished money or necessary items gratuitously, when the husband had already supplied his dependents with necessaries, or when the wife wrongfully lived apart from the husband.[143] Consequently, the doctrine of necessaries had limited practical application because merchants and other providers were exposed to considerable risk when they relied on the husband's credit.

In recent years, the doctrine of necessaries has undergone reevaluation in response to assertions that imposing liability on husbands but not wives violates equal protection principles.[144] Some jurisdictions have reacted by expanding application of the doctrine equally to both spouses. For example, in *North Carolina Baptist Hospitals v. Harris*,[145] the North Carolina Supreme Court adopted a gender-neutral application of the necessaries doctrine. In *Harris*, the court held that a wife could be held liable to a hospital for her husband's necessary medical expenses under the necessaries doctrine. It noted that, in light of the trend towards gender neutrality in other areas of the law, no contemporary reason existed for applying the doctrine only to husbands. Further, the court refused to abolish the doctrine, concluding that it continues to serve beneficial functions, including "the encouragement of health care providers and facilities to provide needed medical attention to married persons and the recognition that marriage involves shared

---

[142] 563 P.2d 1253 (Wash. 1977).

[143] *See* Clark, *supra* note 11, at 265-66.

[144] *See generally* Karol Williams, Comment, *The Doctrine of Necessaries: Contemporary Application as a Support Remedy*, 19 Stetson L. Rev. 661 (1990); Marie T. Reilly, *Me and You Against the World: Marriage and Divorce from Creditors' Perspective, in* Reconceiving the Family: Critique on the American Law Institute's Principles of the Law of Family Dissolution 195, n.30 (Robin Fretwell Wilson ed. 2006).

[145] 354 S.E.2d 471 (N.C. 1987). *See also* Marie T. Reilly, *supra* note 144, at 201 n.28 (collecting statutory and common law adoptions of the gender neutral principle); Mont. Code Ann. § 40-2-210 (2011) (holding both spouses liable for "necessary articles"); *Cooke v. Adams*, 183 So. 2d 925 (Miss. 1966).

wealth, expenses, rights, and duties."[146]

In a similar case, *Jersey Shore Medical Center-Fitkin Hospital v. Estate of Baum*,[147] the New Jersey Supreme Court took a different approach, adopting a rule of primary and secondary liability. In *Jersey Shore*, a hospital sued a wife for payment of her husband's medical expenses under the necessaries doctrine. In a limited extension of the doctrine to wives, the New Jersey Supreme Court stated:

> Interdependence is the hallmark of a modern marriage. The common law rule imposing liability on husbands, but not wives, is an anachronism that no longer fits contemporary society. Under the present rule, even a husband who is economically dependent on his wife would be liable for the necessary expenses of both spouses, while the wife would not be liable for either. In perpetuating additional benefits for a wife when the benefits may not be needed, the rule runs afoul of the equal protection clause.[148]

Although the court refused to apply the necessaries doctrine to the extent that it would impose "unqualified liability" on spouses for each other's debts, it concluded that, absent agreement with the creditor, "the income and property of one spouse should not be exposed to satisfy a debt incurred by the other spouse unless the assets of the spouse who incurred the debt are insufficient."[149] Thus, a spouse who incurs necessary expenses will be primarily liable for repayment of the debt, but the other spouse will be secondarily liable to the extent the incurring spouse is unable to pay.[150]

While a number of other courts have similarly held that the doctrine of necessaries applies equally to both spouses,[151] some courts have rejected the doctrine entirely.[152] For example, in *Connor v. Southwest Florida Regional Medical Center*,[153] the Supreme Court of Florida abrogated the necessaries doctrine, holding that its application to husbands, but not wives, constitutes a denial of equal protection. While the court acknowledged that it could have held the doctrine applicable to both spouses, it refused to impose a duty on wives where none had previously existed, absent a legislative mandate. The Vermont Supreme Court

---

[146] 354 S.E.2d at 474.

[147] 417 A.2d 1003 (N.J. 1980).

[148] *Id.* at 1008.

[149] *Id.* at 1010.

[150] *See* Reilly, *supra* note 144, at 201 n.29; *see also Med. Bus. Associates v. Steiner*, 588 N.Y.S.2d 890 (N.Y. App. Div. 1992).

[151] *See, e.g., Jermunson v. Jermunson*, 592 P.2d 491 (Mont. 1979); *Richland Mem'l Hosp. v. Burton*, 318 S.E.2d 12 (S.C. 1984); *St. Mary's Hospital Med. Ctr. v. Brody*, 519 N.W.2d 706 (Wis. Ct. App. 1994).

[152] *See, e.g., North Ottowa Community Hosp. v. Kieft*, 578 N.W.2d 267 (Mich. 1998).The Supreme Court of Virginia judicially abolished the doctrine as outdated and a violation of equal protection in *Schilling v. Bedford County Mem'l Hosp.*, 303 S.E.2d 905 (Va. 1983), but the Virginia legislature reinstated the doctrine in gender-neutral terms. *See* Va. Code Ann. § 55-37 (2011). *See generally* Elizabeth Jackson, *Equal Protection and Spousal Debt: Novel Application of Necessaries Doctrine*, 11 Stetson L. Rev. 173 (1981).

[153] 668 So. 2d 175 (Fla. 1995).

has adopted the same reasoning, abolishing the necessaries doctrine altogether.[154]

§ 3.11 SPOUSAL SUPPORT DURING SEPARATION

The common law claim for separate maintenance, sometimes referred to as alimony without divorce or separate support, provided another avenue for enforcing the duty of support. The equitable action for separate maintenance permitted a wife to sue her husband for non-support during the spouses' separation while they remained legally married.

In some states, the suit for separate maintenance was statutory. In some instances, it was combined with the concept of divorce from bed and board, also called divorce *a mensa et thoro* or judicial separation, although the two actions remained distinct. The action for separate maintenance was intended merely to provide support for the wife, while the divorce from bed and board technically decreed that the parties would live separate and apart. Little practical difference existed between the actions, as both suits left the parties legally married to each other, unable to remarry anyone else, and both ordered the husband to support the wife.[155]

Historically, courts distinguished between a decree of separate maintenance and a divorce from bed and board. In *Capodanno v. Commissioner of Internal Revenue*,[156] the court decided how a decree of separate maintenance would affect the separated couple's income tax filing status. The court noted that while a separate maintenance decree awarded to a wife recognizes a *de facto* separation based on the husband's fault, it merely enforces the husband's duty to continue supporting her financially. It does not legitimize their living apart but "favors a resumption of cohabitation."[157] The divorce from bed and board, however, "nullifies the marital obligation of cohabitation."[158] Therefore, regardless of the grounds for the separate maintenance decree, the couple remained "married" for tax purposes. *Capodanno* has been superseded by a federal statute that eliminates the difference between separate maintenance and divorce from bed and board for the purpose of federal income taxes.[159]

Although the grounds for the two actions were comparable, they varied from state to state. Traditionally, under either a separate maintenance action or a divorce

---

[154] *Med. Ctr. Hosp. of Vermont v. Lorrain*, 675 A.2d 1326 (Vt. 1996). *See also Medlock v. Fort Smith Serv. Fin. Corp.*, 803 S.W.2d 930 (Ark. 1991); *Condore v. Prince George's County*, 425 A.2d 1011 (Md. 1981). For an account of how "spousal liability varies widely among jurisdictions," see Marie T. Reilly, *In Good Times and in Debt: The Evolution of Marital Agency and the Meaning of Marriage*, 87 Neb. L. Rev. 373, 375 (2008). *See also* Jay M. Zitter, *Necessity, in Action Against Husband for Necessaries*, 19 A.L.R.4th 432 (2008).

[155] *See* Clark, *supra* note 11, at 266-67.

[156] 602 F.2d 64 (3d Cir. 1979).

[157] *Id.* at 67.

[158] *Id.*

[159] *See* 26 U.S.C.A. § 7703(a)(2) (West 2012) ("An individual legally separated from his spouse under a decree of divorce or of separate maintenance shall not be considered as married."); *see also Argyle v. C.I.R.*, 2010 U.S. App. LEXIS 21223 (3d Cir., Oct. 14, 2010).

from bed and board, the wife forfeited her right to support if she was guilty of marital fault.[160] An order for separate maintenance replaced the husband's common law duty of support,[161] and although reconciliation generally terminated a separate maintenance decree, it did not automatically terminate decrees for divorce from bed and board.[162] If the support recipient rejected a good faith offer to reconcile, she could lose the right to bring an action based on desertion if her support was based on a separate maintenance decree, although not if it had been ordered pursuant to a divorce from bed and board.[163]

In some jurisdictions, separate maintenance was intended to be a temporary remedy, while divorce from bed and board traditionally was regarded as permanent.[164] Modern statutes, however, permit or require conversion of the divorce from bed and board into an absolute divorce following a specific period of time or a request for divorce.[165]

Separate maintenance has become important as a source of spousal support while the divorce action is pending. Thus, for example, during the pendency of an action, the court may enter a temporary order for spousal maintenance after a petition for dissolution or legal separation has been filed.[166]

The separate maintenance doctrine has been criticized for imposing the burdens, but not the benefits, of marriage, and some commentators have suggested its only purpose should be to provide relief when one spouse refuses to support the other or when absolute divorce is not an acceptable solution for religious or other reasons.[167] Under contemporary constitutional law principles, separate maintenance must be made available to husbands as well as wives or be subject to invalidation on equal protection grounds.[168]

---

[160] *See Rosenthal v. Rosenthal*, 107 N.W.2d 204 (Wis. 1961); Robert Coleman Brown, *The Duty of the Husband to Support the Wife*, 18 Va. L. Rev. 823, 846 (1932).

[161] *See People ex rel. Comm'rs of Pub. Charities & Correction v. Cullen*, 47 N.E. 894 (N.Y. 1897).

[162] Clark, *supra* note 11, at 267-68 (noting that the parties may petition to have the divorce from bed and board vacated if they reconcile); Va. Code Ann. § 20-120 (2011) (separation remains intact regardless of the parties' reconciliation, until the separation decree is revoked by the decreeing court).

[163] Clark, *supra* note 11, at 267-68.

[164] *See, e.g., Chipman v. Chipman*, 406 P.2d 150 (Or. 1965). *But see Clifford v. Clifford*, 42 Haw. 279 (1958) (either party may convert divorce from bed and board into permanent divorce after thirty days).

[165] *See, e.g.*, Unif. Marriage and Divorce Act § 314, 9A U.L.A. 180 (2011); Va. Code Ann. §§ 20-121, 20-121.02 (2011) (requiring the lapse of one year if the parties have children or six months if there is a separation agreement and no minor children); N.Y. Dom. Rel. Law § 170(5) (McKinney 2011) (living apart for one or more years after grant of decree of judgment of separation is ground for divorce); Mich. Comp. Laws Ann. § 552.7 (2011) (directing the court to enter a decree dissolving the bonds of matrimony rather than a separate maintenance order if a counter-claim for divorce is filed).

[166] *See infra* § 3.12[C]; *Alimony, Maintenance, and other Spousal Support*, 50 State Statutory Surveys, 0080 SURVEYS 11 (2011) (Westlaw).

[167] *See* Clark, *supra* note 11, at 268-69.

[168] *See* Clark, *supra* note 11, at 268.

[A] *Pendente Lite* Statutes

Many state legislatures have enacted pendente lite statutes which force the higher-earning spouse to provide spousal and/or child support for the lower-earning spouse during the pendency of a divorce action. In some states, the order may be made retroactive to the date of filing.[169] A court's determination of temporary spousal or child support is not binding in the final divorce or annulment decree.[170] In states that bar the payment of alimony to recipient spouses after the granting of certain fault-based divorce, the payor spouse often cannot recoup the payment. In states that do not recognize the common law doctrine of separate maintenance, pendent lite statutes often serve as the dependent-spouse's only means of financing the divorce.

§ 3.12 STATUTORY SUPPORT OBLIGATIONS

[A] Spousal and Child Support Statutes

As an additional, but limited, means of enforcing the support obligation, most states have enacted a variety of family expense statutes that codify the spousal duty of support and statutes that impose criminal sanctions for non-support. Family expense and criminal non-support statutes also apply to an equal, and sometimes greater, extent to child support. Equal protection principles now require that these statutes apply equally to both wives and husbands,[171] and federal legislation has significantly augmented child support remedies.[172]

Family expense statutes, often originally enacted in conjunction with the Married Women's Property Acts, provide an additional method for third parties to enforce support obligations.[173] These statutes typically allow a creditor to execute against either spouse's property to collect debts incurred for necessary family expenses.[174] Some statutes create personal liability against the spouse as well.[175] The statutes do not, however, provide a direct remedy for enforcing the duty of support by the spouses themselves.[176] Family expense statutes generally embrace the range of family expenditures included under the necessaries doctrine, although some are more limited. While the types of expenses encompassed by these statutes may vary, courts have found that funeral expenses, legal fees, and, most commonly,

---

[169] *See, e.g.*, Cal. Fam. Code § 4333 (2011).

[170] *See, e.g., Shepherd v. Shepherd*, 200 S.E.2d 893 (Ga. 1973); *Wal-Mart Stores, Inc. v. Alexander*, 868 S.W.2d 322 (Tex. 1993).

[171] *See* Clark, *supra* note 11, at 252; *Beers v. Public Health Trust of Dade County*, 468 So. 2d 995 (Fla. Dist. Ct. App. 1985); *In re Stanton-Rieger*, 25 B.R. 650 (Bankr. Colo. 1982); *Credit Bureau of Santa Monica Bay Dist. v. Terranova*, 93 Cal. Rptr. 538 (Cal. Ct. App. 1971).

[172] *See infra* Chapter 8.

[173] *See* Joan Krauskopf & Rhonda Thomas, *Partnership Marriage: The Solution to an Ineffective and Inequitable Law of Support*, 35 Ohio St. L.J. 558, 571 (1974).

[174] *See* Clark, *supra* note 11, at 257; Mo. Rev. Stat. § 451.260 (2010).

[175] *See, e.g.*, Ill. Ann. Stat. ch. 40, para. 1015 (2011).

[176] *See* Krauskopf & Thomas, *supra* note 173.

medical expenses are included.[177] One court, however, has refused to enforce payment of a promissory note executed for cash and signed by the deceased husband, under the state's family expense statute. It warned that, otherwise, every loan would be susceptible to "minute dissection, tracing every dollar to its ultimate use."[178]

The changing nature of the American family has challenged the application of this doctrine. The Utah Court of Appeals considered whether Utah's Family Expense Statute could be asserted against a non-custodial father by a clinic that had provided medical treatment to his minor children after the parents were divorced. The court concluded that it applied only to intact families.[179] A number of states have addressed this question by statute, imposing a duty of support on the legal parent's cohabitant.[180] The Court of Appeals of Washington concluded that the state's family expense statute only imposes a support obligation on a stepparent when the stepparent has custody of the child.[181] The Washington court also held that a third party must establish the amount of support actually furnished to the child in order to recover against the biological parent.[182]

[B] Criminal Non-Support Statutes

Most criminal non-support statutes are not as broad as the civil family expense statutes and apply only when a spouse is left completely without means of support or without necessary food, clothing, or housing.[183] Criminal non-support statutes typically require desertion, abandonment, or neglect in addition to non-support, and generally do not apply when the spouses are living under the same roof. The purpose of these narrow criminal statutes is to protect the public, not the deserted spouse.[184] Other, more liberal criminal non-support statutes do not require the family to receive public assistance in order to prosecute for non-support.[185]

---

[177] *Davis-Turner Funeral Home v. Chaney*, 573 N.E.2d 1242 (Ohio Mun. Ct. 1991) (funeral expenses within statutory definition of necessaries); *In re Dupont*, 19 Bankr. 605, 607 (E.D.N.Y. 1982) (attorney fees are necessaries under New York law).

[178] *North Shore Community Bank and Trust. Co. v. Kollar*, 710 N.E.2d 106 (Ill. App. 1999).

[179] *Sentry Investigations, Inc. v. Davis*, 841 P.2d 732 (Utah Ct. App. 1992).

[180] *See, e.g.*, Va. Code Ann. § 63.2-510 (2011) (A person is responsible for the support of a child who lives in the same home while the person cohabits with the child's parent as husband and wife). For a further discussion of de facto parenthood, see *infra* § 11.03(d)(5).

[181] *Brewer v. Spencer*, 835 P.2d 267 (Wash. Ct. App. 1992).

[182] *Id.*

[183] Clark, *supra* note 11, at 271. *See, e.g.*, Va. Code Ann. § 20-61 (2011) (providing that a person who willfully fails to support a spouse or child in necessitous circumstances is guilty of a misdemeanor unless the child who is owed support "qualifies for and is receiving aid under a federal or state program for aid to the permanently and totally disabled").

[184] Krauskopf & Thomas, *supra* note 173, at 574.

[185] *See, e.g.*, Conn. Gen. Stat. Ann. § 53-304(a) (2011); Va. Code Ann. § 20-71 (2011) (At any time during the marriage, a spouse can file an action for criminal nonsupport in the juvenile and domestic relations court under Va. Code Ann. § 20-61 (2011) et seq. The court may order temporary spousal support and may enforce the order with contempt.).

The defendant's conduct must be willful and a person cannot be convicted for non-support unless he or she is capable of providing that support.[186] Furthermore, a person cannot be prosecuted for non-support if the complaining spouse has refused to live with the other without cause or in other ways gave the defendant "good excuse" for the failure to support.[187]

Criminal penalties for non-support have been criticized for creating undue hardship and for being self-defeating, because defendants will not be able to provide support for their families if they are jailed.[188] The statutes, however, have the dual purpose of punishing past behavior and acting as an incentive to the defendant to comply with support obligations in the future.[189]

§ 3.13   RIGHTS OF CONSORTIUM

Traditional common law granted the husband rights collectively referred to as "rights of consortium." These "rights" included his wife's services, society, and companionship, as well as an entitlement to sexual relations with his wife.[190] Today, many states now recognize a wife's corresponding rights of consortium with respect to her husband.[191] Contemporary rights of consortium refer to "the total of tangible and intangible relationships prevailing between husbands and wives"[192] and encompass the love, affection, care, services, companionship and society of a spouse.[193]

Most courts recognize a claim for recovery for loss of consortium against a third party. The action is generally limited to legally married parties,[194] and most courts do not allow recovery for injuries incurred prior to marriage or to unmarried cohabiting couples.[195] However, a few cases have recognized claims for loss of

---

[186] *See, e.g., Burris v. State*, 382 N.E.2d 963 (Ind. Ct. App. 1978); *State v. Greer*, 144 N.W.2d 322 (Iowa 1966).

[187] *See* Clark, *supra* note 11, at 273.

[188] *See* Michele Hermann & Shannon Donahue, *Fathers Behind Bars: The Right to Counsel in Civil Contempt Proceedings*, 14 N.M. L. Rev. 275 (1984).

[189] *See* Clark, *supra* note 11, at 270.

[190] *See* Clark, *supra* note 11, at 391. For a modern example of this duty, see La. Civ. Code art. 98 (West 2011). *But see Carey v. Foster*, 221 F. Supp. 185 (E.D. Va. 1963), *aff'd*, 345 F.2d 772 (4th Cir. 1965) (no right of consortium for either spouse at common law).

[191] *See American Export Lines v. Alvez*, 446 U.S. 274 (1980) (41 states and District of Columbia allow either spouse to recover for loss of consortium); D. Richard Joslyn, *Wife's Right of Action for Loss of Consortium*, 36 A.L.R.3d 900 (originally published in 1971). Several states do not recognize a loss of consortium claim by the spouse of an injured party. *See, e.g.*, Kan. Stat. Ann. § 23-205 (1988) (excepting wrongful death actions); Va. Code Ann. § 55-36 (1986 Repl. Pam.).

[192] Clark, *supra* note 11, at 382.

[193] *See Pickens Bond Constr. Co. v. Case*, 584 S.W.2d 21 (Ark. 1979); *Clark v. Ark-La-Tex Auction, Inc.*, 593 So. 2d 870 (La. Ct. App. 1992); *Berger v. Weber*, 267 N.W.2d 124 (Mich. Ct. App. 1978).

[194] *See, e.g., Johnson v. May*, 585 N.E.2d 224 (Ill. App. Ct. 1992) (must be married to injured spouse and prove damages); *Clinquennoi v. Michaels Group*, 577 N.Y.S.2d 550 (N.Y. App. Div. 1991) (wife did not have derivative cause of action for personal injuries suffered by her husband before their marriage).

[195] *See, e.g., Biercevicz v. Liberty Mut. Ins.* Co., 865 A.2d 1267 (Conn. Super. Ct. 2004) (the fiance was not found to be closely related enough to permit recovery as a bystander for emotional distress); *Curry v. Caterpillar Tractor Co.*, 577 F. Supp. 991 (E.D. Pa.1984) (no loss of consortium allowed to 15-year

consortium by cohabiting couples or couples who were engaged but not yet married.[196] For a spouse to recover on a loss of consortium claim against a third party, most courts require proof that the tortfeasor intentionally or negligently harmed the spouse and caused physical injury,[197] although some courts have allowed recovery without physical injury.[198] Punitive damages have sometimes been allowed as part of a claim for loss of consortium where the defendant's conduct was willful or malicious.[199]

Some courts have refused to recognize loss of consortium in wrongful death actions.[200] To avoid the potential double recovery, an increasing number of states require that a single suit combine the injured spouse's own claim for damages with the other spouse's claim for loss of consortium.[201]

In addition to the right of spousal consortium, a father traditionally could sue for the loss of a child's services and earnings.[202] Today "in a substantial minority" of jurisdictions, either parent's interest in the society, companionship, and services of

---

cohabitant and mother of injured party's three children); *Anderson v. Eli Lilly & Co.*, 588 N.E.2d 66 (N.Y. 1991) (husband could not recover for loss of consortium for wife's exposure to DES and resultant injuries prior to marriage); *Miller v. Davis*, 433 N.Y.S.2d 974 (N.Y. Sup. Ct. 1980) (no loss of consortium allowed where injuries required that wedding be delayed).

[196] *See Sutherland v. Auch Inter-Borough Transit Co.*, 366 F. Supp. 127 (E.D. Pa. 1973) (husband allowed damages for loss of consortium where marriage occurred after wife's accident). *Compare Dunphy v. Gregor*, 642 A.2d 372 (N.J. 1994) (permitting recovery for the emotional distress by a cohabitant who witnessed the accident).

[197] *See Johnson v. May*, 585 N.E.2d 224 (Ill. App. Ct. 1992) (spouse may recover from tortfeasor for losses incurred due to other spouse's injury); *Groat v. Town of Glenville*, 418 N.Y.S.2d 842 (Sup. Ct. 1979) (physical injury or physical confinement away from other spouse necessary under tort principles governing loss of consortium damages); *see also* Kevin Lindsey, Note, *A More Equitable Approach to Loss of Spousal Consortium*, 75 Iowa L. Rev. 713 (1990).

[198] *See Molien v. Kaiser Found. Hosps.*, 616 P.2d 813 (Cal. 1980) (husband may recover for loss of consortium based on negligent infliction of emotional distress caused by hospital's erroneous diagnosis of syphilis in wife); *Habelow v. Travelers Ins. Co.*, 389 So. 2d 218 (Fla. Dist. Ct. App. 1980) (wife could maintain action on loss of consortium claim based on "malicious intent to inflict mental anguish" due to insults and abusive conduct directed toward husband).

[199] *See Butcher v. Robertshaw Controls Co.*, 550 F. Supp. 692 (D. Md. 1981). *But see Hammond v. North American Asbestos Corp.*, 435 N.E.2d 540 (Ill. App. Ct. 1982), *aff'd*, 454 N.E.2d 210 (Ill. 1983) (allowing punitive damages for loss of consortium would involve important policy considerations that should be made by supreme court). *See also* Jo-Anne Baio, Note, *Loss of Consortium: A Derivative Injury Giving Rise to a Separate Cause of Action*, 50 Fordham L. Rev. 1344 (1982).

[200] *See Mullen v. Posada del Sol Health Care*, 819 P.2d 985 (Ariz. Ct. App. 1991) (allowable items of injury under wrongful death statute are loss of love, affection, companionship, consortium, personal anguish, and suffering); *Liff v. Schildkrout*, 404 N.E.2d 1288 (N.Y. 1980) (recovery for loss of consortium prior to death permissible, but no statutory authority for such claim after death). *But see Elliot v. Willis*, 447 N.E.2d 1062 (Ill. App. Ct. 1983) (damages for loss of consortium allowable in wrongful death action); *In re Estate of Feld*, 582 N.Y.S.2d 922 (Surr. Ct. 1992) (damages for loss of society not recoverable in wrongful death actions in New York).

[201] *See, e.g.*, Utah Code Ann. § 30-2-11(4)(a) (2011) (making compulsory the joinder of claims by injured spouse and spouse seeking recovery for loss of consortium); *Sharpenter v. Lynch*, 599 N.E.2d 464 (Ill. App. Ct. 1992) (loss of consortium claim accrued at same time husband was injured under sudden and traumatic event rule); *Mease v. Commonwealth*, 603 A.2d 679 (Pa. Commw. Ct. 1992) (widow of bystander who was killed by bullet was not entitled to obtain separate recovery for loss of consortium in wrongful death action); *Nicholson v. Chatham Mem'l Hosp.*, 266 S.E.2d 818 (N.C. 1980).

[202] *See Tinnerholm v. Parke-Davis & Co.*, 285 F. Supp. 432 (S.D.N.Y. 1968), *aff'd*, 411 F.2d 48 (2d Cir.

his or her child is compensable.[203] The law has been more reluctant, however, to extend loss of consortium actions to allow children to recover for injury to a parent.[204]

§ 3.14 RELATIVE RESPONSIBILITY STATUTES

Under common law principles, and in the absence of statutory authority, an adult child has no legal duty to provide for his or her indigent parent's needs. However, a majority of states have enacted relative responsibility statutes, which are derived from the Elizabethan Poor Laws of the sixteenth and seventeenth centuries,[205] requiring adult children to contribute to the support of a needy parent. Some states also have statutes that criminalize a child's failure to support a parent in need.[206]

Relative responsibility statutes usually impose a joint and several duty upon any adult child with sufficient resources, after providing for his or her immediate family, to support parents who are destitute or in necessitous circumstances.[207] A financial responsibility statute generally is enforceable by the parent, but more frequently is applied by an agency seeking reimbursement for services or by denying or altering an elderly person's eligibility for benefits.[208]

Relative responsibility statutes raise policy questions of whether family members or the state should assume responsibility for the elderly. The California Supreme Court addressed these issues in *Swoap v. Superior Court*,[209] a class action case attacking the constitutionality of statutes requiring adult children to reimburse

---

1969); *City of Dalton v. Webb*, 206 S.E.2d 639 (Ga. Ct. App. 1974).

[203] 2 Dan Dobbs, The Law of Torts: Practitioners Treatise Series 842 (2001). *See also Kinsella v. Farmers Ins.*, 826 P.2d 433 (Colo. Ct. App. 1992); *Rogers v. Donelson-Hermitage Chamber of Commerce*, 807 S.W.2d 242 (Tenn. Ct. App. 1990); *Glover v. Norick*, 400 S.E.2d 816 (W. Va. 1990).

[204] *See Murray v. Anthony J. Bertucci Constr. Co.*, 745 F. Supp. 373 (E.D. La. 1990) (child's action for loss of parent's consortium not available under general maritime law).

[205] 43 Eliz. 1 c. 2 (1601). *See also* Usha Narayan, *The Government's Role in Fostering the Relationship Between Adult Children and Their Elder Parents: From Filial Responsibility Laws to . . . What?, A Cross-Cultural Perspective*, 4 Elder L.J. 369, 372 (1996); Jacobus ten-Broek, *California's Dual System of Family Law: Its Origin, Development, and Present Status, Part I*, 16 Stan. L. Rev. 257, 257-58 (1964).

[206] *See* Ann Britton, *America's Best Kept Secret: An Adult Child's Duty to Support Aged Parents*, 26 Cal. W.L. Rev. 351, 354 (1990).

[207] *See* Va. Code Ann. § 20-88 (2011) ("It shall be the joint and several duty of all persons eighteen years of age or over, of sufficient earning capacity or income, after reasonably providing for his or her own immediate family, to assist in providing for the support and maintenance of his or her mother or father, he or she being then and there in necessitous circumstances.").

[208] *See generally* Terrance A. Kline, *A Rational Role for Filial Responsibility Laws in Modern Society?*, 26 Fam. L.Q. 195 (1992); Walton Garrett, *Filial Responsibility Laws*, 28 J. Fam. L. 793, 813 (1980).

[209] 516 P.2d 840 (Cal. 1973). *See also Savoy v. Savoy*, 641 A.2d 596, 598 (Pa. Super. Ct. 1994) ("Accordingly, we affirm the order directing Marcus J. Savoy (Son) to pay $125 per month directly to the medical care providers of Joan M. Savoy (Mother) for her past medical care expenses."), *superseded by statute*, 23 Pa. Cons. Stat. Ann. § 4603 (West 2012), *as recognized in Goforth v. U.S. Dept. of Education*, 466 B.R. 328, 336-37 (W.D. Pa. 2012). *See generally* Allison E. Ross, Note, *Taking Care of Our Caretakers: Using Filial Responsibility Laws to Support the Elderly Beyond the Government's Assistance*, 16 Elder L.J. 167 (2008).

the state for payments made to their elderly parents under a state public assistance program. The court in *Swoap* distinguished cases which had held that the cost of maintaining persons in state institutions could not be arbitrarily assessed to relatives who otherwise had no legal responsibility for the person's care and support, and concluded that California law had long imposed a duty of support upon adult children who were capable of supporting their needy parents. Thus, that duty could be extended to require reimbursement to the state when the state had taken over the responsibility of supporting needy parents without constituting discrimination based on wealth. One justice dissented, arguing that the decision imposed "public expenses on a small class of citizens . . . plac[ing] disproportionate shares of public expenses on various minority groups . . . [and] sanction[ing] a perpetration of a dual system of family law which places special financial burdens on individuals simply because of the poverty of their families."[210]

One rationale supporting relative responsibility laws is the principle of reciprocity in the parent-child relationship. This reasoning, which implies that the child is indebted to his or her parents for their previous support and care, loses its strength when the children in question received disadvantages rather than benefits from their parents. Accordingly, some states' statutes do not impose liability on adult children whose parents willfully neglected or deserted them while they were minors.[211]

Troublesome choice of law questions arise when support is sought on behalf of a needy parent living in a state that has a relative responsibility statute against an adult child who resides in a state without such a statute.[212] Similar problems arise when the defendant's state recognizes a defense, such as abandonment, that is not recognized in the plaintiff's state.[213]

It remains unclear whether a state may require adult children to support their parents without violating federal Medicaid or Medicare statutes and regulations.[214] Largely because of this uncertainty, the number of states retaining and enacting

---

[210] 516 P.2d at 864 (Tobriner, J., dissenting).

[211] *See, e.g.*, Va. Code Ann. § 20-88 (2011) ("This section shall not apply if there is substantial evidence of desertion, neglect, abuse or willful failure to support any such child by the father or mother, as the case may be, prior to the child's emancipation or, except as provided hereafter in this section, if a parent is otherwise eligible for and is receiving public assistance or services under a federal or state program.").

[212] *California v. Copus*, 309 S.W.2d 227 (Tex), *cert. denied*, 356 U.S. 967 (1958). *See also* George Indest, Comment, *Legal Aspects of HCFA's Decision to Allow Recovery from Children for Medicaid Benefits Delivered to their Parents Through State Financial Responsibility Statutes: A Case of Bad Rule Making Through Failure to Comply with the Administrative Procedure Act*, 28 Soc. Sec. Rep. Ser. 728 (1990).

[213] *See Commonwealth v. Mong*, 117 N.E.2d 32 (Ohio 1954).

[214] *See* Katie Wise, *Caring for Our Parents in an Aging World: Sharing Public and Private Responsibility for the Elderly*, 5 N.Y.U.J. Legis. & Pub. Pol'y 563 (2001-02); Robin M. Jacobson, Note, American Health Care Ctr. v. Randall: *The Renaissance of Filial Responsibility*, 40 S.D.L. Rev. 518 (1995); Catherine Doscher Byrd, *Relative Responsibility Extended: Requirement of Adult Children to Pay for Their Indigent Parent's Medical Needs*, 22 Fam. L.Q. 87, 90 (1988). For a pair of cases discussing the requirements of these regulations as to spouses' duty to support, see *In the Matter of Gomprecht*, 652 N.E.2d 936 (N.Y. 1995); *Schweiker v. Gray Panthers*, 453 U.S. 34 (1981).

relative responsibility legislation has fluctuated.[215]

Some commentators have questioned the wisdom of relative responsibility statutes and have recommended their repeal.[216] The underlying policy question of whether the state or adult children should be responsible for needy parents continues to be debated.[217]

§ 3.15   SUPPORT ENFORCEMENT REMEDIES

Actions for contempt, with resulting imprisonment, and other support enforcement remedies provided by the federal child support enforcement acts, may all be utilized when a person fails to support his or her dependents while the marriage remains intact. However, these remedies are most commonly applied in the context of divorce.[218]

In 1996, Congress passed the Personal Responsibility and Work Opportunity Act (PRWORA), also referred to as the 1996 Welfare Reform Act.[219] The PRWORA attempts to make payment of child support more certain and more predictable by processing these cases in bulk rather than individually, by providing greater access to related support information, and by creating automatic enforcement procedures.[220] Recent studies indicate that more stringent support enforcement measures are effective in increasing the amount of child support paid.[221] Because all of these enforcement remedies are most commonly applied in the context of divorced or never-married parents, they are addressed in more detail in Chapter 10.

---

[215] *See* Byrd, *supra* note 214, at 90; Lee Teitelbaum, *Intergenerational Responsibility and Family Obligations: On Sharing*, 1992 Utah L. Rev. 765; Renae Reed Patrick, *Honor Thy Father and Mother: Paying the Medical Bills of Elderly Parents*, 19 U. Rich. L. Rev. 69 (1984).

[216] *See, e.g.*, Robert Whitman & Diane Whitney, *Are Children Legally Responsible for the Support of their Parents?*, 123 Tr. & Est. L.J. 43 (1984).

[217] *See generally* Terrance A. Kline, *A Rational Role for Filial Responsibility Laws in Modern Society?*, 26 Fam. L.Q. 195, 210 (1992); Allison E. Ross, *Taking Care of Our Caretakers: Using Filial Responsibility Laws to Support the Elderly Beyond the Government's Assistance*, 16 Elder L.J. 167, 209 (2008).

[218] *See* § 9.06[F], *infra*, for a discussion of this and other statutes.

[219] 42 U.S.C. § 601 (1996) et. seq.

[220] *See* Linda Elrod, *Child Support Reassessed: Federalization of Enforcement Nears Completion*, 1997 U. Ill. L. Rev. 695, 703.

[221] *Id. See also* Paul K. Leglar, *The Coming Revolution in Child Support Policy: Implications of the 1996 Welfare Act*, 30 Fam. L.Q. 519 (1996).

Chapter 4

MARITAL CONTRACTS AND AGREEMENTS

§ 4.01 INTRODUCTION

Marital property rights and support obligations normally devolve upon the spouses by operation of law at the time of the marriage.[1] Likewise, property and support rights on divorce or dissolution of marriage are generally governed by state statutory and judicial authority at the time the marriage is dissolved.[2]

However, the parties may also create binding economic rights and obligations by contract or agreement: (1) prior to their marriage in the form of a premarital or antenuptial agreement; (2) when a marriage engagement is contracted for and subsequently broken in a minority of states; or (3) in the form of a separation agreement or property settlement agreement at the time of divorce or dissolution of marriage. Indeed, it is estimated that between 80 to 90 per cent of all divorces involve some form of a contractual agreement, which may affect the parties' spousal support rights (or the waiver of such rights), a division of the parties' marital property (or waiver of such rights), and child support and child custody issues (subject to court approval).[3]

The courts therefore have increasingly been asked by the parties to evaluate and enforce their marital contracts, either oral or written, actual or implied, that deal with the economic rights and obligations of the marital partners. For example, in the past, premarital agreements were primarily made by older couples- normally widows and widowers- who were about to be remarried, and who had acquired considerable property from a prior marriage that they wished to control and pass to the children of their first marriage.[4] Premarital agreements today, however, are increasingly being utilized by younger Americans who have acquired, or will acquire, substantial property and, due to a higher probability of divorce or marriage dissolution than in past decades, desire to retain such property as separate property rather than marital property.[5]

---

[1] *See generally supra* Chapter 3.

[2] *See generally infra* Chapters 9-10. Property and support rights for nonmarital relationships and domestic partnerships are discussed in § 2.02

[3] *See* Green & Long, Marriage and Family Law Agreements 213 (1984); Mnookin & Kornhauser, *Bargaining in the Shadow of the Law: The Case for Divorce*, 88 Yale L.J. 950 (1979).

[4] *See generally*, Gamble, *The Antenuptial Contract*, 26 U. Miami L. Rev. 692 (1972); Clark, *Antenuptial Contracts*, 50 U. Colo. L. Rev. 141 (1979).

[5] *See, e.g.*, Swisher, *Divorce Planning in Antenuptial Agreements: Toward a New Objectivity*, 13 U. Rich. L. Rev. 175 (1979); Note, *For Better or For Worse . . . But Just in Case, Are Antenuptial Agreements Enforceable?*, 1982 U. Ill. L. Rev. 531. *See generally* Belcher & Pomeroy, *A Practitioner's*

Premarital agreements may also be utilized by the prospective spouses to provide *more* — rather than less — sharing of income and assets during marriage, or after divorce, than state statutory rules would otherwise require.[6] In addition, some commentators have suggested that premarital contracts also have the potential to improve communication and enhance the commitment of the spouses, both before and during a couple's marriage.[7] For example, Professor Allison Marston states that:

> Prenuptials do not deserve their reputation as the bastion of greed and selfishness in marriage. They can offer more than protection against scheming second wives or social climbing husbands. Rather, prenuptial agreements can promote greater love, communication, and, ultimately, happiness in marriage. A legal framework incorporating an independent counsel requirement would promote fairness and full knowledge by both parties, which increases the potential for prenuptials to be a positive, relation-enhancing experience.[8]

Not all commentators, however, applaud the increased use of marital contracting. Some scholars, for example, oppose the "contractualization" of marriage and divorce because of "the unique nature of the marital relationship, the possibility of irrational and uninformed decision-making at the time of contracting, the likelihood of unforeseen changes in circumstances over the life of the marriage, and the real risk of disadvantage to the economically weaker spouse."[9] Moreover, some feminist scholars argue that premarital and separation agreements invariably harm women by waiving legal and financial protection afforded by state law, and by magnifying an unequal distribution of wealth along gender lines.[10] Other scholars have challenged this view, however, arguing that "emphasizing women's inferior status and bargaining power over women's autonomous right to structure their relations as they see fit reifies the perception that women are the weaker sex and justifies the view that the law — and men — need to protect women from themselves."[11] These scholars suggest that a better approach to empowering women would be to enact procedural and substantive reforms designed to make premarital agreements fairer

---

Guide for Negotiating, Drafting, and Enforcing Premarital Agreements, 37 Real Prop. & Tr. J. 1 (2002).

[6] *See, e.g.*, Guggenheimer, *A Modest Proposal: The Feminomics of Drafting Premarital Agreements*, 17 Women's Rights L. Rep. 147, 204 (1996) (arguing that the drafting norms for premarital agreements should move away from an exclusive focus on competing interests and limiting claims and move "toward a vision of private ordering that is governed by conjoining interests and distributional needs"); *see also* Singer, *The Privatization of Family Law*, 1992 Wis. L. Rev. 1443 (discussing the advantages and disadvantages of a shift from public to private ordering of family law).

[7] *See, e.g.*, Marston, *Planning for Love: The Politics of Prenuptial Agreements*, 49 Stan. L. Rev. 887, 916 (1997).

[8] *Id.* at 916.

[9] Atwood, *Ten Years Later: Lingering Concerns About the Uniform Premarital Agreement Act*, 19 J. Legis. 127, 131 (1993). *See also* Sharp, *Fairness Standards and Separation Agreements: A Word of Caution on Contractual Freedom*, 132 U. Pa. L. Rev. 1399 (1984) (urging greater substantive and procedural fairness review for marital contracts).

[10] *See, e.g.*, Brod, *Premarital Agreements and Gender Justice*, 6 Yale J. L. & Feminism 229 (1994); Tidwell & Linzer, *The Flesh-Colored Band Aid Contracts: Feminism, Dialogue, and Norms*, 28 Houston L. Rev. 791 (1991).

[11] *See, e.g.*, Guggenheimer, *supra* note 6.

from the outset, rather than allowing judges to invalidate such agreements on *ad hoc* grounds of fairness or equity.[12]

Likewise, separation agreements or property settlement agreements on divorce or dissolution of marriage that were once looked upon by various courts and commentators with mistrust and suspicion for allegedly being "in derogation of marriage," or for allegedly "promoting" the procurement of divorce,[13] are now highly favored by family law courts in almost all jurisdictions.[14] Like premarital agreements, separation agreements generally will be upheld by the courts if: (1) there is a full and fair disclosure of the parties' assets and liabilities at the time of contracting; and (2) there is independent legal advice and counsel for both parties, especially if one of the parties is educationally or economically less empowered, such as a traditional house spouse.[15]

Marital agreements — whether they be premarital, postmarital, or separation agreements — therefore allow the parties to agree upon, and privately control, many important aspects of their own marriage and divorce. While such agreements traditionally have been used to limit the parties' economic rights and obligations arising from marriage, they are increasingly being viewed as vehicles to enhance, as well as limit, both the economic and non-economic benefits of marriage. In assessing the desirability of such agreement, and evaluating their validity in any particular case, it may be useful to keep in mind the alternatives in relying on marital agreements as the private ordering of marriage and divorce. As Professors Michael Trebilcock and Rosemin Deshvani observe:

> Whatever the deficiencies of the private ordering process, in every context the hard question must be, compared to what? And the "what" with which actual private ordering regimes must be compared should not be some idealized alternative form of legal ordering, but the available alternative forms of legal ordering as they are actually likely to operate in the real world . . . . [T]he preferences of legislators, judges, bureaucrats, experts, and academics, with all their sundry biases and subjectivities, must be compared with the flawed self-understandings and preferences of individuals attempting to determine their life plans for themselves.[16]

---

[12] *Id.* at 204-07.

[13] *See, e.g.*, J. Madden, Handbook of the Law of Persons and Domestic Relations 331-35 (1931). See also *Dexter v. Dexter*, 371 S.E.2d 816 (Va. Ct. App. 1988), for a historical analysis of this traditional view, and its evolution into the current modern view of judicial promotion and encouragement of marital contracts in general, and separation agreements in particular.

[14] *See, e.g.*, *Drawdy v. Drawdy*, 268 S.E.2d 30, 31 (S.C. 1980) (stating that marital agreements "are praiseworthy products of cooperation between parties seeking a divorce. They also serve to decrease the workload of family courts and thereby enhance judicial efficiency"); *Reynolds v. Reynolds*, 415 A.2d 535, 537 (D.C. 1980) ("This jurisdiction encourages the parties in any marital dispute to resolve by agreement their joint marital interests").

[15] *See generally* Lindey & Parley, Lindey on Separation Agreements and Antenuptial Contracts (1999 rev. ed.); Schlissel, Separation Agreements and Marital Contracts (1986); Green & Long, *supra* note 3.

[16] Trebilcock & Keshvani, *The Role of Private Ordering in Family Law: A Law and Economics Perspective*, 41 U. Toronto L. Rev. 533, 589-90 (1991). *See also* Weisbrod, *The Way We Live Now: A Discussion of Contracts and Domestic Relations*, 1994 Utah L. Rev. 777; Symposium, *Opportunities for and Limitations of Private Ordering in Family Law*, 73 Ind. L.J. 453 (1998). *But see* Judith Younger,

§ 4.02   MARRIAGE PROMISES AND PREMARITAL GIFTS

[A]   Breach of Promise to Marry

An action for breach of promise to marry has existed under the common law for over 300 years. In a breach of promise action, the plaintiff was entitled to recover in contract or tort for injury to his or her feelings, health, and reputation; and damages could be awarded based upon the defendant's wealth, income, and social position. Seduction could also be argued as an "aggravation of damages."[17]

Proof of a broken promise to marry could be circumstantial in this highly emotional area, and thus it afforded "a fertile field for blackmail and extortion."[18] Accordingly, many critics over the past fifty years have advocated the abolition of this fault-based anachronistic action, especially in the era of no-fault divorce, and most states have now abolished breach of promise to marry actions through so-called state "anti-heart balm statutes."[19] Nevertheless, a minority of states still recognize a breach of promise to marry action under the common law.[20]

Although it is well settled under the law that inducing the breach of a business contract can be actionable in tort,[21] most courts have been unwilling to apply this legal theory to a third-party-induced breach of promise to marry. One rationale for denying such relief is that it would prevent parents, relatives, or friends from giving advice to the prospective spouse; another is that it would allow an unsuccessful suitor to sue his or her rival for damages.[22] Similarly, in the majority of jurisdictions, there is no longer an action for alienation of affections by a jilted suitor based upon the conduct of a third party.[23]

[B]   Fraudulent Inducement to Marry Actions

Even though the action for breach of promise to marry has been abolished in the vast majority of states, a party may still have an action against another party for a fraudulent inducement into a marriage contract. For example, if a man

---

Lovers' Contracts in the Courts: Forsaking the Minimum Decencies, 13 Wm. & Mary J. Women & L. 349 (2007) (suggesting that the enforcement of premarital, postmarital, and cohabitation agreements since 2000 are becoming "instruments of oppression").

[17] *See, e.g.,* Keeton et al., Prosser and Keeton on the Law of Torts § 124 (5th ed. 1984).

[18] *Id.*

[19] *See generally* 1 H. Clark, Law of Domestic Relations 1-30 (2d ed. 1987).

[20] According to Green & Long, *supra* note 3, at 102-07, the common law action for breach of promise to marry still exists today in a minority of jurisdictions, including: Georgia, Hawaii, Kansas, Nebraska, North Carolina, Texas, and Washington. Illinois retains this action by statute, but the statute limits recoverable damages only to actual damages. Ill. Ann. Stat. ch. 40 § 1801 *et seq.* See generally *Askew v. Askew,* 28 Cal. Rptr. 2d 284 (Cal. Ct. App. 1994), which provides and excellent background discussion of breach of promise to marry actions and state "anti-heart balm" statutes. *See, e.g., Stanard v. Bolin,* 565 P.2d 94 (Wash. 1977); *Wildey v. Springs,* 47 F.3d 1475 (7th Cir. 1995) (applying Ill. law).

[21] *See generally* Keeton et al., *supra* note 17, at § 129.

[22] *See generally,* Clark, *supra* note 19, at 33-34.

[23] *See generally* Brown, *The Action for Alienation of Affections,* 82 U. Pa. L. Rev. 472, 476 (1934). *But see Cannon v. Miller,* 322 S.E.2d 780 (N.C. Ct. App. 1984), *vacated,* 327 S.E.2d 888 (N.C. 1984).

fraudulently conceals the existence of his prior marital status, and enters into a bigamous second marriage with another woman, that woman can seek compensatory and punitive damages against the man based upon his fraud; and damages can include her mental pain and suffering, as well as lost wages and other economic injuries.[24]

[C] Contracts Restraining or Promoting Marriage

A contract in general restraint of marriage is void as against public policy[25] for two reasons: (1) "the sanctity of the marriage relationship is at the foundation of the welfare of the State,"[26] and (2) the right to marry is a fundamental right.[27]

However, the law will generally permit a partial restraint of marriage, if the specific restraint is shown to be "reasonable" under the circumstances.[28] The "reasonableness" of a restraint of marriage is illustrated by the following examples:

(1) A father promises his 25-year-old son that he will give the son $250,000 in return for the son's promise not to marry for at least ten years. This would be a general restraint of marriage, and not a reasonable one.[29]

(2) An ailing 70-year-old uncle promises to give his 45-year-old niece certain real and personal property in his will if she will remain unmarried, live with him, and take care of him. This would be a reasonable restraint of marriage, and constitute a valid contract.[30]

(3) A paragraph in a will gave a testator's niece "all my real and personal property so long as she remains single and unmarried." This has been held to be a "reasonable" restraint on marriage on the theory that the donee is provided with support or property rights until she marries a "new provider," and therefore it is not a general restraint on marriage.[31]

Contracts promoting marriage are likewise illegal, since marriage should be entered into freely, uninfluenced by third parties who are paid to bring it about.[32] Thus, no action would lie for the collection of any promised fees for procuring a husband or wife by a marriage broker,[33] or by a marriage service agency.[34]

---

[24] *See, e.g., Holcomb v. Kincaid*, 406 So. 2d 650 (La. Ct. App. 1981); *Buckley v. Buckley*, 184 Cal. Rptr. 290 (Cal. Ct. App. 1982); *Humphreys v. Baird*, 90 S.E.2d 796 (Va. 1956); *see also* Annot., 72 A.L.R.2d 956, 981 (Later Case Service).

[25] Restatement (Second) of Contracts § 189 (1981).

[26] *See* 15 Williston on Contracts § 1741 (3d ed. 1972).

[27] *See, e.g., Zablocki v. Redhail*, 434 U.S. 374 (1978).

[28] *See, e.g.,* 6A Corbin on Contracts, § 1474 (1962).

[29] *See* Restatement (Second) of Contracts § 189, Illus. (1981).

[30] *Id. See also Gleason v. Mann*, 45 N.E.2d 280 (Mass. 1942).

[31] *See, e.g., Lewis v. Searles*, 452 S.W.2d 153 (Mo. 1970); *see also* Browder, *Conditions and Limitations in Restraint of Marriage*, 39 Mich. L. Rev. 1288 (1941). According to Annot., 122 A.L.R. 7 (1939), however, this rule has been "eaten out with exceptions."

[32] *See* Williston, *supra* note 26, at § 1289A.

[33] *See, e.g., Jangraw v. Perkins*, 56 A. 532 (Vt. 1903); *Duval v. Wellman*, 26 N.E. 343 (N.Y. 1891).

[D] Premarital Gifts

Disputes frequently arise over who is entitled to an engagement ring or other premarital gifts conditioned on marriage when the engagement is broken. A number of courts follow the traditional rule that the donor of an engagement ring, or the donor of any other gift conditioned on marriage, can recover such a gift only if the engagement is dissolved by mutual agreement, or only if the engagement is unjustifiably broken off by the donee.[35]

Other courts, however, follow the modern view that in the absence of an agreement to the contrary, the engagement ring or other premarital gift conditioned on marriage must be returned to the donor upon the termination of the engagement, regardless of fault.[36] The rationale for this modern view, in the words of one court, is that:

> . . . [I]n most broken engagements there is no real fault as such — one or both of the parties merely changes his [or her] mind about the desirability of the other as a marriage partner. Since the major purpose of the engagement period is to allow a couple time to test the permanency of their feelings, it would seem highly ironic to penalize the donor for taking steps to prevent a possibly unhappy marriage. Just as the question of fault or guilt has become largely irrelevant to modern divorce proceedings, so should it also be deemed irrelevant to the breaking of the engagement.[37]

However, if there is no persuasive evidence that a premarital gift was conditioned on marriage, then such a gift need not be returned to the donor once the engagement is broken off.[38]

§ 4.03 PREMARITAL AGREEMENTS

[A] Traditional Versus Modern Approaches

Premarital agreements, also called antenuptial or prenuptial contracts, are most often utilized when prospective spouses wish to contractually vary, limit, or relinquish certain marital property and support rights that they would otherwise acquire by reason of their impending marriage.

---

[34] *See, e.g., Attorney General v. Marital Endowment Corp.*, 242 N.W. 297 (Mich. 1932) (involving a quo warranto action brought against a company that was promoting marriage for profit).

[35] *See, e.g., White v. Finch*, 209 A.2d 199 (Conn. Cir. Ct. 1964); *De Cicco v. Barker*, 159 N.E.2d 534 (Mass. 1959); Restatement of Restitution § 58 cmt c (1937).

[36] *See, e.g., Lyle v. Durham*, 473 N.E.2d 1216 (Ohio Ct. App. 1984); *Brown v. Thomas*, 379 N.W.2d 868 (Wis. 1985).

[37] *Gaden v. Gaden*, 323 N.Y.S.2d 955, 961-62 (1971).

[38] *See, e.g., Gerard v. Costin*, 215 P. 1011 (Kan. 1923) (premarital gift of land was not conditioned on marriage); *Fortenberry v. Ellis*, 217 So. 2d 792 (La. Ct. App. 1969) (premarital gift of a stereo set was not conditioned on marriage).

However, if a premarital gift was induced by fraud, then it must be returned to the donor. *See, e.g., Earl v. Saks Co.*, 226 P.2d 340 (Cal. 1951) (premarital gift of a fur coat that was induced by fraud).

In the past, premarital agreements were usually made by older couples who were about to be remarried, and who had acquired considerable property from a prior marriage that they wished to control. However, premarital agreements today are increasingly being used by younger Americans who have acquired, or will acquire, substantial property prior to, or during, their first or subsequent marriage — property that they desire to maintain as separate rather than as marital property.[39]

Traditionally, a premarital agreement could only affect property rights on the death of a spouse.[40] Typical premarital agreement provisions might include a release of the distributive shares in each other's estate; the mutual bar of dower and curtesy rights, or a statutory equivalent; the surrender of the right of election to take against the other's estate; and the transfer of money or property to the other, either before the marriage or after. Such an agreement would be judicially recognized as a valid contract only if (1) the premarital agreement provided for full disclosure of the parties' assets or, alternately, a "fair provision" was given to the needy spouse; and (2) independent legal advice of counsel was provided to the less empowered spouse, such as a traditional housewife.[41]

The rationale for this structured approach to determine the validity of a premarital agreement is that after the parties' engagement they are no longer contracting "at arm's length," because a fiduciary relationship has been established that requires full disclosure of the parties' assets, or a fair provision to the other spouse.[42] However, a premarital agreement does not necessarily have to be "fair" to both parties, as long as full disclosure has been made to both parties.[43]

---

[39] *See generally* Gamble, *supra*, note 4; Clark, *supra*, note 4; 3 Lindey on Separation Agreements and Antenuptial Contracts § 90 (2010 rev. ed.).

[40] *See, e.g., Crouch v. Crouch*, 385 S.W.2d 288 (Tenn. Ct. App. 1964); *Smetana v. Smetana*, 726 N.W.2d 887 (S.D. 2007) (holding that a premarital agreement was invalid, because it was only applicable on the death of a party, and did not state it was applicable in the event of divorce); *see also* Annot., 57 A.L.R.2d 942 (1958) (Later Case Service).

[41] *See, e.g., In re Estate of Benker*, 331 N.W.2d 193 (Mich. 1982); *Friedlander v. Friedlander*, 494 P.2d 208 (Wash. 1972); *Batleman v. Rubin*, 98 S.E.2d 519 (Va. 1957) (a "fair provision" should be at least one-third of the husband's worth at the time of contracting, or the presumption of designed concealment is raised). However, the *Battleman* case holding was based upon common law dower and curtesy principles, before augmented estate statutes were enacted in a majority of states, including Virginia. Under this general rule, the burden of proof is initially placed upon the party alleging the invalidity of a premarital agreement. But if there is evidence of nondisclosure of assets (also called overreaching or designed concealment) then the burden of proof shifts, and if this presumption of nondisclosure is not rebutted, then the premarital agreement may be invalidated. *See generally* 3 Lindey on Separation Agreements, *supra* note 39, at § 90-52 to -58.

[42] *Id. See also Cannon v. Cannon*, 865 A.2d 563 (Md. 2005) (holding that the premarital agreement was valid because the wife had adequate knowledge of the assets involved, and entered into the agreement voluntarily); and *Friezo v. Friezo*, 914 A.2d 533 (Conn. 2007) (holding that disclosure requirements in a premarital agreement are satisfied when the parties disclose a general approximation of their income, assets, and liabilities).

[43] *See, e.g., Newman v. Newman*, 653 P.2d 728 (Colo. 1982) (once the tests of full disclosure and lack of fraud or overreaching are met, the parties are free to agree in a premarital agreement to any arrangement for the division of their property, including waiver of any claim to the property of the other); *see also Estate of Moss*, 263 N.W.2d 98 (Neb. 1978); *Del Vecchio v. Del Vecchio*, 143 So. 2d 17 (Fla. 1962); *Pardieck v. Pardieck*, 676 N.E. 2d 359, 363 (Ind. Ct. App. 1997) (holding that if a premarital agreement

A less empowered traditional housewife may still require full disclosure of assets and representation by independent legal counsel.[44] However, if the prospective wife did not have full disclosure of the husband's assets, nor any independent legal advice, but learned of the prospective husband's assets independently, and she had the sophistication and business acumen to understand what she was signing, then the premarital agreement would not necessarily be declared invalid.[45]

Under this traditional approach, however, premarital agreements could not include any contingent divorce planning provisions, because such divorce planning provisions were thought to "encourage" or "promote" the procurement of divorce.[46] Moreover, this traditional rule prohibiting any divorce-planning provisions in premarital agreements resulted in the unfortunate judicial practice of invalidating any divorce planning contingency provisions in premarital agreements that *might* "encourage" or "promote" divorce,[47] which often resulted in voiding the entire premarital agreement itself.[48]

Accordingly, a modern view of divorce planning in premarital agreements began to evolve in some jurisdictions, where contingent divorce-planning provisions in premarital agreements were not judicially declared as invalid *per se*, but were to be tested by the objective intent of the contracting parties themselves.[49]

The rationale behind this modern rule, as explained in the case of *Posner v. Posner*,[50] was that:

> With divorce such a commonplace fact of life, it is fair to assume that many prospective marriage partners whose property and familial situation is such as to generate a valid antenuptial agreement settling their property

---

is clear on its terms, and is not unconscionable, it will be enforced as written); *Moore v. Gillis*, 391 S.E.2d 255, 256-57 (Va. 1990) (similar holding).

[44] *See, e.g., Matson v. Matson*, 705 P.2d 817 (Wash. Ct. App. 1985) (when a premarital agreement attempts to limit or eliminate martial property rights, "equity will zealously and scrupulously examine it for fairness"); *see also* Schembri, *Prenuptial Agreements and the Significance of Independent Counsel*, 17 St. John's J. Legal Comment, 313 (2003).

[45] *See, e.g., Knoll v. Knoll*, 671 P.2d 718 (Or. Ct. App. 1983) (prospective wife was prospective husband's bookkeeper, and she knew, or should have known, what his assets actually were); *Gordon v. Gordon*, 25 So. 3d 615 (Fla. Dist. Ct. App. 2009) (a premarital agreement was not reached under duress or coercion or overreaching because the wife had a high level of education and business acumen); *see also In re Marriage of Bonds*, 5 P.3d 815 (Cal. 2000) (holding that a lack of independent counsel is merely one factor to consider in determining the voluntariness of the unrepresented party's execution of a premarital contract).

[46] *See, e.g., Mulford v. Mulford*, 320 N.W.2d 470 (Neb. 1982); *Duncan v. Duncan*, 652 S.W.2d 913 (Tenn. Ct. App. 1983).

[47] *See, e.g., Fricke v. Fricke*, 42 N.W.2d 500 (Wis. 1950); *In re Marriage of Gudenkauf*, 204 N.W.2d 586 (Iowa 1973); *see also* Annots., 70 A.L.R. 826 (1931), 57 A.L.R.2d 942 (1958) (Later Case Service).

[48] *See generally* Swisher, *supra* note 5.

[49] *Id. See also Posner v. Posner*, 233 So. 2d 381 (Fla. 1970); *Unander v. Unander*, 506 P.2d 719 (Or. 1973); *Frey v. Frey*, 471 A.2d 705 (Md. Ct. Spec. App. 1984); *In re Marriage of Pendleton and Fireman*, 5 P.3d 839 (Cal. 2000) (holding that a waiver of spousal support in a premarital agreement was not contrary to public policy nor per se void or unenforceable).

[50] 233 So. 2d 381 (Fla. 1970).

rights upon the death of either, might want to consider and discuss also —
and agree upon if possible — the disposition of their property and the
alimony rights of the wife [and husband] in the event their marriage,
despite their best efforts, should fail.[51]

Indeed, courts following this modern rule have repeatedly stated that there is
little empirical evidence supporting the traditional view that such divorce planning
provisions in premarital agreements actually invite dispute, encourage separation,
or promote divorce. The possibility is equally arguable that such agreements
promote rather than reduce marital stability by defining the expectations and
responsibilities of the parties.[52]

There is also a second reason why some courts have refused to recognize divorce
planning in premarital agreements, especially when it relates to contingent spousal
support provisions or to a waiver of spousal support:

> The real reason for invalidating such antenuptial contracts seems to be that
> although the [spousal support] provisions may be fair at the time they are
> made, they may not be later when the separation or divorce occurs. The
> wife may thus be left with entirely inadequate support, or the husband with
> an excessively heavy liability to his wife [or vice versa] . . . . Thus, the
> difficulty of forecasting the parties' circumstances so far in the future has
> led [some] courts to disallow antenuptial contracts which attempt to do this
> with respect to support.[53]

An answer to this legitimate concern, however, is that by using an objective
case-by-case evaluation, alimony or spousal support provisions in antenuptial
agreements would be upheld by the court if (1) the contractual terms were fair, and
(2) the contract was made with full disclosure of the parties' worth. Otherwise, as
with separation agreements on divorce in most states, these provisions could be
modified by the court using its equitable powers of judicial review. As the Oregon
Supreme Court has stated this principle:

> We have now come to the conclusion that antenuptial agreements concern-
> ing alimony should be enforced unless enforcement deprives a spouse of
> support that he or she cannot otherwise secure. A provision providing that
> no alimony shall be paid will be enforced unless the spouse has no other
> reasonable source of support. If the circumstances of the parties change,
> the court can modify the decree just as it can modify a decree based upon
> [a separation] agreement made in contemplation of divorce which has a
> provision regarding payment of support.[54]

---

[51] *Id.* at 384. *See also Volid v. Volid*, 286 N.E.2d 42, 46 (Ill. App. Ct. 1972); *Unander v. Unander*, 506
P.2d 719, 720 (Or. 1973); *Osborne v. Osborne*, 428 N.E.2d 810 (Mass. 1981). Indeed, some commentators
have urged that American family law should *require* couples to enter into premarital agreements. *See,
e.g.,* Stake, *Mandatory Planning for Divorce*, 45 Vand. L. Rev. 397 (1992).

[52] *Unander v. Unander*, 506 P.2d 719, 720 (Ore. 1973). *See also Newman v. Newman*, 653 P.2d 728,
732 (Colo. 1982).

[53] *Reiling v. Reiling*, 474 P.2d 327, 328 (Or. 1970) (quoting H. Clark, Law of Domestic Relations 28-29
(1968)).

[54] *Unander v. Unander*, 506 P.2d 719, 721 (Or. 1973), *overruling in part Reiling v. Reiling, supra.*

Consequently, with various courts continuing to apply either the traditional[55] or modern[56] view regarding divorce planning in premarital agreements, there has been a great deal of confusion in many American jurisdictions regarding when the courts *would* recognize certain premarital agreements as valid contracts, and when judicially they would *not.*[57]

For example, a premarital agreement that gave a wife only one-sixth of her husband's estate on the event of his death or their divorce was held to be invalid by the New Hampshire Supreme Court, even though the trial court had held that the premarital agreement was voluntarily entered into by the parties.[58] But on the other hand, the South Carolina Supreme Court upheld the validity of a premarital agreement where a spouse had waived all rights to alimony and attorneys' fees, contending that such agreements are legally valid unless obtained by fraud, duress, or nondisclosure of assets.[59] How can these cases be reconciled?

In an effort to resolve much of this judicial confusion regarding premarital agreements generally, a number of states have adopted the Uniform Premarital Agreement Act.

[B]   The Uniform Premarital Agreement Act

Drafted in 1983, the Uniform Premarital Agreement Act[60] has been adopted by an increasing number of states.[61] The Uniform Premarital Agreement Act is intended to be relatively limited in scope, and does not deal with agreements between unmarried cohabitants, nor does it encompass postnuptial or separation agreements or oral agreements.[62]

---

[55] *See, e.g., Duncan v. Duncan*, 652 S.W.2d 913 (Tenn. Ct. App. 1983).

[56] *See, e.g., Newman v. Newman*, 653 P.2d 728 (Colo. 1982).

[57] *See, e.g.*, Note, *For Better or For Worse . . . But Just in Case, are Antenuptial Agreements Enforceable?*, 1982 U. Ill. L. Rev. 531; Oldham, *Premarital Agreements are Now Enforceable Unless . . .* , 21 Houston L. Rev. 757 (1984).

[58] *In re Estate of Hollett*, 834 A.2d 348 (N.H. 2003) (finding that the premarital agreement was signed under duress, and stating "independent counsel is useless without the ability and time to make effective use of counsel.") *But see In re Marriage of Barnes*, 755 N.E.2d 522 (Ill. Ct. App. 2001) (holding that a threat by husband that he would not marry unless the prospective wife signed a premarital agreement did *not* amount to coercion, and the premarital agreement was held to be binding).

[59] *Hardee v. Hardee*, 585 S.E.2d 501 (S.C. 2003) (finding that both parties were represented by independent legal counsel, and there was no fraud or duress). *But see Lane v. Lane*, 202 S.W.3d 577 (Ky. 2006) (holding that while public policy does not render antenuptial agreements per se invalid, they can be analyzed by the courts as unconscionable, and a trial court judge has broad discretionary power to modify or invalidate antenuptial agreements, especially when circumstances changed over the course of the marriage).

[60] Uniform Premarital Agreement Act (1983), 9B U.L.A. 369 (reprinted in [Reference File] Family Law Reporter, 201:2001 (BNA 1984) [hereafter referred to as the Act].

[61] To date, the Act has been adopted in 28 states including: Arizona, Arkansas, California, Hawaii, Idaho, Illinois, Indiana, Iowa, Kansas, Maine, Montana, Nevada, New Jersey, New Mexico, North Carolina, North Dakota, Oregon, Rhode Island, South Dakota, Texas, and Virginia. Additional states are likely to adopt the Act in the near future.

[62] 9B U.L.A. 369, Prefatory Note.

Section 1 of the Act defines a premarital agreement as "an agreement between prospective spouses made in contemplation of marriage and to be effective upon marriage."[63]

Section 2 of the Act requires that a premarital agreement be in writing and signed by both parties.[64]

Section 3 of the Act deals with its content. Parties to a premarital agreement may contract with respect to: the property of either or both of the parties, whenever or wherever acquired or located; the disposition of property upon separation, marital dissolution, death, or the occurrence or nonoccurrence of any other event; the modification or elimination of spousal support; the making of a will, trust, or other arrangement; the ownership rights and disposition of death benefits from life insurance policies; the choice of law governing the agreement; and "any other matter . . . not in violation of public policy or a statute imposing a criminal penalty." Any child support rights, however, may not be adversely affected by a premarital agreement.[65]

Section 4 of the Act provides that an agreement becomes effective on marriage; and Section 5 states that after marriage, a premarital agreement may be amended or revoked only be a written agreement signed by the parties.[66]

Section 6 is the key operative section of the Act and sets forth the conditions under which a premarital agreement is not enforceable.[67] A premarital agreement is not enforceable if the party against whom enforcement is sought proves that: (1) the party did not execute the agreement voluntarily; or (2) the agreement was unconscionable when it was executed if a party: (i) was not provided with a fair and reasonable disclosure of the property or financial obligations of the other party; (ii) did not voluntarily and expressly waive, in writing, such disclosure; and (iii) did not have adequate knowledge of the property or financial obligations of the other party.[68]

Under the Act, if any provision in the premarital agreement modifies or eliminates spousal support, and causes one party to the agreement to be eligible for support under a program for public assistance at the time of separation or marital dissolution, a court, despite the terms of the agreement, may require the other party to provide support to the extent necessary to avoid that eligibility.[69] Furthermore, any issue of unconscionability of a premarital agreement shall be

---

[63] *Id.* at § 1. Some states subsequently have included postmarital agreements within their state Premarital Agreement Act as well. *See, e.g.*, Va. Code Ann. 20-155 (1987).

[64] 9B U.L.A. 369, at § 2. Nevertheless, an *oral* premarital agreement arguably may still be taken out of the Statute of Frauds through detrimental reliance and part performance under estoppel principles. *See, e.g., T. v. T.*, 224 S.E.2d 148 (Va. 1976); *In re Lord's Estate*, 602 P.2d 1030 (N. M. 1979).

[65] 9B U.L.A. 369, at § 3.

[66] *Id.* at §§ 4, 5.

[67] *Id.* at Prefatory Note.

[68] *Id.* at § 6(a).

[69] *Id.* at § 6(b).

decided by the court as a matter of law.[70]

Although the Uniform Premarital Agreement Act does not expressly require independent legal counsel for the less empowered spouse, a Comment to Section 6 of the Act nevertheless states that:

> . . . Nothing in Section 6 makes the absence of assistance of independent legal counsel a condition for the unenforceability of a premarital agreement. However, lack of that assistance may well be a factor in determining whether the [unconscionability] conditions stated in Section 6 may have existed.[71]

§ 4.04   CONTRACTUAL AGREEMENTS BETWEEN HUSBAND AND WIFE

Since, under the common law, a husband and wife were considered to be one legal entity, spouses were prohibited from contracting with each other. The Married Women's Property Acts,[72] however, removed the wife's contractual incapacity and consequently, in most states today, husbands and wives are now capable of contracting with each other, and may recover for breach of contract against each other.[73] Spousal rights to sue each other also include actions in equity to enforce marital property rights.[74]

Despite this relaxation of the rules regarding interspousal contracts, however, the courts have been reluctant to enforce contracts that relate to altering the spousal duty of support during marriage. For example, courts have refused to enforce contracts in which a husband promised to pay his wife for her household services, under the legal rationale that a wife had a preexisting duty to render such services, and the contract thus failed for lack of consideration.[75] The courts have similarly invalidated spousal contracts where one spouse agreed to devise property to the other spouse in exchange for domestic services or care during the promisor spouse's lifetime.[76]

The common law therefore generally presumed that any services rendered by one spouse to the other spouse were either obligatory or gratuitous, but this presumption could be rebutted by factual evidence demonstrating that such spousal services were *not* intended to be gratuitous.[77] Thus, a spouse would be permitted to prove that certain property acquired during the marriage was held in partnership,

---

[70] *Id.* at § 6(c).

[71] *Id.* at § 6 Comment (citing as authority *Del Vecchio v. Del Vecchio*, 143 So. 2d 17 (Fla. 1962)).

[72] *See infra* § 3.03[B].

[73] *See, e.g., Hamilton v. Hamilton*, 51 So. 2d 13 (Ala. 1950).

[74] *See, e.g., Brobst v. Brobst*, 121 A.2d 178 (Pa. 1956); *see also* McCurdy, *Property Torts Between Spouses*, 2 Vill. L. Rev. 447 (1957).

[75] *See, e.g., Youngberg v. Holstrom*, 108 N.W.2d 498 (Iowa 1961).

[76] *See, e.g., In re Estate of Lord*, 602 P.2d 1030 (N.M. 1979).

[77] *See, e.g., Eggleston v. Eggleston*, 47 S.E.2d 243 (N.C. 1948); *Cooper v. Spencer*, 238 S.E.2d 805 (Va. 1977).

quasi-partnership, joint venture, or in trust — or that a constructive trust should be imposed to prevent unjust enrichment of the title-holding spouse.[78]

Both spouses therefore have the right to enter into partnership agreements or any other business arrangements with each other, and creditors may, or may not, be protected, depending upon the particular form of the business organization.[79]

§ 4.05 POSTNUPTIAL AND SEPARATION AGREEMENTS

After the parties are married, they may contractually agree to buy, sell, or exchange certain property, to dispose of property by will or trust, to determine certain insurance benefits, or to determine certain property and support rights in the event of death, separation, dissolution, or divorce.

If the contracting parties are not contemplating an immediate divorce, then they . would be primarily concerned with existing marital property and support rights, wills and trusts, insurance benefits, or business agreements that normally would take effect during the marriage, or on the death of one or both of the spouses. Although relatively rare in the past, these postnuptial agreements are becoming more common as a result of the current economic climate in the United States, where one spouse may unexpectedly come into great wealth subsequent to the marriage, and may desire to alter the terms of his or her existing marital property and support rights and obligations.[80]

Like premarital agreements, postnuptial agreements can spell out what the dependent spouse claims or waives in the event of divorce or dissolution of marriage. However, although most states have specific laws that govern the creation and enforcement of premarital and separation agreements, only a few state courts and legislatures have adequately dealt with the relatively new concept of postnuptial

---

[78] *See, e.g., McGehee v. McGehee*, 85 So. 2d 799 (Miss. 1956) (upholding a formal, written partnership agreement between the spouses relating to ownership of business assets). *But see Chaachou v. Chaachou*, 135 So. 2d 206 (Fla. 1961). In *Chaachou*, where the couple had no formal partnership agreement with respect to their business property, the court held that any partnership that may have been agreed to "became merged in their larger partnership of marriage, and its terms are now too indistinct to be specifically enforced as such." *Id.* at 214. The court concluded, however, that the husband would be unjustly enriched if he were allowed to retain all the business assets without duly compensating the wife, and the wife was awarded a fraction of the value of the four hotel properties, as well as permanent alimony, a residence, and attorneys' fees.

[79] *See, e.g., Northampton Brewery Corp. v. Lande*, 10 A.2d 583 (Pa. Super. Ct. 1939) (creditor recovered from a family restaurant business that creditor claimed was a partnership, but the wife claimed was held as tenancy by the entireties). *But see Kennedy v. Nelson*, 70 So. 2d 822 (Ala. Ct. App. 1954) (husband, as wife's tenant on her solely owned farm, could not bind his wife for improvements payable to the creditor on a theory of implied agency, despite husband's management of the farm).

However, when a spouse obtains the other spouse's interest in property held as tenants by the entireties during marriage, pursuant to an equitable distribution award on divorce, he or she takes such property subject to any preexisting creditor's interest on the property. *See, e.g., Union Grove Milling & Mfg. Co. v. Faw*, 404 S.E.2d 508 (N.C. Ct. App. 1991).

[80] *See, e.g.*, Desa Philadelphia, *Let's Remake a Deal: When one spouse gets rich, couples now often turn to postnuptial agreements. Are they fair?*, Time Magazine, Apr. 24, 2000, at 56 ("veteran attorneys say the number of mid-marriage agreements has exploded in the last five years, perhaps as much as ten-fold").

agreements. New York and Florida, for example, have ruled that postnuptial agreements are enforceable to the same extent that premarital and separation agreements are enforceable; but North Carolina and Louisiana both require that postnuptial agreements be approved by a judge. And in Hawaii, postnuptial agreements are valid only if the judge deems the contractual terms are fair at the time of signing the agreement *and* at the time of divorce — meaning that a spouse whose wealth has grown substantially since the postnuptial was signed may have to renegotiate the terms of the agreement at the time of the parties' separation.[81]

In a case of first impression, the Massachusetts Supreme Judicial Court held that postnuptial agreements are valid and enforceable, just like premarital agreements, if the following conditions are met: (1) each party had an opportunity to obtain independent legal counsel of his or her choice; (2) there was no fraud, duress, or coercion in obtaining the postmarital agreement; (3) all assets were fully disclosed by both parties; (4) each spouse knowingly agreed in writing to waive the right to an equitable division of marital assets at the time of divorce; and (5) the terms of the postmarital agreement were fair and reasonable both at the time of execution and at the time of divorce.[82] On the other hand, an Ohio court has held that postmarital agreements are *not* valid in Ohio, and therefore a premarital agreement *cannot* be amended after marriage.[83]

Clearly, this is an important area of marital contracting that requires the serious attention of more state courts and legislatures in order to ensure that fundamental fairness exists within the contracting process; and that contractual oppression from a more empowered, wealthier, and overreaching spouse is thereby avoided. Accordingly, if there is a lack of fundamental fairness in drafting a postnuptial agreement, the courts have not hesitated to invalidate such agreements.[84]

Alternately, if the contracting parties were contemplating divorce, or the possibility of a divorce, then their postmarital agreement generally would be drafted in the form of a separation agreement.

[A] Separation Agreements: Necessary Elements

Separation agreements, also called property settlement agreements on divorce, were once looked upon by some courts with suspicion, since such agreements between the spouses to live separate and apart were believed to be in derogation of marriage, by allegedly "promoting" the procurement of divorce.[85]

Today, however, separation agreements are highly favored in almost all jurisdictions,[86] thus allowing a husband and a wife, with the help of their respective

---

[81] *Id.*

[82] *See, e.g., Ansin v. Craven-Ansin*, 929 N.E.2d 955 (Mass. 2010).

[83] *See, e.g., Hoffman v. Dobbins*, 2009 Ohio 5157 (Ct. App.).

[84] *See, e.g., Ewing v. Ewing*, 570 S.E.2d 153 (N.C. Ct. App. 2002); *Estate of Dugger v. Dugger*, 110 S.W.3d 423 (Mo. Ct. App. 2003); *Stoner v. Stoner*, 819 A.2d 529 (Pa. 2003).

[85] For an historical analysis of this traditional rule questioning the validity of separation agreements, see *Dexter v. Dexter*, 371 S.E.2d 816 (Va. Ct. App. 1988). *See also* Madden, *supra* note 13, at 331-35.

[86] *See, e.g., Reynolds v. Reynolds*, 415 A.2d 535, 537 (D.C. 1980) ("This jurisdiction encourages the

attorneys, to contractually agree on a division of the parties' marital property and other assets; to apportion marital debt; to agree on an amount of spousal support, or a waiver of spousal support; to agree on child support and child custody issues, subject to court approval; to determine the disposition of the family residence; to address various insurance coverages, pension plans, or retirement plans; to facilitate tax planning; and to contractually agree on any other related matters regarding the parties' pending divorce or dissolution of marriage.[87]

A voluntary separation agreement between husband and wife offers many benefits over an adversarial court-imposed order. First, the parties themselves know their own needs, assets, problems, and their children's needs much better than a divorce judge does. Second, a separation agreement drafted with a fair and reasonable compromise on both sides usually results in better compliance by both parties than a court-imposed adversarial solution. And third, an enormous amount of time and money can be saved in costly litigation expenses, including attorneys' fees, expert witness fees, and court costs, by using a separation agreement.[88]

Separation agreements, like other marital agreements, are generally recognized and encouraged under state statutory law,[89] and normally will be enforced by the courts.[90] But because the marital relationship imposes a fiduciary duty on each of the parties,[91] and because public policy dictates a requirement of essential fairness in the spouses' negotiations,[92] then most separation agreements require full

---

parties in any marital dispute to resolve by agreement their joint marital interests."); *Drawdy v. Drawdy*, 268 S.E.2d 30, 31 (S.C. 1980) (Separation agreements "are praiseworthy products of cooperation between parties seeking a divorce. They also serve to decrease the workload on family courts and thereby enhance judicial efficiency."); *see also Ford v. Ford*, 68 P.3d 1258 (Alaska 2003); *In re Marriage of Derzy*, 55 P.3d 418 (Montana 2002); *Anderson v. Anderson*, 550 S.E.2d 266 (N.C. Ct. App. 2001); *Cayan v. Cayan*, 38 S.W.3d 161 (Tex. Ct. App. 2000).

[87] *See, e.g.*, Green & Long, *supra* note 3; S. Schlissel, Separation Agreements and Marital Contracts (2010); Lindey & Parley, *supra* note 39; *see also* Haas, *The Rationality and Enforceability of Contractual Restrictions on Divorce*, 66 N.C. L. Rev. 879 (1988); Sean Hannon Williams, *Postnuptial Agreements*, 2007 Wis. L. Rev. 827 (arguing that the availability of a postnuptial agreement benefits both spouses, and is likely to be more equitable than a premarital agreement).

[88] *See generally* Green & Long, *supra* note 3, at 213. *See also* Mnoookin & Kornhauser, *Bargaining in the Shadow of the Law: The Case of Divorce*, 88 Yale L.J. 950 (1979) (stating that divorce cases comprise a very high proportion of all civil cases, and that 80 to 90 percent of these cases are disposed of through separation agreements, with only administrative approval by the courts); Lindey & Parley, *supra* note 15, at § 1.01; Schlissel, *supra* note 15, at §§ 8.01–.02.

[89] *See, e.g.*, N.Y. Dom. Rel. Law § 236 (separation agreements held valid and enforceable); Va. Code Ann. § 20-109.1 (authorizing court approval of separation agreements); *see also* The Uniform Marriage and Divorce Act § 306, 9A U.L.A. 135 (authorizing separation agreements in order to promote the amicable settlement of disputes between spouses).

[90] *See, e.g.*, *LeBert-Francis v. LeBert-Francis*, 194 A.2d 662, 664 (D.C. 1963) (separation agreements should be encouraged, and when made they should be enforced); *see also Dominick v. Dominick*, 463 N.E.2d 564 (Mass. App. Ct. 1984) (a court should presumptively approve a separation agreement unless such an agreement is unconscionable); *Kline v. Kline*, 922 A.2d 261 (Conn. Ct. App. 2007) (when the language of a separation agreement that is incorporated into a divorce decree is clear and unambiguous, it is improper for the court to rewrite the unambiguous portion of the agreement).

[91] *See, e.g.*, Grisham, *A Fiduciary Relationship Between Divorcing Spouses: Impact on Property Settlements*, 13 Community Prop. J. 58 (1986).

[92] *See generally* Sharp, *Fairness Standards and Separation Agreements: A Word of Caution on*

disclosure by each party regarding his or her financial worth.[93]

However, when full disclosure of the parties' financial worth is *not* made, then the separation agreement may be invalidated due to fraud, overreaching [defined as conduct in taking unfair advantage of the other spouse], or designed concealment.[94] For example, in the case of *Selke v. Selke*,[95] a husband's failure to disclose the value of his pension plan to his unrepresented wife warranted voiding both their separation agreement and the divorce decree incorporating the separation agreement. It made no difference that the husband did not know the exact value of his pension plan, because he had access to information regarding its approximate value.[96] A separation agreement may also be voided on grounds of unconscionability.[97]

In the absence of fraud, duress, concealment, overreaching, or unconscionability, a separation agreement normally will be binding on the parties, no matter how ill-reasoned or ill-advised a party may have been in executing it.[98] Thus, separation agreements are held by most courts to be presumptively valid if they are freely and

---

Contractual Freedom, 132 U. Pa. L. Rev. 1399 (1984). *See also Crawford v. Crawford*, 350 N.E.2d 103, 107 (Ill. App. Ct. 1976) (such agreements are enforceable based upon whether they are "reasonably fair and sufficient in light of the station in life and circumstances of the parties").

[93] *See e.g., O'Connor v. O'Connor*, 435 So. 2d 344 (Fla. Dist. Ct. App. 1983); *Golder v. Golder*, 714 P.2d 26 (Idaho 1986); *Williams v. Williams*, 508 A.2d 985 (Md. 1985); *Billington v. Billington*, 595 A.2d 1377 (Conn. 1991); *see also* 1 S. Schlissel, Separation Agreements and Marital Contracts § 8.03–.04 (2011). In a case of first impression, the Massachusetts Supreme Judicial Court, in *Ansin v. Craven-Ansin*, 929 N.E.2d 955 (Mass. 2010), held that before a court can recognize a marital agreement, the judge has to determine: (1) that each party had a chance to obtain legal counsel; (2) that there was no fraud or coercion in obtaining the agreement; (3) that both parties knew about the assets before the agreement was executed; (4) that each spouse agreed in writing to waive the right of a judicial equitable distribution of the assets and other marital rights on divorce; and (5) that the terms of the agreement were fair and reasonable at the time of the contract execution and at the time of the divorce.

[94] *See, e.g., Williams v. Williams*, 508 A.2d 985 (Md. 1985); *Koizim v. Koizim*, 435 A.2d 1030 (Conn. 1980); *Knutson v. Knutson*, 639 N.W.2d 495 (N.D. 2002).

[95] 569 N.E.2d 724 (Ind. Ct. App. 1991).

[96] *Id.*

[97] *See, e.g. Burke v. Sexton*, 814 S.W.2d 290 (Ky. Ct. App. 1991) (a separation agreement requiring the wife to waive all her property interests and spousal support rights in order to receive child support was found to be unconscionable); *Derby v. Derby*, 378 S.E.2d 74 (Va. Ct. App. 1989) (while disagreeing with the trial court that a separation agreement was void due to fraud and duress, the appellate court found that a gross disparity in the parties' property division was shocking and unconscionable). A separation agreement may also be unconscionable if a party was not provided a fair and reasonable disclosure of the other party's assets. *See, e.g., Williams v. Williams*, 508 A.2d 985 (Md. 1985); *Koizim v. Koizim*, 435 A.2d 1030 (Conn. 1980). *But see In re Marriage of Turner*, 803 S.W.2d 655 (Mo. Ct. App. 1991) (the parties' separation agreement was not unconscionable where the husband's representations about the status of his assets, although not entirely accurate, were not so awry as to be fraudulent, and the wife had legal counsel who could have investigated further, but did not). *See also Sims v. Sims*, 685 S.E.2d 869 (Va. Ct. App. 2009) (where the wife, who was disabled and indigent, received only a forgiveness of debt on the marital home, and husband received over $300,000 in assets, the agreement was set aside as unconscionable).

[98] *See, e.g., Reynolds v. Reynolds*, 415 A.2d 535 (D.C. 1980) (in the absence of fraud, duress, concealment or overreaching an agreement is binding no matter how ill-advised a party may have been in executing it); *Lockhart v. Baxter*, 405 S.E.2d 434 (Va. Ct. App. 1991) (the law will not invalidate a separation agreement contract merely because it was ill-reasoned or ill-advised).

understandingly signed by both parties, with full disclosure of the marital assets, regardless of any subsequent allegations of unfairness made by either party.[99] An otherwise valid agreement, therefore, will not be rejected merely because a party had a "change of heart" after the agreement was executed.[100]

Overreaching may occur when one of the parties signing the separation agreement is not represented by independent legal counsel.[101] Most courts and commentators strongly recommend that each party to a separation agreement should have independent legal advice before signing any separation agreement.[102]

However, the lack of independent legal counsel for either party in signing a separation agreement will not always render the agreement invalid and unenforceable. For example, the Washington Supreme Court in *Whitney v. Seattle First National Bank*[103] held that where the separation agreement was fair and reasonable, and where the petitioner had not shown fraud or overreaching, there was no absolute requirement that the wife or husband needed independent legal advice of counsel.[104]

The *Whitney* case notwithstanding, most courts still continue to examine the particular circumstances that led to a party not being represented by independent legal counsel. Such circumstances include the unrepresented party's awareness of the financial circumstances surrounding the agreement, and the unrepresented

---

[99] *See, e.g., Flora v. Flora*, 337 N.E.2d 846 (Ind. Ct. App. 1975); *Dominick v. Dominick*, 463 N.E.2d 564 (Mass. Ct. App.1984); *see also Jennings v. Jennings*, 409 S.E.2d 8 (Va. Ct. App. 1991) (where the court found no unconscionability when the husband, in order to induce his wife to reconcile after she filed suit for divorce, offered to enter into a property settlement agreement which the wife's lawyer prepared and discussed with both parties. The husband signed the agreement after rejecting the recommendation by wife's lawyer that he seek independent legal counsel. After a brief reconciliation, the wife sought a divorce, and the court incorporated the agreement into the final divorce decree. The fact that the husband was an alcoholic and possessed some human frailties did not relieve him of his contractual obligations under the separation agreement).

[100] *See, e.g., Sontag v. Sontag*, 495 N.Y.S.2d 65 (N.Y. App. Div. 1985), *aff'd*, 498 N.Y.S.2d 133 (N.Y. 1986).

[101] *See, e.g., Compton v. Compton*, 612 P.2d 1175, 1183 (Idaho 1980); *Radigan v. Radigan*, 465 N.W.2d 483 (S.D. 1991).

[102] *See, e.g., Craft v. Craft*, 478 So. 2d 258 (Miss. 1985) (where the court held that since both husband and wife were represented by independent legal counsel, that fact constituted strong evidence that each party was advised of his or her respective legal rights and responsibilities under the separation agreement, and that each party knowingly and voluntarily agreed to be bound by the agreement); *see also Murphy v. Murphy*, 239 S.E.2d 597 (N.C. Ct. App. 1977) (similar holding). *But see Smith v. Lewis*, 530 P.2d 589 (Cal. 1975); *Schauer v. Joyce*, 429 N.E.2d 83 (N.Y. 1981). *See also* Green & Long, *supra* note 3, at 217 ("separate representation by retained counsel can go far to protect each side from a variety of possible claims advanced for the purpose of having a separation agreement set aside"); *In re Marriage of Zier*, 147 P.3d 624 (Wash. Ct. App. 2006) (holding that without evidence of coercion or failure of a party to understand a marital agreement, a spouse is not required to have independent legal counsel at the time the agreement was formed).

[103] 579 P.2d 937, 940 (Wash. 1978).

[104] *Id. See also In re Marriage of Gerleman*, 741 P.2d 426 (Mont. 1987). *But see Eltzroth v. Eltzroth*, 679 P.2d 1369 (Or. Ct. App. 1984). *In re Marriage of Bonds*, 5 P. 3d 815 (Cal. 2000) (holding that the lack of independent counsel is only one of many factors to consider in determining the voluntariness of entering into a marital agreement) (premarital agreement).

party's ability to understand the agreement and waive legal counsel.[105]

Another key issue involving separation agreements is whether or not an attorney may represent *both* parties in drafting a separation agreement. The answer is that if there are *any* disputes between the parties regarding spousal or child support, child custody matters, division of the marital assets or the like, then an attorney *cannot* ethically draft a separation agreement for both parties.[106] However, if an attorney is able to maintain his or her neutrality in the matter, and the separation agreement is fair and equitable to both parties, then some courts have held that the separation agreement would not be invalid per se if the attorney who drafted the agreement represented both parties.[107]

Finally, a dilemma may arise if an attorney attempts to represent one spouse in negotiating a separation agreement, but the other spouse refuses to retain independent legal counsel to represent his or her interests. According to one state bar advisory opinion,[108] the attorney for the represented spouse has the following obligations: (1) advise the unrepresented spouse to secure independent counsel; (2) do not state or imply disinterest; (3) advise the unrepresented spouse that you represent the interests of your client only; and (4) advise the unrepresented spouse that his or her interests are, or may be, adverse to those of your client.[109]

[B]   Separation Agreements: Application of Principles

Separation agreements, like other contracts, require valid consideration in order to be enforceable.[110] The exchange of mutual promises, creating bilateral legal rights and obligations between the parties, will normally suffice as consideration for separation agreements.[111]

---

[105] *See, e.g.*, *Levine v. Levine*, 451 N.Y.S.2d 26 (N.Y. 1982); *McClellan v. McClellan*, 451 A.2d 334 (Md. Ct. Spec. App. 1982) *cert. denied*, 462 U.S. 1135 (1982); *Longstreet v. Longstreet*, 566 N.E.2d 708 (Ohio Ct. App. 1989); *see also* Lindey & Parley, *supra* note 15, at §§ 6.01-.06.

[106] *See, e.g.*, ABA Model Rules of Professional Conduct 1.7; ABA Code of Professional Responsibility Disciplinary Rule 5-105(C). *See generally infra* § 8.04.

[107] *See, e.g.*, *Perry v. Perry*, 406 N.Y.S.2d 551, 552 (N.Y. App. Div. 1978) ("While the practice of one attorney representing both parties in the preparation of a separation agreement has been criticized, we agree with the trial court that, in this instance, the attorney managed to preserve neutrality and that the agreement was arrived at fairly, without overreaching by either spouse. Furthermore, the substantive provisions of the agreement are, in toto, fair and equitable."); *accord Levine v. Levine*, 436 N.E.2d 476 (N.Y. 1982); *see also infra* §§ 8.04[A], 8.05.

[108] Va. State Bar Committee on Legal Ethics, Opinion No. 876, reprinted in 13 Fam. L. Rep. 1284 (1987).

[109] *Id.* It would also be a wise practice to give this advice to the unrepresented spouse orally *and* in writing, with a copy for the law office files. *See also Ayers v. Ayers*, 466 So. 2d 979 (Ala. Civ. App. 1985) (unrepresented wife held to the separation agreement drawn up by husband's attorney, which she read and which contained an acknowledgement that the attorney did not represent her).

[110] *See, e.g.*, *Baggs v. Anderson*, 528 P.2d 141 (Utah 1974); *Barnes v. Barnes*, 226 S.E.2d 549 (N.C. Ct. App. 1976).

[111] *See, e.g.*, *Sanchez v. Tilley*, 330 S.E.2d 319 (S.C. Ct. App. 1985); *B.T.L. v. H.A.L.*, 287 A.2d 413 (Del. 1972); *Capps v. Capps*, 219 S.E.2d 901 (Va. 1975).

Separation agreements are required to be in writing in most jurisdictions pursuant to state statutory authority,[112] but various courts have also upheld the enforceability of certain oral separation agreements under general principles of equity.[113] Because most separation agreements are in writing, extrinsic evidence of the parties' intent can only be offered if the agreement is ambiguous,[114] or if there is a mutual mistake of the parties that requires reformation of the contract.[115] The content of a separation agreement therefore is largely determined by the mutual intent of the parties, absent fraud, duress, designed concealment, overreaching, or unconscionability.[116]

Thus, a husband and wife may contractually agree in their separation agreement concerning the division — or waiver — of their respective property rights: whether real or personal, tangible or intangible, marital, community, or separate.[117] In the absence of such an agreement, however, the court would have to classify, value, and distribute the parties' property under applicable equitable distribution or community property statutes.[118]

Likewise, the parties may also contract in their separation agreement regarding the payment — or waiver — of spousal support obligations.[119] And again, in the absence of such an agreement, the court would have to determine any spousal support obligations on divorce under applicable state statutes.[120]

However, contractual provisions regarding child support and child custody are interpreted by the courts in a very different manner from spousal support provisions and from marital property provisions in separation agreements.

Based upon the *parens patriae* power of the state, any child custody or child support provision, and any other provision in a separation agreement affecting the child's welfare, is *always* subject to court review and subject to court modification based upon the child's best interests, despite any provision to the contrary that may exist in a separation agreement.[121]

---

[112] *See, e.g.*, Cal. Civ. Code § 4802; Conn. Gen. Stat. § 46b-66; N.Y. Dom. Rel. Law § 236(B)(3); Tex. Fam. Code § 3.631(a); Va. Code Ann. §§ 20-155, 20-149.

[113] *See, e.g., Richardson v. Richardson*, 392 S.E.2d 688 (Va. Ct. App. 1990); *Gangopadhyay v. Gangopadhyay*, 403 S.E.2d 712 (W. Va. 1991); *Kline v. Kline*, 284 N.W.2d 488 (Mich. Ct. App. 1979); *Kramer v. Kramer*, 339 A.2d 328 (Md. Ct. App. 1975). *But see Jones v. Jones*, 590 S.E.2d 308 (N.C. Ct. App. 2004) (holding that any modification of provisions in a separation agreement must be express and in writing; otherwise the original separation agreement provisions remain in effect and enforceable, because a valid separation agreement cannot be orally modified).

[114] *See, e.g., Lohmann v. Piczon*, 487 A.2d 1386 (Pa. Super. Ct. 1985); *Richheimer v. Richheimer*, 292 N.E.2d 190 (Ill. App. Ct. 1972).

[115] *See, e.g., In re Marriage of Deines*, 608 P.2d 375 (Colo. 1980).

[116] *See supra* § 4.05[A].

[117] *See generally* Lindey & Parley, *supra* note 39, at § 11.01-.63; Schlissel, *supra* note 87, at §§ 20.01-22.29.

[118] *See generally infra* Chapter 9.

[119] *See, e.g.*, Lindey & Parley, *supra* note 39, at § 15A.01-.08; Schlissel, *supra* note 87, at § 19.01-.35.

[120] *See generally infra* § 9.04.

[121] *See, e.g.*, Kan. Stat. Ann. § 60-1610(f) (separation agreements are not modifiable without the parties' consent, except for those provisions relating to children); Ky. Rev. Stat. Ann. § 403.180 (a

The parties' subsequent reconciliation may affect a prior separation agreement. In a majority of jurisdictions, the courts follow the general rule that a bona fide resumption of marital relations would terminate the executory provisions of a separation agreement, while all the executed provisions of a separation agreement would still remain valid.[122]

Although the theoretical underpinnings and practical techniques for drafting a separation agreement are beyond the scope of this treatise, there are a number of helpful resource books on the subject.[123]

---

separation agreement incorporated into a divorce decree is modifiable unless the parties state otherwise, excluding provisions relating to children which are always modifiable); Va. Code Ann. §§ 20-109.1, 20-108 (separation agreements are not modifiable unless the parties so stipulate, but child custody and child support provisions are always modifiable). *See generally* Schlissel, *supra* note 87, at §§ 12.01-12.16, 16.01-.13.

[122] *See, e.g.,* Stegall v. Stegall, 397 S.E.2d 306 (N.C. Ct. App. 1990); *Brazina v. Brazina,* 558 A.2d 69 (N.J. Super. Ct. 1989); *Kaminsky v. Kaminsky,* 364 S.E.2d 799 (W. Va. 1987); *see also Yeich v. Yeich,* 399 S.E.2d 170 (Va. Ct. App. 1990) (reconciliation abrogates the executory portions of a separation agreement, including the waiver of alimony). *But see Jennings v. Jennings,* 409 S.E.2d 8 (Va. Ct. App. 1991) (a separation agreement survived the parties' brief reconciliation); *Vaccarello v. Vaccarello,* 757 A.2d 909 (Pa. 2000) (holding that a subsequent reconciliation of the parties did not invalidate a separation or property settlement agreement that the parties had previously signed).

[123] See, for example, Lindey & Parley, *supra* note 39; Schlissel, *supra* note 87; Green & Long, *supra* note 3; J. Krauskopf, ed. Marital and Nonmarital Contracts (1979); and numerous state-oriented publications. *See also* 7 West's Legal Forms 2d 308-719. Separation agreements also appear in a number of reported cases, including *Greiner v. Greiner,* 399 N.E.2d 571 (Ohio Ct. App. 1979); *Roskein v. Roskein,* 96 A.2d 437 (N.J. Super. Ct. 1953).

Chapter 5

PROCREATION

§ 5.01 INTRODUCTION

The topics covered in this chapter address the legal issues of a fundamental aspect of family life: procreation.

In some areas of procreation, such as assisted conception, the scientific and medical technology and the corresponding legal response is constantly developing and evolving.[1] In other areas of this field, while the medical technology is relatively old, the legal issues involved, such as abortion[2] and contraception,[3] remain very controversial. Even in matters of paternity and legitimacy,[4] paternity testing now has a significant impact on the legal aspects of both proving paternity and providing support for nonmarital as well as marital children.

Although people have had the ability to prevent pregnancy and birth for hundreds of years, medical science has made quantum leaps in the efficacy and safety of these means. However, legal issues regarding contraception have led to the articulation of a fundamental right to privacy in matters of procreation that the Constitution does not specifically mention, but which has been judicially found to exist in the penumbra of other Constitutional rights.[5] In turn, this right of privacy serves as the original legal basis for a limited freedom of choice regarding abortion, an area that has led to one of the greatest political and moral controversies confronting our society today.[6]

Improved means of sterilization, such as vasectomy and tubal ligation via laparoscopy, have allowed individuals to have themselves voluntarily sterilized — and to seek the sterilization of others.[7] The eugenics movement, popular in the first half of the 20th century and fueled by various geneticists and social Darwinists, led to laws that permitted widespread sterilization of the mentally ill and mentally incapacitated. The vast majority of states have repealed these laws, and yet a new concern is rising for the right of incompetent people or their representatives to

---

[1] *See infra* § 5.07.

[2] *See infra* § 5.05.

[3] *See infra* § 5.04.

[4] *See infra* § 5.02.

[5] *See infra* § 5.04.

[6] *See infra* § 5.05.

[7] *See infra* § 5.06.

consent to sterilization.[8]

Assisted conception allows many people who might otherwise be unable to procreate to have children,[9] raising difficult legal issues of paternity and even maternity.[10] For example, what implications do such medical innovations have for inheritance rights or the Rule Against Perpetuities?

Other pressing legal problems arise with surrogate parenting when a couple contracts with a woman to carry a child to term.[11] Issues include whether the rights of the parents differ depending on which method of assisted conception is utilized, the extent of the rights of the surrogate mother (if any) if she decides not to relinquish the child, and whether such contracts should be enforced as written or should instead be prohibited by state law.

§ 5.02 PATERNITY AND LEGITIMACY

[A] Historical Background and Current Perspectives

Under English and American common law, children born out of wedlock have long been subject to different laws and different rights from "legitimate" children. Under the common law, for example, the "illegitimate" child was regarded as *filius nullius* — the son or daughter of no one. Such a child could therefore inherit from no one, and the common law did not impose upon the putative father any legal liability to support his offspring.[12] Indeed, William the Conqueror, who was formerly known as William the Bastard, might have conquered England in 1066, but under the law he had no rights of inheritance or support from either his father or his mother.[13]

In the United States, the laws governing illegitimacy, or bastardy as it was earlier called, generally followed the English common law. Thus, the historical treatment of nonmarital children in America was very harsh, without regard to the needs of the child, with the ultimate result of punishing the child. The rationale offered for such harsh treatment was to protect the exclusivity of the marital unit and to punish adults (particularly women) who engaged in sex outside of marriage.[14]

However, a series of United States Supreme Court decisions between 1968 and 1983 eliminated as unconstitutional most of the categorical legal distinctions between marital and nonmarital children; thus, through a combination of legislative

---

[8] *Id.*

[9] *See infra* § 5.07.

[10] *See generally* Judith Daar, Litowitz v. Litowitz: *Feuding over Frozen Embryos and Forecasting the Future of Reproductive Medicine, in* Health Law & Bioethics 97-119 (Sandra H. Johnson, Joan Krause, Richard Saver & Robin Fretwell Wilson, eds., 2009).

[11] *See infra* § 5.07.

[12] *See, e.g.*, 1 William Blackstone, Commentaries on the Law of England 433-34 (1898).

[13] *See, e.g.*, 2 James Kent, Commentaries on American Law 222 (8th ed. 1852).

[14] *See, e.g.*, Jana Singer, *The Privatization of Family Law*, 1992 Wis. L. Rev. 1443, 1447; Mary Becker, *The Rights of Unwed Parents: Feminist Approaches*, 63 Soc. Serv. Rev. 496 (1989).

enactments and judicial opinions in America, this harsh common law treatment of the nonmarital child has moderated considerably. First, all states have now enacted statutes providing specific support rights to the nonmarital child upon proof of paternity.[15] Second, in almost all states, children born of void or voidable marriages are now deemed to be legitimate by statute.[16] And third, a nonmarital child may now inherit from both parents once paternity has been clearly established.[17] Nevertheless, the legal rights of nonmarital children are not yet co-equal with those of marital children.

Finally, any discussion relating to illegitimacy and paternity matters must note the significant demographic changes in the United States. The rate of nonmarital births in the United States has steadily increased over the past 50 years, despite the greater availability of family planning information, contraceptive devices, and abortion. As of 2006, the total percentage of U.S. births to unwed mothers reached 38.5% and continues to climb, as Figure 5.1 shows.[18]

Figure 5.1

[15] See, for example, the Uniform Parentage Act, 9B U.L.A. 295 (2001) (Supp. 2000), which has been adopted, with modifications, in nine states: Alabama, Delaware, New Mexico, North Dakota, Oklahoma, Texas, Utah, Washington, and Wyoming. Twelve other states have adopted the original 1973 act, but have not adopted the most recent revision as of 2010: California, Colorado, Hawaii, Illinois, Kansas, Minnesota, Missouri, Montana, Nevada, New Jersey, Ohio, and Rhode Island. *See also infra* § 5.02[E]. *See generally* Harry D. Krause, Illegitimacy: Law and Social Policy 19-20 (1971).

[16] *See infra* § 5.02[C].

[17] *See infra* § 5.02[G]. The leading paternity treatise is Sidney B. Schatkin, Disputed Paternity Proceedings (2011).

[18] *See* Carmen Solomon-Fears, *Nonmarital Childbearing: Trends, Reasons, and Public Policy Interventions*, CRS Report for Congress, Nov. 20, 2008, at CRS-21.

The underlying reasons for this dramatic shift are undoubtedly complex. Still, it will be up to the legislator, the jurist, and the family law practitioner to ensure that the nonmarital child's best interests and welfare continue to be legally protected, and to ensure that the social stigma of illegitimacy, which has never been the fault of the child, will no longer continue to be reinforced by archaic legal precedent.

[B] The Presumption of Legitimacy

During the eighteenth and nineteenth century, a common law rule, labeled Lord Mansfield's presumption, was recognized throughout England and America. Under Lord Mansfield's presumption, the "invariable rule" was that "a child born in lawful wedlock is legitimate; unless a physical impossibility of procreation, or of access be proved, or there be strong evidence of non-access."[19] Thus, a child born in marriage is presumed to be the child of the mother's husband, absent extenuating circumstances.

The public policy behind Lord Mansfield's presumption, one of the strongest known in the law,[20] was to legally protect a recognized family and any children born into that family.[21] Accordingly, the burden of proof was on the party claiming that a particular child was nonmarital; but proving a husband's non-access to his wife was extremely difficult under the common law because, under Lord Mansfield's presumption, a wife could not testify to the non-access of her husband.[22] But currently, under the law of most states, a wife is now permitted to testify to the non-access of her husband and, in effect, bastardize her child.[23] Therefore, a moving party today may attempt to rebut this presumption of legitimacy through factors such as lack of access, unavailability, physical

---

[19] *See, e.g., Bowles v. Bingham*, 16 Va. (2 Munf.) 442, 445 (1811). Some courts, however, have held that this presumption could only be rebutted by proof that the mother's husband was impotent or that he was out of the country or "beyond the four seas." *See, e.g., In re Findlay*, 170 N.E. 471 (N.Y. 1930). *See generally* Harry D. Krause, Illegitimacy: Law and Social Policy 9-21 (1971).

[20] *See, e.g., Espree v. Guillory*, 753 S.W.2d 722, 724 (Tex. Civ. App. 1988) (the presumption of legitimacy is one of the strongest presumptions known to the law); *In re Estate of Robertson*, 520 So. 2d 99, 101 (Fla. Dist. Ct. App. 1988) (to overcome the very strong presumption that a child born in marriage is legitimate, the evidence must be clear, strong, and unequivocal).

[21] *See Goodright ex dem Stevens v. Moss*, 2 Cowp. 591, 98 Eng. Rep. 1257 (1777) (Mansfield, L.C.J.).

[22] *See id. at* 1258 ("[I]t is a rule, founded in decency, morality, and policy, that [the husband and wife] shall not be permitted to say after marriage, that they have had no connection, and therefore that the offspring is spurious; more especially the mother, who is the offending party."); *see also* Robert R. LaFortune, Comment, *The Mansfield Rule of Nonaccess*, 21 Wash. & Lee L. Rev. 146 (1964).

[23] However, even in jurisdictions that allow such testimony, the court may require corroborating testimony or other evidence. Schatkin, *supra* note 17, at § 1.06[2][a]. *See also B. v. O.*, 232 A.2d 401 (N.J. 1967); *Gibson v. Gibson*, 153 S.E.2d 189 (Va. 1967). Various courts, however, have held that a third-party putative father has no independent right to bring a paternity suit. *See, e.g., Espree v. Guillory*, 753 S.W.2d 722, 724 (Tex. Civ. App. 1988) ("The presumption of legitimacy of a child born during marriage is one of the strongest presumptions known to law," and "[u]nless the husband or wife deny the husband's paternity and seek and obtain a judgment nullifying the child's legitimate status, no one else may properly do so"). *But also see C.C. v. A.B.*, 550 N.E.2d 365, 370 (Mass. 1990) ("[T]here is no longer any need for a presumption of legitimacy" with regard to a child born to a married woman, and the putative father, who alleges he is the father of such a child, may prove paternity by clear and convincing evidence, instead of rebutting the presumption by proof beyond a reasonable doubt).

impossibility, and blood tests.[24] However, in *Cleo A. E. v. Rickie Gene E.*,[25] on an appeal by the Child Advocate Office, the Court of Appeals of West Virginia refused to allow a couple to stipulate in their divorce decree that one of the children born during marriage was not the child of the husband because the child's best interests would not be served.

In *Michael H. v. Gerald D.*,[26] the United States Supreme Court upheld a California statute that provided that the issue of "a wife cohabiting with her husband, who is not impotent or sterile, is conclusively presumed to be a child of the marriage."[27] The presumption could be rebutted by blood tests only if the husband made a motion within two years from the child's birth or, if the biological father had filed an affidavit acknowledging paternity, by the wife. In *Michael H.*, Carole D. gave birth to a child, Victoria, while she was married to Gerald D., who was listed as the father on the birth certificate and held Victoria out as his daughter. Shortly after the child's birth, Carole informed Michael H., a neighbor with whom she had conducted an adulterous affair, that he was the father. For a several year period during Victoria's first three years, Carole and the child lived with Michael and blood tests indicated a 98.07% probability that Michael was Victoria's father. Michael also held the child out as his own. After Carole parted with Michael, he filed a filiation action to establish his paternity and sought visitation with Victoria. Gerald, who had reconciled with Carole, intervened in the action, claiming, on the basis of the statutory conclusive presumption, that he was Victoria's father.

At the United States Supreme Court, Michael argued that his substantive due process rights were violated because he had established a parental relationship that constituted a constitutionally protected liberty interest. The Court rejected his argument, concluding instead that the marital family is the unit to be protected from claims of third parties, such as Michael, and that the California legislature was free to select that entity as the one to protect. In a persuasive dissent, Justice Brennan, joined by Justices Marshall and Blackmun, argued that the plurality opinion conflicted with the Court's earlier opinions that protected established parent-child relationships between unmarried fathers and their children.[28]

Because the Supreme Court merely upheld the then-existing conclusive statutory presumption of paternity, but did not mandate it, the majority of states have adopted a rebuttable presumption of paternity based on marriage.[29] However,

---

[24] *See, e.g., N.P.A. v. W.P.A.*, 380 S.E.2d 178 (Va. Ct. App. 1989) (the presumption of legitimacy was rebutted by wife's admission that she had sexual intercourse with another man, plus husband's evidence of an HLA human leukocyte antigen blood grouping test that conclusively disproved his paternity); *In re Smith*, 534 N.E.2d 669 (Ill. App. Ct. 1989) (the presumption of legitimacy was overcome by blood test evidence showing 99.99% probability that the putative father, and not the mother's husband, was the father of the child). *See generally* Schatkin, *supra* note 17.

[25] 438 S.E.2d 886 (W. Va. 1993).

[26] 491 U.S. 110 (1989).

[27] Cal. Evid. Code Ann. § 621(a) (West 1995), *repealed by* Cal. Fam. Code §§ 7540-41 (2004) (establishing rebuttable presumption).

[28] 491 U.S. at 136-157 (Brennan, J., dissenting).

[29] *See, e.g., In re Jesusa V.*, 85 P.3d 2 (Cal. 2004) (paternity assigned on basis of policy and logic, not

those states still face questions regarding the circumstances under which the presumption may be rebutted. Some states have required a putative father seeking to rebut the presumption to demonstrate that the best interests of the child would be served.[30] Some states have invalidated their statutes denying a putative father standing to challenge the paternity of the mother's husband.[31]

A number of jurisdictions have used equitable doctrines to deny husbands the right to contest paternity.[32] Courts have also applied equitable principles to prevent mothers from disproving their husbands' paternity.[33] A Michigan court, however, refused to allow a man who was an unmarried cohabitant for five years to rely on equitable doctrines to assert his paternity after the relationship terminated, although he alleged that he had cared for and supported the two children born during the cohabitation. The court held that the equitable doctrines of equitable parenthood and equitable estoppel only applied in the case of divorce, not to unmarried cohabitants, which would undermine the state's interest in promoting marriage.[34] Courts in several states have permitted presumed fathers to disestablish fatherhood upon presentation of genetic evidence.[35]

---

merely proof of biological paternity by competing presumed father, where mother's husband is presumed father); *Stubbs v. Colandrea*, 841 A.2d 361 (Md. Ct. Spec. App. 2004) (best interests of a child does not require genetic paternity testing when mother is married at time of child's birth); *In re Devon M.*, 801 N.E.2d 128 (Ill. App. Ct. 2003) (Uniform Parentage Act allows sanction for refusal to take paternity test only when best interest of child is served); *Witso v. Overby*, 627 N.W.2d 63 (Minn. 2001) (under the state's parentage statute, a man alleging to be the father of a child had a right to compel blood or genetic testing of the mother and child, despite the objection of the child's mother and her husband, the presumed father). The Kansas Supreme Court, in *In re Marriage of Phillips*, 58 P.3d 680 (Kan. 2002), held that the mother of two children born in marriage could not attack an order of joint custody on divorce on the ground that her husband was not the biological father of the children. The court held that in light of the husband's acknowledgment of paternity and his relationship and support of the children, their best interests would not be served by refuting his paternity, especially where there was no evidence of anyone else's paternity.

[30] *See, e.g., Weidenbacher v. Duclos*, 661 A.2d 988, 1000 (Conn. 1995); *In re Paternity of Adam*, 903 P.2d 207 (Mont. 1995), *cert. denied sub nom.* "Bob" v. "Mary," 517 U.S. 1156 (1996).

[31] *See, e.g., State ex rel. Roy Allen S. v. Stone*, 474 S.E.2d 554 (W.Va. 1996) (putative father had a constitutional right to challenge the paternity of the presumptive father, although the constitutional right was subject to waiver); *C.C. v. A.B.*, 550 N.E.2d 365 (Mass. 1990); *Callender v. Skiles*, 591 N.W. 2d 182 (Iowa 1999). *But see Markert v. Behm*, 394 N.W.2d 239 (Minn. Ct. App. 1986) (statute, which denied putative fathers standing to bring paternity actions, did not violate their rights to due process or equal protection; putative father's interest in establishing paternity was outweighed by the need to protect children from the harmful effects of paternity litigation).

[32] *See W. v. W.*, 779 A.2d 716 (Conn. 2001); *Smythe v. Worley*, 899 N.Y.S.2d 365 (N.Y. App. Div. 2010); *Ellison v. Lopez*, 959 A.2d 395 (Pa. Super. Ct. 2008).

[33] *See Fish v. Behers*, 741 A.2d 721 (Pa. 1999). *See generally* Mary R. Anderlik, *Disestablishment Suits; What Hath Science Wrought?*, 4 J. Center for Families, Child. & Cts. 3 (2003).

[34] *Van v. Zahorik*, 597 N.W.2d 15 (Mich. 1999). *See also Killingbeck v. Killingbeck*, 711 N.W.2d 759 (Mich. Ct. App. 2005). But see *In re Nicholas H.*, 46 P.3d 932 (Cal. 2002), in which the court held that the parental status of an unmarried man, who voluntarily took the child into his home and thus became a presumed father under the old UPA, could not be rebutted by biological evidence.

[35] *See In re Marriage of Kates*, 761 N.E.2d 153 (Ill. 2001); *In re M.M.*, 889 N.E.2d 846 (Ind. Ct. App. 2008). *See generally* Alan Stephens, *Admissibility or Compellability of Blood Test to Establish Testee's Nonpaternity for Purpose of Challenging Testee's Parental Rights*, 87 A.L.R.4th 572 (1991).

Although biological paternity alone is currently a sufficient ground for imposing a child support obligation, courts have been considerably more ambivalent about whether the *lack* of a biological connection necessarily precludes the imposition of a child support responsibility. For example, in *Pietros v. Pietros*,[36] the Supreme Court of Rhode Island held that a man who married his wife knowing that she was pregnant with another man's child, and assured her that he would treat the child as his own, was estopped from denying paternity during their subsequent divorce action.[37]

[C] Children of Void and Voidable Marriages

Under the common law, children of void or voidable marriages[38] were illegitimate and, once again, such nonmarital children were deprived of their legal rights due to the parents' unmarried status, rather than due to any wrongdoing on the part of the child.[39] In reaction to this very harsh common law rule, all states have now enacted laws providing that children of void or voidable marriages are legitimate by statute.[40]

These legitimization statutes are liberally construed for remedial purposes,[41] and they would therefore legitimize the children of invalid common law marriages[42] or void bigamous marriages.[43] Likewise, if a marriage were invalidated based upon the husband's insanity, the children of that marriage nevertheless would be marital children under the state statute.[44] However, most state legitimization statutes require a marriage of *some* kind, even though such a marriage is void or voidable. These statutes therefore cannot legitimize a child whose parents lived together in a cohabiting relationship without any pretense of a marriage of any kind.[45] A child

---

[36] 638 A.2d 545 (R.I. 1994).

[37] *See, e.g., Nygard v. Nygard*, 401 N.W.2d 323 (Mich. Ct. App. 1986) (husband held responsible for child support payments, even though child was not his, because wife informed husband of pregnancy and intent to give baby up for adoption before they married, husband asked wife to marry him and agreed to raise the child as his own, the marriage occurred before the child was born, and husband represented himself as the father to hospital personnel). *See generally* Schatkin, *supra* note 17, at § 3.16. The American Law Institute's *Principles of the Law of Family Dissolution* would create a category of persons entitled to full parental rights, known as Parents by Estoppel. *See* ALI *Principles of the Law of Family Dissolution* §§ 2.03, 3.03 (2002).

[38] *See supra* § 2.08[A].

[39] The legal rationale for this severe law was "whatever else depends on the void marriage is void also." 1 Joel Prentiss Bishop, Marriage, Divorce, and Separation 313 (1891).

[40] *See generally* 14 C.J.S. Children out of Wedlock § 2 (2011).

[41] *See, e.g., Kasey v. Richardson*, 462 F.2d 757 (4th Cir. 1972).

[42] *See, e.g., Murphy v. Holland*, 377 S.E.2d 363 (Va. 1989) (an invalid Virginia common law marriage nevertheless legitimized the parties' children under the state statute for inheritance purposes).

[43] *See, e.g., In re Marriage of Seaton*, 133 Cal. Rptr. 3d 50 (Cal. Ct. App. 2011) (children born during a bigamous marriage are considered legitimate even though the marriage was void from inception); *Rance v. Rance*, 587 N.E.2d 150 (Ind. Ct. App. 1992) (if a marriage is bigamous, the children of the marriage would still have the statutory means of obtaining child support).

[44] *See, e.g., Cornwall v. Cornwall*, 168 S.E. 439 (Va. 1933).

[45] *See, e.g., Kasey v. Richardson*, 462 F.2d 757 (4th Cir. 1972); *Grove v. Metropolitan Life Ins. Co.*, 271 F.2d 918 (4th Cir. 1959).

who is legitimized under such state statutes has all the rights of marital children including, but not limited to, inheritance rights, the right to participate under state wrongful death statutes, and the right to receive insurance proceeds.[46]

[D] Constitutional Protection of the Nonmarital Child

The legal status of the nonmarital child has been further normalized since 1968 by the United States Supreme Court, which brought many illegitimacy issues under the protection of federal constitutional law.

For example, in *Levy v. Louisiana,*[47] the Supreme Court held that it was unconstitutional for a state to create a cause of action in favor of a marital child for the wrongful death of a parent while excluding a nonmarital child from the same cause of action. The Court found that nonmarital children were clearly persons within the meaning of the Equal Protection Clause of the United States Constitution, and therefore it would be "invidious to discriminate against them when no action, conduct, or demeanor of theirs is possibly relevant to the harm that was done the mother."[48]

In *Weber v. Aetna Casualty & Surety Co.,*[49] the Supreme Court held that a nonmarital child could also recover under state worker's compensation laws. The Court again invalidated a classification that burdened the nonmarital child for the sake of punishing the illicit relationship of the parents because "visiting this condemnation on the head of an infant is illogical and unjust."[50]

In the seminal case of *Gomez v. Perez,*[51] the Supreme Court held that there was a constitutional duty of *both* parents to support a nonmarital child once paternity had been proved.[52] And in *Trimble v. Gordon,*[53] the Court held that a nonmarital child could inherit from the father as well as the mother once paternity had been proved.[54] Finally, in *Clark v. Jeter,*[55] the Court struck down a Pennsylvania statute limiting the time to bring a support action for nonmarital children to six years, because the statute did not withstand the heightened scrutiny test under the Equal Protection Clause when compared to support rights of marital children.[56]

---

[46] *See* Krause, *supra* note 15, at 11-13.

[47] 391 U.S. 68 (1968).

[48] *Id.* at 72. Although the *Levy* court purportedly applied a rational basis test, arguably today laws that discriminate against nonmarital children must now meet an intermediate scrutiny test. *See, e.g., Clark v. Jeter,* 486 U.S. 456 (1988); *infra* notes 55-56 (and accompanying text).

[49] 406 U.S. 164 (1972).

[50] *Id.* at 175.

[51] 409 U.S. 535 (1973).

[52] *See infra* § 5.02[E].

[53] 430 U.S. 762 (1977).

[54] *See infra* § 5.02[G].

[55] 486 U.S. 456 (1988).

[56] *Id.* A more recently enacted 18-year Pennsylvania statute of limitations for paternity and support actions would presumably withstand such heightened scrutiny since it puts support actions for both nonmarital and marital children on a more equal footing. *See* 23 Pa. Cons. Stat. § 4343(B) (2011).

These Supreme Court cases do not necessarily mean that *any* law that treats nonmarital children differently from marital children would be constitutionally invalid *per se.* For example, in the case of *Mathews v. Lucas,*[57] a Social Security requirement under applicable federal law[58] set out a two-prong test: dependent children could recover benefits only if: (1) they were marital or adopted children of the deceased; or (2) the children lived with the decedent and were dependents in the decedent's household at the time of his death. The nonmarital children of the decedent argued that the denial of benefits in this case violated constitutional due process and equal protection safeguards in that this federal law impermissibly discriminated against nonmarital children. The Supreme Court held otherwise and upheld the federal statute, on the grounds that the statute allowed nonmarital children the opportunity to prove their dependency, and this requirement was rationally related to the purpose of such a statute.[59]

In *Miller v. Allbright,*[60] the Supreme Court rejected an equal protection challenge to an immigration statute that imposed additional requirements for citizenship on nonmarital children born in another country, where the father, rather than the mother, was an American citizen. While nonmarital children born abroad to an American mother and a non-American father automatically acquired citizenship at birth, the child born to a non-American mother and an American father was required to provide formal proof of paternity before attaining the age of 18 in order to qualify for U.S. citizenship. The Court rejected the argument that the statute discriminated on the basis of sex, holding that the biological differences in proving relationship was a legitimate basis for the different rules.

Again, in *Nguyen v. Immigration & Naturalization Serv.,*[61] the Supreme Court upheld 8 U.S.C. § 1409, which imposes different requirements for a child obtaining citizenship based on whether the citizen parent is the mother or the father. The Court held the statute does not violate the Equal Protection Clause because the mother's parentage is clear, while the father's is susceptible to proof. Moreover, the child has a greater opportunity to develop a relationship with the mother: "Paternity can be established by taking DNA samples even from a few strands of hair, years after the birth. Yet scientific proof of biological paternity does nothing, by itself, to ensure contact between father and child during the child's minority."[62]

---

[57] 427 U.S. 495 (1976).

[58] 42 U.S.C. § 402(d)(1).

[59] 427 U.S. 495 (1976). *See also Prudential Ins. Co. v. Moorhead,* 730 F. Supp. 727 (M.D. La. 1989) (statute providing methods for determining inheritance rights of nonmarital children of servicemen was substantially related to important governmental interests of an orderly disposition of property and deterring spurious claims, and thus the statute did not deny due process to a nonmarital child of a serviceman who died before acknowledging paternity).

[60] 523 U.S. 420 (1998).

[61] 533 U.S. 53 (2001).

[62] *Id.* at 67. Before the Supreme Court's decision, at least one court had recognized that the statute discriminates against nonmarital children (as opposed to their parents) since marital children do not have to meet these requirements, regardless of the gender of the citizen parent. See *LeBrun v. Thornburgh,* 777 F. Supp. 1204, 1211 (D.N.J. 1991) ("The statute conditions the retention of citizenship upon an official act by the father of 'illegitimate' children. Courts have long recognized, however, that the rights of one cannot be made contingent upon the act of another."). *But see Catwell v. Attorney Gen. of*

[E] Paternity Grounds and Actions

One of the primary purposes of establishing paternity is to provide for the financial support of nonmarital children. Paternity and support actions can be brought either by the child's mother or by a social service agency. The federal government has required mothers to cooperate with state authorities in establishing paternity in order to obtain public assistance benefits under both the now-abolished Aid to Families with Dependent Children (AFDC) program and the more recent Temporary Assistance to Needy Families (TANF) program that replaced the AFDC program.[63] Although a narrow "good cause" exception exists,[64] primarily for domestic abuse cases, advocates for low-income women have criticized the scope and intrusiveness of the cooperation requirement.[65]

Defenses to paternity and support actions are limited. An unmarried father may not be relieved of his child support obligation because the child's mother became pregnant by deceiving him. In *Murphy v. Meyers*,[66] the Minnesota Court of Appeals denied a putative father's attempt to raise fraud and misrepresentation as affirmative defenses to a paternity and child support action. Although the defendant argued that the child's mother had deceived him by claiming she had been sterilized, the court held that "[t]he purpose of a paternity action is not to punish the father, but rather to impose a duty on the father to support the child, to ensure [that] the mother does not bear full financial responsibility for the child, and to protect the public by preventing the child from becoming a public charge."[67] The court noted that other states had unanimously barred fraud and misrepresentation defenses to such actions. Similarly, in *Matter of L. Pamela P. v. Frank S.*,[68] the court rejected the unwed father's argument that his constitutional right to decide whether to be a father was violated because the child's mother misrepresented to him that she was using birth control. The court held that the needs of the child and the means of the parents are the relevant factors in assigning child support, and noted that the father was not prevented from using contraception himself. However, actions by a nonmarital child against the father in tort or contract, based on breach of a promise to marry, have been unsuccessful. In *Zepeda v. Zepeda*,[69] the court rejected the child's suit, despite noting that the father's actions were morally wrong and perhaps criminally punishable. The court held that such a

---

U.S., 623 F.3d 199, 211 (3d Cir. 2010) (court rejects a challenge to 8 U.S.C. § 1432 based on discrimination against gender and legitimacy).

[63] *See* 42 U.S.C. § 654(29).

[64] 42 U.S.C. § 654(29); 45 C.F.R. § 264.30 (2011).

[65] *See, e.g.*, Lisa Kelly, *If Anybody Asks You Who I Am: An Outsider's Story of the Duty To Establish Paternity*, 3 Am. U. J. Gender & L. 247 (1995).

[66] 560 N.W.2d 752 (Minn. Ct. App. 1997). *See generally* Adrienne D. Gross, *A Man's Right to Choose: Searching for Remedies in the Face of Unplanned Fatherhood*, 55 Drake L. Rev. 1015 (2007); Christopher Bruno, *A Right to Decide Not to Be A Legal Father: Gonzales v. Carhart and the Acceptance of Emotional Harm as a Constitutionally Protected Interest*, 77 Geo. Wash. L. Rev. 141 (2008).

[67] *Id.* at 754 (quoting *Jevning v. Cichos*, 499 N.W.2d 515, 517 (Minn. Ct. App. 1993)).

[68] 451 N.Y.S.2d 766 (N.Y. App. Div. 1982).

[69] 190 N.E.2d 849 (Ill. App. Ct. 1963). *See also* Thomas A. Burns, *When Life Is an Injury: An Economic Approach to Wrongful Life Lawsuits*, 52 Duke L.J. 807 (2003); *infra* § 7.06.

sweeping change in the law was the function of the legislature.

The United States Supreme Court, in *Rivera v. Minnich*,[70] upheld the constitutionality of a preponderance of the evidence standard for determining paternity, distinguishing such actions from proceedings to terminate parental rights, which constitutionally require clear and convincing evidence.[71] A few states still require that paternity be proved by clear and convincing evidence standard, viewing such actions as quasi-criminal.[72]

[1] The Uniform Parentage Act

Under the early common law, a father did not have a legal obligation to support his nonmarital child.[73] However, since the U.S. Supreme Court case of *Gomez v. Perez*,[74] such support for a nonmarital child is now constitutionally mandated once paternity has been proven. Accordingly, in all fifty states today, fathers as well as mothers are compelled to support their nonmarital children under state statutory law.[75]

There is a wide diversity of state parentage statutes, and a detailed study of each state statute is beyond the scope of this treatise. Nevertheless, one of the most influential parentage statutes is the Uniform Parentage Act, originally promulgated in 1973,[76] revised in 2000, and amended in 2002.[77]

The 2002 Uniform Parentage Act, like its predecessors, sets out various methods for establishing the parent-child relationship[78] and provides that a child born to parents who are not married to each other has the same rights as a child of marriage.[79] It creates a presumption of paternity under a number of factual circumstances[80] which can be rebutted only under limited circumstances and within a two-year time period after the birth of the child.[81]

The 2002 Act also allows voluntary acknowledgment of paternity, correlated to the federal Personal Responsibility and Work Opportunity Reconciliation Act of 1996 (PRWORA), discussed *infra* § 9.06[G], and specifies a procedure for such

---

[70] 483 U.S. 574 (1987).

[71] *See Santosky v. Kramer*, 455 U.S. 745 (1982).

[72] *See, e.g., Cattaraugus County Dept. of Soc. Services on Behalf of Katrina M. v. Douglas K.*, 643 N.Y.S.2d 830 (N.Y. App. Div. 1996). Other states have required the higher standard in paternity determinations that take place after the alleged father's death. *See, e.g., Reid v. Flournoy*, 600 So. 2d 1024 (Ala. Civ. App. 1992); *Ross v. Moore*, 758 S.W. 2d 423 (Ark. Ct. App. 1988).

[73] *See, e.g., Allen v. Hunnicutt*, 52 S.E.2d 18 (N.C. 1949).

[74] 409 U.S. 535 (1973).

[75] *See, e.g.*, Krause, *supra* note 15, at 19-20. *See generally* 1 Homer Clark, Law of Domestic Relations 278-358 (2d ed. 1987).

[76] *See supra* note 15.

[77] Uniform Parentage Act, 9B U.L.A. 295 (2002). *See supra* note 15.

[78] *Id.* at § 201.

[79] *Id.* at § 202.

[80] *Id.* at § 204.

[81] *Id.* at § 607.

acknowledgment.[82] Further, the 2002 Act specifies the necessary correlation required to establish or rebut paternity via genetic testing, eliminating the clear and convincing evidence requirement of previous versions.[83]

[2] Jurisdictional Issues

Because a paternity proceeding is normally brought against a putative father for payment of child support, most cases hold that there must be personal jurisdiction over the defendant.[84] Jurisdiction in paternity proceedings may also be based upon a state long-arm statute;[85] and jurisdiction may also exist under the Uniform Interstate Family Support Act (UIFSA). The Uniform Parentage Act also provides that a person who has sexual intercourse within the state thereby submits to the jurisdiction of that state's courts with respect to a child who may have been conceived thereby.[86]

[3] Private Promises and Contracts

It is also important to note that even if a putative father has not been determined to be legally liable for the support of a nonmarital child under the Uniform Parentage Act[87] or a similar state paternity statute, he might still be legally liable for child support under the doctrine of equitable estoppel. For example, in *T. v. T.*,[88] an unwed pregnant woman relied on her boyfriend's oral promise that he would marry her and would support her child as though it were his own. Although this premarital promise to support the child was not in writing to comply with the state statute of frauds,[89] nevertheless the wife's detrimental reliance and partial performance on the husband's oral promise took his promise to support the child out of the

---

[82] *Id.* at Art. 3.

[83] *Id.* at § 201.

[84] *See, e.g., Schilz v. Superior Court*, 695 P.2d 1103 (Ariz. 1985) (personal jurisdiction required); *see also State ex rel. Karr v. Shorey*, 575 P.2d 981 (Or. 1978) (personal jurisdiction could also be based on an agreement acknowledging paternity and providing for the payment of child support).

[85] *See, e.g.*, Va. Code Ann. § 8.01-328.1(A)(8) (West 2011) (Virginia courts would have personal jurisdiction under the state long-arm statute over a defendant who conceived or fathered a child in Virginia); *see also Cochran v. Wallace*, 381 S.E.2d 853 (N.C. Ct. App. 1989) (state statute which subjects a person who participates in an act of sexual intercourse within the state to jurisdiction of the state courts in a paternity matter did not violate the Due Process Clause); *Barber v. Profit*, 576 So. 2d 1168 (La. Ct. App. 1991) (mother's allegation that a child was fathered by the putative father and the parties' stipulation that the child was conceived in the state were sufficient to establish minimum contacts necessary to assert personal jurisdiction pursuant to a state long-arm statute). *But see Garvey v. Mendenhall*, 404 S.E.2d 613 (Ga. Ct. App. 1991) (putative father did not "transact business" in Georgia so as to subject him to personal jurisdiction under the state long-arm statute in a paternity action by making social visits to Georgia); *Freethy v. Maconi*, 2000 Tenn. App. LEXIS 498 (July 31, 2000) (no personal jurisdiction over putative father who had visited Tennessee only once, ten years previously, and where paternity suit was totally unrelated to putative father's profession as a stockbroker licensed in Tennessee).

[86] Unif. Parentage Act § 604, 98 U.L.A. 295 (2002).

[87] *Id.*

[88] 224 S.E.2d 148 (Va. 1976).

[89] Va. Code Ann. § 11-2(5) (West 2011).

statute of frauds, and the husband was estopped to deny the promise.[90]

Likewise, according to the law of most states, if the putative father privately contracts to make child support payments in consideration of the mother's forbearance from bringing a paternity action against him, such a private contract would be legally binding upon the parties, assuming, of course, that the child support contractual provisions are reasonable and adequate.[91] The Uniform Parentage Act[92] also recognizes and authorizes these contracts. However, such a contract may not be enforceable if the consideration for the contract is based upon illicit sexual intercourse that is not severable from other valid consideration.[93] Further, the putative father does not necessarily insulate himself from actions for increased or additional child support by agreeing to a new level of payment or a lump-sum payout.[94]

[F] Scientific Testing in Paternity Proceedings

The development of increasingly sophisticated scientific testing has significantly enhanced the ability to determine paternity. Traditionally, medical or anthropological evidence relating to the alleged parentage of the child was based on tests performed by experts,[95] often involving an alleged family resemblance[96] or blood tests.[97] These tests generally could be used only to *disprove* paternity. In the 1980s, new types of blood and genetic testing, primarily human leukocyte antigen (HLA) typing, emerged, which could exclude more than 98 percent of the male population in most cases, so that the traditional limitations on scientific evidence began to erode.[98] New DNA tests make paternity testing even more accurate. Virtually all states now provide for the introduction of genetic and other blood test

---

[90] *T. v. T.*, 224 S.E.2d 148 (Va. 1976). *But see NPA v. WBA*, 380 S.E.2d 178, 182 (Va. Ct. App. 1989) (court did not allow estoppel because the husband had not knowingly misrepresented that he was the natural father). *See generally*, H. G. Hirschberg, *Liability of mother's husband, not the father of her illegitimate child, for its support*, 90 A.L.R.2d 583 (1963).

[91] *See, e.g., Peterson v. Eritsland*, 419 P.2d 332 (Wash. 1966); *Fiege v. Boehm*, 123 A.2d 316 (Md. 1956); *Haag v. Barnes*, 175 N.E.2d 441 (N.Y. 1961). The holding in *Haag v. Barnes*, however, has been criticized in Albert A. Ehrenzweig, *The Bastard in the Conflict of Laws*, 29 U. Chi. L. Rev. 498 (1962). *But also see Berryhill v. Rhodes*, 21 S.W.3d 188 (Tenn. 2000) (unwed parents' agreement on child support, which provided less support than required under Tennessee's statutory guidelines, violated public policy).

[92] *See supra* note 15.

[93] *See, e.g., Naimo v. La Fianza*, 369 A.2d 987 (N.J. Super. Ct. Ch. Div. 1976).

[94] *See W.S. v. X.Y.*, 676 A.2d 179 (N.J. Super. Ct. App. Div. 1996) (agreed support obligation modifiable on a showing of changed circumstances); *see also* Schatkin, *supra* note 17, at § 29.02[1].

[95] *See, e.g.*, Unif. Parentage Act § 12(4) (1973).

[96] *See, e.g.*, Judge Marvin C. Holz, *The Trial of a Paternity Case*, 50 Marq. L. Rev. 450, 489 (1966-67).

[97] *See, e.g.*, Krause, *Scientific Evidence and the Ascertainment of Paternity*, 5 Fam. L.Q. 252, 270-73 (1971).

[98] *See, e.g., In re the Paternity of J.L.K.*, 445 N.W.2d 673 (Wis. 1989) (results of "DNA fingerprinting" are admissible in a paternity proceeding under a state statute providing for the admission of blood test results and other statistical probabilities of an alleged father's paternity). For a comprehensive discussion of DNA testing in paternity matters, see Schatkin, *supra* note 17, at Chapter 13, *Scientific Aspects of DNA Testing. See also* Jane C. Murphy, *Legal Images of Fatherhood: Welfare Reform, Child Support Enforcement, and Fatherless Children*, 81 Notre Dame L. Rev. 325, n.42 (2005).

evidence for the purpose of affirmatively proving paternity, as well as for the purpose of excluding an alleged father.[99]

Briefly, the accuracy of DNA tests for paternity, called restriction enzyme fragment length polymorphisms, is much higher than HLA blood tests.[100] The major difference between DNA and HLA tests is that DNA tests actually pinpoint the father, while HLA tests involve an exclusion-by-probability method that is often complicated and cumbersome. The sample necessary for a DNA test is also smaller and easier to obtain and the results are much more accurate.[101]

Blood grouping tests have been admitted into evidence in all states to prove or disprove paternity.[102] There are two major blood grouping tests that may be used.[103] First, there is the traditional A, B, O, and AB blood grouping tests with their Rh and Hr factors, which examine red blood cell genetic markers.[104] These tests can establish *nonpaternity* by clear and convincing evidence, but cannot clearly establish paternity.[105]

Among blood grouping tests in paternity actions, the most accurate is the HLA blood grouping tests based upon tissue typing of white blood cells with a cumulative paternity exclusion rate exceeding 99 percent.[106] Moreover, the HLA blood grouping tests can establish a very high degree of probability of paternity inclusion, as well as nonpaternity exclusion.[107] There has been almost universal praise for the HLA paternity tests from state legislatures and courts, and there is also a strong trend toward the admissibility of HLA tests as inclusionary evidence, as well as exclusionary evidence.[108]

---

[99] *See* Schatkin, *supra* note 17, at Chapter 14, *Admissibility of DNA Testing in Individual States*.

[100] For a general discussion of the science underlying DNA and HLA testing, see Laura Gahn, *Genetic Marker Testing, in* Paternity and the Law of Parentage in Massachusetts (2009).

[101] For example, in one paternity case utilizing DNA testing, it was established that the putative father was the father of a nonmarital child by a ratio of 8,077,911 to 1, which would definitely constitute either clear and convincing scientific evidence of paternity or evidence of paternity beyond a reasonable doubt, under applicable state parentage statutes. *In re Baby Girl S.*, 532 N.Y.S.2d 634 (N.Y. Sur. Ct. 1988). *See generally* Murphy, *supra* note 95; Schatkin, *supra* note 17, at Chapter 13, *Scientific Aspects of DNA Testing*.

[102] *See, e.g.*, Unif. Parentage Act §§ 11, 12(3) (1973); Unif. Parentage Act §§ 503, 505 (2011).

[103] *Id. See also* John P. Ludington, *Admissibility and Weight of Blood-Grouping Tests in Disputed Paternity Cases*, 43 A.L.R. 4th 579 (2009).

[104] *See generally* Ludington, *supra* note 103, at § 2[a].

[105] *Id. See also* Schatkin, *supra* note 17, at Chapters 10–11.

[106] *See generally* Ludington, *supra* note 103. *See also* Schatkin, *supra* note 17, at § 3.08 ("HLA tests alone have an average power of exclusion of approximately 93 percent, and can exclude 99 percent of falsely accused men when combined with red cell antigen and/or serum protein testing.").

[107] *See, e.g.*, *Miller v. Kirshner*, 621 A.2d 1326 (Conn. 1993); *Denbow v. Harris*, 583 A.2d 205 (Me. 1990) (a blood test showing a 99.97 percent probability of paternity was admissible in a paternity action); *Braden v. Nash*, 550 So. 2d 866 (La. Ct. App. 1989) (expert testimony about blood test results was admissible even though the expert did not actually perform the tests, and a paternity index of 99.90 percent was sufficiently reliable to be used to support a finding of paternity). *See generally* Schatkin, *supra* note 17, at § 3.08.

[108] *See supra* note 104 (and accompanying text). HLA tests are currently admissible to determine paternity in a majority of jurisdictions. A growing number of states have changed their parentage laws

Despite the development of modern genetic and blood testing evidence, the statistical assumptions and scientific methodology used to assess and present this evidence have created a number of difficulties for the courts.[109] The Wisconsin case of *In re Paternity of M.J.B.*[110] illustrates some of these difficulties, holding that statistics regarding probability of paternity may be introduced only after competent evidence that sexual intercourse occurred between the parties during the period of conception. After explaining the statistical evidence, the court noted that although it is preferable to call an expert witness to explain or attack the tests, the statute does not require such testimony. Other jurisdictions employ various other approaches to the presentation of scientific evidence of paternity. For example, the Oregon Supreme Court held in *Plemel v. Walter*[111] that a range of calculations based on an array of probabilities should be presented, rather than a single figure estimating the probability of paternity.

"Genetic marker" or DNA testing now enables even more certain paternity testing. These tests are admissible in all states when performed by an accredited laboratory.[112] Because it involves many of the same statistical techniques as other types of paternity testing, it raises the same evidentiary concerns, although the fact that each individual's DNA is unique makes the evidence considerably more powerful.[113] Because DNA testing uses molecules that remain stable and testable even after a person's death, it has raised the possibility of accurate paternity testing long after a putative father has died[114] and a number of courts have granted requests for exhumation of bodies to perform DNA tests.[115] Further, comparing the DNA of a close relative of a deceased putative father can help establish paternity posthumously.[116]

---

to accept inclusionary evidence of paternity, as well as exclusionary evidence. *See generally* Jean E. Maess, *Admissibility, Weight and Sufficiency of Human Leukocyte Antigen (HLA) Tissue Typing Tests in Paternity Cases*, 37 A.L.R.4th 167 (2011); Schatkin, *supra* note 17, at § 3.08; S. Joel Kolko, *Admissibility of HLA Test Results to Determine Paternity*, 9 Fam. L. Rep. 4009 (1983). *But see* Schatkin, *supra* note 17, at § 11.06.

[109] *See* Michael I. Meyerson & William Meyerson, *Significant Statistics: The Unwitting Policy Making of Mathematically Ignorant Judges*, 37 Pepp. L. Rev. 771 (2010); Diane E. Hoffmann and Karen H. Rothenberg, *Judging Genes: Implications of the Second Generation of Genetic Tests in the Courtroom*, 66 Md. L. Rev. 858 (2007). *See generally* David L. Faigman, et al., 4 Mod. Sci. Evidence § 32:5 (2010-11).

[110] 425 N.W.2d 404 (Wis. 1988).

[111] 735 P.2d 1209 (Or. 1987).

[112] *See, e.g., Mastromatteo v. Harkins*, 615 A.2d 390 (Pa. Super. Ct. 1992); *Isabella County Dep't of Soc. Services v. Thompson*, 534 N.W.2d 132 (Mich. Ct. App. 1995); *Commonwealth ex rel. Overby v. Flaneary*, 469 S.E.2d 79 (Va. Ct. App. 1996).

[113] *See generally* Nina M. Vitek, Disputed Paternity Proceedings, §§ 13.01-.06 (2011).

[114] *See* Charles Nelson LeRay, *Implications of DNA Technology on Posthumous Paternity Determination: Deciding the Facts When Daddy Can't Give His Opinion*, 35 B.C. L. Rev. 747 (1994); Jill T. Phillips, Comment, *Who is My Daddy? Using DNA to Help Resolve Post-Death Paternity Cases*, 8 Alb. L.J. Sci. & Tech. 151 (1997).

[115] *See, e.g., Lach v. Welch*, 1997 Conn. Super. LEXIS 2218 (Aug. 8, 1997); *In re Estate of Rogers*, 583 A.2d 782 (N.J. Super. Ct. App. Div. 1990); *Batcheldor v. Boyd*, 423 S.E.2d 810 (N.C. Ct. App. 1992); *Wawrykow v. Simonich*, 652 A.2d 843 (Pa. Super. Ct. 1994).

[116] *See Sudwischer v. Estate of Hoffpauir*, 589 So. 2d 474 (La. 1991).

The federal government has become increasingly involved in establishing paternity. In 1993, Congress enacted legislation that requires states participating in federal income security programs to adopt rebuttable or conclusive presumptions of paternity upon genetic testing[117] and requires states to provide for genetic testing of all parties in contested paternity actions, upon the request of any party.[118] Federally funded child support enforcement agencies must also have the power to order genetic tests in appropriate contested cases[119] and certain genetic tests results must be admissible as evidence.[120] Further, states must establish and implement a simplified civil process for voluntary acknowledgment of paternity.[121]

Paternity judgments often raise difficult issues of res judicata, and statutes in a number of states authorize use of DNA testing to override other evidence in paternity cases.[122] One problem arises when an adjudicated father seeks to reopen a paternity judgment on the grounds that newly available scientific evidence demonstrates that he is not the child's biological father. The Court of Appeals of Maryland, Maryland's highest court, addressed that issue in *Tandra S. v. Tyrone W.*,[123] which consolidated two cases in which previously acknowledged and adjudicated paternity actions were challenged after blood tests excluded the paternity of the men. The court held that absent extrinsic fraud that would have prevented an adversarial trial, the paternity judgments were res judicata and could not be vacated. A strong dissent noted that paternity actions, unlike other civil suits, call upon the court to "declare a scientific, biological fact,"[124] which has continuing ramifications; thus, the majority holding "defies common sense."[125] Although the Maryland legislature later amended Maryland's paternity statutes to provide that a paternity declaration may be revised or modified upon scientific evidence,[126] the issue remains unresolved in many other jurisdictions.[127]

An additional issue arises when a child who was the subject of an unsuccessful paternity action later seeks to relitigate the paternity question. Another case from Maryland's highest court, *Jessica G. v. Hector M.*,[128] held that a nonmarital child

---

[117] 42 U.S.C. § 666(a)(5)(G).

[118] 42 U.S.C. § 666(a)(5)(B).

[119] 42 U.S.C. § 666(c)(1)(a).

[120] 42 U.S.C. § 666(a)(5)(F)(I).

[121] 42 U.S.C. § 666(a)(5).

[122] *See, e.g.*, Conn. Gen. Stat. § 46B-172(a)(1) (2011).

[123] 648 A.2d 439 (Md. 1994).

[124] *Id.* at 450.

[125] *Id.* at 452 (Elridge, J., dissenting (*quoting* Md. Ct. Spec. App. in unpublished decision of lower court)).

[126] Md. Fam. Law Code Ann. § 5-1038(a)(2) (2011).

[127] *See Cable v. Anthou*, 699 A.2d 722 (Pa. 1997) (putative fathers cannot be required to re-test for paternity if there is no evidence that prior test was flawed); *St. Ofc. of Child Supp. Enforcement v. Morgan*, 219 S.W.3d 175 (Ark. 2005) (upholding statute requiring state child support enforcement agency to make an adequate showing that an initial paternity test was untrustworthy or defective before ordering a second test).

[128] 653 A.2d 922 (Md.1995).

was not bound by a dismissal with prejudice of an earlier paternity action brought by her mother against the same defendant when blood tests had indicated a 99.97% probability of paternity. Noting the split of authority among state courts, the court held that, in light of the circumstances of this case, the state's strong public policy in according rights to nonmarital children, comparable to those afforded marital children, would be thwarted.[129]

[G] Inheritance Rights

Under the common law, a child born out of wedlock traditionally was not allowed to share in the estate of his or her putative father unless the putative father had included the nonmarital child in a testamentary document. Indeed, in 1971, one of the most important forms of discrimination against the nonmarital child — discrimination regarding the nonmarital child's rights of inheritance — was held *not* to violate the Equal Protection Clause of the United States Constitution in *Labine v. Vincent*.[130]

In *Labine*, the United States Supreme Court held that an acknowledged nonmarital child could not inherit anything from her father under Louisiana law, because where marital children's rights were "socially sanctioned and legally recognized," nonmarital children's relationships were characterized as "illicit and beyond the recognition of the law."[131] Various commentators have criticized the *Labine* decision as an illogical judicial step backward from *Levy v. Louisiana*,[132] on the basis that the Court in *Labine* once again punished the nonmarital child for the sins of the parents.[133]

Fortunately, the Supreme Court again revisited this inheritance rights issue regarding nonmarital children in the 1977 case of *Trimble v. Gordon*.[134] In *Trimble*, the Supreme Court invalidated an Illinois statute on equal protection grounds where the statute provided that an acknowledged nonmarital child could inherit only from his mother and not from his father, while a marital child could inherit from both parents.[135] Although *Trimble v. Gordon* did not expressly overrule *Labine v. Vincent*, it did seriously limit any subsequent application of *Labine*, especially when paternity has been established.[136]

---

[129] *Id.* at 929.

[130] 401 U.S. 532, *reh'g denied*, 402 U.S. 990 (1971).

[131] *Id.* at 538.

[132] 391 U.S. 68 (1968). *See also supra* Figure 5.1 (and accompanying text).

[133] *See, e.g.*, David Hallissey, Note, *Nonmaritals and Equal Protection*, 10 U. Mich. J.L. Ref. 543 (1977); Solangel Maldonado, *Illegitimate Harm: Law, Stigma, and Discrimination Against Nonmarital Children*, 63 Fla. L. Rev. 345 (2011).

[134] 430 U.S. 762 (1977).

[135] *Id.*

[136] Professor Clark believes that *Labine* should be taken as being substantially limited, if not overruled; and the most plausible view of these two cases is that state inheritance rights *may* pass muster if they bar the nonmarital child's inheritance only from and through the father, and then only in those cases in which paternity is in doubt. 1 Clark, Law of Domestic Relations 290 (2d ed. 1987).

However, it is also important to note that the courts have usually upheld state statutes that impose reasonable prerequisites upon a nonmarital child's inheritance rights. The rationale is that because there are no vested rights to succession, a nonmarital child would be subject to reasonable limitations and conditions to such an inheritance as the state legislature may prescribe.

For example, in *Lalli v. Lalli*,[137] the United States Supreme Court upheld the constitutionality of a New York intestate succession statute that allowed a nonmarital child to inherit only if the father's paternity had been established in court. The Supreme Court conceded in *Lalli* that such a statute might be unfair to a nonmarital child who can produce ample evidence of his or her paternity, but has never had the paternity issue formally adjudicated in court. Nevertheless, the statute was held to be constitutional since it was substantially related to the important state interest of providing for a just and orderly disposition of property at death, and therefore did not violate the Equal Protection Clause.[138]

The Supreme Court extended this rationale in *Parham v. Hughes*,[139] when it upheld a Georgia statute that precluded a father who had not legitimated a child from maintaining a wrongful death action arising from the child's death. It concluded that the statute did not invidiously discriminate against men as a class, although mothers did not need to prove maternity. Further, the Court found that the state's "interest in avoiding fraudulent claims of paternity in order to maintain a fair and orderly system of [a] decedent's property disposition" under its wrongful death statute was similar to its legitimate interest in probate actions.[140] However, the Georgia Supreme Court later invalidated, on Equal Protection grounds, Georgia's statute that prevented fathers of nonmarital children from inheriting from their children if they did not treat the child as their own or failed to support the child.[141]

The United States Court of Appeals for the Seventh Circuit held, in *Bennemon v. Sullivan*,[142] that a nonmarital child is eligible for Social Security benefits on account of a deceased parent only if state law so provides, if a written acknowledgment of paternity had been executed, or if a determination by the Social Security Administration indicates that the deceased parent was living with the child at the time of death or was contributing regular and substantial support

---

[137] 439 U.S. 259 (1978).

[138] *Id.* at 275. *See also Estate of McCullough v. Yates*, 32 So. 3d 403 (Miss. 2010) (statute conditioning inheritance rights for a nonmarital child on a prior paternity or legitimacy adjudication, or upon the parents' post-natal marriage, served legitimate state interests and therefore met the constitutional standards of *Trimble v. Gordon*); *In re Estate of Murcury*, 868 A.2d 680 (Vt. 2004) (statute requiring a nonmarital child seeking inheritance from his putative father to establish paternity and file a motion for genetic testing before the child turned 21 did not discriminate against nonmarital children in violation of the constitutional standards expressed in *Trimble v. Gordon*).

[139] 441 U.S. 347 (1979).

[140] *Id.* at 357. Georgia subsequently amended its inheritance statutes to provide additional methods for an unmarried father to establish paternity and become eligible to inherit from his nonmarital child. *See* Ga. Code Ann. § 53-2-4(b) (2011).

[141] *Rainey v. Chever*, 510 S.E.2d 823 (Ga.), *cert. denied*, 527 U.S. 1044 (1999).

[142] 914 F.2d 987 (7th Cir. 1990).

to the child. In *Bennemon*, the child's parents, George Williams and Betty Bennemon, had met one year before Williams's death, during which time Bennemon became pregnant. Testimony from friends stated that the couple was in love and that Williams was excited about becoming a father. Although the two lived separately, Williams subscribed to electrical and telephone service on Bennemon's behalf as she had a bad credit record. While Bennemon was pregnant, Williams was killed. He had never been declared a parent, and the court held that his contribution to the utility payments was insufficient to constitute regular and substantial support. Therefore, the child was denied survivorship benefits.

[H]   Artificial Insemination

Artificial insemination, where a physician artificially inseminates a woman, often with the consent of her husband if she is married, with semen provided by a third-party donor, is a widely accepted means of assisted conception.[143] This topic is dealt with in greater detail in § 5.07[A]. In the absence of a statute, the resulting child would not be the marital issue of the husband, and the husband might therefore argue that the child was nonmarital and that he had no legal obligation to support the child. In such cases, however, whether the child is deemed to be marital or nonmarital, if the husband consented to the artificial insemination, he is normally estopped to deny his support obligations to the child.[144]

Accordingly, a majority of states have now enacted statutes dealing with children born as a result of artificial insemination.[145] These statutes generally provide that any child born to a married woman who was conceived by means of artificial insemination performed by a licensed physician, and with the written consent of the husband, shall be presumed for all purposes to be the marital

---

[143] Normally, state statutes generally exclude the anonymous semen donor from any legal rights or obligations with respect to the resulting child. *See generally*, Michael J. Yaworsky, *Rights and Obligations Resulting from Human Artificial Insemination*, 83 A.L.R.4th 295, § 2[a] (2011). However, a known semen donor may have additional legal rights and obligations to the child if that was the original intent of the parties. *See, e.g., McIntyre v. Crouch*, 780 P.2d 239 (Or. Ct. App. 1989) (a state statute excluding semen donors from parenting rights and obligations would violate a semen donor's constitutional due process rights if he could establish that he and the mother agreed that he should have such rights and responsibilities of fatherhood); *J.R. v. E.C.*, 775 P.2d 27 (Colo. 1989) (state statute providing that semen donors do not have parental rights does not apply when a known semen donor and an unmarried recipient agree that the donor will be treated as the father of the child); *see also infra* note 469.

[144] *See, e.g., Levin v. Levin*, 645 N.E.2d 601 (Ind. 1994) (former husband estopped from denying support obligations where he encouraged wife to attempt artificial insemination, consented both orally and in writing to the procedure, allowed himself to be listed as the father on the birth certificate, held child out as his own during and after the marriage, and had previously paid support after divorce); *Gursky v. Gursky*, 242 N.Y.S. 2d 406 (Sup. Ct. 1963); *People v. Sorensen*, 437 P.2d 495 (Cal. 1968); *L.M.S. v. S.L.S.*, 312 N.W.2d 853 (Wis. Ct. App. 1981).

[145] *See, e.g.*, Cal. Fam. Code § 7613 (West 2011), amended by 2011 Cal. Legis. Serv. Ch. 185 (A.B. 1349) (West 2011); Unif. Parentage Act art. 7 (2000); *see also Changing Realities of Parenthood: The Law's Response to the Evolving American Family and Emerging Reproductive Technologies*, 116 Harv. L. Rev. 2052 (2003); Alexander N. Hecht, Comment and Note, *The Wild Wild West: Inadequate Regulation of Assisted Reproductive Technology*, 1 Hous. J. Health L. & Pol'y 227 (2001). A majority of these statutes, however, do not address the legal status of children born by artificial insemination to unmarried mothers. *See also* Yaworsky, *supra* note 143.

natural child of such husband and wife.[146]

Some courts have held that even when the husband's written consent to artificial insemination is statutorily required, the failure to obtain such written consent does not relieve the husband of the responsibilities of parentage. Therefore, the husband's consent to his wife's impregnation by artificial insemination may be express, or it may be implied from conduct that evidences his knowledge of the artificial insemination procedure and his failure to object.[147]

[I]   Custody Issues

Historically, custody of a nonmarital child was always awarded to the mother. In part this was due to an historical lack of interest on the part of the putative father, and in part to traditional social and moral values that precluded an unwed father from any custodial rights or obligations.

However, an unwed father's custodial right to his nonmarital child began to be recognized in a constitutional sense beginning in 1972 with *Stanley v. Illinois.*[148] In *Stanley*, the United States Supreme Court held that an unwed father could not be deprived of the opportunity to demonstrate his fitness to have custody of his nonmarital children without a due process hearing.

In 1978 in *Quilloin v. Walcott*,[149] the Supreme Court held that a putative father who, for eleven years, had not attempted to establish any relationship with his nonmarital child, could not thereafter exercise any veto power over the child's subsequent adoption by the mother's husband. The test in this case was the best interests of the child, rather than parental fitness.

A year later, in 1979, in *Caban v. Mohammed*,[150] the Court held a New York statute invalid on equal protection grounds because it precluded an unwed father from adopting his own nonmarital children, or from vetoing the adoption of his nonmarital children by a third party. The Court reaffirmed that there must be an ongoing relationship between the unwed father and the nonmarital child in order for the father to exercise his adoption or veto rights.[151]

Finally, in *Lehr v. Robertson*,[152] the Court held that there is a finite time during which the putative father must establish an "opportunity interest" in his

---

[146] *Id.* Many of these state artificial insemination statutes were expanded to cover children conceived by other assisted reproductive technologies. *See, e.g.*, Va. Code Ann. § 20-156 (2011). *See generally infra* § 5.07.

[147] *See, e.g., In re Baby Doe*, 353 S.E.2d 877 (S.C. 1987); *R.S. v. R.S.*, 670 P.2d 923 (Kan. Ct. App. 1983). *But see K.B. v. N.B.*, 811 S.W.2d 634 (Tex. Ct. App. 1991) (husband's oral consent to artificial insemination performed on his wife did not estop him from relying on a state statute requiring that such consent be in writing).

[148] 405 U.S. 645 (1972).

[149] 434 U.S. 246 (1978).

[150] 441 U.S. 380 (1979).

[151] *Id.* This ongoing relationship has been held to constitute an "opportunity interest" of the putative father in the nonmarital child.

[152] 463 U.S. 248 (1983).

nonmarital child. If he fails to establish this interest before a third party begins to legalize a new father-child relationship, then the putative father may lose any legal rights he may have in his nonmarital child.[153]

Lehr appears to mean that the biological relationship only gives the father an opportunity to obtain a constitutionally protected right, but does not address what the biological father must do to exercise that opportunity. The Supreme Court of California, in *In re Adoption of Kelsey S.*,[154] held that a father of a nonmarital child may not constitutionally be denied the right to withhold his consent to his child's adoption when he has not been shown to be unfit. In that case, the petitioner had attempted to establish a relationship and obtain custody of the child, but had been thwarted by the mother, who wanted to place the child for adoption. The court held that the California Code did not anticipate such "constructive" receiving of the child into his home to satisfy the statutory basis for the father's attaining the status of a "presumed father."[155] However, it concluded that there was no substantial relationship between the state's interest in protecting a child and allowing the mother sole control over the child's placement and denying the father the same right; therefore the father's constitutional rights to due process and equal protection were violated. It advised that courts should consider all the factors, including "[t]he father's conduct both *before and after* the child's birth,"[156] in assuming parental responsibilities, and emphasized that only fathers who have "sufficiently and timely demonstrated a full commitment to his parental responsibilities"[157] will be granted the power to veto an adoption. That same court, in *In re Adoption of Michael H.*,[158] denied the right to withhold consent to adoption of an unwed father who had initially agreed with the child's mother to place the child for adoption, and assisted in the arrangements, but changed his mind after the child was born and had been placed with the adoptive parents for several weeks.

These cases still do not resolve the unanswered question of *Lehr*, regarding the rights of an unwed father who is denied an opportunity, through no fault of his own, to develop a relationship with his child. Thus, according to the facts of a particular case, an unwed putative father may or may not be awarded custody or visitation rights of his nonmarital child based upon the best interests of the child.[159]

---

[153] *Id. See also Adoption of G*, 529 A.2d 809 (Me. 1987); *In re Adoption of Stawser*, 522 N.E.2d 1105 (Ohio Ct. App. 1987).

[154] 823 P.2d 1216 (Cal. 1992).

[155] *Id.* at 1223; Cal. Fam. § 8600 (West 2011).

[156] *Id.* at 1236. (emphasis in original).

[157] *Id.*

[158] 898 P.2d 891 (Cal. 1995).

[159] *See generally* Anthony Miller, *The Case for the Genetic Parent: Stanley, Quilloin, Caban, Lehr, and Michael H. Revisited*, 53 Loy. L. Rev. 395 (2007); William Weston, *Putative Father's Right to Custody: A Rocky Road at Best*, 10 Whittier L. Rev. 683 (1989); Daniel C. Zinman, *Father Knows Best: The Unwed Father's Right to Raise his Infant Surrendered for Adoption*, 60 Fordham L. Rev. 971 (1992); Kara L. Boucher & Ruthann M. Macolini, *The Parental Rights of Unwed Fathers: A Developmental Perspective*, 20 N.C. Cent. L.J. 45 (1992).

[J] Claims and Defenses in Paternity Actions

Numerous courts have held, under the doctrine of res judicata, that a final judgment in a paternity matter is generally conclusive on the same parties, and relating to the same issues, in a subsequent paternity proceeding.[160] However, various courts have also held that this res judicata defense as to the mother's and father's interests will not necessarily bar a subsequent action based upon the *child's* interests, since these interests are not necessarily the same.[161]

A statute of limitations in paternity proceedings may also be an issue, since in the past a number of state courts have held that a paternity action may be barred for failure to comply with a state's statute of limitations in bringing such an action.[162] However, state statutes of limitations applied to paternity actions have come under constitutional attack for invidiously discriminating against nonmarital children for the purpose of establishing support or inheritance rights, when no such statute of limitations was applicable in a support or inheritance action for marital children.[163] In *Opinion of the Justices (Supreme Court of New Hampshire)*,[164] the Supreme Court of New Hampshire responded to an inquiry from the state senate regarding a proposed law that would allow child support proceedings when the previous statute of limitations had run. The court answered that the previous one and two year statutes of limitations violated equal protection and that the mere running of that period would not give putative fathers a vested right to assert limitations as a defense to paternity actions. However, where a putative father had already obtained a judgment based on the running of the statute of limitation, res judicata would prevent the state from litigating paternity. The 1984 federal Child Support Enforcement Amendments require states to adopt

---

[160] *See, e.g., Espree v. Guillory*, 753 S.W.2d 722 (Tex. Civ. App. 1988) (a final divorce decree declaring the husband to be the child's father was res judicata on the legal issue); *In re T.S.S.*, 61 S.W.3d 481 (Tex. App. 2001) (final trial court judgment in divorce decree, finding that child was born to the marriage, is equivalent to finding that husband is the father; thus collateral estoppel bars a subsequent paternity suit); *see also State ex rel. Daniels v. Daniels*, 817 P.2d 632 (Colo. Ct. App. 1991) (former husband's failure to raise a defense of nonpaternity during a divorce proceeding in which child support orders were issued barred him from collaterally attacking the determination of paternity which implicitly supported the award of child support incident to that proceeding); *Camps v. Dep't of Health*, 459 So. 2d 1140 (Fla. Dist. Ct. App. 1984); *State ex rel. Partlow v. Law*, 692 P.2d 863 (Wash. Ct. App. 1984).

[161] *See, e.g., In the Matter of the Paternity of SDM*, 882 P.2d 1217, 1225 (Wyo. 1994) (minor child had separate and independent cause of action to initiate a paternity proceeding and was not foreclosed by the application of res judicata, collateral estoppel, judicial estoppel, or laches); *In re State, Div. of Child Support Enforcement, ex rel. NDB*, 2001 WY 118, 35 P.3d 1224 (Wyo. 2001) (absent a prior proceeding to which the child was a party, res judicata, collateral estoppel, judicial estoppel, and laches did not apply to the current proceeding determining paternity of the child) *See generally* Mary R. Anderlik, *Disestablishment Suits: What Hath Science Wrought?*, 4 J. Center for Families, Child. & Cts. 3 (2003).

[162] *See, e.g., Anderson v. Sheffield*, 455 A.2d 63 (Md. Ct. Spec. App. 1983); *Locke v. Zollicoffer*, 608 S.W.2d 54 (Ky. 1980). *See generally* Robert A. Brazener, *Statute of limitations in illegitimacy or bastardy proceedings*, 59 A.L.R.3d 685 (Originally published in 1974).

[163] *See, e.g., Clark v. Jeter*, 486 U.S. 456 (1988) (invalidating a six-year Pennsylvania statute of limitations for paternity actions, and noting that Pennsylvania has now passed a new eighteen-year statute of limitations for such actions); *see also Abrams v. Wheeler*, 468 So. 2d 126 (Ala. 1985); *Dornfeld v. Julian*, 472 N.E.2d 431 (Ill. 1984).

[164] 558 A.2d 454 (N.H. 1989).

18-year statutes of limitations for paternity cases.[165]

The courts are also sharply divided on the issue of whether an indigent defendant in a paternity proceeding is entitled to the assistance of legal counsel at state expense. Some courts have held that the indigent putative father is *not* entitled to legal counsel at the state's expense.[166] The better reasoned view, however, is that fundamental fairness in such an important family law matter requires that an indigent defendant in a paternity proceeding should be provided with legal counsel at the state's expense, because a paternity action is quasi-criminal in nature and can result in consequences of great magnitude.[167]

The United States Supreme Court has held, in *Little v. Streater*,[168] that a Connecticut statute that required anyone seeking a blood test to pay for the test, regardless of indigency, was an unconstitutional denial of due process. The court concluded that because the mother may establish a prima facie showing of paternity based solely on her testimony, and because the father's testimony alone is insufficient to refute her testimony, a father who was indigent and incarcerated at the time of the action had a right to blood testing regardless of his inability to pay under Connecticut's statute, which had "quasi-criminal overtones," since a blood test would provide "exculpatory evidence."[169]

A common law defense frequently used by putative fathers in a paternity action is called *exceptio plurium concubentium*, or the multiple intercourse defense. In order to assert this defense, the alleged putative father must produce evidence that the mother had sexual intercourse during the period of conception with a man or men other than himself. The mother then has the burden of proof to show that only the alleged father could be the biological father of her child.[170]

The multiple intercourse defense, however, has fallen into some disuse, not only due to scientific evidence rebutting this defense, but also due to the increasing

---

[165] 42 U.S.C.A. § 666(a)(5)(A) (2007). As of 2006, one court reported that Maryland and "fourteen States have statutes requiring that a paternity action filed by a parent be brought before the child's eighteenth birthday. Eighteen other States have limitations periods that extend for some relatively brief fixed period beyond majority, but are not open-ended. Sixteen States have no specific time limitations in their paternity statutes . . . although in five of them (Delaware, North Dakota, Texas, Utah, and Wyoming) only the child may bring a paternity action after reaching the age of majority. Thus, in 37 States, there is no open-ended ability for a parent . . . to bring a paternity action on her own behalf." *Trembow v. Schonfeld*, 901 A.2d 825, 835 (Md. 2006) (Footnotes omitted).

[166] *See, e.g., Franks v. Mercer*, 401 So. 2dd 470 (La. Ct. App. 1981); *Tidwell v. Booker*, 225 S.E.2d 816 (N.C. 1976); *State v. Walker*, 553 P.2d 1093 (Wash. 1976).

[167] *See, e.g., Dinkins v. Pearson*, 2008 Conn. Super. LEXIS 1771 (Conn. Sup. Ct. July 10, 2008); *Pruitt v. Pruitt*, 282 N.W.2d 785 (Mich. Ct. App. 1979); *see also Gardner v. Gardner*, 538 A.2d 4 (Pa. Super. Ct. 1988) (only when there is a trial on a disputed issue of paternity is an indigent putative father entitled to legal counsel).

[168] 452 U.S. 1, 9 (1981).

[169] *Id.* at 6, 9. The United States Supreme Court has also held that a state statute that allows establishment of paternity under a preponderance of the evidence standard affords sufficient due process to a putative father. *Rivera v. Minnich*, 483 U.S. 574 (1987).

[170] *See Yarmark v. Strickland*, 193 So. 2d 212 (Fla. Ct. App. 1966); *see also* E. Donald Shapiro & Stewart Reifler, *The DNA Paternity Test: Legislating the Future Paternity Action*, 7 J. L. & Health 1, 13 (1992-93).

reluctance of other men to testify concerning their sexual activities with the mother that may make them equally liable in a paternity suit themselves, or open themselves to criminal prosecution under state fornication or adultery statutes.[171]

Although a paternity action is usually brought against an unwed putative parent, such an action may also be brought as part of a divorce, legal separation, or annulment action. Finally, in the past, the cases were almost unanimous that the death of a putative father normally precludes any paternity or child support action, although a number of more recent decisions have allowed paternity to be proven posthumously.[172]

§ 5.03 PROCREATION AND SEXUAL LIBERTY

The importance of the family in American society has led the United States Supreme Court to acknowledge a number of individual rights involving procreation and sexual liberty. Because the United States Constitution does not specifically address a right to family privacy or personal autonomy regarding an individual's decision whether to have children, the sources of these personal rights are controversial. While some justices see personal rights secured solely by the Due Process Clause, others have found a right to privacy existing by implication from other Constitutional rights. However grounded, the limited freedom of choice with respect to contraception, voluntary sterilization, abortion, and assisted conception are areas that continue to generate political and moral disputes.

[A] The Right to Procreate

The recognition of a fundamental right to procreate originated largely from a line of United States Supreme Court cases relating to parents' rights in raising their children. In 1923, the Supreme Court addressed parental decision-making regarding their children's education in *Meyer v. State of Nebraska.*[173] In *Meyer*, the Court struck down a Nebraska statute that prohibited instruction in certain foreign languages in private schools on the basis that the restriction materially interfered with the power of parents to control the education of their children, as well as with the opportunity of children to acquire knowledge. It found a liberty interest protected by the Fourteenth Amendment that encompasses the right "to marry, establish a home and bring up children."[174]

Two years later, in *Pierce v. Society of Sisters,*[175] the Court held that a state could not require children to attend public, rather than private, schools, finding no reasonable relationship between the statute and a legitimate state purpose. The Court again spoke in broad terms of "the liberty of parents and guardians to direct

---

[171] *See* Shapiro & Reifler, *supra* note 170.

[172] *See, e.g. Harris v. Stewart*, 981 S.W.2d 122 (Ky. Ct. App. 1998); *In re Estate of Wilkins*, 707 N.Y.S.2d 774 (N.Y. Surr. 2000).

[173] 262 U.S. 390 (1923).

[174] *Id.* at 399.

[175] 268 U.S. 510 (1925).

the upbringing and education of children under their control."[176]

When the Court struck down a statute providing for the compulsory sterilization of certain criminals in *Skinner v. Oklahoma*,[177] it expanded the concepts of constitutional protection of families to include marriage and procreation as "fundamental to the very existence and survival of the race" and "involv[ing] one of the basic civil rights of man."[178] The Court later concluded, in *Stanley v. Illinois*,[179] that equal protection principles demanded that an unmarried father could not be deprived of custody of his children with whom he had lived after the mother's death without a showing of unfitness. The Court declared, "The private interest here, that of a man in the children he has sired and raised, undeniably warrants deference and, absent a powerful countervailing interest, protection."[180] Thus, family life and procreation have been recognized as liberties protected by the Due Process Clause of the Fourteenth Amendment.[181]

While on occasion the Court has expanded the concept of family rights to include extended families,[182] its decisions deal primarily with family and procreative rights in the context of marriage and the traditional family. Some states continue to maintain cohabitation statutes that may restrict the rights of single persons.[183]

[B] The Right to Sexual Liberty

Bowers v. Hardwick,[184] decided by the Supreme Court in 1986, for a time delineated the limits of the right of privacy. In *Bowers*, the Court held that the right of privacy did not invalidate state criminal statutes prohibiting sodomy. The Court reasoned that none of the cases dealing with family relationships, procreation, marriage, contraception, and abortion

> bears any resemblance to the claimed constitutional right of homosexuals to engage in acts of sodomy that is asserted in this case. No connection between family, marriage, or procreation on the one hand and homosexual activity on the other has been demonstrated. Moreover, any claim that

---

[176] *Id.* at 534-35.

[177] 316 U.S. 535 (1942). *See also infra* § 5.05[B]. For a rich account of the *Skinner* case, see Victoria F. Nourse, In Reckless Hands (2008).

[178] 316 U.S. at 541.

[179] 405 U.S. 645 (1972).

[180] *Id.* at 651.

[181] *See also Cleveland Bd. of Educ. v. LaFleur*, 414 U.S. 632 (1974); *Wisconsin v. Yoder*, 406 U.S. 205 (1972) (parents' fundamental interest in guiding the religious future and education of their children overrides interest of state in compulsory school attendance).

[182] *See Moore v. City of East Cleveland*, 431 U.S. 494 (1977).

[183] *See, e.g.*, Mich. Comp. Laws Ann. § 750.335 (West 2011) (making "lewdly and lasciviously" cohabitating or associating between unmarried people a misdemeanor offense). For a state-by-state analysis of fornication statutes, see Amanda Connor, *Is Your Bedroom A Private Place? Fornication and Fundamental Rights*, 39 N.M. L. Rev. 507, 521 (2009); "Prohibited Consensual Sexual Activity," 50 State Statutory Surveys: Criminal Laws: Crimes, *available at* 0030 SURVEYS 14 (2007) (Westlaw). For a discussion of *Lawrence v. Texas* and Constitutional protections for intimate sexual relations, see *infra* notes 189-99.

[184] 478 U.S. 186 (1986).

these cases nevertheless stand for the proposition that any kind of private sexual conduct between consenting adults is constitutionally insulated from state proscription is insupportable.[185]

The Court further concluded that the state could legislate against homosexual conduct based on a presumed public belief that such behavior is "immoral and unacceptable."[186]

The dissent argued that what the decision in fact "refused to recognize is the fundamental interest all individuals have in controlling the nature of their intimate associations with others."[187] It would have struck down the statutes under a privacy theory, a claim that would not be addressed again until *Lawrence v. Texas* in 2003.[188]

In *Lawrence*, John Geddes Lawrence and Tyron Garner were convicted of a criminal misdemeanor for participating in "deviate sexual intercourse with another individual of the same sex."[189] Police officers entered Lawrence's apartment where, officers said, Lawrence and Garner were engaging in sodomy. Lawrence and Garner were arrested, charged with deviate sexual intercourse, held overnight, and subsequently tried before a Justice of the Peace, where they entered a plea of *nolo contendere.*[190] At trial, the two contended to no avail that Texas' statute violated equal protection guarantees of both the Fourteenth Amendment and the Texas Constitution.[191] The case ultimately reached the Supreme Court, which found in favor of the defendants, overturning *Bowers v. Hardwick.*[192] The Court began its decision by noting that:

> Liberty protects the person from unwarranted government intrusions into a dwelling or other private places. In our tradition the State is not omnipresent in the home. And there are other spheres of our lives and existence, outside the home, where the State should not be a dominant presence. Freedom extends beyond spatial bounds. Liberty presumes an autonomy of self that includes freedom of thought, belief, expression, and certain intimate conduct. The instant case involves liberty of the person both in its spatial and in its more transcendent dimensions.[193]

The Court found the Texas law unconstitutional because "[t]he State cannot demean [a person's] existence or control their destiny by making their private sexual conduct a crime. Their right to liberty under the Due Process Clause gives

---

[185] *Id.* at 190-91.

[186] 478 U.S. at 196.

[187] *Id.* at 206 (Blackmun, J., dissenting).

[188] 539 U.S. 558 (2003).

[189] Tex. Penal Code Ann. § 21.01(1) (2003) (defining "[d]eviate sexual intercourse" as "(A) any contact between any part of the genitals of one person and the mouth or anus of another person; or (B) the penetration of the genitals or the anus of another person with an object").

[190] 539 U.S. 558. Both men were convicted, fined $200, and assessed court costs of $141.25. *Id.* For a fascinating account of the story behind *Lawrence v. Texas*, see Dale Carpenter, Flagrant Conduct: The Story of *Lawrence v. Texas* (2012).

[191] *See* Tex. Const., Art. 1, § 3(a).

[192] 539 U.S. 558 (2003).

[193] *Id.* at 562.

them the full right to engage in their conduct without intervention of the government. 'It is a promise of the Constitution that there is a realm of personal liberty which the government may not enter,' "[194] notwithstanding the "[s]weeping references . . . [in *Bowers*] to the history of Western civilization and to Judeo-Christian moral and ethical standards" condemning homosexuality.[195] The Court rejected *Bowers'* reading of history, noting that "at the time of the Court's decision [in *Bowers*] 24 States and the District of Columbia had sodomy laws" that "often were being ignored."[196] By 2003, criminal sodomy prohibitions remained in only 13 states, of which only four enforced them solely against same-sex acts.[197] In striking down the Texas law, the Court expressly overruled *Bowers*.

The Court reserved judgment about the limits of this liberty interest in private sexual conduct. It specifically noted that:

> The present case does not involve minors. It does not involve persons who might be injured or coerced or who are situated in relationships where consent might not easily be refused. It does not involve public conduct or prostitution. It does not involve whether the government must give formal recognition to any relationship that homosexual persons seek to enter.[198]

While the full impact of *Lawrence* on these areas continues to play out, at least one commentator has noted that "the *Lawrence* decision has had surprisingly little impact on lower federal courts and state courts," even though "[m]any observers assumed that the *Lawrence* decision would portend a new day for the right to personal and sexual autonomy."[199]

§ 5.04 CONTRACEPTION

Constitutional recognition of a right to procreate led to the more controversial issue of whether a corresponding right *not* to procreate exists, beginning with a line of cases addressing contraception. Although birth control has been practiced for centuries, modern scientific developments have increased the efficacy and availability of contraception. While contraception was at one time a highly controversial issue both socially and legally, today it is generally a well-accepted matter. Contraceptives are commonly used, publicly sold and displayed, and are not prohibited in any state. Nearly one hundred percent of women between the ages of 15 and 44 who have ever engaged in sexual intercourse have used a contraceptive method.[200]

---

[194] *Id.* at 578 (quoting *Planned Parenthood v. Casey*, 505 U.S. 833, 847 (1992)).

[195] *Id.* at 572.

[196] *Id.*

[197] *Id.* at 573.

[198] *Id.* at 578.

[199] J. Kelly Strader, *Resurrecting* Lawrence v. Texas *as a Basis for Challenging Criminal Prosecutions*, 25 Crim. Just. 30, 31 (2010). *See also* Nicole R. Hart, Note, *The Progress and Pitfalls of Lawrence v. Texas*, 52 Buff. L. Rev. 1417 (2004).

[200] W.D. Mosher & J. Jones, U.S. Dept. of Health & Hum. Svcs., Nat. Ctr. for Health Statistics, *Use of contraception in the United States: 1982-2008*, Vital Health Statistics 23(29) (2010), *available at*

[A]   The Right to Contraception

The United States Supreme Court first recognized a right of married people to use contraceptive devices, based on an individual's liberty interest protected by the Due Process clause, in *Griswold v. Connecticut*.[201] In *Griswold*, the Supreme Court invalidated Connecticut statutes that restricted the right of married people to use contraceptives by imposing criminal penalties on their use. The defendants, the director of the Planned Parenthood organization and a physician, had been arrested as accessories to the crime of giving birth control information and advice to married persons and prescribing contraceptives for them.

Although no right of privacy, or even the term "privacy," is mentioned in the Constitution, seven Justices in *Griswold* agreed that Constitutional protection for the right of privacy existed, although they could not agree about its source. Justice Douglas, writing for the Court, found specific guarantees in portions of the Bill of Rights that give rise to "zones of privacy," such as the right of freedom to associate and privacy in one's association.[202] He found that the "penumbra" of these other fundamental and enumerated rights includes the "right of procreation," implicit in the other important decisions delegated to parents in the child-rearing process.[203] He viewed a law forbidding the use of contraceptives, as opposed to regulating their manufacture or sale, as destructive to the marriage relationship, and observed: "Would we allow the police to search the sacred precincts of marital bedrooms for telltale signs of the use of contraceptives? The very idea is repulsive to the notions of privacy surrounding the marriage relationship."[204]

Justice Goldberg, joined by Chief Justice Warren and Justice Brennan, in one of three concurring opinions, found protection for the right of privacy in the inherent nature of the Constitution, especially in the Ninth Amendment concept of reserved rights. Justice Goldberg argued that because of the Ninth Amendment, the people retain other unenumerated rights, a theory that ultimately rests on a very traditional, and today somewhat disfavored, concept of natural law.[205]

In other concurring opinions, Justice White determined that the right of privacy between married persons is protected by the concept of liberty in the Fourteenth Amendment.[206] Justice Harlan found that the Connecticut statute in question infringed on "the Fourteenth Amendment because the enactment violates basic values 'implicit in the concept of ordered liberty.' "[207] Two Justices, Black and

---

http://www.cdc.gov/nchs/data/series/sr_23/sr23_029.pdf.

[201] 381 U.S. 479 (1965).

[202] *Id.* at 484.

[203] *Id. See also supra* § 5.03.

[204] 381 U.S. at 485-86.

[205] *Id.* at 487 (Goldberg, J., Warren, C.J. & Brennan, J. concurring). For a discussion of the Ninth Amendment as it relates to the right of privacy, see Sarah Tupper, Note, *Taking the Ninth: A Victim's Right of Privacy*, 28 Wash. U. J.L. & Pol'y 457 (2008); Calvin R. Massey, *Federalism and Fundamental Rights: The Ninth Amendment*, 38 Hastings L.J. 305 (1987); Lawrence E. Mitchell, *The Ninth Amendment and the "Jurisprudence of Original Intention,"*74 Geo. L.J. 1719 (1986).

[206] 381 U.S. at 502 (White, J. concurring).

[207] 381 U.S. at 500 (quoting *Palko v. Connecticut*, 302 U.S. 319, 325 (1937)).

Stewart, representing the strict constructionist school of constitutional interpretation, declined to rule the Connecticut statute unconstitutional because they could find no express provision of the Constitution that it violated.[208] Both, however, found the statute to be personally repugnant.

In *Eisenstadt v. Baird*,[209] the Supreme Court extended the right to use contraceptives to unmarried persons, striking down a Massachusetts statute which prohibited distribution of contraceptives except upon a physician's prescription to a married person. The defendant in *Eisenstadt* was convicted of giving a woman a package of contraceptive foam following a lecture he had delivered on the subject of contraception at Boston University. The Court held that the statute violated the equal protection rights of unmarried persons, stating, "If the right of privacy means anything, it is the right of the individual, married or single, to be free from unwarranted governmental intrusion into matters so fundamentally affecting a person as the decision whether to bear or beget a child."[210]

In *Carey v. Population Services International*,[211] the Supreme Court struck down a statute that made it a crime to display or advertise contraceptives, for anyone but a pharmacist to sell non-medical contraceptive devices to persons over 16 years of age, and banned the sale of contraceptives to persons under 16. Without prohibiting all regulation of the manufacture and sale of contraceptives, the Court held that the state was unable to demonstrate a compelling interest in limiting their distribution to pharmacists sufficient to justify the burden that the statute placed on an adult's freedom of choice. The restriction on sale of contraceptives to children was also struck, but without a majority opinion. Justice Brennan, writing for four members of the Court, implied that even minors have some rights to freedom of choice in the use of contraceptives.[212] Further, the ban on advertising and display was invalidated because it completely suppressed dissemination of truthful information regarding a lawful activity. Today, "[a]dolescent access to contraception remains a . . . divisive issue, particularly access without parental consent."[213] Multiple states have enacted laws that regulate minors' access.[214] For example, Texas requires parental consent to participate in contraceptive programs that receive state funding, while other states providing contraceptives through their Medicaid programs exclude women under the age of 19.[215]

Lingering questions about the propriety of minors using contraceptives have resurfaced in challenges by parents to both condom distribution programs[216] and

---

[208] *Id.* at 528 (Stewart, J. & Black, J. dissenting).

[209] 405 U.S. 438 (1972).

[210] *Id.* at 453.

[211] 431 U.S. 678 (1977).

[212] *Id.* at 679.

[213] Naomi Cahn & June Carbone, Red Families v. Blue Families: Legal Polarization and the Creation of Culture 179 (2010).

[214] Guttmacher Institute, *State Policies in Brief: Emergency Contraception* (Dec. 2011), *available at* http://www.guttmacher.org/statecenter/spibs/spib_EC.pdf.

[215] Cahn & Carbone, *supra* note 213.

[216] Parents have argued that condom distribution programs violate their rights to privacy and their

abstinence-only sex education in public schools. Both are sure to remain contested terrain in coming years.

[B]   Funding Contraception

Today, the battleground over contraception has shifted from access to funding. While the government cannot forbid access to birth control, it need not "fund access that would make such rights 'meaningful.' "[217] State and federal governments vary in their willingness to fund contraceptives, and some governments have shifted in their willingness over time. For example, early federal regulations tying receipt of federal funding to parental notification of minors' use, which were struck down,[218] have given way to relaxed rules allowing the use of federal funds in family planning through Medicaid waivers.[219]

In 2012, the Obama Administration finalized regulations implementing the new healthcare reform law, the Patient Protection and Affordable Care Act (PPACA),[220] which require nearly all employers and health insurers to cover, as part of their comprehensive healthcare services, sterilization procedures and contraceptives, including emergency contraceptives (EC).[221] The regulations unleashed a "political maelstrom,"[222] with some church leaders asserting that mandated coverage places religious employers "in the untenable position of having to choose between violating the law and violating their consciences."[223] On the other side, women's rights groups praised the Administration for establishing "a major milestone in

---

free exercise of religion, as well as their substantive due process rights. In *Curtis v. School Committee of Falmouth*, 652 N.E.2d 580 (Mass. 1995), the Supreme Judicial Court of Massachusetts held that a condom-availability program did not violate parents' constitutional rights, reasoning that while parents possess a fundamental liberty interest to be free from governmental intrusion in the raising of their children, they have "no right to tailor public school programs to meet their individual religious or moral preferences." *Id.* at 589.

[217] Cahn & Carbone, *supra* note 213, at 176.

[218] In *Planned Parenthood Federation of America v. Heckler*, 712 F.2d 650 (D.C. Cir. 1983), the United States Court of Appeals for the D.C. Circuit invalidated a regulation issued by the Secretary of the Department of Health and Human Services. The regulation required recipients of certain federal funds to order providers to notify parents or guardians when prescribing contraceptives to unemancipated minors. It also required those providers to comply with state laws requiring parental notice or consent, and to consider the eligibility of minors who wish to receive services on basis of their parents' financial resources, rather than their own. The court held that the regulation was invalid because it exceeded statutory authority. It noted that the statute encouraged family participation in their children's decisions, but did not require it.

[219] Guttmacher Institute, *State Policies in Brief: Facts On Publicly Funded Contraceptive Services In The United States* (2011), *available at* http://www.guttmacher.org/pubs/fb_contraceptive_serv.pdf (estimating public expenditures for contraceptives at $1.85 billion in 2006, with Medicaid accounting for 71% of expenditures, state appropriations for 13%, and Title X expenditures for 12%).

[220] Pub. L. No. 111-148, *available at* http://frwebgate.access.gpo.gov/cgi-bin/getdoc.cgi?dbname= 111_cong_public_laws&docid=f:publ148.111.pdf.

[221] *See supra* note 85 (discussing mechanisms of action for ella and Plan B).

[222] Timothy Stoltzfus Jost, "Analysis of the Obama Administration's Updated Contraception Rule," *available at* http://law.wlu.edu/faculty/facultydocuments/jost/contraception.pdf.

[223] *See* Matthew Larotonda, *Catholic Churches Distribute Letter Opposing Obama Healthcare Rule*, A.B.C. News, Jan. 29, 2012, *available at* http://abcnews.go.com/blogs/politics/2012/01/catholic-churches-distribute-letter-opposing-obama-healthcare-rule/.

protecting women's health [because] . . . [c]ontraception is critical preventive health care."[224] The Obama Administration attempted to "accommodate" religious employers by shifting the burden onto insurers, while preserving access to contraceptives. President Obama explained that "if a woman's employer is a charity or a hospital that has a religious objection to providing contraceptive services as part of their health plan, the insurance company — not the hospital, not the charity — will be required to reach out and offer the woman contraceptive care free of charge without co-pays, without hassle."[225] This, too, met with derision from critics.[226]

On June 28, 2012, the U.S. Supreme Court upheld PPACA's individual mandate as a constitutional exercise of Congress's taxing power, while striking down portion of the PPACA's Medicaid expansion as exceeding Congress's authority under the Spending Clause.[227] The sterilization and contraceptive portions of the PPACA were not struck down.

Like the debate over religious exemptions to the contraceptive and sterilization coverage mandate, individual pharmacies and pharmacists have objected on religious grounds to filling prescriptions for EC, sparking a separate firestorm of controversy.[228] Some state legislatures concerned about access to EC have responded with special legislation. For example, Massachusetts directed all hospitals to offer rape victims EC, which 17 states now mandate for victims of sexual assault and rape.[229] A number of states require pharmacists or pharmacies to ensure that all valid prescriptions are filled.[230] Other states have protected the conscientious refusals of both individual pharmacists and pharmacies, bringing them within the scope of traditional abortion conscience clauses that date back to *Roe v. Wade*.[231] As of 2011, six states have passed legislation permitting pharmacists to refuse to fill prescriptions for hormonal contraceptives, including

---

[224] National Women's Law Center, "HHS Decision on Contraceptive Coverage a Major Milestone" (Jan. 20, 2012) *available at* http://www.nwlc.org/press-release/hhs-decision-contraceptive-coverage-important-milestone.

[225] *See* Richard Wolf, *Obama Tweaks Birth Control Rule*, U.S.A. Today, Feb. 10, 2012, *available at* http://content.usatoday.com/communities/theoval/post/2012/02/source-obama-to-change-birth-control-rule/1.

[226] *See, e.g.*, "Unacceptable," Statement of Feb. 27, 2012, *available at* http://www.becketfund.org/wp-content/ uploads/2012/02/Unacceptable-2-27-11am2.pdf (observing that "it is unrealistic to suggest that insurance companies will not pass the costs of these additional services on to the[ir] purchasers" and thus "[i]t is no answer to respond that religious employers are not 'paying' for this aspect of the insurance coverage . . . .").

[227] *See Nat'l Fed'n of Indep. Bus. v. Sebelius*, 132 S. Ct. 2566 (2012).

[228] Robin Fretwell Wilson, Essay, *The Limits of Conscience: Moral Clashes over Deeply Divisive Healthcare Procedures*, 34 Am. J.L. & Med. 41 (2008).

[229] *See* Cati Vanden Breul, *Yale Professors Discuss Morning-After Pill Policies*, Minn. Daily (Minneapolis/St. Paul), Jan. 31, 2005, http://www.mndaily.com/articles/2005/01/31/6300; Guttmacher Institute, *State Policies in Brief: Emergency Contraception* (Dec. 2011), *available at* http://www.guttmacher.org/statecenter/spibs/spib_EC.pdf.

[230] *See, e.g.*, Cal. Bus. & Prof. Code § 733 (2011).

[231] *See* Wilson, *supra* note 228, at 43; *infra* § 5.05.

EC.[232] A number of states have focused on the availability of contraceptives to minors. Twenty-five states require parental approval for minors to consent to EC; some allow only married minors to consent to EC or allow minors to consent only if they have reached a certain age or fulfilled other requirements.[233]

Although the *Griswold* line of cases has concluded the legal debate over the use of contraceptives, the underlying theories of the right of privacy in matters of marriage, procreation, and sexuality remain vital in the continuing evolution of the abortion controversy.

§ 5.05 ABORTION

[A] General Introduction

The issue of abortion has been a topic of constant debate in the United States. The underlying controversy stems from weighing the rights of the unborn against a woman's right to choose whether to bear a child. Historically, abortions were commonly regulated after the time of "quickening," the time at which the mother first felt any movement of the fetus, usually during the fourth or fifth month of pregnancy.[234] Although the performance of an abortion after the quickening stage was a crime, the woman herself was not subject to prosecution.[235]

In 1821, Connecticut became the first state to enact a statute regulating abortion, prohibiting inducement of an abortion by poison in order to protect the mother's health.[236] Physicians led the support for criminalizing abortion because of the high mortality rate of women subjected to abortion methods employed by non-physicians. As the medical profession became more knowledgeable about fetal development, focus shifted to whether a fetus had a right to life.[237] Although numerous statutes were enacted to prohibit abortions during the nineteenth century, they were rarely enforced and illegal abortions were still frequently performed.[238] Abortion laws were more rigorously enforced during the 1950s and early 1960s, until infant deformities caused by an outbreak of German measles and the use of the tranquilizer thalidomide brought the issue of abortion to the forefront, inciting medical and public demands for abortion law reform.[239]

---

[232] Guttmacher Institute, *State Policies in Brief: Minors' Access to Contraceptive Services* (Dec. 2011), *available at* http://www.guttmacher.org/statecenter/spibs/spib_MACS.pdf.

[233] *Id.*

[234] *See* Lawrence H. Tribe, Abortion: The Clash of Absolutes 28 (1990); *see also* Marvin Olasky, Abortion Rites: A Social History of Abortion in America 92-93 (1992) (providing a historical account of the first state law prohibiting abortion in the United States, which punished abortion only when "a woman was 'quick with child' and therefore unmistakably pregnant").

[235] *Id.*

[236] *Id.* at 29. *See also* Olasky, *supra* note 234.

[237] Tribe, *supra* note 234.

[238] *See id.* at 34-35.

[239] *Id.* at 35-38.

By 1967, a number of states began to liberalize their criminal statutes to allow abortion when continuation of the pregnancy would seriously impair the mental or physical health of the mother; when the child was likely to be born with serious mental or physical defects; or when the pregnancy was the result of rape or incest.[240] Yet, legal abortions remained inaccessible to many women because of continued restrictions, bureaucracy, and lack of financial resources.[241]

This would change with the United States Supreme Court's hallmark decision in *Roe v. Wade*,[242] the "essential holding" of which remains in place after a series of United States Supreme Court decisions.[243]

[B] Constitutional Parameters: *Roe v. Wade*

Until the United States Supreme Court first addressed the issue of abortion in 1973 in *Roe v. Wade*,[244] states had the authority to regulate and enforce the conditions under which abortions could be performed. In *Roe*, the Supreme Court overturned a Texas criminal statute that banned abortion except when necessary to save the mother's life. The Court found that the statute unnecessarily infringed on a woman's right to privacy in violation of the Due Process Clause of the Fourteenth Amendment. Justice Blackmun, writing for the majority, extended the earlier interpretation of the Due Process Clause, which already included a woman's fundamental right to bear a child, to a fundamental right of privacy in deciding whether to terminate her pregnancy:

> This right of privacy, whether it be founded in the Fourteenth Amendment's concept of personal liberty and restrictions upon state action, as we feel it is, or, as the District Court determined, in the Ninth Amendment's reservation of rights to the people, is broad enough to encompass a woman's decision whether or not to terminate her pregnancy. The detriment that the State would impose upon the pregnant woman by denying this choice altogether is apparent. Specific and direct harm medically diagnosable even in early pregnancy may be involved. Maternity, or additional offspring, may force upon the woman a distressful life and future. Psychological harm may be imminent. Mental and physical health may be taxed by childcare. There is also the distress, for all concerned, associated with the unwanted child, and there is the problem of bringing a child into a family already unable, psychologically and otherwise, to care for it. In other cases, as in this one, the additional difficulties and continuing stigma of unwed motherhood may be involved. All these are factors the woman and her responsible physician necessarily will consider in consultation.[245]

---

[240] *Id.* at 42.

[241] *Id.* at 43.

[242] 410 U.S. 113 (1973).

[243] *Planned Parenthood of Southeastern Pennsylvania v. Casey*, 505 U.S. 833, 846 (1992). *See infra* § 5.04[C][5] (discussing *Casey*).

[244] 410 U.S. 113 (1973).

[245] *Id.* at 153.

The Court concluded that the right to terminate a pregnancy is not absolute, however, but must be balanced against the state's important interests in safeguarding the mother's health, in maintaining medical standards, and in protecting potential life. The Court applied a two-pronged strict scrutiny test, requiring the state to justify an abortion regulation by first showing that the regulation was necessary and, second, that it was supported by a compelling state interest. Justice Blackmun articulated a trimester system of balancing the competing interests based on the stage of the pregnancy involved. In the first trimester, the woman's decision whether to have an abortion is a medical decision between the woman and her physician, largely private and protected from state interference.[246] During the second trimester, the state's interest in the mother's health becomes compelling and the state has the limited authority to regulate abortions to the extent reasonably related to preservation and protection of the woman's health. Because the Court reasoned that the potential life was entitled to constitutional protection only upon viability, deemed to occur in the third trimester, the state's interest in protecting the fetus becomes compelling then and therefore a state, if it chooses to do so, may enact regulations to protect the fetus after that time. Specifically, the state may prohibit abortions during that final trimester unless the mother's life or health is at stake.[247]

The *Roe v. Wade* decision did not fully satisfy either side of the abortion debate. The choice of viability as the point at which the state may prohibit abortion has been criticized by pro-choice advocates, because the availability of abortion procedures will be undermined as medical and scientific research move the point of viability back further towards the time of conception. Anti-abortion, or "pro-life," advocates, of course, condemn *Roe* for legalizing abortion at all, based on their belief that life begins at the moment of conception and that any abortion is a wrongful taking of a life.

---

[246] *Id.* at 165. The Court made clear, however, that "[t]he State may define the term 'physician,' . . . to mean only a physician currently licensed by the State."). *Id.* at 732-33. In *Mazurek v. Armstrong*, 520 U.S. 968 (1997), the Supreme Court overturned a preliminary injunction against a Montana statute "restricting the performance of abortions to licensed physicians." *Mazurek* at 969. *See also* Samuel W. Calhoun, *Stopping Philadelphia Abortion Provider Kermit Gosnell and Preventing Others Like Him: An Outcome that Both Pro-Choicers and Pro-Lifers Should Support*, 57 Vill. L. Rev. 1 (2012). Subsequently, the Supreme Court of Montana invalidated Montana's physician-only restriction for pre-viability abortions as violating the fundamental right to privacy under Montana's Constitution. *Armstrong v. State*, 989 P.2d 364 (1999).

Like Montana, approximately a dozen states "explicitly recognize a constitutional right to abortion based only on state law and independent of federal law." *See* Ronald Rotunda, Forward *in* Paul Benjamin Linton, Abortion under State Constitutions: A State-by-State Analysis (2008) (providing a comprehensive analysis of state constitutional provisions giving protections to a woman's reproductive decisions that exceed those under the Federal Constitution).

[247] *See* Calhoun, *supra* note 246, at n.180 (noting the "expansive conception of health" in the companion case to *Roe v. Wade*, *Doe v. Bolton*, 410 U.S. 179, 192 (1973), which included "all factors — physical, emotional, psychological, familial, and the woman's age — relevant to the well-being of the patient"). Some commentators suggest that importing *Doe*'s "expansive conception of health into . . . *Roe*'s formulation of when abortion may be prohibited post-viability" would "result[ ], in practice, in the total elimination of the state's power to prohibit post-viability abortions, not just a narrow exception to that power." Calhoun, *supra*, citing Matthew J. Franck, *The Gosnell Case and American Abortion Law*, Nat'l Rev., Feb. 3, 2011, http://www.nationalreview.com/articles/print/258707.

The right of privacy is central to *Roe*. Without this right, a woman has no constitutionally protected interest under *Roe* to balance against the state's interest in protecting potential life. Despite its importance, the majority merely assumed that the right of privacy exists, but did little to establish a theory of constitutional interpretation to support its belief in the existence of the right. Although Justice Blackmun cited numerous cases supporting his view, he mentions the penumbra theory only in passing as it related to *Griswold* and the Ninth Amendment only with respect to Justice Goldberg's concurring opinion in that case.[248]

The holding in *Roe v. Wade* did not provide a formal test for application by the lower courts when reviewing the constitutionality of an abortion regulation. Instead, the *Roe* Court couched its holding in a rigid trimester analysis for determining whether the government had a compelling interest in protecting the health of the woman or fetus. Although the Court did not formally announce its abandonment of the trimester analysis until *Planned Parenthood of Southeastern Pennsylvania v. Casey*,[249] it soon began modifying the *Roe* test and applying, instead, a reasonableness test for determining if an abortion regulation was constitutional.[250]

[C] Constitutional Parameters: The State Response

After *Roe v. Wade*, the United States Supreme Court has had numerous occasions to define the parameters of state authority to regulate abortion. The Court has struck down state and federal statutory attempts to restrict access to abortion in a number of cases and upheld them in others. In 1992, nearly 20 years after *Roe*, the Court in *Planned Parenthood of Southeastern Pennsylvania v. Casey*,[251] formally retreated from the trimester framework set forth in *Roe* in favor of allowing greater state regulation before viability, so long as state regulations do not create an undue burden on a woman's access to abortion. This remains the governing test for evaluating abortion regulations. This section reviews cases following *Roe*, including *Casey*, and notes how *Casey* may affect the holding of earlier decisions.

[1] Rights of the Potential Father

The Supreme Court broadly construed a woman's right to obtain an abortion in 1976 in *Planned Parenthood of Central Missouri v. Danforth*.[252] In *Danforth*, the Court considered the interest of an additional party, the potential father. The dispute centered around a Missouri statute which required the prior written consent of the spouse of a woman seeking an abortion during the first trimester of pregnancy, unless the abortion was necessary to save the mother's life. The Court recognized the father's interest:

---

[248] *See generally* Ronald M. Dworkin, *Unenumerated Rights: Whether and How* Roe *Should be Overruled*, 59 U. Chi. L. Rev. 381 (1992).

[249] 505 U.S. 833 (1992).

[250] *See* Daniel A. Farber & John E. Nowak, *Beyond the* Roe *Debate: Judicial Experience with the 1980's "Reasonableness" Test*, 76 Va. L. Rev. 519, 520-21 (1990).

[251] *See infra* notes 285-89, 322-28 (and accompanying text).

[252] 428 U.S. 52 (1976).

We are not unaware of the deep and proper concern and interest that a devoted and protective husband has in his wife's pregnancy and in the growth and development of the fetus she is carrying. Neither has this Court failed to appreciate the importance of the marital relationship in our society . . . . Moreover, we recognize that the decision whether to undergo or to forego an abortion may have profound effects on the future of any marriage, effects that are both physical and mental, and possibly deleterious.[253]

However, as between the interest of the father and the privacy right of the mother, the Court ruled in favor of the mother: "Inasmuch as it is the woman who physically bears the child and who is the more directly and immediately affected by the pregnancy, as between the two, the balance weighs in her favor."[254] In striking down the statute, the Court concluded: "[W]e cannot hold that the State has the constitutional authority to give the spouse unilaterally the ability to prohibit the wife from terminating her pregnancy, when the [s]tate itself lacks that right."[255]

Later, in *Casey*, the Court again struck down a Pennsylvania abortion provision that required spousal notification except in cases of emergency. Because spousal notification is "likely to prevent a significant number of women from obtaining an abortion," it erected an undue burden on a woman's access to abortion.[256]

[2]   Rights of Minors

The Supreme Court in *Danforth* also extended the fundamental right to choose to have an abortion to minors, striking down a parental consent statute, although it recognized that states have broader powers to protect minors than adults.[257] The Court again directly addressed a parental consent statute in *Bellotti v. Baird* (*Bellotti I*),[258] holding that the Massachusetts parental consent statute was unclear with respect to the authority of parents to veto the decision of a minor child to have an abortion and with respect to the availability of a judicial bypass procedure. In a plurality opinion in *Bellotti v. Baird* (*Bellotti II*),[259] the Court invalidated the Massachusetts statute. Although observing that the constitutional rights of minors, including the right to obtain an abortion, are not co-extensive with the rights of adults, the plurality in *Bellotti II* found that a minor's right to obtain an abortion could be restricted by requiring the consent of a parent only if the state provided a procedure for bypassing the requirement. A minor is entitled to an alternative proceeding in order to show that she is mature and well informed enough to make her own decision about abortion by consulting her physician, regardless of her parents' consent. Even if she is not able to decide for herself, the minor is entitled to show that the abortion would be in her best interest. Thus, a minor's consent

---

[253]   *Id.* at 69-70 (internal citations omitted).

[254]   *Id.* at 71.

[255]   *Id.* at 70 (citing *Eisenstadt v. Baird*, 405 U.S. 438, 453 (1972)).

[256]   505 U.S. 833, 893-95 (1992). *See infra* § 5.04[C][5] (discussing *Casey*).

[257]   428 U.S. 52 (1976).

[258]   428 U.S. 132 (1976).

[259]   443 U.S. 622 (1979).

statute must provide for an alternative to parental permission in order to pass constitutional muster.

Three years later, in *H.L. v. Matheson*,[260] the Court dealt with a statute that required parental notification rather than consent. In *Matheson*, the Court upheld a statute that required a physician to notify a minor's parents, whenever possible, before performing an abortion for a minor. The majority found that notification "furthers a constitutionally permissible end by encouraging an unmarried pregnant minor to seek the help and advice of her parents in making the very important decision whether or not to bear a child."[261] The concurring opinion in *Matheson* stressed that a judicial bypass procedure that followed the guidelines of *Bellotti II* must be included before a notification statute would be found constitutional.[262]

In 1983, in *Akron v. Akron Center for Reproductive Health*,[263] the Court struck down as unconstitutional an Akron ordinance that prohibited "a physician from performing an abortion on a minor pregnant woman under the age of 15 unless he obtains 'the informed written consent' " of a parent or legal guardian or acts pursuant to a court order. Like the statute in *Belotti II*, Akron's ordinance did not create a sufficient procedure for obtaining a judicial order in the absence of parental consent.[264] In 1990, in *Hodgson v. Minnesota*,[265] the Court upheld the most restrictive consent and notice statute it had yet addressed.[266] The Minnesota statute in question required at least 48 hours notice to *both* parents of a minor who sought an abortion, or, in the alternative, a judicial bypass procedure to determine whether the minor was mature enough to give informed consent without parental notification. The majority first considered the two state interests involved: the welfare of pregnant minors and the interest in promoting the role of parents in the care and upbringing of their children. The Court found the two-parent notification portion of the statute constitutionally objectionable because no legitimate state interest was served; however, the majority held that the constitutional impediment was removed by the judicial bypass option, concluding that the interests of immature minors therefore were protected. The Court also held that the 48-hour waiting period was constitutional because it allowed time for parents to consult with their daughters, while imposing only a minimal burden on the right of a minor to decide whether to terminate her pregnancy.[267]

---

[260] 450 U.S. 398 (1981).

[261] *Id.* at 409-10 (quoting *Bellotti v. Baird (Bellotti II)*, 443 U.S. 622, 640-41 (1979)).

[262] 450 U.S. 398 (Powell, J. & Stewart, J. concurring).

[263] 462 U.S. 416 (1983).

[264] *Id.* at 439.

[265] 497 U.S. 417 (1990).

[266] *See generally* Ronald F. Berestka, Jr., Comment, *Constitutional Law — What Ever Happened to a Woman's Fundamental Right to Privacy? Hodgson v. Minnesota, 110 S. Ct. 2926 (1990)*, 25 Suffolk U. L. Rev. 192 (1990).

[267] The Indiana Court of Appeals has held that either parent would qualify as guardian of a child for purpose of consenting to the child's obtaining an abortion when divorced parents had joint legal custody of their sixteen-year-old daughter, because consent of both parents is not required when marriage is intact. *S.H., Appellant-Petitioner v. D.H., Appellee-Respondent*, 796 N.E.2d 1243 (Ind. Ct. App. 2003).

In a companion case to *Hodgson, Ohio v. Akron Center for Reproductive Health*,[268] the Court upheld the judicial bypass procedure of an Ohio abortion statute requiring parental notice and consent. The Court declined to address whether parental notice statutes must contain bypass procedures comparable to those required for parental consent statutes, concluding that the statute in question satisfied the requisites for the more intrusive consent statute.[269]

Finally, in 1992, *Casey* largely laid to rest the question of parental consent and notification. In *Casey*, the Court upheld as constitutional a Pennsylvania requirement that a minor woman under the age of 18 secure the informed consent of one parent or a judicial order authorizing the abortion as in her best interests, except in cases of medical emergency.[270] The Court noted expressly that "a State may require a minor seeking an abortion to obtain the consent of a parent or guardian, provided that there is an adequate judicial bypass procedure."[271]

As of October 2011, "21 states require that at least one parent consent to a minor's abortion, while 11 states require prior notification of at least one parent . . . [and] 5 states require both notification of and consent from a parent prior to a minor's abortion."[272]

[3] Health and Safety Regulations

In *Roe v. Wade*'s companion case, *Doe v. Bolton*,[273] the Supreme Court struck down a provision of the Georgia abortion statute which required that an abortion found necessary by a physician must be performed in a hospital accredited by a particular private agency, that it must be approved by a hospital committee, and that at least two other doctors must concur with the patient's doctor that the abortion is needed. The Court deferred to the medical profession and individual physicians, focusing on the private nature of the physician-patient relationship, and invalidated overly restrictive portions of the statute.

Three years later, in *Danforth*, the Court unanimously upheld a Missouri statutory provision applicable to the first trimester that required a woman to provide her written, informed consent to the abortion.[274] In 1983, *Akron v. Akron*

---

[268] 497 U.S. 502 (1990).

[269] The United States Court of Appeals for the Tenth Circuit invalidated a Colorado statute that required parental notification of a minor's abortion because it failed to provide a health exception. *Planned Parenthood v. Owens*, 287 F.3d 910 (10th Cir. 2002).

[270] 505 U.S. 833, 899 (1992).

[271] *Id.*

[272] Guttmacher Institute, *State Policies in Brief: An Overview of Minors' Consent Law*, (October 1, 2011), *available at* http://www.guttmacher.org/statecenter/spibs/spib_OMCL.pdf (noting also that "[two] states and the District of Columbia explicitly allow all minors to consent to abortion services . . . [six] additional states have parental involvement laws that are temporarily or permanently enjoined . . . [and six] states have no relevant policy or case law").

[273] 410 U.S. 179 (1973).

[274] 428 U.S. 52, 65-67 (1976).

Center for Reproductive Health[275] overturned a city ordinance requiring that a patient be orally informed that an "unborn child is a human life from the moment of conception," and be informed of her pregnancy's status, the fetus's development and possible viability date, and physical complications of abortion, as well as the availability of agencies offering birth control and adoption services.[276] The city ordinance also restricted a physician from performing an abortion for 24 hours after the woman signs the consent form.[277] The Court held unconstitutional the requirement that all abortions after the first trimester be performed in a hospital. The Court found that the regulations failed to promote a woman's health. Further, certain types of abortions early in the second trimester could be safely performed in less expensive clinics. The Court stated that while the regulation may further the state's interest in safe abortions, it actually prevented economically disadvantaged women from obtaining abortions. State legislatures could regulate abortions, but could not depart from accepted medical practices if by "mak[ing] a reasonable effort," the state can "limit the effect of its regulations to the [time period when] its health interest may be furthered."[278]

The Court also struck the informed consent requirement as impermissibly "designed not to inform the woman's consent but rather to persuade her to withhold it altogether" and because it intruded "upon the discretion of the pregnant woman's physician."[279] It struck the 24-hour waiting period because Akron failed to demonstrate "any legitimate state interest [that] is furthered by an arbitrary and inflexible waiting period."[280] Justice O'Connor dissented with respect to the applicable constitutional standard, arguing that strict scrutiny only applies when a regulation is unduly burdensome. She argued that non-burdensome regulations are constitutional if they are rational and logically relate to a legitimate state objective, which would return policy-making authority on abortion issues back to the states. The *Casey* Court would later overrule the holding in *Akron* in part as insufficiently valuing the state's interest in potential life.[281]

In *Planned Parenthood Association v. Ashcroft*,[282] the Court again considered and rejected a requirement that abortions take place in an accredited hospital, but upheld a restriction that a second physician be present during abortions in order to care for a possibly viable fetus. It also upheld a provision requiring the filing of a pathologist's tissue report for abortions.

---

[275] 462 U.S. 416 (1983), overruled in part by *Planned Parenthood of Southeastern Pennsylvania v. Casey*, 505 U.S. 833 (1992). *See infra* § 5.04[C][5].

[276] 462 U.S. at 442, 444.

[277] Id. at 449.

[278] 462 U.S. at 434. In a case decided the same term, the Court upheld a Virginia law requiring all second trimester abortions to "be performed in an outpatient surgical hospital . . . licensed as a 'hospital' by the State." *Simopoulos v. Virginia*, 462 U.S. 506, 515 (1983).

[279] 462 U.S. at 444-45.

[280] *Id.* at 450.

[281] *See Planned Parenthood of Southeastern Pennsylvania v. Casey*, 505 U.S. 833 (1992).

[282] 462 U.S. 476 (1983).

In *Webster v. Reproductive Health Services*, the Court upheld a Missouri statute requiring physicians to advise pregnant women of certain facts when securing informed consent prior to an abortion.[283]

In *Planned Parenthood of Southeastern Pennsylvania v. Casey*,[284] the Court again considered the permissibility of an informed consent requirement, as well as a 24-hour waiting period. The Court reaffirmed "the essential holding" of *Roe* that a woman has the right "to choose to have an abortion before viability and to obtain it without undue interference from the State."[285] It then considered Pennsylvania's informed consent requirement, which included "the provision of specific information by the doctor and [a] mandatory 24-hour waiting period."[286] The Court concluded that if "the information the State requires to be made available to the woman is truthful and not misleading, the requirement may be permissible."[287] The State thus may "further its legitimate goal of protecting the life of the unborn by enacting legislation aimed at ensuring a decision that is mature and informed, even when in so doing the State expresses a preference for childbirth over abortion."[288] Although the 24-hour waiting period would increase costs and the risk of delayed abortions, the Court could not "say that the waiting period imposes a real health risk" or that it constituted "an undue burden."[289]

Since *Casey*, a number of states have enacted regulations purporting to protect or further a woman's health, some challenges to which have yet to run their course.[290] Some regulations are "quite modest,"[291] requiring only that abortion providers submit names of doctors providing abortion services to the relevant state agency — while others are far more expansive — for example, regulating abortion clinics as ambulatory surgical centers — and may have the purpose or effect of "shutting down abortion clinics."[292] In a growing trend, more than a dozen states have enacted laws encouraging or requiring providers to show an ultrasound of the fetus to women considering abortions.[293]

---

[283] 492 U.S. 490 (1989).

[284] 505 U.S. 833 (1992).

[285] *Id.* at 846. *See also infra* § 5.04[C][5].

[286] 505 U.S. at 881. The Court specifically overruled *Akron* and *Thornburgh v. American College of Obstetricians and Gynecologists*, 476 U.S. 747 (1986): "To the extent *Akron I* and *Thornburgh* find a constitutional violation when the government requires, as it does here, the giving of truthful, non-misleading information about the nature of the procedure, the attendant health risks and those of childbirth, and the 'probable gestational age' of the fetus, those cases go too far." *Id.* at 882.

[287] *Id.* at 882.

[288] *Id.* at 883.

[289] *Id.* at 886-87.

[290] *See generally* Calhoun, *supra* note 246.

[291] *Id.* at n.34 (discussing proposed laws that passed Florida's Senate but not its House).

[292] *Id.* at n.38 and accompanying text (citing Virginia's 2011 law and articulated motives for the law).

[293] *See* Guttmacher Institute, *State Policies in Brief: Requirements for Ultrasound* (Dec. 2011), *available at* http://www.guttmacher.org/statecenter/spibs/spib_RFU.pdf (stating that "[six] states mandate that an abortion provider perform an ultrasound on each woman seeking an abortion, and require the provider to offer the woman the opportunity to view the image . . . [nine] states require that a woman be provided with the opportunity to view an ultrasound image if her provider performs the

[4]   Funding and Facilities

In order to qualify for federal Medicaid funds, states must create plans establishing standards for determining the extent of medical assistance they will provide to indigents.[294] Several states established plans that would cover only medically required abortions. On several occasions, the Supreme Court has addressed the extent, if any, to which states must authorize the use of public funds or facilities to provide abortions to women who are unable to pay.[295]

In *Maher v. Roe*,[296] the Supreme Court addressed a claim that a state plan that would not fund non-therapeutic abortions through Medicaid had erected an unconstitutional barrier to the right to abortion. The Court upheld the state's decision, construing *Roe v. Wade* to guarantee the freedom to choose to have an abortion, not the right to obtain one. Retreating from a strict scrutiny analysis, the Court framed its decision in terms of protecting women from unduly burdensome interference with their freedom to decide whether to end a pregnancy. The Court held that the plan did not interfere with that freedom. Observing that states are not required to pay any medical expenses of indigents, the Court concluded that states are not prohibited from making value judgments favoring childbirth over abortion and may allocate public funds accordingly. Justice Brennan, dissenting, viewed the Court's opinion as revealing "a distressing insensitivity to the plight of impoverished pregnant women," resulting in the indigent having no realistic possibility of exercising their constitutional right to choose an abortion.[297]

The Court upheld similar funding restrictions in *Beal v. Doe*[298] and *Poelker v. Doe*,[299] companion cases to *Maher*. In *Beal*, the Court concluded that states have broad discretion to decide what medical treatment is reasonably necessary and need not fund non-essential abortions. In *Poelker*, the Court held that a city hospital may refuse public hospital services for abortions.[300]

Three years after *Roe*, Congress restricted the use of federal Medicaid funds for abortion through the Hyde Amendment.[301] In *Harris v. McRae*,[302] the Court upheld the Hyde Amendment which allowed funding for some medically necessary

---

procedure as part of the preparation for an abortion . . . [and five] states require that a woman be provided with the opportunity to view an ultrasound image").

[294] *See* 42 U.S.C. §§ 300-300a-6.

[295] *See generally* Gayle Binion, *Reproductive Freedom and the Constitution: The Limits on Choice*, 4 Berkeley Women's L.J. 12, 14-20 (1988-90).

[296] 432 U.S. 464 (1977).

[297] *Id.* at 483 (Brennan, J., dissenting).

[298] 432 U.S. 438 (1977).

[299] 432 U.S. 519 (1977).

[300] The United States Court of Appeals for the Eighth Circuit later distinguished *Poelker* in *Nyberg v. City of Virginia*, noting a "fundamental difference between providing direct funding to effect the abortion decision and allowing staff physicians to perform abortions at an existing publicly owned hospital," and upheld an injunction compelling a city hospital to permit staff physicians to perform paid abortions if they so chose. 667 F.2d 754, 758 (8th Cir. 1982).

[301] Pub. L. No. 94-439, § 209, 90 Stat. 1434 (1976).

[302] 448 U.S. 297 (1980).

abortions where the woman's health was endangered.[303]

In 1989, for the first time with a reconstituted bench after *Roe*, the Supreme Court in *Webster v. Reproductive Health Services*[304] addressed a legislative ban on the use of public funds and facilities for counseling and performing abortions. *Webster*, a class action suit opposing a Missouri statute which placed restrictions on abortions, addressed the constitutionality of a statute containing the funding restriction, as well as a legislative declaration that a fetus has protectable interests in life, health, and well-being from the moment of conception. The statute also included requirements that physicians perform tests to determine the development of a fetus and to advise pregnant women of certain facts to constitute informed consent prior to an abortion.

The Court upheld all of these restrictions as constitutional and repudiated the strict scrutiny standard. Chief Justice Rehnquist, announcing the judgment and delivering the plurality opinion, attacked "the rigid *Roe* framework [as] hardly consistent with the notion of a Constitution cast in general terms," and faulted *Roe* for the confusing and inconsistent subsequent decisions and legislation.[305] Chief Justice Rehnquist complained that "[t]he key elements of the *Roe* framework — trimesters and viability — are not found in the text of the Constitution or in any place else one would expect to find a constitutional principle."[306] He further questioned the designation of viability as the point at which the state's interest in protecting human life becomes compelling, arguing that such an interest is equally compelling throughout pregnancy. The Court acknowledged that its decision expanded state authority to avoid the restrictions of the trimester analysis and to enact additional abortion regulations. *Webster* thus severely narrowed the application of *Roe v. Wade* without expressly overruling it, although the plurality, joined by Justice Scalia, urged overruling it entirely.[307]

In 1991, in *Rust v. Sullivan*,[308] Title X grantees and supervising physicians challenged the facial validity of new regulations limiting the ability of federal Title X fund recipients to engage in abortion-related activities.[309] The regulations prohibited Title X projects from providing counseling regarding abortion and from providing referrals for abortion as a method of family planning; broadly forbade

---

[303] Later, Congress revised the Hyde Amendment to limit federally funded abortions to circumstances in which the mother's life would be endangered if the pregnancy went to term. *See* Pub. L. No. 97-377, § 204, 96 Stat. 1894 (1982). Today, the Hyde Amendment restricts the use of federal funding for abortion services "except in cases of rape or incest, or when the life of the woman would be endangered." Omnibus Appropriations Act, 2009, PL 111-8, 123 Stat. 524.

[304] 492 U.S. 490 (1989).

[305] *Id.* at 518.

[306] *Id.*

[307] *See generally* Walter Dellinger & Gene B. Sperling, *Abortion and the Supreme Court: The Retreat from* Roe v. Wade, 138 U. Pa. L. Rev. 83 (1989).

[308] 500 U.S. 173 (1991).

[309] Title X of the Public Health Service Act, 84 Stat. 1506 (1970), as amended, 42 U.S.C. §§ 300-300a-6. Title X provides federal funding for family-planning services. Grants and contracts under Title X must be made pursuant to regulations that the Secretary of the Department of Health and Human Services issues. Title X also provides that "[n]one of the funds appropriated under this subchapter shall be used in programs where abortion is a method of family planning." 42 U.S.C. § 300a-6.

Title X projects from engaging in any activities that "encourage, promote or advocate abortion as a method of family planning"; and required that Title X projects be "physically and financially separate" from these forbidden types of activities.[310] The Court refused to invalidate the regulations because they constituted a plausible construction of the statute and did not interfere with Congress's express intent.

The Court in *Rust* held that the regulations did not violate the First Amendment by impermissibly discriminating on the basis of opinion; rather, they were legitimate decisions on program funding intended to encourage activities to benefit the public. The Court noted that the regulations prohibited abortion-related activities only as a "method of family planning" and did not prevent Title X projects from otherwise engaging in such activities.[311] The Court distinguished between denying benefits and refusing to allocate public funds for a specific purpose. Finally, it held that a woman's right to choose to have an abortion was not impinged upon because her lack of access to abortion counseling from a Title X project "leaves her in no different position than she would have been if the Government had not enacted Title X."[312]

Justice Blackmun, joined by Justice Marshall, and in part by Justices Stevens and O'Connor, dissented. Justice Blackmun argued that the regulations were "clearly viewpoint-based" and an unconstitutional condition upon public employment.[313] Justice O'Connor would have reversed solely on the basis that the regulations were not a reasonable interpretation of the statute.[314]

In the era of federal healthcare reform, the question of funding for abortion has cropped up anew — this time over required health plan coverage for emergency contraceptives that some charge may act as abortifacients in limited circumstances.

While the Patient Protection and Affordable Care Act (PPACA) was still under consideration,[315] concerns were raised that it would circumvent the general proscription of the use of federal funding for abortion services contained in the Hyde Amendment. In response to these concerns, President Barack Obama signed an executive order "Ensuring Enforcement and Implementation of Abortion Restrictions in the Patient Protection and Affordable Care Act."[316] The Executive Order established "an adequate enforcement mechanism to ensure that Federal funds are not used for abortion services (except in cases of rape or incest, or when the life of the woman would be endangered), consistent with "the longstanding Federal statutory restriction in the Hyde Amendment."[317]

---

[310] *Rust*, 500 U.S. at 180.

[311] *Id.* at 178 (quoting 42 U.S.C. § 300a-6).

[312] *Id.* at 202.

[313] *Id.* at 209.

[314] *Id.* at 224-25.

[315] Pub. L. No. 111-148, 124 Stat. 119 (2010), *amended by* Health Care and Education Reconciliation Act of 2010, Pub. L. No. 111-152, 124 Stat. 102, *available at* http://frwebgate.access.gpo.gov/cgi-bin/getdoc.cgi?dbname=111_cong_public_laws&docid=f:publ148.111.pdf.

[316] Executive Order 13535 (Mar. 24, 2010).

[317] *Id.*

Implementing PPACA, the Departments of Health and Human Services, Labor, and Treasury have issued an "interim final rule" under PPACA requiring all employers (with the exceptions of churches) and health insurers to cover sterilization procedures and contraceptives, including emergency contraceptives which some charge may act sometimes as abortifacients.[318] Some members of the faith community urged broader religious exemptions from the coverage mandate so they would not be forced to "choose between violating the law and violating their conscience[s]."[319] In response, the Obama Administration proffered its much-criticized "accommodation" for religious employers, which would require "the insurance company — not the [objecting religious employer] — . . . to reach out and offer the woman contraceptive care free of charge without co-pays, without hassle."[320] As of June 2012, the White House has indicated that notwithstanding continued criticism, the President's accommodation "set[s] out [the Administration's] policy."[321]

[5] *Casey's* Re-evaluation of *Roe v. Wade*

In 1992, nearly 20 years after *Roe v. Wade*, five members of the Supreme Court reaffirmed the central principles of *Roe*, while upholding most of a highly restrictive Pennsylvania abortion statute in *Planned Parenthood of Southeastern Pennsylvania v. Casey*.[322] In an opinion co-authored by Justices O'Connor, Kennedy, and Souter, the Court first reaffirmed "the essential holding" of *Roe*:

> It must be stated at the outset and with clarity that *Roe's* essential holding, the holding we reaffirm, has three parts. First is a recognition of the right of the woman to choose to have an abortion before viability and to obtain it without undue interference from the State. Before viability, the State's interests are not strong enough to support a prohibition of abortion or the imposition of a substantial obstacle to the woman's effective right to elect the procedure. Second is a confirmation of the State's power to restrict abortions after fetal viability, if the law contains exceptions for pregnancies

---

[318] *See generally* Robin Fretwell Wilson, *The Calculus of Accommodation: Contraception, Abortion, Same-Sex Marriage, and Other Clashes between Religion and the State*, 53(4) Boston College Law Review 1417, 1454-59 (2012).

[319] *See* Larotonda, *supra* note 223.

[320] *See supra* note 225.

[321] *See Obama Chief of Staff: No More Compromise, Contraceptive Rule Is Done Deal* (Feb. 12, 2012), http://www.foxnews.com/politics/2012/02/12/obama-chief-staff-no-more-compromise-contraceptive-rule-is-done-deal/. Since the Obama Administration signaled its unwillingness to compromise further, the Department of Justice has asked the United States District Court for the Western District of Pennsylvania to dismiss a suit challenging the coverage mandate because "the administration is working on an amendment to address the religious objections."

See Brian Bowling, *Feds ask judge to dismiss 'morning-after' lawsuit*, Pittsburgh Tribune Review, May 1, 2012, http://triblive.com/home/1292708-74/college-lawsuit-drugs-says-amendment-geneva-administration-coverage-department-federal (arguing also that the plaintiffs "cannot satisfy the imminence requirement for standing"). For a list of suits challenging PPACA, see *HHS Mandate Information Central*, The Becket Fund for Religious Liberty, http://www.becketfund.org/hhsinformationcentral.

[322] 505 U.S. 833 (1992).

that endanger the woman's life or health. And third is the principle that the State has legitimate interests from the outset of the pregnancy in protecting the health of the woman and the life of the fetus that may become a child. These principles do not contradict one another; and we adhere to each.[323]

As noted above, the Court struck down a spousal notification provision but upheld a minimum 24-hour waiting period for informed consent after a physician advises the patient about the nature and risks of the procedure, estimated gestational age of the fetus, information describing the fetus, and alternatives to abortion.[324] The Court also upheld provisions that impose a reporting requirement for abortion providers and define "medical emergency" as a condition that requires an immediate abortion to prevent the woman's death or a serious risk of substantial and irreversible impairment of a major bodily function, provided that the definition is construed broadly enough to include several enumerated conditions, like preeclampsia. The Court also approved a parental consent provision, with judicial bypass, for minors seeking abortion. The *Casey* Court reasoned that although the state may demonstrate concern for the life of the unborn, its interest in that life may only override the woman's right to terminate her pregnancy once the fetus is viable. It recognized "the urgent claims of the woman to retain the ultimate control over her destiny and her body, claims implicit in the meaning of liberty. Liberty must not be extinguished for want of a line that is clear."[325] The Court concluded that "the line should be drawn at viability,"[326] which it defined as "the time at which there is a realistic possibility of maintaining and nourishing a life outside the womb, so that the independent existence of the second life can in reason and all fairness be the object of the state protection that now overrides the rights of the woman."[327] However, it rejected the trimester framework as unnecessary to accomplish its objective.[328] After *Casey*, the state's legitimate interests in fetal life from a pregnancy's outset are limited when an abortion restriction, pre-viability, creates an "undue burden" but the State may regulate abortions post viability so long as it provides an exception for those abortions that are necessary to preserve the life or health of the woman. Thus, the undue burden framework carves out greater scope for state regulation of abortion, if the State so chooses, than *Roe* did.

---

[323] 505 U.S. at 846.

[324] *See supra* § 5.05[C][2], [3].

[325] *Id.* at 869.

[326] *Id.* at 870.

[327] *Id.*

[328] The Tennessee Supreme Court, in *Planned Parenthood of Middle Tennessee v. Sundquist*, 38 S.W.3d 1 (Tenn. 2000), relied on the state constitution to reject *Casey's* "undue burden" test and adopt a strict scrutiny test to analyze stringent state abortion laws, to assure that they are narrowly tailored to further state interests. For a state-by-state analysis of state constitutional protections for abortions conferring protections for a woman's reproductive decisions that exceed those under the Federal Constitution, see Paul Benjamin Linton, Abortion under State Constitutions: A State-by-State Analysis (2008).

[6]   Partial Birth Abortion and Infants Born Alive

In *Stenberg v. Carhart*,[329] a divided Supreme Court, 5 to 4, found unconstitutional a Nebraska statute criminalizing most partial-birth abortions because it lacked any exception for preservation of the mother's health as required by *Casey*. Further, the Court held that the statute imposed an undue burden on a woman's right to choose abortion. This statute was especially problematic because it applied both pre- and post-viability and was directed only to the method of performing abortions, not preserving a life.

Seven years later, in *Gonzales v. Carhart*,[330] the Court upheld the federal Partial-Birth Abortion Ban Act of 2003.[331] In enacting the law, Congress stated that it had found partial-birth abortions were never medically necessary, and therefore there was no need to include an exception for the woman's health.[332] Congress provided an exception for the life of the mother, however, and targeted a narrower set of procedures than the Nebraska law invalidated in *Stenberg*. The Court concluded that the federal ban did not impose an undue burden on a woman's right to an abortion;[333] indeed, the law allowed for other types of late-term abortion procedures.[334] Harkening back to *Roe v. Wade*, the Court found the evaluation of abortion to be a balancing act between the privacy rights of the mother and the State's interest in preserving the health of the child.[335] In this instance, the Court found that for the late-term abortions proscribed by the ban, the balance favored the State's interest.[336]

One year before, in 2002, Congress enacted the Born-Alive Infants Protection Act of 2002 (BAIPA),[337] which directs that the words "person," "human being," "child," and "individual" shall include every infant who is born alive (defined in BAIPA to include infants who survive an induced abortion) at any stage of development, when determining the meaning of any Act of Congress or of any ruling, regulation, or interpretation of the various U.S. administrative bureaus and agencies. In 2005, the U.S. Department of Health and Human Services (HHS) issued Program Instructions to agencies administering or supervising child abuse prevention and treatment programs, explaining that state child abuse reporting laws must include born-alive infants in the state's procedures for responding to allegations of medical neglect.[338] HHS also issued revisions to its Medicare and

---

[329]   530 U.S. 914 (2000).

[330]   550 U.S. 124(2007).

[331]   Pub. L. No. 108-105, 117 Stat. 1201 (2003) (codified at 18 U.S.C. § 1531 (2011)).

[332]   Pub. L. No. 108-105 at § 2(13).

[333]   550 U.S. at 147.

[334]   *Id.*

[335]   *Id.* at 145.

[336]   *Id.* at 147.

[337]   Pub. L. No. 107-207, 116 Stat. 926 (2002) (codified at 1 U.S.C. § 8 (2011)).

[338]   *See* U.S. Dept. of Health & Hum. Svcs., Admin. on Children, Youth and Families, *Program Instruction: CAPTA and the Born-Alive Infants Protection Act of 2002, available at* http://www.acf.hhs.gov/programs/cb/laws_policies/policy/pi/2005/pi0501.pdf.

Medicaid State Operations Manual's complaint procedures for providers,[339] explaining how BAIPA affects a provider's duties under the Emergency Medical Treatment and Active Labor Act of 1986 (EMTALA)[340] to screen a born-alive infant for emergency medical conditions, to admit the infant for services, to stabilize the infant, or to transfer the infant as required by EMTALA.

Mirroring BAIPA, a number of states have attempted to enact "Personhood Amendments" to construe the word "person" to confer on unborn children "all the rights, privileges, and immunities available to other persons" under state law, "subject only to the Constitution of the United States, and decisional interpretations thereof by the United States Supreme Court."[341] As of 2011, no state had enacted such an amendment. Opponents fear such measures would provoke suits challenging abortion rights, make emergency contraceptives illegal, and deter physicians from offering certain services, like in-vitro fertilization.[342] At the very least, personhood amendments likely would bring fetuses within the scope of criminal law protections.[343]

[7] Abortion Demonstrations and Conscientious Objections

The abortion debate has sparked demonstrations on both sides of the issue. Most of the litigation about these demonstrations has involved anti-abortion demonstrations. The United States Supreme Court in *Bray v. Alexandria Women's Health Clinic*[344] overturned a decision of the United States Court of Appeals for the Fourth Circuit which held that blocking access to abortion clinics interfered with the right to interstate travel and constituted trespass and public nuisance under Virginia law.[345] Writing for the majority, Justice Scalia rejected the right to travel argument, reasoning that the only restriction of movement that would have resulted from the proposed demonstrations would have been in the limited area of the abortion clinics.[346]

---

[339] *See* Dept. of Health & Hum. Svcs., Ctrs. for Medicare and Medicaid Svcs., *State Operations Manual*, ch.5, *available at* https://www.cms.gov/manuals/downloads/som107c05.pdf.

[340] 42 U.S.C. § 1395dd. *See also* U.S. Dept. of Health & Hum. Svcs., Ctrs. for Medicare and Medicaid Svcs., *EMTALA Overview* (2011), *available at* https://www.cms.gov/emtala/.

[341] *See, e.g.*, Virginia H.B. No. 1440, *available at* http://leg1.state.va.us/cgi-bin/legp504.exe?111+ful+ HB1440H1+pdf. As of 2011, similar bills have been introduced in nine states. *See* http:// gopchoice.wordpress.com/2011/02/16/2362/ (listing efforts in Florida, Georgia, Iowa, Mississippi, Montana, North Dakota, Oklahoma, Texas, and Virginia).

[342] Associated Press, *Mississippi defeats life at conception ballot initiative*, USA Today, Nov. 8, 2011, http://www.usatoday.com/news/politics/story/2011-11-08/Mississippi-Abortion-Amendment/51129886/1. Some bills specifically provide that assisted conception will not be affected. *See* Virginia H.B. No. 1440 § 7, *supra* note 341.

[343] Fetuses already receive legal protection in some states. *See, e.g.*, *State v. McKnight*, 576 S.E.2d 168 (S.C. 2003) (defining persons to include fetuses for purposes of state's homicide by child abuse statute); *see also infra* § 7.06.

[344] 506 U.S. 263 (1993).

[345] *See Nat'l Org. for Women v. Operation Rescue*, 914 F.2d 582 (4th Cir. 1990).

[346] *Bray*, 506 U.S. at 276-77.

In response to *Bray*, Congress enacted the Freedom of Access to Clinic Entrances Act of 1994 (FACE).[347] FACE criminalizes violence, the threat of violence, and obstruction at the entrances of abortion clinics, in an attempt to prevent violence generated by the abortion protest movement.[348] The constitutionality of FACE has been upheld in the federal courts.[349]

Additionally, the Supreme Court has reaffirmed a woman's right to "unfettered ingress to and egress from [clinics]" in *Madsen v. Women's Health Center, Inc.*[350] Again, in 1997, in *Schenck v. Pro-Choice Network of Western N.Y.*,[351] the Court held that a preliminary injunction could be granted against demonstrations at an abortion clinic in order to guarantee free access and upheld a fixed 15-foot buffer zone from the entrance to the clinic, although it declined to uphold a similar floating buffer.

Abortion objections take the form of not only demonstrations, but also individual refusals to facilitate an abortion. Since 1973, a federal law known as the Church Amendment has allowed "health-care personnel to refuse to provide or assist with abortion, sterilization, and other procedures if doing so would violate their 'religious beliefs or moral convictions.' "[352] Nearly every state in the nation carves out similar conscience protections for abortion.[353] Notwithstanding these explicit protections, a number of healthcare providers have brought suit, alleging that they were threatened or coerced into assisting with abortions despite their stated religious objections.

In May, 2009, Cathy Cenzon-DeCarlo, a nurse, sued Mt. Sinai Hospital in New York, claiming that she was coerced into assisting with a late-term abortion in violation of the Church Amendment.[354] Mt. Sinai responded by asking that the case be dismissed, asserting that the Church Amendment did not confer a private right of action and the U.S. District Court for the Eastern District of New York agreed, dismissing the suit.[355] The Office of Civil Rights within HHS subsequently opened

---

[347] Pub. L. No. 103-259, 108 Stat. 694 (1994) (codified at 18 U.S.C. § 248 (2011)).

[348] *See* Helen R. Franco, Comment, *Freedom of Access to Clinic Entrances Act of 1994: The Face of Things to Come?*, 19 Nova L. Rev. 1083 (1995).

[349] *See U.S. v. Gregg*, 226 F.3d 253 (3d Cir. 2000). At least one federal judge has found abortion objectors not guilty of criminal contempt after being enjoined not to obstruct clinic access, reasoning that the objectors lacked the requisite willfulness for a violation because they "acted out of a sense of conscience and sincere religious conviction." *See United States v. Lynch*, 952 F. Supp. 167, 169 (S.D. N.Y. 1997).

[350] 512 U.S. 753, 769 (1994).

[351] 519 U.S. 357 (1997).

[352] Robin Fretwell Wilson, *Empowering Private Protection of Conscience*, 9 Ave Maria L. Rev. 101, 102 (2010).

[353] For a listing of these states, see Robin Fretwell Wilson, *Matters of Conscience: Lessons for Same-Sex Marriage from the Healthcare Context, in* Same-Sex Marriage and Religious Liberty: Emerging Conflicts, app. 299-310 (Douglas Laycock, Anthony R. Picarello, Jr. & Robin Fretwell Wilson, eds., 2008).

[354] Wilson, *supra* note 352, at 104.

[355] *Cenzon-DeCarlo v. Mt. Sinai Hosp.*, No. 09-CV-3120 (RJD), 2010 U.S. Dist. LEXIS 3208 (E.D.N.Y., Jan. 15, 2010).

an investigation.[356] DeCarlo filed a separate lawsuit in state court that is currently on appeal.[357]

In a second case, a group of nurses filed suit against the University of Medicine and Dentistry of New Jersey (UMDNJ) for "demanding that the Nurses must assist abortions in violation of their religious objections . . . illegally coerc[ing] some of the Nurses to train to assist abortions . . . and . . . scheduling . . . others to do so . . . [in] violation of federal and state law."[358] The federal District Court issued a temporary restraining order enjoining UMDNJ from forcing the nurses to assist in training or abortion services.[359] The case was fully resolved by settlement on the record "memorializing" the parties' agreement that, except when the mother's life is at risk and there is no other non-objecting staff available to assist, nurses with conscientious objections will not have to assist with abortions. In such rare cases, "the only involvement of the objecting plaintiffs would be to care for the patient until such time as a non-objecting person can get there to take over the care."[360]

As these cases illustrate, the abortion debate is far from over, and lower court cases addressing the extent of permissible restrictions on abortion will continue to make their way to the Supreme Court.

§ 5.06 VOLUNTARY AND INVOLUNTARY STERILIZATION

Like contraception and abortion, voluntary sterilization of a competent person involves the right to control one's reproductive capacity by not having children. Sterilization has become a commonly used method of birth control, but in contrast to other methods of contraception, sterilization should be considered permanent. Vasectomy of a male is a relatively simple operation performed by severing the canal that carries the sperm, preventing its inclusion in the semen, and thus preventing pregnancy. Female sterilization procedures are somewhat more complicated. Usually either tubal ligation, in which the fallopian tubes are tied, or salpingectomy, in which they are severed, is employed to prevent passage and fertilization of the ova. Both male and female procedures are relatively safe and do not interfere with the ability to engage in sexual intercourse.[361]

---

[356] *See also* Kaithianne Boniello, *Federal Probe of Nurse's Abort Suit*, N.Y. Post, June 20, 2010, *available* *at* http://www.nypost.com/p/news/local/federal_probe_of_nurse_abort_suit_6fjeTK9PMueTeNt E0afJAK. *See generally* Wilson, *supra* note 352, at 104.

[357] *See Cenzon-DeCarlo v. The Mount Sinai Hospital*, Nos. 2011-02282 and 2011-07705 (N.Y. App. Div., Apr. 12, 2010).

[358] *Danquah v. Univ. of Med. and Dentistry of N.J.*, No. 2:11-cv-06377-JLL-MAH, Pls.' Verif. Compl. at paras. 1, 2 (D.N.J., Oct. 31, 2011).

[359] *Id.*, at TRO (D.N.J., Nov. 3, 2011).

[360] *See id.* at Transcript of Proceedings, at 5, (D.N.J., Dec. 22, 2011). U.S. District Court Judge Linares "retain[ed] jurisdiction of this matter to ensure that the terms of the agreement are in fact followed." *Id.*

[361] *See* Homer J. Clark, Jr., *supra* note 72, at 214.

While contraception, abortion, and voluntary sterilization deal with the right to not have children, involuntary sterilization implicates the right to reproduce despite state interests in medically terminating that ability. The problems in this area have arisen because of developments in medical technology that enable the sterilization of people cheaply and efficiently, and because of the scientific or pseudo-scientific view that the mentally handicapped, mentally ill, or those convicted of a crime will have offspring similar to themselves and that society can benefit from eugenically controlling reproduction.

[A] Voluntary Sterilization

The right of competent adults to be voluntarily sterilized presumably has been resolved by *Griswold v. Connecticut.*[362] Voluntary sterilization is legal in the vast majority of states, provided that informed consent is obtained from the patient. No state interest or interest of an unconceived child arises to balance against the right of a competent adult to choose voluntary sterilization.

One case, *Hathaway v. Worcester City Hospital,*[363] involving a woman with eight children whose health would be endangered by further child-bearing, recognized a right to a "therapeutic sterilization" in a public hospital. However, the *Hathaway* rationale, based on *Roe v. Wade,*[364] may no longer be persuasive in light of the Supreme Court's holding in *Poelker v. Doe*[365] that there is no constitutional right to obtain a non-therapeutic abortion in a public hospital which provides public care for childbirth.[366]

More recently, in *Conservatorship of Valerie N.,*[367] the California Supreme Court recognized a positive right to sterilization for developmentally disabled persons. There, parents of a 29-year-old Down Syndrome daughter, Valerie, sought permission to authorize a salpingectomy or similar procedure that would permanently sterilize their daughter, a request denied by the probate court. Valerie lived at home but had made "inappropriate" sexual advances toward men, had rejected birth control pills, which made her ill, and was unable to apply a diaphragm safely.[368] The California Supreme Court affirmed the probate court's denial because the record did "not support a conclusion that sterilization [was] necessary to Valerie's habilitation," nor that less intrusive means were unavailable to Valerie.[369] The court did, however, authorize Valerie's parents to file a renewed petition without prejudice to make the requisite showing.[370]

---

[362] *See supra* § 5.04.

[363] 475 F.2d 701 (1st Cir. 1973).

[364] 410 U.S. 113 (1973). *See supra* § 5.05[B].

[365] 432 U.S. 519 (1977). *See supra* note 226 (and accompanying text).

[366] *But see Nyberg v. City of Virginia,* 667 F.2d 754 (8th Cir. 1982) (city could not prohibit staff physicians from performing abortions for paying patients at the sole hospital in the community).

[367] 40 Cal. 3d 143 (1985).

[368] *Id.* at 147-50.

[369] *Id.* at 148.

[370] *Id.* at 169. The California legislature subsequently amended the California Probate Code to provide for "those persons with developmental disabilities who, despite those disabilities, are capable of

A number of cases dealing with voluntary sterilization have involved medical malpractice actions addressing the liability of a physician for negligent performance of a voluntary sterilization resulting in the birth of a child.[371] Causes of actions have been framed in terms of "wrongful conception" or "wrongful pregnancy," which claim that negligent sterilization resulted in the birth of an unplanned or unwanted child; "wrongful birth," which alleges that a physician's inadequate counseling failed to give parents the option of avoiding conception or terminating pregnancy to prevent the birth of a child with genetic defects; and "wrongful life" claims brought on behalf of the child born with an impairment.[372] When negligence is proven, most courts allow direct damages, such as expenses of pregnancy, lost wages, pain and suffering, medical expenses for childbirth, and a second sterilization procedure, but have denied recovery for the expenses of raising and educating a non-handicapped child.[373] A few cases have additionally allowed parents to recover the costs of raising the child to adulthood.[374]

[B] Involuntary Sterilization

Involuntary sterilization deals with the converse issue: whether a person has a constitutional right to maintain the ability to procreate, despite countervailing interests of the state in mandating sterilization. Legal challenges to involuntary sterilization initially arose in response to scientific or pseudo-scientific theories,

---

engaging in sexual activity yet who, because of those disabilities, are unable to give the informed, voluntary consent necessary to their fully exercising the right to procreative choice, which includes the right to choose sterilization." *See* Cal. Prob. Code § 1950 (2011).

[371] *See generally* James Bopp, Jr., et al., *The "Rights" and "Wrongs" of Wrongful Birth and Wrongful Life: A Jurisprudential Analysis of Birth Related Torts*, 27 Duq. L. Rev. 461 (1989).

[372] *See infra* § 7.06; *Miller v. Rivard*, 585 N.Y.S.2d 523 (N.Y. App. Div. 1992); Martha C. Romney & Dorothy Duffy, *Medicine and Law: Recent Developments*, 25 Tort & Ins. L.J. 351, 356-59 (1990). The Ohio Supreme Court decided two cases on the same day that deal with children with birth defects. In *Simmerer v. Dabbas*, 733 N.E.2d 1169 (Ohio 2000), the court dealt with a case in which a child was born with heart defect and died after fifteen months, after the mother's negligent sterilization. The court treated the case as a wrongful pregnancy action, focusing on appropriate damages and concluding that the child's condition was not a "reasonably foreseeable result" of the physician's negligence so that damages were not recoverable. *Id.* at 1173. In *Hester v. Dwivedi*, 733 N.E.2d 1161 (Ohio 2000), which dealt with a child born with spina bifida after physicians failed to inform the parents of prenatal testing, the court rejected the parents' claim of wrongful life, finding that the negligence elements of damages and causation were not present and that the defendant's negligence did not cause the defect. *See also* Debra E. Batten, Note, McAllister v. Ha: *Wrongful Conception or Misconception?*, 34 Wake Forest L. Rev. 915 (1999).

[373] *See infra* § 7.06; *see also, e.g., Rouse v. Wesley*, 494 N.W.2d 7 (Mich. Ct. App. 1992); *Girdley v. Coats*, 825 S.W.2d 295 (Mo. 1992); *Johnson v. Univ. Hospitals*, 540 N.E.2d 1370 (Ohio 1989).

[374] *See infra* § 7.06; *see also Burke v. Rivo*, 551 N.E.2d 1 (Mass. 1990) (damages include costs of pregnancy, wife's lost earning capacity, medical expenses of delivery and care following birth, cost of care for other children while wife was incapacitated, cost of second sterilization procedure, husband's loss of consortium, wife's pain and suffering in connection with pregnancy, birth, and second sterilization operation, and emotional distress sustained as a result of the unwanted pregnancy, where parents wished to avoid having more children for economic reasons); *Lovelace Med. Ctr. v. Mendez*, 805 P.2d 603 (N.M. 1991) (no offset for intangible emotional benefits which will be received in raising the child; parents not required to mitigate damages by either having an abortion or placing the child for adoption because neither is an "ordinary or reasonable measure" within the meaning of the law relating to mitigation of damages).

now discredited, that the mentally handicapped, mentally ill, and certain convicted criminals will bear offspring with the same characteristics.[375] Involuntary sterilization actions generally arise from requests by institutions or parents responsible for people who are incapable of caring for themselves but are capable of reproduction.[376]

In the early 1900s the government began an effort to segregate those with mental retardation, mental illness, epilepsy and other "undesirable" conditions into state institutions.[377] Some states took even more drastic action, authorizing by statute the sterilization of the genetically "unfit."[378] Use of governmental power to institutionalize and sterilize persons with disabilities was based largely on then-popular theories of heredity, such as positive eugenics, the science of improving the characteristics and qualities of the human race by careful selection of parents, and its corollary, negative eugenics, which advocates attempting to prevent the reproduction of unfavorable traits.[379] Indiana enacted the first sterilization law in 1907, and by 1921, thousands of sterilizations had been performed.[380]

[1] *Buck* and *Skinner*

In the 1927 case of *Buck v. Bell*, the United States Supreme Court upheld a Virginia statute authorizing salpingectomy of institutionalized, mentally retarded female residents and vasectomy of males in certain circumstances.[381] The plaintiff, 18-year-old Carrie Buck, was described in Justice Holmes's majority opinion as "a feeble-minded white woman who was committed to the State Colony. She is the daughter of a feeble-minded mother in the same institution and the mother of an illegitimate feeble-minded child"[382] — characterizations that are greatly disputed today.[383]

After noting that the plaintiff had been afforded ample procedural protections, the Court upheld the statute on the grounds that, like compulsory vaccination, involuntary sterilization of Carrie Buck advanced the public good:

> We have seen more than once that the public welfare may call upon the best citizens for their lives. It would be strange if it could not call upon those who already sap the strength of the State for these lesser sacrifices, often not felt to be such by those concerned, in order to prevent our being swamped

---

[375] *See generally* Paul A. Lombardo, Three Generations, No Imbeciles: Eugenics, the Supreme Court, and Buck v. Bell 53-57 (2008) (describing early critiques).

[376] *Id.* at 267-68.

[377] *See* Stewart R. Hakola & Joseph F. Lavey, *Forty-Three Million Strong: An Overview of Civil Rights Protections for Persons with Disabilities*, 70 Mich. B.J. 548, 548 (1991).

[378] *See generally* Elyce Ferster, *Eliminating the Unfit — Is Sterilization the Answer?*, 27 Ohio St. L.J. 591(1966).

[379] *See generally* Lombardo, *supra* note 375.

[380] Ferster, *supra* note 378, at 593-94. *See also* Philip Reilly, The Surgical Solution: A History of Involuntary Sterilization in the United States 164 (1991).

[381] 274 U.S. 200 (1927).

[382] *Id.* at 205.

[383] *See* Lombardo, *supra* note 101.

with incompetence. It is better for all the world, if instead of waiting to execute degenerate offspring for crime, or to let them starve for their imbecility, society can prevent those who are manifestly unfit from continuing their kind. The principle that sustains compulsory vaccination is broad enough to cover cutting the Fallopian tubes . . . *Three generations of imbeciles are enough.*[384]

The dominant basis of the *Buck* decision was the eugenic theory, since discredited.[385] *Buck* did not address a constitutional right to procreate because it was decided prior to cases describing procreation as a fundamental right. Fortunately, later social and medical thought has influenced modern courts to reject the eugenic view and replace it with a much greater concern for the disabled.[386] Today, the statute at issue in *Buck* would likely be viewed as encroaching upon individuals' reproductive autonomy, although it may survive constitutional challenge if the statute was found to use "narrowly tailored means to achieve a compelling government interest."[387]

The Supreme Court's opinion in *Skinner v. Oklahoma*,[388] written by Justice Douglas in 1942, marked a change in position and the development of a fundamental right to procreate. The petitioner in *Skinner* was incarcerated for his third offense involving moral turpitude[389] and the Attorney General of Oklahoma sought to have him sterilized under the state's Habitual Criminal Sterilization Act. The Court struck down the statute,[390] basing its decision upon the Equal Protection Clause because it found that the statute differentiated based on the type of crime committed.[391] Most importantly, the classification was held to be subject to strict scrutiny because the legislation

involves one of the basic civil rights of man. Marriage and procreation are fundamental to the very existence and survival of the race. The power to sterilize, if exercised, may have subtle, far-reaching and devastating effects.

---

[384] 274 U.S. at 207 (emphasis added).

[385] Lombardo, *supra* note 101, at xi. The historical record suggests that the description of Carrie Buck as an imbecile and mental defective was a "legal sham" resting on "manufactured evidence"; moreover, evidence exists to indicate that *Buck* was a collusive suit intended to gain support for the Virginia statute and the eugenic movement. *See id.*; Paul Lombardo, *Three Generations, No Imbeciles: New Light on* Buck v. Bell, 60 N.Y.U. L. Rev. 30 (1985).

[386] *See generally* Elizabeth Scott, *Sterilization of Mentally Retarded Persons: Reproductive Rights and Family Privacy*, 1986 Duke L.J. 806.

[387] *See Vaughn v. Ruoff*, 253 F.3d 1124, 1129 (8th Cir. 2001) (citing *Buck v. Bell*, 274 U.S. 200, 207-08 (1927)).

[388] 316 U.S. 535 (1942).

[389] Professor Lombardo explains that "Skinner had committed three felonies," which included thefts valued at $25 or more. Lombardo, *supra* note 98, at 225.

[390] *Id.* at 224 (noting that "offenses arising out of the violation of the prohibitory laws, revenue acts, embezzlement, or political offenses" did not result in sterilization).

[391] *Id.* at 230 (quoting Justice Douglas that a statute which sterilizes "those who have thrice committed grand larceny with immunity for those who are embezzlers is a clear, pointed, unmistakable discrimination").

In evil or reckless hands it can cause races or types that are inimical to the dominant group to wither and disappear.[392]

Skinner recognized the individual's interest in the freedom to procreate, thus extending the right to privacy as it relates to sexual matters. *Skinner* did not, however, hold that all statutes authorizing involuntary sterilization are unconstitutional *per se*; it was decided under an equal protection analysis and held that statutes permitting sterilization would be subjected to strict scrutiny.[393]

[2] Modern Sterilization Issues

Whether sterilization may ever be imposed as punishment for a crime remains uncertain. One California case has held that conditioning a woman's probation for conviction of robbery on her not becoming pregnant without being married was improper because the condition was not reasonably related to the crime or to future criminal behavior.[394] A later California case held that a condition of probation for conviction of felony child abuse, which prohibited the defendant from conceiving a child, was overbroad, despite its relation to the crime committed. An alternative that was less subversive of the fundamental right to procreate must be imposed.[395] The California legislature has repealed a statute that authorized sterilization of certain sex offenders and replaced it with a provision that allows the court to impose hormonal chemical treatment in addition to other punishments; alternatively, if the criminal voluntarily undergoes permanent surgical sterilization, he can avoid the chemical treatment.[396]

One court has upheld the constitutionality of a temporary prohibition on procreation as condition of probation. In *State v. Oakley*,[397] the Wisconsin Supreme Court upheld a prohibition of procreation unless the defendant demonstrated that he had the ability to support and is supporting his existing children.[398] However, the Indiana Court of Appeals accepted a defendant's argument, in *Trammell v. State*,[399] that a non-procreation condition on probation did not serve any rehabilitative purpose, doing nothing to improve defendant's parenting skills or her prenatal condition should she later become pregnant.

The Arizona Supreme Court has held that conditioning a more lenient criminal punishment for child abuse on the defendants' sterilizations was impermissible absent statutory authority. It noted, however, that had the defendants voluntarily

---

[392] 316 U.S. at 541. Because the Court had "not the slightest basis for inferring that the line [between larceny and embezzlement] has any significance in eugenics nor that the inheritability of criminal traits follows the neat legal distinctions which the law has marked between those two offenses," the Court found the classification unconstitutional. Lombardo, *supra* note 375, at 230.

[393] Ronald D. Rotunda & John E. Nowak, Treatise on Constitutional Law: Substance and Procedure § 18.27, 569 (3d ed. 1999).

[394] *See People v. Dominguez*, 64 Cal. Rptr. 290 (Cal. Ct. App. 1967).

[395] *See People v. Pointer*, 199 Cal. Rptr. 357 (Cal. Ct. App. 1984).

[396] Cal. Penal Code § 645 (West 2011).

[397] 629 N.W.2d 200 (Wis. 2001).

[398] *See also State v. Kline*, 963 P.2d 697 (Ore. Ct. App. 1998) (same result).

[399] 751 N.E.2d 283 (Ind. Ct. App. 2001).

submitted to sterilization, the court could have considered that fact in sentencing.[400]

A number of states retain some form of statutory authorization for involuntary sterilization.[401] Although the trend among the states is to abolish these statutes,[402] other states have judicially determined that sterilization may be ordered in appropriate cases.[403]

Sterilization of the mentally disabled or mentally ill remains an important legal issue. Because of *Skinner's* recognition of a right to procreate, as well as the discrediting of the eugenic theory and changing conceptions of mental retardation, most contemporary cases and commentary have concluded that sterilization of the mentally handicapped cannot be presumptively acceptable.[404] This view was reflected in *North Carolina Ass'n for Retarded Children v. State*:[405]

> Most competent geneticists now reject social Darwinism and doubt the premise implicit in Mr. Justice Holmes' incantation that ". . . three generations of imbeciles is enough." [P]revalent medical opinion views with distaste even voluntary sterilization for the mentally retarded and is inclined to sanction it only as a last resort and in relatively extreme cases. In short, the medical and genetical experts are no longer sold on sterilization to benefit either retarded patients or the future of the Republic.[406]

Disabled persons are now entitled to the same fundamental procreative rights as others, and because of their mental disability, a higher burden of proof should be required before subjecting them to sterilization.[407]

Although voluntary sterilization of the mentally disabled or mentally ill is permissible if it is performed with informed consent, it is often difficult to assess an individual's capacity to consent and the nature of the information which must be given. A number of states have statutes establishing procedures for determining the

---

[400] *Smith v. Superior Court*, 725 P.2d 1101 (Ariz. 1986). *See also* Emily Campbell, *Birth Control as a Condition of Probation for those Convicted of Child Abuse: A Psycholegal Discussion of Whether the Condition Prevents Future Child Abuse or is a Violation of Liberty*, 28 Gonz. L. Rev. 67 (1992-93).

[401] *See, e.g.*, Colo. Rev. Stat. Ann. § 27-10.5-130 (West 2011); Ga. Code Ann. § 31-20-3 (2011); Idaho Code §§ 39-3901-39-3915 (2011).

[402] *See* Lombardo, *supra* note 375, at 270 (suggesting most laws have been repealed or significantly amended); *McKinney v. McKinney*, 805 S.W.2d 66 (Ark. 1991) (holding Arkansas' involuntary sterilization statute unconstitutional).

[403] *See, e.g.*, *In re Matejski*, 419 N.W.2d 576 (Iowa 1988); *In re Truesdell*, 304 S.E.2d 793 (N.C. Ct. App. 1983), *modified & aff'd*, 329 S.E.2d 630 (N.C. 1985); *see also* Nowak & Rotunda, *supra* note 393, at § 18.27, 567-68.

[404] *See* Scott, *supra* note 386, at 834-40.

[405] 420 F. Supp. 451 (M.D.N.C. 1976).

[406] *Id.* at 454.

[407] *See, e.g.*, *Conservatorship of Valerie N.*, 707 P.2d 760 (Cal. 1985) (conservators not entitled to demand sterilization because such proceedings impermissibly deprive developmentally disabled persons of privacy and liberty); *Motes v. Hall County Dept. of Family & Children Svcs.*, 306 S.E.2d 260 (Ga. 1983) (due process requires "clear and convincing evidence" to authorize sterilization); *In re Debra B.*, 495 A.2d 781 (Me. 1985) (mother failed to prove clearly and convincingly that daughter was physiologically capable of procreation).

circumstances in which sterilization of a handicapped individual is permissible.[408] In the absence of statutory authority, a number of courts have held that sterilization cannot be ordered,[409] although other courts have concluded that they possess equitable jurisdiction to order such sterilizations.[410]

Several tests have been applied for determining when sterilization of the handicapped should be ordered, including the best interests test, the substituted judgment test, and the medical necessity test.[411] The best interests test sustains sterilization if it is in the best interest of the patient and of society.[412] Under the substituted judgment test, the idea is that an incompetent's inability to exercise a fundamental right should not result in a loss of the person's constitutional interests; thus, the court is tasked with determining what the incompetent would choose if he or she were competent, substituting that judgment for its own.[413] The medical necessity test requires a medical expert to determine that sterilization is essential to preserve the life or health of the patient.[414]

The courts have applied these tests strictly. A compelling state interest should be established before interference with a person's bodily integrity and procreative rights is authorized.[415] If the person is a sexually active mentally disabled person who is unwilling to or incapable of controlling procreation by other contraceptive means and is likely to produce a handicapped child or would be unable to care for the child because of the degree of retardation, authorization of sterilization has been

---

[408] *See* Lombardo, *supra* note 375, at 267-68. Lombardo contrast states that provide extensive due process "before a court may order surgery for someone unable to give informed consent" — which includes a showing that the person to be sterilized is sexually active now or is likely to be, that no reasonable alternative method of contraception is available, and that sterilization does "not pose an unreasonable risk to the life or health of the patient and the patient [is] permanently incapable of raising a child, after considering "as completely as possible the wishes of the patient," as Virginia does — with states that have less protective involuntary sterilization statutes. For example, Arkansas "permits sterilization by court order of 'incompetents' who are unable to care for themselves 'by reason of mental retardation, mental illness, imbecility, idiocy or other mental incapacity.' . . . In cases of 'obvious hardship,' three physicians can certify, pursuant to the wishes of a guardian, that 'a sterilizing procedure is justified' without going to court at all."

[409] *See, e.g., In re S.C.E.*, 378 A.2d 144 (Del. Ch. 1977); *In re D.D.*, 408 N.Y.S.2d 104 (N.Y. App. Div. 1978).

[410] *See, e.g., In re Moe*, 432 N.E.2d 712 (Mass. 1982); *Wentzel v. Montgomery Gen. Hosp.*, 447 A.2d 1244 (Md. 1982), *cert. denied*, 459 U.S. 1147 (1983); *In re C.D.M.*, 627 P.2d 607 (Alaska 1981); *In re Sallmaier*, 378 N.Y.S.2d 989 (N.Y. Sup. Ct. 1976); *see also Wyatt v. Aderholt*, 368 F. Supp. 1383 (M.D. Ala. 1974); Eric M. Jaegers, Note, *Modern Judicial Treatment of Procreative Rights of Developmentally Disabled Persons: Equal Rights to Procreation and Sterilization*, 31 U. Louisville J. of Fam. L. 947 (1992); Maura McIntyre, Note, Buck v. Bell *and Beyond: A Revised Standard to Evaluate the Best Interests of the Mentally Disabled in the Sterilization Context*, 2007 U. Ill. L. Rev. 1303.

[411] *See generally* Scott, *supra* note 386.

[412] *See In re C.D.M.*, 627 P.2d 607 (Alaska 1981); *In re Hayes*, 608 P.2d 635 (Wash. 1980); *In re Eberhardy*, 307 N.W.2d 881 (Wis. 1981).

[413] *See In re Grady*, 405 A.2d 851 (N.J. Super. Ct. App. Div. 1979), *vacated and remanded on other grounds*, 426 A.2d 467 (N.J. 1981).

[414] *See In re A.W.*, 637 P.2d 366 (Colo. 1981); *In re Moe*, 432 N.E.2d 712 (Mass. 1982).

[415] *See generally* Scott, *supra* note 386; John A. Robertson, *Procreative Liberty and the Control of Conception, Pregnancy, and Childbirth*, 69 Va. L. Rev. 405(1983).

held to be constitutional.[416]

The Washington Supreme Court asserted its equitable jurisdiction to order a nonconsensual sterilization in the absence of a controlling statute in *In re Guardianship of Hayes*.[417] It adopted a best interests analysis, which balances the court's power against the individual's right to procreate. However, the plurality in *Hayes* failed to reach a consensus regarding when the individual's best interests would be served, and held that the minor's mother failed to show by clear and convincing evidence that the child's best interests would be served by undergoing involuntary sterilization.[418]

Some courts, however, limit the inquiry to the mentally disabled person's best interests, not the interests of caretakers or others. Thus, in *Estate of C.W.*,[419] the Superior Court of Pennsylvania upheld a lower court decision determining that "a guardian with authority to consent to a tubal ligation should be appointed for C.W., a 24-year-old mute woman with a mental age of 3-5."[420] The court stated that

> because sterilization necessarily results in the permanent termination of the intensely personal right of procreation, the trial judge must take the greatest care to ensure that the incompetent's rights are jealously guarded. [I]n making the decision of whether to authorize sterilization, a court should consider *only* the best interest of the incompetent person, not the interests or convenience of the individual's parents, the guardian or of society.[421]

The court found that sterilization was in the best interests of C.W.[422]

---

[416] *See North Carolina Ass'n for Retarded Children v. North Carolina*, 420 F. Supp. 451 (M.D.N.C. 1976).

[417] 608 P.2d 635 (Wash. 1980).

[418] The same type of analysis has been applied in cases dealing with mandated abortion when the risks of pregnancy and childbirth outweigh the risk of an abortion. For example, in *In the Matter of D.D.*, 394 N.Y.S.2d 139 (N.Y. Sur. Ct. 1977), the guardian of a severely mentally retarded woman sought authority from the court to consent to an abortion for the ward. The appellate court rejected a medical necessity test and applied a best interest analysis, holding that absent proof that the guardian was not acting in the best interests of the ward, the court had no basis for denying the requested authority for consent.

[419] 640 A.2d 427 (1994).

[420] *Id.* at 427.

[421] *Id.* at 428 (quoting *Matter of Terwilliger*, 450 A.2d 1376 (Pa. Sup. Ct. 1982)).

[422] *Id.* at 439. The court referenced "a non-exclusive list of 'guidelines'" for determining an incompetent's best interests with regard to sterilization, which included:

> . . . (2) The possibility that the incompetent person will experience trauma or psychological damage if she becomes pregnant or gives birth, and, conversely, the possibility of trauma or psychological damage from the sterilization operation . . . (3) The likelihood that the individual will voluntarily engage in sexual activity or be exposed to situations where sexual intercourse is imposed upon her . . . (4) The inability of the incompetent person to understand reproduction or contraception and the likely permanence of that inability . . . (7) The ability of the incompetent person to care for a child, or the possibility that the incompetent may at some future date be able to marry and, with a spouse, care for a child . . . (8) Evidence that scientific or medical advances may occur within the foreseeable future which will make possible either improvement of the individual's condition or alternative and less drastic sterilization procedures . . . [and] (9) A demonstration that the proponents of sterilization are

In *In re Grady*,[423] the New Jersey Supreme Court, exercising equitable jurisdiction in the absence of a controlling statute, adopted a substituted judgment test to authorize sterilization of a twenty-year-old woman afflicted with Down's Syndrome. The court recognized that exercise of its power to allow sterilization potentially violated the woman's right to procreate and it expressly disavowed the eugenic theory. After examining the United States Supreme Court decisions dealing with privacy and contraception, the *Grady* court concluded that these decisions support a personal right to control contraception, including the right to choose voluntary sterilization. The court reasoned that an individual's incompetence should not prevent exercise of this right and held that the court may employ its judicial power to exercise a fundamental right in cases where limited mental capacity renders a person's own right to choose meaningless.

Similarly, in *In re Moe*,[424] the mother of an adult mentally retarded woman filed a petition seeking an order for sterilization of her daughter. The Supreme Court of Massachusetts, before exercising its equitable jurisdiction to order sterilization, held that a guardian cannot validly consent to sterilization because the operation irreversibly extinguishes the ward's fundamental right to procreate. However, the court found that the doctrine of substituted judgment requires it to determine whether the incompetent would have chosen sterilization if she were competent. The court stressed that the personal rights implicated in a parent's or guardian's petition for sterilization require the judge to exercise the utmost care in reviewing all the evidence when determining whether the ward would consent to sterilization if competent.

Some states look first to substituted judgment and, lacking clear evidence, then to the incompetent person's best interests. For instance, in *In re Estate of K.E.J.*, the Appellate Court of Illinois addressed the appeal of V.H., a guardian who had unsuccessfully petitioned the lower court for an involuntary sterilization of her ward, K.E.J., "a 29-year-old mentally disabled woman."[425] The court affirmed the denial of permission to sterilize K.E.J., finding that

> guardians are to apply a substituted judgment standard, where they attempt to discern what the ward would have wished if she were competent, and then substitute that judgment for their own . . . . If there is clear and convincing evidence to demonstrate the course of action that the ward would have taken if competent, then those wishes take precedence over any best interests analysis . . . . [I]f the guardian is unable to determine such wishes "after reasonable efforts to discern them," then the guardian should instead act to further the ward's best interests.[426]

---

seeking it in good faith and that their primary concern is for the best interests of the incompetent person rather than their own or the public's convenience.

Id. at 428-29 (citing *Matter of Terwilliger*, 450 A.2d 1376 (Pa. Sup. Ct. 1982)).

[423]   426 A.2d 467 (N.J. 1981).

[424]   432 N.E.2d 712 (Mass. 1982).

[425]   887 N.E.2d 704, 708 (2008).

[426]   *Id.* at 720.

The court determined that V.H. had not established that the sterilization procedure was in the best interest of K.E.J.[427]

Most states have repealed their non-consensual sterilization statutes or held them unconstitutional over the past two decades. Only a handful of states retain statutes authorizing involuntary sterilization of particular individuals. Statutes compelling sterilization of the mentally retarded or criminal sex offenders may be constitutionally flawed,[428] although numerous cases have upheld sterilization statutes. The issue of sterilization has generated extensive literature and most recent commentary reflects dissatisfaction with laws that promote sterilization.[429]

§ 5.07 ASSISTED CONCEPTION

Assisted conception poses great challenges to the legal system by enabling people to have children when they might otherwise be unable to do so.[430] It has been argued that legal protection should be afforded not only to conception and childbirth but also to the right to the use of assisted reproduction techniques like artificial insemination, in vitro fertilization, and surrogacy to become pregnant or to be a parent.[431] On the other hand, some have contended that freedom to have sex without reproduction does not guarantee the freedom to reproduce without sex.[432] While artificial insemination has been employed for generations in this country, recent decades have witnessed the development of even more advanced means of aiding procreation. Such procedures include in vitro fertilization (IVF), cryopreservation of embryos, gamete interfallopian transfer (GIFT), zygote intrafallopian

---

[427] *Id.* at 722.

[428] *See, e.g., In re Thompson*, 169 N.Y.S. 638 (N.Y. Spec. Term), *aff'd*, 171 N.Y.S. 1094 (1918) (violation of state's police power); *Davis v. Berry*, 216 F. 413 (S.D. Iowa 1914) (statute constituted cruel and unusual punishment and failed to provide adequate procedural due process protections), *rev'd as moot*, 242 U.S. 468 (1917); *Haynes v. Lapeer Circuit Judge*, 166 N.W. 938 (Mich. 1918) (violation of equal protection standards).

[429] *See, e.g.,* Scott, *supra* note 386; Lombardo, *supra* note 375; Rebecca M. Gould, *Procreation: A Choice for the Mentally Retarded*, 23 Washburn L.J. 359 (1984); Susan Stefan, *Whose Egg is it Anyway?: Reproductive Rights of Incarcerated, Institutionalized, and Incompetent Women*, 13 Nova L. Rev. 405 (1989); Janice L. Ricks & Sophia F. Dziegielewski, *Involuntary Sterilization and the Mentally Retarded, Revisited*, 2 Hum. Rts. Rev. 125 (2000).

[430] *See, e.g.,* Judith Daar, Reproductive Technologies & the Law (1st ed. 2006).

[431] *See Carey v. Population Services Int'l*, 431 U.S. 678, 685 (1977) (decision whether to bear a child is fundamental to individual autonomy); *Eisenstadt v. Baird*, 405 U.S. 438, 453 (1972) ("If the right of privacy means anything, it is the right of the *individual*, married or single, to be free from unwarranted governmental intrusion into matters so fundamentally affecting a person as the decision whether to bear or beget a child") (emphasis in original); *see also Davis v. Davis*, 842 S.W.2d 588 (Tenn. 1992) (while the outer limits of the privacy right are not delineated, the decision whether to bear a child is at the heart of protected choices).

[432] *See* Jennifer L. Rosato, *The Children of ART (Assisted Reproductive Technology): Should the Law Protect Them From Harm?*, 2004 Utah L. Rev. 57; Catherine A. Clements, *What about the Children? A Call for Regulation of Assisted Reproductive Technology*, 84 Ind. L.J. 331 (2009); John A. Robertson, *Procreative Liberty and the Control of Contraception, Pregnancy and Childbirth*, 69 Va. L. Rev. 405 (1983) (also tracing history of procreative rights from birth control to women's decision whether to reproduce or not). *Compare* Glenn Cohen, *Right Not to be a Genetic Parent?* 81 So. Cal. L. Rev. 1115 (2008).

transfer (ZIFT), gamete donation, embryo donation, traditional surrogacy, and gestational surrogacy.[433] Indeed, by 2009, "more than 3 million individuals [world-wide could] trace their conception to in vitro fertilization, with nearly 3 in every 100 births in the United States . . . attributable to some form of assisted conception."[434] These procedures are used by infertile individuals, individuals who do not want to pass a genetic defect on to their offspring, and fertile individuals who are not living in traditional heterosexual relationships. One reason for the growth of assisted reproductive technology is the increased incidence of infertility, which has been attributed in part to delayed childbearing.[435] In addition, many infertile persons and individuals living in non-traditional family relationships desire a child with a genetic or biological link to them.[436] Another major impetus is the litany of difficulties many couples or individuals face in adopting a child.[437]

Perhaps the most significant issue raised by any assisted conception technique is, as Professor Harry Krause urged early on, "the child's legal status."[438] Indeed, numerous commentators have emphasized that any legislative responses to assisted conception techniques should focus primarily on the interests of the children who will be conceived.[439] But, as Professor Krause also indicated, many courts and

---

[433] *See* Lori B. Andrews & Lisa Douglass, *Symposium on Biomedical Technology and Health Care: Social and Conceptual Transformations, Alternative Reproduction*, 65 S. Cal. L. Rev. 623 (1991).

[434] Judith F. Daar & Robert G. Brzyski, *Genetic Screening of Sperm and Oocyte Donors: Ethical and Policy Implications*, 302(15) JAMA 1702-04 (2009).

[435] *See* U.S. Dept. of Health & Human Svcs., Centers for Disease Control and Prevention, *Fertility, Family Planning, and Reproductive Health of U.S. Women: Date from the 2002 National Survey of Family Growth*, Vital Health Stat. 23(25)at 22, 108 (tbl. 69) (2005), *available at* http://www.cdc.gov/nchs/data/series/sr_23/sr23_025.pdf (using "the standard medical definition of infertility [which classifies] a married couple . . . as 'infertile' if they have not used contraception and not become pregnant for 12 months or more" and finding that the "[p]ercent of married childless women 15-44 years of age who are infertile is 15-29 years: 11.0% . . . 30-34 years: 16.9% . . . 35-39 years: 22.6% . . . 40-44 years: 27.4%"); *see also* Robin Fretwell Wilson, *Keeping Women in Business (and Family)*, in Rethinking Business Management 103 (Samuel Gregg & James R. Stoner, eds., 2008) ("For women over 30, the relatively slim chances of pregnancy, 30%, begin to decline by 3.5% each year, ebbing to 12.5% by age 35 and 2% by age 40. By 45, it's nearly impossible for a woman to conceive using her own eggs. Men face shrinking odds of conceiving after 35 as well."); Michele Goodwin, *Assisted Reproductive Technology and the Double Bind: The Illusory Choice of Motherhood*, 9 J. Gender Race & Just. 1 (2005) (explaining reasons for delayed child bearing).

[436] Andrews & Douglass, *supra* note 433, at 626.

[437] Individuals who want to parent alone and same-sex couples seeking a child face significant barriers to adopting. *See* David M. Brodzinsky, *Adoption by Lesbians and Gays: A National Survey of Adoption Agency Policies, Practices, and Attitudes*, Evan B. Donaldson Adoption Institute,http://www.adoptioninstitute.org/whowe/Gay%20and%20Lesbian%20Adoption1.html.

[438] Harry D. Krause, *Artificial Conception: Legislative Approaches*, 19 Fam. L.Q. 185, 193 (1985).

[439] *Compare* Ilana Hurwitz, *Collaborative Reproduction: Finding the Child in the Maze of Legal Motherhood*, 33 Conn. L. Rev. 127, 169-74 (2000) (arguing for recognition of a "best interests of the child" standard), *and* Browne C. Lewis, *Three Lies and a Truth: Adjudicating Maternity in Surrogacy Disputes*, 49 U. Louisville L. Rev. 371 (2011), *with* Vanessa S. Browne-Barbour, *Bartering for Babies: Are Preconception Agreements in the Best Interests of Children?*, 26 Whittier L. Rev. 429 (2004) (arguing that statutory requirements that "parties . . . obtain prior court approval of their preconception agreements, among other things, to protect the best interest of the child . . . may protect the interest of the parties; however, these agreements are not and cannot be based upon a true best interest of the child analysis"), *and* Mimi Yoon, *The Uniform Status of Children of Assisted Conception Act: Does it*

legislatures have also struggled to show respect for the interests of the adult parties involved, who may include the donor of the semen, the donor of the ovum, the woman who carries the child to term, and the couple who intends to parent the resulting child.[440] Some policymakers and commentators favor recognizing the gestational mother;[441] others advocate an intent test in deciding parentage;[442] while still others argue for or against the genetic relationship itself as a sufficient basis for allocating parenthood.[443]

[A]   Artificial Insemination

Artificial insemination may be accomplished by several relatively simple medical procedures. Artificial insemination by donor (AID) involves impregnation of a woman by syringe, using the semen of a donor who is not the patient's husband or, more recently, partner. AID is a potential solution for couples where the male partner is infertile. Both non-profit and commercial sperm banks have been established to freeze and store semen for later use. Homologous artificial insemination (AIH) entails a similar procedure using the semen of a woman's husband or partner.[444]

Initially, when sperm from a third-party donor was used, legal questions arose concerning paternal responsibility.[445] The Uniform Parentage Act (UPA), promulgated in 1973, provided that if a married woman was artificially inseminated with a third-party donor's semen under the supervision of a licensed physician and with the consent of her husband, a child so conceived would be legally treated as

---

Protect the Best Interests of the Child in a Surrogate Arrangement?, 16 Am. J.L. & Med. 525 (1990).

[440] *Id.*

[441] *See, e.g.*, Anne Goodwin, *Determination of Legal Parentage in Egg Donation, Embryo Transplantation, and Gestational Surrogacy Arrangements*, 26 Fam. L.Q. 275, 291 (1992).

[442] *See, e.g.*, Erin Y. Hisano, Comment, *Gestational Surrogacy Maternity Disputes: Refocusing on the Child*, 15 Lewis & Clark L. Rev. 517 (2011) (arguing that "[i]f, after weighing each woman's connection and traits, the court still finds that each woman is equally fit to care for the child, the court may use pre-conception intent as a tiebreaker . . . . [I]ntent is the fairest solution because courts should recognize and preserve the pre-conception intent as indicated by both the commissioning party and the gestational surrogate"); Martha J. Stone, Comment, *Tick . . . Tick . . . Tick: As Biological Clocks Wind Down, the Laws Governing Inheritance and Parental Rights Issues Heat up*, 43 S. Tex. L. Rev. 233 (2001).

[443] *Compare, e.g.*, Jeffrey M. Place, *Gestational Surrogacy and the Meaning of "Mother": Johnson v. Calvert, 851 P.2d 776 (Cal. 1993)*, 17 Harv. J. L. & Pub. Pol'y 907, 908 (1994) (urging that "a genetic definition of motherhood is best suited for surrogacy cases"), *and* Amanda E. de Vito, Comment, *Establishing and Rebutting Maternity: Why Women are at a Loss Despite the Advent of Genetic Testing*, 74 Alb. L. Rev. 1873 (2010-11), *with* John Lawrence Hill, *What Does It Mean to Be A "Parent"?: The Claims of Biology as the Basis For Parental Rights*, 66 N.Y.U.L. Rev. 353, 418 (1991) ("[T]he genetic relationship, in itself, should be accorded very little moral weight in the determination of parental status."); Jennifer S. Hendricks, *Essentially a Mother*, 13 Wm. & Mary J. Women & L. 429, 431 (2007) (arguing that "proposals for determining parentage [that] range from the purely genetic to the purely contractual . . . denigrate the non-genetic aspects of biological reproduction . . . commodify gestation and create perverse incentives to use riskier rather than safer reproductive technology").

[444] *See* Charles P. Kindregan, Jr. & Maureen McBrien, Assisted Reproductive Technology: A Lawyers Guide to Emerging Law and Science (2006); Gaia Bernstein, *The Socio-Legal Acceptance of New Technologies: A Close Look at Artificial Insemination,*77 Wash. L. Rev. 1035 (2002).

[445] *See supra* § 5.02[H].

the natural child of the husband.[446] The sperm donor in such an authorized procedure is legally regarded not to be the natural father of a child conceived pursuant to the Act.[447] The Act fails, however, to address the parentage issues that arise when parties use artificial insemination in less formal settings. As of 2010, 12 states still had statutes modeled after the 1973 Uniform Parentage Act provisions.[448]

The UPA was updated in 2000, and amended in 2002.[449] The 2000 version of the UPA loosened the restriction to only married women, providing that "a donor is not a parent of a child conceived by means of assisted reproductive technology," whether or not the mother is married.[450]

Assisted conception procedures and consent forms generally attempt to preserve the donor's anonymity.[451] Many recipients prefer to use an anonymous donor to ensure that the donor will not interfere in the parent-child relationship. The primary fear of sperm donors — future financial responsibility for the child — has been ameliorated in states that have adopted statutes providing either that the husband of the sperm recipient is the legal father or that state affirmatively that the donor will have no legal relationship to the child.[452] However, confidentiality poses risks to children created with donor gametes who develop a genetic defect. The American Society for Reproductive Medicine recommends that confidential

---

[446] Unif. Parentage Act, *Artificial Insemination*, § 5, 9B U.L.A. 301 (1987). *See also Jackson v. Jackson*, 739 N.E.2d 1203, 1206 (Ohio Ct. App. 2000); *R.S. v. R.S.*, 670 P.2d 923 (Kan. Ct. App. 1983); *L.M.S. v. S.L.S.*, 312 N.W.2d 853 (Wis. 1981).

[447] Unif. Parentage Act § 5(b) (providing that a sperm donor who is not married to the mother "is treated in law as if he were not the natural father").

[448] For a list of state adopters of each version, see *supra* note 15.

[449] Uniform Parentage Act (2000) (last amended or revised in 2002). A second uniform act, the Uniform Status of Children of Assisted Conception Act, has been adopted by two states, North Dakota and Virginia. Unif. Status of Children of Assisted Conception Act (1988).

[450] Unif. Parentage Act § 702 (2010) (last amended or revised in 2002). *See also* 2 Ann M. Haralambie, Handling Child Custody, Abuse and Adoption Cases 55 (3d ed. 2009) (citing UPA § 702 (2000)).

[451] *See, e.g.*, Vanessa L. Pi, Note, *Regulating Sperm Donation: Why Requiring Exposed Donation is not the Answer*, 16 Duke J. Gender L. & Pol'y 379 (2009). *But also see* Michelle Dennison, *Revealing Your Sources: The Case for Non-Anonymous Gamete Donation*, 21 J.L. & Health 1 (2008).

[452] *See, e.g.*, Ala. Code § 26-17-702 (2011) ("A donor who donates to a licensed physician for use by a married woman is not a parent of a child conceived by means of assisted reproduction. A married couple who, under the supervision of a licensed physician, engage in assisted reproduction through use of donated eggs, sperm, or both, will be treated at law as if they are the sole natural and legal parents of a child conceived thereby."); Fla. Stat. Ann. § 742.14 (2011) ("The donor of any egg, sperm, or preembryo, other than the commissioning couple or a father who has executed a preplanned adoption agreement . . . shall relinquish all maternal or paternal rights and obligations with respect to the donation or the resulting children."); N.M. Stat. Ann. § 40-11A-702 (effective Jan. 1, 2010) ("Donors of eggs, sperm or embryos are not the parents of a child conceived by means of assisted reproduction."); Va. Code Ann. § 20-158(A)(3) (2008) ("A donor is not the parent of a child conceived through assisted conception, unless the donor is the husband of the gestational mother."); *see also* Christina M. Eastman, Comment, *Statutory Regulation of Legal Parentage in Cases of Artificial Insemination by Donor: A New Frontier of Gender Discrimination*, 41 McGeorge L. Rev. 371, 380 (2010) (noting that the present version of § 702 of the UPA "provides that 'donors are eliminated from the parental equation'" (quoting official comment)). As of 2010, statutes in thirteen states — Alabama, Colorado, Connecticut, Delaware, Florida, Idaho, New Mexico, North Dakota, Texas, Utah, Virginia, Washington, and Wyoming — protect third-party sperm and egg donors alike from parental responsibility for offspring. *Id.* at nn.74, 75.

records be kept on gamete or embryo donors and be made available to the recipient or child in accordance with the parties' advance agreement about how and when donor information will be released.[453]

Confidentiality of semen donors also presents the risk of incest between half-siblings or between a sperm donor and his unknown daughter.[454] Other concerns include apprehension about insufficient screening of donors, the possibility of transmitting an infectious disease or genetic disorder,[455] and lack of regulation of facilities and screening.[456]

Obtaining consent of the recipient's husband is critical for assuring financial support for the child. In *In re Baby Doe*,[457] a wife was artificially inseminated with the knowledge of her husband, who was unable to father children. After conception, but before the birth of the child, the couple separated and the husband sought an order declaring that he was not the child's father in order to avoid child support obligations. Noting that most decisions have been relatively uniform in assigning paternal responsibility to the husband when his conduct evidences consent to the artificial insemination, the court stated that a husband's consent to his wife's impregnation by artificial insemination need not be express, but may be implied

---

[453] American Society for Reproductive Medicine, *Informing Offspring of Their Conception by Gamete Donation*, 81 Fertility & Sterility 527 (2004), *available at* http://www.sart.org/uploadedFiles/ ASRM_Content/News_and_Publications/Ethics_Committee_Reports_and_Statements/informing_ offspring_donation.pdf.

[454] Donor sibling registries have emerged, in part, to assist donor-conceived children to avoid "accidental incest." *See* http://www.donorsiblingregistry.com. While such risks may seem remote, one attorney in 2011 learned that he has at least 75 children as a result of donating to a Virginia sperm bank, a figure he expects will grow to 120 to 140 children. *See* Debra Cassens Weiss, *Lawyer Learns He Has at Least 75 Children*, ABA J., Sept. 27, 2011, *available at* http://www.abajournal.com/news/article/ lawyer_learns_he_has_at_least_75_children. Some have advocated for mandatory listing of donors on a national gamete donor registry. *See* J. Graham, *When a disease is donated: mom's quest to warn daughter's offspring goes to the heart of a thorny debate on sperm, egg donors*, Chi. Trib., Mar. 27, 2008, at A1; Naomi Cahn, *Necessary subjects: the need for a mandatory national donor gamete registry*, 12 DePaul J. Healthcare Law 203 (2008); Michelle Dennison, *Revealing Your Sources: The Case for Non-Anonymous Gamete Donation*, 21 J.L. & Health 1 (2008). Other commentators have called for greater regulation, such as limiting the number of children fathered by any single donor, as Great Britain, France, and Sweden do. *See* Naomi Cahn, Test Tube Families: Why the Fertility Markets Need Legal Regulation 114-29 (2009); Annette Baran & Reuben Pannor, Lethal Secrets 167-72 (1989) (calling for a limit on donors to no more than three offspring). Other authors feel the risk of future incest is minimal in our large, transient society. Andrews & Douglass, *supra* note 433, at 661.

[455] In May 2005, the U.S. Food and Drug Administration began screening biologics, including eggs and sperm, for certain infectious diseases and genetic disorders. Donated gametes have been linked to the transmission of a number of disorders, including "hypertrophic cardiomyopathy, . . . autosomal dominant polycystic kidney disease, cystic fibrosis, and severe congenital neutropenia." Judith F. Daar & Robert G. Brzyski, *Genetic Screening of Sperm and Oocyte Donors: Ethical and Policy Implications*, 302(15) JAMA 1702, 1703-04 (2009) (arguing that the present system is one of "no or low screening" which should be reformed to add "baseline genetic screening to current [FDA] regulations and [to] establish[ ] a voluntary registry of gamete donors"). The possibility that by donating gametes, one might transmit a genetic disease is unlikely to occur to most gamete donors, who are typically "unmarried men and women in their 20s and early 30s who are not parents. Individuals in this demographic group typically do not contemplate their own genetic health, let alone that of their offspring, until faced with their own childbearing decisions." *Id.*

[456] Andrews & Douglass, *supra* note 433, at 656.

[457] 353 S.E.2d 877 (S.C. 1987).

from conduct demonstrating his knowledge of the procedure and his failure to object. The court held that "a husband who consents for his wife to conceive a child through artificial insemination, with the understanding that the child will be treated as their own, is the legal father of the child born as a result of the artificial insemination and will be charged with all the legal responsibilities of paternity, including support."[458] The husband was thus responsible for support of the child due to his knowledge of and assistance in his wife's efforts to conceive through artificial insemination.

The husband's consent estops him from later denying paternity and assures that children conceived through artificial insemination will have parents who remain responsible for them, especially financially. In *L.M.S. v. S.L.S.*,[459] the Wisconsin Court of Appeals held that where the husband had consented to his wife's impregnation by artificial insemination, he had the legal duties and responsibilities of a father, including support. It concluded that a person who "participates in the arrangement for the creation of a child cannot consider" the subsequent relationship to be "a temporary relation to be assumed and disclaimed at will."[460] Rather, "[s]uch an arrangement imposes an obligation to support the child for whose existence he is responsible."[461]

Similarly, when a husband consented orally, but not in writing, to his wife's insemination and had no contact with the treating physician immediately prior to successful insemination, the Kansas Court of Appeals, in *R.S. v. R.S.*,[462] held the husband responsible for the resulting child and the child's support. The *R.S.* court concluded that a husband who consents to his wife's insemination with another's sperm is estopped from denying paternity, unless the husband establishes by clear and convincing evidence that such consent was withdrawn prior to the wife becoming pregnant.

The question of paternity was raised in a less conventional setting in *Karin T. v. Michael T.*,[463] in which the respondent had been born a female but changed her identity to male, then married a woman. The couple had two children by artificial insemination prior to the parties' separation, after which the Department of Social

---

[458] 353 S.E.2d at 878.

[459] 312 N.W.2d 853 (Wis. Ct. App. 1981).

[460] *Id.* at 855.

[461] *Id.*

[462] 670 P.2d 923 (Kan. Ct. App. 1983). *Compare In Re Marriage of A.C.H. and D.R.H.*, 210 P.3d 929 (Or. Ct. App. 2009) (imposing duty of support on husband who consented, albeit not in writing, to participation in wife's artificial insemination). The converse is also true — husbands who do not consent will not be liable for support to any child who results. *See In Re Marriage of Witbeck-Wildhagen*, 667 N.E.2d 122 (Ill. App. Ct. 1996).

[463] 484 N.Y.S.2d 780 (N.Y. Fam. Ct. 1985). The issue of consent has also arisen in the context of a criminal prosecution for non-support. *See People v. Sorenson*, 437 P.2d 495 (Cal. 1968). In *Sorenson*, a father who had been convicted of criminal non-support disputed his conviction, arguing that he was not the child's father because his wife had conceived the child through AID. The court stated "One who consents to the production of a child cannot create a temporary relation to be assumed and disclaimed at will, but the arrangement must be of such character as to impose an obligation of supporting those for whose existence he is directly responsible . . . [I]t is safe to assume that without defendant's active participation and consent the child would not have been procreated." *Id.* at 499.

Services filed a support action on behalf of the children. The New York court held that, in view of the agreement that the respondent signed as father of the children, the children were marital children of the respondent, who had waived any rights to disclaim them.

A husband's consent may also estop the wife from denying him parental rights. In *Lone v. Lone*, a husband's after-the-fact consent to assisted conception by his wife substantially complied with statutory requirements, warranting a joint custody award.[464]

The legal father of a child conceived through AID obtains the same rights to custody, visitation, and other parenting prerogatives as a natural father. In *In re Adoption of Anonymous*,[465] a couple divorced after the birth of a child conceived through consensual artificial insemination by a third-party donor. Their divorce decree declared the child to be a child of the marriage. After the wife's remarriage, her new husband petitioned to adopt the child and the former husband refused. The court held that a child born of consensual artificial insemination during a valid marriage is a legitimate child of the marriage, entitled to the same rights and privileges of a child naturally conceived during marriage. A husband who consents to his wife's artificial insemination by semen of a third-party donor is the parent of the child so conceived and his consent is required in order for the child to be adopted by another.[466]

Because physicians typically use only sperm from anonymous donors, most known-donor cases stem from instances of self-insemination by single women or lesbian couples, who request sperm from a friend or acquaintance and perform the insemination themselves.[467] These private arrangements fail to comply with the common statutory requirements that the woman be married and inseminated under the supervision of a licensed physician.[468] A myriad of issues have arisen from such arrangements, with different courts resolving them in different ways.

For example, known donors have sought to be declared the child's father, with mixed results. A pair of Texas cases illustrates the divergent outcomes. In 2005, a Texas Court of Appeals in Houston held that despite the exclusion of sperm donors

---

[464]   912 P.2d 290 (N.M. Ct. App. 1996).

[465]   345 N.Y.S.2d 430 (N.Y. Sur. Ct. 1973).

[466]   *See K.B. v. J.R.*, 887 N.Y.S.2d 516, 525 (N.Y. Sup. Ct. 2009).

[467]   *See, e.g.*, Dawn R. Swink, *Caveat Vendor: Potential Progeny, Paternity, and Product Liability Online*, 2007 B.Y.U. L. Rev. 857, 869 n.69 (describing the ease of ordering donor sperm online and "hav[ing] vials shipped to the client's home for self-insemination"); Daniel Wikler & Norma J. Wikler, *Turkey-baster Babies: The Demedicalization of Artificial Insemination*, 69 Milbank Q. 5, 5-6 (1991) (noting that "[a]lthough the number of women who have performed self-insemination can only be estimated, it is surely greater than those involved in surrogacy, in vitro fertilization, and surrogate embryo transfer combined"); Harvey L. Fiser & Paula K. Garrett, *It Takes Three, Baby: The Lack of Standard, Legal Definitions of "Best Interest of the Child" and the Right to Contract for Lesbian Parents*, 15 Cardozo J. L. & Gender 1, 4 (2008) (noting that self-insemination "goes against a primary condition of the 1973 UPA requiring physician intervention" and that, in states whose statutes are modeled on the earlier version of the UPA, self-insemination "may create legal issues when parties attempt to terminate any possible parentage rights of the donor"); *see also Jhordan C. v. Mary K.*, 224 Cal. Rptr. 530 (Cal. Ct. App. 1986), *infra* note 334.

[468]   *See supra* note 446; Haralambie, *supra* note 450, at 17.

from the state code's definition of "alleged father," the code did "not exclude sperm donors from the definition of a man 'whose paternity is to be adjudicated,'" and therefore, a known donor could bring action to adjudicate his parentage under the UPA.[469] By contrast, in 2006, a Texas Court of Appeals in San Antonio held that an unmarried sperm donor did not have standing to pursue a paternity determination of the child ultimately born through assisted reproduction because he had not signed an acknowledgment of paternity.[470]

Known donors have also sought visitation. In *C.M. v. C.C.*,[471] an unmarried woman used a donor's sperm to artificially inseminate herself. The New Jersey court acknowledged the sperm donor as the natural father of the child and granted him visitation rights. Similarly, in *Jhordan C. v. Mary K.*,[472] Mary and her female partner mutually agreed that Jhordan would be the sperm donor for artificial insemination of Mary and that the two women would raise the child. No written contract was executed concerning Jhordan's status, although he maintained continuous contact with Mary throughout her pregnancy and after the birth of the child. When Jhordan requested visitation, Mary refused, and Jhordan brought an action to establish paternity and visitation rights. The trial court declared Jhordan the legal father, ordered him to pay child support, and granted him visitation, but denied him any input into decision-making for the child. Upon Mary's appeal, the California Court of Appeals affirmed, holding that a statute denying paternal rights to a sperm donor when artificial insemination is performed according to statutory procedures does not apply to sperm donors who provide the semen directly to the child's mother.

One of the difficulties with awarding rights to or imposing obligations on known donors is the notion that guides many courts, namely that a child can have only two legal parents.[473] But "with the use of assisted reproductive technologies . . . it is possible for a child to have more than two legal parents, and there are instances in which the adults involved envision parental roles for more than two adults."[474] Some courts have concluded that such arrangements may in fact be beneficial, and have awarded parental rights to more than two people.[475] In 2007, a Pennsylvania

---

[469] *In re Sullivan*, 157 S.W.3d 911 (Tex. App. 2005). *See also Tripp v. Hinckley*, 290 A.D.2d 767 (N.Y. App. Div. 2002) (donor listed on birth certificate may seek visitation); *Breit v. Mason*, 718 S.E.2d 482 (Va. Ct. App. 2011) (finding that unmarried father of child conceived by assisted conception, who acknowledged paternity and provided support to the child, with whom he lived, was not barred from asserting paternity), *cert. granted*, 2012 Va. LEXIS 141 (June 11, 2012).

[470] *In re H.C.S.*, 219 S.W.3d 33 (Tex. App. 2006).

[471] 377 A.2d 821 (N.J. Super. Ct. App. Div. 1977).

[472] 224 Cal. Rptr. 530 (Cal. Ct. App. 1986).

[473] *See* Melanie B. Jacobs, *More Parents, More Money: Reflections on the Financial Implications of Multiple Parentage*, 16 Cardozo J. L.& Gender 217 (2010). See also California Senate Bill 1476, vetoed by Governor Edmund G. Brown Jr. on September 30, 2012, *available at* http://www.leginfo.ca.gov/cgi-bin/postquery?bill_number=sb_1476&sess=CUR&house=B&author=leno, which would have permitted, under limited circumstances, a child to have more than two legal parents if doing so was in the best interest of the child.

[474] *Id.* at 218.

[475] *Id.*

court found "that it was possible to establish legal support obligations for three parents."[476]

Claims for support have succeeded when the donor and recipient of sperm have not complied with statutory requirements for the "cut-off" of the donor's parental duties. Thus, in *In the Matter of Parentage of J.M.K. and D.R.K.*,[477] the Washington Supreme Court reversed a lower court ruling that a married man who donated semen to his lover's physician for her to conceive a child by IVF while they were together, but was unaware when she used the semen to conceive and give birth to a second child, was not the father of the children under a statute exempting semen donors. The court held the donor liable for child support for both children, finding that his "numerous photographs, letters and cards" negated the possibility that he was an "anonymous" donor, as required by the statute to be legally regarded not to be the legal father of the children.[478]

The degree to which parties can bargain around these background rules remains an open issue. In *Ferguson v. McKiernan*,[479] the mother and the sperm donor, with whom she had previously had an intimate relationship, entered into an oral agreement wherein he agreed to provide the sperm for IVF in a clinical setting while relinquishing any right to visitation with the resultant child. In return, the mother agreed to release him from any obligation for any child conceived. As a result of IVF treatments, the mother gave birth to twin sons and eventually sought child support five years after their birth.[480] The trial court ruled that the contract was unenforceable, as the legal rights at stake were not actually held by either parent, but instead belonged to the children, and therefore could not be negotiated prior to their existence. The Supreme Court of Pennsylvania subsequently reversed[481] the trial court decision, holding that the agreement was indeed enforceable and that such agreements did not contravene public policy "in the face of the evolving role played by alternative reproduction technologies in contemporary American society."[482]

Similarly, in *Lamaritata v. Lucas*,[483] a Florida appeals court reversed an order granting visitation rights to a known sperm donor, even though the parties' contract allowed for it, because a sperm donor retains no legal parental rights under Florida law. However, parties to a contract that is not enforced may have remedies in tort.[484]

---

[476] *Id.* at 218-19 (citing *Jacob v. Shultz-Jacob*, 923 A.2d 473 (Pa. Super. Ct. 2007)).

[477] *In re Parentage of J.M.K.*, 119 P.3d 840 (Wash. 2005).

[478] *Id.* at 848.

[479] 855 A.2d 121 (2004).

[480] *Id.* at 122.

[481] 940 A.2d 1236 (Pa. 2007).

[482] *Id.* at 1245.

[483] 823 So. 2d 316 (Fla. Dist. Ct. App. 2002).

[484] In a 2000 California appellate case, *Dunkin v. Boskey*, 98 Cal. Rptr. 2d 44 (Cal. Ct. App. 2000), an unmarried man who had been denied the opportunity to establish paternity was later allowed to recover damages based on unjust enrichment. The man, who was sterile due to testicular cancer, had entered into a written contract with his female cohabitant to become the father of a child to be conceived by artificial

The ability to preserve sperm for later use has raised a number of thorny questions of who controls its use and disposition, as well as what duties of support flow to a child conceived by "posthumous insemination by cryopreserved semen or posthumous implantation of a cryopreserved embryo."[485] The question of custody arose in *Hecht v. Superior Court.*[486] There, an attorney who committed suicide left his semen by will to his long-time cohabitant, who wished to be impregnated by the semen. The decedent's children opposed the impregnation and wanted the sperm destroyed. The California Court of Appeals upheld the testamentary disposition, concluding that the decedent's interest in his cryogenically preserved sperm was property over which the probate court had jurisdiction and that public policy would not prohibit artificial insemination of an unmarried woman, nor would posthumous artificial insemination violate any public policy.

Posthumous insemination also raises difficult questions about the resulting child's entitlement to survivor's benefits since the genetic parent has pre-deceased the child. The 2000 version of the UPA authorizes posthumous assisted reproduction if the deceased parent "consented in a record that if assisted reproduction were to occur after death, the deceased individual would be a parent of the child."[487] In *Estate of Kievernagel*,[488] the California Court of Appeals denied a widow's request for her deceased husband's frozen sperm, where he had signed an agreement with the company storing his sperm calling for its destruction upon his death.[489] The court observed that

> there is only one gamete-provider. The material at issue is Joseph's sperm, not a preembryo. Only Joseph had 'an interest, in the nature of ownership, to the extent that he had decision-making authority as to the use of his sperm for reproduction.' The disposition of Joseph's frozen sperm does not

---

insemination of his partner. The male partner was designated the father of the child on her birth certificate, cared for the child on a daily basis, and held her out as his own. Two years later, the parties terminated their relationship and the mother and child moved out of state. After the man's action to establish a parental relationship was dismissed, he brought an action based on breach of contract. The court held that the written contract did not assert the same rights as the paternity suit and therefore could go forward.

[485] Haralambie, *supra* note 450, at 36. *See generally* Christina C. Lawrence, Note, *Procreative Liberty and the Preembryo Problem: Developing a Medical and Legal Framework to Settle the Disposition of Frozen Embryos*, 52 Case W. Res. L. Rev. 721 (2002); Laura S. Langley & Joseph W. Blackston, *Sperm, Egg, and a Petri Dish: Unveiling the Underlying Property Issues Surrounding Cryopreserved Embryos*, 27 J. Legal Med. 167 (2006); Katherine Poste Gunnison, Note, *Poaching the Eggs: Courts and the Custody Battles over Frozen Embryos*, 8 J. L. & Fam. Stud. 275 (2006).

[486] 20 Cal. Rptr. 2d 275 (Cal. Ct. App. 1993).

[487] Uniform Parentage Act (2000) § 707 (Revised 2002). *See generally* Browne C. Lewis, *Dead Men Reproducing: Responding to the Existence of Afterdeath Children*, 16 Geo. Mason L. Rev. 403 (2009); Kathryn Venturatos Lorio, *Conceiving the Inconceivable: Legal Recognition of the Posthumously Conceived Child*, 34 ACTEC J. 154 (2008); Michael K. Elliott, *Tales of Parenthood from the Crypt, The Predicament of the Posthumously Conceived Child*, 39 Real Prop. Prob. & Tr. J. 47 (2004); Margaret Ward Scott, *A Look at the Rights and Entitlements of Posthumously Conceived Children: No Surefire Way to Tame the Reproductive Wild West*, 52 Emory L. J. 963 (2003).

[488] 166 Cal. App. 4th 1024 (Cal. Ct. App. 2008).

[489] *Id.* at 1025.

implicate Iris's right to procreative autonomy. That would be so only if she could show that she could become pregnant only with Joseph's sperm.[490]

In *Astrue v. Capato*,[491] the United States Supreme Court held that a child conceived after the genetic father's death, through sperm collected prior to his death, was not eligible to receive Social Security Survivor Benefits.[492] In this case, Robert Capato was diagnosed with esophageal cancer in 1999, shortly after marrying his wife, Karen. Knowing that treatments for cancer could render Robert sterile, the couple decided to have his sperm preserved to have children later. The couple conceived a child in 2001 without the use of the frozen sperm. Robert died in 2002. Eighteen months after his death Karen gave birth to twins as a result of fertility treatments with her husband's frozen sperm. She then filed for Social Security Survivor Benefits after their birth. The Social Security Administration (SSA) denied her request and she sued in federal district court. The district court affirmed the SSA's decision, but the United States Court of Appeals for the Third Circuit reversed. The United States Supreme Court granted certiorari and overturned the Third Circuit's decision. The Supreme Court gave *Chevron* deference to the SSA's determination and found SSA's interpretation of the statute was "attuned to the statute's text and its design to benefit primarily those supported by the deceased wage earner in his or her lifetime."[493] As a consequence of *Capato*, children conceived prior to, but born after the genetic father's death may be ineligible for Social Security survivor benefits.

The courts have limited the procreative ability of prisoners. In *Goodwin v. Turner*,[494] an inmate sought habeas corpus relief after denial of his request to artificially inseminate his wife. Goodwin requested artificial insemination because of his concern that his wife's age at the time of his scheduled release date would increase her chances of bearing a child with birth defects.[495] The court first recognized that procreation has consistently been recognized as a fundamental right;[496] however, the court denied Goodwin's request by finding the prison regulation prohibiting inmate procreation was rationally related to legitimate

---

[490] *Id.* 1032-33 (quoting *Hecht v. Superior Court*, 20 Cal. Rptr. 2d. 275, 283 (Cal. Ct. App. 1993)). *See also Woodward v. Commissioner of Social Security*, 760 N.E.2d 257 (Mass. 2002) (twin girls born two years after their father's death were eligible for Social Security survivor benefits upon establishment of genetic relationship; evidence showed deceased father had clearly consented to support of any child posthumously conceived). *See generally* Michael R. Soules, *Commentary: Posthumous Harvesting of Gametes — A Physician's Perspective*, 27 J. L. Med. & Ethics 362 (1999); Carson Strong, *Ethical and Legal Aspects of Sperm Retrieval after Death or Persistent Vegetative State*, 27 J. L. Med. & Ethics 347 (1999).

[491] 132 S.Ct. 2021 (2012).

[492] A number of states agree that generally, a posthumously conceived child does not qualify as a decedent's survivor. *See, e.g., Woodward v. Comm'r of Social Sec.*, 760 N.E.2d 257 (Mass. 2002) (posthumously conceived child may only qualify as decedent's survivor if mother establishes the child's genetic relationship with the decedent, that the decedent consented to reproduce posthumously, and that decedent consented to support any resulting child).

[493] *Id.*, at 2026.

[494] 908 F.2d 1395 (8th Cir. 1990).

[495] *Id.* at 1397.

[496] *Id.* at 1398 (citations omitted).

penological interests. However, in *Gerber v. Hickman*,[497] the United States Court of Appeals for the Ninth Circuit held that the right to procreate is "fundamentally inconsistent with incarceration" and, therefore, the court did not have to inquire whether a prison regulation banning artificial insemination was related to a legitimate penological interest.[498]

[B] In Vitro Fertilization

The first "test tube baby," Louise Brown, born in England in 1978, provoked medical, legal, and ethical debate over the implications of IVF.[499] IVF, along with embryo transfer, may facilitate child bearing for women otherwise unable to conceive or may allow the embryo of one couple to be carried by a gestational surrogate who will deliver the child.[500] IVF with embryo transfer is widely used by women who have gynecological problems that prevent conception and by couples with male infertility.[501] Conception by IVF is "a process whereby (usually multiple) ova are placed in a medium to which sperm are added for fertilization, the zygote thus produced then being introduced into the uterus and allowed to develop to term."[502] Because the rate of pregnancy following IVF is related to the number of embryos placed in the uterus, most clinics stimulate the ovary with drugs in order to produce multiple ova for fertilization.[503] After the ova and sperm are fertilized and the embryos reach the proper stage of development, they are implanted in the uterus of the woman who will carry the child until birth.[504]

When multiple embryos result, options for the couple and their physician include (a) re-implanting all the fertilized embryos to enhance the possibility of pregnancy, (b) implanting some and freezing others to use in the future if the initial transplantation fails, or (c) implanting some and making others available to another couple, rather than destroying the excess embryos and perhaps risking prosecution.[505]

---

[497] 291 F.3d 617 (9th Cir. 2002).

[498] *See* Adam M. Breault, Note, *"Onan's Transgression": The Continuing Legal Battle over Prisoners' Procreation Rights*, 66 Alb. L. Rev. 289 (2002).

[499] *See* Lisa C. Ikemoto, Johnson v. Calvert: *Technology, Family, and Commerce, in* Health Law & Bioethics 79 (Sandra H. Johnson, Joan H. Krause, Richard S. Saver & Robin Fretwell. Wilson, eds., 2009).

[500] *See infra* § 5.07[C][2].

[501] *See generally* W. Droegemueller, et al., Comprehensive Gynecology (1987).

[502] "Fertilization," Stedman's Medical Dictionary 147560 (27th ed. 2000).

[503] *See* Ikemoto, *supra* note 499. IVF industry and advocacy groups have, in some instances, successfully lobbied to prevent statutory limits on the number of eggs that may be fertilized. Partially in response to media attention directed at "Octomom" Nadya Suleman, who gave birth to octuplets through IVF in 2009, the Georgia Legislature attempted to pass such a limiting bill. The bill was defeated in April 2009. *See* Resolve: The National Infertility Association, "The National Infertility Association and Supporters Defeat Dangerous Georgia Bill," Apr. 9, 2009, *available at* http://www.resolve.org/about/resolve-the-national-infertility-association-and-supporters-defeat-dangerous-georgia-bill.html.

[504] *See Smith v. Hartigan*, 556 F. Supp. 157, 159 n.4 (N.D. Ill. 1983) (describing in vitro fertilization as a six-step procedure).

[505] *See* George J. Annas & Sherman Elias, *In Vitro Fertilization and Embryo Transfer: Medicolegal Aspects of a New Technique to Create a Family*, 17 Fam. L.Q. 199, 208-10 (1983). In part to address such

As the question of embryo disposition illustrates, medical progress quickly outstripped legal response to and regulation of IVF procedures,[506] posing many unanswered questions relating to disposition of unused embryos, as well as the more foundational issues of paternity, maternity, and the rights and obligations of the various parties involved. One court presciently cautioned:

> In this era of artificial insemination, surrogate parenting and in-vitro fertilization, legal rights of a non-biological parent may become fixed by virtue of the parties' actions and the developmental relationship of the child with the parent. To permit one parent to revoke the parentage of the other parent, once those rights have been legally determined, in the absence of fraud, by invoking a blood test, invites chaos to the child's emotional well-being and legal status.[507]

This section surveys the many issues raised by IVF, together with the differing responses by courts and legislatures.

[1] Legality of and Access to In Vitro Fertilization in General

The legality of IVF procedures was raised in *Smith v. Hartigan.*[508] In *Smith*, the Smiths had discussed the possibility of IVF with a physician who determined that the procedure was the only means available for Mrs. Smith to conceive children. Because of concern that the Illinois abortion statute contained a prohibition relating to IVF, the doctor was reluctant to perform the procedure. The Smiths and the physician filed a suit challenging the constitutionality of the Illinois statute stating that "[a]ny person who intentionally causes the fertilization of a human ovum by a human sperm outside the body of a living human female shall, with regard to the human being thereby produced, be deemed to have the care and custody of [the] child,"[509] subject to prosecution for child abuse if harm ensued, with an exception

---

issues, a number of states have enacted "embryo adoption" statutes in recent years. *See, e.g.*, Ga. Code Ann. §§ 19-8-40 to -43 (2012); Okla. Stat. tit. 10, § 556 (2012); La. Rev. Stat. Ann. § 9:130 (2011) ("An in vitro fertilized human ovum is a juridical person which cannot be owned by the in vitro fertilization patients who owe it a high duty of care and prudent administration. If the in vitro fertilization patients renounce, by notarial act, their parental rights for in utero implantation, then the in vitro fertilized human ovum shall be available for adoptive implantation . . . . The in vitro fertilization patients may renounce their parental rights in favor of another married couple, but only if the other couple is willing and able to receive the in vitro fertilized ovum. No compensation shall be paid or received by either couple to renounce parental rights. Constructive fulfillment of the statutory provisions for adoption in this state shall occur when a married couple executes a notarial act of adoption of the in vitro fertilized ovum and birth occurs."). *See generally* Polina M. Dostalik, Note, *Embryo "Adoption"? The Rhetoric, the Law, and the Legal Consequences*, 55 N.Y.L. Sch. L. Rev. 867 (2010/2011).

[506] A number of states now provide statutory immunity for IVF providers. *See, e.g.*, La. Rev. Stat. § 9:132 (2011) ("Strict liability or liability of any kind . . . shall not be applicable to any physician, hospital, in vitro fertilization clinic, or their agent who acts in good faith in the screening, collection, conservation, preparation, transfer, or cryopreservation of the human ovum fertilized in vitro for transfer to the human uterus. Any immunity granted by this Section is applicable only to an action brought on behalf of the in vitro fertilized human ovum as a juridical person.").

[507] *Commonwealth ex rel. Coburn v. Coburn*, 558 A.2d 548, 552-53 (Pa. Super. Ct. 1989).

[508] 556 F. Supp. 157 (N.D. Ill. 1983).

[509] *Id.* at 159.

for lawful termination of pregnancy. The plaintiffs claimed that the IVF provision failed to give adequate notice to physicians of the type of conduct that was prohibited, violating their constitutional rights to privacy, and was void for vagueness.

Partially in reliance on the state's concession that it had never initiated nor intended to pursue any prosecution against the doctor for engaging in such a procedure, the court dismissed the action for lack of controversy, concluding that it would be inappropriate for it to render a decision on the constitutionality of the challenged provision. The court held that the IVF provision did not absolutely prohibit the act of causing IVF because the statute did not prohibit the procedure sought by the plaintiffs. The Illinois abortion statute was later amended to specifically exclude the performance of IVF.[510]

A class action by a group of physicians engaged in reproductive technology later challenged the Illinois abortion statute in *Lifchez v. Hartigan*,[511] resulting in a portion of the statute being declared unconstitutional. The statute's prohibition against intentional experimentation upon human fetuses, unless the experimentation was therapeutic to the fetus, was held to be void for vagueness for failing to define "experimentation" and "therapeutic." Furthermore, because the statute prohibited embryo transfer and chorionic villi sampling,[512] the court held that the statute interfered with a woman's right to attempt to bear a child or become informed of potential birth defects, activities protected under the right to privacy.[513]

[2] Leftover "Pre-Embryos" and the Right Not to Parent

Fertilized ova that had not yet been implanted have raised the question of whether a party who initially consents to assisted conception may withdraw that consent. This controversy arose in *Davis v. Davis*.[514] In *Davis*, a married couple, Mary Sue and Junior Davis, decided to have children by IVF and nine of the wife's ova were fertilized with the husband's sperm. Efforts to implant two of the ova were unsuccessful and seven fertilized ova were frozen for prospective future implantation. At the time, neither spouse anticipated their forthcoming divorce action, which commenced a "custody" battle over the preserved embryos.

The trial court found that the frozen embryos were "human beings" from the moment of fertilization and awarded custody of the seven fertilized ova to Mary Sue.[515] It directed that she be afforded the opportunity to bring the children to term through implantation. The Tennessee Court of Appeals reversed, finding a consti-

---

[510] 720 Ill. Comp. Stat. 510/6 (2011).

[511] 735 F. Supp. 1361 (N.D. Ill. 1990).

[512] This is a sampling of the "vascular processes of the chorion of the embryo entering into the formation of the placenta." "Villus," Stedman's Medical Dictionary 436090 (27th ed. 2000).

[513] The statute continues to prohibit experimentation on a fetus produced by IVF "unless such experimentation is therapeutic to the fetus thereby produced," and criminalized intentional violation. 720 Ill. Comp. Stat. 510/6 (2011).

[514] 842 S.W.2d 588 (Tenn. 1992). *See also* Judith Daar, *supra* note 203.

[515] *Davis v. Davis*, 1989 Tenn. App. LEXIS 641 (Cir. Ct., Sept. 21, 1989), *rev'd*, 1990 Tenn. App. LEXIS 642 (Sept. 13, 1990).

tutionally protected right in Junior Davis not to father a child when no pregnancy had yet occurred. On remand, it ordered the trial court to award joint custody and an equal right to disposition of the embryos to the parties, who had both since remarried.[516]

Upon Mary Sue's request for review, the Tennessee Supreme Court agreed that the parties had the sole decision-making authority over the embryos.[517] Because they could not agree, the court balanced their interests and decided that the woman's interest in donating the embryos to a childless couple was outweighed by the man's constitutionally protected right to avoid procreation.[518] The court added that if the woman herself sought to use the embryos and was unable to achieve parenthood by any other means, the balancing of their relative interests would be closer. The court stated that while each case must be decided on its own merits, the party objecting to procreation should usually prevail, if the other party has a reasonable possibility of becoming a parent by other means. Absent an agreement regarding the disposition of the embryos, the court concluded that the clinic where the embryos were stored should dispose of them.[519]

Davis is typical of frozen embryo cases, nearly "all of which favor the party wishing to avoid procreation."[520] In *J.B. v. M.B.*,[521] the New Jersey Supreme Court ruled that, in a divorce proceeding, disposition of cryopreserved preembryos, which were created in connection with an in vitro fertilization procedure, should be determined by the party wishing to avoid procreation. The parties to the divorce had had a child through in vitro fertilization. The wife, who wanted the preembryos destroyed, contended that if the preembryos were successfully implanted, she would be forced to become a biological parent. Her husband, on the other hand, was capable of having other children; thus, his right to procreate was not lost if he was denied the opportunity to use or donate the preembryos. The court noted that the parties had not entered into a contract regarding disposition of the cryopreserved pre-embryos. The court affirmed the wife's right to prevent implantation of the preembryos and ordered them destroyed.

A party who changes his or her mind on the cusp of the procedure will prevail, too. In a 2006 case, *Roman v. Roman*,[522] a husband withdrew his consent for the implantation of his wife's eggs fertilized with his sperm the day before the

---

[516] 1990 Tenn. App. LEXIS at *9.

[517] 842 S.W.2d 588, 603 (Tenn. 1992), *rev'd in part*, 1990 Tenn. App. LEXIS 642 (Tenn. Ct. App. Sept. 13, 1990).

[518] By this time, Mary Sue had shifted her earlier position of wanting to use the embryos herself. *Id.* at 590.

[519] 842 S.W.2d at 603, *cert. denied*, 507 U.S. 911 (1993). On a petition to rehear the case from Junior Davis, the Tennessee Supreme Court specifically prohibited the clinic from following its "usual procedure . . . to donate surplus pre-embryos to a childless couple for procreational purposes. Such a disposition is *not* authorized under the opinion, because it is the very outcome that Junior Davis has sought to avoid, and one which we have held to be constitutionally unavailable over his objection." 1992 Tenn. LEXIS 622, *3-4 (Nov. 23, 1992).

[520] *See* Judith Daar, *supra* note 430, at 104, tbl. 5.1 (cataloging cases).

[521] 783 A.2d 707 (N.J. 2001).

[522] 193 S.W.3d 40 (Tex. Ct. App. 2006).

procedure, citing concerns about the marital relationship. The couple agreed to freeze the embryos, which were later ordered destroyed by the Texas Court of Appeals pursuant to the couple's contract terms governing cryopreservation on divorce. Not surprisingly, the most common condition under which embryo disputes arise is divorce of the intended parents.[523]

The right to not parent appears to prevail even where one party agreed by contract to do so. Generally courts attempt to enforce certain contract terms.[524] In the 2000 case of *A.Z. v. B. Z.*,[525] a former wife was enjoined from having embryos implanted when her ex-husband objected after the parties' divorce. The court held that an unambiguous written agreement that had allocated a frozen preembryo to the wife if the parties separated was unenforceable where one party has reconsidered their decision.[526]

A notable exception to this pattern came in the 2012 case, *Reber v. Reiss.*[527] There, the Superior Court of Pennsylvania held that when there was no specific agreement regarding the disposition of frozen pre-embryos created by the husband and wife upon divorce, the husband's interest in avoiding procreation was outweighed by the wife's interest in using the embryos. The court's decision turned on the fact that the wife was unable to have children by other means and was willing to fully support the children financially, while still allowing the husband to have parental rights and visitation.[528]

While the right not to parent arises most often when frozen embryos survive the adults' relationship, questions of paternity have also arisen. In the Texas case of *In*

---

[523] *See* Judith Daar, *supra* note 10, at 105; *see also* Karissa Hostrup Windsor, Note, *Disposition of Cryopreserved Preembryos after Divorce*, 88 Iowa L. Rev. 1001 (2003); Angela K. Upchurch, *The Deep Freeze: A Critical Examination of the Resolution of Frozen Embryo Disputes through the Adversarial Process*, 33 Fla. St. U. L. Rev. 395 (2005).

[524] *See also Kass v. Kass*, 696 N.E.2d 174 (N.Y. 1998) (court should enforce agreements where the potential parents provide for the disposition of frozen pre-embryo); *J. B. v. M.B. and C.C.*, 783 A.2d 707 (N.J. 2001) (court applied balancing test in absence of formal, unambiguous agreement, honoring wife's wish to prevent implantation of frozen preembryos after couple divorced).

[525] 725 N.E.2d 1051 (Mass. 2000). *See also In re Marriage of Witten*, 672 N.W.2d 768, 783 (Iowa 2003) (where a party has changed their mind, it would violate public policy for the court to enforce a prior agreement about the use or disposition of embryos, and "no transfer, release, disposition, or use of the embryos can occur without the signed authorization of both donors. If a stalemate results, the status quo [will] be maintained . . . . The . . . embryos [will be] stored indefinitely unless both parties can agree to destroy the fertilized eggs.").

[526] *See* Helene S. Shapo, *Frozen Pre-Embryos and the Right to Change One's Mind*, 12 Duke J. Comp. & Int'l L. 75 (2002).

[527] 2012 PA Super 86 (Pa. Super. Ct. 2012).

[528] The growing number of unused embryos housed by IVF clinics around the country has led the creation of embryo adoption programs to facilitate the use or storage of unused embryos. *See* Heather Johnson Kukla, *Embryonic Stem Cell Research: An Ethical Justification*, 90 Geo. L.J. 503, 526-530 (2002) (identifying embryo adoption as a viable option to meet the "mandate for respect" required when dealing with the extraneous embryos produced during fertility treatments). Embryo Adoption has also become an area of significant commercial activity as well. *See, e.g.*, The Embryo Adoption Awareness Center, *available at* http://adoptembryos.org/; The National Embryo Donation Center, *available at* http://www.embryoadoption.org/; *see also supra* note 166.

re O.G.M.,[529] the court found sufficient evidence to support a grant of paternity to a former husband for a child born through IVF from a frozen pre-embryo conceived during marriage but implanted into former wife after divorce. The former husband was the child's biological father, was named as the father on the birth certificate, filed a statement of paternity, consented to the procedure, and was paying child support for the child. Since the former wife was unmarried at time of the child's birth, and no writing set out the parties' agreement as to the child, denying paternity rights to the father would have bastardized the child, which was against the child's best interest and public policy.

[3] Same-Sex Relationships

Same-sex partnerships and marriages present unique issues for deciding whether a partner will be recognized as a legal parent. In many instances, the same-sex partner is neither the biological parent of the child nor the presumed parent as a result of marriage. As a consequence, he or she may face tremendous difficulty in seeking parental rights. The partner must first meet the threshold for standing and then show his or her entitlement to parental rights.

Questions of standing arose in the case of *Latham v. Schwerdtfeger*.[530] There, the court held that the doctrine of *in loco parentis* provided the basis for standing when the plaintiff, a former domestic partner, sued the natural mother for custody and visitation of two minor children born during the course of the couple's same-sex relationship.

Like standing, the question of parental rights is equally thorny. In *K.M. v. E.G.*,[531] the California Supreme Court declined to decide parentage based upon intent, as it did with a gestational surrogacy agreement in *Johnson v. Calvert*, discussed below. In *K.M.*, a woman "donated" her eggs to her lesbian partner, with whom she was registered in domestic partnership, so that her partner could bear a child by IVF. The couple's relationship ended after the birth of twin daughters. K.M. filed a petition to establish a parental relationship with the children as their biological parent because "[s]he donated her egg to respondent, the gestational mother of the children."[532] E.G. moved to dismiss the petition arguing that, although she and K.M. "were lesbian partners who lived together until [the] action was filed," K.M. had "explicitly donated her ovum under a clear written agreement by which she relinquished any claim to offspring born of her donation."[533]

The trial court dismissed K.M.'s petition and the California Court of Appeal affirmed. The California Supreme Court, however, reversed. Despite K.M.'s written waiver of right to any resulting children, executed at the time of the donation, K.M.'s genetic relationship to the children constituted evidence of a mother-child relationship under the Uniform Parentage Act. K.M. did not intend simply to donate her

---

[529] 988 S.W.2d 473 (Tex. Ct. App. 1999).

[530] 802 N.W.2d 66 (2011).

[531] 117 P.3d 673 (2005).

[532] *Id.* at 675.

[533] *Id.*

eggs, but rather designed her donation so that her partner could give birth to a child that would be raised in their joint home.

The court distinguished *Johnson*, discussed *infra*, in which the intent test was applied to decide parentage in a contest between a married couple and the gestational surrogate they employed. *Johnson* was distinguishable because in *Johnson* "the child could have two mothers, leaving the child with three parents," while here, there were only two potential parents and *both* could be the children's mothers:

> Unlike in *Johnson*, their claims are not mutually exclusive. K.M. acknowledges that E.G. is the twins' mother. K.M. does not claim to be the twins' mother *instead of* E.G., but *in addition to* E.G., so we need not consider their intent in order to decide between them . . . [The] *Johnson* intent test does not apply when '[t]here is no "tie" to break.' Rather, the parentage of the twins is determined by application of the UPA. E.G. is the twins' mother because she gave birth to them and K.M. also is the twins' mother because she provided the ova from which they were produced.[534]

[4] Third-Party Issues

IVF has generated litigation against fertility clinics and intermediates, too.[535]

York v. Jones[536] concerned the determination of the rights and duties of medical facilities and personnel involved in IVF. In *York*, a husband and wife successfully brought a breach of contract action against a medical college to obtain possession of their potential child, which had been cryo-preserved at a pre-zygote stage, after the college had refused to consent to a transfer to a different institution. The federal district court held that the parties' agreement constituted a bailment that limited the college's rights to exercise control over the fertilized ova.[537]

Medical malpractice cases, and products liability and warranty claims, may also possibly result if ovum, sperm, or embryos are defective.[538] These theories were put

---

[534] *Id.* at 143, (quoting *In re Marriage of Moschetta*, 25 Cal. App. 4th 1218, 1224 (1994)).

[535] *See, e.g., Egert v. Connecticut Gen. Life Ins. Co.*, 900 F.2d 1032 (7th Cir. 1990) (challenging carrier's decision that insured's in vitro fertilization was not covered under employee health insurance plan); *Official Comm. of Equity Sec. Holders v. Mabey*, 832 F.2d 299 (4th Cir. 1987), *cert. denied*, 485 U.S. 962 (1988) (holding that order to create emergency treatment for reconstructive surgery or in vitro fertilization for Dalkon Shield claimants violates Bankruptcy Code provisions governing preferential treatment of unsecured creditors).

[536] 717 F. Supp. 421 (E.D. Va. 1989).

[537] In 2001, President Bush refused to federally fund stem cell research that would have destroyed frozen preembryos donated for research, while allowing support for research on existing lines of cells. *See* Katharine Q. Seelye with Frank Bruni, *The President's Decision: The President: A Long Process That Led Bush to His Decision*, N.Y. Times, Aug. 11, 2001, at A1.

[538] *See, e.g.,* Jennifer M. Vagle, Comment, *Putting the "Product" in Reproduction: The Viability of a Products Liability Action for Genetically Defective Sperm*, 38 Pepp. L. Rev. 1175 (2011); Suriya E. P. Jayanti, Comment, *Guarantors of our Genes: Are Egg Donors Liable for Latent Genetic Disease?*, 58 Am. U. L. Rev. 405 (2008); J. Brad Reich & Dawn Swink, *You Can't Put the Genie Back in the Bottle: Potential Rights and Obligations of Egg Donors in the Cyberprocreation Era*, 20 Alb. L.J. Sci. & Tech. 1 (2010); Ikemoto, *supra* note 499.

to the test in *Donovan v. IDant Laboratories*,[539] when a child born with a genetic condition known as Fragile X sued the fertility clinic. The court found that "the sale of sperm is considered a product and is subject to strict liability,"[540] but that the plaintiff could not bring claims of negligence, negligent misrepresentation, strict liability, and breach of warranty because they are "essentially claims for wrongful life."[541] All claims in *Donovan* were eventually dismissed, but this case opened the door for courts to contemplate similar claims in the future.

In *Moon v. Michigan Reproductive Services & IVF Center P.C.*,[542] doctors told single women seeking IVF that they would not perform the procedures on unmarried women. The Michigan Court of Appeals found this marital discrimination to be a violation of the Civil Rights Act,[543] which "prohibit[s] doctors and medical facilities from refusing to form a doctor-patient relationship based solely on the patient's protected status."[544]

In his article *Discrimination Out of Dismissiveness: The Example of Infertility*,[545] Professor David Orentlicher argues that refusal to cover fertility treatments, including IVF, are a form of discrimination. Changing "views of fertility and reproduction in western society" determine the societal perspective of the "value" of reproduction and have turned "infertility from an obvious disability into a condition that may be viewed by many as non-disabling." In order to protect the "interests of persons with infertility and anyone else who might be subject to discrimination on the basis of dismissiveness, it is critical to ensure that public policy recognizes the possibility of discrimination from dismissiveness as it shapes antidiscrimination theory." Orentlicher focuses on medical insurance as a source of evidence "for the view that infertility is not seen as a disability . . . [as it is the] longstanding practice [of] healthcare plans [not to] cover the costs of IVF and other similar procedures to help infertile couples have children."

Courts are divided over whether specific insurance contracts cover IVF treatments. In *Kinzie v. Physician's Liability Insurance Co.*,[546] the court held that IVF was not a medically necessary procedure within the meaning of the insurance policy. This case was distinguished by *Ralston v. Connecticut General Life Insurance Company*,[547] in which the court held that IVF inducing pregnancy was "treatment for a 'sickness' " and was therefore covered by the insurance policy.

---

[539] 625 F. Supp. 2d 256 (E.D. Pa. 2009).

[540] *Id.* at 273.

[541] *Id.* at 276.

[542] 810 N.W.2d 919 (2011).

[543] *Id.* at 921.

[544] *Id.*

[545] David Orentlicher, *Discrimination Out of Dismissivness: The Example of Infertility*, 85 Ind. L.J. 143 (2010).

[546] 750 P.2d 1140 (1987).

[547] 617 So. 2d 1379 (1993).

Concerns over coverage for IVF and similar treatments have been addressed by many state legislatures.[548] Currently, 15 states have passed laws that require insurers to cover or offer coverage for infertility diagnosis and treatment. Of those 15 states, only three (California, New York, and Louisiana) have specifically excluded coverage of IVF in their statutes. With continuing increases in the use of IVF to combat infertility, state and federal courts will probably see more cases regarding insurance coverage for IVF treatments in the future. However, until a clear result can be seen, these issues will have to be addressed on an individual basis, with consideration given to the jurisdiction, the insurer, and the specific medical problems.[549]

As the technologies are refined, additional issues inevitably will surface.

[C] Surrogate Motherhood

Two methods of surrogacy exist: traditional surrogacy and gestational surrogacy, although the former is almost never performed today.[550] These methods may be used by heterosexual couples or same-sex partners. In traditional surrogacy, a heterosexual or lesbian couple may use a surrogate mother when the woman (or both) cannot contribute genetically or gestationally to reproduction. The same is true for male same-sex partners who desire to have a child. Sperm may be supplied by the male partner in the couple (if there is a male partner) to inseminate a surrogate mother who agrees to bear the child and then give the child to the couple to raise; alternatively, a donor may provide semen.

By contrast, gestational surrogacy may be used when a woman is able to provide an ovum but unable to carry a fetus. Male same-sex partners desiring to have a child may also elect to use an egg from a donor rather than the surrogate, for reasons explained below. As with traditional surrogacy, semen may also be supplied by a third-party donor. The fertilized ovum is then implanted in the gestational surrogate, who has contracted with the intended (or genetic) parents to carry the child through birth and then release the child to them. Thus, with gestational surrogacy, the couple that plans to raise the child may both be genetic parents, whose sperm and ova are fertilized in vitro, or one or neither of them may be genetically related to the resulting child.

Although surrogacy has typically been used by heterosexual couples, over time the pool of individuals who use such arrangements has expanded to include "single women who desire to become pregnant, by lesbian partners who desire to rear a

---

[548] 50 State Statutory Surveys, Health Care: Mandated Benefits: *Mandated Coverage for Infertility Treatment*, 0100 SURVEYS 37 (Westlaw).

[549] *See* Valarie Blake, *It's an ART not a Science: State-Mandated Insurance Coverage of Assisted Reproductive Technologies and Legal Implications for Gay and Unmarried Persons*, 12 Minn. J.L. Sci. & Tech. 651 (2011); Note, *In Vitro Fertilization: Insurance and Consumer Protection*, 109 Harv. L. Rev. 2092 (1996).

[550] Andrews & Douglass, *supra* note 433, at 630-31. For a general overview of the subject, see also Susan Markens, Surrogate Motherhood and the Politics of Reproduction (2007), and Carla Spivak, *The Law of Surrogate Motherhood in the United States*, 58 Am. J. Comp. L. 97 (2010).

child genetically related to one of them, or by homosexual men who desire to father a child through use of a surrogate."[551]

Artificial insemination and IVF have transformed surrogacy into a global business.[552] The surrogate mother may be motivated by the desire to help a childless couple, or she may be enticed by the money she is paid for the service. Usually a professional intermediary or fertility clinic facilitates the surrogacy contract, often with similarly mixed motives.

Despite its apparent simplicity, both the process and the contract involved are quite complex.[553] Generally, the intermediary advertises for both potential parents and surrogates, interviews both, and often offers legal and psychological counseling. The intermediary matches the intended parents with the surrogates, prepares contracts between the parties and between them and itself, sets the fees, and arranges for the assisted conception process (whether artificial insemination or IVF), as well as the transfer of the child.

[1] Traditional Surrogacy

In a traditional surrogacy arrangement, the contract usually runs between one partner in the couple (traditionally, the husband in a married couple) and the surrogate mother. The contract is framed as a service contract, not a contract to provide a child, because contracts to sell children are void as against public policy.[554] For the same reason, the other partner in the couple (traditionally, the wife) is excluded from the contract. In the classic case of a married, heterosexual couple, the husband agrees to provide semen, to pay a fee to the surrogate mother and to the intermediary,[555] and to accept the child with any birth defects that cannot be discovered during the pregnancy. The surrogate mother, whose husband may also be a party to the contract, agrees to be artificially inseminated, to bear the child, to relinquish it upon birth, to forego all rights that she has to the child, and to consent to the child's adoption by the wife. The intermediary agrees to introduce the parties

---

[551] Haralambie, *supra* note 450, at 4.

[552] For a variety of perspectives on this issue, *see, e.g.*, Margaret Ryznar, *International Commercial Surrogacy and its Parties*, 43 J. Marshall L. Rev. 1009 (2010) (examining "the rights, interests, and obligations of the parties to a surrogacy . . . [and] the various opportunity costs of international commercial surrogacy"); Elizabeth Anderson, *Why Commercial Surrogate Motherhood Unethically Commodifies Women and Children*, 8 Health Care Anal. 19 (2000); Hugh V. McLachlan & Kim Swales, *Commercial Surrogate Motherhood and the Alleged Commodification of Children: A Defense of Legally Enforceable Contracts*, 72 Law & Contemp. Probs. 91 (2009); J. Brad Reich & Dawn Swink, *Outsourcing Human Reproduction: Embryos and Surrogacy Services in the Cyberprocreation Era*, 14 J. Health Care L. & Pol'y 241 (2011) (discussing the impact of the internet upon assisted conception and arguing that it has created a " 'wild west and largely unregulated" market for embryos and surrogacy services).

[553] *See, e.g.*, Abigail Lauren Perdue, *For Love or Money: An Analysis of the Contractual Regulation of Reproductive Surrogacy*, 27 J. of Contemp. Health L. & Pol'y 279 (2011); Brock A. Patton, Note, *Buying a Newborn: Globalization and the Lack of Federal Regulation of Commercial Surrogacy Contracts*, 79 U.M.K.C. L. Rev. 507 (2010).

[554] *See, e.g.*, Kelly A. Anderson, *Certainty in an Uncertain World: The Ethics of Drafting Surrogacy Contracts*, 21 Geo. J. Legal Ethics 615 (2008); Avi Katz, *Surrogate Motherhood and the Baby-Selling Laws*, 20 Colum. J. L. & Soc. Probs. 1, 1-3 (1986).

[555] *See, e.g.*, Jennifer L. Watson, Note, *Growing a Baby for Sale or Merely Renting a Womb: Should Surrogate Mothers be Compensated for their Services?*, 6 Whittier J. Child & Fam. Advoc. 529 (2007).

and make all the arrangements. The contract is usually a form prepared by the intermediary and the other parties may or may not have legal advice.

Cases and statutory reforms over several decades have approved key elements of these transactions. For example, in *Surrogate Parenting Associates, Inc. v. Commissioner ex. rel. Armstrong*,[556] the Kentucky Supreme Court held that the surrogacy business does not violate the state's law prohibiting child brokering and refused to revoke the corporate charter of a surrogate motherhood intermediary. The court found "fundamental differences between the surrogate parenting procedure . . . and the buying and selling of children."[557] Although the statute was intended to prevent "baby brokers from overwhelming an expectant mother or the parents of a child with financial inducements to part with the child,"[558] the court held that the procedure in issue involved merely a contract to bear a yet unconceived child, which assists persons who are unable to conceive in the ordinary manner. The court reasoned:

> The essential consideration[s] for the surrogate mother when she agrees to the surrogate parenting procedure are *not* avoiding the consequences of an unwanted pregnancy or fear of the financial burden of child rearing. On the contrary, the essential consideration is to assist a person or couple who desperately want a child but are unable to conceive one in the customary manner to achieve a biologically related offspring.[559]

The court concluded that any ban on surrogate parenting procedures was a matter for the legislature.

Litigation involving surrogacy issues most commonly arises when one party seeks to avoid fulfilling the contract terms. Special difficulties exist when the child has already been born or at least conceived. While problems of paternity and support would arise if the father attempted to breach the contract, the usual difficulty is that the surrogate mother refuses to relinquish the child. In resolving the matter, conflicts develop between contract law and the laws of custody and adoption that govern the parent-child relationship.

Proponents of a contractual approach advocate specific enforcement of surrogacy agreements in recognition that adults are free to contractually bind themselves, absent fraud, duress, unconscionability, or overreaching.[560] Refusing to enforce

---

[556] 704 S.W.2d 209 (Ky. 1986), *superseded by statute*, 1994 Ky. Laws Ch. 242 (H.B. 191) (1994). Ky. Rev. Stat. § 199.590 now states that no "person, agency, institution, or intermediary shall . . . be a party to a contract or agreement which would compensate a woman for her artificial insemination and subsequent termination of parental rights to a child born as a result of that artificial insemination" and "[a] person, agency, institution, or intermediary shall not receive compensation for the facilitation of contracts or agreements as proscribed by this subsection. Contracts or agreements entered into in violation of this subsection shall be void." Ky. Rev. Stat. § 199.590(4) (2011).

[557] 704 S.W.2d.at 211.

[558] *Id.*

[559] *Id.* at 211-12.

[560] *See* Hugh V. McLachlan & Kim Swales, *Commercial Surrogate Motherhood and the Alleged Commodification of Children: A Defense of Legally Enforceable Contracts*, 72 Law & Contemp. Probs. 91 (2009). *But also see* Elizabeth Anderson, *Why Commercial Surrogate Motherhood Unethically*

surrogacy contracts may be paternalistic and as offensive as denying married women the right to contract.[561]

Opponents of a contractual approach argue that such contracts are illegal because they violate the public policy against child-selling.[562] They further allege that they tend to exploit the poor.[563] Opponents urge that the surrogate mother has all the rights of a natural mother, so that protections surrounding adoption should apply — meaning that the surrogate mother's parental rights cannot be terminated except on statutory grounds. If the surrogate mother's rights are not forfeited, the wife cannot adopt the child. Moreover, because the father does not lose his rights either, the issue becomes one of child custody, which usually applies the "best interests of the child" standard.[564] In ordinary custody disputes, if custody is granted to one natural parent, the other party is normally given visitation rights.

Surrogate motherhood drew national attention during the litigation of *In re Baby M*.[565] *Baby M* highlights both the demand for surrogate motherhood and the legal problems that can arise under three areas of law: contracts, adoptions, and child custody.

In the *Baby M* case, William Stern had entered into a formal surrogacy contract with Mary Beth Whitehead and her husband Richard, in which Mrs. Whitehead agreed to be artificially inseminated with Stern's semen. In addition to numerous assurances relating to the potential pregnancy, Mrs. Whitehead further agreed not to form a parent-child relationship with the child, to surrender custody to Stern immediately upon the child's birth, and to terminate her own parental rights. Richard Whitehead also agreed to relinquish any rights to the child and do anything necessary to rebut the presumption of paternity. Stern agreed to pay Mrs. Whitehead $10,000 for her services, plus her uninsured medical expenses. He further contracted to pay $7,500 to a corporate intermediary.[566]

After the birth of the child, whom Stern and his wife named Melissa, Mrs. Whitehead became severely distraught at the prospect of turning the child over to the Sterns and terminating her own parental rights to allow Mrs. Stern to adopt the child. After a series of changes in physical custody of Melissa, both voluntary and forced, the Sterns brought suit to enforce the surrogacy contract and to compel Mrs. Whitehead to surrender the infant to them, to restrain her from interfering

---

Commodifies Women and Children, 8 Health Care Anal. 19 (2000).

[561] *See, e.g.*, Christine L. Kerian, *Surrogacy: A Last Resort Alternative for Infertile Women or a Commodification of Women's Bodies and Children?*, 12 Wisc. Women's L.J. 113 (1997).

[562] *See, e.g.*, Vanessa S. Browne-Barbour, *Bartering for Babies: Are Preconception Agreements in the Best Interests of Children?*, 26 Whittier L. Rev. 429 (2004); Anderson, *supra* note 560.

[563] *See, e.g.*, Ruby L. Lee, Note, *New Trends in Global Outsourcing of Commercial Surrogacy: A Call for Regulation*, 20 Hastings Women's L.J. 275 (2009); Jennifer Rimm, Comment, *Booming Baby Business: Regulating Commercial Surrogacy in India*, 30 U. Pa. J. Int'l L. 1429 (2009); Usha Rengachary Smerdon, *Crossing Bodies, Crossing Borders: International Surrogacy between the United States and India*, 39 Cumb. L. Rev. 15 (2008-09).

[564] *See infra* § 11.03[A].

[565] *In re Baby M*, 525 A.2d 1128 (N.J. Super. Ct. Ch. Div. 1987), *aff'd in part and rev'd in part*, 537 A.2d 1227 (N.J. 1988), *remanded to* 542 A.2d 52 (N.J. Sup. Ct. Ch. Div. 1988).

[566] 525 A.2d at 1158.

with their custody, and to terminate her parental rights. The superior court upheld the contract, awarded Stern sole custody, and authorized the adoption by Mrs. Stern. Mrs. Whitehead appealed.[567]

The New Jersey Supreme Court found the surrogacy contract invalid on both legal and public policy grounds. It found "the payment of money to a 'surrogate' mother illegal, perhaps criminal, and potentially degrading to women."[568] Despite the care taken to frame the contract as one for services, it conflicted with laws that strongly prohibit payment in conjunction with adoption cases. The court observed that laws prohibiting baby selling are intended to prevent "the exploitation of all parties involved" and to advance "the best interests of the child."[569]

The court also found that the agreement for termination of Mrs. Whitehead's parental rights conflicted with statutory provisions requiring proof of unfitness or abandonment prior to termination of parental rights or an order of adoption. Additionally, the provision for irrevocable consent to surrender the child contravened state law with respect to private placement adoptions.[570]

The contract also violated public policy by allocating custody prior to the child's birth, without regard to the child's best interests. Such terms have the potential to exploit the poor and detract from the requisite voluntariness for a binding agreement. They also could have unknown adverse impacts on the natural and adoptive parents as well as the child.[571]

Finally, the court held that the right of procreation did not entitle the natural father and his wife to custody of the child. However, in light of extensive expert testimony, it concluded that the best interests of Melissa justified a custody award to Stern, with Mrs. Whitehead entitled to visitation, on terms to be determined on remand.[572]

On remand, the trial court held that Melissa's best interests would be furthered by "unsupervised, uninterrupted, liberal visitation with her [natural] mother," who had since divorced and remarried.[573] The court found no credible evidence or expert opinion suggesting that the child would suffer any harm from continued and expanded visitation with her natural mother. The court found that Mary Beth Whitehead (now Gould) had attained family stability with her new husband and had accepted that she would never have custody of Melissa. Moreover, Melissa had a warm and loving relationship with her mother and had demonstrated no separation anxiety during supervised visitation.[574] In order to promote communication and cooperation between the parties, the court decided to appoint a mental health professional and direct the parties to participate in counseling. Lastly, the court

---

[567] *Id.* at 1144-46, 1175-76.

[568] 537 A.2d at 1234.

[569] *Id.* at 1242.

[570] *Id.* at 1244, 1246.

[571] *Id.* at 1246-50.

[572] *Id.* at 1251-53, 1261-64.

[573] 542 A.2d at 53.

[574] *Id.* at 53-54.

restrained and enjoined the parties from publicly discussing their relationships with the child, or her personal activities, or from selling any movie rights they may have concerning "Baby M" without prior approval of the court.[575]

Although the court in *Baby M* would allow surrogate motherhood where the surrogate gratuitously volunteers to carry the child and is given the right to change her mind and assert her parenthood, such an arrangement may lack the consideration necessary for a valid contract.

Other jurisdictions similarly have concluded that non-gratuitous surrogacy contracts are invalid. In *Doe v. Kelley*,[576] the Michigan Court of Appeals held that the state's adoption law, which prohibited the payment of money other than for expenses in connection with adoption, applied to surrogacy contracts, despite any fundamental interest in bearing or begetting a child. Michigan has since enacted a Surrogate Parenting Act, which declares surrogate contracts void, makes them unlawful when entered into for compensation, and provides for placement of children born pursuant to surrogacy arrangements.[577] In a declaratory action brought by infertile couples and potential surrogate mothers, the Michigan Court of Appeals held the Act constitutionally valid.[578] The Court of Appeals found that the due process clauses of the State and Federal Constitutions, together with penumbral rights emanating from specific guarantees in the Bill of Rights, protect individual decisions in matters of procreation from unjustified intrusion by the state. However, it concluded that the state had compelling interests sufficient to warrant intrusion into the protected matter of childbearing that justified the invalidation of surrogacy contracts.

Some courts have concluded that the terms of a surrogacy contract requiring the surrogate mother to surrender custody and terminate her parental rights are not void, but merely voidable.[579] While expressing strong moral and ethical reservations about surrogacy contracts in general, a New York court upheld a contract which provided for a $10,000 payment to a surrogate mother and held that the best interests of the child take precedence over any agreement between the parties. It further urged the state legislature to review the question of surrogacy contracts. In a subsequent case,[580] however, the New York Family Court, noting that proposed legislation had not been passed, concluded that the state's adoption statutes prohibited payment in excess of actual medical and related expenses in connection with childbirth, and held that surrogacy contracts are void.[581] It ruled that it would only accept surrender and termination of the natural mother's parental rights if she would "swear under oath before this [C]ourt that she [had] not and [would] not request, accept, or receive the $10,000 promised to her in exchange for surrender of

---

[575] *Id.* at 54-55.

[576] 307 N.W.2d 438 (Mich. Ct. App. 1981), *cert. denied*, 459 U.S. 1183 (1983).

[577] Pub. Act No. 199 (1988), codified at Mich. Comp. Laws §§ 722.851-722.863 (2011).

[578] *Doe v. Attorney Gen'l*, 487 N.W.2d 484 (Mich. Ct. App. 1992).

[579] *In re Adoption of Baby Girl L.J.*, 505 N.Y.S.2d 813 (N.Y. Surr. Ct. 1986).

[580] *In re Adoption of Paul*, 550 N.Y.S.2d 815 (N.Y. Fam. Ct. 1990).

[581] *Id.* at 816-18.

her child."[582] It further required the prospective adoptive parents to likewise swear not to compensate any party in exchange for the child.

State legislatures have taken a variety of approaches to the propriety and desirability of surrogate parenting arrangements. Some make surrogate parenting contracts void. For example, New York enacted legislation that regulates surrogate parenting contracts and declares such contracts "contrary to the public policy of this state, and . . . void and unenforceable."[583] It prohibits payment of any direct or indirect remuneration in connection with any surrogacy contract, including the assistance by a third party, while excepting otherwise authorized payments in connection with adoption or "reasonable and actual medical fees and hospital expenses for artificial insemination or IVF services incurred by the mother in connection with the birth of the child."[584] New York's law sets out civil penalties for violation of its terms.[585] It further establishes proceedings regarding parental rights, status, and obligations and includes a provision that forbids the court from considering the birth mother's participation in a surrogacy contract adversely with respect to her claims to custody.[586] Other states, like Louisiana[587] and Nebraska,[588] prohibit such contracts, while yet others pronounce surrogacy arrangements as illegal baby buying or selling.[589]

A number of states permit surrogacy contracts.[590] Some states simply apply their general artificial insemination statutes to surrogacy situations, creating a presumption of parentage in surrogacy arrangements as is done with artificial insemination.[591]

Some states have adopted a comprehensive statutory scheme dealing with broadly defined types of assisted conception and their implications.[592] Virginia law,

---

[582] *Id.* at 818-19.

[583] N.Y. Sess. Laws Ch. 308 (1992), N.Y. Dom. Rel. §§ 122 - 124 (McKinney 2011).

[584] N.Y. Dom. Rel. at § 123(1)(b).

[585] *Id.* at § 123 (2)(a), (b).

[586] *Id.* at § 124.

[587] La. Rev. Stat. Ann. § 9:2713 (2011).

[588] Neb.Rev.St. § 25-21, 200 (2011).

[589] *See, e.g.*, Mich. Comp. Laws §§ 722.851-722.861 (2011) (authorizing prison sentences of up to five years and / or fines of up to $50,000 for certain parties who "induce[ ], arrange[ ], procure[ ], or otherwise assist[ ] in the formation of a surrogate parentage contract for compensation."); *see also Doe v. Att'y Gen'l*, 487 N.W.2d 484, 486-87 (Mich. Ct. App. 1992) ("[U]nbridled surrogacy for profit could encourage the treatment of babies as commodities. Whatever sense of idealism that may motivate a fertile woman into hosting a pregnancy for an infertile couple is rent asunder by the introduction of the profit motive. It could be only a matter of time before desirable, healthy babies would come to be 'viewed quantitatively, as merchandise that can be acquired, at market or discount rates.' " (quoting Shari O'Brien, *Commercial Conceptions: A Breeding Ground for Surrogacy*, 65 N.C. L. Rev. 127, 144 (1986))).

[590] *See, e.g.*, Fla. Stat. Ann. §§ 742.14 to 742.17 (West 2011); Nev. Rev. Stat. Ann. §§ 126.045, 127.287 (West 2010). N.H. Rev. Stat. Ann. §§ 168-B:1 to 168-B:32 (2011); Va. Code Ann. §§ 20-156 to 20-165 (West 2011).

[591] *See, e.g.*, Ark. Code Ann. §§ 9-10-201to 9-10-202 (West 2011); Ark. Code Ann. § 9-10-201 (2011) (creating a presumption).

[592] Uniform Status of Children of Assisted Conception Act, 1991 Va. Acts Ch. 600 (1991), Va. Code Ann. §§ 20-156 to 20-165 (2011).

for instance, defines the parentage of a child conceived by assisted conception, deals with death and divorce of a party prior to the child's birth,[593] and validates and establishes a procedure for court approval of surrogacy contracts,[594] as well as for termination of surrogacy contracts.[595] The statutes regulate the rights of parties to unapproved surrogacy contracts[596] and prohibit surrogacy brokers.[597]

Several other states have enacted legislation directed at some of the issues involved in surrogacy arrangements. Some state statutes have declared surrogacy contracts void;[598] others invalidate only surrogacy contracts for compensation.[599] The Nevada Code completely excepts surrogate contracts from its provisions prohibiting payment in adoptions, but limits payments to "the medical and necessary living expenses related to the birth of the child as specified in the contract."[600] In *Soos v. Superior Court*,[601] the Arizona Court of Appeals struck down a statute prohibiting surrogacy and awarding the children of an illegal surrogacy arrangement to the surrogate mother.

The Uniform Status of Children of Assisted Conception Act, promulgated in 1988, offers two alternatives to model surrogacy statutes. Both take strong stands against open-market surrogacy.[602] Alternative A allows surrogacy if there has been judicial approval, and provides requirements for counseling, home study, and fitness.[603] Alternative B simply voids surrogacy contracts and favors the gestational mother if a child is conceived.[604]

If contract law is applied to resolve surrogacy issues, additional dilemmas arise if the father and his wife are found to be unfit or are discovered to possess qualities repugnant to the surrogate mother after the contract is signed.[605]

Like IVF, surrogate parenting agreements may also raise problems of paternity, which is comprehensively dealt with in other contexts by statutory schemes in most states, usually including procedures for establishing paternity and presumptions as to paternity.[606] The paternity issue could arise in a surrogacy context if the

---

[593] *Id.* at § 20-158.

[594] *Id.* at §§ 20-159, 20-160.

[595] *Id.* at § 20-161.

[596] *Id.* at § 20-162.

[597] *Id.* at § 20-165.

[598] *See, e.g.*, N.Y. Dom. Rel. Law §§ 121-124 (McKinney 2011).

[599] *See, e.g.*, Ky. Rev. Stat. Ann. § 199.590(2), 199.990 (Baldwin 2011); La. Rev. Stat. Ann. § 9:2713 (West 2011); Wash. Rev. Code Ann. §§ 26.26.230-26.26.240 (West 2011).

[600] Nev. Rev. Stat. § 126.045 (2010).

[601] 897 P.2d 1356 (Ariz. Ct. App. 1995).

[602] Unif. Status of Children of Assisted Conception Act (2010).

[603] *Id.* §§ 5-6, 8.

[604] *Id.* § 5(b).

[605] *See generally* David D. Meyer, *Parenthood in a Time of Transition: Tensions between Legal, Biological, and Social Conceptions of Parenthood*, 54 Am. J. Comp. L. 126 (2006); George J. Annas & Sherman Elias, *In Vitro Fertilization and Embryo Transfer: Medicolegal Aspects of a New Technique to Create a Family*, 17 Fam. L.Q. 199 (1983).

[606] *See supra* § 5.02[B], [F].

surrogate mother breached her promise to relinquish the child and sought to acquire child support or to establish the paternity of her husband or another man.

The biological father of the child also may attempt to establish paternity. A Michigan court addressed such a situation in *Syrkowski v. Appleyard*,[607] in which a married man with no other children sought a filiation order and entry of his name as natural and legal father of the child born through artificial insemination with his sperm. The surrogate mother cooperated in his action and her husband had consented in writing to the surrogacy arrangement. The Attorney General intervened, arguing that the Paternity Act, which allows a father to assert paternity of a child born out of wedlock, did not control because of the rebuttable presumption that the mother's husband was the father of the child. The trial court agreed, concluding that the Paternity Act was not intended to encompass monetary transactions of this nature. The Michigan Supreme Court reversed, deciding that the father could use the Act to establish paternity, that the presumption could be rebutted in a paternity action, and that the term "out of wedlock" included circumstances where the child resulted from a relationship of the wife and someone other than the husband, including a surrogacy arrangement.

Unresolved surrogacy issues will continue to develop, although the field has largely shifted away from traditional surrogacy to gestational surrogacy, which raises its own distinct issues.

[2] Gestational Surrogacy

Gestational surrogacy shares many features with IVF and traditional surrogacy — the key difference being the use of a third-party egg, which is fertilized and implanted into the gestational surrogate.[608] Although the egg may add considerable expense to an already-expensive procedure,[609] the advantages to the intended parents of a gestational surrogacy arrangement are readily apparent from court decisions emphasizing that the gestational surrogate, "whose pregnancy does not involve her own egg, [occupies] a different legal position from a traditional surrogate, whose pregnancy does involve her own egg."[610]

The 2002 surrogacy arrangement between James Flynn, Eileen Donich, Jennifer Rice, and Danielle and Douglas Bimber is illustrative. It unleashed a storm of multi-state litigation. Flynn, a 62-year-old Ohio mathematics professor, and his 60-year-old fiancée, dentist Eileen Donich, wished to have children and made arrangements through a private company with egg donor Jennifer Rice, gestational surrogate Danielle Bimber, and her husband, Douglas.[611] In Pennsylvania, where

---

[607] 362 N.W.2d 211 (Mich. 1985).

[608] Ardis L. Campbell, *Determination of status as legal or natural parents in contested surrogacy births*, 77 A.L.R.5th 567, § 2(a) (2000) (gestational surrogacy is defined as an "arrangement wherein a woman's eggs can be retrieved and inseminated with her partner's sperm and transferred to the uterus of another woman for gestation and birth").

[609] *See* Ikemoto, *supra* note 499.

[610] *Id.* at 742.

[611] Robert E. Rains, *What the Erie "Surrogate Triplets" can Teach State Legislatures about the Need to Enact Article 8 of the Uniform Parentage Act* (2000), 56 Clev. St. L. Rev. 1, 3-5 (2008).

the Bimbers resided and the three resulting children were born, the trial court awarded the Bimbers primary custody of the triplets produced by the surrogacy.[612] James Flynn, the sperm donor and intended father, was granted partial custody and ordered to pay child support to the Bimbers, who supported themselves on Danielle's occasional part-time work and Douglas' self-employment as an appliance repairman earning approximately $9,600 per year.[613] The egg donor, Jennifer Rice, was denied visitation rights. On appeal, the Pennsylvania Superior Court decided the case on issues of standing and reversed the termination of egg donor Rice's parental rights and directed that the intended father, Flynn, be awarded full physical and legal custody.[614] However, the surrogacy contract stipulated Ohio law would govern disputes over the contract's execution. In an earlier decision in *J.F. v. D.B.*,[615] the Ohio Court of Appeals had rejected the trial court's decision in *Flynn*, noting that:

> [T]he legal analysis utilized by the Pennsylvania court is questionable under both Ohio and Pennsylvania precedent. To wit, a married woman bore a child during marriage and, with the marriage still in effect, the court granted a third-party to the marriage partial custody of the child and ordered him to pay the married couple child support for that child. Ordinarily, a child born during a marriage is presumed to be the child of the husband. This is a strongly guarded presumption in Ohio. In Pennsylvania, this presumption is even stronger than in Ohio: "the presumption is *irrefutable* where the mother, child and husband live together as an intact family, with the husband assuming parental responsibility." Mrs. Bimber was then and is now married to Douglas Bimber. Flynn never engaged in coitus with Mrs. Bimber; doctors fertilized Rice's embryos in a lab and impregnated Mrs. Bimber by surgically implanting the resulting zygotes into her uterus. In fact, Flynn and Mrs. Bimber had no relationship at all, beyond the arms-length surrogacy-contract negotiation. The Pennsylvania *court* created a father-and-mother relationship.[616]

The Ohio Court of Appeals held that the surrogacy contract was enforceable, that the Bimbers breached the agreement, and that Flynn was entitled to reimbursement pursuant to the contract and reimbursement by the Bimbers of all child support payments.[617] On appeal, the Ohio Supreme Court held that a gestational surrogacy contract prohibiting the gestational surrogate from asserting parental rights did not violate public policy.[618] The court highlighted the fundamental distinction between traditional and gestational surrogacy in stating "the obvious fact that a gestational surrogate, whose pregnancy does not involve her own egg, may have a different legal position from a traditional surrogate, whose pregnancy

---

[612] *J.F. v. D.B.*, 66 Pa. D. & C. 4th 1 (Pa. Ct. Com. Pl. 2005).

[613] Rains, *supra* note 611, at 4. Under the terms of the surrogacy arrangement, Flynn ultimately paid the Bimbers a total of $24,000. *Id.* at 5.

[614] *J.F. v. D.B.*, 897 A.2d 1261, 1281 (Pa. Sup. Ct. 2006).

[615] 848 N.E.2d 873 (2006), *rev'd on other grounds by* 879 N.E. 2d 740 (2007).

[616] *Id.* at 876 (internal citations omitted) (emphasis in original).

[617] *Id.* at 880-81.

[618] 879 N.E.2d 740, 741-42 (2007). The Ohio Supreme Court affirmed, in relevant part.

does involve her own egg . . . [W]e draw no conclusions about, traditional surrogates and Ohio's public policy concerning them."[619]

Surrogacy raises the thorny issue of who is a child's mother — the genetic mother, the gestational surrogate, or the intended mother? The California case, *Johnson v. Calvert*,[620] may be the first case to explore how to determine who a child's mother is with the same degree of scrutiny that courts have used to determine paternity. In *Johnson*, Anna Johnson had offered herself as a gestational surrogate to Mark Calvert and his wife Crispina, who had undergone a hysterectomy but retained intact ovaries. Anna, Mark, and Crispina signed a contract stating that an embryo created by Mark and Crispina would be implanted in Anna and the child born would be given to Mark and Crispina as their child. After Anna agreed to relinquish all parental rights in return for $10,000 plus a $200,000 life insurance policy, the couple's fertilized ova was implanted in Anna.

After several disputes among the parties, Anna threatened to refuse to give up the child if the balance of the payments was not made, and Mark and Crispina sought a declaration that they were the legal parents. As a result of blood tests after the child's birth, the trial court found Mark and Crispina to be the genetic, biological, and natural parents. It held that the contract was legal and enforceable, precluding any parental and visitation rights in Anna. The Court of Appeal affirmed, and the Supreme Court of California granted review. Rejecting a constitutional or policy analysis, the court decided the issue under the Uniform Parentage Act. Noting that the Act recognizes both genetic relationship and the act of giving birth as methods of establishing paternity, the court held that where both were undisputed — as here — the parties' intentions as expressed in the surrogacy contract should control. It rejected Anna's arguments that the contract was invalid under either the adoption laws or public policy grounds, holding that the contract was for Anna's services, not the sale of a child and that Anna had entered the contract knowingly and intelligently. The court concluded that concern that surrogacy contracts tend to exploit or dehumanize women, especially those of lower economic means, would be more appropriately addressed by the legislature. A strong dissent by Justice Kennard urged the application of a best interests of the child standard. In later cases, the California Supreme Court has explained that the "intent test does not apply when '[t]here is no "tie" to break.' "[621]

Likewise, in *Anna J. v. Mark C.*,[622] the court ruled that a woman who contracted to serve as the gestational mother had no statutory or constitutional right to be declared the child's parent.

A New York court arrived at the opposite conclusion under similar facts in *Andres A. v. Judith N.*[623] A married woman, Luz Elena A., sought a determination that she was the biological mother of twins born to Judith N. pursuant to a

---

[619] *Id.* at 742.

[620] 851 P.2d 776 (Cal. 1993) (en banc). For a fascinating account focusing on the race of the parties in *Johnson*, see Ikemoto, *supra* note 499.

[621] *See also K.M. v. E.G.*, 117 P.3d 673 (Cal. 2005), discussed *supra*.

[622] 234 Cal. App. 3d 1557 (1991).

[623] 591 N.Y.S.2d 946 (N.Y. Fam. Ct. 1992).

gestational surrogacy arrangement. In the arrangement, Judith agreed to become pregnant with Luz Elena's ova which had been fertilized by the sperm of Luz Elena's husband, Andres A. The parties agreed that Luz Elena and Andres were the biological parents of the children, but, in an uncontested filiation proceeding, the court held that the state's artificial insemination law precluded it from declaring Luz Elena the mother of the children.[624] It noted that she was not without a remedy, however, since she could seek to adopt the children.

Despite this case, many same-sex couples find gestational surrogacy attractive because both partners can be recognized as the legal parents of the resulting child. In *Raftopol v. Ramey*,[625] for example, the court declared that partners in a same-sex domestic partnership having a valid agreement with a gestational surrogate, who agreed to release putative parental rights upon birth of the child, could be declared the legal parents of the child, even though one partner was not biologically related to the child.

Regardless of whether surrogacy contracts are deemed invalid, the courts have focused on the best interests of the child born through a surrogacy arrangement. In *In re Marriage of Buzzanca*,[626] the California Court of Appeals held that parties who divorced after entering into a surrogacy contract were the legal parents of a child born to the surrogate and were responsible for the child's support, although neither was a biological parent of the child and the third-party surrogate carried and gave birth to the child. Despite the former husband's disclaimer of responsibility, the court treated him the same as a husband who consents to artificial insemination.[627]

Because same-sex couples often must rely on gestational surrogacy to create a genetic or biological tether between each one and the child, these arrangements frequently yield unique questions. For example, a Florida case, *T.M.H. v. D.M.T.*, involved two women in a same-sex partnership who conceived a child by one partner donating her egg and the other partner receiving that egg through IVF treatments so as to be the gestational mother. After the relationship deteriorated, the gestational mother fled the country with the child and the biological mother filed a petition seeking return of the child and a declaration of maternity. Initially her petition was denied because a Florida statute required her to sign away her maternal rights when she donated her ova. The appeals court, however, held that the statute requiring the egg donor to relinquish maternal rights violated the biological mother's constitutionally protected parental rights since the ova was donated with intent to raise the child with her partner.

---

[624] The court found that the presumption of paternity of Judith N.'s husband had been successfully rebutted and declared Andres the father of the children. *Id.* at 950.

[625] 12 A.3d 783 (Conn. 2011). For a very interesting account focusing on the race of the parties in *Johnson*, see Ikemoto, *supra* note 499.

[626] 72 Cal. Rptr. 2d 280 (Ct. App. 1998).

[627] *See generally* Linda S. Anderson, *Adding Players to the Game: Parentage Determinations when Assisted Reproductive Technology is used to Create Families*, 62 Ark. L. Rev. 29 (2009); Marsha Garrison, *Law Making for Baby Making: An Interpretive Approach to the Determination of Legal Parentage*, 113 Harv. L. Rev. 835 (2000).

Like IVF, frozen embryos intended for use with a gestational surrogate can occupy a central position in a contentious and highly charged divorce action. In *Litowitz v. Litowitz*,[628] the intended mother moved for reconsideration of the trial court's decision to award the embryos to her husband. The IVF contract stated "I agree that the [sperm] specimen can only be used by me for the purposes of artificial insemination, in vitro fertilization or assisted reproductive technique involving my lawful spouse,"[629] while the egg donor contract incorporated the egg donor's written declaration that, "[i]n the event that the court fails to award the [preembryos] to [the intended mother], I insist that the court award the [preembryos] to me or return the eggs to me in accordance with the contract."[630]

Arguing for the primacy of the donor contract, the intended mother maintained that the court should not consider the IVF contract since it implicated procreation but did not include the egg donor as a necessary party.[631] The intended father asked the court to uphold the terms of the IVF contract, focusing particularly upon the term quoted above. Since the couple had separated, he argued, the intended mother was no longer his "lawful spouse," his consent to proceed with further IVF had effectively been withdrawn, and he alone should control the use of the remaining "specimen" and its products.[632]

The Court of Appeals rejected the intended mother's argument, finding that "the egg donor is not a party to the . . . dissolution" and that the "contract provision deals with ownership and disposition of the *eggs*. The eggs, however, no longer exist. They have been fertilized and are now preembryos. Thus, the egg donor's request . . . even if properly before the court, cannot be met."[633] Focusing on the constitutional right to procreate, the Court of Appeals determined that such right exists only in scenarios involving genetic reproduction; since the intended mother "did not contribute any gametes to the embryos . . . she does not have a constitutional right to procreate. But [the intended father] is a progenitor and, therefore, he has a constitutional right not to procreate."[634] Further,

> [i]f any of the preembryos becomes a child in a setting where [the intended father] has contact with the child, he will be thrust into a lifetime parenting role. And if [he] has the right to control whether the preembryos continue on to life, he can surely exercise this right for the purpose of avoiding parenthood . . . . [T]he financial and psychological consequences flow from the long-term obligations of parenting, not the brief act of procreating . . . . [U]nder these circumstances, [he] can exercise his right not to procreate in a limited way that allows the preembryos to develop but avoids placing him in the unwanted parenting role.[635]

---

[628] 10 P.3d 1086 (Wash. Ct. App. 2000), *rev'd*, 48 P.3d 261 (Wash. 2002) (en banc).

[629] *Id.*

[630] 10 P.3d 1089-90. *See also* Daar, *supra* note 430, at 105.

[631] Daar, *supra* note 430, at 106.

[632] *Id.*

[633] 10 P.3d at 1093, n.13.

[634] *Id.* at 1092.

[635] *Id.* at 1092-93.

In an eight to one decision, the Supreme Court of Washington reversed the Court of Appeals' award of the frozen embryos to the intended father. It held the parties to IVF contract term specifying the embryos were to be thawed if they remained in cryopreservation for five years after they were initially frozen.[636] The parties later agreed in a settlement that the embryos would be offered to another patient who would remain anonymous.[637]

Unlike sperm donation, egg donation does not follow the model of total donor relinquishment, in particular because eggs normally are used immediately upon retrieval and while still fresh. Typically, "a couple or individual will select the donor from a profile booklet, and the donor will be consulted as to her willingness to donate to a particular recipient. [Unlike sperm donors, egg donors may] reserve the right to direct [their] eggs exclusively to the selected recipient."[638]

---

[636] 48 P.3d 261 (Wash. 2002), *amended by* 53 P.3d 516 (2002), *cert. denied*, 537 U.S. 1191 (2003).

[637] Daar, *supra* note 430, at 108.

[638] Daar, *supra* note 10, at 101.

Chapter 6

ADOPTION[1]

§ 6.01 ADOPTION AND TERMINATION OF PARENTAL RIGHTS

[A] Introduction and Overview

Adoption is the statutory process by which existing parental rights and responsibilities with respect to a child are extinguished and a new parent-child relationship is created. Adoption is best understood as a two step process, although both steps may be accomplished in the same proceeding. The first step involves termination of all rights in the child of the parent or anyone else having a legal relationship with the child. The second and final step is the creation of a new parent-child relationship with its attendant rights and responsibilities.

Generally, termination of parental rights will occur in one of two ways. A natural parent may voluntarily relinquish parental rights, most often through the execution of a surrender to a licensed child care agency or consent to a private or independent adoption. Alternatively, a state agency may seek termination of parental rights in a judicial proceeding. In this latter case, most states require a showing of unfitness, such as abandonment, abuse, or persistent neglect.

With increasing frequency, termination of the rights of a biological mother has been found to be unnecessary, particularly in cases that involve "second parent" adoptions. Illustrative is the opinion and decision of the Supreme Court of Vermont in *Adoption of B.L.V.B.*,[2] a case involving two women who had lived together as partners in a monogamous and committed relationship for several years. One of the parties twice gave birth after artificial insemination with the sperm of an anonymous donor. The probate court, despite lack of opposition, refused to approve the adoption of the child by the mother's partner under the conventional statutory mandate that required termination of the biological parent's rights. Thus, the issue before the court was "whether Vermont law requires the termination of a natural mother's parental rights if her children are adopted by a person to whom she is not married."[3] The court pointed out that the primary concern of the state's adoption statute is promotion of the welfare of children, and held that "when the family unit is comprised of the natural mother and her partner, and the adoption is in the best interests of the children, terminating the natural mother's rights is unreasonable

---

[1] John C. Eller, Esq., Contributing Editor.

[2] 628 A.2d 1271 (Vt. 1993).

[3] *Id.* at 1272.

and unnecessary."[4] In *Adoption of Tammy*,[5] the Supreme Judicial Court of Massachusetts reached the same conclusion when faced with similar facts, and courts in several other states have approved adoptions in these circumstances.[6]

[B] Involuntary Termination of Parental Rights

[1] Introduction

Termination of parental rights, whether consensually or involuntarily is, like adoption, a creature of statute. Even in cases where adoption is not contemplated or possible, statutes authorizing involuntary termination enable the courts to sever the ties between children and parents who neglect or harm them.[7] Typical statutory grounds for termination of parental rights include abandonment, child abuse, neglect or dependency, non-support, incarceration of the parent, and a parent's mental illness.[8] Generally, termination of parental rights will require a showing of the parent's unfitness in one form or another, and most states also require a demonstration by the preponderance of the evidence that termination will serve the best interests of the child.[9]

[2] Statutory Requirements

At first glance, variations in the language of statutes authorizing termination of parental rights appear bewildering. A close examination of the statutes reveals, however, that the requirements in many jurisdictions are similar. The grounds for involuntary termination set out in the Uniform Adoption Act are illustrative and typical, and provide:

> In addition to any other proceeding provided by law, the relationship of parent and child may be terminated by a court order issued in connection with an adoption proceeding under this Act on any ground provided by other law for termination of the relationship, and in any event on the ground (1) that the minor has been abandoned by the parent, (2) that by reason of the misconduct, faults, or habits of the parent or the repeated and continuous neglect or refusal of the parent, the minor is without proper parental care and control, or subsistence, education, or other care or control necessary for his physical, mental, or emotional health or morals,

---

[4] *Id.*

[5] 619 N.E.2d 315 (Mass. 1993) (noting that "[t]he Legislature obviously did not intend that a natural parent's legal relationship to its child be terminated when the natural parent is a party to the adoption").

[6] *See, e.g.*, *Sharon S. v. Superior Court*, 73 P.3d 554 (Cal. 2003) (analogizing second parent adoption to stepparent adoption); *In re Jacob*, 660 N.E.2d 397 (N.Y. 1995) (approving second parent adoption for both same-sex partners and unmarried heterosexual couples); *see also* Julie Shapiro, *A Lesbian-Centered Critique of Second-Parent Adoptions*, 14 Berkeley Women's L. J. 17 (1999); Alona R. Croteau, Comment, *Voices in the Dark: Second Parent Adoptions when the Law is Silent*, 50 Loy. L. Rev. 675 (2004); Christopher Colorado, Note, *Tying the Braid of Second-Parent Adoptions — Where Due Process Meets Equal Protection*, 74 Fordham L. Rev. 1425 (2005).

[7] *See* H. Clark, The Law of Domestic Relations in the United States 888 (2d ed. 1988).

[8] *See* Joan H. Hollinger, Adoption Law and Practice, § 4.04 (Matthew Bender).

[9] *Id.* at § 4.04[1][a].

or, by reason of physical or mental incapacity the parent is unable to provide necessary parental care for the minor, and the court finds that the conditions and causes of the behavior, neglect, or incapacity are irremediable or will not be remedied by the parent, and that by reason thereof the minor is suffering or probably will suffer serious physical, mental, moral, or emotional harm, or (3) that in the case of a parent not having custody of a minor, his consent is being unreasonably withheld contrary to the best interest of the minor.[10]

[3]   Constitutional Considerations

In 1981 and in 1982, the United States Supreme Court addressed two related questions that involved termination of parental rights. In the earlier case, *Lassiter v. Department of Social Services*,[11] the Court held that there was no requirement under the Constitution that counsel be appointed for an indigent parent in every proceeding for termination of parental rights. Rather, the Court held, the decision whether due process requires the appointment of counsel for parents in proceedings for the termination of parental rights should be left to the trial court, subject to appellate review.

In deciding whether the due process requirement of fundamental fairness required appointment of counsel in these proceedings, the Court gleaned from its earlier holdings the principle that the presumption that counsel must be appointed for an indigent litigant arises only when deprivation of physical liberty may result. The court then reviewed the other elements of due process, as reflected in its decision in *Mathews v. Eldridge*,[12] namely, the private interest at stake, the interest of the government, and the risk that the procedures used will lead to erroneous decisions. Having balanced these interests against each other and weighed them against the presumption, the Court concluded that the trial court's failure to appoint counsel in the case before it did not violate due process.

State courts have not slavishly adhered to the teaching of *Lassiter.* In *M.E.K. v. R.L.K.*,[13] for example, the Court of Appeal of Florida held that "[i]n the area of termination of parental rights," the due process clause of the Florida Constitution "provides higher due process standards than the federal due process clause" and guarantees to indigent parents the right to court-appointed counsel.[14] Most states now guarantee counsel for indigent parents in termination proceedings, either by statute or through judicial decisions.[15] Several state courts have also ruled that if

---

[10]   Unif. Adoption Act § 19(c), 9 U.L.A. 217 (1999).

[11]   452 U.S. 18 (1981).

[12]   424 U.S. 319 (1976).

[13]   921 So. 2d 787 (Fla. Dist. Ct. App. 2006). *See also V.F. v. State*, 666 P.2d 42 (Alaska 1983) (holding that the due process clause of the Alaska Constitution guarantees indigent parents the right to appointed counsel in proceedings for the termination of parental rights).

[14]   921 So. 2d at 790.

[15]   *See, e.g., In re I.B.*, 933 N.E.2d 1264 (Ind. 2010) (parents whose parental rights are being terminated against their will have the right to appointed counsel if they are indigent); Ala. Code § 12-15-305(b) (2012) ("In dependency and termination of parental rights cases, the respondent parent, legal guardian, or legal custodian shall be informed of his or her right to be represented by counsel and,

counsel is provided for an indigent parent at the trial court level, counsel must also be available if the parent appeals an order terminating parental rights. In *Santosky v. Kramer*,[16] the Court considered the standard of proof required in proceedings for termination of parental rights. Applying the factors in *Mathews v. Eldridge*,[17] the Court held that New York's fair preponderance of the evidence standard in termination proceedings violated the Due Process Clause, and that the constitutionally required standard is clear and convincing evidence.[18]

In *Adoption of Kelsey S.*,[19] the California Supreme Court held that a state statutory scheme violated federal constitutional guarantees of equal protection and due process to the extent that it permitted mothers unilaterally to preclude biological fathers from achieving the status of presumed father. Under California law, a man who met certain conditions was deemed the presumed father, and his consent was then required for a third-party adoption to take place. In *Kelsey*, where the mother planned to place the child for such an adoption, petitioner was the undisputed natural father of an out-of-wedlock child and, after the child's birth, he initiated an action to establish his parental relationship with the child and to obtain custody. The parents were not cohabiting and the mother denied the father any opportunity to exercise actual custody of the child, thus denying him a basis for attaining the status of presumed father. As the court noted, under the extant statutory scheme

> [the] system . . . leads to irrational distinctions between fathers. Based solely on the mother's wishes, a model father can be denied presumed father status, whereas a father of dubious ability and intent can achieve such status by the fortuitous circumstance of the mother allowing him to come into her home, even if only briefly — perhaps a single day . . . . Under the statutory scheme, two fathers who are by all accounts equal in their ability and commitment to fulfill their parental missions can be treated differently based solely on the mothers' decisions whether to allow the father to become a presumed father.[20]

---

if the juvenile court determines that he or she is indigent, counsel shall be appointed where . . . [they are] unable for financial reasons to retain [their] own counsel."); *see also* Hollinger, *supra* note 8, at § 2.10; Vivek Sankaran, A National Survey on a Parent's Right to Counsel in Termination of Parental Rights and Dependency Cases (unpub. manuscript), *available at* http://www.law.umich.edu/centersandprograms/ccl/specialprojects/Documents/National%20Survey%20on%20a%20Parent's%20Right%20to%20Counsel.pdf.

[16] 455 U.S. 745 (1982).

[17] 424 U.S. at 335.

[18] In *Santosky*, the Court noted its "historical recognition that freedom of personal choice in matters of family life is a fundamental liberty interest protected by the Fourteenth Amendment" and explained that "[t]he fundamental liberty interest of natural parents in the care, custody, and management of their child does not evaporate simply because they have not been model parents or have lost temporary custody of their child to the State. Even when blood relationships are strained, parents retain a vital interest in preventing the irretrievable destruction of their family life. If anything, persons faced with forced dissolution of their parental rights have a more critical need for procedural protections than do those resisting state intervention into ongoing family affairs. When the State moves to destroy weakened familial bonds, it must provide the parents with fundamentally fair procedures." 455 U.S. at 753-54.

[19] 823 P.2d 1216 (Cal. 1992).

[20] *Id.* at 1235.

Since the statutory scheme applied divergent standards between a "wholly acceptable father who wants to nurture [the child], but whose parental rights can be terminated under the best-interest standard because the mother has precluded [him] from attaining presumed father status," and "a presumed father [who] is highly questionable in every respect . . . [but can] withhold consent absent proof by clear and convincing evidence that he is unfit," the court held the statutory scheme violated federal constitutional guarantees of equal protection and due process.[21]

[4]   Grounds for Termination of Parental Rights

[a]   Abandonment

Statutes that govern termination of parental rights generally list abandonment as one of the grounds. Frequently, there is a requirement of failure to communicate with the child for a specified period of time, failure to provide support, or other evidence of intent to relinquish parental claims to the child.[22] The elements of the California statute are typical. The statute authorizes an action to free from parental custody a person

> [who] has been left without provision for the child's identification by the child's parent or parents . . . [or] in the care and custody of another person for a period of six months without any provision for the child's support, or without communication from the parent or parents, with the intent on the part of the parent or parents to abandon the child . . . [or] one parent has left the child in the care and custody of the other parent for a period of one year without any provision for the child's support, or without communication from the parent, with the intent on the part of the parent to abandon the child.[23]

> The failure to provide identification, failure to provide support, or failure to communicate is presumptive evidence of the intent to abandon. If the parent or parents have made only token efforts to support or communicate with the child, the court may declare the child abandoned by the parent or parents.[24]

The Minnesota statute similarly authorizes the court to terminate a parent's right to an abandoned child. The statute presumes abandonment when a parent has had no contact "with the child on a regular basis and [has] not demonstrated

---

[21] *Id.* at 1236.

[22] *See, e.g.*, Mich. Comp. Laws § 712A.19b(3)(f)(ii) (2012) (a parent with "the ability to visit, contact, or communicate with the minor, [who] has regularly and substantially failed or neglected, without good cause, to do so for a period of 2 years or more"); P.R. Laws Ann. tit. 31, § 634a(4)(b) (2009) (failure "to provide a reasonable amount for the support of the minor according to his/her financial means"); 23 Pa. Cons. Stat. § 2511(a)(1) (2012) (parent, for a period of at least six months, "has evidenced a settled purpose of relinquishing parental claim to a child or has refused or failed to perform parental duties").

[23] Cal. Fam. Code § 7822(a)(1)-(a)(3) (2012).

[24] Cal. Fam. Code § 7822(b) (2012).

consistent interest in the child's well-being" for six months.[25] Also, for the presumption of abandonment to obtain, the social service agency must have made "reasonable efforts to facilitate contact, unless the parent establishes that an extreme financial or physical hardship or treatment for mental disability or chemical dependency or other good cause prevented the parent from making contact with the child."[26] While abandonment is a statutory ground for termination of parental rights in any number of states,[27] the statutes frequently do not define the term abandonment or provide examples of what conduct will constitute abandonment.

Lack of parental contact might not constitute abandonment if its cause is not within the parent's control. In *In re T.M.R.*,[28] for example, the California Court of Appeal acknowledged that sporadic efforts at communication or communications in the face of threatened legal action may be considered only token. Nevertheless, the court reversed the trial court's order terminating the parental rights of a mother who was incarcerated. The court noted that the mother wrote to the children twice a month and sent them birthday and Christmas cards, the only means of communication available to her.

Similarly, in *State in Interest of M.C.*,[29] the Utah Court of Appeals upheld a juvenile court's conclusion that a finding of abandonment is not justified when the parent is incarcerated and under court orders not to contact their children or the children's guardian. The court concluded that "involuntary confinement of a parent excuses that parent from maintaining contact with his or her children, but only to the extent the parent is precluded, by directive or by circumstances, from maintaining contact during the period of incarceration."[30] Applying the generally recognized principle that conduct constituting abandonment must be willful, the court noted that "although the acts leading to [the mother's] incarceration were voluntary, [her] resulting incarceration does not represent willful conduct justifying termination of her parental rights,"[31] and "where official acts prevent a parent from maintaining contact with a child, unfitness . . . cannot be proven by such lack of contact standing alone . . . . We do not believe that the [state] should be permitted to prevent a parent from contacting her children and then claim that the parent is unfit solely because she did not do so."[32]

---

[25] Minn. Stat. Ann. § 260C.301 subd. 2(a)(1) (2012), *amended by* 2012 Minn. Laws Ch. 216 (S.F. No. 1675).

[26] *Id.*

[27] *See, e.g.*, Ariz. Rev. Stat. § 8-533(B)(1) (2012); Colo. Rev. Stat. § 19-3-604(1)(a)(i) (2012); N.Y. Soc. Serv. Law § 384-b(4)(b) (2012); *see also* U.S. Dept. of Health and Human Services, Grounds for Involuntary Termination of Parental Rights (Feb. 2010), *available at* http://www.childwelfare.gov/systemwide/laws_policies/statutes/groundtermin.pdf.

[28] 116 Cal. Rptr. 292 (Cal. Ct. App. 1974).

[29] 940 P.2d 1229 (Utah Ct. App. 1997).

[30] *Id.* at 1235.

[31] *Id.*.

[32] *Id.* (quoting *In re Taylor*, 334 N.E.2d 194, 197 (Ill. App. Ct. 1975)).

In an Alaska case, *Adoption of V.M.C.*,[33] the state's highest court found that a father who left his child in his mother's care in order to seek employment in another state had not abandoned the child.

In *In re Adoption of Baby E.A.W.*,[34] the Supreme Court of Florida addressed the certified question whether an out-of-wedlock father had abandoned the child, which would free her for adoption without parental consent. The question before the court was whether the trial court could properly consider lack of emotional support or emotional abuse of the mother in evaluating the statutory factor or "conduct of the father towards the child during the pregnancy."[35] The court answered the question in the affirmative and affirmed the trial court's finding of abandonment.

[b]   Child Abuse, Neglect and Dependency

Termination of parental rights may result from abuse or persistent neglect of a child. The opinion of the Colorado Court of Appeals in *People ex rel. C.R.*[36] sets out a scenario that is not atypical. At the time of the termination proceeding in *C.R.*, the children were in the custody of the county department of social services, the three youngest children having been adjudicated as neglected or dependent because of child abuse, and the mother having been found incompetent to care for the oldest child. The finding of neglect or dependency was based on evidence that a man with whom the mother was cohabiting had inflicted injuries on the children over an extended time period, and that she did not seek medical or other assistance for the children.

The court affirmed the trial court's termination of the mother's parental rights in a subsequent dispositional hearing. The court held:

> In decreeing termination of parental rights, a trial court must find that the conditions which resulted in the earlier determination of dependency will in all probability continue into the future, and that under no reasonable circumstances would the welfare of the children be served by a continuation of the parent-child relationship.[37]

The court in *C.R.* also noted that a trial court properly may infer that a non-abused child lacks proper care from evidence of the mistreatment of the other children. The decision of the Wyoming Supreme Court in *In re M.L.M.*[38] reflects this principle, observing that abuse by a stepfather or some other person is evidence of a mother's neglect if she takes no steps to stop the abuse or remove the child from the abusive environment.[39] Courts in other states have terminated parental rights based on the failure of a parent, typically a mother, to protect a child from abuse

---

[33] 528 P.2d 788 (Alaska 1974).

[34] 658 So. 2d 961 (Fla. 1995).

[35] *See* Fla. Stat. § 63.032(1) (Supp. 1992).

[36] 557 P.2d 1225 (Colo. Ct. App. 1976).

[37] *Id.* at 1227-28.

[38] 682 P.2d 982 (Wyo. 1984).

[39] *Id.* at 987. *See also* A. Haralambie, Handling Child Custody, Abuse and Adoption Cases §§ 13:8-9, 22 (3d ed. 2011).

from a husband or other member of the household.[40] In some cases, parents have faced criminal charges for failure to protect a child from abuse under such circumstances.[41]

[c]   Failure to Provide Child Support

The failure of a parent to provide support is frequently a ground for involuntary termination of parental rights. The influential Uniform Adoption Act lists among those whose consent is not required for adoption of a child "a parent of a child in the custody of another, if the parent for a period of at least one year has failed significantly without justifiable cause . . . to provide for the care and support of the child as required by law or judicial decree."[42] The Minnesota statute, while its language is more elaborate, is to the same effect, authorizing termination of parental rights upon the finding of the following condition:

> That the parent has substantially, continuously, or repeatedly refused or neglected to comply with the duties imposed upon that parent by the parent and child relationship, including but not limited to providing the child with necessary food, clothing, shelter, education, and other care and control necessary for the child's physical, mental, or emotional health and development, if the parent is physically and financially able, and either reasonable efforts by the social services agency have failed to correct the conditions that formed the basis of the petition or reasonable efforts would be futile and therefore unreasonable.[43]

The decision of the Supreme Court of Alaska in *In re J.J.J.*,[44] a leading case, is frequently cited as an illustration of the elements required for involuntary termination of parental rights on the ground of non-support. The trial court in *J.J.J.* held that under the controlling statute the stepfather could adopt a seven-year-old boy without the biological father's consent because the father had, for a twelve month period, "failed significantly without justifiable cause to provide support required by judicial decree."[45]

In its affirmance, the court held that the father's "sporadic partial payments" of court-ordered support did not "preclude a finding of significant failure to provide child support," and that child support payments should be "substantial or regular

---

[40] *See. e.g., In the Interest of B.R.S.*, 402 S.E.2d 281 (Ga. Ct. App. 1991) (mother's parental rights terminated after she failed to protect her children from emotional and physical abuse by her husband, who she knew was prone to violence and who had previously harmed her and her children); *In re K.H.*, 895 N.E.2d 809 (Ohio 2008) (mother's parental rights terminated when she continued to cohabit with the father, who was a pedophile); *In re H.R.C.*, 781 N.W.2d 105 (Mich. Ct. App. 2009) (mother's parental rights terminated after she failed to prevent, and then concealed, her husband's sexual abuse of her daughter).

[41] *See, e.g., State v. Legg*, 623 N.E.2d 1263 (Ohio Ct. App. 1993) (sustaining mother's conviction for child endangering where she testified she was aware her husband was severely beating her son but took no action to stop the abuse).

[42] Unif. Adoption Act § 6(a)(2), 9 U.L.A. 154-55 (2009).

[43] Minn. Stat. § 260C.301 subd. 1(b)(2) (2012), *amended by* 2012 Minn. Laws Ch. 216 (S.F. No. 1675).

[44] 718 P.2d 948 (Alaska 1986).

[45] *Id.* at 949.

and constitute a material factor" in child support.[46] The resistance of the former wife to the father's interest in visitation with the boy did not excuse failure to support him.

[d]   Unfitness

Unfitness as a ground for termination of parental rights encompasses a vast array of parental conduct, including some of the grounds previously discussed, such as abuse, persistent neglect, failure to protect a child when a parent has the duty to do so, and the like.[47] In *In re Adoption of Michael J.C.*,[48] the prospective adoptive parents sought termination of the parental rights of the mother of an infant girl who sought to withdraw consent to adoption. The court reviewed evidence in the record that the child's mother had physically abused her own mother and children for whom she was a baby sitter. There was also evidence of alcohol abuse and illegal drug use, including hospitalization for a drug overdose, and treatment in a mental hospital after suicide threats.

Furthermore, she had engaged in promiscuous sexual intercourse at the age of sixteen, and had a history of violent exhibitions of temper toward friends and family members. She maintained an insanitary apartment that her landlord described as uninhabitable. The court concluded:

> [W]hen a parent has demonstrated a continued inability to conduct his or her life in a fashion that would provide a safe environment for a child, whether that child is living with the parent or not, and the behavior of the parent is irremediable as supported by clear and competent evidence, the termination of parental rights is justified.[49]

In *New Jersey Division of Youth and Family Services v. A.W.*,[50] the New Jersey Supreme Court cautioned that a court analyzing parents' ability to care for their children should determine only whether the parents foreseeably can cease to harm their children, rather than determining that the parents are themselves unfit or "the victims of social circumstances beyond their control."[51] The court observed that "[p]arents are not to be adjudged unfit because they lack resources or intelligence, but only by reason of conduct detrimental to the physical or mental health of the child, specifically in the form of actual or imminent harm."[52] Absent such a showing, children may not be removed from their parents.

---

[46] *Id.* at 954 (internal quotations omitted).

[47] *See generally* Haralambie, *supra* note 39, at §§ 13:7-182; Hollinger, *supra* note 8, at § 2.10[1].

[48] 486 A.2d 371 (Pa. 1984).

[49] *Id.* at 375.

[50] 512 A.2d 438 (N.J. 1986).

[51] *Id.* at 447.

[52] *Id.* at 451.

[e] Mental or Physical Disability of the Parent

In some jurisdictions, statutes authorize termination of parental rights when a parent is unable to care for a child because of mental illness or retardation. The Uniform Adoption Act permits a court to dispense with parental consent to adoption by "a parent judicially declared incompetent or mentally defective if the Court dispenses with the parent's consent."[53] The California statute is of similar effect, authorizing the court to declare free from parental custody and control a child "[w]hose parent or parents have been declared by a court of competent jurisdiction . . . to be developmentally disabled or mentally ill . . . ."[54]

In *In re K.F.*,[55] Iowa's Supreme Court affirmed a judgment terminating the parental rights of a mother who suffered from paranoid schizophrenia. The court noted that "mental disability, standing alone, is not a sufficient reason for the termination of the parent-child relationship."[56] It is, however, "a proper factor to consider and, when it contributes to a person's inability to parent, may be determinative on the issue" of whether the child's best interests require termination of parental rights.[57] Also illustrative is the opinion in *New Jersey Division of Youth and Family Services v. B.G.S.*,[58] in which a New Jersey appellate court affirmed the trial court's termination of the parental rights of a mother who abused alcohol and drugs, and who also suffered from bipolar disorder and polysubstance dependency.

[f] Best Interests of the Child

Although the cases do not always say it explicitly, it is obvious that termination of parental rights and adoption should be in the best interests of the child — a standard which focusses on the child's needs rather than on parental rights.[59] At the same time, however, the cases make it clear that conduct that is harmful to the child or that reflects what may be deemed "unfitness" will be weighed in the determination of what constitutes the child's best interest. The Supreme Court of Rhode Island, in *In re Kristina L.*,[60] set out the generally prevailing principle:

> Parental unfitness and the best interest of the child are not unrelated concepts. Concern for the best interests of the child is "not inconsistent with a respect for parental rights with which no agency of the state may

---

[53] Unif. Adoption Act § 6(a)(6), 9 U.L.A. 155 (2009).

[54] Cal. Fam. Code § 7826(a) (2012).

[55] 437 N.W.2d 559 (Iowa 1989).

[56] *Id.* at 560.

[57] *Id.*

[58] 677 A.2d 1170 (N.J. Super. Ct. 1996).

[59] *See generally* Haralambie, *supra* note 39, at § 1:7 (noting that in "focusing on the best interests of the child, courts have emphasized external conditions more than the psychological needs of the child," but that [c]ourts are [also] becoming more sensitive to all of the child's interests, emotional as well as psychological"); Hollinger, *supra* note 8, at § 1.01[2][b] (noting that "[t]he legal conclusion that an adoption is warranted ultimately rests on a judicial evaluation of the personal and psychological dynamics of the relationship between the child and the adopting parents").

[60] 520 A.2d 574 (R.I. 1987).

interfere on arbitrary or irrational grounds." . . . The inability of parents to provide the basic necessities of life for their children is certainly not in the child's best interest. However, even though it may be in a child's best interest to live with a family of comfortable means rather than a poorer family, this standard may not justify the state's intervention into a family relationship absent a finding of parental unfitness.[61]

In sum, it is only after a determination of parental unfitness that the best interests of the child will outweigh other considerations in a proceeding for termination of parental rights.

[C]   Independent or Private Adoption

The adoption of children may be accomplished in every jurisdiction through state licensed child care agencies. In a number of states, however, adoptions may occur independent of agencies licensed to care for and place children. In such independent adoptions, the child's birth parent and prospective adoptive parents may know each other prior to adoption and arrange for the adoption through direct placement without an intermediary. More frequently, however, an adoption intermediary brings together the birth parent and the prospective adoptive parents, culminating in a private placement adoption.[62]

Independent adoptions sometimes are referred to as "gray market" adoptions, a term that purportedly is meant "to indicate that independent adoptions often fall into a gray area of the law, somewhere between the highly regulated agency adoptions and the patently illegal baby selling of black market adoptions."[63] As one commentator has succinctly and correctly observed:

> A black market adoption differs from a legal private placement or gray market adoption only in that the intermediary receives a disallowable fee. Since it is so easy to cross the line between a permitted private placement and an illegal black market sale of a child, the threat of a black market adoption is greater with independent adoptions.[64]

As is generally the case with adoption and termination of parental rights, the states take a variety of approaches to independent adoptions. In the vast majority of jurisdictions, a parent may place a child with unrelated prospective adoptive parents either directly or with an intermediary's assistance. Only about four states

---

[61] *Id.* at 581 (citations omitted).

[62] *See* Gustafson, Note, *Regulating Adoption Intermediaries: Ensuring that the Solutions Are No Worse Than the Problem*, 3 Geo. J. Legal Ethics 837, 842 (1990); Kimberly D. Krawiec, *Altruism and Intermediation in the Market for Babies*, 66 Wash. & Lee L. Rev. 203 (2009).

[63] Bernadette W. Hartfield, *The Role of the Interstate Compact on the Placement of Children in Interstate Adoption*, 68 Neb. L. Rev. 292, 304 (1989). On distinguishing between lawful and unlawful placements, see generally Hollinger, *supra* note 8, at § 1.05[3][c]; Melinda Lucas, *Adoption: Distinguishing Between Gray Market and Black Market Activities*, 34 Fam. L.Q. 553 (2000). *See also* 2 Am. Jur. 2d *Adoption* § 54 (2012).

[64] Barbara L. Atwell, *Surrogacy and Adoption: A Case of Incompatibility*, 20 Colum. Hum. Rts. L. Rev. 1, 13-14, n.62 (1988). *See also* Lucas, *supra* note 63; Carol S. Silverman, *Regulating Independent Adoptions*, 22 Colum. J.L. & Soc. Probs. 323 (1988).

bar independent adoptions and limit authorization for adoption placements to state agencies or state licensed private agencies.[65]

Those states in the majority that permit private placement have sought to prevent profiteering in adoption placements by the enactment of laws or regulations that limit compensation payable to intermediaries who arrange adoption placements.[66] In some instances, states have prescribed criminal sanctions for the violation of statutory procedures governing adoption placement.[67]

An array of often conflicting regulations govern independent adoptions in the several states. Some states, for example, require a home study to be conducted by an approved social worker, while others require no such study.[68] There are also conflicting approaches among the states with respect to such issues as whether the birth mother must receive mandatory counseling; whether prospective adoptive parents may advertise that they wish to adopt a child; whether birth parents and adoptive parents may share identifying information; and the time within which a consent may be signed or revoked.[69]

Without exception, states that permit independent adoption placement do not permit a person to profit from the placement.[70] As one commentator has noted, "if

---

[65] U.S. Dept. of Health & Human Services, Administration for Children and Families, *Who May Adopt, Be Adopted, or Place a Child for Adoption?* 4 (Jan. 2012), *available at* http://www.childwelfare.gov/systemwide/laws_policies/statutes/parties.pdf.

[66] Ahilemah Jonet, *Legal Measures to Eliminate Transnational Trading of Infants for Adoption: An Analysis of Anti-Infant Trading Statutes in the United States*, 13 Loyola L.A. Int'l & Comp. L.J. 305, 307 (1990). *See also* Jorge L. Carro, *Regulation of Intercountry Adoptions: Can the Abuses Come to an End?*, 18 Hastings Int'l & Comp. L. Rev. 121 (1994); Gabriela Marquez, *Transnational Adoption: The Creation and Ill Effects of an International Black Market Baby Trade*, 21 J. Juv. L. 25 (2000); U.S. Dept. of Health & Human Services, Administration for Children and Families, "Regulation of Private Domestic Adoption Expenses" (Mar. 2010), *available at* http://www.childwelfare.gov/systemwide/laws_policies/statutes/expenses.pdf.

[67] Jonet, *supra* note 66, at 307. For a state-by-state discussion of criminal sanctions, *see generally* Hollinger, *supra* note 8, at app. 1-A, question XII; Kristine Cordier Kanezis, *Criminal Liability of One Arranging for Adoption of Child Through Other Than Licensed Child Placement Agency*, 3 A.L.R.4th 468 (2011).

[68] *See* Gustafson, *supra* note 62, at 843; *see also, e.g.*, N.C. Gen. Stat. §§ 48-2-501(a), 502(a) (2012) ("Whenever a petition for adoption of a minor is filed, the court shall order a report . . . made to assist the court to determine if the proposed adoption of the minor . . . is in the minor's best interest . . . . [Preparing the report] shall [include] a personal interview with each petitioner in the petitioner's residence and at least one additional interview with each petitioner and the adoptee"); Okla. Stat. tit. 10, §§ 7505-5.1, -5.3 (2012) ("[O]nly a person for whom a favorable written preplacement home study has been prepared may accept custody of a minor for purposes of adoption . . . . A home study . . . must include . . . a home visit . . . and [v]erification that the home is a healthy, safe environment in which to raise a minor").

[69] *See* Gustafson, *supra* note 62, at 843.

[70] *See* Atwell, *supra* note 64, at 27-29; *see also, e.g.*, Colo. Rev. Stat. § 19-5-213(1)(a) (2012) ("No person shall offer, give, charge, or receive any money or other consideration or thing of value in connection with the relinquishment and adoption, except attorney fees and such other charges and fees as may be approved by the court"); La. Rev. Stat. Ann. § 14:286(A), (D) (2011) ("[I]t shall be unlawful for any person to sell or surrender a minor child to another person for money or anything of value, or to receive a minor child for such payment of money or anything of value"; "A person convicted . . . shall be punished by a fine not to exceed fifty thousand dollars or imprisonment with or without hard labor for

the attorney, physician, or other intermediary who arranges an independent adoption were permitted to profit from the transaction, the temptation would arise to place the child with adoptive parents who would pay the highest price for the child rather than with parents who would act in the child's best interest."[71]

There is general agreement that it is ethically improper for a lawyer to represent both the birth parent and the prospective adoptive parents in a private placement adoption. In *Matter of Petrie*,[72] the Supreme Court of Arizona upheld disciplinary sanctions imposed on a lawyer who violated conflict of interest rules by representing multiple clients in a private adoption. The lawyer in *Petrie* established an attorney-client relationship with the child's natural mother, and subsequently with two different prospective adoptive couples. The court noted that while the parties to an independent adoption proceeding generally do not have an adversary relationship, there is nevertheless the potential for conflicts of interest. The court stated:

> Despite the spirit of cooperation often present in an adoption, conflict of interest situations are likely to arise for an attorney involved in the proceedings. First, the interests of potential adoptive parents of the same child are always adverse to one another . . . .
>
> Second, and perhaps less apparent, the interests of the adoptive parents may be adverse to the interests of the natural parents. The decision to give the baby up for adoption is often a difficult one to make. The natural parents' attorney has a duty to provide them with counsel about such matters as paternity issues, economic matters, and the legal effect of signing the consent to adopt.[73]

Criminal sanctions may also apply to unauthorized private placement adoptions.[74] For example, in *Galison v. District of Columbia*,[75] the appellant was a New York lawyer whose associate was contacted by a Florida lawyer who stated that he had not been able to arrange for an adoption in Florida of the expected child of a Florida resident. The expectant mother was willing to travel only as far as the District of Columbia, where Galison met her. After the woman's change of heart, Galison persuaded her to proceed with the adoption and that she would be paid $2000 in addition to her medical and living expenses. Ultimately, Galison was

---

not more than ten years, or both"); S.D. Codified Laws § 25-6-4.2 (2012) ("Any person who offers, gives, or receives any money or other consideration or thing of value in connection with the placing of any child for adoption, or relating to the consent to adoption, or with the petition for adoption except such charges as are approved by the court and fees charged by agencies licensed pursuant to [statute], is guilty of a Class 6 felony").

[71] *Id.* at 29.

[72] 742 P.2d 796 (Ariz. 1987).

[73] *Id.* at 800.

[74] For a state-by-state discussion of criminal sanctions, *see generally* Hollinger, *supra* note 8, at app. 1-A, question XII; Kamezis, *supra* note 67.

[75] 402 A.2d 1263 (D.C. Ct. App. 1979). *See also Combs v. Commonwealth*, 520 S.E.2d 388 (Va. Ct. App. 1999) (upholding wife's convictions for soliciting and conspiracy to solicit in connection with a placement or adoption; wife's husband, in her presence, tried repeatedly to obtain money from numerous people in return for placing their child for adoption and wife failed to object to his offers or to his remark that he was not going to "give the baby away free" because he could "make thousands of dollars off the baby.").

convicted of the District statute that proscribed placement of children by other than a licensed child-placing agency.

[D] Agency Adoption

In every state, children may be placed for adoption by either state agencies or by private agencies licensed by the state to undertake child care and child placement.[76] Ordinarily, children will come into the care and custody of an authorized agency through either involuntary termination of parental rights in a judicial proceeding, or voluntary relinquishment of parental rights through execution of a document commonly known as a surrender. Under either method of placement, the child generally will be eligible for adoption.

As a leading commentator has pointed out, adoption statutes contain few restrictions as to what persons are eligible to adopt, including age and residence requirements in some states, and generally requiring only that they be adults, and for married persons that both husband and wife join in the adoption petition.[77] The rationale offered for this state of affairs is the intent to rely on adoption agencies to screen out prospective adoptive parents who are unsuitable.[78] The writer concludes:

> Since particular adoption agencies may have many standards or rules of thumb respecting the qualifications of prospective adoptive parents, this gives the agencies considerable legal power over the grant or denial of adoptions. The agency's refusal to place a child with prospective adoptive parents, although it may theoretically be reviewable by the courts, as a practical matter will seldom be challenged.[79]

In *Scott v. Family Ministries*,[80] a prospective adoptive parent mounted a successful challenge to the policies of an authorized adoption agency.[81] Richard Scott, a physician, sought to adopt a Cambodian child who was in the custody of Family Ministries, a California licensed adoption agency that served the evangelical Protestant community and placed children only in evangelical Protestant homes. Although he signed the agency's required statement of faith, he was informed that he was not qualified to adopt because he was an Episcopalian, and not an evangelical Protestant.

---

[76] *See generally* Adoption, 50 State Survey (Lexis 2012).

[77] Clark, *supra* note 7, at 908.

[78] *Id.*

[79] *Id.*

[80] 135 Cal. Rptr. 430 (Cal. Ct. App. 1976).

[81] *See also McLaughlin v. Pernsley*, 693 F. Supp. 318, 319 (E.D. Pa. 1988), *aff'd*, 876 F.2d 308 (3d Cir. 1989) (granting preliminary injunction to plaintiffs where social services agency, "pursuant to their policy against cross-racial long-term foster care placements and adoptions," removed child from the care of plaintiffs). *See generally* Jehnna Irene Hanan, Comment, *The Best Interest of the Child: Eliminating Discrimination in the Screening of Adoptive Parents*, 27 Golden Gate U. L. Rev. 167 (1997); Kimberly A. Collier, Comment, *Love v. Love Handles: Should Obese People be Precluded from Adopting a Child Based Solely Upon Their Weight?*, 15 Tex. Wesleyan L. Rev. 31 (2008).

The California Court of Appeal affirmed the trial court's judgment granting injunctive relief. In the course of its opinion the court noted that the adoption laws of almost all states embody religious considerations. The California statute, like those in a number of other states, provides for religious matching, which "requires or gives preference to adoption by parents of the same faith as that of the natural parents of the child or of a religion for which the natural parents express a preference."[82] The court observed:

> The process preserves constitutionality by placing the state in a neutral position in which parentage or parents and not the state determines the religion of the home into which the child is to be adopted . . . . It recognizes the common law right of a natural parent to control the religious upbringing of his child.[83]

The court noted that because of the significant role that private licensed adoption agencies play under the California statutory scheme and the extent to which the state delegates to those agencies the governmental function of performing tasks leading to judicially approved adoptions, the activities of the agencies constitutes state action. Accordingly, the court held that in order to make the California statute constitutional, it must be interpreted as precluding the imposition of religious requirements upon prospective adoptive parents beyond the religious matching provisions of the applicable statute.[84]

Some courts maintain that agencies have an affirmative duty to disclose to adoptive parents all relevant information about a child's genetic propensities and risks of disease, at least to the extent that information is known or discoverable through reasonable diligence.[85] In *Roe v. Jewish Children's Bureau of Chicago*,[86] the Appellate Court of Illinois allowed negligence and fraudulent misrepresentation claims to go forward against an adoption agency. The adopting parents told the agency "they would only accept . . . a child whose parents were normal mentally, intellectually, and emotionally, and who had no history of psychiatric problems" and were told falsely by the agency that the mother had no such problems, despite her "history of emotional problems including psychiatric hospitalization."[87] Shortly after the adoption, the appellants learned from medical professionals that the child was "suffering from a psychiatric disorder with features of autism and schizophrenia."[88] Still later, they learned from the biological father of the birth mother's history of mental problems. The court concluded that:

---

[82] *Scott*, 135 Cal. Rptr. at 437. *See also Dickens v. Ernesto*, 281 N.E.2d 153 (N.Y. 1972).

[83] *Scott*, 135 Cal. Rptr. at 437.

[84] *See generally* Hollinger, *supra* note 8, at § 3.06[3].

[85] *See generally* Haralambie, *supra* note 39, at § 14:18; Marianne Brower Blair, *Lifting the Genealogical Veil: A Blueprint for Legislative Reform of the Disclosure of Health-Related Information in Adoption*, 70 N.C. L. Rev. 681 (1992); Marianne Brower Blair, *Getting the Whole Truth and Nothing But the Truth: The Limits of Liability for Wrongful Adoption*, 67 Notre Dame L. Rev. 851 (1992).

[86] 790 N.E.2d 882 (Ill. App. Ct.), *appeal denied*, 803 N.E.2d 500 (Ill. 2003).

[87] 790 N.E.2d 882 at 887.

[88] *Id.*

[A]n adoption agency interjects itself into a process that alters permanently the structure of families and affects fundamental human relationships . . . . An adoption creates a parent-child relationship where none existed before and alters forever the lives of both the child and the adoptive parents . . . . [A] fraudulent or negligent misrepresentation claim against an adoption agency is viable when the agency makes a false statement that affects the adoptive parents' right to make an informed decision.[89]

[E]   Consent

[1]   Who Must Give Consent?

In every state, the statute governing adoption requires the consent of the mother of a minor child before a petition to adopt is granted. Also required is the consent of the father of the child if he was married to the child's mother at the time of the child's conception or birth. Such persons whose consent is required may, of course, relinquish their parental rights voluntarily, or may have those rights terminated involuntarily in a judicial proceeding.[90] If a child's parents are both deceased or both have been deprived of their rights through involuntary termination or voluntary surrender, the child cannot be adopted without their legal guardian's consent or the consent of an agency or individual authorized by the court to withhold or grant consent.[91]

Historically, the consent of the father of a child born out of wedlock was not required. Following a series of decisions by the Supreme Court of the United States, however, it is now well established that the consent of the father of an out — of — wedlock child is required in a variety of circumstances. Unlike birth mothers, these fathers must establish their right to consent. Among the ways of doing so are formal acknowledgement or judicial establishment of paternity, or by showing under the applicable statute that they have established a relationship with the child that is entitled to recognition.[92]

---

[89] *Id.* at 894, 896.

[90] *See supra* § 6.01[B].

[91] On consent, see generally Hollinger, *supra* note 8, at § 2.02, and Haralambie, *supra* note 39, at § 14:11.

[92] *See, e.g.*, Ariz. Rev. Stat. § 8-106.01(A) (2012) ("A person who is seeking paternity, who wants to receive notice of adoption proceedings and who is the father or claims to be the father of a child shall file notice of a claim of paternity and of his willingness and intent to support the child to the best of his ability with the state registrar of vital statistics . . ."); Neb. Rev. Stat. § 43-104.02 (2012) ("A Notice of Objection to Adoption and Intent to Obtain Custody shall be filed with the biological father registry . . . (1) within five business days after the birth of the child or (2) if notice is provided after the birth of the child (a) within five business days after receipt of the notice . . . or (b) within five business days after the last date of any published notice . . ."); Fla. Stat. § 63.062(2)(a)(1) (2012), *amended by* 2012 Fla. Sess. Law Ch. 2012-81 (for a child placed with adoptive parents more than six months after the child's birth, the consent of an unmarried, biological father is only required if, among other requirements, the father has "developed a substantial relationship with the child, taken some measure of responsibility for the child and the child's future, and demonstrated a full commitment to the responsibilities of parenthood by providing reasonable and regular financial support to the child in accordance with [his] ability, if not prevented from doing so by the person or authorized agency having lawful custody of the child").

[2]   Consent of the Unwed Father

In a series of four cases, the United States Supreme Court has established the contours of the rights of fathers of children born out of wedlock to consent to their adoption.[93] In the seminal case, *Stanley v. Illinois*,[94] the court considered the constitutionality of an Illinois statutory scheme that presumed that every father of a child born out of wedlock was unfit to have custody of his children. The father in *Stanley* had lived with the children for all of their lives, and had lived with their mother intermittently for 18 years. When the mother died, the children were declared wards of the state.

The Court held that under the Due Process Clause, Stanley was entitled to a hearing as to his fitness, and that the state could not presume that he, and unwed fathers generally, were neglectful and unsuitable parents. The Court also held that denying a hearing for unwed fathers while extending that right to all other parents whose custody of their children was challenged violated the Equal Protection Clause of the Constitution.

Although adoption was not involved in *Stanley*, the Court made a brief reference to the subject in footnote 9 to its opinion:

> We note in passing that the incremental cost of offering unwed fathers an opportunity for individualized hearings on fitness appears to be minimal. If unwed fathers, in the main, do not care about the disposition of their children, they will not appear to demand hearings. If they do care, under the scheme here held invalid, Illinois would admittedly at some later time have to afford them a properly focused hearing in a custody or adoption proceeding. Extending opportunity for hearing to unwed fathers who desire and claim competence to care for their children creates no constitutional or procedural obstacle to foreclosing those unwed fathers who are not so inclined. The Illinois law governing procedure in juvenile cases . . . provides for personal service, notice by certified mail, or for notice by publication when personal or certified mail service cannot be had or when notice is directed to unknown respondents under the style of "All whom it may Concern." Unwed fathers who do not promptly respond cannot complain if their children are declared wards of the State. Those who do respond retain the burden of proving their fatherhood.[95]

Largely in response to this footnote, a number of states amended their adoption statutes to require notice to unwed fathers.[96]

---

[93] *See generally* Ardis L. Campbell, *Rights of Unwed Father to Obstruct Adoption of his Child by Withholding Consent*, 61 A.L.R.5th 151 (2012); Laura Oren, *Thwarted Fathers or Pop-Up Pops? How to Determine when Putative Fathers can Block the Adoption of their Newborn Children*, 40 Fam. L.Q. 153 (2006).

[94] 405 U.S. 645 (1972).

[95] 405 U.S. at 657 n.9.

[96] *See, e.g., K.D. v. Gift of Life Adoptions, Inc.*, 17 So. 3d 1244 (Fla. Dist. Ct. App. 2009) (termination of father's parental rights reversed, where father's failure to file with the state's putative father registry occurred because the adoption agency did not provide notice of the planned adoption at least thirty days before filing the termination petition, as required by statute; father was thus denied timely notice and

Some six years after *Stanley*, in *Quilloin v. Walcott*,[97] the court addressed an unwed father's rights in the adoption context, ruling on the constitutionality of a Georgia statute that authorized adoption of a child born out of wedlock over the objection of the natural father. The statute in question required only the mother's consent to adoption of an out of wedlock child, but permitted the father to veto the adoption if he had legitimated the child in accordance with Georgia law. After the mother and her new husband had filed an adoption petition, the father attempted to block the adoption, secure visitation rights, and legitimate the child. The Georgia courts ruled that the adoption was in the best interests of the child.

The Court held that application of a "best interests of the child" standard did not violate due process or equal protection. On the question of due process, Mr. Justice Marshall, writing for a unanimous Court, observed:

> [T]his is not a case in which the unwed father at any time had, or sought, actual or legal custody of his child. Nor is this a case in which the proposed adoption would place the child with a new set of parents with whom the child had never before lived. Rather, the result of the adoption in this case is to give full recognition to a family unit already in existence, a result desired by all concerned, except appellant. Whatever might be required in other situations, we cannot say that the State was required in this situation to find anything more than that the adoption, and denial of legitimation, were in the "best interests of the child."[98]

The Court also rejected the appellant's equal protection challenge to the statute, holding that the state could properly recognize the differences in commitment to a child's welfare between an unwed father like appellant and a divorced father who bore responsibility to the child during marriage.

The parties in *Caban v. Mohammed*[99] lived together and held themselves out as husband and wife for more than five years, although they were never legally married. Two children were born during the relationship and the father, whose name was on the birth certificate, lived with them and contributed to their support. When the parties separated, the mother took the children and married another man. For the next two years the father visited or maintained contact with the children. Subsequently, the New York Surrogate's Court granted a petition by the mother and her new husband, over the father's objection, to adopt the children. The Court acted pursuant to the New York statutory scheme, which permitted an unwed mother, but not an unwed father, to withhold consent to a child's adoption.

The Supreme Court upheld the father's equal protection challenge to the statute, holding that its gender based distinction bore no substantial relation to an important governmental interest. In support of its conclusion, the Court observed that "maternal and paternal roles are not invariably different in importance," and pointed out that "[e]ven if unwed mothers as a class were closer than unwed fathers to their newborn infants, this generalization concerning parent-child relations

---

opportunity to meet the statutory requirements to preserve his parental rights).

[97] 434 U.S. 246 (1978).

[98] *Id.* at 255.

[99] 441 U.S. 380 (1979).

would become less acceptable as a basis for legislative distinctions as the age of the child increased."[100] Further, where the father has not participated in the rearing of his child, the equal protection clause does not preclude the state from withholding his power to veto his child's adoption.

The unwed father in *Lehr v. Robertson*[101] had lived with the mother prior to the child's birth but not afterward, and did not provide financial support. Subsequently, she married another man, and when the child was two years old, the mother and her new husband commenced adoption proceedings. A month later, the father filed a petition seeking a declaration of his paternity and orders for support and visitation. Soon afterward, he learned of the pending adoption proceeding and immediately sought to have it stayed pending determination of his paternity action. The state court informed him that it had signed the adoption order, and then dismissed the paternity petition.

The Supreme Court in *Lehr* rejected the unwed father's due process claim. After reviewing and discussing its earlier holdings in the area, the Court stated:

> The difference between the developed parent-child relationship that was implicated in *Stanley* and *Caban*, and the potential relationship involved in *Quilloin* and this case, is both clear and significant. When an unwed father demonstrates a full commitment to the responsibilities of parenthood by "com[ing] forward to participate in the rearing of his child," . . . his interest in personal contact with his child acquires substantial protection under the due process clause. At that point, it may be said that he "act[s] as a father toward his children." . . . But the mere existence of a biological link does not merit equivalent constitutional protection.[102]

The Court pointed out that after *Stanley*, New York had enacted a statutory scheme that gives notice automatically to seven categories of unwed fathers likely to have assumed responsibility for their children's care. The father in *Caban*, if he had sent a postcard to the state's putative father registry, could have guaranteed that he would receive notice of the adoption proceeding.

The Court in *Lehr* also rejected the unwed father's equal protection claim, factually distinguishing the case before it from *Caban*. The court noted that in *Lehr* the child's mother had continuous custody of the child and the father did not establish a custodial, personal, or financial relationship. The Court concluded that "[i]f one parent has an established custodial relationship with the child and the other parent has either abandoned or never established a relationship, the Equal Protection Clause does not prevent a State from according the two parents different legal rights."[103] Subsequent to the Court's decision in *Lehr*, state courts have variously interpreted statutes that require notice to unwed fathers and their opportunity to be heard in adoption proceedings. In *Adoption of Kelsey S.*,[104] for

---

[100] *Id.* at 389.

[101] 463 U.S. 248 (1983).

[102] *Id.* at 261 (citations omitted).

[103] *Id.* at 267-68 (citations omitted).

[104] 823 P.2d 1216 (1992).

example, the Supreme Court of California held that the father of an out of wedlock child "who has come forward to grasp his parental responsibilities" and diligently attempts to obtain custody once aware of the mother's pregnancy or the child's birth, cannot be denied his right to withhold the adoption of his child by third parties unless shown to be unfit to rear the child.[105] In *Robert O. v. Russell K.*,[106] however, New York's highest court adopted a standard that is not so generous for the father of an out-of-wedlock child. The father in *Robert O.* learned from the mother that he was the father of a child seventeen months after the child's birth and some ten months after adoption of the child was finalized. Even though he sought custody promptly after he became aware of these circumstances, the court denied him a remedy, noting that the requirement of promptness in asserting parental rights is measured by the life of the baby, rather than by the father's awareness.[107]

[3] Consent of Minor Parent

Ordinarily, the fact that the biological parent of a child is a minor is of no consequence with respect to the ability to give valid consent. State adoption statutes typically validate the consent of minor parents in the absence of fraud or duress. The Virginia statute, for example, provides that "[a] birth parent who has not reached the age of eighteen shall have legal capacity to give consent to adoption and perform all acts related to adoption, and shall be as fully bound thereby as if the birth parent had attained the age of eighteen years."[108] In *Norfolk Division of Social Services v. Unknown Father*,[109] the Court of Appeals of Virginia upheld a

---

[105] *Id.* at 1236. *See also, e.g.*, *In re Matter of Raquel Marie X.*, 559 N.E.2d 418 (N.Y. 1990) (statute which requires the father of an out-of-wedlock child to openly and continuously live with the mother for six months prior to the child's placement for adoption, in order to have the right of consent to adoption, violates the Equal Protection Clause of the U.S. Constitution). *But see, e.g.*, *Adoption of Michael H.*, 898 P.2d 891 (Cal. 1995) (narrowing the standard of *Kelsey S.* by "conclud[ing] that an unwed father has no federal constitutional right to withhold consent to an at-birth, third party adoption . . . unless he shows that he promptly came forward and demonstrated as full a commitment to his parental responsibilities as the biological mother allowed and the circumstances permitted within a short time after he learned or reasonably should have learned that the biological mother was pregnant with his child."); *In re Adoption of T.B.*, 232 P.3d 1026 (Utah 2010) (statue stating that an unwed natural father may only acquire the right to consent by satisfying strict requirements does not violate equal protection, even though it requires him to "(1) initiate paternity proceedings; (2) file notice that he has commenced paternity proceedings with the state registrar of vital statistics; (3) file a sworn affidavit with the district court stating that he is willing and able to take full custody of the child, setting forth his plans to care for the child, and agreeing to a court order of child support and payment of medical expenses; and (4) offer to assist, and actually assist, with expenses associated with the pregnancy and birth").

[106] 604 N.E.2d 99 (1992).

[107] *But see In re Termination of Parental Rights of Biological Parents of Baby Boy W.*, 988 P.2d 1270 (Okla. 1999) (due process was violated when natural mother and adoption agency "deprived [the] Natural Father of the chance to grasp his parental opportunity interest" by failing to provide him with notice of the pregnancy and birth; natural father did not learn of child until the pre-adoption termination proceedings); *In re Baby Girl B.*, 261 P.3d 558 (Kan. Ct. App. 2011) (termination of natural father's parental rights for abandonment and failure to support the mother during pregnancy requires natural father's actual knowledge of the pregnancy).

[108] Va. Code Ann. § 63.2-1202(B) (2012), *amended by* 2012 Va. Laws Ch. 424.

[109] 345 S.E.2d 533 (Va. Ct. App. 1986). *See also In re J.N.*, 95 P.3d 414, 420 (Wash. Ct. App. 2004) (minor mother failed to provide "clear, cogent, or convincing evidence that that her foster mother, her social worker, or [the state social services agency] applied duress to force her to relinquish her parental

minor's agreement that surrendered her child to an agency for adoption, holding that there was not the requisite clear and convincing evidence of fraud or duress.

In *Kathy O. v. Counseling & Family Services*,[110] fifteen-year-old parents filed a habeas corpus petition seeking the return of their child whom they had surrendered for adoption. The Appellate Court of Illinois upheld the surrender, noting that the evidence was clear and convincing that the parents knew the legal effect of the document they signed and that there was neither fraud nor duress by the agency.

While status as a minor will not impair the ability to consent to adoption of one's child, some states also require the consent of the minor's parents. The Michigan statute is illustrative. In the section describing persons who are authorized to consent to adoption, the statute provides: "If the parent of the child to be adopted is an unemancipated minor, that parent's consent is not valid unless a parent, guardian, or guardian ad litem of that minor parent has also executed the consent."[111]

[4] Revocation of Consent

The law relating to revocation of consent to adoption is not easily summarized but in most jurisdictions, absent fraud, duress, or mutual consent, a consent is deemed irrevocable.[112] The subject is addressed in some, but by no means all state adoption statutes. The Virginia statute, for example, provides as follows: "Parental consent to an adoption . . . shall be revocable prior to the final order of adoption (i) upon proof of fraud or duress or (ii) after placement of the child in an adoptive home, upon written, mutual consent of the birth parents and prospective adoptive parents or the child-placing agency."[113]

The Uniform Adoption Act provides that

> a relinquishment of parental rights with respect to a child, executed under this section, may be withdrawn by the parent, and a decree of a court terminating the parent and child relationship . . . may be vacated by the Court upon motion of the parent, if the child is not on placement for adoption and the person having custody of the child consents in writing to the withdrawal or vacation of the decree.[114]

---

rights"; "No fraud exists when an agency accurately tells the mother of alternatives to caring for her child or renders advice on adoption"); *J.K. ex rel. D.K. v. M.K.*, 5 P.3d 782, 792 (Wyo. 2000) (minor father failed to prove duress and failed to provide clear and convincing evidence of fraud where, as a result of statements made by a social services worker, he "signed the [consent and relinquishment] documents under the mistaken belief that he could revoke his consent within the next six months").

[110] 438 N.E.2d 695 (Ill. App. Ct. 1982). *But see Janet G. v. N.Y. Foundling Hospital*, 403 N.Y.S.2d 646, 655 (N.Y. Fam. Ct. 1978) (minor mother's surrender of child for adoption "was not a voluntary, was not an informed and was not a knowing surrender under the circumstances" where mother, at the time of surrender, was not given the opportunity to seek legal advice, was not told that she did not have to make a decision about surrendering her child at that time, and was not provided required counseling by state agents about alternatives to surrendering her child for adoption).

[111] Mich. Comp. Laws Ann. § 710.43(4) (West 2012).

[112] *See generally* Haralambie, *supra* note 39, at § 14:13; Hollinger, *supra* note 8, at § 8.02.

[113] Va. Code Ann. § 63.2-1204 (2012).

[114] Unif. Adoption Act § 19(g), 9 U.L.A. 218 (2009).

In some jurisdictions, the statute provides for a time within which there may be revocation. The Georgia statute, for example, states: "A person signing a surrender . . . shall have the right to withdraw the surrender by written notice . . . within ten days after signing; and the surrender document shall not be valid unless it so states . . . . After ten days, a surrender may not be withdrawn."[115] *Yopp v. Batt*[116] is also illustrative of typical principles relating to revocation of consent. In this case, the Supreme Court of Nebraska examined relinquishment of consent in a closed private adoption. The court noted that the rights of the relinquishing parent are not entirely extinguished until the formal adoption of the child, and that an adoption in Nebraska cannot take place until at least six months after the child is relinquished. Also, the court conceded that the law was not clear with respect to who has legal rights to the child during the period between relinquishment and adoption. Nevertheless, in the case before it, the court concluded that the mother, even before the child's birth, had firmly stated that she did not want to keep the child. Also, she made her decision independently and without influence by any other person. Accordingly, her relinquishment was valid.[117]

[F] Subsidized Adoptions and Children With Special Needs

Federal legislation has driven state legislation that encourages the adoption of those who are frequently referred to as hard-to-place children. Under the applicable federal statute, in order for a state to qualify for federal payments for foster care and adoption assistance, the state must provide financial assistance to adoptive parents of children with special needs.[118] For a child to be considered a child with special needs, the State must determine, among other things,

> that there exists with respect to the child a specific factor or condition (such as ethnic background, age, or membership in a minority or sibling group, or the presence of factors such as medical conditions or physical, mental, or emotional handicaps) because of which it is reasonable to conclude that the

---

[115] Ga. Code Ann. § 19-8-9(b) (2012).

[116] 467 N.W. 2d 868 (Neb. 1991).

[117] For other examples of attempts to withdraw consent in which the relinquishment was held valid, see, e.g., *In re Baby Girl P.*, 188 S.W.3d 6 (Mo. Ct. App. 2006) (mother who was neither under duress nor subject to misrepresentations gave valid consent, despite claims she orally withdrew consent in Spanish before trial court accepted the consent); *C.G. v. Guardian Ad Litem Program*, 920 So. 2d 854 (Fla. Dist. Ct. App. 2006) (mother's consent and surrender to an adoption agency was not conditional upon particular prospective parents consummating the adoption and remained valid and binding); *Youngblood v. Jefferson County Div. of Family and Children*, 838 N.E.2d 1164 (Ind. Ct. App. 2005) (previous drug use and suicide attempt did not render mother incompetent to give knowing and voluntary consent, where consent was given in court while represented by counsel).

[118] *See* 42 U.S.C. §§ 670, 671, 673 (2012). For a more detailed examination of the structure, operation, and eligibility requirements of the federal adoption assistance program, see Seth A. Grob, *Adoption Subsidies: Advocating for Children with Special Needs*, 7 U.C. Davis J. Juv. L. & Pol'y 83 (2003); U.S. Dept. of Health & Human Services, Administration for Children and Families, Child Welfare Policy Manual ch. 8 (2012), *available at* http://www.acf.hhs.gov/cwpm/programs/cb/laws_policies/laws/cwpm/policy.jsp?idFlag=8.

child cannot be placed with adoptive parents without providing adoption assistance . . . and medical assistance . . . .[119]

The Model Act for Adoption of Children With Special Needs,[120] published by the Department of Health and Human Services in 1981, notes in its introduction that because of barriers to adoption, thousands of children remain in institutional or foster care. The Act describes among its express purposes identification of children with special needs and removal of barriers to their adoption, and recruitment of adoptive families for such treatment.

The District of Columbia Subsidized Adoption Statute is illustrative of state legislation pursuant to the federal initiative. The statute authorizes the payment of adoption subsidies to adoptive families, defined to include single persons, for children with special needs who would otherwise "in all likelihood go without adoption."[121] The statute further provides:

> The amount and duration of adoption subsidy payments may vary according to the special needs of the child, and may include maintenance costs, medical dental and surgical expenses, psychiatric and psychological expenses, and other costs necessary for his care and well-being. A subsidy may be paid on a long-term basis to help a family whose income is limited and is likely to remain so; on a time-limited basis to help a family meet the cost of integrating a child into the family over a specified period of time; or on a special services basis to help a family meet a specific anticipated expense or expenses when no other resource appears to be available.[122]

The New York statute authorizing subsidies for the adoption of children provides for monthly payments for the care of handicapped or hard to place children who have been placed for adoption or adopted.[123] The statute also permits payments for non-recurring adoption expenses of adoptive parents of a child with special needs who adopts through an authorized agency,[124] and for medical subsidies.[125]

[G] Adult Adoption

All states permit adult adoptions, which the parties may seek for a variety of reasons — to formalize extant but informal familial relationships, to create inheritance rights, or to provide access to benefits available only to members of a legal family.[126] However, states vary on whether adult adoption requires a showing of the intent to create or to continue an authentic parent-child relationship.[127]

---

[119] 42 U.S.C. § 673(c)(2).

[120] 46 Fed. Reg. 50,022 (1981).

[121] D.C. Code § 4-301(b)(1) (2012).

[122] *Id.* § 4-301(e)(1).

[123] N.Y. Soc. Serv. Law § 453 (2012).

[124] *Id.* § 453-a.

[125] *Id.* § 454.

[126] For a more detailed discussion of adult adoption,see generally Hollinger, *supra* note 8, at § 1.05[2][f].

[127] *See, e.g.*, Ohio Rev. Code Ann. § 3107.02(B) (West 2012) (barring other special circumstances (e.g.,

In *In re Adoption of Robert Paul P.*,[128] the New York Court of Appeals affirmed a judgment denying the petition of a 57-year-old homosexual male to adopt a 50-year-old male with whom he shared a relationship. The Court discussed at some length the purpose of adult adoptions. The court began with the fundamental proposition that in New York, as in other states, the parent and child relationship may be established by law under an adoption statute, resulting in the adopted child enjoying all the incidents of that relationship as would a natural child, despite the absence of blood ties.

The court firmly rejected the use of adoption as a "quasi-matrimonial vehicle to provide nonmarried partners with a legal imprimatur for their sexual relationship, be it heterosexual or homosexual."[129] Among the reasons an adult adoption would be appropriate in the eye of the Court are perpetuation of the family name by a childless individual, ties of filial affection, or the desire of a stepparent to adopt the adult children of a spouse.[130]

Cases concerning adult adoption most often involve the effect of such an adoption on the disposition of estates, and typically require a parent and child relationship when approving the adoption of an adult.[131] In *Adoption of Swanson*,[132] however, the Supreme Court of Delaware declined to recognize this requirement. In *Swanson*, the petitioner, who was 66 years of age, sought to adopt his companion of 17 years, who was 51 years old. Their apparent motive was to prevent claims on their estates by distant members of their respective families and to take advantage of the reduced inheritance tax rate available for natural and adopted children under Delaware law. The family court dismissed their petition because there was no parent-child relationship between the petitioner and the

---

mental retardation; total or permanent disability), an adult may only be adopted where "the adult had established a child-foster caregiver, kinship caregiver, or child-stepparent relationship with the petitioners as a minor, and the adult consents to the adoption"). *But see In re Adoption of Swanson*, 623 A.2d 1095 (Del. 1993) (state statutes do not require a pre-existent parent-child relationship for an adult adoption to be granted, and such an adoption for purposes of estate planning is neither invalid nor against public policy). *See also* Cal. Fam. Code § 9328(b) (2012) (requiring a court to find the adoption will be in the best interests of *both* parties and in the public interest before granting an adult adoption).

[128] 471 N.E.2d 424 (N.Y. 1984).

[129] *Id.* at 425. *But see In re Adoption of Elizabeth P.S.*, 509 N.Y.S.2d 746 (N.Y. Fam. Ct. 1986) (Forty-nine-year-old nun permitted to adopt forty-eight-year-old woman because "their relationship is totally devoid of any sexual overtones").

[130] *Id.* at 427. For more on the rationales behind adult adoptions, particularly those which are economic, see generally Sarah Ratliff, Comment, *Adult Adoption: Intestate Succession and Class Gifts Under the Uniform Probate Code*, 105 Nw. U. L. Rev. 1777 (2011).

[131] *See, e.g., Faville v. Burns*, 960 N.E.2d 99 (Ill. App. Ct. 2011) (Trial Order) ("The adoption of an adult solely for the purpose of making him an heir . . . under the terms of [an existing] testamentary instrument . . . is an act of subterfuge. . . . [which] does great violence to the intent and purpose of our adoption laws and should not be permitted" (*quoting Cross v. Cross*, 532 N.E.2d 486, 488-89 (1988)); *In re Hallahan*, 2007 Phila. Ct. Com. Pl. LEXIS 256 (Pa. Com. Pl. July 11, 2007) (trial order) ("[T]he adult adoptees . . . ha[ve] the burden of establishing that they had a parent-child relationship with [the decedent] during the period of their minority and that their adoption was not effected to secure an inheritance"). *But see In re Trust Created by Nixon*, 763 N.W.2d 404, 410 (Neb. 2009) (finding "no clear indication that the public policy behind the Nebraska adoption statutes is to prevent the use of adoption to create inheritance rights").

[132] 623 A.2d 1095 (Del. 1993).

prospective adoptee. After an extensive review of cases denying or upholding such adoptions, the court held that the applicable statute did not require such a relationship and, accordingly, reversed the family court decision and directed the family court to issue an adoption decree.

[H] Equitable Adoption

Equitable adoption does not involve a lawful adoption pursuant to state statute resulting in a parent and child relationship for all purposes. One commentary has provided the following serviceable definition: " 'Equitable adoption' allows a child, under certain circumstances, to inherit property from foster parents, or from other adults who have acted in a parental capacity."[133] In a wrongful death suit, *Coon v. American Compressed Steel, Inc.*,[134] the Missouri Court of Appeals upheld the trial court's determination that the appellant had equitably adopted her fiance's son, and thus was a proper party to bring suit. In the course of its decision, the court pointed out that equitable adoption requires proof by "evidence so clear, cogent, and convincing as to leave no room for reasonable doubt" and that "if the plaintiff relies solely on circumstantial evidence, that evidence must be consistent only with the existence of the equitable adoption and inconsistent with any other reasonable hypothesis leaving nothing to conjecture."[135] The majority of states have recognized equitable adoption, sometimes called adoption by estoppel, virtual adoption, or de facto adoption,[136] typically for the purpose of securing inheritance or other statutory rights.

[I] Second-Parent Adoption

An increasing number of lesbian, gay, bisexual, or transgender individuals seek to adopt. Most frequently, these are individuals in a relationship with the adoptee's natural parent who participate in raising the child, and wish to become the child's "second parent" or "co-parent" without affecting or ending the extant legal relationship between the natural parent and the child.[137] While similar in some respects to step-parent adoptions, second-parent adoptions may involve unmarried

---

[133] Peter Nash Swisher, Anthony Miller & Helene S. Shapo, Family Law: Cases, Materials, and Problems 704 (3d ed. 2012). For a more detailed discussion of the concept of equitable adoption, see Michael J. Higdon, *When Informal Adoption Meets Intestate Succession: The Cultural Myopia of the Equitable Adoption Doctrine*, 43 Wake Forest L. Rev. 223 (2008); William G. Reeves, *Inheritance by Equitable Adoption: An Overview of Theory and Proof*, 57 J. Mo. B. 130 (2001); Tracy Bateman Farrell, *Modern Status of Law as to Equitable Adoption or Adoption by Estoppel*, 122 A.L.R.5th 205 (2012).)

[134] 207 S.W.3d 629 (Mo. Ct. App. 2006).

[135] *Id.* at 634.

[136] *See* Higdon, *supra* note 133.

[137] *See generally* Courtney G. Joslin & Shannon Price Minter, Lesbian, Gay, Bisexual and Transgender Family Law § 5:3 (2011). *See also* Christine Metteer Lorillard, *Placing Second-Parent Adoption Along the "Rational Continuum" of Constitutionally Protected Family Rights*, 30 Women's Rts. L. Rep. 1 (2008); Colorado, *supra* note 6; Jason N.W. Plowman, Note, *When Second-Parent Adoption is the Second-Best Option: The Case for Legislative Reform as the Next Best Option for Same-Sex Couples in the Face of Continued Marriage Inequality*, 11 Scholar 57 (2008); Jane S. Schacter, *Constructing Families in a Democracy: Courts, Legislatures, and Second-Parent Adoption*, 75 Chi-Kent L. Rev. 933 (2000).

partners and frequently arise from situations in which the partners have been co-parenting a planned child from birth.[138] Beyond the emotional and psychological benefits to the child, the natural parent, and the adopting parent, second-party adoption provides the child with the added security of a second legal parent and protects the second parent from loss of their rights in the child in the event of death or incapacity of the natural parent or the termination of the parents' relationship.[139]

States divide over whether second-parent adoptions are permissible. In at least thirty states and the District of Columbia,[140] trial or appellate courts have allowed second-parent adoptions and a few states allow them by statute.[141] In a small minority of states, second-parent adoptions have been explicitly prohibited by statute or through judicial decisions.[142] As in other types of adoption, in deciding whether to grant a second-parent adoption the court will place enormous weight on its determination of the child's best interest.[143] The underlying rationale for approving second-parent adoptions was clearly articulated by the New York Surrogate's Court in *In re Adoption of Garrett*:

> It is undeniable that the area of adoption law has undergone a significant transformation in recent years whereby same-sex couples were deemed eligible to adopt, and unmarried heterosexual couples were also permitted to adopt. . . . Notably . . . , all of these decisions have been predicated on the rationale that the relationship between the proposed adoptive parents is the functional equivalent of the traditional husband-wife relationship, albeit between same-sex couples or unmarried partners.[144]

---

[138] *See* Joslin & Minter, *supra* note 137, at § 5:3.

[139] *See generally* Hollinger, *supra* note 8, at § 3.06[6].

[140] *See id.* at appx. 1-A.

[141] *See, e.g.*, Vt. Stat. Ann. tit. 15A, § 1-102(b) (2012) ("If a family unit consists of a parent and the parent's partner, and adoption is in the best interest of the child, the partner of a parent may adopt a child of the parent").

[142] *See, e.g., Boseman v. Jarrell*, 704 S.E.2d 494 (N.C. 2010) (state legislature "did not vest our courts with subject matter jurisdiction to create the type of adoption attempted here [second-parent adoption]"; thus, district court's "adoption decree . . . is void *ab initio*"); *In re Adoption of Luke*, 640 N.W.2d 374, 377 (Neb. 2002) (under adoption statute, "a single adult person [can] adopt only when the child had been relinquished" by the natural parent; thus, second-parent adoptions are not permissible); Miss. Code Ann. § 93-17-3(5) (2012), *amended by* 2012 Miss. Laws WL No. 234 ("Adoption by couples of the same gender is prohibited"). *But see, e.g., Fla. Dept. of Families and Children v. Adoption of X.X.G.*, 45 So. 3d 79, 85 (Fla. Ct. App. 2010) (Florida Adoption Act provisions "categorically exclud[ing] a homosexual person from adopting" served no rational purpose and violated the equal protection clause of the state constitution).

[143] *See, e.g., M.A.T. v. G.S.T.*, 989 A.2d 11, 17 (Pa. Super. Ct. 2010) (lower court's conclusion that "the [homo]sexual orientation of a parent will have an adverse effect on the child, and that the traditional heterosexual household is superior to that of the household of a parent involved in a same sex relationship" is "based upon unsupported preconceptions and prejudices . . . . Such preconceptions and prejudices have no proper place in child custody cases, where the decision should be based exclusively upon a determination of the best interests of the child . . .").

[144] 841 N.Y.S.2d 731, 732 (N.Y. Sur. Ct. 2007).

[J] Open Adoption

In recent years, "open" adoption has become more widespread. In an open adoption, some post-adoption contact occurs between the natural parents and the child or the traditional confidentiality between the natural parents and the adoptive family is abrogated.[145] Such arrangements between the parties are ratified by inclusion in the order of adoption of a provision directing such continuing contact and / or visitation.[146] Electing for an open adoption does not, however, change the fundamental outcome of the adoption process — the adoptive parents still become the new, and only, legal parents of the child and the parental rights of the natural parents are terminated. Courts will not treat a visitation agreement as consideration for entering into an open adoption,[147] and generally will not allow the adoption to be set aside due to violations of the contact agreement.[148] Whether to allow an open adoption, or to enforce contact or visitation agreements, is determined by the court on the basis of the best interests of the child.[149]

Traditionally, few, if any, states provided explicit statutory authority for courts to grant open adoptions. As a consequence, courts often struggled to reconcile the idea that adoptive parents were entitled to raise their children as they saw fit and to allow contacts between adoptees and the natural parents if they so wished, and the theory that the traditional post-adoption exclusion of natural kin from further participation in the child's life would allow adoptive parents to raise children free of interference and as "naturally" as possible.[150] While some courts proved willing to countenance such agreements, others rejected them because of a lack of express

---

[145] *See generally* Haralambie, *supra* note 39, at § 14:23; Hollinger, *supra* note 8, at § 13.02; Leigh Gaddie, Comment, *Open Adoption*, 22 J. Am. Acad. Matrim. Law. 499 (2009); Amy L. Doherty, *A Look at Open Adoption*, 11 J. Contemp. Legal Issues 591 (2000); Tammy M. Somogye, Comment, *Opening Minds to Open Adoption*, 45 U. Kan. L. Rev. 619 (1997).

[146] *See generally* 2 Am. Jur. 2d *Adoption* § 2 (2012).

[147] *See, e.g., In re M.B.*, 921 N.E.2d 494, 500 (Ind. 2009) (statute authorizing open adoptions did not authorize trial court to grant post-adoption contact rights to birth mother as a condition precedent to her consent to termination of her parental rights; visitation proviso "contravened both Indiana statutory law and public policy" and was void *ab initio*); *see also* Haralambie, *supra* note 39, at § 14:23.

[148] *See* Unif. Adoption Act § 3-707(c), 9 U.L.A. 98 (1999) ("The validity of a decree of adoption issued under this [Act] may not be challenged for failure to comply with an agreement for visitation or communication with an adoptee"); *In re Adoption of S.K.L.H.*, 204 P.3d 320, 327 (Alaska 2009) ("[P]ost-decree disputes about details of an open adoption cannot be grounds to set aside an adoption decree. If the parties cannot resolve post-decree disputes about the boundaries of a biological parent's relationship with an adopted child, these boundaries can be determined by the court."). *But see In re Matter of Adoption of Brunner*, 1993 Ohio App. LEXIS 1418 (Mar. 11, 1993) (in intrafamily adoption, natural mother's consent was invalid; trial court erred in finding consent was "knowingly given and free from duress" where "despite repeated attempts to impress upon appellant that adoption severed all her parental rights, appellant nonetheless understood, based on her parents' promises, that [the child] would remain her son, legally as well as in fact" and "appellant considered the matter to be more in the nature of a custody arrangement than an adoption").

[149] *See, e.g., In re Adoption of S.K.L.H.*, 204 P.3d 320, 327 (Alaska 2009) ("[T]he contours of an open adoption are subject to the best interests of the child, regardless of the detail and content of an agreement by the parties" (citation omitted)); *Michaud v. Wawruck*, 551 A.2d 738, 742 (Conn. 1988) (visitation agreement did not violate public policy where it was "openly and lovingly negotiated, in good faith, in order to promote the best interest of the child").

[150] *See* Hollinger, *supra* note 8, at § 13.02[1].

statutory authority[151] or because of public policy considerations, chiefly that allowing such contacts would undermine the integrity of the new adoptive family.[152]

Increasingly, states have amended their statutes to explicitly authorize and shape the contours of open adoptions. Arizona's open adoption statute[153] is fairly representative,[154] and provides for the enforcement of written, court-approved agreements regarding communications between birth parents, adoptive parents, and child adoptees. The court may not approve such an agreement without the approval of the prospective adoptive parents, any birth parents who are parties to the agreement, and, where the adoptee is in the custody of a state agency, a representative of that agency.[155] In keeping with many open adoption statutes, Arizona's also provides that the court may not approve such an agreement without a finding that its provisions are in the best interests of the child, and that the court may take into account the child's wishes if he or she is at least twelve years old.[156] The agreement must state that an adoptive parent may terminate the contact if, at any time, the adoptive parent comes to believe the contact is no longer in the child's best interests, and the court will retain jurisdiction to modify an order if it finds it is necessary to serve the child's best interests and the adoptive parents agree to the modification or "exceptional circumstances" have arisen to justify

---

[151] *See, e.g., State ex rel. Kaylor v. Bruening*, 684 N.E.2d 1228, 1232 (Ohio 1997) (holding that while lower court "possessed basic statutory jurisdiction to grant visitation to a natural parent in a divorce, dissolution, legal separation, or child support proceeding, [adoption statute] patently and unambiguously divested [the court] of jurisdiction to proceed on the biological mother's motions relating to visitation following the adoption decree terminating [her] parental rights"); *In re Adoption of C.H.*, 548 N.W.2d 292, 297 (Minn. Ct. App. 1996), *aff'd in part, rev'd in part*, 554 N.W.2d 737 (Minn. 1996) (open adoption order reversed because "Minnesota law does not recognize 'open adoptions' ").

[152] *See generally* 2 Am. Jur. 2d *Adoption* § 166 (2012). *See also Hill v. Moorman*, 525 So. 2d 681, 681-82 (La. Ct. App. 1988) (agreement allowing natural parent to visit her child post-adoption is unenforceable, because "[a]n agreement providing for visitation by a third party would impair the adoptive parents' rights . . . . [and] might also impair the new parent-child relationship with very undesirable consequences"); *In re Adoption of Child by W.P.*, 748 A.2d 515, 523 (N.J. 2000) (holding that "the primary purpose of the termination of rights . . . is to "protect adoptive parents from post-adoption disruptions in their relationship with adoptive children, by natural parents" and that "[e]ven arrangements . . . entered into with mutual consent permitting continued contact between biological relatives and the adopted child, cannot be judicially enforced given the potential for disruption of the child's family life . . . and the fact that under the adoption laws the adoptive parents' rights are paramount" (quotations and citations omitted)).

[153] Ariz. Rev. Stat. § 8-116.01 (2012).

[154] *See also* Ind. Code § 31-19-16-2 (2012), *amended by* 2012 Ind. Legis. Serv. P.L. 128-2012 (S.E.A. 287) (West) (a court may grant contact privileges if: it determines that the best interests of the child would be served; the child is at least two years old and the court finds "there is a significant emotional attachment between the child and the birth parent"; each adoptive parent consents; the adoptive and birth parents file an executed agreement with the court; state agents or the guardian *ad litem* recommends the agreement; and consent is obtained from the child if the child is at least 12); Minn. Stat. § 259.58 (2012) (if it finds it is in the best interests of a minor adoptee, a court may approve a written agreement between adoptive parents and a birth relative or foster parents; a birth parent must approve in writing of an agreement between adoptive parents and any other birth relative or foster parent; failure to comply with the agreement is not grounds for setting aside the adoption decree or revoking consent; the court may not modify the agreement unless it finds it necessary to serve the best interests of the child, and the parties agree or exceptional circumstances have arisen.)

[155] Ariz. Rev. Stat. § 8-116.01(B) (2012).

[156] *Id.* at subsec. D.

modification.[157] Failure to comply with such a court-approved agreement is not grounds for setting aside an adoption decree, revoking a written consent to an adoption, or the relinquishment of parental rights.[158]

Legitimating open adoption has been rationalized on a number of grounds. Though traditional concerns about interfering with the relationship between the adopting parents and the child remain, there is an increasing awareness of the psychological and emotional benefits that can inure to adopted children who remain in contact with, or knowledgeable about, their blood relations. As the Supreme Court of South Dakota explained, in *People in Interest of S.A.H.*,[159]

> The most compelling argument for open adoption is founded on the psychological needs of the child. A child has an important need to know his ancestral, religious, ethnic and cultural background. Shrouding a child's past in secrecy may retard emotional development and self-identity. The adopted child may have a strong need or desire to know his natural parents. The natural parents may be unable to raise or care for the child but the best interests of the child may dictate that those parents have a role in the child's life.[160]

As the court noted, there may well be instances in which natural parents are perfectly capable of playing a positive role in the life and development of their child,[161] but circumstances simply render them unable to provide adequate care — for example, as a consequence of chronic ill health or straitened economic circumstances. Some birth parents may prove more willing to voluntarily surrender their parental rights when they know they will not be entirely barred from contact with their children, and when older children are adopted, ongoing contact with members of their birth family may help ease the transition into a new home and family.[162] Contact with siblings,[163] or with birth parents or grandparents[164] in

---

[157] *Id.* at subsecs. C, G, H.

[158] *Id.* at subsec. F.

[159] 537 N.W.2d 1 (1995), *overturned on other grounds by legislative action*, 1997 S.D. Laws Ch. 153.

[160] *Id.* at 7 (internal citations omitted).

[161] *See, e.g., Groves v. Clark*, 982 P.2d 446, 448 (Mont. 1999) (upholding lower court's finding that child's best interests would be served by regular telephone contact and weekend visitation with birth mother, where evidence showed that the child lived with the birth mother for three years prior to adoption, had developed a bond with her, and would "likely . . . suffer from issues of abandonment, identity, and grieving unless appropriate visitation" was granted). *But see, e.g., In re Adoption of Greta*, 729 N.E.2d 273, 282 (Mass. 2000) (trial court erred in finding the child's interests would be served by ordering "occasional visits with her mother to address [the child's] curiosity regarding her mother's welfare, [and] to know that she is 'alright'," where trial court found there was "no significant relationship to maintain" and "no observable bond" between mother and child; "There is nothing to suggest that, if [the child] is curious about her birth mother's well-being, the only mechanism for satisfying that curiosity is through twice yearly visits with the biological mother extending years into the future.").

[162] *See generally* Haralambie, *supra* note 39, at § 14:23.

[163] *See, e.g., In re D.C.*, 4 A.3d 1004, 1021 (N.J. 2010) ("[adult] siblings can petition for visitation with their brothers and sisters who have been adopted by non-relatives, subject to the avoidance of harm standard"); *In re Adoption of Vito*, 728 N.E.2d 292 (Mass. 2000) (it is inherent in the authority of the court to allow post-adoption sibling visitation). *But see, e.g., Degrenier v. Reid*, 716 N.E.2d 667, 669-70 (Mass. App. Ct. 1999) ("The tensions between finality of an adoption, fair play to siblings, and the

step-parent adoptions, may also serve the best interests of the adopted child.

[K]   Effects of Adoption

Simply stated, the general rule today is that the law will treat the parent and child relationship between an adopted child and the adoptive parent precisely as it would if the child were the parent's natural or birth child. In *In re Estate of Rose Zestrow*,[165] the Wisconsin Supreme Court reviewed the provisions of a Wisconsin adoption statute, which, in language typical of such statutes, provided:

> After the order of adoption is entered the relationship of parent and child between the adopted person and his natural parents, unless the natural parent is the spouse of the adoptive parent, shall be completely altered and all the rights, duties and other legal consequences of the relationship shall cease to exist.[166]

The court read the language literally as changing the status of an adopted person, but held that it did not bar a testatrix from transferring property by will to her grandnephews, as she had intended. In *In re Estate of Holt*,[167] a testamentary disposition was not involved, but the issue was whether an adopted child could inherit from her natural grandmother. The Supreme Court of New Mexico held that because the child's natural father had predeceased the grandmother, and the adoption by her stepfather occurred prior to the grandmother's death, the adopted child could not inherit from her grandmother. Similarly, in *In re Estate of Carlson*,[168] the Court of Appeals of Minnesota held that two brothers who were

---

recognized importance of the sibling relationship, are not easily reconcilable . . . . [But] absent legislation to the contrary, an adoptive parent's decision not to allow sibling visitation should remain inviolate, even if that decision is unwise." (citations omitted)).

[164] Approximately one-third of states have revised their statutes to explicitly allow grandparents, during the pendency of step-parent adoption proceedings, to seek visitation orders. *See* Hollinger, *supra* note 8, at §§ 13.02, 1303; *see also* Mich. Comp. Laws § 722.27b (2012); Tenn. Stat. §§ 36-6-303(2), 307 (2012) ("[G]randparents . . . may be granted reasonable visitation rights" upon a finding that such visitation would be in the child's best interest, the grandparents would "adequately protect the child from further abuse or intimidation by the perpetrator or any other family member," and the grandparents were not implicated in criminal or abusive acts toward the child or their own child; consideration of the child's best interests shall encompass all pertinent matters, including "the length and quality of the prior relationship between the child and the grandparent and the role performed by the grandparent," "existing emotional ties of the child to the grandparent," the child's preference if the child is found to be of "sufficient maturity to express a preference," and "the effect of hostility between the grandparent and the parent of the child manifested before the child").

[165] 166 N.W.2d 251 (Wis. 1969).

[166] *Id.* at 253.

[167] 622 P.2d 1032 (N.M. 1981). *See also In re Medeiros Testamentary Trust & Life Ins. Trust*, 96 P.3d 1098 (Haw. 2004) (adoption of granddaughter by her stepfather excluded her from being considered her natural father's issue, for purposes of inheriting from the trust estate of her natural grandfather); *Ellis v. West ex rel. West*, 971 So. 2d 20 (Ala. 2007) (children were severed from their natural lineage for purposes of intestate succession when, following their mother's death, they were adopted by their paternal grandmother and her husband).

[168] 457 N.W.2d 789 (Minn. Ct. App. 1990). *But see In re Estate of Yount*, 845 So. 2d 724 (Miss. Ct. App. 2003) (natural half-brother of decedent was a wrongful death beneficiary and heir at law of decedent even though natural half-brother had been adopted by a third party).

adopted after the death of their parents could not inherit from the estate of a third brother who died intestate and who was not adopted, because the adoption statute cut off inheritance rights of blood relatives.

Chapter 7

UNIQUE FAMILY ISSUES

§ 7.01 INTRODUCTION

Once a family unit has been established, some troubling legal questions still remain concerning the proper roles of, and interrelationships between, the parents and the state in regulating the supervision, education, medical care, and upbringing of children and providing for their general welfare. For example, assuming that there is a constitutionally protected right of privacy within the American family, should the parents always serve as the ultimate authority for their child's welfare, or at some point must the State intervene when this parenting function is perceived to be inadequate or harmful to the child?[1] And assuming that the State does in fact have a legitimate role in protecting the best interests of the child, at what point should this state interest be manifested, and at what point should this state interest be limited or curtailed?[2] Additionally, what are the legal rights of an abused spouse or child, and what legal remedies are available to a family member who has been injured through the tortious or criminal action of another family member?

This chapter will analyze these important family law issues,[3] exploring the interplay and tensions involving parental authority to raise children,[4] children's rights as individuals, and state responsibility to protect spouses and children.[5]

---

[1] *See, e.g., Darryl H. v. Coler*, 801 F.2d 893, 894-95 (7th Cir. 1986) (where the court was attempting to resolve and reconcile the "fundamental constitutional values: the privacy rights of the child; the privacy rights of the family in the important area of childrearing; and the obligation and right of responsible government to deal effectively with the stark reality of child abuse in our society").

[2] *See, e.g.*, Laurence Tribe, American Constitutional Law 1418 (2d. ed. 1988) ("Once the State, whether acting through its courts or otherwise, has 'liberated' the child — and the adult — from the shackles of such intermediate groups as the family, what is to defend the individual against the combined tyranny of the State and her own alienation?"); *see also* McCarthy, *Parents, Children, and the Courts: The Confused Constitutional Status and Meaning of Parental Rights*, 22 Ga. L. Rev. 975 (1988).

[3] *See infra* §§ 7.02[B], 7.03, 7.04, 7.05, 7.07, 7.08[B], 7.09; Woodhouse, *"Who Owns the Child?": Meyer and Pierce and the Child as Property*, 33 Wm. & Mary L. Rev. 995 (1992) (arguing that it makes sense to locate the parental right to control children in the liberty clause of the Fourteenth Amendment only if children are viewed as the "property" of their parents); Lawrence, *Substantive Due Process and Parental Rights: From* Meyer v. Nebraska *to* Troxel v. Granville, 8 J.L. & Fam. Stud. 71, 111 (2006).

[4] *See infra* §§ 7.02[B], 7.03, 7.06, 7.08[B], 7.09, 7.10.

[5] *See infra* §§ 7.01, 7.02, 7.03, 7.05, 7.07, 7.08[A]-[B], 7.09.

§ 7.02 INTRAFAMILY TORT IMMUNITY AND LIABILITY

[A] Interspousal Tort Actions

Under the early common law, because a wife's legal identity merged into that of her husband under a "unity of person" doctrine,[6] neither spouse was able to bring a tort action against the other. By the late 1800s, however, all states had adopted the Married Women's Property Acts,[7] which allowed the wife to bring an action against her husband for tortious acts against her *property* interests, including recoveries based upon wrongful conversion, trespass to land, fraud, and negligent injury to her property.[8] And because this "unity of person" doctrine was abolished for property interests under the Married Women's Property Acts, the husband also possessed these same property rights against his wife.[9]

The Married Women's Property Acts, however, did *not* destroy the spousal immunity doctrine when it came to *personal*, rather than property, torts.[10] The rationale for this interspousal tort immunity doctrine generally was based upon two major premises: (1) that such an action would destroy the "peace and harmony" of the marital home; and (2) that such an action might encourage fraud and collusion between the spouses when the tort injury was covered by insurance.[11]

Today, under withering criticism from courts and commentators,[12] interspousal tort immunity has been largely eliminated out of concern for injured spouses.[13]

---

[6] *See, e.g.*, 1 Blackstone, Commentaries on the Law of England 445 (3d ed. 1884).

[7] *See supra* §§ 3.02[B], 4.03.

[8] *See, e.g., Hubbard v. Ruff*, 103 S.E.2d 134 (Ga. Ct. App. 1958); *Vigilant Ins. Co. v. Bennett*, 89 S.E.2d 69 (Va. 1955), *overruled by Surratt v. Thompson*, 183 S.E.2d 200 (Va. 1971) (extending the right to bring an action to personal injuries sustained in an automobile accident). *See generally* 1 Dobbs, The Law of Torts: Practitioner Series § 279 at 751 (2001 & Supp. 2007).

[9] *See, e.g., Madget v. Madget*, 85 Ohio App. 18, 40 Ohio Op. 37, 87 N.E.2d 918, 55 Ohio L. Abs. 450 (1st Dist. Hamilton County 1949).

[10] *See, e.g., Thompson v. Thompson*, 218 U.S. 611 (1910). A criminal act, however, by one spouse against the other spouse or children, could still be prosecuted as long as the action was criminal rather than civil in nature. *See, e.g., Goode v. Martinis*, 361 P.2d 941 (Wash. 1961).

[11] *See, e.g., Bonkowsky v. Bonkowsky*, 431 N.E.2d 998 (Ohio), *cert. denied*, 457 U.S. 1135 (1982), *overruled by Shearer v. Shearer*, 480 N.E.2d 388 (Ohio 1985); *Robeson v. International Indem. Co.*, 282 S.E.2d 896 (Ga. 1981); *Shoemake v. Shoemake*, 407 S.E.2d 134 (Ga. Ct. App. 1991); *Gates v. Gates*, 587 S.E.2d 32 (Ga. 2003) (reaffirming the doctrine of interspousal tort immunity in Georgia; *see also* Kelson, *The Doctrine of Interspousal Immunity: Does It Still Exist in Utah?*, 3 J. L. & Fam. Stud. 161 (2001).

[12] *See, e.g., Merenoff v. Merenoff*, 388 A.2d 951 (N.J. 1978) (there is no danger of domestic tranquility being disturbed by a negligence action brought by one spouse against the other spouse who carries indemnity insurance, and the courts can police possible insurance fraud in marital tort claims without having to ban the claim entirely); Siegel, *"The Rule of Love": Wife Beating as Prerogative and Privacy*, 105 Yale L.J. 2117 (1996); 1 Clark, Law of Domestic Relations 632 (2d ed. 1987) ("The kindest thing to be said about these policy arguments is that they are frivolous."); *see also* Johnson, *Interspousal Tort Immunity: The Rule Becoming the Exception*, 27 Howard L.J. 995 (1984); Barker, *Spousal Immunity and Domestic Torts*, 15 Am. J. Trial Advoc. 625 (1992).

[13] For example, in *Counts v. Counts*, 266 S.E.2d 895 (Va. 1980), a husband was seriously injured in an unsuccessful murder-for-hire scheme instituted by his wife. His tort action against the wife, however, was barred by the interspousal tort immunity doctrine since it "contribute to the destruction of [the] marriage." *Id.* at 898. Negative reaction to the *Counts* case, and to interspousal tort immunity in general,

Consequently, a number of states have abolished interspousal immunity by judicial decision or statute.[14] Only a fraction of jurisdictions today retain some form of interspousal tort immunity.[15]

Interspousal tort liability actions have been brought for the infliction of sexually transmitted diseases,[16] invasion of privacy,[17] and domestic violence.[18] Courts and commentators, however, are divided on the desirability of recognizing tort claims based on the infliction of emotional distress during marriage and other intimate relationships.[19]

---

culminated a year later in a Virginia statute that abolished the doctrine completely. Va. Code Ann. § 8.01-220.1 (West 2011). *See also Waite v. Waite*, 618 So. 2d 1360 (Fla.1993) (husband attacked wife with machete; on certification to the Florida Supreme Court, the court concluded that interspousal immunity no longer existed as a part of Florida's common law, allowing possible recovery by wife from homeowner's policy); Wayne D. Foster, Annotation, *Modern Status of Interspousal Tort Immunity in Personal Injury and Wrongful Death Actions*, 92 A.L.R.3d 901 (1980 & Supp. 2009).

[14] *See, e.g.*, Va. Code Ann. § 8.01-220.1 (2011); Haw. Rev. Stat. § 572-28 (1993 & Supp. 2005); 750 Ill. Comp. Stat. 65/1 (2009); N.C. Gen. Stat. § 52-5 (2009); *Asplin v. Amica Mut. Ins. Co.*, 394 A.2d 1353 (R.I. 1978) (the rule is abrogated for motor vehicle torts; and when the death of either spouse occurs, there is no longer any family harmony to disrupt); *Burns v. Burns*, 518 So. 2d 1205 (Miss. 1988) (interspousal tort immunity abolished in a tort suit arising out of damages for husband beating wife); *Bozman v. Bozman*, 830 A.2d 450 (Md. 2003) (abolishing interspousal tort immunity in Maryland as contrary to prevailing societal norms).

[15] As of 2004, eight states limit the basis upon which spouses may sue one another. *See* Jill Elaine Hasday, *The Canon of Family Law*, 57 Stan. L. Rev. 825, n.32 (2004) (observing that, "spouses can sue each other only for negligent torts [in Delaware], or only for intentional torts [in Utah], or only for torts arising from a motor vehicle accident [in Nevada and Vermont], or only for torts that do not implicate 'marital or nuptial privileges, consensual acts and simple, common domestic negligence,' [in New Jersey] or only for torts that do not involve 'personal injuries between married persons [that] will not justify a recovery of damages, [in Massachusetts]" and that some states do not allow interspousal suits unless the parties were separated at the time the tort occurs or had filed for divorce prior to the suit [citing Georgia and Louisiana]").

[16] *See, e.g.*, *S.A.V. v. KGV.*, 708 S.W.2d 651 (Mo. 1986) (allowing wife's claim against her husband for negligently transmitting herpes); *John B. v. Superior Court*, 38 Cal. 4th 1177 (2006) (allowing discovery in wife's claim against husband that he exposed her to HIV). *See generally* Krohse, Note, *No Longer Following the Rule of Thumb — What to Do with Domestic Torts and Divorce Claims*, 1997 U. Ill. L. Rev. 923, 929; Oyler, *Interspousal Tort Liability for Infliction of a Sexually Transmitted Disease*, 29 J. Fam. L. 519 (1990-91); Fayerweather, Note, *Homeowner's Insurance Coverage of Negligent Transmission of Sexually Transmitted Disease*, 31 B.C. L. Rev. 1209 (1990).

[17] *See Miller v. Brooks*, 123 N.C. App. 20 (1996).

[18] *See generally* Scherer, *Tort Remedies for Victims of Domestic Abuse*, 43 S.C. L. Rev. 543 (1992). *See also infra* § 6.08.

[19] *See, e.g.*, *Twyman v. Twyman*, 855 S.W.2d 619 (Tex. 1993); *see also* Evans, Note, *Wrongs Committed During a Marriage: The Child That No Area of the Law Wants to Adopt*, 66 Wash. & Lee L. Rev. 465 (2009); Wilson, *Beyond the Bounds of Decency: Why Fault Continues to Matter to (Some) Wronged Spouses*, 66 Wash. & Lee L. Rev. 503 (2009) (discussing how the difficulties raised by dual proceedings argue for some ability to consider fault in the marriage); Krause, *Propter Honoris Respectum: On the Danger of Allowing Marital Fault to Re-emerge in the Guise of Torts*, 73 Notre Dame L. Rev. 1355 (1998); Wriggins, *Domestic Violence Torts*, 75 S. Cal. L. Rev. 121 (2001) (proposing mandatory insurance coverage of intentional torts during the marriage which ordinarily are not covered by insurance); Ellman & Sugarman, *Spousal Emotional Abuse as a Tort?*, 55 Md. L. Rev. 1268 (1996) (exploring arguments for and against the recognition of such a tort action, and arguing that spousal abuse not be recognized as a tort unless the abusive behavior is also criminal). *See generally* Spector, *Marital Torts: The Current Legal Landscape*, 33 Fam. L. Q. 745 (1999).

The abolition of interspousal tort immunity in many states has prompted many insurance companies to insert a "family exclusion" or "household exclusion" clause in their liability insurance policies, with particular application to automobile and homeowner's liability insurance. These clauses generally provide that liability insurance coverage will *not* apply to any member of the insured's family living in the same household.[20]

Some courts have held that such a "family exclusion" clause is a valid exercise of an insurer's legitimate contractual right to limit its liability, and therefore is not contrary to state public policy.[21] Other courts, however, have held that a "family exclusion" clause is contrary to public policy since all victims of negligence, including family members, should be able to recover from a tortfeasor.[22]

Complex choice of law issues may arise if, for example, a husband and wife are domiciled in one state, which has abolished interspousal tort immunity, and they are involved in an automobile accident caused by the negligence of one spouse and the other spouse is seriously injured in a state that still recognizes the doctrine of interspousal tort immunity. Under traditional conflict of laws principles, the law of the state where the injury occurred generally determines whether one spouse can sue the other in tort,[23] and a minority of states still follow this rule.[24] A majority of states, however, in determining whether or not the spouses can sue one another in tort, often apply the law of the state of the parties' domicile or the state which has the "most significant relationship" with the action.[25]

---

[20] *See generally* Martinez, Insurance Law 843-50 (6th ed. 2010); Ashdown, *Intrafamily Immunity, Pure Compensation, and the Family Exclusion Clause*, 60 Iowa L. Rev. 239 (1974).

[21] *See, e.g., Transamerica Ins. Co. v. Henry by Henry*, 563 N.E.2d 1265 (Ind. 1990); *Farmers Ins. Exch. v. Cocking*, 29 Cal. 3d 383 (1981) (explaining that most insurers are disadvantaged without a "family exclusion" clause by the lack of a true adversary); *Linehan v. Alkhabbaz*, 398 So. 2d 989 (Fla. Dist. Ct. App. 1981); Jonathan M. Purver, Annotation, *Validity, Construction, and Application of Provision of Automobile Liability Policy Excluding from Coverage Injury or Death of Member of Family or Household of Insured*, 46 A.L.R.3d 1024 (1972) (partially superseded by 52 A.L.R.4th 18).

[22] *See, e.g., Farmers Ins. Exch. v. Dotson*, 913 P.2d 27 (Colo. 1996) (named insured exclusion void as contrary to public policy); *State Farm Mutual Insurance Co. v. Schwartz*, 933 F.2d 848 (10th Cir. 1991) (affirming judgment that a "household exclusion" in an auto policy violated Oklahoma public policy given its laws requiring compulsory auto liability insurance); *Jennings v. GEICO*, 488 A.2d 166 (Md. 1985); *Bishop v. Allstate Ins. Co.*, 623 S.W.2d 865 (Ky. 1981); *see also* Martin J. McMahon, Annotation, *Validity, Under Insurance Statutes, of Coverage Exclusion for Injury to or Death of Insured's Family or Household Members*, 52 A.L.R.4th 18 (1987 & Supp. 2009).

[23] Restatement (First) of Conflict of Laws § 384 (1934).

[24] *See Hataway v. McKinley*, 830 S.W.2d 53, 56 (Tenn. 1992) (listing 15 states still following the traditional approach); *see also McMillan v. McMillan*, 253 S.E.2d 662 (Va. 1979); *Yates v. Lowe*, 348 S.E.2d 113 (Ga. Ct. App. 1986). *See generally* W. E. Shipley, Annotation, *Conflict of Laws as to Right of Action Between Husband and Wife or Parent and Child*, 96 A.L.R.2d 973 (1964).

[25] *See* Restatement (Second) of Conflict of Laws §§ 145-46, 169 (1971); *see also Heinze v. Heinze*, 742 N.W.2d 465 (Neb. 2007); *Henry v. Henry*, 229 S.E.2d 158 (N.C. 1976); *Brooks v. Sturiano*, 497 So. 2d 976 (Fla. Dist. Ct. App. 1986).

[B] Child and Parent Tort Actions

Although the early common law recognized a "unity of identity" doctrine between a husband and wife, no such doctrine applied to a parent and minor child. Accordingly, a child — emancipated or not — could sue his or her parent for breach of contract or for torts affecting property, and an emancipated child could sue his or her parent for personal injury torts.[26]

Personal injury tort actions brought by unemancipated minors, however, have historically been subject to a parent-child tort immunity doctrine, which was recognized throughout the United States beginning in the late 1800s and based on the rationale of preserving family harmony. For example, in the 1905 case of *Roller v. Roller*,[27] the Washington Supreme Court held that a daughter could not sue her father for rape under the doctrine of parent-child tort immunity, since such litigation "seems abhorrent to the idea of family discipline."[28]

As a result of many court decisions similar to *Roller*, various courts[29] and commentators[30] increasingly expressed criticism of the parent-child tort immunity doctrine. Today, the majority of states have abrogated the doctrine either partially or completely.[31]

However, jurisdictions that have limited the immunity differ as to where the line should be drawn. Some states, for example, have totally abolished the parent-child tort immunity doctrine in favor of a "reasonable parent" standard.[32] Other states maintain a distinction between torts occurring in the exercise of parental discretion and authority, where the parent-child immunity doctrine would continue to exist, and other kinds of tortious parental activity that would not be protected by the parent-child immunity doctrine.[33] For example, if a child is injured in an

---

[26] *See, e.g.*, Dobbs, *supra* note 8, at § 280; McCurdy, *Torts Between Parent and Child*, 5 Vill. L. Rev. 521 (1960); Allan E. Korpela, *Liability of Parent for Injury to Unemancipated Child Caused by Parent's Negligence*, 41 A.L.R.3d 904 (1972) (superseded by 6 A.L.R.4th 1066).

[27] *Roller v. Roller*, 79 P. 788 (Wash. 1905).

[28] *Id.* at 789.

[29] *See, e.g.*, *Karam v. Allstate Ins. Co.*, 436 N.E.2d 1014 (Ohio 1982) (although critical, the *Karam* court ultimately upheld parent-child immunity. However, it was quickly overruled and the immunity abolished by *Dorsey v. State Farm Mut. Auto. Ins. Co.*, 457 N.E.2d 1169 (Ohio 1984)). *See also Rousey v. Rousey*, 528 A.2d 416 (D.C. 1987).

[30] *See, e.g.*, Hollister, *Parent-Child Immunity: A Doctrine in Search of Justification*, 50 Fordham L. Rev. 489 (1981-82); Ross, Note, *The Parental Tort Immunity Doctrine Applied to Wrongful Death Actions: A Rule Without Reason*, 13 S. Ill. U. L.J. 175 (1988); Dean, *It's Time to Abolish North Carolina's Parent-Child Immunity, but Who's Going to Do It?*, 68 N.C. L. Rev. 1317 (1990); Haley, *The Parental Tort Immunity Doctrine: Is It a Defensible Defense?*, 30 U. Rich. L. Rev. 575 (1996).

[31] *See generally* Romualdo P. Eclavea, *Liability of Parent for Injury to Unemancipated Child Caused by Parent's Negligence — Modern Cases*, 6 A.L.R.4th 1066 (1981).

[32] *See, e.g.*, *Broadbent v. Broadbent*, 907 P.2d 43 (Ariz. 1995); *Hartman v. Hartman*, 821 S.W.2d 852 (Mo. 1991); *Rousey v. Rousey*, 528 A.2d 416 (D.C. 1987); *Gibson v. Gibson*, 479 P.2d 648 (Cal. 1971); *Kirchner v. Crystal*, 474 N.E.2d 275 (Ohio 1984); *see also* Restatement (Second) of Torts § 895G (1979); Note, *Defining the Parent's Duty After Rejection of Parent-Child Immunity*, 33 Vand. L. Rev. 775 (1980).

[33] *See, e.g.*, *Goller v. White*, 122 N.W.2d 193 (Wis. 1963); *Sears, Roebuck & Co. v. Huang*, 652 A.2d 568, 572 (Del. 1995) (citation omitted); *Cates v. Cates*, 619 N.E.2d 715, 728-29 (Ill. 1993); *Smith v. Smith*, 646

automobile accident caused by the negligence of a parent, because such a negligent act does *not* involve parental discretion or authority, the parent *can* be held liable for the child's injuries in certain jurisdictions.[34] However, if the child is injured while the parent is exercising parental discretion and authority, even in the realm of a parent's negligent supervision of the child, then the parent would *not* be held liable for the child's injuries.[35] Some courts that still recognize the parent-child tort immunity doctrine have nevertheless found that when parental conduct is so outrageous, egregious, and intentional, far exceeding mere negligence, a tort action by the child against the parent is justified and should be actionable.[36]

Whether the parent-child immunity doctrine applies to a grandparent or other person acting *in loco parentis* usually depends on whether or not there was a true *in loco parentis* relationship,[37] or whether the defendants were only temporary custodians of the child.[38]

If a child is injured by the negligence of a parent while the parent is acting within the course of his or her employment, and the child is barred from suing the parent in tort under the parent-child immunity doctrine, the courts are split as to whether the child may sue the parent's employer. Some courts hold that if a child cannot sue the parent, then the child would not be able to sue the parent's employer since the employer's liability is derivative.[39] Other courts, however, would allow a tort action against the employer based upon the doctrine of *respondeat superior*, even if the parent was immune under the doctrine.[40]

N.W.2d 412, 415 (Iowa 2002); *Lewis v. W. Am. Ins. Co.*, 927 S.W.2d 829, 832 (Ky. 1996); *Broadwell v. Holmes*, 871 S.W.2d 471, 476-77 (Tenn. 1994); *Holodook v. Spencer*, 324 N.E.2d 338 (N.Y. 1974).

[34] *See, e.g., Unah v. Martin*, 676 P.2d 1366 (Okla. 1984); *Ard v. Ard*, 414 So. 2d 1066 (Fla. 1982); *Black v. Solmitz*, 409 A.2d 634 (Me. 1979).

[35] *See, e.g., Haddrill v. Damon*, 386 N.W.2d 643 (Mich. Ct. App. 1986); *Wagner v. Smith*, 340 N.W.2d 255 (Iowa 1983).

[36] *See, e.g., Mitchell v. Davis*, 598 So. 2d 801 (Ala. 1992) (parent-child immunity upheld as to negligence claims but not wantonness); *Ex parte Spurgeon*, 82 So. 3d. 663 (Ala. 2011) (parental immunity doctrine does not bar claims of wantonness); *Doe v. Holt*, 418 S.E.2d 511 (N.C. 1992) (parent-child immunity doctrine does not bar recovery for injuries suffered as a result of a parent's willful and malicious conduct); *Calhoun v. Eagan*, 681 A.2d 609 (Md. Ct. Spec. App. 1996), *vacated on other grounds*, 698 A.2d 1097 (Md. 1997) (applying this exception to allow a wrongful death suit on behalf of the children against the father, based on allegations that the father deliberately or recklessly killed the children's mother).

[37] *See, e.g., Lawber v. Doil*, 547 N.E.2d 752 (Ill. App. Ct. 1989) (stepfather stood *in loco parentis* and was immune from suit); *Maddox v. Queen*, 257 S.E.2d 918 (Ga. Ct. App. 1979) (grandparents stood *in loco parentis* and were immune under the doctrine). B*ut see C.M.L. ex rel Brabant v. Republic Servs.*, 800 N.E.2d 200 (Ind. Ct. App. 2003) (a stepparent must take some action, such as adopting a stepchild, in order to be protected by the parental immunity doctrine); *Arnold v. Arnold*, 2002 Tenn. App. LEXIS 107 (Feb. 7, 2002) (when both father and grandfather were present when a two-year-old was injured by an engine, the father was immune to claims of negligent supervision, but the grandfather was not).

[38] *See, e.g., Gulledge v. Gulledge*, 367 N.E.2d 429 (Ill. App. Ct. 1977) (grandparents, as mere custodians of the child, did not come under the parent-child immunity doctrine).

[39] *See, e.g., Pullen v. Novak*, 99 N.W.2d 16 (Neb. 1959); *Sherby v. Western Bros. Trans. Co.*, 421 F.2d 1243 (4th Cir. 1970) (applying Maryland law).

[40] *See, e.g., Begley v. Kohl & Madden Co.*, 254 A.2d 907 (Conn. 1969); *Littleton v. Jordan*, 428 S.W.2d 472 (Tex. Civ. App. 1968). *See generally* B. H. Glenn, Annotation, *Liability of Employer for Injury to Wife or Child of Employee Through Latter's Negligence*, 1 A.L.R.3d 677 (1965).

The courts have been unable to reach agreement on whether or not a parent should be able to sue his or her children in tort.[41] Similarly, the courts are split as to whether minor brothers or sisters can sue each other for tortious injuries.[42]

Finally, conflict exists over whether a child may sue his or her mother for prenatal injuries brought about through the mother's negligence or other conduct. The traditional rule was that under a "unity of person" rationale, a child who was born alive did not have a cause of action for prenatal injuries.[43] However, the modern majority rule now allows a child to sue his or her mother for prenatal injuries;[44] thus children born with drug addiction or fetal alcohol syndrome based upon the mother's prenatal actions are increasingly able to hold their mothers legally accountable.[45]

§ 7.03 PARENTAL DISCIPLINE OF A CHILD

A parent, or a person acting *in loco parentis*, has the legal right and authority to discipline, punish, or chastise his or her child, but such discipline or punishment cannot exceed due moderation, nor be used as a cloak for violence or malevolence on the part of the parent.[46] Thus, where a question is raised as to whether the parental discipline or punishment has been moderate or excessive, the trier of fact must make the ultimate determination, considering, among other things, the age and conduct of the child; the nature of the child's misconduct; the means of punishment; and the damage inflicted upon the child.[47]

---

[41] *Compare Kirtz v. Kirtz*, 447 A.2d 492 (Md. Ct. Spec. App. 1982), *with Silva v. Silva*, 446 A.2d 1013 (R.I. 1982) *and Ertl v. Ertl*, 141 N.W.2d 208 (Wis. 1966) (a parent is legally capable of suing his or her child in tort). *See also* J. A. Tyler, Annotation, *Right of Parent or Representatives to Maintain Tort Action Against Minor Child*, 60 A.L.R.2d 1284 (1958) (superseded by 62 A.L.R.3d 1299).

[42] *See, e.g., Midkiff v. Midkiff*, 113 S.E.2d 875 (Va. 1960) (since an infant (age 17 at time of incident), is generally liable for his or her own torts, it is not against public policy to permit an unemancipated minor to sue his or her minor sibling in tort). *But see Smith v. Sapienza*, 417 N.E.2d 530 (N.Y. 1981). *See also* Irwin J. Schiffres, Annotation, *Family Relationship Other Than That of Parent and Child or Husband and Wife Between Tortfeasor and Person Injured or Killed as Affecting Right to Maintain Action*, 81 A.L.R.2d 1155 (1962).

[43] *See, e.g., Stallman v. Youngquist*, 531 N.E.2d 355 (Ill. 1988); *Egbert v. Wenzl*, 260 N.W.2d 480 (Neb. 1977).

[44] *See, e.g., Grodin v. Grodin*, 301 N.W.2d 869 (Mich. Ct. App. 1980); *Bonte v. Bonte*, 616 A.2d 464 (N.H. 1992). *See generally* Thomas M. Fleming, Annotation, *Right of Child to Action Against Mother for Infliction of Prenatal Injuries*, 78 A.L.R.4th 1082 (1990).

[45] *See generally* Beale, *Can I Sue Mommy? An Analysis of a Woman's Tort Liability for Prenatal Injuries to her Child Born Alive*, 21 San Diego L. Rev. 325 (1984); Oberman, *Rethinking the Problems of Pregnant Women Who Use Drugs*, 43 Hastings L.J. 505 (1992); Bopp & Gardner, *AIDS Babies, Crack Babies: Challenges to the Law*, 7 Issues L. & Med. 3 (1991). *See also infra* § 7.06.

[46] *See, e.g., Commonwealth v. Diehl*, 385 S.E.2d 228 (Va. Ct. App. 1989) (a parent becomes criminally liable for punishment to a child which exceeds due moderation, even though a parent has a right to discipline his or her child).

[47] *See, e.g., People v. Green*, 2011 IL App (2d) 91123, ¶ 24 ("[T]he degree of injury inflicted upon a child is not the exclusive or determinative factor in evaluating whether the discipline exceeded the bounds of reasonableness . . . [;] other factors to consider include the likelihood of future punishment that might be more injurious, the psychological effects of the discipline on the child, and whether the parent was calmly attempting to discipline the child or whether the parent was lashing out in anger."); *Harbaugh v.*

For example, in the case of *In re Edward C.*,[48] a California appellate court held that even though the First Amendment to the United States Constitution severely limits the power of the State to interfere with parental rights in directing the upbringing of their children, the parents' religious beliefs that God and the Bible ordained excessive discipline by beating and whipping children cannot justify jeopardizing the health and safety of such children, nor be tolerated by the State.[49]

§ 7.04 PARENTAL LIABILITY FOR A CHILD'S ACT

Under the common law, a parent was not liable for his or her child's wrongful acts unless the parent authorized the child's tortious acts, such as in a vicarious master-servant relationship, or a principal-agent relationship.[50] Thus, in the absence of a state statute to the contrary, a parent would not be liable for any injury or damage inflicted upon a third party by his or her child.[51]

However, an increasing number of states have now passed specific statutes making the parents civilly liable in tort[52] if their child willfully causes personal

---

Commonwealth, 167 S.E.2d 329 (Va. 1969). *See generally* H. D. Warren, *Criminal Liability for Excessive or Improper Punishment Inflicted on Child by Parent, Teacher, or One in Loco Parentis*, 89 A.L.R.2d 396 (1963). *See also* Dyslin & Thomsen, *Religiosity and Risk of Perpetrating Child Physical Abuse: An Empirical Investigation*, 33 J. Psychol. & Theology 291 (2005) (child abuse researchers distinguish child abuse from corporal punishment as "entail[ing] more extreme forms of physical aggression," such as "being hit with a fist, burned, or choked"); Strauss & Yodanis, *Corporal Punishment by Parents*, 2 U. Chi. L. Sch. Roundtable 35, 37 (1995) (noting that most Americans believe that "a good spanking is sometimes necessary" to discipline children); Gelles & Cornell, *supra* note 119, at 44 (indicating that physical punishment is used by 84% to 97% of all parents at some time in their children's lives). Some commentators have defended the use of physical punishment by parents, arguing that such disciplinary measures are both effective and constitutionally protected. *See, e.g.*, John Rosemond, To Spank or Not to Spank 13 (1994); *People v. Green*, 2011 IL App (2d) 91123 (the right to corporally punish one's own children is derived from the constitutional right to privacy). Other studies suggest that corporal punishment during childhood may be associated with higher levels of dysfunctional and aggressive behavior in adulthood, including adult domestic violence and physical abuse of children. *See, e.g.*, Chiancone, *Corporal Punishment: What Lawyers Need to Know*, 16 Child Law Practice 1 (1997); Straus & Yodanis, *supra*. However, the distinction between reasonable physical punishment and actionable child abuse is not always so obvious. *See, e.g.*, *In the Interest of J.P.*, 692 N.E.2d 338 (Ill. Ct. App. 1998); *see also In the Interest of T.A.*, 663 N.W.2d 225 (S.D. 2003) (holding that the spanking of a twelve-year-old boy by his stepfather constituted child abuse and neglect, despite the fact that state statutory authority recognizes and condones corporeal punishment of children).

48 178 Cal. Rptr. 694 (Cal. Ct. App. 1981).

49 *Id. See also infra* § 7.08[B]. Empirical studies show that "[r]eligious observance weakly protect[s] individuals from family violence, but . . . family violence still occurs in religious communities." Robin Fretwell Wilson, *The Perils of Privatized Marriage, in* Marriage and Divorce in a Multi-Cultural Context: Reconsidering the Boundaries of Civil Law and Religion 269 (Joel A. Nichols, ed. 2011).

50 *See, e.g.*, *Bell v. Hudgins*, 352 S.E.2d 332 (Va. 1987). *But see* Va. Code Ann. § 8.01-44 (2011) which allows for recovery against parents for intentional torts of children up to a limit; *Lanterman v. Wilson*, 354 A.2d 432 (Md. 1976); *Ross v. Souter*, 464 P.2d 911 (N.M. 1970).

51 *See generally* Wade R. Habeeb, Annotation, *Parents' Liability for Injury or Damage Intentionally Inflicted by Minor Child*, 54 A.L.R.3d 974 (1973).

52 *See* Andrew C. Gratz, *Increasing the Price of Parenthood: When Should Parents Be Held Civilly Liable for the Torts of Their Children?*, 39 Hous. L. Rev. 169, 191 (2002) (indicating that every state but New Hampshire has some form of parental liability statute); *see also* Restatement (Second) of Torts § 316 (1979) (recommending that parents be liable for their own negligence, resulting in personal injury

injury,[53] or if their child willfully destroys or vandalizes property,[54] up to a statutory limit.[55]

§ 7.05   MEDICAL CARE FOR THE CHILD AND THE SPOUSE

The general rule with respect to medical and psychiatric care for children is that the parents ultimately decide whether care is to be provided for the child, and what that care is to be.[56] This general rule, however, is not absolute. Parents still owe their minor children the legal duty of providing adequate medical care, and their failure to provide it could lead to prosecution for child abuse or manslaughter.[57]

Although parents have substantial authority to determine their child's medical care, the state, under a *parens patriae* doctrine, is permitted to override certain parental decisions concerning medical care for the child when the child's welfare and best interests demand it.[58] The difficult legal problem arises when determining at what point parental authority for the medical care of a child should cease, and at what point the state should take over the social and legal responsibility to protect the welfare of the child.[59]

Although most of these difficult judicial decisions are normally made on a case-by-case basis, there is general agreement that when the medical treatment

---

or property damage intentionally inflicted by their minor child on third parties); *Crisafulli v. Bass*, 38 P.3d 842 (Mont. 2001) (adopting the Restatement and holding a parent liable for negligently allowing their child to ride a bike into a bystander).

[53] *See, e.g., Gilbert v. Floyd*, 168 S.E.2d 607 (Ga. Ct. App. 1969) (a child's malicious stabbing of a guest with a butcher knife made the parents liable under a Georgia statute). *But see Owens v. Ivey*, 525 N.Y.S.2d 508 (N.Y. City Ct., Rochester 1988) (finding New York's Parental Liability Act invalid on constitutional grounds as establishing a bill of attainder in an intentional assault action by the parents' daughter against another teenage girl).

[54] *See, e.g., Frost v. Taylor*, 649 S.W.2d 264 (Mo. Ct. App. 1983) (parents' 15-year-old shot and killed plaintiff's dog without provocation).

[55] *See, e.g., Buie v. Longspaugh*, 598 S.W.2d 673 (Tex. Civ. App. 1980) (the parents were liable under state statute for their son's vandalism up to $5,000 per act, for a total of $15,000); *Johnson v. Dempsey*, 901 P.2d 615 (1995) (upholding a parental limit of $2,500 per child when three siblings caused almost $30,000 in damage). *See generally* Habeeb, *supra* note 51.

[56] 3 Haralambie, Handling Child Custody, Abuse and Adoption Cases § 18:3 (3d ed. 2009); Hughes, *The Death of Children by Faith-Based Medical Neglect*, 20 J.L. & Religion 247, 248 (2004-05).

[57] Haralambie, *supra* note 56, at § 18.3; Barrett, Annotation, *Homicide: Failure to Provide Medical or Surgical Attention*, 100 A.L.R.2d 483 (1965). *See, e.g., Matter of Faridah W.*, 180 A.D.2d 451 (N.Y. 1992) (finding medical neglect when a mother refused to consent to surgery for an adolescent girl suffering from spina bifida, when the surgery would prevent the child from being on dialysis for the remainder of her life); *Commonwealth v. Barnhart*, 497 A.2d 616 (Pa. Super. Ct. 1985) (parents were convicted of manslaughter of their child by withholding medical treatment, despite their religious beliefs).

[58] Haralambie, *supra* note 56, at § 18:3 (3d ed. 2009).

[59] *See generally* Haralambie, *supra* note 56, at § 18:3 n.9 (collecting cases showing that "[w]here the medical condition is life-threatening, and the risks of withholding the proposed treatment are much greater than the risks associated with the treatment, courts are more likely to find medical neglect and order the recommended treatment"); Vorys, *The Outer Limits of Parental Autonomy: Withholding Medical Treatment from Children*, 42 Ohio St. L.J. 813 (1981).

involves little risk to the child, but a failure to provide such treatment would substantially endanger the child's life or health, the state may step in and a court may order such medical treatment over the parents' medical, ethical, or religious objections.[60]

On the other hand, the courts have been more reluctant to order medical treatment for a child over parental objections when the medical treatment involves a substantial risk to the child or when the absence of treatment would be unlikely to increase the probability of harm to the child.[61]

If the state does not intervene with medical treatment, and the child is seriously harmed or dies, the parents may be held criminally responsible.[62] However, a number of states have enacted faith healing exceptions to their criminal neglect statutes.[63] In general, these exceptions protect parents from certain kinds of legal

---

[60] Zitter, Annotation, *Power of Court or Other Public Agency to Order Medical Treatment over Parental Religious Objections for Child Whose Life is Not Immediately Endangered*, 21 A.L.R.5th 248 (1994) ("The broad principle has been enunciated, in a wide range of cases, that, in a proper case, the state may, through a court or otherwise, intervene to insure that a child is given medical treatment necessary for the protection of its life or limb — including treatment for mental or emotional ills — where the custodian of the child has unreasonably refused to allow such treatment, and that the exercise of the state's power to protect the lives and health of its children over the objections of their custodians is not violative of the constitutional right to freedom of religion where such objections are based on religious grounds."). *See also, e.g.*, *In re McCauley*, 565 N.E.2d 411 (Mass. 1991) (authorizing life saving blood transfusions for eight-year-old girl suffering from leukemia ordered over the religious objections of her parents); *Matter of Cabrera*, 552 A.2d 1114 (Pa. Super. Ct. 1989) (overriding the parents' religious objections and ordering a transfusion for a child with sickle-cell anemia).

[61] *See, e.g.*, *In re Phillip B.*, 156 Cal. Rptr. 48, 51 (Ct. App. 1979) (finding where the parents refused to consent to high-risk surgery for a Downs Syndrome child, that "[s]everal relevant factors must be taken into consideration before a state insists upon medical treatment rejected by the parents. The state should examine the seriousness of the harm the child is suffering or the substantial likelihood that he will suffer serious harm; the evaluation for the treatment by the medical profession; the risks involved in medically treating the child; and the expressed preferences of the child. Of course, the underlying consideration is the child's welfare and whether his best interests will be served by the medical treatment"); *Newmark v Williams/DCPS*, 588 A.2d 1108 (Del. 1991) (holding that the state could not order cancer treatments for a three-year-old over the parents' religious objections, even if the child would die within months if untreated, when the treatment itself had a low probability of success, 40 percent, and would itself be risky and life-threatening); *Commonwealth v. Barnhart*, 497 A.2d 616, 626 (Pa. Super. Ct. 1985); *see also* Zitter, *supra* note 60; Williams, Annotation, *Power of Court or Other Public Agency to Order Medical Treatment for Child over Parental Objections Not Based on Religious Grounds*, 97 A.L.R.3d 421 (1980).

[62] Barrett, *supra* note 57; *Walker v. Superior Court*, 763 P.2d 852 (Cal. 1988) (parents' sincere religious convictions were not a defense to manslaughter charges stemming from their decision to withhold medical treatment from their child). *See also* Trescher & O'Neill, *Medical Care for Dependent Children: Manslaughter Liability of the Christian Scientist*, 109 U. Pa. L. Rev. 203 (1960); Ingram, *State Interference with Religiously Motivated Decisions on Medical Treatment*, 93 Dick. L. Rev. 41 (1988). In a recent case, 11-year-old Madeline Kara Neumann died on March 23, 2008 from untreated diabetes. Her parents "just thought it was a spiritual attack and . . . prayed for her." The father said that "given the same set of circumstances with another child, he would not waiver in his faith and confidence in the healing power of prayer." Bill Glauber, *Parents Charged in Diabetes Death*, Apr. 29, 2008, *available at* http://www.jsonline.com/news/wisconsin/29556929.html; Colby Robertson, *After two days, jury finds Dale Neumann guilty*, WASW.com, Aug. 1, 2009, *available at* http://www.waow.com/Global/story.asp?S=10832105. Wisconsin exempts faith-healing from child abuse charges, but not from homicide charges. In 2009, Kara's mother and father were convicted of second-degree reckless homicide. *Id.*

[63] Haralambie, *supra* note 56, at §§ 7.11, 18.3 (summarizing statutes). The federal Child Abuse

liability when they provide faith healing to their children in accordance with their good faith religious beliefs, but have been sharply criticized for doing so.[64] However, the scope and effect of these faith healing exemptions varies significantly from state to state, especially when the child's life or health is at serious risk.[65]

Some jurisdictions recognize a common law or statutory exception to parental consent for medical treatment of a "mature minor." These exceptions generally permit children of a certain age or demonstrated maturity to participate in decisions about their medical care.[66] Many states allow minors to make decisions about certain health care services, such as contraceptive services, treatment of sexually transmitted infections, and prenatal services, without parental involvement.[67]

Another legal, medical, and ethical problem involves the medical care of children who are born with serious birth defects. The law makes no exception for the necessary medical treatment of a child with serious birth defects,[68] and a parent or physician who withholds such medical treatment may well risk criminal and civil sanctions.[69]

Prevention and Treatment Act ("CAPTA") originally required states to exempt faith-based denials from child abuse laws in order to receive federal funding. Congress later amended CAPTA to permit, but not require, such exemptions. Wilson, *supra* note 49, at 258.

[64] Wilson, *supra* note 49, at 258-61 (documenting the chilling costs for children of the state's wholesale delegation to parents of the choice to treat); Marci A. Hamilton, God vs. the Gavel: Religion and the Rule of Law 32-33 (2005) ("The result [of exemptions and parental failure to treat] is suffering, unnecessary death, and the martyrdom of children who have not been permitted to reach adulthood when they could make an informed choice to live or die for their religious beliefs."); James Dwyer, *The Children We Abandon: Religious Exemptions to Child Welfare and Education Laws as Denials of Equal Protection to Children of Religious Objectors*, 74 N.C. L. Rev. 1321 (1996) (arguing that religious exemptions deny children of parents who believe in faith-healing equal protection of the law); Kent Greenawalt, *The Rule of Law and the Exemption Strategy*, 30 Cardozo L. Rev. 1513, 1529 (2009) (discussing whether criminal liability will serve as a deterrent and suggesting that the question is a complex one).

[65] *See generally* Rosato, *Putting Square Pegs in a Round Hole: Procedural Due Process and the Effect of Faith Healing Exemptions on the Prosecution of Faith Healing Parents*, 29 U.S.F. L. Rev. 43 (1994); Monopoli, *Allocating the Costs of Parental Free Exercise: Striking a New Balance Between Sincere Religious Belief and a Child's Right to Medical Treatment*, 18 Pepp. L. Rev. 319 (1993).

[66] *See* Will, *My God, My Choice: The Mature Minor Doctrine and Adolescent Refusal of Life-Saving or Sustaining Medical Treatment Based upon Religious Beliefs*, 22 J. Contemp. Health L. & Pol'y 233 (2006); Rosato, *Let's Get Real: Quilting a Principled Approach to Adolescent Empowerment in Health Care Decision-Making*, 51 DePaul L. Rev. 769 (2002).

[67] Guttmacher Institute, *State Policies in Brief: An Overview of Minors' Consent Law* (2012), *available at* http://www.guttmacher.org/statecenter/spibs/spib_OMCL.pdf.

[68] *See generally* 29 U.S.C. § 794 (1973) (hospitals and health care programs cannot discriminate against the handicapped); 45 C.F.R. § 84.55 (2005) (infant care review commissions); 42 U.S.C. § 5106a(b) (2010) (requiring states to establish "procedures for responding to the reporting of medical neglect including instances of withholding of medically indicated treatment from infants with disabilities who have life-threatening conditions"); 45 C.F.R. § 1340.15(b) (2011) (defining withholding of medically indicated treatment). In 2002, Congress enacted the Born-Alive Infant Protection Act, which reaffirmed the commitment to treating disabled infants. *See supra* § 5.05.

[69] These federal statutes were largely enacted as a result of the Indiana Baby Doe case and the New York Baby Jane Doe case where the parents in both these controversial cases refused to consent to life-saving medical treatment and surgery for their severely disabled newborn children. *See generally* Angell, *Handicapped Children: Baby Doe and Uncle Sam*, 309 New Eng. J. of Med. 443 (1983); Mathieu,

The duty of one spouse to pay the necessary medical expenses for his or her spouse is also recognized in the vast majority of states, either by state statute or under the common law doctrine of necessaries.[70]

Less clear is when the state can intercede in the treatment of spouses. For example, it is unclear when, if ever, a state court should order a caesarean operation, purportedly to protect the life of the fetus, over the objections of the mother.[71]

In response to difficult questions regarding whether a state's interest in preserving life may override a competent adult's right to refuse medical treatment, a growing body of state law now allows a competent adult to refuse such medical treatment under "living will" statutes and Natural Death Acts.[72] In the absence of such legislation, uncertainty continues about the circumstances in which a spouse, parent, or other family member may remove medical life support systems from an incompetent loved one. This controversial legal, medical, and ethical dilemma continues to be debated from the earlier case involving Karen Ann Quinlan[73] and

---

The Baby Doe Controversy, 1984 Ariz. St. L.J. 605; Annas, *The Case of Baby Jane Doe: Child Abuse or Unlawful Federal Intervention?*, 74 Am. J. Pub. H. 727 (1984). *See also* Shapiro, *Medical Discrimination Against Children With Disabilities: A Report of the U.S. Commission on Civil Rights*, 6 Issues L. & Med. 285 (1990). For more recent discussions, see Fine, *Government as God: An Update on Federal Intervention in the Treatment of Critically Ill Newborns*, 34 New Eng. L. Rev. 343 (2000); Nelson et al., *Forgoing Medically Provided Nutrition and Hydration in Pediatric Patients*, 23 J.L. Med. & Ethics 33, 40-41 (1995).

[70] *See, e.g.*, Va. Code Ann. § 55-37 (2011); *see also Mem'l Hosp. v. Hahaj*, 430 N.E.2d 412 (Ind. Ct. App. 1982); *Marshfield Clinic v. Discher*, 314 N.W.2d 326 (Wis. 1982); Zitter, Annotation, *Modern Status of Rule That Husband is Primarily or Solely Liable for Necessaries Furnished Wife*, 20 A.L.R.4th 196 (1983). *But see Sharon Clinic v. Nelson*, 394 N.Y.S.2d 118 (N.Y. County Ct. 1977) (nontherapeutic elective abortion did not come under the doctrine of necessaries). *See also supra* § 3.10.

[71] *See, e.g.*, V. Chandis & T. Williams, *The Patient, the Doctor, the Fetus, and the Court-Compelled Cesarean: Why Courts Should Address the Question Through a Bioethical Lens*, 25 Med. & L. 729 (2006); Finer, *Toward Guidelines for Compelling Cesarean Surgery: Of Rights, Responsibility, and Decisional Authenticity*, 76 Minn. L. Rev. 239 (1991); Harmon, *Falling Off the Vine: Legal Fictions and the Doctrine of Substituted Judgment*, 100 Yale L.J. 1 (1990); Williams, In re A.C.: *Foreshadowing the Unfortunate Expansion of Court-Ordered Cesarean Sections*, 74 Iowa L. Rev. 287 (1988). In *In re A.C.*, 533 A.2d 611 (D.C. 1987), a three-judge motions panel initially upheld the decision of the trial court judge to allow a caesarean delivery of the fetus over the mother's objection, who was terminally ill *in extremis*. The child and mother died shortly thereafter. However, upon rehearing the case en banc, the appeals court vacated the trial court's order because the judge did not properly apply a "substituted medical judgment test" to ascertain the mother's intent. The court of appeals emphasized "that it would be an extraordinary case indeed in which a court might ever be justified in overriding the patient's wishes and authorizing a major surgical procedure such as a caesarean section." *In re A.C.*, 573 A.2d 1235, 1252 (D.C. 1990).

[72] *See generally* Johnson, *Quinlan and Cruzan: Beyond the Symbols, in* Health Law and Bioethics (Sandra Johnson, Joan Krause, Richard Saver & Robin Fretwell Wilson, eds. 2009). *See also, e.g.*, *John F. Kennedy Mem'l Hosp. v. Bludworth*, 452 So. 2d 921 (Fla. 1984) (a terminally ill patient may consent to terminate extraordinary life support systems that are keeping him alive, and an incompetent person may further express this intent through a prior "living will"); *In re Conroy*, 486 A.2d 1209 (N.J. 1985) (a competent adult has the right to refuse medical treatment and be free from medical intervention even at the risk of death, and this right to an individual's self-determination, which outweighs any state interest in preserving life or safeguarding the integrity of the medical profession, should not be affected by the patient's medical condition or prognosis).

[73] *In re Quinlan*, 355 A.2d 647 (N.J), *cert. denied*, 429 U.S. 922 (1976) (parents of Karen Ann Quinlan

Nancy Cruzan, to the controversy over Terri Schiavo's long drawn-out death.[74]

In the *Cruzan* case, Nancy Cruzan was in a persistent vegetative state as a result of an automobile accident, and her parents sought to remove her nasogastric feeding tube and permit her to die of natural causes.[75] In a sharply divided 4-3 decision, the Missouri Supreme Court held that a patient's right to privacy is not absolute, and the interest of the State of Missouri in preserving life could outweigh any privacy interest. In balancing these interests, and applying a clear and convincing evidence standard, the Missouri Supreme Court held that Nancy Cruzan's parents could not withdraw Nancy's food or water since they had not met Missouri's clear and convincing evidence standard that Nancy would have made such a decision herself.[76]

The United States Supreme Court affirmed the Missouri Supreme Court, but with two important qualifications. First, the Court ruled that artificial feeding is a form of medical treatment that may be terminated to fulfill a person's desire to die with dignity. Second, the Court held that Missouri's requirement that a patient's desire to have medical treatment withdrawn must be proven by clear and convincing evidence was not facially unconstitutional.[77] Nevertheless, the Supreme Court did not *require* a clear and convincing evidentiary standard, and in fact most states today do not apply this higher Missouri evidentiary standard to surrogate medical decision-making.[78]

---

who sought to remove extraordinary medical life support systems from their unconscious adult daughter, who was in an irreversible coma; refusal of medical treatment may now include the removal of artificial life-prolonging devices such as a respirator or a nasogastric feeding tube). *See, e.g., Corbett v. D'Alessandro*, 487 So. 2d 368 (Fla. Dist. Ct. App. 1986).

[74] Johnson, *supra* note 72; *Cruzan v. Director, Mo. Dept. of Health*, 760 S.W.2d 408 (Mo. 1988), *aff'd*, 497 U.S. 261 (1990).

[75] For a compelling account of the Cruzans' legal battle, see Colby, Long Goodbye: The Deaths of Nancy Cruzan (2002).

[76] *Id.* The Missouri Supreme Court criticized the New Jersey *Quinlan* decision, *supra*, as allegedly departing from "previously accepted norms." *Cruzan v. Harmon*, 760 S.W.2d 408, 422 (Mo. 1988) (quoting Alexander, *Death by Directive*, 28 Santa Clara L. Rev. 67, 82 (1988)). *But see* Weinberg, *Whose Right is it Anyway? Individualism, Community, and the Right to Die: A Commentary on the New Jersey Experience*, 40 Hastings L.J. 119 (1988).

[77] Ultimately the Cruzans marshaled sufficient evidence of Nancy's wishes to satisfy this standard in a proceeding in which the State did not oppose the withdrawal of her feeding tube. Johnson, *supra* note 72, at 69.

[78] *See, e.g., In re Conroy*, 486 A.2d 1209 (N.J. 1985); *see also* Stewart, *Right to Die, But . . .* , 76 A.B.A. J. 36-40 (Sept. 1990), where even legal counsel for the Missouri Attorney General's Office described the Missouri clear and convincing evidentiary rule in *Cruzan* as "an aberration," and opined that most other states will *not* follow its example. *Id.* at 40. Accordingly, the vast majority of states have now enacted important surrogate medical decision making statutes in this area utilizing a preponderance of the evidence test, rather than a clear and convincing evidence standard. *See generally* Symposium, *Cruzan and the Right to Die*, 25 Ga. L. Rev. 1253 (1991); Grant & Cleaver, *A Line Less Reasonable: Cruzan and the Looming Debate over Active Euthanasia*, 2 Md. J. Contemp. Legal Issues 99 (1991); Peters, *The State's Interest in the Preservation of Life: From* Quinlan to Cruzan, 50 Ohio St. L.J. 891 (1989); Fentiman, *A New Framework for Substitute Decision Making for Incompetent, Incurably Ill Adults*, 57 Geo. Wash. L. Rev. 801 (1989).

§ 7.06   WRONGFUL DEATH, WRONGFUL BIRTH, WRONGFUL LIFE, AND WRONGFUL CONCEPTION

Under state wrongful death and survival statutes, the surviving spouse and children of the deceased would normally qualify as the primary class of beneficiaries, and if there were none in that class, then the parents, brothers, and sisters of the deceased would qualify as the statutory beneficiaries.[79]

Regarding the term "deceased," 35 states and the District of Columbia now recognize that an unborn fetus constitutes a "person" under state wrongful death and survival statutes.[80] The traditional common law rule, however, did not recognize a stillborn or viable unborn child as a "person" under state wrongful death or survival statutes.[81] In almost all jurisdictions that have considered the question, a tort remedy for "wrongful birth" is also actionable if a child is born with a severe illness, handicap, or genetic abnormality that was negligently misdiagnosed by the attending physician.[82] The recoverable damages may include extraordinary expenses — "those over and above the ordinary expense of child rearing,"[83] and damages for the parents' mental distress.[84] A few states have also recognized claims

---

[79] *See generally* Dobbs, *supra* note 8, at § 298. *See also* Barnett, Annotation, *Fact That Tortfeasor Is Member of Class of Beneficiaries as Affecting Right to Maintain Action for Wrongful Death*, 95 A.L.R.2d 585 (1964); Scheafer, Annotation, *Effect of Death of Beneficiary upon Right of Action Under Death Statute*, 13 A.L.R.4th 1060 (1982).

[80] Speiser, Recovery for Wrongful Death § 7:40 (4th ed. 2011) (noting that some states limit recovery to the death of a stillborn child or the viable fetus, while others exclude recovery for pre-embryos). *But see, e.g.*, Tex. Civ. Prac. & Rem. Code §§ 71.001(4), 71.003 (2011) (defining "individual" to include unborn children "at every stage of gestation" for purposes of all wrongful death claims except those against physicians and health care providers); *Fort Worth Osteopathic Hosp., Inc. v. Reese*, 148 S.W.3d 94 (Tex. 2004) (holding that the statutory bars on parents' recovery for wrongful death of a stillborn child did not violate the Equal Protection Clause because the latter does not protect the unborn); *Jeter v. Mayo Clinic Arizona*, 121 P.3d 1256 (Ariz. Ct. App. 2005) (holding that a cryopreserved eight-cell pre-embryo, three days old, is not a person for wrongful death claims); *Ryan v. Brown*, 827 N.E.2d 112 (Ind. Ct. App. 2005) (holding that, under the Indiana Wrongful Death of a Child statute, the child must be stillborn to bring a wrongful death claim). *See also* Loquist, *The Wrongful Death of a Fetus: Erasing the Barrier Between Viability and Nonviability*, 36 Washburn L.J. 259 (1997); Shapiro, Annotation, *Right to Maintain Action or to Recover Damages for Death of Unborn Child*, 84 A.L.R.3d 411 (1978).

[81] *See, e.g.*, Speiser, *supra* note 80, at § 7:40; *Lawrence v. Craven Tire Co.*, 169 S.E.2d 440 (Va. 1969); *see also supra* § 5.05[A].

[82] In a wrongful birth case, the claim prompting recovery is that the child, but for the physician's negligent diagnosis, would not have been born because the mother would have terminated or avoided the pregnancy. Dobbs, *supra* note 8, at § 291.

[83] *Id.* § 292.

[84] *Id.* (noting that some courts allow damages for emotional harm to both parents or the mother alone, while other courts are unwilling to permit such damages or limit recovery with offset rules or bystander requirements). *See, e.g.*, *Procanik v. Cillo*, 478 A.2d 755 (N.J. 1984). In this case a child was born with congenital birth defects caused by rubella, which had not been properly diagnosed by the physician. The claim of the parents for extraordinary medical care and emotional distress was found to be actionable. *See also Naccash v. Burger*, 290 S.E.2d 825 (Va. 1982) (finding actionable a claim for medical damages and damages for the parents' emotional distress against a physician who had negligently failed to discover that the fetus was affected with Tay-Sachs disease). *See generally* Weinman, Note, *Birth Related Torts: Can They Fit the Malpractice Mold?*, 56 Mo. L. Rev. 175 (1991); Weber, Note, *The Question of Prospective Damage Claims for Genetic Injury in Wrongful Life Cases*, 23 Ind. L. Rev. 753 (1990); 3 M. Minzer, et al., Damages in Tort Actions, ch. 18 (1981). *Cf. Arche v. United*

by the child for "wrongful life," but limit recovery to "medical expenses" the parent would recover for wrongful birth.[85] Some states recognize a related claim for a "wrongful pregnancy" or "wrongful conception."[86]

For example, if a doctor negligently performs a voluntary sterilization,[87] such as a vasectomy on the husband or a salpingectomy or tubal ligation on the wife, and the result is a healthy, bouncing baby, the doctor may be liable for negligence. In such wrongful pregnancy or conception cases, most courts disallow recovery of the cost of raising the healthy child until the age of majority, concluding the child's birth is no injury at all or that the cost of a healthy child, after accounting for the benefits, are simply unknowable.[88] Some courts have, however, allowed recovery for the mother's pain in delivering the child and her emotional distress for the unplanned pregnancy.[89] A few states have allowed recovery of the cost of raising a healthy child until the age of majority, when the parents sought to avoid the child's birth for economic reasons, offset by the benefit to the parents of having a child.[90] In "wrongful conception" cases, in which a genetically damaged child resulted, courts appear more willing to award damages without an offset.[91]

§ 7.07 REGULATION OF A CHILD'S EDUCATION

The conflicting interests of parents, their children, and the state are very much in evidence with compulsory education laws, which have been enacted in all states and require children to be sent to school, usually between the ages of five and seventeen.[92] Generally, these state compulsory education statutes require that a minor child attend a public school or be provided with appropriate equivalent education, such as a state approved private school[93] or approved home schooling

---

States, 798 P.2d 477 (1990) (limiting recovery of damages to the child's minority and then recognizing a claim only when the child has "such gross deformities" that she will never "function as a normal human being").

[85] Most courts "reject this claim altogether," but those that recognize it limit recovery to "medical expenses" recoverable by the parent for wrongful birth, although damages recouped by child may be measured by the child's life expectancy and not merely her minor years, as it would be for the mother's or parents' recovery. Dobbs, *supra* note 8, at § 292.

[86] *Id.* § 291.

[87] *See also supra* § 5.06.

[88] *See, e.g., Sherlock v. Stillwater Clinic*, 260 N.W.2d 169 (Minn. 1977). For "wrongful life" cases that were held to be actionable, see *Turpin v. Sortini*, 643 P.2d 954 (Cal. 1982); *Harbeson v. Parke-Davis*, 656 P.2d 483 (Wash. 1983). *See also* Kelly, *The Rightful Position in "Wrongful Life" Actions*, 42 Hastings L.J. 505 (1991); Tucker, *Wrongful Life: A New Generation*, 27 J. Fam. L. 673 (1989); Minzer, *supra* note 84, at Ch. 18.

[89] Dobbs, *supra* note 8, at § 292.

[90] *Id. See also, e.g., Berman v. Allan*, 404 A.2d 8 (N.J. 1979); *Miller v. Johnson*, 343 S.E.2d 301 (Va. 1986). *See generally* Tucker, *supra* note 88; Bopp, Bostrom & McKinney, *The "Rights" and "Wrongs" of Wrongful Birth and Wrongful Life: A Jurisprudential Analysis of Birth Related Torts*, 27 Duq. L. Rev. 461 (1989); Roberts, *Distinguishing "Wrongful" from "Rightful" Life*, 6 J. Contemp. Health L. & Pol'y 59 (1990); Berenson, *The Wrongful Life Claim*, 64 Tul. L. Rev. 895 (1990).

[91] Dobbs, *supra* note 8, at § 293 n.12.

[92] *See generally* T. Van Geel, The Courts and American Education Law (1987).

[93] In *Pierce v. Society of Sisters*, 268 U.S. 510, 534 (1925), the United States Supreme Court ruled that

instruction.[94]

Noncompliance with state compulsory education laws may lead to the filing of misdemeanor charges against the parents and the initiation of juvenile court proceedings against the children for their truancy.[95]

A related problem some courts have faced is that of parents attempting to exempt their children from compulsory state education laws for religious reasons, citing *Wisconsin v. Yoder*[96] as their authority. However, most courts have read *Yoder* narrowly and distinguished it as applying only to Amish children and other self-contained religious communities of long standing.[97]

Another legal issue addressed by the courts has been the issue of corporal punishment in the schools. For example, in *Ingraham v. Wright*,[98] the United States Supreme Court held that the paddling of a Florida junior high school student did not constitute cruel or unusual punishment, and the imposition of reasonably necessary corporal punishment for discipline and classroom control was not tortious, even without the consent of the child's parents. Moreover, notice or a hearing prior to any corporal punishment was not required under *Ingraham*.[99] However, if the corporeal punishment was so unnecessary, malicious, or atrocious as to amount to a brutal abuse of power, then the student may be able to recover for

---

a state cannot compel all its students to be educated in public schools. Nevertheless, it did recognize "the power of the state reasonably to regulate all schools, to inspect, supervise, and examine them, their teachers and pupils; [and] to require that all children of proper age attend some school."

[94] *See generally* Robin Cheryl Miller, Annotation, *Validity, Construction, and Application of Statute, Regulation, or Policy Governing Home Schooling or Affecting Rights of Home-Schooled Students*, 70 A.L.R.5th 169 (1999); Burgess, *The Constitutionality of Home Education Statutes*, 55 UMKC L. Rev. 69 (1986-87); Knight, *The Case for Allowing Home Education*, 18 Tex. Tech L. Rev. 1261 (1987). As to whether parents have a constitutionally protected right to educate their children at home, the courts have reached varying conclusions. *Compare Mazaenic v. North Judson-San Pierre School Corp.*, 614 F. Supp. 1152, 1160 (N.D. Ind. 1985), *aff'd*, 798 F.2d 230 (7th Cir. 1986) (holding that parents have "a constitutional right to educate [their] children in an educationally proper home environment"), *with Null v. Board of Educ.*, 815 F. Supp. 937, 939-40 (S.D. W. Va. 1993) (holding that parents do *not* have a fundamental constitutional right to direct their children's education, but only a general liberty interest subject to reasonable state regulation). Today, however, all 50 states allow home schooling, and the number of children educated at home has increased significantly. *See* Kimberly A. Yuracko, *Education Off the Grid: Constitutional Constraints on Homeschooling*, 96 Cal. L. Rev. 123 (2008) (estimating the number of homeschooled children as between 1.2 and 2 million); Likasik, *The Latest Home Education Challenge: The Relationship Between Home Schools and Public Schools*, 74 N.C. L. Rev. 1913 (1996); *see also* MacMullan, *The Constitutionality of State Home School Statutes*, 39 Vill. L. Rev. 1309 (1994) (discussing various types of state home schooling regulations).

[95] *See generally* Haralambie, *supra* note 56, at § 12:16; Clark, *supra* note 12, at 571-80; *see also In Re Amanda K*, 13 A.D.3d 193 (N.Y. 1st Dep't 2004).

[96] *Wisconsin v. Yoder*, 406 U.S. 205 (1972). In *Yoder*, the United States Supreme Court exempted Amish children from Wisconsin's compulsory education laws because post-eighth-grade education violated Amish religious tenants.

[97] *See, e.g., Duro v. District Attorney*, 712 F.2d 96 (4th Cir. 1983); *see also Burrow v. State*, 669 S.W.2d 441 (Ark. 1984); *State v. Morrow*, 343 N.W.2d 903 (Neb. 1984). State approved home schooling, however, is legally recognized in all 50 states. *See* Yuracko, *supra* note 94.

[98] 430 U.S. 651 (1977).

[99] *Id. See also* Rosenberg, Note, Ingraham v. Wright: *The Supreme Court's Whipping Boy*, 78 Colum. L. Rev. 75 (1978).

violation of his or her civil rights under 42 U.S.C. § 1983, and for violation of his or her substantive due process rights.[100] Recently, scholars have also debated corporal punishment in the context of the U.N. Convention on the Rights of the Child,[101] although courts have yet to follow their lead.

Student free expression and school dress codes have also provoked legal disputes. A number of cases attempt to define parents' and student's rights vis-à-vis the state. *Tinker v. Des Moines Independent School District*[102] represents the high-water mark of student free expression cases. *Tinker* involved children suspended from school for wearing black armbands to protest the Vietnam War. Siding with the students against school officials, the United States Supreme Court famously announced: "It can hardly be argued that either students or teachers shed their constitutional rights to freedom of speech or expression at the schoolhouse gate."[103] *Tinker*'s "material disruption" test erred on the side of a student's right to free expression so long as there was no "material or substantial interference with school work or discipline . . . or the rights of others."[104] However, *Tinker*'s progeny have since diminished its expansive holding. In *Bethel School District No. 403 v. Fraser*, the Court held that students' First Amendment rights "are not automatically coextensive with the rights of adults in other settings."[105] In *Hazelwood School District v. Kuhlmeier*, the Court further refined *Tinker* by articulating the "legitimate pedagogical concern" test: "Educators do not offend the First Amendment by exercising editorial control over the style and content of student speech in school-sponsored expressive activities so long as their actions are reasonably related to a legitimate pedagogical concern."[106] A more recent court decision found that a school could censor student speech that promotes drug use even though it occurred at an off-campus assembly.[107] Despite this apparent narrowing of student rights, courts have been hopelessly divided on how much proof the school system must demonstrate in order to uphold school dress codes governing student grooming, appearance, and permitted dress.[108]

---

[100] *See, e.g., Hall v. Tawney*, 621 F.2d 607 (4th Cir. 1980) (West Virginia student was severely paddled and subsequently hospitalized with permanent injuries to her lower back and spine). Corporal punishment of less severity that is still unreasonable may also result in a tort action by the student against the school officials for personal injuries. *See generally* James A. Rapp, Education Law § 9.10[7] (2011); M. McCarthy & N. Cambrone-McCabe, Public School Law: Teachers' and Students' Rights (3d ed. 1992).

[101] *See, e.g.,* Andre R. Imbrogno, *Corporal Punishment in America's Public Schools and the U.N. Convention on the Rights of the Child: A Case for Nonratification*, 29 J.L. & Educ. 125 (2000) (arguing against ratification of the Convention because of corporal punishment's deep historical roots and popular support); Alice Farmer & Kate Stinson, *Failing the Grade: How the Use of Corporal Punishment in U.S. Public Schools Demonstrates the Need for U.S. Ratification of the Children's Rights Convention and the Convention on the Rights of Persons with Disabilities*, 54 N.Y.L. Sch. L. Rev. 1035 (2010) (arguing that the United States needs to ban corporal punishment to comply with treaty obligations).

[102] *Tinker v. Des Moines Independent School District*, 393 U.S. 503 (1969).

[103] *Id.* at 506.

[104] *Id.* at 511.

[105] 478 U.S. 675, 685 (1986).

[106] 484 U.S. 260, 273 (1988).

[107] *Morse v. Frederick*, 551 U.S. 393 (2007).

[108] *Compare Massie v. Henry*, 455 F.2d 779 (4th Cir. 1972), *and Breen v. Kahl*, 419 F.2d 1034 (7th Cir.

Search and seizure issues involving public schools have drawn increased attention in recent years, reflecting the unfortunate and pervasive problems of illegal drugs, weapons, and alcohol on school grounds. In several cases, students have asserted that warrantless searches conducted by school officials violated their Fourth Amendment constitutional rights. However, in *New Jersey v. T.L.O.*,[109] the United States Supreme Court held that although the Fourth Amendment's prohibition against unreasonable search and seizures applied to school officials, the school officials' substantial interest in maintaining discipline required an "easing" of warrant and probable cause requirements that are normally imposed on other public officials. Thus, the Court in *T.L.O.* held that the legality of school searches should depend on the "reasonableness, under all the circumstances, of the search" which is based upon a two-prong test: (1) are there reasonable grounds for suspecting that the search will turn up evidence that the student has violated, or is violating, either the law or the rules of the school? and (2) are the measures adopted reasonably related to the objectives of the search and not excessively intrusive in light of the age and sex of the student and the nature of the infraction?[110]

With respect to expulsion and suspension from school, the United States Supreme Court in *Goss v. Lopez*[111] held that minimum due process requirements must be met before a student can be suspended from school, even for a short period of time. The Court recognized that a student's state-created property right to an education is protected by the Fourteenth Amendment and cannot be impaired unless the student has notice of the charges and an opportunity to refute them.[112] *A fortiori* these same procedural safeguards should apply when a student is expelled from school.[113]

The Supreme Court also has dealt with private, as well as public schools that attempt to discriminate based upon race, gender, or religious beliefs.[114]

1969) (dress codes held unconstitutional), *with King v. E. Side Union High Sch. Dist.*, 445 F.2d 932 (9th Cir. 1971), *and Jackson v. Dorrier*, 424 F.2d 213 (6th Cir. 1970) (dress codes held constitutional). The United States Supreme Court, wisely or unwisely, refused to grant certiorari in any of these cases. *See generally* Karen A. Haase, *School Regulation of Exotic Body Piercing*, 79 Neb. L. Rev. 976 (2000); Cheryl Miller, Annotation, *Validity of Regulation by Public-School Authorities as to Clothes or Personal Appearance of Pupils*, 58 A.L.R.5th 1 (1998); Rapp, *supra* note 100, at § 9.04[8][c]-[d].

[109] *New Jersey v. T.L.O.*, 469 U.S. 325 (1985).

[110] *Id.* at 341-42. *See also Safford Unified Sch. Dist. No. 1 v. Redding*, 557 U.S. 364 (2009) (divided court held that a strip search of 13-year-old girl was not justified even though the assistant principal's suspicion of drug contraband was reasonable). *See generally*, M. McCarthy & N. Cambron-McCabe, *supra*, note 100; Rapp, *supra* note 100, at § 9.08.

[111] 419 U.S. 565 (1975).

[112] *Id.*

[113] *See, e.g., Dunn v. Tyler Indep. Sch. Dist.*, 460 F.2d 137 (5th Cir. 1972).

[114] *See, e.g., Runyon v. McCrary*, 427 U.S. 160 (1976) (a private school case interpreting 42 U.S.C. § 1981, which states that all persons shall have the same right to make and enforce contracts as white citizens); *Mississippi Univ. for Women v. Hogan*, 458 U.S. 718 (1982) (a male student desired to attend a state-supported all-female nursing school); *Bob Jones Univ. v. United States*, 461 U.S. 574 (1983) (a sectarian private school prohibited interracial dating and marriage); *see also* Van Geel, supra note 92, at 15-63.

Courts have been reluctant to enforce private contractual agreements dealing with the religious education of children, such as a premarital, postmarital, or separation agreement providing that the children should be raised in a particular religious faith. If both parties mutually agree to a certain religious education and upbringing for their children, then there is no legal controversy to settle. But if the custodial parent subsequently decides not to honor his or her previous agreement, then the court normally cannot compel compliance with the prior agreement.[115] Therefore, religious education decisions concerning children can be modified in light of the child's best interests, and are normally left to the discretion of the custodial parent or the court even if the parents previously entered into a contractual agreement to the contrary.[116]

§ 7.08 DOMESTIC VIOLENCE

Under the early common law, a disciplinary "rule of thumb" allowed the husband a legal right to inflict "moderate personal chastisement" upon his wife and children, provided that he used a stick no larger around than his thumb.[117] Although this archaic and outrageous common law rule is now prohibited under state law,[118] for many years both law enforcement officials and the courts largely ignored allegations of domestic violence, which now includes any intentional or reckless act that causes physical injury to another family member.[119]

One traditional response to domestic abuse by a battered spouse or child was a tort action, but such an action did not constitute a legal remedy in those jurisdictions recognizing the doctrine of intrafamily tort immunity.[120] Moreover, traditional tort remedies did not provide physical protection, nor immediate relief for the battered spouse or child in the midst of repeated violent acts. Similarly, state criminal assault statutes also failed to adequately protect the battered spouse or child due to delayed police response to domestic violence calls, as well as the unfortunate *de facto* policy of many law enforcement agencies treating victims of domestic assault differently than victims of non-domestic assaults.[121]

---

[115] *See, e.g., Hackett v. Hackett,* 150 N.E.2d 431 (Ohio Ct. App. 1958); *Stanton v. Stanton,* 100 S.E.2d 289 (Ga. 1957); *Lundeen v. Struminger,* 165 S.E.2d 285 (Va. 1969).

[116] *See generally* Jordan C. Paul, Comment, *"You Get the House. I Get the Car. You Get the Kids. I Get their Souls." The Impact of Spiritual Custody Awards on the Free Exercise Rights of Custodial Parents,* 138 U. Pa. L. Rev. 583 (1989).

[117] 3 Va. L. Reg. 241 (1917).

[118] *See infra* § 7.08[A], [B].

[119] *See generally* M. Straus, et al., Behind Closed Doors: Violence in the American Family (1980). *See also* Gelles & Cornell, Intimate Violence in Families 1 (2d ed. 1990) ("People are more likely to be killed, physically assaulted, hit, beaten up, slapped, or spanked in their own homes by other family members than anywhere else, or by anyone else, in our society.").

[120] *See supra* § 7.02; *see also* Siegel, *"The Rule of Love": Wife Beating as Prerogative and Privacy,* 105 Yale L.J. 2117 (1996); Scherer, *Tort Remedies for Victims of Domestic Abuse,* 43 S.C. L. Rev. 543 (1992); Dalton, *Domestic Violence, Domestic Torts, and Divorce Constraints and Possibilities,* 31 New Eng. L. Rev. 319 (1997).

[121] *See, e.g.,* Oppenlander, *Coping or Copping Out: Police Service Delivery in Domestic Disputes,* 20 Criminology 449 (1982).

Since the mid-1970s, however, states have given increased attention to the serious implications of intrafamily violence. In 2011, the Bureau of Justice Statistics reported that rates of nonfatal and fatal intimate violence had declined from 1993 to 2005,[122] but that intimate partner violence represented 22% of all the nonfatal violent victimizations of females aged 12 or older.[123] Nearly a third (30%) of female homicides were committed by their intimate partners.[124] A December 14, 2011, survey by the Centers for Disease Control and Prevention found that "[o]n average, 24 people per minute are victims of rape, physical violence, or stalking by an intimate partner in the United States."[125] The incidence of rape may be subject to underreporting, as the federal government has only recently expanded the Uniform Crime Report's definition of rape to include oral and anal penetration of any victim regardless of gender.[126] The Report had previously limited forcible rape to vaginal penetration by a penis.[127]

Legal responses to family violence have changed dramatically over the past several decades, and the vast majority of states have responded to this domestic violence crisis by enacting serious domestic abuse legislation that provides, among other remedies, for a temporary restraining order against the abusive spouse.[128]

According to two leading scholars:

In the last twenty years, litigation, legislation, activism, and, to a lesser extent, social services for battered women have proliferated. In that time, society has moved from virtual denial of the existence of domestic violence to a somewhat grudging acknowledgment that it is a pervasive and serious problem with legal, sociological, and psychological dimensions. Fundamental changes in civil and criminal law and practice have resulted in battered women becoming more visible in the legal system: protective restraining orders are now available in every state; many states have amended their custody statutes to provide for consideration of domestic violence in custody cases; policies for arrest of batterers are increasingly common;

---

[122] Catalano, Intimate Partner Violence in the United States 1 (U.S. Department of Justice, Bureau of Justice Statistics 2007).

[123] *Id.* (noting that "both females and males who were separated or divorced individuals were at greater risk of nonfatal intimate partner violence while persons who were married or widowed reported the lowest risk of violence").

[124] *Id.*

[125] Centers for Disease Control and Prevention, Press Release, *Sexual Violence, Stalking, and Intimate Partner Violence Widespread in the US*, Dec. 14, 2011, *available at* http://www.cdc.gov/media/releases/2011/p1214_sexual_violence.html. *But see CDC Survey: 1 in 4 Women Attacked by Partner*, AP, Dec. 14, 2011, *available at* http://news.yahoo.com/survey-1-4-women-attacked-intimate-partner-225334654.html ("One expert called the new report's estimate on attempted rape 'extremely high' with 1 in 5 women saying they were victims. About half of those cases involved intimate partners. No documentation was sought to verify the women's claims, which were made anonymously.").

[126] Press Release, U.S. Department of Justice, *Attorney General Eric Holder Announces Revisions to the Uniform Crime Report's Definition of Rape*, Jan. 6, 2012, *available at* http://www.justice.gov/opa/pr/2012/January/12-ag-018.html.

[127] *Id.*

[128] *See generally* Cook, *Domestic Abuse Legislation in Illinois and Other States: A Survey and Suggestions for Reform*, 1983 U. Ill. L. Rev. 261.

prosecutors' offices have begun to prosecute domestic violence cases; and public defenders have begun to recognize the relevance of battering to some of their clients' defenses.[129]

[A] Spousal Abuse

The vast majority of states have now recognized that there had been inefficient enforcement of state criminal statutes dealing with spousal abuse or abuse of an intimate partner,[130] and these states therefore have provided alternative civil remedies to deter what is essentially criminal behavior.[131] Unlike tort actions against the abusive spouse, these civil protective restraining orders also protect the abused spouse from further violent acts, and often provide financial support as well as physical protection.[132] Civil protection orders thus grant immediate relief to victims of domestic abuse by enjoining batterers from further violence against their partners, and usually provide further relief by evicting the batterer from a shared residence, providing for temporary relief of children, limiting the batterer's visitation rights, ordering the payment of child and spousal support, and requiring the batterer to attend mandatory counseling sessions.[133] In addition, a number of state protection order statutes authorize the award of monetary damages to compensate victims for the economic costs of domestic violence.[134]

---

[129] Cahn & Meier, *Domestic Violence and Feminist Jurisprudence: Toward a New Agenda*, 4 B.U. Pub. Int. L.J. 339, 339 (1995). *See also* Wriggins, *Domestic Violence Torts*, 75 S. Cal. L. Rev. 121 (2001); Al-Hibri, *An Islamic Perspective on Domestic Violence*, 27 Fordham Int'l L.J. 195 (2003); Decasas, *Protecting Hispanic Women: The Inadequacy of Domestic Violence Policy*, 24 Chicano-Latino L. Rev. 56 (2003); Collins, *Same-Sex Domestic Violence*, 4 J.L. Soc'y 99 (2002); *Symposium: Integrating Responses to Domestic Violence*, 47 Loyola L. Rev. 1 (2001); *Symposium: Together: Bridging the Gaps in the Legal Response to Domestic Violence*, 14 Hastings Women's L.J. 1 (2003); Spiropoulos, *Prefatory Note and Comments to the Uniform Interstate Enforcement of Domestic Violence Protection Order Act*, 35 Fam. L. Q. 205 (2001).

[130] Although spousal abuse problems are most commonly referred to in terms of the "battered wife," husbands are also assaulted by their wives. *See, e.g.*, Michele C. Black et al., *The National Intimate Partner and Sexual Violence Survey: 2010 Summary Report*, National Center for Injury Prevention and Control, Centers for Disease Control and Prevention (2011); Mary Z. Silverzweig, *Domestic Terrorism: The Debate and Gender Divides*, 12 J.L. & Fam. Stud. 251 (2010). National crime statistics, however, indicate that more than 80% of heterosexual partner violence reported to law enforcement authorities is perpetrated by men against women. *See, e.g.*, Molly Dragiewicz & Yvonne Lindgren, *The Gendered Nature of Domestic Violence: Statistical Data for Lawyers Considering Equal Protection Analysis*, 17 Am. U. J. Gender Soc. Pol'y & L. 229 (2009). Although domestic violence is no longer the single largest cause of injury to women in the United States, intimate partner homicides still account for almost half of all murders of women in the United States. *See, e.g.*, Jacquelyn C. Campbell, et al., *Assessing Risk Factors for Intimate Partner Homicide*, 250 NIJ Journal 16 (2003). *Cf.* Kelly, *Disabusing the Definition of Domestic Abuse: How Women Batter Men and the Role of the Feminist State*, 30 Fla. St. U. L. Rev. 791 (2003) (concluding that existing gender-based definitions of domestic violence must be challenged in theory and practice).

[131] *See, e.g.*, "Domestic Violence," 50 State Statutory Surveys: Criminal Laws: Crimes, *available at* 0030 SURVEYS 7 (Westlaw).

[132] *See, e.g.*, Ariz. Rev. Stat. Ann. § 13-3602 (2011); Va. Code Ann. § 16.1-279.1 (2011).

[133] *See, e.g.*, "Protective Orders," 50 State Statutory Surveys: Family Law: General, *available at* 0080 SURVEYS 19 (Westlaw).

[134] *See, e.g.*, Del. Code Ann. tit. 10, § 1045 (West 2010); *see also Wine v. Quezada*, 379 N.J. Super. 287 (Ch. Div. 2005); *Powell v. Powell*, 547 A.2d 973 (D.C. 1988); Klein & Orloff, *Providing Legal Protection*

The purpose of this domestic abuse legislation, therefore, is to provide immediate protection to an abused spouse or other intimate partner by allowing a court to enjoin the violent spouse or partner from further assaulting, molesting, or in any other way harming the abused victim. Violations of these court orders usually result in a contempt penalty ranging from six months to one year in prison.[135]

Many victims of domestic violence are often followed and threatened by their abusers, both before and after being attacked. At one time, the law offered little recourse for these acts of intimidation. Since 1990, however, virtually all states have enacted statutes that criminalize such stalking behavior. These state anti-stalking statutes typically define stalking as the "willful, malicious, and repeated following and harassing of another person," and most state anti-stalking statutes require both threatening behavior and a continuing course of conduct.[136] Also, 18 jurisdictions today have implemented the Uniform Interstate Enforcement of Domestic-Violence Protection Orders that allows for closer interstate cooperation when one state issues a protective order.[137]

Unfortunately, no matter what spousal abuse remedy is sought, delayed police response to domestic violence calls still presents a major problem. The belief that many police agencies respond to domestic violence calls with a minimum of intervention and arrests has been confirmed in various research studies.[138]

---

for Battered Women: An Analysis of State Statutes and Case Law, 21 Hofstra L. Rev. 801 (1993); Finn, *Statutory Authority in the Use and Enforcement of Civil Protection Orders Against Domestic Abuse*, 23 Fam. L.Q. 43 (1989); Niemi-Kiesilainen, *The Deterrent Effect of Arrest in Domestic Violence: Differentiating Between Victim and Perpetrator Response*, 12 Hastings Women's L.J. 283 (2001).

[135] *See generally* Cook, *Domestic Abuse Legislation in Illinois and Other States*, 1983 U. Ill. L. Rev. 261; Waits, *The Criminal Justice System's Response to Battering: Understanding the Problem, and Forging the Solutions*, 60 Wash. L. Rev. 267 (1985). *But see* Topliffe, *Why Civil Protection Orders Are Effective Remedies for Domestic Violence but Mutual Protective Orders Are Not*, 67 Ind. L.J. 1039 (1992). *See also* Chiu, *Confronting the Agency in Battered Mothers*, 74 S. Cal. L. Rev. 1223 (2001); Kohn, *Why Doesn't She Leave? The Collision of First Amendment Rights and Effective Court Remedies for Victims of Domestic Violence*, 29 Hastings Const. L.Q. 1 (2001); Cole & Buel, *Safety and Financial Security for Battered Women*, 7 Geo. J. Poverty on L. & Pol'y 307 (2000); Brandl & Muer, *Domestic Abuse in Later Life*, 8 Elder L.J. 297 (2000); Hodges, *Trouble in Paradise: Barriers to Addressing Domestic Violence in Lesbian Relationships*, 9 L. & Sex 311 (1999-2000).

[136] *See generally* "Stalking," 50 State Statutory Surveys: Criminal Law: Crimes, *available at* 0030 SURVEYS 16 (Westlaw). *See* Thomas L. Hafemeister, *If All You Have Is a Hammer: Society's Ineffective Response to Intimate Partner Violence*, 60 Cath. U. L. Rev. 919, 976-77 (2011). Some state anti-stalking statutes have been constitutionally challenged for vagueness or First Amendment overbreadth. *Compare State v. Bryan*, 910 P.2d 212 (Kan. 1996) (state anti-stalking statute struck down as unconstitutionally vague because statutory terms lacked definition and there was no objective standard), *and Commonwealth v. Kwiatkowski*, 637 N.E.2d 854 (Mass. 1994) (use of statutory phrase "repeatedly follows or harasses" was unconstitutionally vague), *with State v. Culmo*, 642 A.2d 90 (Conn. Super. Ct. 1993) (state anti-stalking statutory language was upheld as constitutional since it was "narrowly tailored to serve significant governmental interests"), *and Staley v. Jones*, 239 F.3d 769 (6th Cir. 2001) (also rejecting a vagueness challenge to a state anti-stalking statute). *See also* Bjerregaard, *Stalking and the First Amendment: A Constitutional Analysis of State Stalking Laws*, 32 Crim. L. Bull. 307 (1996); *State v. Zatkovich*, 52 P.3d 36 (Wash. Ct. App. 2002) (holding that an exceptionally long prison sentence for stalking was supported by a finding of domestic violence along with the stalking offense).

[137] Unif. Interstate Enforcement of Domestic-Violence Prot. Orders, 9.U.L.A. 233 (Supp. 2011).

[138] *See, e.g.*, Oppenlander, *Coping or Copping Out: Police Service Delivery in Domestic Disputes*, 20

Accordingly, a number of battered women have brought lawsuits against their local police departments; if an injured spouse can prove an administrative pattern of police neglect in domestic violence cases, then a cause of action may lie against the local police department and the municipality pursuant to 42 U.S.C. § 1983, as well as a violation of the Equal Protection Clause of the Fifth and Fourteenth Amendments to the Constitution based upon the nonperformance or malperformance of official duties by the defendant police officers.[139]

As a result of this delayed or trivialized police response to domestic violence, advocates for battered women have demanded that more states and municipalities enact mandatory arrest and no-drop prosecution policies.[140] But mandatory arrest statutes and no-drop prosecution policies have generated controversy. Supporters of mandatory arrest policies argue that, by reducing police discretion, mandatory arrest policies ensure that police officers will not trivialize domestic violence or make decisions about arrests on a discriminatory or otherwise illegitimate basis. Moreover, by physically removing the abuser, arrest provides immediate protection for the victim, affords her time away from her batterer to evaluate her situation, and further empowers her by demonstrating that she can take effective action to stop the abuse.[141] Critics of mandatory arrest laws counter that under a mandatory arrest regime, a victim's call to the police is tantamount to a request for arrest, and although some victims may be encouraged to summon help because they will be assured of at least temporary incarceration of their abuser, other victims who do

---

Criminology 449, 451-63 (1982); *see also* Battered Women 13 (D. Moore ed., 1979).

[139] *See, e.g.*, *Town of Castle Rock, Colo. v. Gonzales*, 545 U.S. 748 (2005); *Watson v. City of Kansas City*, 857 F.2d 690 (10th Cir. 1988); *Balistreri v. Pacifica Police Dept.*, 901 F.2d 696 (9th Cir. 1988); *see also* Niji Jain, *Engendering Fairness in Domestic Violence Arrests: Improving Police Accountability Through the Equal Protection Clause*, 60 Emory L.J. 1011 (2011); Milena Shtelmakher, *Police Misconduct and Liability: Applying the State-Created Danger Doctrine to Hold Police Officers Accountable for Responding Inadequately to Domestic-Violence Situations*, 43 Loy. L.A. L. Rev. 1533 (2010); Schuerman, *Establishing a Tort Duty for Police Failure to Respond to Domestic Violence*, 34 Ariz. L. Rev. 355 (1992); Buzawa & Buzawa, Domestic Violence: The Criminal Justice Response 75 (1990); Niemi-Kiesilainen, *supra* note 134; Juthani, *Police Treatment of Domestic Violence and Sexual Abuse: Duty to Protect vs. Fourth Amendment Privacy Issue*, 59 N.Y.U. Ann. Surv. Am. L. 51 (2003); Hickman & Simpson, *Fair Treatment or Preferred Outcome? The Impact of Police Behavior on Victim Reports of Domestic Violence Incidents*, 37 Law & Soc'y Rev. 607 (2003); Symposium, *Bridging the Gaps in the Legal Response to Domestic Violence*, 14 Hastings Women's L.J. 1 (2003). *But see* Epstein, *Procedural Justice: Tempering the State's Response to Domestic Violence*, 43 Wm. & Mary L. Rev. 1843 (2002) (suggesting that those concerned with victims' safety must also address abusers' perceptions of fairness in order to increase their compliance with legal directives).

[140] *See, e.g.*, Hoctor, *Domestic Violence as a Crime Against the State: The Need for Mandatory Arrest in California*, 85 Cal. L. Rev. 643 (1997) (arguing that domestic violence is not simply an assault on a particular intimate partner, but it is an offense against the state as well); Sara R. Benson, *Failure to Arrest: A Pilot Study of Police Response to Domestic Violence in Rural Illinois*, 17 Am. U. J. Gender Soc. Pol'y & L. 685, 690 (2009) (observing that states enacted mandatory arrest laws hoping to deter future incidents of violence and to avoid liability for a failure to protect victims of domestic violence victims). *But see* Corsilles, *No-Drop Policies in the Prosecution of Domestic Violence Cases: Guarantee to Action or Dangerous Solution?*, 63 Fordham L. Rev. 853 (1994). *See also* Han, *Mandatory Arrest and No-Drop Policies: Victim Empowerment in Domestic Violence Cases*, 23 B.C. Third World L.J. 159 (2003); Ko, *Civil Restraining Orders for Domestic Violence: The Unresolved Question of "Efficacy,"* 11 S. Cal. Interdisc. L.J. 361 (2002).

[141] *See, e.g.*, *Developments in the Law: Legal Responses to Domestic Violence*, 106 Harv. L. Rev. 1528, 1537-38 (1993).

not want their batterer arrested may be discouraged from calling the police.[142] In addition, when arrest is mandatory, women who strike their batterers in self-defense risk being arrested along with, or instead of, their abusers. Instructing police officers to arrest only the primary physical aggressor may alleviate the problems associated with dual arrests, but it is not always so easy to determine whom that is, particularly if spousal abuse is on-going. Some criminologists also have questioned whether arrest alone actually deters future battering.[143] But other observers urge the adoption of more, rather than less, vigorous law enforcement strategies, including a commitment to arrest, prosecution, and more severe sentencing practices.[144]

Until the mid-1990s, legal efforts to combat domestic violence took place almost exclusively at the state and local level, and federal involvement was limited to providing modest amounts of funding for battered women's shelters and other victim services. In 1994, however, Congress enacted a major domestic violence initiative — the Violence Against Women Act (VAWA).[145] VAWA contains a wide range of provisions designed to enhance the enforcement of laws against domestic violence. In particular, VAWA's funding provisions encourage states to implement mandatory arrest or pro-arrest policies, and coordinate the enforcement, prosecution, and judicial responsibility for domestic violence cases.[146]

---

[142] *Id.* at 1538.

[143] *See, e.g.*, Sherman, *The Influence of Criminology on Criminal Law: Evaluating Arrests for Misdemeanor Domestic Violence*, 83 J. Crim. L. & Criminology 1 (1992) (discussing various studies); *see also* Jane Aiken & Katherine Goldwasser, *The Perils of Empowerment*, 20 Cornell J.L. & Pub. Pol'y 139 (2010) (arguing that norm changing strategies that make communities "interested third part[ies]" rather than "bystander[s]" to domestic violence are more likely to reduce domestic violence).

[144] *See, e.g.*, Lerman, *The Decontextualization of Domestic Violence*, 83 J. Crim. L. & Criminology 217 (1992); Mitchell, *Contemporary Police Practice in Domestic Violence Cases: Arresting the Abuser: Is It Enough?*, 83 J. Crim. L. & Criminology 241 (1992). *But see* Hanna, *No Right to Choose: Mandated Victim Participation in Domestic Violence Prosecutions*, 109 Harv. L. Rev. 1849 (1996).

[145] Violence Against Women Act of 1994, Pub. L. No. 103-322, 108 Stat 1796 (reauthorized as a part of the Victims of Trafficking and Violence Protection Act of 2000, 22 U.S.C. §§ 7101-10 (2006), funding law enforcement, civil legal services, and shelter services for victims of violence and again in 2006 (Pub. L. No. 109-162, 119 Stat. 2960) to provide increased funding for legal services, medical services, and housing options for other categories of victims, like elderly victims and disabled victims). Although not reauthorized as of July 30, 2012, funding for VAWA programming is annually reauthorized in appropriations bills. *See* 158 Cong. Rec. S2762 (daily ed. Apr. 26, 2012) (statement of Sen. Grassley), *available at* http://www.gpo.gov/fdsys/pkg/CREC-2012-04-26/pdf/CREC-2012-04-26-pt1-PgS2761-2.pdf ("First, I hope a consensus version of the Violence Against Women Act will be reauthorized. If a consensus bill doesn't pass, no rights of women or anyone else will be affected if the bill does not pass because, contrary to the statements made, there would be no cutbacks of services. The Violence Against Women Act — the bill before us — is an authorization bill only, not an appropriations bill. This bill does not allow the expenditure of one dime because that result occurs through the appropriations process. Appropriators can and will fund the Violence Against Women Act programs regardless of whether this bill is reauthorized. This is exactly what happened over the past year."); Russell Berman, *Boehner names GOP conferees on stalled Violence Against Women Act*, July 30, 2012, *available at* http://thehill.com/homenews/house/241053-boehner-names-gop-conferees-on-long-stalled-violence-against-women-act.

[146] *See generally* Goldfarb, *The Civil Rights Remedy of the Violence Against Women Act: Legislative History, Policy Implications and Litigation Strategy*, 4 J. Law & Policy 391 (1996); Norse, *Where Violence, Relationship, and Equality Meet: The Violence Against Women's Act Civil Rights Remedy*, 11 Wis. Women's L.J. 1, 13 (1996).

VAWA also established several new federal causes of action. First, the Act creates a new federal crime of interstate domestic violence, which punishes a person who travels across a state line with the intent of injuring, harassing, or intimidating a spouse or intimate partner, and who commits a crime of violence in the course of, or as a result of, such interstate travel.[147] The Act also criminalizes travel across a state line with the intent to engage in conduct that violates the provisions of a protection order,[148] and (until invalidated by the United States Supreme Court) allows a person victimized by gender-motivated violence to obtain injunctive and monetary relief, including both compensatory and punitive damages from the perpetrator of the violence.[149]

A number of commentators, however, have criticized VAWA's civil rights remedy as unnecessary and inconsistent with federalism principles. Opponents of the VAWA remedies have argued that defining gender-motivated violence as a civil rights violation raises serious questions about the federal courts' capacity to manage their caseload, the need for federalization of a traditional state responsibility, and the appropriate role that federal courts should play. They have voiced specific concerns regarding the "overfederalization" of domestic violence crimes, and the ability of federal law enforcement to do "the kind of on-site policing that the federal system has never been very good at."[150]

The courts have agreed with this criticism of VAWA. In the case of *Brzonkala v. Virginia Polytechnical Institute and State University*,[151] a former university student brought a VAWA action against other students who allegedly raped her. The United States Court of Appeals for the Fourth Circuit found that the civil rights remedy contained in VAWA was unconstitutional because Congress exceeded its powers under the Commerce Clause, and Section 5 of the Fourteenth Amendment.[152] The United States Supreme Court subsequently affirmed this ruling in *U.S. v. Morrison*,[153] which held that "(1) [the] Commerce Clause did not

---

[147] 18 U.S.C. § 2261 (2011).

[148] 18 U.S.C. § 2265 (2011).

[149] *See* 42 U.S.C. §§ 13701, 13981 (2011) (invalidated in *U.S. v. Morrison*, 529 U.S. 598 (2000)). *See, e.g., U.S. v. Helem*, 186 F.3d 449 (4th Cir. 1999).

[150] *See, e.g.*, Brassler, *The Federalization of Domestic Violence: An Exercise in Cooperative Federalism or A Misallocation of Federal Judicial Resources?*, 48 Rutgers L. Rev. 1139, 1141-42 (1996); Kadish, *The Folly of Overfederalization*, 46 Hastings L.J. 1247, 1249 (1995). At a Congressional hearing, Representative Neal Smith shared Chief Justice William Rehnquist's remarks in a Congressional hearing, quoting Rehnquist as criticizing VAWA's private right of action is "so sweeping that it could involve the federal courts in a whole host of domestic disputes." 138 Cong. Rec. E746, E747746, 747 (Mar. 19, 1992).

[151] *Brzonkala v. Virginia Polytechnic Inst. and State University*, 169 F.3d 820 (4th Cir. 1999) (en banc).

[152] *Id.* This decision has been criticized in that the Fourth Circuit's opinion, which concluded that gender-based violence is "too remote" both from interstate commerce and state action to give Congress authority to act under the Commerce Clause or Section Five of the Fourteenth Amendment, has been criticized as "rest[ing] on an unwarranted adherence to traditional notions of privacy that are damaging to women." *See, e.g.*, Goldfarb, *Violence Against Women and the Persistence of Privacy*, 61 Ohio St. L.J. 1 (2000).

[153] *U.S. v. Morrison*, 529 U.S. 598, 598 (2000) (Christy Brzonkala, Petitioner). *But see* Resnick, *The Programmatic Judiciary: Lobbying, Judging, and Invalidating the Violence Against Women Act*, 74 S.

provide Congress with [the] authority to enact the civil remedy provision of VAWA," and "(2) [the] enforcement clause of [the] Fourteenth Amendment did not provide Congress with [the] authority to enact" the civil remedy provision of VAWA either.

Another legal problem relating to spousal abuse is whether or not a battered wife who subsequently kills her husband should be allowed to raise as a defense, or to mitigate a sentence, "battered women's syndrome" which produces severe stress and anxiety. Not surprisingly, the courts have split on this controversial issue.[154]

Although domestic violence is difficult to measure, various studies suggest that it is an extensive problem, and one that strikes American families regardless of their economic class, race, national origin, or educational background.[155] Most commentators agree that those domestic abuse victims who do identify themselves are only the tip of the iceberg.[156] As will be discussed in the next sections, "domestic violence often co-occurs with physical and sexual child abuse."[157] [158]

Cal. L. Rev. 269 (2000); Block, *The Strange Career of VAWA: Chief Justice Rehnquist and the Shift from "Political" to "Constitutional" Federalism*, 16 J. Law & Pol'y 499 (2000); Anderson, *Women Do Not Report the Violence They Suffer: Violence against Women and the State Action Doctrine*, 46 Vill. L. Rev. 907 (2001) (all critical of the *Morrison* decision).

[154] *Compare Hawthorne v. State*, 408 So. 2d 801 (Fla. Dist. Ct. App. 1982), *Smith v. State*, 277 S.E.2d 678 (Ga. 1981), *and State v. Anaya*, 438 A.2d 892 (Me. 1981) (all admitting such evidence), *with State v. Griffiths*, 610 P.2d 522 (Idaho 1980), *People v. White*, 414 N.E.2d 196 (Ill. App. Ct. 1980) *and State v. Thomas*, 423 N.E.2d 137 (Ohio 1981) (refusing to admit such evidence). *See also* Meszaros, *Achieving Peace of Mind: The Benefits of Neurobiological Evidence for Battered Women Defendants*, 23 Yale J.L. & Feminism 117 (2011); Note, *The Use of Expert Testimony in the Defense of Battered Women*, 52 Colo. L. Rev. 587 (1981); Note, *Does Wife Abuse Justify Homicide*, 24 Wayne L. Rev. 1705 (1978); Note, *Partially Determined Imperfect Self-Defense: The Battered Wife Kills and Tells Why*, 34 Stan. L. Rev. 615 (1982). *But see* Dowd, *Dispelling the Myths about the "Battered Woman's Syndrome": Toward a New Understanding*, 19 Fordham Urb. L.J. 567 (1992); Lenkevich, *Admitting Expert Testimony on Battered Woman Syndrome in Virginia Courts*, 6 Wm. & Mary J. Women & L. 297 (1999) (analyzing self-defense law in Virginia before and after *Peeples v. Commonwealth*); Orr, *Weland v. State and the Battered Spouse Syndrome: The Toothless Tigress Can Now Roar*, 2 Fla. Coastal L.J. 125 (2000) (concluding that Florida women can now assert the battered women defense when they use deadly force against a batterer).

[155] *See generally* Catalano, *supra* note 122.

[156] *See generally* National Coalition Against Domestic Violence, *Domestic Violence Facts* (2007); Truman, *National Crime Victimization Survey: Criminal Victimization*, 2010 (U.S. Department of Justice 2011); U.S. Commission on Civil Rights, Battered Women: Issues of Public Policy (1978); Domestic Violence: The Changing Criminal Justice Response (Buzawa & Buzawa eds., 2003).

[157] Lyon & Mechanic, *Domestic Violence and Child Protection: Confronting the Dilemmas in Moving From Family Court to Dependency Court*, *in* Handbook of Children, Culture & Violence 29-30 (Dowd et al., eds., Sage Press 2006) ("One review of 31 studies spanning over two decades found a median co-occurrence of 40% between domestic violence and child physical abuse."); *see also* Bragg, *Child Protection in Families Experiencing Domestic Violence* 7 (U.S. Department of Health and Human Services 2003), *available at* http://www.childwelfare.gov/pubs/usermanuals/domesticviolence/ domesticviolence.pdf.

[158] *See generally* U.S. Commission on Civil Rights, Battered Women: Issues of Public Policy (1978); Domestic Violence: The Changing Criminal Justice Response (Buzawa & Buzawa ed. 1992).

[B] Child Abuse

Child abuse and neglect[159] has always existed in the United States, but important articles regarding battered children written by concerned physicians in the 1960s[160] brought widespread public attention to this serious and continuing problem.[161] Consequently, child abuse and neglect remedial statutes and protective services now exist in all states. Since child abuse generally occurs in the privacy of the family home,[162] these legal remedies can only become effective when evidence of the child's mistreatment comes to light through child abuse reporting acts adopted in all fifty states.[163]

What counts as child abuse or neglect varies from state to state,[164] but generally child abuse and neglect will encompass physical abuse, sexual abuse, emotional abuse (including medical neglect), and failure to educate or supervise a child.[165]

---

[159] Child abuse and neglect has been defined broadly in some states as consisting of physical injury, sexual abuse, or mistreatment. *See, e.g.* Ala. Code 1975 § 26-14-1 (2011). Other state statutes are more specific, defining child abuse as any physical injury inflicted on a child by other than accidental means including, but not limited to severe bruising, lacerations, fractured bones, burns, internal injuries, sexual intercourse on contact, or any other injury constituting great bodily harm. *See, e.g.*, Wis. Stat. Ann. § 48.981 (2011).

[160] *See* Kempe, et al., *The Battered Child Syndrome*, 181 JAMA 17 (1962); C. Kempe & R. Helfer, The Battered Child (3d ed. 1980); *see also* Diana Russell, The Secret Trauma: Incest in the Lives of Girls and Women (1986); Gelles & Cornell, *supra* note 119, at 33-35.

[161] *See, e.g.*, Davis, *Child Abuse: A Pervasive Problem of the 80s*, 61 N.D.L. Rev. 193 (1985); Meyers, *The Legal Response to Child Abuse: In the Best Interests of Children?*, 24 J. Fam. L. 149 (1986).

[162] *See* Wilson, *The Cradle of Abuse: Evaluating the Danger Posed by a Sexually Predatory Parent to the Victim's Siblings*, 51 Emory L.J. 242 (2002); Wilson, *Children at Risk: The Sexual Exploitation of Female Children After Divorce*, 86 Cornell L. Rev. 253 (2011).

[163] Child Welfare Information Gateway, *Mandatory Reporters of Child Abuse and Neglect: Summary of State Laws* (U.S. Department of Health and Human Services 2010), *available at* http://www.childwelfare.gov/systemwide/laws_policies/statutes/manda.pdf. *Compare* Va. Code Ann. § 63.2-1509 (2011) (certain enumerated persons, including physicians, nurses, teachers, and law enforcement officials must report suspected child abuse; and any other person may report suspected child abuse), *with* Md. Code Ann., Fam. Law § 5-705 (2011) (mandatory reporting requirements are expanded to include all persons). *See also* Weithorn, *Protecting Children from Exposure to Domestic Violence: The Use and Abuse of Child Mistreatment Statutes*, 53 Hastings L.J. 1 (2001) (urging new collaborative relationships between child protection and domestic violence agencies); *Smith v. M.D.*, 130 Cal. Rptr. 2d 315 (Ct. App. 2003) (holding that the state Child Abuse and Neglect Reporting Act does not apply to minor children who report their own sexual abuse).

[164] Child Welfare Information Gateway, *Definitions of Child Abuse and Neglect* (U.S. Department of Health and Human Services 2011), *available at* http://www.childwelfare.gov/systemwide/laws_policies/statutes/define.pdf.

[165] Haralambie, *supra* note 56, at § 12:1; Wilson, *The Cradle of Abuse*, *supra* note 175, at 283 (noting how restrictive definitions of emotional abuse are, which "permit jurisdiction over children 'at substantial risk of suffering severe emotional damage' but only if 'evidenced by severe anxiety, depression, withdrawal, or untoward aggressive behavior toward self or others' "). For a helpful chart showing kinds of maltreatment, see Sedlak, et al., *Fourth National Incidence Study of Child Abuse and Neglect (NIS-4): Report to Congress*, Table 2.1: Typology for Classifying Alleged Maltreatment (U.S. Department of Health and Human Services, Administration for Children and Families 2010), *available at* http://www.acf.hhs.gov/programs/opre/abuse_neglect/natl_incid/reports/natl_incid/nis4_report_congress_full_pdf_jan2010.pdf.

Some have argued for even more expansive definitions of neglect.[166]

The number of child abuse and neglect reports is significant. The Fourth National Incidence Study of Child Abuse and Neglect (NIS-4), "the last congressionally mandated, periodic effort of the United States Department of Health and Human Services . . . [to give] updated estimates of the incidence of child abuse and neglect in the United States," found that CPS "investigated the maltreatment of only 32% of children who experienced Harm Standard maltreatment and of 43% of those whose maltreatment fit the Endangerment Standard."[167] Many child abuse reports come from professionals, including educators, law enforcement and justice officials, medical and mental health professionals, social service professionals, and child care providers. Although nearly two-thirds of all reports to CPS agencies in 2009 were not "substantiated," over 700,000 children were victims of substantiated child maltreatment in 2009.[168]

For some children, state intervention comes too late. According to the NIS-4, an estimated 1,256,600 children experienced maltreatment during 2005-06,[169] or one child in every 58 in the United States.[170] Forty-four percent, or an estimated 553,300 children, were abused; 61% or an estimated 771,700 children were neglected; 58% experienced physical abuse or approximately 323,000 children; 24%, or an estimated 135,300 children, were sexually abused; and 27%, or an estimated 148,500 children, were emotionally abused.[171] Among children who were neglected, nearly one-half of neglected children "experienced educational neglect (46% of neglected children, or an estimated 360,500 children), more than one-third were physically neglected (38%, or an estimated 295,300 children), and one-fourth were

---

[166] James G. Dwyer, *No Place for Children: Addressing Urban Blight and its Impact on Children Through Child Protection Law, Domestic Relations Law and "Adult-Only" Residential Zoning*, 62 Ala. L. Rev. 887 (2011) (suggesting that housing a child in a very unhealthy and dangerous neighborhood constitutes neglect).

[167] Sedlak et al., *Fourth National Incidence Study of Child Abuse and Neglect (NIS-4): Report to Congress* (U.S. Department of Health and Human Services, Administration for Children and Families 2010), *available at* http://www.acf.hhs.gov/programs/opre/abuse_neglect/natl_incid/reports/natl_incid/nis4_report_congress_full_pdf_jan2010.pdf.

[168] Administration on Children, Youth, and Families, Children's Bureau, *Child Maltreatment 2009* (U.S. Department of Health and Human Services 2010). *See also* English et al., *Factors That Influence the Decision Not to Substantiate a CPS Referral Phase II: Mail and Telephone Surveys of Child Protective Services Social Workers*, 72 Table 28 (showing that an unsubstantiated CPS referral is not same as a false referral) (Department of Social and Health Services, Children's Administration 2002).

[169] Measured by the stringent Harm Standard definition, which "generally requires that an act or omission result in demonstrable harm in order to be classified as abuse or neglect." Sedlak et al., *Fourth National Incidence Study of Child Abuse and Neglect (NIS-4): Report to Congress, Executive Summary* 3 (U.S. Department of Health and Human Services, Administration for Children and Families 2010), *available at* http://www.acf.hhs.gov/programs/opre/abuse_neglect/natl_incid/reports/nis_execsumm/nis4_report_exec_summ_pdf_jan2010.pdf.

[170] Sedlak et al., *Fourth National Incidence Study of Child Abuse and Neglect (NIS-4): Report to Congress, Executive Summary* 5 (U.S. Department of Health and Human Services, Administration for Children and Families 2010), *available at* http://www.acf.hhs.gov/programs/opre/abuse_neglect/natl_incid/reports/nis_execsumm/nis4_report_exec_summ_pdf_jan2010.pdf.

[171] *Id.*

emotionally neglected (25%, an estimated 193,400 children)."[172]

Child abuse reporting acts generally provide that certain designated persons such as physicians, nurses, teachers, social workers, childcare workers, and law enforcement officials have an affirmative duty to report any suspected child abuse or neglect to the proper state authorities.[173] Any other person who suspects that a child is abused or neglected may also make a complaint, and such a person is normally immune from any civil or criminal liability if the complaint was made in good faith.[174]

Every state child abuse statute also provides for the establishment of CPS agencies, which may investigate allegations of abuse and neglect. They further allow a protective service worker, law enforcement official, or physician to take a child into protective custody for a certain period of time, without prior approval of the parents, whenever the circumstances of the child are such that remaining with the parent, or person responsible for the child's care, appears to present an imminent danger to the child's life or health.[175]

Such removal proceedings are referred to as proceedings for dependency, children in need of protective services (CHIPS), children in need of care (CINC), or children in need of assistance (CINA).[176]

A number of remedies are available to the court following an adjudication of dependency, including: leaving the child with his or her parents subject to supervision; placing the child in the custody of a relative or another suitable person; placing the child in a foster home; placing the child with a state agency; or committing the child to a state institution.[177] In cases of abuse within a family, some jurisdictions also explicitly authorize removal of the alleged offender from the

---

[172] *Id.* at 6 (under an Endangerment Standard of maltreatment, nearly 3 million children, or one in 25 children, experienced maltreatment in 2005-06 in the United States).

[173] Haralambie, *supra* note 56, at App. 17-1 (reprinting the American Medical Association Diagnostic and Treatment Guidelines on Child Physical Abuse and Neglect, which indicate that "Physicians and other professionals providing services to children are required by state law to report suspected incidents of child abuse and neglect").

[174] Social workers responding to a report also receive immunity in a number of jurisdictions when acting upon "an objectively reasonable suspicion of abuse." Wilson, *Sexually Predatory Parents and the Children in Their Care: Remove the Threat, Not the Child, in* Handbook of Children, Culture & Violence 47 (Nancy Dowd, Dorothy Singer & Robin Fretwell Wilson, eds. 2006).

[175] *See, e.g., State v. Poehnelt*, 722 P.2d 304 (Ariz. 1985); *People v. Schwartz*, 678 P.2d 1000 (Colo. 1984) (holding that child abuse reporting obligations generally take precedence over the physician/patient privilege); *see also* Mosteller, *Child Abuse Reporting Laws and Attorney Client Confidence: The Reality and the Specter of Lawyer as Informant*, 42 Duke L.J. 203 (1992).

[176] Haralambie, *supra* note 56, at § 12:1.

[177] Haralambie, *supra* note 56, at § 12:30. *See, e.g., In re D.D.*, 653 N.W.2d 359 (Iowa, 2002) (two siblings were found to be Children in Need of Assistance requiring continued court supervision based upon evidence of sexual misconduct by the father toward daughter and her friend); *In re T.S.*, 74 P.3d 1009 (Kan. 2003) (court ordered placement of child with his father upon determination that child was in need of care after a sibling was found dead of hypothermia at the mother's residence); *In re Andrew A.*, 815 A.2d 931 (Md. Ct. App. 2003) (the actual neglect of an infant is not needed under Maryland law since the state statute recognizes that a finding can be based upon a "substantial risk of harm").

home, rather than the child.[178]

Once the state takes a child into protective custody, it then acquires an affirmative obligation to look after that child's safety.[179] However, in the controversial case of *DeShaney v. Winnebago County*,[180] the United States Supreme Court held that there was no state liability when a child was *not* taken into state custody, even though a state social worker had feared for the child's life if he remained with his father at home.[181]

A parent still has the legal right to discipline his or her child for misbehavior,[182] but child abuse statutes become applicable in cases of excessive punishment and overly severe discipline.[183]

Conversely, the non-offending parent who is able to prevent an injury to his or her child, but fails to do so, may also be guilty of child abuse and neglect.[184] For example, in *Smith v. State*,[185] a mother watched as her boyfriend drowned, kicked, and beat her four-year-old son Eric to death because Eric could not correctly spell the word "butterfly." Although she repeatedly pleaded for the boyfriend to stop, he did not respond. At her trial on child abuse and manslaughter charges, the mother's attorney argued that she was meek, timid, and dependent on her boyfriend, and was therefore unable to stop him. However, the court held that the mother had a duty to remove her child from any situation of danger; she had knowingly placed her son in that situation, and allowed him to remain in it. The mother was therefore convicted of child abuse and manslaughter.[186]

---

[178] Wilson, *supra* note 187 (discussing Hawaii, Kentucky, Maine, New York, Tennessee, Texas, and Guam). *See also, e.g.*, 19 Guam Code Ann. § 13316 (2011); N.Y. Fam. Ct. Act § 842 (2011).

[179] *See, e.g., Vonner v. State Dep't of Pub. Welfare*, 273 So. 2d 252 (La. 1973) (state agency was held vicariously liable when a foster child was beaten to death by the foster mother); *Doe v. New York City Dep't of Soc. Services*, 709 F.2d 782 (2d Cir. 1983) (state agency was liable under 42 U.S.C. § 1983 for negligently failing to supervise plaintiff child's placement in a foster home where she was sexually abused). *But see Langton v. Maloney*, 527 F. Supp. 538 (D. Conn. 1981) (state social workers are entitled to a good faith immunity in civil rights actions if they acted in good faith, both objectively and subjectively). *See e.g.*, Marcus, *The Neglectful Parens Patriae: Using Child Protective Laws to Defend the Safety Net*, 30 N.Y.U. Rev. L. & Soc. Change 255 (2006); Dine, *Protecting Those Who Cannot Protect Themselves: State Liability for Violation of Foster Children's Right to Safety*, 38 Cal. W. L. Rev 507 (2002).

[180] 489 U.S. 189 (1989).

[181] *Id.*

[182] *See supra* § 7.03.

[183] *See, e.g., In re Edward C.*, 178 Cal. Rptr. 694 (Cal. Ct. App. 1981) (religion cannot be used as a justification for excessive discipline that jeopardizes the health or safety of a child); *State v. Campbell*, 306 N.W.2d 272 (Wis. 1981) (throwing a baby against a wall constituted child abuse, even though no injury was alleged in the complaint); *see also supra* § 7.05 (summarizing faith-based exceptions to child abuse and neglect laws).

[184] Haralambie, *supra* note 56, at § 16:2 ("If a parent is unwilling or unable to protect the child from the sexual abuse, that parent contributes to the child's risk. [CPS] workers often remove children from their homes when the non-abusing parent does not protect the child."). At least as to sexual abuse, most non-offending mothers never knew of the abuse and most are "very" or "mostly" protective once they find out. Wilson, *supra* note 187, at 39, 44.

[185] 408 N.E.2d 614, 617 (Ind. Ct. App. 1980).

[186] *Id. See also State v. Williams*, 670 P.2d 122 (N.M. 1983) (even if a mother could not stop her

In many instances of domestic violence in the family, a child witnesses the abuse of a parent. It is estimated that between "10 and 20% of all children are at risk for exposure to domestic violence."[187] Such witnessing "may form the basis for a 'failure to protect' petition before the juvenile court that hears dependency cases."[188]

Finally, should drug or alcohol abuse by a pregnant woman constitute child abuse when the child is born addicted to drugs or is born with fetal alcohol syndrome?[189] Although some courts have held that the word "child" in child abuse and child endangerment statutes does not include an unborn child or fetus,[190] other courts have found that an unborn child is indeed a "person" under the Child Abuse Act,[191] or that the parent's substance abuse is probative of future neglect[192] and therefore that such a child therefore has a legal right to begin life with a sound mind and body under the protection of the state.[193] Some states child abuse

---

husband from beating their daughter, that did not prevent her from seeking help, and therefore the mother could be convicted of child abuse); *Commonwealth v. Cardwell*, 515 A.2d 311 (Pa. Super. Ct. 1986) (a mother was guilty of child abuse when she was aware that the husband had sexually abused the child over a period of time, and she took only feeble and ineffective actions to protect the child); *State ex rel J.W.*, 779 So. 2d 961 (La. Ct. App. 2001) (holding that the state had sufficient reason to find children in need of care after a mother's boyfriend had beaten her youngest child to death); *In re Jam J.*, 825 A.2d 902 (D.C. 2003) (in this case, a trial court correctly found that a mother neglected her children by not protecting them from her abusive boyfriend; but since the trial court judge did not allow the mother or boyfriend to examine the children, nor allow the children to testify, perhaps outside the presence of the mother and boyfriend, these neglect findings were vacated on procedural grounds). Failure to protect claims against non-offending parents is very controversial. *See* Cahn, *Child Witnessing of Domestic Violence*, *in* Handbook of Children, Culture, and Violence (Nancy Dowd, Dorothy Singer & Robin Fretwell Wilson, eds. 2006).

[187] Cahn, *supra* note 199.

[188] *Id.* at 11. *See also*, Child Welfare Information Gateway, *Child Witnesses to Domestic Violence: Summary of State Laws* (U.S. Department of Health and Human Services 2009), *available at* http://www.childwelfare.gov/systemwide/laws_policies/statutes/witnessdvall.pdf.

[189] Haralambie, *supra* note 56, at § 18:2 ("Prenatal drug and alcohol exposure may constitute physical neglect, at least once the child is born."); *See generally* James G. Hodge, Annotation, *Prosecution of Mother for Prenatal Substance Abuse Based on Endangerment of or Delivery of Controlled Substance to Child*, 70 A.L.R.5th 461 (1999).

[190] *See, e.g., Reyes v. Superior Court*, 141 Cal. Rptr. 912 (Cal. Ct. App. 1977); *see also In re Unborn Child of Starks*, 18 P.3d 342 (Okla. 2001) (holding that a fetus, whether viable or nonviable, did not fall under the definition of a child under Oklahoma's Children in Need of Supervision statute, so a trial court lacked jurisdiction to take custody of the fetus after the mother had been arrested for methamphetamine use); *Reinesto v. Superior Court of State In and For County of Navajo*, 894 P.2d 733 (Ariz. Ct. App. 1995) (fetus not considered a child for purpose of abuse statute).

[191] *See, e.g., State v. McKnight*, 576 S.E.2d 168 (S.C. 2003); *Matter of Smith*, 492 N.Y.S.2d 331 (N.Y. Fam. Ct. 1985); *see also* La. Child Code Ann. art. 603(16) (2008) ("Neglect includes prenatal neglect.").

[192] *In re Troy D.*, 215 Cal. App. 3d 889 (1989).

[193] *See, e.g., Matter of Baby X*, 293 N.W.2d 736 (Mich. Ct. App. 1980); *Whitner v. State*, 492 S.E.2d 777 (S.C. 1977), *cert. denied*, 523 U.S. 1145 (1998); Nev. Rev. Stat. § 432B.330(4) (2008) ("[C]hild may be in need of protection if he is identified as being affected by prenatal illegal substance abuse or as having withdrawal symptoms resulting from prenatal drug exposure."). *But see State ex rel. Angela M.W. v. Kruzicki*, 561 N.W.2d 729 (Wis. 1997) (dismissing protective custody of mother). *See generally* Denison, Note, *The Efficacy and Constitutionality of Criminal Punishment for Maternal Substance Abuse*, 64 S. Cal. L. Rev. 1103 (1991); Barrett, Note, *Prosecuting Pregnant Addicts for Dealing to the Unborn*, 33 Ariz. L. Rev. 221 (1991); Smith & Dabiri, *Prenatal Drug Exposure: The Constitutional Implications of*

statutes explicitly encompass prenatal exposure to both illegal and legal drugs as grounds for reporting or removal.[194] There is a longstanding controversy over whether to prosecute a mother for homicide when a fetus is killed through tortious criminal behavior.[195]

[C] Spousal Rape

Under a common law rule, which is still the law in many states,[196] a husband who forcibly rapes his wife could not be prosecuted for that crime.[197] The origin of this common law rule dates back to unsupported dicta of Lord Hale, who was Chief

---

Three Governmental Approaches, 2 Seton Hall Const. L.J. 53 (1991); Oberman, *Sex, Drugs, Pregnancy, and the Law: Rethinking the Problems of Pregnant Women Who Use Drugs*, 43 Hastings L.J. 505 (1992).

Some commentators have argued that the state should intervene more aggressively before birth, to protect a developing fetus from serious or well-defined dangers. *See, e.g.*, Chan, *S.O.S. From the Womb: A Call for New York Legislation Criminalizing Drug Use During Pregnancy*, 21 Fordham Urb. L.J. 199 (1993); Dougherty, *The Right to Begin Life With Sound Body and Mind: Fetal Patients and Their Mothers*, 63 U. Det. L. Rev. 89 (1985). Some courts have criticized trial courts for acting too precipitously. *See, e.g.*, *T.H. v. Dep't of Health & Rehabilitative Services*, 661 So. 2d 403 (Fla. Dist. Ct. App. 1995) (rejecting bi-monthly precautionary drug testing of mother pregnant with an adjudicated dependent child). Some recent medical studies suggest that long-term effects on children of prenatal exposure to cocaine may be less devastating than previously believed. *See* Schempf, Illicit Drug Use and Neonatal Outcomes: a Critical Review, 62(11) Obstetrical & Gynecological Survey (2007) (reviewing the epidemiologic literature on the neonatal impact of marijuana, opiate, and cocaine use and finding cocaine use is most consistently related to fetal growth decrements and dose-response effects but faulting studies for largely failing to control for associated social, psychosocial, and contextual factors). Evidence continues to mount that maternal alcohol abuse during pregnancy poses a significant threat to the health and well-being of a developing fetus. *See, e.g.*, U.S. Department of Commerce, *Fetal Alcohol Syndrome — Diagnosis, Epidemiology, Prevention, and Treatment* (1996); *See, e.g.*, P.K. Jaudes, E. Ekwo, J. Van Voorhis, Association of Drug Abuse and Child Abuse, 19/9 Child Abuse & Neglect 1065 (1995).

Other commentators have expressed concern that most women who have been prosecuted for using drugs during pregnancy have been poor and women of color. *See, e.g.*, Roberts, *Representing Race: Unshackling Black Motherhood*, 95 Mich. L. Rev. 938 (1997); Roberts, *Punishing Drug Addicts Who Have Babies: Women of Color, Equality, and the Right to Privacy*, 104 Harv. L. Rev. 1419 (1991).

[194] Me. Rev. Stat. Ann. tit. 22, § 4004-B (2008) ("[D]epartment shall act to protect infants born identified as being affected by illegal substance abuse or suffering from withdrawal symptoms resulting from prenatal drug exposure, whether or not the prenatal exposure was to legal or illegal drugs, regardless of whether or not the infant is abused or neglected."); Me. Rev. Stat. Ann tit. 22 § 4011-B(1) (2008) ("[H]ealth care provider involved in the delivery or care of an infant who the provider knows or has reasonable cause to suspect has been born affected by illegal substance abuse or is suffering from withdrawal symptoms resulting from prenatal drug exposure, whether or not the prenatal exposure was to legal or illegal drugs, shall notify the department of that condition in the infant" but the statute "may not be construed to establish a definition of 'abuse' or 'neglect.'"). For a state-by-state analysis of parental drug use as child abuse, see Child Welfare Information Gateway, *Parental drug use as child abuse*, Dep't of HHS, Children's Bureau (2012), *available at* http://www.childwelfare.gov/systemwide/laws_policies/statutes/drugexposed.pdf.

[195] *See generally* Alan S. Wasserstrom, Annotation, *Homicide Based on Killing of Unborn Child*, 64 A.L.R.5th 671 (1998).

[196] Walsh, Annotation, *Criminal Responsibility of Husband for Rape, or Assault to Commit Rape, on Wife*, 24 A.L.R.4th 105 (1983).

[197] *See, e.g.*, *State v. Kennedy*, 616 P.2d 594 (Utah 1980). As of 2003, 24 states and the District of Columbia have abolished marital immunity for rape by statute. Anderson, *Marital Immunity, Intimate Relationships, and Improper Inferences: A New Law on Sexual Offenses by Intimates*, 54 Hastings L.J. 1465, 1557 n.8 (Arkansas, Colorado, Delaware, Florida, Georgia, Indiana, Kentucky, Maine, Massachu-

Justice of the Court of King's Bench from 1671 to 1675. Lord Hale made an extrajudicial declaration that by consenting to marry, a wife grants consent to intercourse with her husband from "which she cannot retract."[198] Some commentators, however, have suggested that the marital rape exemption was derived from the traditional definition of rape as "unlawful" carnal knowledge without consent, while intercourse between a husband and wife is not unlawful, no matter what the surrounding circumstances may be.[199]

It was not until the early 1980s that the questionable reasoning behind this common law rule came under critical scrutiny by legal commentators[200] and by the courts, specifically in the landmark *Smith* and *Chretien* cases.[201] A growing number of states have followed the *Smith* and *Chretien* precedents, holding that an estranged wife can now unilaterally revoke her implied consent to marital sex when she has manifested her intent to terminate the marital relationship by living separate and apart from her husband, and when she conducts herself in a manner that establishes a *de facto* end to the marriage, even though the parties have not yet obtained a divorce.[202]

Many states, however, still prohibit prosecution of a husband for the rape of his wife while they are still living together.[203] At least six states permit prosecution of

---

setts, Missouri, Montana, Nebraska, New Hampshire, New Jersey, New Mexico, North Carolina, North Dakota, Oregon, Pennsylvania, Texas, Utah, Vermont, West Virginia, and Wisconsin). *See also, e.g.*, Ark. Code Ann. § 5-14-103 (2011); N.H. Rev. Stat. Ann. § 632-A:5 (2011). Case law in four other states provides that there is no marital exception to rape. *See, e.g.*, *Warren v. State*, 255 Ga. 151 (1985).

[198] 1 Hale, History of Pleas of the Crown 629 (1847).

[199] For example, Model Penal Code Section 213.1 still defines the act of rape as sexual intercourse between a male and a female "not his wife." *See also* Lafave, Criminal Law: Hornbook Series § 17.4(D) (5th ed. 2010); *People v. Liberta*, 64 N.Y.2d 152, 162 (1984) (discussing "the assumption . . . before the marital exemption was codified, that a man could not be guilty of raping his wife"); *Lane v. State*, 348 Md. 272 (1997) (holding that if parties continue to live together, the marital exemption applies to rape offenses unless actual force is used); Walsh, *supra* note 196, at 108-11.

[200] *See generally* Pracher, *The Marital Rape Exemption: A Violation of a Woman's Right to Privacy*, 11 Golden Gate U. L. Rev. 717 (1981); Bearrows, *Abolishing the Marital Exemption for Rape: A Statutory Proposal*, 1983 U. Ill. L. Rev. 201. *See also* Walsh, *supra* note 196.

[201] *See Smith v. State*, 426 A.2d 38 (N.J. 1981) (husband was convicted of raping his estranged wife when the parties were living separate and apart at the time of the attack); *Commonwealth v. Chretien*, 417 N.E.2d 1203 (Mass. 1981) (husband was convicted of raping his wife where the attack occurred after the wife had been granted an interlocutory divorce, but before entry of the final divorce decree).

[202] *See, e.g.*, *People v. Brown*, 632 P.2d 1025 (Colo. 1981); *Weishaupt v. Commonwealth*, 315 S.E.2d 847 (Va. 1984); *People v. Hawkins*, 407 N.W.2d 366 (Mich. 1987); *see also* Walsh, *supra* note 196. *But see State v. Getward*, 365 S.E.2d 209 (N.C. 1988).

[203] Walsh, *supra* note 196. As of 2011, courts in 23 states (Alabama, California, Colorado, Illinois, Indiana, Kansas, Louisiana, Maryland, Michigan, Missouri, Montana, Nevada, New Hampshire, New Mexico, New York, North Carolina, Oklahoma, Oregon, Pennsylvania, South Carolina, Texas, Utah, and West Virginia) have upheld the marital rape exemption. *Id.* at § 4[b]. *But see* Jessica Klarfeld, *A Striking Disconnect: Marital Rape Law's Failure To Keep Up With Domestic Violence Law*, 48 Am. Cr. L.R. 1819 (2011) (noting that "[a]lthough every state legislature has formally abolished its marital rape exemption, reminders of the exemption still remain in the statutory law of several states," in the form of "decreased sentences for the accused, proof of force and/or resistance, and shorter time frames by which a woman has to report a rape by her husband, ultimately making spousal rape more difficult to prosecute").

husbands who rape their wives during the marriage when living apart.[204] More than half the jurisdictions in the United States have abolished the marital rape exemption entirely and, therefore, recognize sexual assault of a spouse or intimate partner as a form of domestic violence.[205] However, as of 2011, 127 countries still do not consider marital rape a crime.[206]

§ 7.09   CHILDREN IN NEED OF SUPERVISION

Most states have enacted statutes dealing with so-called "status offenses" that normally involve children under the age of eighteen who habitually disobey and disregard their parents' lawful guidance and discipline, run away from home, or are habitually truant from school.[207] State legislation concerning such "ungovernable" children gives a court jurisdiction over their conduct, even though such conduct does not specifically amount to a violation of state criminal law. These state statutes dealing with Children in Need of Supervision (CHINS) therefore provide state support for parental authority over ungovernable children in non-criminal matters.[208] Some jurisdictions use alternate terms such as Minors Requiring Authoritative Intervention (MRAI)[209] or Person in Need of Supervision (PINS).[210]

Some commentators have criticized CHINS statutes for permitting all kinds of harmless conduct to be prosecuted by the courts, for often failing to investigate the underlying reasons behind the child's conduct, and for allowing the courts to deal ineffectively with ungovernable children when that role ought to be the responsibility of other community organizations.[211] In addition, commentators have criticized these statutes (as well as the juvenile system generally) for having a

---

[204] *See* Note, *Sexism and the Common Law: Spousal Rape in Virginia,* 8 Geo. Mason L. Rev. 369, 370 (1986). For example, Virginia's criminal statute provides that a person is guilty of rape if, by force, threat, or intimidation, he or she has sexual intercourse with his or her spouse against the spouse's will if, at the time of the offense, the spouses were living separate and apart, or the defendant caused serious physical injury to the spouse by the use of force or violence. Va. Code Ann. § 18.2-61 (B) (West 2011).

[205] *See generally* West, *Marital Rape, Equality, Theory and the Promise of the Fourteenth Amendment,* 42 Fla. L. Rev. 45 (1990); Schelong, *Domestic Violence and the State: Responses to and Rationales for Spousal Battering, Marital Rape, and Stalking,* 78 Marq. L. Rev. 79 (1994). *See., e.g.,* Anderson, *Marital Immunity, Intimate Relationships, and Improper Inferences: A New Law on Sexual Offenses by Intimates,* 54 Hastings L.J. 1465 (2003); Walsh, *supra* note 196.

[206] Bennhold, *In Norway, Gender Equality Does Not Extend to the Bedroom,* N.Y. Times, Oct. 24, 2011, *available at* http://www.nytimes.com/2011/10/25/world/europe/in-norway-gender-equality-does-not-extend-to-the-bedroom.html?_r=1&emc=eta1.

[207] *See generally,* Nancy E. Dowd, Justice for Kids: Keeping Kids Out of the Juvenile Justice System (2011).

[208] *See, e.g., L.A.M. v. State,* 547 P.2d 827 (Alaska 1976) (the purpose of CHINS is to vindicate the parents' right to custody to their child, and to protect the child against the harms resulting from running away or rejecting parental supervision); *see also* Gregory, *Juvenile Court Jurisdiction Over Noncriminal Behavior: The Argument Against Abolition,* 39 Ohio St. L.J. 242 (1978).

[209] 705 Ill. Comp. Stat. Ann. 405/3-3 (West 2012).

[210] N.Y. Fam. Ct. Act § 712(a) (McKinney 2010).

[211] *See, e.g.,* Rosenberg & Rosenberg, *The Legacy of the Stubborn and Rebellious Son,* 74 Mich. L. Rev. 1097 (1976); Note, *Ungovernability: The Unjustifiable Jurisdiction,* 83 Yale L.J. 1383 (1974).

disproportionate impact on minority youth.[212] Regardless of the criticisms, most state CHINS statutes have withstood constitutional attacks for their alleged vagueness and overbreadth.[213]

Generally speaking, a child under the age of 18 will be considered to be "beyond the control" of his or her parents or legal guardian, and classified as a minor in need of supervision under state CHINS statutes, if he is incorrigible, a frequent runaway, or his acts posed serious hazards to himself or others.[214] For example, in *In re Snyder*,[215] evidence that a minor was adamant about refusing to return home, had established a pattern of refusing to obey her parents, and on two occasions had fled her home, was sufficient to support a finding of loss of parental power and control, and subjecting the minor to state CHINS jurisdiction. But in *In re D.J.B.*,[216] the court held that, although evidence that a minor is beyond the control of his parents may be predicated on a single act if sufficiently serious, nevertheless evidence in this case that a minor left home without parental consent was not of such a nature as to be indicative of the loss of parental control.[217]

If a child is found to be in need of supervision under state CHINS jurisdiction, a number of remedies are available to the court including: leaving the child with his or her parents, with or without a protective order, or an order for medical or psychiatric treatment and counseling; placing the child on probation, or under the supervision of a social worker; placing the child in the custody of a relative or another suitable person; placing the child in a foster home; placing the child with a state agency; or committing the child to a state institution.[218] However, courts have disagreed on whether a child in need of supervision, as a status offender, should be

---

[212] *See, e.g.*, Gabriella Celeste & Patricia Puritz, *The Children Left Behind: An Assessment of Access to Counsel and Quality of Representation in Delinquency Proceedings in Louisiana*, 30 S.U. L. Rev. 395, 484-86 (2003) (citing statistics and anecdotal evidence of disparate impact); Scott R. Hechinger, *Juvenile Life Without Parole: An Antidote to Congress's One-Way Criminal Law Ratchet?*, 35 N.Y.U. Rev. L. & Soc. Change 408, 487-89 (2011) (citing statistics showing that minority youth are disproportionately serving life sentences without parole). *See generally* Dorothy Roberts, *Shattered Bonds: The Color of Child Welfare* (2002) (discussing the influence of race permeating America's child welfare system).

[213] *See, e.g., Blondheim v. State*, 529 P.2d 1096 (Wash. 1975).

[214] *See, e.g., In re Polovchak*, 454 N.E.2d 258, 263 (Ill. 1983) (citing examples of a frequent runaway, a minor beyond her parents' control, and a habitually truant minor).

[215] 532 P.2d 278 (Wash. 1975).

[216] 96 Cal. Rptr. 146 (Ct. App. 1971).

[217] *Compare Matter of Morrison*, 442 N.Y.S.2d 43 (N.Y. Fam. Ct. 1981) (repeated acts, or evidence of habitual conduct, is required to come within the statute), *with In re David S.*, 91 Cal. Rptr. 261 (Ct. App. 1970) (a single serious act, such as a 14-year-old boy running away 600 miles from home and attempting to cross the border into Mexico, may show that a child was beyond the control of his parents).

[218] *See* Clark, *supra* note 12, at 361-69; *see also In re Sonya LL.*, 53 A.D.3d 727 (N.Y. 3d Dep't 2008) (affirming Family Court's order placing the respondent in the custody of the Department of Social Services after a month in diversion program and provision of seven distinct services, including anger management, failed to change respondent's behavior and she continued to pose a threat to her mother); *In re Polovchak*, 97 Ill. 2d 212 (1983) (affirming lower court ruling that appellant minor was not "beyond the control" of his parents and thus did not qualify as a minor requiring authoritative intervention despite his refusal to return with his parents to their home in the Ukraine and ordering minor's release to his parents upon their return to the country).

placed in the same state institutions housing juvenile delinquents who have committed serious crimes.[219]

§ 7.10 FAMILY RIGHTS VERSUS INDIVIDUAL RIGHTS

Throughout this chapter, and throughout this text, there has been ample evidence of a dramatic and fundamental change in the way our society, and our courts, view the American family.[220] Traditionally, the American family unit was highly valued as the fundamental cornerstone of our society,[221] and state legislatures and courts were reluctant to intervene in family affairs on behalf of individual family members. Two basic reasons have been suggested for this traditional opposition to state intervention in family matters. First, many courts perceived that such intervention would be ineffective, and second, the specter of governmental intrusion should not invade the traditional right to family privacy, which had been so deeply ingrained in American social and legal consciousness.[222]

In 1965, the United States Supreme Court held that marital privacy was a constitutional right in *Griswold v. Connecticut*,[223] but this new constitutional right to marital privacy rapidly became not just a family right, but an individual right as well.[224]

Thus, according to Professor Jane Rutherford, despite the new commitment to the constitutional right to privacy, individualism prevailed when individualism and privacy conflicted, and the courts increasingly were willing to intrude on marital privacy rights to further the goal of individual independence.[225]

Professor Carl Schneider argues that the rise of individual legal rights over family rights means that when the law makes moral decisions, it now transfers them to individuals rather than to families, thus sustaining the image of the family as a

---

[219] *See, e.g., State ex rel. Harris v. Calendine*, 233 S.E.2d 318 (W. Va. 1977) (juvenile status offenders must be helped and not punished, and incarceration of status offenders in prison-like facilities along with children guilty of criminal conduct would inflict a constitutionally disproportionate penalty upon status offenders). *But see Vann v. Scott*, 467 F.2d 1235 (7th Cir. 1972) (applying Illinois law) (incarceration of runaway juveniles in training schools with delinquents who had committed serious crimes was not unconstitutional under a Illinois law which authorized a finding of delinquency whenever a minor violated a lawful court order).

[220] *But see* Jill Elaine Hasday, *The Canon of Family Law*, 57 Stan. L. Rev. 825, 834-48 (2004) (arguing that the differences between the common law regime and today are overstated); Vivian Hamilton, *Principles of U.S. Family Law*, 75 Fordham L. Rev. 31, 45 (2006) (arguing that "biblical traditionalism" remains a driving force on various family law issues).

[221] *See, e.g., Maynard v. Hill*, 125 U.S. 190, 205 (1888); *see also supra* §§ 1.02[A], 1.03.

[222] *See* Schneider, *Moral Discourse and the Transformation of the American Family*, 83 Mich. L. Rev. 1803, 1837-38 (1985).

[223] 381 U.S. 479 (1965) (overturning a Connecticut statute prohibiting contraceptives to married couples based upon a constitutional right to marital privacy).

[224] *See, e.g., Eisenstadt v. Baird*, 405 U.S. 438 (1972) (use of contraceptives by unmarried individuals); *Roe v. Wade*, 410 U.S. 113 (1973) (a woman's right to privacy of her body in abortion decisions).

[225] Rutherford, *Beyond Individual Privacy: A New Theory of Family Rights*, 39 U. Fla. L. Rev. 627, 636-37 (1987).

collection of discrete individuals rather than a unified family entity.[226] Moreover, a major problem involved with the fundamental right to privacy is that although most Americans believe that this right should exist, they do not all agree on exactly what should be included within this right. For example, Professor Robert Mnookin gives the illustration that liberals generally consider sexuality to be a private sphere, but view economics as a public sphere; whereas conservatives generally believe in private economic enterprise, yet favor regulation of such sexual matters as abortion and homosexuality.[227]

In an attempt to incorporate and synthesize the traditional view of family privacy rights with a more recent judicial emphasis on individual rights, Professor Rutherford persuasively argues for a new theory of family rights. This theory recognizes: (1) that fundamental family rights belong both to the family as a group, and to each individual family member; and (2) that when competing rights need to be accommodated, the rights of the objectively weaker party should take priority over the privacy rights of the family. These competing rights, however, would only arise in an adversarial context against other people or against the government.[228] Thus, the modern American family, as a viable legal entity, could arguably continue to coexist with, and nurture, its individual family members under its mutually supportive legal and constitutional safeguards.

The alternative to a strong and viable family structure may be grave. As Professor Laurence Tribe warns, "Once the State, whether acting through its courts or otherwise, has 'liberated' the [individual] from the shackles of such intermediate groups as the family, what is to defend the individual against the combined tyranny of the State and [his or] her own alienation?"[229]

---

[226] Schneider, *Moral Discourse and the Transformation of American Family Law*, 83 Mich. L. Rev. 1803, 1858 (1985).

[227] Mnookin, *The Public/Private Dichotomy*, 130 U. Pa. L. Rev. 1429, 1430 (1982).

[228] Rutherford, *Beyond Individual Privacy: A New Theory of Family Rights*, 39 U. Fla. L. Rev. 627, 643-44 (1987).

[229] Tribe, *supra* note 2, at 988 (1978).

Chapter 8

DIVORCE GROUNDS AND DEFENSES

§ 8.01 INTRODUCTION

Divorce, or dissolution of marriage, is the legal termination of a valid marriage. Divorce actions not only affect the parties' legal status, but involve the resolution of the essentials of marriage, including the division of marital property, the continued support of dependent family members, and the custody of children.

[A] Historical Background

Early Hebrew, Greek, and Roman societies afforded a right to divorce only to the husband, who could repudiate and divorce his wife for no reason and without legal or public intervention.[1] However, after the Punic Wars, Roman divorce law was liberalized to permit either the husband or the wife to divorce at will. During that time, marriages for limited and temporary purposes were common, often solely for economic or political reasons, and the Roman divorce rate reached alarming proportions. In 18 B.C. Caesar Augustus attempted to restrict divorce by enacting the *Lex Julia de Adulteris*, making adultery a crime and requiring a divorcing party to execute a written statement renouncing the marriage. In that period, Roman law also required a mandatory property settlement on divorce. The settlement directed the husband to return the wife's dowry or other premarital property if he divorced his wife on minor grounds or was at fault himself, which discouraged husbands from divorcing wealthy wives. On divorce, the Roman husband was usually awarded custody of any children of the marriage.[2]

Divorce law in England, and subsequently in the United States, evolved from different sources. Early English law assimilated the rather informal Anglo-Saxon custom of bride purchase, along with the husband's sole right to divorce. The extremely influential Medieval Church doctrine later replaced these customs. Under the doctrine of the Roman Catholic Church and its ecclesiastical courts, and later the Church of England, marriage was regarded as a holy sacrament that created an indissoluble bond. Accordingly, absolute divorce, also designated divorce *a vinculo matrimonii* or a divorce from the bonds of marriage, was not permitted under canon law, although influential individuals sometimes were able to have their marriages annulled based on specific marital impediments.[3] Permanent separation, or divorce *a mensa et thoro* (divorce from bed and board), was allowed upon certain

---

[1] *See* Joyce Green, et al., Dissolution of Marriage 6-7 (1986 & Supp. 1991).

[2] *Id.* at 7-10.

[3] *Id.* at 11-14. *See generally* Lawrence Stone, The Road to Divorce: England 1530-1987 (1990).

fault grounds, but neither party could remarry under that type of decree.[4]

During the Protestant Reformation, activists rebelled against the many perceived abuses of, and inconsistencies in, divorce law under the canon law and its ecclesiastical courts. These reformers argued that marriage and divorce should be regulated by secular legislative authority and by courts of equity, rather than by the Church. They further contended that absolute divorce should be granted upon specified marital fault grounds such as adultery, cruelty, or desertion, in addition to recognizing those grounds as the basis for the traditional divorce *a mensa et thoro*.[5]

The English law has been a dominant force in the establishment of American divorce law. Influenced by these Protestant reformers, the American colonies refused to adopt an ecclesiastical court system. Primarily in the New England colonies, colonial legislatures were given the authority to establish divorce grounds. In other areas, mostly in the southern and middle colonies, this authority was granted to the courts of equity.[6] Today, every state in this country regulates its divorce grounds and procedures by statute and designates specific state courts as the forum for divorce proceedings.[7]

[B]   Fault Grounds for Divorce and the No-Fault Revolution

Historically, public policy in the United States has placed considerable value on the institution of marriage and has discouraged divorce except in extreme circumstances. Regulation of both marriage and divorce in this country has reflected this perspective. A 1945 Virginia case, *Jacobs v. Jacobs*, illustrates the prevailing judicial philosophy of the mid-20th century. The Virginia supreme court declared that it could not guarantee a happy relationship, but would only cancel the parties' errors of judgment upon a serious, statutory marital breach.[8]

This country, as well as earlier societies, traditionally regarded divorce as a statutory remedy available exclusively to an innocent spouse whose partner has caused the breakdown of the marriage by committing some enumerated type of egregious marital fault. American law borrowed the traditional fault grounds which English law had developed for application in divorce *a mensa et thoro* and applied those grounds to absolute divorce. Under this system, a guilty spouse could not obtain a divorce, nor would a court award a divorce when both spouses were found to have contributed to the marital breakdown. Accordingly, the grounds for marriage dissolution originally were narrow and few. Adultery, extreme cruelty, and desertion by a spouse commonly were considered by most state legislatures to constitute serious enough injuries for awarding the innocent spouse a divorce. The

---

[4] *See infra* § 8.03[B][1].

[5] *See* Green, *supra* note 1, at 13-14.

[6] *Id.* at 14-15.

[7] *See generally* Nelson Blake, The Road to Reno (1962); Homer Clark, The Law of Domestic Relations in the United States § 15.1 (2d ed. 1987); Green, *supra* note 1, at 4-53; Max Rheinstein, Marriage Stability, Divorce, and the Law (1972); Walter Wadlington, *Divorce Without Fault Without Perjury*, 52 Va. L. Rev. 32 (1966).

[8] 35 S.E.2d 119 (Va. 1945).

statutory lists of marital fault became expanded in many states to include insanity, conviction of a crime, habitual drunkenness and drug addiction, and other perceived evils.[9]

Because divorce itself was discouraged, very strict and specific proof of fault was required for dissolving a marriage. Unlike other civil actions, the plaintiff in a divorce case could not merely receive a default judgment without proof that the other spouse had in fact committed the enumerated wrongs. A divorce case could be dismissed for insufficient evidence, and many jurisdictions employed divorce referees to assure that the alleged facts had actually occurred. As a result, many couples in unhappy marriages fabricated fault grounds and resorted to perjury, often with the assistance of legal counsel. Others left the jurisdiction to obtain a divorce in a state with more liberal divorce laws.[10] The subversion of state divorce laws led to corruption of the legal system and disrespect for divorce attorneys and their practices.

Critics of the fault-based divorce system in the fields of both law and the social sciences long contended that divorce should be viewed as a regrettable but necessary legal consequence of a failed marriage. Furthermore, those critics argued, the breakdown of the marital relationship usually resulted from the incompatibility and irreconcilable differences of both spouses, rather than the unilateral "fault" of one "guilty" spouse. No convincing data existed to demonstrate that liberal divorce grounds would generate unstable marriages or that strict divorce laws prevented or reduced the incidence of marital discord. By the second half of this century, a strong movement had formed, demanding that the legal system allow failed marriages to be dissolved in a peaceful and honest manner.[11]

Widespread divorce law reform began in the United States in the 1960s and 1970s, culminating in what has been referred to as the "divorce revolution."[12] No-fault divorce legislation began in 1966 when a California Governor's Commission recommended that divorce grounds be limited to "irremediable breakdown" and insanity. That recommendation became the law of California in 1969.[13]

Noting a "virtual unanimity as to the urgent need for basic reform," and describing the fault-based divorce ground system as "an unfortunate device which adds to the bitterness and hostility of divorce proceedings,"[14] the National Conference of Commissioners on Uniform State Laws proposed the Uniform Marriage and Divorce Act [UMDA] in 1970.[15] The UMDA attempts to "reduce the adversary trappings of marital litigation" and encourages divorcing parties "to make amicable settlements of their financial affairs," in part by designating the no-

---

[9] *See generally* 2 Chester G. Vernier, American Family Laws: A Comparative Study of the Family Law of the Forty-eight American States, Alaska, the District of Columbia, and Hawaii 70-71 (1932).

[10] *See, e.g.*, Blake, *supra* note 7.

[11] *See, e.g.*, Max Rheinstein, *The Law of Divorce and the Problem of Marriage Stability*, 9 Vand. L. Rev. 633 (1956); *see also* Rheinstein, *supra* note 7.

[12] *See* Lenore Weitzman, The Divorce Revolution (1985).

[13] Cal. Civ. Code § 2310 (West 2010).

[14] Prefatory Note, Unif. Marriage and Divorce Act, 9A part I U.L.A. 159 (1998).

[15] Unif. Marriage and Divorce Act, 9A part I U.L.A. 159 (1998).

fault ground of irretrievable breakdown of marriage as the sole ground for divorce.[16] The American Bar Association approved the UMDA and recommended its passage by the states in 1974.

Section 302 of the UMDA currently provides that a court shall enter a decree of dissolution of marriage when it finds that the marriage is "irretrievably broken." The Act mandates that legal conclusion when either the parties have lived separate and apart for more than 180 days or there exists "serious marital discord" adversely affecting the attitude of one or both of the parties toward the marriage.[17]

By 1985, all states had adopted some form of no-fault divorce, either by designating a no-fault ground as the exclusive basis for divorce or by adding such a provision to existing fault grounds. Currently, some 15 states have adopted irreconcilable differences or irretrievable breakdown as the sole ground for divorce, while an additional 20 states list one of those grounds in addition to traditional fault-based grounds. The remaining states provide for a no-fault type divorce based on living separate and apart for a stated period of time, in addition to traditional fault-based grounds.[18]

[C] Current Divorce Concerns and Statistics

Although divorce was once relatively rare in the United States, it is now commonplace. During the decade between 1970 and 1980, the divorce rate more than doubled, and more than a million divorces were granted each year,[19] a figure that has remained fairly constant throughout the 1990s and 2000s.[20] An estimated one-half or more of American marriages are estimated to end in divorce.[21] The average duration of marriage is seven years[22] and remarriage of divorced persons accounts for nearly one-half of the marriages in this country.[23] The continuing high divorce rate is one of the most dramatic alternations in contemporary American family life.[24]

According to one judge, "Approximately half of all the civil cases heard in the major state courts involve domestic matters . . . . It is not surprising, therefore,

---

[16] *Id.* at 147, 149.

[17] 9A U.L.A. § 302 (1987).

[18] *See* Linda D. Elrod & Robert G. Spector, *A Review of the Year in Family Law: Working Toward More Uniformity in Laws Relating to Families*, 44 Fam. L.Q. 469 (2011).

[19] Bureau of the Census, U.S. Dep't of Commerce, Statistical Abstract of the United States: 1991 at 86-89 (111th ed. 1991).

[20] *See* Laura Gatland, *Putting the Blame on No-Fault*, 83 A.B.A. J. 50, 51 (Apr. 1997).

[21] Statistical Abstract of the United States, Table No. 133, at 89 (1990); Bureau of Census, U.S. Dep't of Commerce, Studies in Marriage and the Family, Special Studies Series P-23, No. 162, at 4 (June 1989).

[22] Bureau of the Census, U.S. Dep't of Commerce, Statistical Abstract of the United States: 1991 at 88 (111th Ed. 1991). *See also* U.S. Dep't of Commerce, Current Population Reports Series P-70 (2009), *available at* www.census.gov/prod/2011pubs/p70-126.pdf.

[23] First time marriages for both the bride and groom represented fewer than 54% of all marriages in each year from 1981-87. Bureau of the Census, U.S. Dep't of Commerce, Statistical Abstract of the United States: 1991 at 87 (111th Ed. 1991).

[24] Terry Arendell, Mothers and Divorce: Legal, Economic, and Social Dilemmas 1 (1986).

that a state civil court's most important function, at least with respect to the number of lives touched, is in the resolution of family matters."[25]

With no-fault divorce now available in all states, divorce litigation has largely shifted from moral issues to economic controversies, primarily property division and child and spousal support, and to child custody disputes. Large law firms are increasingly involved in family law practice with their more prosperous clients, whose divorce actions often require corporate and tax advice as well as the more traditional aspects of family law.[26]

Most divorcing Americans, however, are not affluent, and some commentators have criticized the negative financial impact of no-fault divorce legislation on persons in lower economic brackets. Sociologist Lenore Weitzman, for example, has documented the severe economic impact of no-fault divorce on women and children. Weitzman concluded that gender-neutral rules have falsely assumed that women are equally capable of earning adequate livings as their former husbands following divorce. The results have deprived divorced women, especially older homemakers and those with small children, of the legal and financial benefits that the old law provided.[27] While Weitzman does not advocate a return to the traditional fault-based divorce system, she urges that the new law reflect "a continuous process of correction and refinement . . . to follow through on the road to fairness, equity, and equality in the legal process of divorce."[28]

Uncomplicated, no-fault divorce has also been charged with having a negative impact on children of divorced parents. Without significant safeguards, no-fault laws may contribute to long-term psychological damage to the children of divorce.[29]

[D] The Continuing Debate Over Fault Factors in Contemporary Divorce Actions

Even though all states have now enacted some form of no-fault divorce, only 15 states have adopted irreconcilable differences as the sole ground for divorce. However, 32 other states have retained traditional fault-based grounds for divorce, in addition to providing a no-fault alternative, and in approximately 30 states, fault still remains one of various statutory factors in determining spousal support, division of marital property, or both on divorce.[30]

---

[25] Richard Neely, The Divorce Decision: The Legal and Human Consequences of Ending a Marriage 1 (1984).

[26] *See* Mark Diamond, *Big Firms Get in on Divorce Action*, 74 A.B.A. J. 60 (Aug. 1988).

[27] Weitzman, *supra* note 12.

[28] *Id.* at 401. *See also* Michael Redman, *Coming Down Hard on No-Fault*, 10 Fam. Advoc. 6 (no. 2, 1987); Donald C. Schiller, *Dueling Over Issues of Fault-Fault Undercuts Equity*, 10 Fam. Advoc. 10 (no. 2, 1987).

[29] *See* Robert Cochran & Paul Vitz, *Child Protective Divorce Laws: A Response to the Effects of Parental Separation on Children*, 17 Fam. L.Q. 327 (1983); Judith Wallerstein & Sandra Blakeslee, Second Chances: Men, Women and Children A Decade After Divorce (1989); Elizabeth Scott, *Rational Decision-Making About Marriage and Divorce*, 76 Va. L. Rev. 9, 29 (1990).

[30] *See* Elrod & Spector, *supra*, note 18.

The American Law Institute recently proposed a financially-based *Principles of the Law of Family Dissolution*[31] that strongly argue for the total abolition of all fault-based factors and all non-financial losses in divorce or dissolution of marriage.[32] ALI Reporter Ira Ellman argues, for example, that fault factors on divorce "no longer serve any viable function in a marital dissolution action," and "the potentially valid functions of a fault principle are better served by the tort and criminal law," and "attempting" to serve them through a fault rule risks serious distortion in the resolution of the dissolution action."[33] Other commentators, however, question whether this refusal to take into account non-financial losses on divorce undervalues a woman's noneconomic contributions to the marriage,[34] or whether punishment for egregious marital behavior can realistically be relegated to a tort or criminal law action.[35] Thus, while there are many commentators, and the American Law Institute, arguing for a total abolition of all fault-based factors on divorce,[36] there are other commentators who have argued that fault factors still serve a legitimate function in contemporary American divorce law.[37]

---

[31] ALI, *Principles of the Law of Family Dissolution*, § 506 cmt. e (2001).

[32] The ALI *Principles* advocate a number of recommendations pertaining to spousal support, division of marital property, child custody, and other crucial areas impacting divorce or dissolution of marriage. Recent symposia discussing and analyzing the ALI *Principles* include: *Gender Issues on Divorce: Commentaries on the American Law Institute's Principles of the Law of Family Dissolution*, 8 Duke J. Gender L. & Pol'y 1 (2001); *The ALI Family Dissolution Principles: Blueprint to Strengthen or Deconstruct Families?*, 2001 B.Y.U. L. Rev. 857; *Symposium on the American Law Institute's Principles of the Law of Family Dissolution*, 4 J. L. & Fam. Studies 1 (2002).

[33] Ira Ellman, *The Place of Fault in a Modern Divorce Law*, 28 Ariz. St. L.J. 773, 807-08 (1996). Other commentators who forcefully argue for the abolition of noneconomic fault factors in divorce or dissolution of marriage include: Norman Lichtenstein, *Marital Misconduct and the Allocation of Financial Resources on Divorce: A Farewell to Fault*, 54 U.M.K.C. L. Rev. 1 (1985); Herma Hill Kay, *Equality and Difference: A Perspective on No-Fault Divorce and its Aftermath*, 56 U. Cinn. L. Rev. 1 (1987); Lawrence Friedman, *A Dead Language: Divorce Law and Practice Before No-Fault*, 86 Va. L. Rev. 1497 (2000); and Rhona Bork, *Taking Fault with New York's Fault-Based Divorce: Is the Law Constitutional?*, 16 St. John's J. Legal Comment 165 (2002).

[34] *See, e.g.*, Katharine Silbaugh, *Gender and Nonfinancial Matters in the ALI Principles of the Law of Family Dissolution*, 8 Duke J. Gender L. & Pol'y 203 (2001); *see also* June Carbone, *Economics, Feminism, and the Reinvention of Alimony*, 43 Vanderbilt L. Rev. 1463 (1990).

[35] *See, e.g.*, Peter Nash Swisher, *The ALI Principles: A Farewell to Fault — But What Remedy for the Egregious Marital Misconduct of an Abusive Spouse?*, 8 Duke J. Gender L. & Pol'y 213, 227-30 (2001); *see also* Robert Spector, *Marital Torts: The Current Legal Landscape*, 33 Fam. L. Q. 745, 762-63 (1999).

[36] *See supra* note 33 (and accompanying text); *see also* Ira Ellman & Sharon Lohr, *Marriage as Contract, Opportunistic Violence, and Other Bad Arguments for Fault Divorce*, 1997 U. Ill. L. Rev. 719.

[37] *See, e.g.*, Barbara Bennett Woodhouse, *Sex, Lies, and Dissipation: The Discourse of Fault in a No-Fault Era*, 82 Georgetown L. J. 2525 (1994); Adriaen Morse Jr., *Fault: A Viable Means of Re-Injecting Responsibility in Marital Relations*, 30 U. Rich. L. Rev. 605 (1996); Jana Singer, *Husbands, Wives, and Human Capital: Why the Shoe Won't Fit*, 31 Fam. L. Q. 119 (1997); Peter Nash Swisher, *Reassessing Fault Factors in No-Fault Divorce*, 31 Fam. L. Q. 269 (1997); Swisher, *supra* note 35. *See generally* Herbie DiFonzo & Ruth Stern, *Family Law in the Twenty-First Century: The Winding Road from Form to Function: A Brief History of Contemporary Marriage*, 21 J. Am. Acad. Matrim. Law. 1 (2008) (detailing the historical emergence of the no-fault divorce process and discussing the effects of no-fault divorce on the modern institution of marriage).

In summary, the no-fault divorce revolution is still undergoing reassessment, refinement, and modification in an attempt to meet the current and future needs of our changing society.

§ 8.02　JURISDICTION AND VENUE

[A]　Divorce Jurisdiction in General

Family law jurisdiction, including jurisdiction of divorce, is governed by state statutes and administered by state courts.[38] Under the "domestic relations exception" to federal subject matter jurisdiction, the federal courts have no jurisdiction over family law matters, despite the existence of diversity of citizenship. The domestic relations exception is a judicially created doctrine first pronounced by the United States Supreme Court in *Barber v. Barber*[39] in 1858 and developed through a long line of cases.[40] The courts have made some exceptions to the domestic relations exception on occasion.[41]

In *Jagiella v. Jagiella*,[42] the Court of Appeals for the Fifth Circuit held that the federal district court had jurisdiction to grant judgment for alimony and child support arrearages. It further held that the court had properly dismissed the former husband's counterclaim for modification of child support and visitation and damages for alienation of the children's affection and infliction of mental anguish by his former wife, because these claims would necessitate inquiry into the marital or parent-child relationship.

The United States Supreme Court limited the scope of the exception in *Ankenbrandt v. Richards*,[43] a 1992 case which dealt with a tort action based on alleged child abuse. The Court reviewed the basis for the limitation of federal court jurisdiction, noting that no Constitutional restrictions existed. It questioned the historical rationale that because no ecclesiastical courts were recognized in the United States, divorce was not considered an action "of a civil nature at common law or equity" under the original Judiciary Act.[44] It acknowledge, however, that policy considerations continue to support the rule, such as a lack of family law expertise on the part of federal court judges and judicial economy. Although it expressed unwillingness to completely set aside a rule that has been recognized for over a century, the Court held that the domestic relations exception applied only to

---

[38] *See supra* § 1.03.

[39] 62 U.S. (21 How.) 582 (1858).

[40] *See, e.g., In re Burrus*, 136 U.S. 586, 593-94 (1890); *Solomon v. Solomon*, 516 F.2d 1018 (3d Cir. 1975).

[41] *See, e.g., Spindel v. Spindel*, 283 F. Supp. 797 (E.D.N.Y. 1968) (federal court jurisdiction to resolve question of fraudulent divorce decree); *Lloyd v. Loeffler*, 694 F.2d 489 (7th Cir. 1982) (parent's claim for damages for concealment of child); *Crouch v. Crouch*, 566 F.2d 486 (5th Cir. 1978) (private contract to pay money between persons long since divorced).

[42] 647 F.2d 561 (5th Cir. 1981).

[43] 504 U.S. 689 (1992).

[44] *See Barber v. Barber*, 62 U.S. (21 How.) 582, 605 (1858) (dissenting opinion); *Ohio ex rel. Popovici v. Agler*, 280 U.S. 379 (1930).

the traditional areas of family law: divorce, alimony, and child custody decrees.

In response to an alternative argument based on abstention, the Court also emphasized that federal abstention should rarely be invoked unless proceedings are pending in state courts or in a case involving "elements of the domestic relationship even when the parties do not seek divorce, alimony, or child custody."[45]

> This would be so when a case presents "difficult questions of state law bearing on policy problems of substantial public import whose importance transcends the result in the case then at bar." . . . Such might well be the case if a federal suit were filed prior to effectuation of a divorce, alimony, or child custody decree, and the suit depended on a determination of the status of the parties. Where, as here, the status of the domestic relationship has been determined as a matter of state law, and in any event has no bearing on the underlying torts alleged, we have no difficulty concluding that . . . abstention is inappropriate . . . .[46]

The *Ankenbrandt* decision is likely to generate considerable future litigation concerning the extent to which the domestic relations exception remains applicable.[47]

[B]   The Domiciliary Requirement

Although divorce law is a state law matter, the United States Supreme Court has delineated some special rules for divorce jurisdiction, primarily to specify which divorce decrees must be afforded full faith and credit. The Court has held that domicile of one or both spouses is *sufficient* to confer divorce jurisdiction to a state court, stating that "each state, by virtue of its command over its domiciliaries and its large interest in the institution of marriage, can alter within its own borders the marriage status of the spouse domiciled there."[48] Nonetheless, other than by dicta in a series of mid-twentieth century cases, it has never squarely held that domicile is *necessary*, nor that it is the *sole* basis for divorce jurisdiction.[49]

Because marriage is a status, based on contract, the Court has viewed divorce as essentially an *in rem* action, regarding the "marriage" itself as an entity present in the state whenever either of the spouses is present. Mere presence alone, however, is insufficient to confer divorce jurisdiction, and the state which regulates the marriage or terminates the status must have a substantial nexus with that marriage. State law generally requires that the nexus to be established by the domicile of one or both of the spouses as a requisite for proper assertion of divorce jurisdiction.

---

[45] *Ankenbrandt*, 504 U.S. at 689.

[46] *Id.* at 2216 (citation omitted).

[47] *See, e.g., Lannan v. Maul*, 979 F.2d 627 (8th Cir. 1992) (federal district court erred in dismissing child's claim against deceased father's estate to recover proceeds of life insurance policy according to terms of property settlement agreement).

[48] *Williams v. N. Carolina*, 317 U.S. 287, 299 (1942) (*Williams I*).

[49] *See Williams v. N. Carolina*, 325 U.S. 226 (1945) (*Williams II*), *rehearing denied*, 325 U.S. 895 (1945); *Alton v. Alton*, 207 F.2d 667 (3d Cir.), *dismissed as moot*, 347 U.S. 610 (1954).

"Domicile" is generally defined as the place where a person is physically present with the intent of making that place his or her home.[50] While a person may have more than one "residence," or place where he or she resides, "domicile" connotes a subjective intent to remain more or less permanently or indefinitely.[51] Unnecessarily confusing the issue, many states use the term "residence" rather than "domicile" in their divorce jurisdiction statutes. However, in interpreting the jurisdictional requirements for divorce, a statutory reference to "residence" is usually construed to mean "domicile."[52]

In *In re Marriage of Kimura*,[53] both spouses were Japanese citizens. The husband came to the United States on a temporary visa, and the wife remained in Japan. The husband moved to Iowa, and after one year, filed for divorce in that state. The wife challenged the jurisdiction of the court and also argued that the matter should be dismissed on forum non conveniens grounds. The Iowa Supreme Court upheld the state's assertion of jurisdiction and concluded that the divorce could be granted on the basis of the husband's domicile within the state. It noted, however, that its jurisdiction was limited to terminating the marriage and did not extend to determination of the other issues related to the dissolution.

A state's jurisdictional requirement of domicile is a critical issue in any divorce action. As a general rule, divorce jurisdiction cannot be waived and may be asserted at any time during a divorce proceeding. Lack of jurisdiction may be the basis for a subsequent collateral attack on a prior divorce decree.[54] A valid divorce cannot be granted if the forum court does not have jurisdiction over the marriage or if the defendant did not receive notice sufficient to satisfy constitutional due process standards.[55] Similarly, if a divorce decree is entered without proper jurisdiction or upon insufficient notice, the decree is void and has no legal effect. Such a decree may be attacked at any time, although equitable defenses may apply.[56]

The domiciliary requirement for divorce jurisdiction has been criticized as obsolete and irrelevant in our current transient society with no-fault divorce options.[57] At the same time, because some form of no-fault divorce is presently available in all American jurisdictions, the problems that migratory divorces once

---

[50] *See Fiske v. Fiske*, 290 P.2d 725 (Wash. 1955).

[51] *See* Restatement (Second) of Conflict of Laws §§ 70-72 (1971).

[52] *See, e.g., Cooper v. Cooper*, 74 Cal. Rptr. 439 (Cal. Ct. App. 1969); *Raybin v. Raybin*, 430 A.2d 953 (N.J. Super. Ct. App. Div. 1981). *But see Garrison v. Garrison*, 246 N.E.2d 9 (Ill. App.Ct. 1969). *See generally* Willis Reese & Robert Green, *That Elusive Word "Residence"*, 6 Vand. L. Rev. 561 (1953).

[53] 471 N.W.2d 869 (1991).

[54] *See, e.g., Hartman v. Hartman*, 412 N.E.2d 711 (Ill. App. Ct. 1980); *see also* Restatement (Second) of Judgments §§ 11, 12, 69 (1982).

[55] *See supra* § 8.02.

[56] *See supra* § 8.02[J].

[57] *See, e.g.*, Helen Garfield, *The Transitory Divorce Action: Jurisdiction in the No-Fault Era*, 58 Tex. L. Rev. 501, 544 (1980) (suggesting that "the problem today is not so much migratory divorce as migratory people," and recommending a proposed Uniform Divorce Jurisdiction Act which would provide as the basis for divorce jurisdiction the mere presence of both parties in a state for bilateral divorces, and a brief period of presence or simple residence in the forum state for ex parte, unilateral divorces).

posed are diminished. Therefore, it is questionable whether requiring merely physical presence rather than domicile would serve any compelling social need. Because significant connections continue to be required between an individual and the state with respect to state and local police protection, property rights, rights of inheritance, taxes, voting rights, education, and employment, such a nexus may be equally relevant with respect to the parties' marital status.[58]

Some legal commentators have contended that mere domicile as a basis for divorce jurisdiction in unilateral ex parte divorces is an insufficient nexus and may constitute an unconstitutional violation of the absent spouse's due process rights.[59] In *Shaffer v. Heitner*,[60] the Supreme Court stated that "in order to justify an exercise of jurisdiction *in rem*, the basis for jurisdiction must be sufficient to justify exercising jurisdiction over the interests of persons in a 'thing.'" However, Professor Clark has pointed out that while *Shaffer* stated that both *in rem* and *in personal* cases require minimum contacts to satisfy due process requirements, the Court disclaimed any intention of changing jurisdictional rules based upon status. Therefore, it is not likely that *Shaffer* and subsequent cases alter the jurisdictional rules for divorce.[61]

Although domicile provides a sufficient basis for a state court to assert jurisdiction in a divorce case, the United States Supreme Court has held that states may additionally impose a durational residency requirement without unconstitutionally discriminating against residents who have recently moved to the state and seek a divorce there. In *Sosna v. Iowa*,[62] Carol Sosna had moved from New York, the marital domicile, to Iowa, where she sought dissolution of her marriage to Michael Sosna. Although Michael was personally served when he visited the couple's children in Iowa, the Iowa court dismissed the action for lack of jurisdiction under an Iowa statute that required a divorce petitioner to have been an Iowa resident for one year. Noting that the vast majority of states impose durational residency requirements for divorce, the Supreme Court upheld the statute.

> A decree of divorce is not a matter in which the only interested parties are the State as a sort of "grantor," and a plaintiff such as appellant in the role of "grantee." Both spouses are obviously interested in the proceedings, since it will affect their marital status and very likely their property rights. Where a married couple has minor children, a decree of divorce would usually include provisions for their custody and support. With consequences of such moment riding on a divorce decree issued by its courts,

---

[58] *See, e.g., Boddie v. Connecticut*, 401 U.S. 371, 376 (1971).

[59] *See, e.g.*, E. Roy Hawkens, *The Effect of* Shaffer v. Heitner *on the Jurisdictional Standard in Ex Parte Divorces*, 18 Fam. L.Q. 311 (1984); Sheila Cunningham, Note, *Jurisdiction in the Ex Parte Divorce: Do Absent Spouses Have a Protected Due Process Interest in Their Marital Status?*, 13 Memphis St. U.L. Rev. 205 (1983).

[60] 433 U.S. 186, 207 (1977).

[61] Clark, *supra* note 7, at 424. *See also In re Marriage of Rinderknecht*, 367 N.E.2d 1128 (Ind. Ct. App. 1977) (domicile of one of the spouses in a state is a sufficient minimum contact to meet the requirements of *Shaffer*).

[62] 419 U.S. 393 (1975).

Iowa may insist that one seeking to initiate such a proceeding have the modicum of attachment to the State required here.[63]

The Court further recognized a state interest in "avoiding officious intermeddling in matters in which another State has a paramount interest, and minimizing the susceptibility of its own divorce decrees to collateral attack."[64] Furthermore, Ms. Sosna was not prevented from divorcing in Iowa, but was merely delayed in obtaining access to its courts until she fulfilled the durational residency requirement.

Although the concept of domicile as the exclusive basis for divorce jurisdiction remains open to debate,[65] state law currently considers domicile essential for divorce. While a few states have no durational requirement but require only a bona fide residency or domicile,[66] most states additionally impose a durational requirement ranging from six weeks[67] to one year.[68] The most common durational requirement for divorce is six months.[69]

An important exception to the general jurisdictional requirements for divorce involves military personnel and their spouses. Approximately twenty states, as well as the Uniform Marriage and Divorce Act, additionally confer divorce jurisdiction over members of the armed forces who are stationed in the state for a specified period of time.[70] Because of the mobile nature of the military, servicemen and women and their spouses might otherwise be unable to establish domicile or meet the residency requirements of the jurisdiction of their current station. Although the state of their pre-military domicile may continue to assert jurisdiction to grant divorces to absent military personnel, that state may have little current connection with the serviceperson may be a distant and inconvenient forum.[71] Although one state has declared its special military jurisdictional statute unconstitutional,[72] the United States Supreme Court has upheld other statutes that confer special benefits

---

[63] *Id.* at 406-07.

[64] *Id.* at 407.

[65] *See, e.g., Williams v. N. Carolina*, 325 U.S. 226, 239-60 (1945) (*Williams II*) (Rutledge, Black & Douglas dissenting); Edward Stimson, *Jurisdiction in Divorce Cases: The Unsoundness of the Domiciliary Theory*, 42 A.B.A. J. 222 (1956); Russell Weintraub, *An Inquiry into the Utility of "Domicile" as a Concept in Conflicts Analysis*, 63 Mich. L. Rev. 961 (1965).

[66] *E.g.*, Alaska Stat. § 01.10.055 (1998); S.D. Codified Laws Ann. § 25-4-30 (1999).

[67] *E.g.*, Idaho Code § 32-701 (1996); Nev. Rev. Stat. Ann. § 125.020 (Michie 1998).

[68] *E.g.*, Conn. Gen. Stat. Ann. § 46b-44 (West 1995); Iowa Code Ann. § 598.6 (West 1996); N.Y. Dom. Rel. L. § 230 (McKinney 1999).

[69] *See* Timothy Walker, *Family Law in the Fifty States: An Overview*, 25 Fam. L.Q. 417, 441 (1992).

[70] *See, e.g.*, Unif. Marriage and Divorce Act § 302(a), 9A part I U.L.A. 200 (1998); *see also* Pearson, Annotation, *Validity and Construction of Statutory Provisions Relating to Jurisdiction of Court for Purpose of Divorce for Servicemen*, 73 A.L.R. 3d 431 (1976 & Supp. 1992).

[71] *See Johnson v. Johnson*, 53 Cal. Rptr. 567 (Cal. Ct. App. 1966) (change of residence required by military service will not change domicile, absent clear intent); *see also In re Marriage of Thornton*, 185 Cal. Rptr. 388 (Cal. Ct. App. 1982) (divorce jurisdictional requirements may be met without domicile of either spouse in unique circumstance by residency of one spouse, unavailability of better forum, property within the jurisdiction, and site of last marital home).

[72] *Viernes v. Dist. Court of Fourth Judicial Dist.*, 509 P.2d 306 (Colo. 1973) (other "significant contacts" in addition to stationing in state necessary).

to veterans against equal protection attacks, based on the legitimate longstanding policy to compensation veterans for past contributions.[73]

Relatedly, the Soldiers' and Sailors' Civil Relief Act permits stay of continuance in any divorce and related family law matter to military personnel stay who are prevented from being present and participating in the scheduled proceedings due to their military service.[74]

Whether a court has jurisdiction to enter a divorce decree is especially important in determining whether other states must recognize the divorce as valid pursuant to full faith and credit principles. The validity of a decree may depend largely on whether the divorce was granted in a bilateral or ex parte proceeding.

[C] Venue

Jurisdictional rules for divorce determine whether any court in a particular state has authority to hear the case and to grant a valid divorce decree. Venue, on the other hand, governs the appropriate place *within* the state for bringing the divorce action. Venue statutes generally require filing a divorce action in the county of the parties' last marital domicile, in the county where the defendant resides, or, if the defendant's location is unknown or is out-of-state, in the county where the plaintiff resides.[75] Other venue statutes provide for alternatives, such as the county of the parties' last domicile, the county where the defendant resides, or, if the defendant is out of state or the defendant's whereabouts are unknown, the county where the plaintiff resides.[76]

While jurisdictional requirements may not be waived in a divorce proceeding, some states have held that venue rules may be waived.[77] However, in other states, venue statutes in divorce proceedings have been interpreted as mandatory and jurisdictional, thus not waivable.[78] If venue statutes may not be waived in a divorce action, the validity of the divorce decree may be affected.

[D] Service on the Defendant

Due process requires that service of process on the defendant in a divorce action be made in strict compliance with state statutes. If the defendant is not properly served in a manner reasonably calculated to give notice, the divorce may be

---

[73] *See Regan v. Taxation with Representation*, 461 U.S. 540 (1983) (tax exemption for veterans' lobbying groups does not violate equal protection); *see also United States v. Hampshire*, 95 F.3d 999 (10th Cir. 1996) *cert. denied*, 519 U.S. 1084 (1997) (state court order under Child Support Recovery Act did not violate soldier's due process rights or his right to attorney under Soldier's and Sailor's Relief Act, because father was absent without leave (AWOL)).

[74] 50 U.S.C.A. §§ 501, 521. *See also Lackey v. Lackey*, 278 S.E.2d 811 (Va. 1981). *See generally* Annotation Soldiers' and Sailors' Civil Relief Act of 1940 as Amended as Affecting Matrimonial Actions, 54 A.L.R.2d 390 (1957 & Supp. 1992).

[75] *See, e.g.*, Cal. Civ. Code § 2320 (West 1994); *In re Marriage of Dick*, 18 Cal. Rptr. 2d 743 (Ct. App. 1993); *see also Dunn v. Dunn*, 577 So. 2d 378 (Miss. 1991).

[76] *See, e.g.*, Va. Code Ann. § 8.01-261 (Michie 1995).

[77] *See, e.g., Nelms v. Nelms*, 108 S.E.2d 529 (N.C. 1959); *Kelley v. Kelley*, 263 S.W.2d 505 (Tenn. 1953).

[78] *See, e.g., Gerdel v. Gerdel*, 313 A.2d 8 (Vt. 1973).

attacked and invalidated for lack of adequate notice.[79]

A United States District Court applied this principle in *Breuer v. Sullivan*,[80] overturning an administrative law judge's conclusion that he must recognize a divorce decree valid for purposes of a woman's claim for widow's benefits under the Social Security Act. In light of the woman's testimony that she had never received a copy of the 1958 divorce summons or complaint, the District Court Judge held that, on remand, the administrative law judge must determine the claimant's marital status before deciding her eligibility for benefits.

A divorce plaintiff's false representations of lack of knowledge of the defendant's whereabouts may constitute a fraud sufficient to invalidate the divorce.[81] Similarly, if the notice to the defendant fails to indicate that the plaintiff is also seeking a division of marital property in the divorce action, the service may be adequate for granting the divorce but inadequate to confer jurisdiction to distribute property.[82]

[E] Bilateral Divorces

A bilateral divorce is a divorce proceeding in which both spouses are subject to the jurisdiction of the forum state court. A divorce is bilateral when both of the spouses the are domiciliaries of the forum state or when both are subject to the forum state's personal jurisdiction because of consent, appearance, or application of a long-arm statute. A bilateral divorce and decree may not be collaterally attacked by the parties themselves nor, generally, by third parties, including other states.[83] In a bilateral divorce action, the court may resolve all the incidents of the marriage, including support and property rights, as well as terminate the parties' marital status.[84]

[F] Ex Parte Divorces

An ex parte or unilateral divorce is a divorce proceeding in which the court of the forum state has personal jurisdiction in the over only one of the spouses. While the United States Supreme Court has held that the domicile of one spouse is sufficient for the forum court to litigate the status of marriage and to grant a

---

[79] It is now generally recognized in most states that the defendant in a divorce action must be given due process notice of the divorce suit and an opportunity to be heard, and if the defendant's whereabouts are unknown and cannot be discovered by reasonable diligence, then notice by publication is required. *See, e.g., Atherton v. Atherton*, 181 U.S. 155 (1901); *Williams v. North Carolina* [I], 317 U.S. 287 (1942); Restatement (Second) of Conflict of Laws § 69 (1971). *See generally* Clark, *supra* note 7, at 81-108.

[80] 18 Fam. L. Rep. (BNA) 1439 (D.N.M. 1991).

[81] *See, e.g., Ford v. Whelan*, 288 N.W. 737 (Wis. 1930).

[82] *See In re Marriage of Campbell*, 683 P.2d 604 (Wash. Ct. App. 1984).

[83] *See infra* § 8.02[J].

[84] *See, e.g., Sherrer v. Sherrer*, 334 U.S. 343 (1948); *Newport v. Newport*, 245 S.E.2d 134 (Va. 1978); *Wilson v. Wilson*, 732 N.E.2d 841 (Ind. Ct. App. 2000); *see also Zeolla v. Zeolla*, 908 A.2d 629 (Me. 2006) (holding that because the trial court had personal jurisdiction over the parties in a divorce action, it also had jurisdiction to distribute all the marital property, including property located out-of-state; *Shao v. Ma*, 861 N.E.2d 788 (Mass. App. Ct. 2006) (similar holding).

divorce,[85] the forum state does not have jurisdiction to resolve the economic incidents of the marriage without personal jurisdiction over the party whose rights are to be affected.[86] Problems involving ex parte divorces most commonly arise in the context of migratory divorces, although the same problems may be encountered when one or both parties have moved from the state of the last marital domicile for purposes other than obtaining a divorce.

[G] Migratory Divorces

The classic migratory divorce cases, in which one spouse leaves the state of the marital domicile to obtain a divorce in another jurisdiction, serve as useful examples of the structure of divorce jurisdiction and the principles controlling recognition of divorce decrees by other states. Although the availability of no-fault divorce in all 50 states has greatly decreased the incentive for a spouse to go out-of-state to procure a divorce, some individuals still may attempt to obtain a divorce in another state or a foreign country that has more lenient jurisdictional requirements, a shorter waiting period, or less stringent substantive standards, or to avoid the publicity that may arise in the forum state.[87]

[1] Sister State Divorces

The Full Faith and Credit Clause of the United States Constitution requires states to recognize valid divorce decrees entered by the courts of other states.[88] However, because each state has developed specific divorce laws based on its own public policy, confusion historically resulted as to the circumstances in which one state must recognize a divorce decree from a sister state and when that state may legally refuse to recognize such a decree. Because many parties who obtain migratory divorces subsequently remarry, and because substantial property and support rights are determined on divorce, both the parties and the states themselves have a strong interest in ensuring that their divorce decrees will be recognized in all states.

The United States Supreme Court first addressed the issue of migratory divorce in the 1906 case of *Haddock v. Haddock*.[89] In *Haddock*, the husband had obtained a divorce in a state where he had established a bona fide domicile after wrongfully leaving his wife in the state of the marital domicile. The Court held that the state of the marital domicile was not obligated to recognize the ex parte divorce decree. The *Haddock* decision remained the law until 1942, when the Supreme Court decided the seminal ex parte divorce case of *Williams v. North Carolina* [*Williams I*].[90]

---

[85] *Williams v. N. Carolina*, 317 U.S. 287 (1942) (*Williams I*). *See supra* § 8.02[B].

[86] *See infra* § 8.02[F].

[87] *See* Philip Adams & Stephen Adams, *Ethical Problems in Advising Migratory Divorce*, 16 Hastings L.J. 60, 99 (1964).

[88] Article IV § 1, U.S. Constitution (requiring states to give full faith and credit to the public acts, records, and judicial proceedings of every other state).

[89] 201 U.S. 562 (1906).

[90] 317 U.S. 287 (1942).

In *Williams*, Mr. Williams and Mrs. Hendrix left their respective spouses in North Carolina and traveled to Las Vegas, Nevada, where, after fulfilling Nevada's six weeks residency requirement, they both obtained divorces. Although neither of their North Carolina spouses was personally served in Nevada nor entered an appearance there, they received notice of the divorce complaints and summonses in North Carolina. Mr. Williams and Mrs. Hendrix then married each other in Nevada and returned to North Carolina. Relying on *Haddock*, the State of North Carolina tried and convicted them of bigamous cohabitation, despite their argument that the Nevada divorce decree and remarriage should be recognized in North Carolina.[91]

In *Williams I*, an opinion written by Justice Douglas, the Supreme Court overruled *Haddock* and held that an ex parte divorce, based on proper jurisdiction and with adequate due process notice to the other spouse, must be given full faith and credit by another state, even though the public policies of the two states might conflict. Moreover, the Court held that domicile of the plaintiff would supply the basis for jurisdiction in an ex parte divorce. Because no evidence in the record in the North Carolina proceeding indicated that Mr. Williams and Mrs. Hendrix were *not* domiciled in Nevada, Justice Douglas stated that the Court "must assume that petitioners had a bona fide domicile in Nevada, not that the Nevada domicile was a sham."[92] The case was reversed and remanded back to the North Carolina court.

Upon remand, North Carolina again upheld the bigamy convictions on the basis that the petitioners had not in fact been domiciled in Nevada, therefore the divorces had no legal validity in North Carolina. In 1945, the appeal again reached the Supreme Court in *Williams v. North Carolina [Williams II]*.[93] In a decision written by Justice Frankfurter, the Court reaffirmed the *Williams I* doctrine that an ex parte divorce based upon the domicile of only one spouse, with proper due process to the non-appearing spouse, must be recognized by other states under the Full Faith and Credit Clause. However, although the Nevada court's finding of a Nevada domicile "was entitled to respect and more," the Court held that North Carolina was not bound by the Nevada jurisdictional finding of domicile[94] and could subsequently reexamine the facts to determine whether the parties had actually acquired a Nevada domicile. Thus, under *Williams II*, a sister state court may inquire into the factual basis for jurisdiction and refuse to recognize an ex parte divorce if it concludes that the divorcing court did not have adequate jurisdiction to grant the divorce because no true domicile had been established.[95] The Williams' conviction of bigamous cohabitation was therefore affirmed.

---

[91] *See generally* Thomas Reed Powell, *And Repent at Leisure: An Inquiry into the Unhappy Lot of Those Whom Nevada Hath Joined Together and North Carolina Hath Put Asunder*, 58 Harv. L. Rev. 930 (1945).

[92] 317 U.S. at 302.

[93] 325 U.S. 226 (1945).

[94] *Id.* at 233.

[95] *See, e.g., Manasseri v. Manasseri*, 504 N.Y.S.2d 140 (N.Y. App. Div. 1986) (finding husband's move to Nevada a sham when he moved with only two suitcases and golf clubs soon after dismissal of New York divorce action, despite his registering to vote and acquiring driver's license in Nevada).

The Iowa Supreme Court applied the *Williams II* doctrine in *Cooper v. Cooper,*[96] when it determined that an ex parte Nevada divorce decree was based on proper jurisdiction. The husband in *Cooper* had left Iowa, the marital domicile, after a lengthy marriage and moved to Nevada where he lived for three months, obtained a license to practice medicine, worked at a medical center, rented an apartment, opened a bank account, and obtained a driver's license. A Nevada court granted him a default judgment of divorce, after which he moved back to Iowa, remarried, and subsequently died. Denying the first wife's claim that the divorce and remarriage were invalid, the court held that she had failed to prove by clear, satisfactory, and convincing evidence that the husband did not have the requisite intent to establish a domicile in Nevada.

A state court's determination regarding the validity of another state's divorce decree under the *Williams II* doctrine may not bind subsequent states. Subsequent states may re-examine the factual issue of domicile, resulting in a divorce decree that is considered valid in some states but not in others.[97]

On occasion, courts have issued injunctions against a spouse's obtaining a divorce in another state when it appears likely that the spouse does not intend to establish domicile in the new state.[98]

While the *Williams I* and *Williams II* doctrines apply generally to ex parte divorces, bilateral migratory divorces involve some different concerns. A new issue arises when neither spouse is domiciled in the divorcing state, but both submit to the court's jurisdiction by personal or general appearance. The Supreme Court first dealt with the issue of bilateral migratory divorce in the 1948 case of *Sherrer v. Sherrer.*[99]

The *Sherrer* case involved a husband and wife who both had been Massachusetts domiciliary before Mrs. Sherrer moved to Florida and commenced a divorce action there. Mr. Sherrer, through his attorney, made a general appearance in the Florida divorce action, but did not challenge his wife's allegations that she was a Florida domiciliary during the proceedings. The Florida court found that Mrs. Sherrer was a Florida domiciliary and Mr. Sherrer did not appeal the divorce in a Florida appellate court.

Subsequently, Mr. Sherrer attacked the validity of the Florida divorce in a Massachusetts court, alleging that Mrs. Sherrer's domicile in Florida was a sham and that the Florida court did not have jurisdiction to grant a valid divorce. Despite his argument that Massachusetts should not recognize the decree under the *Williams II* doctrine, the Supreme Court upheld the validity of the Florida divorce and stated that Massachusetts must recognize the decree.

---

[96] 217 N.W.2d 584 (Iowa 1974).

[97] *See Colby v. Colby*, 369 P.2d 1019 (Nev.), *cert. denied*, 371 U.S. 888 (1962); *see also* Recent Developments, 15 Stan. L. Rev. 331 (1963); Restatement (Second) of Judgments § 15 (1982). *But see, e.g., Sutton v. Leib*, 342 U.S. 402 (1952); *Layton v. Layton*, 538 S.W.2d 642 (Tex. Civ. App. 1976).

[98] *See Monihan v. Monihan*, 264 A.2d 653 (Pa. 1970); *Stambaugh v. Stambaugh*, 329 A.2d 483 (Pa. 1974); *see also* Annotation, *Injunction Against Suit in Another State or Country for Divorce or Separation*, 54 A.L.R.2d 1240 (1957 & Supp. 1992).

[99] 334 U.S. 343 (1948).

The distinction between *Sherrer* and the *Williams* cases is that Mr. Sherrer had submitted to the jurisdiction of the Florida court by entering an appearance in the divorce action, making it a bilateral, rather than an ex parte, divorce. He had therefore participated in the bilateral Florida divorce proceeding and had the opportunity to dispute the jurisdictional issue, which he failed to do. The Supreme Court held that because Mr. Sherrer had his day in court on the merits of the case, he was precluded from relitigating the issue under the doctrine of res judicata or estoppel by judgment.[100] The practical effect of the *Sherrer* decision was to limit the scope of the *Williams II* decision to jurisdictional challenges of ex parte divorces.[101]

The Court in *Sherrer* did not hold that divorces are valid without domicile of either party, but rather foreclosed collateral attack by a party who participated in a bilateral divorce. It remains uncertain, therefore, whether the domicile state of one or both of the divorcing parties may itself collaterally attack a bilateral migratory divorce in a proceeding such as a bigamy or adultery prosecution.[102]

[2] Foreign Country Divorces

Although the Full Faith and Credit Clause requires recognition of valid sister state migratory divorce decrees,[103] migratory divorces granted in foreign countries are not shielded by this constitutional mandate. Instead, state courts apply the discretionary principle of comity in determining whether to recognize such divorces. The Supreme Court has defined comity as

> neither a matter of absolute obligation, on the one hand, nor of mere courtesy and good will, upon the other. But it is a recognition which one nation allows within its territory to legislative, executive, or judicial acts of another nation, having due regard both to international duty and convenience, and to the rights of its own citizens or of other persons who are under the protection of its laws.[104]

Comity is generally interpreted to mean merely that a state is not obligated to apply foreign law.[105] Consequentially, a state may decide not to afford comity to a foreign divorce when it is contrary to the state's public policy or prejudicial to its interests.[106] Circumstances in which state courts typically refuse to grant comity to foreign divorce decrees include insufficient proof or lack of finality of a foreign judgment; lack of subject matter or personal jurisdiction or insufficient notice or opportunity to be heard; clear mistake of fact or law made by the foreign court or

---

[100] Id. at 352.

[101] *See also Aldrich v. Aldrich*, 378 U.S. 540 (1964) (relitigation of a mistake of law or a mistake of fact in divorce decree barred by res judicata). *See generally* John R. McDonough, Jr., *Mr. Justice Jackson and Full Faith and Credit on Divorce Decrees: A Critique*, 56 Colum. L. Rev. (1956).

[102] *See infra* § 8.02[J].

[103] *See supra* § 8.02[E][1].

[104] *Hilton v. Guyot*, 159 U.S. 113, 163-64 (1895).

[105] *See Growe v. Growe*, 138 N.W.2d 537 (Mich. Ct. App. 1965).

[106] *See, e.g., Watson v. Blakely*, 748 P.2d 984 (N.M. Ct. App. 1987).

procurement of the foreign judgment by fraud; and contravention of the public policy of the recognition forum.[107]

In *Mayer v. Mayer*,[108] the North Carolina Court of Appeals analyzed whether foreign country migratory divorces should be recognized under comity principles. In *Mayer*, a husband seeking to avoid alimony challenged the validity of his marriage by attacking his wife's Dominican divorce from her first husband. Although the court ultimately held that the second husband, who had assisted the wife in procuring the foreign divorce, was estopped from attacking the decree,[109] it denounced foreign divorces that are not based on sufficient jurisdiction.

The *Mayer* court found that the divorce decree offended the state's public policy "against hasty dissolution of marriages" and rejected the wife's contention that the Dominican ground of "irreconcilable differences" was substantially equivalent to North Carolina's divorce ground based on a one year's separation. It refused to

> . . . sanction a procedure by which citizens of this State with sufficient funds to finance a trip to the Caribbean can avoid our legislature's judgment on the question of divorce. To hold otherwise would be to flout our law; it would permit domiciliaries of North Carolina to submit their marital rights and obligations to the contrary policies and judgments of a foreign nation with which they have no connection.[110]

Similar reasoning has led the overwhelming majority of American states to refuse to recognize foreign divorce decrees without a domiciliary requirement. An American court is likely to deny recognition, regardless of the purported validity of the divorce in the country awarding it, unless at least one of the spouses was a good-faith domiciliary of that country at the time the divorce was rendered, and regardless of whether the foreign divorce was procured bilaterally, ex parte, or by mail order.[111]

Although no states recognize ex parte or mail-order migratory foreign divorces, a few American jurisdictions have recognized bilateral foreign divorces based solely on both parties' physical presence in the foreign jurisdiction, despite a lack of domicile.[112] For example, in the New York case of *Rosenstiel v. Rosenstiel*,[113] New York couples were allowed to evade the then strict New York divorce laws by obtaining foreign divorces. The *Rosenstiel* decision has been strongly criticized by

---

[107] *See* Courtland H. Peterson, *Res Judicata and Foreign Country Judgments*, 24 Ohio St. L.J. 291, 308-10 (1963).

[108] 311 S.E.2d 659 (N.C. Ct. App. 1984), *appeal denied*, 321 S.E.2d 140 (N.C. 1984).

[109] *See infra* § 8.02[J].

[110] 311 S.E.2d at 666.

[111] Peter Nash Swisher, *Foreign Migratory Divorces: A Reappraisal*, 21 J. Fam. L. 9, 22-33 (1982-83). *See also Kugler v. Haitian Tours Inc.*, 293 A.2d 706 (N.J. Super. Ct. Ch. Div. 1972) (Haitian divorce); *Basiouny v. Basiouny*, 445 So. 2d 916 (Ala. Civ. App. 1984) (Egyptian divorce).

[112] *See, e.g., Yoder v. Yoder*, 330 A.2d 825 (Conn. Super. Ct. 1974) (Mexican divorce); *Hyde v. Hyde*, 562 S.W.2d 194 (Tenn. 1978) (Dominican Republic divorce).

[113] 209 N.E.2d 709 (N.Y. 1965), *cert. denied*, 384 U.S. 971 (1966).

commentators as overriding state public policy as declared by the New York legislature.[114]

On the other hand, the Connecticut court, in *Yoder v. Yoder*,[115] found "no repugnancy" between Mexican and Connecticut divorce grounds and granted comity to a Mexican divorce based on irretrievable breakdown in the marriage. However, *Yoder* did not involve a claim that the Mexican court lacked jurisdiction to enter the divorce decree.[116]

In the past, Americans frequently procured easy, 24-hour divorces in Mexico.[117] In 1971, however, Mexican law was amended to require aliens to become residents for at least six months prior to obtaining a divorce, making Mexican divorces less available to American citizens. Nevertheless, Mexican divorces continue to generate litigation because of the distinction between "residence" and "domicile" and because of the potential for forged Mexican residency certificates.[118]

The Dominican Republic and Haiti have now replaced Mexico as favored locations for Americans seeking quick divorces. Neither country has either a residency or domicile requirement.[119] "Divorce tour packages" are advertised in prominent periodicals, and solicitations by Haitian and Dominican divorce lawyers are sometimes mailed directly to American attorneys.[120]

These practices were successfully attacked in *Kugler v. Haitian Tours*[121] when the New Jersey attorney general brought an action under the Consumer Fraud Act against Haitian Tours, Inc., for selling travel packages to Haiti for the purpose of assisting clients to obtain a divorce in that country, which did not require domicile of either party. Although the package did not express any views as to the validity or recognition of the Haitian divorce in this country, the court held that their sale constituted a fraud, because the divorces were worthless and did not accomplish the purpose for which they were purchased.

Various countries have attempted to alleviate the problems involved in the recognition of foreign country divorces by adopting the Hague Convention on the Recognition of Divorce and Legal Separations.[122] The Hague Convention authorizes jurisdiction for divorce or legal separation based upon the "habitual residence"

---

[114] *See* David P. Currie, *Suitcase Divorce in the Conflict of Laws: Simmons, Rosensteil and Borax*, 34 U. Chi. L. Rev. 26, 57-62 (1966); Comment, *Mexican Bilateral Divorce*, 61 Nw. U. L. Rev. 584, 608 (1966).

[115] 330 A.2d 825 (Conn. Super. Ct. 1974).

[116] *See also Bruneau v. Bruneau*, 489 A.2d 1049 (Conn. App. Ct. 1985).

[117] *See, e.g.*, David P. Currie, *supra* note 114; W. Barton Leach, *Divorce by Plane Ticket in the Affluent Society — With a Side Order of Jurisprudence*, 14 Kans. L. Rev. 549 (1966).

[118] *See* J. Gareth Miller, *Mexican Divorces Revisited*, 84 Case & Com., No. 4 at 43 (1979).

[119] *See Blair v. Blair*, 643 N.E.2d 933 (Ind. Ct. App. 1994) (refusing to recognize husband's ex parte Dominican divorce).

[120] *See generally* Peter Nash Swisher, *supra* note 111; Robert Steuk, Note, *Isle of Hispaniola: American Divorce Haven?*, 5 Case W. Res. J. Int'l L. 198 (1973); James Fulton, Note, *Caribbean Divorce for Americans: Useful Alternative or Obsolescent Institution?*, 10 Cornell Int'l L.J. 116 (1976).

[121] 293 A.2d 706 (N.J. Super. Ct. App. Div. 1972).

[122] 978 U.N.T.S. 399 (1975).

(including, but not limited to "domicile") of either spouse or when the petitioner is a national of that state. Approximately 14 countries, including the United Kingdom, have adopted the Hague Convention. However, the United States is not a signatory to this Convention, which, therefore, is not binding law in this country.[123]

[H]   The Divisible Divorce Doctrine

Although a valid ex parte divorce is entitled to full faith and credit in all sister states with respect to termination of the marital status of the parties,[124] a court may not create, extinguish, or modify the financial incidents of marriage, such as spousal and child support and marital property division, without personal jurisdiction over the defendant.[125] The Supreme Court limited the *Williams I* doctrine when it announced the principle of "divisible divorce" in *Estin v. Estin*[126] in 1948.

In *Estin*, Mrs. Estin, a New York domiciliary, had been awarded a decree of legal separation, including an order for spousal support, in 1943, one year after her husband had left her. In 1945, Mr. Estin obtained an ex parte Nevada divorce, which made no provision for spousal support. When Mr. Estin ceased making support payments, Mrs. Estin brought an action in New York for support arrearages against Mr. Estin. Mr. Estin appeared in the New York action and argued that under the *Williams I* doctrine the subsequent Nevada ex parte divorce decree legally extinguished the earlier New York separation decree.

After examining the conflicting interests of Nevada and New York, the Supreme Court held that although a divorcing state has a valid interest in determining the legal status of the marriage, the state of the former marital domicile also has an interest in preventing an abandoned spouse from becoming a public charge. The Court reconciled these interests by holding that although an ex parte divorce may terminate the marital status, it does not necessarily result in the termination of all the financial incidents of the marriage. It held that Mrs. Estin's prior New York judgment was a property interest that could not be affected by a Nevada court without personal jurisdiction over Mrs. Estin.[127] Hence, the Court created the concept of "divisible divorce," validating ex parte divorces as to the parties' status, but refusing to allow marital support or property rights to be altered without personal jurisdiction over both parties.[128]

In 1957, in *Vanderbilt v. Vanderbilt*,[129] the Supreme Court extended the concept of divisible divorce to situations in which one spouse obtains an ex parte divorce when the other does not have a pre-existing support order. In *Vanderbilt*, the

---

[123] *See* John Nichols, *Recognition and Enforcement: American Courts Look at Foreign Decrees*, 9 Fam. Advoc. 9 (Spring 1987); David Cavers, *Habitual Residence: A Useful Concept?*, 21 Am. U. L. Rev. 475 (1972).

[124] *See supra* § 8.02[D].

[125] Jurisdictional rules pertaining to child custody are different. *See infra* § 10.02.

[126] 334 U.S. 541 (1948).

[127] *Id.* at 548.

[128] *See also* Green, *supra* note 1, at 163-64.

[129] 354 U.S. 416 (1957).

couple had separated in California after a four-year marriage; the wife moved to New York, and the husband subsequently obtained an ex parte Nevada divorce decree which declared that both parties were "freed and released from the bonds of matrimony *and all the duties and obligations thereof.*"[130] The next year, the wife instituted an action in New York, seeking a separation and alimony from Mr. Vanderbilt. The husband contended that the Nevada decree both terminated the marriage and extinguished any duty of support.

The Supreme Court held that it was not material that the wife did not have a preexisting support order, as the wife in *Estin* had. The Nevada court had no power to extinguish any of the wife's rights to support without personal jurisdiction over her, nor could a court without jurisdiction over the husband order him to pay support. Thus, the Nevada decree was void to the extent that it purported to terminate the non-appearing party's support rights.

The Supreme Court constrained the divisible divorce doctrine to some extent in *Simons v. Miami Beach First National Bank*[131] in 1965. In *Simons*, the husband had moved to Florida where he obtained an ex parte divorce after Mrs. Simons had obtained a New York legal separation decree which included spousal support. Mr. Simons continued to pay the spousal support until his death in Florida some years later. When Mrs. Simons filed an election to take dower rights as a surviving spouse in the Florida probate proceedings, the Supreme Court held that under Florida law, dower rights in Florida property may be legally extinguished by an ex parte divorce under the divisible divorce doctrine. The distinction was that the wife in *Simons* sought property benefits granted to surviving spouses, which were created by the law of the divorcing state and depended on the claimant's marital status.

The United States District Court for the Southern District of New York reached a similar conclusion in *Kahn v. Kahn.*[132] It held that a former wife could not challenge an ex parte sister state divorce decree in order to obtain retirement benefits under her former husband's pension plan. The court noted that although the divorce court could not directly deprive the wife of property rights without personal jurisdiction, it could terminate her spousal status, upon which her claim to the pension benefits depended.

Most states have interpreted the divisible divorce doctrine to mean that neither marital support nor property rights can be modified or extinguished without personal jurisdiction over both parties,[133] although a court may refuse to order spousal support if the petitioner moved to the forum state after the divorce.[134] In *Newport v. Newport,*[135] the Supreme Court of Virginia held that a Virginia court with jurisdiction over the husband could awarded the wife alimony after the

---

[130] *Id.* (emphasis added).

[131] 381 U.S. 81 (1965).

[132] 801 F. Supp. 1237 (S.D.N.Y. 1992).

[133] *See, e.g., Newport v. Newport*, 245 S.E.2d 134 (Va. 1978); Unif. Marriage and Divorce Act § 208(1) (1987); *see also* Clark, *supra* note 7, at 452.

[134] *See Loeb v. Loeb*, 152 N.E.2d 36 (N.Y. 1958).

[135] 245 S.E.2d 134 (Va. 1978).

husband's ex parte Nevada divorce. It noted that although spousal support is a duty incident to marriage, it survives an absolute ex parte divorce and may be granted in an independent suit. A minority of states, however, have held that an ex parte divorce granted in another state may extinguish spousal support that a spouse might ordinarily be able to assert on divorce, because the duty of spousal support and the power to order a continuation of that duty via alimony derives from a valid marriage. Once that marital status is terminated, the court has no authority to order support.[136]

[I] Long-Arm Statutes

To minimize the problems associated with the concept of divisible divorce, many states have enacted long-arm statutes specifically designed to enable assertion of personal jurisdiction over both spouses in divorce actions.[137] These statutes are intended to enable the forum court to determine related marital support and property rights in a divorce action even when the defendant spouse no longer resides in the state at the time of the divorce.

To assure constitutional "minimum contacts" necessary for a valid assertion of such long-arm jurisdiction, many of these statutes require the spouses to have maintained a marital domicile within the state at the time of their separation. Thus, a brief stay in the state during any period of time will not be sufficient for valid assertion of long-arm jurisdiction.[138]

In *Hine v. Clendenning*,[139] the Supreme Court of Oklahoma held that personal jurisdiction could be exercised over an absent husband in an action for divorce, support and attorney fees, pursuant to the state's long-arm statute. The couple had been married in Oklahoma and had resided in the state during two periods of their marriage, and the husband had obtained a medical license and registered to vote in Oklahoma. Although the couple later moved to California when the husband entered the Air Force, the husband continued to vote in Oklahoma. He later demanded that the wife return to her parents' home in Oklahoma and refused to allow her to return to California. In light of these facts and the interest of the state in assuring financial relief for its residents in divorce actions, the court concluded that the husband had maintained sufficient minimum contacts to satisfy the constitutional requirements for assertion of jurisdiction.

Even when a state long-arm statute does not specifically apply to divorce, states have sometimes applied more general long-arm statutes to assert jurisdiction in

---

[136] *See, e.g., Hudson v. Hudson*, 344 P.2d 295 (Cal. 1959); *Stambaugh v. Stambaugh*, 329 A.2d 483 (Pa. 1974); *Morphet v. Morphet*, 502 P.2d 255 (Or. 1972); *Burton v. Burton*, 376 S.W.2d 504 (Tenn. Ct. App. 1963). *Compare* Restatement (Second) of Conflict of Laws § 77 cmt. f (1971), *with* Clark, *supra* note 7, at 452-53.

[137] *See, e.g.*, Me. Rev. Stat. tit. 14 § 704-A(2)(G) (1980); Va. Code Ann. § 8.01-328.1(A)(9) (1992); Wis. Stat. Ann. § 801.05(11) (West 1994).

[138] *See, e.g., Thompson v. Thompson*, 657 S.W.2d 629 (Mo. 1983); *see also Kulko v. Superior Court*, 436 U.S. 84 (1978) (discussed *infra* § 9.02[E]).

[139] 465 P.2d 460 (Okla. 1970).

divorce or related family law matters.[140] To avoid constitutional challenges, however, the defendant's connections with the forum state must not only fall within the actions described in the state's long-arm statute, but must fulfill the constitutional "minimum contacts" requirements.[141]

[J] Collateral Attack and Estoppel

Whether a divorce decree may be collaterally attacked may depend on whether the divorce action was ex parte or bilateral and on the identity of the person challenging that decree in a subsequent action. If an ex parte divorce is invalid under the *Williams I* or *Williams II* doctrine,[142] the party who obtained the invalid decree may be estopped by his or her conduct to deny its invalidity. The non-appearing defendant, however, is not estopped from attacking the invalid ex parte decree unless he or she remarried in reliance on the decree or benefitted in other ways from assuming the validity of that decree.[143] Under the *Sherrer* doctrine of res judicata or estoppel by judgment, neither party can thereafter collaterally attack a bilateral divorce, even if based on invalid jurisdiction, due to estoppel by conduct and estoppel by judgment.[144]

The overwhelming majority of American states refuse to recognize foreign country divorces, regardless of the decree's validity in the nation awarding it, unless at least one of the spouses was a bona fide domiciliary of that country at the time the divorce was rendered.[145] A minority of states recognize foreign country bilateral divorces not based on domicile under a theory of comity, but all states, on that same theory, refuse to recognize foreign country ex parte or mail-order divorces without a domicile requirement. However, even though these divorces are legally invalid, certain estoppel defenses may nevertheless bar the parties from collaterally attacking the decree.

Although courts in this country are likely to deny comity to a foreign country migratory divorce decree and consider the decree void, the spouse who obtained the foreign divorce generally will be estopped from denying its validity.[146] In

---

[140] *See, e.g., Ross v. Ross,* 358 N.E.2d 437 (Mass. 1976) (execution of separation agreement constitutes purposefully availing oneself of privilege of conducting activities in state); *Poindexter v. Willis,* 231 N.E.2d 1 (Ill. App. Ct. 1967) (support for non-marital child). *But see Janni v. Janni,* 611 S.W.2d 785 (Ark. 1981) (long-arm statute did not extend to confer jurisdiction over child support on divorce when acts of husband occurred in other state, despite commission of act which caused harmful consequences in Arkansas); *Boyer v. Boyer,* 383 N.E.2d 223 (Ill. 1978) (failure of defendant to make alimony payments ordered by foreign decree not commission of tortious act in Illinois). *See also* Green, *supra* note 1, at 141-43; Clark, *supra* note 7, at 448.

[141] *See infra* § 9.02[E].

[142] *See supra* § 8.02[E][1].

[143] *See* Restatement of Conflict of Laws § 112 (1934); Restatement (Second) of Conflict of Laws § 74 cmt. b (1971).

[144] *See supra* notes 79-82 (and accompanying text).

[145] *See supra* § 8.02[G][2].

[146] *See, e.g., Contra Costa Country ex rel. Petersen v. Petersen,* 451 N.W.2d 390 (Neb. 1990); *Lowenschuss v. Lowenschuss,* 579 A.2d 377 (Pa. Super. Ct. 1990).

Perrin v. Perrin,[147] a defendant husband appealed the decision of the District Court of the Virgin Islands that granted the wife a divorce and custody. The wife had obtained a divorce decree in Mexico six months earlier, where she had appeared personally and the husband appeared by a duly empowered attorney and filed a consenting answer. The appellate court reversed the District Court, holding that the husband's motion to dismiss for lack of subject matter jurisdiction, holding that there was no marriage to dissolve because it had already been dissolved in the Mexican proceeding. Recognizing that domicile of one of the spouses in the foreign country is usually required, such proceedings should be recognized as a matter of comity where no public policy is offended. Because the wife had initiated the earlier Mexican proceeding as a bilateral divorce, she was precluded from denying the validity of that proceeding.

Similarly, if a subsequent spouse of a party actively helps procure the invalid decree, estoppel by conduct may also prevent that spouse from later repudiating the divorce.[148] For example, the court in *Mayer v. Mayer*,[149] applied the doctrine of "quasi-estoppel," or estoppel by conduct, to bar a husband from attacking his wife's earlier Dominican divorce which he had helped her obtain. It held that despite the state's strong policy against foreign divorces, "it would be even more inimical to our law and to our public policy, to permit [the husband] to avoid his marital obligations by acting inconsistently with his prior conduct."[150] The court emphasized that the estoppel did not validate the foreign divorce, rather

> [t]here is a difference, however, between declaring a marriage valid and preventing one from asserting its invalidity. The theory behind the equitable estoppel doctrine is not to make legally valid a void divorce or to make an invalid marriage valid, but rather, to prevent one from disrupting family relations by allowing one to avoid obligations as a spouse.[151]

Thus, the doctrine of equitable estoppel merely forecloses the attacking party from asserting its invalidity.[152] The same void divorce might still be collaterally attacked by the state or by another interested third party.

In many states, estoppel by conduct and other equitable doctrines, such as laches or unclean hands, may effectively bar the party attacking the decree from obtaining a judgment of invalidity. The result is the modern concept of "practical" recognition of a divorce decree which would otherwise have no legal effect. Similarly, if the person attacking a void divorce is "taking a position inconsistent with his past

---

[147] 408 F.2d 107 (3d Cir. 1969). *See also, e.g., Mayer v. Mayer*, 311 S.E.2d 659 (N.C. Ct. App. 1984), *appeal denied*, 321 S.E.2d 140 (N.C. 1984); *Spellens v. Spellens*, 317 P.2d 613 (Cal. 1957); *Bruneau v. Bruneau*, 489 A.2d 1049 (Conn. App. Ct. 1985).

[148] *See, e.g., Mayer v. Mayer*, 311 S.E.2d 659 (N.C. Ct. App. 1984), *appeal denied*, 321 S.E.2d 140 (N.C. 1984); *Spellens v. Spellens*, 317 P.2d 613 (Cal. 1957); *Bruneau v. Bruneau*, 489 A.2d 1049 (Conn. App. Ct. 1985).

[149] 311 S.E.2d 659 (N.C. Ct. App. 1984), *appeal denied*, 321 S.E.2d 140 (N.C. 1984). *See supra* § 8.02[E][2].

[150] *Id.* at 669.

[151] *Id.* at 663.

[152] *Accord Kazin v. Kazin*, 405 A.2d 360 (N.J. 1979).

conduct, or if the parties to the action have relied on the divorce, and if, in addition, holding the divorce invalid will upset relationships or expectations formed in reliance upon the divorce, then estoppel will preclude calling the divorce in question."[153] Moreover, these same equitable principles may bar a third party, such as a subsequent spouse of a party who obtained a foreign divorce, from later attacking the decree and, consequently, the validity of the later marriage.[154]

Some states, however, have refused to follow this modern trend. A more conservative approach was taken by the Louisiana court in *Everett v. Everett*,[155] which rejected any estoppel defense in holding a bilateral Dominican divorce invalid, thus permitting the wife to pursue a Louisiana divorce on adultery grounds.

Even within the same jurisdiction, courts have been inconsistent in their approaches to an estoppel defense. Three different estoppel theories have been used, often within the same jurisdiction. Under the "traditional" rule, neither the domiciliary state nor the parties themselves are bound by any estoppel defense.[156] Under the "practical recognition" or "sociological" view, a person who has obtained a void divorce, or who has assisted in obtaining a void divorce, will be precluded from attacking the validity of that divorce, if, under the circumstances, it would be inequitable to do so.[157] Under the "status versus property right" doctrine, an estoppel defense is denied in an action to determine marital status, but may apply when the action deals with a related marital property right or spousal support.[158]

Regardless of whether the parties themselves are estopped from challenging an invalid divorce decree, uncertainty remains whether the state of domicile itself may collaterally attack a void divorce, such as in a bigamy or adultery prosecution.[159] Most of the cases holding that the state was not barred were decided before the *Sherrer* case,[160] and some recent commentators now believe that the state may not collaterally attack a bilateral divorce decree, regardless of its actual lack of validity.[161]

Interested third parties, other than the spouses or the state, on occasion have attempted to collaterally attack an invalid divorce decree. For example, in *Johnson*

---

[153] Homer H. Clark, Jr., *Estoppel Against Jurisdictional Attack on Decrees of Divorce*, 70 Yale L.J. 45, 57 (1960).

[154] *See, e.g., Zwerling v. Zwerling*, 244 S.E.2d 311 (S.C. 1978) (second husband, who knew of wife's bilateral Mexican divorce from first husband, could not attack validity of his subsequent marriage).

[155] 345 So. 2d 586 (La. Ct. App. 1977).

[156] *See, e.g., Everett v. Everett*, 345 So. 2d 586 (La. Ct. App. 1977); *In re Estate of Steffke*, 222 N.W.2d 628 (Wis. 1974).

[157] *See, e.g., Sherrer v. Sherrer*, 334 U.S. 343 (1948); *Kazin v. Kazin*, 405 A.2d 360 (N.J. 1979); *see also supra* note 79 (and accompanying text).

[158] *See, e.g., Caldwell v. Caldwell*, 81 N.E.2d 60 (N.Y. 1948); *Rabourn v. Rabourn*, 385 P.2d 581 (Alaska 1963).

[159] *See, e.g., Zenker v. Zenker*, 72 N.W.2d 809 (Neb. 1955); *State v. DeMeo*, 118 A.2d 1 (N.J. 1995). *Compare* David Currie, *supra* note 114, at 54-55 n. 130, *with* Albert Ehrenzweig, Conflict of Laws 253 (1962).

[160] *See, e.g., Lipham v. State*, 22 S.E.2d 532 (Ga. Ct. App. 1942).

[161] *See* Eugene Scoles & Peter Hay, Conflict of Laws § 15.11 (1982).

v. Muelberger,[162] a daughter by a man's first marriage attacked the validity of her deceased father's Florida divorce from his second wife based on the latter's sham domicile in Florida. Had she been successful, the daughter, who was the sole beneficiary under her father's will, would have inherited his entire estate by establishing that his third marriage was bigamous and void, preventing his third wife from claiming a statutory share. The United States Supreme Court held that where the parties to the divorce themselves could not have collaterally attacked the decree, children or other strangers to the divorce proceedings were similarly barred by res judicata or estoppel by judgment under the *Sherrer* doctrine.[163]

§ 8.03   DIVORCE GROUNDS AND DEFENSES

[A]   Introduction

The role of traditional fault grounds for divorce, as well as their impact on the economic incidents of marriage, has declined significantly since the adoption of no-fault statutory grounds for divorce in all states. Nevertheless, traditional fault grounds remain important for several reasons. First, no-fault grounds have been enacted as an alternative, not a replacement, to fault grounds in the majority of states. Second, fault remains a factor in awarding spousal support or dividing marital property in many states. And third, family law remains in transition, and although some commentators believe no-fault laws, with additional safeguards for dependent spouses and children, ultimately will prevail,[164] others maintain that fault still serves a legitimate role in some aspects of dissolution.[165] Each state's legislature must determine for itself what role, if any, marital fault should play in divorce proceedings in its state.[166]

[B]   Fault Grounds for Divorce

[1]   Bed and Board Divorces and Absolute Divorces

Although the grounds for divorce are completely statutory in the United States, those grounds evolved from the English ecclesiastical law and from equitable rules. Until recently, English law did not recognize absolute divorce, or divorce from the bonds of matrimony, which terminates the parties' marital status. Rather, when

---

[162] 340 U.S. 581 (1951).

[163] *See also Evans v. Asphalt Roads & Materials, Inc.*, 72 S.E.2d 321 (Va. 1952) (under common law rule, son of a deceased employee could not collaterally attack validity of his father's Nevada divorce unless son had a pre-existing interest at time of divorce; worker's compensation benefits considered mere expectancy, not pre-existing interest). *But see Old Colony Trust v. Porter*, 88 N.E.2d 135 (Mass. 1949) (third-party interest does not always need to be pre-existing at time of divorce).

[164] *See, e.g.*, Ellman, *supra* note 33; Lichtenstein, *supra* note 33; Kay, *supra* note 33.

[165] *See, e.g.*, Woodhouse, *supra* note 37; Singer, *supra* note 37; Swisher, *supra* note 37. *See generally* § 8.01[D] *supra.*

[166] *See generally* Harvey Golden & Michael Taylor, *Fault Enforces Accountability*, 10 Fam. Advoc. 11, 12 (Fall 1987); Abrams, *The Effect of Marital Misconduct on Monetary Awards* 57 Fla. Bar J. 95 (Feb. 1983).

certain serious marital problems arose, the innocent party could be granted a divorce from bed and board, or divorce *a mensa et thoro*, which amounted to a legal separation.

The divorce from bed and board, still recognized in about half the American states today, is a judicial decree which orders the spouses to live separate and apart, but does not affect their marital status and, thus, neither spouse is free to remarry. Because the parties remain legally married, the marital duty of support continues, and in this respect the action for divorce from bed and board differs little from an action for separate maintenance or alimony without divorce.[167] In some states, statutes that authorize divorce from bed and board also allow the court to divide property and enter child custody decrees.[168]

If the parties reconcile, they may have the decree of divorce from bed and board terminated. Under some statutes, if the parties fail to reconcile, the decree for divorce from bed and board may be converted into an absolute divorce after a specific time has elapsed.[169]

American law, influenced by the Protestant reformers, has always taken a more liberal view of divorce than English law, and statutes permitting absolute divorce were enacted during the colonial period. Although judicial separations were not favored, they were sometimes allowed. Most importantly, however, American law borrowed the traditional English grounds of adultery, cruelty, and desertion, which had been developed in the actions of divorce from bed and board and separate maintenance, and applied those grounds to actions for absolute divorce. After the American Revolution, many states modified those traditional grounds and often added additional statutory grounds.[170]

[2] Adultery Grounds

Adultery, a traditional fault ground, is currently a ground for divorce in approximately 29 states.[171] Adultery is generally defined as sexual intercourse by either spouse with someone other than their spouse. Such actions may constitute adultery although the spouses are living separate and apart, as long as the marriage has not been legally dissolved.[172] Even in situations where the parties have entered into a separation agreement, adulterous behavior may provide grounds for divorce. For example, in *Hanger v. Hanger*,[173] the wife had admitted to her husband that she was having an affair. They thereafter entered into a separation agreement providing in pertinent part that the husband waived his right to sue for divorce on grounds of adultery. After the wife began to cohabit with another man, the husband had an adulterous affair, upon which the wife based an action for divorce. The court held

---

[167] *See supra* § 3.11. *See generally* Clark, *supra* note 7, at 266.

[168] Clark, *supra* note 7, at 267.

[169] *See, e.g.*, Unif. Marriage & Divorce Act § 314, 9A part II U.L.A. 75 (1998); N.Y. Dom. Rel. L. § 170(5) (1977).

[170] *See* Clark, *supra* note 7, at 406-09.

[171] *See* [Reference File — State Divorce Laws] Fam. L. Rep. (BNA) 400ii (2001).

[172] *See, e.g.*, *Clark v. Clark*, 644 S.W.2d 681 (Tenn. Ct. App. 1982).

[173] Civ. No. D1382-74 (D.C. Super. Ct., Aug. 31, 1974).

that a separation agreement would not allow the parties to avoid claims of adultery because the adultery is an offense against the institution of marriage which the parties cannot contract away. Furthermore, the husband could not raise the wife's previous adultery because of the agreement, and the wife obtained a divorce based on grounds of the husband's adultery.

Some jurisdictions also regard sexual intercourse with a person of the same sex as adultery.[174] Some courts have held that sexual activities short of intercourse may constitute adultery.[175]

Adultery cases frequently involve problems of proof because there are seldom any eyewitnesses to the act. Adultery may be proved by circumstantial evidence, but the standard of proof varies from a preponderance of the evidence in many states to clear and convincing evidence or beyond a reasonable doubt in others states.[176] In *Patzschke v. Patzschke*,[177] the Maryland Court of Appeals upheld a divorce granted to the husband on grounds of the wife's adultery.[178] The court held that circumstantial evidence which clearly establishes that the accused spouse had both the disposition and the opportunity to commit the offense is sufficient. In *Patzschke*, a pattern of unusual behavior by the wife, substantiated by private detectives' observations, although not wholly conclusive of adulterous behavior, was believable and adequate.[179]

---

[174] *See, e.g., Bales v. Hack*, 509 N.E.2d 95 (Ohio Ct. App. 1986) (although homosexuality is not a specifically enumerated ground for divorce, it could constitute adultery or extreme cruelty); *M.V.R. v. T.M.R.*, 454 N.Y.S.2d 779 (N.Y. Sup. Ct. 1982) (extramarital homosexual act may be grounds for divorce, but has no relevance in equitable distribution of property, where fault may not be introduced). *But see In re Blanchflower*, 834 A.2d 1010 (N.H. 2003) (holding that a married person's sexual relationship with a person of the same sex does not constitute adultery as to allow a fault ground under the state's divorce statute).

[175] *See, e.g., Menge v. Menge*, 491 So. 2d 700 (La. Ct. App. 1986) (wife's admission of having had oral sex but not coitus fell under definition of adultery).

[176] *Compare Westervelt v. Westervelt*, 258 N.E.2d 98 (N.Y. 1970) (evidence of spouse's cohabitation with another insufficient to prove adultery), *and Seemann v. Seemann*, 355 S.E.2d 884 (Va. 1987) (evidence that defendant wife had spent ten nights in room with adult male insufficient to prove adultery when wife testified that she had not slept with the man due to her strong religious beliefs), *with Everett v. Everett*, 345 So. 2d 586 (La. Ct. App. 1977) ("Courts are a bit more sophisticated today and infer that people do what comes naturally when they have the opportunity."). *See also Hughes v. Hughes*, 531 S.E.2d 645 (Va. Ct. App. 2000) (holding that the trial court had no substantial proof of alleged sexual acts; since even though the wife conceded her open cohabitation and romantic relationship with another man, she testified that there was no sexual intercourse). *But see Watts v. Watts*, 581 S.E.2d 224 (Va. Ct. App. 2003) (in this case husband had secret meetings with a woman, embraced her in public, and confessed to his wife about his infatuation with the woman. This was held sufficient to prove adultery because of husband's covert activity and lack of a plausible explanation).

[177] 238 A.2d 119 (Md. 1968).

[178] *See Lickle v. Lickle*, 52 A.2d 910 (Md. 1947) (evidence that husband and another, married, woman, vacationed together and shared a hotel room registered to him and his family, that he visited her regularly at her home in four separate residences, spent the night with her several times a week and was at her house most of the time, in addition to her husband's testimony that he was serving in military duty overseas at the time and his wife had refused to have sexual relations with him for more than two years, was sufficient circumstantial evidence of adultery).

[179] *Id. See also Brown v. Brown*, 665 S.E.2d 174 (S.C. Ct. App. 2008) (holding that a wife committed adultery where she admitted meeting her paramour for lunches, calling him frequently, and having a sexual relationship with him, although the couple's rendezvous always stopped short of intercourse).

In addition to difficult problems of proof, many jurisdictions also recognize a complex assortment of defenses to adultery.[180] The fact that the spouse was intoxicated at the time of the adulterous acts, however, is not a defense to adultery.[181] Although the plaintiff in a divorce case may not have sufficient evidence to prove adultery, the same facts may constitute cruelty as a ground for divorce.[182]

[3]　Cruelty Grounds

Prior to the enactment of no-fault statutes, the traditional fault ground of cruelty was the most commonly utilized ground for divorce in the United States. Cruelty, sometimes designated cruel and inhuman treatment, is currently a ground for divorce in about 28 states.[183] Cruelty typically has been defined as bodily harm, or reasonable apprehension of bodily harm, that endangers life, limb, or health, and renders marital cohabitation unsafe or improper.[184]

Traditionally, cruelty required successive acts of ill-treatment over an extended period of time. A single act of physical cruelty ordinarily did not provide a basis for divorce unless the act was so severe and atrocious that it endangered life or inflicted serious bodily harm, or caused reasonable apprehension of serious danger in the future.[185]

The ground of cruelty has been liberalized to a great extent over the past few decades. In states which retain cruelty as a ground for divorce, most courts today recognize mental, as well as physical, cruelty.[186] In *Hughes v. Hughes*,[187] the Louisiana Court of Appeals considered the sufficiency of evidence necessary to sustain a separation from bed and board based on mental cruelty. The wife's allegations of the husband's cold and indifferent treatment, threats, and generally abusive behavior, were substantiated by the parties' only child, and the court found sufficient mental harassment to sustain her action and defeat the husband's counterclaim that the wife had abandoned him.

---

[180] *See, e.g., Surbey v. Surbey*, 360 S.E.2d 873 (Va. Ct. App. 1987), (discussed *infra* § 8.03[F]).

[181] *See Miller v. Miller*, 116 A. 840 (Md. 1922).

[182] *See, e.g., Bales v. Hack*, 509 N.E.2d 95 (Ohio Ct. App. 1986) (although homosexuality not specifically enumerated ground for divorce, it could constitute adultery or extreme cruelty).

[183] *See* [Reference File — State Divorce Laws] Fam. L. Rep. (BNA) 400(ii) (2001).

[184] *See, e.g., Brady v. Brady*, 476 N.E.2d 290 (N.Y. 1985); *see also Thomson v. Thomson*, 661 S.E.2d 130 (S.C. Ct. App. 2008) (granting wife a divorce on the ground of physical cruelty where the husband acknowledged there was a great deal of physical violence during the wife's high risk pregnancy).

[185] *See, e.g., Gibson v. Gibson*, 322 S.E.2d 680 (S.C. App. 1984); *Bolin v. Bolin*, 99 S.W.3d 102 (Tenn. Ct. App. 2002) (husband's act of chasing son with a firearm, and ultimately causing his death, was a valid reason to find that it was unsafe for wife to cohabit with husband, and was cruel and inhumane). *But see Reed v. Reed*, 839 So. 2d 565 (Miss. Ct. App. 2003) (one single isolated physical attack was not enough to constitute cruelty).

[186] *See, e.g., Stewart v. Stewart*, 550 S.E.2d 86 (W. Va. 2001) (holding that a husband's continuing to be seen in public with a blond after his wife had objected constituted mental cruelty); *see also Freas v. Freas*, 822 N.Y.S.2d 798 (App. Div. 2006) (holding that the trial court had wide discretion to grant the wife divorce on grounds of cruel and inhuman treatment, which included husband's lack of communication, a continuing affair with another, and failure to participate in marital counseling as examples of a "systematic pattern of emotional neglect").

[187] 326 So. 2d 877 (La. Ct. App. 1976).

In *Brady v. Brady*,[188] the New York court concluded that the conduct constituting cruel and inhuman treatment may partially depend on the length of the marriage. It noted that although isolated acts of mistreatment might be considered substantial misconduct in a marriage of short duration, similar conduct might indicate only "transient discord" in a long-term marriage and a higher degree of proof would be demanded. The court found that such a standard was especially important when a spouse would be ineligible to receive alimony if he or she was at fault in the divorce. Although the law no longer precluded alimony because of marital misconduct, the court held that the duration of the marriage remained relevant and that the alleged actions must be viewed in the context of the entire marriage, including its duration, before deciding if those actions properly can be designated cruel and inhuman. Despite the broad discretion of the trial court, it cannot grant a divorce based on cruelty merely because it concludes that the marriage is "dead."

In *Muhammad v. Muhammad*,[189] however, the Mississippi Supreme Court determined that a divorce may be obtained on cruelty grounds without proof that intolerable conditions had been caused by the offending spouse, but rather that they were inseparable from the marital relationship itself. In *Muhammad*, the couple had converted to the Black Muslim religion and moved from Michigan to the University of Islam in Mississippi. The wife was extremely dissatisfied with the living conditions at the University, including the regulation of family relations, diet, personal mobility, and privacy, and returned to Michigan with the children after two years and sought a divorce. The court reasoned that one of the primary considerations in granting a divorce on cruelty grounds is whether the nonoffending spouse finds the situation intolerable, with any change in those circumstances being unforeseeable.

Divorces based on cruelty have included such diverse acts as a spouse's insistence on "excessive, unnatural, or otherwise unreasonable" sexual intercourse,[190] refusal to engage in "reasonable" sexual intercourse,[191] mistreatment and abuse of children,[192] and transvestitism or transsexualism.[193] Similarly, verbal and physical abuse, non-support, homosexuality, drunkenness or use of drugs, false accusations of infidelity or criminal misconduct, and general marital unkindness have supported divorce actions based on cruelty.[194] If a spouse's cruelty forces the other spouse out of the marital home, the offending spouse may be guilty of constructive desertion as well as cruelty.[195]

---

[188] 476 N.E.2d 290 (N.Y. 1985).

[189] 622 So. 2d 1239 (Miss. 1993).

[190] *See Thomason v. Thomason*, 332 S.W.2d 148 (Tex. Civ. App. 1959).

[191] *See Mante v. Mante*, 309 N.Y.S.2d 944 (N.Y. App. Div. 1970).

[192] *See Halderman v. Halderman*, 326 A.2d 908 (Pa. Super. Ct. 1974).

[193] *See Steinke v. Steinke*, 357 A.2d 674 (Pa. Super. Ct. 1976). *See* James White, *Symposium: One Hundred Years of Uniform State Laws, Ex Proprio Vigore*, 89 Mich. L. Rev. 2096 (1991).

[194] *See* White, *supra* note 193.

[195] *See Day v. Day*, 501 So. 2d 353 (Miss. 1987); *Weatherspoon v. Weatherspoon*, 246 P.2d 581 (Or. 1952).

Not all allegations of mistreatment rise to the level of cruelty, however. In *Benscoter v. Benscoter*,[196] the husband petitioned for divorce based on grounds of cruelty, alleging that his wife of 16 years, who had been diagnosed with multiple sclerosis a year earlier, had complained about, and blamed him for, their having four sons and no daughters, and was sporadically verbally abusive. The court found that because the husband had tolerated verbal abuse and complaints for many years prior to filing for divorce, his "condition could not have been intolerable nor his life so burdensome as he now alleges," and that the wife's alleged behavior was not the "course of conduct" required by law.[197] The court concluded that the wife's ill health explained and excused her actions. Further, evidence of the husband's extramarital affair made him a non-innocent party and, therefore, not entitled to a divorce on cruelty grounds.

[4] Desertion Grounds

Desertion, sometimes designated abandonment, is another traditional fault ground for divorce that is currently recognized in approximately 30 states.[198] The ground of desertion has been defined as the breaking off of marital cohabitation with an intent to end the marriage on the part of the deserting spouse. It thus involves a voluntary separation by one spouse from the other, with the intent not to resume marital cohabitation, and without justification or the consent of the other spouse.[199] A separation by mutual consent is not desertion by either party.[200] In *Gottlieb v. Gottlieb*,[201] the Virginia Court of Appeals held that a spouse who reasonably fears for his or her life or health by remaining in the home and has unsuccessfully taken reasonable measures to eliminate the danger has not deserted the other spouse by leaving the household.

In the past, a husband could divorce his wife for desertion if she failed to accompany him wherever he chose to live. The Court of Appeals of Louisiana held that a statute defining desertion in this manner violates equal protection in *Crosby v. Crosby*,[202] a case in which a wife had been denied alimony for desertion under this statute.

In *Reid v. Reid*,[203] the Virginia Court of Appeals reversed the divorce court's conclusion that a wife, as a matter of law, had not intended to desert the marriage when she informed her husband that she wanted a separation and left the marital home. Although she claimed she wanted to show her husband the seriousness of their marital problems, stemming from sexual inactivity, lack of meaningful

---

[196] 188 A.2d 859 (Pa. Super. Ct. 1963).

[197] *Id.* at 860.

[198] *See* [Reference File — State Divorce Laws] Fam. L. Rep. (BNA) 400ii (2001).

[199] *See, e.g., Bergeron v. Bergeron*, 372 So. 2d 731 (La. Ct. App. 1979); *In re Marriage of Jones*, 412 N.E.2d 1122 (Ill. App. Ct. 1980).

[200] *See, e.g., Day v. Day*, 501 So. 2d 353 (Miss. 1987) (living separate and apart prior to divorce did not constitute desertion).

[201] 448 S.E.2d 666 (Va. Ct. App. 1994).

[202] 434 So. 2d 162 (La. Ct. App. 1983).

[203] 375 S.E.2d 533 (Va. Ct. App. 1989).

communication, and her husband's excessive work habits and lack of involvement with their children, the court held that her complaints were not attributable solely to the conduct of the husband, but rather to their different personalities and the husband's efforts to financially support his family. Additionally, the fact that the wife filed for divorce two months after leaving the marital home supported its conclusion that she had not intended only a temporary separation.

Actions that fall short of physically leaving the marital home may constitute constructive desertion. For example, one recent case held that the wife's wilful withdrawal of sexual privileges from her husband without just cause and her breach and neglect of her other marital duties, such as doing her husband's laundry, cleaning, preparing meals, and failing to help alleviate her husband's financial problems, which destroyed the couple's home life, gave the husband sufficient evidence of desertion.[204] Constructive desertion may also operate as a defense to the other spouse's divorce action.[205]

[5] Other Miscellaneous Fault Grounds

At various times, states have recognized numerous other statutory fault grounds for divorce, including conviction of a crime, drunkenness, or drug addiction. In *Husband D. v. Wife D.*,[206] the court construed the husband's allegations that the wife had been habitually drunk for over two years as a petition for divorce based on statutory grounds of "habitual intemperance . . . so destructive of the marriage relation that the petitioner cannot reasonably be expected to continue in that relation."[207] The trial court had found the parties were both alcoholics and granted the divorce. The appellate court reversed because the parties frequently drank together before and during the marriage and the difference between their drinking habits was one of degree only. Although it found that the defenses of condonation and connivance did not apply, it held that the doctrine of recrimination barred the divorce, because only an injured or innocent party may obtain a divorce. The court further found that the wife's behavior did not have a sufficiently adverse effect on the husband's life, as he admitted that she adequately maintained the household; therefore, it denied him a decree of divorce.

Some states have authorized divorce on grounds of insanity;[208] however, in others, insanity may constitute a defense to a fault-based divorce because of a lack of intent to commit a marital offense.[209] In *Anonymous v. Anonymous*,[210] a wife unsuccessfully defended her husband's divorce action on grounds of adultery based on her insanity. The wife's psychiatrist testified that the wife did not or could not

---

[204] *See Jamison v. Jamison*, 352 S.E.2d 719 (Va. Ct. App. 1987).

[205] *Alphin v. Alphin*, 424 S.E.2d 572 (Va. Ct. App. 1992).

[206] 383 A.2d 302 (Del. Fam. Ct. 1977). *See also In re Sarvela*, 910 A.2d 1214 (N.H. 2006) (holding that the phrase "habitual drunkenness" as a ground for divorce in New Hampshire did not include prescription drug abuse).

[207] 13 Del. Code Ann. tit. 13, § 1503(5) (1999).

[208] *See* Idaho Code § 32-603(7) (1996).

[209] *See* Clark, *supra* note 7, at 534.

[210] 236 N.Y.S.2d 288 (N.Y. Sup. Ct. 1962).

appreciate the wrongfulness of her behavior because of her mental illness. The court held that the spouse asserting an insanity defense must overcome a presumption of sanity by a preponderance of the evidence. Although the wife had testified that she attempted to resist the adulterous affair, but felt compelled to continue, the court concluded that she appreciated the wrongfulness of her actions, and therefore had not overcome the presumption of sanity.

[C] Defenses to Fault-Based Divorce

The traditional system of fault-based divorce generated a number of defenses to the various fault-based divorce grounds. The rationale underlying fault-based divorce was that only an innocent party could obtain a divorce, so if the parties connived or colluded to bring about a fault-based divorce, or if both spouses were guilty of serious marital misconduct, then neither party was entitled to a fault-based divorce. Current state no-fault divorce statutes do *not* recognize these traditional fault-based defenses. However, to the extent that fault-based divorce grounds still exist in a significant number of states today, one or more of these fault-based defenses may still be applicable whenever a party chooses to bring a fault-based divorce action, rather than a no-fault divorce.

Four traditional defenses to fault-based divorce were commonly available: connivance, collusion, condonation, and recrimination. Some states recognized additional statutory or common law defenses. Justification also constituted a defense to the divorce ground of desertion. In some jurisdictions, certain types of marital fault were deemed more serious than others; in other states, particular defenses were available only with respect to specific fault grounds, but not to other grounds.

[1] Connivance

Connivance occurs when one spouse procures or consents to the other spouse's commission of a marital fault. The defense of connivance has also been based on the equitable clean hands doctrine.[211]

Connivance was primarily applied as a defense to a divorce brought on grounds of adultery, but could apply to other fault grounds as well.[212] For example, a husband and wife who mutually agreed that the husband would commit adultery or desert the wife to furnish grounds for the wife to bring a divorce action engaged in connivance. The wife would not be entitled to a divorce, as she could not complain of something to which she has consented.

Hiring an agent to seduce a defendant spouse also may constitute connivance.[213] Connivance has been broadly interpreted to include instances in which a spouse knows of the other's inclination to commit a marital offense but does nothing to

---

[211] *See, e.g., Fonger v. Fonger*, 154 A. 443 (Md. 1931).

[212] Clark, *supra* note 7, at 521.

[213] *See generally* Marvin M. Moore, *An Analysis of Collusion and Connivance Bars to Divorce*, 36 UMKC L. Rev. 193 (1968).

prevent it. In the 1920 case of *Sargent v. Sargent*,[214] a defense of connivance was successfully raised against the husband's charges that his wife had engaged in adulterous behavior with their chauffeur. The court found that the petitioner had reason to suspect that his wife was inclined towards an illicit relationship with the chauffeur, but did nothing to prevent it. Rather, the husband continued to employ him, left the parties alone in the home at night, and engaged detectives to report to him. The court noted, "He did not even warn her against intimacy with Simmons, but he left her in danger, and did nothing whatever to withdraw her from Simmons' evil influence."[215] It concluded that the husband wanted the wife to commit the offense and, therefore, he had implicitly consented to it.[216]

[2] Collusion

Collusion is a fraud upon the divorce court by the husband and wife, committed by their alleging false evidence of a marital offense in order to obtain a divorce. The defense was related to the theory that, traditionally, only the injured spouse could be granted a divorce and that injury had to be established by the evidence.[217] However, while the parties' mutual desire for a divorce generally did not amount to collusion unless some fraud was actually perpetrated upon the court,[218] an agreement that one spouse would sue for divorce and the other would not defend has been deemed collusion.[219] In *Fuchs v. Fuchs*,[220] for example, the wife agreed to a default judgment of divorce in exchange for sole custody of the parties' child, then later moved to set aside the judgment. The court granted her motion, based on collusion, holding that the state has a strong interest in the regulation of divorce and a collusively obtained default judgment attempts to subvert the state's interest.

When collusion was discovered at trial, the court could simply deny the divorce and dismiss the case. When collusion was uncovered after a divorce had been finalized, the court could subsequently vacate the divorce decree.[221] If one of the parties had remarried or become dissatisfied with the economic aspects of the divorce, however, vacating the decree would effectively reward one of the wrong-doers, and courts have tended to refuse relief, invoking equitable theories of estoppel, clean hands, or *in pari delicto*.[222]

---

[214] 114 A. 428 (N.J. Super. Ct. Ch. Div. 1920).

[215] *Id.* at 438.

[216] *Id. See also Hollis v. Hollis*, 427 S.E.2d 233 (Va. Ct. App. 1993) (holding that wife's connivance in husband's adultery was established by her encouraging his extramarital affair).

[217] *See* Clark, *supra* note 7, at 522.

[218] *See* Moore, *supra* note 213.

[219] Clark, *supra* note 7, at 523.

[220] 64 N.Y.S.2d 487 (N.Y. Sup. Ct. 1946).

[221] *See generally* John S. Bradway, *Collusion and the Public Interest in the Law of Divorce*, 47 Cornell L.Q. 372 (1962); Note, 47 Cornell L.Q. 459 (1962).

[222] Clark, *supra* note 7, at 524.

[3]   Condonation and Cohabitation

Condonation is the conditional forgiveness of a marital fault by the aggrieved spouse, with the understanding that the offence will not be reported. Condonation, in effect, places the offending spouse on temporary probation. If the marital fault is repeated or the spouse exhibits conduct that indicates an intention not to perform the terms of the condonation in good faith, the defense is nullified and the divorce ground is revived, even if the later conduct would have been insufficient to provide grounds for divorce in and of itself.[223]

Although condonation may be express or implied, the general rule is that the innocent spouse's knowledge of the marital fault is necessary for a condonation defense to apply.[224] Continued or resumed cohabitation, or resumption of sexual intercourse, with knowledge of the marital offense, historically led to a presumption of condonation. A 1960 English case, *Willan v. Willan*,[225] employed this principle, denying a husband a divorce based on cruelty when he had sexual intercourse with his wife, allegedly at her insistence, on the day the couple separated.[226] When applied to isolated acts of intercourse, condonation has been criticized as discouraging attempts at reconciliation.[227] The New York Appellate Division took this approach in *Haymes v. Haymes*,[228] concluding that a six week attempted reconciliation period was insufficient to preclude a wife from pursuing an otherwise valid claim of abandonment.

[4]   Recrimination

Under the doctrine of recrimination, if *both* spouses are guilty of marital misconduct, then any fault-based divorce action must be dismissed, because traditionally a divorce could only be granted to an innocent spouse. Under the recrimination doctrine, both spouses are *in pari delicto* under the "clean hands" rule.[229]

Application of the doctrine of recrimination has led to egregious results. For example, in *Rankin v. Rankin*,[230] both parties had been physically and verbally abusive to each other. The husband presented evidence that the wife had threatened to kill him, both by car and by knife, had thrown hot water on him, called him names, refused to have children, and spit in his face, among other things; the wife claimed that the husband had kicked and beat her, causing serious injuries, and threatened

---

[223] *Wood v. Wood*, 495 So. 2d 503 (Miss. 1986).

[224] *See generally* F. Eugene Reader, *Knowledge or Belief as a Prerequisite for Condonation*, 21 Minn. L. Rev. 408 (1936).

[225] 2 All E.R. 463 (1960).

[226] *But see contra Lawrence v. Lawrence*, 956 So. 2d 251 (Miss. Ct. App. 2006) (holding that simply engaging in the act of sexual intercourse with a spouse after an extramarital affair was *not* condonation of the affair for purposes of asserting adultery as the ground for divorce).

[227] Clark, *supra* note 7, at 526-27.

[228] 646 N.Y.S.2d 315 (App. Div. 1996).

[229] *See generally* J. G. Beamer, *Doctrine of Recrimination in Divorce Proceedings*, 10 UMKC L. Rev. 213 (1942).

[230] 124 A.2d 639 (Pa. Super. Ct. 1956).

to kill her. The court held that neither spouse was entitled to a divorce based on indignities to the person when neither party was innocent. It concluded:

> The fact that married people do not get along well together does not justify a divorce. Testimony which proves merely an unhappy union, the parties being high strung temperamentally and unsuited to each other and neither being wholly innocent of the causes which resulted in the failure of their marriage, is insufficient to sustain a decree.[231]

Similarly, in *Kucera v. Kucera*,[232] the North Dakota Supreme Court reversed the granting of a divorce on the basis of recrimination. The wife had been pregnant by another man at the time of the marriage, but contended that the husband knew, and adopted the baby at its birth. Both parties indicated that it was doubtful that the marriage would work, but married to give the child a name, and agreed to divorce after a year. After a second child was born, the parties did not engage in sexual relations for a two year period, and the wife resumed a relationship with the father of her first child. The trial court granted a divorce to the wife, on her allegations of grievous mental suffering, and held that insufficient evidence of the wife's adultery existed. However, Supreme Court held that the husband's allegations did justify a claim of desertion on his behalf, and because both parties had demonstrated sound fault grounds for divorce, the doctrine of recrimination preclude the granting of a divorce to either party.

Under similar circumstances, where the wife had committed adultery after the parties had separated and was able to demonstrate the husband's cruel and inhuman treatment, including verbal abuse, excessive jealousy, apparent infidelity, and causing the closure of the wife's beauty shop, the Mississippi Supreme Court, in *Parker v. Parker*,[233] upheld the court's decision to grant the wife a divorce despite the doctrine of recrimination. The Court reasoned that the traditional justifications of the defense were not applicable in this chase, because marital stability could no longer be promoted and the wife's economic security had already been seriously undermined, and the denial of divorce would perpetuate a bad marriage.

Professor Clark has censured the doctrine of recrimination as an "outrageous legal principle" that "prevents the dissolution of those very marriages most appropriate for dissolution, insuring that warring spouses may never form happier attachments."[234] Fortunately, the doctrine of recrimination has been abolished in most states, and where it still officially exists, it is rarely applied.[235]

---

[231] *Id.* at 644.

[232] 117 N.W.2d 810 (N.D. 1962).

[233] 519 So. 2d 1232 (Miss. 1988).

[234] Clark, *supra* note 7, at 527.

[235] Clark, *supra* note 7, at 528. *But see Merrick v. Merrick*, 627 N.Y.S.2d 884 (N.Y. Sup. Ct. 1995), *aff'd*, 636 N.Y.S.2d 1006 (N.Y. App. Div. 1996) (applying a recrimination defense to adultery grounds).

[5]   Justification

A divorce action based on grounds of desertion may be defended against on the basis of justification. A spouse may be justified in leaving the marital home due to the misconduct of the other spouse. Although some courts have required this misconduct to be equivalent to a specific ground for divorce or "constructive desertion," other courts have simply demanded that the provoking conduct "is inconsistent with the marriage relationship or makes it impossible to continue cohabitation with due regard to safety, health, or self-respect."[236] Adultery and cruelty could never be defended by justification.

[6]   Other Defenses

To prevent against the possibility of connivance and collusion of the parties, many states historically required third-party corroboration of the divorce ground.[237] Today, in light of no-fault grounds for divorce, lack of corroboration rarely, if ever, bars a divorce.

In addition to the traditional ground of collusion, other types of fraud on the court may result in dismissal of the divorce action or subsequent invalidation of a divorce decree. Broadly speaking, any fraud that affects a judicial proceeding may be a fraud on the court.[238] For instance, the Ohio Supreme Court, in *Coulson v. Coulson*,[239] held that when an attorney's conduct and misrepresentations to the court and to the wife in a divorce action prevented the wife from adequately presenting her case, his conduct interfered with the functioning of the judicial system and constituted a fraud on the court, providing the basis for vacating the divorce decree. At the same time, a fraud between the parties themselves does not necessarily constitute a fraud on the court; in the situation, the defrauded party may need to seek redress from the other party or by a motion for relief from judgment.[240]

Insanity has sometimes been asserted as a defense to a fault grounds divorce, based on the argument that the defendant spouse lacked sufficient capacity to appreciate the wrongfulness of the conduct. In *Simpson v. Simpson*,[241] the Tennessee Supreme Court held that the testimony by the husband's physician, that the husband was suffering from paranoid schizophrenia when he verbally and physically assaulted his wife, was insufficient to demonstrate an insanity defense to her divorce brought on grounds of cruelty and inhuman treatment.

---

[236] Note, *Constructive Desertion — A Broader Basis for Breaking the Bond*, 51 Iowa L. Rev. 108, 120 (1965). *See also Breschel v. Breschel*, 269 S.E. 2d 363 (Va. 1980) (spouse who reasonably believes health would be endangered by remaining in home, and has unsuccessfully taken reasonable measure to eliminate danger without breaking off cohabitation, not legally at fault in leaving).

[237] Vernier, *supra* note 9, at 142, n.22.

[238] *See* 11 Charles Alan Wright & Arthur Miller, Federal Practice and Procedure (1973) 253, § 2870.

[239] *Coulson v. Coulson*, 448 N.E.2d 809 (Ohio 1983).

[240] *See* Fed. R. Civ. P. 60(B).

[241] 716 S.W.2d 27 (Tenn. 1986).

When a party had knowledge of a defense and could have raised it during the divorce proceeding itself, res judicata will prevent subsequent collateral attack.[242] Similarly, even jurisdictional defenses and issues relating to fraud upon the court may be barred by equitable defenses such as laches or estoppel.[243]

A minority of states have statutes of limitation for bringing a divorce based on specific fault grounds.[244] These statutes frequently apply only to divorces based on grounds of adultery.

[D] Divorce Based upon Living Separate and Apart

Approximately half the states authorize divorce based on living separate and apart for a specified period of time. These statutes are generally regarded as a form of no-fault divorce because the parties are not required to prove the reasons for the separation. Some of these statutes preceded the widespread enactment of no-fault divorce grounds in general, although many of the earlier versions have since been liberalized.

The specified period of separation for divorce based on living separate and apart varies from sixty days to three years, although periods of six to eighteen months are the most frequently employed.[245] The Uniform Marriage and Divorce Act provides that a marriage may be dissolved if the parties have lived separate and apart for more than 180 days preceding the commencement of the suit.[246]

Mere physical separation alone is insufficient for obtaining a divorce based on grounds of living separate and apart; at least one of the parties must intend to dissolve the marital relationship and must clearly manifest or communicate this intention. In *Sinha v. Sinha*,[247] the husband originally came to the United States to pursue an advanced decree in 1976, while his wife remained in India because of her inability to obtain a visa. For the first two years of their separation, the couple corresponded regularly and the husband professed his love for his wife. In August 1979, three years after his arrival in this country, the husband filed for divorce. The first divorce action was dismissed due to the husband's relocation and he filed a new action, alleging that the parties had lived separate and apart for the requisite three years under Pennsylvania law. The court found that the husband first revealed his intention to terminate the marriage upon filing the initial divorce complaint, not when the couple became physically separated. The court noted, "The demands placed on marriage by modern society will often force a spouse to leave the marital abode for long periods of time. These separations should not to be interpreted as

---

[242] *See supra* § 8.02[C] (bilateral divorce).

[243] *See supra* § 8.02[J]; *see also* Clark, *supra* note 7, at 551-59.

[244] *See, e.g.*, N.Y. Dom. Rel. L. § 171(3) (1999) (5 years for adultery actions); Va. Code Ann. § 20-94 (Michie 1995) (5 years for adultery, sodomy, or buggery).

[245] *See* Linda Elrod & Robert G. Spector, *A Review of the Year in Family Law*, 30 Fam. L.Q. 765, 807 (1997).

[246] Unif. Marriage and Divorce Act § 302, 9A part I U.L.A. 200 (1998).

[247] 526 A. 2d 765 (Pa. 1987).

an intent to terminate the marriage."[248] Thus, to satisfy the statutory requirement of living separate and apart, the separation period will not commence until it is clear that at least one of the parties intends to dissolve the marriage. Otherwise, the other spouse would be denied a chance to attempt reconciliation.

The period of separation must be uninterrupted, and the parties may not cohabit during that period. Some older cases held that any voluntary resumption of sexual relations, even casual or isolated instances, during the statutory separation period interrupts the period of separation.[249] Because this approach thwarts attempts at reconciliation and risks manipulation, most modern decisions have concluded that resumption of the marital relationship itself, with its corresponding rights and responsibilities, must occur before the ground for divorce is destroyed.[250]

In some circumstances, living in separate dwellings will be insufficient to constitute living separate and apart if the couple in other respects continues their relationship as before. For example, in *Ellam v. Ellam*,[251] the court held that the husband was not entitled to a divorce on grounds of separation when the couple maintained the appearances of marriage. Although the husband slept at his mother's home every night and the couple did not have sexual intercourse during this time, the husband ate his meals, watched television, and kept his vehicle and dog at the marital residences. The court concluded that "the substantial number of the many elements and ties which go into and make up the marital relationship and bind the parties together" precluded them from living separate and apart within the meanings of the divorce statute.

Likewise, in *Bennington v. Bennington*,[252] the Ohio Court of Appeals held that the time during which the husband lived in a travel van located on the same premises as the marital home did not count toward the period of living separate and apart. During that time the husband had no intention of abandoning the marriage, and went regularly into the home to assist his disabled wife. He asserted that he moved into the van because the wife kept the home excessively hot and took 15 to 20 minutes to open the door for him when he returned from work. The court held that because there was no cessation of marital duties, the couple was not actually living separate and apart in the marital sense.

Conversely, some courts have concluded that when a husband and wife occupy separate portions of the same house and have little contact with each other, they may have been "constructively" separated for the requisite time period.[253] Constructive separation may be a sensible approach when the couple's financial

---

[248] *Id.* at 766.

[249] *See Pitts v. Pitts*, 282 S.E.2d 488 (N.C. Ct. App. 1981) (overruled by N.C. Gen. Stat. § 52-10.2 (1999), which provides: "Isolated incidents of sexual intercourse . . . shall not constitute resumption of marital relations").

[250] *See Thomas v. Thomas*, 483 A.2d 945 (Pa. Super. Ct. 1984); *Petachenko v. Petachenko*, 350 S.E.2d 600 (Va. 1986).

[251] 333 A.2d 577 (N.J. Super. Ct. 1975).

[252] 381 N.E.2d 1355 (Ohio Ct. App. 1978).

[253] *See, e.g., In re Marriage of Uhls*, 549 S.W.2d 107 (Mo. Ct. App. 1977).

circumstances make their living in separate households prohibitive.

A small minority of states provide that the separation required under living separate and apart divorce grounds must be voluntary and by mutual consent of the parties. Thus, if one spouse is mentally incapacitated at the time of separation, the requisite voluntariness for separation would not be present and a divorce on this ground could not be granted.[254] Furthermore, a lack of mutual consent to separate might result in the non-consenting spouse bringing an action for desertion against the separating spouse.

However, a majority of states that have a living separate and apart ground for divorce do not require that the separation be mutual and voluntary, and these statutes therefore approximate a no-fault alternative. Nevertheless, an *intent* to separate for purposes of ending the marriage must still be shown to avoid "instant divorces" and to allow an opportunity for reconciliation.[255]

In *Bruce v. Bruce*,[256] the Court of Appeals of North Carolina held that the facts which constitute a separation ground for divorce must be pleaded and proved even though they are uncontested by the defendant spouse, because of the general rule prohibiting default judgments in divorce actions. That court further held that traditional defenses such as recrimination would not be applicable in an action for divorce on grounds of living separate and apart.

[E] No-Fault Divorce Grounds

Approximately 18 states have abolished all fault grounds for divorce and have substituted a no-fault statute as the sole and ground for divorce or dissolution of marriage; the remaining states have combined traditional fault grounds with statutes providing for no-fault divorce.[257] Some no-fault statutes are worded in terms of "irretrievable breakdown" of the marriage, while others are expressed in terms such as "irreconcilable differences," "incompatibility," "living separate and apart," or "mutual consent."[258]

Incompatibility was one of the first forms of no-fault divorce, although it was construed narrowly in earlier cases. The courts often struggled with the factual question of whether a couple was incompatible to the extent that a divorce was warranted. For example, in *Husband W. v. Wife W.*,[259] the Delaware Supreme Court reversed a trial court's refusal to grant a divorce to a husband who had presented evidence of a separation of almost one and a half years. The separation

---

[254] *See, e.g., Adams v. Adams*, 402 So. 2d 300 (La. Ct. App. 1981).

[255] *See, e.g., Hooker v. Hooker*, 211 S.E.2d 34 (Va. 1975) (although couple physically separated earlier, husband was not entitled to divorce until two years after the time at which he could additionally prove intention to terminate marriage); *see also Frey v. Frey*, 821 A.2d 623 (Pa. Super. 2003) (the date of the parties' separation was the date the husband filed the divorce complaint, although he continued to spend subsequent time at the marital residence).

[256] 339 S.E.2d 855 (N.C. Ct. App. 1986).

[257] *See* [State Divorce Laws], Fam. L. Rep. (BNA) (1989).

[258] *See* Walker, *supra* note 69, at 439-40.

[259] 297 A.2d 39 (Del. 1972).

followed numerous violent quarrels involving personal injury, which frequently involved the police and the family court. The trial court found that the husband had not satisfied his burden of proving that no reasonable possibility of reconciliation existed.

Some states will not grant a no-fault divorce absent mutual consent of the parties. For example, in *Marriage of Mitchell*,[260] The Missouri Court of Appeals held that if one party denies under oath that the marriage is irretrievable broken the petitioner must satisfy the court that one of five alternative facts exist, relating to the respondent's behavior or that they have satisfied the provisions for living separate and apart. The Missouri Court of Appeals reiterated this position in *Nieters v. Nieters*,[261] concluding that husband's unsubstantiated evidence of the couple's differences in child rearing attitudes and the wife's donation of money to television evangelists failed to establish that the marriage was irretrievably broken.

States vary as to whether a petitioner seeking a no-fault divorce must present factual evidence proving the no fault ground or whether a simple sworn allegation is sufficient. Some states apply a subjective test to determine whether the parties themselves believe that they cannot continue living together as husband and wife. In *Riley v. Riley*,[262] the Florida Court of Appeals interpreted the state's new "irretrievable breakdown" statute to require a judicial inquiry into the circumstances in order to ascertain that the parties could no longer live together and that no reasonable effort could effect a reconciliation. The court continued the proceedings for three months to enable an attempt at reconciliation or consultations with professional counselors before the dissolution would be granted.

Other jurisdictions implement an objective standard based on the court's perception of the facts.[263] In *Hagerty v. Hagerty*,[264] the Minnesota Court refused to engraft an exception onto its dissolution statute based on discord and irretrievable breakdown. The husband in *Hagerty* filed for divorce after the wife requested that he seek treatment for alcoholism and asked him to leave the marital home. The trial court granted the divorce, finding that the husband's alcoholism was the principle cause of the marital discord which had adversely affected the husband's attitude. The wife appealed, arguing that the marriage was salvageable if the husband obtained treatment. The appellate court affirmed, holding that because the statute did not contain a provision for a separate determination of the likelihood of reconciliation, nor did public policy require such an inquiry, the

---

[260] 545 S.W.2d 313 (Mo. App. 1976).

[261] 815 S.W.2d 124 (Mo. Ct. App. 1991). *See also Simpson v. Strong*, 234 S.W.3d 567 (Mo. Ct. App. 2007) (holding that where there was insufficient evidence to show that the marriage was irretrievably broken, the court could still grant a legal separation).

[262] 271 So. 2d 181 (Fla. Dist. Ct. App. 1972).

[263] *See, e.g., Dunn v. Dunn*, 511 P.2d 427 (Or. Ct. App. 1973). *Compare Grotelueschen v. Grotelueschen*, 318 N.W.2d 227 (Mich. Ct. App. 1982) (after moving out of home and living with another woman, husband argued that marriage was irretrievably broken and no reconciliation was possible, while wife believed that marriage could still be saved), *with In re Baier's Marriage*, 561 P.2d 20 (Colo. Ct. App. 1977) (wife stated she no longer like or trusted husband, but husband stated that the marriage was satisfactory and wife's problems could be overcome with counseling).

[264] 281 N.W.2d 386 (Minn. 1979).

established fact of breakdown would not be defeated. In *Desrochers v. Desrochers*,[265] The New Hampshire Supreme Court stated that although inquiry into the particular circumstances of the couple's relationship is important in deciding whether to grand a divorce, based on irremedial break down, the length of separation and the determination and persistence of the party seeking the divorce is evidence to be considered.

Section 302 of the Uniform Marriage and Divorce Act provides that the marriage may be dissolved as "irretrievably broken" if there is an evidentiary finding that the parties have lived separate and apart for more than 180 days preceding the commencement of the suit *or* if there is "serious marital discord adversely affecting the attitude of one or both parties toward the marriage."[266] A marriage may be terminated under such a statute despite one spouse's opposition to absolute divorce or preference for a divorce from bed and board.[267]

In jurisdictions that have supplemented rather than replaced fault grounds with no-fault divorce, conflicts may arise when one spouse seeks a divorce based on a no-fault statute and the other on a fault ground. The no-fault ground will not necessarily override the fault ground, and the courts may need to determine the cause of the marital breakdown and award the divorce accordingly.[268] *Williams v. Williams*,[269] a Virginia case, emphasizes that the trial court has extensive discretion in determining which of conflicting grounds should be the basis of a divorce degree. In *Williams* the husband argued on appeal that, in light of his proof of the wife's adultery, the court should not have granted the divorce on grounds of one year separation. The husband's motive was that adultery would bar the wife from permanent maintenance and support.[270] In addition to affirming the granting of the divorce on no-fault grounds, the Virginia Court of Appeals noted that a finding of adultery is not necessarily an absolute bar on a spousal support award, nor to a recovery of fees and costs.[271]

[F] Effect of Fault on Property Division and Spousal Support

Obtaining a divorce based upon no-fault grounds does not automatically mean that marital property will be distributed and spousal support will be awarded on a no-fault basis.[272] Courts are almost equally divided on the question of whether

---

[265] 347 A.2d 150 (N.H. 1975).

[266] 9A U.L.A. 96, 120 (1979).

[267] *See Husting v. Husting*, 194 N.W.2d 801 (Wis. 1972); *In re Halford's Marriage*, 528 P.2d 119 (Or. Ct. App. 1974); *Colabianchi v. Colabianchi*, 646 S.W.2d 61 (Mo. 1983). *But see* Tenn. Code Ann. § 36-4-103 (1984). *See also* Homer Clark, *Divorce Policy and Divorce Reform*, 42 U. Colo. L. Rev. 403 (1971).

[268] *See, e.g., Ebbert v. Ebbert*, 459 A.2d 282 (N.H. 1983); *Robertson v. Robertson*, 211 S.E.2d 41 (Va. 1975).

[269] 415 S.E.2d 252 (Va. Ct. App. 1992).

[270] Va. Code § 20-107.1 (listing adultery as the sole fault ground for precluding spousal support).

[271] *See also Hammonds v. Hammonds*, 597 So. 2d 653 (Miss. 1992) (alimony should not have been denied solely because of adulterous behavior).

[272] *See generally* Allen Parkman, No-Fault Divorce — What Went Wrong (1992).

legislation adopting no-fault grounds for divorce, as either an exclusive or an alternate ground, also requires that they adopt no-fault property distribution and spousal support principles. A total lack of uniformity exists among states as to whether fault continues to be a relevant factor in dividing marital property or awarding spousal support. While some jurisdictions permit or require consideration of fault or relative merits in formulating financial awards,[273] other states have expressly excluded fault as a factor in determining spousal support or dividing marital property.[274]

Some courts have held that when a divorce is granted on a no-fault ground, facts that might have supported an alternative fault ground are necessary to bar a dependent spouse from receiving alimony. For example, in the Virginia case of *Surbey v. Surbey*,[275] the husband filed for divorce, alleging that the wife's cruel conduct amounted to constructive desertion, which had forced him to leave the marital residence. The wife counterclaimed, arguing that the husband deserted her without causes and that he additionally was guilty of adultery prior to and after their separation. The husband denied the charges, pled condonation as a defense to adultery, and later alleged that the wife had also committed adultery, which she denied. The evidence, supported by detective reports on behalf of both parties, established misconduct by both the husband and the wife. The trial court concluded that because both parties were at fault and were guilty of adultery after their separation, recrimination barred each from using the ground of adultery as basis for divorce, and the divorce was granted on grounds of separation.

The husband in *Surbey* appealed the court's awarding spousal support to the wife, arguing that she should be barred because of her adultery. The Virginia Court of Appeals upheld the award, noting that while post-separation adultery may give a deserting party grounds for divorce, it is unnecessary to determine which party caused the separation which ultimately became the basis for the divorce. Furthermore, because both parties were guilty of adultery, the doctrine of recrimination prevented either from obtaining a divorce on that ground. Therefore, the wife was not barred from receiving spousal support, because neither party's duty of support would be affected absent a finding of fault that would have constituted independent grounds for divorce.

Subsequent to *Surbey*, the Virginia Code was amended to provide that divorces granted on grounds of cruelty, desertion, and conviction of a felony would not constitute an absolute bar to spousal support, but evidence supporting those grounds could be considered factors in determining the amount of support awarded. Adultery remains the only fault ground that would comprise an absolute bar to spousal support, unless "manifest injustice" would occur if support were denied.[276]

---

[273] *See, e.g., Sparks v. Sparks*, 485 N.W.2d 893 (Mich. 1992); *see also* Woodhouse, *supra* note 37; Swisher, *supra* note 37.

[274] *See generally* Ellman, *supra* note 33; proposed ALI *Principles of the Law of Family Dissolution* (2001).

[275] 360 S.E.2d 873 (Va. Ct. App. 1987).

[276] Va. Code Ann. § 20-107.1 (Michie 1995).

In *Tenner v. Tenner*,[277] a wife who committed adultery during marriage and would be barred from receiving maintenance raised the defense of the mental illness of Multiple Personality disorder as an excuse, claiming that it was not the same person who married her husband who had committed adultery, although they occupied the same body. The Kentucky Supreme Court reversed the appellate court, holding that the wife had not demonstrated by a preponderance of the evidence that she had not been able to appreciate the wrongfulness of her conduct, and reinstated the trial court's judgment denying her claim for maintenance.

A minority of courts have concluded that enactment of no-fault grounds for divorce has no effect on the traditional bases for awarding alimony, child support, custody, property division, or attorney's fees. Although a trial judge is not required to take fault into consideration in all cases, it may, in its discretion, regard all the facts and circumstances regarding the marriage and the causes for its dissolution. In *Grosskopf v. Grosskopf*,[278] the Wyoming Supreme Court aligned itself with this minority view and denied the wife alimony in light of the extent to which her actions contributed to the break-up of the marriage, despite the fact that the husband was awarded a no-fault divorce based on grounds of irreconcilable differences.

One rationale for considering marital fault relevant in determining spousal support and property division is that although divorce is governed by statute, it is essentially an equitable proceeding and, therefore, the conduct of the parties is always relevant.[279] Some courts regard marital fault as more relevant in awarding spousal support than in distributing marital property.[280]

Other jurisdictions refuse to consider marital fault in determining spousal support and property division on theory that the actual financial needs and abilities of the parties, rather than their marital conduct or misconduct, should control those awards.[281] Thus, in *In re Koch*[282] the court rejected a wife's claim for spousal support based on injuries sustained in a physical confrontation with her husband, absent an actual need arising from her physical condition. Some courts have made exceptions, however, when a spouse's conduct has been outrageous or egregious.[283]

---

[277] 906 S.W.2d 322 (Ky. 1995).

[278] 677 P.2d 814 (Wyo. 1984).

[279] *See, e.g., Robinson v. Robinson*, 444 A.2d 234, 236 (Conn. 1982) (a spouse "whose conduct has contributed substantially to the breakdown of the marriage should not expect to receive financial kudos for his or her misconduct"); *Williamson v. Williamson*, 367 So. 2d 1016, 1018 (Fla. Dist. Ct. App. 1979) ("A spouse who invokes the jurisdiction of a court of equity to resolve his or her marital difficulties must submit to the equitable doctrines that he who seeks equity must stand before the court with 'clean hands' . . .").

[280] *See* Elrod & Spector, *supra* note 18, Charts 1 & 5.

[281] *See generally* Lichtenstein, *supra* note 33.

[282] 648 P.2d 406 (Or. Ct. App. 1982).

[283] *Compare D'Arc v. D'Arc*, 395 A.2d 1270 (N.J. Super. Ct. Ch. Div. 1978), *cert. denied*, 451 U.S. 971 (1981), *with In re Marriage of Cihak*, 416 N.E.2d 701 (Ill. App. Ct. 1981).

[G] "Economic Fault"

Most states' statutes take into account both the economic and non-economic contributions of the parties to the marriage when equitably distributing marital property or awarding spousal support on divorce.[284] Even in jurisdictions where traditional grounds of marital fault are not to be considered in dividing property or awarding support, the waste or dissipation of marital assets, or "economic fault," usually is considered relevant in resolving the financial incidents of divorce, although it is often difficult to distinguish between marital fault and economic fault.

Allegations of economic fault may arise when one spouse has "consumed, given away or otherwise transferred, mismanaged, converted or otherwise adversely affected property that, had it been before the court, would have been subject to equitable distribution."[285] Professor Lewis Becker has noted a conflict between the policy of protecting spouses from conduct of the other party that diminishes the amount of property available for equitable distribution and protecting spouses from undue restrictions on the use of their own property. He also warns of an increased risk of perjury if economic fault is considered a factor in property division.[286]

Many courts consider dissipation of marital assets as a factor in determining the shares of remaining property.[287] Dissipation may also be a factor supporting a larger share of marital property when the other spouse has squandered his or her own nonmarital property.[288] Some courts limit consideration of dissipation to actions occurring after the marital relationship has broken down;[289] others look to the motive or nature of the expenditures.[290] In light of the diversity of approaches applied by various courts and other deficiencies in the law, Professor Becker has recommended a nonrestrictive standard for evaluating dissipation, involving a general duty of good faith that does not include expenditures for family support unless a spouse secures an unfair benefit from the use of jointly held funds when he or she had individual funds. He further would except expenditures made with the consent or acquiescence of the other spouse.[291]

[H] Divorce Practice and Procedure

Although divorce law originated in equality and in the ecclesiastical courts, today it is primarily statutory. In general, divorce cases are treated like other civil cases, and, in the absence of a special statutory provisions or local rules, the rules

---

[284] See infra § 10.12.

[285] Lewis Becker, *Conduct of a Spouse That Dissipates Property Available for Equitable Property Distribution: A Suggested Analysis*, 52 Ohio St. L.J. 95, 96 (1991).

[286] *Id.* at 97.

[287] See, e.g., *Lenczycki v. Lenczycki*, 543 N.Y.S.2d 724 (N.Y. App. Div. 1989); *Booth v. Booth*, 371 S.E.2d 569 (Va. Ct. App. 1988).

[288] See *In re Marriage of Cecil*, 560 N.E.2d 374 (Ill. App. Ct. 1990).

[289] See *In re O'Neill*, 563 N.E.2d 494 (Ill. 1990).

[290] See Becker, *supra* note 285, at 106-111.

[291] *Id.* at 125-132.

of civil procedure apply. Considerable variation exists among jurisdictions as to the specific rules governing divorce procedure.[292]

The party petitioning for divorce must pay a filing fee and pay the costs of service of process on the defendant. In *Boddie v. Connecticut*,[293] the Supreme Court held that these fees must be waived if the plaintiff is indigent. *Boddie* left open the questions of what constitutes indigency and whether an indigent litigant has a constitutional right to counsel. States have varied as to when a party to a divorce proceeding is entitled to court appointed counsel.[294]

In general, only the spouses are appropriate parties to a divorce action, although third parties may be joined in issues other than the granting of the divorce itself if they have an interest in the case, such as the disposition of marital property.[295] Furthermore, a number of states authorize the appointment of a guardian ad litem to protect the interests of the parties' children in divorce actions.[296]

Most courts allow liberal discovery in divorce cases as long as the information is relevant.[297] Discovery may be particularly important in the property division stage of divorce, especially when the couple has considerable assets.

During pending divorce litigation, a divorce court may grant support pendente lite for a dependent spouse and children of the marriage, as well of attorneys' fees.[298] It may also order injunctions to protect the property interests of the spouses and to protect the spouses and children from physical abuse or interferences during the course of the divorce process.[299]

Despite the existence of no-fault divorce, most courts require the petitioner to appear before the court and will not grant a divorce based solely on affidavits. In *Manion v. Manion*[300] the New Jersey Supreme Court held that when the defendant husband neglected to answer or appear, the trial court erred in entering a default judgment of divorce, holding that it is essential that the non-defaulting party appear before the courts to answer any questions it must have. In *In re Marriage of McKim*,[301] the California Supreme Court held that although the general rule was to require appearance, in exceptional cases, an affidavit or the testimony of competent witnesses could be used to establish proof of irreconcilable difference. In this case, the court determined that it would be an unnecessary hardship to deny the wife's divorce because she was unaware that the trial court could, in its discretion, require her appearance, especially in light of the fact that

---

[292] *See generally* Clark, *supra* note 7, at 529-30.

[293] 401 U.S. 371 (1971).

[294] *See, e.g., Flores v. Flores*, 598 P.2d 893 (Alaska 1979) (denial of counsel to indigent party in child custody case would be fatal to mother's action; court appointed counsel from private bar).

[295] *See* Clark, *supra* note 7, at 532.

[296] *See, e.g.*, Cal. Civ. Code § 4606 (1990); Wis. Stat. Ann. § 767.045 (1993).

[297] *See Roussos v. Roussos*, 434 N.Y.S.2d 600 (N.Y. Sup. Ct. 1980).

[298] *See infra* §§ 9.04[A], 9.06[B].

[299] *Id. See generally* Clark, *supra* note 7, at 536-39.

[300] 363 A.2d 921 (N.J. Super. 1976).

[301] 493 P.2d 868 (Cal. 1972).

the defaulting husband had appeared and gave sparse testimony that the couple had irreconcilable differences.

Approximately one-half of the states have statutes creating some form of court-ordered conciliation or mediation prior to divorce, in which the spouses meet with a third-party counselor to discuss their marital differences.[302] Under some statutes, this conciliation or mediation process is wholly voluntary, while other statutes, empower the court to order mandatory participation by the spouses, especially when minor children are involved.[303]

In most jurisdictions, divorce cases are tried before a judge without a jury,[304] although a minority of states permit the parties to demand a jury trial.[305] The court may conduct the trial in private if necessary to protect the privacy of the parties and their children, as long as the parties are not deprived of a fair trial.[306]

A few states grant interlocutory decrees of divorce that do not become final until a specified time period has elapsed.[307] In some of these jurisdictions, the divorce automatically becomes final, while in others, the court must enter a final decree.[308] Because the parties remain married during this interlocutory period, problems arise if either spouse attempts to remarry or dies before the decree is finalized.[309]

Death of either party during the divorce action usually results in the automatic abatement of the action.[310] Some courts, however, have continued to divide property if the divorce action was bifurcated and the decree dissolving the marriage was already entered.[311]

[I] Appellate Review

State Rules of Civil Procedure establish the time limitation for filing an appeal from a divorce case, as well as other cases. Except for attacks on the courts' jurisdiction to enter the divorce decree,[312] once the time for appeal expires, the

---

[302] *See infra* § 8.05 [A].

[303] *See generally* Linda Silberman & Andrew Shepard, *Court-Ordered Mediation in Family Disputes: The New York Proposal*, 14 N.Y.U. Rev. L. & Soc. Change 741 (1986); Nancy Maxwell, *Keeping the Family Out of Court: Court-Ordered Mediation of Custody Disputes under the Kansas Statutes*, 25 Washburn L.J. 203 (1986); Lincoln Clark & Jane Orbeton, *Mandatory Mediation of Divorce: Maine's Experience*, 69 Judicature 310 (Feb.-Mar. 1986); Susan Kuhn, *Mandatory Mediation: California Civil Code Section 4607*, 33 Emory L.J. 733 (1984).

[304] *See, e.g.*, Unif. Marriage and Divorce Act § 302(a)(4), 9A part I U.L.A. 200 (1979); Mich. Com. Laws Ann. § 25.92 (1984).

[305] *See, e.g.*, N.Y. Dom. Rel. Law § 173 (1999); Texas Fam. Code Ann. § 6.703 (West 1998).

[306] *See* Clark, *supra* note 7, at 541.

[307] *See, e.g.*, Cal. Civ. Code Ann. §§ 4512, 4514 (1997); Mass. Gen. Laws Ann. ch. 208, § 21(1998).

[308] *See* Clark, *supra* note 7 at 545.

[309] *Id.* at 545-46.

[310] *See, e.g.*, *Howard v. Howard*, 364 N.E.2d 464 (Ill. App. Ct. 1977); *State ex rel. Rivera v. Conway*, 741 P.2d 1380 (N.M. 1987).

[311] *See, e.g.*, *In re Allen (Allen v. Graham)*, 10 Cal. Rptr. 2d 916 (Cal. Ct. App. 1992), *review granted*, 839 P.2d 983 (Cal. 1992); *Kinsler v. Superior Court*, 175 Cal. Rptr. 564 (Cal. Ct. App. 1981).

[312] *See supra* § 8.02.

divorce itself and other related issues addressed by the divorce decree will be considered res judicata and not susceptible to later attack, unless appropriate motions are filed based on limited grounds available for reopening judgments such as fraud, mistake, or newly discovered evidence.[313]

In general, the decision of the trial court in a divorce case will not be overturned absent an abuse of discretion or an error in the interpretation or application of law by the trial court judge.[314] A few states, however, direct de novo consideration of the facts of specific issues in divorce cases.[315]

§ 8.04 ETHICAL ISSUES FOR THE FAMILY LAWYER

All the ethical obligations that otherwise pertain to the practice of law, such as the duty to exercise reasonable care, skill, and diligence, obviously apply equally to divorce practice.[316] However, a number of ethical issues particularly concern family law practitioners,[317] and the American Academy of Matrimonial Lawyers has recently adopted Standards of Conduct that exceed the ethical requirements of the ABA and state bar ethical codes.[318] Attorney misconduct in a divorce action may cause a court to vacate a divorce decree, and also may result in a substantial malpractice action and professional discipline, including suspension or disbarment.[319]

[A] Dual Representation in Divorce Proceedings

Divorcing couples frequently request that one attorney represent both spouses in their divorce action. While their primary motive may be to avoid the expense of hiring separate counsel, they also may have agreed to the general terms of their

---

[313] *See, e.g.*, Fed. R. Civ. P. 60.

[314] *See, e.g., Burhoop v. Burhoop*, 380 N.W.2d 254, (Neb. 1986); *Schwandt v. Schwandt*, 471 N.W.2d 176 (S.D. 1991); *see also Thomson v. Thomson*, 661 S.E.2d 130 (S.C. Ct. App. 2008) (holding that husband's affirmative defense of condonation to his cruelty was raised for the first time on appeal, and was never argued in the trial court proceeding, so this defense could not be argued on appeal).

[315] *See, e.g.*, Tenn. Code Ann. § 36-6-101 (1996) (authorizing de novo review of custody cases); Neb. Rev. Stat. § 42-366-(7) (reissue 1998) (decree can limit modification or prohibit review of terms, except for child custody and support).

[316] *See* Model Rules of Professional Conduct 1.1 (2d ed. 1982); *see also Smith v. Lewis*, 530 P.2d 589 (Cal. 1975) (failure to research wife's interest in husband's pension benefits); *Morris v. Geer*, 720 P.2d 994 (Colo. Ct. App. 1986) (failure to properly value marital property and failure to reopen and prosecute after discovery of fraud); *Ziegelheim v. Apollo*, 607 A.2d 1298 (N.J. 1992) (attorney advising client on divorce settlement held to same standard of professional care required in other legal tasks); *Rodgers v. Davenport*, 331 S.E.2d 389 (Va. 1985) (client's allegations that attorney settled action for child support arrearages without her consent sufficient to overturn summary judgment for attorney).

[317] *See generally* Richard Crouch, *Ethics Aspects of Family Law Practice*, 25 Trial 63 (Apr. 1989); Norman Robbins, *Family Law Ethics*, 4 Am. J. Fam. L. 117 (Summer 1990).

[318] American Academy of Matrimonial Lawyers, *Bounds of Advocacy: Standards of Conduct* (1991). A number of states continue to adhere to the ABA's Model Code of Professional Responsibility, although many have adopted the newer ABA Model Rules of Professional Conduct.

[319] *See generally* Nathan Crystal, *Ethical Problems in Marital Practice*, 30 S.C.L. Rev. 321 (1979); *Trend Analysis, The "Changed Landscape" of Divorce Practice as Ethical Minefield*, 3 Fam. L. Rep. (BNA) 4031(1977).

divorce or anticipate no serious disagreements, or both may have a great deal of confidence in the attorney. Whether such dual representation is ethical depends primarily on whether any present or potential disputes exist between the spouses, regarding spousal or child support, child custody, division of marital property, or other matters.[320] Issues of confidentiality also make dual representation problematic.

The ABA Model Code of Professional Responsibility permits an attorney to represent multiple clients only if it is clear that the attorney can adequately and objectively represent the interest of each client.[321] The lawyer must fully explain the implications of representing both spouses to each and accept or continue employment only upon their consent.[322] Thus, if the interests of the clients conflict or if any dispute between the parties later arises, the attorney cannot adequately represent either party and must withdraw from the case.[323] In *Board of Overseers of the Bar v. Dineen*,[324] an attorney, Dineen, was suspended for failing to withdraw from a divorce case due to a conflict of interests. Dineen originally agreed to represent both parties so long as there were no contested issues. During the pendency of the action, the wife was hospitalized for alcoholism and asked Dineen to continue the proceedings. Dineen subsequently began representing the husband exclusively and requested that custody of the parties' children be awarded to the husband because of the wife's alcoholism. After the wife moved to have Dineen withdraw and he refused, the state bar brought disciplinary proceedings against him, resulting in his suspension. The Supreme Court Maine upheld the suspension, holding that his use of the information of the wife's alcoholism communicated by her Dineen during the existence of an attorney-client relationship, along with his refusal to withdraw from representing the husband, clearly violated a number of rules of professional ethics.

The majority of states consider divorce as inherently involving conflicting legal issues between the spouses and regard representation of both spouses as improper.[325] Some commentators have argued for an absolute prohibition of dual representation in divorce cases under the rationale that the "friendly" or "uncontested" divorce is actually a myth because all divorces have significant areas of disagreement.[326] *Lange v. Marshall*,[327] in which a jury awarded a former wife damages based on attorney negligence, illustrates this concern. In *Lange*, the

---

[320] *See, e.g., Jensen v. Jensen*, 557 P.2d 200 (Idaho 1976) (attorney purporting to represent both parties must adequately protect the interests of each spouse).

[321] *See* Model Code of Professional Responsibility EC 5-14-BC-17 (1980); Disciplinary Rule 5-105(C); Model Rules of Professional Conduct 1.7.

[322] Model Code of Professional Responsibility EC 5-16; Disciplinary Rule 5-105(c); Model Rules of Professional Conduct 1.7.

[323] Model Code of Professional Responsibility EC 5-15. *See also* Model Rules of Professional Conduct 2.2.

[324] 500 A.2d 262 (Me. 1985), *cert. denied*, 476 U.S. 1141 (1986).

[325] *See, e.g.*, Ethics Comm. of the Miss. State Bar, Op. 80 (1983); Comm. on Professional Ethics, State Bar of Wisconsin, Op. E-84-3 (1984).

[326] *See Trend Analysis, supra* note 319, at 4034-36.

[327] 622 S.W.2d 237 (Mo. Ct. App. 1981).

attorney had agreed to represent both parties, who were his personal friends, if they could agree on the terms of the divorce. During the divorce discussions, the wife was admitted to a psychiatric ward and, upon her release, signed the settlement agreement which the defendant attorney had drafted for them. When the trial judge delayed judgment, the defendant attorney withdrew and both parties sought separate counsel. The wife later received a more favorable settlement and filed a negligence action against the first attorney, alleging that he had failed to inquire into her husband's financial status, to negotiate a better settlement or advise her that she could obtain a better settlement through litigation, and to fully and fairly disclose her marital property, custody, and maintenance rights. Although the appellate court reverse the jury award for failure to prove damages proximately caused by attorney's negligence, *Lange* illustrates the potential hazards of dual representation.

Even if no dispute arises during the divorce action itself, one may occur later. For example, in *Ishmael v. Millington*[328] an attorney who had previously represented the husband in other matters prepared a divorce complaint and a property settlement agreement for the wife. After the court approved the agreement and entered a divorce decree, the wife sued the attorney for malpractice for failing to properly ascertain the actual value of the property covered by the agreement. The court cautioned:

> Divorces are frequently uncontested; the parties may make their financial arrangements peaceably and honestly . . . The husband may then seek out and pay an attorney to escort the wife through the formalities of adjudication, . . . Even in that situation the attorney's professional obligations do not permit his descent to the level of a scrivener. The edge of danger gleams if the attorney has previously represented the husband. A husband and wife at the brink of division of their marital assets have an obvious divergence of interests. Representing the wife in an arm's length divorce, an attorney of ordinary professional skill would demand some verification of the husband's financial statement; or, at a minimum, [would] inform the wife that the husband statement was unconfirmed, that wives may be cheated, [and] that prudence called for investigation and verification. Deprived of such disclosure, the wife cannot make a free and intelligent choice. Representing both spouses in an uncontested divorce situation (whatever the ethical implications), the attorney's professional obligations demand no less. He may not set a shallow limit on the depth to which he will represent the wife.

Purporting to represent both parties in a divorce proceeding may also lead to allegations of fraud on the court and the vacating of a prior divorce decree. For example, in *Coulson v. Coulson*[329] the husband requested his corporate counsel to draft a separation agreement and handle his divorce. The attorney merely drafted the agreement as dictated to him, then purported to represent the wife, but never advised her or the court that his representation was limited. At the divorce hearing, the attorney advised the wife that the settlement was fair and reasonable, and the

---

[328] 50 Cal. Rptr. 592 (Cal. Ct. App. 1966).

[329] 448 N.E.2d 809 (Ohio 1983).

separation agreement was incorporated into the divorce decree. More than two years later, the wife filed a motion seeking relief from the judgment, alleging fraud on the court. Affirming that the judgment should be vacated, the Ohio Supreme Court held that:

> when an attorney files and signs a divorce complaint, purporting to represent the plaintiff in the action even though he drafted the complaint and accompanying separation agreement at the direction of and upon the terms dictated by the defendant in the same action, and he represents to the court that he is plaintiff's counsel and that the separation agreement, which he had not examined for fairness and equity, is fair and equitable, and the court, in reliance on these representations, proceeds to approve the divorce and incorporate the separation agreement into the judgment, which it would not have done hand it known of the arrangement between the attorney and the defendant, the attorney perpetrates a fraud upon the court, and a trial court does not abuse its discretion in granting relief from judgment . . .[330]

Thus, a divorce decree procured by an attorney's misrepresentations about his or her client may be set aside as a fraud on the court. An attorney's participation in a fraudulent divorce proceeding may also provide a ground for a disciplinary action for suspension or disbarment.[331]

If both spouses consent to dual representation, preferably in writing and after full disclosure of the dangers, some states do not consider dual representation in an uncontested divorce action to be unethical per se.[332] Some courts have also required that the attorney discuss the implications of a separation agreement and consider whether it fair to both parties.[333] In *Klemm v. Superior Court of Fresno County*,[334] an attorney, Bailey, had agreed to represent both parties pro bono because they were personal friends. The couple agreed to the terms of their divorce, and their agreement stated that the wife did not seek and that the husband did not want to pay child support. Upon a court-ordered investigation, the District Attorney's office recommended that the husband pay $50 a month child support, because the wife was receiving AFDC payments. Bailey attempted to represent both parties again at the support hearing; however, no written waivers of representation were filed, and the evidence conflicted as to whether the wife wished Bailey to continue representing her. At a subsequent support hearing, Bailey produced a written waiver from both the husband and wife, but the court refused Bailey's motion to allow her to represent both parties. The parties filed a writ of mandate to order the court to allow continued dual representation. The appellate court held that an attorney may

---

[330] *Id.* at 813.

[331] *See, e.g., In re Hockett*, 734 P.2d 877 (Or. 1987); *see also* Model Code of Professional Responsibility DR 7-102(A)(4)-(7).

[332] *See, e.g., Levine v. Levine*, 436 N.E.2d 476 (N.Y. 1982); *Klemm v. Superior Court* 142 Cal. Rptr. 509 (Cal. Ct. App. 1977); *see also* Ethics Comm. of the Board of Professional Responsibility of the Supreme Ct. of Tennessee, Formal Ethics Opinion No. 81-F-16 (1981).

[333] *See Blum v. Blum*, 477 A.2d 289 (Md. Ct. Spec. App. 1984); *In re Marriage of Eltzroth*, 679 P.2d 1369 (Or. Ct. App. 1984).

[334] 142 Cal. Rptr. 509 (Cal. Ct. App. 1977).

represent both parties if they agree on all the issues and consent in writing to representation of both and there is no actual conflict. It remanded the case for determination of the validity of the waivers.

If either spouse is financially disadvantaged or dependent, that spouse should have independent legal counsel.[335] When the opposing party is represented by a lawyer, an attorney must not communicate with that party on the subject matter without prior consent of that person's lawyer unless otherwise required by law.[336]

Representation of both spouses in a divorce action also raises problems of confidentiality. The parties must waive their attorney-client privilege and the attorney may later be forced to testify to damaging information if the divorce becomes contested.[337]

[B] Confidential Information

Both the Model Code and the Model Rules impose a high duty of confidentiality on attorneys in order to facilitate appropriate representation and to encourage persons to obtain necessary counsel.[338] Unless the client consents to disclosure, virtually anything the client tells the lawyer must be kept confidential, except for information necessary to respond to a client's allegations of the attorney's misconduct or ineffective representation and certain communications regarding the client's criminal or fraudulent intentions.[339] While the ABA Code permits the attorney to reveal confidential information relating to the client's intention to commit a crime and the information necessary to prevent the crime,[340] the Model Rules provide that "[a] lawyer may reveal such information to the extent the lawyer reasonably believes necessary: (1) to prevent the client from committing a criminal act that the lawyer believes is likely to result in imminent death or substantial bodily harm; . . ."[341] Because of the difficulty in demonstrating that the information is actually subject to disclosure, without actually revealing it, the court should conduct a preliminary *in camera* investigation of a limited nature before requiring disclosure.[342]

An ethical dilemma regarding privileged communications may arise if an attorney learns of a clients fraud or other misconduct through client communications, such as intentional concealment of substantial assets.[343] The ABA Code of Professional Responsibility provides that a lawyer who receives

---

[335] *See* Crystal, *supra* note 319, at 329-30.

[336] Model Code of Professional Responsibility DR 7-104(A)(1).

[337] *See* Model Rules of Professional Conduct 1.6; Crystal, *supra* note 319, at 325-32.

[338] *See* Model Code of Professional Responsibility DR 4-101; Model Rules of Professional Conduct 1.6.

[339] *Id.*

[340] Model Code of Professional Responsibility DR 4-101(C)(3).

[341] Model Rules of Professional Conduct, Rule 1.6(b)(1).

[342] *See United States v. Zolin*, 491 U.S. 554 (1989); *In re Decker*, 606 N.E.2d 1094 (Ill. 1992) (attorney's refusal to disclose whereabouts of client who allegedly abducted child).

[343] *See generally* Crystal, *supra* note 319, at 348-53.

information clearly establishing that his or her client has perpetuated a fraud upon a person or tribunal shall promptly "call upon his client to rectify the same;" if the client refuses or is unable to do so, the attorney "shall reveal the fraud to the affected person or tribunal, except when the information is protected as a privileged communication."[344] Further, the attorney may be required to withdraw from continuing representation of the client.[345] Similarly, the attorney must reveal a fraud on the court committed by person other than the client.[346]

Confidentiality issues may also arise when a lawyer has previously represented one or both spouses in other legal matters.[347] If there is a substantial possibility that knowledge acquired in a earlier representation could be used against the former client in the subsequent divorce, the lawyer may be disqualified from representing either spouse in the divorce action.[348]

For example, in *Woods v. Superior Court of Tulare County*,[349] the California Court of Appeal held that, absent consent or waiver, an attorney who had represented the family business should be disqualified from representing one of the spouses in a divorce action, despite conflicting evidence concerning whether the attorney actually had obtained confidential information from the other spouse. The court emphasized that potential, as well as actual, adversity to a former client created a conflict and that an attorney for a family corporation must be impartial among all the shareholders and decline to represent either side to avoid the appearance of impropriety.

Similarly, in *In re Braun*,[350] an attorney was disciplined for representing the wife in divorce action after discussing a potential reconciliations with both parties and later conferring with the husband alone about possible representation. Although the attorney alleged that no confidential information was exchanged in his meeting with the husband and withdrew as the wife's counsel after the husband complained, the court held that attorneys may be disciplined for acts which give rise to the appearance of impropriety even if no confidential information was actually revealed.

---

[344] Model Code of Professional Responsibility DR 7-102(B)(1) (1974). *See also* Model Rules of Professional Conduct 3.3, cmt.

[345] *See* Model Code of Professional Responsibility DR 2-110.

[346] Model Code of Professional Responsibility DR 7-102(B)(2).

[347] *Cf. In re Boyle*, 611 A.2d 618 (N.H. 1992) (attorney serving as guardian ad litem for children in custody action violated ethical rules by undertaking to represent children's father is criminal case).

[348] *See In re Conduct of Jayne*, 663 P.2d 405 (Or. 1983) (representation of husband in dissolution proceeding after previous representation of wife in various other matters constituted violation of ethical obligation to preserve confidences and secrets of clients and of duty to refuse to accept employment on behalf of client if exercise of independent professional judgment of lawyer on behalf of another client would be impaired; public reprimand warranted). *But see Rush v. Rush*, 574 So. 2d 808 (Ala. Civ. App. 1990) (attorney's previous representation of husband in another matter did not meet substantial relationship test for disqualification); *Gause v. Gause*, 613 P.2d 1257 (Alaska 1980) (wife's motion to disqualify husband's attorney's law firm in divorce action denied because two prior occasions of representation did not raise substantial possibility of knowledge being gained to detriment of wife).

[349] 197 Cal. Rptr. 185 (Cal. Ct. App. 1983).

[350] 227 A.2d 506 (N.J. 1967).

On some occasion, courts have demanded termination of the attorney-client privilege when failure to disclose perpetrates a fraud on the court and when the best interest of children need to be considered. In *Bersani v. Bersani*,[351] the wife moved with the children and failed to tell the husband of her whereabouts. The wife's attorney knew of her location but would not disclose any information based on the attorney-client relationship. After the husband was granted custody of the children, the wife's counsel continued to argue the privilege, on the basis that the custody was a separate issue. The court held that the issue of custody was inextricably intertwined with the attorney-client privilege issue and counsel's withholding information constituted a fraud on the court, compelling counsel to reveal the whereabouts of the wife and children.

[C]   Attorney Fees on Divorce

An attorney must not charge excessive fees in a divorce action. Whether a fee is reasonable depends on factors such as the time expended on the case, the attorney's individual skill and professional reputation, the nature and complexity of the case, the usual charges, and the benefit to the client.[352] When a fee is questioned, the trial court normally has the discretion to determine its reasonableness.[353]

In *Moses v. Moses*,[354] The Pennsylvania appellate court held that an attorney involved a divorce case must remain cognizant of how much of the time he is billing is actually necessary to achieve the desired results. An attorney cannot expect to be reimbursed by one spouse for an inordinate number of hours spent tending to the emotional need of the other spouse. In *Moses*, the bill reflected 121 hours spent over a period of 56 days, often at strange hours and involving discussions based on the attorney's personal relationship with the couple. The settlement reached through these efforts was a weekly support award of $275, and the couple did not divorce. The court held that an attorney must balance a number of factors in determining the number of hours to spend with a client, and that these facts did not necessitate such a fee.

The prevailing general rule is that contingent fee arrangements, in which the client agrees to pay a percentage the amount recovered, are not proper in divorce litigation.[355] Fees contingent upon obtaining a divorce, upon the amount of alimony, or a portion of a lump sum settlement in lieu of alimony are often considered to be void as against public policy, because an attorney would obtain an interest in discouraging the couple's reconciliation and because support payments may not be

---

[351]   565 A.2d 1368 (Conn. 1989).

[352]   *See Reid v. Reid*, 562 N.Y.S.2d 981 (N.Y. App. Div. 1990).

[353]   *See, e.g.*, *Ransom v. Ransom*, 429 N.E.2d 594 (Ill. App. Ct. 1981); *In re Matter of Kinast*, 357 N.W.2d 282 (Wis. 1984); *see also* Stuart Speiser, Attorneys Fees § 8.2 (1973 & Supp. 1992).

[354]   1 Fam. L. Rep. (BNA) 2604 (July 22, 1975), *aff'd*, 344 A.2d 912 (Pa. Super. Ct. 1975).

[355]   *See* ABA Code of Professional Responsibility EC 2-20; Model Rules of Professional Conduct 1.5(d)(1); *Thompson v. Thompson*, 319 S.E.2d 315 (N.C. Ct. App. 1984), *rev'd on other grounds*, 328 S.E.2d 288 (N.C. 1985). *But see* Kathleen Southern, *Professional Responsibility — Contingent Fees in Domestic Relations Actions: Equal Freedom to Contract for Domestic Relations Bar*, 62 N.C.L. Rev. 381(1984).

assigned.[356] It has also been suggested that because divorce clients are often distraught, they may be more likely to allege that contingent fees were obtained through undue influence and overreaching, ultimately to the detriment of the legal profession.[357]

Contingent fee agreements in child support cases raise additional policy questions. In *Davis v. Taylor*,[358] the court held that the portion of an award of over $45,000 for attorneys' fees that was based on a contingent-fee contract was void because it "alters and disrupts the judicial formulation and structuring of the support award."[359] Statutes allowing the award of reasonable legal fees enable parties to bring support actions when they otherwise lack the financial means to employ counsel. Such statutes protect the best interests of the child by assuring that the opposing party will be met on fair terms. The court concluded, "To allow a contingent-fee contract based on a percentage of a child support award would upset the equilibrium between judicially-monitored support schedules and judicially-monitored awards of attorneys' fees for plaintiffs who could not otherwise afford adequate legal representation."[360]

The issue of contingent fees most commonly arises in connection with attempted collection of support or property division payments, often long after the divorce itself has been granted. The decisions on their appropriateness in this context are inconsistent.[361] In *Meyers v. Handlon*,[362] the Indiana Court of Appeals held that contingent fee agreements are not allowed in divorce cases, despite the fact that the defendant attorneys were hired after the divorce had been granted and they were not in a position to promote divorce. The court concluded that all questions relating to marriage and property rights arising therefrom are part of the divorce action, and the contingent fee arrangement was void and unenforceable as a violation of public policy.

[D]   Sexual Relations with a Divorce Client

The ethical implications of an attorney engaging in sexual relations with a divorce client recently have generated considerable concern. Courts have found that repeated attempts to exploit the attorney-client relationship and the resulting trust produced therein may take "particular advantage of clients whose

---

[356] *See McCrary v. McCrary*, 764 P.2d 522 (Okla. 1988); *see also* Speiser, *supra* note 353 at § 2:6 (1973 & Supp. 1992).

[357] *See Thompson v. Thompson*, 319 S.E.2d 315 (N.C. Ct. App. 1984), *rev on other grounds*, 328 S.E.2d 288 (N.C. 1985).

[358] 344 S.E.2d 19 (N.C. Ct. App. 1986).

[359] *Id.* at 22.

[360] *Id.*

[361] *Compare Licciardi v. Collins*, 536 N.E.2d 840 (Ill. App. Ct. 1989) (contingency fee contract not valid in post-divorce modification of property divisions), *with Roberds v. Sweitzer*, 733 S.W.2d 444 (Mo. 1987) (contingent fee arrangement not improper in action to set aside property division), *and Gross v. Lamb*, 437 N.E.2d 309 (Ohio Ct. App. 1980) (contingency fee not improper where client could not afford hourly fee of experienced domestic relations lawyer). *See also* Kathleen Southern, *supra* note 355.

[362] 479 N.E.2d 106 (Ind. App. 1985).

matrimonial difficulties placed them in a highly vulnerable emotional state."[363] Engaging in a sexual relationship with a divorce client may destroy the chance for reconciliation and may prevent the attorney from properly exercising independent judgment.[364]

However, in the absence of any specific ethical prohibition and lack of evidence that the attorney took advantage of the professional relationship, the court in *Edwards v. Edwards*,[365] held that an attorney is not compelled to withdraw from representation of a client with whom he is sexually involved. In *Edwards*, the attorney was nonetheless required to withdraw from the case once he was named as a witness in the husband's counter-claim for divorce based on the wife's adultery.[366]

The seriousness of an ethical issue posed by an attorney's sexual relations with a divorce client depends on the particular jurisdiction and the facts of each case. On one hand, for example, an Illinois court of appeals held that an attorney's sexual relationship with his divorce client did not constitute malpractice in the absence of allegations of inadequate representation, exchange of sexual favors for legal services, or actual damages.[367] On the other hand, the Supreme Court of Rhode Island, in *In re DiSandro*, found that engaging in a consensual sexual relationship with a divorce client was unethical and would warrant public censure. That court noted,

> [A]ny attorney who practices in the area of domestic relations must be aware that the conduct of the divorcing parties, even in a divorced based on irreconcilable differences . . . may have a significant impact on that client's ability to secure child custody and/or may materially affect the client's rights regarding distribution of marital assets. An attorney who engages in sexual relations with his or her divorce client places that client's rights in jeopardy. The lawyer's own interest in maintaining the sexual relationship creates an inherent conflict with the obligation to represent the client properly.

More serious sanction may also be brought against an attorney who has sexual relations with his or her divorce client, as *Committee on Professional Ethics and Conduct of the Iowa State Bar v. Hill*,[368] illustrates. In *Hill*, a client, K.C., who was unemployed and a drug addict, contacted attorney Hill for representation in a divorce and custody action. Hill agreed to represent her, although she had no money. K.C. offered to engage in sexual intercourse with Hill in exchange for money. Although Hill offered to extend K.C. a personal loan if she did not wish to engage sex, she declined because she had no means of repayment. Hill gave her

---

[363] *Matter of Bowen*, 542 N.Y.S.2d 45 (N.Y. App. Div. 1989).

[364] *See Colorado v. Zeilinger*, 814 P.2d 808 (Colo. 1991).

[365] 567 N.Y.S.2d 645 (N.Y. App. Div. 1991).

[366] *See also Suppressed v. Suppressed*, 565 N.E.2d 101 (Ill. App. Ct. 1990) (attorney's sexual relationship with divorce client not malpractice in absence of allegations of inadequate representation, exchange of sexual favors for legal services, or actual damages).

[367] *Id.*

[368] 436 N.W.2d 57 (1989).

money and they had sexual intercourse in his office.

K.C. later underwent treatment for chemical dependency, reconciled with her husband, and the divorce action was dismissed. Upon a complaint to the Grievance Commission, Hill was found to have violated his ethical obligations and the commission recommended that he be suspended from practice. The Supreme Court of Iowa, holding that Hill had violated the high standards of ethical conduct and that such conduct reflects negatively on the legal profession, and suspended Hill's license to practice indefinitely with no possibility of reinstatement for three months.

The California State Bar became the first in the country to enact rules forbidding attorney-client sexual relations in specified circumstances, although it refused to enact a complete ban[369] While neither the ABA Model Rules of Professional Conduct or the Model Code of Professional Responsibility forbid sexual relations with clients, the ABA Standing Committee on Ethics and Professional Responsibility has advised against such conduct, warning that the attorney may be lured into other conduct that may result in violation of other ethical rules.[370]

[E]   Candor Toward the Court and Withdrawal from the Case

Both the ABA Model Rules and the Model Code of Professional Conduct contain various rules governing a lawyer's relationship with the court and behavior in court. Under various formulations, lawyers' obligations include duties not to make false statements of material law or fact to a court, to disclose material facts necessary to avoid assisting a criminal or fraudulent act by a client, and to not offer false evidence or perjured testimony.[371] A lawyer must withdraw from representing a client for any or no reason, and a client may hire and fire attorneys at will.[372] A lawyer who withdraws or is discharged must give reasonable notice to the client, allow time for the client to employ other counsel, deliver paperwork and property to which the client is entitled, and refund any advance but unearned fees.[373] Mandatory withdrawal is required when further representation will result in violation of rules of professional conduct, the law or when the lawyer's physical or mental health material impairs the ability to represent the client.[374] *Matza v. Matza*[375] illustrates a case where client misconduct justifies attorney withdrawal, where the attorney withdrew because he feared that his client would commit perjury or submit fraudulent documents in court.

---

[369] Cal. Ethics Rule 3-120(B) (1992).

[370] ABA Comm. on Ethics and Professional Responsibility, Formal Op. 92-354 (1992).

[371] *See, e.g.*, Model Rules of Professional Conduct 3.3; Model Code of Professional Responsibility DR 7-102.

[372] *See, e.g., In re Cooperman*, 611 N.Y.S.2d 465, 468 (N.Y. 1994).

[373] *See* Model Code of Professional Responsibility DR 2-110; Model Rules of Professional Conduct 1.16.

[374] *Id.*

[375] 627 A.2d 414 (Conn. 1993).

Lawyers have also been disciplined for professional misconduct in the context of their own divorces, including failing to pay spousal or child support[376] and failing to make an adequate financial disclosure of marital property.[377] Similarly, a lawyer spouse who purports to represent both parties by convincing the other spouse that independent counsel is unnecessary may have breached a confidentiality fiduciary relationship and the divorce decree may be set aside.[378]

[F] Pro Se Divorces

Over the past two decades, the number of pro se litigants in divorce cases has grown rapidly. A 1993 ABA study of divorce filings in one Arizona county, known for its user-friendly court system, found that in almost 90% of divorce cases, at least one party was unrepresented and in more than 50% of the cases, both parties were unrepresented.[379]

If one spouse is not represented by counsel, the attorney must not give that person the impression that the attorney is disinterested and must make reasonable efforts to assure that the unrepresented party understands the attorney's role of representing the other spouse.[380] Other than advising the other party to obtain counsel, the lawyer must not give advice to the unrepresented party if that person's interests could conflict with the client's interests.[381] The lawyer must not make any inaccurate or misleading statements of law to the unrepresented spouse.[382]

An unrepresented spouse may later attack the validity of a divorce decree and the fairness of a separation agreement if the attorney violated these ethical principles. *Adkins v. Adkins*[383] depicts an egregious case of attorney misconduct against an unrepresented opposing party. In *Adkins* the wife had threatened her husband that she would get a lawyer who would force him out of the marital home, obtain all his property, and require him to pay her for the rest of his life if he refused to comply with her wishes regarding a divorce. The husband, who had little education or knowledge of his legal rights, believed her. The wife subsequently retained an attorney, Franchshessa Bixler, who requested that the husband come to her office. She discouraged the husband from hiring his own lawyer and misrepresented his legal rights, then induced him to sign a marital settlement agreement which gave the wife most of parties' property, created an obligation for the husband to pay alimony, and assessed him with the wife's attorney's fees and all outstanding debts. The husband signed the documents without the opportunity to read or understand them after Bixler convinced him he would do worse if litigation was necessary.

---

[376] *See, e.g., In re Warren*, 888 S.W.2d 334, 336-37 (Mo. 1994).

[377] *See, e.g., In re Finnerty*, 641 N.E.2d 1323, 1327 (Mass. 1994).

[378] *See Webb v. Webb*, 431 S.E.2d 55, 61 (Va. Ct. App. 1993).

[379] ABA Standing Committee On Delivery of Legal Services, Self-Representation in Divorce Cases 33 (1993).

[380] Model Rules of Professional Conduct 4.3.

[381] *See* Model Code of Professional Responsibility DR 7-104(A)(2).

[382] Model Rules of Professional Conduct 4.1.

[383] 186 Cal. Rptr. 818 (Cal. Ct. App. 1982).

After the divorce decree was entered, the husband in *Adkins* received notification of a proceeding to hold him in contempt for failure to pay spousal support. He then sought independent legal advice for the first time and instituted an action which resulted in vacating the judgment and rescinding the marital settlement agreement. In upholding the invalidation of the divorce and settlement agreement, the California Court of Appeals held that the documents had been obtained by fraud and that the wife and her attorney had deceived and prevented the husband from knowing his rights and asserting them in court.

In a similar case, *Tenneboe v. Tenneboe*,[384] the unrepresented husband filed a motion to set aside a property settlement agreement drafted by the wife's attorney, on grounds of misrepresentation and overreaching. The husband signed an agreement providing for alimony and child support payments of $700 per week when he netted just over $800 a week, working seven days a week. He later testified that when he signed the agreement, he protested that the payments were more than he could handle, but the wife's attorney told him he could go back to court at a future time to have the payments modified, but did not inform him he would need to show a substantial change in income. Additionally, the agreement gave the wife most of the couple's assets. The Florida Court of Appeals concluded that the agreement left the husband impoverished and the that unless separate counsel represents both parties, the parties relationship remains nonadversarial and each party has a fiduciary type responsibility to the other. The court held that the husband had provided enough evidence on misrepresentation and overreaching to allow him to have the property settlement set aside.

In response to the growth of pro se divorce litigants, a number of court systems have hired staff or developed programs designed to provide information and assistance to these self-represented parties. These programs range from simplified form pleading and instruction books to group classes and telephone hot-lines.[385]

While some have applauded the rise of pro se divorce as a necessary alternative to the high cost of attorney representation, others have voiced concern about the dangers of self-representation and about the quality of some of the programs developed to assist pro se litigants.[386] The increase in pro se divorce litigants also poses an ethical dilemma for attorneys, since individuals who self-represent may seek limited attorney services for specific issues or aspects of a case. Traditionally, the establishment of an attorney-client relationship encompassed full service representation for an entire matter and could result in significant malpractice exposure. Recently, several commentators have proposed for notion of unbundled legal services, or discrete task representation as an alternative to this traditional full-service model, under which clients could contract for specific tasks or aspects of the divorce.[387] Unfortunately, existing ethical and malpractice rules fail to address the situation of an attorney who handles only discrete parts of a case,

---

[384] 558 So. 2d 470 (Fla. App. 1990).

[385] *See* Robert B. Yegge, *Divorce Litigants Without Lawyers*, 28 Fam. L.Q. 407, 412-16.

[386] *See* Elizabeth McCulloch, *Let Me Show You How: Pro Se Divorce Courses and Client Power*, 48 Fla. L. Rev. 481 (1996).

[387] *See* Forrest S. Mosten, *Unbundling of Legal Services and the Family Lawyer*, 28 Fam. L.Q. 421 (1994).

making such unbundled representation a risky undertaking.

In response to the cost of attorneys' fees, do-it-yourself, pro se divorces have become increasingly popular, assisted with pre-packaged "divorce kits."[388] Because of simplification of divorce proceedings due to no-fault legislation, various groups, including "feminists, family law reformers, consumer activists, and entrepreneurs" have supported pro se divorce, largely to protest the pricing practices of the bar.[389] Bar associations have assailed pro se divorce kits on the basis that they may mislead the lay public and result in serious problems, especially with respect to marital support and property rights.[390]

Although some decisions have upheld the commercial sale of these divorce kits,[391] such methods have been successfully attacked as the unauthorized practice of law.[392] In *State Bar v. Cramer*,[393] a non-attorney was held in civil contempt of court for continuing to sell divorce kits after having been permanently enjoined from holding herself out to the public as qualified to render advice and services and from furnishing forms and documents. The court found that her advertising, conferring with and advising clients, and preparing and filing documents constituted the unauthorized practice of law.

[G]   Representing Children

Most states permit, but do not require, the appointment of counsel to represent children in contested divorce or custody proceeding.[394] Considerable disagreement exists, however, regarding the appropriate role of a child's attorney. Conflict exists over whether the attorney should be a zealous of the child's wishes, or whether the attorney should make an independent assessment of the child's best interests and present that position to the court. The Supreme Court of Wyoming, in *Clark v. Alexander*,[395] examined the roles of guardian ad litem and acknowledge a hybrid role, which necessitates a modification of the Rules of Professional Conduct. Some commentators have rejected the hybrid approach and advocate that the attorney's role is the same as with adult clients.[396]

---

[388] *See* Project, *The Unauthorized Practice of Law and Pro Se Divorce: An Empirical Analysis*, 86 Yale L.J. 104 (1976); Patricia Winks, *Divorce Mediation: A Nonadversary Procedure for the No-Fault Divorce*, 19 J. Fam. L. 615, 625 (1980-81).

[389] Project, *supra* note 388, at 109.

[390] *See, e.g., In re Marriage of Eller*, 552 P.2d 30 (Colo. Ct. App. 1976) (wife waived right to support in "divorce kit" separation agreement; later sought support from husband).

[391] *See Oregon State Bar v. Gilchrist*, 538 P.2d 913 (Or. 1975) (publishing, advertising, and sales of "divorce kits," without personal contact with customers, not "practice of law," although consultation, explanation, or advice does constitute such practice and may be enjoined).

[392] *See Delaware State Bar v. Alexander*, 386 A.2d 652 (Del. 1978) (injunction to prohibit divorce reform group from engaging in unauthorized practice of law); *Florida State Bar v. Stupica*, 300 So. 2d 683 (Fla. 1974) (publication of "divorce kit" including explanations, instruction, and advice on use of forms to secure no-fault divorce constitutes unauthorized practice of law).

[393] 249 N.W.2d 1 (Mich. 1976).

[394] *See* Ann Haralambie, The Child's Attorney 2 (1993).

[395] 953 P.2d 145 (1998).

[396] *See, e.g., Proceedings of the Conference on Ethical Issues in the Legal Representation of Children:*

§ 8.05   ALTERNATIVE DISPUTE RESOLUTION

Traditional adversarial divorce litigation often is an expensive, time-consuming, and emotionally-laden process. With the advent of no-fault divorce grounds, the use of alternative dispute resolution (ADR) techniques, particularly divorce mediation and arbitration, has greatly increased, largely because of their potential to reduce the emotional and financial burdens that so often accompany divorce. Especially when the parties have children, peaceful resolution of divorce issues is considered particularly important in avoiding any additional stress and psychological damage that children may suffer.[397]

Divorce mediation and arbitration allow the parties to resolve their differences regarding child and spousal support, division of marital property, and child custody in a private, cooperative and non-adversarial manner. Use of divorce mediation and arbitration, based on no-fault alternatives, therefore "reflects a preference for private ordering over public name calling, [and] for resolution over retribution."[398]

Nevertheless, although ADR is not necessarily appropriate in all situations, divorce mediation and arbitration may be valuable alternatives to traditional divorce litigation. Divorce mediation and arbitration techniques and processes continue to be refined and are gaining increasing understanding and acceptance by the practicing bar and the courts.[399]

[A]   Divorce Mediation

Divorce mediation is a process in which the parties to a divorce are assisted by an impartial, professional third party mediator in reaching an agreement with respect to divorce related matters such as spousal and child support, custody, and property division.[400] Divorce mediation differs from conciliation in that the mediator does not attempt to reconcile the parties, but aids them in procuring a divorce settlement agreement with minimal adversarial hostility and economic expense. One commentator has described the basic features of mediation as "contracting, gathering and analyzing data, generating and evaluating options, negotiating, and drafting agreements."[401]

Recommendations of the Conference, 64 Ford. L. Rev. 1301(1996); *Representing Children: For Attorneys and Guardians Ad Litem in Custody or Visitation Proceedings (With Commentary)*, 13 J. Am. Acad. Matrim. Law 1 (1995); *see also* Peter Margulies, *The Lawyer As Caregiver: Child Client's Competence in Context*, 64 Ford. L. Rev. 1473 (1996).

[397]   *See* Hugh McIsaac, *Reducing the Pain of a Child Custody Struggle*, 14 Fam. Advoc. 26 (Spr. 1992).

[398]   Winks, *supra* note 388, at 615.

[399]   *See, e.g.*, John Fiske, *Divorce Mediation: An Attractive Alternative to Advocacy*, 20 Suffolk U.L. Rev. 55 (1986); Debra Moss, *Enter the Divorce Mediator: Family Mediation is Gradually Gaining Acceptance*, 73 A.B.A. J. 27 (Aug. 1987); Richard Salem, *The Alternate Dispute Resolution Movement: An Overview*, 40 Arb. J. 3 (1985); Jessica Pearson & Nancy Thoennes, *Divorce Mediation: An Overview of Research Results*, 19 Colum. J.L. & Soc. Probs. 451 (1985).

[400]   *See, e.g.*, Joan Kelly, *Who Should Be the Mediator?*, 14 Fam. Advoc. 19 (Spring 1992) (comparing three models of divorce mediation); Joan Blades, *Family Mediation: Cooperative Divorce Settlement* (1985).

[401]   Kelly, *supra* note 400, at 21.

Several states mandate mediation in certain contexts, most commonly, in disputed child custody cases.[402] For instance, the California Civil Code expressly provides for mediation in child custody or visitation cases.[403] It further requires standards of practice which include providing for the best interests of the child and safeguarding the child's rights to frequent, continuing contact with both parents, easing the transition of the family by enumerating the factors be considered in decisions regarding the child's future, and conducting negotiations in a manner that will equalize the power relationships of the parties.[404]

Absent formal requirements for mediation in state statutes, local rules, or state supreme court rules, a court may order mediation, in its discretion, in a disputed custody case when a reasonable basis exists.[405] In most instances however, divorce mediation is a voluntary arrangement that requires the approval of both spouses.

As divorce and custody mediation has grown in popularity, it has also become increasingly professionalized. In the mid-1980s, both the Family Law Section of the American Bar Association and the Association of Family and Conciliation Courts issued model standards of practice for divorce and family mediators.[406] The standards require a mediator to define and describe the mediation process and its costs before beginning mediation, not to disclose voluntarily information acquired during mediation without the prior consent of both parties, to be impartial, and to assure that the parties have sufficient information and knowledge for making decisions. The mediator must discontinue or end mediation when continuation would injure or prejudice one or both participants, and advise each party to obtain independent legal review before reaching agreement.[407] A number of states have also adopted practice standards and/or minimum qualifications for mediators.[408]

Questions exist regarding whether divorce mediation is the practice of law, and, if so, whether non-lawyers are prohibited from mediating family disputes. If not, it is unclear what ethical rules and standards govern the conduct of lawyer-mediators.[409] If mediation does constitute the practice of law, then lawyer-mediators risk violating ethical rules, especially constraints on dual representation;

---

[402] *See, e.g.,* Cal. Civ. Code § 3155-77 (West Supp. 1998); N.C. Gen. Stat. § 50-13.1 (1999); *see also* Dane E. Gashen, *Note & Comment, Mandatory Custody Mediation: The Debate Over Its Usefulness Continues,* 10 Ohio St. J. On Disp. Resol. 469, 469, 472-73 (1995).

[403] Cal. Civ. Code § 3155 (West Supp. 1998).

[404] *Id.*

[405] *See, e.g., Biel v. Biel,* 336 N.W.2d 404 (Wis. 1983).

[406] Family Law Section of the ABA, *Standards of Practice for Family Mediators,* 17 Fam. L.Q. 455 (1984); AFCC Model Standards of Practice for Divorce and Family Mediators, *reprinted in* Divorce Mediation: Theory and Practice 403 (Jay Folberg & Ann Milne, eds. 1988).

[407] *See* Thomas Bishop, *Outside the Adversary System: An ADR Overview,* 14 Fam. Advoc. 16 (Spring 1992).

[408] *See* Stephen G. Bullock & Linda Rose Gallagher, *Surveying the State of the Mediative Art: A Guide to Institutionalizing Mediation in Louisiana,* 57 La. L. Rev. 885, 930-36 (1997) (reporting that as of 1993, twenty states had adopted qualifications for practicing as a mediator and that three states have recently adopted ethical rules for mediators).

[409] *See, e.g.,* Carrie Menkel-Meadow, *Is Mediation the Practice of Law?,* 14 Alternatives to the High Cost of Litis. 1, 60 (1996); Bruce Meyerson, *Lawyers Who Mediate Are Not Practicing Law,* 14 Alternatives to the High Cost of Litis. 74 (1996).

although the ABA Model Rules of Professional Conduct recognize a professional role as "intermediary," and permit this role under certain conditions.[410]

Confidentiality remains a problem which statutes in only a minority of states have addressed.[411] The ABA Standards suggest that the parties agree in writing "not to require the mediator to disclose to any third party any statements made in the course of mediation."[412] If the mediation process breaks down, however, one of the parties may attempt to introduce such evidence in court in subsequent litigation and an agreement regarding confidentiality may be unenforceable.[413]

California enacted mandatory pre-hearing mediation in child custody and visitation disputes and permitted the mediator to make a recommendation to the court if the parties were unable to agree.[414] To implement the statute, the local court had adopted a rule or policy that required a mediator to make recommendations, but not to state the reasons for the recommendations, and prohibited cross-examination by the parties, in order to assure the confidentiality of the mediation proceedings. The California Court of Appeal held in *McLaughlin v. Superior Court for San Mateo County*[415] that the rule violated the parties' right to cross-examine witnesses. It concluded that the trial court should not receive a recommendation from a mediator on any contested issue on which agreement had not been reached unless the court first enters a protective order guaranteeing the parties the right to have the mediator testify and be cross-examined, unless those rights are waived.

Total neutrality, fairness, and impartiality of mediators may not always be realistically possible when one of spouses has superior educational and business knowledge or other strong negotiating advantages. The ABA Standards do not, however, equate impartiality with neutrality, and they stress that the mediator must be concerned with fairness in order to avoid an unreasonable result. Some commentators indicate that a mediator may need to balance the parties' negotiating skills, even while retaining an appearance of neutrality.[416] Such balancing or "empowering" of the more vulnerable spouse might objectively constitute representation of multiple clients under the ABA Code of Professional Responsibility, and the divorce mediator may risk legal and ethical problems resulting from dual representation.[417]

---

[410] A.B.A. Model Rule 2.2.

[411] *See, e.g.*, Cal. Fam. Code § 3177 (1994).

[412] Bishop, *The Standards of Practice for Family Mediators: An Individual Interpretation and Comments*, 17 Fam. L.Q. 455, 456 (1984).

[413] *See id.* at 465.

[414] Cal. Fam. Code § 3183 (1994).

[415] 189 Cal. Rptr. 479 (Cal. Ct. App. 1983).

[416] *See, e.g.*, Blades, *supra* note 400; *see also* Richard Crouch, *Divorce Mediation and Legal Ethics*, 16 Fam. L.Q. 219 (1982) (discussing differences in dual representation in mediated versus litigated divorce).

[417] *See supra* § 8.04[A].

The status and the duties of the mediator are not always entirely clear. In *Lange v. Marshall*[418] the court held that an attorney who had represented the plaintiff and her husband as a mediator rather than an advocate was not liable for negligence in failing to inquire into the financial position of the husband and negotiate a better settlement for the wife or advise her of her rights to marital property, custody and maintenance or to advise her that she would get a better settlement if she litigated. Because both spouses repudiated the mediated agreement, obtained separate counsel, and litigated the divorce action, the court held that the wife failed to establish any damages proximately by the lawyer-mediator's conduct.

One of the claimed advantages of mediation is its potential for reducing the costs of divorce. However, because a lawyer-mediator cannot represent either party in a subsequent divorce or other legal action and because each party should also obtain independent legal counsel before signing a mediated agreement, three lawyers, rather than the usual two, may be required.[419] Conversely, if mediation breaks down, each party will need to obtain individual counsel. Thus, mediation risks adding one more tier to the divorce process and increasing, rather than reducing, the expense.[420]

The role of attorneys and judges as mediators, as opposed to trained lay counselors and mental health professionals, remains controversial.[421] Using an interdisciplinary team of mental health professionals and lawyer mediators may prove beneficial in assisting the parties in dealing with the interrelationship of the legal, emotional, and economic issues involved in divorce.[422] Non-lawyer mediators may lack the background to understand the legal ramifications of decisions made by the spouses in areas such as spousal and child support rights, child custody issues tax implications, and property division.[423] The non-lawyer mediator risks charges of unauthorized practice of law and may be disadvantaged by the lack of a confidentiality privilege.

ADR, however, has not been fully embraced without serious reservations and criticism.[424] The extent to which a mediator may give legal information or advice to either or both parties has raised ethical questions concerning conflicts of interest

---

[418] 622 S.W.2d 237 (Mo. Ct. App. 1981).

[419] *See* Kevin Mazza, *Divorce Mediation*, 14 Fam. Advoc. 40, 42-43 (Spring 1992).

[420] *See* Richard Crouch, *Mediation and Divorce: The Dark Side is Still Unexplored*, 4 Fam. Advoc. 27, 33 (Winter 1982). *But see* Jessica Pearson & Nancy Thoennes, *Mediation and Divorce: The Benefits Outweigh the Costs*, 4 Fam. Advoc. 26 (Winter 1982).

[421] *See* Kelly, *supra* note 400.

[422] *See* Linda Silberman, *Professional Responsibility Problems of Divorce Mediation*, 16 Fam. L.Q. 107, 128-31 (1982); Folberg, *Divorce Mediation — A Workable Alternative*, 1982 ABA Nat'l Conf. on Alternate Means of Family Dispute Resolution 39-40.

[423] *See* Silberman, *supra* note 422, at 123.

[424] *See, e.g.*, Penelope Bryan, *Killing Us Softly: Divorce Mediation and the Politics of Power*, 40 Buff. L. Rev. 441 (1992); Trina Grillo, *The Mediation Alternative: Process Dangers for Women*, 100 Yale L.J. 1545 (1991); Mazza, *supra* note 419; Connie Beck & Bruce Sales, *A Critical Reappraisal of Divorce Mediation Research and Policy*, 6 Psychol. Pub. Policy & L. 989 (2000); Marsha Freedman, *Divorce Mediation: Sweeping Conflicts under the Rug: Time to Clean House*, 78 U. Det. Mercy L. Rev. 67 (2000).

and confidentiality, and a lack of standards and guidelines regulating mediation has caused concern. Mediation has been criticized for forfeiting the protections of the adversarial process and for being less advantageous to a party who is more inclined to compromise or is in a weaker economic position.[425] Feminist commentators, in particular, have cautioned that mediation may disadvantage women.[426] Other scholars have suggested that the informality and emphasis on consensus that characterizes mediation may reinforce racial and ethnic hierarchies, as well as gender inequalities.[427] Many scholars and mediators believe that mediation is unsuited and dangerous for cases involving domestic violence.[428] Balancing both the advantages and disadvantages of divorce mediation, most commentators and a growing number of judges and practitioners recognize the mediation process as a valuable alternative to traditional adversarial divorce litigation in offering a workable resolution to an individual family's unique needs.[429] Supporters of mediation stress that it encourages parents to put their children's needs first, helps them to develop communication and problem solving skill that can facilitate post-divorce co-parenting, and avoid the trauma, bitterness, and costs associated with trial.[430]

[B] Arbitration

Approximately half the states have adopted the Uniform Arbitration Act.[431] Arbitration, which is widely used in settling various labor law and commercial law disputes, is also being used in many states to settle divorce disputes.[432]

Arbitration resembles the adversarial judicial process to the extent that the parties voluntarily submit their disputes to an impartial decision-maker, but arbitration avoids the delay and expense often associated with using a traditional judicial forum. Arbitration awards are normally binding on the parties and are affirmed by a court, unless they were fraudulently procured or the arbitrator did

---

[425] See, e.g., Crouch, supra note 416; Crouch, supra note 420; Andrew Morrison, Is Divorce Mediation the Practice of Law? A Matter of Perspective, 75 Cal. L. Rev. 1093 (1987); William Weston, Divorce Mediation: Cheaper for Your Client But Dangerous for You, 4 Compleat Law. 40 (Spring 1987).

[426] See Jana B. Singer, The Privatization of Family Law, 1992 Wis. L. Rev. 1443, 1540-48.

[427] See, e.g., Isabelle R. Gunning, Diversity Issues in Mediation: Controlling Negative Cultural Myths, 1995 J. Disp. Resol. 55, 70; Richard Delgado, et al., Fairness and Formality: Minimizing the Risk of Prejudice in Alternative Dispute Resolution, 1985 Wis. L. Rev. 1359.

[428] See, e.g., Mary Pat Treuthart, In Harms Way? Family Mediation and the Role of the Attorney Advocate, 23 Golden Gate U. L. Rev. 717 (1993); see also Nancy Ver Steegh, Yes, No, and Maybe: Informed Decision Making About Divorce Mediation in the Presence of Domestic Violence, 9 William & Mary J. Women & L. 145 (2003).

[429] See Russell Coombs, Noncourt-Connected Mediation and Counseling in Child Custody Disputes, 17 Fam. L.Q. 469-95 (1984); Joshua Rosenberg, In Defense of Mediation, 33 Ariz. L. Rev. 467 (1991).

[430] See Nancy S. Palmer & William D. Palmer, Family Mediation: Good for Clients, Good for Lawyers, The Compleat Law. 32, 33 (Fall 1996); see also Andrew Schepard, An Introduction to the Model Standards of Practice for Family and Divorce Mediation, 35 Fam. L. Q. 1 (2001); Joan Kelly, Issues Facing the Family Mediation Field, 1 Pepp. Disp. Resol. L. J. 37 (2000).

[431] 7 U.L.A. 201 (1985).

[432] See generally Andre Imbrogna, Arbitration as an Alternative in Divorce Litigation: Redefining the Judicial Role, 31 Cap. U. L. Rev. 413 (2003).

not act in an impartial manner.[433] Although courts have approved agreements to arbitrate spousal support and property issues, arbitration of divorce issues relating to children remains controversial.

Arbitration may be conducted before a single arbitrator chosen by either the parties or a designated third party, or by an impartial tripartite board appointed under the guidelines of the American Arbitration Association (AAA), or by a panel consisting of two designees appointed by the parties and a third member chosen by the designees or a third party.[434] The AAA, one of numerous arbitration organizations, is a well-known national nonprofit agency that conducts arbitration and mediation work throughout the United States. Judicare, another organization that conducts arbitration and "minitrials," uses retired judges for its work.

Most commonly, an agreement to arbitrate rather than litigate certain issues will be included in the parties' separation agreement, but a pre-marital agreement may also contain an arbitration provision. The agreement should specify that the arbitration will be final and binding, and set out the arbitration procedure. The agreement should defer the procedure for selecting the arbitrator and scheduling the time and place of arbitration. The parties may also agree to enlarge their rights to review and appeal.

Arbitration affords procedural flexibility and may be quicker and less expensive than litigation. Clear definition of issues that may be arbitrated is crucial, however, because arbitration is based on the parties' agreement, and the arbitrator may not exceed the scope of the contractual authority.[435] Lack of specificity resulted in litigation in *Bowmer v. Bowmer*,[436] in which a former wife sought to stay arbitration on the issue of whether the husband's support obligation could be decreased. The Bowmer's separation agreement contained a clause reading: "Any claim. dispute or misunderstanding arising out of or in connection with this Agreement, or any breach hereof, or any default in payment by the Husband, or any matter herein made the subject matter of arbitration, shall be arbitrated." In deciding that the arbitration clause did not pertain to support modification, the New York Court of Appeals declared that "unless the agreement to arbitrate expressly and unequivocally encompasses the subject matter of the particular dispute, a party cannot be compelled to forego the right to seek judicial relief and instead submit to arbitration."[437] Because the separation agreement specifically delineated other issues that were to be arbitrable and contained a detailed formula for calculating support, the court held that the arbitration clause was not intended to encompass support modification. Subsequent to *Bowmer*, the American

---

[433] *See, e.g.,* Unif. Arbitration Act §§ 12-13.

[434] *See generally* Green, *supra* note 1 at 187-92; 2 Lindey & Parley, Separation Agreements and Antenuptial Contracts § 29 (1992); Janet Maleson Spencer & Joseph P. Zammit, *Mediation-Arbitration,* 1976 Duke L.J. 911.

[435] *See* Koritzinsky, et al., *The Benefits of Arbitration,* 14 Fam. Advoc. 45 (Spring 1992). *See, e.g., In re Marriage of Woods,* 142 P.3d 1072 (Or. Ct. App. 2006) (holding that the husband was entitled to a trial *de novo,* because the arbitration was not binding, since the parties agreed to binding arbitration on the assumption that Oregon law allowed them to appeal the decision in court).

[436] 406 N.E.2d 760 (N.Y. 1980).

[437] *Id.* at 762.

Arbitration Association recommended inclusion of support modification and enforcement in its standard arbitration provision.[438]

Disadvantages of arbitration include the lack of discovery procedures and the inapplicability of the rules of evidence and other procedural safeguards. Arbitrators do not have the power to enforce their awards, nor to enter divorce decrees, although the Uniform Arbitration Act provides for confirmation by a court in a judgment or decree unless the court vacates or modifies the arbitration award.[439]

Although most courts have approved, in general, of arbitration provisions dealing with spousal support and property rights,[440] courts generally afford less weight to similar provisions concerning child support and custody.[441] Neither the parties nor the arbitrator may deprive the court of the power to enforce or modify orders for alimony, child support, or to hold a party in contempt.[442]

In *Faherty v. Faherty*,[443] the former wife sought a court order establishing the amount of past-due alimony, child support, and property division payments and compelling discovery of the husband's business records. The husband successfully filed a cross-motion to compel arbitration of the arrearages and to reduce future payments, pursuant to an arbitration agreement in the parties' separation agreement. After extensive arbitration, the arbitrator set the amount of the arrearages and denied the husband's request for reduction of future alimony and child support. When the court confirmed the arbitration award, the husband challenged the validity of the arbitration clause, arguing that arbitration of alimony and child support violates public policy, and attempted to overturn confirmation of the award.

In upholding the confirmed arbitration award, the New Jersey Supreme Court found no reason to prohibit binding arbitration of spousal support, since parties are free to settle those matters by contract. It observed that arbitration has proven to be an effective and highly desirable method of resolving disputes:

> the advantages of arbitration of domestic disputes include reduced court congestion, the opportunity for resolution of sensitive matters in a private and informal forum, reduction of the trauma and anxiety of marital litigation, minimization of the intense polarization of the parties that often occurs, and the ability to choose the arbitrator.[444]

---

[438] *See also* Lindey & Parley, *supra* note 434, at § 29.

[439] Unif. Arbitration Act § 11, 7 U.L.A. 264 (1997). *See also* Koritzinsky, et al., *supra* note 435, at 46.

[440] *See Spencer v. Spencer*, 494 A.2d 1279 (D.C. 1985).

[441] *Compare Fence v. Fence*, 314 N.Y.S.2d 1016 (N.Y. Fam. Ct. 1970), *Nestel v. Nestel*, 331 N.Y.S.2d 241 (N.Y. Sup. Ct. 1972), *and Biel v. Biel*, 336 N.W.2d 404 (Wis. 1983), *with Sheets v. Sheets*, 254 N.Y.S.2d 320 (N.Y. Sup. Ct. 1964), *Faherty v. Faherty*, 477 A.2d 1257 (N.J. 1984), *and Crutchley v. Crutchley*, 293 S.E.2d 793 (N.C. 1982). *See also* Unif. Arbitration Act § 12(a), 7 U.L.A. 280 (1997).

[442] *See Fence v. Fence*, 314 N.Y.S.2d 1016 (N.Y. Fam. Ct. 1970).

[443] 477 A.2d 1257 (N.J. 1984).

[444] *Id.* at 1262.

It tempered its support of arbitration with public policy considerations involving child support and custody conflicts. Although it refused to prohibit arbitration of child support and custody matters entirely, it held that courts should review those arbitrated decisions more closely because of the courts' responsibility for protecting the best interest of children. In reviewing child support awards, the court should review any award that reduces or refuses to increase child support which affects the substantial best interests of the child. Without reaching the question of child custody, which was not before the court, it advised that the same reasoning may apply to those cases.

The Superior Court of Pennsylvania, in *Miller v. Miller*,[445] directly confronted the issue of an agreement to arbitrate child custody. In *Miller*, the parties had agreed that the father would have custody of the children and that if any dispute over the children could not be resolved by mediation, that they would submit to binding mediation. When the mother sought a modification of custody, the parties were unable to mediate the issue and the matter was submitted to arbitration, which was decided in favor of the mother. The father refused to relinquish custody and the mother attempted to have the arbitrators' decision enforced as a court order. The trial judge, who had originally entered the divorce decree which incorporated the parties agreement, struck the provisions calling for binding arbitration of custody and refused to enter the arbitrators' award. Upon appeal, the superior court agreed that arbitration is generally a favored remedy, but held that a custody determination is subject to court review based on its responsibility to examine the best interest of the child. Accordingly, it concluded that the trial court erred in striking the arbitration provisions as void as against public policy, but that court was not bound to confirm the arbitration.

One commentator has observed that the AAA rules do not require an arbitrator to determine child-related issues under the standard of the best interest of the child, and has encouraged parties to include such directions in the arbitration agreements.[446] With appropriate safeguards, arbitration may prove as effective in dealing with child support and custody issues as it has in other family law matters.

[C] Collaborative Law

Collaborative law is a relatively new form of alternative dispute resolution (ADR). Collaborative law differs from mediation and arbitration in that it does not involve the use of neutrals in the decision-making process. Instead, each party is represented by an attorney trained in collaborative law, and assisted by financial and mental health professionals or "coaches" as the need may arise. The parties, with the help of their respective attorneys, engage in direct problem-solving negotiations with one another in the context of conferences between husband and wife and their respective attorneys, in generating creative ideas and negotiated solutions and settlements.

----

[445] 620 A.2d 1161 (Sup. Ct. Penn. 1993).

[446] Philbrick, *Agreements to Arbitrate Post-Divorce Custody Disputes*, 18 Col. J.L. & Soc. Prob. 419, 453-54 (1985).

The collaborative family law process relies on voluntary disclosure of all relevant information from both parties, and in addition to a retainer agreement, the parties and their attorneys also sign a "disqualification agreement" stating that each lawyer is only retained to represent his or her client in the collaborative process, and cannot represent either party in any subsequent litigation against the other party.

The proposed Uniform Collaborative Law Act, adopted in 2009 by the National Conference of Commissioners on Uniform State Laws, makes a "disqualification clause" mandatory in order to obtain the protections of the Act. The Act provides that a "collaborative lawyer is disqualified from appearing before a tribunal to represent a party in any proceeding related to a collaborative matter."[447] Only two exceptions to this general rule are allowed: (1) a collaborative lawyer may appear before a tribunal to "seek or defend an emergency order to protect the health, safety, welfare, or interest of a party [or household member] if a successor lawyer is not immediately available to represent that person"; and (2) a collaborative lawyer may "ask a tribunal to approve an agreement resulting from the collaborative law process."[448]

Although a comprehensive discussion and critique of collaborative family law is beyond the scope of this treatise, there are a number of excellent source books and articles to introduce the family law student and practitioner to collaborative law theory and practice.[449]

---

[447] Unif. Collaborative Law Act § 9 (2009).

[448] *Id. See generally* Herbie DiFonzo, *From Dispute Resolution to Peacemaking: A Review of Collaborative Divorce Handbook — Helping Families Without Going to Court by Forrest S. Mosten*, 44 Fam. L.Q. 95 (2010).

[449] *See, e.g.,* Pauline Tesler, Collaborative Law: Achieving Effective Resolution in Divorce Without Litigation (2d ed. 2008); Janis Pritchard, et al., Collaborative Practice Handbook (2002); Sheila Gutterman, Collaborative Law: A New Model for Dispute Resolution (2004); *see also* Joshua Isaacs, *A New Way to Avoid the Courtroom: The Ethical Implications Surrounding Collaborative Law*, 18 Geo. J. Legal Ethics 833 (2005); Forrest S. Mosten, Collaborative Divorce Handbook: Helping Families Without Going to Court (2009).

Chapter 9

SPOUSAL AND CHILD SUPPORT ON DIVORCE

§ 9.01 INTRODUCTION

Spousal support or maintenance, traditionally called alimony, was originally based on a husband's duty to support his wife after a divorce from bed and board. In the United States, alimony was later made available after absolute divorce as a continuation of the duty of support arising from the marriage. Alimony was based primarily on fault and was available only to innocent wives whose husbands had caused the marriage to fail. In this sense, alimony functioned as a type of damages remedy for breach of the marriage contract.[1] With the advent of no-fault divorce, the role of fault in alimony began to decline, although not entirely disappear,[2] replaced by greater emphasis on the needs of the wife and the husband's ability to pay. This change in focus led many states to replace the term "alimony" with "support" or "maintenance," although the terms are often used synonymously.

In 1979, the United States Supreme Court held in *Orr v. Orr*[3] that divorce statutes which authorized alimony payments only to needy wives, but not to needy husbands, constituted gender-based discrimination in violation of the Equal Protection Clause of the Fourteenth Amendment. The *Orr* court held that the "old notion" that "generally it is the man's primary responsibility to provide a home and its essentials" could no longer justify a statute that discriminated on the basis of gender.[4] "No longer is the female destined solely for the home and the rearing of the family, and only the male for the marketplace and the world of ideas."[5] *Orr* thus extended alimony rights on divorce to needy or dependent spouses of either gender. As a practical matter, however, when alimony is granted at all, it is much more commonly awarded to wives than to husbands.[6] According to the U.S. Census Bureau, although the percentage of alimony recipients who are male rose by 50% between 2001 and 2006, men still only represented 3.14% of all recipients in 2011.[7]

---

[1] *See* Jana B. Singer, *Divorce Reform and Gender Justice*, 67 N.C. L. Rev. 1103, 1106 (1989) (noting that statistics indicate that only a small minority of women were awarded alimony under the fault-based regime).

[2] *See supra* § 8.01[B], [C].

[3] 440 U.S. 268 (1979).

[4] *Id.* at 279-80 (quoting *Stanton v. Stanton*, 421 U.S. 7, 10 (1975)).

[5] *Id.* at 280 (quoting with approval *Stanton v. Stanton*, 421 U.S. 7, 14-15 (1975)).

[6] Anita Raghavan, *Men Receiving Alimony Want a Little Respect: Modern Males Say Living off the Ex-Wife is No Cause for Shame*, Wall St. J., Apr. 1, 2008, at A1.

[7] U.S. Dept. of Commerce, Bureau of the Census, *Current Population Survey, 2011 Annual Social and Economic Supplement*, Table 4 (2011). The Census Bureau's *Current Population Survey* is based

In practice, only a small percentage of divorced women are awarded alimony today, and even fewer actually receive alimony.[8] The Census Bureau reported that in 1989 only 15.5% of divorced or separated women were awarded spousal support.[9] Many courts are reluctant to award much, if any, alimony, believing they should encourage nonwage earning spouses to obtain work outside the home and become self-supporting.[10] For the decade ending in 2006, the overall number of individuals reporting alimony income fell by 17%, and in 2009 the Census Bureau found that only 349,000 individuals were reporting alimony payments from their former spouses as income.[11] The stereotypical image of an ex-wife who is "living in luxury" on the proceeds of her ex-husband's labor is rarely reflected in the real world.[12]

Divorce can have a substantial financial impact on divorced spouses, usually women, who have not worked outside the home during marriages of long duration and on parents who have custody of small children (again, usually mothers). While sociologists disagree about the extent to which wives as a group experience a substantial change in their economic circumstances after divorce, all agree that most experience at least some decline in resources.[13]

The authority to grant spousal support or alimony upon divorce is statutory in nature. All states authorize alimony or support awards upon divorces, although the

---

upon a monthly survey of 57,000 U.S. households that are carefully and scientifically selected to represent the nation as a whole. Of the households surveyed in March 2011, in which an adult reported receiving alimony income, 96.86% of recipients were women and only 3.14% of recipients were men.

[8] *See* Cynthia Lee Starnes, *Mothers as Suckers: Pity, Partnership, and Divorce Discourse*, 90 Iowa L. Rev. 1513, 1516 n.7 (2005); *see also* Patricia A. Cain, *Taxing Families Fairly*, 48 Santa Clara L. Rev. 805, 827 n.85 (2008); Singer, *supra* note 1, at 2426 n.14; Marsha Garrison, *Good Intentions Gone Awry: The Impact of New York's Equitable Distribution Law on Divorce Outcomes*, 57 Brook. L. Rev. 621 (1991).

[9] U.S. Dept. of Commerce, Bureau of the Census, *Child Support and Alimony: 1989*, Rep. P60-173, Table L (1991). For a state-level analysis of this issue, see Women's Law Center of Maryland, Inc., *Families in Transition: A Follow-up Study Exploring Family Law Issues in Maryland* iii (2006), *available at* http://www.wlcmd.org/pdf/publications/FamiliesInTransition.pdf.

[10] *See, e.g., Ventimiglia v. Ventimiglia*, 307 A.D.2d 993, 995 (N.Y. 2003); *In re Marriage of Roppe*, 64 P.3d 1145, 1147 (Or. Ct. App. 2003).

[11] *Supra* note 6; U.S. Dept. of Commerce, Bureau of the Census, *Statistical Abstract of the United States: 2012* (131st ed.), Table 542: Number of People With Income by Specified Sources of Income: 2009 (2011), *available at* www.census.gov/compendia/statab/2012/tables/12s0542.xls.

[12] *See generally* Clark, The Law of Domestic Relations in the United States 619-22 (2d ed. 1987); *see also* Margaret Brinig, *Unhappy Contracts: The Case of Divorce*, 1 Rev. L. & Econ. 241 (2005).

[13] *Compare* Lenore Weitzman, The Divorce Revolution: The Unexpected Social and Economic Consequences for Women and Children in America (1985) (concluding that divorcing wives' incomes drop by 73% after divorce, while divorcing men experience a rise in their income by 42%), *and* James McLindon, *Separate but Unequal: The Economic Disaster of Divorce for Women and Children*, 21 Fam. L.Q. 351, 352 (1987) (arguing that "the economic outlook for women divorcing under . . . no-fault statutes [is] grim indeed"), *with* Philomila Tsoukala, *Gary Becker, Legal Feminism, and the Costs of Moralizing Care*, 16 Colum. J. Gender & L. 357, 358-59 n.4 (2007) (noting that "Weitzman's figures have been widely discredited after it was discovered that there were transcription errors in her data set. The rise and drop in post-divorce men's and women's incomes after correcting the errors was calculated at 10% and 27%, respectively"), *and* Sanford L. Braver, *The Gender Gap in Standard of Living After Divorce: Vanishing Small?*, 33 Fam. L.Q. 111, 131 (1999) (arguing that the gender gap in post-divorce incomes has been "seriously overestimated . . . because we have ignored . . . the effect of unequal taxes and of sharing children's expenses").

statutory factors for both eligibility and amount vary considerably from state to state.[14]

Courts in all states are statutorily authorized to provide for the support of the parties' minor children in divorce actions.[15] Although both parents are generally responsible for providing child support,[16] women remain more likely to receive custody, and thus child support, than men.[17]

A large number of divorced and non-custodial fathers fail to comply with court-ordered child support obligations, causing much of the welfare dependency in female-headed households and impoverishment of children.[18] In 2007, for example, only about three-quarters of all women who were due child support actually received a portion of the child support payments owed and less than half received the full amount due.[19] Overall, from 2008 through 2010, only about 62% of support due was actually paid to recipients.[20] Such distressing statistics led to the enactment of federal and state remedies, such as the Child Support Enforcement Amendments of 1984.[21]

The family law practitioner must be familiar with all the available spousal support remedies on divorce and support remedies both for marital and non-marital children, and their equally important enforcement mechanisms.

---

[14] *See, e.g.,* "Alimony, Maintenance, and Other Spousal Support," tbl.1, 50 State Statutory Surveys: Family Law: Divorce and Dissolution, *available at* 0080 SURVEYS 11 (Westlaw).

[15] *See* "Determination of Child Support Required for High and Low Income Families," 50 State Statutory Surveys: Family Law: Child Custody and Support, *available at* 0080 SURVEYS 4 (2011) (Westlaw); 27C C.J.S. *Divorce* § 1084 (2011); *see also* Donna Schuele, *Origins and Development of the Law of Parental Child Support*, 27 J. Fam. L. 807 (1988-89).

[16] *See infra* § 9.06[A]; *see also* "Determination of Child Support Required for High and Low Income Families," 50 State Statutory Surveys: Family Law: Child Custody and Support, *available at* 0080 SURVEYS 4 (2011) (Westlaw); 27C C.J.S. *Divorce* § 1084 (2011).

[17] *Supra* note 7, at Table 4.

[18] *See* Teresa Amott, *Working for Less: Single Mothers in the Workplace, in* Women as Single Parents 106-08 (Elizabeth Mulroy ed., 1988); Jessica Pearson & Nancy Thoennes, *Supporting Children After Divorce: The Influence of Custody on Support Levels and Payments*, 22 Fam. L.Q. 319 (1988) (quoting Hoffman, *Marital Instability and the Economic Status of Women*, 14 Demography 67 (1977)).

[19] *See* U.S. Dep't of Commerce, Bureau of the Census, *Custodial Mothers and Fathers and their Child Support: 2007*, Rep. P60-237, Table 1 (2009) (76.6% of custodial mothers who were due child support received some payment and 47.1% of custodial mothers actually received the full child support payments due).

[20] U.S. Dep't of Health & Human Services, Administration for Children & Families, Office of Child Support Enforcement, *Child Support Enforcement FY 2010: Preliminary Report* (2011), *available at* http://www.acf.hhs.gov/programs/cse/pubs/2011/reports/preliminary_report_fy2010/.

[21] *See* 42 U.S.C. § 654 (1996); *infra* § 9.06[F][4].

§ 9.02   JURISDICTION FOR SPOUSAL AND CHILD SUPPORT

[A]   The Doctrine of Continuing Jurisdiction

A court must have personal jurisdiction over a defendant in order to create, modify, or extinguish marital support or property rights or obligations.[22] Once a court has asserted personal jurisdiction over the parties in an action for spousal or child support, most jurisdictions view any subsequent support actions as part of one continuing process which began in the original divorce or support decree.[23] Because all jurisdictions recognize the doctrine of continuing jurisdiction, a court may subsequently modify an alimony award entered by another state if it has jurisdiction over both parties and if the award was modifiable in the jurisdiction that originally ordered support.[24] However, the interstate applicability of the continuing jurisdiction doctrine has been affected by the enactment of the Uniform Interstate Family Support Act, discussed in § 9.06.

[B]   The Doctrine of Divisible Divorce

As discussed previously in § 8.02[H], although a court only needs to have personal jurisdiction over one of the parties to validly terminate the marital status under the doctrine of divisible divorce,[25] it must have jurisdiction over both parties to determine any support or marital property rights.[26] Thus, a valid *ex parte* divorce decree may be entered without affecting or eliminating the parties' rights and duties with respect to support.[27]

---

[22] *See, e.g., Auman v. Auman*, 653 P.2d 688 (Ariz. 1982); *Boyd v. Boyd*, 340 S.E.2d 578 (Va. Ct. App. 1986); Restatement (Second) Conflict of Laws § 77 (1971). *See generally* Robert C. Casad & William B. Richman, Jurisdiction in Civil Actions, § 9-4 (3d ed. 1998). For discussion of jurisdiction on divorce, see *supra* § 8.02.

[23] *See, e.g., Campbell v. Campbell*, 357 So. 2d 129 (Miss. 1978); *Sauls v. Sauls*, 577 P.2d 771 (Colo. Ct. App. 1977). The Restatement (Second) of Conflict of Laws § 26 (1971) states: "If a state obtains judicial jurisdiction over a party to an action, the jurisdiction continues throughout all subsequent proceedings which arise out of the original claim. Reasonable notice and reasonable opportunity to be heard must be given the party at each new step in the proceeding."

[24] *See, e.g., Brisco v. Brisco*, 355 So. 2d 506 (Fla. Dist. Ct. App. 1978); *Lumpkins v. Lumpkins*, 495 P.2d 371 (N.M. 1972).

[25] *See supra* § 8.02[H]. Similarly, a court may lack personal jurisdiction over a party but nevertheless may enter a valid protective order against him or her. *See, e.g., Hemenway v. Hemenway*, 992 A.2d 575 (N.H. 2010) (though wife failed to demonstrate sufficient facts to establish the court's personal jurisdiction over her husband, the court had subject matter jurisdiction to issue a protective order); *see also* Casad & Richman, *supra* note 22, at § 9-2.

[26] *See, e.g., Vanderbilt v. Vanderbilt*, 354 U.S. 416 (1957); *Scharer v. Scharer*, No. FA010451858, 2001 Conn. Super. LEXIS 2722 (Sept. 17, 2001); *Lofton v. Lofton*, 924 So. 2d. 596, 601 (Miss. Ct. App. 2006); *Russ v. Russ*, 530 S.E.2d 469 (Ga. 2000). For full discussion of the divisible divorce doctrine, see *supra* § 8.02[F].

[27] *See Hayes v. Hayes*, 351 S.E.2d 590 (Va. Ct. App. 1986) (holding that wife's right to support survived divorce decree); *Komorous v. Komorous*, 467 A.2d 1039 (Md. Ct. Spec. App. 1983) (following foreign *ex parte* divorce decree, wife could obtain temporary alimony pending litigation for permanent alimony); *see also* Casad & Richman, *supra* note 22, at § 9-2[4] n.98.

The converse is also true: a court can have jurisdiction to enter a valid support order without having jurisdiction to grant a divorce.[28] Since personal jurisdiction may always be established through personal service in the forum state, some plaintiffs have attempted to lure defendants into the forum state for service of process. So long as the court can find some indication the defendant entered the forum state of his or her own free will or had minimum contacts with the forum state independent of any fraudulent inducement, the validity of service will be upheld.[29] Courts are divided over whether a defendant may contest a divorce proceeding through a form of limited appearance which does not constitute consent to jurisdiction for support, property, or custody proceedings.[30]

A small minority of states, however, will not order spousal support once the marital status has been terminated because the duty of support arises from marriage and continuation of that duty in the form of alimony presupposes an existing duty.[31] Child support, however, may be ordered at any time because the parent-child relationship is not affected by the marital status of the parties.[32]

[C]   Interstate Enforcement Legislation

The Uniform Interstate Family Support Act (UIFSA), promulgated in 1992 and last amended in 2008, has been enacted in all states and the District of Columbia as a condition for a state's receipt of welfare block grants under the 1996 Federal Welfare Reform Act. UIFSA replaces the earlier and more cumbersome Uniform Reciprocal Enforcement of Support Act (URESA) and its replacement version, the Revised Uniform Enforcement of Support Act (RURESA). UIFSA sets out jurisdictional standards and enforcement mechanisms for obtaining and collecting support when the parties reside in different states, or in different areas of the same state, allowing support actions to be initiated against an absent obligor even

---

[28] *See, e.g., Rogers v. Rogers*, 97 S.W.3d 429 (Ark. Ct. App. 2003) (court's lack of jurisdiction to grant divorce, due to inability to corroborate residency, did not negate court's subject matter jurisdiction over spousal and child support).

[29] *See, e.g., Hammett v. Hammett*, 74 A.D.2d 540, 541 (N.Y. 1980) (support petitioner enticed defendant to visit her apartment in the forum state, where defendant was served, but service was valid since defendant regularly visited the forum state and did not dispute that his presence on that occasion was for separate personal reasons); *Blackson v. Blackson*, 579 S.E.2d 704, 711-12 (Va. Ct. App. 2003) (no indicia of fraudulent inducement where husband, informed by wife of her intent to keep their children in the forum state, traveled to the forum state to try and take children home with him); *Swarts v. Dean*, 766 P.2d 1291, 1292 (Kan. Ct. App. 1989) (personal service on husband during exercise of visitation rights held valid); *see also* Casad & Richman, *supra* note 22, at § 9-2[4][a][i].

[30] *See, e.g., Spak v. Specht*, 628 N.Y.S.2d 207 (App. Div. 1995) (appearance in filiation proceeding subjected defendant to jurisdiction for child support proceedings); *Scott v. Scott*, 451 N.W.2d 876 (Mich. Ct. App. 1990) (bringing suit to modify out-of-state custody award waived jurisdiction for former spouse's support claim). *But see, e.g., Puhlman v. Turner*, 874 P.2d 291 (Alaska 1994) (party seeking to enforce out-of-state divorce decree visitation provisions not subject to personal jurisdiction for action to modify decree's support provisions); *In re Marriage of Wallick*, 524 N.W.2d 153 (Iowa 1994) (attempt to enforce out-of-state support decree through the Uniform Reciprocal Enforcement of Support Act did not submit party to personal jurisdiction for proceeding to modify support); *see also* Casad & Richman, *supra* note 22, at § 9-2[4][a][ii].

[31] *See* Clark, *supra* note 12, at 452-54.

[32] *Id.* at 456, 711-13.

without a previous support order. The details of UIFSA are discussed in § 9.06[C], *infra*.

[D] State Long-Arm Statutes

Generally, a person seeking support may also utilize a state's long-arm statute to enforce or modify spousal and child support obligations.[33] *Soule v. Soule*[34] was among the first cases to apply a long-arm statute to allow a spouse to obtain a divorce with alimony after the other spouse had moved to another state. Similarly, in *Lozinski v. Lozinski*,[35] the Supreme Court of West Virginia approved use of the state's long-arm statute on the basis that the father's failure to support his children qualified as a tortious act under the statute. Therefore, it concluded that service on the West Virginia Secretary of State was an acceptable form of process over the father who was then located in Florida. A number of states now have special long-arm statutes which authorize extending jurisdiction over an absent spouse for purposes of awarding or modifying support, although some of those statutes require continued residence by the spouse seeking such support.[36] UIFSA adds additional bases for asserting jurisdiction over an absent parent.[37]

[E] Child Support Jurisdiction: The *Kulko* Case

Child support jurisdiction, like jurisdiction for spousal support, is based on personal jurisdiction over the obligor. In *Kulko v. Superior Court*,[38] the United States Supreme Court held that the mere fact that the child is living in the forum state is insufficient for asserting personal jurisdiction over the parent, even if the parent sent the child or acquiesced to the child's moving to that state. In *Kulko*, the parties had lived in New York for most of their marriage and their two children were born there. The parties entered into a written separation agreement which provided that the children would remain in New York with their father during the

---

[33] For a complete discussion of the use of long-arm statutes in divorce actions, see *supra* § 8.02[G]. *See, e.g.*, Mass. Gen. Laws Ann. ch. 223A, § 3(h) (West 2011); Tex. Fam. Code Ann. § 6.305 (West 2011).

[34] 14 Cal. Rptr. 417 (Cal. Ct. App. 1961).

[35] 408 S.E.2d 310 (W.Va. 1991).

[36] *See* "Personal Jurisdiction," 50 State Statutory Surveys: Civil Laws: Civil Procedure, *available at* 0020 SURVEYS 10 (Westlaw). Some statutes require that the forum state must have been the locus of the "matrimonial domicile," while others speak more generally of the plaintiff and defendant having lived there "in the marital relationship." See, e.g., the statutes of Georgia, Maine, and Michigan, and the statutes of Indiana, New Mexico, and Tennessee, respectively. *See also* Casad & Richman, *supra* note 22, at § 9-2[4][a][iv] nn120, 121. Other statutes allow the assertion of long-arm jurisdiction under "any constitutional basis" clauses, even when the forum state was never a marital domicile or was not the couple's last marital domicile. *See, e.g., Carney v. Dahlmann*, 624 A.2d 197 (Pa. Super. Ct. 1993) (even though former husband lived in another state and support order against him was issued there, county of former wife's residence and last family residence pre-divorce was the appropriate venue for support enforcement action); *State ex. rel. Houk v. Grewing*, 586 N.W.2d 224, 227 (Iowa 1998) (mother's Iowa residence at the time her child was born, together with her receipt of state public assistance for the child, were sufficient for state to assert jurisdiction under long-arm statute in child support proceeding); *see also* Casad & Richman, *supra* note 22, at § 9-2[4][a][iv].

[37] *See* UIFSA § 401(b).

[38] 436 U.S. 84 (1978).

school year, but would spend holidays and summer vacations with their mother, who had moved to California. The father agreed to pay child support for the periods when the mother had physical custody. She obtained a divorce in Haiti, which incorporated the separation agreement.

A year after the parents' divorce, one of the children requested that she be allowed to remain in California with her mother following the Christmas vacation. The father consented and bought her a one-way ticket. Several years later, the other child decided he also wanted to live with his mother; the mother sent him a plane ticket without consulting the father. After the second child's arrival in California, the mother brought an action in California to modify custody and increase the child support obligation. The father appeared specially to object to the state's assertion of personal jurisdiction over him; his motion was denied. On appeal, he renewed his argument only with respect to the child support action. The California Court of Appeals held that the court had jurisdiction based on its long-arm statute, finding that the father had "caused an effect" in the state. The California Supreme Court affirmed, holding that the exercise of jurisdiction was reasonable because the father had "purposely availed himself" of the "benefits and protection" of California's laws by consenting to his daughter's living in that state.[39]

The United States Supreme Court reversed, holding that when a state asserts jurisdiction to order or modify child support, the obligor must have sufficient contacts with the forum state to satisfy due process standards of fairness and substantial justice. The Court concluded that the father did not have sufficient minimum contacts with California and that allowing that state to enter a judgment against him would "sanction a result that is neither fair, just, nor reasonable."[40] The Court noted that the father's agreement to allow the children to live in California with their mother, "in the interest of family harmony and his children's preferences," could "hardly be said to have 'purposefully availed himself' of the 'benefits and protections' of California's laws."[41] Nor was the exercise of jurisdiction warranted by the financial benefit he received from his daughter's presence in that state for a large portion of the year, as any decrease in his expenses was due to the child's absence from his household rather than her presence in California. Additionally noting that the mother was not without a remedy, since she could bring an action for modification of child support in the New York courts, the Court concluded that the father's single act of acquiescing in the child's choice of residence "is surely not one that a reasonable parent would expect to result in the substantial financial burden and personal strain of litigating a child-support suit in a forum 3,000 miles away . . . ."[42] *Kulko* thus limits the extent to which long-arm statutes may be applied to obtain jurisdiction for awarding or modifying child support orders.[43]

---

[39] *Id.* at 94 (quoting *Shaffer v. Heitner*, 433 U.S. 186, 216 (1977)).

[40] *Id.* at 92.

[41] *Id.* at 94 (quoting *Shaffer v. Heitner*, 433 U.S. at 216).

[42] *Id.* at 97.

[43] *But see Daknis v. Burns*, 278 A.D.2d 641, 643 (N.Y. 2000) (stipulation to a foreign court order transferring custody to out-of-state former spouse, together with consent to a simultaneous forum state

The Supreme Court later reaffirmed the rule that personal service on a defendant within the forum state continues to constitute a valid basis for personal jurisdiction, despite a defendant's lack of other connections with the state. In *Burnham v. Superior Court of California*,[44] the wife and children had moved to California while the husband remained in New Jersey.[45] When the husband went to California on business, he visited the children in that state and was served with a summons and divorce petition. The husband asserted that the California court lacked personal jurisdiction over him because he lacked sufficient contacts with that state. The Court held that the minimum contacts requirement applies only when jurisdiction is sought over a defendant who is not physically present within the forum state. It declared that jurisdiction over nonresidents who are physically present in a state is one of "the most firmly established principles of personal jurisdiction in American tradition."[46] Under the *Burnham* analysis, a parent who is personally served within the forum state may be required to litigate support issues in that state.

§ 9.03 SPOUSAL SUPPORT FACTORS AND JUDICIAL DISCRETION

While alimony was traditionally based on fault concepts, which extended the husband's duty to support his wife after the marriage ended due to his fault, the decline of the role of fault, along with the recognition of gender-neutral principles, has caused most states to shift their focus in awarding alimony.[47] Today alimony, commonly designated spousal support or maintenance, is generally based on need

---

order of custody, constituted more than mere acquiescence to child's change of residence under the *Kulko* standard and were sufficient "acts" to confer personal jurisdiction).

[44] 495 U.S. 604 (1990).

[45] Although the couple had agreed that the wife would file for divorce in California, the husband later filed in New Jersey, but the wife was not served in that action. After unsuccessfully demanding that the husband honor the agreement, the wife filed for divorce in California. *Id.* at 608.

[46] *Id.* at 610. *See generally* Peter Hay, *Transient Jurisdiction, Especially Over International Defendants: Critical Comments on* Burnham v. Superior Court of California, 1990 U. Ill. L. Rev. 593.

[47] Although fault has been sidelined by many states and by professional organizations like the American Law Institute, the debate over what role, if any, fault should play continues to rage. *Compare* Norman A. Katter, Conduct, Fault, and Family Law 5, 55 (1987) (arguing that a code of marital conduct should be established under the law and that violators should be financially penalized upon divorce), *and* Barbara Bennett Woodhouse, *Sex, Lies, and Dissipation: The Discourse of Fault in a No-Fault Era*, 82 Geo. L.J. 2525, 2567-68 (1994) (with comments by Katharine T. Bartlett) (arguing law should "reclaim[ ] the power of fault" and "reward family-centric, caring conduct, rather than turn a blind eye to abuse and exploitation"), *and* Lynn D. Wardle, *Beyond Fault and No-Fault in the Reform of Marital Dissolution Law, in* Reconceiving the Family: Critique on the American Law Institute's *Principles of the Law of Family Dissolution* 9 (Robin Fretwell Wilson ed., 2006) (hereinafter "Reconceiving the Family") (arguing that fault is integral to marital dissolution decisions and proceedings and thus it is "irrational and impractical" for the law to ignore fault), *with* Ira Mark Ellman & Sharon Lohr, *Marriage as Contract, Opportunistic Violence, and Other Bad Arguments for Fault Divorce*, 1997 U. Ill. L. Rev. 719 (challenging the idea that the reintroduction of fault-based divorce will encourage improved marital conduct and rejecting the argument that no-fault divorce has contributed to an increase in domestic violence). Approximately half of all states no longer allow consideration of fault in determining spousal support awards. *See* Linda D. Elrod & Robert G. Spector, *A Review of the Year in Family Law*, 42 Fam. L.Q. 713, Chart 1 (2009).

and is regarded as a means for providing necessary support to dependent former spouses.[48] Even if a custodial parent must work outside the home after divorce, his or her earning power may not be sufficiently adequate to support both the custodial parent's needs and those of their children. Alimony may be an appropriate vehicle for supplementing that income. Alimony is frequently viewed as a temporary measure to allow a spouse to obtain the necessary education or work skills in order to re-enter the job market and become self-supporting.[49]

[A]   General Factors

The statutory factors for determining spousal support differ considerably from state to state,[50] and a number of groups have attempted to guide courts' discretion in calculating alimony awards or determining which alimony factors are, or should be, important.[51] Some states' statutes authorize alimony in broad terms, granting the judge discretion to award it when it is, for example, "equitable" or "just and proper," and allow the courts to develop more precise standards.[52] Many other states, however, have statutes that list mandatory and permissible factors for consideration in alimony awards.[53]

---

[48] *See generally* Joan Krauskopf, *Maintenance: A Decade of Development*, 50 Mo. L. Rev. 259 (1985). The American Law Institute, scholars, and practitioners have articulated a number of alternative rationales for spousal support, including compensation for losses. *See* ALI, *Principles of the Law of Family Dissolution* § 5.02 (2011) (refocusing alimony from a need basis to an emphasis on "compensatory spousal payments" for financial losses according to equitable principles and without regard to marital misconduct; losses include "loss of earning capacity arising from a spouse's disproportionate share of caretaking responsibilities," "losses that arise from the changes in life opportunities and expectations caused by the adjustments . . . [made] over the course of a long marital relationship," and "disparities in the financial impact of a short marital relationship on the spouses' post-divorce lives, as compared to their situation prior to marriage"); *see also* Katharine B. Silbaugh, *Money as Emotion in the Distribution of Wealth at Divorce, in* Reconceiving the Family, *supra* note 47, at 234 (describing the ALI's spousal support framework as "incoherent" in their treatment of non-financial matters and criticizing their general separation of the financial aspects of divorce from the emotional and personal aspects of marriage); Starnes, *supra* note 8 (critiquing the ALI alimony model and advocating a "marital partnership" approach that would focus on income-sharing during the minority of marital children); June Carbone, *Income Sharing: Redefining the Family in Terms of Community*, 31 Hous. L. Rev. 359 (1994) (advocating income-sharing and treating ex-spouses' post-divorce income as "family income").

[49] *See infra* § 9.04[C].

[50] *See* Mary Kay Kisthardt, *Re-thinking Alimony: The AAML's Considerations for Calculating Alimony, Spousal Support, or Maintenance*, 21 J. Am. Acad. Matrimonial Law 61 (2008); *see also* 27B C.J.S. Divorce §§ 879-90 (2011); 24A Am. Jur. 2d. Divorce and Separation §§ 681-95, 767-68 (2011).

[51] *See, e.g.*, Report, American Acad. of Matrimonial Lawyers, *Considerations when Determining Alimony, Spousal Support, or Maintenance*, Mar. 9, 2007, *available at* http://www.aaml.org/sites/default/files/AAML-ALI-REPORT-Final%205-02-07.pdf (recommending formulas and deviation factors for calculating duration and amount of alimony awards); ALI, *Principles of the Law of Family Dissolution: Analysis and Recommendations* §§ 5.05-.07 (2002); *see also* Virginia R. Dugan & Jon A. Feder, *Alimony Guidelines: Do they Work?*, 25 Fam. Advoc. 20 (2003); Christopher W. Nicholson, Maryland Alimony Factors Chart 2008 (unpublished manuscript) (on file with author) (cross-referencing the courts' employment of statutory alimony factors in eighteen recent cases).

[52] *See, e.g.*, Ala. Code § 3-2-51 (West 2011); N.M. Stat. Ann. § 40-4-7(A) (West 2011).

[53] *See, e.g.*, Alaska Stat. § 25.24.160 (2011); Cal. Fam. Code § 4320 (West 2011).

A number of states require a two-step determination in awarding spousal support: first, the court must decide whether the spouse is *eligible* for support; and second, it must calculate the appropriate *amount* of support to be ordered.[54] The Uniform Marriage and Divorce Act limits eligibility to a spouse who lacks property sufficient for his or her reasonable needs *and* who is unable to support himself or herself through appropriate employment *or* is a custodian of a child such that it would be inappropriate for the parent to work outside the home.[55] In applying such a standard for eligibility, the court in *Neal v. Neal*[56] concluded that a spouse must not only demonstrate insufficient income, but also show that he or she is incapable of employment in order to qualify for spousal maintenance. The court held that because the wife, who had custody of two school-age children and worked part-time as a cleaning person, did not prove that she was physically unable to work full time, she failed to satisfy the requirements for receiving maintenance.

This approach may impose severe hardships on an older spouse who has never worked outside the home or who has been out of the labor force for many years.[57] Some states, while limiting support to a spouse who is "dependent" on the supporting spouse, have interpreted dependency to mean that the party must merely be incapable of maintaining the accustomed standard of living.[58]

If a spouse is qualified to receive alimony, various factors may be applied to determine the appropriate amount of the award. Those factors are generally based on the financial needs of the party seeking support; the earning capacity, assets, and ability of the defendant spouse to pay; and the standard of living established during the marriage. Typical factors include the duration of the marriage; the ability of the dependent spouse to secure job-related education and training; the age, physical, and mental condition of each party; and each party's contribution to or dissipation of marital assets, including homemaking services.[59]

In recent years, some states have recognized a "fairness objective" in addition to the "support objective" when fashioning maintenance awards.[60] The court in *In re Marriage of LaRocque*[61] held that the trial court erred in awarding limited term alimony of $1,500 per month for five months, then $1,000 a month for 13 months.

---

[54] *See, e.g.*, Unif. Marriage and Divorce Act § 308 (West 2010).

[55] *Id.* To date, the Uniform Marriage and Divorce Act has been adopted by Arizona, Colorado, Illinois, Kentucky, Minnesota, Missouri, and Montana. *See* Unif. Marriage and Divorce Act: References and Annotations (West 2011).

[56] 570 P.2d 758 (Ariz. 1977).

[57] *See, e.g., Abuzzahab v. Abuzzahab*, 359 N.W.2d 12, 14 (Minn. 1984) (Wahl, J., dissenting); *see also* Weitzman, *supra* note 13.

[58] *See Williams v. State of North Carolina*, 261 S.E.2d 849 (N.C. 1980).

[59] *See* Unif. Marriage and Divorce Act § 308 (West 2010).

[60] *See, e.g.*, Nev. Rev. Stat. § 125(1), (2) (West 2011) (court may award alimony "as appears just and equitable" and "[s]hall, to the extent practicable, make an equal disposition of the community property . . . except that the court may make an unequal disposition . . . as it deems just if the court finds a compelling reason to do so and sets forth in writing the reasons for making the unequal disposition"); *see also Rodriguez v. Rodriguez*, 13 P.3d 415, 416 (Nev. 2000); Carol Rogerson, *Spousal Support After* Moge, 14 Can. Fam. L.Q. 281 386-87 (1997).

[61] 406 N.W.2d 736 (Wis. 1987).

The wife had received a bachelor's degree the year of the couple's marriage and had been employed in several capacities including secretary, clerk, and teacher. During most of the parties' twenty-five-year marriage, however, she was a homemaker and cared for the couple's five children. The husband received a law degree during the marriage and was employed as an attorney and later as a judge, earning $60,000 per year at the time of divorce.

The *LaRocque* court held that the state's alimony statute was intended to assure a fair and equitable financial arrangement, as well as to provide support according to the parties' needs and earning capacities. In addition, it held that the trial court should consider the feasibility of the spouse becoming self-supporting at a standard of living reasonably comparable to that enjoyed during marriage, as well as the length of time necessary to acquire such ability. The court should measure a reasonable maintenance award in terms of the marital lifestyle rather than the average annual earnings of the parties over the duration of the marriage. A reasonable starting point is to consider an equal division of the parties' total income.[62]

[B]   Fault as a Factor in Spousal Support

Because of the decreased importance of marital fault in divorce and the corresponding emphasis on need, compensation, or other rationales for awarding spousal support, approximately half the states have entirely eliminated consideration of marital misconduct in ordering support.[63] The remaining states, however, still recognize marital fault either as a factor in determining the amount of spousal support or as an absolute bar to spousal support.[64]

Even when fault is not an enumerated factor for determining the appropriate amount of support, some courts have determined that misconduct should remain relevant. For example, in *Williams v. Williams*,[65] the North Carolina Supreme Court noted that despite the statutory omission of fault as a factor for determining a spouse's dependency or the amount of support to be ordered, the state retained statutes that conditioned receipt of alimony on the supporting spouse's committing one of ten specific acts. It further disqualified a dependent spouse from receiving alimony for committing any of those acts. The court concluded that because divorce works an economic hardship on both parties:

> the burden of contending with diminished assets should, in all fairness, fall on the party primarily responsible for the breakup of the economic unit . . . . Sound public policy would dictate that the party who violated that binding [marriage] contract should continue to bear its financial burden

---

[62] Post *LaRocque*, Wisconsin courts have used an equal split of total income as a starting point in determining spousal maintenance. However, in *King v. King*, 590 N.W.2d 480 (Wis. 1999), the court held that there is no legal entitlement to maintenance.

[63] *See* Peter Nash Swisher, *Marriage and Some Troubling Issues with No-Fault Divorce*, 17 Regent U. L. Rev. 243, 248 (2004-05); Elrod & Spector, *supra* note 47, at Chart 1.

[64] *Id.* at 248. *See also supra* § 8.03[F]. In over forty states, courts may also consider parties' economic misconduct in determining property division. *See* Elrod & Spector, *supra* note 47, at Chart 1 (2009).

[65] 261 S.E.2d 849 (N.C. 1980).

where he or she can reasonably do so and where that is necessary to prevent a relatively greater economic hardship on the party without fault.[66]

Other courts have held that while fault may be properly considered to compensate a spouse for actual injuries incurred because of the other's misbehavior or to bear the economic burden of divorce, it may not be used to punish a spouse. In *Taylor v. Taylor*,[67] the court held that alimony could not be used as a "substitute for a money judgment in a personal injury case," where the husband had physically abused the wife during their marriage, although he could be required to pay her medical and dental expenses resulting from his abuse.[68]

Because a trial court has wide discretion in determining both a spouse's eligibility for spousal support and the amount to be awarded in an individual case, awards are often inconsistent and unpredictable. A trial court's alimony decision will not be overturned by an appellate court absent abuse of discretion or a misapplication of the statutory standards.[69]

§ 9.04 FORMS OF SPOUSAL SUPPORT

[A] Temporary Spousal Support *Pendente Lite*

During a period of separation, while a divorce action is pending but prior to a divorce decree, a dependent spouse may petition the court for temporary spousal support, or support *pendente lite*.[70] *Pendente lite* support may provide for daily necessities during the interim, including medical expenses, preserve a spouse's assets, prevent the other spouse from controlling all the parties' income and assets, provide suit money, and decrease the financial burden of family, friends or the

---

[66] *Id.* at 858–59. North Carolina statutes now incorporate the *Williams* holding about spousal misconduct as a factor in determining the appropriate amount of support. Section 50-16.3A(b), adopted in 1995, states that "The court shall exercise its discretion in determining the amount, duration, and manner of payment of alimony . . . consider[ing] all relevant factors, including: (1) The marital misconduct of either of the spouses. Nothing herein shall prevent a court from considering incidents of post date-of-separation marital misconduct as corroborating evidence supporting other evidence that marital misconduct occurred during the marriage and prior to date of separation . . . ." N.C. Gen. Stat. Ann. § 50-16.3A (West 2011).

[67] 378 So. 2d 1352 (Fla. Dist. Ct. App. 1980).

[68] Increasingly, current or recently divorced spouses bring tort suits against one other. Typically these suits seek compensation for assault and battery, but plaintiffs have also prevailed in suits alleging "intentional infliction of emotional distress, . . . fraud, . . . tortious infliction of a venereal disease, wiretapping, abuse of process, and tortious interference in custodial relations." Robert G. Spector, *Marital Torts: The Current Legal Landscape*, 33 Fam. L.Q. 745, 760-61 (1999). *See also* Michelle L. Evans, Note, *Wrongs Committed During a Marriage: The Child that No Area of the Law Wants to Adopt*, 66 Wash. & Lee L. Rev. 465 (2009); Benjamin Shmueli, *Tort Litigation Between Spouses: Let's Meet Somewhere in the Middle*, 15 Harv. Negot. L. Rev. 195 (2010).

[69] *See, e.g., Brooks v. Brooks*, 498 S.E.2d 461, 462 (Va. Ct. App. 1998) (citing *Dodge v. Dodge*, 343 S.E.2d 363, 367 (Va. Ct. App. 1986)); *Clark v. Clark*, 696 P.2d 1386 (Kan. 1985); *Rosenberg v. Rosenberg*, 497 A.2d 485 (Md. Ct. Spec. App. 1985); *Quick v. Quick*, 290 S.E.2d 653 (N.C. 1982).

[70] *See generally* Kathleen Kay, *Alimony* Pendente Lite *and Earning Capacity*, 45 La. L. Rev. 79 (1984).

public, upon whom the dependent spouse may otherwise rely.[71] Disadvantages of seeking temporary support include limited time for discovery, lack of a hearing in some jurisdictions, and the potential that the amount of temporary support awarded may unduly influence a final award.[72] Courts have upheld temporary *pendente lite* support orders for payments to a spouse to continue her education which she had commenced prior to the filing of a divorce petition[73] and for making mortgage payments while the divorce is pending.[74]

In *In re Marriage of Burlini*,[75] the California Court of Appeals held that spousal support guidelines are to be used only for awarding temporary spousal support, as a separate statute determines the award of permanent spousal support. The court observed that temporary support is intended to maintain the parties' standard of living as closely as possible to the status quo during the pendency of the divorce action. Permanent support, on the other hand, is meant to provide long-term financial assistance, when necessary, as determined after dissolution and division of property. The court encouraged the continued use of guidelines for temporary support orders, absent unusual facts, to promote consistency by proportionately dividing the family income.

[B] "Permanent" Spousal Support

Alimony following divorce was traditionally ordered as a series of specified periodic payments for an indefinite period of time. Periodic support or alimony, often called "permanent" alimony, is not literally "permanent" because, absent a separation agreement to the contrary, it generally terminates on the death of either former spouse, on the remarriage of the recipient, or sometimes even upon the continued cohabitation of the recipient.[76] It also can be modified upward or

---

[71] *See, e.g.*, Ark. Code Ann. § 9-11-809(d) (2011) (spousal support may be awarded during divorce proceedings or a separation period); Fla. Stat. § 61.071 (2011) (courts may award suit money); Ga. Code Ann. § 19-6-3 (2011) (courts may award support for litigation expenses "as the condition of the parties and the facts of the case may justify"); S.D. Codified Laws § 25-4-38 (2011) (during a pending divorce action, "the court may in its discretion require one spouse to pay as alimony any money necessary to support the other spouse or the children of the parties, or to prosecute or defend the action"); Wyo. Stat. Ann. § 20-2-111 (2011) ("[T]he court may require either party to pay any sum necessary to enable the other to carry on or defend the action and for support and the support of the children of the parties during its pendency."); *see also* Alimony, Maintenance, and Other Spousal Support, tbl.1, 0080 SURVEYS 11 (2010) (Westlaw).

[72] *See* Melvyn Frumkes, *Temporary Alimony — The Importance of Itemizing Daily Expenses*, 25 Trial 36, 37 (1989). Some jurisdictions provide that temporary maintenance awards may not dictate subsequent permanent maintenance awards. *See, e.g.*, Colo. Rev. Stat. § 14-10-114(2)(d) (2011).

[73] *See McNulty v. McNulty*, 500 A.2d 876 (Pa. Super. Ct. 1985).

[74] *See Taylor v. Taylor*, 364 S.E.2d 244 (Va. Ct. App. 1988). *See generally* Zitter, *Excessiveness or Adequacy of Money Awarded as Temporary Alimony*, 26 A.L.R.4th 1218 (2011).

[75] 191 Cal. Rptr. 541 (Cal. Ct. App. 1983).

[76] *See, e.g.*, Unif. Marriage and Divorce Act § 316(b), 9A U.L.A. 183 (1998); Mo. Rev. Stat. § 452.075 (2011) ("[T]he remarriage of the former spouse shall relieve the spouse obligated to pay support from further payment of alimony . . . from the date of the remarriage, without the necessity of further court action."); Wash. Rev. Code § 26.09.170(2) (2011) ("Unless otherwise agreed in writing or expressly provided in the decree the obligation to pay future maintenance is terminated upon the death of either party or the remarriage of the party receiving maintenance or registration of a new domestic partnership

downward on motion of either party upon proof of a significant change of circumstances.[77]

A spouse is most likely to be awarded permanent alimony if the spouse is older, without significant job skills, and is unlikely to become self-supporting, especially when the marriage has been long-term. The Arizona Court of Appeals addressed this concept in *Rainwater v. Rainwater*,[78] in which the husband appealed an award to the wife of $1,900 per month for 3 years or until one year after the wife completed her bachelor's degree, whichever occurred first, followed by $1,200 a month until her death or remarriage. The husband argued that Arizona law permitted spousal maintenance only for a finite, transitional, rehabilitative term unless the recipient is permanently unable to become self-sustaining. The court decided that although the policy goal of a fixed term maintenance award is to promote a diligent effort to become self-sustaining, this goal must be balanced with the likelihood that the receiving spouse will be able to support herself in a manner reasonably approximating the standard of living during marriage. At the end of their 22 year marriage, the wife was 42 and working as a secretary while she pursued a college degree. During much of the marriage she had worked full time outside the home, helping to support the husband while he worked toward an engineering degree. She had contributed socially and emotionally to the husband's career, while maintaining the home and raising their two now-grown children. The husband earned more than $100,000 a year at the time of divorce. The court concluded that the wife could not foreseeably expect to maintain her standard of living without ongoing support from the husband at a level reasonably within his ability to provide.

By contrast, later that same year, the Arizona Court of Appeals, in *Hughes v. Hughes*,[79] applied the same standard it set out in *Rainwater* but denied permanent spousal maintenance because the wife presented no evidence that she would eventually not be able to generate her own earnings. In addition, the marriage was relatively short, there was no evidence that their standard of living increased during the marriage, or that the wife made any contribution to the husband's education or earning capacity, and she received a half interest in the husband's business when the marriage ended.

In 2010, the New York Supreme Court Appellant Division concluded that the trial court "providently exercised its discretion in awarding the 69-year old [wife] nondurational maintenance." The trial court considered "the standard of living of the parties during the marriage, the distribution of marital property, the age and health of the parties, the present and future earning capacity of both parties, the ability of the party seeking maintenance to become self-supporting, and the fact that the plaintiff was the primary homemaker and caregiver for the parties'

---

of the party receiving maintenance."); 31 P.R. Laws Ann. § 385 (2008) ("Alimony shall be revoked through judicial decision . . . if the divorced spouse entitled to such alimony contracts a new marriage or lives in public concubinage."). *See generally* Alimony, Maintenance, and Other Spousal Support, tbl.1, 0080 SURVEYS 11 (2010) (Westlaw).

[77] *See infra* § 9.05.

[78] 869 P.2d 176 (Ariz. Ct. App. 1993).

[79] 869 P.2d 198 (Ariz. Ct. App. 1993).

children during their lengthy marriage."[80]

Some states that had placed a time limitation on alimony, such as New Hampshire (which had limited alimony to three years), have since authorized their courts to issue orders for indefinite alimony.[81] Courts have also vacated awards of rehabilitative alimony and remanded back to the trial court for consideration of whether any disparity that existed between the parties' standards of living was so unconscionable as to warrant permanent alimony.[82] Many states also authorize "lump sum" support payments, also referred to as "alimony in gross" or "alimony in solido."[83] Although lump sum alimony is defined in terms of a definite, specific sum, it may be payable in a series of installments for a designated time. Alimony payable in a lump sum may closely resemble property division payments, and despite its different theoretical basis, difficult categorization problems may arise when enforcement is sought.[84]

[C] "Rehabilitative" Spousal Support

Because a large proportion of married women now work outside the home, some jurisdictions disfavor permanent alimony, regarding it as a "pension" to the recipient, and prefer to make spousal support awards, if at all, for a limited period of time.[85] A number of states now have a presumption or a preference for "rehabilitative" or "transitional" alimony, limited to definite time periods in an attempt to encourage the recipient to become self-supporting or to re-adjust to

---

[80] *Rodriguez v. Rodriguez*, 70 A.D.3d 799, 802 (N.Y. 2010). *See also Chamberlain v. Chamberlain*, 615 N.W.2d 405 (Minn. App. 2000) (upholding an award of permanent alimony of $2,400 per month to a 50-year-old woman in good health and employed as a teacher, on the basis that the state's maintenance statute requires consideration of the standard of living during marriage, and the couple lived a lavish lifestyle for twenty years).

[81] *See* N.H. Rev. Stat. § 458:19(I) (2011); *Canaway v. Canaway*, 13 A.3d 320, 324 (N.H. 2010) (noting that "[u]nder the prior version of [New Hampshire statute] RSA 458:19, alimony automatically expired after three years . . . and the party seeking a renewal or an extension had the burden of showing that justice required a renewal or extension . . . . However, the current version of RSA 458:19 authorizes the court to issue indefinite alimony orders").

[82] *See, e.g., Simonds v. Simonds*, 886 A.2d 158, 165 (Md. Ct. Spec. App. 2005).

[83] *See, e.g., Winokur v. Winokur*, 365 S.E.2d 94 (Ga. 1988); *Washburn v. Washburn*, 677 P.2d 152 (Wash. 1984).

[84] *See infra* § 9.06[F]. In some states, different rules govern the termination and modification of lump-sum alimony. *Compare Barrett v. U.S.*, 74 F.3d 661 (1996) (payor's obligation to pay lump-sum alimony did not terminate upon death) *with Springer v. Comm'r*, 86 T.C.M. (CCH) 127 (2003) (except as otherwise agreed by the parties or ordered by the court, liability to make "alimony in gross" payments terminates on the death of either party or the remarriage of payee spouse; such payments do not constitute a vested right to the payee spouse).

[85] *See also Quamme v. Bellino*, 652 N.W.2d 360 (N.D. 2002) (spousal support may be required for an indefinite period to maintain a spouse who cannot be adequately retrained to achieve economic independence, although temporary spousal support to rehabilitate a disadvantaged spouse is preferred); 2011 Mass. Acts ch. 124 (2011) (Alimony Reform Act abolishing most lifetime support payments when payor reaches retirement age or payee begins living with another romantic partner, and establishing a formula for alimony based on the length of the marriage). *See generally* Joan Krauskopf, *Rehabilitative Alimony: Uses and Abuses of Limited Duration Alimony*, 21 Fam. L.Q. 573 (1988).

single status.[86]

Rehabilitative alimony is intended to provide both spouses with some measure of predictability concerning their present and future needs and obligations, as well as to encourage the recipient to find employment or to undertake the education or training that will lead to future employment.[87] Rehabilitative alimony may be available for educational and cost of living expenses for both spouses.[88]

In *Pfohl v. Pfohl*,[89] both the wife and husband appealed from the trial court's awarding the husband $30,000 in lump sum alimony when the husband had previously received $200,000 in assets as gifts from the wife. The wife had a net worth of $4,250,000, and the couple had enjoyed a high standard of living based on the wife's contributions during the nine-year marriage. Noting that Florida's no-fault divorce law permitted alimony to be awarded to a husband under the same criteria as to a wife, the court held that the husband had shown both the wife's ability to pay and his own need, in light of the standard of living enjoyed during the marriage. The husband was 37 years old and in good health, but was mentally impaired and unemployed, with limited skills. Furthermore, the wife had insisted that the husband quit his job as a toy salesman so he could devote all his time to her and the family. Rehabilitative alimony was appropriate to supplement the husband's other means until he could become self-supporting.

The Appellate Court of Connecticut reached a similar conclusion in *Kovalsick v. Kovalsick*,[90] a case in which the spouses enjoyed an equal level of education but the husband historically earned five times more than the wife and the wife had never earned more than $25,000 per year during the marriage. The trial court awarded the wife neither marital property nor rehabilitative or time-limited alimony, despite no evidence at trial that she could earn more than her historical salary during the marriage without additional training and education. Moreover, the trial court ordered the wife to pay the entirety of the parties' marital debt. On appeal, the court found that if the financial orders were not modified and the wife continued to be responsible for the full marital debt, but did not receive any marital property and was not able to increase her earning capacity, it was "reasonably foreseeable" that "she could well be [placed] in dire financial straits."[91] The court held that the order denying any alimony at all constituted an abuse of discretion and reversed and remanded for reconsideration of the trial court's financial orders.

---

[86] *See, e.g., Taylor v. Taylor*, 504 N.Y.S.2d 698 (N.Y. App. Div. 1986); *Stevenson v. Stevenson*, 511 A.2d 961 (R.I. 1986).

[87] *See also Kulakowski v. Kulakowski*, 468 A.2d 733 (N.J. Super. Ct. Ch. Div. 1982); *Turner v. Turner*, 385 A.2d 1280 (N.J. Super. Ct. App. Div. 1978), *criticized by Arnold v. Arnold, infra* note 105.

[88] *See, e.g., Horton v. Horton*, 62 So. 3d 689, 692 (Fla. Dist. Ct. App. 2008) (affirming award of rehabilitative alimony for tuition expenses but instructing the trial court, on remand, to award rehabilitative alimony "commensurate with her rehabilitative plan so she can establish the capacity for self-support").

[89] 345 So. 2d 371 (Fla. Dist. Ct. App. 1977).

[90] 7 A.3d 924 (Conn. App. Ct. 2010).

[91] *Id.* at 930.

Rehabilitative alimony has been described as a device to " 'equalize the burdens of divorce or to restore an economically disadvantaged spouse to independent status by providing a disadvantaged spouse an opportunity to acquire an education, training, work skills, or experience to become self-supporting.' "[92] Thus, rehabilitative alimony may be appropriate when a spouse has been awarded a large amount of marital property,[93] when the marriage was of short duration,[94] or when the spouse is "young enough and able" to eventually increase his or her earning power.[95] In *In re Marriage of Wilson*,[96] the court noted that limited-term alimony may be proper in a short term, second marriage when the spouse is incapable of becoming self-supporting due to an injury incurred during the marriage, and affirmed termination of alimony after 58 months following a 70-month marriage. By contrast, a New Jersey appellate court, in *Cox v. Cox*,[97] concluded that while limited-duration alimony is meant for short marriages, in long-term marriages limited-duration alimony is inappropriate if it fails to account for the spouse's long-term contributions to the marriage.

Factors considered in awarding rehabilitative alimony vary by state, but may include such things as

> demonstrated need during the post-divorce economic readjustment period; the parties' station in life; the length of the marriage and the ages of the spouses; the earning capacity of the parties as well as their physical condition and financial means; the accustomed style of living of the parties; evidence of a spouse's own income-producing capacity and the time needed to make the post-divorce transition for self-support.[98]

---

[92] *Becker v. Becker*, 799 N.W.2d 53, 63 (N.D. 2011) (*quoting Paulson v. Paulson*, 783 N.W.2d 262 (N.D. 2010)). *See also Clapp v. Clapp*, 653 A.2d 72 (Vt. 1994) (upholding a one-year award of maintenance to the wife based on an equalization of the parties' incomes is within trial court's discretion; the Vermont Supreme Court had previously rejected a permanent maintenance award based on the equalization approach).

[93] *See Hathaway v. Hathaway*, 791 N.Y.S.2d 631 (App. Div. 2005) (upholding limited-duration rehabilitative maintenance to husband of only $1,000 per month when, among other things, husband received relatively high property award); *Wagner v. Wagner*, 728 N.W.2d 318 (N.D. 2007) (wife should receive rehabilitative maintenance in the amount of $5,000 per month for five years after being awarded net property valued at over $765,000, which was roughly $200,000 more than awarded to husband); *Crabtree v. Crabtree*, 16 S.W.3d 356 (Tenn. 2000) (wife's award of $2,500 monthly rehabilitative alimony for five years was justified where, among other things, wife received $373,000, which equates to 45% of the marital property, including the marital home).

[94] *Carlson v. Carlson*, 722 P.2d 222 (Alaska 1986) (though marriage only lasted one year, award of two years' rehabilitative alimony was proper to assist relatively unskilled wife while she trained as a bookkeeper). *See also* Russell G. Donaldson, *Power to Modify Spousal Support Award for a Limited Term*, 62 A.L.R.4th 180 (2011).

[95] *Jaffy v. Jaffy*, 965 So. 2d 825, 828 (Fla. Dist. Ct. App. 2008) (award of permanent, periodic alimony rather than rehabilitative alimony was inappropriate where wife was college educated, young enough to become self-supporting, and trial court premised its award on wife's "deranged" lack of interest in working).

[96] 247 Cal. Rptr. 522 (Ct. App. 1988).

[97] 762 A.2d 1040 (N.J. App. Div. 2000).

[98] *Hutchings v. Hutchings*, 250 P.3d 324, 327 (Okla. 2011) (*citations omitted*).

Some courts require the recipient spouse to "present the court with an education plan that identifies a career goal, a degree program aimed at realizing that goal, and a time frame during which the degree may be earned through reasonable diligence."[99] At least one court has upheld an award of rehabilitative alimony that included a $5,000 "incentive" payment from husband to wife upon the wife's completing of a program for educational or vocational study.[100]

The Supreme Court of North Dakota, in *Van Klootwyk v. Van Klootwyk*,[101] noted that two concepts of rehabilitative spousal support have been developed: a "minimalist" doctrine, which seeks to educate and retrain the recipient for minimal self-support, and an "equitable" doctrine, which attempts to enable the disadvantaged spouse to obtain "adequate" self-support in light of the standard of living during the marriage. Under the latter, the recipient may be eligible for rehabilitative support regardless of whether she is employed full-time, and should not be disqualified because she began her economic self-rehabilitation by education or training during the marriage. This is especially warranted where the parties accumulated few assets during the marriage. A strong dissent would have denied the wife rehabilitative alimony because of her attainment of an education and career during marriage and because the husband's living expenses were higher.

Early in its development, some commentators regarded the use of rehabilitative alimony as potentially dangerous because trial courts, "in their zeal to restrict alimony and under the influence of the notion that most married women today work outside the home, will award rehabilitative alimony when the wife has no realistic expectation of earning enough to support herself in an acceptable [manner]."[102] These dangers were realized in *Otis v. Otis*.[103] The court upheld an award of alimony that terminated after four years, despite the fact that the wife had not worked during the couple's 25-year marriage since the birth of their child. Quoting a 1978 law review article, the court observed that statutory changes in the state's law of alimony were a reflection that:

> [T]raditionally spousal support was a permanent award because it was assumed that a wife had neither the ability nor the resources to become self-sustaining. However, with the mounting dissolution rate, the advent of no-fault dissolution, and the growth of the women's liberation movement, the focal point of spousal support determinations has shifted from the sex of the recipient to the individual's ability to become financially independent.[104]

---

[99] *Cartee v. Cartee*, 239 P.3d 707, 713 (Alaska 2010) (*quoting Tybus v. Holland*, 989 P.2d 1281, 1288 (Alaska 1999)). *See also Westberry v. Westberry*, 777 So. 2d 1087 (Fla. Dist. Ct. App. 2001) (absent evidence of a rehabilitation plan, trial court could not award rehabilitative alimony).

[100] *Giardina v. Giardina*, 987 So. 2d 606 (Ala. Civ. App. 2008).

[101] 563 N.W.2d 377 (N.D. 1997).

[102] *See* Clark, *supra* note 12, at 650-51.

[103] 299 N.W.2d 114 (Minn. 1980), *superseded by statute*, S.F. No. 378, 1982 c. 535 § 1, *as recognized in Gales v. Gales*, 553 N.W.2d 416, 418 (Minn. 1996).

[104] *Id.* at 116 (citation omitted).

Although the husband's income exceeded $120,000 per year, the court held that the limited alimony award satisfied the state's new statutory standards. Some jurisdictions that initially embraced rehabilitative alimony have since tempered their enthusiasm, noting that

> [s]uch a [time] limitation has been characterized euphemistically as "rehabilitative alimony" by matrimonial judges who have employed such a technique as a means of encouraging a wife to seek employment and self-support . . . . The avowed purpose of encouraging a spouse to seek employment . . . may be achieved . . . by molding the quantum of the alimony award to a spouse. In the absence of unusual facts, however, which support a cut-off date for alimony payments, such a technique should be avoided. There are other available methods of setting reasonable alimony based upon all the circumstances of the case including the provisions for equitable distribution . . . . Normally there would be no rational basis for an arbitrary termination date in light of our law permitting modification by increase or decrease because of a change of circumstances.[105]

Likewise, to safeguard against harsh consequences, some courts have concluded that permanent, rather than rehabilitative, alimony must be awarded when the spouse is older, is without significant job skills or work history, has medical problems, or is otherwise unlikely to be able to become self-supporting.[106] For example, in *Lash v. Lash*[107] the Florida Court of Appeals held that, in light of the husband's substantial salary as an executive, an award of rehabilitative, rather than permanent, alimony was improper when inequities would result due to the wife's medical problems and absence from the job market for most of the parties' 26-year marriage. Other courts have held that rehabilitative alimony is proper only when the recipient can obtain employment at compensation which provides a standard of living roughly commensurate to that established during marriage.[108]

In many instances, rehabilitative alimony awards have spanned nearly a decade or more, allowing it to serve many of the same functions as permanent alimony. For instance, in the case of *In re Marriage of Becker*,[109] the Supreme Court of Iowa awarded rehabilitative alimony to the wife for ten years in the amount of $8,000 per month for the first three years, and $5,000 per month for the remaining seven years. The court calculated her standard of living to be $6,980 per month during the marriage, but awarded the wife higher payments for the initial term to update her education and resume the career she abandoned after having children. The court determined the remaining seven years of support were necessary so she would have "time to develop her earning capacity past an entry-level position."[110]

---

[105] *Arnold v. Arnold*, 401 A.2d 261, 262-64 (N.J. Super. Ct. App. Div. 1979).

[106] *See In re Marriage of Morrison*, 573 P.2d 41 (Cal. 1978); *see also* Md. Code Ann., Fam. Law § 11-106(c) (2011).

[107] 307 So. 2d 241 (Fla. Dist. Ct. App. 1975).

[108] *See, e.g., Bagan v. Bagan*, 382 N.W.2d 645 (N.D. 1986); *In re Marriage of Carney*, 462 N.E.2d 596 (Ill. App. Ct. 1984).

[109] 756 N.W.2d 822 (Iowa 2008).

[110] *Id.* at 827. *See also Duff v. Kearns-Duff*, 792 N.W.2d 916 (N.D. 2010) (upholding award to husband

Several jurisdictions recognize a role for rehabilitative alimony to smooth the transition from married life to single life, even apart from the need for further education or training.[111] Thus, Florida courts will award "bridge-the-gap" alimony.[112] This award can assist a spouse "with any legitimate, identifiable, short-term need"[113] and may be used for "reorientation."[114]

---

of $9,000 per month for two years followed by declining awards over the next seven years, rather than an award of permanent support, in order to provide husband with the opportunity to finish his education and become self-supporting); *Porter v. Porter*, 769 A.2d 725 (Conn. App. Ct. 2001) (upholding rehabilitative alimony for wife for fourteen-year period where the court considered statutory criteria in awarding time-limited alimony, and intended to give wife an opportunity to develop marketable skills while the couple's children were in college when wife could focus full-time on her career); *Ruane v. Ruane*, 865 N.Y.S.2d 632 (App. Div. 2008) (concluding that trial court "providently exercised" its discretion in awarding wife $6,000 per month in maintenance for eight years, in order to allow wife reasonably sufficient time to become self-sufficient while maintaining a semblance of her pre-divorce standard of living); *Johnson v. Johnson*, 580 A.2d 503, 506 (Vt. 1990) (upholding a rehabilitative alimony award of $1,500 per month for ten years, where wife supported herself as a teacher with an earning potential of $17,700 per year, which was above the poverty line, but "insufficient to meet her reasonable needs . . . in light of the standard of living established during the marriage"); *In re Marriage of Gillis*, 227 P.3d 809 (Or. Ct. App. 2010) (concluding that where 52-year-old wife possessed an earning capacity no greater than $20,000 per year and worked as homemaker during the marriage, while husband earned $205,000 per year, including retirement contributions, it was just and equitable to award wife eight years of spousal support until she could draw upon her retirement accounts without penalty).

[111] *Demont v. Demont*, 67 So. 3d 1096, 1098 (Fla. Dist. Ct. App. 2011) (upholding award to wife of $4,000 per month for two years where wife was capable of obtaining full-time work, but would be totally dependent upon husband's financial support until she obtained secure full-time employment, the couple's expensive marital home remained unsold, and the parties faced a declining economy); *Liebrecht v. Liebrecht*, 58 So. 3d 415, 418 (Fla. Dist. Ct. App. 2011) (upholding lump-sum, nonmodifiable gap-bridging alimony instead of permanent, periodic alimony where wife, who had been out of the workforce for thirteen years, had "reasonable level of earning capacity and should be able to obtain employment sufficient to become self-supporting," but would need some time to become self-sufficient). *See also Barner v. Barner*, 716 So. 2d 795, 799 (Fla. Dist. Ct. App. 1998) (upholding award to wife of $1,800 per month of "bridge-the-gap" alimony for two-and-one-half years after a twenty-four year marriage, where wife owned valuable timberland but had no means of support until the timber could be sold upon reaching maturity in the future because her assets were not immediately capable of liquidation); *Kanouse v. Kanouse*, 549 So. 2d 1035, 1036 (Fla. Dist. Ct. App. 1989) (award to wife of $1,500 per month for five years was inadequate to enable her to "bridge the gap" between her earning capacity during the marriage and the time at which she would be able to "[re]establish[ ] herself in the market place" by developing her own law practice and maximizing her capacity for self-support).

[112] *See Bell v. Bell*, 68 So. 3d 321, 327 (Fla. Dist. Ct. App. 2011) (" '[B]ridge-the-gap' alimony is intended to smooth the transition between a higher standard of marital living and the standard that a spouse can provide for herself, and [is] typically awarded for a very short period of time. . . . It is meant for situations where the court finds that permanent alimony is not appropriate, and where no rehabilitation is requested or needed . . . . It should be used to assist a spouse with legitimate, identifiable, short-term needs under such circumstances in which an award is reasonable and the other spouse has the ability to pay. Bridge-the-gap alimony is most appropriately awarded in instances where the receiving spouse is already employed, possesses adequate employment skills, and requires no further rehabilitation other than a brief time to ease the transition to single life." (internal citations omitted)).

[113] *See Liebrecht v. Liebrecht*, 58 So. 3d 415, 418 (Fla. Dist. Ct. App. 2011) (requiring also that "a lump sum award is reasonable and . . . the other spouse has the ability to pay the award") (*quoting Borchard v. Borchard*, 730 So. 2d 748, 753 (Fla. Dist. Ct. App. 1999)).

[114] *See Gallant v. Gallant*, 945 P.2d 795, 801 (Alaska 1997) ("[R]eorientation alimony is essentially transitional and may be awarded for brief periods to provide support pending the sale of marital property or to enable a spouse to get a job appropriate to the spouse's existing skills. . . . [G]iven the transitional purposes of reorientation alimony, it is difficult to imagine circumstances under which an

[D]   New or Hybrid Forms of Alimony

Because many modern alimony statutes authorize alimony only when a spouse can demonstrate need,[115] a number of states have recognized new forms of alimony to compensate a spouse for contributions to the other spouse's education or career development. These awards, which are based on statute,[116] contract, or equitable principles, permit compensation when little divisible property has been accumulated, but one spouse has obtained valuable career assets not categorized as property, partially as a result of the other's contributions.[117] These new awards, frequently denominated "reimbursement" or "restitutional" alimony, are hybrids of alimony and property division, as they combine features of both doctrines.

In *Pyeatte v. Pyeatte*,[118] the Arizona Court of Appeals rejected a wife's contract claim that she had put the husband through three years of law school based on his agreement that he would then put her through graduate school. When the husband sought a divorce after completing law school and entering the bar, the wife sought damages for breach of contract. The court denied her claim, holding that the agreement was insufficiently defined in terms of time, place, and cost of performance, and lacked other material provisions. However, it acknowledged that the wife could obtain restitution, based on an equitable theory of quasi-contract, to prevent the husband's unjust enrichment. It limited the award on remand to her financial contributions to the husband's living expenses and direct educational expenses, not to exceed the amount of benefit she had anticipated.

Some courts have authorized similar awards even when the contributing spouse does not intend to pursue further education. In *Gallant v. Gallant*,[119] the Supreme Court of Alaska upheld an award to the wife of "extended spousal support" intending to provide for the wife's significant "period of time out of the job market," help alleviate the balance between her expenses and income, and support her

---

award of reorientation alimony extending for longer than one year would be justified" (internal citations omitted)).

[115] *See, e.g.*, *McDermott v. McDermott*, 628 P.2d 959 (Ariz. Ct. App. 1981) (wife unable to demonstrate need because she had supported couple as teacher while husband obtained education; court awarded her $500 per month for up to 33 months as matter of equity, provided that she attended school); *see also* Unif. Marriage and Divorce Act § 308(a) (2010) (making need a prerequisite for the award of alimony). The Uniform Marriage and Divorce Act, approved by the National Conference of Commissioners on Uniform State Laws in 1970 and revised and amended in 1971 and 1973, has to date been adopted only in Arizona, Colorado, Illinois, Kentucky, Minnesota, Missouri, Montana, and Washington.

[116] *See, e.g.*, Ariz. Rev. Stat. § 25-319(A)(3) (2011); Cal. Civ. Code § 4320 (West 2011); La. Civ. Code Ann. art. 121 (2011); *see also Clemons v. Clemons*, 960 So. 2d 1068 (La. Ct. App. 2007); *In re Marriage of Watt*, 214 Cal. App. 3d 340 (Ct. App. 1989).

[117] *See, e.g.*, *In re Marriage of Thornley*, 838 N.E.2d 981 (Ill. App. Ct. 2005) (finding proper award of maintenance in gross when one spouse supports the other to obtain a license or degree); *see also infra* § 10.08; William M. Howard, *Spouse's Professional Degree or License as Marital Property for Purposes of Alimony, Support, or Property Settlement*, 3 A.L.R.6th 447 (2011) (describing treatment of contributions to enhanced earning capacity).

[118] 661 P.2d 196 (Ariz. Ct. App. 1983).

[119] 945 P.2d 795 (Alaska 1997). *See also DeLa Rosa v. DeLa Rosa*, 309 N.W.2d 755 (Minn. 1981); *infra* note 123 (and accompanying text).

payments of past and future medical bills. In *In re Marriage of Francis*,[120] the Iowa Supreme Court approved an award, framed in terms of "reimbursement" alimony, which allowed the wife some return on her investment in addition to her direct contributions. The court permitted consideration of the future earning capacity of the husband who had completed his medical degree and residency while the wife supported him and their two children by running an in-home day care business. The court stated:

> [A]limony has traditionally taken the place of support that would have been provided had the marriage continued. A calculation of future earning capacity, in a case like the present one, essentially represents a value placed on the income to be derived from the advanced degree achieved during the marriage. The amount that would have been the student spouse's contribution to the future support of the parties is logically tied, if not wholly determined by, future earning capacity. Thus, the court's duty to look at the future earning capacity of the spouses tracks more closely with a concern for loss of anticipated support, reimbursable through alimony, than through division of as-yet-unrealized tangible assets.[121]

In deciding whether reimbursement alimony should be due, some courts examine whether the supporting spouse "benefited during the marriage from the increased earning power of [the supported spouse] following the completion of [their] education."[122] Other courts have limited reimbursement alimony to actual contributions to living expenses and direct educational expenses after subtracting the supporting spouse's own living expenses and the supported spouse's own contributions.[123]

Professor Ira Ellman has argued that because spouses often make sacrifices to their own earning capacity based on decisions to benefit the marital community, new principles of alimony should be developed in order to recompense the contributing spouse's reliance interests. He advocates recovery on divorce for losses in earning capacity in order to ensure that marital sharing principles result in sharing the costs, as well as the benefits, of marriage.[124] The ALI *Principles of the Law of*

---

[120] 442 N.W.2d 59 (Iowa 1989).

[121] *Id.* at 63. These awards may also be denominated "rehabilitative alimony." *See, e.g., Heinz v. Heinz*, 632 N.W.2d 443 (N.D. 2001) (award to wife of rehabilitative spousal support of $700 per month for eight years, followed by permanent support of $400 per month, because wife missed opportunities and lost her advantage in the work force while the husband earned a master's degree as a teacher during their lengthy marriage); *Nuveen v. Nuveen*, 795 N.W.2d 308 (N.D. 2011); *Stone v. Stone*, 488 S.E.2d 15 (W. Va. 1997).

[122] *See, e.g., Bourgeois v. Bourgeois*, 818 So. 2d 1005 (La. Ct. App. 2002); Howard, *supra* note 117; *see also* Cal. Fam. Code § 2641 (2011).

[123] *See DeLa Rosa v. DeLa Rosa*, 309 N.W.2d 755 (Minn. 1981) (wife worked as a teacher and at other jobs while the husband pursued his undergraduate and medical degrees; before husband completed his medical degree, he filed for dissolution and the trial court awarded restitution to the wife for the financial support she had provided; the Minnesota Supreme Court approved the concept of reimbursement, but remanded the judgment for a reduction of the award after establishing a formula to calculate reimbursement).

[124] *See* Ira Ellman, *The Theory of Alimony*, 77 Cal. L. Rev. 1, 3 (1989). Whether to recast alimony as compensation for lost earning capacity has sparked considerable academic debate. *See, e.g.,* June

Family Dissolution adopted this approach, characterizing spousal support as "compensatory [spousal] payments."[125] The *Principles* view alimony as a vehicle for compensating a spouse for certain types of financial losses that were incurred due to family care responsibilities and have negative post-divorce consequences for a spouse. Section 5.07 recommends that the duration of compensatory awards be proportionate to the length of the marriage.[126] Under this view, the obligation to share "losses from dissolution" arises not from "an exchange of promises, from the 'marriage ceremony alone' or from any particular 'conception of marriage' " but "from the fact that 'over time . . . the parties' lives become entwined.' "[127]

The Supreme Court of Montana, in *In re Marriage of Williams*,[128] expressly approved a support award designed to compensate a spouse for foregone career opportunities. In *Williams*, the wife had a bachelor's degree at the time of marriage, but remained home to raise the couple's six children and had been out of the job market for eighteen years, while the husband was engaged in the practice of law. The court calculated the wife's career losses in terms of her lost retirement benefits and salary differential due to her absence from work outside the home, and held that these factors were appropriate in determining her reasonable needs and ability to support herself through appropriate employment.[129]

The Vermont Supreme Court considered an income sharing approach to alimony in *Delozier v. Delozier*.[130] In that case the family court had awarded permanent monthly maintenance to a wife in an undetermined amount to be calculated by annually dividing equally the parties' combined income. The court held that in some long-term marriages, permanent alimony may be appropriate to approximate the parties' marital standard of living, but regarded the use of formulas with disfavor, in that they modify support payments without regard to modification standards and

---

Carbone, *Back to the Future: The Perils and Promise of a Backward-Looking Jurisprudence, in* Reconceiving the Family, *supra* note 47; Silbaugh, *supra* note 48; Katherine Shaw Spaht, *Postmodern Marriage as Seen Through the Lens of the ALI's "Compensatory Payments," in* Reconceiving the Family, *supra* note 47; Carl E. Schneider, *Rethinking Alimony: Marital Decisions and Moral Discourse*, 1991 B.Y.U. L. Rev. 197; Lee E. Teitelbaum, *The Family as a System: A Preliminary Sketch*, 1996 Utah L. Rev. 537.

[125] *Principles of the Law of Family Dissolution* § 5.07 cmt. b (2000). Professor Ellman is one of three reporters for the ALI *Principles*.

[126] Compensation would be due without regard to "fault" in the marriage. *See Principles of the Law of Family Dissolution* § 5.04 cmt. b (2011). As Professor Carbone notes, "The [ALI] *Principles* concerning spousal support, which require couples to share the 'losses' that arise at dissolution, would reflect a societal insistence that a wealthier spouse provide for a destitute partner . . . . [But] [c]onsider, for example, an executive husband and a homemaker wife filing for divorce after the wife informs the husband that her casual affair has persuaded her that she no longer loves him. If couples were informally surveyed, they might agree that in such a case the wife who decides to call it quits without cause should be held responsible for the consequences of the dissolution." Carbone, *supra* note 124, at 211.

[127] Carbone, *supra* note 124, at 220 (quoting *Principles of the Law of Family Dissolution* § 5.04 cmt. c (2011)).

[128] 714 P.2d 548 (Mont. 1986).

[129] *See also* Joan Williams, *Is Coverture Dead? Beyond a New Theory of Alimony*, 82 Geo. L. J. 2227 (1994); Jana B. Singer, *Alimony and Efficiency: The Gendered Costs and Benefits of the Economic Justification for Alimony*, 82 Geo. L.J. 2423 (1994) (examining the economic opportunities forgone by a child-rearing spouse, and the corresponding enhancement of their partner's earning capacities).

[130] 640 A.2d 55 (Vt. 1994).

are not responsive to the needs of the parties. In this case, in which the former wife was relatively young, in good health, and was pursuing a career as a registered nurse, the court determined that rehabilitative support and compensatory alimony was appropriate, and temporary income equalization was permissible. The court authorized the trial court to leave the details of the equalization formula to be worked out with an accountant.

Notwithstanding these decisions, courts have been reluctant to consult the *Principles* on this issue, and when they do, often accord them negative treatment.[131]

§ 9.05   MODIFICATION OF SPOUSAL SUPPORT

Most states authorize modification of future payments of spousal support or alimony by statute.[132] Generally, only periodic alimony may be modified; lump sum alimony, like property division, is not modifiable. In general, the party seeking modification must show a change of circumstances that is sufficiently substantial or material to justify either an increase or decrease in the amount originally ordered. A minority of states, following the Uniform Marriage and Divorce Act, have adopted a higher standard, which provides in part:

> (a) . . . [T]he provisions of any [divorce] decree respecting maintenance or support may be modified only as to installments accruing subsequent to the motion for modification and only upon a showing of changed circumstances *so substantial and continuing as to make the terms unconscionable* . . . .

> (b) Unless otherwise agreed in writing or expressly provided in the decree, the obligation to pay future maintenance is terminated upon the death of either party or the remarriage of the party receiving maintenance . . . .[133]

Unless an order modifying spousal support has been entered, the majority of states regard each installment of alimony as final and non-modifiable when it becomes due. An alimony installment that is final and non-modifiable has the status of a final judgment and is entitled to full faith and credit in all other states.[134] Accrued alimony installments or arrearages cannot be modified retroactively, and future alimony payments may be modified prospectively only after a motion has been filed and the other party served with notice.

In a minority of jurisdictions, however, retroactive modification of alimony arrearages is permitted, either by statute or judicial decision.[135] If accrued alimony

---

[131] *See* Michael R. Clisham & Robin Fretwell Wilson, *American Law Institute's* Principles of the Law of Family Dissolution, *Eight Years After Adoption: Guiding Principles or Obligatory Footnote?*, 42 Fam. L.Q. 573 600-04 (2008) (discussing empirical analysis of judicial citations to the *Principles* and noting that provisions on compensatory spousal payments merited only 8.08% of all citations to the *Principles*, and received negative treatment in more than a quarter (28.57%) of citations).

[132] *See, e.g.*, Fla. Stat. Ann. ch. 61.14 (2011). *See generally* Alimony, Maintenance, and Other Spousal Support, tbl.1, 0080 SURVEYS 11 (2010) (Westlaw); Donaldson, *supra* note 94.

[133] Unif. Marriage and Divorce Act § 316, 9A U.L.A. 102 (2010) (emphasis added). The Uniform Marriage and Divorce Act has been adopted only in a handful of states. *See supra* note 115.

[134] *See, e.g.*, *Sistare v. Sistare*, 218 U.S. 1 (1910); *Corliss v. Corliss*, 549 P.2d 1070 (N.M. 1976).

[135] *See generally* Emile F. Short, *Retrospective Increase in Allowance for Alimony, Separate*

arrearages are retroactively modifiable, other states need not afford them full faith and credit because they are not final judgments. When full faith and credit does not prohibit modification, other state courts apply comity principles and consider modification issues under the standards of the state which originally granted the alimony.[136]

Alimony may be modified when the original decree did not sufficiently provide for the spouse or children. Such modifications are permissible regardless of whether the obligation arose in a written separation agreement or a court order, but require a showing of changed circumstances.[137]

Some states allow the parties to agree that a court cannot modify a spousal support award.[138] Courts in a minority of jurisdictions have interpreted separation agreements under traditional contract principles and refused to allow modification of contractual spousal support unless the parties agree.[139] In *In re Marriage of Mass*,[140] the court distinguished between court-ordered support and contractual support. It held that the husband's contractual agreement to pay alimony did not merge into the divorce decree and that his obligation would not terminate under statutory provisions that terminated alimony upon remarriage of the recipient. Child support, however, is always modifiable based on a *bona fide* change of circumstances when it is in the child's best interests, regardless of whether it is based on a court order or private agreement.[141]

Before a modification is justified, the moving party must prove that the circumstances of either or both of the parties have substantially changed. The alleged change in circumstances must have occurred since the last hearing. In *Herndon v. Herndon*,[142] the husband, a chiropractor, had previously been granted a reduction in both his child support and alimony obligations based on the appreciation of the wife's assets and his own health problems involving his hands. The trial court denied his later petition for termination of alimony because it found no sufficient change of circumstances since the previous hearing, the husband's hand condition had not changed and, although the wife's assets had appreciated, their increase in value was due to inflation, which had also affected her costs of raising the child. The husband was not currently practicing chiropraxis, but maintained his licenses in Arizona and California and had not shown he was unable

---

Maintenance, or Support, 52 A.L.R.3d 156 (2011). *See also* N.Y. Dom. Rel. Code §§ 236, 244 (2011); *Fainberg v. Rosen*, 278 A.2d 630 (Md. Ct. Spec. App. 1971).

[136] *See Alig v. Alig*, 255 S.E.2d 494, 497 (Va. 1979).

[137] *See, e.g., Lepis v. Lepis*, 416 A.2d 45 (N.J. 1980).

[138] *See generally* Alimony, Maintenance, and Other Spousal Support, tbl.1, 0080 SURVEYS 11 (2010) (Westlaw) (indicating which states allow parties to a premarital agreement to contract regarding the modification of spousal support). *See also Moseley v. Mosier*, 306 S.E.2d 624 (S.C. 1983) (providing parties with the ability to contract regarding alimony in divorce settlement agreements and, as long as the agreement unambiguously stipulates that the terms may not be altered and is approved by the family court, it binds the court and the parties to those terms).

[139] *See, e.g., Parrillo v. Parrillo*, 336 S.E.2d 23 (Va. 1985).

[140] 431 N.E.2d 1 (Ill. App. Ct. 1981).

[141] *See id.; Drummond v. Drummond*, 495 P.2d 994 (Kan. 1972). *See infra* § 9.06[E].

[142] 305 N.W.2d 917 (S.D. 1981).

to maintain a practice. The Supreme Court of South Dakota affirmed, concluding that the trial court had not abused its discretion.

Determining a legitimate and sufficient change of circumstances that warrants an increase, decrease, or termination of spousal support has generated considerable litigation.[143] Modification will generally be authorized if the recipient's needs or the payor's ability to pay changes because of circumstances beyond the party's control; these may include when either party dies, if the recipient remarries, or, in some states, if the recipient cohabits with another (if such events are not terminating events under the statute).[144]

A substantial increase in the recipient's cost of living, including additional expenses for the parties' children, may constitute grounds for an increase in spousal support.[145] Similarly, a recipient's continuing illness or a significant mental or physical impairment normally constitutes a *bona fide* change of circumstances. However, if the payee's elevated need was due to a voluntary change in lifestyle, courts are hesitant to increase support.[146]

A number of courts have held that when the payor's financial position greatly improves after divorce, the alimony recipient is only entitled to support at the level enjoyed during the marriage and will not be granted an increase in spousal support based solely on the payor's increased ability to pay.[147] Other courts, however, have held that the payor spouse's post-divorce wealth should be shared by the recipient spouse.[148] For example, in *Naylor v. Naylor*,[149] the Utah Supreme Court emphasized that the earnings and financial assets of the husband, who was a surgeon, had increased dramatically since the divorce while the ex-wife's financial status and employment as a hairdresser had not changed. Although alimony had originally been ordered for only five years, the court relied on its statutory power to modify support, regardless of the parties' previous agreement or stipulation. It found that

---

[143] *See generally* James R. Higgins, Jr., Note, *Modification of Spousal Support: A Survey of a Confusing Area of Law*, 17 J. Fam. L. 711 (1979).

[144] *See, e.g., Lepis v. Lepis*, 416 A.2d 45 (N.J. 1980). *But see Reveal v. Reveal*, 798 N.E.2d 1132 (Ohio Ct. App. 2003) (concluding where ex-husband knew ex-wife would be eligible to collect retirement benefits at age 59½, yet agreed to pay her alimony until her remarriage or death, that wife's eligibility for retirement benefits was not a substantial change of circumstances not contemplated by parties).

[145] *Naylor v. Naylor*, 700 P.2d 707 (Utah 1985); *Siegel v. Siegel*, 102 Cal. Rptr. 613 (Cal. Ct. App. 1972).

[146] *See, e.g., Sistrunk v. Sistrunk*, 235 So. 2d 53 (Fla. Dist. Ct. App. 1970).

[147] *See, e.g., In re Marriage of Hoffmeister*, 236 Cal. Rptr. 543 (Cal. Ct. App. 1987); *see also In re Marriage of Smith*, 274 Cal. Rptr. 911 (Cal. Ct. App. 1990) (increase of support to marital standard of living unwarranted where husband worked excessive hours and couple lived beyond means during marriage).

[148] *See, e.g., In re Marriage of Geis*, 512 N.E.2d 1354 (Ill. App. Ct. 1987); *Lott v. Lott*, 302 A.2d 666 (Md. Ct. Spec. App. 1973); *Bedell v. Bedell*, 583 So. 2d 1005, 1007 (Fla. 1991) ("Thus, we hold that a substantial increase in the financial ability of the paying spouse, standing alone, may justify but does not require an order of increased alimony.").

[149] 700 P.2d 707 (Utah 1985). *See also Schwarz v. Schwarz*, 5 A.3d 548 (Conn. App. Ct. 2010) (affirming increase in alimony obligation where payor experienced increase in gross income of 20 percent per year and increase in net income of over 13 percent per year); *Mahoney v. Mahoney*, 567 N.W.2d 206 (N.D. 1997) (husband's extraordinary ability to produce income, wife's minimal income and need for ongoing rehabilitative alimony to complete a two-year internship, and reduction of husband's support obligation together provided sufficient basis for extending husband's support obligation).

the parties' earlier expectations that the wife's income would increase had failed to materialize and, along with increased costs of raising the parties' child, this constituted a sufficient change of circumstances to warrant a four-year extension of the alimony as well as an increase in the amount.

If the payor's income substantially declines after the divorce, through no fault of his or her own, an alimony award may be reduced.[150] An involuntary loss of employment, a physical or mental handicap, or attainment of mandatory retirement age may be sufficient to authorize a decrease in an alimony obligation.[151] In *Rome v. Rome*,[152] the parties had stipulated that the husband would pay the wife $1,000 a month in spousal support when they ended their 32-year marriage. Three months later, the husband sought a reduction of support because he had lost his job. The trial court lowered the amount to $100 a month and established a sliding scale correlated to his future income for subsequent support. Although the husband presented undisputed evidence that he had been fired without cause, the appellate court questioned the sincerity of his efforts to find new employment and reversed the order because of the trial court's refusal to continue the matter for reassessment of the husband's efforts to obtain employment.

If the payor voluntarily reduces his or her income by taking a lower paying job, or no job at all, many courts have held that modification of alimony is not justified. In *Ellis v. Ellis*,[153] both parties appealed the trial court's reduction of the husband's alimony obligation. After the parties' divorce, the husband had remarried, assumed financial responsibility for his new mother-in-law, and voluntarily retired from his job. The Iowa Supreme Court held that the modification of alimony was improper in light of the husband's voluntary retirement and plans for the future, remarking that the husband "equates self-interest with good faith."[154] The court reinstated the alimony to its original amount, declaring:

> We do not dispute the sincerity of his wish to leave his employment and move to a warmer climate. We do not doubt his desire to see his present wife continue her education. Nor do we question his devotion to their child and his mother-in-law. Although the record indicates his health problems are not as serious as he makes them out to be, we do not think they are imaginary. However, he is not free to plan his future without regard to his obligation to his first wife. He cannot arbitrarily freeze her out of his future. Similar obligations in and apart from family life compel many persons to maintain employment which may be difficult, undesirable and even physically or mentally painful.[155]

---

[150] *See, e.g., Smith v. Smith*, 419 A.2d 1035 (Me. 1980).

[151] *See, e.g., Marriage of Kowski*, 463 N.E.2d 840 (Ill. App. Ct. 1984).

[152] 167 Cal. Rptr. 351 (Cal. Ct. App. 1980).

[153] 262 N.W.2d 265 (Iowa 1978).

[154] *Id.* at 267. Courts will also consider the reasons behind a payor's loss of income. *See, e.g., Murphy v. Murphy*, 759 N.W.2d 710 (Neb. Ct. App. 2008) (payor's misconduct on multiple occasions placed him in a "resign or be fired" position and led to his termination as a deputy sheriff, meriting denial of his petition for downward modification of his alimony and child support obligations).

[155] 262 N.W.2d at 267.

Voluntary or early retirement may nonetheless be a factor, although not necessarily determinative, in deciding whether to reduce the alimony.[156] For example, in *Ebach v. Ebach*,[157] the Supreme Court of North Dakota found no material change of circumstances warranting modification of the husband's spousal support obligation where the husband voluntarily retired at age 62, was financially secure and of average health for his age, and during the divorce had contemplated retiring at age 65. Moreover, the wife in *Ebach* suffered from multiple sclerosis. Similarly, the New Jersey Supreme Court in *Deegan v. Deegan*[158] denied the husband's motion to terminate alimony when he voluntarily retired at age 60 because of an attractive retirement package, a suspicion that he would soon be laid off due to lack of work, and his job had become increasingly difficult because of its physical demands. The court held that even if a former spouse retires in good faith, it must balance the advantage of a new life for the retiring party and the disadvantage to the payee spouse. Here, the wife relied on the alimony in order to survive. The court further cautioned that issues of early retirement or voluntary changes in life should be addressed at the time of divorce and that "[n]o thoughtful matrimonial lawyer should leave an issue of this importance to chance and subject his or her client to lengthy future proceeding[s]."[159]

In some cases, courts will look to other sources of payment rather than terminate support. Thus, in *Acker v. Acker*,[160] a divorced husband moved to terminate his alimony obligation after accepting early retirement, arguing he no longer had the ability to pay his former spouse $3,000 per month in accordance with their settlement agreement. The trial court denied his petition and the appeals court and the Supreme Court of Florida affirmed, holding that he had sufficient funds with which to pay continuing support, including pension benefits that were equitably distributed to him. Likewise, in some circumstances the courts may look not only at the payor's actual income but at the payor's potential earning capacity as well.[161] However, the payor should be left with sufficient income to pay his or her own reasonable needs.[162]

---

[156] *Compare Pimm v. Pimm*, 601 So. 2d 534 (Fla. 1992) (retirement constitutes a change in circumstance that the court may consider when determining the modification of an existing alimony obligation), *with Smith v. Smith*, 419 A.2d 1035 (Me. 1980) (retirement of payor spouse for primary purpose of avoiding alimony does not of itself bring about substantial change in payor's circumstances needed to justify reduction in alimony). *See generally* Jane Massey Draper, *Retirement of Husband as Change of Circumstances Warrantying Modification of Divorce Decree — Early Retirement*, 36 A.L.R.6th 1 (2011).

[157] 700 N.W.2d 684 (N.D. 2005).

[158] 603 A.2d 542 (N.J. Super. Ct. App. Div. 1992).

[159] *Id.* at 546. *See also Olsen v. Olsen*, 557 P.2d 604 (Idaho 1976) (husband petitioned for modification of alimony and child support when his earnings declined after he retired from the active practice of medicine; the court denied his petition in consideration of the parties' correlative needs and abilities, citing husband's Social Security income, pension, substantial trust fund, and admission that he would return to active practice if necessary, while the wife's income was reduced due to mandatory retirement, leaving her with insufficient means to meet her expenses even with the continued alimony).

[160] 904 So. 2d 384 (Fla. 2005).

[161] *See, e.g., Schuler v. Schuler*, 416 N.E.2d 197 (Mass. 1981). *But see In re Marriage of Dixon*, 683 P.2d 803 (Colo. Ct. App. 1983).

[162] *Compare Payne v. Payne*, 363 S.E.2d 428 (Va. Ct. App. 1987) (MBA husband who worked as

A payor spouse who retires at the customary age will often be entitled to a hearing on a petition to modify alimony,[163] but retirement at the customary age may not itself be dispositive.[164] A payor spouse who wishes to make a career change to a lower paying job may continue to be burdened with alimony payments based on his or her previous higher salary. While some courts focus on the payor's good faith motives and may allow modification under the circumstances,[165] others balance the benefit to the supporting spouse against the detriment to the supported spouse.[166] A third approach affords priority to the needs of the former spouse and children, refusing to adjust support payments based on lower pay and effectively locking the payor into the position held at the time of the divorce.[167]

Courts have had mixed responses to petitions for reduction of spousal support based on the payor's remarriage and the additional expenses of a new family and children.[168] On the one hand, the obligor has new legal duties of support to the later family which is equally deserving of protection; on the other, the changed circumstances are voluntary and the payor should not be able to unilaterally manipulate pre-existing obligations to a former spouse.[169]

---

hospital administrator and family counselor), *with Butler v. Butler*, 227 S.E.2d 688 (Va. 1976) (neurosurgeon who worked in hospital staff position).

[163] *Silvan v. Sylvan*, 632 A.2d 528 (N.J. Super. Ct. App. Div. 1993).

[164] *See, e.g., Pierce v. Pierce*, 916 N.E.2d 330, 340 (Mass. 2009) (former husband sought termination of his alimony obligation after voluntarily retiring at the customary age of 65; while the lower court reduced but did not eliminate the husband's obligation, the Supreme Judicial Court declined to create a rebuttable presumption that any alimony obligation should terminate upon a payor spouse's retirement; voluntary retirement at a customary age is simply one factor for courts to consider alongside other factors comprising the totality of the circumstances, such as, here, the payee spouse's recent loss of employment).

[165] *See, e.g., Woolf v. Woolf*, 901 So. 2d 905 (Fla. Dist. Ct. App. 2005) (modifying child support and alimony payments of former husband who lost his job due to an economic downturn, the loss of his rainmaking partner, and the loss of many of his firm's clients; while there were jobs available for attorneys with the former husband's skills, all required a substantial client base the husband no longer possessed). *In re Meegan*, 13 Cal. Rptr. 2d 799 (Cal. Ct. App. 1992) (reduction of spousal support proper where former husband quit his job in good faith to become a priest).

[166] *Storey v. Storey*, 862 A.2d 551 (N.J. Super. Ct. App. Div. 2004) (a decision to modify alimony should balance the advantages and disadvantages of a pre-retirement career change that reduces earnings; while some reasons for change are entitled to substantial weight — e.g., one's health, loss of a professional license, a lack of work in one's field, or the need to care for a child — other reasons merit less weight because they are not statutorily recognized — e.g., changing careers to attain better working conditions or due to the desire for a less demanding job).

[167] *See, e.g., Wolcott v. Wolcott*, 735 P.2d 326 (N.M. Ct. App. 1987) (voluntary career change, resulting in major reduction of income, was not in good faith and thus not a substantial change in circumstances justifying modification). *See generally* David Giacalone, *The Dropout Ex-Husband's Right to Reduce Alimony and Support Payments*, 1 Fam. L. Rep. 4065 (1975).

[168] *Compare Peterka v. Peterka*, 675 N.W.2d 353 (Minn. Ct. App. 2004) (payor was not entitled to have the expenses associated with his support of a new family considered when determining his ability to pay maintenance when supported spouse was receiving a maintenance award below the parties' marital standard of living), *with Lewis v. Lewis*, 248 P.2d 1061 (Idaho 1952) (responsibility to second family and to father properly considered in modification of child support).

[169] *See, e.g., Martin v. Martin*, 698 S.E.2d 491 (N.C. Ct. App. 2010) (denying alimony modification to a husband who made excessive, voluntary expenditures including paying for an adult son's mortgage when he was under no obligation to make such payments); *Cowie v. Cowie*, 564 So. 2d 533 (Fla. Dist. Ct.

Remarriage of the recipient former spouse usually results in an automatic termination of alimony, often dictated by statute. In the absence of a statute or a provision in the divorce decree, the payor generally will need to bring an action for modification or termination, although remarriage will often raise a prima facie case of changed circumstances sufficient to extinguish a former spouse's alimony obligation. The Massachusetts Supreme Court adopted this position in *Keller v. O'Brien*,[170] reversing a trial court determination that because the wife was still in need of support, her remarriage did not constitute a material change of circumstances. The court held that alimony is not automatically terminated upon remarriage, but remarriage does create a prima facie case of termination absent extraordinary circumstances. The mere fact that the wife was unable to continue her previous standard of living based on her new husband's income was insufficient to continue the alimony.

In *Peterson v. Peterson*,[171] the divorce decree required the husband to pay alimony to the wife of $1,000 per month for seven years, and then $500 per month for ten years unless she were to die or remarry, at which time the alimony would cease. Two years after the divorce, the wife remarried and the husband petitioned to have his duty extinguished. The wife argued that the alimony provision required the husband to pay alimony for the first seven years regardless of her remarriage, that the alimony was an integral part of the property settlement of the divorce decree, and that extenuating circumstances existed in that her current husband was unable to support her. The South Dakota Supreme Court held that unless specified in a divorce decree to the contrary, spousal support will be extinguished upon remarriage. It further held that the ability of a new spouse to support the former recipient is not a factor that will justify continuation of alimony payments, adding that "it is 'illogical and unreasonable' that a spouse should receive support from a present spouse and a former spouse at the same time."[172] Jurisdictions likewise split over whether remarriage or the death of the payor will terminate rehabilitative alimony.[173]

App. 1990) (payor's difficulty in paying alimony did not warrant modification in the amount of alimony due where difficulty arose from payor's voluntary creation of obligations due to remarriage and purchase of a new home). *Cf. infra* § 9.06[E].

[170] 652 N.E.2d 589 (Mass. 1995). *See also In re Marriage of Rubey*, 996 P.2d 1006, 1009 (Or. Ct. App. 2000) (concluding that when the supported spouse remarried and elected not to seek certification that would allow her to reenter workforce the purposes of an alimony award to permit a supported spouse to gain employment had "either been satisfied or obviated," and that the payor met his burden of showing that the income now available to his ex-wife after her remarriage "provide[s] her with the same or greater level of income than the original award of spousal support").

[171] 434 N.W.2d 732 (S.D. 1989).

[172] *Id.* at 736 (quoting *Marquardt v. Marquardt*, 396 N.W.2d 753, 754 (S.D. 1986)). *But see Gibb v. Sepe*, 690 N.W.2d 230 (N.D. 2004) (where the divorce agreement incorporated the parties' settlement agreement, stating that the husband would pay the wife $3,000 per month until she was 65 if she did not remarry and $1,000 per month until she was 65 if she did remarry, there was no material change in circumstances warranting modification of the husband's support obligation even though wife's subsequent marriage greatly improved her circumstances so that she and her new husband had a combined income of $528,815).

[173] *See, e.g., Owens v. Owens*, 241 S.W.3d 478 (Tenn. Ct. App. 2007) (finding that rehabilitative alimony to wife could be modified as circumstances required but would not terminate upon husband's death where husband earned $12,000 to $13,000 per month, wife had spent the last twenty-five years primarily as a

Although remarriage of the recipient usually terminates that party's right to receive support or alimony from a former spouse,[174] many courts refuse to reinstate an alimony award if the latter marriage is annulled.[175] The payor may have detrimentally relied on the appearance of the recipient's remarriage, not its validity, and should not be penalized by the former spouse's decision to seek its invalidation. Furthermore, many states now authorize the award of alimony in annulment actions as well as in divorce cases.[176]

A number of states permit modification or termination of spousal support if the recipient cohabits or enters into a civil union with another person, sometimes additionally requiring that the cohabitation be "conjugal" or of a marriage-like relationship.[177] Although cohabitation does not generally create a legal duty of support, as a practical matter, cohabitants are likely to share living expenses, thus potentially justifying the modification or termination of spousal support. Further, some decisions appear to be based on moral judgments that an unmarried cohabitant no longer deserves continued support from a former spouse.[178]

Absent a governing statute, most states do not automatically regard cohabitation as a basis for modification or termination, but instead will weigh the economic impact of the living arrangement and its effect upon the recipient's continued need for support by the former spouse.[179] The court in *Gayet v. Gayet*[180] adopted an

---

homemaker and parent, and wife had reacquired her real estate license but faced an uncertain economic future); Haw. Rev. Stat. § 580-51(a) ("All rights to receive . . . support and maintenance shall automatically terminate . . . after the date of the [payee's] remarriage, unless the final decree or order, or an agreement of the parties approved by the final decree or order, provides specifically for the payments to continue after such remarriage."). *See generally* Gary L. Young, Jr., *Alimony as Affected by Recipient Spouse's Remarriage in Absence of Controlling Specific Statute*, 47 A.L.R.5th 129 (2011).

[174] *See Woodward v. Woodward*, 229 N.W.2d 274 (Iowa 1975) (no single factor controls whether an award constitutes alimony for purpose of termination upon recipient's remarriage).

[175] *Compare Denberg v. Frischman*, 264 N.Y.S.2d 114 (N.Y. App. Div. 1965) (no revival of alimony upon annulment), *with DeWall v. Rhoderick*, 138 N.W.2d 124 (Iowa 1965) (resumption of alimony following annulment). *See also In re Cargill*, 843 P.2d 1335 (Colo. 1993) (adopting an equitable middle position to determine reinstatement on facts and equities of each case). *See generally* Louanne S. Love, *The Way We Were: Reinstatement of Alimony After Annulment of Spouse's "Remarriage,"* 28 J. Fam. L. 289 (1989-90).

[176] *See, e.g.,* Cal. Fam. Code § 2254 (West 2011); Conn. Gen. Stat. Ann. § 46b-60 (West 2011).

[177] *See, e.g.,* Ga. Code Ann. § 19-6-19(b) (2011) (voluntary cohabitation of alimony recipient with a third party in a "meretricious relationship" shall be grounds for modification of alimony); Fla. Stat. § 61.14 (2011) (alimony may be reduced or terminated where the recipient has entered into a "supportive relationship" with a person who resides with them and who is not related to them by blood or consanguinity); N.J. Stat. Ann. 2A:34-25 (2011) (permanent and limited duration alimony shall terminate upon the date of the recipient's entry into a new marriage or civil union); 31 P.R. Laws Ann. § 385 (2008) ("Alimony shall be revoked through judicial decision . . . if the divorced spouse entitled to such alimony contracts a new marriage or lives in public concubinage."). *But see Elliott v. Rogers*, 775 So. 2d 1285 (Miss. Ct. App. 2000) (living outside marriage with sexual partner after divorce is not itself grounds to terminate periodic alimony). *See also* Evan J. Langbein, *Post-Dissolution Cohabitation of Alimony Recipients: A Legal Fact of Life*, 12 Nova L. Rev. 787 (1988); J. Thomas Oldham, *Cohabitation by an Alimony Recipient Revisited*, 20 J. Fam. L. 615 (1981-82).

[178] *See, e.g., Bentzoni v. Bentzoni*, 442 So. 2d 235 (Fla. Dist. Ct. App. 1983); *Bisig v. Bisig*, 469 A.2d 1348 (N.H. 1983).

[179] *See, e.g., Payne v. Payne*, 206 S.W.3d 379 (Mo. Ct. App. 2006) (finding no substantial change of circumstances in ex-wife's financial needs and resources warranting the termination of ex-husband's

economic test to determine the effect of cohabitation on alimony. It examined the competing policies of terminating alimony upon remarriage and the former spouse's interest in "privacy, autonomy, and the right to develop personal relationship[s] free from governmental sanctions."[181] It concluded that only the actual economic effect of cohabitation, and not the former spouse's conduct as a cohabitant, should determine the duration of support. The trial court should modify alimony either when a third party contributes to the recipient's support or when a third party resides with the recipient without contributing to household expenses.

Where recipient's structure their relationships to avoid the appearance of cohabitation, courts will look to the substance of the relationship and whether it provides "mutual support." Thus, in *Martin v. Martin*,[182] the chancellor terminated the ex-husband's alimony obligation where the ex-wife and her fiancé mutually supported one another and the fiancé provided in-kind services to the ex-wife that were not insubstantial. To avoid the appearance of cohabitation and thus to continue receiving her alimony, the ex-wife had structured her relationship with her fiancé so that the two maintained separate residences. Absent a financial impact, however, some courts conclude that conditioning a recipient's support on not cohabiting goes too far. In *Melletz v. Melletz*,[183] the parties specified in their divorce settlement agreement that the wife's alimony would be suspended if the wife cohabited with an unrelated male. The appellate court applied the *Gayet* economic impact test to hold that a husband attaching conditions to the alimony unrelated to the wife's financial status undermined the very purpose of alimony, noting that matters of personal preference, residence, or occupation, insofar as they do not reflect changes in the income, expenses, or other matters of recognized mutual concern, simply are not the business of a former spouse.

Modification is not warranted where, despite cohabitation, the supported spouse's financial needs remain unchanged. The Supreme Court of Nevada addressed this factual question in *Gilman v. Gilman*,[184] which consolidated two cases.

---

alimony obligation where, although ex-wife's boyfriend resided with ex-wife, he lived with her rent-free, and although the boyfriend earned approximately $1,800 per month for part-time work, he contributed only $200 monthly toward ex-wife's expenses). Some states presume that cohabitation entails material financial support warranting modification. *See, e.g., Wallace v. Wallace*, 12 So. 3d 572 (Miss. Ct. App. 2009) (concluding supported spouse did not overcome the presumption of mutual financial support due to cohabitation). *See generally* Alimony, Maintenance, and Other Spousal Support, tbl.1, 0080 SURVEYS 11 (2010) (Westlaw).

[180] 456 A.2d 102 (N.J. 1983).

[181] *Id.* at 103 (citing *State v. Saunders*, 381 A.2d 333 (1977)). Some states treat only conjugal relationships as triggering possible modification. *See, e.g., In re Marriage of Thornton*, 867 N.E.2d 102 (Ill. App. Ct. 2007) (concluding that where supported spouse allowed former husband's brother to stay in her basement because he had nowhere else to stay, and where she and the brother led separate lives, there was no ground for terminating former husband's maintenance obligation). Conjugal relationships need not be with a person of the opposite sex. *See, e.g., Stroud v. Stroud*, 641 S.E.2d 142 (Va. Ct. App. 2007) (finding that supported ex-wife's relationship with girlfriend constituted cohabitation).

[182] 751 So. 2d 1132 (Miss. Ct. App. 1999).

[183] 638 A.2d 898 (N.J. App. Div. 1994).

[184] 956 P.2d 761 (Nev. 1998). *See also Pearson v. Pearson*, 606 N.W.2d 128 (N.D. 2000) (former wife's cohabitation with her male partner was not material change in her circumstances justifying change in spousal support where she was not entitled to support from her male partner).

In one case, the divorce decree made no reference to cohabitation. In the other case, the parties' negotiated agreement, approved by the court, stipulated that spousal support would terminate upon the death or remarriage of the wife, and the court would consider the issue if the wife cohabitated with a man who significantly contributed to her support. The court, approving of what it referred to as the majority rule, adopted an economic needs test, which requires a showing that the recipient's financial needs actually decreased because of the cohabitation. Finding that neither former husband had proved such change of circumstances, the court upheld the trial courts' denials of the modification petitions. One judge dissented with respect to decrees that do not mention cohabitation, arguing that a marriage type relationship should result in a rebuttable presumption of a change of circumstances.

Likewise, where a supported spouse shares a residence with a paramour because he or she cannot afford other housing, courts may find insufficient evidence of cohabitation warranting termination of support. Thus, in *Campbell v. Campbell*,[185] the ex-wife rented a bedroom in the home of a man she was dating and occasionally had sexual relations with. Wife was unable to afford independent housing after her ex-husband received the marital residence as part of a legal separation. She intended to move into her own apartment as soon as it became financially possible. In this instance, the court found insufficient evidence of cohabitation required to prevent an award of alimony or to terminate one

When a non-cohabitation restriction is part of the parties' agreement, courts often construe them narrowly. For example, the Supreme Judicial Court of Massachusetts in *Bell v. Bell*[186] determined that a former husband's contractual obligation to pay alimony had ended upon the wife's cohabitation and dismissed a contempt complaint brought for his failure to make alimony payments. The parties' separation agreement provided that the husband would pay alimony for fifteen years or until the wife died, remarried or lived "with a member of the opposite sex so as to give the outward appearance of marriage."[187] The court interpreted the term to provide for termination of alimony if the wife lived as though she was married, despite additional provisions in the separation agreement that neither party would interfere with the other's personal liberty and each would be free of any criticism or restraint by the other.

Similarly, courts have narrowly construed statutory grounds permitting termination for continued cohabitation. Thus, in *Fiddie v. Fiddie*,[188] the South Carolina Court of Appeals found the evidence insufficient to support a finding that the wife

---

[185] 41 So. 3d 775 (Ala. Civ. App. 2009), *overruled on other grounds by A.B. v. J.B.*, 40 So. 3d 723 (Ala. Civ. App.), *cert. denied*, 41 So. 3d 786 (Ala. 2010).

[186] 468 N.E.2d 859 (Mass. 1984).

[187] *Id.* at 860. *See also Barr v. Barr*, 922 S.W.2d 419 (Mo. Ct. App. 1996) (no error in terminating ex-husband's maintenance obligation where parties' dissolution decree stated maintenance would cease upon ex-wife's "conjugal cohabitation" with an adult male for a period of 60 days, where an adult male spent 10-12 nights per month at the ex-wife's home, kept personal belongings there, and had sexual relations with ex-wife, even though he did not comingle funds with her or contribute to household expenses and he and ex-wife did not hold themselves out as married).

[188] 681 S.E.2d 42 (S.C. Ct. App. 2009).

continuously cohabited for 90 days, which would allow termination of alimony, because there was uncontroverted evidence that the wife stayed with at least three people other than her male companion every month that was in question.[189] Some courts have barred claims for past-due spousal support or alimony based on laches or waiver if the recipient unreasonably delayed bringing the action.[190] Most courts, however, have not been receptive to such defenses for two reasons: first, if the spousal support award was ordered by the court, the court has not waived its enforceability, even if the recipient arguably has; second, a long delay does not amount to laches unless the payor can clearly demonstrate detrimental reliance on the delay.[191]

Whether temporary or rehabilitative alimony may be extended when the recipient has not improved his or her earning capacity has troubled courts. Although rehabilitative alimony resembles lump sum alimony to the extent that it is ordered as a liquidated sum for a specific period of time, some courts have allowed modification if the recipient has been unable to become self-supporting despite his or her best efforts.[192] Other courts have refused to permit modification of rehabilitative alimony.[193]

In *Hecker v. Hecker*,[194] the wife was awarded ten years of temporary spousal maintenance. During those years, she worked part-time so she could retain flexibility to meet the needs of the children. When the maintenance was scheduled to end, the former wife claimed she would be without sufficient means to provide for her own support. The court-appointed referee found that former wife's inability to improve her earning capacity constituted a substantial change of circumstances and modified the award to one of permanent maintenance. The appeals panel reversed and remanded to the district court to address why the former wife's rehabilitation

---

[189] *See also Myers v. Myers*, 231 P.3d 815 (Utah Ct. App. 2010) (evidence was insufficient to establish former wife formed relationship resembling marriage with foster brother's son, as required to establish cohabitation, even where they had a boyfriend-girlfriend relationship including sex, yet they did not establish a common household, share expenses, or share space and meals).

[190] *See, e.g., Clark v. Chipman*, 510 P.2d 1257 (Kan. 1973) (claim barred by laches after five-year delay).

[191] *See, e.g., Brock v. Cavanaugh*, 468 A.2d 1242 (Conn. App. Ct. 1984) (six-year delay not barred by laches); *Richardson v. Moore*, 229 S.E.2d 864 (Va. 1976) (25-year delay not barred by laches). *See generally* George L. Blum, *Laches or Acquiescence as Defense, So as to Bar Recovery of Arrearages of Permanent Alimony or Child Support*, 2003 A.L.R.5th 9 (2011).

[192] *See, e.g., In re Marriage of Morrison*, 573 P.2d 41 (Cal. 1978); *In re Marriage of Webb*, 156 Cal. Rptr. 334 (Cal. Ct. App. 1979). Some jurisdictions allow the recipient to petition for further support while others reserve jurisdiction over the question. *Compare Bellefeuille v. Bellefeuille*, 636 N.W.2d 195 (N.D. 2001) (before rehabilitative support ends, and if the circumstances merit, recipient may apply for further support or for the court to retain jurisdiction over the matter), *with Smith v. Smith*, 609 S.E.2d 844 (W. Va. 2004) (wife could seek modification or extension of award if she was unable to meet rehabilitative plan).

[193] *See, e.g., Liebrecht v. Liebrecht*, 58 So. 3d 415, 418 (Fla. Dist. Ct. App. 2011) (upholding lump-sum, nonmodifiable gap-bridging alimony instead of permanent, periodic alimony where wife had "reasonable level of earning capacity and should be able to obtain employment sufficient to become self-supporting," yet had been out of the workforce for thirteen years and would need some time to achieve self-sufficiency).

[194] 568 N.W.2d 705 (Minn. 1997). *See generally* Donaldson, *supra* note 94.

efforts were unsuccessful. The court found that she had failed to make any reasonable effort toward rehabilitation and attributed to her the income that her reasonable efforts would have produced. Even with the attributed income, however, former wife would be unable to meet her monthly expenses and the court held that she was not precluded from receiving further maintenance if she failed to become self-supporting through her diligent efforts. It awarded her permanent maintenance amounting to the difference between her monthly expenses and the attributed income.

§ 9.06 CHILD SUPPORT

[A] Basic Concepts

Child support has changed radically during the past four decades. Congress has mandated that states enact child support guidelines in order to receive federal funds, in an attempt to increase the uniformity, efficiency and levels of child support awards.

Despite nationwide enactment, child support guidelines continue to differ considerably among the states. Child support enforcement mechanisms have also been enacted to increase support collection, and both state and federal statutes have established new jurisdictional rules to stabilize jurisdiction disputes.

Although earlier common law imposed a primary duty of support on the father, holding the mother only secondarily liable, states today regard the duty to support a child as gender neutral.[195] For example, in *Rand v. Rand*,[196] the Court of Appeals of Maryland held that the trial court's allocation of 92% of the child support obligation to the father was erroneous in light of the state's Equal Rights Amendment. The mother, who had sought an increase in child support to finance the child's college education, earned over $16,000, while the father's annual income exceeded $27,000. Faced with the mother's contention that she should be responsible only to the extent the father was financially incapable of providing support, the court held that the child support obligation is now borne by both parents in a ratio corresponding to their respective financial resources.

Further, the law requires individuals to support their children regardless of whether the parents were ever married to each other.[197] The child support

---

[195] *See* Harry D. Krause, Child Support In America: The Legal Perspective 4 (1981); *see also Carole K. v. Arnold K.*, 380 N.Y.S.2d 593 (N.Y. Fam. Ct. 1976) (striking down statute requiring fathers, but not mothers, to pay child support); *In re Aguilar*, 145 Cal. Rptr. 197 (Cal. Ct. App. 1978) (imposing primary criminal liability upon father, but only secondary liability upon mother, for willful failure to support minor children violates equal protection guarantee of federal and state constitutions). Courts have even imposed child support obligations on minor children who father a child. *See Evelyn v. Shire*, No. 242681, 2004 Mich. App. LEXIS 756 (Mich. App. Feb. 19, 2004) (finding fourteen-year-old father liable for child support despite being victim of sex abuse act by twenty-one-year-old woman).

[196] 374 A.2d 900 (Md. 1977), *modified by statute*, Md. Code Fam. Law § 12-201 (2011), as recognized by *Voishan v. Palma*, 609 A.2d 319 (Md. 1992).

[197] *See, e.g., Mercer City Dep't of Soc. Servs. v. Alf M.*, 589 N.Y.S.2d 288 (N.Y. Fam. Ct. 1992).

obligation may continue after termination of parental rights.[198] The duty of child support is commonly codified under the subjects of divorce or dissolution and paternity,[199] although some states have a generalized family support statute.[200]

The common law imposed no duty of support on stepparents, except when the stepparent voluntarily assumes the duty of support as part of assimilating the child into the stepparent's family.[201] The voluntary decision to support a stepchild is usually terminable at will and does not extend beyond the end of the marriage to the child's parent,[202] except in unusual cases in which the stepparent is estopped from denying the duty because his or her conduct induced the child's reliance and dependence.[203] A number of states have enacted legislation that requires stepparents to support their spouses' children in certain circumstances.[204] These statutes are primarily aimed at reducing or eliminating the child's eligibility for state welfare benefits.[205]

The Supreme Court of Washington has held that stepparent responsibility statutes may impose a duty of support on parties who were married prior to the enactment of the legislation in *Washington Statewide Organization of Stepparents v. Smith*.[206] The *Smith* decision also upheld the constitutionality of the statute, refuting claims that the statute violated equal protection principles by not imposing similar duties on unmarried cohabitants.

Traditionally, the amount of a person's child support obligation was determined on a case-by-case basis and took into account the particular needs of the child and the ability of the parents to provide for those needs. For example, the Uniform Marriage and Divorce Act directs courts to consider all relevant factors, except marital misconduct, in awarding child support, including:

1) the financial resources of the child;

2) the financial resources of the custodial parent;

3) the standard of living the child would have enjoyed had the marriage not been dissolved;

---

[198] *See In re Stephen Tyler R.*, 584 S.E.2d 581 (W.Va. 2003).

[199] *See, e.g.*, Unif. Marriage and Divorce Act § 309 (2010); Unif. Parentage Act § 15 (2010).

[200] *See, e.g.*, Cal. Fam. Code § 3900 (West 2011).

[201] *See* Margaret M. Mahoney, Stepfamilies and the Law (1994); Clark, *supra* note 12, at 264.

[202] *See* Clark, *supra* note 12, at 264.

[203] *See Tirey v. Tirey*, 806 N.E.2d 360 (Ind. App. 2004) (claiming non-parent may be liable for continued child support when he insisted on paying support for six years to continue visitation privileges); *M.H.B. v. H.T.B.*, 498 A.2d 775 (N.J. 1985). *But see Knill v. Knill*, 510 A.2d 546 (Md. 1986); *NPA v. WBA*, 380 S.E.2d 178 (Va. Ct. App. 1989).

[204] *See, e.g.*, N.Y. Soc. Serv. Law § 101 (McKinney 2011) (making stepparents responsible for the care of children under the age of 21); Va. Code Ann. § 63.2-510 (2011) (stipulating that stepparents are liable for support of stepchildren residing with them in the same home, for as long as stepparent cohabits with spouse as man and wife).

[205] *See* Clark, *supra* note 12, at 263.

[206] 536 P.2d 1202 (Wash. 1975).

4)   the physical and emotional condition of the child and his educational needs; and

5)   the financial resources and needs of the noncustodial parent. [207]

A broad range of a parent's financial resources may be considered in setting child support awards. Most types of assets and income are appropriate sources, including alimony payments,[208] income from overtime, bonuses, and night shift differential,[209] and rent collected by a support obligor.[210] State child support guidelines often broadly define "income" for purposes of determining the amount of child support in an individual case.[211] In the absence of a statute, an appropriate definition of available "income" could include wages, salary, commissions, bonuses, payments to an independent contractor, dividends, capital gains, gifts, prizes, awards, partnership profits, disability benefits, workers' compensation benefits, veterans and social security benefits, annuities, awards in civil suits, interest, rents, royalties, real and personal property, insurance proceeds, trust income, inheritance rights, severance pay, unemployment compensation, and pension or retirement benefits.[212]

For some time, the courts were divided on the issue of whether a support obligor could be required to use disability payments to satisfy a support obligation.[213] In 1987, the United States Supreme Court held in *Rose v. Rose*[214] that federal law does not preempt a state's right to hold a disabled veteran in contempt for failure to pay support when his only means of payment were his disability payments from the Veteran's Administration for compensation relating to service-related injuries, despite express statutory provisions that the benefits were not subject to attachment or other forms of seizure.[215] The Court, although noting that the legislative history of the provisions was sparse, concluded that Congress intended the anti-attachment provisions to "avoid the possibility of the Veterans' Administration . . . being placed in the position of a collection agency" and to "prevent the deprivation and depletion of the means of subsistence of veterans

---

[207]   Unif. Marriage and Divorce Act § 309 (2010).

[208]   *See Hyde v. Hyde*, 618 A.2d 406 (Pa. Super. Ct. 1992), *overruling, Steinmetz v. Steinmetz*, 554 A.2d 83 (Pa. Super. Ct. 1989).

[209]   *See In re Pins*, 19 Fam. L. Rep. (BNA) 1046 (Iowa Ct. App. Oct. 27, 1992); *In re Marriage of Pettit*, 493 N.W.2d 865 (Iowa Ct. App. 1992).

[210]   *See Kipper v. Kipper*, 542 N.Y.S.2d 617 (N.Y. App. Div. 1989).

[211]   *See, e.g.*, N.M. Stat. Ann. § 40-4-11.1(c) (West 2011); N.Y. Dom. Rel. Law § 240(1-b)(e) (McKinney 2011); Va. Code Ann. § 20-108.1(G) (2011).

[212]   *See, e.g.*, Robert M. Horowitz, et al., Remedies Under the Child Enforcement Amendments of 1984, 112-30 (1985).

[213]   *Compare In re Marriage of Robinson*, 651 P.2d 454 (Colo. Ct. App. 1982), superseded by statute, Colo. Rev. Stat. Ann. § 14-10-115(11)(II)(c) (West 2011), as recognized in *In re Marriage of Wright*, 924 P.2d 1207, 1209 (1996) (Social Security disability and retirement payments for minor children may be credited toward father's obligation to pay child support), *with Douglas v. Donovan*, 534 F. Supp. 191 (D.C. Dist. Ct. 1982), *vacated as moot*, 704 F.2d 1276 (1983) (Federal Employee's Compensation Act benefits are not subject to attachment or garnishment for enforcement of child support or alimony payments).

[214]   481 U.S. 619 (1987).

[215]   38 U.S.C. § 5301(a)(1) (1992).

dependent upon these benefits as the main source of their income."[216] The Court held that neither purpose would be frustrated by allowing a state court to hold a child support obligor in contempt for failing to pay child support:

> The contempt proceeding did not turn the Administrator into a collection agency; the Administrator was not obliged to participate in the proceeding or to pay benefits directly to appellee. Nor did the exercise of state-court jurisdiction over appellant's disability benefits deprive appellant of his means of subsistence contrary to Congress' intent, for these benefits are not provided to support appellant alone.[217]

When disability benefits are paid directly to a child as a result of the parent's disability, some jurisdictions credit the amount toward the disabled parent's child support obligation.[218]

[B] Temporary Child Support *Pendente Lite*

Just as temporary alimony may be ordered prior to a final divorce decree,[219] child support orders *pendent lite* may be entered during the course of divorce litigation to assure that the children are provided for during the interim.[220] The state's interest in protecting children enables a court to order child support regardless of whether a parent seeks it in a divorce action.[221]

Many courts will also enter *pendente lite* child custody orders, temporary restraints on disposition of the parties' marital assets, and temporary non-molestation orders against a spouse who has made physical threats to the other spouse or children.[222] *Pendente lite* orders are temporary, by definition, and thus are nonbinding in a subsequent divorce proceeding.[223]

[C] Statutory Child Support Guidelines

The traditional case-by-case method of awarding child support incorporates a multitude of factors and provides judges with substantial discretion in determining the appropriate level of the award. Child support awarded through this method lacked uniformity, both within and amongst the states, and was generally considered to be inadequate. The insufficiency in child support amounts, inefficient determination of awards, and inconsistent treatment of similarly situated parties

---

[216] 481 U.S. at 630, quoting S. Rep. No. 94-1243, at 147-48 (1976).

[217] *Id. See also State v. Blankenship*, 935 So. 2d 793 (La. Ct. App. 2006) (father's federal Social Security disability benefits and veterans' disability benefits may be considered in setting the amount of child support).

[218] *See, e.g., Rosenberg v. Merida*, 697 N.E.2d 987 (Mass. 1998) (concluding that non-custodial parent receiving Social Security disability benefits should receive credit against child support obligations in the amount paid by the SSA to his minor children due to his disability); Va. Code Ann. § 20-108.2(C) (2011).

[219] *See supra* § 9.04[A].

[220] *See, e.g.,* Ohio Rev. Code § 3109.05 (Baldwin 2011).

[221] *See* Clark, *supra* note 12, at 711-12.

[222] *See, e.g.,* Cal. Fam. Code § 3011 (West 2011).

[223] *See, e.g., Shepherd v. Shepherd*, 200 S.E.2d 893 (Ga. 1973).

led Congress to enact legislation in 1984 that required all states to develop child support determination guidelines.[224] The legislation does not require adoption of any particular type of guideline and therefore, the standards and resulting orders continue to vary considerably from one state to another.[225] However, the guideline amount of child support must be presumptive, and a written finding of fact that the amount would be unjust or inappropriate is required to overcome that presumptive amount.[226] States are required to review their guidelines periodically.[227] Child support guidelines have been upheld under Constitutional attacks.[228]

Despite variation among jurisdictions, several general formulas commonly have been adopted, including the percentage of income method, income share models, and the Delaware Melson formula.[229] Other formulas, such as an income equalization approach, have been proposed and have generated considerable commentary but have not been widely adopted.[230] Each approach considers unique factors and strikes a different compromise between equity and simplicity.[231]

The percentage of income or "obligor" model bases the child support amount on the income of the obligor and the number of children, without consideration of the custodial parent's income or any extraordinary expenses of the child.[232] Percentage

---

[224] Pub. L. No. 98-378, 42 U.S.C. 667 (2011). *See also infra* § 9.06[F][4].

[225] *See generally* Laura W. Morgan, Child Support Guidelines: Interpretation and Application (2011); Marsha Garrison, *Child Support: Guidelines and Goals*, 33 Fam. L. Q. 157 (1999); Robert J. Williams, *Guidelines for Setting Levels of Child Support Orders*, 21 Fam. L.Q. 281 (1987); Linda Balisle, *New Formulas to Fairness*, 10 Fam. Advoc. 16 (Spring 1988); Diane Dodson, *A Guide to the Guidelines*, 10 Fam. Advoc. 4 (Spring 1988); Karen A. Getman, *Changing Formulas for Changing Families*, 10 Fam. Advoc. 46 (Spring 1988). *But see* Laura W. Morgan & Mark C. Lino, *A Comparison of Child Support Awards Calculated Under States' Child Support Guidelines with Expenditures on Children Calculated by the U.S. Department of Agriculture*, 33 Fam. L. Q. 191 (1999) (finding that outside of low-income groups, there is little difference in economic awards produced by each type of child support guideline).

[226] 42 U.S.C. § 667(b)(2) (2011).

[227] 42 U.S.C. § 667(a) (2011).

[228] *See, e.g., Keck v. Harris*, 594 S.E. 2d 367 (Ga. 2004) (not invalid under Supremacy Clause); *Ward v. McFall*, 593 S.E.2d 340 (Ga. 2004) (failure to review every four years pursuant to federal mandate does not make guidelines unconstitutional); *Stillman v. State*, 87 P.3d 200 (Colo. App. 2003) (guidelines upheld after challenge based on equal protection, privacy, and due process).

[229] *See* National Conference of State Legislatures, Child Support Guideline Models by Model Type, *available at* http://www.ncsl.org/issues-research/human-services/guideline-models-by-model-type.aspx (updated June 2012); Nancy Thoennes, Patricia Tjaden & Jessica Pearson, *The Impact of Child Support Guidelines on Award Adequacy, Award Variability, and Case Processing Efficiency*, 25 Fam. L.Q. 325 (1991).

[230] *See* Morgan, *supra* note 225, at § 1.03[a], n.34 (noting that no state has adopted the "equal living standards" model); Sharon J. Badertscher, *Ohio's Mandatory Child Support Guidelines: Child Support or Spousal Maintenance?*, 42 Case W. Res. L. Rev. 297 (1992); Mark J. Connor, *Resolving Child Support Issues Beyond the Scope of AR 608-99*, 132 Mil. L. Rev. 67 (1991); Peter Leehy, *The Child Support Standards Act and the New York Judiciary: Fortifying the 17 Percent Solution*, 56 Brook. L. Rev. 1299 (1991).

[231] *See generally* Williams, *supra* note 225.

[232] *See, e.g.,* 750 ILCS 5/505 (Smith-Hurd 2011). There are two variants of this model, based on a flat percentage of income and a varying percentage of income. The latter reduces the percentage of income devoted to child support as income increases. For a complete list of states using each approach, see Morgan, *supra* note 225, at tbl. 1-3.

guidelines vary as to their definitions of the types of income available for child support. Unlike most flat percentage guidelines, the well-known Wisconsin percentage of income model accounts for shared or split physical custody and later children of the obligor.[233]

The Supreme Court of North Dakota, in *Eklund v. Eklund*,[234] upheld its state's percentage of income guidelines, rejecting the father's argument that the Department of Human Services had exceeded its delegated authority in adopting such guidelines. Despite the fact that an income shares model might be fairer, the percentage of income model was found to be less complex, and easier to use, and in most cases resulted in little or no difference in child support awards.

The income shares model, variations of which have been adopted by an overwhelming majority of states,[235] takes into account the incomes of both parents in an attempt to approximate the standard of living the child would have enjoyed if the parents had remained together.[236] Under this method, a basic child support amount is arrived at using the parents' combined incomes and estimated child-rearing expenditures, and is then supplemented to reflect actual child-care expenses and extraordinary needs of the child. The parents are required to contribute to that obligation on a pro-rata basis of their incomes, with the custodial parent simply retaining the amount assessed against him or her. Alterations may be made for split and shared custody arrangements,[237] and the formula may be adapted to assure that the obligor has sufficient remaining funds for self-support, at least at the poverty level. Schedules can be varied to correspond to the ages of the children, based on the notion that the cost of raising a child increases as the child grows older.[238]

In *P.O.P.S. v. Gardner*,[239] the United States Court of Appeals for the Ninth Circuit upheld the constitutionality of the Washington State Child Support Schedule, which applies an income shares approach. The plaintiffs, Parents Opposed to Punitive Support (P.O.P.S.), argued that the guideline amounts were so high that they effectively prevented some noncustodial parents from remarrying, and thus infringed on their fundamental right to marry. P.O.P.S. also argued that noncustodial parents become so frustrated by the schedule that they spend less time with their children. The court rejected these claims, noting that courts were authorized to deviate from the formula if a parent would be burdened. As to the

---

[233] *See, e.g., Molstad v. Molstad*, 535 N.W.2d 63 (Wis. App. 1995); *Prosser v. Cook*, 519 N.W.2d 649 (Wis. App. 1994).

[234] 538 N.W.2d 182 (N. D. 1995). For a summary of other constitutional challenges to child support guidelines, see generally Morgan, *supra* note 225, at § 1.04.

[235] *See, e.g.*, Colo. Rev. Stat. Ann. § 14-10-115 (West 2011); Va. Code Ann. §§ 20-108.1, 20-108.2 (2011). For a complete list of states using this approach, see Morgan, *supra* note 225, at tbl. 1-3.

[236] *See* Thoennes, Tjaden & Pearson, *supra* note 229, at 327-28.

[237] *See, e.g.*, Va. Code Ann. § 20-108.2 (2011); *Kammueller v. Kammueller*, 672 N.W.2d 594 (Minn. App. 2003) (increasing parenting time not sufficient to decrease child support); *Colonna v. Colonna*, 855 A.2d 648 (Pa. 2004) (concluding that child support may be payable to non-custodial parent if necessary to equalize ability to exercise visitation).

[238] *See* Me. Rev. Stat. Ann. tit. 19-A c. 694 § 2006 (2011).

[239] 998 F.2d 764 (9th Cir. 1993).

plaintiff's Equal Protection claim, the court held that the schedule does not discriminate, and that, in any event, children of noncustodial parents are not a suspect class.

The Oregon Supreme Court approved a variation of the income shares model in *Smith v. Smith*,[240] calculating a parent's child support obligation as the fraction of the payor's income divided by the combined incomes of both parents, multiplied by the needs of the children. To determine the children's needs, the court must consider the standard of living they would have enjoyed but for the divorce, as well as the child's physical and emotional condition, educational needs and capacity, age, and the child's own financial resources and earning ability. After calculating the obligation pursuant to this formula, the court must additionally consider: the interrelationship of the child support with any awards of property and spousal support; indirect forms of child support, including medical care, insurance, and trusts; the income of each spouse's current domestic partner or spouse; each parent's assets, including equity in real or personal property; the existence of, and support obligations to, each parent's other dependents; and special hardships of each parent. Because of the variables involved, this form of an income shares model continues to require a case-by-case evaluation.

The Delaware, or Melson, formula is based on the principle that the basic needs of the children must be met before the parent should be allowed to retain any income beyond that necessary to satisfy the parent's minimum needs.[241] It further presumes that excess income should be shared to allow children to benefit from an absent parent's higher standard of living. Applying the Melson formula involves a series of complex calculations. First, the court determines each parent's available income and then deducts from that figure the amount required to meet the individual parent's subsistence needs. The level of need depends upon whether the parent lives alone, or is married or cohabiting. Any remaining income is then applied to the child support obligation.

The Melson formula then requires calculation of the children's basic subsistence support requirements, based on the number of children, with adjustments for the custodial arrangement, and including necessary additional child-rearing expenses. This obligation is pro-rated between the parents, with a standard of living allowance awarded from any remaining income.[242] In *Child Support Enforcement Agency v. Doe*,[243] the Hawaii Court of Appeals upheld the guidelines against a challenge based on equal protection due a father's three other children. The court noted that the guidelines permitted the father to show exceptional circumstances warranted deviation from the presumptive amount.

---

[240] 626 P.2d 342 (Or. 1981) (en banc). For a summary of other constitutional challenges to child support guidelines, see generally Morgan, *supra* note 225, at § 1.04.

[241] *See* Thoennes, Tjaden & Pearson, *supra* note 229, at 328-29.

[242] *See generally* Williams, *supra* note 225. Only Delaware, Hawaii, and Montana presently use this approach. *See also* Morgan, *supra* note 225, at tbl. 1-3 (providing state-by-state comparison of support guideline models).

[243] 91 P.3d 1092 (Haw. Ct. App. 2004).

Childcare and extraordinary medical expenses are encompassed in child support guidelines. Several different methods are utilized, including deducting the cost from the income of the parent who incurs the expense, adding the cost to the basic child support obligation and dividing proportionately between the parents, and considering the expenses a factor for deviating from the presumptive award.[244]

The guidelines actually adopted by different states vary considerably in their details, regardless of the model upon which they are based. Guidelines vary in their definitions of applicable income,[245] which has been described as the "most important piece of information."[246] Some states have detailed statutory provisions defining income for child support purposes,[247] and case law has included as income such sources as deferred compensation,[248] severance pay,[249] disability payments,[250] personal injury awards,[251] retirement income,[252] certain gifts, loans, and inheritances,[253] and Social Security benefits.[254]

Most states require a minimum amount of support to be paid.[255] However, because children are generally entitled to support consistent with the parents' ability to pay, questions concerning "reasonable" limits on child support obligations arise when a parent has an unusually large income. States generally resolve this

---

[244] See Morgan, *supra* note 225, at § 3.02[b].

[245] See Morgan, *supra* note 225 at §§ 2.03[a] (Supp. 2009), 2.03[b] (Supp. 2010) (noting that states are about evenly split as to whether net or gross income should be used).

[246] L. Gold-Bikin & L. Hammond, *Determination of Income*, Child Support Guidelines: The Next Generation (U.S. Dep't of Health & Human Svcs., Ofc. of Child Support Enforcement (1994).

[247] See, e.g., Md. Code Ann., Fam. Law § 12-201 (West 2011); Minn. Stat. Ann. §§ 518A.29-32 (West 2011).

[248] See In re Marriage of Berger, 88 Cal. Rptr. 3d 766 (Ct. App. 2009) (husband was a company's chief executive officer with ability to elect for his salary to be deferred; trial court required the amount he elected to defer be included as actual earnings for support determinations); *Posey v. Tate*, 656 N.E.2d 222 (Ill. App. Ct. 1995).

[249] See, e.g., *Berry v. Berry*, 898 A.2d 1100 (Pa. Super. Ct. 2006) (including severance pay in calculation of obligor's income).

[250] See *State v. Blankenship*, 935 So. 2d 793 (La. Ct. App. 2006) (including veteran's benefits in calculation of income).

[251] See *In re Jerome*, 843 A.2d 325 (N.H. 2004); *In re Fain*, 794 P.2d 1086 (Colo. Ct. App. 1990); *Tulloch v. Flickinger*, 616 A.2d 315 (Del. 1992).

[252] See *Shelton v. Shelton*, 225 P.3d 693 (Idaho 2009).

[253] See *In re Marriage of Rogers*, 802 N.E.2d 1247 (Ill. App. 2003) (including annual gifts and loans from parents in income); *In re A.M.D.*, 78 P.3d 741 (Colo. 2003) (en banc) (including monetary inheritance in income).

[254] See *Com. ex rel. Morris v. Morris*, 984 S.W.2d 840 (Ky. 1998) (finding no conflict between statute allowing Social Security Supplemental Security Income (SSI) benefits' to be included in calculations of gross income, for purposes of determining support obligation, and federal SSI anti-attachment statute); *In re Lee*, 486 N.W.2d 302 (Iowa 1992). *But see* Va. Code Ann. § 20-108.2 (2011); *Burns v. Edwards*, 842 A.2d 186 (N.J. Super. Ct. App. Div. 2004) (federal SSI benefits not income). *See generally* Angela F. Epps, *To Pay or not to Pay, That is the Question: Should S.S.I. Recipients be Exempt from Child Support Obligations?*, 34 Rutgers L. J. 63 (2002).

[255] See, e.g., Cal. Fam. Code § 4055 (West 2011) (providing formula to establish minimum amount of support to be ordered); Va. Code Ann. § 20-108.2 (2011) (establishing minimum amount of support to be ordered).

issue in one of three ways: by providing a formula in the statutory guidelines for arriving at the amount due from the high-income parent;[256] by presumptively applying the highest amount provided in the guidelines, subject to deviation for the child's special needs and standard of living before divorce;[257] or by setting aside the guidelines in favor of case-by-case examinations.[258] Courts describe their approaches variously as capturing a child's needs or as permitting the child to share in the parent's wealth as the child would have in an intact family. Thus, in *White v. Marciano*,[259] the California Court of Appeal held that when the child has a wealthy parent, "the child is entitled to, and therefore 'needs,' something more than the bare necessities of life." Although the non-custodial parent's standard of living, in addition to his or her income, is relevant, the court will not make a detailed inquiry into the parent's lifestyle.

Similarly, in *Voishan v. Palma*,[260] the Court of Appeals of Maryland refused to infer a cap on child support when the parents' combined income exceeds $10,000 a month. It held that the children should enjoy a standard of living comparable to that which they would have had the parents remained married, and refused to impose an artificial ceiling on child support awards.[261] Likewise, the Illinois Court of Appeals upheld a monthly child support award of $8,500 where the father was a professional basketball player, concluding that although the child's living expenses

---

[256] *See, e.g.*, Va. Code Ann. § 20-108.2 (2011).

[257] *See, e.g.*, *In re Marriage of Krieger and Walker*, 199 P.3d 450 (Wash. Ct. App. 2008) (concluding that support awards above the maximum guidelines amount are not limited to those with extraordinary needs when parents' combined monthly income exceeded $7,000).

[258] *See, e.g.*, *Wright v. Wright*, 19 So. 3d 901, 906 (Ala. Civ. App. 2009) (" 'When the combined adjusted gross income exceeds the uppermost limit of the child support schedule, the amount of child support awarded must rationally relate to the reasonable and necessary needs of the child, taking into account the lifestyle to which the child was accustomed and the standard of living the child enjoyed before the divorce, and must reasonably relate to the obligor's ability to pay for those needs' " (*quoting Anonymous v. Anonymous*, 617 So. 2d 694, 697 (Ala. Civ. App. 1993))))). Other courts have held that when a parent's income exceeds the maximum listed in the guidelines, the court should use evidence of special circumstances, such as the realistic needs of the children, the obligor's ability to satisfy these needs, the financial condition of both parents, and a parent's new spouse. *See, e.g.*, *Peterson v. Peterson*, 434 N.W.2d 732 (S.D. 1989); *see also Nash v. Mulle*, 846 S.W.2d 803 (Tenn. 1993) (placing burden of showing increased need on the recipient parent). *See generally* Morgan, *supra* note 225, at tbl. 4-7 (showing state-by-state treatment of high-income parents).

[259] 235 Cal. Rptr. 779 (Cal. Ct. App. 1987).

[260] 609 A.2d 319 (Ct. App. Md. 1992).

[261] *See also McGowin v. McGowin*, 991 So. 2d 735 (Ala. Civ. App. 2008) (finding child support award set at a level commensurate with a combined annual income of $120,000 to be inadequate in light of husband's income of over $480,000 per year); *In re Marriage of Wittgrove*, 16 Cal. Rptr. 3d 489 (Cal. Ct. App. 2004) (concluding that what constitutes the reasonable needs for a child varies with the parties' circumstances); *Mehra v. Mehra*, 819 S.W.2d 351 (Mo. 1991) (en banc); *Cassano v. Cassano*, 651 N.E.2d 878 (N.Y. 1995). Other courts worry that forced sharing of the parent's wealth may produce "an inappropriate windfall to the child or even in some cases infring[e] on the legitimate right of either parent to determine the appropriate lifestyle of a child." *Strahan v. Strahan*, 953 A.2d 1219, 1224 (N.J. Super. Ct. App. Div. 2008). *See also In re Marriage of Bush*, 547 N.E.2d 590, 597 (Ill. App. Ct. 1989) (finding that the guideline support amount of $30,000 a year, or 20% of the father's income, was excessive and a deviation from that amount to 6%, or $800 per month, was justified, observing that the child support guidelines were "not intended to create windfalls but, rather, adequate support payments for the upbringing of the children").

were $1,000 a month, the child would have enjoyed a higher standard of living if their parents lived together. The court added that it was not necessary to place funds in trust.[262]

Some states set a maximum limit on child support, based on the theory that the child would not necessarily have received the benefit of the parent's excess income in an intact family. In *State v. Hall*,[263] the Minnesota Court of Appeals held that the trial court did not abuse its discretion in declining to deviate from statutory child support guidelines that provided for a maximum of $1,000 monthly support when an obligor's net income is $4,000 or above, despite the obligor's actual monthly income of $116,000 and the mother's meager resources. The court found that the child's actual personal expenses did not exceed $1,000 a month and held that it would be inappropriate to increase the mother's own standard of living indirectly by means of child support.

A court may depart from the statutory guidelines only upon express findings of fact that the presumptive amount will be unjust or provide inadequate support of the child.[264] In *Kowalzek v. Kowalzek*,[265] the Minnesota Court of Appeals held that a mechanical calculation based solely on the child living with a parent and a mere general reference to "all the circumstances of this case" were insufficient to justify an order substantially below the guideline amount.

An upward departure from the guideline amount may be appropriate when the child needs private schooling and the parent has the ability to pay for it. Several factors may be considered in determining a child's need, including the child's past history and performance in private school, the availability of adequate public schools, the child's religious background, and the child's emotional and physical needs.[266]

---

[262] *In re Keon C.*, 800 N.E.2d 1257 (Il. App. 2003).

[263] 418 N.W.2d 187 (Minn. Ct. App. 1988). *See also Ratliff v. Ratliff*, 5 So. 3d 570, 587 (Ala. Civ. App. 2008) (holding that when the parties have a combined adjusted gross income exceeding the top income listed under the statutory guidelines table, the child support awarded must "rationally relate to the reasonable and necessary needs of the child, taking into account the lifestyle to which the child was accustomed and the standard of living the child enjoyed before the divorce, and must reasonably relate to the obligor's ability to pay for those needs" (*quoting Dyas v. Dyas*, 683 So. 2d 971, 973-74 (Ala. Civ. App. 1995)).

[264] Family Support Act of 1988, Pub. L. 100-485, Title I, Subtitle A, § 103, 102 Stat. 2343 (1988) (mandating that guidelines provide for a rebuttable presumption that guideline amounts of support are correct and requiring written finding that application of guidelines "would be unjust or inappropriate in a particular case" to rebut presumption). Some states provide for deviation when the parent cannot work. *See, e.g.*, Va. Code Ann. § 20-108.2(B) (2011) (allowing deviation from the basic child support amount mandated by the statutory guidelines table when "parents [are] unable to pay child support because they lack sufficient assets from which to pay child support and who, in addition, are institutionalized in a psychiatric facility; are imprisoned for life with no chance of parole; are medically verified to be totally and permanently disabled with no evidence of potential for paying child support, including recipients of Supplemental Security Income (SSI); or are otherwise involuntarily unable to produce income").

[265] 360 N.W.2d 423 (Minn. Ct. App. 1985). Some states bar downward deviation from the minimum award provided in the guidelines. *See, e.g.*, Morgan, *supra* note 225, at § 4.07[c][ii], tbl. 4-8.

[266] *In re Barrett*, 841 A.2d 74 (N.H. 2004). *See also Estevez v. Superior Court*, 27 Cal. Rptr. 2d 470 (Cal. Ct. App. 1994) (where a parent has an extraordinarily high income, it may not be necessary to compel discovery of all financial information to calculate the presumptive guideline amount of child

If a parent is voluntarily unemployed, or not employed to full earning capacity, every jurisdiction allows the court to impute income based on the parent's potential earnings rather than actual income.[267] In *Henderson v. Smith*,[268] the Supreme Court of Idaho examined when it is appropriate to impute income. In *Henderson*, the child's biological father, an attorney, was ordered to pay child support under the state's guidelines based on the average income of attorneys in the area, rather than on his actual income. The court noted that "[t]he determination of income and expenses from an individual who is self employed should be carefully reviewed to determine the level of gross income to satisfy a child support obligation. This gross income for the self employed parent may differ from a determination of business income for tax purposes."[269] The court held that an underemployed parent's potential income may be calculated by factoring in his employment history, qualifications, and job availability in the community. Similarly, in *In re Marriage of Paulin*[270] the California Court of Appeals found that the child support obligation of a mother who had remarried and voluntarily ended her employment could be based on her earning capacity because she failed to produce documented efforts to find comparable employment. The court held that this indicated an unwillingness, rather than an inability, to work. The Supreme Judicial Court of Maine overturned a trial court's decision to modify a father's child support obligation based on his current actual income in *Harvey v. Robinson*,[271] when the father voluntarily retired from the National Guard and returned to college, with aspirations of eventually attending medical school. Despite the conclusion that the father had left his full-time employment in good faith, the court held that his good faith did "not ameliorate the dramatic effect on the children,"[272] which must be balanced against his decision. The court suggested that the father could work full time and attend school part time in order to fulfill his parental responsibilities, and remanded for reconsideration of child support based on his current earning capacity. A strong dissent noted that consideration of earning capacity is not mandatory and that the trial court's decision should not be overturned absent an abuse of discretion.

In *Goldberger v. Goldberger*,[273] the Court of Special Appeals of Maryland dealt with imputing the income of a father of six who was a permanent Torah/Talmudic student, and had been throughout the entire marriage. The father had been supported by donations from others for support, and the trial court based his earning capacity on the average of contributions for the previous three years.

---

support when such discovery would be unduly burdensome and oppressive and when the parent has stipulated that he is able and willing to pay any reasonable amount of child support based on his stipulated income); *Downing v. Downing*, 45 S.W.3d 449 (Ky. Ct. App. 2001) (where a parent's income is extraordinarily high, the trial court may cap the child support amount to reflect the child's reasonable needs and the standard of living during the marriage).

[267] *See* Morgan, *supra* note 225, at § 2.04[a]; Va. Code Ann. § 20-108.1(B)(3) (2011) (making unemployment or underemployment a factor for deviation from support guidelines).

[268] 915 P.2d 6 (Idaho 1996).

[269] *Id.* at 13 (citing Idaho Child Supp. Guidelines § 6(a)(2)).

[270] 54 Cal. Rptr. 2d 314 (Cal. Ct. App. 1996).

[271] 665 A.2d 215 (Me. 1995).

[272] *Id.* at 218.

[273] 624 A.2d 1328 (Md. Ct. Spec. App. 1993).

While agreeing that the father was "voluntarily impoverished," and that his child support obligation should be calculated on his earning capacity, the appellate court concluded that the trial court erred in assuming that his earning potential should be based on his ability to raise funds during the course of the custody litigation. It remanded to the trial court to hear testimony and make findings regarding his earning capacity, and then determine whether the amount presumed under the guidelines should be altered.

Other courts have held that participation in a strike is not a voluntary reduction of income,[274] and that incarceration alone is insufficient to demonstrate a parent's inability to pay child support.[275]

Courts frequently face the question of whether the income of a parent's new spouse or an obligation to support other children should be taken into account in determining child support. In *In re Marriage of Wood*,[276] the California Court of Appeal held that amendments to the state's statute prohibiting consideration of the income earned by a parent's subsequent spouse — "except in an extraordinary case where excluding that income would lead to extreme and severe hardship to any child" — prevented the trial court from examining the income of the mother's new husband, a wealthy man, although the earlier statute allowed consideration of a new spouse's income.[277] The court held that an impact on the former wife and children's standard of living was insufficient, and that the new spouse's income could only be considered when the children were negatively affected. Other courts have been willing to consider a new spouse's income, particularly when statutory authority to do so exists.[278] Some courts, however, flatly refuse to consider spousal income.[279] Income of a cohabitant seems even less relevant to a former spouse's child support obligation.[280]

All states consider the obligation to support other children in calculating child support, although different methods are applied.[281] Although the rationale for considering other support obligations is that all children are worthy of support, some states require or permit a deduction from the parent's income for child support paid for other children,[282] which generally results in a preference for first

---

[274] *See, e.g., Rawlings v. Rawlings*, 460 S.E.2d 581 (Va. Ct. App. 1995).

[275] *See, e.g., Thomasson v. Johnson*, 903 P.2d 254 (N.M. Ct. App. 1995); *see also* Ann Cammett, *Deadbeats, Deadbrokes, and Prisoners*, 18 Geo. J. on Poverty L. & Pol'y 127, 151-52 (2011).

[276] 44 Cal. Rptr. 2d 236 (Cal. App. 1995).

[277] Cal. Fam. Code § 4057.5(a)(1), (a)(2) (West 2011).

[278] *See, e.g., Flanagan v. Flanagan*, 673 So. 2d 894 (Fla. Dist. Ct. App. 1996); *LaForge v. La Forge*, 649 So. 2d 151 (La. Ct. App. 1995).

[279] *See, e.g., In re Marriage of Hardiman*, 889 P.2d 1354 (Or. Ct. App. 1995).

[280] *See, e.g., Jackson v. Jackson*, 907 P.2d 990 (Nev. 1995). Empirically, cohabiting couples pool resources less often than marital couples. *See generally* Marsha Garrison, *Marriage Matters: What's Wrong with the A.L.I.'s Domestic Partnership Proposal, in* Reconceiving the Family, *supra* note 47, at 305.

[281] *See* Morgan, *supra* note 225 at § 3.04[a].

[282] *See, e.g.*, Va. Code Ann. § 20-108.2(C)(4) (2011); *Flanagan v. Flanagan*, 673 So. 2d 894 (Fla. Dist. Ct. App. 1996).

families. In *Feltman v. Feltman*,[283] the Supreme Court of South Dakota rejected a father's claim that the support guidelines violate the equal protection rights of children born in subsequent marriages by giving support priority to children of the first marriage. The court held that the guidelines survived a rational relationship standard of review, and that the guidelines prevented the standard of living of the children of a first marriage from suffering due to voluntary acts of the noncustodial parent, such as a subsequent remarriage and support of additional children from that marriage.

Other states regard the obligation to other children as a factor in deviating from the guideline amount, and typically give both families equal status.[284] The Supreme Court of Wyoming applied such a standard in *Hasty v. Hasty*,[285] in which it concluded that although the presumptive amount of child support should be calculated only with respect to the child in question, the court then may consider the parent's responsibility to other children as a factor in deciding whether to deviate from the guideline amount.

The federal regulations also require states to adopt expedited judicial or administrative methods for establishing and enforcing child support awards.[286] States may delegate child support determinations to administrative hearing officers. The federal regulations further require that states periodically review their child support guidelines and adjust them to reflect current economic conditions.[287]

The use of guidelines has improved the efficiency of child support adjudication. Their implementation has increased voluntary settlement and reduced court and agency time in resolving disputed cases because of increased predictability.[288]

[D]   Duration of the Child Support Obligation

Absent a written agreement to the contrary, a parent's obligation to support his or her child usually ends when the child reaches the age of majority (commonly age 18) or graduates from high school.[289] In the past, some states specified a younger

---

[283]   434 N.W.2d 590 (S.D. 1989).

[284]   *See, e.g., State ex rel. English v. Troisi*, 659 So. 2d 658 (Ala. Civ. App. 1995); *Burch v. Burch*, 916 P.2d 443 (Wash. Ct. App. 1996).

[285]   828 P.2d 94 (Wyo. 1992).

[286]   45 C.F.R. § 303.101(b) (2011). *See also infra* § 9.06[F][4].

[287]   45 C.F.R. § 303.4(c) (2011).

[288]   Williams, *supra* note 225, at 324.

[289]   *See, e.g.,* Morgan, *supra* note 225, at tbl. 4-6 (giving state-by-state comparison of when child support terminates for children reaching the age of majority); National Conference of State Legislatures, Termination of Support — Age of Majority, *available at* http://www.ncsl.org/issues-research/human-services/termination-of-child-support-age-of-majority.aspx (updated June 2012). Morgan notes that in many jurisdictions, support obligations continue until the child graduates from high school or turns nineteen, whichever occurs first. The District of Columbia, Indiana, Mississippi, and New York are among the jurisdictions requiring parents to support their children until the age of 21. *Id*; N.Y. Dom. Rel. L. § 240 (2011); *Stokes v. Maris*, 596 So. 2d 879, 882 (Miss. 1992) (trial court "had no authority to order child support in any form, whether regular, college expenses, or otherwise, to continue in effect" after the child turned twenty-one). Hawaii and Missouri extend the duty of support until age twenty-three and

age of majority for females than for males, based on the notion that girls tend to mature and marry earlier and that boys need a good education or training to prepare them for the eventual responsibility of supporting a family.[290] In the 1975 case of *Stanton v. Stanton*,[291] the United States Supreme Court declared such gender-based classifications unconstitutional on equal protection grounds.

The parent's duty of child support may end before the child attains the age of majority if the child becomes legally emancipated by validly marrying, entering the United States military service, or becoming otherwise self-sufficient.[292] If a child leaves home and becomes self-supporting, courts have the discretion to deem the child emancipated because of changed circumstances which justify modification of support.[293] Some states have statutes which establish a judicial procedure for emancipation.[294]

If an emancipated child becomes unemancipated — for instance by termination of the minor child's marriage — the parents' obligation of support may be reinstated.[295] Correspondingly, some courts have held that a minor child who willfully places himself or herself out of the parents' control may lose the right to support.[296] In *Roe v. Doe*,[297] the Court of Appeals of New York, the highest court in New York, held that a father was not required to continue supporting his daughter when she disobeyed her father's demands that she live in the college dormitory. The court held that where a minor is old enough to work and in full possession of her faculties, and voluntarily and without cause abandons the parent's home, against the will of the parent and for the purpose of avoiding parental control, she forfeits the right to demand support.

Either by statutory interpretation or by application of common law principles, most jurisdictions extend the legal duty of child support beyond the child's minority if the child is mentally or physically handicapped, disabled, or becomes a ward of the state.[298] Some courts have revived the parental duty of support when a

---

twenty-two, respectively, if the child attends college or vocational school. *See* Morgan, *supra* note 225, at tbl. 4-6 (giving state-by-state comparison).

[290] *See Stanton v. Stanton*, 517 P.2d 1010 (Utah 1974), *rev'd*, 421 U.S. 7 (1975).

[291] 421 U.S. 7 (1975).

[292] *See, e.g.*, Va. Code Ann. §§ 16.1-333, 334 (West 2011).

[293] *See, e.g., In re Marriage of O'Connell*, 146 Cal. Rptr. 26 (Cal. Ct. App. 1978) (judicial decree of emancipation insufficient to end parental support obligation). *But see Butrum v. Roman*, 803 N.E.2d 1139 (Ind. App. 2004) (daughter not emancipated when she moved in with boyfriend and got a job because she had applied for school and was not yet self-supporting).

[294] *See, e.g.*, Cal. Fam. Code §§ 7120-23 (West 2011).

[295] *See Eyerman v. Thias*, 760 S.W.2d 187 (Mo. Ct. App. 1988) (annulment of daughter's marriage during her minority reinstated parent's duty of child support).

[296] *See, e.g., Dept. of Human Serv. v. Marshall*, 859 So. 2d 387 (Miss. 2003) (concluding that only extreme actions against supporting parent may forfeit child's right to support); *In re Sandlin*, 831 P.2d 64 (Or. Ct. App. 1992) (child not ineligible to receive support because of cohabitation with man).

[297] 272 N.E.2d 567 (N.Y. 1971).

[298] *See, e.g., Eccleston v. Bankosky*, 780 N.E.2d 1266, 1274 (Mass. 2003) (where a financially dependent minor female became a ward of the state because her parents were found unfit, trial court possessed power to impose post-minority financial support on the child's non-custodial parent who

child becomes disabled after reaching the age of majority.[299] However, in a minority of states, the courts have refused to extend the parental obligation beyond the literal statutory term, despite the child's mental or physical incapacity. For instance, in *Baril v. Baril*,[300] the Maine Supreme Court held that it was powerless to extend a father's child support obligation beyond the eighteenth birthday of his handicapped daughter when the controlling statute merely described the parent's duty as continuing until a child reaches the age of majority.

The duty of child support traditionally ended upon the death of either the child or the parent. In recent years, some statutes and judicial decisions have extended the parent's duty to support after the parent's death.[301] In such cases, a support order may be entered against the estate of the deceased parent. Section 316(c) of the Uniform Marriage and Divorce Act permits such child support to be modified, revoked, or commuted to a lump-sum payment when appropriate.[302]

Life insurance is an appropriate vehicle for dealing with post-death support problems whether or not the jurisdiction recognizes survival of the child support obligation.[303] Parents can agree by contract that the supporting parent will maintain life insurance designating the child or custodial parent as the beneficiary. Absent a contract, some courts have held that a court may not order a parent to maintain life insurance.[304] In other jurisdictions, courts may order such policies as part of an overall support award.[305]

States are divided on the issue of whether a court may require a divorced parent to continue child support beyond the age of majority while the child continues his or her education or to pay for the cost of college if the parent has the financial ability to do so.[306] In *Childers v. Childers*,[307] the Washington Supreme Court

---

possessed the financial ability to provide such support); *Grapin v. Grapin*, 450 So. 2d 853 (Fla. 1984) (common law); *Brown v. Brown*, 474 A.2d 1168 (Pa. Super. Ct. 1984) (common law); *Miller v. Miller*, 660 P.2d 205 (Or. Ct. App. 1983) (statute); *Hight v. Hight*, 284 N.E.2d 679 (Ill. App. Ct. 1972) (statute). *See generally* National Conference of State Legislatures, Termination of Child Support — Exception for Adult Children with Disabilities, *available at* http://www.ncsl.org/issues-research/human-services/termination-of-child-support-exception-for-adult.aspx (updated June 2012).

[299] See *Blaner v. Blaner*, No. 2003-T-0042, 2004 WL 1559721 (Ohio Ct. App. July 9, 2004) (no abuse of discretion in not terminating father's child support obligation when daughter turned eighteen, graduated from high school, and seven months later developed health problems that rendered her unable to work and thus still dependent upon her parents); *Towery v. Towery*, 685 S.W.2d 155 (Ark. 1985). *See generally* Noralyn O. Harlow, *Postmajority Disability as Reviving Parental Duty to Support Child*, 48 A.L.R. 4th 919 (2011).

[300] 354 A.2d 392 (Me. 1976). *See also Streb v. Streb*, 774 P.2d 798 (Alaska 1989) (upholding lower court award of continuing child support payments for a handicapped adult child).

[301] *See, e.g.*, 750 ILCS 5/510 (c) (Smith-Hurd 2011); *Bailey v. Bailey*, 471 P.2d 220 (Nev. 1970). *But see Hirst v. Dugan*, 611 A.2d 616 (N.H. 1992) (no claim against estate of unwed father in absence of pre-existing support order).

[302] 9A U.L.A. 102 (1998).

[303] *See* David A. Bratt, Note, *Child Support, Life Insurance and the Uniform Marriage and Divorce Act*, 67 Ky. L.J. 239 (1978).

[304] *See, e.g., Hudson v. Aetna Life Ins. Co.*, 545 F. Supp. 209 (E.D. Mo. 1982).

[305] *See Thomas v. Studley*, 571 N.E.2d 454 (Ohio Ct. App. 1989); *Kulmacz v. New York Life Ins. Co.*, 466 A.2d 808 (Conn. Super. Ct. 1983); *Wallace v. Wallace*, 371 S.W.2d 918 (Tex. Civ. App. 1963).

[306] *Compare Zetterman v. Zetterman*, 512 N.W.2d 622 (Neb. 1994) (when considering an action for

concluded that a parent may be required to support a child beyond the age of majority while the child pursues a college education. It construed its child support statute as basing its obligation on dependency, not minority, which therefore ends upon the child's emancipation, not majority. In determining that the facts indicated that the children in question remained dependent while they continued their college educations, the court declared, "[W]e think it reasonable to assume that a medical doctor, himself with years of higher education which brings him a higher than average income, would willingly treat his sons as dependents if they chose and showed an aptitude for college, but for the fact of the divorce."[308] The court noted that although married parents are not obligated to support their children through college, in fact, most "choose willingly to make financial sacrifices for their children's education," regardless of their age.[309] Children from divorced families deserve additional protection to compensate for the disadvantages they experience because of the divorce. Thus the parent's duty of support following divorce may include providing a college education if the child displays an aptitude and the parent will not suffer a significant hardship.

Another line of cases has refused to interpret similar statutes to require post-majority child support for children attending college.[310] In *In re Marriage of Plummer*,[311] the Colorado Supreme Court reversed a trial court's order requiring a father to continue supporting his twenty-one-year-old daughter who was in her third year of college. Although Colorado's statutory duty of support terminates upon the child's "emancipation," the court noted that emancipation generally is presumed to occur upon reaching the age of majority. When the child is incapable of self-support because of mental or physical handicap, the presumption is defeated. The court refused to extend that reasoning "to require an award of child support payments when a capable, able-bodied young adult chooses to attend college after reaching the age of majority."[312]

---

the dissolution of child support after the child reaches the age of majority, if either parent objects the court may not order continued support), *with Hutchinson v. Hutchinson*, 397 A.2d 1218 (Pa. Super. Ct. 1979) (both parents required to assist child attending college). *See generally* National Conference of State Legislatures, Termination of Support — College Support Beyond the Age of Majority, *available at* http://www.ncsl.org/issues-research/human-services/termination-of-support-college-support.aspx (updated June 2012); Morgan, *supra* note 225, tbl. 4-6.1 (giving state-by-state treatment of the duty to provide college support); Carol R. Goforth, *The Case for Expanding Child Support Obligations to Cover Post-Secondary Educational Expenses*, 56 Ark. L. Rev. 93 (2003); Kathleen Conrey Horan, *Post-minority Support for College Education — A Legally Enforceable Obligation In Divorce Proceeding?*, 18 N.M. L. Rev. 153 (1988).

[307] 575 P.2d 201 (Wash. 1978).

[308] *Id.* at 205-06.

[309] *Id.* at 207.

[310] *See Ex Parte Barnard*, 581 So. 2d 489 (Ala. 1991) (court denied mother's petition for postminority education support, holding that it lacked jurisdiction over two of the three children who had reached the age of majority before the petition was filed). *Compare Ex Parte Bayliss*, 550 So. 2d 986 (Ala. 1989) (where application is made before child attains the age of majority, trial court may award support for postminority education out of the property and income of either or both parents).

[311] 735 P.2d 165 (Colo. 1987).

[312] *Id.* at 167.

The Supreme Court of Pennsylvania held that a state statute allowing a court to order separated, divorced, or unmarried parents to provide equitably for their children's college educations while imposing no obligation on married parents, was an unconstitutional violation of the Equal Protection clause because the state had no legitimate purpose for discriminating between children of unmarried parents and children of married parents.[313] A dissenting opinion argued that the act was supported by a legitimate state interest in that it sought to redress the negative effects of divorce on children. It urged that equal protection would not be compromised by an attempt to equalize the situations of children in intact families and non-intact families.[314] However, a parent's estate may not be liable for college expenses when the parent dies before the child completes college.[315]

As of 2010, a dozen states had enacted legislation expressly authorizing support awards for college expenses.[316] These statutes have been challenged on constitutional grounds, with varying success.[317] For example, the South Carolina Supreme Court first struck on equal protection grounds the ability of courts to force parents under child support orders to pay for the education of adult children — when other parents are not forced to do so — and two years later overruled the earlier decision. Specifically, in the 2010 case *Webb v. Sowell*,[318] the court held that long-standing precedent under *Risinger v. Risinger*[319] — allowing family courts to order continued child support for majority-aged children attending college — was unconstitutional. The court found that the *Risinger* decision was "focused on the interests of the child," when it should have "examine[d] the rights of the parents."[320] The court then found that the statute at issue violated both the federal and state equal protection guarantees because there was "no rational basis for the varied treatment of [parents under child support orders] as compared to those parents who are not."[321] Two years later, however, the court reversed itself again in *McLeod v. Starnes*,[322] finding that the *Webb* court erred because it applied a

---

[313] *Curtis v. Kline*, 666 A.2d 265 (Pa. 1995).

[314] *Id.* at 272.

[315] *In re Estate of Sanders*, 2004 Tenn. App. LEXIS 184 (Tenn. Ct. App., Mar. 25, 2004).

[316] These states are Alabama, Connecticut, Hawaii, Illinois, Indiana, Iowa, Massachusetts, Missouri, New York, North Dakota, Oregon, and Washington. *See* Morgan, *supra* note 225, at § 4.05[d], n.85.

[317] *Compare Johnson v. Louis*, 654 N.W.2d 886 (Iowa 2002) (statute authorizing a court to order postsecondary educational child support for children of divorce but not for children whose parents had never married did not violate equal protection principles because "the educational benefit is a quid pro quo for the loss of stability resulting from divorce," while children whose parents never married each other are not similarly situated) *and Monroe v. Monroe*, 23 Fam. L. Rep. (BNA) 1302 (D.C. Super. Ct., Apr. 21, 1997) (rejecting equal protection challenge and upholding constitutionality of statute providing for support for college expenses), *with Curtis v. Kline*, 666 A.2d 265 (Pa. 1995) (holding unconstitutional a statute which required divorced, separated, or unmarried parents to provide their adult children with support for post-secondary education because the statute discriminated against children of intact marriages who may be in need of funds for post-secondary education).

[318] 692 S.E.2d 543 (2010).

[319] 253 S.E.2d 652 (1979).

[320] *See Webb*, *supra* note 318, at 545.

[321] *Id.*

[322] 723 S.E.2d 198 (S.C. 2012).

standard closer to strict scrutiny instead of the rational basis standard used when no suspect classification is alleged. The court found that the state's treatment of college expenses for children of divorce has a rational basis, "minimiz[ing] any economic and educational disadvantages to children of divorced parents."[323]

The degree of support may be measured by the "reasonable necessaries of the child's college expenses"[324] or by the amount necessary for the child to attend high school and four years of college, where there is evidence that "the characteristics of the child indicate that he or she will benefit from college, . . . demonstrates the ability to do well, or at least make satisfactory grades, . . . the child cannot otherwise go to school, . . . and the parent has the financial ability to help pay."[325] When examining child support arrangements for post-secondary education of majority aged children, a court should consider the child's ability to fund such education through scholarships, financial aid, employment, or their own funds, in congress with each parent's financial circumstances and the child's educational potential.[326]

Even in jurisdictions where the court has no power to award post-majority child support, most states permit the parents to extend the obligation contractually.[327] When contractual provisions for post-majority support or for payment of educational expenses are incorporated into a divorce decree, some jurisdictions allow those terms to be enforced as part of the court decree itself, even though the children have reached the age of majority.[328] However, a parent's estate may not be liable for college expenses when the parent dies before the child completes college.[329]

[E] Modification of Child Support

The traditional standard for modification of child support has been the changed circumstances test. Under this standard, a court may modify child support prospectively if material or substantial changed circumstances warrant an increase or decrease.[330] Section 316(a) of the Uniform Marriage and Divorce Act adopts a

---

[323] *Id.* (quoting *Kujawinski v. Kujawinski*, 376 N.E.2d 1382, 1390 (Ill. 1978)).

[324] *Entrekin v. Entrekin*, 627 So. 2d 955, 957 (Ala. Civ. App. 1993) (*citing Thrasher v. Wilburn*, 574 So. 2d 839, 841 (Ala. Civ. App. 1990)).

[325] *West v. West*, 419 S.E.2d 804, 806 n.2 (S.C. Ct. App. 1992).

[326] *See, e.g., In re Marriage of Steele*, 502 N.W.2d 18 (Iowa Ct. App. 1993); *In re Marriage of Murphy*, 592 N.W.2d 681 (Iowa 1999); *Passemato v. Passemato*, 427 Mass. 52, 691 N.E.2d 549 (1998).

[327] *See, e.g., H.P.A. v. S.C.A.*, 704 P.2d 205 (Alaska 1985); *Nichols v. Tedder*, 547 So. 2d 766 (Miss. 1989).

[328] *See Jameson v. Jameson*, 306 N.W.2d 240 (S.D. 1981). *But see Noble v. Fisher*, 894 P.2d 118 (Idaho 1995) (absent an independent agreement, neither statutes nor case law impose a duty of college support; father agreed in separation agreement to pay half of college expenses and the agreement, merged into the divorce decree, was unenforceable as a contract). However, a court need not order funds to be set aside for future college costs when parents agree to pay for college expenses. *See Lang v. Koon*, 806 N.E.2d 956 (Mass. App. 2004).

[329] *Supra* note 264.

[330] *See, e.g.*, Idaho Code Ann. § 32-709(1) (2011) ("The provisions of any decree respecting maintenance or support may be modified . . . only upon a showing of a substantial and material change

higher standard for modification of child support awards, requiring that the changed circumstances be "so substantial and continuing as to make the terms unconscionable."[331] The changed circumstances, which may justify a modification of support, can affect the child, the supporting parent, the custodial parent, or a combination of the parties. A change in the child's circumstances frequently relates to increased need due to medical care, special education, or training. Some courts have held that the changed circumstances test is not applicable where there is no previous child support order.[332]

The non-custodial parent's substantial increase in income may authorize an increase in child support based on the notion that the child is entitled to share in the parent's standard of living. In *Graham v. Graham*,[333] the court held that an increase in the parent's ability to pay child support may alone constitute a material change in circumstances justifying an increase in support. The *Graham* court rejected the view that the needs of the recipients must also increase to support an upward modification, reasoning that a decrease in the payor's income may support a downward modification. "To adopt such a distinction would mean that children would have to bear the burden of a lowered standard of living when their parent's income declined but could not share the benefit when that parent's resources grew."[334]

Similarly, a substantial decline in the supporting parent's income may justify a decrease in child support if the parent becomes unable to furnish the amount previously ordered.[335] However, a voluntary decrease in salary may be deemed insufficient to warrant a reduction of child support. In *Antonelli v. Antonelli*,[336] the Supreme Court of Virginia held that a father who changed employment that resulted in a reduction of income, was not entitled to reduce his child support obligation because he had failed to demonstrate that his current inability to pay was not brought about by his own voluntary act or neglect. Although it was not determined whether the father had changed employment to frustrate the feasibility or enforceability of the support obligation, the court held that the father assumed the risk of not being able to pay when he moved from a salaried position to a commissioned one. Because a custodial parent's income is also a consideration in child support, changes in that parent's income or family circumstances may also warrant modification.

---

of circumstances."); Miss. Code Ann. § 93-5-23 (2011).

[331] Unif. Marriage and Divorce Act § 316 (2010). For a list of adopting states, see *supra* note 115.

[332] *See Warren v. Hart*, 747 P.2d 511 (Wyo. 1987).

[333] 597 A.2d 355 (D.C. 1991). *But see Yeatman v. Gortney*, 562 So. 2d 258 (Ala. Civ. App. 1990) (increased income alone does not support modification); *Hanson v. Hanson*, 397 N.W.2d 656 (S.D. 1986) (finding modification of child support order improper where the court found no change in circumstances other than father's increased income).

[334] 597 A.2d at 358. *See also Kerby v. Kerby*, 60 P.3d 1038, 1043 (Okla. 2002) (where the combined income of the parents exceeds the statutory guidelines table for child support, a "significant increase" in one parent's income constitutes a "material change of circumstances allowing the court to review the existing child support award" without showing a change in the children's needs).

[335] *See Guyton v. Guyton*, 602 A.2d 1143 (D.C. 1992).

[336] 409 S.E.2d 117 (Va. 1991).

In the past, some courts have allowed child support to be modified retroactively, to reduce the amount of arrearages, upon proof that it was impossible for the obligor to make the payments when they were due.[337] Under current federal law, states are not permitted to allow modification of past due unpaid support payments.[338] *Price v. Price,*[339] a decision of the Kentucky Supreme Court, illustrates that this rule may have harsh results. In *Price*, the mother was awarded custody of the couple's child in 1987 and the father was ordered to pay $1400 a month in child support. Three years later, the parents agreed to change the child's residence to the father's home because of behavioral problems the child was experiencing. When the child moved to the father's house, the father stopped paying child support. Over a year later, the mother filed a motion to compel the father to pay child support payments from the date of the child's move. The father filed for modification of child support and a legal change in custody. The trial court held that requiring the father to pay the arrearages would be unfair, and the decision was upheld by the appeals court. The Kentucky Supreme Court held that the trial court had no power to relieve the father of his child support obligations because the child support statute provides that payments may be modified only as to installments due after the filing of a motion for modification. Furthermore, because the courts are without authority to forgive accrued child support, they cannot enforce a private oral agreement between the parties to do the same thing.

As discussed earlier in the section on establishing guideline support obligations,[340] career changes by a parent have generated much of the litigation concerning modification of child support. When an obligor parent voluntarily changes employment that substantially decreases his or her income, that party may seek a decrease in the child support obligation. Some courts find a voluntary career change which drastically reduces the parent's income a suspicious circumstance.[341] Others have emphasized that because a married parent has the option of changing the economic lifestyle of the family, it would be inequitable for a divorced parent to be denied that same flexibility.[342] Other courts attempt to

---

[337] *See In re C.S.S. (Grant),* 18 Fam. L. Rep. (BNA) 1366 (N.Y. Fam. Ct. May 13, 1992); *Schoenfeld v. Marsh,* 614 A.2d 733 (Pa. Super. Ct. 1992).

[338] *See* 42 U.S.C. § 666(a)(9)(C) (West 2011). However, a court may retroactively increase the amount of support a parent was previously directed to pay where a material change in circumstances occurs affecting the child's welfare and necessitating the custodial parent's expenditure of sums beyond the existing support obligation. *See Strowmatt v. Rodriguez,* 897 N.E.2d 500 (Ind. Ct. App. 2008). Moreover, a court may order a retroactive modification of child support when the payor is estopped from opposing the increase. *See Winters v. Winters,* 87 P.3d 1005 (Mont. 2004). In some states, child support modification may relate back to the date on which a petition to modify was filed. *See, e.g., Van Wieren v. Van Wieren,* 858 N.E.2d 216 (Ind. Ct. App. 2006).

[339] 912 S.W.2d 44 (Ky. 1995).

[340] *See supra* § 9.06[C].

[341] *See Devault v. Waller,* 494 N.W.2d 92 (Minn. Ct. App. 1992); *In re Marriage of McKeever,* 583 P.2d 30 (Or. Ct. App. 1978).

[342] *Compare, e.g., Woolf v. Woolf,* 901 So. 2d 905 (Fla. Dist. Ct. App. 2005) (modifying child support and alimony payments of former husband who lost his job due to an economic downturn, the loss of his rainmaking partner, and the loss of many of his firm's clients; while there were jobs available for attorneys with the former husband's skills, all required a substantial client base the husband no longer possessed), *with Curtis v. Curtis,* 442 N.W.2d 173 (Minn. Ct. App. 1989) (husband acted in bad faith in

balance the payor's and child's competing interests, with the child's needs taking precedence.[343]

In *Rome v. Rome*,[344] the Montana Supreme Court held that the appellant's change of jobs and remarriage did not sufficiently alter his ability to pay the previously ordered child support amount. It refused, however, to adopt a standard that would automatically foreclose modification when the payor voluntarily brings about the conditions that reduce the ability to pay. Instead, the court held that a judge should consider all the circumstances, including whether the change in income was intentional.

While courts are reluctant to effectively lock a parent into his or her job, they sometimes base the parent's obligation on the obligor's earning capacity rather than actual income.[345] In *Weiser v. Weiser*,[346] the husband, a patent lawyer, left the law firm at which he had been employed shortly before the couple's separation and established a practice on his own, reducing his income by about one half. The wife appealed the sum awarded for support of her and the parties' three children, arguing that the husband's earning potential and the family's standard of living, rather than his current income, should be considered. Acknowledging that there was no evidence that he had deliberately decreased his income to defeat his support obligation, the court observed that the husband had not reduced his own standard of living. It stated:

> Appellee's change in employment resulted in an income reduction of more than one half. It is also a fact that as a partner in the law firm he could control the draw and his weekly income of $340 may not accurately reflect his new earnings. It is for these reasons that we feel the award is inadequate. Most certainly he has the right to establish his own business but not at the expense of his family whose life style he created based on $40,000 per year income which now must be changed to meet the new conditions while he continues to enjoy his usual high standard.[347]

---

terminating his employment of more than 10 years; no reduction of support or forgiveness of arrears), *and Daigre v. Daigre*, 527 So. 2d 9 (La. Ct. App. 1988) (father's voluntary change in circumstances in leaving real estate business and entering law school was reasonable and not an attempt to avoid support obligations, and thus a reduction in child support was warranted).

[343] An increase or decrease in the payor's income is recognized as a change in circumstance that would support a modification of maintenance; however, a decrease in income resulting solely from retirement does not necessarily justify modifying support. *See, e.g., Lissner v. Marburger*, 926 A.2d 890 (N.J. Super. Ct. Ch. Div. 2007) (concluding that voluntary retirement at age 61 did not warrant modification in payor's child support obligation when payor would receive 70 percent of his average salary during retirement, and while payor would benefit from a reduced workload, the reduction was not outweighed by the impact on the child of reduced support, as to which the payor presented no evidence).

[344] 621 P.2d 1090 (Mont. 1981).

[345] *See, e.g., Morille-Hinds v. Hinds*, 928 N.Y.S.2d 727, 729 (N.Y. App. Div. 2011).

[346] 362 A.2d 287 (Pa. Super. Ct. 1976).

[347] *Id.* at 290. Courts will also consider the reasons behind a payor's loss of income. In *Murphy v. Murphy*, 759 N.W.2d 710 (Neb. Ct. App. 2008), payor's repeated misconduct as a deputy sheriff placed him in a "resign or be fired" position and led to his termination, meriting denial of his petition for downward modification of his alimony and child support obligations.

The court ordered a modification to increase the amount of the husband's support obligation.[348]

In *In re Marriage of McCord*,[349] the Colorado Court of Appeals held that the trial court could find that the father was voluntarily unemployed and imputed income to increase child support when the father had quit his job after winning the state lottery. It rejected the father's arguments that the mother must show an increased need on the part of the child and that his decision to resign from his job was a good faith career choice.

The remarriage of either parent frequently prompts an action seeking modification of child support.[350] The income of a new spouse may increase the parent's ability to support the child and justify an adjustment of the parent's support obligation. In *Yost v. Yost*,[351] the Idaho Supreme Court concluded that the remarriage of the custodial parent requires consideration of the new marital community's financial resources, not merely the parent's individual income, because of the nature of community property in that state.

Jurisdictions are also divided on the effect of a parent's acquiring new family obligations. Some jurisdictions have held that obligations owed to later children justify a decrease in the supporting parent's previous child support responsibility because all children deserve equal support.[352] Other courts have expressed the conventional opinion that a supporting parent starts a new family at his or her own risk and so have refused to reduce child support when new children arrive.[353] Some states' child support guidelines accommodate preexisting child support obligations by excluding those amounts actually paid from a parent's income.[354]

---

[348] *See also Van Offeren v. Van Offeren*, 19 Fam. L. Rep. (BNA) 1123 (Wis. Ct. App. 1992) (unnecessary to show bad faith in refusing to decrease child support when father shirked his obligation by leaving job in order to start new business).

[349] 910 P.2d 85 (Colo. Ct. App. 1995).

[350] *See generally*, Simon R. Fodden, *Poor Relations: The Effect of Second Families on Child Support*, 3 Can. J. Fam. L. 207 (June 1980).

[351] 735 P.2d 988 (Idaho 1987).

[352] *See* Va. Code Ann. § 20-108.2(C)(4) (2011) ("Where a party to the proceeding has a natural or adopted child or children in the party's household or primary physical custody, and the child or children are not the subject of the present proceeding, there is a presumption that there shall be deducted from the gross income of that party [an] amount . . . that represents that party's support obligation based solely on that party's income as being the total income available for the natural or adopted child or children in the party's household or primary physical custody, who are not the subject of the present proceeding. Provided, however, that the existence of a party's financial responsibility for such a child or children shall not of itself constitute a material change in circumstances for modifying a previous order of child support in any modification proceeding. Any adjustment to gross income under this subsection shall not create or reduce a support obligation to an amount which seriously impairs the custodial parent's ability to maintain minimal adequate housing and provide other basic necessities for the child, as determined by the court."); *see also In re Michael M.*, 561 N.Y.S.2d 870 (N.Y. Fam. Ct. 1990); *Martin v. Martin*, 430 N.E.2d 962 (Ohio Ct. App. 1980).

[353] *See, e.g., Meyers v. Bohrer*, 176 So. 2d 3 (La. Ct. App. 1965); *Oregon ex rel. State of New York v. Hasbun*, 556 P.2d 166 (Or. Ct. App. 1976).

[354] *See, e.g.*, Va. Code Ann. § 20-108.2(C)(4) (2011); Col. Rev. Stat. Ann. § 14-10-115(3)(a) (West 2011).

The problem is more complex when a support obligor adopts the children of a new spouse. In *Berg v. Berg*,[355] a father was found in contempt when he stopped making support payments to his first wife and two children after he adopted the three children of his new wife. The court ruled that although it was irrelevant whether the acquisition of new children resulted from birth or adoption, the trial court should examine the father's good faith when considering the additional financial obligations he voluntarily incurred.[356]

When a new family includes stepchildren, the effect on previous child support obligations may depend on whether a stepparent has a legal obligation to those children. In *Ainsworth v. Ainsworth*,[357] the court concluded that courts have discretion to deviate from statutory child support guidelines in consideration of expenses associated with subsequent families even in the absence of court orders. In the absence of a legal duty to support stepchildren, however, the court held that remarriage along with the acquisition of stepchildren does not necessarily justify a reduction in child support owed to a previous family, although the court must consider all relevant factors to avoid an inequitable result.[358]

Jurisdictions remain divided on the question of whether a support obligor's incarceration justifies a reduction in child support. The majority of courts have held that modification is appropriate when the incarcerated obligor lacks the assets to satisfy the support obligation.[359]

However, a growing number of courts have adopted a "no justification" rule, holding that a parent's current inability to pay does not warrant modification when it results from voluntary conduct that led to imprisonment.[360] A third approach simply treats incarceration as one factor which may be considered in deciding whether to grant a modification.[361]

Jurisdictions also differ on whether a child's attendance at college warrants modification of the original child support award. Some allow a motion to modify the

---

[355] 359 A.2d 354 (R.I. 1976).

[356] *See also Mack v. Mack*, 749 P.2d 478 (Haw. Ct. App. 1988).

[357] 574 A.2d 772 (Vt. 1990), superseded by statute, Vt. Stat. Ann. tit. 15, § 656a, as recognized in *Tetreault v. Coon*, 708 A.2d 571 (Vt. 1998).

[358] *See also Openshaw v. Openshaw*, 639 P.2d 177 (Utah 1981). *Compare* Va. Code Ann. § 20-108.2(C)(4) (2011).

[359] *See Pierce v. Pierce*, 412 N.W.2d 291 (Mich. Ct. App. 1987); *Foster v. Foster*, 471 N.Y.S.2d 867 (N.Y. App. Div. 1984).

[360] *See, e.g., State v. Tenny*, 493 N.W.2d 824 (Iowa 1992); *Knights v. Knights*, 522 N.E.2d 1045 (N.Y. 1988) (where a payor's current financial hardship is solely the result of his wrongful conduct culminating in a felony conviction and imprisonment, the "changed financial circumstances" warrant neither a reduction of payor's child support obligation nor a suspension in the accrual of support payments during the period of incarceration); *State v. Nelson*, 587 So. 2d 176, 178 (La. Ct. App. 1991) (a voluntary act cannot be used to justify extinction of a protected right such as child support).

[361] Cammett, *supra* note 275. *See also Sanders v. State*, 67 P.3d 323 (Nev. 2003); *In re Marriage of Hari*, 804 N.E.2d 144, 148 (Ill. App. Ct. 2004) (in exercising its discretion, a court should consider all relevant factors, including the assets of the incarcerated payor; the reason payor entered prison; the length of incarceration; and payor's potential for work release).

original divorce judgment to include expenses and support for a child in college, even after the child reaches majority.[362]

Whether deviation from the guideline constitutes a sufficient change in circumstances has become a dominant issue under statutory child support guidelines. Federal rules require states to adopt provisions that make any inconsistency between the support order and the guideline grounds for modification.[363] States have adopted quantitative standards of ten to thirty percent and/or a fixed dollar value, which allow modification to occur as soon as the deviation between an actual support order and the current guideline amount reaches that percentage and/or fixed dollar value.[364] Additionally, parties can include escalator clauses in their marital settlement agreements, which automatically increase the amount of support upon certain circumstances.[365]

[F] Enforcement of Spousal and Child Support Orders

While obtaining a spousal support award or an adequate child support order can pose its own difficulties, enforcing an existing order can be even more problematic.[366] Although in the past, about one-third of total child support owed was not paid, under current legal reforms more than 76% of custodial mothers due child support in 2007 received some payment and 47% received the full amount owed.[367] However, from 2008 through 2010 only about 62% of the total amount due in child support was actually paid to recipients.[368] Both state and federal governments have established a number of mechanisms for increasing the amount of support that actually reaches the hands of the intended recipients when the obligor does not voluntarily comply with the support obligation. While governmental interest in support enforcement has focused largely on child support, most of the same remedies are available for collection of spousal support as well.

---

[362] *See, e.g., Newburgh v. Arrigo*, 443 A.2d 1031 (N.J. 1982); *see also supra* § 9.06[D].

[363] 45 C.F.R. § 303.8(b)(1)(i), (f) (2011).

[364] *See* Morgan, *supra* note 225, at § 5.03[b] (1996 & 2010 Supp). *E.g.*, Alabama, 10%; Arkansas, 20% or $100 per month in gross income; California, 30% or $50, whichever is greater; Illinois, 20% or $10, whichever is less; Georgia, 15% and $25. *Id.*

[365] *See, e.g., Stigler v. Stigler*, 48 So. 3d 547 (Miss. 2009) (finding enforceable an escalator clause in divorce decree which increased father's child support obligations when his adjusted gross income increased, despite imposing a greater support amount than the guidelines would otherwise impose, where both parties agreed to the clause). *But see Perez v. Perez*, 882 So. 2d 537 (Fla. Dist. Ct. App. 2004) (order that husband's child support obligation would increase after he ceased paying wife rehabilitative alimony was not appropriate, where adjustment would not take place for four years, at which time the income of the parties may have changed).

[366] For a listing of State Child Support Oversight Entities, see National Conference of State Legislatures, State Child Support Oversight Entities, *available at* http://www.ncsl.org/issues-research/human-services/state-child-support-oversight-entities.aspx (updated June 2012).

[367] Wash. Post, Dec. 3, 2003, at A6; U.S. Dep't of Commerce, Bureau of the Census, *Custodial Mothers and Fathers and their Child Support: 2007*, Rep. P60-237, Table 1 (2009).

[368] U.S. Dep't of Health & Human Services, Administration for Children & Families, Office of Child Support Enforcement, *Child Support Enforcement FY 2010: Preliminary Report* (2011), *available at* http://www.acf.hhs.gov/programs/cse/pubs/2011/reports/ preliminary_report_fy2010/.

[1] Support Arrearage Issues and Defenses

In most states, unpaid and past due installments of either alimony or child support are considered final judgments.[369] Support installments that are final judgments may not be modified retroactively and may be enforced by execution without further legal action.[370] In the past, a few jurisdictions permitted modification of accrued alimony installments.[371] Even fewer allowed retroactive modification of child support, although some states have permitted modification of past due payments in extreme circumstances when necessary to prevent severe hardship to the obligor.[372] This practice is now prohibited by federal law.[373] In some states, if the child support obligation arose by contractual agreement between the parents, such as in a divorce settlement agreement, the debt for arrearages must be reduced to judgment and then remedies available for non-payment of a debt are available for collecting the arrearages.[374] Therefore, good practice dictates that private settlement agreements be merged into the decree of divorce to give those support obligations the status of court orders. Even when reduction to judgment is required, the proceeding is generally regarded as a continuation of the original divorce action and, thus, no re-assertion of personal jurisdiction over the defendant is necessary.[375]

Once a support payment has become a final judgment, it accrues interest. States vary with respect to the applicable statute of limitations on past due child support,[376] and methods for collecting arrearages differ greatly among the states.[377]

Inability to pay generally will not serve as a defense in an action for arrearages,[378] although it may render such an action impractical. An obligor who becomes

---

[369] See, e.g., Britton v. Britton, 671 P.2d 1135 (N.M. 1983).

[370] See Clark, supra note 12 at 672, 725.

[371] Id. at 672.

[372] Id. at 725.

[373] 45 C.F.R. § 303.8(b)(1)(i), (f) (2011).

[374] See Keltner v. Keltner, 589 S.W.2d 235 (Mo. 1979) (en banc).

[375] See Clark, supra note 12 at 672-73.

[376] See Carter v. Carter, 611 A.2d 86 (Me. 1992) (statute of limitations for civil actions does not preclude claim for child support arrearages); Thurman v. Thurman, 777 N.E.2d 41 (In. 2002) (applying statute of limitations for enforcement of child support to calculation of arrearage where statute of limitations required that action to collect past due support be brought not later than 10 years after child is emancipated or reaches age 18); Skolak v. Skolak, 895 N.E.2d 1241 (In. 2008) (applying statute that judgment and decrees expire if not satisfied in 20 years to dismiss state action to collect child support payments); Cloutier v. Turner, 34 A.3d 1146 (Me. 2012) (holding that statute of limitations under paternity statute limiting liability to preceding "6 year period" did not bar action to recover past due support).

[377] See 37 Am. Jur. Trials § 639.

[378] In People v. Likine, 492 Mich. 367 (2012), a divided Michigan Supreme Court held that an individual charged with felony non-payment of support may defend herself using the common-law defense of impossibility, notwithstanding the state law provision precluding a defense based on inability to pay under Michigan Compiled Laws Annotated Section 750.165. A defendant must show not only that she "cannot pay, but that [hers] are among the exceptional cases in which it was not reasonably possible to obtain the resources to pay." Id. at 402.

unable to pay spousal or child support because of loss of employment or other circumstances is not permitted to simply stop paying, but must bring an action to modify the support obligation due to changed circumstances. It may be worthwhile to initiate the enforcement process if there is a chance that the obligor may acquire money in the future. A debt for arrearages is enforceable against the estate of a deceased obligor, and some states allow the estate of a deceased support recipient to collect arrearages.[379]

[2]   State Enforcement Remedies

[a]   Contempt Proceedings

Contempt proceedings are a common method of enforcing spousal and child support, available in virtually all states once a support decree has been entered.[380] Decrees based on agreement are also subject to enforcement by contempt.[381] The court's contempt power may be statutory[382] or may stem from the court's equitable powers to enforce its orders and injunctions.

In *In re Marriage of Ramos*,[383] the ex-husband, a surgeon with an income of approximately $300,000 a year and assets over $20 million, was held in contempt for his failure to pay his ex-wife $175,000 due on a lump-sum maintenance award. On appeal, the Illinois Court of Appeals first concluded that a settlement agreement which is incorporated into a judgment is enforceable through contempt proceedings under state statutes and further noted that the availability of other means of support and alternative remedies for enforcement do not preclude a proceeding for contempt. It then held that the trial court's conclusion that the contempt was willful was supported by ample evidence of the appellant's assets and transactions, and was not rebutted by his general testimony that he was unable to pay.

The Wisconsin Supreme Court, in *Dennis v. Dennis*,[384] upheld a trial court's decision to hold a father in contempt for his failure to seek work as ordered and his failure to make minimal child support payments. The court noted that the trial court had not ordered the husband to take a different job, but only to seek other work in order to allow the court to make an accurate and informed finding as to his

---

[379] *See, e.g., Kay v. Vaughan*, 165 S.E.2d 131 (Ga. 1968); *In re Estate of Nielsen*, 445 N.W.2d 780 (Iowa 1989); *Spiliotis v. Campbell*, 431 N.E.2d 591 (Mass. App. Ct. 1982); *Estate of Carpenter v. Carpenter*, 220 S.W.3d 263 (Ar. 2005); *Elkins v. Kokocinski*, 2000 Mass. App. Div. 103 (Ma. 2000); *but see Cohan v. Feuer*, 810 N.E.2d 1222 (Ma. 2004) (stipulation modifying original divorce decree that alimony to wife would continue until her death or remarriage was insufficient to overcome presumption that alimony obligation ends on obligor's death).

[380] *See, e.g.*, Cal. Fam. Code § 290 (West 2011); N.Y. Dom. Rel. Law § 245 (McKinney 2011); *see also* Unif. Marriage and Divorce Act § 311(d) (2010).

[381] *See, e.g., Keltner v. Keltner*, 589 S.W.2d 235 (Mo. 1979) (en banc); *In re Marriage of Sager*, 249 P.3d 91 (Ok. 2010); *Sheahan v. Sheahan*, 721 S.W.2d 81 (Mo. 1986).

[382] *See, e.g.*, Cal. Fam. Code § 290 (West 2011); N.Y. Dom. Rel. Law § 245 (McKinney 2011); Unif. Marriage and Divorce Act § 311(d) (2010).

[383] 466 N.E.2d 1016 Ill. App. Ct. (1984), *cert. denied*, 471 U.S. 1017 (1985).

[384] 344 N.W.2d 128 (Wis. 1984).

earning ability upon which to make a fair child support award.

Incarceration for non-payment of a support debt has been held exempt from state constitutional provisions prohibiting imprisonment for failure to pay a debt because a support debt derives from the duty of support, provides maintenance for the recipient, and fulfills public policy goals.[385] While failure to pay alimony or spousal support falls within the category of debts exempted from the constitutional ban, failure to make payments due under a property settlement provision generally is not punishable by contempt.[386] However, property division awards that assume the function of support sometimes have been held to be enforceable by contempt.[387] Contempt proceedings may also be brought to enforce legal fees and court costs. Courts have also allowed attorneys' fees to be awarded against defendants in contempt actions brought for failure to pay support.[388]

Contempt proceedings may be either criminal or civil actions. Criminal contempt imposes a punishment for violation of a court order. Because of the criminal nature of the action, a defendant is entitled to constitutional protection guaranteed by the Due Process Clause. Civil contempt, on the other hand, is intended to enforce compliance with the support order and to collect arrearages by coercing the obligor to comply with the court order. If the obligor refuses to comply, he or she may be jailed; while the obligor is incarcerated, a government agency often provides support to the needy ex-spouse and children. Imprisonment is impermissible if the obligor is unable to pay; therefore, the key feature of civil contempt is that the obligor must have the ability to purge himself of the contempt by payment of the amount owed.[389] Ordinarily, this means that the obligor's inability to pay is an excuse for nonpayment, although it will not defeat an action to collect arrearages. Moreover, the court may hold the obligor in contempt for refusing to sell assets to satisfy the support obligation.

It is often difficult to distinguish between civil and criminal contempt actions because both forms of contempt actions relate to the non-payment of a support

---

[385] *See, e.g., Bradley v. Superior Court*, 310 P.2d 634 (Cal. 1957); *McAlear v. McAlear*, 469 A.2d 1256 (Md. 1984); *West v. West*, 101 S.E. 876 (Va. 1920); *Seablom v. Seablom*, 348 N.W.2d 920 (N.D. 1984), superseded by statute, N.D. Cent. Code Ann. § 14-05-25.1 (West 2011), as recognized in *Kautzman v. Kautzman*, 618 N.W.2d 500, 503 (N.D. 2000). *See generally* 24A Am. Jur. 2d Divorce and Separation § 1067 (2012).

[386] *McAlear v. McAlear*, 469 A.2d 1256 at 1272-73 (Md. 1984), *Rosenberg v. Rosenberg*, 452 So. 2d 620 (Fla. Dist. Ct. App. 1984) (relationship between former spouses as to rights under property settlement agreement is one of debtor and creditor, barring use of contempt proceeding to enforce rights); *Coleman v. Coleman*, 539 N.E.2d 34 (Ind. Ct. App. 1989) (remedy is execution, not contempt); *Attilli v. Attilli*, 722 A.2d 268 (R.I. 1999) (contempt not available where agreement was not merged into the divorce decree).

[387] *See, e.g., McAlear v. McAlear*, 469 A.2d 1256 (Md. 1984); *Haley v. Haley*, 648 S.W.2d 890 (Mo. Ct. App. 1982); *Hall v. Hall*, 838 P.2d 995 (N.M. Ct. App. 1992), *cert. denied*, 838 P.2d 468 (N.M. 1992); *Hanks v. Hanks*, 334 N.W.2d 856 (S.D. 1983), *Walton v. Walton*, 789 S.W.2d 64 (Mo. Ct. App. 1990), *Minor v. Minor*, 901 S.W.2d 163 (Mo. Ct. App. 1995).

[388] *See, e.g., Hartt v. Hartt*, 397 A.2d 518 (R.I. 1979), *Wertkin v. Wertkin*, 763 So. 2d 465 (Fla. Dist. Ct. App. 2000).

[389] *See Mead v. Batchlor*, 460 N.W.2d 493 (Mich. 1990), abrogated on other grounds by *Turner v. Rogers*, 131 S.Ct. 2507 (2011); *Napoli v. Napoli*, 689 So. 2d 1192 (Fl. 1997); *Mallardi v. Jenne*, 721 So. 2d 380 (Fl. 2008).

order and either may result in a fine or imprisonment. In *Feiock v. Feiock*,[390] the United States Supreme Court dealt with the problem of differentiating between civil and criminal contempt in the course of evaluating the constitutionality of a California contempt statute, deemed "quasi-criminal" in nature by the state courts. California's statute allowed the defendant to prove his inability to pay the ordered support as a defense, but did not allocate the burden of proving his ability to comply with the order to the state as an element of its case. The Court held that although a label may provide guidance, it is the substance of the action and the type of relief sought that determine whether the contempt is civil or criminal in nature and, consequently, the extent of the procedural safeguards necessary. The Court noted that civil contempt is brought for the benefit of the complainant, while criminal contempt seeks to vindicate the authority of the court. Further, if the defendant may be imprisoned until he performs some affirmative act, the action is civil, but if the sentence is for a definite period, it is criminal. If a fine is imposed, it is civil if it is remedial and payable to the complainant, but criminal if punitive and payable to the court. If the defendant may avoid paying the fine by performing some act, the contempt action is civil. However, a court may not impose punishment in a civil contempt proceeding "when it is clearly established that the alleged contemnor is unable to comply with the terms of the order," and "once a civil contemnor complies with the underlying order, he is purged of the contempt and is free."[391]

Civil contempt does not necessarily require all the due process protections afforded criminal defendants. In *Turner v. Rogers*,[392] the United States Supreme Court held that the Due Process Clause of the Fourteenth Amendment does not automatically require states to provide counsel to indigent, noncustodial parents facing civil contempt proceedings for non-payment of child support orders. Even if the non-paying party faces incarceration of up to one year, the state is under no obligation to provide free representation.[393] However, the Court attached an "important caveat" to the decision: "namely, that the [s]tate must nonetheless have in place alternative procedures that assure a fundamentally fair determination of the critical incarceration-related question, whether the supporting parent is able to comply with the support order."[394] The Court described a set of substitute procedural safeguards "which, if employed together, can significantly reduce the risk of an erroneous deprivation of liberty," including: notice to the defendant that defendant's ability to pay is a critical issue in the contempt proceeding; use of a pre-hearing form to elicit relevant financial information from the defendant; an opportunity at the hearing for the defendant to respond to statements and questions about defendant's financial status; and requiring an express finding by the court that the defendant has the ability to pay.[395] However, the Court "[did] not claim that [these] are the only possible alternatives" and noted that "sometimes

---

[390] *Feiock v. Feiock*, 485 U.S. 624 (1988).

[391] *Id.* at 638 n.9, 633.

[392] 131 S.Ct. 2507 (2011).

[393] *Id.* at 2520.

[394] *Id.* at 2512.

[395] *Id.* at 2519.

assistance other than purely legal assistance (here, say, that of a neutral social worker) can prove constitutionally sufficient."[396]

[b]   Other State Law Remedies

Most states authorize a broad range of other remedies for enforcing support obligations. These methods include discovery of assets, execution liens, liens on real property, attachment, garnishment, sequestration, and the appointment of a receiver. Courts traditionally have had the power to order the support obligor to provide security for future support in the form of a bond, insurance policy, cash, or other property. These security measures are becoming more common since federal law, discussed below, now encourages states to employ such methods.

Imposing liens on the obligor's property is another common support enforcement procedure.[397] The courts are split as to whether a divorce decree containing a spousal or child support order automatically becomes a lien in the absence of any specific statutory authority.[398] Most courts consider such liens to be appropriate only when there is evidence that the obligor intends to be uncooperative or is likely to convey or conceal assets.[399]

A number of state statutes also provide for attachment of the obligor's property for non-payment of spousal or child support obligations.[400] Alternatively, an uncooperative support obligor may be required to provide some form of security assuring compliance with these obligations.[401]

Traditional garnishment procedures are available for enforcing spousal and child support obligations. Since the enactment of federal-state child support enforcement remedies in the 1970s, 1980s, and 1990s,[402] income withholding, or

---

[396] *Id.*

[397] *See generally* Jeffrey Ball & Virginia Sablan, Effective Use of Liens in Child Support Cases (1990).

[398] *Compare Prior v. Prior,* 447 A.2d 1155 (R.I. 1982), *with In re Marriage of Daniel,* 639 S.W.2d 650 (Mo. Ct. App. 1982). *See also* C.T. Drechsler, Annotation, *Decree for periodical payments for support or alimony as a lien or the subject of a declaration of lien,* 59 A.L.R. 2d 656; 24A Am. Jur. 2d Divorce and Separation §§ 812, 932 (2011).

[399] *See, e.g., White v. White,* 429 So. 2d 730 (Fla. Dist. Ct. App. 1983).

[400] *See, e.g.,* N.C. Gen. Stat. § 50-16.7(e) (2010).

[401] *See, e.g.,* N.Y. Dom. Rel. Law § 243 (McKinney 2011); Va. Code Ann. § 20-114 (West 2011).

[402] Family Support Act of 1974 (Title IV-D of the Social Security Act), 42 U.S.C. §§ 651-65 (2011) (requiring states that receive funds under the Aid to Families with Dependent Children program to establish and enforce child support obligations); Child Support Enforcement Amendments of 1984 (CSEA), 42 U.S.C. §§ 651-67 (2011) (requiring states to strengthen enforcement by providing for the imposition of liens and withholding from the wages and tax refunds of delinquent payors); Family Support Act of 1988, 42 U.S.C. §§ 654, 666-67 (2011) (requiring states to establish presumptive, rather than advisory, child support guidelines); Omnibus Budget Reconciliation Act of 1990, 42 U.S.C. §§ 664, 666 (2011) (permanently requiring the Internal Revenue Service, upon the request of a state, to collect child support arrearages of $500 or more); Child Support Recovery Act of 1992, 18 U.S.C. § 228 (2011) and 42 U.S.C. § 3796cc (2011) (criminalizing willful failure to pay support for a child resident in another state, where past-due support has remained unpaid for over one year or exceeds $5,000); the Full Faith and Credit for Child Support Orders Act of 1994 (FFCCSOA), 28 U.S.C. § 1738B (2011) (requiring each state to enforce other states' child support orders and prohibiting modification of other states' orders

wage assignment, procedures have been streamlined.[403] Many of these expedited techniques may apply to spousal support, as well as child support collection, especially if the spousal support was intended, at least in part, to provide funds for children in the recipient's custody.

A number of states have enacted statutes authorizing the refusal, suspension, or revocation of state licenses of delinquent child support obligors. These statutes include any state license, including driver's, hunting and fishing, and professional licenses, such as membership in a state bar.[404]

All of these mechanisms demonstrate the state's broad power to enforce child support orders through various avenues, both coercive and punitive, although some methods go too far. A prominent example of this is the Wisconsin statute that prevented child support debtors from remarrying until arrears were paid, which was struck by the U.S. Supreme Court in *Zablocki v. Redhail* on equal protection grounds, citing the fundamental right to marry.[405]

[3]   Interstate Enforcement

[a]   Traditional Interstate Enforcement

Final judgments of one state are enforceable in all other states under the Full Faith and Credit Clause of the United States Constitution.[406] Finality, however, is essential to invoking full faith and credit; therefore, interstate enforcement of alimony and child support traditionally depended on whether the decree was final.

Although the United States Supreme Court held in *Barber v. Barber*[407] that periodic installments of alimony are entitled to full faith and credit as the installments mature, it later concluded in *Lynde v. Lynde*[408] that alimony payable in the future is not a final judgment for a fixed sum and does not qualify for the same recognition. In *Sistare v. Sistare*,[409] the Court elaborated, concluding that

---

unless certain jurisdictional requirements are satisfied); Bankruptcy Reform Act of 1994, 11 U.S.C. § 523(a)(5), (15) (2011) (enabling creditor spouse to prevent discharge of obligations in bankruptcy); Personal Responsibility and Work Opportunity Reconciliation Act of 1996 (PRWORA), 42 U.S.C. §§ 652-666 (2011) (mandating the creation of state and federal support case and new hire registries; requiring the adoption of the Uniform Interstate Family Support Act; authorizing liens on professional and occupational licenses; and expanding the services of the Federal Parent Locator Service); Deadbeat Parents Punishment Act of 1998, 18 U.S.C. § 228 (2012) (amending the Child Support Recovery Act of 1992 to provide harsher punishment for chronic failure to pay child support); Deficit Reduction Act of 2005, § 7310 (Pub. L. No. 109-17) (creating an additional fee when the state assists with child support collection).

[403] *See infra* § 9.06[F][4][a].

[404] *See, e.g.,* Tex. Fam. Code Ann. § 232.003 (2011); *see also State Department of Revenue v. Beans,* 965 P.2d 725 (Alaska 1998) (state statute suspending driver's license of delinquent child support obligor is constitutional to the extent it is applied to obligors who have the ability to pay).

[405] *Zablocki v. Redhail,* 434 U.S. 374 (1978).

[406] Art. IV, Sec. 1, 28 U.S.C. § 1738 (2011).

[407] 62 U.S. 582 (1858).

[408] 181 U.S. 183 (1901).

[409] 218 U.S. 1 (1910).

future alimony installments were entitled to full faith and credit to the same extent as arrearages if the recipient's right was "vested" and could not be canceled or modified by the original court, even if the order was not reduced to a money judgment.

The United States Supreme Court later recognized the possibility that the court that originally ordered the alimony may have the authority to retroactively modify its award,[410] and therefore, a sister state need only give the order the same recognition that the state which issued the order would give it. Because child support orders are always prospectively modifiable, the full faith and credit requirement does not prevent another state from modifying an original decree, although the same inquiry regarding retroactive modification of spousal support arrearages arises in enforcement of child support arrearages.[411]

Historically, enforcement of a judgment for child support or alimony arrearages in another state required the cumbersome process of filing a suit on the judgment in the rendering state and establishing the judgment in the sister state. To facilitate enforcement of judgments, 47 states, the District of Columbia, and the U.S. Virgin Islands have adopted the Uniform Enforcement of Foreign Judgments Act.[412] The Act establishes a simplified procedure for the registration of foreign judgments, which are defined as "any judgment, decree, or order of a court of the United States or of any other court which is entitled to full faith and credit in this state."[413] The court in which the judgment is registered then treats and regards the judgment in the same manner as it does its own judgments.

The Uniform Enforcement of Foreign Judgments Act has been held to be constitutionally applicable to periodic support payments.[414] When a past-due support payment is regarded as a final judgment of the state that ordered the support, it is entitled to full faith and credit and may not be modified by a state in which the decree is later registered, although it may be modified prospectively upon showing of a sufficient change of circumstances.[415] A decree that was subject to retroactive modification in the state that entered the decree is not entitled to full faith and credit, however.[416]

The traditional method of enforcement must be used in states that have not

---

[410] *Griffin v. Griffin*, 327 U.S. 220 (1946).

[411] *See, e.g., Elkind v. Byck*, 439 P.2d 316 (Cal. 1968); *Banton v. Mathers*, 309 N.E.2d 167 (Ind. Ct. App. 1974).

[412] Unif. Enforcement of Foreign Judgments Act, *Table of Jurisdictions*, 13 U.L.A. pt. I 155, at 58-59 (2002 & Supp. 2011). *See also* Unif. Law Commission, *Legislative Fact Sheet: Enforcement of Foreign Judgments Act*, http://www.nccusl.org/LegislativeFactSheet.aspx?title=Enforcement of Foreign Judgments Act (last visited Oct. 13, 2011). California, Massachusetts, and Vermont have yet to ratify the Act; legislation to do so was introduced in the Massachusetts General Court in 2011. *Id.. See also* H.B. 1277, 187th Gen. Ct. of Mass. (2011).

[413] 13 U.L.A. § 1 (2011).

[414] *See, e.g., Willhite v. Willhite*, 546 P.2d 612 (Okla. 1976).

[415] *Holley v. Holley*, 568 S.W.2d 487 (Ark. 1978) (en banc) (action to register Kansas divorce decree with vested alimony arrearages).

[416] *See Overman v. Overman*, 514 S.W.2d 625 (Mo. Ct. App. 1974) (action to register Tennessee divorce that could be retroactively modified).

adopted the Uniform Enforcement of Foreign Judgments Act. In either case, multiple suits will be necessary to enforce arrearages as they accrue. The Uniform Reciprocal Enforcement of Support Act and its revisions has supplemented these traditional methods, and facilitates continued collection of support as well as arrearages.

[b]   The Uniform Reciprocal Enforcement of Support Acts

Prior to the enactment of the Uniform Reciprocal Enforcement of Support Act (URESA) of 1958 and its 1968 revision, the Revised Uniform Enforcement of Support Act (RURESA),[417] support obligors found it relatively easy to avoid payment of their support obligations by crossing state lines. Most recipients lacked the financial means to enforce interstate judgments. URESA and RURESA were enacted to simplify, expedite and lower the cost of enforcing spousal and child support payments, whether the parties resided in different states or areas of the same state and in some cases, in foreign jurisdictions.[418] These statutes allowed interstate establishment of support orders in addition to enforcement of existing orders.[419] Variations of these statutes have been enacted in every U.S. state and territory, as well as several Canadian provinces.[420]

Despite Congress' best intentions, URESA and RURESA were plagued by various problems. The Acts' procedures were cumbersome because most actions require involving multiple states. Further, the Acts were ambiguous regarding modification actions and conflicting child support orders.[421] Delays and difficulties with implementation further limited the Acts' success.[422]

[c]   The Uniform Interstate Family Support Act

Dissatisfaction with the Acts led to a thorough revision that began in 1988, ultimately resulting in the Uniform Interstate Family Support Act (UIFSA).[423] The federal Personal Responsibility and Work Opportunity Reconciliation Act of

---

[417] Rev. Unif. Reciprocal Enforcement of Support Act, 9C U.L.A. 81 (2001 & Supp. 2011).

[418] *See* Carl A. Gallageher, Note, *Uniform Reciprocal Enforcement of Support Act*, 20 Washburn L.J. 409 (1981).

[419] *See, e.g., State of Iowa ex rel. Petersen v. Miner*, 412 N.W.2d 832 (Neb. 1987).

[420] *See* Gallageher, *supra* note 418.

[421] Revised Unif. Reciprocal Enforcement of Support Act, § 11 (2011).

[422] *See* John J. Sampson & Paul M. Kurtz, *UIFSA: An Interstate Support Act for the 21st Century*, 27 Fam. L. Q. 85 (1993).

[423] 9 U.L.A. pt. I-B 281 (2005). In accordance with the provisions of the Personal Responsibility and Work Opportunity Reconciliation Act of 1996, *infra*, UIFSA was adopted by every U.S. jurisdiction by 1998. *Id.* at 2011 Supp. 74. A revision in 2001 included amendments clarifying jurisdictional issues in modification proceedings; specifying procedures for the reconciliation of multiple orders; and expanding UIFSA to cover enforcement of support orders from non-U.S. jurisdictions. *Id.* at 75-76; 9 U.L.A. pt. I-B 159 (2005). *See also* National Center for State Courts, *UIFSA Proposed Revisions, available at* http://www.ncsc.org/services-and-experts/government-relations/child-support-enforcement/uifsa-proposed-revisions.aspx. The 2001 revisions had been adopted by 23 jurisdictions by 2011 (Ariz., Cal., Colo., Conn., Del., D.C., Idaho, Ill., Me., Md., Miss., Neb., Nev., N.M., Okla., R.I., S.C., Tex., Utah, Va.,

1996 (PRWORA) required all states to adopt UIFSA by January 1, 1998, or lose federal funding for state welfare programs.[424]

UIFSA expands personal jurisdiction to its constitutional limits, which allows a custodial parent or state agency attempting to establish or collect support the maximum opportunity to do so without resorting to the two-state proceedings of RURESA. It permits a state to exercise long-arm jurisdiction based on limited contacts relating to the child in question, including a child residing in the state as a result of the individual's acts or directives and an individual engaging in sexual intercourse in the state if the child may have been conceived by that act.[425] Although UIFSA retains RURESA's two-state proceeding, there should less need to rely upon these procedures because of the expanded grounds for asserting personal jurisdiction under UIFSA.

UIFSA applies the law of the forum state, simplifying the more complicated approach of RURESA. When arrearages exist, the forum court may need to apply the law of other states.[426]

To eliminate the problem of conflicting support orders under RURESA, UIFSA applies a one-order system. One child support order is entered and that order maintains continuing validity. To control issues of conflicting orders, UIFSA severely limits when a petition can be filed in one state if a pleading has already been filed in another state.[427] A state has "continuing, exclusive jurisdiction over a child support order . . . as long as this State remains the residence of the obligor, the individual obligee, or the child."[428] The state issuing the initial order has jurisdiction to modify that order as long as the child and obligee are present.[429]

In *LeTellier v. LeTellier*,[430] the Tennessee Supreme Court held that Tennessee courts did not have jurisdiction to modify a child support order entered in the

---

Wash., W. Va., and Wyo.). 9 U.L.A. pt. I-B 168. In 2008, a further series of amendments were proposed to implement the provisions of the Hague Convention on the International Recovery of Child Support and Other Forms of Family Maintenance, signed by the U.S. in November, 2007. 9 U.L.A. pt. I-B 72, 76-77 (2011 Supp.). By 2011, 10 states had enacted the 2008 amendments (Fla., Me., Mo., Nev., N.M., N.D., R.I., Tenn., Utah, and Wis.) and three others (Haw., Minn., and Wash.) and Puerto Rico had introduced the legislation. *See* Uniform Law Commission, *Legislative Fact Sheet — Interstate Family Support Act Amendments (2008)*, *available at* http://uniformlaws.org/LegislativeFactSheet.aspx?title=Interstate Family Support Act Amendments (2008).

[424] Pub. L. No. 104-193, 110 Stat. 2105 § 321, codified at 42 U.S.C. § 666(f) (2011).

[425] UIFSA § 201, 9 U.L.A. pt. I-B 487 (2010). *See also State ex rel. Mahoney v. St. John*, 964 P.2d 1242 (Wyo. 1998) (valid exercise of jurisdiction under UIFSA long-arm provision to collect child support over a resident of Wyoming when the defendant had lived as a family in Washington with the child and mother during a short-lived marriage before returning on his own to Wyoming).

[426] UIFSA § 202. *See also Child Support Enforcement v. Brenckle*, 675 N.E.2d 390 (Mass. 1997) (in child support enforcement case decided by the trial court on the same day that the state's URESA statute was repealed and replaced by UIFSA, court held that UIFSA was intended to apply retroactively, but in any event, the father was also liable for $107,365 in back child support under URESA).

[427] *Id.* at § 204.

[428] *Id.* at § 205(a).

[429] *Id.* at § 206(b).

[430] 40 S.W.3d 490 (Tenn. 2001).

District of Columbia after the mother and child had moved to Tennessee and the father had moved to Virginia. Although the order was properly registered in Tennessee, without personal jurisdiction over the absent parent UIFSA would permit only a petitioner who did not reside in the state to seek modification in the state. The court further found that the Full Faith and Credit for Child Support Orders Act of 1994 (FFCCSOA) and UIFSA do not conflict in this respect, therefore it did not need to rule on preemption.[431]

UIFSA actions may be brought by either state agencies[432] or private attorneys.[433] Interstate enforcement usually begins with registration of a support order in the state where enforcement is sought. After registration, it is enforced by a tribunal of the state where it is registered, applying either local support enforcement mechanisms or those imposed by UIFSA itself.[434]

A major feature of UIFSA is that modification by an enforcing state is extremely limited. The original jurisdiction has the exclusive power to modify unless that state has lost jurisdiction because the child and the custodial parent have left. If the issuing state loses jurisdiction, another state may modify the order if it has jurisdiction over both parties. Once another state has validly modified a support order under UIFSA, it becomes the only enforceable order.[435] The North Carolina Court of Appeals interpreted this section in *Welsher v. Rager*,[436] when it reversed a trial court decision that refused to continue child support under a New York order. The father had argued that his duty to support the children ended when they turned 18. However, under New York law, a child is not emancipated until age 21. The North Carolina appellate court held that UISFA, which North Carolina had enacted, requires that a support order be interpreted according to the law of the state where it was issued; the father was bound by the New York law which requires him to support his children until they attain the age of 21.

In *P.A.N. v. R.N.*,[437] the Delaware Family Court also interpreted the difference between URESA and UIFSA. The parties were divorced in New York and their separation agreement specified that child support would be paid at a set amount until the youngest child became emancipated. When the eldest child reached the age of majority, the father requested and was awarded a decrease in support payments by the Delaware Family Court. Upon the mother's petition for review de novo, the court noted that although URESA permits the coexistence of two or more valid child support orders, UIFSA requires that an order issued by a court of the current home state must be recognized as the sole, controlling order. Because the mother and children continued to reside in New York, the court held that the earlier New York order would be recognized rather than the subsequent Delaware order. However, the Delaware courts had no authority to enforce the New York

---

[431] Pub. L. No. 103-383, 108 Stat. 4064, codified at 28 U.S.C. § 1738B (2011).

[432] UIFSA at § 307(a).

[433] *Id.* at § 309.

[434] *Id.* at §§ 601-04.

[435] *See id.* at §§ 205, 206, 605-08.

[436] 491 S.E.2d 661 (N.C. Ct. App. 1997).

[437] 1996 Del. Fam. Ct. LEXIS 139 (Nov. 8, 1996).

order because the mother had never requested Delaware registration of the New York order. Once she registered her order in Delaware, that court would have the power of enforcement.

UIFSA contains streamlined enforcement features. It allows a support order to be mailed directly to an employer in another state, eliminating the need for a hearing unless the payor actively seeks one.[438] Further, a party seeking to enforce a support order or an income withholding order may send the necessary documents to the support enforcement officer of another state.[439]

UIFSA is enhanced by FFCCSOA.[440] Under FFCCSOA, full faith and credit must be afforded to support orders that are consistent with express standards, which are identical to those required to establish the validity of an order under UIFSA.

[4] Federally Mandated Support Enforcement Remedies

The federal government's involvement in child support has not been limited to requiring adoption of child support guidelines. Over the past several decades, federal concern with child support has increased exponentially. In addition to concern for the welfare of children, Congress was alarmed by the enormous costs of welfare programs, which were largely driven by parents' failure to fulfill their child support obligations. These considerations led to federal legislation intended to directly confront the problems associated with enforcing child support orders. The lack of enforcement was a drain on public funds and eventually became a national crisis, prompting Congress to enact Title IV-D of the Social Security Act[441] in 1974. Title IV-D creates a program for establishing child support obligations as well as coordinating federal and state processes to increase collection efficiency. The program, administered by the Federal Office of Child Support Enforcement and partially funded with federal funds, requires states to establish plans to improve child support enforcement. Federal law also authorizes the revocation of the passport of a person who owes more than $2500 in child support arrearages.[442] The constitutionality of this statute has been upheld by several federal courts of appeals.[443]

The original Act required states to establish specific child support enforcement plans in order to continue receiving federal funding for family assistance programs.[444] The original Act required states to establish programs, administered by state IV-D agencies, to use existing state mechanisms for setting and enforcing child support orders, as well as for proving paternity, for families receiving welfare

---

[438] UIFSA at § 501.

[439] *Id.* at § 502.

[440] Pub. L. No. 103-383, 108 Stat. 4064, codified at 28 U.S.C. § 1738B (2011).

[441] 42 U.S.C. §§ 651-65 (2011).

[442] 42 U.S.C. § 652(k).

[443] *See Weinstein v. Albright*, 261 F.3d 127 (2d Cir. 2001); *Eunique v. Powell*, 302 F.3d 971 (9th Cir. 2002).

[444] *See generally* Diane Dodson & Robert M. Horowitz, *Child Support Enforcement Amendments of 1984: New Tools for Enforcement*, 10 Fam. L. Rptr. 3051 (BNA) (1984).

benefits, then known as Aid to Families with Dependent Children (AFDC) and now known as Temporary Assistance to Needy Families (TANF).[445]

Although child support collection improved under the original act, noncompliance remained high, and state efforts focused almost exclusively on collection from parents whose families received welfare benefits. To increase the effectiveness of the programs, Congress, a decade later, enacted the Child Support Enforcement Amendments of 1984 (CSEA).[446] These amendments required states to legislate specific mechanisms for improving their child support enforcement programs to intensify interstate enforcement and to equalize treatment of families that receive no welfare with those receiving such benefits. In addition to mandating longer statutes of limitations on paternity actions, the CSEA ordered states to adopt procedures for (a) mandatory income tax withholding, (b) offsets to state income tax refunds, (c) guarantees to assure support (such as liens, bonds, and securities), and (d) reporting arrearages to credit agencies, and federal income tax offsets in non-welfare cases.[447] Many of the resulting state statutes apply to enforcement of spousal support as well as child support.

[a]   Income Withholding

One of the most important enforcement techniques mandated by the CSEA is income withholding, an expedited form of the traditional remedy of garnishment. The CSEA requires that all support orders issued or modified by a state included, at minimum, a conditional provision for wage withholding when the support payments are in arrears.[448] The withholding mandated by the CSEA does not limit states from reaching broader forms of income, it is only the basic requirement. States can authorize further withholding from any source of income, including commissions, bonuses, disability and retirement benefits.[449] Enforcement of these withholdings may be initiated as soon as the obligor is in arrears of an amount equal to one month's support.[450] The CSEA's enforcement power has been extended by the Child Support Act of 1988, which mandates that states include automatic wage assignments in all new or modified child support orders.[451]

The procedures for income withholding dictated by Congress are mandatory with respect to obligees represented by the state IV-D agency, but state legislatures may elect to apply the same system to privately represented or pro se obligees. The compulsory provisions allow the withholding action to be commenced without further court or administrative order, and notice need only be sent to the

---

[445] 42 U.S.C. § 654(4)(A).

[446] Pub. L. 98-378, §, 98 Stat. 1305 (Aug. 16, 1984). *See also* Harry B. O'Donnell, Note, *Title I of the Family Support Act of 1988 — The Quest for Effective National Child Support Enforcement Continues*, 29 J. Fam. L. 149 (1990-91).

[447] *Id.*

[448] 42 U.S.C. §§ 666(a)(8), (b)(2), (b)(3) (2011). Note that private settlement agreements not incorporated or merged into a court decree are exempt from this requirement, but provisions requiring withholdings may be voluntarily inserted by the parties.

[449] *See* Dodson & Horowitz, *supra* note 444, at 3054.

[450] 42 U.S.C. § 666(b)(3)(B) (2011).

[451] Pub. L. No. 100-485, 102 Stat. 2343.

obligor once the withholding decision has been made. While the withholding must be accomplished in accordance with procedural due process, the obligor may contest only on the limited ground of "mistakes of fact," which includes errors in the amount of current support due or of arrearages or mistaken identity of the obligor.[452] Contested withholding actions must be resolved within 45 days. The CSEA contemplates that states will develop a clearinghouse to monitor support payments and facilitate accounting, which would reduce the number of contested actions.[453]

Withholding is accomplished by sending notice to the obligor's employer or other source of income, directing that a specified amount be withheld from the employee's pay. The employer is liable for failure to comply and is prohibited from taking retaliatory action against the employee on account of the withholding.

The CSEA requires withholding of an amount equal to the current support obligation and an additional amount to be applied toward the arrearage, plus a fee paid to the employer. The Consumer Credit Protection Act[454] limits the amount that may be withheld to 50 to 65 percent of the employee's disposable earnings, depending on whether the obligor has a second family to support and on whether the arrearages arose more than twelve weeks previously. States must give child support withholding priority over the rights of other creditors. Except in limited, specified circumstances, the withholding continues once the arrearages have been paid in order to assure a reliable continuation of support.[455]

States must provide the enforcement agencies of other states access to their withholding systems to enable out-of-state support obligees to reach the earnings of obligors within the state. Child support enforcement agencies now have access to an obligor's social security number,[456] as well as numerous other tracing devices. Information regarding certain amounts of unpaid support obligations must be reported to credit reporting agencies on their request.[457]

[b]   Security for Payments

The CSEA further requires states to adopt procedures for securing support payments by liens, bonds, and other securities. These devices may be particularly useful when the obligor is self-employed or has income or assets that are otherwise inaccessible through the withholding provisions.[458] The judge or administrative agency has discretion regarding the type and amount of security required in an individual case.

---

[452] H. Rep. No. 527 at 33.

[453] *See* Dodson & Horowitz, *supra* note 444, at 3054.

[454] 15 U.S.C. § 1673(b) (2011).

[455] 42 U.S.C. § 666(b) (2011).

[456] 42 U.S.C. § 653(b) (2011).

[457] 42 U.S.C. § 666(a)(7) (2011).

[458] *See* Dodson & Horowitz, *supra* note 444, at 3055.

[c]   Income Tax Refund Intercepts

The CSEA also broadened the scope of tax refund intercepts for collection of past-due child support. Under this mechanism, any federal income tax refund due an obligor may be sent to the relevant state agency for distribution to the obligee.[459] Under the earlier act, the intercept was only available to welfare recipients and was usually limited to the amount owed to state agencies.[460] The CSEA extends the intercept mechanism to non-welfare recipients, but only the state IV-D agency may initiate the procedure; thus, private obligees must enlist the assistance of the agency. Only arrearages, not current support, may be collected through the intercept, and it may be used only after other remedies have been exhausted. However, the amount collected is not limited by the Consumer Credit Protection Act.[461] The procedures for implementing the tax refund intercept are complex, requiring that the obligor receive prior notice, procedural due process protections and an opportunity to contest the amount owed. States which impose state income taxes are also required to develop state income tax refund intercept mechanisms.[462]

The United States Supreme Court held in *Sorenson v. Secretary of the Treasury*[463] that the intercept device may be used to confiscate tax refunds due to the earned-income credit as well as overpayment of taxes, resolving a split of authority among the federal circuits. In *Sorenson*, the delinquent obligor father had remarried and had a new child. The father and his new wife, who brought the action because she had earned most of the family's income, were due a tax refund of approximately $1400, partly attributable to overpayment of taxes and partly to the earned-income credit.[464] The IRS notified the couple that $1100 of the refund was being paid to the State of Washington, which had been assigned the mother's right to the child support arrearages under the AFDC program. The Court acknowledged the important goals of the earned-income credit,[465] but concluded that Congress could deem that alleviating the " 'devastating consequences for children and the taxpayers' of the epidemic of nonsupport" was a more compelling objective and upheld the lower court's view that the credit refund could be intercepted.[466]

---

[459]   42 U.S.C. § 664(a)(1).

[460]   *See id.* at 3056.

[461]   15 U.S.C. § 1673(b)(1)(A) (2012).

[462]   42 U.S.C. § 666(a)(3)(a) (2012).

[463]   475 U.S. 851 (1986).

[464]   The earned-income credit gives low-income workers supporting children living with them a tax credit of their earned income for the taxable year, up to $5751 for tax year 2011; unlike most other credits, it is refundable. *See* United States Internal Revenue Service, *Preview of 2011 E.I.T.C. Income Limits, Maximum Credit Amounts and Tax Law Updates, available at* http://www.irs.gov/individuals/article/0,,id=233839,00.html (last updated Jan. 3, 2011).

[465]   The credit is intended to encourage low-income persons to work and to provide them relief from rising costs of living, as well as to stimulate the economy. 475 U.S. at 864 (Stevens, J., dissenting).

[466]   *Id.* at 864-65, quoting Hearings before the Senate Committee on Finance on Spending Reduction Proposals, 97th Cong., 1st Sess., pt. 1, p. 34 (1981) (statement of Secretary Schweiker).

[d]   Child Support Guidelines

The CSEA requires that all states establish specific child support guidelines, in the form of schedules or formulas, for determining basic child support obligations. Although guideline schemes vary amongst the states,[467] they generally provide for extraordinary medical or dental expenses and child-care costs due to employment of the custodial parent. The 1998 amendments to the Social Security Act requires state child support guidelines to be applied as a rebuttable presumption, permitting deviation from the guidelines only upon express findings of fact that their application would be unjust or inappropriate in a given case.[468] The amendments also established minimum review standards: state guidelines must be reviewed for appropriateness at least once every four years by an appropriate state agency and all individual child support awards once every three years.

[e]   Parent Locator Service

Federal law[469] requires state child support enforcement programs to operate a Parent Locator Service (PLS), interconnected with other state and federal PLS programs, to trace child support obligors who have deserted their families or moved to an unknown location. The PLS accepts location requests from IV-D agencies in both welfare and non-welfare cases. Non-welfare custodial parents or their private attorneys seeking federal location assistance may request the state PLS to obtain federal PLS location information for a small fee.[470]

Location requests forwarded to the federal PLS should state the following: the absent parent's full name; any last-name alias; the parent's social security number, if known; whether the parent is or has been a member of the armed forces, and the branch of service, if known; whether the parent is a federal employee; and whether the parent is receiving any federal compensation or benefits. If the parent's social security number is unknown, the state PLS must send additional identifying data, including the absent parent's date and place of birth, mother's maiden name, and father's full name. Upon receipt of a location request, the federal PLS will conduct a computer search of federal departments and agencies to learn the absent parent's social security number, last known address, and place of employment.[471]

When attempting to locate an absent parent for child support purposes, the PLS may obtain new mailing addresses and information from the post office system,[472] credit bureaus,[473] previous employers,[474] public information on file with the state Department of Motor Vehicles, state employment commissions and law

---

[467] *See generally supra* § 9.06[C].

[468] 42 U.S.C.A. § 667 (2011).

[469] 42 U.S.C. § 654(8) (2012).

[470] 42 U.S.C. § 654 (2011).

[471] *See* Horowitz, et al., *supra* note 212, at 112-30.

[472] 39 C.F.R. § 265.6(d)(1) (2011).

[473] 15 U.S.C. § 1681b(a)(4)(A) (2011).

[474] 45 C.F.R. § 303.100(d)(3), (e)(i)(x) (2011).

enforcement divisions, and the Internal Revenue Service.[475]

[f]   The Child Support Recovery Act of 1992

The Child Support Recovery Act of 1992[476] (CSRA) made the willful failure to pay child support a federal crime. In order for an obligor to be criminally liable, the child must reside in another state and the support obligation must have been determined by a court or administrative process order[477] — in addition to being of a certain dollar amount and having been outstanding for a specified length of time. The willful failure to pay child support, if such obligation remains unpaid or amounts to more than $5,000, is punishable with fines and/or imprisonment for up to six months.[478] The punishment for a subsequent offense increases to fines and/or imprisonment for up to two years. Congress amended the CRSA in 1998 with the Deadbeat Parents Punishment Act (DPPA),[479] which criminalized interstate or foreign travel with the intent to evade a support obligation if the obligation remains unpaid for more than one year or amounts to more than $5,000,[480] or the willful failure to pay child support if the support obligation remains unpaid for more than two years or accumulates to greater than $10,000.[481] Finally, the CRSA required the court to order restitution for the total amount of unpaid support.[482]

The constitutionality of the statute was upheld by the United States Court of Appeals for the 10th Circuit in *United States v. Hampshire*.[483] The defendant in *Hampshire*, who conditionally pled guilty and was sentenced to two years probation and ordered to pay $38,804 in restitution, challenged his conviction on the grounds that the Child Support Recovery Act violates the Commerce Clause. The court noted that while several district courts have held the CSRA unconstitutional, a number have upheld its constitutionality on the basis that nonpayment of child support involves payment of a debts and constitutes economic activity or commerce; that nonpayment of child support in general has a substantial impact on commerce; and that the requirement that the delinquent parent and child live in different states provides an interstate nexus.[484] The court held that Congress had a rational basis for concluding that the child support

---

[475]   26 U.S.C. §§ 6103(1)(6)(A) (2011).

[476]   18 U.S.C. § 228 (2011).

[477]   *Id.* at § 228(f)(3).

[478]   *Id.* at § 228(a)(1), (c)(1).

[479]   *Id.* at § 228(a)(3).

[480]   *Id.* at § 228(a)(2), (c)(2).

[481]   *Id.* at § 228(a)(3), (c)(2).

[482]   *Id.* at § 228(d).

[483]   95 F.3d 999 (10th Cir. 1996), *review denied*, 519 U.S. 1084 (1997).

[484]   The statutory presumption at 18 U.S.C. § 228(b) that "[t]he existence of a support obligation that was in effect for the time period charged in the indictment or information creates a rebuttable presumption that the obligor has the ability to pay the support obligation for that time period" has been held unconstitutional by a number of courts. *See, e.g., U.S. v. Edelkind*, 2006 U.S. Dist. LEXIS 41056 (W.D. La., May 18, 2006); *U.S. v. Casey*, 2006 U.S. Dist. LEXIS 35702 (D. Neb., Feb. 3, 2006); *U.S. v. Pillor*, 387 F. Supp. 2d 1053 (N.D. Cal. 2005); *U.S. v. Morrow*, 368 F. Supp. 2d 863 (C.D. Ill. 2005); *U.S. v. Grigsby*, 85 F. Supp. 2d 100 (D.R.I. 2000).

delinquencies have a substantial impact on interstate commerce and upheld the CSRA.

Defendants may be convicted under the DPPA even if they lacked the ability to pay the full amount if they did not pay the portion they could afford.[485] The CSRA has survived numerous challenges to its constitutionality,[486] although the United States Court of Appeals for the Second Circuit, in *U.S. v. Kerley*, limited its application by holding that an indictment on multiple counts for failure to pay child support is duplicatous where only a single child support order covering multiple children is in effect.[487]

[g]   The Personal Responsibility and Work Opportunity Reconciliation Act of 1996

The Personal Responsibility and Work Opportunity Reconciliation Act of 1996[488] (PRWORA) replaced the older AFDC entitlements with block welfare grants to the states distributed under the TANF program, and removed the federal guarantee for child welfare, shifting the primary responsibility to the states. At the same time, it provided important provisions for collecting child support. It established a national system for tracking employment which required reporting of new hires, required states to adopt UIFSA, allowed enforcement agencies access to governmental sources of information for tracking delinquent parents, and permited military persons to be located immediately. PRWORA afforded enforcement agencies access to private records, applied modern case management techniques to child support enforcement, including computer matching, and required states to adopt expedited procedures.[489] PRWORA facilitated international support enforcement by establishing procedures for recognizing orders of reciprocating countries.

In *Kansas v. United States*,[490] the State of Kansas brought suit protesting the changes in child support enforcement policy required by PRWORA as too costly, onerous, and difficult to administer, as well as infringing on the state's ability to determine its own laws. The United States Court of Appeals for the Tenth Circuit upheld the Act's constitutionality and concluded that it was not unduly coercive because of the amount of federal funding at stake. Rather, it found that PRWORA was a "reasoned attempt by Congress to ensure that its grant money is used to

---

[485] *See United States v. Mattice*, 186 F.3d 219 (2d Cir. 1999); *United States v. Mathes*, 151 F.3d 251 (5th Cir. 1998); *see also United States v. Davis*, 588 F.3d 1173 (8th Cir. 2009).

[486] *See, e.g., United States v. Parker*, 108 F.3d 28 (3d Cir. 1997); *United States v. Bailey*, 115 F.3d 1222 (5th Cir. 1997); *United States v. Faasse*, 265 F.3d 475 (2001) (en banc) (holding that the CRSA was within Congress' power to regulate a "thing" in interstate commerce); *United States v. Pillor*, 387 F. Supp. 2d 1053 (N.D. Cal. 2005).

[487] 544 F.3d 172 (2nd Cir. 2008). *See generally* Kurtis A. Kemper, *Validity, Construction, and Application of the Child Support Recovery Act of 1992*, 147 A.L.R. Fed. 1 (2005).

[488] Pub. L. No. 104-193, 110 Stat. 2105.

[489] *See* Linda D. Elrod, *Child Support Reassessed: Federalization of Enforcement Nears Completion*, 1997 U. Ill. L. Rev. 695.

[490] 214 F.3d 1196 (3d Cir. 2000).

further the state and federal interest in assisting needy families, in part through improved child support enforcement."[491]

[h]   Deadbeat Parents Punishment Act of 1998 and the Deficit Reduction Act of 2005

Since PRWORA, there have been two federal child support enforcement initiatives. In 1998, Congress enacted the Deadbeat Parents Punishment Act of 1998 making it a felony (1) to travel between states with the intent of evading child support payments or (2) if child support arrearages have existed for over two years or are greater than $10,000.[492]

The federal Deficit Reduction Act of 2005 ("DRA") required state child support enforcement offices to collect mandatory fees if the state collects at least $500 for recipients who are not on public assistance, to support the work of the state office. States are permitted to retain the fee from the child support collected, to charge the recipient or recover the fee from the absent parent, or simply pay the fee out of the state's own budget.[493] For families on public assistance, the DRA also permitted states to give more of the child support collected to the recipient, rather than keeping those funds to support the state's administrative work — a new "family first" policy.[494]

§ 9.07   FEDERAL TAX CONSEQUENCES OF CHILD AND SPOUSAL SUPPORT

The tax implications of divorce were greater under previous tax law when the uppermost marginal income tax rate was higher and there was a greater differential between the highest and lowest rates, and thus more opportunity for income shifting from a spouse in a higher bracket to one in a lower bracket. Nevertheless, the tax implications of divorce continue to have a significant effect on divorcing parties and their influence should be considered in negotiating the structure of a separation agreement.[495]

Furthermore, the tax ramifications of divorce are complex because many of the former tax provisions continue to apply to divorce decrees entered prior to the enactment of the present tax laws, resulting in a "current divorce tax system [that] is a confusing conglomeration of four different models."[496] Family law practitioners

---

[491] *Id.* at 1204. *See also* Louis Kaplow & Steven Shavell, *Fairness Versus Welfare*, 114 Harv. L. Rev. 961 (2001); Stacy L. Brustin, *The Intersection Between Welfare Reform and Child Support Enforcement: D.C.'s Weak Link*, 52 Cath. U. L. Rev. 621 (2003).

[492] 18 U.S.C. § 228 (2012).

[493] The Deficit Reduction Act of 2005, § 7310 (Pub. L. No. 109-17).

[494] *Id.*

[495] *See generally* Michelle Drumbl, *Decoupling Taxes & Marriage: Beyond Innocence and Income Splitting*, 4 Colum. J. Tax. L. 1 (2012); Leon Gabinet, et al., Tax Aspects of Marital Dissolution (2d ed. 1997); Garrison Lepow, *Nobody Gets Married for the First Time Anymore — A Primer on the Tax Implications of Support Payments in Divorce*, 25 Duq. L. Rev. 43 (1986).

[496] Beverly I. Moran, *Welcome to the Fun House: The Incredible Maze of Modern Divorce Taxation*,

thus must be familiar with both prior and present tax laws, and they must also keep abreast of proposed and anticipated changes in those laws.

[A]   Alimony or Spousal Support Payments

Since 1942,[497] the Internal Revenue Code (IRC) has treated alimony or spousal support as taxable income to the recipient spouse[498] and deductible from the gross income of the payor spouse,[499] provided that the payments comply with specific statutory qualifications. The payor spouse may deduct alimony payments in computing adjusted gross income;[500] thus the deduction is available regardless of whether the payor spouse itemizes or takes the standard deduction.

Prior to the 1984 Deficit Reduction Act, the IRC prevented property division payments that were disguised as alimony from qualifying as alimony for tax purposes. Under the old IRC, the payment needed to stem from a duty of spousal support, not a division of property, pursuant to a divorce decree, separation decree, or written instrument incident to divorce.[501] The purported distinction between alimony and property division generated considerable litigation, especially as the difference between the two concepts blurred at the state family law level.

Furthermore, the payments had to be paid on a periodic basis, although the IRC failed to define that term.[502] Lump sum settlements payable in installments were periodic only if the payment period was greater than 10 years;[503] alimony payable for a shorter time was periodic if it could be modified or terminated because of the death of either spouse, the remarriage of the recipient, or a change in circumstances.[504]

The Deficit Reduction Act of 1984[505] (the "1984 Act") and Tax Reform Act of 1986[506] simplified the alimony rules and eliminated the support and periodicity requirements for qualification as alimony. In order for payments to be deductible to the payor and includable income to the payee, IRC § 71 now requires the following:

(1) The payments must be in cash, not in other property.[507]

---

26 Harv. J. Legis. 117, 118 (1989) (examining the history of divorce taxation and its implications).

[497]   *See* Eleanor S. Rich, *Alimony Taxation After the Tax Reform Act of 1986*, 6 B.U. J. Tax L. 67, 67-68 (1988) (examining the historical tax treatment of alimony payment).

[498]   I.R.C. § 71 (2011).

[499]   I.R.C. § 215 (2011).

[500]   *See* I.R.C. § 62(a)(10) (2011).

[501]   I.R.C. § 71 (1954) (amended in 1984).

[502]   *Id.*

[503]   Treas. Reg. § 1.71-1(d)(4) (1960).

[504]   Treas. Reg. § 1.71-1(d)(3) (1960).

[505]   Deficit Reduction Act of 1984, Pub. L. No. 98-369, 98 Stat. 494 (1984).

[506]   Tax Reform Act of 1986, Pub. L. No. 99-514, 100 Stat. 2085 (1986).

[507]   I.R.C. § 71(b)(1) (2011). Checks and money orders qualify as cash payments, and rent, mortgage, tax, or tuition payments made on behalf of the recipient may qualify as alimony. *See, e.g.*, Treas. Reg. § 1.71-1T(a), Q&A (5), (6).

(2) The payments must be received by, or on behalf of, a spouse under a divorce decree or separation agreement.[508]

(3) The divorce or separation instrument must not expressly state that the payments shall *not* be treated as alimony for tax purposes.[509]

(4) The spouses may not be "members of the same household" when the payments are made.[510]

(5) The payments must terminate upon the death of the recipient, with no substitute payments imposed on the payor spouse after the recipient's death.[511] Unless the payments were part of a court order and state law automatically terminates the payments on the recipient's death, the instrument must expressly provide for such discontinuation.[512]

(6) The spouses cannot file a joint income tax return.[513]

(7) The payments cannot represent child support.[514]

To prevent parties from "front-loading," or disguising property settlement payments as alimony to obtain a large tax benefit in the years immediately following divorce, the 1984 Act further devised a "recapture" rule.[515] The recapture rule applied whenever annual payments exceeding $10,000 decreased by more than $10,000 during any year over the six-year period following divorce. If excess payments were recaptured, the payor was required to re-compute the over-payments as income and the recipient was granted a corresponding deduction.[516]

The Tax Reform Act of 1986 modified the recapture rule and retained certain earlier limitations on qualification as alimony for tax purposes.[517] The provisions currently apply a statutory formula to payments made during the first three years after the alimony or separate maintenance agreement.[518] If, under the formula, the payments decrease by a certain amount within the first two years, then the payor must recapture the calculated "excess payment" amounts as income in the third year.[519] As under the old rule, the recipient receives a corresponding deduction.[520]

---

[508] I.R.C. § 71(b)(1)(A) (2011).

[509] I.R.C. § 71(b)(1)(B) (2011).

[510] I.R.C. § 71(b)(1)(C) (2011). If the payments are made pursuant to a separation agreement but the parties are not yet legally separated or divorced and one spouse is preparing to leave the household and does so within one month of the payments in question, the payments may qualify. I.R.C. § 71(f)(5)(A) (2011).

[511] I.R.C. § 71(b)(1)(D) (2011).

[512] *See* Treas. Reg. § 1.71-1T, Q&A (12).

[513] *See* I.R.C. § 71(e) (2011).

[514] *See* I.R.C. § 71(c)(1) (2011).

[515] I.R.C. § 71(c)(2) (1984) (amended in 1986).

[516] *See* Rich, *supra* note 494 at 69-70 (examples of operation of recapture rule).

[517] *See generally* Moran, *supra* note 496, at 158-61; Rich, *supra* note 494, at 71-81.

[518] I.R.C. § 71(f) (2011).

[519] I.R.C. § 71(f)(1)(A) (2011). Note that the statutory calculation serves as a guide for statutory payments that will not be subject to the recapture rule. The current recapture rules apply to payments

The amounts paid in the fourth year and beyond are not subject to recapture rules.

The recapture rules do not apply to temporary support orders,[521] to payments to extend for a minimum of three years that are calculated as a fixed percentage of income of the payor's property, business, or compensation for employment or self-employment,[522] or to payments that cease upon the recipient's death.[523]

[B]   Child Support Payments

Child support payments are not deductible for the payor nor included as income to the recipient.[524] In the past, pursuant to *Commissioner v. Lester*,[525] child support payments could be treated as alimony if the instrument establishing the payments was carefully drafted to avoid fixing a sum certain as child support and by incorporating the child support into an alimony payment. The 1984 Act abrogated *Lester* and greatly reduced the opportunity to structure child support as deductible alimony. The current law regards payments as nondeductible child support if the payments to the recipient will be reduced on the occurrence of an event or contingency relating to the child or at a time that clearly can be associated with such contingency.[526] Applicable contingencies include events such as the child's reaching a specific age, marrying, or leaving school.[527] If, however, the payments are reduced on contingencies unrelated to the child, such as the remarriage of the former spouse, the payments may be treated as alimony, if they otherwise qualify.[528]

Whether payments are alimony or child support continues to raise questions, especially when payments to a former spouse are made in an undifferentiated lump sum. Because the taxpayer has the burden of proving that the tax commissioner's determinations are erroneous, results in individual cases may appear inconsistent. For example, in *Roosevelt v. Commissioner of Internal Revenue*,[529] the Tax Court held that an unallocated family allowance, which had no portion specifically designated as child support, was taxable to the former wife as alimony. However, in *Folberg v. Commissioner of Internal Revenue*,[530] the Tax Court held, under similar facts, that an unallocated payment to the former spouse was child support and, therefore, was not deductible to the husband.

---

under instruments executed after December 31, 1986, and to earlier instruments modified after that date for the express purpose of meeting the current requirements. Tax Reform Act of 1986, 26 U.S.C. § 1843(c)(2)(3) (1986).

[520] I.R.C. § 71(f)(1)(B) (2011).

[521] I.R.C. § 71(f)(5)(B) (2011).

[522] I.R.C. § 71(f)(5)(C) (2011).

[523] I.R.C. § 71(f)(5)(A) (2011).

[524] *See* Rich, *supra* note 494, at 73-75; *see also* I.R.C. § 71(c)(1) (2011).

[525] 366 U.S. 299 (1961).

[526] I.R.C. § 71(c) (2011).

[527] *See* T.D. 7973, 1984-2, C.B. 176.

[528] *See supra* § 9.07[A].

[529] 70 T.C.M. (CCH) 612, T.C.M. (RIA) 95,430 (1995).

[530] 64 T.C.M. (CCH) 1527, T.C.M. (RIA) 92,713 (1992).

[C] Dependency Exemption for Children

Prior to 1984, the parent providing more than fifty percent of a child's support was entitled to claim the child as a dependent.[531] If the divorce decree specified that the non-custodial parent would take the exemption and the non-custodial parent furnished at least $600 of the child's support, the exemption could be allocated to that parent.[532] Similarly, if the non-custodial parent provided at least $1,200 in child support and the custodial parent could not establish that he or she furnished a greater amount, the non-custodial parent received the exemption.[533]

The dependency exemption rules have been simplified in the current IRC, providing that the parent who has custody of a child for the majority of the calendar year is entitled to both a dependency exemption and the child tax credit if the child receives over half of his or her support from the divorced or separated parents.[534] In cases of joint custody, the actual residence of the child controls.

If the custodial parent signs a written statement disclaiming the right to the exemption for a specified year and the non-custodial parent attaches that statement to the tax return, the noncustodial parent may claim the exemption.[535] The waiver can be executed on a yearly basis or made applicable to all years until the child reaches the age of majority. The non-custodial parent also may claim the exemption under a pre-1985 divorce or separation agreement that allocated the exemption to that parent if the parent provided at least $600 in support for the child.[536]

Some jurisdictions have held that the divorce court may allocate the dependency exemption without the agreement of the parties and order a custodial parent to execute a waiver.[537] Other courts have concluded that federal law has preempted

---

[531] I.R.C. § 151(e)(1)(A) & (B) (1954) (amended in 1984).

[532] I.R.C. § 152(e)(2)(A) (1954) (amended in 1984).

[533] *Id.* at § 152(e)(2)(B).

[534] I.R.C. § 152(e)(1) (2011). In 2008, the U.S. Treasury Department finalized guidelines for determining which parent qualifies as the custodial parent. Treas. Reg. § 1.152-4(d) provides that, absent special circumstances, the "custodial parent is the parent with whom the child resides for the greater number of nights during the calendar year . . . . [A] child resides with a parent for a night if the child sleeps (i) at the residence of that parent (whether or not the parent is present); or (ii) in the company of the parent, when the child does not sleep at a parent's residence ([e.g.], the parent and child are on vacation together)." The regulations address certain special circumstances, such as when a parent works at night. Treas. Reg. § 1.152-4(d)(5). A child who resides with each parent for an equal number of nights during the calendar year and is in the custody of one or both parents for more than half the calendar year may be claimed as a dependent by the parent "with the higher adjusted gross income for the calendar year" and that parent will be "treated as the custodial parent." Treas. Reg. § 1.152-4(d)(4).

[535] I.R.C. § 152(e)(2) (2011). The written statement must be provided on I.R.S. Form 8332, "Release/Revocation of Release of Claim to Exemption for Child by Custodial Parent." Prior to tax year 2009, the noncustodial parent could simply attach the divorce or separation agreement instead of Form 8332. As of tax year 2009, the I.R.S. will accept only Form 8332 as the waiver.

[536] I.R.C. § 152(e)(3)(A) (2011).

[537] *See State ex rel. Pathammavong v. Pathammavong*, 679 N.W.2d 749 (Neb. 2004); *Bojarski v. Bojarski*, 41 A.3d 544 (Me. 2012); *Fenner v. Fenner*, 599 So. 2d 1343 (Fla. Dist. Ct. App. 1992); *Singer v. Dickinson*, 588 N.E.2d 806 (Ohio 1992). *See generally* David J. Benson, *The Power of State Courts to Award the Federal Dependency Exemption Upon Divorce*, 16 U. Dayton L. Rev. 29 (1990); Joseph L.

that option.[538]

A parent may also be entitled to a child care credit for certain employment-related child care expenses for a qualified child who is under the age of 15 or is incapable of self-care, regardless of allocation of the dependency exemption.[539] Furthermore, both parents can treat a child as a dependent for purposes of deducting medical expenses as long as the parents have actually paid the medical expense and meet certain other criteria.

[D] Deductibility of Legal Fees

In general, attorney fees incurred in a divorce or divorce related actions are not deductible expenses. Personal living expenses and family expenses are not deductible,[540] while expenses incurred for producing income or managing, preserving, or maintaining property for the production of income are deductible.[541] The deductibility of attorney fees in a divorce case depends upon which category the fees are allocated to, and claims for alimony and property may overlap both categories. In *United States v. Gilmore*, the United States Supreme Court held that assignment of attorney fees to either of these categories depends on whether the fees "arise[] in connection with the taxpayer's profit-seeking activities," rather than the effect on the party's property.[542] If the nature of the claim or defense arises from the marital relationship, not from income producing activity, the fee is non-deductible.[543] However, fees for advice regarding the tax implications of divorce have been held to be deductible if they are segregated from the rest of the divorce services rendered by the attorney.[544]

[E] Other Divorce Related Taxation Issues

[1] Transfer of Property

Before 1984, the transfer of appreciated property from one spouse to the other pursuant to a divorce settlement could trigger recognition of the built-in gain on the property for tax purposes. Under *United States v. Davis*,[545] a transfer made as part of a property division was treated as a taxable event, on the theory that the transaction amounted to a sale of the asset in exchange for the release of the transferee's marital claims. The transferor was required to pay tax on the difference between the tax basis of the asset and its fair market value. The recipient received

---

Landenwich, *Divorce and Amended Section 152(e) of the Internal Revenue Code: Do State Courts Have the Power to Allocate Dependency Exemptions?*, 29 J. Fam. L. 901 (1990-91).

[538] *See Varga v. Varga*, 434 N.W.2d 152 (Mich. Ct. App. 1988); *Echele v. Echele*, 782 S.W.2d 430 (Mo. Ct. App. 1989).

[539] I.R.C. § 21 (2011).

[540] I.R.C. § 262(a) (2011).

[541] I.R.C. § 212(1), (2) (2011).

[542] 372 U.S. 39, 48 (1963).

[543] *See* Clark, *supra* note 12, at 704-05.

[544] *See Munn v. United States*, 455 F.2d 1028 (Ct. Cl. 1972); Rev. Rul. 72-545, 1972-2 C.B. 179.

[545] 370 U.S. 65 (1962).

a basis measured by the fair market value of the property at the time of transfer, but was not required to include its value as income. One commentator has noted:

> While the *Davis* decision made theoretical tax sense, it made no practical sense. It frequently imposed a heavy tax burden at the worst possible time — when a couple's finances were in disarray and every available dollar was needed to finance the transition from one household into two. The taxable transfer was essentially involuntary because it was compelled by marital property law. Finally, the transfer produced no cash with which to pay the tax.[546]

However, equal divisions of community property were not treated as taxable, and courts and legislatures in non-community property jurisdictions soon began to adopt measures to effectuate the same result in those states. The result was "[a] deplorable state of confusion and complexity" in both types of jurisdictions, often catching divorcing parties and their lawyers unaware.[547]

Current IRC section 1041 was enacted in 1984 to provide that property transfers between spouses during marriage or between spouses or former spouses incident to divorce are nontaxable transactions. Therefore, the transferor incurs no gain or loss and the transferee maintains the previous or "carryover" basis, without including the value as income.[548] To qualify, the transfer must occur within one year after the marriage ends or must be "related to the cessation of the marriage,"[549] which Treasury Regulations have defined as occurring pursuant to a divorce or separation instrument within six years after the marriage ends.[550] Certain transfers to third parties on behalf of a spouse may also qualify for such treatment.[551] If the property has appreciated, the recipient spouse will be taxed on the gain upon making a taxable disposition, such as a sale, of the asset. Therefore, an attorney must also be attentive to the future tax consequences of property transferred between spouses incident to divorce, as those future tax consequences affect the present value of the property.[552]

---

[546] Michael Asimow, *The Assault on Tax-Free Divorce: Carryover Basis and Assignment of Income*, 44 Tax L. Rev. 65, 67 (1988).

[547] *Id.* at 68.

[548] I.R.C. § 1041 (2011). The general rule does not apply where the transferor is a nonresident alien. I.R.C. § 1041(d) (2011).

[549] I.R.C. § 1041(c)(2) (2011).

[550] T.D. 7973, 1984-2, C.B. 170.

[551] Treas. Reg. § 1.1041-1T(c), A-9 (2011).

[552] So, for example, if transferor spouse owns stock worth 100x with a basis of 10x, and stock worth 100x with a basis of 90x, those stocks are not of equal value to the transferee spouse. All other things being equal, the transferee spouse would prefer to take the high-basis stock because upon sale there will be a lower resulting tax liability. *See generally* Roland Hjorth, *The Effect of Federal Tax Consequences on Amount of Property Allocated to Spouses In State Court Dissolution Proceedings*, 24 Fam. L.Q. 247 (1990).

[2]   Head of Household Status

A divorced or separated parent who has custody of a child usually will be entitled to the status of "Head of Household," which permits that party to be taxed at a lower filing rate.[553] The parent may be entitled to head of household status regardless of the allocation of the dependency exemption. To qualify, the parent must pay more than half of the cost of maintaining a household for himself or herself and a child or a specified other dependent. When the parents have more than one child and each parent has custody of at least one child, both parents may qualify for head of household status.[554]

An abandoned spouse may also claim head of household status without divorce. That spouse must file a separate return, the abandoning spouse may not have resided in the same household for the last six months of the year, and the household must have been the primary residence of a dependent child.[555] Head of household status is also available if the residence is the principal home for a dependent married child[556] or the taxpayer's parent.[557]

[3]   Joint Returns

Marital status is determined on the last day of the year for purposes of eligibility for filing joint income tax returns.[558] Divorce or legal separation, but not informal separation, terminates the taxpayer's ability to file joint returns.

Joint filers are jointly and severally liable for the tax.[559] To alleviate the hardship that joint and several liability may impose when one spouse was unaware of the other's significant understatement of tax liability, Congress created and later expanded provisions for "innocent spouse relief."[560] An individual who is granted relief under these provisions will be relieved of liability for any deficiency or unpaid tax, including any accompanying penalties and interest.[561]

---

[553] *See* I.R.C. § 1(b) (2011). For example, a taxpayer filing as head of household is subject to the 15% income tax rate for the first $29,600 of income, whereas a taxpayer filing as an unmarried individual would receive the 15% rate for only the first $22,100 of income.

[554] I.R.C. § 2(b) (2011).

[555] *See* I.R.C. §§ 2(c), 7703(b) (2011).

[556] I.R.C. § 2(b)(1)(A)(i) (2011).

[557] I.R.C. § 2(b)(i)(B) (2011).

[558] I.R.C. § 6013(d)(1)(A) (2011).

[559] I.R.C. § 6013(d)(3)(2011).

[560] I.R.C. § 6015 (2011).

[561] *See, e.g.*, *Bozick v. C.I.R.*, 99 T.C.M. (CCH) 1242, *12 (2010) (spouse entitled to innocent spouse relief for deficiencies which her husband failed to pay before his death when spouse had signed a joint return only after "having been browbeaten into doing so by her husband and after having filed a separate return"); *see also* Drumbl, *supra* note 495; Richard C.E. Beck, *The Failure of Innocent Spouse Reform*, 51 N.Y.L. Sch. L. Rev. 929 (2006/2007); Lily Kahng, *Innocent Spouses: A Critique of the New Tax Laws Governing Joint and Several Tax Liability*, 49 Vill. L. Rev. 261 (2004); Svetlana G. Attestatova, Comment, *The Bonds of Joint Tax Liability Should Not Be Stronger Than Marriage: Congressional Intent Behind Section 6015(c) Separation of Liability Relief*, 78 Wash. L. Rev. 831 (2003).

[4]   The Family Home

In 1997, the Taxpayer Relief Act made important changes in taxation of gain on the sale of family homes, perhaps most importantly by providing for a tax-free sale of most families' homes.[562] After May 7, 1997, gain on the sale of a family home is taxable only to the extent that gain exceeds $250,000 for an individual[563] or $500,000[564] for a couple if the home is sold in a year during which the couple files a joint tax return. Qualifying homes must have been the couple's principal residence for two of the preceding five years.[565] The act also applies when one spouse is granted the exclusive use of the house following a divorce. When the house is later sold and the proceeds divided, the spouse who did not have possession will be treated as having possession for purposes of the exclusion.[566] This exclusion may be used every two years.[567]

[5]   Retirement Plans

When a pension benefit is assigned to a spouse following a divorce pursuant to a Qualified Domestic Relations Order, the payee is taxed in the same manner as the original participant would have been, and no additional tax liability is incurred because of the assignment.[568] Annuities are taxed at the time of distribution, and only to the extent they were not previously taxed.[569] Similarly, lump-sum payments of original non-deductible contributions are not taxed, and special rules avoid some of the harsh tax consequences of a single-year payment on a lump-sum distribution.[570] Alternatively, lump-sum payments can be rolled over into an Individual Retirement Account (IRA) or another qualified tax deferred retirement plan.[571]

[6]   Stock Transfers and Redemptions

The transfer of stocks and bonds incident to divorce does not trigger tax consequences, and capital gains tax will not be incurred until the time that the recipient sells the stock.[572] The original basis of the stock carries over. The rule applies to transfers of stock in closely held corporations as well as publicly traded stock.

When a family business is awarded to the proprietor spouse, an offsetting award to the other spouse upon divorce is not taxable, regardless of whether it is paid in

---

[562] I.R.C. § 121 (2011).

[563] I.R.C. § 121 (b)(1) (2011).

[564] I.R.C. § 121(b)(2) (2011).

[565] I.R.C. § 121(b)(2)(A)(ii) (2011).

[566] I.R.C. § 121(d)(3)(B) (2011).

[567] I.R.C. § 121(b)(3)(A) (2011).

[568] *See* Marjorie A. O'Connell, *Taxation of Employee Benefits: Qualified and Nonqualified Retirement Plans and Deferred Compensation Arrangements*, 30 Fam. L.Q. 91 (1996).

[569] *See* I.R.C. § 72 (2011).

[570] *See* I.R.C. § 402(e)(1)(B) (2011).

[571] *See* I.R.C. § 402(c)(1) (2011).

[572] *See* I.R.C. § 1041(a)(2) (2011).

the form of other assets or a note. If the business is a closely held corporation, the matter may be complicated if a buyout is accomplished with corporate funds, called a stock redemption. Courts continue to differ regarding the tax consequences of a stock redemption, because the transfer of shares is to the corporation, and is not a transaction between the spouses. Courts often apply substance over form in determining the application of IRC section 1041.[573]

[7] Federal Estate and Gift Taxes

Gift taxes are not imposed on transfers made in connection with divorce actions if the transfer is ordered in the divorce decree, is made according to the terms of a property settlement agreement, or provides child support.[574] The transfer must be made within a period two years prior to or one year after the divorce.[575]

Similar provisions effectuate the same result for estate tax purposes. An obligation of a deceased spouse to transfer property to a former spouse shall be treated as a deductible obligation of the deceased spouse's estate, if the transfer is made in settlement of the transferee's marital or property rights pursuant to a divorce decree or separation agreement.[576]

§ 9.08 BANKRUPTCY

Shared income, while sufficient to maintain a single household, may be woefully inadequate to support the two households resulting from divorce. Divorce expenses may further burden, and even cripple, one or both of the former spouses, leading to the not uncommon filing of bankruptcy shortly after a divorce. Bankruptcy may affect the post-divorce financial obligations between former spouses.[577]

---

[573] *See* I.R.C. § 1041(2011). In *Arnes v. United States*, 981 F.2d 456 (1992)]*Arnes I*], the United States Court of Appeals for the Ninth Circuit held that such a transfer of shares to the corporation amounted to a transfer to the proprietor spouse, triggering the non-recognition provision of IRC section 1041 (which does not recognize gain on the transfer of property to a spouse incident to divorce). Thus, Section 1041 operated to exempt the transfer from tax consequences to the transferor spouse. The key to the court's analysis was the husband's personal obligation to purchase the stock under the divorce instrument. Therefore, the transaction did not constitute a recognizable gain to the non-proprietor spouse. While under this theory, the proceeds paid by the corporation to the transferor spouse arguably should have constituted a constructive dividend to the proprietor spouse, the Tax Court in *Arnes v. Commissioner*, 102 T.C. 522 (1994) [*Arnes II*], determined that the proprietor spouse did not receive any dividend in the transaction. *See* Paul J. Buser & Thomas R. White, *Stock Redemptions In Marital Separation Agreements: Unsteady Steps for the Unprepared*, 30 Fam. L.Q. 41 (1996).

[574] I.R.C. § 2516 (2011).

[575] *Id.*

[576] I.R.C. §§ 2043(b)(2), 2053(e), 2516 (2011).

[577] *See generally* Margaret Howard, Cases and Materials on Bankruptcy (5th ed. 2011); Lynne F. Riley & Maria C. Furlong, *Intersection of Divorce and Bankruptcy: BAPCPA [Bankruptcy Abuse and Prevention Act] and Other Developments*, 2010 Ann. Surv. of Bankr. Law 15 (2010); David C. Hoskins & Ellen R. Weiner, *Bankruptcy and Divorce: What Divorce Counsel Should Know about Bankruptcy*, 37 Colo. Law. 35 (2008).

A primary, underlying objective of bankruptcy law is to give an honest "but unfortunate" debtor a "fresh start."[578] The United States Supreme Court has described the fresh start as "a new opportunity in life . . . unhampered by the pressure and discouragement of pre-existing debt."[579] Accordingly, one of the most important features of bankruptcy law is to grant the debtor a discharge of most pre-bankruptcy debts, releasing the debtor from continued liability on those debts and preventing creditors from attempting to collect against them personally.[580] However, not all debts are subject to discharge; countervailing policies, deemed superior to the "fresh start" policy, demand that debtors remain liable for certain debts even after bankruptcy.[581] Protecting a debtor's present or former family members has long been regarded as one of those overriding policy-based exceptions from discharge.[582] As one leading authority has pointed out, "[t]aken together, these provisions make support claimants the most favored creditors in bankruptcy."[583]

[A]   Support Obligations

Until 1994, bankruptcy law protected only support debts from the obligor's bankruptcy. The exception from discharge for family support debts originally was formulated by the United States Supreme Court in a trilogy of cases at the beginning of this century,[584] Congress codified the exception in 1903, and the text of the support exception remained essentially unchanged until the enactment of the current Bankruptcy Code in 1978.[585]

The current Bankruptcy Code prevents discharge of debts owed "for a domestic support obligation."[586] In addition, the Bankruptcy Code prevents discharge of other family-related obligations (primarily obligations to divide property)[587] owed

> to a spouse, former spouse, or child of the debtor and not of the kind described in paragraph (5) [for a domestic support obligation] . . . that is incurred by the debtor in the course of a divorce or separation or in connection with a separation agreement, divorce decree or other order of a

---

[578] *See Local Loan Co. v. Hunt*, 292 U.S. 234, 244 (1934).

[579] *Id.*

[580] 11 U.S.C. § 524(a) (2011).

[581] 11 U.S.C. § 523(a) (2011) (exceptions from discharge in Chapter 7 cases); 11 U.S.C. § 1141(d)(2) (2011) (exceptions from discharge in Chapter 11 cases, cross-referencing and incorporating by reference § 523 for individual debtors); 11 U.S.C. § 1328 (2011) (exceptions from discharge in Chapter 13 cases). *See also* 11 U.S.C. § 522(c)(1) (2011) (allowing enforcement against debtor's exempt property for support obligations covered by § 523(a)(5) (2011)).

[582] *See generally* Charles Jordan Tabb, The Law of Bankruptcy (2d ed. 2009).

[583] Howard, *supra* note 577, at 690.

[584] *Wetmore v. Markoe*, 196 U.S. 68 (1904); *Dunbar v. Dunbar*, 190 U.S. 340 (1903); *Audubon v. Scufeldt*, 181 U.S. 575 (1901).

[585] Bankruptcy Act, ch. 487, 32 Stat. 797, 798 (1903). Section 17a(2) (later § 17a(7)) excepted from discharge those debts "for alimony due or to become due, or for maintenance or support of wife or child."

[586] 11 U.S.C. § 523(a)(5) (2011). A "domestic support obligation" is defined in 11 U.S.C. § 101(14A) (2011).

[587] Howard, *supra* note 577, at 688.

court of record, or a determination made in accordance with State or territorial law by a governmental unit.[588]

Thus, the debtor's obligation to pay spousal and child support, whether accrued arrearages or future payments, will not be discharged by the bankruptcy, although the obligation may be stayed during the proceeding's pendency.[589] Certain property related debts are also nondischargeable. Prior to the enactment of 11 U.S.C. section 523(a)(15) in 1994, debts that were classified as property division rather than support were discharged and extinguished, except to the usually insignificant extent they were paid off in the bankruptcy action.[590]

Determining the proper classification of a debt as either a support obligation or a property division for bankruptcy purposes was once a difficult process that generated substantial litigation.[591] Now, however, this determination is "less critical" since the 2005 amendment of 11 U.S.C. section 523(a)(15) removed previously extant affirmative defenses and made "all property settlements arising out of separation or divorce nondischargeable."[592]

Whether a debt is one for support under Section 523(a)(5) or represents a property settlement under Section 523 (a)(15) remains relevant to its treatment upon bankruptcy because Section 523(a)(5)debts are not discharged in Chapter 13 proceedings and may be enforced against exempt property, whereas Section 523(a)(15) debts enjoy neither benefit.[593] While courts may refer to state law or private agreements in determining the proper classification of a debt, ultimately federal bankruptcy law, which focuses upon the underlying nature of the debt,

---

[588] 11 U.S.C. § 523(a)(15) (2011).

[589] As Professor Howard notes, 11 U.S.C. § 523(a)(5) and (a)(15) work "in tandem" with a number of related code provisions to address stays and issues of exemption and priority:

[Section] 362(b)(2), excepting from the automatic stay actions to establish paternity, to obtain or modify a support order, or to collect spousal or child support from non-state property; § 507(a)(1), providing first priority for domestic support obligations; § 522(c), making exempt property liable for nondischargeable support obligations; § 522(f)(1)(A), barring avoidance of judicial liens that secure domestic support obligations; and § 547(c)(7), excepting payments for domestic support obligations from preference avoidance.

[In addition,] debtors must be current on domestic support obligations in order to confirm any reorganization plan, §§ 1129(a)(14), 1225(a)(7), [and] 1325(a)(8), or to receive a discharge in Chapters 12 or 13, §§ 1225(a) [and] 1328(a); information about pending bankruptcy cases must be sent to support claimants, as well as to state child support agencies, §§ 704(a)(10), 1106(a)(8), 1202(b)(6), [and] 1302(b)(6); and a debtor's failure to pay postpetition support obligations may constitute cause for conversion or dismissal of a case under Chapters 11, 12 and 13, §§ 1112(b)(4)(P), 1208(c)(10) [and] 1307(c)(11).

Howard, *supra* note 577, at 689-90.

[590] *See* Tabb, *supra* note 582, at § 10.20, pp. 990-92 (noting that the 1994 amendments made both property settlement debts and "hold harmless" agreements nondischargeable; under a "hold harmless" arrangement, the debtor spouse agrees to pay certain marital debts and to hold the non-debtor spouse harmless from those debts); *see also* Douglas G. Baird, The Elements of Bankruptcy 18-19 (2006).

[591] For an historical examination of the significance of such determinations, see Tabb, *supra* note 582, at 991. *See also* Sheryl L. Scheible, *Defining "Support" Under Bankruptcy Law: Revitalization of the "Necessaries" Doctrine*, 41 Vand. L. Rev. 1 (1988).

[592] *See* Tabb, *supra* note 582, at 991.

[593] *Id.*

controls the issue of dischargeability.[594] Bankruptcy courts "borrow heavily from state domestic relations law" when categorizing a debt for bankruptcy purposes.[595] The bankruptcy court is often guided by "a long laundry list of factors" generally considered relevant by state courts in determining whether to grant support.[596] Those factors include, but are not limited to

> the nature of the obligations assumed (provision of daily necessities indicates support); the structure and language of the parties' agreement or the court's decree; whether other lump sum or periodic payments were also provided; length of the marriage; the existence of children from the marriage; relative earning powers of the parties; age, health and work skills of the parties; the adequacy of support absent the debt assumption; and evidence of negotiation or other understandings as to the intended purpose of the assumption.[597]

Bankruptcy courts generally concur that some version of an "intent" test should be used to determine the nature of a marital debt.[598] Although the exact formulation of the intent test is not uniform, the analysis requires the bankruptcy court to discern whether the parties themselves, in a negotiated settlement agreement, or the divorce court, in a litigated case, intended the debt to constitute support.[599] Intent, however, is frequently ambiguous and disputed, so the bankruptcy courts commonly balance the recipient spouse's needs against the supporting spouse's ability to pay. The reasonableness of the payments is measured by the marital standard of living and the spouses' circumstances at the time of the divorce. Thus, if a debt *functioned* as support, the bankruptcy courts generally conclude that the requisite intention was present.[600] Because support is based on relative need, every disputed case will require an individualized investigation.

Debts that are labeled property division or were created pursuant to a property division may still be categorized as support obligations covered by Section 523(a)(5).[601] Conversely, the fact that an obligation was labeled a support obligation

---

[594] *See Bieluch v. Cook*, 216 F.3d 1071 (2d Cir. 2000); *Long v. West (In re Long)*, 794 F.2d 928 (4th Cir. 1986); *Shaver v. Shaver*, 736 F.2d 1314, 1316 (9th Cir. 1984).

[595] Tabb, *supra* note 582, at 992. *See, e.g., Harrell v. Sharp (In re Harrell)*, 754 F.2d 902 (11th Cir. 1985); *Pauley v. Spong (In re Spong)*, 661 F.2d 6 (2d Cir. 1981); *Yeates v. Yeates (In re Yeates)*, 44 B.R. 575 (Bankr. D. Utah 1984), *aff'd*, 807 F.2d 874 (10th Cir. 1986).

[596] Tabb, *supra* note 582. *See Long v. Calhoun (In re Calhoun)*, 715 F.2d 1103, 1107-08 (6th Cir. 1983).

[597] *Long v. Calhoun*, 715 F.2d at 1108, n.7. *See also Goin v. Rives (In re Goin)*, 808 F.2d 1391 (10th Cir. 1987).

[598] *See, e.g., Yeates v. Yeates (In re Yeates)*, 807 F.2d 874, 878 (10th Cir. 1986); *Smith v. Smith (In re Smith)*, 131 B.R. 959 (Bankr. E.D. Mich. 1991).

[599] *See, e.g., Marker v. Marker (In re Marker)*, 139 B.R. 615 (Bankr. W.D. Pa. 1992); *In re Brody*, 3 F.3d 35, 38 (2nd Cir. 1993) ("All evidence, direct or circumstantial, which tends to illuminate the parties' subjective intent is relevant").

[600] *See, e.g., Daulton v. Daulton (In re Daulton)*, 139 B.R. 708 (Bankr. C.D. Ill. 1992); *In re Sampson*, 997 F.2d 717, 726 (10th Cir. 1993) (because debtor's obligation "effectively function[ed] as the former spouse's source of income at the time of the divorce, it [was], in substance, a support obligation").

[601] *See, e.g., Singer v. Singer (In re Singer)*, 787 F.2d 1033 (6th Cir. 1986). Courts generally will look behind the labels to determine the true nature of a debt. In *In re Singer*, the court concluded that a debtor's agreement to pay his former wife $800 a month for five years, then $400 a month for the next

would not necessarily prevent it from being treated as a property division covered by Section 523(a)(15).[602] While "the label placed on the debt by the parties themselves or by the state court is not controlling," some courts place considerable importance upon clear and unambiguous language.[603]

To count as a nondischargeable support obligation under Section 523(a)(5), the debt must be "established or subject to establishment" through "(i) a separation agreement, divorce decree, or property settlement agreement; (ii) an order of a court of record; or (iii) a determination made in accordance with applicable nonbankruptcy law by a governmental unit."[604] Thus, contractual agreements to pay post-majority child support have been found to constitute nondischargeable support despite the absence of a state law duty to provide such support.[605] However, the limitation to property settlement agreements, divorce decrees, and court or government orders means that debts owed to persons who were never validly married to the debtor, such as debts owed under "palimony" agreements or to putative spouses, are dischargeable.[606] Likewise, "common law support obligations not embodied in one of the cited vehicles, as well as other contractual debts for necessaries and the like not part of an actual separation or property settlement agreement," are dischargeable.[607]

Domestic support obligations also cover debts owed to someone other than a spouse, former spouse, child of the debtor (or the child's parent, legal guardian, or responsible relative), or governmental unit.[608] Frequently, the debtor will have agreed to or been ordered to make payments to a third party. These cases raise a preliminary question of whether a debt owed to a third party, or to a party to whom such a debt has been voluntarily assigned for purposes of collection, may still be

---

five years was support, despite the fact that the parties' separation agreement labeled the payments a release of property rights. Even in situations in which alimony would not have been authorized under state law, the payments may be considered "in the nature of alimony, maintenance, or support" for bankruptcy purposes. 11 U.S.C. § 101(14A)(B). *See also Benich v. Benich (In re Benich)*, 811 F.2d 943 (5th Cir. 1987); *Balvich v. Balvich (In re Balvich)*, 135 B.R. 323 (Bankr. N.D. Ind. 1991).

[602] *See, e.g., Roberts v. Poole*, 80 B.R. 81 (Bankr. N.D. Tex. 1987).

[603] Tabb, *supra* note 582, at 992. *See, e.g., Long v. West (In re Long)*, 794 F.2d 928 (4th Cir. 1986) (holding that when an debt is designated alimony, although the label is not controlling, that designation is a significant factor in classifying a litigated award).

[604] 11 U.S.C. § 101(14A)(C) (2011).

[605] *See Harrell v. Sharp (In re Harrell)*, 754 F.2d 902 (11th Cir. 1985) (debtor's obligation, under separation agreement, to pay son's educational expenses through college and graduate school was nondischargeable); *Boyle v. Donovan*, 724 F.2d 681 (8th Cir. 1984) (debtor's agreement, in a property settlement agreement incorporated into divorce decree, to pay for son's college education was a nondischargeable support obligation rather than a dischargeable property settlement).

[606] *See Niermeyer v. Doyle, (In re Doyle)*, 70 B.R. 106 (Bankr. 9th Cir. 1986) (nonmarital relationship between creditor and debtor is not the type of family arrangement creating family duties entitled to protection under the Bankruptcy Code); *see also In re Magee*, 111 B.R. 359 (M.D. Fla. 1990) (debt for support of debtor's illegitimate children not dischargeable, despite fact that mother was not debtor's former spouse because discharge would frustrate congressional intent that debtor should not be able to avoid child support obligations); Madison Grose, *Putative Spousal Support Rights and the Federal Bankruptcy Act*, 25 UCLA L. Rev. 96 (1977).

[607] Tabb, *supra* note 582, at 992.

[608] 11 U.S.C. § 101(14A)(D) (2011).

excepted from discharge under Section 523(a)(5).[609]

Section 523(a)(5) has been narrowly interpreted to mean that it is not necessary that the former spouse directly receive payment from the debtor; rather, the debtor's obligations to pay third parties for the benefit of a dependent may constitute nondischargeable support.[610] Some bankruptcy cases have also concluded that the provision does not apply when an assignment was made solely for the purpose of collection.[611]

Obligations to make specified future payments to third parties for the direct benefit of the former spouse or children, such as medical, educational, and insurance expenses, or payment of specified living costs, such as rent, mortgage payments, and utility bills, are usually analyzed in the same manner as debts payable directly to the spouse. In this context, courts generally disregard the fact that the actual recipient of the payments does not fall within the statutory definition of a dependent.[612] In *In re Osterberg*,[613] the court concluded that the former husband's assumption of marital debts was essential to the wife's economic security and was nondischargeable maintenance and support.

Court orders and separation agreements also frequently obligate a divorcing person to pay a dependent spouse's divorce-related expenses. When determining the dischargeability of an obligation to pay attorney's fees, bankruptcy courts often apply the same criteria used to classify direct support obligations.[614] Because state courts generally award attorney's fees on the basis of the spouse's need, bankruptcy courts consider these fees sufficiently related to support to escape discharge if "there is a significant disparity in earning power between the debtor and nondebtor former spouse and . . . the nondebtor former spouse will not have sufficient funds to meet her monthly expenses if the legal fees debt is discharged and the nondebtor former spouse is required to pay the entire amount of such fees."[615] Similarly, courts have found attorney's fees for drafting documents in pre-divorce support actions, for post-divorce enforcement of decrees, or for defending modification actions to be nondischargeable.[616]

---

[609] *See* 11 U.S.C. § 101(14A)(A), (D) (2011).

[610] *See, e.g., Edwards v. Edwards (In re Edwards)*, 31 B.R. 113 (Bankr. N.D. Ga. 1983).

[611] *See Brodsky v. Daumit (In re Daumit)*, 25 B.R. 371 (Bankr. D. Md. 1982). *But see Crawford v. Crawford (In re Crawford)*, 8 B.R. 552 (Bankr. D. Kan. 1981) (court-ordered attorney's fees payable to wife, otherwise classified as support, dischargeable when assigned to attorney).

[612] *See Williams v. Holt (In re Holt)*, 40 B.R. 1009 (Bankr. S.D. Ga. 1984).

[613] 109 B.R. 938 (Bankr. D.N.D. 1990).

[614] *See generally* Diane M. Allen, *Debts for Alimony, Maintenance, and Support as Exceptions to Bankruptcy Discharge*, 69 A.L.R. Fed. 403, § 6 (2011). *See also Pauley v. Spong (In re Spong)*, 661 F.2d 6 (2d Cir. 1981); *Bodrey v. Bodrey (In re Bodrey)*, 31 B.R. 589 (Bankr. M.D. Tenn. 1983).

[615] *In re Butler*, 308 B.R. 1, 23 (Bankr. S.D. N.Y. 2004) (citations omitted). *See also Senkel v. Fahland (In re Fahland)*, 110 B.R. 431 (Bankr. E.D. Mo. 1990) (payment need not be directly payable to ex-spouse in order to qualify as nondischargeable).

[616] *See, e.g., In re Butler*, 308 B.R. 1 (Bankr. S.D. N.Y. 2004) (obligation to pay attorney's fees awarded in divorce decree does not escape discharge if it is only tangentially related to an award for maintenance and support; such an obligation is a nondischargeable support award if it reflects a balancing of the debtor's and the non-debtor's financial needs); *In re Palomino*, 355 B.R. 349 (Bankr. S.D. Fla. 2006)

Many of the same courts that refuse discharge of attorney's fees take a much narrower view of other divorce-related debts. For example, bankruptcy courts have allowed discharge of certain marital debts comprising medical expenses and collection agency bills where the debtor's ex-spouse failed to show that the debtor's obligation under the divorce decree to pay the expenses was "support," rather than a desire to equalize the distribution of the marital estate, since a larger portion of the marital assets had also been awarded to the debtor.[617] Courts have justified discharge in such cases by classifying the debt as one owed to a party other than a dependent. Other courts have considered the substance of the debt and its relationship to support without regard to the identity of the payee.[618]

Difficult practical problems arise when a spouse has agreed to, or was ordered to, assume sole responsibility for a debt incurred jointly by the spouses during marriage.[619] Both former spouses have a continuing legal obligation to the joint creditor irrespective of an agreement made at the time of divorce; the assumption of the debt by one spouse is a secondary agreement that does not alter the underlying joint obligation to the third party creditor. Absent the creditor's release of the non-debtor spouse, the assumption by the debtor merely indemnifies the spouse.[620] Thus, two debts are involved in the bankruptcy action: the debt owed directly to the third-party creditor, which is likely to be discharged to the extent it is unsecured; and the debt owed to the former spouse, which may receive differential treatment depending on whether it is classified as a support or a property division debt.[621]

Even before the 1994 amendments making hold harmless agreements nondischargeable,[622] courts had little difficulty concluding that the debtor may not be relieved of continuing liability to the spouse for an assumption simply because the underlying debt is owed to a third party when an express "hold-harmless" or indemnity clause is present.[623] The courts have differed, however, when the debt assumption fails to provide an indemnity clause. While many cases simply have held that an assumption itself implies an agreement to indemnify the former spouse for

---

(finding debtor's obligation to pay attorney's fees incurred by ex-wife to be a nondischargeable support obligation, where the obligation was assumed in connection with the parties' settlement agreement about child support and orders arising from the debtor's failure to meet court-ordered obligations for child support).

[617] *See In re Kimball*, 253 B.R. 920, 926 (Bankr. D. Idaho 2000); *see also Harrod v. Harrod (In re Harrod)*, 16 B.R. 711, 714 (Bankr. W.D. Ky. 1982) (psychologist's fees incurred in custody hearings and fees of accountants hired to evaluate spousal assets are dischargeable).

[618] *See e.g., In re Levin*, 306 B.R. 158 (Bankr. D. Md. 2004) (guardian ad litem fees for debtor's minor children treated as nondischargeable child support). *See, e.g., Peters v. Hennenhoeffer (In re Peters)*, 133 B.R. 291 (Bankr. S.D.N.Y. 1991) (guardian ad litem fee incurred in custody dispute nondischargeable).

[619] *See* Peter C. Alexander, *Building "A Doll's House": A Feminist Analysis of Marital Debt Dischargeability in Bankruptcy*, 48 Vill. L. Rev. 381 (2003).

[620] *See Williams v. Williams (In re Williams)*, 703 F.2d 1055, 1057 (8th Cir. 1983); *Stevens v. French (In re French)*, 19 B.R. 255 (Bankr. M.D. Fla. 1982); *Sledge v. Sledge (In re Sledge)*, 47 B.R. 349, 352 (Bankr. E.D. Va. 1981).

[621] *See supra* note 593 (and accompanying text).

[622] 11 U.S.C. § 523(a)(15) (2011).

[623] *Id.*

liability,[624] a number of courts refused to extend the exception further and have granted discharge in the absence of an express hold-harmless provision, regardless of the effect of the debt's discharge on the dependents.[625]

[B] Property Division Debts

The 1994 amendment to the Bankruptcy Code added Section 523(a)(115), making property division debts nondischargeable. In order to avoid discharge under Section 523(a)(15), a debt must arise out of a divorce related agreement or court order, and must not be a domestic support obligation.[626] As noted above, classification as a property debt may still matter in some instances.[627]

Section 523(a)(15) also strengthens the hold harmless clause in marital settlement agreements, as the clause may protect other previously dischargeable obligations.

[C] Marital Liens

Although the bulk of bankruptcy cases involving family law issues address the discharge of either support or property obligations, the two areas of law overlap in other ways as well.[628] Another controversial issue involves the effect of bankruptcy on liens securing debts originating in divorce.

The United States Supreme Court addressed the question of whether a debtor in a bankruptcy action may avoid a judicial lien imposed upon the debtor's exempt

---

[624] *See, e.g., Lewis v. Lewis (In re Lewis)*, 39 B.R. 842 (Bankr. W.D.N.Y. 1984); *Jensen v. Jensen (In re Jensen)*, 17 B.R. 537 (Bankr. W.D. Mo. 1982).

[625] *See, e.g., Lineberry v. Lineberry (In re Lineberry)*, 9 B.R. 700 (Bankr. W.D. Mo. 1981).

[626] Domestic support obligations are a separate exception covered by § 523(a)(5); for discussion of this, see *supra* § 9.08[A].

[627] Prior to further substantial revisions to Section 523 in 2005, property debts were nondischargeable unless the debtor did not have the ability to pay or the "benefit [of discharge] to the debtor . . . outweigh[ed] the detrimental consequences to the creditor, the former spouse, or child." 11 U.S.C. § 523(a)(15). The exceptions seemed to raise affirmative defenses to the nondischargeability, and courts were conflicted as to where the burden of proof for each element should be allocated. *See* Bernice B. Donald & Jennie D. Latta, *The Dischargeability of Property Settlement and Hold Harmless Agreements In Bankruptcy: An Overview of § 523(a)(15)*, 31 Fam. L.Q. 409, 420-21 (1997). In *In re Patterson*, 1997 U.S. App. LEXIS 33664 (6th Cir., Nov. 24, 1997), the Court of Appeals for the Sixth Circuit held that the bankruptcy court had not erred when it concluded that the debtor did not meet his burden of proving an inability to pay his debt to his former wife, despite his evidence that his expenditures and child support payments exceeded his income and that he had injured his hand, which restricted his work. The bankruptcy court had found the evidence regarding the injury unpersuasive, and found that the debtor currently had excess income and thus an ability to pay the court ordered debt. In analyzing the balancing of the detriments test, the court held that the debt should not be discharged if the debtor's standard of living would be greater than or approximately equal to the former spouse's if the debt is not discharged. Some courts responded to the balancing test necessary prior to 2005 under § 523(a)(15) by allowing a partial discharge of the debt. *See, e.g., In re Greenwalt*, 200 B.R. 909, 914 (Bankr. W.D. Wash. 1996); *In re Comisky*. 183 B.R. 883, 884 (Bankr. N.D. Cal. 1995). Other cases rejected this approach, because the code did not mention the potential for partial discharge. *See, e.g., In re Haines*, 210 B.R. 586, 592 (Bankr. S.D. Cal. 1997); *In re Florez*, 191 B.R. 112, 115 (Bankr. N.D. Ill. 1995).

[628] *See generally* Janet Chubb, *Divorce and Bankruptcy: A Dangerous Liaison*, 4 Am. J. of Fam. L. 339 (1990).

property to secure an obligation owed to a former spouse. In *Farrey v. Sanderfoot*,[629] husband and wife had owned the marital home as joint tenants in common, each possessing an undivided one-half interest in the property.[630] The divorce court awarded the husband full title to the home, while granting the wife a cash award of half the marital estate[631] and a lien upon the home to secure the payment of the award.

The husband then filed a voluntary Chapter 7 bankruptcy action in the months following the divorce. He claimed the home as exempt property and attempted to avoid the wife's lien by invoking section 522(f)(1), a code provision that allows the debtor to avoid the fixing of judicial liens that impair an exemption. The bankruptcy court denied his motion; however, the district court reversed and the Seventh Circuit affirmed.[632]

The Supreme Court in turn reversed, holding that in order to avoid lien fixing under section 522(f)(1), the debtor's intent in the contested property must pre-date the lien.[633] The Court found that the divorce decree extinguished the husband's prior interests in the home and replaced it with a new fee simple interest subject to the wife's lien.[634] The husband's interest could not have pre-dated the lien, and accordingly, the court denied his motion to avoid the fixing of the lien under section 522(f)(1).[635] The Court's decision implied that a debtor may at least partially avoid a judicial lien in cases where a divorce decree simply conveyed a property interest from one spouse to another. Congress attempted to remedy this problem by first distinguishing judicial liens for nondischargeable domestic support obligations from other voidable judicial liens,[636] and then excepting from discharge judicial liens that secured any domestic support obligations.[637] Thus, when a judicial lien is created concurrently with or prior to the debtor's obtaining an interest in the property on which the lien is imposed, the lien cannot be destroyed in the bankruptcy action.[638] Neither the 1994 nor the 2005 amendments contradict *Farrey* and thus timing remains critical, so practitioners must be mindful that judicial liens imposed as part of a divorce action still risk being avoided in bankruptcy if they attach to a pre-existing or concurrent property interest of the debtor.[639] The result

---

[629] 500 U.S. 291 (1991).

[630] *Id.* at 291.

[631] *Id.* at 293 (division reflected the Wisconsin statutory presumption of an equal division of the marital estate).

[632] *Id.* at 291.

[633] *Id.*

[634] *Id.* at 299. The Court further found that the divorce decree replaced the parties' preexisting interests with new interests, created simultaneously with the decree. *Id.* at 299-300.

[635] *Id.* at 301.

[636] 11 U.S.C. § 522(f)(1). *See* Tabb, *supra* note 582, at § 9.8, p. 922.

[637] 11 U.S.C. § 523(a)(5). *See* Tabb, *supra* note 582, at § 9.8, p. 922.

[638] *See generally* Phyllis A. Klein, Comment, *"A Fresh Start With Someone Else's Property": Lien Avoidance, The Homestead Exemption and Divorce Property Divisions Under Section 522(f)(1) of the Bankruptcy Code*, 59 Fordham L. Rev. 423 (1990).

[639] *See* Tabb, *supra* note 582, at § 9.8, p. 922.

may vary depending on the underlying state marital property law.[640]

[D]　Automatic Stay

The Bankruptcy Code's automatic stay provisions, which bar most debt collection actions and suspend law suits against the debtor during the bankruptcy action,[641] provide yet another potential conflict with family law. Actions establishing or modifying domestic support obligations, as well as paternity determination and other domestic relations actions, are excepted from the stay.[642] However, collection of domestic support obligations are only permitted to the extent that these support obligations are satisfied from assets that are not property of the bankruptcy estate.[643] Because this exception to the stay also turns on classifying certain obligations as support, if collection of support might violate the automatic stay, the recipient should seek relief from the stay in the bankruptcy court.[644]

[E]　Exempt Property

Bankruptcy law and family law may also intersect when the recipient of divorce-related payments files a bankruptcy. For instance, the right to receive alimony, support, or maintenance "reasonably necessary for the support of the debtor and any dependent of the debtor" is exempt and thus is not available for payment of the debtor's debts in the bankruptcy case.[645] In determining what constitutes "reasonable need," courts consider a number of factors, such as "the debtor's other

---

[640] *Compare In re Donovan*, 137 B.R. 547 (Bankr. S.D. Fla. 1992) (divorce attorney's lien attached prior to client's ex-wife's interest in marital home; not avoidable by debtor-wife), *with Parrish v. McVay (In re Parrish)*, 144 B.R. 349 (Bankr. W.D. Tex. 1992) (lien attaching to debtor's separate property; avoidable). *See generally* Tabb, *supra* note 582, at § 9.10, p. 931 ("While judicial liens do not attach to exempt property at all in many states, they do . . . in some jurisdictions. In those states, the lien attaches, but simply is not enforceable by foreclosure as long as the property retains its exempt character. In those states, then, there would be a judicial lien on exempt property that could be avoided under § 522(f)(1)(A).").

[641] 11 U.S.C. § 362(a) (2011). *See also Robbins v. Robbins (In re Robbins)*, 964 F.2d 342 (4th Cir. 1992) (stay lifted to allow equitable distribution to proceed in state court). *See generally* Henry J. Sommer, *The Automatic Stay Packs a Punch*, 14 Fam. Advoc. 50 (Winter 1992); Michaela M. White, *Spousal and Child Support Payment Provisions in Chapter 13 Plans*, 16 Cap. U. L. Rev. 369 (1987).

[642] 11 U.S.C. § 362(b)(2) (2011) (excepting the commencement or continuation of civil actions or proceedings to establish paternity, to establish or modify an order for domestic support obligations, concerning child custody or visitation, regarding domestic violence, or for the dissolution of a marriage so long as it does not determine the division of property that is property of the estate).

[643] 11 U.S.C. § 362(b)(2)(B) (2011). As Professor Tabb explains, while the "family debt creditor is stayed from collecting against property of the estate," she "is free to pursue the debtor's assets, which the debtor obtains either by exemption, abandonment, or from postpetition earnings." Tabb, *supra* note 582, at § 3.14, p. 286.

[644] 11 U.S.C. § 362(d)(1) (2011).

[645] 11. U.S.C. § 522(d)(10)(D) (2011). Because "states may 'opt out' of the federal exemptions and limit resident debtors to the state and non-bankruptcy federal exemptions [under § 522(b)(2)] . . . § 522(d) is in effect in only 16 states." Tabb, *supra* note 582, at § 9.3, p. 890. *See also* 11 U.S.C. § 522(c)(1) (2011) (allowing domestic support obligations to be enforced against obligor debtor's otherwise exempt property).

anticipated income, the debtor's projected expenses, [and] the debtor's age and health . . . . Courts focus on the basic needs and responsibilities of the debtor and the debtor's dependents, and do not attempt to maintain the debtor in the lifestyle to which they were accustomed."[646] Although the problems of classification of debts owed to a debtor by a former spouse could also arise in the exemption context, virtually no litigation has occurred on the right to exempt such payments.

Family law attorneys should be informed about bankruptcy law so they are able to structure divorce settlements that anticipate the possibility of later bankruptcy and to deal with the many family law issues that arise when, in fact, bankruptcy occurs. Pre-divorce bankruptcy planning may also be valuable when financial problems and marital problems coincide.[647]

---

[646] Tabb, *supra* note 582, at § 9.3, p. 895.

[647] *See* W. Jefferson Giles, III, *Till Debt Do Us Part: Prebankruptcy Planning for Your Divorce Client*, 14 Fam. Advoc. 23 (Winter 1992).

Chapter 10

EQUITABLE DISTRIBUTION OF PROPERTY

§ 10.01 INTRODUCTION

Prior to the widespread adoption of equitable distribution statutes throughout the United States, a spouse was entitled to receive the property held in his name upon dissolution of marriage. Simply stated, except for the small minority of states in which community property principles were in force, title to property was the controlling factor. A leading commentator has summarized the common law approach to property division upon marriage dissolution as follows:

> Under the common law no property rights arise during marriage by virtue of the marriage itself. Since the Married Women's Property Acts were enacted giving the wife control over her separate property, there has been a complete separation of assets. Only at death, through dower, curtesy and, more recently, statutory forced shares, does one spouse acquire any interest in the property of the other by operation of law . . . . At [the time of divorce] the common law recognized no property interests by virtue of the marriage alone. In the absence of a statute, the courts of many states . . . had no power to order transfers or divisions of property.[1]

Wirth v. Wirth[2] is frequently cited as a shocking illustration of the harshness and injustice of the common law approach to disposition of property acquired during the marriage through the joint efforts and mutual endeavors of the spouses. In *Wirth,* during twenty-two years of marriage the husband gave his earnings to the wife, who pooled them with her own to support the family, paid bills and made investments. In time, the husband started a savings program, telling the wife that it was for the two of them. During most of the marriage, the wife used her salary for household expenses and family support while the husband invested part of his earnings in his own name.

The court rejected the wife's claim, based on a constructive trust theory, to half ownership of the marital home, titled in the husband's name, and half of his life insurance. The court found that there was no promise or arrangement in the husband's stated intention to save for the two of them or in any of the parties' conduct thereafter during the marriage.

---

[1] Joan M. Krauskopf, *A Theory for "Just" Division of Marital Property in Missouri*, 41 Mo. L. Rev. 165, 167-68 (1976) (citations omitted).

[2] 326 N.Y.S.2d 308 (N.Y. App. Div. 1971).

§ 10.02   COMMUNITY PROPERTY ORIGINS

Equitable distribution of property in the United States is an outgrowth of the systems of community property introduced into the Western Hemisphere by Spanish and French settlers.[3] A leading treatise describes the theory that underlies community property as follows:

> Equality is the cardinal precept of the community property system. At the foundation of this system is the principle that all wealth acquired by the joint efforts of the husband and wife shall be common property; the theory of the law being that, with respect to marital property acquisitions, the marriage is a community of which each spouse is a member, equally contributing by his or her industry to its prosperity, and possessing an equal right to succeed to the property after its dissolution.[4]

A community property system has long existed in eight states: Arizona, California, Idaho, Louisiana, Nevada, New Mexico, Texas, and Washington. Under community property law, the property that a spouse owned at the time of the marriage, together with property acquired during marriage by gift or inheritance, remained that person's separate property.[5] Also, unless there was an agreement to the contrary between the spouses, all property acquired during the marriage was the property of both spouses, regardless of whose effort had led to its acquisition.[6] This system grew out of the principle that "upon their marriage, the husband and wife become partners in future business transactions with each devoting his or her own time and talent, as joint entrepreneurs, in furtherance of that enterprise."[7]

In 1983, the National Conference of Commissioners on Uniform State Laws approved the Uniform Marital Property Act (UMPA).[8] The UMPA adopts a partnership concept of marriage, based on the principle of shared ownership of property during the marriage. Professor William S. Reppy, Jr., a distinguished scholar who has written extensively on community property law, describes the UMPA as a community property act, albeit not a typical one.[9] Wisconsin, by enacting the UMPA with minor modifications[10] has joined the ranks of community property states.

---

[3] Norvie L. Lay, *Community Property: Its Origin and Importance to the Common Law Attorney*, 5 J. Fam. L. 51 (1965).

[4] William Q. DeFuniak & Michael J. Vaughn, Principles of Community Property 2-3 (1971).

[5] Lay, *supra* note 3, at 54-55.

[6] *Id.*

[7] *Id.*

[8] Unif. Marital Prop. Act §§ 1-26, 9A U.L.A. 110 (1998).

[9] William A. Reppy, *The Uniform Marital Property Act: Some Suggested Revisions for a Basically Sound Act*, 21 Hous. L. Rev. 679 (1984).

[10] Wis. Stat. Ann. §§ 766.001-.097.

§ 10.03 CHARACTERIZING PROPERTY FOR THE PURPOSE OF EQUITABLE DISTRIBUTION

In cases involving the equitable distribution of property upon dissolution of marriage, the courts face three basic tasks. First, they must undertake classification of assets, identifying those that are subject to distribution and those that will remain the separate property of each spouse. The second task is valuing those assets that are subject to distribution and, in some instances, those that will be assigned separately to one of the spouses. The third task is deciding on a distribution that will be equitable, just and fair.[11] In this section, we turn to the first of these subjects, characterization or classification.

The statutes of each state provide the rules for classifying property subject to distribution on dissolution of marriage. Equitable distribution statutes in a slim majority of states, and particularly those statutes most recently enacted, employ a dual property system for classification of assets. Dual property jurisdictions make a distinction between marital property, which is subject to distribution, and separate property, which is assigned to the spouse having title.[12]

[A] Dual Property Equitable Distribution Jurisdictions

In dual property states, marital property is generally defined to include all property acquired by either spouse (or party) subsequent to or during the marriage. Property acquired before the marriage is generally defined as separate property. There is, however, considerable variation in statutory language. A basic variation lies in the approach to the definition of marital property.

The first most common statutory approach defines marital property and then lists exceptions. The second defines marital property and then explicitly defines separate or nonmarital property. Although the precise wording is different in these two types of dual property statutes, the substance or effect is the same. That is, both types of statutes limit distribution to marital property, and the exceptions listed in the first group of statutes are generally equivalent to the definitions of nonmarital or separate property in the second group. Also, although dual property statutes explicitly limit distribution to marital property, in a few jurisdictions the courts under some circumstances have included property acquired in contemplation of marriage as eligible for distribution.[13]

---

[11] *See, e.g., Rothman v. Rothman*, 320 A.2d 496, 503 (N.J. 1974); *Lancellotti v. Lancellotti*, 481 A.2d 7, 10 (R.I. 1984).

[12] *See, e.g.*, Colo. Rev. Stat. § 14-10-113(2); 750 Ill. Comp. Stat. Ann. 5/503; Mo. Ann. Stat. § 452.330; N.Y. Dom. Rel. Law § 236 pt. B.

[13] The decisions suggest that when the parties acquire property shortly before their marriage with the intent that it be used as the family residence, the courts are willing to divide the property on the theory that it was acquired in contemplation of marriage. The courts in most cases appear to be reluctant, however, to so classify and distribute property acquired during premarital cohabitation; in such cases, the courts generally adopt a literal interpretation of the statutory definition of marital property. *See In re Marriage of Altman*, 530 P.2d 1012 (Colo. App. 1974) ("Where . . . a family residence is selected and acquired within a few days of the parties' marriage in contemplation of that marriage, and the equity accumulated therein results from contributions by both parties, . . . the court [may treat] the residence and all equity obtained therein as marital property."); *Stallings v. Stallings*, 393 N.E.2d 1065

Under either statutory approach in dual property jurisdictions, the most common categories of separate or nonmarital property are:

1. Property acquired by gift, bequest, devise, or descent;

2. Property acquired in exchange for separate property;

3. The increase in value (appreciation) of separate property;

4. Property excluded by a valid agreement between the parties;

5. Property acquired by a spouse after a decree of legal separation.

Whether a jurisdiction defines marital property and lists exceptions or contains a definition of marital property followed by explicit definitions of separate property, lawyers must carefully examine the applicable statute. Although most statutes include the items commonly listed as separate property, they are found in differing combinations with varying additions and omissions. The New York statute, for example, includes within the meaning of the term "separate property" compensation for personal injuries and excludes the increase in value of separate property attributable to the contributions or efforts of the other spouse.[14]

Some courts, in the absence of clear statutory guidance, have had to address the question of when property is no longer "acquired during the marriage." In *Ghia v. Ghia*,[15] the trial court dismissed the wife's application for post final judgment relief, in which she claimed that the husband's winning Massachusetts lottery prize of $120,000 was marital property. The Supreme Court of Rhode Island, noting that the husband had won the prize after an interlocutory judgment of divorce but prior to the final judgment determined that the lottery prize was marital property. The court's decision in *Ghia* is consistent with other cases in which, although the property was received after divorce, the right to receive it was acquired during the marriage.

(Ill. App. Ct. 1979) (real estate, purchased in contemplation of marriage with the intent that it would be the family home, was marital property); *see also In re Marriage of Ohrt*, 507 N.E.2d 160 (Ill. App. Ct. 1987). Other courts, however, have declined to classify property acquired by a spouse during premarital cohabitation as marital property, finding their conclusions to be compelled by the applicable equitable jurisdiction statute. *See, e.g., Grishman v. Grishman*, 407 A.2d 9 (Me. 1979) ("We cannot expand the definition the Legislature has provided to encompass property to which the husband took title before this couple were married."); *Id.* at 12; *Cummings v. Cummings*, 376 N.W.2d 726 (Minn. Ct. App. 1985); *Wilen v. Wilen*, 486 A.2d 775 (Md. Ct. Spec. App. 1985). The ALI *Principles of the Law of Family Dissolution* adopt a conventional dual property equitable distribution scheme, with one startling exception: the *Principles* provide that "Property acquired during a relationship between the spouses that immediately preceded their marriage, and which was a domestic partner relationship . . . is treated as if it were acquired during the marriage." *See* ALI *Principles of the Law of Family Dissolution* § 4.03(6) (2000). *See generally*, J. Thomas Oldham, *ALI Principles of Family Dissolution: Some Comments*, 1997 U. Ill. L. Rev. 801.

[14] N.Y. Dom. Rel. Law § 236(B)(d)(2), (3).

[15] 609 A.2d 945 (R.I. 1992).

[B] All Property Equitable Distribution Jurisdictions

A slim minority of equitable distribution states do not distinguish between marital property and separate property for purposes of property distribution upon dissolution of marriage. Although there are substantial variations in the language of the statutes in those jurisdictions, the result is essentially the same. The Montana statute is illustrative. It provides in broad terms that the court must "finally equitably apportion between the parties the property and assets belonging to either or both, however and whenever acquired and whether the title thereto is in the name of the husband or wife or both."[16] The Connecticut statute, framed in somewhat more economical language, achieves the same result by providing that the court "may assign to either the husband or wife all or any part of the estate of the other."[17] Despite the fact that all property in these jurisdictions is subject to division upon dissolution of marriage, the lawyer who represents either party in a divorce proceeding must be aware of the nature and origins of the property to which each party holds title, and must be familiar with the statutory factors the court must consider in making an equitable distribution. These circumstances may influence the manner in which the property is distributed. In Montana, for example, although the statute provides for the distribution of all property, it lists a number of factors the court must consider in disposing of certain kinds of property that would in most cases be classified as separate property in a dual property jurisdiction. The kinds of property listed are property acquired prior to marriage or its increased value; property acquired by gift, bequest, devise, or descent or its increased value; and property acquired in exchange for such property or acquired subsequent to legal separation. In distributing such property, the court must consider certain contributions to the marriage by the other spouse.[18]

In addition to making the nature and origin of the property a relevant consideration in distribution, all property statutes typically contain other factors that the court must consider in dividing property between the spouses. Taken together, the statutes contain a dazzling array of factors in combinations that defy classification. Accordingly, it cannot be overemphasized that the lawyer or student must pay careful attention to the explicit statutory provisions in a given jurisdiction.[19]

---

[16] Mont. Code Ann. § 40-4-202(1).

[17] Conn. Gen. Stat. Ann. § 46b-81(a).

[18] *See* Mont. Code Ann. § 40-4-202(1).

[19] A few examples are illustrative. The North Dakota statute simply requires the court to "make such equitable distribution of the real and personal property of the parties as may seem just and proper . . . having regard to the circumstances of the parties respectively." N.D. Cent. Code § 14-05-24(1). "When a divorce is granted, the court shall make an equitable distribution of the property and debts of the parties." *Id.* The Hawaii statute requires the court to consider "the respective merits of the parties, the relative abilities of the parties, the condition in which each party will be left by the divorce, the burdens imposed upon either party for the benefit of the children of the parties, . . . and all other circumstances of the case." Haw. Rev. Stat. § 580-47(a). The statute in Vermont lists twelve explicit relevant factors that the court may consider. Vt. Stat. Ann. tit. 15, § 751(b).

§ 10.04   CHARACTERIZING PROPERTY AS MARITAL OR SEPARATE: CHANGE IN CLASSIFICATION

A significant set of issues confronted by courts and practitioners in dual property jurisdictions concerns the circumstances, events, or transactions that may cause a change in the character of property from separate property to marital property, and on occasion from marital to separate. Generally, this change in character or classification affects property that was wholly or partly acquired prior to marriage.

[A]   The Marital Property Presumption

The equitable distribution statutes of several states contain a presumption that all property acquired by either party during marriage is marital property, regardless of how title is held.[20] For the most part these statutes explicitly provide that the presumption may be overcome by a showing that the property was acquired by a method listed in the exceptions to the definition of marital property. The presence or absence of this presumption in a statute does not appear to affect the burden of proof, which rests upon the party who seeks to show that property is separate or nonmarital. Depending on the wording of the statute, the party must prove either that the property was acquired in a manner listed in an exception or that the property was acquired in a manner described in the definition of separate property.

The fact that the marital property presumption is not set out explicitly in the statute of a given jurisdiction does not necessarily mean that the courts of a given state have not adopted it. The Supreme Court of New Jersey, for example, judicially created the presumption without reliance on statutory authority.[21]

[B]   Judicial Development of Classification Rules

To deal with issues of characterization and changes in characterization of property, the courts in equitable distribution jurisdictions with dual property statutes have adopted or developed several basic rules or theories. These include inception of title, source of funds, and transmutation.

[1]   Inception of Title

The inception of title rule derives from community property law and currently prevails in community property states. According to inception of title, property is classified as of the time that title is first taken. A typical case involves the husband's purchase of real property prior to marriage, making a down payment and giving a note payable in installments and secured by a mortgage. During the marriage mortgage payments are made with funds that are marital property. The wife will have no cognizable claim to equitable distribution on divorce. Once the property acquires the status of separate property, that status does not change, regardless of

---

[20] *See, e.g.,* Colo. Rev. Stat. § 14-10-113(3); Del. Code. Ann. tit. 13, § 1513(c); Fla. Stat. Ann. § 61.075(8); 750 Ill. Comp. Stat. Ann. 5/503(b)(1); Ky. Rev. Stat. Ann. § 403.190(3); Minn. Stat. § 518.003 (subd. 3b); Mo. Rev. Stat. § 452.330(3); 23 Pa. Cons. Stat. § 3501(b); Va. Code Ann. § 20-107.3(A)(2).

[21] *See Painter v. Painter,* 320 A.2d 484 (N.J. 1974).

the application of marital funds to satisfy indebtedness or eliminate an encumbrance.

Although the inception of title rule was adopted in a series of opinions by intermediate appellate courts in Missouri, it did not gain favor in other equitable distribution states. The Supreme Court of Missouri ultimately rejected inception of title[22] and adopted the source of funds theory.[23] Inception of title continues to be of some significance for the practitioner in a dual property state. Conceptually, it is the point of departure for the development of the currently evolving source of funds approach for the characterization of property for the purposes of equitable distribution.

[2] Source of Funds

Courts in a number of dual property states have explicitly rejected the inception of title theory. Rather than classifying property in accordance with the time of obtaining title, these courts have looked to the source of each contribution as payments are made. The decision of the Maryland Court of Special Appeals in a leading case, *Harper v. Harper*,[24] is illustrative. The court in *Harper* framed the issue before it in two parts. The first question was whether a parcel of real property purchased by the husband under a land installment contract and paid for in part prior to the marriage and in part during marriage was marital property. The second question was whether the marital home erected on the property during marriage was marital property.

In a lengthy and scholarly opinion, the court reviewed decisions from Maine, Missouri and Illinois, as well as those from a number of community property states. Explicitly rejecting the inception of title and transmutation[25] theories, the court stated:

> We conclude that . . . the appropriate analysis to be applied is the source of funds theory. Under that theory, when property is acquired by the expenditure of both nonmarital and marital property, the property is characterized as part nonmarital and part marital. Thus, a spouse contributing nonmarital property is entitled to an interest in the property in the ratio of the nonmarital investment to the total nonmarital and marital investment in the property. The remaining property is characterized as marital property and its value is subject to equitable distribution. Thus, the spouse who contributed nonmarital funds, and the marital unit that contributed marital funds each receive a proportionate and fair return on their investment.[26]

---

[22] *See Hoffmann v. Hoffmann*, 676 S.W.2d 817 (Mo. 1984).

[23] *See infra* § 10.04[B][2].

[24] 448 A.2d 916 (Md. 1982). *But see Gordon v. Gordon*, 923 A.2d 149, 178 (Md. Ct. Spec. App. 2007) (holding that the need to "trace the source of the funds is no longer applicable to real estate titled as tenants by the entireties."

[25] *See infra* § 10.04[B][3].

[26] *Harper*, 448 A.2d at 929.

In applying the source of funds theory, the Maryland court followed the teaching of the Supreme Judicial Court of Maine in *Tibbetts v. Tibbetts*,[27] defining the statutory term "acquired" to mean "the on-going process of making payment for property,"[28] making the classification of property dependent on the source of each contribution as payments are made, rather than the time of obtaining title. A number of other equitable distribution states have used similar reasoning in adopting the source of funds theory.[29]

[3] Transmutation

Like the inception of title rule,[30] the transmutation doctrine has its origins in the law of community property. Broadly stated, transmutation involves the process, based on the intent of the parties, by which separate property is altered in character and becomes marital or community property. Also, but less frequently, marital property may be transmuted to separate property. When the evidence shows the parties' intent to change the character of the property, the courts generally have reclassified the property based on this intent, often without explicit reference to "transmutation."

Courts faced with the task of distributing marital property in divorce proceedings frequently hold that separate assets may be so commingled with marital property that they do not retain their identity as separate, but are transmuted to marital property.

Transmutation may also be based on donative intent. In *Quinn v. Quinn*[31] for example, the Supreme Court of Rhode Island upheld the lower court's division of property based on transmutation, citing the transmutation doctrine as consistent with the partnership theory of marriage. The court classified as marital property the proceeds from the sale of real estate that the husband had inherited. The court justified its reasoning on the grounds that the proceeds had been placed into a joint account and that later some of the funds were used to purchase property in which the husband and wife held a joint tenancy. The court also held that investment securities, which were partly purchased with inherited funds, were marital property. The court held that "[w]hen marital and nonmarital assets are commingled and then exchanged for other property, the newly acquired asset is marital property."[32]

Divorce courts in recent years have accepted the transmutation doctrine with increasing frequency.[33]

---

[27] 406 A.2d 70 (Me. 1979).

[28] *Harper*, 448 A.2d at 929.

[29] *See, e.g., Gregg v. Gregg*, 474 So. 2d 262 (Fla. Dist. Ct. App. 1985); *Brandenburg v. Brandenburg*, 617 S.W.2d 871 (Ky. Ct. App. 1981); *Hoffmann v. Hoffmann*, 676 S.W.2d 817 (Mo. 1984); *Wade v. Wade*, 325 S.E.2d 260 (N.C. Ct. App. 1985).

[30] *See supra* § 10.04[B][1].

[31] 512 A.2d 848 (R.I. 1986).

[32] *Id.* at 853.

[33] *See, e.g., Umber v. Umber*, 591 P.2d 299 (Okla. 1979); *Kendall v. Kendall*, 367 S.E.2d 437 (S.C. Ct. App. 1988).

[C]   Tracing

A party may, in some jurisdictions, defeat the characterization of property as marital property by "tracing" separate property into assets acquired during the marriage. As one court has stated, "[t]he tracing of funds is a procedure which allows the court to find that property which would otherwise fall within the definition of marital property is actually nonmarital property under one of the exceptions."[34] Tracing is a difficult procedure, particularly in long marriages or where liquid assets rather than real property are involved. The party seeking to identify the property as separate has the burden to prove that separate property was given in exchange for marital assets. Tracing has been criticized as discouraging the partnership theory of marriage by rewarding the spouse who carefully accounts for what is his or hers. Courts that prefer to "expand the scope of the divisible marital estate" can limit the success of tracing by finding that separate property has commingled with or transmuted into marital property.[35]

In *Chenault v. Chenault*[36] the Supreme Court of Kentucky rejected the assertion that a party seeking to prove through tracing the nonmarital character of property must do so with documentary evidence and with almost mathematical precision. The court observed:

> While such precise requirements for nonmarital asset-tracing may be appropriate for skilled business persons who maintain comprehensive records of their financial affairs, such may not be appropriate for persons of lesser business skills or persons who are imprecise in their record-keeping abilities. This problem is compounded in a marital union where one spouse is the recorder of financial detail and the other is essentially indifferent to such matters. Moreover, such a requirement may promote marital disharmony by placing a premium on the careful maintenance of separate estates.[37]

§ 10.05   APPRECIATION OF SEPARATE PROPERTY DURING MARRIAGE

As discussed, in dual property states, property acquired before the marriage is generally defined as separate property.[38] Other categories of property may also be defined as separate under a variety of statutory provisions.[39] A number of dual property statutes deal with the question of whether the increase in value of property acquired before marriage, or otherwise classified as separate, is treated as separate property or marital property. In some states, the increase in value, or amount of appreciation, is classified as marital property. In others, the increase in

---

[34] *In re Marriage of Scott*, 407 N.E.2d 1045 (Ill. App. Ct. 1980).

[35] *See* J. Thomas Oldham, *Tracing, Commingling and Transmutation*, 23 Fam. L.Q. 219, 249 (1989).

[36] 799 S.W.2d 575 (Ky. 1990).

[37] *Id.* at 578.

[38] *See supra* § 10.03[A].

[39] *Id.*

value is treated as separate property. Even in these latter jurisdictions, however, the treatment accorded to appreciation may depend on whether or not the increase in value is attributable, in whole or in part, to the contribution of the nontitled spouse. Again, even if the applicable statute designates the increase in value of separate property as separate, some jurisdictions, applying the source of funds rule, have classified the appreciation as marital because of spousal contributions to separate property.[40]

When characterizing the increase in value of property, courts frequently make a critical distinction between active appreciation and passive appreciation. In *Rogers v. Rogers*,[41] the Supreme Court of Appeals of West Virginia, applying that state's equitable distribution statute, provided typical and serviceable definitions. The court defined passive appreciation of separate property as an increase "which is due to inflation or to a change in market value resulting from conditions outside the control of the parties," and which is not subject to equitable distribution.[42] Active appreciation, on the other hand, is an increase that "results from . . . an expenditure of funds which are marital property, including an expenditure of such funds which reduces indebtedness against separate property, extinguishes liens, or otherwise increases the net value of separate property, or . . . work performed by either or both of the parties during the marriage."[43] Active appreciation of separate property will be classified under this approach as marital property eligible for distribution on marriage dissolution. Accordingly, in *Rogers*, where the increase in value of separate property was attributable solely to illegal mining underneath the property, the court held that the appreciation was the result of market factors beyond the parties' control and, therefore, not distributable as marital property.

As we have noted, the characterization of the increase in value of property during marriage may also depend upon whether the appreciation is caused, in whole or in part, by contributions by the nontitled or non owning spouse. In several states, the applicable statute explicitly classifies as marital property appreciation attributable to the contributions or efforts of the nonowner.[44] Courts applying such statutes have not reached consistent results when determining whether a spouse's indirect contributions, such as homemaker services, will qualify. In *Brandenberg v. Brandenberg*,[45] for example, the court held that the only contributions to be considered with respect to the increase in value were marital funds or nonmarital funds of the nontitled spouse. Other efforts or contributions, such as homemaker contributions, although they were to be considered in dividing marital property, were not to be considered with respect to the increase in value of nonmarital property.

---

[40] *See, e.g., Hoffmann v. Hoffmann*, 676 S.W.2d 817 (Mo. 1983); *Hall v. Hall*, 462 A.2d 1179 (Me. 1984).

[41] 405 S.E.2d 235 (W. Va. 1991).

[42] *Id.* at 239. *See* W. Va. Code § 48-2-1(f)(6).

[43] *Id. See* W. Va. Code § 48-2-1(e)(2); *see also Middendorf v. Middendorf*, 696 N.E.2d 575 (Ohio 1998).

[44] *See, e.g.*, Ky. Rev. Stat. Ann. § 403.190(2)(e); N.Y. Dom. Rel. Law § 236(B)(d)(3); S.C. Code Ann. § 20-3-630(A)(5); Tenn. Code Ann. § 36-4-121(b)(2); W. Va. Code § 48-2-1(e)(2).

[45] 617 S.W.2d 871 (Ky. Ct. App. 1981).

In *Price v. Price*,[46] a leading case, the New York Court of Appeals took a sharply different view with respect to contributions to the appreciation of separate property in the indirect form of homemaker services. *Price* involved a husband who received a large amount of stock in a family corporation by gift and subsequently became the sole owner of the corporation when its outstanding shares were redeemed. The wife gave up her outside employment upon the birth of their first child to devote all of her efforts to being a homemaker and parent. The dispute arose concerning the appreciation of the stock of the corporation.

Relying on the economic partnership theory of marriage, the court stated:

> The Equitable Distribution Law reflects an awareness that the economic success of the partnership depends "not only upon the respective financial contributions of the partners, but also on a wide range of non-remunerated services to the joint enterprise, such as homemaking, raising children and providing the emotional and moral support necessary to sustain the other spouse in coping with the vicissitudes of life outside the home" (*see* Governor's Memorandum, McKinney's Session Laws of N.Y., 1980, p. 1863).[47]

In keeping with the active appreciation-passive appreciation distinction,[48] the court held:

> As a general rule, however, where the appreciation is not due, in any part, to the efforts of the titled spouse but to the efforts of others or to unrelated factors including inflation or other market forces, as in the case of a mutual fund, an investment in unimproved land, or in a work of art, the appreciation remains separate property, and the nontitled spouse has no claim to a share of the appreciation.[49]

Other courts have applied statutory provisions governing increases in value of separate property in the identical manner as the court in *Price*. In *Goderwis v. Goderwis*[50] for example, the husband devoted virtually all of his time during the course of an 18-year marriage to an auto repair business that he had started before the marriage. The Supreme Court of Kentucky affirmed a holding that the increase in value of the business during the marriage was marital property. After noting that increases in value due to general economic conditions are not marital property, the court held that the opposite is true when the increase is the result of the joint efforts of the parties. The court explicitly recognized indirect contributions of the nontitled spouse, stating: "The efforts of the parties may include the contribution of one

---

[46] 503 N.E.2d 684 (N.Y. 1986).

[47] *Id.* at 687.

[48] *See supra* notes 41-43 (and accompanying text).

[49] 503 N.E.2d at 690. *See also Hartog v. Hartog*, 647 N.E.2d 749 (NY 1995); S.C. Code Ann. § 20-3-630(A)(5) (includes in definition of nonmarital property "any increase in value in nonmarital property, except to the extent that the increase resulted directly or indirectly from efforts of the other spouse during marriage").

[50] 780 S.W.2d 39 (Ky. 1989).

spouse as a primary operator of the business and the other spouse as primarily a homemaker."[51]

The equitable distribution statutes of several states do not state directly whether the increase in value during marriage of separate property is to be treated as marital or separate. A number of court decisions in these states, however, have addressed the issue, reaching results generally consistent with the decisions discussed in this section that rely on explicit statutory provisions.[52]

In *Cockrill v. Cockrill*,[53] the Supreme Court of Arizona, a community property state, rejected the husband's assertion that the increase in value of a farm operation that the husband owned before marriage was separate property, and also declined to classify it as community property. Refusing to accept the all or none doctrine from other jurisdictions, the court held that "when the value of separate property is increased the burden is upon the spouse who contends that the increase is also separate property to prove that the increase is the result of the inherent value of the property itself and is not the product of the work effort of the community."[54] Accordingly, the court remanded the case to the trial court for apportionment of the increase in value between the husband's separate property and the community property.

§ 10.06   GIFTS AND INHERITANCES

[A]   Statutory Approaches

Statutes in the vast majority of dual property states explicitly classify gifts and inheritances (generally, property acquired by bequest, devise or descent) as separate or nonmarital property. In a slight majority of all property jurisdictions the equitable distribution statutes are silent with respect to property acquired by gift or inheritance. Courts interpreting these statutes have permitted distribution of such property in a variety of circumstances.[55] In other all property jurisdictions, the typical statutory treatment of gifts and inheritances is to include them among the factors the court must consider in dividing the marital estate or to list their source of acquisition as a factor. The Indiana statute is illustrative of this latter approach, providing in pertinent part:

> The court shall presume that an equal division of the marital property between the parties is just and reasonable. However, this presumption may be rebutted by a party who presents relevant evidence, including evidence

---

[51] *Id.* at 40.

[52] *See, e.g., Mol v. Mol*, 370 A.2d 509 (N.J. Super. Ct. App. Div. 1977); *Palmer v. Palmer*, 455 N.E.2d 1049 (Ohio Ct. App. 1982); *Templeton v. Templeton*, 656 P.2d 250 (Okla. 1982); *Plachta v. Plachta*, 348 N.W.2d 193 (Wis. Ct. App. 1984).

[53] 601 P.2d 1334 (Ariz. 1979).

[54] *Id.* at 1336.

[55] *See, e.g., Ahlo v. Ahlo*, 619 P.2d 112 (Haw. Ct. App. 1980); *In re Marriage of Jenks*, 656 P.2d 286 (Or. 1982); *Goehry v. Goehry*, 354 N.W.2d 192 (S.D. 1984).

concerning the following factors, that an equal division would not be just and reasonable:

. . .

(2) The extent to which the property was acquired by each spouse:

(A) before the marriage; or

(B) through inheritance or gift.[56]

[B] Judicial Treatment

Among a variety of issues the courts have addressed in connection with the characterization of gifts and inheritances, the most commonly encountered and significant involve (1) acquisition by gift or inheritance by either spouse from a third party, (2) transfers to the spouses jointly, (3) interspousal transfers, and (4) whether or not an asset is a gift.

[1] Gifts or Inheritances From a Third Party to Either Spouse

Under various statutory formulations, the courts have generally held that gifts or inheritances from a third party to one of the spouses are nonmarital or separate property. The Appellate Court of Illinois, for example, reached this result under a statute that contains the presumption, set out in a number of dual property statutes, that all property acquired by either spouse during the marriage is marital property.[57] The court concluded that acquisition of property by gift was a method of acquisition that overcomes the presumption of marital property.[58]

The decision of the Supreme Court of Alaska in *Julsen v. Julsen*[59] is also instructive, holding that an inheritance received during marriage was not distributable, even though the Alaska statute provides for "division between the parties of their property . . . whether joint or separate, acquired only during marriage . . . ."[60] The court noted that the decision was consistent with its "view of equitable distribution in general, which recognizes the partnership theory of marriage and considers the mutual effort and tangible contributions of the parties rather than the mere existence of the marital relationship."[61] In *Gaulrapp v. Gaulrapp*,[62] the husband and wife each received gifts during the marriage. The Supreme Court of North Dakota held that it was error to exclude from the marital estate gifts to the wife that were in cash and not segregated from other marital assets. The court

---

[56] Ind. Code Ann. § 31-15-7-5; Wyo. Stat. Ann. § 20-2-114 (1986) (requiring the court to consider "the party through whom the property was acquired").

[57] *See supra* § 10.04[A].

[58] *In re Marriage of Cook*, 453 N.E.2d 1357 (Ill. App. Ct. 1983).

[59] 741 P.2d 642 (Alaska 1987).

[60] Alaska Stat. § 25.24.160(a)(4) (Supp. 1988).

[61] *Julsen*, 741 P.2d at 648 (citations omitted). *See also Van Newkirk v. Van Newkirk*, 325 N.W.2d 832 (Neb. 1982).

[62] 510 N.W.2d 620 (N.D. 1994).

noted that both the length of the marriage and the origins of the property were relevant and that "redistribution of gifted property may often be equitable in long-term marriages."[63]

[2] To the Spouses Jointly

Almost invariably, the courts treat transfers to the spouses jointly through gift or inheritance as property eligible for equitable distribution upon marriage dissolution in both all property and dual property jurisdictions, reaching the same result under varying statutory formulations.[64] The decision in *Forsythe v. Forsythe*,[65] a leading case, is illustrative. The trial court in *Forsythe* set aside to the wife property, the source of which was a gift from the wife's parents to the parties as husband and wife. Reversing, the Missouri Court of Appeals accepted the husband's claim that a gift to both husband and wife was marital property subject to distribution. The court noted that the Missouri statute defined marital property to mean "all property acquired by either spouse subsequent to the marriage," listing as one of the exceptions "property acquired by gift, bequest, devise, or descent."[66] The statute also contained a marital property presumption.[67] After reviewing the intent and purpose of the statute, the court concluded:

> The purpose of [the statutory provision] which by mention exempts from division only a gift to *either* spouse is to treat as marital property a gift to *both* spouses. From this we conclude that the integral Act intends for the court to divide and settle title to all property which has come to the spouses by virtue of the marriage relation.[68]

[3] Interspousal Transfers

Cases addressing the transfer of property between the spouses contain a variety of approaches. Interspousal transfers are likely to result in the characterization of the transferred property as marital in cases where one spouse transfers property into joint tenancy or tenancy by the entirety.

A common statutory formulation explicitly characterizes such transfers as marital property. In *In re Marriage of Deem*,[69] the husband and wife took title as joint tenants to property acquired during the marriage with the wife's separate

---

[63] *Id.* at 62.

[64] *See, e.g., In re Marriage of Wendt*, 339 N.W.2d 615 (Iowa Ct. App. 1983) (holding that gift to both parties is jointly acquired property, divisible in the same way as other jointly held marital assets); *Van Newkirk v. Van Newkirk*, 325 N.W.2d 832 (Neb. 1982) (reaffirming earlier authority that gifts or inheritances acquired by one of the parties were ordinarily not part of the marital estate, but holding that a gift to both husband and wife is includable); *Darwish v. Darwish*, 300 N.W.2d 399 (Mich. Ct. App. 1980) (holding that wedding gifts that were to be enjoyed and used jointly should be considered the same as property purchased jointly by the spouses).

[65] 558 S.W.2d 675 (Mo. Ct. App. 1977), *aff'd*, 591 S.W.2d 222 (Mo. Ct. App. 1979).

[66] Mo. Rev. Stat. § 452.330(2)(1).

[67] Mo. Rev. Stat. § 452.330(3).

[68] *Forsythe*, 558 S.W.2d at 678 (emphasis in original).

[69] 463 N.E.2d 1317 (Ill. App. Ct. 1984).

funds. Subsequently, the spouses transferred the property to the wife by warranty deed. The husband argued on appeal that there was insufficient evidence to prove that the transfer was a gift and, therefore, nonmarital property. The court, noting the marital property presumption in the Illinois statute, held that the party seeking to exclude property acquired during the marriage from distribution has the burden of proving by clear and convincing evidence that the property was a gift. Considering that the deed itself was not sufficient to prove a gift, the court ordered the property to be treated as marital on remand.[70]

In *Roig v. Roig*,[71] however, where the trial court included in the marital estate the value of jewelry and furs that the husband and his aunt had given to the wife, the Supreme Court of Appeals of West Virginia reversed. The court held that "it was obviously the intent of the legislature to allow one spouse to transfer property to the other spouse by irrevocable gift and thereby remove assets so transferred from inclusion in the marital estate."[72] The court cautioned, however, that in every instance the spouse claiming the gift has the burden of proof.[73] In *O'Neill v. O'Neill*,[74] the husband presented jewelry and other personal items to his wife on her birthday, at Christmas, and on other occasions, all of which items were paid for from the husband's salary. The Kentucky Court of Appeals noted that classification turns on the pertinent facts in each case, including the source of the purchase money, the donor's intent, the status of the marriage and the like. Accordingly, because the husband had purchased the items as an investment, hoping that an increase in value could be turned to cash for the children's education, the items were not a gift.

The Supreme Judicial Court of Maine, in *Carter v. Carter*,[75] classified an interspousal transfer of the husband's separate property as marital property. In *Carter*, the husband conveyed to himself and his wife, by joint tenancy warranty deed, certain real property that he had acquired before marriage. The court held that the statutory gift exception to marital property was not applicable to transfers from one spouse to the spouses jointly. Absent clear and convincing evidence to the contrary, the conveyance demonstrated an intention to transfer the property to the marital estate.

Property acquired with marital funds is likely to be characterized as marital property, regardless of a subsequent interspousal transfer. In *McArthur v. McArthur*,[76] a case of first impression, the Supreme Court of Georgia held that property acquired during marriage remains marital property, despite any subsequent transfers between the spouses. In *McArthur*, the parties purchased with joint funds a house that became the marital home. The house was titled in the husband's name

---

[70] *See also In re Marriage of Severns*, 416 N.E.2d 1235 (Ill. Ct. App. 1981).

[71] 364 S.E.2d 794 (W. Va. 1987).

[72] *Id.* at 798.

[73] *See* W. Va. Code § 48-3-10 (1984).

[74] 600 S.W.2d 493 (Ky. Ct. App. 1980).

[75] 419 A.2d 1018 (Me. 1980).

[76] 353 S.E.2d 486 (Ga. 1987).

at the time of purchase. Subsequently, he deeded the property to the wife and title remained in her name.

The wife contended that the house was a gift to her and, therefore, separate property. The husband argued that he intended no gift, nor did he intend to give up his equitable interest in the home. Having reviewed the judicial treatment of interspousal gifts in several other jurisdictions, the court embraced the view of the District of Columbia Court of Appeals in *Hemily v. Hemily*,[77] looking "to the source of the money with which the 'gift' was purchased. Thus, if a gift from one spouse to another was purchased with marital funds, the 'gift' remains marital property subject to equitable division."[78]

The courts of Missouri and Pennsylvania, in varying factual contexts, have classified interspousal transfers as marital property. In *Dildy v. Dildy*,[79] the Missouri Court of Appeals classified as marital property stocks that the husband transferred as an inter vivos gift to himself and his wife as joint tenants. Similarly, the Superior Court of Pennsylvania held, under a statute excepting gifts from distribution and containing a marital property presumption, that bonds placed by the husband in joint ownership with his wife were subject to distribution.[80]

[4] Was There a Gift?

In determining how transfers of property by gift should be classified for the purpose of equitable distribution, lawyers and courts must occasionally face the question of whether, as a matter of definition, a transfer is a gift at all.

McGlone v. McGlone[81] sharply presents the question. The case concerned a grant from the Veterans Administration (VA) to the husband, a totally disabled career serviceman who was confined to a wheelchair. The husband received the grant during marriage. The parties used the funds in part to defray the costs of constructing and designing special features of the marital residence to accommodate the husband's physical handicaps. The divorce court found that the grant was marital property subject to division. On appeal, the Supreme Court of Kentucky, having reviewed the federal statute that entitled the husband to the grant, concluded that the grant was not awarded for military service but was made pursuant to an authorization for the VA to make gifts to veterans with disabilities similar to the husband's. The court held that the grant was a gift within the meaning of the Kentucky statute and, accordingly, should have been classified as nonmarital property.

In the course of interpreting the New Jersey statute, which excepts gifts from equitable distribution, the Superior Court of New Jersey has identified the hallmarks of a gift. The court noted that "[a] 'gift' is a transfer without consideration, . . . requiring an unequivocal donative intent on the part of the donor, actual

---

[77] 403 A.2d 1139 (D.C. 1979).

[78] *McArthur*, 353 S.E.2d at 488, n.3.

[79] 650 S.W.2d 324 (Mo. Ct. App. 1983).

[80] *Madden v. Madden*, 486 A.2d 401 (Pa. Super. Ct. 1984).

[81] 613 S.W.2d 419 (Ky. 1981).

or symbolic delivery of the subject matter of the gift, and an absolute and irrevocable relinquishment of ownership by the donor."[82] Consistent with this definition, the Missouri Court of Appeals has held that a conveyance of real property that was conditioned upon lifetime care for the decedent was a contract for services rather than a gift.[83]

§ 10.07   PERSONAL INJURIES AND WORKERS' COMPENSATION

[A]   Introduction

Equitable distribution jurisdictions have reached varying results in the treatment of compensation for personal injuries or workers' compensation benefits. In any given jurisdiction, however, for the most part, the courts afford these two types of assets similar treatment. Therefore, we treat them here as a single subject. Equitable distribution statutes generally contain no explicit reference to the treatment or characterization of personal injury claims and awards or workers' compensation. The New York statute is a notable exception. In its definition of "separate property," the statute includes "compensation for personal injuries."[84]

[B]   Approaches to Classification

There are two predominant approaches to the division of personal injury awards, commonly described as the mechanistic approach and the analytic or purpose approach. The analytic approach originated in community property states. Under this method of classification, recovery for lost wages and for medical expenses paid out of marital funds is deemed distributable marital property. Recoveries for pain and suffering or for the injury itself, on the other hand, are classified as nonmarital or separate property. The mechanistic approach was adopted in a number of the earlier decisions in dual property states. This method does not divide the personal injury claim or award into component parts.

The highest courts of several states have considered the characterization of personal injury and workers' compensation proceeds. The decisions suggest a trend toward preference for the analytic approach. The decision of the Supreme Court of Appeals of West Virginia in *Hardy v. Hardy*,[85] a case of first impression, is instructive. In *Hardy*, the husband and wife recovered separate judgments for injuries to the husband and for loss of consortium and nursing services by the wife. In the subsequent divorce proceeding, the wife asserted that the husband's personal injury award was marital property subject to equitable distribution.

The court noted that several early decisions in a number of states had concluded that a personal injury award was marital property. As the court observed, these

---

[82] *Sleeper v. Sleeper*, 446 A.2d 1220, 1222 (N.J. Super. Ct. App. Div. 1982) (citations omitted).

[83] *Cochenour v. Cochenour*, 642 S.W.2d 402 (Mo. Ct. App. 1982).

[84] N.Y. Dom. Rel. Law § 236(B)(1)(d)(2) (2012).

[85] 413 S.E.2d 151 (W. Va. 1991).

decisions "were generally based upon a purely mechanical reading of statutory definitions of marital and separate property."[86] That is, under the mechanistic approach adopted in these decisions, if an award was acquired during the marriage and did not fall within an explicit exception to the definition of marital property or within the definition of separate property, it was marital property.[87]

Ultimately rejecting the mechanistic approach, the court in *Hardy* observed that in recent years an increasing number of state courts "have classified personal injury settlements under a framework referred to as the analytical, or purpose, approach, which draws a distinction between the economic loss suffered by the marital partnership and the economic and personal loss suffered by each individual spouse and asks what a personal injury award was intended to replace."[88] Accordingly, the court in *Hardy* concluded that a personal injury recovery should be characterized based on its purpose. The court held:

> [To] the extent that its purpose is to compensate an individual for pain, suffering, disability, disfigurement, or other debilitation of the mind or body a personal injury award constitutes the separate nonmarital property of an injured spouse. However, economic losses, such as past wages and medical expenses, which diminish the marital estate are distributable as marital property when recovered in a personal injury award or settlement. The burden of proving the purpose of part or all of a personal injury recovery is on the party seeking a nonmarital classification.[89]

The Supreme Court of Oklahoma, consistent with the trend noted, followed the analytical approach with respect to a workers' compensation award, holding in *Crocker v. Crocker*[90] that the award was marital property "only to the extent to which it reimburses the couple for loss of income during the marriage."[91] It is separate property, however, insofar as it is compensation for loss of the injured spouse's post-divorce earnings, even though the injury occurred during marriage.[92]

---

[86] *Id.* at 154.

[87] *See, e.g., Clayton v. Clayton*, 760 S.W.2d 875 (Ark. 1988); *In re Marriage of Fjeldheim*, 676 P.2d 1234 (Colo. App. 1983); *In re Marriage of Burt*, 494 N.E.2d 868 (Ill. App. Ct. 1986); *Nixon v. Nixon*, 525 S.W.2d 835 (Mo. Ct. App. 1975); *Platek v. Platek*, 454 A.2d 1059 (Pa. Super. Ct. 1982); *Bero v. Bero*, 367 A.2d 165 (Vt. 1976); *Richardson v. Richardson*, 407 N.W.2d 231 (Wis. 1987).

[88] *Hardy*, 413 S.E.2d at 154.

[89] *Id.* at 156.

[90] 824 P.2d 1117 (Okla. 1991).

[91] *Id.* at 1118.

[92] *Id. See also Bandow v. Bandow*, 794 P.2d 1346 (Alaska 1990) (applying analytic approach to annuity given in settlement of medical malpractice claim); *Weisfeld v. Weisfeld*, 545 So. 2d 1341 (Fla. 1989) (applying analytic approach to workers' compensation award); *Kirk v. Kirk*, 577 A.2d 976 (R.I. 1990) (applying analytic approach to personal injury settlements and workers' compensation benefits).

§ 10.08 LICENSES, DEGREES AND ENHANCED EARNINGS

[A] Overview

The overwhelming majority of courts that have addressed the issue have concluded that a professional license or degree is not marital property. The highest court of only one state, New York, has reached a contrary result, and panels of the Michigan Court of Appeals are split on the question. With these exceptions, the courts unanimously have declined to characterize a degree or license as property.

Many courts, however, using a variety of theories, have provided remedial relief in one form or another to the "non-degreed" or supporting spouse. The relief has generally consisted of reimbursement of funds spent for the education or support of the degree-earning spouse, or consideration of the spousal contribution in a maintenance award or in the division of marital property. Also, some courts have held, or recognized in dicta, that enhanced earning capacity is a appropriate consideration in the distribution of marital property on marriage dissolution.

[B] Statutory Treatment

For the most part, equitable distribution statutes are silent with respect to the characterization or treatment of professional licenses or degrees. There are a few exceptions. The North Carolina statute, in its definition of "separate property," provides: "All professional licenses and business licenses which would terminate on transfer shall be considered separate property."[93] The Indiana statute states, in pertinent part:

> If the court finds there is little or no marital property, the court may award either spouse a money judgment not limited to the property existing at the time of final separation. However, this award may be made only for the financial contribution of one (1) spouse toward tuition, books, and laboratory fees for the postsecondary education of the other spouse.[94]

In Ohio, among the factors that the court must consider in awarding spousal support is "[t]he contribution of each party to the education, training, or earning ability of the other party, including, but not limited to, any party's contribution to the acquisition of a professional degree of the other party."[95]

[C] Degree or License Not Property

In re Marriage of Graham,[96] a landmark decision of the Supreme Court of Colorado, presents on its facts what has become virtually the paradigmatic case of the treatment of licenses and degrees for the purpose of the equitable distribution of property. In *Graham*, the parties were divorced after a relatively brief marriage (six years), during which they accumulated no significant marital assets. The

---

[93] N.C. Gen. Stat. § 50-20(b)(2).

[94] Ind. Code Ann. § 31-15-7-6.

[95] Ohio Rev. Code § 3105.18(C).

[96] 574 P.2d 75 (Colo. 1978).

husband attended school for about three and a half years of the marriage, earning a bachelor's degree and a master's degree while the wife worked full time. The wife contributed 70 percent of the spouses' finances, which were devoted both to family expenses and to the husband's education. The trial court found that the husband's education was jointly held property in which the wife had a property right and valued the husband's MBA degree at $82,836. Of this, the court awarded the wife $33,134, payable in monthly installments of $100. The Colorado court of appeals reversed and remanded, and certiorari was granted.

Affirming the judgment denying the wife relief, the Supreme Court of Colorado observed in a passage so frequently quoted as to become the pervasive rationale in subsequent license or degree cases:

> An educational degree, such as an M.B.A., is simply not encompassed even by the broad views of the concept of "property." It does not have any exchange value or any objective transferable value on an open market. It is personal to the holder. It terminates on death of the holder and is not inheritable. It cannot be assigned, sold, transferred, conveyed, or pledged. An advanced degree is a cumulative product of many years of previous education, combined with diligence and hard work. It may not be acquired by the mere expenditure of money. It is simply an intellectual achievement that may potentially assist in the future acquisition of property. In our view, it has none of the attributes of property in the usual sense of that term.[97]

In a lengthy and carefully reasoned opinion, the Supreme Court of New Jersey, in *Mahoney v. Mahoney*,[98] stated a variety of reasons why the value of a professional degree (MBA) earned during marriage was not property for the purposes of equitable distribution. The court pointed out that although "New Jersey courts have subjected a broad range of assets and interests to equitable distribution including vested but unmatured private pensions," the Supreme Court had "never subjected to equitable distribution an asset whose future monetary value is as uncertain and unquantifiable as a professional degree or license."[99]

Citing the decision in *Graham* with approval, the court observed that distribution of a professional degree would involve distributing the earning capacity relating to speculative future earnings. Further, valuation of the degree at the threshold of the holder's career "would involve a gamut of calculations that reduces to little more than guesswork."[100] Finally, miscalculation of the value of the license or degree would result in unfairness, with the finality of the property division precluding any remedy.[101] Accordingly, although the court enunciated several theories under which the supporting spouse might receive remedial relief,[102] it adopted the overwhelming majority view excluding a license of degree from equitable distribution.

---

[97] *Id.* at 77.

[98] 453 A.2d 527 (N.J. 1982).

[99] *Id.* at 531.

[100] *Id.* at 532.

[101] *Id.*

[102] *See supra* § 9.08[E].

The opinions of the highest courts of other jurisdictions, while often not as carefully or thoroughly reasoned as *Mahoney*, have not departed significantly from the principle enunciated in *Graham*, that a license or degree is not property.[103] In several states, where the issue of classification of a professional license or degree has not yet reached the highest court, trial courts and intermediate appellate courts have, with rare exceptions, reached the same conclusion, denying distribution of licenses or degrees.[104] The only dissent from this unanimous view among appellate courts is found in several decisions from Michigan, where panels of the Court of Appeals have taken contrary views on the question.[105]

[D] Degree or License as Marital Property

In *O'Brien v. O'Brien*,[106] the New York Court of Appeals held that a medical license was marital property within the meaning of the state's equitable distribution statute and was, therefore, subject to equitable distribution. *O'Brien* is the first and only unequivocal holding to this effect by the highest court of any state.[107]

In *O'Brien*, after about two and a half years of marriage, the parties moved from New York to Guadalajara, Mexico, where the husband became a full-time medical student. While he completed three years of medical school, the wife worked at teaching and tutoring and contributed her earnings to meet the parties'

---

[103] *See, e.g., Nelson v. Nelson*, 736 P.2d 1145 (Alaska 1987); *Wilson v. Wilson*, 741 S.W.2d 640 (Ark. 1987); *In re Marriage of Francis*, 442 N.W.2d 59 (Iowa 1989); *Sweeney v. Sweeney*, 534 A.2d 1290 (Me. 1987); *Drapek v. Drapek*, 503 N.E.2d 946 (Mass. 1987); *Ruben v. Ruben*, 461 A.2d 733 (N.H. 1983); *Nastrom v. Nastrom*, 262 N.W.2d 487 (N.D. 1978); *Stevens v. Stevens*, 492 N.E.2d 131 (Ohio 1986); *Hubbard v. Hubbard*, 603 P.2d 747 (Okla. 1979); *Hodge v. Hodge*, 520 A.2d 15 (Pa. 1986); *Helm v. Helm*, 345 S.E.2d 720 (S.C. 1986); *Wehrkamp v. Wehrkamp*, 357 N.W.2d 264 (S.D. 1984); *Martinez v. Martinez*, 818 P.2d 538 (Utah 1991); *Downs v. Downs*, 574 A.2d 156 (Vt. 1990); *Hoak v. Hoak*, 370 S.E.2d 473 (W. Va. 1988); *Haugan v. Haugan*, 343 N.W.2d 796 (Wis. 1984); *Grosskopf v. Grosskopf*, 677 P.2d 814 (Wyo. 1984).

[104] *See, e.g., Jones v. Jones*, 454 So. 2d 1006 (Ala. Civ. App. 1984); Wisner v. Wisner, 631 P.2d 115 (Ariz. Ct. App. 1981); *Wright v. Wright*, 469 A.2d 803 (Del. Fam. Ct. 1983); *Hernandez v. Hernandez*, 444 So. 2d 35 (Fla. Dist. Ct. App. 1983); *In re Marriage of Weinstein*, 470 N.E.2d 551 (Ill. App. Ct. 1984); *Wilcox v. Wilcox*, 365 N.E.2d 792 (Ind. Ct. App. 1977); *Moss v. Moss*, 639 S.W.2d 370 (Ky. Ct. App. 1982); *Riaz v. Riaz*, 789 S.W.2d 224 (Mo. Ct. App. 1990); *Beeler v. Beeler*, 715 S.W.2d 625 (Tenn. Ct. App. 1986).

[105] *See infra* § 10.08[D].

[106] 489 N.E.2d 712 (N.Y. 1985).

[107] Panels of the Court of Appeals of Michigan are divided on the question of whether a license or degree may be distributed as a marital asset. In *Woodworth v. Woodworth*, 337 N.W.2d 332 (Mich. Ct. App. 1983), the court held that in some circumstances the spouse of a degree holder is "entitled to share in the fruits of the degree." *Id.* at 335. *But see Watling v. Watling*, 339 N.W.2d 505 (Mich. Ct. App. 1983) (distinguishing the facts in *Woodworth* and declining to award the supporting spouse any part of the husband's dentistry degree); *Olah v. Olah*, 354 N.W.2d 359 (Mich. Ct. App. 1984) (holding that a degree is not a marital asset, but awarding permanent alimony to wife who supported husband through medical school). More recent cases continue to reflect this apparent disagreement. The court cited *Woodworth* with approval in *Postema v. Postema*, 471 N.W.2d 912 (Mich. Ct. App. 1991); *Beckett v. Beckett*, 463 N.W.2d 211 (Mich. Ct. App. 1990); *Lewis v. Lewis*, 448 N.W.2d 735 (Mich. Ct. App. 1989); and *Wiand v. Wiand*, 443 N.W.2d 464 (Mich. Ct. App. 1989). Cases adopting the reasoning of *Watling* include *Rickel v. Rickel*, 442 N.W.2d 735 (Mich. Ct. App. 1989); *Krause v. Krause*, 441 N.W.2d 66 (Mich. Ct. App. 1989); and *Sullivan v. Sullivan*, 438 N.W.2d 309 (Mich. Ct. App. 1989).

expenses. They then returned to New York, where the husband completed his last two semesters of medical school and his internship and the wife returned to a former teaching position. The husband began a divorce proceeding two months after obtaining his license to practice medicine.

The trial court awarded the wife $188,800, representing 40 percent of the value of the husband's medical license, payable in eleven annual installments.[108] The intermediate appellate court, by a divided vote, determined that the husband's medical license was not marital property.[109]

Before the New York Court of Appeals, the husband did not argue that his medical license was separate property and excluded from equitable distribution for that reason. Rather, he asserted that the license was "not property at all, but represents a personal attainment in acquiring knowledge."[110] The court squarely rejected this argument, stating:

> Neither contention is controlling because decisions in other States rely principally on their own statutes and the legislative history underlying them, and because the New York Legislature deliberately went beyond traditional property concepts when it formulated the Equitable Distribution Law . . . . Instead, our statute recognizes that spouses have an equitable claim to things of value arising out of the marital relationship and classifies them as subject to distribution by focusing on the marital status of the parties at the time of acquisition. Those things acquired during marriage and subject to distribution have been classified as "marital property" although, as one commentator has observed, they hardly fall within the traditional property concepts because there is no common law property interest remotely resembling marital property.[111]

The court concluded: "The determination that a professional license is marital property is also consistent with the conceptual base upon which the statute rests."[112] Despite the decision in *O'Brien*, the law remains well settled elsewhere that a license or degree is not marital property. No court that has subsequently addressed the question has adopted the reasoning or reached the same result as the New York Court of Appeals. Courts in other states have, however, devised a variety of remedies designed to avoid the gross unfairness that a contrary result in *O'Brien* would have entailed.[113]

Trial courts and intermediate appellate courts in New York have applied the principle of *O'Brien* liberally, holding that a variety of licenses, degrees, and certificates are marital property.[114] Moreover, in *Elkus v. Elkus*,[115] the New York

---

[108] *O'Brien*, 452 N.Y.S.2d 801 (N.Y. Sup. Ct. 1982).

[109] *O'Brien*, 485 N.Y.S.2d 548 (N.Y. App. Div. 1985).

[110] *O'Brien*, 489 N.E.2d at 715.

[111] *Id.*

[112] *Id.* at 716.

[113] *See infra* § 10.08[E].

[114] *See, e.g., Savasta v. Savasta*, 549 N.Y.S.2d 544 (N.Y. Sup. Ct. 1989) (medical board certification); *Anderson v. Anderson*, 545 N.Y.S.2d 335 (N.Y. App. Div. 1989) (nursing home license); *Morimando v.*

Supreme Court, Appellate Division, reversed a trial court determination that an opera singer's career or celebrity status was not marital property. The court found that "to the extent the [husband's] contributions and efforts led to an increase in value of the [wife's] career, this appreciation was a product of the marital partnership, and, therefore, marital property subject to equitable distribution."[116] Alternatively, to make New York's treatment of licenses and degrees, and by extension enhanced earnings, consistent with the law almost everywhere else, will require legislative action.

[E] Alternative Remedies for the Supporting Spouse

[1] Overview

The overwhelming majority of courts have determined that a professional license or degree is not marital property, or, indeed, property at all. Many courts have recognized, nevertheless, the inherent unfairness in a situation when one spouse contributes earnings to support the other spouse's professional education, only to be rewarded, shortly after graduation, with a divorce decree. Accordingly, the courts have devised several remedies for the supporting spouse. The most common forms of relief are reimbursement for funds expended for the education or support of the degree-holding spouse and consideration of the supporting spouse's contribution when a maintenance award of property distribution is determined.

Courts sometimes purport to compensate the supporting spouse in professional license or degree cases by taking that spouse's contribution into account as a factor either in awarding maintenance or in dividing property. Indeed, equitable distribution statutes in some states list the contributions of one spouse to the education of the other spouse among the factors the court must consider in making a property division. It is questionable whether this is an effective or satisfactory resolution of the problem. In these cases, the degree-holding spouse is typically at the threshold of a professional career and has limited income, and there is virtually no property available for distribution. Furthermore, depending on the circumstances of the case, the statute in a given jurisdiction may or may not authorize a maintenance award.

In some instances, courts have made a lump-sum award to the supporting spouse hardly reflective of the value of the degreed spouse's education and enhanced earning capacity, or have declined to compensate the supporting spouse at all.

Morimando, 536 N.Y.S.2d 701 (N.Y. App. Div. 1988) (certificate as a physician's assistant); *McAlpine v. McAlpine*, 539 N.Y.S.2d 680 (N.Y. Sup. Ct. 1989) (fellowship in Society of Actuaries); *McGowan v. McGowan*, 535 N.Y.S.2d 990 (N.Y. App. Div. 1988) (master's degree).

[115] 572 N.Y.S.2d 901 (N.Y. App. Div. 1991).

[116] *Id.* at 901. *See also Golub v. Golub*, 527 N.Y.S.2d 946 (N.Y. Sup. Ct. 1988) (finding no rational basis for distinguishing between celebrity status and a degree, license or other income generating special skill).

[2] Reimbursement or Rehabilitation

In the landmark case *In re Marriage of Graham*,[117] the Supreme Court of Colorado set out principles that courts in other jurisdictions have often followed, occasionally with variations. The court observed:

> A spouse who provides financial support while the other spouse acquires an education is not without a remedy. Where there is marital property to be divided, such contribution to the education of the other spouse may be taken into consideration by the court . . . . Further, if maintenance is sought and a need is demonstrated, the trial court may make an award based on all relevant factors . . . . Certainly, among the relevant factors to be considered is the contribution of the spouse seeking maintenance to the education of the other spouse from whom the maintenance is sought.[118]

This remedy did not apply in the *Graham* case itself, however, because the wife had not sought maintenance.

Almost ten years later, in *In re Marriage of Olar*,[119] the Supreme Court of Colorado considered whether it should overrule *Graham* or whether the wife should receive maintenance, taking into consideration her contribution to the husband's education. The court acknowledged the harsh and frequently unfair results under *Graham* when one spouse postpones educational and career goals to support and contribute to those of the other spouse. Nevertheless, after an extensive review of decisions in other jurisdictions, the majority of which follow the position in *Graham*, the court reaffirmed its holding in the earlier case that an educational degree is not marital property.

Having reaffirmed its *Graham* decision, even while recognizing the "potential for injustice" in this result, the court explored possible remedies for the supporting spouse under the maintenance statute, which permitted maintenance only for a spouse who "[l]acks sufficient property . . . to provide for his reasonable needs"[120] and "[i]s unable to support himself through appropriate employment . . . ."[121] The court construed this language broadly and remanded the case to the trial court for reconsideration of a maintenance award.

The Supreme Court of Vermont in *Downs v. Downs*,[122] a case of first impression, agreed explicitly with the decision of the Colorado court in *Olar*, construing similar statutory language to permit courts to consider the future value of a professional degree as a relevant factor for consideration in making an equitable maintenance award. Again the Supreme Court of Iowa, while adhering to earlier decisions that an advanced degree or professional license is not a divisible marital asset, held in *In*

---

[117] 574 P.2d 75 (Colo. 1978).

[118] *Id.* at 78 (citations omitted).

[119] 747 P.2d 676 (Colo. 1987).

[120] Colo. Rev. Stat. § 14-10-114(1)(a) (1987).

[121] *Id.* at (1)(b).

[122] 574 A.2d 156 (Vt. 1990).

re Marriage of Francis[123] that the enhanced earning capacity resulting from the degree or license was a factor to be considered in dividing property and awarding alimony.[124] In *Lowery v. Lowery*,[125] the Supreme Court of Georgia reached the same conclusion. Consistent with this view, the Supreme Court of Pennsylvania in *Bold v. Bold*,[126] held that the supporting spouse should receive "equitable reimbursement to the extent that his or her contribution to the education, training or increased earning capacity of the other spouse exceeds the bare minimum legally obligated support . . . ."[127]

§ 10.09 PROFESSIONAL GOODWILL

Closely held business interests, especially professional practices, frequently present problems of both characterization and valuation. This section will consider the various ways in which the courts have addressed characterization or classification questions, and then will address several approaches to valuation.

The courts have often struggled with the problem of whether to classify the goodwill of these enterprises as a marital asset subject to distribution upon dissolution of marriage. Generally, the courts have opted for one of three basic approaches. Some courts have declined to recognize goodwill as a marital asset. Others recognize goodwill and assign it a value, as difficult as the task may be. In a third group of cases, the courts hold that professional goodwill is divisible if it is independent of the individual practitioner.

[A] Goodwill: Definitions and Basic Concepts

Goodwill, an intangible asset of a business or professional practice, is often considered by the courts even though a precise definition does not exist. Early in the nineteenth century, Lord Eldon defined goodwill as "nothing more than the probability that the old customers will resort to the old place."[128] The most frequently cited modern definition of goodwill is that of Mr. Justice Story, who wrote:

> [G]ood-will may be properly enough described to be the advantage or benefit, which is acquired by an establishment, beyond the mere value of the capital, stock, funds, or property employed therein, in consequence of the general public patronage and encouragement, which it receives from constant or habitual customers, on account of its local position, or common celebrity, or reputation for skill or affluence, or punctuality, or from other

---

[123] 442 N.W.2d 59 (Iowa 1989).

[124] *See also In re Marriage of Lalone,* 469 N.W.2d 695 (Iowa 1991).

[125] 413 S.E.2d 731 (Ga. 1992).

[126] 574 A.2d 552 (Pa. 1990).

[127] *Id.* at 556.

[128] *Cruttwell v. Lye,* 34 Eng. Rep. 129, 134 (Ch. 1810).

accidental circumstances or necessities, or even from ancient partialities or prejudices.[129]

Also frequently cited is Judge Cardozo's observation in *In re Brown*,[130] that "[m]en will pay for any privilege that gives a reasonable expectancy of preference in the race of competition. Such expectancy may come from succession in place or name or otherwise to a business that has won the favor of its customers. It is then known as good will."[131] Despite scholarly criticism of such definitions as confusing and unsound,[132] these or similar definitions persist in the case law and continue to be cited and relied upon by the courts.

[B] Classification of Professional Goodwill

[1] Community Property Influences

California courts have long held that professional goodwill should be considered an asset subject to division on divorce, and courts in Arizona and Washington have held to the same effect. The Texas courts, however, strongly reject this view. Courts in several equitable distribution jurisdictions have relied heavily on the reasoning and result reflected in one or the other of these conflicting judicial approaches.

In *Golden v. Golden*,[133] the California Court of Appeal decided the issue squarely and unequivocally, holding that the goodwill of the husband's medical practice was a community asset and should be considered in determining the award made to the wife. The court took pains to distinguish between the situation in divorce and that in which a firm is being dissolved and concluded:

> [I]n a matrimonial matter, the practice of the sole practitioner husband will continue, with the same intangible value as it had during the marriage. Under the principles of community property law, the wife, by virtue of her position of wife, made to that value the same contribution as does a wife to any of the husband's earnings and accumulations during marriage. She is as much entitled to be recompensed for that contribution as if it were represented by the increased value of stock in a family business.[134]

The court's observation has obvious applicability to the analogous principle, underlying the law of equitable distribution, of marriage as an economic partnership.[135]

---

[129] Joseph Story, Commentaries on the Law of Partnership § 99 at 170 (6th ed. 1868).

[130] 150 N.E. 581 (N.Y. 1926).

[131] *Id.* at 582 (citation omitted).

[132] *See, e.g.*, James T. Friedman, *Professional Practice Goodwill: An Abused Value Concept*, 2 J. Am. Acad. Matrim. L. 23 (1986) ("Publications by attorneys may accurately record and analyze case law development across the country, but case law generally is not grounded on sound economic theory or valid value concepts.").

[133] 75 Cal. Rptr. 735 (Cal. Ct. App. 1969).

[134] *Id.* at 738.

[135] *See also In re Marriage of Fleege*, 588 P.2d 1136 (Wash. 1979); *Mitchell v. Mitchell*, 732 P.2d 208 (Ariz. 1987).

Other courts in community property jurisdictions reject the proposition that professional goodwill is divisible on divorce as a community asset. In *Nail v. Nail*,[136] the Supreme Court of Texas held that the goodwill of the husband's practice could not be said to be a vested or earned property right that qualified as property divisible by a court decree. The court stated:

> It did not possess value or constitute an asset separate and apart from his person, or from his individual ability to practice his profession. It would be extinguished in the event of his death, or retirement, or disablement, as well as in the event of the sale of his practice or the loss of his patients, whatever the cause.[137]

[2] Classification of Goodwill for Equitable Distribution

In determining whether the goodwill of a professional practice is an asset eligible for distribution upon dissolution of marriage, the courts in equitable distribution jurisdictions often rely heavily on decisions in community property states. There are three conflicting views. The courts of one group of states have followed the lead of California and found professional goodwill to be distributable property. To the contrary, in a number of states the decisions are consistent with those of the Texas courts, holding that professional goodwill is personal to the holder and not distributable as a marital asset. In several other states, the courts have adopted still a third approach to the classification of goodwill, holding that goodwill may or may not be divisible, depending on its marketability.

[a] Professional Goodwill as Divisible Property

New Jersey was the first equitable distribution state to give extensive consideration to the classification of goodwill as a marital asset. In *Stern v. Stern*,[138] although classification was not in dispute, the Supreme Court of New Jersey acknowledged the existence of goodwill in a professional partnership. The court noted that although ethical considerations barred the sale of the goodwill of a law firm, its existence and value could be proved in a given case.[139] The goodwill of a lawyer in his solely owned professional corporation came directly before the Supreme Court of New Jersey in *Dugan v. Dugan*.[140] In a thorough and wide-ranging opinion, the court, citing authority from California and other jurisdictions, held that an attorney's goodwill in his wholly owned professional corporation was subject to equitable distribution.

The Colorado Court of Appeals in *In re Marriage of Nichols*,[141] a case of first impression in that state, held that the goodwill of the husband's dental practice was

---

[136] 486 S.W.2d 761 (Tex. 1972).

[137] *Id.* at 764. *See also Pearce v. Pearce*, 482 So. 2d 108 (La. Ct. App. 1986).

[138] 331 A.2d 257 (N.J. 1975).

[139] *Id.* at 261, n.5.

[140] 457 A.2d 1 (N.J. 1983).

[141] 606 P.2d 1314 (Colo. App. 1979).

distributable on divorce. Setting out the rationale for this approach to the question, the court observed:

> Professional practices that can be sold for more than the value of their fixtures and accounts receivable have saleable goodwill. A professional, like any entrepreneur who has established a reputation for skill and expertise, can expect his patrons to return to him, to speak well of him, and upon selling his practice, can expect that many will accept the buyer and will utilize his professional expertise. These expectations are a part of goodwill, and they have a pecuniary value.[142]

In *Hanson v. Hanson*,[143] the Supreme Court of Missouri, after an extensive review of conflicting authorities in both equitable distribution and community property states, held that the goodwill of a professional practice is a marital asset that may be divided in a proceeding for dissolution of marriage. The court carefully distinguished professional goodwill from future earning capacity and the reputation or professional skill of the practitioner. The court stated: "We define goodwill within a professional setting to mean the value of the practice which exceeds its tangible assets and which is the result of the tendency of clients/patients to return to and recommend the practice irrespective of the reputation of the individual practitioner."[144] The highest courts and intermediate appellate courts in the majority of jurisdictions that have confronted the question have come to the conclusion that professional goodwill is a divisible marital asset.[145]

In what appears to be the furthest extension of the recognition of professional goodwill, a New Jersey intermediate appellate court upheld the trial court's recognition of "celebrity goodwill" as marital property. In *Piscopo v. Piscopo*,[146] the court analogized the goodwill flowing from the husband's celebrity status to the professional goodwill that the state's Supreme Court had recognized in *Dugan v. Dugan*,[147] defined as ". . . essentially reputation that will probably generate future business."[148]

---

[142] *Id.* at 1315.

[143] 738 S.W.2d 429 (Mo. 1987).

[144] *Id.* at 434.

[145] *See, e.g., In re Marriage of Hull*, 712 P.2d 1317 (Mont. 1986); *Ford v. Ford*, 782 P.2d 1304 (Nev. 1989); *In re Marriage of Keyser*, 820 P.2d 1194 (Colo. App. 1991); *Russell v. Russell*, 399 S.E.2d 166 (Va. Ct. App. 1990); *Clark v. Clark*, 782 S.W.2d 56 (Ky. Ct. App. 1990).

[146] 557 A.2d 1040 (N.J. Super. Ct. App. Div. 1989).

[147] 457 A.2d 1 (N.J. 1983).

[148] *Id.* at 3. Courts in New York also have recognized celebrity status as marital property. The New York decisions do not analogize to professional goodwill, but find celebrity status to be indistinguishable from the licenses or degrees involved in *O'Brien v. O'Brien*, 489 N.E.2d 712 (N.Y. 1985), and its progeny. *See Elkus v. Elkus*, 572 N.Y.S.2d 901 (N.Y. App. Div. 1991); *Golub v. Golub*, 527 N.Y.S.2d 946 (N.Y. Sup. Ct. 1988); *supra* § 10.08[D].

[b]   Professional Goodwill Not Divisible

The leading case in an equitable distribution state holding that professional goodwill is not marital property is *Holbrook v. Holbrook*,[149] decided by the Wisconsin Court of Appeals. After reviewing myriad authorities from other jurisdictions, the court concluded:

> We are not persuaded that the concept of professional goodwill as a divisible marital asset should be adopted in Wisconsin. We are not obliged nor inclined to follow the twisted and illogical path that other jurisdictions have made in dealing with this concept in the context of divorce.
>
> The concept of professional goodwill evanesces when one attempts to distinguish it from future earning capacity. Although a professional business's good reputation, which is essentially what goodwill consists of, is certainly a thing of value, we do not believe that it bestows on those who have an ownership interest in the business, an actual, separate property interest. The reputation of a law firm or some other professional business is valuable to its individual owner to the extent that it assures continued substantial earnings in the future. It cannot be separately sold or pledged by the individual owners. The goodwill or reputation of such a business accrues to the benefit of the owners only through increased salary.[150]

The court in *Holbrook* then analogized professional goodwill to an educational degree or its increased earning capacity, which the court in an earlier case had held was not marital property.[151] Further, the court found "a disturbing inequity in compelling a professional practitioner to pay a spouse a share of intangible assets at a judicially determined value that could not be realized by a sale or another method of liquidating value."[152] Finally, the court noted that the goodwill or reputation of the husband's law partnership was reflected in the husband's salary and that to treat the law firm's goodwill as a separate, divisible asset would be "double counting."[153] The fact that he was a partner was, however, a proper factor for consideration in the division of assets or the determination of support.

The decision of the Wisconsin Court of Appeals in *Holbrook* continues to be enormously influential in cases in other states holding that professional goodwill is

---

[149] 309 N.W.2d 343 (Wis. Ct. App. 1981). In *McReath v. McReath*, 789 N.W.2d 89 (Wis. Ct. App. 2010), the court clarified its decision in *Holbrook*, noting:

> Thus, the key to *Holbrook* is understanding that it addresses professional goodwill that cannot be sold. At most, Holbrook supports the proposition that *non-salable* professional goodwill is not a divisible asset. *Holbrook* does not contain a blanket holding that professional goodwill may never be treated as divisible property. In *Holbrook*, we did not, as we do here, address a situation in which the evidence and fact finding show that some portion of professional goodwill is salable.

Id. at 94.

[150] *Id.* at 354.

[151] *See De Witt v. De Witt*, 296 N.W.2d 761 (Wis. Ct. App. 1980).

[152] *Holbrook*, 309 N.W.2d at 355.

[153] *Id.*

not a distributable marital asset. In *Powell v. Powell,*[154] for example, the Supreme Court of Kansas, having reviewed conflicting decisions from other jurisdictions, quoted *Holbrook* at length and held that a physician's professional practice does not have goodwill but is personal to and entirely dependent upon the professional. Similarly, and more recently, the Supreme Court of Oklahoma in *Travis v. Travis,*[155] a case of first impression, quoted *Holbrook* with approval in holding that a law practice had no goodwill value for the purpose of dividing property at divorce.[156]

[c]   Professional Goodwill Divisible if Independent of Individual

Courts in a small but increasing minority of jurisdictions take a third approach to the characterization of professional goodwill, declining to adopt a rigid rule. The Supreme Court of Nebraska, in *Taylor v. Taylor,*[157] was the first court to adopt this approach. In *Taylor,* the court held that the husband's medical practice did not have goodwill as a divisible asset. Unlike other courts so holding, however, the Nebraska court declined to announce a firm and unvarying rule. The court concluded that to be distributable property, "goodwill must be a business asset with value independent of the presence or reputation of a particular individual, an asset which may be sold, transferred, conveyed, or pledged."[158] The court cautioned, however, that it was neither stating nor implying that a professional practice may never have goodwill as a salable business asset.

In a case in which the goodwill of the husband's medical practice was at issue, the Supreme Court of Arkansas in *Wilson v. Wilson*[159] noted approvingly the *Taylor* court's observations and concluded accordingly: "Thus, whether goodwill is marital property is a factual question and a party, to establish goodwill as marital property and divisible as such, must produce evidence establishing the saleability or marketability of that goodwill as a business asset of a professional practice."[160]

A Maryland court's decision in *Prahinski v. Prahinski,*[161] applying the approach in *Taylor* to the husband's law practice, is also instructive. The court in *Prahinski* defined "true goodwill" as "not simply a *possibility* of future earnings, but a *probability* based on existing circumstances"[162] and observed that "goodwill is a marketable and transferrable asset."[163] The court noted that even if the goodwill of a law practice cannot ethically be sold, it may still have value. The court concluded

---

[154] 648 P.2d 218 (Kan. 1982).

[155] 795 P.2d 96 (Okla. 1990).

[156] *See also In re Marriage of Zells,* 572 N.E.2d 944 (Ill. 1991); *Donahue v. Donahue,* 384 S.E.2d 741 (S.C. 1989); *Sonek v. Sonek,* 412 S.E.2d 917 (N.C. Ct. App. 1992).

[157] 386 N.W.2d 851 (Neb. 1986).

[158] *Id.* at 858-59.

[159] 741 S.W.2d 640 (Ark. 1987).

[160] *Id.* at 647.

[161] 540 A.2d 833 (Md. Ct. Spec. App. 1988), *aff'd,* 582 A.2d 784 (Md. 1990) (lawyer's goodwill not marital property).

[162] *Id.* at 841 (emphasis in original).

[163] *Id.*

that "if there is true goodwill in an attorney's practice, separable from his individual future earning capacity, then a value can be placed on it."[164] The court determined that on the facts in the case before it, the wife could not make a showing that goodwill existed as an asset distinct from the husband's continued presence and reputation.

Since the decision of the Supreme Court of Nebraska in *Taylor*, courts in other jurisdictions increasingly have followed its commonsensical and persuasive approach and applied its teaching in a variety of circumstances. The Supreme Court of Alaska in *Richmond v. Richmond*,[165] for example, held that only marketable goodwill may be included in the marital estate, and that the goodwill of a sole practitioner was not marketable and, therefore, not an asset subject to distribution in a divorce proceeding. Again, the Supreme Court of Florida in *Thompson v. Thompson*[166] citing *Taylor* with approval, held that goodwill is divisible if it was developed during the marriage and exists separate and apart from the individual's reputation.[167] In *Yoon v. Yoon*,[168] the Supreme Court of Indiana reached a similar result with respect to the division at divorce of the goodwill value of a business or professional practice. The court reviewed decisions that had addressed the issue in several jurisdictions, and concluded that "enterprise goodwill" is divisible while "personal goodwill" was nothing more than enhanced earning capacity and was, therefore, not subject to distribution. Holdings in a number of courts reflect this trend toward recognition of professional goodwill as a divisible marital asset only if it is independent of the individual practitioner.[169]

[C] Valuation

Valuation of professional practices and other closely held business interests is without question one of the most difficult problems that courts and lawyers face in connection with the equitable distribution of property on dissolution of marriage. There are few principles that are uniformly or unvaryingly reliable. The form of the enterprise — whether a sole proprietorship, a partnership, or a closely held corporation — is generally not controlling and most often not of particular significance. In most cases, and certainly when the enterprise is financially or structurally complex, valuation requires the testimony of experts. This is not to suggest, however, that valuation involves valid and reliable scientific methods. All too frequently, well-qualified experts, purporting to use identical methods of valuation, reach widely variant conclusions as to the value of the same assets. There is as much conflict over the value of goodwill as there is with respect to its classification.[170] Nevertheless, appellate courts uniformly hold that the difficulty of

---

[164] *Id.*

[165] 779 P.2d 1211 (Alaska 1989).

[166] 576 So. 2d 267 (Fla. 1991).

[167] *See also Ombres v. Ombres*, 596 So. 2d 956 (Fla. 1991).

[168] 711 N.E.2d 1265 (Ind. 1999).

[169] *See, e.g., Fexa v. Fexa*, 578 A.2d 1314 (Pa. Super. Ct. 1990); *McCabe v. McCabe*, 575 A.2d 87 (Pa. 1990); *Hollander v. Hollander*, 597 A.2d 1012 (Md. Ct. Spec. App. 1991).

[170] *See supra* § 10.09[B].

establishing value does not relieve trial courts of the obligation to do so.

Valuation contemplates the determination of fair market value, commonly defined as "the price at which the property would change hands between a willing buyer and a willing seller when the former is not under any compulsion to buy and the latter is not under any compulsion to sell, both parties having reasonable knowledge of relevant facts."[171]

Determining the fair market value of a closely held corporation (and by analogy, other closely held business interests) is problematic. Because sales of such corporations are infrequent, no market of willing buyers and sellers exists.

The methods or approaches to valuation in the following discussion should be considered as representative or illustrative, not all-inclusive. As long as the method of valuation chosen by a trial court is fair and reasonable and is supported by the evidence, a reviewing court is unlikely to reject it.

[1] Book Value

A number of courts have expressed skepticism with respect to exclusive reliance on book value in valuing shares of closely held corporations. The Superior Court of New Jersey, in *Lavene v. Lavene*,[172] cogently described the limitations of book value as a method of valuation:

> There are probably few assets whose valuation imposes as difficult, intricate and sophisticated a task as interests in close corporations. They cannot be realistically evaluated by a simplistic approach which is based solely on book value, which fails to deal with the realities of the goodwill concept, which does not consider investment value of a business in terms of actual profit, and which does not deal with the question of discounting the value of a minority interest.[173]

The courts do not, however, categorically and without exception reject book value as the measure of value. The circumstances of the case may justify its acceptance.[174]

[2] Capitalization of Excess Earnings

There is widespread agreement that earnings are the most important factor in valuation of the stock of an operating company, and these are sometimes the sole factor used in determining value.[175] The courts generally accept the fact that "at least in the case of an operating company with consistent earnings, asset value has markedly less importance in valuation than does earnings,"[176] and occasionally,

---

[171] Rev. Rul. 59-60, 1959-1 C.B. 237.

[172] 372 A.2d 629 (N.J. Super. Ct. App. Div.), *cert. denied*, 379 A.2d 259 (N.J. 1977).

[173] *Id.* at 633. *See also Nehorayoff v. Nehorayoff*, 437 N.Y.S.2d 584 (N.Y. Sup. Ct. 1981).

[174] *See, e.g., In re Marriage of Messerle*, 643 P.2d 1286 (Or. Ct. App. 1982), *review denied*, 648 P.2d 853 (Or. 1982); *Whaley v. Whaley*, 436 N.E.2d 816 (Ind. Ct. App. 1982).

[175] Ruth R. Longenecker, *A Practical Guide to Valuation of Closely Held Stock*, 122 Tr. & Est. 32, 33 (1983).

[176] *Id.* at 32 (citations omitted).

"earnings have even been the only factor used to determine value."[177]

Earnings having been determined, capitalization of excess earnings is frequently employed as a method of valuation. This method involves applying to the earnings of the corporation a capitalization rate or multiplier that reflects the stability of past corporate earnings and the predictability of future earnings.[178]

Courts frequently adopt this approach in evaluating the goodwill of professional corporations. As the court noted in *Poore v. Poore*[179] in a frequently cited passage:

> Under this approach, the value of goodwill is based in part on the amount by which the earnings of the professional spouse exceed that which would have been earnings by a person with similar education, experience, and skill as an employee in the same general locale . . . . It has also been suggested that the value of goodwill be based on one year's average gross income of the practice or a percentage thereof . . . .[180]

The trial court should then determine and average the net income before taxes of the professional for approximately five years, compare this average with the employee norm and multiply the excess amount by an appropriate capitalization factor.

[3] Buy-Sell Agreements

A serviceable description of buy-sell agreements is as follows:

> A buy-sell agreement usually provides for the business entity or remaining principal's purchase of the withdrawing parties' shares at a predetermined price. Such an agreement is restrictive in nature as it alienates the transferability of the shares. Those agreements are usually entered into to meet the business-planning objectives such as protection from outsiders, prevention of changes in ownership, economic security and estate tax purposes.[181]

Such arrangements frequently appear as partnership agreements and in connection with other forms of closely held business interests. Generally, the courts take such agreements into account in arriving at a valuation of these interests but do not consider them as binding.[182]

---

[177] *Id.* at 33.

[178] *See* Joseph D. Hartwig, *Valuing an Interest in a Closely Held Business for the Purpose of Buy/Sell Agreements and for Death Tax Purposes*, 26 S. Cal. Inst. on Fed. Tax'n. 215 (1974).

[179] 331 S.E.2d 266 (N.C. Ct. App. 1985).

[180] *Id.* at 271-72.

[181] Gary N. Skoloff, *A Matrimonial Attorney's Alert: Beware of Buy-Sell Agreements*, 7 Nat'l. L.J., Sept. 10, 1984, at 16 (citing Desmond & Kelly, Business Valuation Handbook 239 (1980)).

[182] *See, e.g., Amodio v. Amodio*, 509 N.E.2d 936, 937 (N.Y. 1987); *Kaye v. Kaye*, 478 N.Y.S.2d 324, 328 (N.Y. App. Div. 1984) ("A bona fide buy-sell agreement which predates the marital discord, while not conclusive, may also prove an invaluable aid"); *Stern v. Stern*, 331 A.2d 257 (N.J. 1975).

[4] Discount for Minority Interest

Among the factors affecting the fair market value of the stock of closely held corporations is the size of the block of stock being valued. A minority interest in an enterprise that others control may be of significantly less value than the liquidation value of the shares. This lack of control significantly reduces the value of the minority shareholder's stock.[183] Accordingly, courts in a number of equitable distribution jurisdictions discount the value of a minority interest in valuing and distributing interests in closely held corporations upon marriage dissolution.

§ 10.10   PENSIONS AND RETIREMENT BENEFITS

[A] Overview

With the possible exception of the marital home, pensions or retirement benefits are the most significant asset available for distribution in many marriage dissolution proceedings. Consequently, there is a large body of cases dealing with the treatment of pensions. Courts have struggled to classify and value pensions, sometimes with little statutory guidance. The majority of courts in equitable distribution jurisdictions hold that all pensions, including military retirement benefits, are distributable as marital property. A few decisions, however, have treated pensions somewhat less expansively, distinguishing between vested and nonvested benefits.

The majority of equitable distribution statutes are silent with respect to the treatment of pensions and other forms of retirement benefits. Those statutes that do address the question reflect two basic approaches. They either classify pensions or retirement benefits as marital or separate property[184] or list these assets among the factors the divorce court must consider when making a property distribution.[185] The statutes offer no guidance with respect to the valuation or equitable distribution of these assets.

[B] Basic Terms and Concepts

Pensions are generally either defined contribution plans or defined benefit plans. A defined contribution plan provides a separate account for each participating employee into which specified periodic contributions are made.[186] Interest in the invested assets and appreciation are allocated to each employee's account, and the employee, upon retirement, "is entitled to an amount equal to the cumulative value of his share."[187]

---

[183] *See* Alan L. Feld, *The Implications of Minority Interest and Stock Restrictions in Valuing Closely-Held Shares*, 122 U. Pa. L. Rev. 934, 934-36 (1974).

[184] *See, e.g.*, Fla. Stat. Ann. § 61.075(6)(a)(d); N.C. Gen. Stat. § 50-20(b)(1).

[185] *See, e.g.*, Iowa Code § 598.21(5)(i).

[186] *See Rosenberg v. Rosenberg*, 497 A.2d 485, 493 (Md. Ct. Spec. App. 1985).

[187] *Id.* at 494.

Defined benefit plans provide a fixed monthly (or annual) amount for the employee upon retirement and for the rest of his or her life. The employer, under such plans, does not maintain a separate account for each employee. Most state retirement systems are defined benefit plans.

A further distinction involves whether a plan is contributory or noncontributory, terms that describe the method of the plan's funding. In a contributory plan, employees make payments into the plan, whereas under a noncontributory plan, the employer makes all the payments or contributions. Most commonly, both the employer and the employee, generally through payroll deductions, make contributions under the plan. Both defined contribution plans and defined benefit plans may be contributory or noncontributory, nominally funded by the employee, the employer, or both.

Valuation and distribution of pension benefits may be affected significantly by whether they are vested or nonvested and whether they are mature or nonmatured. Generally, pension benefits are said to be vested when the employee's discharge or voluntary termination of employment would not forfeit benefits.[188] Once pension benefits are vested, in order to receive them the employee need only survive until retirement age.[189] Nonvested pension benefits, on the other hand, "are contingent upon the employee continuing his employment with the employer or organization sponsoring the plan."[190] Pension benefits are said to be matured when the employee, upon retirement, has an unconditional right to receive payment.[191]

[C] Characterization of Pension Benefits

The overwhelming majority of courts that have addressed the issue hold that pensions, whether or not vested, are marital property insofar as the rights are acquired during the marriage. In some states, the courts have ruled only with respect to vested pensions.

[1] Majority View — All Pensions Marital Property

The leading case holding that pension benefits are marital property whether vested or nonvested is *In re Marriage of Brown*,[192] decided by the Supreme Court of California, a community property jurisdiction. Courts in a substantial number of equitable distribution jurisdictions have followed the result in Brown and often adopted its reasoning. Accordingly, the case warrants more than cursory attention.

The court in *Brown* overruled its own decision, some thirty years earlier in *French v. French*,[193] that nonvested pension rights were not property but a mere expectancy and, therefore, not subject to division upon divorce as community

---

[188] *See Damiano v. Damiano*, 463 N.Y.S.2d 477, 480 (N.Y. App. Div. 1983).

[189] *Id.*

[190] *Id.*

[191] *Id.*

[192] 544 P.2d 561 (Cal. 1976).

[193] 112 P.2d 235 (Cal. 1941).

property. The husband's employer in *Brown* maintained a noncontributory pension plan under which the employee could forfeit his rights if discharged before accumulating a minimum number of "points." The trial court held that because the husband's rights were not fully vested, they were not divisible as community property. Reversing, the Supreme Court of California noted that pension benefits were not merely an expectancy, but were a form of deferred compensation for service rendered and thus were property. In a frequently quoted passage, the court observed:

> We conclude that *French v. French* and subsequent cases erred in characterizing nonvested pension rights as expectancies and in denying the trial courts authority to divide such rights as community property. This mischaracterization of pension rights has, and unless overturned, will continue to result in inequitable division of community assets. Over the past decades, pension benefits have become an increasingly significant part of the consideration earned by the employee for his services. As the date of vesting and retirement approaches, the value of the pension right grows until it often represents the most important asset of the marital community. . . . A division of community property which awards one spouse the entire value of this asset, without any offsetting award to the other spouse, does not represent that equal division of community property contemplated by [the statute].[194]

Since the California court's decision in *Brown*, the highest courts or intermediate appellate courts of several states have ruled to the same effect in a variety of circumstances. Although appellate courts in some jurisdictions have yet to decide the question, the clear trend is to hold that nonvested as well as vested pensions are marital property. In some cases, even when the pension benefits are vested, the language of the decisions and their reliance on *Brown* make clear their application to nonvested pensions as well.[195]

After surveying the law in a number of community property and equitable distribution jurisdictions, the New York Supreme Court, Appellate Division in *Damiano v. Damiano*[196] stated the generally prevailing view that "pension benefits belonging to either spouse attributable to employment during the marriage, whether those benefits are vested or nonvested, and whether the plan is contributory or noncontributory constitute marital property subject to equitable distribution upon divorce."[197]

---

[194] *Brown*, 544 P.2d 561, 566 (Cal. 1976) (citation omitted).

[195] *See, e.g., Laing v. Laing*, 741 P.2d 649 (Alaska 1987); *Robert C.S. v. Barbara J.S.*, 434 A.2d 383 (Del. 1981); *Janssen v. Janssen*, 331 N.W.2d 752 (Minn. 1983); *Carpenter v. Carpenter*, 657 P.2d 646 (Okla. 1983).

[196] 463 N.Y.S.2d 477 (N.Y. App. Div. 1983).

[197] *Id.* at 481. *See also Cohen v. Cohen*, 937 S.W.2d 823 (Tenn. 1996) (holding that retirement benefits that accrue during the marriage are marital property, whether vested or unvested).

[2]   Classification of Pensions — Minority View

A minority of courts have not explicitly accepted the teaching of the decision in *In re Marriage of Brown*.[198] In *Kirkman v. Kirkman*,[199] for example, the Supreme Court of Indiana declined to approve distribution of pension or retirement benefits that were not vested, having held in an earlier case that vested benefits were distributable property.[200]

[D]   Valuation and Distribution of Pensions

There are three basic approaches to the division of pension benefits that have been characterized as marital property. The first, and the one the courts have usually preferred, is to determine the present value of the pension benefits, taking into account contingencies such as vesting, maturity, and mortality, and to award the nonemployee spouse a lump sum or other assets as an offset. Second, the court may award the nonemployee spouse a specific share or percentage of the pension benefits, if, as, and when received. Finally, the court may defer distribution, reserving jurisdiction until the time the employed spouse actually begins to receive benefits under the pension plan. This latter method usually eliminates the need for the court to value the pension during the course of the divorce proceeding.

The decision of the Superior Court of Pennsylvania in *Braderman v. Braderman*[201] provides an excellent overview of the selection and application of methodology for the valuation and distribution of retirement benefits. In *Braderman*, the husband was in receipt of monthly benefits from the State Employees Retirement System. After determining that the husband's vested and matured benefits were marital property, the court turned to the questions of valuation and distribution of those benefits.

The immediate offset method "divides the benefits at the time the equitable distribution order is entered by assigning a present value to them."[202] Having determined this present value, the court must calculate the portion earned during the marriage, and then proceed as follows.

> This present value must then be multiplied by the "coverture" fraction to reach the present value of the entitlement which was acquired during the marriage. The "coverture" fraction represents that portion of the value of the benefits attributable to the marriage. The numerator of the fraction reflects the total period of time the employee spouse participated in the plan during the marriage, and the denominator is the total period the employee participated in the benefits program . . . . Next, the court must determine how the sum available for equitable distribution should be apportioned between the spouses . . . . After determining the non-employee spouse's interest in the benefits, the court awards these benefits

---

[198]   544 P.2d 561 (Cal. 1976).

[199]   555 N.E.2d 1293 (Ind. 1990).

[200]   *See In re Marriage of Adams*, 535 N.E.2d 124 (Ind. 1989).

[201]   488 A.2d 613 (Pa. Super. Ct. 1985).

[202]   *Id.* at 619.

to the employee spouse and offsets this award by distributing other marital property or by ordering payment to the non-employee spouse.[203]

In some jurisdictions, while recognizing that present value is generally accepted as the proper test for determining the value of pension benefits, contingencies such as disability or early retirement cannot be accurately calculated under this rule. In *In re Rolfe v. Rolfe*,[204] the Supreme Court of Montana responded to such concerns, stating:

> The division of retirement benefits upon receipt is commonly known as the "time rule . . . ." Under this method, the marital interest is represented by a fraction, the numerator of which is the length of the employee's service during the marriage, and the denominator is the employee's total length of service. This fraction is then applied to each benefit payment, lump or periodic, to determine the portion earned during the marriage. Although the extent of the marital interest is determined as of the date of the dissolution, the benefit factors to be applied to the pension credits earned during the marriage are those in effect at retirement. Thus, the non-employee spouse is entitled to increases or accruals on her interest because of the delay in receiving those payments.[205]

Under the reserved jurisdiction (or deferred distribution) method of awarding pension benefits, the court retains jurisdiction until the pension benefits reach maturity or pay status. Under this method, as previously stated, it is not necessary to calculate the present value. Instead, "the 'coverture' fraction is applied to the benefits when they enter pay status since there are too many variables projected into the future."[206]

A number of courts have expressed a preference for reducing pension benefits to present value and disposing of them in the course of the divorce proceeding.[207] The rationale for this preference is that it settles the pension distribution question and avoids continued strife and hostility between the spouses. In *Moore v. Moore*[208] the Supreme Court of New Jersey cogently summarized the potential problems under an alternative method of distribution:

> Under the "deferred distribution" approach the parties, the court, and the employer of the pensioner may continue to be embroiled in controversy. On actual receipt of the benefits by the pensioner a determination of the proper percentage of each pension payment to be distributed to the non-employee spouse must be made. The non-employee spouse must keep contact with

---

[203] *Id. See generally* Skoloff, *How to Evaluate and Distribute Employee Benefits in Divorce*, Nat'l L.J., Feb. 13, 1984, at 25. *See also McDermott v. McDermott*, 552 A.2d 786 (Vt. 1988) (holding that failure of trial court to use coverture fraction in calculating present value of husband's retirement benefits attributable to marriage was abuse of discretion).

[204] 766 P.2d 223 (Mont. 1988).

[205] *Id.* at 226.

[206] *Braderman*, 488 A.2d at 619.

[207] *See, e.g., Morlan v. Morlan*, 720 P.2d 497 (Alaska 1986); *Hodgins v. Hodgins*, 497 A.2d 1187 (N.H. 1985).

[208] 553 A.2d 20 (N.J. 1989).

the employee spouse to determine the official date of retirement. Additionally, the non-employee spouse will have to be constantly vigilant to ensure that proper revised beneficiary forms are filed with the employer and that agreed proper benefits are chosen at retirement. For instance, if the employee spouse remarries and changes the beneficiary of the plan, his new wife may receive the benefit.[209]

Despite the frequently expressed judicial preference for reduction of pension benefits to present value and distribution at the time of the dissolution proceeding, the decisions generally make it clear that once pensions are characterized as marital property, their treatment is within the discretion of the court. The way in which this discretion is exercised depends on the facts of the case and the circumstances of the spouses.

[E]   Disability Benefits

The courts in equitable distribution jurisdictions have not addressed the treatment of disability pensions with great frequency. Decisions in this area, compared with those involving retirement benefits, are relatively sparse. The courts take several basic and distinct approaches to disability benefits. Some courts hold that disability benefits are subject to equitable distribution and do not distinguish them, in this respect, from retirement benefits. Simply stated, these courts hold that disability payments are marital property, finding no meaningful distinction between annuities payable upon disability and those payable on longevity.[210]

Under a second approach, the nonpensioned spouse may be entitled to an equitable distribution of a disability pension only to the extent that the pension matches the benefits that the previously employed spouse would have received upon retirement. Courts adopting this approach view disability payments as subject to equitable distribution only to the extent that they represent what would be payable upon retirement and are, therefore, indistinguishable from a longevity retirement benefit.

The decision of the Superior Court of Pennsylvania in *Ciliberti v. Ciliberti*[211] is illustrative, holding that a true disability pension is not marital property subject to equitable distribution. The court noted that the purpose of such benefits is the compensation of the employee spouse for lost earning capacity, replacing future income that the employee cannot earn because of disability. The court cautioned, however, that when a portion of the disability pension represents retirement benefits, that amount remains marital property subject to equitable distribution.[212]

---

[209] *Id.* at 26.

[210] *See, e.g., Morrison v. Morrison*, 692 S.W.2d 601 (Ark. 1985); *Lookingbill v. Lookingbill*, 483 A.2d 1 (Md. 1984); *Watson v. Watson*, 379 N.W.2d 588 (Minn. Ct. App. 1985).

[211] 542 A.2d 580 (Pa. Super. Ct. 1988).

[212] *See also Mylett v. Mylett*, 558 N.Y.S.2d 160 (N.Y. App. Div. 1990).

The third approach holds that disability payments are not distributable as marital property.[213] In *Christmas v. Christmas*,[214] the Supreme Court of Oklahoma offered a persuasive rationale for this conclusion. The court observed that retirement pensions, which insure against survival beyond the age of retirement, function as substitutes for life savings. Absent retirement coverage, savings of the additional wages received would be joint property earned during marriage. Disability benefits, however, are insurance against wage losses from disability prior to superannuation, and when received after divorce "replace post-coverture wages that would be the earner's separate property."[215] Therefore, the court concluded, "while retirement pensions replace joint property, disability benefits replace separate property. This difference in the replacement nature of the benefits requires that disability benefits be classified as the disabled worker's separate property."[216]

[F] Federal Pensions

The Supremacy Clause of the United States Constitution forbids states from interfering with federal authority. Although family law traditionally has been a state matter for most purposes, the Supremacy Clause may still be invoked when a federal interest is at stake. Such a federal interest is involved in some federal pensions.

In *Hisquierdo v. Hisquierdo*,[217] for example, the Supreme Court struck down a state court ordered property division of a Railroad Retirement pension. The Court found that the state court order determining that the benefits were community property would do major damage to federal interests. The decision was based on the two provisions of the Act that stated that the benefits were not assignable and could not be anticipated.[218] Subsequently, *Hisquierdo* was overruled in part by a 1983 amendment that allows some railroad retirement benefits to be classified as either community or marital.

The remainder of benefits under the Railroad Retirement Act remain preempted and state courts cannot consider these benefits when making a property division.[219]

[G] Qualified Domestic Relations Orders (QDROs)

State courts also must deal with the application of state domestic relations laws to private pensions that are regulated by the federal Employee Retirement Income Security Act of 1974 (ERISA).[220] As originally enacted, ERISA prohibited

---

[213] *See, e.g., Sherman v. Sherman*, 740 S.W.2d 203 (Mo. Ct. App. 1987).

[214] 787 P.2d 1267 (Okla. 1990).

[215] *Id.* at 1268.

[216] *Id.*

[217] 439 U.S. 572 (1979).

[218] 45 U.S.C. § 231 (1986).

[219] *See Belt v. Belt*, 398 N.W.2d 737 (N.D. 1987).

[220] 29 U.S.C. § 1003(a)(1) (2012).

assignment or alienation of benefits under pension plans subject to the Act.

The Retirement Equity Act of 1984 (REA)[221] now provides that if a state court accepts a Qualified Domestic Relations Order (QDRO), the pension benefits may be assigned. A "qualified domestic relations order" is one "which creates or recognizes the existence of an alternate payee's right to, or assigns to alternate payee the right to, receive all or a portion of the benefits payable with respect to a participant under a [pension or retirement] plan."[222]

A QDRO must specify the name and last known mailing address of the participant and each alternate payee designated by the court order, and the amount or percentage of benefits each alternate payee is to receive when the benefits are to be distributed. The QDRO must also specify the number of payments or the period for which the order is effective, and identify which retirement or pension plan the order applies to. Upon receipt of a domestic relations order, the pension plan administrator must notify the participant and alternate payee, and if within 18 months the domestic relations order is determined to be a qualified domestic relations order (QDRO), the plan administrator will distribute the money to the alternate payee. If, however, the domestic relations order is found not to be a qualified domestic relations order, the plan administrator must pay the pension proceeds to the person who would have received the money if there had been no order in the first place.[223]

[H]   Military Retirement Benefits

On June 26, 1981, the Supreme Court of the United States held, in *McCarty v. McCarty*,[224] that federal law bars state courts from dividing military retirement pay under state community property laws. Although the decision explicitly addressed division in community property states, its language and principles clearly apply to the division of marital property in equitable distribution states generally. The Court in *McCarty* posed the issue as "whether, upon the dissolution of a marriage, federal law precludes a state court from dividing military nondisability retired pay pursuant to state community property laws."[225] The Court concluded that the federal supremacy clause barred states from dividing or distributing military retirement benefits in divorce proceedings.

In response to the decision in *McCarty*, Congress enacted the Uniformed Services Former Spouses Protection Act (USFSPA),[226] effective January 1, 1983. The effect of the act is to place state courts in the position they were in prior to the decision in *McCarty*, enabling them to apply state law in determining whether military retirement pay is divisible on divorce. The statute provides, in part:

---

[221]   29 U.S.C. § 1056 (2012).

[222]   29 U.S.C. § 1056(d)(3)(B)(i) (2012).

[223]   *See generally* I.R.C. § 414(p)(2)-(7) (2008).

[224]   453 U.S. 210 (1981).

[225]   *Id.* at 211.

[226]   10 U.S.C. § 1408 (2012).

Subject to the limitations of this section, a court may treat disposable retired pay payable to a member for pay periods beginning after June 25, 1981, either as property solely of the member or as property of the member and his spouse in accordance with the law of the jurisdiction of such court.[227]

The USFSPA, then, permits state courts to treat military retirement benefits as property subject to distribution but it does not require them to do so. The determination is within the province of the state courts. A majority of state courts addressing the question hold that military retirement pensions are marital property. A small minority of courts have held that military retirement benefits are not distributable.

Military pensioners may be eligible to receive tax exempt disability benefits, but must waive a corresponding portion of their retirement payments to avoid double compensation. The Uniformed Services Former Spouse's Protection Act (Act) authorizes states to treat military retirement pay as divisible property excluding any amount waived in order to receive disability benefits.

In *Mansell v. Mansell*,[228] parties entered into a settlement agreement prior to the Act's passage. The agreement provided for the wife to receive 50% of the husband's military pension including the portion waived to receive veterans disability benefits. The husband's modification petition was denied by the lower and intermediate appellate courts. The Supreme Court reversed and remanded holding that states may not treat military pay waived to receive veteran's benefits as divisible property.

The Court noted that the Act exemplifies "one of those rare instances where Congress has directly and specifically legislated in the area of domestic relations."[229] The holding was based on a plain meaning reading of the Act and an interpretation by the Court that the legislature intended to create new benefits for spouses but also to limit the state court's discretion and thereby protect military retirees.

§ 10.11   VALUATION OF ASSETS: GENERAL PRINCIPLES

Valuation of assets is a critical step in an equitable distribution proceeding. After the court has determined what property is eligible for distribution, a value must be placed on that property so that an equitable allocation can be made between the spouses.[230]

There is a clear consensus among appellate courts that the valuation of assets is within the trial court's discretion and that those courts' findings will not be disturbed on appeal absent an abuse of that discretion. In *Hertz v. Hertz*,[231] the

---

[227] 10 U.S.C. § 1408(c)(1) (2012).

[228] 490 U.S. 581 (1989).

[229] *Id.* at 587.

[230] *See Rothman v. Rothman*, 320 A.2d 496, 503 (N.J. 1974).

[231] 229 N.W.2d 42 (Minn. 1975).

Supreme Court of Minnesota set out the basic principal in language that is typical and characteristic of the cases generally:

> Assigning a specific value to an asset is a finding of fact; disputes as to asset valuation are to be addressed to the trier of fact, and conflicts are to be resolved in that court . . . .

> Furthermore, valuation is necessarily an approximation in many cases, and it is only necessary that the value arrived at lies within a reasonable range of figures. Thus, the market valuation determined by the trier of fact should be sustained if it falls within the limits of credible estimates made by competent witnesses even if it does not coincide exactly with the estimate of any one of them.[232]

§ 10.12 FAIR AND EQUITABLE DISTRIBUTION

[A] Introduction

Courts undertaking the equitable distribution of property pursuant to divorce face three tasks. The first task, classification or characterization, requires determination of which assets of the spouses are subject to division and distribution. Second, a trial court must place a value on the assets, both those that are distributable and those, if any, that remain the property of one spouse or the other. The final task, of course, is to make a fair division of the distributable assets.

Most equitable distribution statutes set out a list of factors that trial courts must consider when distributing property. In a few states, where the statutes do not contain factors, appellate courts have developed them for the guidance of trial courts. In *Ferguson v. Ferguson*,[233] for example, the Supreme Court of Mississippi, without guidance from the legislature, enunciated guidelines similar to the factors in several states in order to assist chancellors in the division of marital property. No particular factors are intended to be more important than any others. Thus, in the final analysis, judicial discretion is the hallmark of equitable distribution of property on divorce.

A much debated point is whether equal division is the most equitable.[234] The question is far from resolved and perhaps never will be. In a small minority of states, the statutes contain a presumption of equal division of marital property. In a few others, the courts have created a fifty-fifty starting point for division, even while rejecting a presumption of equal division. Some courts reject altogether both presumptions of equal division and starting points.

Also, with some frequency courts will decline to make substantial property distributions in marriages that are of short duration. In *Rose v. Rose*,[235] for

---

[232] *Id.* at 44 (citation omitted).

[233] 639 So. 2d 921 (Miss. 1994).

[234] *See, e.g.,* Henry H. Foster, *Commentary on Equitable Distribution*, 26 N.Y.L. Sch. L. Rev. 1 (1981).

[235] 755 P.2d 1121 (Alaska 1988).

example, the Supreme Court of Alaska adopted this approach, stating that "in marriages of short duration, where there has been no significant commingling of assets between the parties, the trial court may, without abusing its discretion, treat the property division as an action in the nature of recission, aimed at placing the parties in, as closely as possible, the financial position they would have occupied had no marriage taken place."[236]

[B] Factors in Equitable Distribution

As noted, most equitable distribution statutes require that the trial court consider a variety of explicit factors in arriving at a fair and equitable division of marital property. Absent statutory factors, courts have enumerated factors similar to those that are statutorily mandated elsewhere. Generally, judicial application of the factors is mandatory, often with the additional requirement that the trial court set forth written reasons for its determinations on property distribution or to indicate the factors on which it relied.

Several states have adopted the provisions of the 1970 version of the Uniform Marriage and Divorce Act (UMDA) to control the disposition of property. The Act requires that the court consider all relevant factors, including:

(1) contribution of each spouse to acquisition of marital property, including contribution of a spouse as homemaker;

(2) value of the property set aside to each spouse;

(3) duration of the marriage; and

(4) economic circumstances of each spouse when the division of property is to become effective including the desirability of awarding the family home or the right to live therein for reasonable periods to the spouse having custody of any children.[237]

The UMDA factors are by no means exclusive or exhaustive, and additional factors appear in various combinations and with variations in language in statutes in the several jurisdictions. An additional factor in an increasing number of jurisdictions is the contribution of a spouse to the education, training, or increased earning power of the other spouse.[238] Also, in a considerable number of states, the list of factors concludes with a catchall provision, authorizing the court to consider any other factors deemed relevant, just, or proper, in addition to those expressed in the statute.[239]

---

[236] *Id.* at 1125.

[237] Unif. Marriage and Divorce Act § 307, 9A U.L.A. 240 (1973).

[238] *See, e.g.,* Iowa Code § 598.21(5)(e); 23 Pa. Cons. Stat. § 3502(a)(4).

[239] *See, e.g.,* N.Y. Dom. Rel. Law § 236(B)(5)(d)(14) (2012) ("any other factor which the court shall expressly find to be just and proper").

[C] Equal Division and Starting Points

The statutes of several states contain a presumption that property subject to distribution shall be divided equally. The language of the Arkansas statute is illustrative, requiring that "marital property shall be distributed one-half (½) to each person unless the court finds such a division to be inequitable. In that event the court shall make some other division that the court deems equitable" after considering nine listed factors.[240]

In a number of other states, courts have held that the equal division of marital property is presumptively equitable or is an appropriate starting point when undertaking equitable distribution at divorce. These courts have so held without the benefit of statutory guidance or mandates to this effect. Most such courts caution, however, that the adoption of a fifty-fifty starting point by no means reflects a presumption of equal division. Rather, the determination of what distribution is fair, just, and equitable is a matter within the sound discretion of the trial court.

It is not uncommon for courts to abstain from significant property divisions in marriages of short duration. Typifying this approach is *Rose v. Rose.*

[D] Dissipation of Assets and Marital Misconduct

[1] Overview[241]

There is general agreement that dissipation of assets is a relevant factor in the equitable distribution of property. In fact, in most states, the equitable distribution statute lists dissipation among the factors the court is required to consider when making a property division. There is somewhat less agreement, however, about what conduct constitutes dissipation of assets. To establish dissipation, the burden of proof is generally on the party charged. Remedies for the adversely affected party range from inclusion of the value of the dissipated assets in the marital estate to consideration of a party's dissipation of assets as a factor in the ultimate property distribution.

There is considerably less agreement about the relevance in equitable distribution of marital misconduct or fault that is not economic in nature. In some jurisdictions, the statutes require that fault be considered, while others proscribe its consideration. In still other states, the statutes are silent and the courts decide the issue by applying general equitable principles.

[2] What Conduct Constitutes Dissipation?

The courts have not adopted a uniform definition of dissipation to determine what actions or inactions by a spouse that diminish the amount of property available for division are sufficient to affect the ultimate distribution. Whether or not a spouse's

---

[240] Ark. Code Ann. § 9-12-315.

[241] *See generally* Lewis Becker, *Conduct of a Spouse That Dissipates Property Available for Equitable Property Distribution: A Suggested Analysis*, 52 Ohio St. L.J. 95 (1991).

conduct constitutes dissipation depends on the facts of the particular case.[242] The Supreme Court of Illinois has detailed the elements that constitute dissipation of assets. Courts in other states frequently cite or rely on Illinois authority when addressing this issue. In *In re Marriage of O'Neill*,[243] the court stated: "[T]he term 'dissipation'. . . refers to the 'use of marital property for the sole benefit of one of the spouses for a purpose unrelated to the marriage at a time that the marriage is undergoing an irreconcilable breakdown . . . .' "[244]

The courts have departed on occasion from the general requirement that dissipation, to be cognizable as a factor in distribution, must occur during the breakdown of the marriage.[245] Also, a requirement of intent to dissipate assets is often implied or mentioned explicitly by courts. In *Robinette v. Robinette*,[246] for example, the Court of Appeals of Kentucky stated:

> We believe the concept of dissipation, that is, spending funds for a nonmarital purpose, is an appropriate one for the court to consider when the property is expended (1) during a period when there is a separation or dissolution impending, and (2) where there is a clear showing of intent to deprive one's spouse of his or her proportionate share of the marital property.[247]

[3] Burden of Proof

The courts are in general agreement that the party against whom dissipation is charged has the burden of proving the legitimacy of his or her expenditure of marital funds. The opinion of the Appellate Court of Illinois in *In re Marriage of Smith*[248] presents a useful paradigm. In *Smith*, the trial court awarded the wife some 63 percent of the marital property, having concluded that the husband had dissipated marital assets.

On appeal, the husband asserted that the trial court's finding of dissipation was not supported by the evidence, implying that it was the wife's obligation to prove how the husband had spent the funds. Squarely rejecting this position, the court stated the following general principle: "[T]he person charged with dissipation is under an obligation to establish by clear and specific evidence how the funds were spent. General and vague statements that funds were spent on marital expenses or to pay bills are inadequate to avoid a finding of dissipation."[249]

---

[242] *In re Marriage of Sevon*, 453 N.E.2d 866 (Ill. App. Ct. 1983).

[243] 563 N.E.2d 494 (Ill. 1990).

[244] *Id.* at 498-99 (citation omitted).

[245] *See, e.g.*, *In re Marriage of Kaplan*, 500 N.E.2d 612 (Ill. App. Ct. 1986).

[246] 736 S.W.2d 351 (Ky. Ct. App. 1987).

[247] *Id.* at 354.

[248] 471 N.E.2d 1008 (Ill. App. Ct. 1984).

[249] *Id.* at 1013. *See also Manaker v. Manaker*, 528 A.2d 1170 (Conn. App. Ct. 1987); *Robinette v. Robinette*, 736 S.W.2d 351 (Ky. Ct. App. 1987); *In re Marriage of Roehrdanz*, 410 N.W.2d 359 (Minn. Ct. App. 1987).

[4] Remedies for Dissipation

In seeking to compensate or make whole the innocent party in cases involving spousal dissipation of assets, the courts have not taken a uniform approach. Some courts hold that dissipation justifies including in the marital estate assets that are no longer in existence at the time when the equitable distribution of property is ordered. In other jurisdictions, however, the courts find such awards to be improper.

The Appellate Court of Illinois stated the commonly prevailing principle in *In re Marriage of Partyka*[250] as follows: "Where a party has dissipated marital assets, the court may charge the amount dissipated against his or her share of the marital property so as to compensate the other party."[251] In accordance with this principle, courts in several states have included in the marital estate dissipated assets no longer in existence.[252]

Not all courts find authority to include dissipated, and therefore nonexistent, assets in the marital estate. In *Lippert v. Lippert*,[253] for example, the Supreme Court of Montana held that although the state's equitable distribution statute required the court to consider dissipation, the power of the trial court did not extend to assets not in existence. As an alternative to the award of nonexistent assets, the court may take into account a party's dissipation of assets as a factor in the ultimate distribution of whatever marital property remains.

[5] Marital Misconduct or Fault

It is clear that dissipation of assets, a kind of economic fault, is invariably a factor that the courts consider when dividing property. One cannot say the same for marital misconduct, commonly referred to simply as fault. In the overwhelming majority of states, either spouse can have the marriage dissolved without proving marital fault on the part of the other spouse. With respect to the aspect of the divorce proceeding involving distribution of assets, however, there is no such clear consensus.

State legislatures generally take one of five basic approaches to the issue. Some states follow the approach of the UMDA, which requires the division of the spouses' property "without regard to marital misconduct."[254] A number of states have adopted identical language in their equitable distribution statutes.[255] Statutes in the second group explicitly command that the court consider "the conduct of the parties during the marriage"[256] or "the respective merits of the parties"[257] when making an

---

[250] 511 N.E.2d 676 (Ill. App. Ct. 1987).

[251] *Id.* at 680.

[252] *See, e.g., Berish v. Berish*, 432 N.E.2d 183 (Ohio 1982); *Sharp v. Sharp*, 473 A.2d 499 (Md. Ct. Spec. App. 1984).

[253] 627 P.2d 1206 (Mont. 1981).

[254] Unif. Marriage and Divorce Act § 307, 9A U.L.A. 288 (1998).

[255] *See, e.g.*, 750 Ill. Comp. Stat. Ann. 5/503 (West 2012); Minn. Stat. § 518.58; 23 Pa. Cons. Stat. § 3502(a).

[256] *See, e.g.*, Mass. Ann. Laws ch. 208, § 34; Mo. Rev. Stat. § 452.330(1)(4).

[257] *See, e.g.*, Vt. Stat. Ann. tit. 15, § 751(b)(12).

equitable distribution of property.

A few states take a third approach, requiring trial courts to consider only misconduct that causes or leads to the breakdown of the marriage or to divorce.[258] Fourth, some statutes contain a so-called catchall factor. In New York, for example, the court must consider, in addition to thirteen other listed factors, "any other factor which the court shall expressly find to be just and proper."[259] Under such formulations, the extent, if any, to which marital misconduct is a factor in property division is a matter for judicial interpretation. Accordingly, in *O'Brien v. O'Brien*,[260] New York's highest court stated:

> Except in egregious cases which shock the conscience of the court, . . . [marital fault] is not a "just and proper" factor for consideration in the equitable distribution of marital property . . . . That is so because marital fault is inconsistent with the underlying assumption that a marriage is in part an economic partnership and upon its dissolution the parties are entitled to a fair share of the marital estate, because fault will usually be difficult to assign and because introduction of the issue may involve the courts in time-consuming procedural maneuvers relating to collateral issues . . . .[261]

Under the ALI *Principles*, adopting the prevailing standard in the majority of states, courts are not permitted to take into account fault or marital misconduct when making an equitable distribution of marital property.[262]

Finally, some statutes are silent with respect to marital misconduct or fault. Here, again, the courts must determine whether or not fault is relevant in dividing property. Interpreting such a statute in *Painter v. Painter*,[263] the Supreme Court of New Jersey held that marital fault is not an appropriate factor to consider in the equitable distribution of marital assets. The Supreme Court of Arkansas, on the other hand, in *Stover v. Stover*,[264] interpreting a statute in which fault was not a factor, approved the trial court's consideration of the fact that the wife was convicted of criminal conspiracy to cause her husband's murder.

[E]   Marital Debts and Liabilities

In the strict sense, debts or liabilities of the spouses existing at the time of divorce are not assets or property. Nonetheless, legislatures and courts in many equitable distribution states generally analyze the characterization and distribution of debts in the same manner as they do assets. Most commonly, debts or liabilities are listed among the factors that the trial court is required to consider

---

[258] *See, e.g.*, Conn. Gen. Stat. § 46b-81; Va. Code Ann. § 20-107.3(E)(5).

[259] N.Y. Dom. Rel. Law § 236B(5)(d)(14) (2012).

[260] 489 N.E.2d 712 (N.Y. 1985).

[261] *Id.* at 719.

[262] *See* ALI *Principles of the Law of Family Dissolution* at 66-67; *see also* Ira Mark Ellman, *The Place of Fault in a Modern Divorce Law*, 28 Ariz. St. L.J. 773 (1996).

[263] 320 A.2d 484 (N.J. 1974).

[264] 696 S.W.2d 750 (Ark. 1985).

when making an equitable distribution of property.[265] In jurisdictions in which the statutes do not mention the subject, the courts must formulate principles to govern the treatment of debts and liabilities in order to ensure property divisions that are just and equitable.

Judicial decisions on the subject reflect two fundamental views. In a few states, appellate courts hold that the trial court must allocate debts and liabilities when making an equitable distribution of marital property.[266] In a greater number of states, the courts hold that although the allocation of debts and liabilities is not required, it is the better practice. As the Missouri Court of Appeals pointed out in *N.J.W. v. W.E.W.*:[267]

> A debt owed by the spouses does not constitute "property" owned by them. The failure of the decree to provide as to payment of debts is therefore not a fatal defect, although the better practice would be to do so and thereby reduce subsequent dispute and contention.

> The existence and extent of debts does, of course, affect the fairness of the way in which assets are divided.[268]

[F]   The Marital Home

In many cases, perhaps most, the marital home, homestead, or family residence is the most valuable asset of the divorcing spouses. It is usually acquired during the marriage and clearly falls within the category of marital property. The overriding concern in cases concerning the marital home is what constitutes a fair and equitable distribution in light of statutory and other factors and the circumstances of the case and the parties. In approximately a third of the states, there is statutory treatment of the marital home. The statutes explicitly authorize trial courts to award exclusive use and possession of the marital home to the spouse having custody of any children.[269]

Decisions treating the marital home fall into two basic categories. In many cases, the courts order use and occupancy by the custodial spouse, followed by sale of the home and division of the proceeds when the child is emancipated or the custodial spouse remarries. In a second group of cases, the courts make an award of the marital home or order its sale and an equitable division of the proceeds at the time of divorce. It is apparently within the courts' inherent equity powers to award possession of the marital home to the custodial spouse, whether or not there is explicit statutory authority. Such an award is also appropriate, when just and equitable, under the catchall factor listed in a number of equitable distribution

---

[265] *See, e.g.*, Ark. Code Ann. § 9-12-315(a)(1)(A)(vii); 750 Ill. Comp. Stat. Ann. 5/503 (2012); Minn. Stat. § 518.58; N.C. Gen. Stat. § 50-20(c)(1); Va. Code § 20-107.3(E)(7) (2012).

[266] *See, e.g., In re Marriage of Johnson*, 299 N.W.2d 466 (Iowa 1980).

[267] 584 S.W.2d 148 (Mo. Ct. App. 1979).

[268] *Id.* at 151.

[269] *See, e.g.*, Colo. Rev. Stat. § 14-10-113(1)(c) (including among the statutory factors in property division "[t]he economic circumstances of each spouse at the time the division of property is to become effective, including the desirability of awarding the family home or the right to live therein for reasonable periods to the spouse with whom any children reside the majority of the time.").

statutes. By and large, as the Supreme Court of South Carolina remarked in *Herring v. Herring*,[270] "[t]he best interests and needs of the child are paramount."[271]

---

[270] 335 S.E.2d 366 (S.C. 1985).

[271] *Id.* at 369.

Chapter 11

CHILD CUSTODY AND VISITATION

§ 11.01 INTRODUCTION

The issues of child custody and visitation addressed in this chapter arise most frequently in the context of divorce, but also may occur in disputes between parents who have not married each other. When the parents' marital or non-marital relationship breaks down, courts will ordinarily award physical/residential custody of the couple's children to one of the parents. The noncustodial parent generally will be granted visitation rights. Visitation may be viewed as a limited form of custody, at least to the extent that the noncustodial parent has the authority to make decisions relating to the child during visitation.

For some period of time, frequently in response to legislative mandates, courts looked to joint custody as an alternative to the traditional award of sole custody with visitation. In principle, joint custody arrangements afford parents shared responsibility for major decisions relating to their children after divorce. As a practical matter, however, joint custody arrangements often resemble sole custody with visitation, in that one of the parents has primary physical custody of the child or children.

Whatever the form of custody, judicial discretion is the hallmark of child custody decision making. The trial court's broad discretion "enables [it] to explore every aspect of the litigants' circumstances so that its custody determination will reflect the child's best interests."[1] Such broad discretion obviously carries the potential for subjective decisions that may be tainted by personal bias or lack of understanding of child development.

§ 11.02 CHILD CUSTODY JURISDICTION

Child custody jurisdiction refers to the authority of a court to resolve a custody dispute. Although child custody jurisdiction issues arise in a number of contexts, including adoption, neglect proceedings, and actions to terminate parental rights, most custody jurisdiction disputes arise during proceedings related to divorce. Moreover, these issues most frequently arise when one party attempts to have a custody decree modified, although they sometimes surface as part of an initial custody determination at the time of divorce. The problem exists largely because custody decrees are not considered final judgments, but may be modified in order to safeguard the best interests of the child upon changed circumstances.

---

[1] *Berman v. Berman*, 270 N.W.2d 680, 683 (Mich. Ct. App. 1978).

Interstate jurisdictional conflicts generally arise when a noncustodial parent seeks a modification of custody while the child is with that parent either legally, during visitation or with the consent of the custodial parent, or illegally, when the noncustodial parent refuses to return the child after visitation or abducts the child.[2] Jurisdictional disputes ensue in these situations not only because of the natural desire of parents to have custody of their children, but also because of a strong tendency of state courts to assert their own jurisdictional power.

Jurisdiction to resolve child custody matters has always been the domain of the state courts, and state courts gradually expanded the limits of their own jurisdictional requirements for resolving custody matters. During the 20th century, the increased mobility of the American population contributed to forum shopping and parents abducting their children as disappointed parents attempted to obtain more favorable forums for their custody actions. In an attempt to discourage such behavior, considered detrimental to the children involved, both state and federal governments have responded over the past several decades by enacting legislation. By the early 1980's, all states had adopted versions of Uniform Child Custody Jurisdiction Act (UCCJA). However, these uniform acts were only the first wave of legislation aimed at solving the problem of competing child custody orders. In 1980, Congress enacted the Parental Kidnapping Prevention Act (PKPA) to remedy perceived problems with custody orders under the state UCCJAs. Since the PKPA, every state (except Massachusetts) has replaced its UCCJA with the Uniform Child Custody Jurisdiction and Enforcement Act (UCCJEA). The UCCJEA, like the PKPA, sought to fix practical problems associated with the application of state UCCJAs.[3] Finally, the international community grappled with child custody issues, particularly international kidnapping, in the widely-adopted Hague Convention on the Civil Aspects of International Child Abduction[4] (which was implemented in the United States by the International Child Abduction Remedies Act).[5] Each of these legislative (and diplomatic) efforts intend to create stability for custody decrees and to assure that custody litigation occurs in an optimal forum. This section will explore the history behind these acts, how they interact with one another, and whether they achieve their stated policy objectives. It begins with a quick snapshot of differences between the UCCJA, UCCJEA, and PKPA in Figure 11.1, followed by a more in-depth discussion of each.

---

[2] "Single mothers . . . often are not aware of the importance of a custody order — they believe they already have legal custody, since they have physical custody and were never married to the father." Nancy S. Erickson, *The Parental Kidnapping Prevention Act: How Can Nonmarital Children Be Protected?*, 18 Golden Gate U. L. Rev. 17 (1988). *See also* Patricia Hoff, et al., Interstate Child Custody Disputes and Parental Kidnapping: Policy, Practice, and Law app. IV, 2-17 (1982) ("There are many cases where the mother has de facto custody which has been uncontested by the father."). For the PKPA to operate to prevent "child snatching," the parent with physical custody must have a custody order. For an annual Percentage of United States Births to Unwed Mothers, see *supra* Ch. 5, Fig. 5.1.

[3] For a complete list of the variations between state UCCJEAs, see "Personal Jurisdiction," 50 State Statutory Surveys: Civil Laws: Civil Procedure, 0020 SURVEYS 10 (Westlaw).

[4] Hague Convention on the Civil Aspects of International Child Abduction, Oct. 25, 1980, 19 I.L.M. 1501.

[5] International Child Abduction Remedies Act, 42 U.S.C. § 11601 *et seq.*

Figure 11.1

	UCCJA	UCCJEA	PKPA
Where the statute applies:	Adopted in whole or part by Massachusetts and Puerto Rico (although bills to adopt the UCCJEA are pending in both legislatures). Also applies to modifications of orders made under older state UCCJAs.	Adopted in whole or part by 49 states, the District of Columbia and U.S. Virgin Islands.	Preempts state law when there is a conflict.
When the statute applies:	**Applies to:** • Initial custody determination; • Visitation; • Modification; • Adoption; AND • Dependency in child neglect cases	**Applies to:** • Divorce; • Separation; • Neglect; • Abuse; • Dependency; • Guardianship; • Paternity; • Termination of parental rights; *and* • Protection from domestic violence Note: Unless modified by an individual state, UCCJEA does not apply to adoptions. It also does not apply to custody proceedings involving Native American children when governed by the Indian Child Welfare Act.	**Applies when:** • An interstate conflict arises over enforcement and recognition of custody decrees, including adoptions; • Does not apply to initial custody proceedings; • When its statutory requirements are met, states <u>must</u> afford another state's custody order full faith and credit.
Bases for jurisdiction:	• "Home state" jurisdiction; • "Significant Connection" jurisdiction; • "Emergency" jurisdiction; *and* • "Default" jurisdiction Note: Physical presence of the child in the state is not enough to confer jurisdiction.	Preference for "home state" jurisdiction. The UCCJEA considers other bases for jurisdiction only if home state jurisdiction does not exist. Note: Physical presence of the child in the state is not enough to confer jurisdiction.	Lists 4 possible bases for jurisdiction modeled after the UCCJA. But like the UCCJEA, the PKPA has a statutory preference for "home state" jurisdiction. The other 3 bases can only be used if no state has "home state" jurisdiction.
Jurisdiction over the Parties	UCCJA does not require personal jurisdiction over the parties, only subject matter jurisdiction.	UCCJEA does not require personal jurisdiction over the parties, only subject matter jurisdiction.	• Requires federal subject matter jurisdiction, although federal courts traditionally will defer to state courts. • Does not require personal jurisdiction
Continuing Jurisdiction	Interpreted to allow concurrent jurisdiction to modify a custody order in both a child's new home state and in the state where the initial order originated.	UCCJEA gives exclusive continuing jurisdiction to the court that entered the initial custody decree. Matches the PKPA's approach.	Once a state has exercised jurisdiction, it retains "exclusive" jurisdiction until every party to the custody action has left the original state.
Emergency Jurisdiction	Provides an equal basis for jurisdiction with the other 3 bases under the UCCJA. A court can claim continuing jurisdiction after issuing an order based on emergency jurisdiction.	Unlike the UCCJA, a state with emergency jurisdiction can only claim continuing jurisdiction if no other state has "home state" jurisdiction and every other state declines jurisdiction.	The UCCJEA and the PPKA view emergency jurisdiction similarly.

	UCCJA	UCCJEA	PKPA
Enforcement	The UCCJA imposes a basic duty on one state to enforce another state's custody orders; but lacks specific enforcement provisions. The UCCJA left the question of how to enforce to other areas of state law.	Above and beyond its jurisdictional provisions, the UCCJEA provides enforcement provisions lacking in the UCCJA: • Expedited enforcement hearings; • Enhanced court remedies; • Duty to enforce another state's valid custody order; • Civil enforcement of custody order.	The PKPA is enforced like other Federal criminal laws.
Full Faith and Credit		An order under the UCCJEA receives full faith and credit only if all relevant parties are given notice and reasonable opportunity to be heard.	When the PKPA's statutory requirements are met, states must afford another state's custody order full faith and credit.

[A] Traditional Rules

Until the late 1960s, the traditional approach, reflected in the First Restatement of the Conflict of Laws, was that child custody jurisdiction was based on the child's domicile.[6] Additionally, the United States Supreme Court recognized few constitutional limitations on the states' jurisdiction to resolve jurisdictional custody disputes. In *New York ex rel. Halvey v. Halvey*,[7] the Court held that because a state with original jurisdiction can modify its own custody decree, and because a state need not give a sister-state's judgment greater recognition than its own, the Full Faith and Credit Clause does not prevent modification of a custody decision by another state that has grounds for jurisdiction. In light of *Halvey's* broad authorization for custody modification, many state courts began to exert their powers liberally, sometimes finding changed circumstances sufficient for adjusting custody rights merely because the child was living in a different state. The result was a system in which a parent unhappy with a custody decision in one state could remove the child to another state and seek a modification. In addition to the child's domicile, state courts began asserting custody jurisdiction based on the domicile of one or both parents or the physical presence of the child.[8] The Supreme Court compounded the problem in the 1953 case of *May v. Anderson*,[9] concluding that a custody decree that was not based on personal jurisdiction over the respondent was not entitled to full faith and credit.

Not only did the traditional approach encourage forum shopping, but it frequently resulted in a form of kidnapping by a parent who impermissibly

---

[6] *See* Restatement (First) of Conflict of Laws § 117 (1934).

[7] 330 U.S. 610 (1947).

[8] For historical accounts of this "seize and run" period of the law, see Sheldon A. Vincenti, *The Parental Kidnapping Prevention Act: Time to Reassess*, 33 Idaho L. Rev. 351, 355 (1997). *See also* Cristopher L. Blakesley, *Child Custody Jurisdiction and Procedure*, 35 Emory L.J. 291 (1986); Russell M. Coombs, *Interstate Child Custody: Jurisdiction, Recognition, and Enforcement*, 66 Minn. L. Rev. 711 (1982).

[9] 345 U.S. 528 (1953). *Compare infra* § 11.02[B] (reviewing widely adopted statutes like the UCCJA and the PKPA which do not require personal jurisdiction over a respondent in child custody cases).

retained the child after visitation or removed the child to another state in order to relitigate the custody question. The incidence of such abuses led to legislative action by both state governments — in the form of state UCCJAs and its successors state UCCJEAs — and the federal government through the PKPA.

[B]   The Uniform Child Custody Jurisdiction Act and the Uniform Child Custody Jurisdiction and Enforcement Act

The UCCJA,[10] promulgated in 1968, was adopted by all states with some internal variations by the early 1980s. By 2011, the UCCJA had been replaced with its 1997 revision, the UCCJEA, in all states and territories except for Massachusetts and Puerto Rico, where legislatures in both were considering it as of 2012.[11] The purpose of the UCCJA, as well as the UCCJEA, is not only to create uniformity in child custody jurisdiction practices among states, but also to "avoid jurisdictional competition and conflict with courts of other states in matters of child custody which have in the past resulted in the shifting of children from state to state with harmful effects on their well-being."[12] Both acts strive to provide a uniform basis for child custody decisions that is not as inflexible as the First Restatement's domicile standard, and, at the same time, discourages the competition among jurisdictions that the domicile standard encouraged.

The drafters of the UCCJA envisioned it applying to a wide variety of custody proceedings: initial custody, visitation, modification, and dependency in child neglect cases.[13] Some state legislatures altered the individual state's UCCJA, for example, by excluding dependency actions from the scope of the state act.[14] By contrast, many state courts have held the UCCJA applicable to adoptions and other issues involving child placement.[15]

The UCCJEA expands the UCCJA's definition of "Child-custody proceeding" to include "a proceeding for divorce, separation, neglect, abuse, dependency, guardianship, paternity, termination of parental rights, and protection from domestic violence," but excludes a "proceeding involving juvenile delinquency,

---

[10] *See generally* Brigette M. Bodenheimer, *Progress Under the Uniform Child Custody Jurisdiction Act and Remaining Problems: Punitive Decrees, Joint Custody, and Excessive Modifications*, 65 Cal. L. Rev. 978 (1977).

[11] *See* 9 Unif. L. Ann. (Part 1A) 649 (1999); Nat'l Conf. of Comm'rs on Unif. St. Laws, *available at* http://www.nccusl.org/Shared/docs/UCCJEAadoptions.pdf. For a comprehensive overview of the UC-CJEA and a comparison with the UCCJA, see Patricia Hoff, *The ABC's of the UCCJEA: Interstate Child-Custody Practice Under the New Act*, 32 Fam. L. Q. 267 (1998).

[12] UCCJA § 1(a)(1). *See also* UCCJEA § 101 comment (containing identical text).

[13] UCCJA § 2(3) & official cmt.

[14] UCCJA § 2 cmt. (listing the following states: New Hampshire, New Mexico and New York).

[15] *See, e.g., Stubbs v. Weathersby*, 833 P.2d 1297 (Or. Ct. App. 1992) (Oregon joins majority of states holding that UCCJA applies to adoptions); *see also* Greg Waller, *When the Rules Don't Fit the Game: Application of the Uniform Child Custody Jurisdiction Act and the Parental Kidnapping Prevention Act to Interstate Adoption Proceedings*, 33 Harv. J. on Legis. 271 (1996); Bernadette W. Hartfield, *The Uniform Child Custody Jurisdiction Act and the Problem of Jurisdiction in Interstate Adoption: An Easy Fix?*, 43 Okla. L. Rev. 621 (1990).

contractual emancipation, or enforcement."[16] It also excludes adoptions — deferring to the Uniform Adoption Act — and proceedings pertaining to the authorization of emergency medical care for a child.[17] The UCCJEA spells out its applicability in permanent, temporary, initial, and modification contexts.[18] The UCCJEA also applies to adjudications of custody and visitation arising in the context of protection from domestic violence.[19] The UCCJA and UCCJEA attempt to fulfill their comprehensive goals by promoting cooperation of various state courts through facilitating the exchange of information among courts.

The ultimate goal is to ensure that custody decisions are rendered in the state best equipped to determine the best interests of a particular child. As noted *infra* § 11.02[B][1], the UCCJA encourages custody litigation in the state with the closest connection to the child and the family by recognizing alternate bases for assertion of custody jurisdiction. The UCCJA prefers the state with the most evidence pertaining to the child's welfare. It sets out mechanisms for enforcing existing custody decrees and avoiding re-litigation to the extent feasible, and establishes guidelines for state courts to decline jurisdiction in deference to a more appropriate forum. By contrast, the UCCJEA prefers the child's home state.

A tension exists between the UCCJA's goals of achieving stability of custody decrees and creating a system with sufficient flexibility to accommodate the best interests of the child in a mobile society. Indeed, one court has commented, "A close reading of the [UCCJA] discloses a schizophrenic attempt to bring about an orderly system of decision and at the same time to protect the best interests of the children who may be immediately before the court."[20]

The UCCJEA amends the UCCJA to solve some of the problems that arose under the UCCJA and to conform to the federal Parental Kidnapping Prevention Act and the Violence Against Women Act (VAWA).[21]

---

[16] UCCJEA § 102(4). Paternity actions that raise no custody or visitation questions may fall outside the UCCJEA. *See Harshberger v. Harshberger*, 724 N.W.2d 148 (N.D. 2006).

[17] UCCJEA § 103. Several states include adoption within the state's enactment of the UCCJEA. *See, e.g.,* D.C. Code § 16-4601.01(4) (2008) (including adoption); N.M. Stat. Ann. § 40-10A-102(4) (2008) (defining "child custody proceeding" to include termination of parental rights when filed alone or together with an adoption proceeding). In a 2004 case, *In People ex rel. A.J.C.*, 88 P.3d 599, 600 (Colo. 2004), the Colorado Supreme Court held that the UCCJEA will not apply to custody applications filed after failed adoptions.

[18] UCCJEA § 102(3).

[19] UCCJEA § 102(4).

[20] *In re Marriage of Settle*, 556 P.2d 962, 968 (Or. 1976).

[21] *See* Ron W. Nelson, *The UCCJA and the UCCJEA: A Side-by-Side Comparison*, 10/12 Divorce Litig. 233 (1998). Domestic violence protection orders, including those addressing custody, are entitled to full faith and credit "only if there has been notice and a reasonable opportunity to be heard." *See* UCCJEA § 204 & official cmt. Under the Uniform Interstate Enforcement of Domestic Violence Protection Orders Act (2000, 2002), domestic violence protection orders may be registered and enforced.

[1] Jurisdictional Prerequisites

The UCCJA and the UCCJEA both set forth bases for jurisdiction and require the parties to provide enough information in their pleadings or attached affidavit for the court to determine that it has appropriate jurisdiction.[22] This section first reviews the UCCJA's jurisdictional prerequisites — both because the UCCJA continues, as of 2011, to be the governing law in two jurisdictions and because the PKPA provides that full faith and credit will be given to certain orders only when made consistently with then-governing local law, which in many cases will be the UCCJA. This section then discusses the differences between the UCCJA and the now more widely-adopted UCCJEA. Finally, this section examines how state UCCJAs and UCCJEAs interact with the federal Parental Kidnapping Prevention Act and international Hague Convention on the Civil Aspects of International Child Abduction.

The UCCJA contains four bases for jurisdiction in custody actions: (1) "home state" jurisdiction, (2) "significant connection" jurisdiction, (3) "emergency" jurisdiction, and (4) "default" jurisdiction.

A court has "home state" jurisdiction when it qualifies as the home state at the time the action is commenced and is otherwise competent to hear the case.[23] The UCCJA defines "home state" as "the state in which the child immediately preceding the time involved lived with his parents, a parent or a person acting as parent, for at least 6 consecutive months."[24] If the child is less than six months old, the state where the child lived from birth with any of the named persons is considered the home state.[25] Temporary absence of any of the named persons counts toward the requisite time period.[26] Home state jurisdiction continues to exist when the state has been the home state within the previous six months and a parent or custodian still lives in the state, even though the child has been removed from the state by a person contesting custody.[27]

Home state jurisdiction is based on the theory that a court in the state of the usual residence of the child and a parent or a person acting as a parent is likely to have access to the most information regarding the proper custody of the child.[28] The concept of "home state" establishes jurisdiction in the vast majority of custody decisions. In a sense, it serves as a less rigid substitute for domicile, while providing

---

[22] UCCJA § 9; UCCJEA § 209(a), (e) (making such information subject to local law governing confidentiality and providing for information to be sealed when disclosure would put the safety or liberty of a party or child at risk).

[23] UCCJA § 3(a)(1). *See also* UCCJEA § 201.

[24] UCCJA § 2(5). *See also* UCCJEA § 102(7) (giving a similar definition).

[25] UCCJA § 2(5).

[26] *Id.* This is also true of the UCCJEA. *See* UCCJEA § 102(7).

[27] UCCJA § 3(a)(1). *See also* UCCJEA § 201(a)(1) (while the UCCJA extended the home state concept to a child absent from the state because of her removal or retention by a party, under the UCCJEA, the reason for the child's absence is irrelevant). *But see Powell v. Stover*, 165 S.W.3d 322 (Tex. 2005) (concluding that for purposes of determining home-state jurisdiction, the court must take into account the child's physical presence in another state).

[28] *See, e.g., In re B.R.F.*, 669 S.W.2d 240 (Mo. Ct. App. 1984).

a firmer foundation for jurisdiction than mere physical presence.

The UCCJA's second jurisdictional ground, "significant connection," exists if:

> [I]t is in the best interest of the child that a court of this State assume jurisdiction because (i) the child and his parents, or the child and at least one contestant, have a significant connection with this State, and (ii) there is available in this State substantial evidence concerning the child's present or future care, protection, training, and personal relationships.[29]

Significant connection jurisdiction requires more than a mere conclusion that the exercise of jurisdiction would be in the child's best interest. It demands both a significant connection with the state and substantial evidence relating to the child available in the state.

Even though the UCCJA's significant connection jurisdiction was intended to serve as an alternative, not an exception to, home state jurisdiction, it creates a dangerous loophole that potentially could be used whenever a parent desires to litigate outside the home state. If a parent assembles facts sufficient to establish a significant connection before the other parent brings a custody action in the home state, the forum court will have considerable discretion in asserting jurisdiction on this ground.[30] Much of the litigation arising under the UCCJA has resulted from the manner in which the court interprets the significant connection test. Some courts have taken an extremely broad view of that test, placing great emphasis on the substantial evidence present in the forum state.[31] Provisions of the PKPA attempt to resolve these issues, but many state courts still liberally construe the UCCJA to grant themselves jurisdiction.[32]

The third jurisdictional basis under the UCCJA is "emergency" jurisdiction. It exists when the child is physically present in the state and has been abandoned or "it is necessary in an emergency to protect the child because he has been subjected to or threatened with mistreatment or abuse or is otherwise neglected [or dependent]."[33] Emergency jurisdiction should be exercised only in extraordinary circumstances, such as situations in which the child faces imminent harm.[34] Some courts have held that exercise of emergency jurisdiction under the UCCJA is a temporary measure which exists only until the state with more substantial contacts

---

[29] UCCJA § 3(a)(2).

[30] *See Pomraning v. Pomraning*, 682 S.W.2d 775 (Ark. Ct. App. 1985) ("Fact that wife and children had lived in state for shorter period than that required to establish it as their 'home state' did not preclude jurisdiction over custody issue."); *Smith v. Superior Ct.*, 137 Cal. Rptr. 348 (Cal. Ct. App. 1977).

[31] *See, e.g., Allison v. Superior Ct.*, 160 Cal. Rptr. 309 (Cal. Ct. App. 1979) ("By reason of significant connection of parents and children with California, and availability of substantial evidence in California on children's personal relationships, California court possessed jurisdiction to make child custody determination even though children had resided with father in Texas for 18 months prior to outbreak of controversy between parents.").

[32] *See infra* § 11.02[C].

[33] UCCJA at § 3(a)(3).

[34] *See O'Gwynn v. Hebert*, 878 A.2d 119, 125 (Pa. Super. Ct. 2005); *McDow v. McDow*, 908 P.2d 1049, 1051 (Alaska 1996) (citing with approval *Benda v. Benda*, 565 A.2d 1121, 1124 (N.J. Sup. Ct. App. Div. 1989)); *Swan v. Swan*, 796 P.2d 221, 222 (Nev. 1990).

is able to consider the custody question.[35] This is the stance adopted by the UCCJEA.[36]

Finally, a fourth basis for jurisdiction under the UCCJA arises when the state serves as the "default" jurisdiction. This ground allows a court to assert jurisdiction only when no other ground exists.[37] The UCCJEA also provides for "default" jurisdiction.[38]

The UCCJEA seeks to resolve some of the problems created by the UCCJA's alternative bases for jurisdiction. Under the UCCJA, more than one state may have statutory authority to decide a custody case, although only one should exercise that jurisdiction. Courts have often reached divergent conclusions as to which state has the strongest connection, and therefore, the best claim to jurisdiction. The UCCJEA gives priority to home state jurisdiction and eliminates the "best interest" prong of the significant connection jurisdiction.[39] With the UCCJEA's jurisdictional preference for home state jurisdiction, most jurisdictional conflicts will be eliminated except in the rare situation where no home state exists.[40]

The UCCJEA also severely curtails emergency jurisdiction.[41] Emergency jurisdiction is dropped from the UCCJEA as a third basis for initial jurisdiction and replaced by a new section 204, which covers all features of emergency jurisdiction. The UCCJEA thus assures that, in most cases, only one state will have jurisdiction, because only one state can be the home state of a particular child.[42] Under both the

---

[35] *See, e.g.*, *State ex rel. D.S.K.*, 792 P.2d 118 (Utah Ct. App. 1990).

[36] *See infra* note 41 (and accompanying text discussing emergency jurisdiction).

[37] UCCJA § 3(a)(4).

[38] UCCJEA § 201(a)(4).

[39] UCCJEA § 201 & official cmt.

[40] *See Welch-Doden v. Roberts*, 42 P.3d 1166 (Ariz. Ct. App. 2002) (state deferred to Oklahoma under UCCJEA as home state because it had been home state within preceding six months and had not been replaced by another home state). A home state may not exist when, for instance, an infant younger than six months is born in one state but then taken to another state. *See, e.g.*, *Doe v. Baby Girl*, 657 S.E.2d 455 (S.C. 2008) (finding infant born in Illinois but placed for adoption in South Carolina when four days old had no home state but significant connections to South Carolina); *In re Brown*, 203 S.W.3d 888 (Tex. App. 2006) (finding significant connection jurisdiction by Missouri courts, where child's parents were airline pilots with homes in both Missouri and Texas, because the mother filed divorce and custody petitions six hours before the father filed in Texas, thus precluding Texas courts from considering the case).

[41] UCCJEA §§ 201(2), 204. Under the UCCJEA, "emergency jurisdiction" operates only on a temporary basis until a court having jurisdiction under the UCCJEA's other provisions issues an order. UCCJEA § 204(b). *See, e.g.*, *Dalessio v. Gallagher*, 997 A.2d 283 (N.J. App. Div. 2010) (providing that the New Jersey court's temporary emergency order would govern until the child's home state issued further orders).

[42] In *In re Amberley D.*, 775 A.2d 1158 (Me. 2001), the Maine Supreme Court upheld the exercise of jurisdiction in a child guardianship case although the child's mother did not have notice of the hearing. The child was fifteen years old at the time and had fled across state lines from her mother. Because there was no outstanding custody order, the PKPA did not apply, and the UCCJEA defers to state law on notice requirements to out-of-state persons. Maine state law allowed the court to waive notice when a minor is over fourteen years old. Further, no home state existed under either the PKPA or the UCCJEA because the child had not been in one state for a six-month period prior to the hearing. Therefore the court concluded that Maine could exercise jurisdiction under the significant connection basis.

UCCJA and the UCCJEA, the physical presence of the child or a party is not, in itself, sufficient to confer custody jurisdiction.[43] While the presence of the child is preferable, it is not required for jurisdiction over matters concerning custody, except under the emergency basis for jurisdiction.[44]

Neither act requires personal jurisdiction over the respondent in a custody action. Although the Supreme Court's plurality opinion in *May v. Anderson*[45] literally stands for the proposition that a custody decree is not entitled to full faith and credit unless there is personal jurisdiction over the respondent, and has been construed to mean that child custody orders are void without personal jurisdiction,[46] the Court's later opinion in *Shaffer v. Heitner*[47] carved out an exception for cases determining status. The continued vitality of *May*'s holding appears doubtful[48] and many courts have either limited *May* or simply ignored it.[49] One way of circumventing the personal jurisdiction requirement is to regard custody actions as merely determinations of status, which do not require *in personam* jurisdiction.[50] However, some commentators contend that dispensing with personal jurisdiction over a parent in a custody dispute deprives the parent of procedural due process.[51]

[2] Restraints on Jurisdiction

A number of restraints on jurisdiction exist under both acts. Under the UCCJA, the mere existence of a ground for custody jurisdiction is insufficient to justify a court's exercise of its authority. If a custody proceeding concerning a child is pending in a court which is exercising jurisdiction substantially conforming to the UCCJA, another court is forbidden from asserting its jurisdiction unless the first court stays its action.[52] The UCCJA further directs the court to examine available information to determine whether proceedings may be pending in another state and

---

[43] UCCJA § 3(b); UCCJEA § 201(c).

[44] UCCJA § 3(c); UCCJEA § 204(a).

[45] 345 U.S. 528 (1953). *See supra* note 5 (and accompanying text).

[46] *See Kulko v. Superior Ct.*, 436 U.S. 84 (1978), *reh. den.*, 438 U.S. 908 (1978). Importantly, the custodial parent in *Kulko* also sought to modify the New York custody award in California, something the Supreme Court had never suggested would be a denial of due process for a California court to have done. *See* Robert C. Casad & William B. Richman, Jurisdiction in Civil Actions § 9-2 (2011).

[47] 433 U.S. 186 (1978).

[48] *See* Rhonda Wasserman, *Parents, Partners, and Personal Jurisdiction*, 1995 U. Ill. L. Rev. 813; Barbara A. Atwood, *Child Custody Jurisdiction and Territoriality*, 52 Ohio St. L. J. 369 (1991); Brigitte M. Bodenheimer & Janet Neeley-Kvarme, *Jurisdiction Over Child Custody and Adoption After* Shaffer *and* Kulko, 12 U.C. Davis L. Rev. 229 (1979).

[49] *See, e.g.*, *In re Marriage of Leonard*, 175 Cal. Rptr. 903 (Cal. Ct. App. 1981); *Morrell v. Giesick*, 610 P.2d 1189 (Mont. 1980); *Goldfarb v. Goldfarb*, 268 S.E.2d 648 (Ga. 1980).

[50] *See In re Marriage of Schuham*, 458 N.E.2d 559 (Ill. App. Ct. 1983); *see also* Bodenheimer & Neeley-Kvarme, *supra* note 48.

[51] *See* Helen Garfield, *Due Process Rights of Absent Parents in Interstate Custody Conflicts: A Commentary on* In re Marriage of Hudson, 16 Ind. L. Rev. 445 (1983).

[52] UCCJA § 6(a). *See also In re C.A.D.*, 839 P.2d 165 (Okla. 1992) (Oklahoma court required to defer jurisdiction to Texas court, because the Texas proceeding was pending when the Oklahoma action was filed, the Texas proceeding conformed with the UCCJA, and the Texas court refused to stay its proceedings).

to inquire of the officials in that state.[53] Similar provisions prohibiting simultaneous proceedings are found in the UCCJEA.[54]

Both the UCCJA and the UCCJEA permit a court to decline jurisdiction *sua sponte* or upon motion of a party or representative of the child if it determines that another state provides a more appropriate forum.[55] Both acts list factors that may be considered and provide for the exchange of information with the court in another jurisdiction before deciding whether to retain jurisdiction or to dismiss or stay the action.[56]

[3] Recognition and Enforcement of Custody Decrees

Both the UCCJA and UCCJEA require states to recognize and enforce properly rendered child custody determinations of other states.[57] Both acts extend recognition to properly rendered custody decrees of foreign countries,[58] and the UCCJEA, unlike the UCCJA, includes an optional provision that extends recognition to custody determinations made by Indian tribal courts to the same extent as those made by state courts.[59]

Under the UCCJA, states are forbidden from modifying sister-state custody decrees unless (a) the forum court itself has jurisdiction under one of the four bases of the UCCJA *and* (b) it appears to the forum court that the state which initially entered the custody order no longer has such jurisdiction or has declined to assume jurisdiction to modify its decree.[60] The UCCJA's modification provision provides that the court that entered the original decree did not need to continue to possess the same type of jurisdictional basis it initially had; rather, it needed only to possess any one of the four bases for assertion of jurisdiction.[61] Many courts interpreted this provision to allow concurrent jurisdiction to modify in both a child's new home state and in the original state, based on significant connection jurisdiction.

---

[53] UCCJA § 6(b).

[54] UCCJEA § 206.

[55] UCCJA § 7(a), (b); UCCJEA § 207. Because the UCCJEA is a subject matter jurisdiction statute, jurisdiction can be raised by the court at any time. *See, e.g., Rosen v. Rosen*, 664 S.E.2d 743 (W. Va. 2008).

[56] UCCJA § 7(c)-(i); UCCJEA § 207(b).

[57] UCCJA § 13; UCCJEA § 202. The UCCJA and the UCCJEA define a child custody determination similarly. The UCCJEA defines it as "a judgment, decree, or other order of a court providing for the legal custody, physical custody, or visitation with respect to a child. The term includes a permanent, temporary, initial, and modification order. The term does not include an order relating to child support or other monetary obligation of an individual." UCCJEA § 102(3). *See also* UCCJA § 2(2). Some courts construe a "custody determination" to require an actual custody order. *See Foster v. Wolkowitz*, 785 N.W.2d 59 (Mich. 2010) (finding an acknowledgment of paternity not to be a custody determination conferring continuing exclusive jurisdiction).

[58] UCCJA § 23; UCCJEA § 105.

[59] UCCJEA § 104. *See also* Lesley M. Wexler, *Tribal Court Jurisdiction in Dissolution-Based Custody Proceedings*, 2001 U. Chi. Legal F. 613; Barbara Ann Atwood, *Identity and Assimilation: Changing Definitions of Tribal Power Over Children*, 83 Minn. L. Rev. 930 (1999).

[60] UCCJA § 14(a)(1), (2).

[61] *See Greenlaw v. Smith*, 869 P.2d 1024 (Wash. 1994) (Washington continued to have jurisdiction after mother and children moved from state because father continued to live there and evidence existed there).

Under the UCCJA conflicts regarding modification proceedings often arose, leading to uncertainty with respect to a decree's validity. To remedy this problem the UCCJEA replaced the old rule with one giving exclusive continuing jurisdiction to the court that entered the original custody decree.[62] So long as the original custody determination was made consistently with the UCCJEA,[63] the court issuing the original decree retains exclusive continuing jurisdiction until it determines that:

> (1) neither the child, nor the child and one parent, nor the child and a person acting as a parent have a significant connection with the [original] state and that substantial evidence is no longer available in the state concerning the child's care, protection, training, and personal relationships; or (2) a court of [the original] state or a court of another state determines that the child, the child's parents, and any person acting as a parent do not presently reside in [the original] state.[64]

Unlike the UCCJA rule, the UCCJEA provides that only the original court may make the determination of whether that court has significant connection jurisdiction.[65] An original court that has lost exclusive, continuing jurisdiction may modify its determination "*only if* it has jurisdiction to make an initial determination" under the UCCJEA.[66]

The UCCJEA also provides that when the original court no longer has jurisdiction, the new state may modify the custody order taking into account the home state preference for jurisdiction. If an enforcement proceeding has been initiated in another state, the court *may* communicate with that state, and if a modification action has commenced in another state, the court *must* communicate immediately with the other state.[67] The UCCJEA imposes the same basic duty to enforce valid custody decrees as the UCCJA. The UCCJEA also creates a new expedited enforcement remedy: a warrant for taking immediate physical custody of the child if a risk of danger or abduction exists.[68] It also provides for the registration in one state of custody determinations issued in another state.[69]

---

[62] UCCJEA § 202.

[63] *See Consford v. Consford*, 271 A.D.2d 106 (N.Y. App. Div. 2000) (court need not defer to earlier custody determination obtained without proper jurisdiction); *Czupil v. Jernigan*, 286 S.W.3d 753 (Ark. Ct. App. 2008) (finding no exclusive jurisdiction where continuing jurisdiction was premised on a void child-custody determination); *see also Jorgensen v. Vargas*, 627 N.W.2d 550 (Iowa 2001).

[64] UCCJEA § 202.

[65] UCCJEA § 203. *See also In re Forlenza*, 140 S.W.3d 373, 379 (Tex. 2004) ("Clearly, exclusive jurisdiction continues in the decree-granting state as long as a significant connection exists or substantial evidence is present.").

[66] UCCJEA § 202(b) (emphasis added). *See also Novatny v. Novatny*, 872 N.E.2d 673 (Ind. Ct. App. 2007) (finding no jurisdiction to modify an original Indiana custody order after the parties moved to other states).

[67] UCCJEA § 206.

[68] UCCJEA §§ 208-10.

[69] UCCJEA § 304.

[4] Effect of a Party's Conduct on Jurisdiction

Both the UCCJA and UCCJEA contain provisions for a court to decline jurisdiction because of a party's conduct in the custody dispute, although the specifics of their provisions differ. Under the UCCJA, if the petitioner for an *initial* custody decree has "wrongfully taken the child from another state or has engaged in similar reprehensible conduct," the court is authorized, but not required, to decline jurisdiction when it is "just and proper under the circumstances."[70] In a UCCJA action to *modify* another state's custody decree, however, the court is prohibited from exercising its jurisdiction "if the petitioner, without consent of the person entitled to custody, has improperly removed the child from the physical custody" of that person or "has improperly retained the child after a visit or other temporary relinquishment of physical custody," unless the interests of the child require that the court exercise its jurisdiction.[71] The court may also decline to exercise its jurisdiction for other violations of any existing custody decree of another state if it is "just and proper under the circumstances."[72] If a court dismisses an action because of wrongful conduct, it may assess "necessary travel and other expenses, including attorneys' fees, incurred by other parties or their witnesses" against the petitioner.[73]

Although the UCCJA does not require an actual violation of a custody decree, or even the existence of a custody decree, for a court to decline jurisdiction based on a party's "wrongful" taking of the child from the other parent, courts have been somewhat reluctant to decline jurisdiction based on parental misconduct. In *Morgan v. Morgan*,[74] an Alaska trial court accepted jurisdiction even though a Virginia court had already entered a custody decree in favor of a father who had removed a couple's children from Washington to Virginia before any custody action was filed. The Alaska Supreme Court overturned the trial court, reasoning that the father had not "wrongfully" transported the children from Washington to Virginia because both parents were equally entitled to custody prior to any court action and therefore the Alaska trial court should have declined jurisdiction.[75]

Of course, if a court exercises jurisdiction based on misconduct this may result in a case being decided by a less optimal forum. Five years after *Morgan*, the Alaska Supreme Court held that its trial court should have refused to decide a custody case brought by a mother who had removed the children from Ohio to Alaska after an Ohio court entered a temporary order granting custody to the father pursuant to the couple's own agreement.[76]

---

[70] UCCJA § 8(a).

[71] *Id. See also In re Marriage of Settle*, 556 P.2d 962, 967 (Or. 1976) (court equated time spent in forum state with children's best interest and declined to refuse jurisdiction based on wrongful conduct); *In re Custody of Ross*, 630 P.2d 353 (Or. 1981) (state does not lose jurisdiction merely because of a wrongful, unilateral removal of the child).

[72] UCCJA § 8(b).

[73] *Id.* at § 8(c).

[74] 666 P.2d 1026 (Alaska 1983).

[75] *Id.* at 1029.

[76] *Stokes v. Stokes*, 751 P.2d 1363 (Alaska 1988).

The UCCJEA has completely refashioned the UCCJA's "wrongful conduct" provisions, replacing them with one rule for both initial and modification proceedings, subject to emergency jurisdiction and other provisions of state law.[77] Under the UCCJEA's new provision, a court is required to reject jurisdiction if a person pursuing a custody action has engaged in "unjustifiable conduct," subject to three exceptions.[78] "Unjustifiable conduct" is not defined in the UCCJEA, although it has been suggested that acting in "a reprehensible manner, such as by removing, secreting, retaining, or restraining a child," will constitute unjustifiable conduct.[79] Cases decided under the UCCJA's Section 8 may also be instructive in defining unjustifiable conduct.[80]

[C] The Parental Kidnapping Prevention Act of 1980

Although the UCCJA marked an improvement over the traditional, domicile-based approach to custody jurisdiction, not all states had adopted the UCCJA by the end of the 1970s. States that had enacted state UCCJAs frequently altered provisions or interpreted the state UCCJA in a manner that undermined its purposes. As a result, forum shopping and parental kidnapping continued. Congress decided to intervene by enacting legislation that would specify which types of custody decrees must be afforded full faith and credit, as well as the circumstances that would allow states to modify an outstanding custody decree of another state.

The result was the 1980 Parental Kidnapping Prevention Act. While the PKPA contains provisions that criminalize parental kidnapping[81] and authorize parent locator services,[82] its major impact is to set federal standards for recognition of custody decrees.[83] To the extent that the PKPA conflicts with state law like the UCCJA, state law is preempted.[84] The UCCJEA is intended to avoid such conflicts, largely by adopting the PKPA's statutory home-state preference.[85]

---

[77] UCCJEA § 208.

[78] UCCJEA § 208 (providing three exceptions to the UCCJEA's unjustifiable conduct rule: (1) the parties acquiesce to the court's jurisdiction, even though the party's unjustifiable conduct would have ordinarily forced the court to reject jurisdiction; (2) the "alternative" court that would otherwise have jurisdiction says the other state is more the appropriate forum; or (3) no other state would have jurisdiction if the court rejected jurisdiction based on the party's unjustifiable conduct).

[79] *See* Patricia Hoff, *supra* note 11, at 286.

[80] *See id.*

[81] 18 U.S.C. § 1073.

[82] 42 U.S.C. § 663.

[83] 28 U.S.C. § 1738A. *See also Meade v. Meade*, 812 F.2d 1473, 1475-76 (4th Cir. 1987).

[84] *See, e.g., Scott v. Somers*, 903 A.2d 663 (Conn. App. Ct. 2006); *In re Marriage of Wiseman*, 737 N.E.2d 325 (Ill. App. 2000); *Murphy v. Woerner*, 748 P.2d 749 (Alaska 1988); *Greenlaw v. Smith*, 869 P.2d 1024 (Wash. 1994); *see also* Coombs, *supra* note 8, at 826-34.

[85] UCCJEA § 201.

[1] Scope of Application

The PKPA is concerned only with interstate enforcement and recognition of custody decrees. The PKPA does not dictate the terms for exercising initial custody jurisdiction nor does it prohibit states from recognizing decrees that do not conform to the PKPA. Rather, it sets out criteria which, if complied with, will result in a custody decree that must be afforded full faith and credit.[86] It further forbids states from modifying custody decrees of other states that were entered consistently with the PKPA, except under specified conditions.[87] To constitute a custody determination that must be afforded full faith and credit, the court entering the decree must have jurisdiction under its own laws, whether the UCCJA or the UCCJEA, and the PKPA.[88]

[2] Similarities and Differences between the Federal and State Statutes

The relationship between the PKPA and the UCCJA is complex, and Congress failed thoroughly to consider the interrelationship of the two.[89] The acts correspond in many features, but differ in others.

The PKPA sets out four bases for jurisdiction modeled after the UCCJA.[90] However, the PKPA, and now the UCCJEA, establish a statutory preference for home state jurisdiction, and the UCCJA's three alternate bases — significant connection, emergency, and default jurisdiction — are to be exercised only if it is apparent that no other state has home state jurisdiction.[91]

The Washington State Court of Appeals addressed this home state preference in *In re Marriage of Murphy.*[92] In *Murphy,* the parties had lived together with their two children in several states, until the husband abandoned the family in Arizona and moved to Ohio. The mother and children later moved to Washington. The husband subsequently filed for divorce in Ohio and requested that the Ohio court determine parental rights. Although the mother argued in a motion in the Ohio court that Ohio lacked jurisdiction because it was not the home state (which the husband conceded), the court denied her motion. The spouses entered into an agreement, which awarded the wife custody of the children, with liberal visitation to

---

[86] 28 U.S.C. § 1738A.

[87] 28 U.S.C. § 1738A(d) (providing that the state with initial jurisdiction consistent with the PKPA retains continuing jurisdiction to modify its order if a child or any contestant remains in the state and the state has jurisdiction under its own laws, whether the UCCJA or UCCJEA). In this instance, no other state may modify the issuing court's order until the original state declines jurisdiction. 28 U.S.C. § 1738A(f).

[88] 28 U.S.C. § 1738A(c). Thus, if an initial decree or an order modifying an initial decree are not entitled to PKPA protection, the case would proceed under the UCCJA or UCCJEA and local law. *See, e.g., In re Jorgensen,* 627 N.W.2d 550 (Iowa 2001).

[89] *See* Homer Clark, Law of Domestic Relations 476-94 (2d ed. 1988).

[90] The PKPA was amended in 1998 to apply to visitation as well as custody. H.R. Res. 4164, 105th Cong. (1998) (enacted) amending 28 U.S.C. § 1738A.

[91] 28 U.S.C. § 1738A(c)(2)(B)(i). *See also* UCCJEA § 201(a).

[92] 952 P.2d 624 (Wash. Ct. App. 1998).

the husband, and stipulated jurisdiction in Ohio. The wife later claimed that she entered into this agreement under duress, in fear of losing custody of the children.

Subsequently, the mother returned to the Washington court, asking it to assume jurisdiction, which the trial court denied. The Court of Appeals reversed and remanded, relying on the home state preference in the PKPA. The court concluded that although the PKPA did not give the home state exclusive jurisdiction in an initial custody hearing, if a home state exists, other states need not accord full faith and credit to a custody decree based on another jurisdictional ground. Because the jurisdictional ground for the Ohio decree was not evident from the record, the Washington court held that it was impossible to determine the basis for its assertion for jurisdiction, and remanded the case to the trial court for a determination of whether the decree was the type that must be recognized by the Washington court. The court in *Murphy* apparently overlooked the fact that even if the PKPA did not require recognition of the Ohio decree, Washington's own version of the UCCJA would require recognition if the Ohio decree were based on *any* valid jurisdictional basis, not merely on home state jurisdiction.

The PKPA and both the UCCJA and UCCJEA contain provisions for notice and the opportunity to be heard.[93] Neither the UCCJA nor the UCCJEA requires a court to have personal jurisdiction over a parent to determine child custody. Both acts restrict courts from exercising custody jurisdiction when a custody proceeding is pending in another state which is exercising jurisdiction consistent with the provisions of the acts,[94] but the PKPA does not have an independent provision denying full faith and credit to orders when the child has been wrongfully taken.[95] However, because the PKPA requires a court to have jurisdiction under its own state law as well as federal law, the no "wrongful conduct" or no "unjustifiable conduct" criteria for declining jurisdiction will still apply to state courts.[96]

Similarly, inconvenient forum provisions appear in both the UCCJA and the UCCJEA,[97] but not the PKPA. Courts may apply the inconvenient forum provision of the acts despite the lack of a similar provision in the PKPA.[98] Likewise, the UCCJA and UCCJEA extend recognition to custody decrees of foreign countries, a procedural mechanism lacking in the PKPA.[99]

The PKPA prohibits a court of another state from modifying a custody decree unless it has jurisdiction itself and the court of the original state either no longer

---

[93] 28 U.S.C. § 1738A(e); UCCJA § 4; UCCJEA § 205. *See also Schuyler v. Ashcraft*, 680 A.2d 765 (N.J. Super. Ct. App. Div. 1996) (concluding, where an original decree relinquished jurisdiction after six months, that a Florida court failed to give mother notice when it extended its jurisdiction and subsequently modified the original decree; therefore New Jersey, the new home state, could modify the Florida court's orders); *Lutes v. Alexander*, 421 S.E.2d 857 (Va. Ct. App. 1992).

[94] 28 U.S.C. § 1738A(g); UCCJA § 6; UCCJEA § 206.

[95] 28 U.S.C. § 1738A(g).

[96] *See supra* § 11.2[B][4].

[97] *See* UCCJA § 7; UCCJEA § 207.

[98] *See Patricia R. v. Andrew W.*, 467 N.Y.S.2d 322 (N.Y. Fam. Ct. 1983).

[99] UCCJA § 23; UCCJEA § 105.

has jurisdiction or has declined to exercise such jurisdiction to modify the decree.[100] In addition, like the UCCJEA, under the PKPA the court that entered an initial custody determination consistent with the statute continues to retain jurisdiction as long as it has jurisdiction under its own laws, and the state "remains the residence of the child or of any contestant."[101] By contrast, the UCCJA does not specifically recognize continuing jurisdiction based on the continued residence of a party.

In an attempt to determine which of two outstanding custody decrees is valid, parties sometimes have sought resolution in the federal courts. The United States Supreme Court denied litigants a federal forum as a tie-breaker for conflicting state court decrees in *Thompson v. Thompson*,[102] holding that the PKPA does not furnish an implied private cause of action to resolve a "jurisdictional stalemate."[103]

Thompson involved a California court's decree that modified an earlier award of joint custody to an award of sole custody to the mother when she moved to Louisiana. The decree was to be effective only until the California court received a more detailed report from a court investigator. Before the report was filed with the California court, the mother sought permanent recognition and enforcement in Louisiana of the temporary California decree. The Louisiana court granted her motion and awarded her sole custody. Subsequently, the California court awarded sole custody to the father based on its investigative report. The father eventually filed an action in federal district court seeking a declaration of validity of his California decree and invalidity and injunction of the Louisiana decree.

The father's action was dismissed by the United States District Court for the Central District of California, a decision affirmed by both the United States Court of Appeals for the Ninth Circuit and the United States Supreme Court. The Supreme Court found that Congress did not intend to create a federal private cause of action when it enacted the PKPA but, instead, had deliberately rejected the notion of extending diversity jurisdiction to enforcement of custody orders. Noting that "ultimate review remains available in the [Supreme] Court for truly intractable jurisdictional deadlocks," the Court refused to presume that either state was unable or unwilling to enforce the provisions of the PKPA.[104] The Court concluded:

> State courts faithfully administer the Full Faith and Credit Clause every day; now that Congress has extended full faith and credit requirements to child custody orders, we can think of no reason why the courts' administration of federal law in custody disputes will be any less vigilant. Should state courts prove as obstinate as petitioner predicts, Congress may choose to revisit the issue. But any more radical approach to the problem will have to await further legislative action; we "will not engraft a remedy on a

---

[100] 28 U.S.C. § 1738A(f). *Compare* UCCJA § 14a, *with* UCCJEA § 202. *See also Walter v. Walter*, 589 N.Y.S.2d 104 (N.Y. App. Div. 1992).

[101] 28 U.S.C. § 1738A(d).

[102] 484 U.S. 174 (1988).

[103] *Id.* at 177.

[104] *Id.* at 187.

statute, no matter how salutary, that Congress did not intend to provide."[105]

While proper application of both the PKPA and the UCCJA should prevent conflicting custody decrees, Professor Clark has noted that "[i]f anything, the injection of the PKPA into the continuing jurisdiction issue has amplified the confusion already evident under the UCCJA."[106] As noted above, the UCCJEA strives to resolve that confusion.

Both the UCCJA and PKPA have been held by most courts which have addressed the issue to apply to adoptions and terminations of parental rights,[107] while the UCCJEA defers to the Uniform Adoption Act.[108] The UCCJEA does, however, apply to neglect, abuse, dependency, wardship, guardianship, termination of parental rights and domestic violence cases.[109]

[3]   Personal Jurisdiction

Like the UCCJA and UCCJEA, the PKPA does not require personal jurisdiction over the respondent. As noted earlier, the Supreme Court's 1953 plurality decision in *May v. Anderson*[110] means that full faith and credit will not be given to a custody decree unless there is personal jurisdiction over the respondent. *May* implies that all custody decrees without such jurisdiction are void. The framers of the UCCJA, UCCJEA, and PKPA have never grappled directly with this question and the issue has not been directly addressed by the Supreme Court again. However, in 1990, in *Burnham v. Superior Court*,[111] Justice Scalia, writing for the plurality in dictum, assumed that personal jurisdiction is necessary for child custody.[112] The unresolved personal jurisdiction question raises serious issues relating to the best interest of the child if the Court were to conclude that custody decisions or modifications could not be made if a parent were absent.

[D]   The Hague Convention on International Child Abduction

Enforcement of child custody rights becomes even more complex when a child is taken to a foreign country or brought into the United States from another country. While the UCCJA and UCCJEA's provisions apply to recognition of custody

---

[105]   *Id.* at 187 (citing *California v. Sierra Club*, 451 U.S. 287, 297 (1981)).

[106]   Clark, *supra* note 89, at 485.

[107]   *See, e.g., Souza v. Superior Court*, 238 Cal. Rptr. 892 (1987) ("Under the Uniform Child Custody Jurisdiction Act and Parental Kidnapping Prevention Act, which were applicable in [the California] adoption proceeding, California court should have deferred to primary jurisdiction of Hawaii."); *In re Baby Girl Clausen*, 502 N.W.2d 649 (Mich. 1993); *In re Adoption of Child by T. W. C.*, 636 A.2d 1083 (N.J. Super. Ct. App. Div. 1994). *But see State in re R.N.J.*, 908 P.2d 345 (Utah App. 1995).

[108]   UCCJEA § 103. *But see supra* note 17 (explaining extension of UCCJEA to adoption by some states).

[109]   UCCJEA § 102(4).

[110]   345 U.S. 528, 533-34 (1953) (discussed *supra* § 11.02[A]).

[111]   495 U.S. 604 (1990).

[112]   *See also* Atwood, *supra* note 48, at 371-72.

decrees of other countries,[113] neither act has application to custody disputes which are litigated in foreign forums. In response to the increasing problem of international child abductions, in 1988 the United States joined a number of nations as a party to the Hague Convention on the Civil Aspects of International Child Abduction (the "Hague Convention").[114] The United States implemented the Hague Convention by enacting the International Child Abduction Remedies Act (ICARA).[115] Congress also made it a federal felony for a parent to wrongfully remove or retain a child outside the United States in the International Parental Kidnapping Act (IPKA).[116]

The Hague Convention was intended to decrease the incidence of international child abduction. For countries that have ratified it, the Hague Convention provides for the prompt return of a child under 16 years old,[117] who has been wrongfully removed or retained, back to the country of his or her "habitual residence" without an adjudication on the merits of the custody dispute.[118] Once "wrongful removal" is established,[119] the child must be returned unless the defendant establishes one of four principal defenses:[120] that (1) the proceeding was brought more than one year from the removal and the child has become settled in the new environment;[121] (2)

---

[113] UCCJA § 23 (comment lists Missouri, New Mexico, Ohio, and South Dakota as omitting this provision); UCCJEA § 105 (providing that recognition is not required when custody laws of another country violate "fundamental principles of human rights"). The UCCJEA also refers to the Hague Convention specifically in Sections 301, 302 and 315. For a discussion of the UCCJEA and the Hague Convention, see *Strout v. Campbell*, 864 So. 2d 1275 (Fla. Ct. App. 2004).

[114] *See also* Symposium, *The Past and Promise of the 1980 Hague Convention on the Civil Aspects of International Child Abduction*, 33 N.Y.U. J. Intl. L. & Pol'y (2000). For more information on the Hague Convention, including its full text and a list of adopting countries, see www.hcch.net.

[115] International Child Abduction Remedies Act, 42 U.S.C. § 11601 *et seq.*

[116] 42 U.S.C. § 11601 (1988); 18 U.S.C. § 1204 (1994). *See also* Susan Kreston, *Prosecuting International Parental Kidnapping*, 15 Notre Dame J. L. Ethics & Pub. Pol'y 533 (2001). Many child abductors are mothers attempting to seek protection from domestic violence. It has been suggested that the Convention fails to adequately address domestic abuse cases. The IPKA § 1204 provides as a defense to international parental kidnapping charges that the defendant was fleeing from domestic violence. *See* Merle H. Weiner, *International Child Abduction and the Escape from Domestic Violence*, 69 Fordham L. Rev. 593 (2000).

[117] The age requirement has been strictly construed by U.S. Courts. *See Abbott v. Abbott*, No. A-06-CV-359-LY (W.D. Tex., Feb. 10, 2012). The child in dispute was taken by his mother from Chile to the United States. The father sued for his son's return to Chile under the Hague Convention. The United States District Court for the Western District of Texas decided in favor of the mother, and was affirmed by the United States Court of Appeals for the Fifth Circuit. The Supreme Court reversed the trial court's order and remanded. However, during this legal process the child in question turned 16 years old. On remand, the District Court dismissed under Fed. R. Civ. P. 12(c). The court held that it lacked jurisdiction under the Hague Convention because the child was no longer under the age of 16. *Id. See also infra* notes 144–47 (discussing *Abbott*).

[118] Hague Convention art. 1. For a list of ratifying countries, together with reservations by each country, see http://www.hcch.net/index_en.php?act=conventions.status&cid=24. The Hague Convention has no application to disputes involving other countries. *See, e.g., de Silva v. Pitts*, 481 F.3d 1279, 1284 (10th Cir. 2007) (concluding Hague Convention was inapplicable to a case involving Sri Lanka because Sri Lanka is not a Convention signatory).

[119] Hague Convention art. 3. If the removal or retention is not wrongful, no return is required. *Id.*

[120] *See infra* notes 136–37, 150 (discussing the child's wishes as grounds for denying return).

[121] Hague Convention art. 12.

the person seeking return consented or acquiesced to the removal;[122] (3) the child would face a grave risk of physical or psychological harm, or an intolerable situation, if returned;[123] or (4) return would endanger human rights and fundamental freedoms.[124] All of the defenses are interpreted narrowly; the first two must be proven by a preponderance of the evidence, while the second two must be shown by clear and convincing evidence.[125]

In *Blondin v. Dubois*,[126] a mother conceded that she had wrongfully removed the children from France and had even forged their father's signature to do so, but argued a "grave risk" defense citing physical abuse from their father. The court concluded that all ameliorative measures that might allow the children to be returned while still protecting them must be fully analyzed, and it remanded the case to the district court. The court specifically noted the possibility that the children might be placed temporarily with a third party in their country of habitual residence.[127]

Subject to these limited defenses, return of a child to her country of "habitual residence" is mandatory if the petitioner files an application within one year of the

---

[122] Hague Convention art. 13(a).

[123] Hague Convention art. 13(b). Grave risk is often raised as a defense in cases alleging spousal or child abuse. *See* Weiner, *supra* note 116, at 634; *see also Danaipour v. McLarey*, 286 F.3d 1 (1st Cir. 2002) (sexual abuse constitutes grave harm); *Rodriguez v. Rodriguez*, 33 F. Supp. 2d 456 (D. Md. 1999) (grave risk of harm established by children's well-founded fear of harm, regardless of whether actual abuse had occurred); *Walsh v. Walsh*, 221 F.3d 204 (1st Cir. 2000) (adequate grave risk of harm defense established where mother was a domestic violence victim and father repeatedly violated court orders). Courts have rejected grave risk defenses premised on emotional harm to the child from being returned to their country of habitual residence or of merely remaining in an impoverished country. *See England v. England*, 234 F.3d 268 (5th Cir. 2000) (psychological harm resulting from return not sufficient); *Cuellar v. Joyce*, 596 F.3d 505, 508-09 (9th Cir. 2010) (reversing an order denying return of child to Panama, where child had lived in a "slum-like" neighborhood "beyond the end of the road" in a home with "no indoor running water, no climate control, no refrigeration, and very little furniture" and where residents "use a nearby creek and outhouse for waste disposal," noting that people across the world live in similar circumstances so that if this constituted a grave risk of harm, "parents in more developed countries would have unchecked power to abduct children from countries with a lower standard of living").

[124] Hague Convention art. 20.

[125] *See* 42 U.S.C. § 11603(e)(2) (setting forth the burdens of proof); 42 U.S.C. § 11601(a)(4) (describing the exceptions to return as narrow); *Friedrich v. Friedrich*, 78 F.3d 1060, 1067 (6th Cir. 1996) ("All four of these exceptions are 'narrow,' . . . [It is] not a basis for avoiding return of a child merely because an American court believes it can better or more quickly resolve a dispute.").

[126] 189 F.3d 240 (2d Cir. 1999).

[127] Petitioners may not always succeed in showing that precautionary measures will prevent grave risk to the child upon return. *See Blondin v. Dubois*, 238 F.3d 153, 162 (2d Cir. 2001) (*Blondin II*) (concluding that French authorities could not eliminate risk to the child because nothing could ensure that the child's return to France would not cause traumatic stress to recur). Courts are split as to whether the abducted-from country's capacity to provide protection to the child upon return may properly be considered. *Compare Friedrich v. Friedrich*, 78 F.3d 1060 (6th Cir. 1996) (concluding that a grave risk of harm will be demonstrated when the court in the country of habitual residence is incapable of providing or unwilling, for whatever reason, to provide the child adequate protection), *with Baran v. Beaty*, 526 F.3d 1340, 1347 (11th Cir. 2008) (finding that a parent may show grave risk of harm without providing evidence that the home country is unable or unwilling to offer protection to the child, but that courts may consider such evidence in the decision to deny return.).

wrongful removal or retention.[128] The Hague Convention itself does not define "habitual residence," which has been developed by case law. In *Feder v. Evans-Feder*,[129] the United States Court of Appeals for the Third Circuit adopted a "settled purpose" test for determining the child's habitual residence. In that case, the parties had lived with their son in Pennsylvania for the child's first three and a half years, until the father accepted a job in Australia. The mother reluctantly agreed to move to Australia, where they bought a house, enrolled the child in nursery school, and otherwise exhibited an intent to remain in that country. The mother was unhappy, and decided to leave her husband and return to the United States with their son after five months, but she told her husband she was going to visit her family. Within a month, the mother filed for divorce in Pennsylvania, seeking custody of the child, among other things. The father was served with the complaint when he went to visit them while on a business trip to the United States. Upon returning to Australia, the father sought and received a declaration from the Family Court of Australia under the Hague Convention, which found that the child and parents were habitual residents of Australia immediately before the mother retained the child in the United States, that the father had been exercising his rights to joint custody, and that the mother's retention of the child was wrongful under the Hague Convention. The father then filed a petition pursuant to the Hague Convention in the United States, requesting the child's return.

The U.S. District Court denied his petition, concluding that the father had failed to prove that the child's habitual residence had changed from the United States to Australia, focusing on the period of time that the child had lived in the United States prior to the move to Australia. The United States Court of Appeals for the Third Circuit reversed, agreeing that there must be a degree of settled purpose, either specific or general, but concluding that the father had demonstrated that purpose. The court reasoned:

> [W]e believe that a child's habitual residence is the place where he or she has been physically present for an amount of time sufficient for acclimatization and which has a "degree of settled purpose" from the child's perspective. We further believe that a determination of whether any particular place satisfies this standard must focus on the child and consists of an analysis of the child's circumstances in that place and the parents' present, shared intentions regarding their child's presence there.[130]

Consequently, the court concluded that both parents did what people who intend to reestablish themselves and their children generally do. Despite the mother's lack

---

[128] Hague Convention arts. 12, 13. Some courts toll the one-year period when a child is abducted and her whereabouts are concealed from the petitioning parent. *See Perez v. Garcia*, 198 P.3d 539 (Wash. Ct. App. 2009).

[129] 63 F.3d 217 (3d Cir. 1995). *See also Silverman v. Silverman*, 338 F.3d 886, 898 (8th Cir. 2003) (observing that the "[f]ederal courts are agreed that 'habitual residence' must encompass some form of 'settled purpose.'").

[130] *Feder v. Evans-Feder*, 63 F.3d 217, 224 (3d Cir. 1995). In a later Third Circuit case, the court concluded that the parties' custody agreement evidenced the intent to abandon the United States "for at least two years." *Whiting v. Krassner*, 391 F.3d 540, 550 (3d Cir. 2004).

of intent to remain permanently in Australia, a settled purpose to live as a family in that country was established.

The United States Court of Appeals for the Sixth Circuit reached a similar conclusion in the converse situation, in *Friedrich v. Friedrich*,[131] in which the child was born in Germany to a German father and an American mother, where they lived as a family until the mother removed the child to the United States. The court concluded that the child's habitual residence was in Germany, despite the mother's evidence that the child had United States citizenship, that his permanent address on United States documentation was in Ohio, and his mother intended to return to the United States with the child upon her discharge from the military.[132]

The United States Court of Appeals for the Ninth Circuit interpreted the term "habitual residence" slightly differently in *Mozes v. Mozes*.[133] In *Mozes*, the father consented to the mother's taking their children from Israel to California for a limited period of time. The mother decided not to return to Israel and the couple was divorced in California. The father later filed a petition in federal court to have the children returned to Israel under the Hague Convention. The court regarded the relevant inquiry as whether the child has abandoned a prior habitual residence. It concluded that it is not merely a question of whether the children had become "settled" in a new environment; rather, it depends on whether a new forum has supplanted the old one as the "locus of the children's family and social development."[134] A parent's simple consent to the children's presence in another jurisdiction is insufficient to make this showing; a shared intent to abandon previous

---

[131] 983 F.2d 1396, 1401 (6th Cir. 1993).

[132] On remand, the mother was ordered to return the child to Germany. She appealed, arguing that the father had not been "exercising" custody rights at the time she removed the child and further alleged that the child faced a grave risk of harm if returned. In *Friedrich v. Friedrich (II)*, 78 F.3d 1060 (6th Cir. 1996), the court held that the court in the abducted-to country has jurisdiction to decide the merits of the abduction claim but not the merits of the underlying custody dispute, reasoning that the Hague Convention was intended to restore the situation to the pre-abduction status quo. It concluded that the father's placing the mother and child's belongings in an outside hallway during an argument on the night of removal did not constitute a termination of parental rights under German law, liberally defining "exercise" of custodial rights as whenever the parent with *de jure* custody rights keeps or attempts to keep regular contact with child. Determining the adequacy of a parent's exercise of custodial rights is too close to deciding the merits of a custody dispute and, therefore, should be decided by the country of habitual residence. The court held that if a person has valid custody rights under the law of the country of habitual residence, that person cannot fail to "exercise" those rights unless there is clear and unequivocal evidence of an act of abandonment. The court further held that a "grave risk" of harm is more than the adjustment problems likely to be experienced by the child upon return.

[133] 239 F.3d 1067 (9th Cir. 2001).

[134] *Id.* at 1084. In a later Ninth Circuit case, the court asked "whether the children's lives have become firmly rooted in their new surroundings [during their father's four-year military assignment so that] returning the children to Germany [would] be tantamount to sending them home?" *Holder v. Holder*, 392 F.3d 1009, 1019 (9th Cir. 2004). *See also Koch v. Koch*, 450 F.3d 703, 715 (7th Cir. 2006) (concluding that a "shared" subjective wish to someday return to the United States did not suffice for the U.S. to continue to be the country of habitual residence); *Ruiz v. Tenorio*, 392 F.3d 1247, 1252 (11th Cir. 2004) (asking whether the parties " 'entitled to fix the place of the child's residence' " developed a settled intention to abandon the prior country of residence, together with sufficient time for the child to become acclimated to the new country (quoting *Mozes v. Mozes*, 239 F.3d 1067, 1076 (9th Cir. 2001)).

habitual residence must be demonstrated.[135]

Some courts take the child's perspective as central in determining habitual residence. In *Karkkainen v. Kovalchuk*,[136] the United States Court of Appeals for the Third Circuit found that an 11-year-old child possessed "the material and psychological wherewithal" for her parents to allow her to decide where she would reside after a nine-week visit with her father in the United States. The Sixth and Seventh Circuits have likewise emphasized that a "child's habitual residence is the nation where, at the time of their [sic] removal, the child has been present long enough to allow acclimatization, and where this presence has a 'degree of settled purpose from the child's perspective.' "[137]

The Hague Convention requires countries to establish a Central Authority to assist in locating and returning children who have been abducted across international boundaries.[138] A pre-existing custody order is not required if the petitioning party is the child's parent.[139]

The Central Authority must first seek a voluntary return of the child before initiating legal action.[140] The obvious problem with this provision is that the runaway parent is given notice that his or her whereabouts are known and an opportunity to further conceal the child. If legal proceedings occur, the court must find a breach of custodial rights; after this finding is made, the Central Authority must return the child to the other country immediately. However, if the proceeding to return the child is initiated more than one year after the child's removal, the new country may decline to return the child if there is proof that the child has been integrated into the new home.[141]

---

[135] *See also Harkness v. Harkness*, 577 N.W. 2d 116 (Mich. Ct. App. 1998) (habitual residence not necessarily last place child lived); *Gitter v. Gitter*, 396 F.3d 124, 134 (2d Cir. 2005) ("[T]he court should inquire into the shared intent of those entitled to fix the child's residence (usually the parents) at the latest time that their intent was shared."); *Barzilay v. Barzilay*, 600 F.3d 912, 920-21 (8th Cir. 2010) ("Any idea that parents could contractually determine their children's habitual residence is also at odds with the basic purposes of the Hague Convention" and thus parents cannot stipulate to the child's residence, thereby removing the question from the court's review).

[136] 445 F.3d 280 (3d Cir. 2006).

[137] *Robert v. Tesson*, 507 F.3d 981, 993 (6th Cir. 2007) (quoting *Feder v. Evans-Feder*, 63 F.3d 217, 224 (6th Cir. 2007). *See also Kijowska v. Haines*, 463 F.3d 583, 588 (7th Cir. 2006) (citing *Karkkainen v. Kovalchuk*, 445 F.3d 280, 291-92 (3d Cir. 2006)).

[138] The Department of State is the Central Authority in the United States. *See* Exec. Order No. 12,648, 53 Fed. Reg. 30,637 (1988).

[139] Hague Convention art. 3.

[140] Hague Convention arts. 7(c), 10.

[141] Hague Convention art. 12. As one court has noted, "it is not the mere passage of time which determines the issue or the [Hague] Convention would have so provided. Rather, there must also be evidence that the children are in fact settled in or connected to the new environment so that, at least inferentially, return would be disruptive with likely harmful effects." *In re Robinson*, 983 F. Supp. 1339, 1345 (D. Colo. 1997). *See also In re Koc*, 181 F. Supp. 2d 136, 152 (E.D.N.Y. 2001) ("Among the factors considered by the courts in determining whether a child is settled in her new environment are the age of the child, the stability of the child's residence in the new environment, whether the child attends school or day care consistently, whether the child attends church regularly, the stability of the mother's employment, and whether the child has friends and relatives in the new area.").

A country is not required to return the child if the parent seeking return was "not actually exercising the custody rights at the time of removal or retention, or had consented to or subsequently acquiesced in the removal or retention" of the child.[142] Thus, a person with visitation rather than custody rights has no right of return of the child under the Hague Convention, but may seek access to the child.[143]

Because so much hinges on the exercise of custody rights, a number of questions have arisen about whether an individual has custody rights in a child, which may arise from judicial determination, administrative decision, or operation of law. In *Abbott v. Abbott*,[144] the United States Supreme Court held that the *ne exeat* right under Chilean law is a custody right under the Hague Convention. The Court found any suggestion that a *ne exeat* right is a mere " 'righ[t] of access' " [to be] illogical and atextual."[145] The Court explained that:

> The [Hague] convention defines "rights of access" as "includ[ing] the right to take a child for a limited period of time to a place other than the child's habitual residence," Art. 5(b), Treaty Doc., at 7, and ICARA defines that same term as "visitation rights," § 11602(7). The joint right to decide a child's country of residence is not even arguably a "right to take a child for a limited period of time" or a "visitation righ[t]." Reaching the common-sense conclusion that a *ne exeat* right does not fit these definitions of "rights of access" honors the [Hague] Convention's distinction between rights of access and rights of custody.[146]

Moreover, the Court pointed out that international case law and "[s]cholars agree that there is an emerging international consensus that *ne exeat* rights are rights of custody."[147]

As noted above, important exceptions to the Hague Convention allow the other country to retain the child if "there is a grave risk that his or her return would expose the child to physical or psychological harm or otherwise place the child in an intolerable situation"[148] or if the child's return "would not be permitted by the fundamental principles of the requested State relating to the protection of human

---

[142]   Hague Convention art. 13(a).

[143]   Hague Convention art. 21. *See also, e.g., Ibarra v. Quintanilla Garcia*, 476 F. Supp. 2d 630 (S.D. Tex. 2007) (reading the parties' divorce decree to award custody to the mother with visitation to the father, as giving the father no custody rights within the meaning of the Hague Convention).

[144]   130 S. Ct. 1983 (2010).

[145]   *Id.* at 1992.

[146]   *Id.* at 1992, 1997. *See also Bader v. Kramer*, 445 F.3d 346 (4th Cir. 2006) (concluding that German law confers on both parents joint custody until a competent court enters a different order and remanding the case for determination of whether the father was exercising those joint custody rights); *Whallon v. Lynn*, 230 F.3d 450 (1st Cir. 2000) (finding divisible custody rights under Mexican law of physical custody and *patria potestas*, with the latter "independent" from mere visitation rights, giving the father custody rights under the Hague Convention).

[147]   *Abbott v. Abbott*, 130 S. Ct. 1983 (2010). For a postscript to *Abbott*, see *supra* note 117.

[148]   Hague Convention art. 13(b). *See also supra* note 123 (and accompanying text); Caroline LeGette, *International Child Abduction and the Hague Convention: Emerging Practice and Interpretation of the Discretionary Exception*, 25 Tex. Int'l L. J. 287 (1990).

rights and fundamental freedoms."[149] Another exception gives the foreign authority the discretion to defer to the child's wishes if the child is of sufficient age and maturity.[150] A conflicting custody order entered in the child's present location does not constitute a defense, however.[151] A decision to return the child is not a decision on the merits of the custody issue, although the authorities may initiate a legal action regarding visitation rights.[152]

The Hague Convention merely supplements existing procedures and does not preclude persons from pursuing alternate legal or administrative remedies.[153] It does, however, require any court with notice of the unauthorized removal of a child to stay any custody action initiated by the alleged abductor until the matter has been resolved under the Hague Convention.[154] State and federal courts have concurrent jurisdiction to decide actions for return or visitation under the Hague Convention.[155]

The United States declined to adopt a provision that the countries themselves bear the costs of actions without charge to the applicant, except the expense of private legal counsel and travel expenses. ICARA awards "necessary expenses" to the successful petitioner unless the award would be "clearly inappropriate,"[156] although the Hague Convention would make such awards discretionary.[157]

In addition to the potential expense of invoking the Hague Convention, continuing problems include the inability of state authorities to locate the abducted children and the removal of children to non-member countries.[158] Despite these inherent obstacles, the Hague Convention has been hailed as "remarkably successful in achieving its goals,"[159] although a number of challenges remain.[160]

---

[149] Hague Convention art. 20.

[150] Hague Convention art. 13. The "age and maturity" exception applies narrowly. *See* 42 U.S.C. § 11601(a)(4) (2011). *Compare, e.g., Leites v. Mendiburu,* 2008 U.S. Dist. LEXIS 1677 (M.D. Fla., Jan. 7, 2008) (finding 13-year-old to be bright, articulate and mature and crediting her objection to returning to Argentina because she viewed her home in the United States as a calmer environment with better opportunities), *with Lopez v. Alcala,* 547 F. Supp. 2d 1255 (M.D. Fla. 2008) (finding a seven-year-old not sufficiently mature to require her views to be taken into account).

[151] Hague Convention art. 17.

[152] Hague Convention art. 16.

[153] 42 U.S.C. § 11603(h).

[154] Hague Convention art. 16.

[155] *See* Hague Convention art 18; *see also* Weiner, *Navigating the Road Between Uniformity and Progress: The Need for Purposive Analysis of the Hague Convention on the Civil Aspects of International Child Abduction,* 33 Colum. Human Rights L. Rev. 275 (2002).

[156] 42 U.S.C. § 11607(b)(3).

[157] Hague Convention art. 26.

[158] *See* LeGette, *supra* note 148, at 288-89.

[159] *Id.* at 288.

[160] *See, e.g.,* Melissa S. Wills, *Interpreting The Hague Convention on International Child Abduction: Why American Courts Need to Reconcile the Rights of Non-Custodial Parents, the Best Interests of Abducted Children, and the Underlying Objectives of The Hague Convention,* 25 Rev. Litig. 423 (2006); Linda Silberman, *Interpreting the Hague Abduction Convention: In Search of a Global Jurisprudence,* 38 U.C. Davis L. Rev. 1049 (2005); Anastacia M. Greene, *Seen and Not Heard?: Children's Objections*

§ 11.03 FACTORS IN DISPUTED CHILD CUSTODY CASES

[A] The Best Interests of the Child

The prevailing standard in child custody adjudications is the best interest of the child. Modern statutes generally reflect this standard. In some jurisdictions, the legislature has provided little guidance to the courts, merely setting out the "best interest" standard in broad terms. The Arkansas statute governing the award of custody of children of the marriage on divorce, for example, simply requires that the award "shall be made without regard to the sex of the parent but solely in accordance with the welfare and best interests of the children."[161]

In other states, reflecting an approach that is increasingly more common, if not typical, the statute sets out a detailed list of relevant factors that define the best interests of the child or that the trial court must consider in making its determination. The Minnesota statute is illustrative, requiring the court to consider and evaluate the following factors:

(1) the wishes of the child's parent or parents as to custody;

(2) the reasonable preference of the child, if the court deems the child to be of sufficient age to express preference;

(3) the child's primary caretaker;

(4) the intimacy of the relationship between each parent and the child;

(5) the interaction and interrelationship of the child with a parent or parents, siblings, and any other person who may significantly affect the child's best interests;

(6) the child's adjustment to home, school, and community;

(7) the length of time the child has lived in a stable, satisfactory environment and the desirability of maintaining continuity;

(8) the permanence, as a family unit of the existing or proposed custodial home;

(9) the mental and physical health of all individuals involved;

(10) the capacity and disposition of the parties to give the child love, affection, and guidance, and to continue educating and raising the child in the child's culture and religion or creed, if any;

(11) the child's cultural background; and

(12) the effect on the child of the actions of an abuser, if related to domestic

---

Under The Hague Convention On International Child Abduction, 13 U. Miami Int'l & Comp. L. Rev. 105 (2005).

[161] Ark. Code Ann. § 9-13-101 (1987). *See also* Ala. Code § 30-3-1 (1975) (providing that on divorce the court may give custody of children of the marriage "to either father or mother, as may seem right and proper, having regard to the moral character and prudence of the parents and the age and sex of the children").

abuse, . . . that has occurred between the parents.[162]

In *Maxfield v. Maxfield*,[163] the Supreme Court of Minnesota, affirming the award of custody of three children to the mother, discussed in detail the way in which the enumerated statutory factors relate to the best interests of the child standard. The court stated:

> In applying the bests interests analysis, we recognize much must be left to the discretion of the trial court. Some statutory criteria will weigh more in one case and less in another and there is rarely an easy answer. Yet, . . . the golden thread running through any best interests analysis is the importance, for a young child in particular, of its bond with the primary parent as this relationship bears on the other criteria, such as the need for "a stable, satisfactory environment and the desirability of maintaining continuity" and "mental and physical health of all individuals involved." Usually this relationship "should not be disrupted without strong reasons.[164]

[B] Doctrinal Presumptions

Just as state legislatures have enacted factors in attempts to define the content of "best interests of the child," the prevailing standard in cases involving child custody,[165] the courts also have struggled to enunciate factors in an attempt to give "best interests" a reliable and precise meaning. In furtherance of this end, courts reviewing child custody cases have developed over time, but sometimes subsequently rejected, a number of presumptions intended to aid in determining best interests. Among the most common are the tender years presumption, the natural parent presumption, and the primary caretaker presumption. Preference for the natural parent has been attenuated to some extent by the acceptance of some courts of the concept of psychological parenthood.

[1] The Tender Years Presumption

Among the earliest presumptions that courts adopted in attempting to reach custody determinations consistent with the best interests of the child was the tender years doctrine, which favored placement of young children with their mothers. The court in *Freeland v. Freeland*[166] tersely stated the rationale underlying the doctrine: "Mother love is a dominant trait in even the weakest of women, and as a general thing surpasses the paternal affection for the common offspring, and, moreover, a child needs a mother's care even more than a father's."[167] Thus, the

---

[162] Minn. Stat. Ann. § 518.17 (1990) (the statute also precludes the use of "one factor to the exclusion of all others"; explicitly bars use of the primary caretaker factor as a presumption in determining best interests; and requires detailed findings on each factor and an explanation of how the factors led to the court's best interest determination. When the parties seek joint custody, the court must consider additional listed factors).

[163] 452 N.W. 2d 219 (Minn. 1990).

[164] *Id.* at 222.

[165] *See supra* § 11.03[A].

[166] 159 P. 698 (Wash. 1916).

[167] *Id.* at 699.

court noted judicial reluctance to deprive a mother of custody absent a clear showing that she is so unfit as to endanger her children's welfare.

While modern courts have largely rejected the tender years doctrine on constitutional and other grounds, some have done so grudgingly. In *DeCamp v. Hein*,[168] for example, the court considered a gender neutral amendment to the Florida custody statute requiring that fathers be given the same consideration as mothers in determining the child's primary residence, regardless of the child's age. The court rejected the trial court's view that the statute had totally abolished the tender years doctrine. Rather, the court held that the statutory mandate to consider all relevant facts in custody matters required some consideration of the tender years doctrine. Accordingly, the court held that common sense required that girls aged one and three years should reside with their mother.

In later cases, the Florida District Court of Appeal implicitly distanced itself from any implication that it was not in agreement with the view that the tender years doctrine had been effectively abolished.[169] Finally, in *Charradi v. LaVoie*,[170] the court further clarified its views, holding that the tril court could not consider the age or sex of a child a separate factor when determining who should be the primary residential parent, but could consider those factors with relation to other relevant statutory factors that affect the child's interests.

Simply stated, although remnants of the tender years doctrine appear occasionally in contemporary decisions, it is now largely a historical anachronism, as are the stereotypical views that supported it. The opinion of the Supreme Court of Alaska in *Johnson v. Johnson*[171] is illustrative. The court in *Johnson* held that use of the tender years doctrine was not a permissible criterion for the state's trial courts to use. The court held that the age of children in a custody dispute is only one factor, to be weighed against others in making a best interests determination, and that the tender years doctrine was inconsistent with the statutory "best interests" requirement.[172]

While the court in *Johnson* found it unnecessary to reach the father's contention that the trial court's use of the tender years doctrine violated his right to equal protection, courts in other jurisdictions have invoked the 14th Amendment of the United States Constitution as a basis for rejecting the doctrine. In *Ex parte Devine*, for example, the Supreme Court of Alabama undertook a detailed and thoughtful examination of the history of the tender years presumption and a reexamination of the doctrine in light of pronouncements relating to gender discrimination by the Supreme Court of the United States.[173] The court concluded that "the tender years

---

[168] 541 So. 2d 708 (Fla. Dist. Ct. App. 1989).

[169] *See Kuutti v. Kuutti*, 645 So. 2d 80 (Fla. Dist. Ct. App. 1994).

[170] 662 So. 2d 751, 753 (Fla. Dist. Ct. App. 1995).

[171] 564 P.2d 71 (Alaska 1977).

[172] *Id.* at 75. *See also In re Marriage of Bowen*, 219 N.W.2d 683 (Iowa 1974); *State ex rel. Watts v. Watts*, 350 N.Y.S.2d 285 (N.Y. Sup. Ct. 1973).

[173] The court reviewed the Supreme Court's holdings in *Reed v. Reed*, 404 U.S. 71 (1971) (striking down a provision of the Idaho probate code that gave men preference over women for appointment as estate administrators); *Frontiero v. Richardson*, 411 U.S. 677 (1973) (overturning a federal statutory

presumption represents an unconstitutional gender-based classification which discriminates between fathers and mothers in child custody proceedings solely on the basis of sex."[174]

[2] The Natural Parent Presumption

Custody disputes between a child's natural or biological parent and another arise occasionally in divorce proceedings, but more often in other contexts. Generally, to overcome statutory or judicially created preferences for the natural parent will require circumstances such as unfitness, abandonment or the like, but the courts have not been entirely consistent in adhering to this standard. In *Bennett v. Jeffreys*,[175] the natural mother sought custody of an eight-year-old girl from a friend of the child's grandmother to whom she had entrusted the child shortly after birth. In the course of its opinion, New York's highest court resoundingly endorsed its preference for the natural parent in disputed custody matters, stating:

> Absent extraordinary circumstances, narrowly categorized, it is not within the power of a court, or, by delegation of the Legislature or court, a social agency, to make significant decisions concerning the custody of children, merely because it could make a better decision or disposition. The state is *parens patriae* and always has been, but it has not displaced the parent in right or responsibility. Indeed, the courts and the law would, under existing constitutional principles, be powerless to supplant parents except for grievous cause or necessity . . . .[176]

The court noted, however, exceptions to parental rights "created by extraordinary circumstances, illustratively, surrender, abandonment, persisting neglect, unfitness, and unfortunate or involuntary disruption of custody over an extended period of time."[177] Only when such extraordinary circumstances are present may the court inquire into and base its custody determination on the best interests of the child. In the case before it, the court found that the mother's protracted separation from the child, lack of her own established household, her unwed state and the child's attachment to the custodian were extraordinary circumstances. Accordingly, the court remanded the case to the trial court for an inquiry into the best interests of the child.

On remand, the trial court awarded custody to the foster mother, basing its decision in large part on the testimony of a psychiatrist that a psychological parent-child relationship[178] had developed between the child and the foster mother.[179] Thus, it appears that in the view of some courts, a natural parent

---

presumption of dependency extended to spouses of male but not female members of the armed forces); and *Orr v. Orr*, 440 U.S. 268 (1979) (invalidating a state statute imposing the obligation to pay alimony on husbands, but not wives), among others.

[174] *Devine*, 398 So. 2d at 686. *See also Pusey v. Pusey*, 728 P.2d 117 (Utah 1986).

[175] 356 N.E.2d 277 (N.Y. 1976).

[176] *Id.* at 281.

[177] *Id.*

[178] *See* J. Goldstein, et al., Beyond the Best Interests of the Child (1973).

[179] *Bennett v. Marrow*, 399 N.Y.S.2d 697 (N.Y. App. Div. 1977).

presumption or preference will be rebutted by proof that a third party has become the child's psychological parent.

In *Guardianship of Philip B.*,[180] the court elaborately described and applied the psychological parent concept in awarding custody to a third party over the objections of a child's natural parents. The child involved, born with Down's Syndrome, was placed by his parents in a residential facility for developmentally disabled children. Over time, the child developed a close and caring relationship with a volunteer worker at the facility and her family, while the natural parents simultaneously developed a pattern of physical and emotional detachment from their son. Describing the right of parents to custody of their children as fundamental, the court noted that a custody award to a nonparent required a finding that custody to the parent would be detrimental to the child and that custody to the nonparent would be in the child's best interests. Purporting to apply this standard, the court approved the trial court's finding that an award of custody to the child's natural parents would be harmful to the child "in light of the psychological or 'de facto' parental relationship established between him and [the nonparents]."[181]

Although a few courts have expressly relied on psychological parenthood in reaching decisions in custody cases, the concept has by no means achieved universal approval, and some courts have explicitly rejected it.[182] In any event, well before the concept was enunciated, the courts often enough identified factors or circumstances that would overcome the presumption favoring a fit parent. In *Painter v. Bannister*,[183] for example, after the death of his wife, the father voluntarily gave custody of his son to the child's maternal grandparents. Four years later, the father was unsuccessful in his attempt to regain custody. The court acknowledged the presumption of parental preference, but nevertheless awarded custody to the grandparents, noting the child's positive development in their care, the stability and security of their home, and a father-son relationship that the child had established with his grandfather.

In sum, the decisions make clear that the preference for the natural parent in custody proceedings is a strong one, although it may be rebutted in a variety of circumstances. The Supreme Court of Kansas, in *In re Guardianship of Williams*,[184] acurately stated that [n]ot only is the parental preference doctrine one of long standing in Kansas, it is also the rule, in one form or another, in a majority of the jurisdictions in this country.[185] Accoringly the court concluded that it would "adhere to the rule that absent highly unusul or extraordinary circumstances the prental preference doctrine is to be applied in a custody dispute over minor children when the dispute is between a natural parent who has not been found unfit and a

---

[180]   188 Cal. Rptr. 781 (Cal. Ct. App. 1983).

[181]   *Id.* at 789.

[182]   *See generally* Richard E. Crouch, *An Essay on the Critical and Judicial Reception of Beyond the Best Interests of the Child*, 13 Fam. L.Q. 49 (1979).

[183]   140 N.W.2d 152 (Iowa 1966).

[184]   869 P.2d 661 (Kan. 1994).

[185]   *Id.* at 669-70.

nonparent"[186]. Again, in a case in which the child's father died several years after his divorce from the child's mother, a Florida court noted that the right of a fit natural parent to custody in a dispute with a third party was "older than the common law itself," and awarded custody to the mother over the stepparent who had been married to the deceased father.[187] Conversely, the Supreme Court of Idaho held that where a child has a long-term relationship with a stepparent, the best interest test is appropriate and the natural parent presumption does not preclude its application.[188]

[3]   The Primary Caretaker Presumption

As discussed, modern courts for the most part have rejected the tender years doctrine in favor of gender neutral decision making, either as a matter of policy or based on the view that the doctrine is violates the right to equal protection under the United States Constitution.[189] The primary caretaker presumption, while gender neutral on its face, may compel the same results as would obtain under the tender years doctrine. Obviously, and as might have been anticipated, it is usually the mother of the child who will meet the definitional requirements of primary caretaker.

The decision of the Supreme Court of Appeals of West Virginia in *Garska v. McCoy*[190] is the leading articulation of the primary caretaker presumption. The case arose in the context of a legislative amendment eliminating gender based presumptions in awarding custody, which was enacted in response to an earlier case that had announced a strong maternal presumption for children of tender years.[191] The court held that "there is a presumption in favor of the primary caretaker parent, if he or she meets the minimum, objective of being a fit parent . . . , regardless of sex."[192]

Conceding the difficulty of enumerating all of the factors that will identify the primary caretaker parent, the court, nevertheless, listed certain criteria as requiring consideration, stating:

> In establishing which natural or adoptive parent is the primary caretaker, the trial court shall determine which parent has taken primary responsibility for, *inter alia*, the performance of the following caring and nurturing duties of a parent: (1) preparing and planning of meals; (2) bathing, grooming and dressing; (3) purchasing, cleaning and care of clothes; (4) medical care, including nursing and trips to physicians; (5) arranging for social interaction among peers, after school, *i.e.*, transporting to friends'

---

[186] *Id.* at 670.

[187] *Webb v. Webb*, 546 So. 2d 1062, 1065 (Fla. Dist. Ct. App. 1989).

[188] *Stockwell v. Stockwell*, 775 P.2d 611 (Idaho 1989). *See also Prawdzik v. Hiner*, 454 N.W.2d 399 (Mich. Ct. App. 1990) (awarding custody of child to parental grandparents with whom child had lived for five years in preference to the child's mother).

[189] *See supra* § 11.03[B][1].

[190] 278 S.E.2d 357 (W. Va. 1981).

[191] *See J.B. v. A.B.*, 242 S.E.2d 248 (W. Va. 1978).

[192] *Id.* at 362.

houses or, for example, to girl or boy scout meetings; (6) arranging for alternative care, *i.e.*, babysitting, day-care, etc.; (7) putting child to bed at night, waking child in the morning; (8) disciplining, *i.e.*, teaching general manners and toilet training; (9) educating, *i.e.*, religious, cultural, social, etc; and (10) teaching elementary skills, *i.e.*, reading, writing and arithmetic.[193]

In *Burchard v. Garay*,[194] the Supreme Court of California sharply criticized a trial court's decision awarding custody to the father of an out of wedlock child because of his better economic position. The trial court also referred to the fact that the mother worked and placed the child in day care, while the father's new wife could care for the child at home. The reviewing court summarily rejected the unfair assumption that working mothers cannot provide care, nurturance and continuity of attention, particularly where the working mother has been the primary caregiver. The court found all of the grounds relied on by the trial court as insignificant, compared to the fact that the mother had been the child's primary caretaker from birth until the date of trial.

Consideration of the primary caretaker factor does not necessarily raise it to the level of a presumption. The Supreme Court of North Dakota in *Wolf v. Wolf*[195] noted that the best interests and welfare of the child remains the governing standard for trial courts in child custody determinations. Stating what would appear to be the rule in most jurisdictions, the court observed that "the primary caretaker factor is not a presumptive rule but only one of many considerations to be evaluated by the trial court in making its finding as to the best interest of the child."[196] In 1991, the West Virginia legislature repealed the state's primary caretaker provisions and adopted a statutory scheme derived from a standard enunciated by the American Law Institute.[197] The ALI standard allocates custodial responsibility in accordance with the proportion of time that each of the parents spent performing caretaking functions in the past.[198]

[C] The Effect of Parental Conduct on Custody Determinations

The conduct of a parent that will most often affect custody is sexual conduct, sometimes disguised by references to "lifestyle." Courts generally will consider a parent's heterosexual conduct outside of marriage or homosexual conduct as one factor to be considered in a custody determination, rather than as constituting unfitness *per se.* Nevertheless, cases involving lesbian or gay male custodians who

---

[193] *Id.* at 363. *See also Pikula v. Pikula*, 374 N.W.2d 705, 713 (Minn. 1985).

[194] 724 P.2d 486 (Cal. 1986).

[195] 474 N.W.2d 257 (N.D. 1991).

[196] *Id.* at 258.

[197] *See* ALI, *Principles of the Law of Family Dissolution* § 2.09 (2002) (hereinafter ALI *Principles*).

[198] *See generally* Elizabeth S. Scott, *Pluralism, Parental Preference and Child Custody*, 80 Cal. L. Rev. 615 (1992).

maintain live-in or other relationships with persons of the same sex often enough provoke judicial high dudgeon.[199]

[1] Statutory Provisions Relating to Parental Conduct

In some states, the statutes governing custody explicitly identify parental conduct among the factors a court must consider in arriving at a determination reflecting the best interests of the child. The Minnesota statute, for example, contains a range of factors involving parental conduct, but directs that "[t]he court shall not consider the conduct of a proposed custodian that does not affect the custodian's relationship to the child."[200] In Alabama the court must consider, among other things, "the moral character and prudence of the parents."[201] In the District of Columbia, the statute identifies "race, color, national origin, political affiliation, sex or sexual orientation" as factors that alone should not be determinative of custody or visitation.[202] This language clearly does not preclude the trial judge from considering these factors.

[2] Judicial Approaches

Decisions that address the relevance of a parent's sexual conduct to fitness for custody often reflect varying judicial views of what constitute appropriate moral standards. The appellate court's framing of the question presented in *Feldman v. Feldman*[203] reflects an astute recognition of this truism. The court stated: "The issue presented is whether the [lower] court's determination, cloaked in the rubric 'best interests of the child,' was, in fact, based upon its subjective moral judgment rejecting and in effect severely punishing this sexually-liberated divorced woman for her life-style and personal beliefs."[204]

In *Feldman*, the court below transferred custody of two children, aged six and nine, from their mother, with whom they had lived since birth, to their father. At the hearing, it appeared that the mother had in the home a copy of "Screw," a sexually explicit magazine, together with letters with explicit photographs attached, solicited through an advertisement that the wife and her boyfriend had placed in the magazine. Evidence at the hearing also established that the mother's sex life did not affect the children, who were in a happy, cheerful, and comfortable home, and were well provided for emotionally and physically. Nevertheless, without finding the mother unfit, the hearing court awarded custody to the father based on its view that the mother's life-style indicated a "desire to experiment sexually."[205]

---

[199] *See generally* Donald H. Stone, *The Moral Dilemma: Child Custody When One Parent is Homosexual or Lesbian*, 23 Suffolk U. L. Rev. 711 (1989).

[200] Minn. Stat. Ann. § 518.17 (1990).

[201] Ala. Code § 30-3-1 (1975).

[202] D.C. Code Ann. § 16-914 (1981).

[203] 358 N.Y.S.2d 507 (N.Y. App. Div. 1974).

[204] *Id.* at 509.

[205] *Id.* at 509-10.

Awarding custody to the mother, the appellate court observed that "amorality, immorality, sexual deviation and what we conveniently consider aberrant sexual practices do not *ipso facto* constitute unfitness for custody."[206] The court also cited precedents that absolved sexually active unmarried men from moral censure and found no rational basis for imposing a more stringent standard on divorced women.

In *Jarrett v. Jarrett*,[207] however, the Supreme Court of Illinois was far less solicitous of the right of a divorced woman, engaged in a nonmarital sexual relationship, to retain custody of her three daughters. Despite the absence of any evidence whatsoever that the custodial mother's open cohabitation with a male had any adverse effect on the children, who were healthy and well cared for, the court affirmed the trial court's transfer of custody to the father. The court reasoned that the relevant standard of conduct was expressed in the provisions of the criminal code that sanctioned open and notorious cohabitation or sexual intercourse with a nonspouse as fornication. Accordingly, the court concluded:

> [The mother's] disregard for existing standards of conduct instructs her children, by example, that they, too, may ignore them . . . , and could well encourage the children to engage in similar activity in the future. That factor, of course, supports the trial court's conclusion that their daily presence in that environment was injurious to the moral well-being and development of the children.[208]

In sharp contrast to *Jarrett* is the opinion of the Supreme Court of Vermont in *Hansen v. Hansen*,[209] a case in which the trial court, at divorce, awarded physical custody of the parties' son and daughter, aged eight and five years, to the father. The trial court based its decision in part on the mother's continuing what had begun as an extramarital affair that had caused the breakup of the marriage. The reviewing court reversed the award and remanded for a new hearing. The court found an abuse of discretion by the trial court in basing its award on factors unrelated to the best interests of the children, in that the decision was not supported by any findings that the mother's misconduct affected them. Similarly, in *Hanhart v. Hanhart*,[210] the Supreme Court of South Dakota held that the trial court did not abuse its discretion in awarding custody to the child's adulterous mother, noting that the mother's affair had not had a deleterious impact on the children, and that fault is not relevant to custody determinations "except to the extent it is relevant to prove unfitness of the parent."[211]

The Supreme Court of Virginia in *Roe v. Roe*[212] posed the question of "whether a child's best interests are promoted by an award of custody to a parent who carries

---

[206] *Id.* at 510.

[207] 400 N.E.2d 421 (Ill. 1979).

[208] *Id.* at 424 (citations omitted).

[209] 562 A.2d 1051 (Vt. 1989).

[210] 501 N.W. 2d 776 (S.D. 1993).

[211] *Id.* at 777.

[212] 324 S.E.2d 691 (Va. 1985).

on an active homosexual relationship in the same residence as the child."[213] The court concluded not only that a custody award to such a parent was not in the child's best interests, but also that such an award constituted an abuse of judicial discretion.

When the parents in *Roe* were divorced, they agreed on custody to the mother. Some two years later, the father took over the child's care because of the mother's illness. Several years later the mother sought custody of the nine year old child, having learned that the father was living with a homosexual lover. The trial court granted joint legal custody to the parents, and provided that the child should live with the mother during summer vacation and with the father during the school year. The trial court found that the child was happy and well adjusted, and there was no evidence that the father's conduct had affected her adversely. Nevertheless, the order contained a condition that the father not share his bed or bedroom with any male friend or lover while the child was in residence.

The Virginia Supreme Court reversed and granted sole custody to the mother, relying on an earlier case that removed custody from an otherwise fit custodial mother who maintained an open, adulterous relationship with a male lover. Noting that sexual relations between homosexuals were punishable as a felony, the court concluded that "[t]he father's continuous exposure of the child to his immoral and illicit relationship renders him an unfit and improper custodian as a matter of law."[214] In addition to the change in custody, the court ordered that all visitation "in the father's home or in the presence of his homosexual lover" should cease.[215]

A decade later, in *Bottoms v. Bottoms*,[216] the court of Appeals of Virginia overturned a trial court's award to his grandmother on the ground that the child's parent was unfit because she was living in an open lesbian relationship with another woman and engaged in the illegal act of sodomy. The court held that the presumption favoring a natural parent over a third party, in this case the grandmother, was not rebutted merely because of the mother's lesbian relationship. On appeal, the Supreme Court of Virginia construed the facts differently and, without articulating a clear legal standard, reversed the judgment of the court of appeals.[217]

Although the approach of the Virginia Supreme Court in *Roe* was antagonistic to judicial recognition of the legitimacy of homosexual relationships, courts in other states have taken a more expansive position toward a custodial parent's intimate relationship with a person of the same sex. In *S.N.E. v. R.L.B.*,[218] for example, a father sought a change in custody from the mother, who was living with a female companion, on the grounds that she was a lesbian, was emotionally unstable, and

---

[213] *Id.* at 691.

[214] *Id.* at 694.

[215] *Id.*

[216] 444 S.E. 2d 276 (Va. Ct. App. 1994), *reversed* 457 S.E. 2d 102 (Va. Ct. App. 1995).

[217] *See Bottoms v. Bottoms*, 457 S.E. 2d 102 (Va. 1995). *See also* Peter N. Swisher & Nancy D. Cook, Bottoms v. Bottoms: *In Whose Best Interest? Analysis of a Lesbian Mother Child Custody Dispute*, 34 U. Louisville J. Fam. L. 843 (Fall 1995-96).

[218] 699 P.2d 875 (Alaska 1985).

held radical political views. The Supreme Court of Alaska emphasized that for parental conduct to be relevant to a custody award, an adverse effect on the child must result from the parental conduct. Citing *Palmore v. Sidoti*,[219] the court stated, "[s]imply put, it is impermissible to rely on any real or imagined social stigma attaching to Mother's status as a lesbian."[220]

Similarly, in *Conkel v. Conkel*,[221] the Court of Appeals of Ohio affirmed a trial court's order granting overnight visitation for a father who was living with a male friend with whom he maintained a sexual relationship. The child's mother argued that the children's sexual development could be influenced by the father's sexual orientation, that they might contract AIDS, and that they would "suffer the slings and arrows of a disapproving society."[222] Citing *Palmore*, the court stated, "[t]his court cannot take into consideration the unpopularity of homosexuals in society when its duty is to facilitate and guard a fundamental parent-child relationship."[223]

[D]   Relative Considerations Between Fit Parents

[1]   The Gender of the Parents

As discussed, the tender years presumption, favoring maternal custody of young children, no longer prevails.[224] In some states, statutes that govern child custody contain an explicit mandate that courts maintain an attitude of gender neutrality. The Arkansas statute, for example, provides that in divorce actions custody of the children "shall be made without regard to the sex of the parent but solely in accord with the welfare and best interests of the children."[225] Accordingly, in *Fox v. Fox*,[226] the Arkansas Court of Appeals reversed an award of custody to the mother in light of the trial court's view that young girls should be with their mothers. The court noted the statutory abolition of gender based presumptions and emphasized that custody questions must be determined on an individual basis.[227]

The Indiana statute includes "the age and sex of the child" among the factors that a trial judge must consider when determining custody.[228] In *Warner v. Warner*,[229] the Court of Appeals of Indiana affirmed the trial court's award of

---

[219] 466 U.S. 429 (1984) (concluding that the effects of racial prejudice did not justify removing a child from Caucasian custodial mother who had married an African American man). *See infra* § 11.03[D][3].

[220] *S.N.E.*, 699 P.2d at 875.

[221] 509 N.E.2d 983 (Ohio Ct. App. 1987).

[222] *Id.* at 984.

[223] *Id.* at 987.

[224] *See supra* § 11.03[B][1].

[225] Ark. Code Ann. § 9-13-101 (1987). *See also* N.Y. Dom. Rel. Law § 240(1) (1988) (enacting a "best interests of the child" standard and providing that "[i]n all cases there shall be no prima facie right to the custody of the child in either parent").

[226] 788 S.W.2d 743 (Ark. Ct. App. 1990).

[227] *See also Pusey v. Pusey*, 728 P.2d 117 (Utah 1986) (disavowing "those cases that continue to approve, even indirectly, an arbitrary maternal preference").

[228] Ind. Code Ann. § 31-17-2-8(1) (2001).

[229] 534 N.E.2d 752 (Ind. Ct. App. 1989).

custody to the father of a four year old boy. The court took into account a psychologist's testimony that the father was able to provide the young child with the important "nurturing usually attributable to a mother."[230] The psychologist also stressed the importance of being able to identify with a parent of the same sex as a child gets older.[231] Accordingly, the court found no abuse of discretion in granting custody to the father.

[2]   The Child's Preference in Custody Determinations

[a]   Statutory Treatment

Taking a variety of approaches, a number of states have determined by statute the question of what role the child's preference plays in a custody determination. The Minnesota statute is illustrative, allowing the court to interview the child in chambers "to ascertain the child's reasonable preference as to custodian, if the court deems the child to be of sufficient age to express a preference."[232] The court is required to permit counsel to be present and to ask reasonable questions at the interview, either directly or through the court.[233]

The Illinois statute similarly allows the court to interview the child in chambers, with counsel present unless the parties agree otherwise, and requires the presence of a court reporter whose record of the interview is made a part of the record in the case.[234] The Georgia statute gives a child who is 14 or older the right to select the custodial parent, and the child's selection controls unless the parent selected is determined to be unfit for custody.[235]

[b]   Judicial Approaches

It is clear from the statutes that the trial court must first determine whether a child is mature enough to state a preference for one or the other parent. Also, the court must decide how much weight should be given to the child's preference, and how to determine it reliably. The Supreme Court of Rhode Island addressed these questions in *Goldstein v. Goldstein.*[236]

The child in *Goldstein* was a 9 1/2-year-old girl. The trial judge questioned the child in open court, where the child voiced difficulty in saying with which parent she wanted to live. Subsequently, in chambers, the child conceded that she preferred her father, but could not say so in the presence of her parents. The reviewing court held that there was no abuse of discretion in awarding custody to the father, and rejected the mother's contention that the trial court had allowed the child's preference to control its decision.

---

[230]   *Id.* at 754.

[231]   *Id.*

[232]   Minn. Stat. Ann. § 518.166 (1990).

[233]   *Id.*

[234]   *See* 750 Ill. Comp. Stat. 5/604(a) (2012).

[235]   *See* Ga. Code Ann. § 19-9-3(a)(5) (1991).

[236]   341 A.2d 51 (R.I. 1975).

The court noted that the child was very intelligent for her age. Further, legislative policy setting 14 as the minimum age at which a child may nominate a preferred guardian was merely one factor among other relevant considerations weighed by the trial court. The court concluded that the factors favoring each parent were "so nearly in a state of equipoise" that the trial court did not abuse his discretion in giving substantial weight to the child's preference.[237]

The Supreme Court of Wyoming, in *Yates v. Yates*[238] neatly summarized the factors that the trial court should consider with respect to the child's preference in custody matters. Noting that as the child grows older, his preference should receive more weight, the court stated:

> In determining the weight to be given a child's preference several factors should be considered: the age of the child; the reason for the preference; the relative fitness of the preferred and non-preferred parent; the hostility, if any of the child to the non-preferred parent; the preference of other siblings; and whether the child's preference has been tainted or influenced by one parent against the other.[239]

An interview is not necessarily the only way or the best way for a court to determine a child's wishes with respect to custody. In *In re Marriage of Susen*,[240] the mother argued on appeal that the trial court's decision not to interview a child of kindergarten age was a violation of the statutory mandate that the court consider the child's wishes.[241] The court noted that while the statute requires consideration of the wishes of the child, it does not require that the court interview the child. In light of the testimony of all of the witnesses that the child loved and had a good relationship with both parents, the trial court's award of shared legal and physical custody was not an abuse of discretion.

In *Miller v. Miller*,[242] the Supreme Court addressed the custodial preferences of the three children of the parties to a divorce proceeding in a most unusual way. Having received a telephone call from one of the children, an attorney agreed to undertake pro bono representation of the child and his siblings. Construing statutory civil procedure requirements and having examined whether the children's claims were entitled to constitutional recognition, the court rejected the proposition that the children's preference should have primacy in a custody determination. To the contrary, the court observed,

> The best interest standard set forth in [the applicable statute] appropriately makes the preference of the child only one of many factors that the court must consider. The exclusion of children as parties in the divorce of their parents, and the related possibility that there will be no forceful advocacy for the custodial preference of the children, does not increase the

---

[237] *Id.* at 53.

[238] 702 P. 2d 1252 (Wyo. 1985).

[239] *Id.* at 1255.

[240] 788 P.2d 332 (Mont. 1990).

[241] *See* Mont. Code Ann. § 40-4-212(1)(b) (1991).

[242] 677 A.2d 64 (Me. 1996).

risk of erroneous custody determinations that disserve the best interests of children. The guardian ad litem is already an advocate for the best interest of the children in all of its complex dimensions. The narrow focus of an attorney for the children, who would be obligated to carry out their preferences regardless of the wisdom of such a course, might well increase the likelihood of a custody determination that is not in the best interest of the children.[243]

[3] Race

Ordinarily, courts have broad discretion in making child custody awards and may consider a variety of factors, many of which are frequently delineated in statutes.[244] Subsequent to the decision of the United States Supreme Court in *Palmore v. Sidoti*,[245] however, it is clear that race may not be the determinative factor in awarding custody of children.

In *Palmore*, when the parties, both Caucasians, were divorced, a Florida court awarded custody of their three year old daughter to the mother. Subsequently, the court granted the father's petition to modify custody based on changed circumstances, in that the mother had first cohabited with and then married a Black man. The court found both parents fit.

Nevertheless, the court concluded that because the child would be vulnerable to peer pressure and social stigmatization as part of an interracial household, her best interests would be served by living with her father.

The Supreme Court rejected the Florida court's reasoning as impermissibly resting on race alone and, therefore, violative of the Equal Protection Clause. The Court concluded:

> The question . . . is whether the reality of private biases and the possible injury they might inflict are permissible considerations for removal of an infant child from the custody of its natural mother. We have little difficulty concluding that they are not. The Constitution cannot control such prejudices but neither can it tolerate them. Private biases may be outside the reach of the law, but the law cannot, directly or indirectly, give them effect.[246]

Thus, the Court concluded that the effects of racial prejudice would not justify a racial classification removing a child from a natural mother found to be an appropriate custodian.[247]

Subsequent to the decision of the Court in *Palmore*, state courts have become quite skittish about taking race into consideration at all in custody contests between

---

[243] *Id.* at 69 (citations omitted).

[244] *See supra* § 11.03[A].

[245] 466 U.S. 429 (1984).

[246] *Id.* at 433.

[247] See Twila L. Perry, *Race and Child Placement: The Best Interests Test and the Cost of Discretion*, 29 J. Fam. L. 51 (1990-91), for an excellent discussion of *Palmore* and related questions.

fit parents. An exception is the judgment of the Supreme Court of South Dakota in *Jones v. Jones*.[248] In Jones, the mother of the child argued that the trial court had awarded the children to the husband because he, having suffered prejudice as a Native American, could better help the children, who were biracial with Native American features, to deal with the prejudice that they would encounter. The appellate court affirmed the custody award to the father, and concluded:

> To say, as [the mother] argues, that a court should never consider whether a parent is willing and able to expose to and educate children on their heritage, is to say that society is not interested in whether children ever learn who they are. *Palmore* does not require this, nor do the constitutions of the United States or the State of South Dakota.[249]

Accordingly, the court held "that it is proper for a trial court, when determining the best interests of a child in the context of a custody dispute between parents, to consider the matter of race as it relates to a child's ethnic heritage and which parent is more prepared to expose the child to it."[250] Contrary to the result in *Jones* and like cases, the ALI *Principles*, if adopted, would bar judicial consideration in custody proceedings of the race of a child, parent, or any household member.[251]

[4] Religion

As is the case with race, consideration of religion in child custody determinations implicates constitutional issues. In *Pater v. Pater*,[252] the Supreme Court of Ohio described the impact of the Constitution on child custody determinations, observing that "a domestic relations court may consider the religious practices of the parents in order to protect the best interests of a child . . . . However, the United States Constitution flatly prohibits a trial court from ever evaluating the merits of religious doctrine or defining the contents of that doctrine."[253] Cases addressing the relevance of religion in child custody matters . . . generally adhere to this principle.

Illustrative is *Quiner v. Quiner*,[254] a leading case decided in California in 1967 that involved a custody dispute between the fit parents of a two-year-old boy. The parents were divorced following the wife's decision to remain affiliated with their religious group, which had become isolated to the greatest extent possible from the outside world and its influences.

At the time *Quiner* was decided, the statutory tender years presumption[255] in California would have placed the child with his mother, and the custodial parent was entitled to determine the child's religion. Having found that either parent would provide for the child's physical needs, the court examined the factor of mental

---

[248] 542 N.W. 2d 119 (S.D. 1996).

[249] *Id.* at 123.

[250] *Id.* at 123-24.

[251] ALI, *Principles of the Law of Family Dissolution* § 212(1)(a) (2002).

[252] 588 N.E.2d 794 (Ohio 1992).

[253] *Id.* at 797.

[254] 59 Cal. Rptr. 503 (Cal. App. Dep't Super. Ct. 1967).

[255] *See supra* § 11.03[B][1].

welfare, defined to include "the opportunities for intellectual, character and personality growth, and the development of those social graces and amenities without which one cannot live comfortably or successfully in a complex, integrated society."[256]

After an exhaustive survey of ways in which the religious practices of the mother's group could adversely affect a young child's development by isolating him from the rest of society, the court concluded that custody in the mother was "more than likely to retard his mental growth and personality development, would be inimical to his welfare, and would severely handicap him in later years in his struggle to achieve his goals of social and economic attachment."[257] The court cited ample precedents to support the constitutionality of its decision, upholding the state's interest in protecting children's welfare and best interests over the parents' rights to control religious practices.

In *In re Marriage of Hadeen*,[258] the Court of Appeals of Washington considered whether religious acts could be a determinative factor in a custody award and if so, the required test for protection of both the children's interests and the parents' religious freedom. The parents in *Hadeen* belonged to a fundamentalist Christian sect that required of its members total loyalty and subservience; condoned strict discipline of children, including beating, fasting and isolation; and fostered hostility toward non-members. When the spouses separated, the father left the church. The trial court awarded him custody of the four youngest of five children, observing that custody in the mother would cut him off from the contact his children needed.

On appeal, the mother of the children argued successfully that the trial court's decision violated her right freely to exercise her religion under the First Amendment because there was no showing that her religion adversely affected the children's welfare. The appellate court reversed and remanded, stating that "religious decisions and acts may be considered in a custody decision only to the extent that those decisions or acts will jeopardize the temporal mental health or physical safety of the child."[259] This standard is met, the court held, by showing "a reasonable and substantial likelihood of immediate or future impairment" of the child's mental or physical well-being.[260]

The parents in *In re Marriage of Gershowitz*[261] agreed to a joint custody arrangement for their son. The trial court decided that when the boy reached school age he should reside primarily with one parent to avoid interruption of his education by multiple transfers of custody. The child's father objected to the trial court's selection of the mother as primary physical custodian, arguing that the child's continued upbringing in the Jewish faith and way of life would be undermined. The Supreme Court of Montana affirmed, holding that the trial court's decision correctly reflected the child's best interests and was constitutionally sound. Reflecting the

---

[256] *Quiner*, 59 Cal. Rptr. at 527.

[257] *Id.* at 532.

[258] 619 P.2d 374 (Wash. Ct. App. 1980).

[259] *Id.* at 382.

[260] *Id.*

[261] 779 P.2d 883 (Mont. 1989).

conventional wisdom, the court observed:

> The First Amendment guarantees religious liberty, and the right of parents to direct the religious upbringing of their children . . . . [C]ourts will not debate the merits of different religions or show preference to any religious faith. However, courts will examine religious practices which interfere with the child's general welfare . . . . A question of religious education must be strictly limited to the context of the best interests of the minor child.[262]

The court noted that under the applicable Montana statute the custodial parent determines the child's religious training, and that in the case before it, "an award of custody for the purpose of religious education should not dominate other elements which comprise the best interests" of the child.[263]

In *In re Marriage of Wang*,[264] the Supreme Court of Montana considered another custody challenge related to one parent's religious beliefs. The court rejected the mother's assertion that the trial court was required to make specific findings with respect to the husband's church affiliation and how his religious involvement affected the child's best interest. Over a strong dissent, the court held that a review of the entire record demonstrated that both parents were suitable and that the trial court's findings were supported by credible evidence.

In *Leppert v. Leppert*,[265] the Supreme Court of South Dakota reversed the trial court's award of custody of five children to their mother, despite a law guardian's report stating that because of her beliefs the mother's parenting was physically and emotionally extremely dangerous to the children. The court in *Leppert* clearly and cogently set out the reigning principle with respect to the impact of a parent's religion on the best interests of the child. The court observed:

> Although we agree with the district court that [the mother] must not be discounted from consideration as a custodial parent simply because of her religious *beliefs*, this does not mean her religiously motivated *actions*, which are emotionally and physically harmful to the children, should be ignored when determining the children's best interests. Such a holding would immunize from consideration all religiously motivated acts, no matter what their impact on the children.[266]

State courts continue to struggle to develop and apply an appropriate standard for consideration of religion in child custody determinations in a variety of factual circumstances. In *Kendall v. Kendall*,[267] for example, at the time of marriage, the plaintiff husband was Jewish and the wife was Catholic, and the parties agreed to

---

[262] *Id.* at 885.

[263] *Id. See also Pater v. Pater*, 588 N.E.2d 794, 801 (Ohio 1992) (adopting "the majority rule that a court may not restrict a non-custodial parent's right to expose his or her child to religious beliefs, unless the conflict between the parents' religious beliefs is affecting the child's general welfare").

[264] 896 P.2d 450 (Mont. 1995).

[265] 519 N.W. 2d 287 (N.D. 1994).

[266] *Id.* at 290.

[267] 687 N.E.2d 1228 (1997). *See generally*, Schneider, *Religion and Child Custody*, 25 U. Mich. J. L. Ref. 879 (1992).

raise their children in accordance with the Jewish faith. Subsequently, after the birth of three children, the father joined a fundamentalist Christian church that taught that non-believers would be damned in hell, and a few years later the mother adopted Orthodox Judaism. Having undertaken a comprehensive review of relevant decisions in other states, the Supreme Judicial Court of Massachusetts determined that court intervention was proper only where there was a showing of harm to the child so substantial as to warrant limitations on a parent's religious beliefs.

[5] Physical Condition of the Custodial Parent

The Uniform Marriage and Divorce Act includes among the factors a court shall consider in determining custody in accordance with the best interest of the child "the mental and physical health of all individuals involved."[268] Statutes in some states also include this factor.[269] Decisions involving the mental or emotional fitness of prospective custodians, primarily in intermediate appellate courts, are largely dependent on the unique facts in the individual cases.[270]

The decision of the Supreme Court of California in *In re Marriage of Carney*[271] is a paradigmatic case addressing the weight to be given to the physical disability of a parent seeking custody. The father in *Carney*, pursuant to a written agreement with the mother, had cared for their two boys for almost five years prior to the commencement of a marriage dissolution action. During this entire time the mother resided some 3,000 miles away in New York and neither visited the children nor contributed to their support. Shortly before the dissolution action began, the father was paralyzed as the result of injuries sustained in an automobile accident.

The trial judge awarded custody to the mother, noting that sports and other physical activities are an important aspect of a father-son relationship. The trial judge concluded that because the father could do nothing more for the children than talk to them and teach them, "[i]t wouldn't be a normal relationship between father and boys."[272] Reversing the award to the mother, the Supreme Court of California stated that while the health or physical condition of parents is relevant in determining the child's best interests, it is ordinarily a factor of minor importance. The court then set forth the following standard for evaluating the suitability for child custody of a physically disabled parent:

> [I]f a person has a physical handicap it is impermissible for the court simply to rely on that condition as prima facie evidence of the person's unfitness as a parent or of probable detriment to the child; rather, in all cases the court must view the handicapped person as an individual and the family as a whole. To achieve this, the court should inquire into the person's actual and potential physical capabilities, learn how he or she has adapted to the

---

[268] U.M.D.A. § 402(5), 9A U.L.A. 561 (1988).

[269] *See, e.g.*, Minn. Stat. Ann. § 518.17(9) (1990).

[270] *See, e.g., In re Marriage of Lewin*, 231 Cal. Rptr 433, 437 (Cal. Ct. App. 1986) (finding the mother's unfounded allegations that the father used drugs and sexually abused his daughter to be "outrageous conduct" supporting an award of custody to the father).

[271] 598 P.2d 36 (Cal. 1979).

[272] *Id.* at 41.

disability and manages its problems, consider how the other members of the household have adjusted thereto, and take into account the special contributions the person may make to the family despite — or even because of — the handicap. Weighing these and all other relevant factors together, the court should then carefully determine whether the parent's condition will in fact have a substantial and lasting adverse effect on the best interests of the child.[273]

Having rejected the trial court's "conventional sex-stereotypical thinking,"[274] the court pointed out that public policy, reflected in a number of legislative enactments, supports the total integration of disabled people into society. This includes participation in the "responsibilities and satisfactions of family life, [the] cornerstone of our social system."[275]

The decision of the Supreme Court of Idaho in *Moye v. Moye*[276] reflects an approach that is entirely consistent with that of the California court in *Carney.* Among the factors that an Idaho court must consider when making a custody determination is "[t]he mental and physical health and integrity of all individuals involved."[277] In *Moye,* the mother's epilepsy, somewhat controlled by medication, manifested itself in seizures, post-seizure lack of energy, migraine headaches and the need for nine to ten hours sleep each night. The reviewing court found that this evidence did not sufficiently support the trial court's conclusion that the best interests of two pre-school children would be served by awarding custody to the father. The court observed that an abuse of discretion may occur not only when there is insufficient evidence to support the trial court's conclusion, but also when the court places undue emphasis on a single factor, such as the physical condition of a parent. In either case, the court fails to support its conclusion that a particular custody award serves the interests and welfare of a child. Subsequent to the decision in *Moye,* the Idaho legislature amended the applicable statute so as to require the trial court to consider the "charater and circumstances of all individuals involved."[278]

With increasing frequency, courts face issues relating to custodial fitness of persons infected with human immunodeficiency virus (HIV), which causes acquired immune deficiency syndrome (AIDS).[279] The decision of the Court of Appeals of Indiana in *Stewart v. Stewart*[280] is illustrative. The father in *Stewart* sought a change of custody from the mother, alleging that she was not properly caring for their daughter.[281] After hearing testimony that the father tested positive for the

---

[273] *Id.* at 42.

[274] *Id.*

[275] *Id.*

[276] 627 P.2d 799 (Idaho 1981).

[277] Idaho Code § 32-717 (1983).

[278] *See* Idaho Code § 32-717(e) (2003).

[279] *See generally* Nancy B. Mahon, Note, *Public Hysteria, Private Conflict: Child Custody and Visitation Disputes Involving an HIV Infected Parent,* 63 N.Y.U. L. Rev. 1092 (1988).

[280] 521 N.E.2d 956 (Ind. Ct. App. 1988).

[281] See *infra* § 11.06 for a discussion of modification of child custody awards.

HIV virus, the trial court terminated his visitation rights, ruling that he presented a physical danger to the child.

The Indiana Court of Appeals carefully reviewed medical evidence that no cases of transmission of the AIDS virus through "household contact" had been reported, even when the household member had developed AIDS.[282] Accordingly, the court held that termination of the father's visitation was an "extreme and unwarranted action."[283]

New York courts addressing this question have reached similar results. In *Doe v. Roe*,[284] the maternal grandparents sought custody of two minor children from their custodial father and moved for an order to compel him to submit to a test for AIDS. Citing the leading case of *Carney v. Carney*,[285] the court noted that the proper inquiry is whether a debilitating condition has a detrimental effect on the child. Further, the court observed, the potentially shortened life span of a person with AIDS would not justify removal of children from a long term caretaker with whom they have strong bonds of love and affection.[286]

§ 11.04   JOINT CUSTODY

[A]   Introduction and Overview

Traditional awards of sole custody, even with liberal visitation in the non-custodial parent, may result in, or at least have the appearance of elevating the status of one parent over the other. Recently, courts and legislatures have looked to joint custody as an alternative that, at least in theory, permits parents to share responsibility and decision making on an equal basis. A reading of the cases reveals that there are those who question whether shared parenting arrangements between divorced couples actually fulfill the ideas embodied in the concept of joint custody.

As is the case with sole custody, the courts weigh various factors to determine whether joint custody is the preferable arrangement. The overall objective, however, is constant. It is the best interests and welfare of the child that forms the framework within which the factors are considered. The question is not whether a particular number of factors is present. Rather, each case turns on its individual facts and circumstances.

---

[282] 521 N.E.2d at 963-64.

[283] *Id.*

[284] 526 N.Y.S.2d 718 (N.Y. Sup. Ct. 1988).

[285] 598 P.2d 36 (Cal. 1979).

[286] *See also Anne D. v. Raymond D.*, 528 N.Y.S.2d 775 (N.Y. Sup. Ct. 1988) (holding that husband's allegations that wife engaged in a series of extra-marital affairs were not sufficient basis to require her to undergo HIV blood test for AIDS in connection with custody determination); *Steven L. v. Dawn J.*, 561 N.Y.S.2d 322 (N.Y. Fam. Ct. 1990) (holding that positive HIV test did not warrant change of custody from mother whose physical condition did not impair her caretaking ability of affect the child's physical or psychological well being).

As the court in a leading case has accurately observed, "[t]he inability of courts and commentators to agree on what is meant by the term 'joint custody' makes difficult the task of distilling principles and guidelines from a rapidly growing body of literature and case law."[287] Although a precise definition has proved elusive, two concepts are embodied within the definition — legal custody and physical custody. In *Beck v. Beck*,[288] the Supreme Court of New Jersey has provided a useful articulation of these concepts:

> Under a joint custody arrangement legal custody — the legal authority and responsibility for making "major" decisions regarding the child's welfare — is shared at all times by both parents. Physical custody, the logistical arrangement whereby the parents share the companionship of the child and are responsible for "minor" day-to-day decisions, may be alternated in accordance with the needs of the parties and the children.[289]

Although the language of the decisions may vary, the conceptual difference between physical custody and legal custody is critical.

[B]   Statutory Joint Custody Provisions

State legislatures have taken a variety of approaches to joint custody. The scope and language of statutes governing the matter vary greatly from state to state. The examples below are illustrative of typical approaches, but are by no means comprehensive or exhaustive.

Adopting a common approach, the Florida statute sets out a presumption in favor of joint custody, stating that "[t]he court shall order that the parental responsibility for a minor child be shared by both parents unless the court finds that shared parental responsibility would be detrimental to the child."[290] Similarly, the Louisiana statute contains a rebuttable presumption that joint custody is in the best interests of the child.[291]

In sharp contrast to the approach in Florida and Louisiana, Massachusetts reflects an entirely neutral approach with respect to the form of custody awards. The statute permits sole or shared awards of legal or physical custody, provides that absent misconduct the parents' rights are equal, and declares that "[t]here shall be no presumption either in favor of or against shared legal or physical custody at the time of the trial on the merits."[292]

The Iowa statute sets out a preference for a custody award that will maximize the child's opportunity for emotional and physical contact with both separated or divorced parents. To that end, the statute directs the courts to "consider the denial

---

[287]   *Taylor v. Taylor*, 508 A.2d 964, 966 (Md. 1986).

[288]   432 A.2d 63 (N.J. 1981).

[289]   *Id.* at 66. *See also McCarty v. McCarty*, 807 A.2d 1211 (Md. Spec. App. 2002) (defining joint physical custody and legal custody and emphasizing the difference between the two meanings); Elizabeth E. Scott & Andrew P. Derdeyn, *Rethinking Joint Custody*, 45 Ohio St. L.J. 455 (1984).

[290]   Fla. Stat. Ann. § 61.13.2 (1985 & Supp. 1993).

[291]   La. Civ. Code Ann. art. 131 (Supp. 1993).

[292]   Mass. Gen. Laws ch. 208 § 31 (Cum. Supp. 1990).

by one parent of the child's opportunity for maximum contact with the other parent, without just cause, a significant factor in determining the proper custody arrangement."[293] Although such "friendly parent" provisions are intended to encourage cooperation between the parents, it is obvious that they may also discourage a parent from opposing a joint custody arrangement out of fear of losing custody.

There is some evidence, admittedly scant, that the legislative tide in favor of joint custody may be turning. The legislatures of both California and Utah have repealed legislative joint custody presumptions that had been in effect in those states.[294] And in May 2012, the Governor of Minnesota vetoed a bill that would have created a joint custody presumption in his state.[295]

[C] Judicial Treatment of Joint Custody

It is not possible to identify a universal standard that courts employ in deciding when joint custody is appropriate. As discussed, the child's best interests are paramount. In seeking to achieve this objective in joint custody, the courts generally consider the ability of the parents to communicate with each other and reach shared decisions affecting the child's welfare.

In *Beck v. Beck*,[296] the Supreme Court of New Jersey declined to establish a presumption in favor of joint custody, recognizing that such an arrangement would be appropriate infrequently. The initial inquiry is "whether the children have established such relationships with both parents that they would benefit from joint custody."[297] At a minimum, the court suggested, both parents must be fit, which means psychologically and physically able to fulfill the parental role. Further, each must be willing to accept custody, although the parents' opposition to joint custody does not preclude the court from ordering that arrangement. Finally, the trial court should examine such practical considerations as the parties' financial status, their geographical proximity, and the age and number of children,[298] and must accord due weight to the preference of children of "sufficient age and capacity."[299]

New York's highest court reviewed a joint custody determination in *Braiman v. Braiman*,[300] holding that joint custody is not appropriate when the parents are "embattled and embittered."[301] The court concluded:

> There are no painless solutions. In the rare case, joint custody may approximate the former family relationships more closely than other custodial arrangements. It may not, however, be indiscriminately substi-

---

[293] Iowa Code Ann. § 598.41 (1992).

[294] *See* Utah Code Ann. § 30-3-10.2 (2001).

[295] *See* http:/governor.state.mn.us.

[296] 432 A.2d 63 (N.J. 1981).

[297] *Id.* at 71.

[298] *Id.* at 72.

[299] *Id.* at 73.

[300] 378 N.E.2d 1019 (N.Y. 1978).

[301] *Id.* at 1021.

tuted for an award of sole custody to one parent. Divorce dissolves the family as well as the marriage, a reality that may not be ignored.[302]

The view of Maryland's highest court, as set out in *Taylor v. Taylor*,[303] is not inconsistent with that of the New York court in *Braiman*. In the Maryland court's view, the parents' capacity to communicate and reach shared decisions affecting the child's welfare is clearly the most important factor in the determination of whether an award of joint legal custody is appropriate, and is relevant as well to a consideration of shared physical custody. Rarely, if ever, would joint legal custody be awarded in the absence of a record of mature conduct on the part of the parents evidencing an ability to effectively communicate with each other concerning the best interest of the child, and then only when it is possible to make a finding of a strong potential for such conduct in the future.[304]

Noting that no enumeration of appropriate factors in a joint custody is all-inclusive, the court considered as relevant factors, among others, fitness of the parents, the relationship between the child and each parent, the preference of a child of suitable age and discretion, the potential disruption of the child's school and social life, the geographical proximity of the parents' homes, the demands of parental employment, the number and ages of the children and the parents' financial status.[305]

In *Squires v. Squires*,[306] the Supreme Court of Kentucky considered "whether parties who are found to be good parents will endeavor to place the interest of their child uppermost should be denied joint custody due to their hostility and refusal to cooperate with one another."[307] The court in *Squires* noted that joint custody and sole custody do not require a significantly different analysis; in either case the court must look at all the relevant factors in order to determine a result that comports with the best interest of the child. Thus, there is no requirement of agreement between the parties and willingness to cooperate at the time when the court determines custody. The court pointed out that such a requirement would permit the parent opposed to joint custody "to dictate the result by his or her own belligerence and would invite contemptuous conduct."

Accordingly, the court held that the trial court, after considering the application of statutory standards for a custody award must weigh the likelihood of future parental cooperation. The court continued:

> Thereafter, we believe a trial court should look beyond the present and assess the likelihood of future cooperation between the parents. It would be shortsighted to conclude that because parties are antagonistic at the time of their divorce, such antagonism will continue indefinitely. Emotional maturity would appear to be a dependable guide in predicting future

---

[302] *Id.* at 1022. *See also Dodd v. Dodd*, 403 N.Y.S.2d 401 (N.Y. Sup. Ct. 1978).

[303] 508 A.2d 964 (Md. 1986).

[304] *Id.* at 971.

[305] *Id.* at 973-74. *See also In re Marriage of Weidner*, 338 N.W.2d 351, 355-58 (Iowa 1983).

[306] 854 S.W. 2d 765 (Ky. 1993).

[307] *Id.* at 767.

behavior. By cooperation we mean willingness to rationally participate in decisions affecting the upbringing of the child. It should not be overlooked that to achieve such cooperation, the trial court may assist the parties by means of its contempt power and its power to modify custody in the event of a bad faith refusal of cooperation.[308]

The court in *Squires* took pains to point out that it was not endorsing a preference for joint custody, but that under current law "joint custody must be awarded the same dignity as sole custody and trial courts must determine which form would serve the best interest of the child."[309]

§ 11.05 VISITATION

[A] Right of Noncustodial Parent to Visitation

In essence, under the traditional approach of awarding sole custody to one of the parents, visitation rights are a corollary to custody awards. Any number of issues may arise in connection with post-divorce disputes relating to visitation. Typical are questions that involve schedules, transportation costs, the impact on visitation of a custodial parent's relocation, and behavioral problems in children resulting from ongoing conflict between the parents.[310]

As in the case of an initial custody determination, trial courts have considerable discretion in determining visitation for noncustodial parents that is in the best interests of the child. As one court has cogently put it, "[a] noncustodial parent's right of visitation is a natural right and should be denied only under extraordinary circumstances, which would include, among other things, a showing that the visitation would harm the child."[311]

One example of parental conduct that may result in the denial of visitation is drug or alcohol addiction.[312] On occasion, courts have considered the visitation rights of noncustodial parents who are incarcerated. In *Suttles v. Suttles*,[313] for example, a father who was imprisoned for shooting his father-in-law and abducting his son requested reasonable visitation rights. The court held that although incarceration alone does not preclude visitation, it was inappropriate in this case in light of the father's violent behavior.[314]

---

[308] *Id.* at 769.

[309] *Id.* at 768-69.

[310] *See Sterbling v. Sterbling*, 519 N.E.2d 673 (Ohio Ct. App. 1987).

[311] *Id.* at 676.

[312] *See, e.g., Soltis v. Soltis*, 470 So. 2d 1250 (Ala. Civ. App. 1985) (denying visitation to mother who was addicted to ethyl alcohol and engaged in violent behavior in child's presence). *But see Roberts v. Roberts*, 371 A.2d 689, 694 (Md. Ct. Spec. App. 1977) (reversing a decree that terminated a mother's visitation rights because of alcohol abuse, stating that even an "errant parent" has a right of reasonable access to a child in the absence of injury to the child's welfare).

[313] 748 S.W.2d 427 (Tenn. 1988).

[314] *See also In re Marriage of Brewer*, 760 P.2d 1225 (Kan. Ct. App. 1988) (rejecting claim that denial of visitation abridged father's constitutional rights and holding that although incarceration alone may not

[1]   Illustrative Statutes

State statutes that govern custody often contain explicit provisions relating to visitation rights of the noncustodial parent. The Colorado statute, for example, entitles the parent not granted custody of the child to reasonable visitation rights unless there is a finding by the court that visitation "would endanger the child's health or significantly impair his emotional development."[315] Curiously, the Colorado statute sets out a list of crimes which, if committed by the custodial parent, may result in divestment of visitation rights.

The statute governing custody in Illinois similarly provides that the parent not granted custody of a child is entitled to reasonable visitation rights unless a hearing reveals that visitation would seriously endanger the child physically, mentally, morally, or emotionally.[316] The statute also contains procedures for enforcing visitation where there has been "visitation abuse," meaning that one party has denied visitation rights to the other, or that a party has exercised visitation rights in a manner that is harmful to either the child or the child's custodian.[317]

[2]   Enforcement of Visitation

[a]   Statutory Remedies

The statutes of some states contain explicit remedial provisions for failure to permit visitation or other disputes concerning visitation. In Colorado, for example, upon an allegation of noncompliance with a visitation order the court may set a hearing or require the parties to seek mediation. Upon proof of noncompliance, the court may impose additional terms or conditions, require the posting of a bond to assure future compliance, require makeup visitation, find the violator in contempt and impose a fine or jail sentence, or schedule a modification hearing.[318]

The Alaska statute creates a cause of action against the custodian for money damages of $200 for each wilful and inexcusable failure to permit court ordered visitation.[319] In Michigan, the statute sets out a highly structured and detailed makeup visitation policy, administered by the office of the friend of the court, in cases of wrongful denial of visitation to a noncustodial parent.[320]

---

foreclose visitation rights, tender ages of children and lengthy estrangement from father made visitation in a prison setting contrary to their best interests). *But see McCurdy v. McCurdy*, 363 N.E.2d 1298 (Ind. Ct. App. 1977) (holding that visitation of imprisoned father with four- and seven-year-old children can mutually benefit parent and child in that children need to appreciate the reality of the situation, and visitation might have rehabilitative effect on father).

[315] Colo. Rev. Stat. § 14-10-129 (2001).

[316] 750 Ill. Comp. Stat. 5/607 (2001).

[317] *Id.* at 5/607.1.

[318] Colo. Rev. Stat. Ann. § 14-10-129.5 (1987).

[319] Alaska Stat. § 25.20.140 (1992).

[320] Mich. Comp. Laws Ann. § 552.642 (1988).

[b]   Judicial Remedies

A variety of remedies are available to the noncustodial parent whose visitation rights are thwarted by the parent who has custody of the child. In *Smith v. Smith*,[321] for example, the custodial mother appealed unsuccessfully from an order finding her in contempt and sentencing her to 5 days in a correctional facility for failing to abide by the father's visitation schedule established by the trial court. The appellate court rejected the mother's argument that all she need do to comply with the trial court's order was to encourage visitation with the father. The children, aged 5 and 8, were too young to "affirmatively and independently" refuse to have visitation with their father.[322] Under these circumstances, and absent evidence of harm to the children from visitation, the court found that the custodial parent had a duty to "follow the court order that she deliver the children to the [father] for purposes of visitation."[323]

Generally, in instances where the child's lack of cooperation results in frustration of the noncustodial parent's visitation rights, the courts will carefully scrutinize the child's unwillingness to visit in light of the possibility of influence by the custodial parent. Obviously, enforcement of visitation is likely to be difficult or nearly impossible when an older child refuses to cooperate.[324]

The custodial mother's persistent and extreme interference with her former husband's visitation rights resulted in a change of custody in *Egle v. Egle*.[325] The mother's conduct included physically evading the children's father and alienating them from him. The court observed that although, as a general rule, a change of circumstances is required before custody is changed, "[a] showing of sabotage or deliberate frustration of visitation rights provides an alternative ground for a change of custody and obviates the need to show a change of circumstances."[326] Accordingly, the court concluded that in such instances it would serve the best interests of the children to change their custody "to the parent who is more likely to honor the other parent's (and the children's) rights."[327]

In *Schutz v. Schutz*,[328] the Supreme Court of Florida addressed the assertion by the child's mother, the custodial parent, that the trial court's order that she do all

---

[321]   434 N.E.2d 749 (Ohio Ct. App. 1980).

[322]   *Id.* at 752.

[323]   *Id. See also Prater v. Wheeler*, 322 S.E.2d 892, 894 (Ga. 1984) (holding that although 14-year-old may select custodian under Georgia law, visitation is parent's natural right. To permit children to refuse visitation "would permit, if not encourage, custodial parents to vent their spite for their former mates by pressuring, directly or indirectly their children to make such an election").

[324]   *See, e.g., In re Two Minor Children*, 249 A.2d 743 (Del. 1969) (refusing to force 16-year-old to visit her mother, because enforcement would be impossible). *See generally* Steven L. Novinson, *Post-Divorce Visitation: Untying The Triangular Knot*, 1983 U. Ill. L. Rev. 121 (1983).

[325]   715 F.2d 999 (5th Cir. 1983).

[326]   *Id.* at 1016.

[327]   *Id.* at 1017. *See also Rosenberg v. Rosenberg*, 504 A.2d 350 (Pa. Super. Ct. 1986) (holding that automatic transfer of custody is not an appropriate remedy for interference with visitation, and that normal means of enforcement is through contempt proceeding).

[328]   581 So. 2d 1290 (Fla. 1991).

that was in her power to create a loving feeling toward their father violated her first amendment rights. The court, purporting to "balance the mother's right to free expression against the state's parens patriae interest in assuring the well-being of the parties' minor children"[329] stated:

> [W]e read the challenged portion of the order at issue to require nothing more of the mother than a good faith effort to take those measures necessary to restore and promote the frequent and continuing positive interaction (e.g., visitation, phone calls, letters) between the children and their father and to refrain from doing or saying anything likely to defeat that end. There is no requirement that [the mother] express opinions that she does not hold, a practice disallowed by the first amendment.[330]

Conventional civil remedies may not always be available in connection with disputes involving visitation. In *Gleiss v. Newman*,[331] for example, a noncustodial mother sought to recover damages against her former husband for the tort of intentional infliction of emotional distress arising from his interference with her rights of visitation. Having looked to the law of other jurisdictions that have declined to recognize such claims, the court held that no such cause of action exists.

As the court noted, several reasons of public policy support its decision. Allowing suits of this kind may encourage claims for "petty infractions" before courts that are already overburdened with visitation disputes.[332] Further, there are other remedies available for interference with visitation rights, including contempt proceedings, proceedings to enforce visitation rights, and proceedings to modify custody. Finally, recognition of a claim for compensatory and punitive damages is contrary to the child's best interests. It "would alter the focus from determining visitation consistent with the child's best interests to parental compensation."[333]

[B] Restrictions on Visitation

There are occasions when the courts will approve restrictions on noncustodial parents' exercise of visitation rights. Disputes appear to arise most frequently with respect to the religious training of children and the noncustodial parent's sexual conduct. In *Zummo v. Zummo*,[334] a Pennsylvania appellate court vacated a trial court order barring a noncustodial parent from taking his children during visitation periods to religious services that were inconsistent with the custodial mother's faith. Refusing to impose restricted visitation, the court found that the parents' earlier agreement and practice of bringing up the children in the Jewish faith did not control. The court rejected the argument that inconsistent religious teachings would result in substantial physical or emotional harm to the children.

---

[329] *Id.* at 1293.

[330] *Id.* at 1292.

[331] 415 N.W.2d 845 (Wis. Ct. App. 1987).

[332] *Id.* at 846.

[333] *Id.* at 846-47.

[334] 574 A.2d 1130 (Pa. Super. Ct. 1990).

Based on similar reasoning, a New Jersey trial court in *Brown v. Szakai*[335] refused to require a father to observe Jewish dietary laws during visitation with his children. The court balanced the right of the custodian to control the religious upbringing of the children against the goal of promoting a good relationship with the father through "appropriate unrestricted visitation."[336] Citing with approval authority from other jurisdictions, the court concluded that absent a showing of harm to the children it would not impose on the noncustodial parent the burden of carrying out the custodial parent's religious instructions.[337]

As is the case with initial custody determinations,[338] courts from time to time have reviewed the sexual conduct of noncustodial parents in connection with visitation. In *DeVita v. DeVita*,[339] for example, a New Jersey appellate court in a questionable decision upheld a restriction that a father's weekend visitation with his seven children, aged eight to twenty, not take place in the presence of a female friend. The court conceded that there was no showing of harm to the children, but recognized "that in the mother's view the moral welfare of the child is possibly endangered if the trial judge's restriction is not upheld."[340] The court also observed "that her views are not contrary to those of a substantial body of the community."[341]

In a case with facts similar to those in *DeVita*, the court in *Kelly v. Kelly*,[342] adopted an arguably more enlightened view, purporting to distinguish *DeVita* and holding that the court must consider the best interests of the child, and not only a custodian's "moral outrage," when determining visitation arrangements. Taking note of the testimony of psychiatric experts, the court concluded that the children's welfare would be served by a continuation of overnight visitation with their father, despite the presence of his female companion.

Similarly, in *In re Marriage of Cabalquinto*,[343] the mother refused to allow the child visitation in the father's home out of state because the father resided with a homosexual lover. The court cited the rule in several states that "homosexuality in and of itself is not a bar to custody or to reasonable rights of visitation."[344] To hold otherwise would be to base visitation on a parent's sexual orientation rather than the best interests of the child.

---

[335] 514 A.2d 81 (N.J. Super. Ct. Ch. Div. 1986).

[336] *Id.* at 83.

[337] *Id.* at 84. *But see LeDoux v. LeDoux*, 452 N.W.2d 1, 5 (Neb. 1990) (upholding an order prohibiting a Jehovah's Witness father from exposing the children during visitation to religious practices inconsistent with the custodial mother's Catholic faith. Noting that the children and the father-child relationship were being harmed by participation in the father's religion, the court stated that while the custodial parent ordinarily controls the children's religious training, it is constitutionally permissible for courts to restrict religious practices in the best interest of the children through narrowly tailored orders).

[338] *See supra* § 11.03[C].

[339] 366 A.2d 1350 (N.J. Super. Ct. App. Div. 1976).

[340] *Id.* at 1354.

[341] *Id.*

[342] 524 A.2d 1330 (N.J. Super. Ct. Ch. Div. 1986).

[343] 669 P.2d 886 (Wash. 1983).

[344] *Id.* at 888.

[C]   Visitation and Child Support

In most states, child support obligations and visitation rights are treated separately and one is not tied to the other. In a few states there is a statutory link between visitation and child support, while in others statutes explicitly bar the denial of visitation for failure to pay child support. Cases that address the issue generally take a similar approach.

[1]   Illustrative Statutes

The Oregon statute is unusual, in that it links child support and visitation and enables the court to modify either provision when a person having custody of a child denies visitation rights.[345] The statute in Kentucky provides that when children entitled to support are receiving public assistance, neither parent may use matters concerning custody or visitation as a reason for failing to pay child support.[346] The Minnesota statute is an excellent example of a logical and principled approach to this issue:

> Failure by a party to make support payments is not a defense to: interference with visitation rights; or without the permission of the court or the noncustodial parent removing a child from this state. Nor is interference with visitation rights or taking a child from this state without permission of the court or the noncustodial parent a defense to nonpayment of support. If a party fails to make support payments, or interferes with visitation rights, or without permission of the court or the noncustodial parent removes a child from this state, the other party may petition the court for an appropriate order.[347]

[2]   Case Law

The cases that follow reflect quite typical fact patterns and judicial determinations with respect to the relationships between child support obligations and visitation rights. In *Kemp v. Kemp*,[348] after the custodial mother terminated all contact between her son and his father, the father discontinued support payments. The mother then sought suspension of visitation rights and a contempt citation against the father for nonpayment of child support, and the father sought to hold her in contempt for noncompliance with the visitation order. The trial court suspended both visitation and child support, and the intermediate appellate court reversed both determinations.

When the case reached the Maryland Court of Appeals, the court held that one and a half years having passed since the last hearing on visitation, changed

---

[345]   Or. Rev. Stat. § 107.431(1) (2001).

[346]   Ky. Rev. Stat. Ann. § 205.770 (1991).

[347]   Minn. Stat. Ann. § 518.612 (2001). *See generally* Carolyn E. Taylor, Note, *Making Parents Behave: The Conditioning of Child Support and Visitation Rights*, 84 Colum. L. Rev. 1059 (1984) (criticizing courts that link child support and visitation for creating a remedy that adversely affects the parties involved).

[348]   411 A.2d 1028 (Md. 1980).

circumstances required a new hearing on that issue. The court directed the trial judge on remand to base a visitation decision on the best interests of the child, cautioning that "he should . . . only deny visitation if the evidence clearly demonstrates the existence of extraordinary circumstances requiring such drastic action."[349]

In *Cooper v. Cooper*,[350] a noncustodial father sought termination of child support and relief from any obligation to pay for the college education of his two minor children, alleging that the children refused to visit him. The court reviewed allegations that the mother deliberately influenced the children to refuse visitation through behavior characterized as "psychological warfare." Remanding, the court held that termination was within the trial court's authority under extreme and unusual circumstances.

[D]   Visitation by Third Parties

The common law rule, generally favoring natural parents in the absence of a showing of unfitness, did not provide for visitation by third persons.

In recent years, however, legislatures throughout the country have enacted statutes that permit courts to grant visitation rights to grandparents in a variety of circumstances. In some states, the statutes extend visitation rights to other third parties, including stepparents, siblings, so called de facto parents, and others who have established relationships with the child. Although grandparent visitation is the only species of third party visitation that the United States Supreme Court has addressed,[351] a number of courts have applied state constitutional provisions far more broadly.

[1]   The Common Law Rule

The decision by a California appellate court in *Odell v. Lutz*[352] is illustrative of the common law rule regarding visitation by parties other than the parents. The plaintiff in this case sought to visit her 8-year-old granddaughter, her deceased daughter's child, over the objection of the child's father, who had remarried. The court held that while parental rights are not absolute and are subject to the state's power to protect the child from parental abuse, it would be unconstitutional to interfere with the "natural liberty of parents to direct the upbringing of their children."[353]

Again, in a decision typical of those addressing the question, the Court of Appeals of North Carolina adhered to the traditional rule that grandparents' love for a child does not give them the right to enforce visitation. Although ties of love and affection between children and grandparents are desirable, this is no justification for interference with the parent-child relationship.

---

[349] *Id.* at 1031-32 (citation omitted).

[350] 375 N.E.2d 925 (Ill. App. Ct. 1978).

[351] 530 U.S. 57 (2000).

[352] 177 P.2d 628 (Cal. Dist. Ct. App. 1947).

[353] *Id.* at 629.

[2] Third Party Visitation Statutes

A dazzling variety of legislative enactments across the country currently provide for visitation by grandparents, and in not a few instances other third parties are also authorized to seek visitation. The California statute is among the most liberal. It directs the court to order reasonable visitation rights to the noncustodial parent in the absence of detriment to the child, and also gives the court discretion to award visitation to "any other person having an interest in the welfare of the child."[354] Similarly, the Connecticut statute authorizes the trial court to grant visitation rights "to any person," pursuant to a petition that includes allegations that "(1) a parent-like relationship exists between the person and the minor child, and (2) denial of visitation would cause real and significant harm."[355]

The Oregon provision is also broad in scope, although it contains some limiting language, authorizing petitions for visitation rights to any person "who has established emotional ties creating a parent-child relationship or an ongoing personal relationship with a child . . . ."[356] The right to petition extends but is not limited to stepparents, foster parents, grandparents and relatives by blood or marriage.

In some states, the statutory right of third parties to petition for visitation is more limited. In both Louisiana and New Jersey, for example, the right is afforded only to siblings and grandparents of children whose parents are deceased, divorced or legally separated.[357] Similarly, the Alaska statute allows visitation by a grandparent or other person when one or both parents of the child are deceased.[358]

[3] Grandparent Visitation

Grandparents generally enjoy a statutory right to petition for visitation.[359] The reported cases reflect varying degrees of success when custodial parents have challenged this right. In *Kudler v. Smith*,[360] for example, a Colorado appellate court affirmed the trial court's termination of visitation with the grandparents of the children's deceased mother. Observing that the grandparents had maligned, criticized and undermined the father during visits with the children, the court held that termination of visitation was in the children's best interest.

In *In re Visitation of Gasteau*,[361] the child's divorced father, after the mother's remarriage, voluntarily terminated his parental rights to allow adoption by the stepfather. The Court of Appeals of Indiana reversed the lower court's order

---

[354] Cal. Fam. Code § 3100(a) (2001).

[355] See Conn. Gen. Stat. Ann. § 46b-59 (2012).

[356] Or. Rev. Stat. § 109.119 (1999).

[357] *See* La. Rev. Stat. Ann. § 344 (2001); N.J. Stat. Ann. § 9:2-7-1 (1993).

[358] Alaska Stat. § 25.24.150 (1992).

[359] *See supra* § 11.05[D][2]. *See generally* Catherine A. McCrimmon & Robert J. Howell, *Grandparents' Legal Rights to Visitation in the Fifty States and the District of Columbia*, 17 Bull. Am. Acad. Psychiatry & L. 355 (1989).

[360] 643 P.2d 783 (Colo. Ct. App. 1981).

[361] 585 N.E.2d 726 (Ind. Ct. App. 1992).

dismissing the grandmother's visitation petition on the ground that termination of the father's parental rights also terminated the grandmother's derivative rights. The court held that the legislature, in enacting the Grandparent Visitation Rights Act,[362] intended that grandparents' visitation rights survive adoption of the child by a stepparent.

Recent cases in some jurisdictions have subjected grandparent visitation statutes to constitutional scrutiny. In *King v. King*,[363] for example, the Supreme Court of Kentucky upheld the constitutionality of a statute upon which the trial court relied in ordering visitation by a child's grandfather over the objection of the married parents of the child. In the course of an extensive disquisition in support of its judgment, the court stated:

> This statute seeks to balance the fundamental rights of the parents, grandparents and the child. At common law, grandparents had no legal rights to visitation. However, the [legislature] . . . determined that, in modern day society, it was essential that some semblance of family and generational contact be preserved. If a grandparent is physically, mentally and morally fit, then a grandchild will ordinarily benefit from contact with the grandparent . . . *The grandparent can be invigorated by exposure to youth, can gain an insight into our changing society, and can avoid the loneliness which is so often a part of an aging parent's life. These considerations by the state do not go too far in intruding into the fundamental rights of parents.*[364]

A dissenting opinion in *King* described the court's opinion as "mak[ing] little pretense of constitutional analysis," depending on "the sentimental notion of an inherent value in visitation between grandparent and grandchild," and worst of all, reaching the "conclusion that a grandparent has a 'fundamental right' to visitation wit a grandchild."[365] Nevertheless, the Supreme Court of Missouri, in *Herndon v. Tuhey*,[366] upheld the that state's grandparent visitation statute with copious comments from and in full agreement with *King*.

Some state courts, however, have invalidated grandparent visitation statutes under the applicable state constitutions or the federal constitution. In *Hawk v. Hawk*,[367] for example, the Supreme Court of Tennessee held that the state's grandparent visitation statute was unconstitutional. The court in *Hawk*, reviewed a number of Supreme Court decisions, stated that although it is "often expressed as a 'liberty' interest, the protection of 'childrearing autonomy' reflects the Court's larger concern with privacy rights for the family.[368] Also, the court was not persuaded by the grandparents' argument that a finding that visitation is in a child's best interest creates a compelling state interest. Rather, the court concluded that

---

[362] *See* Ind. Code § 31-1-11.7 (Supp. 1992).

[363] 828 S.W. 2d 630 (Ky. 1992).

[364] *Id.* at 632 (citation omitted) (emphasis added).

[365] *Id.* at 633 (Lambert, J., dissenting).

[366] 857 S.W. 2d 203 (Mo. 1993).

[367] 855 S.W. 2d 573 (Tenn. 1993).

[368] *Id.* at 578.

under both the Tennessee and federal constitutions, state interference with the right of a parent to raise a child must be based on a showing of harm to the welfare of the child.[369]

In *Troxel v. Glanville*,[370] the United States Supreme Court for the first time considered the constitutionality of a state grandparent visitation statute. Affirming a decision of the Washington Supreme Court, the Court held that the state's visitation statute, as applied, infringed on "the fundamental right of parents to make decisions concerning the care, custody, and control of their children."[371] The Washington statute provided: "Any person may petition the court for visitation rights at any time including, but not limited to custody proceedings. The court may order visitation rights for any person when visitation may serve the best interests of the child whether or not there has been any change of circumstances."[372]

Justice O'Connor, in an opinion joined by a plurality of the Court, found the Washington statute to be "breathtakingly broad" and noted that it "effectively permits any third party seeking visitation to subject any decision by a parent concerning visitation of the parent's children to state-court review."[373] In its decision, the plurality addressed only the extraordinarily broad statute before it and explicitly declined consideration of "the primary constitutional question passed on by the Washington Supreme Court — whether the Due Process Clause requires all nonparental visitation statutes to include a showing of harm or potential harm to the child as a condition precedent to granting visitation."[374] Subsequently, the Washington legislature amended the statute.[375] Time will tell whether *Troxel* will have a significant impact on the myriad state grandparent visitation statutes.[376]

[4] Stepparent Visitation

There is a relative paucity of reported cases that involve visitation rights of stepparents. Not all courts have been persuaded, however, that allowing visitation by stepparents "opens the door to the butcher, the baker and the candlestick maker to a right to a hearing on visitation' rights."[377] Thus, in *Evans v. Evans*,[378] Maryland's highest court rejected a lower court decision limiting statutory visitation rights to biological parents, adoptive parents and grandparents. The court also held that in loco parentis status need not be established for stepparent visitation to be granted, although it may be a relevant factor in determining the best interests of the child.

---

[369] *Id.* at 580-81.

[370] 530 U.S. 57 (2000).

[371] *Id.* at 66-67.

[372] Wash. Rev. Code § 26.10.160(3) (1994).

[373] *Troxel*, 530 U.S. at 66-67.

[374] *Id.* at 73.

[375] *See* Wash. Rev. Code § 26.10.160 (2012).

[376] *See generally* John DeWitt Gregory, *Defining the Family in the Millennium: The* Troxel *Follies*, 32 U. Mem. L. Rev. 687 (2002).

[377] *Simpson v. Simpson*, 586 S.W.2d 33, 36 (Ky. 1979) (Stephenson, J., dissenting).

[378] 488 A.2d 157 (Md. 1985).

More typically, however, state courts have held that in loco parentis status is a significant factor when a stepparent seeks to be awarded visitation rights. In *Spells v. Spells*,[379] for example, perhaps the first reported appellate case to apply the in loco parentis doctrine to favor a stepparent seeking visitation over the biological parent's objection, the Pennsylvania Superior Court stated:

> [W]hen a stepparent is "in loco parentis" with his stepchildren, courts must jealously guard his rights to visitation. Of course, the paramount concern in any child custody or visitation dispute is the welfare and best interests of the child. But the hearing court must permit a stepparent to establish what his relationship to the child is and to demonstrate that his interest in visitation should be protected.[380]

The former stepparent in *Simmons v. Simmons*[381] was ineligible to petition for visitation under a Minnesota statute that permits reasonable visitation rights when a child has resided with a person for at least two years.[382] Although the petitioner had lived with his stepson for only 18 months before divorcing the child's mother, he was successful, nevertheless, in establishing his right to visitation. The court held that a former stepparent who was in loco parentis to his former stepchild may have a common law right to visitation, and that nothing in the statute specifically repealed, restricted, or abridged a non-parent's common law rights of visitation.

[5] "De Facto Parent" Visitation

The claims that the California Court of Appeal addressed in *Nancy S. v. Michele G.*[383] are typical of those asserted by persons who seek legal recognition as "de facto parents" or "co-parents" for the purpose of obtaining rights to visitation. The court declined to recognize any of the theories under which the lesbian former partner claimed visitation rights with two children.

The children were conceived through artificial insemination during the parties' relationship. After the parties separated and came to disagree about a custody arrangement, the biological mother, Nancy S., sought a declaration under the Uniform Parentage Act that her former partner was not a parent and was, therefore, entitled to visitation only if the biological mother consented. Michele G. then sought an order for shared custody and visitation which the court denied, holding that Michele lacked standing to pursue visitation and awarding sole custody to Nancy.

Michele then argued that she was a de facto parent, defined as one who assumes the role of parent from day to day and fulfills the child's physical and psychological needs. While conceding that Michele might be a de facto parent under California law, the court ruled that this status does not give one the right to visitation over the objection of the biological parent. The court similarly rejected Michele's theory that

---

[379] 378 A.2d 879 (Pa. Super. Ct. 1977).

[380] *Id.* at 883.

[381] 486 N.W.2d 788 (Minn. Ct. App. 1992).

[382] *See* Minn. Stat. § 257C.08 (2002).

[383] 279 Cal. Rptr. 212 (Cal. Ct. App. 1991).

the common law in loco parentis doctrine gave her rights to seek custody and visitation equal to those of the biological parent, declining to extend the doctrine to give a nonparent the same rights as a parent in a custody dispute. Lastly, after finding the doctrine of equitable estoppel inapplicable, the court concluded:

> [E]xpanding the definition of a "parent" in the manner advocated by appellant could expose other natural parents to litigation brought by child-care providers of long standing, relatives, successive sets of stepparents or other close friends of the family . . . . By deferring to the Legislature in matters involving complex social and policy ramifications far beyond the facts of the particular case, we are not telling the parties that the issues they raise are unworthy of legal recognition. To the contrary, we intend only to illustrate the limitations of the courts in fashioning a comprehensive solution to such a complex and socially significant issue.[384]

In *Alison D. v. Virginia M.*,[385] the parties shared child care and support duties toward a child conceived by artificial insemination pursuant to their agreement. After the women separated, the biological mother eventually ended all contact between her former companion and the child. The New York Court of Appeals held that the petitioner was not a parent within the meaning of the applicable statute and, therefore, lacked standing to petition for a hearing regarding visitation. The court noted that the petitioner had no right to "limit or diminish the right of the concededly fit biological parent to choose with whom her child associates."[386] The court further observed:

> Traditionally, in this State it is the child's mother and father who, assuming fitness, have the right to the care and custody of the child, even in situations where the nonparent has exercised some control over the child with the parent's consent. To allow the courts to award visitation — a limited form of custody — to a third person would necessarily impair the parents' right to custody and control.[387]

Courts in other jurisdictions have rendered decisions similar to that of New York's highest court in *Alison D.* More recently, however, a number of courts have rejected an approach that strictly construes the applicable statute. In *In re Custody of H.S.H.K.*,[388] for example, the Supreme Court of Wisconsin, departing from its own decision in an earlier case, recognized visitation rights for lesbian partners of legal parents. Even though the Wisconsin visitation statute did not apply to the case before it, the court concluded that the legislature did not intend the visitation statute "to be the exclusive provision on visitation," nor that it "supplant or preempt the courts' long standing equitable power to protect the best interest of a child by ordering visitation in circumstances not included in the statute."[389]

---

[384] *Id.* at 219.

[385] 572 N.E.2d 27 (N.Y. 1991).

[386] *Id.* at 29. *See also In re Interest of Z.J.H.*, 471 N.W.2d 202 (Wis. 1991).

[387] *Id.* at 29 (citations omitted).

[388] 533 N.W. 2d 419, 420 (Wis. 1995).

[389] *Id.* at 424-25 (emphasis supplied).

Similarly, in *E.N.O. v. L.M.M.*,[390] the Supreme Judicial Court of Massachusetts reached the same result. Even though there was no statutory authority to award visitation, and even though the court recognized the amorphousness of the best interest of the child standard, the court concluded that the authority to award visitation could be found in the equity jurisdiction of the trial court. The Supreme Court of New Jersey surveyed case law in other jurisdictions and ruled to the same effect in *V.C. v. M.J.B.*[391]

§ 11.06 MODIFICATION OF CHILD CUSTODY

[A] Introduction and Overview

A change in child custody almost invariably involves the potential for conflict between two important principles. The need for finality of judgments or decrees complements the desire for continuity and stability in child custody arrangements. At the same time, however, it is essential that ongoing custody arrangements continue to provide for the best interests of the child. The standard that generally governs modification of child custody, requiring a showing of materially changed circumstances and that modification is in the best interest of the child, reflects these ostensibly competing principles.[392]

The Colorado statutory provisions governing modification of sole custody and joint custody are illustrative, taking into account both the need for continuity and stability, and concern for the child's best interests. In this jurisdiction, once a motion to modify a custody decree is filed, whether it is granted or not, no subsequent modification motions may be filed unless the court finds that the child's emotional or physical well-being is endangered.[393] Further, the court may not modify a prior sole custody absent a finding, based on facts that have arisen since the prior decree or were unknown at the time of its issuance, that there has been a change in circumstances and that modification will serve the child's best interests.[394] Additionally, a prior custody arrangement will not be disturbed unless the custodian agrees or the child has been "integrated into the family of the petitioner" and the custodian consents to that arrangement, or the present arrangement poses a danger to the child's emotional or physical welfare such that the potential harm of a custody change is less than the potential benefit to the child.[395]

Regardless of the disposition of a prior motion for modification of joint custody, no such motion may be filed within two years, unless the court finds cause for a

---

[390] 711 N.E. 2d 886 (Mass. 1999).

[391] 748 A. 2d 539 (2000).

[392] *See generally* Joan G. Wexler, *Rethinking the Modification of Child Custody Decrees*, 94 Yale L.J. 757 (1985) (discussing the standards for modification of custody decrees and proposing a more restrictive standard for modification and greater use of social science data).

[393] Colo. Rev. Stat. Ann. § 14-10-131 (1999).

[394] *Id.*

[395] *Id.*

hearing or the parties stipulate to the change.[396] The party seeking modification must prove by a preponderance of the evidence that the change is indicated.[397]

[B] Judicial Standards for Modification of Custody Decrees

In *Burchard v. Garay*,[398] the mother of a child born out of wedlock cared for the child for two years while the father denied paternity and neither visited the child nor furnished support. After the mother established paternity in a court proceeding, both parents filed petitions for exclusive custody. The trial court awarded custody to the father, in accordance with its view of the child's best interests.

On appeal, the Supreme Court of California examined the function of the changed circumstance rule in child custody cases. The court concluded that the rule does not require a change of circumstances where no prior custody decree exists, but affirmed "the importance of stability in custody arrangements, placing the burden upon the person seeking to alter a long-established arrangement."[399] The court noted that in most cases the result will be the same whether the court applies a changed circumstance or a best interest test because of the importance of the child's need for stability and continuity.

The Supreme Court of New Hampshire, in *Perrault v. Cook*,[400] provided elaborate reasons for the importance of requiring a substantial and material change of circumstances before altering an existing custody arrangement. The court observed:

> In a custody proceeding . . . the focus is on the welfare of the child. The stability of family relationships is recognized as an essential ingredient in nurturing the healthy psychological development of a child . . . . The shuffling of a child back and forth between a father and mother can destroy his sense of security, confuse his emotions, and greatly disrupt his growth as an individual. . . . Accordingly, the party to whom custody of a child has been given pursuant to a divorce decree has a much higher interest in maintaining the status quo for the purpose of protecting the child from psychological injury. The relationship established by the custody award should not be disturbed unless the moving party demonstrates that the circumstances affecting the welfare of the child have been so greatly altered that there is a strong possibility the child will be harmed if he continues to live under the present arrangement.[401]

---

[396] *Id.*

[397] *Id.*

[398] 724 P.2d 486 (Cal. 1986).

[399] *Id.* at 804.

[400] 322 A.2d 610 (N.H. 1974).

[401] *Id.* at 612. *But see In re Choy*, 919 A2d 801 (N.H. 2007) (noting that the amended New Hampshire statute makes no reference to a change in circumstances and concluding that the legislature intentionally chose not to require the petitioner to plead and prove a change in circumstance in order to obtain relief).

With the increasing emphasis on joint custody,[402] courts must now consider with some frequency petitions seeking modification of this arrangement. In *King v. King*,[403] for example, when the child was eight years old, the divorce court awarded joint physical custody, with primary residence in the mother's home. Four years later, the trial court granted the father's motion to amend the decree and award him sole custody. In its affirmance, the Supreme Court of Rhode Island held that the child's substantially increased age at a critical time of his life was a sufficient change of circumstances to warrant reopening the prior custody order. In *In re Marriage of Birnbaum*,[404] however, California court held that the trial court's change of the child's joint custody residential arrangement was not a change in custody. Therefore, no showing of a change in circumstances was required.

§ 11.07   RELOCATION OF CUSTODIAL PARENT

[A]   Statutory Restrictions

Statutes in a number of states, of which the following are illustrative, impose residential restrictions on custodial parents. The New Jersey statute prohibits removal of a child who is a native of New Jersey or who has resided there for five years without the consent of both parents or a court order issued upon good cause.[405] The statute in Nevada provides that a parent having custody or joint custody must petition the court for permission to move out of the state if the other parent does not consent to the move; noncompliance may be a factor if the noncustodial parent or other joint custodial parent requests a change of custody.

[B]   Court Ordered Limitations on Relocation by a Custodial Parent

In *Schwartz v. Schwartz*,[407] the Supreme Court of Nevada, in a case of first impression interpreted that state's "anti-removal" statutory provisions.[408] The child's father, the residential custodian, sought the court's permission to move from Nevada to Pennsylvania to be near his family, where he could provide better care for the child. In establishing guidelines for the removal of children from the state, the court relied heavily on the criteria adopted by the Chancery Division of the Superior Court of New Jersey in *D'Onofrio v. D'Onofrio*,[409] a leading and frequently cited case in the area.

The court required that the custodial parent show that both the children and the custodial parent would realize an "actual advantage" in moving so far from the

---

[402]   *See supra* § 11.04.

[403]   333 A.2d 135 (R.I. 1975).

[404]   260 Cal. Rptr. 210 (Cal. Ct. App. 1989).

[405]   N.J. Stat. Ann. § 9:2-2 (1993).

[407]   812 P.2d 1268 (Nev. 1991).

[408]   *See supra* § 11.07[A].

[409]   365 A.2d 27 (N.J. Super. Ct. Ch. Div.), *aff'd*, 365 A.2d 716 (N.J. Super. Ct. App. Div. 1976).

current residence as virtually to preclude weekly visitation.[410] Once this requirement is met, the court must weigh several additional factors, including (1) the extent to which it is likely that the move will improve the children's and the custodial parent's quality of life; (2) whether the custodial parent has honorable motives, not intended to impede visitation rights; (3) whether the custodial parent will comply with the court's visitation orders after removal; (4) whether the noncustodian's motives in resisting removal are honorable, and not designed to obtain financial advantages; and (5) whether reasonable visitation can be accomplished at the distance contemplated. When alternative reasonable visitation is possible and removal affords a clear advantage, the court will not deny relocation solely to preserve weekly visitation.

In *DeCamp v. Hein*,[411] a Florida court similarly adopted the New Jersey relocation test set out in *D'Onofrio*. In *DeCamp*, the children's mother physically separated from her husband and moved from Florida to her birthplace in New Jersey to be near her relatives, and there secured employment and housing. In a subsequent Florida divorce decree, the court granted custody to the mother, but required that the children reside in Florida near their father. The appellate court found these requirements incompatible and, relying on the guidelines in *D'Onofrio*, held that the wife could retain custody of the children and move to New Jersey.

As the court in *DeCamp* observed, in deciding the children's best interest in cases involving the relocation of a custodial parent, "[t]here can be no bright line test," and the court must examine all the facts and circumstances.[412] Thus, in *Lozinak v. Lozinak*[413] the Pennsylvania Superior Court affirmed an award of physical custody to the mother on the condition that she remain in Pennsylvania, with the father to have custody if she moved to Iowa. The court found that the mother offered no reasons, "economic, educational, religious, health or emotional," to justify moving a child from Pennsylvania, where the child had an extended family, the time and attention of both parents and an excellent environment.[414]

Similarly, in *Carpenter v. Carpenter*,[415] the Supreme Court of Virginia affirmed an order enjoining a custodial mother from moving from Virginia to New York, where she would be near to her family and anticipated substantially improved employment opportunities. The court accepted the lower court's conclusions that removal to New York would not be in the children's best interests because they benefited from the care of both parents in Virginia, and the mother's employment plans were entirely speculative. Also, "the cultural and educational advantages in New York City were not significantly greater than the cultural, educational and

---

[410] *Schwartz*, 812 P.2d at 1271. In *Cooper v. Cooper*, 491 A.2d 606 (N.J. 1984), the New Jersey Supreme Court required that a custodial parent must establish, inter alia, a real advantage from a move. The court modified this requirement in *Holder v. Polanski*, 544 A.2d 852, 855 (N.J. 1988) (holding that "a custodial parent may move with the children of the marriage to another state as long as the move does not interfere with the best interests of the children of the visitation rights of the non-custodial parent").

[411] 541 So. 2d 708 (Fla. Dist. Ct. App. 1989).

[412] *Id.* at 712.

[413] 569 A.2d 353 (Pa. Super. Ct. 1990).

[414] *Id.* at 355.

[415] 257 S.E.2d 845 (Va. 1979).

recreational advantages in Tidewater Virginia."[416]

For many years, the New York courts applied a different and arguably stricter rule in determining whether to permit removal of a child to another jurisdiction. In *Aldrich v. Aldrich*,[417] the court stated that "[i]t is now hornbook law that exceptional circumstances must exist before the visitation rights of a noncustodial parent may be diminished or denied."[418] In *Tropea v. Tropea*,[419] the New York Court of Appeals departed from this long standing approach to the custodial parent's relocation. The court held "that each relocation request must be considered on its own merits with due consideration of all the relevant facts and circumstances and with predominant emphasis being placed on what outcome is most likely to serve the best interests of the child."[420] The court was careful to point out that among the significant factors that must be considered are the rights of custodial and non custodial parents. But "it is the rights and needs of the children that must be accorded the greatest weight, since they are innocent victims of their parents decision to divorce and are the least equipped to handle the stresses of the changing family situation."[421]

In *Burgess v. Burgess*,[422] the Supreme Court of California also overruled prior law created by the appellate courts that favored the noncustodial parent. The court stated:

> [I]n a matter involving immediate or eventual relocation by one or both parents, the trial court must take into account the presumptive right of a custodial parent to change the residence of the minor children, so long as the removal would not be prejudicial to their rights or welfare . . . . The showing required is substantial. We have previously held that a child should not be removed from prior custody of one parent and given to the other "unless the material facts and circumstances occurring subsequently are of a kind to render it essential or expedient for the welfare of the child that there be a change.' "[423]

The decisions in *Tropea* and *Burgess*, rendered by the highest courts of New York and California respectively, may well signal a trend toward near universal acceptance of the best interest of the child standard in cases involving relocation by the custodial parent.

---

[416] *Id.* at 848.

[417] 516 N.Y.S.2d 328 (N.Y. App. Div. 1987).

[418] *Id.* at 329.

[419] 665 N.E. 2d 145 (N.Y. 1996).

[420] *Id.* at 150.

[421] *Id.*

[422] 913 P. 2d 473 (Cal. 1996).

[423] *Id.* at 478, 482.

§ 11.08   INTERFERENCE WITH CHILD CUSTODY

[A]   State Criminal Sanctions

Statutes in many states provide for punishment for the act of interference with custody by a noncustodial parent. The statutes, of which the following are illustrative examples, generally supplement criminal kidnapping provisions.

In Colorado, the offense of violation of custody, a felony, is committed when a person, including a natural parent or foster parent who knows he "has no privilege to do so," takes or entices a child from the parent or legal guardian or violates a custody order with the intent of depriving the parent or legal custodian of custody.[424] The offender's reasonable belief that the conduct was necessary to protect the child is an affirmative defense.[425] The California statute similarly contains criminal sanctions against a person having a custodial right to a child. It punishes maliciously taking the child with the intent to deprive another of custody rights without good cause relating to the child's protection.[426] Violation of the provision carries fines of $1000 to $10,000 or imprisonment from one year in the county jail to three years in state prison.[427]

In Arizona, the status of the person who interferes with custody or visitation determines the level of the offense. That is, a parent or a parent's agent who violates the statute commits a felony of a lower grade than a parent who engages in the same conduct.[428] Again, if the parent or the parent's agent safely returns the child before being arrested, the offense is a misdemeanor.[429]

The definition of "simple kidnapping" in the Louisiana Criminal Code includes:

> The intentional taking, enticing or decoying away and removing from the state, by any parent of his or her child, from the custody of any person to whom custody has been awarded by any court of competent jurisdiction of any state, without consent of the legal custodian, with intent to defeat the jurisdiction of the said court over the custody of the child.[430]

Simple kidnapping is punished by a fine up to $5,000, imprisonment for up to five years, or both.[431] In Louisiana, interference with child custody is an offense separate and distinct from simple kidnapping, and is punishable by a fine of up to

---

[424]   Colo. Rev. Stat. § 18-3-304 (2001).

[425]   *Id.*

[426]   Cal. Penal Code § 278 (2007).

[427]   *Id.*

[428]   Ariz. Rev. Stat. Ann. § 13-1302 (1989). A person commits custodial or visitation interference under the statute "if, knowing or having reason to know that he has no legal right to do so, such person knowingly takes, entices or keeps from lawful custody or specified visitation any child less than 18 years of age or incompetent, entrusted by authority of law to the custody of another person or institution." *Id.*

[429]   *Id.*

[430]   La. Rev. Stat. Ann. § 14:45(A)(4) (1986).

[431]   La. Rev. Stat. § 14:45(B) (1992).

$500, six months imprisonment, or both.[432]

[B]   Tortious Interference With Custody

In *Wood v. Wood*,[433] the Supreme Court of Iowa recognized a cause of action for tortious interference with custody.[434] In so doing, the court pointed out that it was joining the majority of jurisdictions that had considered the question in following the Restatement of Torts, which provides that "[o]ne parent may be liable to the other parent for the abduction of his own child if by judicial decree the sole custody of the child has been awarded to the other parent."[435] A strong dissent in *Wood* argues vigorously against establishment of a cause of action in tort for interference with custody. The dissent asserts that the decision of the court will generate excessive litigation for already overburdened courts, and that pursuit of a tort remedy will be contrary to the best interests of children and their families as a "new weapon for the arsenal of litigants engaging in marital or post-marital warfare."[436]

Arguably, the court's decision in *Kajtazi v. Kajtazi*[437] verifies the dissenter's dire predictions in *Wood*. In *Kajtazi*, the child's father, with help from his other relatives, removed his child from the country without the consent or knowledge of the mother, who was the temporary custodian. The court held the defendants liable to the child for false imprisonment and intentional infliction of emotional distress, and awarded punitive damages based on the defendants' malicious and intentional disregard of the child's rights. The mother recovered damages for "loss of services of the child, the parent's wounded feelings and for the expenses incurred in attempting to recover the child," together with punitive damages and compensation for intentional infliction of emotional distress.

§ 11.09   MEDIATION OF CHILD CUSTODY DISPUTES

As alternative dispute resolution has increasingly taken hold in connection with matrimonial and family issues,[438] a number of state legislatures have enacted provisions authorizing mediation of custody and visitation matters. In Kansas, for example, the statute permits the court to order mediation of contested child custody

---

[432]   La. Rev. Stat. § 14:45.1 (1992).

[433]   338 N.W.2d 123 (Iowa 1983).

[434]   *See generally* Richard A. Campbell, *Note, The Tort of Custodial Interference — Toward A More Complete Remedy to Parental Kidnappings*, 1983 U. Ill. L. Rev. 229 (arguing that tort liability for custodial interference, because it is the only remedy that gives compensation to the custodial parents, is an important component in solving the problem of kidnapping).

[435]   Restatement (Second) of Torts § 700 (1977). *See also Fenslage v. Dawkins*, 629 F.2d 1107, 1109 (5th Cir. 1980) (awarding compensatory and punitive damages to a custodial mother against the child's father and others who conspired to keep the child from the mother, and noting that the Texas Supreme Court would follow the Restatement's principles).

[436]   *Id.* at 127.

[437]   488 F. Supp. 15 (E.D.N.Y. 1978).

[438]   *See supra* § 8.08.

or visitation questions upon the motion of either party or on its own motion.[439] If mediation is ordered, the statute directs that the court or hearing officer take into account the parties' choice of a specific mediator, whether the proposed mediator has relationships with the parties or any interests that might result in a conflict of interest or bias, and the proposed mediator's training and experience, including knowledge of child development, community resources, and relevant state law.[440]

The California Civil Code contains what are perhaps the most elaborate and comprehensive custody mediation provisions of any jurisdiction. In custody or visitation matters, the statute mandates that mediation be scheduled prior to or concurrently with the setting a hearing.[441] The provision states explicitly that its purpose is to "reduce acrimony" between the parties and to encourage an agreement that will assure "close and continuing contact" between parents and their children.[442] The mediator must strive for a settlement that is in the children's best interests, and has the authority to exclude counsel from the proceeding, interview the children, and meet separately with the parties.[443]

---

[439] Kan. Stat. Ann. § 23-602 (2000).

[440] *Id.*

[441] Cal. Fam. Code § 3161 (2011).

[442] *Id.*

[443] *Id.*

TABLE OF CASES

[References are to pages.]

[References are to pages.]

[References are to pages.]

[References are to pages.]

E

[References are to pages.]

[References are to pages.]

[References are to pages.]

[References are to pages.]

[References are to pages.]

L

[References are to pages.]

M

[References are to pages.]

[References are to pages.]

[References are to pages.]

[References are to pages.]

[References are to pages.]

[References are to pages.]

[References are to pages.]

[References are to pages.]

[References are to pages.]

[References are to pages.]

INDEX

[References are to sections.]

[References are to sections.]

[References are to sections.]

[References are to sections.]

[References are to sections.]

[References are to sections.]